BY THE EDITORS OF
CONSUMER GUIDE®
AND JAY A. BROWN

RATING THE MOVIES

FOR HOME VIDEO, TV, AND CABLE

BEEKMAN HOUSE

Manufactured in the U.S.A.
8 7 6 5 4 3 2 1

This edition published by Beekman House,
Distributed by Outlet Book Company, Inc.,
A Random House Company,
225 Park Avenue South, New York, New York 10003

ISBN 0-517-05654-2

Acknowledgement: The Editors of CONSUMER GUIDE® wish to thank the Motion Picture Association of America for supplying MPAA ratings information.

CONTENTS

ALPHABETICAL MOVIE LISTINGS

Lana Turner

Clint Eastwood

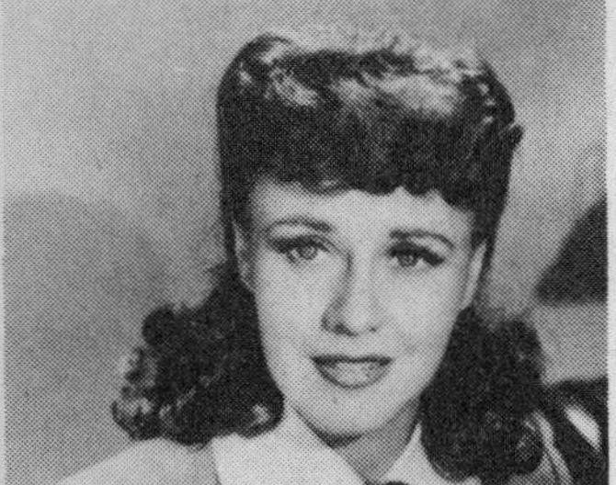
Ginger Rogers

John Wayne

Eddie Murphy

Bette Davis

Sylvester Stallone

Diane Keaton

AN INTRODUCTION TO RATING THE MOVIES

The advent of cable TV and the introduction of the videocassette recorder has meant riches for movie lovers. Each week scores of films are shown on regular and cable television channels; thousands more are available on Beta and VHS videocassettes, so that you're not even restricted by television programming but can schedule your viewing as you please. What's more, movie viewing has never been so inexpensive. For the price of less than one movie ticket, you and your family or friends can rent a movie to watch together on the VCR in your own home.

Sounds wonderful. And it is. But there's one drawback: How do you know which movies are really worth watching? Can you judge a film's worth by its publicity? Not necessarily. What about the movie critics' reviews or the reactions of your friends and colleagues? Critical reaction and word-of-mouth provide an important measure of guidance on well-known movies, but there are thousands of movies now available that you know little or nothing about—classics filmed before you were born, perhaps; or minor movies that never got the attention they deserved; or foreign movies that showed up briefly at an art house and disappeared before you caught up with them. That's why you need *Rating the Movies.* This comprehensive guide to over 3900 movies (new and old; great and not so great; forgotten, best forgotten, and never to be forgotten) is designed specifically to help you make the best use of your viewing time—and of the money you spend on building a movie library of videocassettes. This book is filled with facts and critical comments about motion pictures from the 1930s to the 1990s. You'll find just about every movie that's now being shown on network, cable, or pay TV. What's more, each film has been marked as to its availability on videocassette. The symbol ✇ indicates that you will be able to find this film in most video stores. Additionally, the symbol 🗨® means that the videotape version of a film is available with closed captions for the hearing-impaired.

Remember that not all films are available in all video stores. In recent years, video companies have begun the practice of placing certain titles on moratorium. That is, titles are taken off the sell-through market for an indefinite period. These titles are often still available for rental in some stores or libraries. Thus, despite their scarcity, these titles are marked with a video symbol in *Rating the Movies.*

Although our emphasis is on more recent movies—which are the ones most likely to appear on network or cable TV—there's extensive coverage of the movies that have made history since talking pictures began. In fact, this new and revised edition of *Rating the Movies* owes a lot to reader input from earlier editions of the book . . . you reminded us of movies you felt should be included—among them some true classics—and we've put in as many as we had space for.

In the course of revising this book, our reviewers have also revised their opinions of a number of movies. It sometimes happens that a film that is received with wild enthusiasm when it first appears does not stand the test of time—watch it when the fuss has died down, and you wonder what the excitement was all about. Conversely, movies that receive little critical acclaim on first viewing may improve, like wine, with age; repeated viewings reveal subtlety and depth that went unrecognized the first time around. So we consider it part of our responsibility to reflect these changes in viewer response to certain films.

THE STAR RATING SYSTEM

The key to *Rating the Movies* is CONSUMER GUIDE's® four-star rating system. The ratings have been assessed by experienced film historians who know and love movies. But even so, you're not going to agree with every rating. Movie viewing and film criticism are both subjective processes, and one person's film of the year may put someone else to sleep in the first reel. What the star ratings will do, though, is give you a fair, carefully considered analysis of the impact and overall quality (or lack of it) of a particular film.

This is how the star rating system works: The top, four-star (★★★★) rating tells you that this film meets exceptionally high standards of performance, direction, and production. A four-star rating also indicates that the film is engrossing and enjoyable (using the term "enjoyable" loosely, because some fine films can be emotionally demanding—perhaps "satisfying" would be a better word). Four stars also suggest, in most cases, that the film has something to say or is significant in the history of cinema; it's not just empty entertainment. Three and a half stars (★★★½) and three stars (★★★) indicate that a film is well worth watching and of generally high quality but doesn't for one reason or another match up to our four-star criteria. Two and a half stars (★★½) indicates an average film—a rating that can have either a negative or a positive connotation. A Hollywood blockbuster with a big-name cast that receives a two-and-a-half-star rating would suggest that the film was a disappointment. It did not live up to the expectations of critics and audiences. On the other hand, if that same star rating is assigned to a low-budget genre or exploitation film—a type of movie notorious for poor production values and bad acting—then two and a half stars would suggest that the film might have something to offer most viewers. A two-star movie (★★) is a fair film; it's of limited interest but may suffer from a thin plot, poor characterizations, or weak acting or direction. Don't expect a great movie. One-and-a-half-star (★½) and one-star (★) ratings indicate a movie that's unlikely to hold your interest or provide you with much satisfaction. Skip it unless you've got nothing better to do. If a film is given (**no stars**), we consider watching it a waste of time. Such a film is most often in very poor taste, and we wouldn't want to recommend it to anyone. Occasionally, however, such a rating may indicate a "golden turkey"—a film so bad it almost takes on a charm of its own.

THE MOVIE REVIEWS

The format in which the movie reviews are presented has been designed to give you all the important facts about the film, along with critical comments to help you decide if the film is one that you will enjoy. Here are a few notes on how the format works.

Title. All titles are listed alphabetically. Most movies have only one title. Once in a while, however, a film will have an alternate title or will have been released in another country under a different name. Alternate titles are listed alphabetically and refer you to the title under which the review appears.

Foreign films are often listed under their original-language titles. Foreign films that begin with an article, such as *La Dolce Vita* and *La Cage aux Folles,* are alphabetized by the second word in that title, just as a title in English would not be alphabetized by the word "The." For example, *La Dolce Vita* is listed between *The Dogs of War* and *A Doll's House. La Cage aux Folles* and its sequels, *La Cage aux Folles II* and *La Cage aux Folles 3: The Wedding,* are listed in the C's.

Year of release. The year that appears immediately following the title usually refers to the year the film was first released theatrically in any country. Occasionally, readers may notice that another reference book or source will list a different year from that given in *Rating the Movies* for a certain film. This discrepancy may occur, for instance, when a film has been kept off the market for a year or two after it is completed, and the other reference source has listed its year of production rather than its year of release. It might also occur when a foreign film is released in the United States after its release in the country of origin, and the other source lists only American release dates for its entries, rather than first release dates.

Review. Under the movie title appears a list of the film's leading actors; supporting actors may also be mentioned in the course of the review. The director is named either in the review or at the end of it. The review itself tells you what the film is about and adds critical comments on performances, direction, script, and production values. Foreign-language films are indicated by referring to their language of origin—for example, "Originally filmed in French."

MPAA Rating. In the latter part of 1968, the Motion Picture Association of America (MPAA) introduced a rating system to enable people to judge what kind of audience a movie was meant for—and whether or not it was okay to take the kids to see it. The classification system now consists of five categories: "G" means "General Audiences"; people of any age may be admitted to see the film. "PG" indicates "Parental Guidance"; some material may not be suitable for children. "PG-13" strongly suggests parents give special guidance to children under 13. "R" indicates "Restricted"; a person under 17 requires an accompanying parent or adult guardian. "X" indicates "no one under 17 admitted (age limit may vary in certain areas)."

Most films released theatrically in the United States since 1968 carry an MPAA rating, and some older rereleases may also be MPAA-rated. Some films released after 1968, including many foreign films that are sold directly to television or videocassette, may not have been submitted to the MPAA. These post-1968 films are designated by **(no MPAA rating)**; you should read the reviews carefully to determine their suitability. For instance, *The Evil Dead,* which contains several gory scenes of mutilation and violence, is unrated. Also, some films have been released in more than one version. For example, *Caligula,* originally rated "X," was later released in an "R" version. Periodically, the MPAA updates their ratings to fit the changing times. For example, *Midnight Cowboy* was originally rated "X" upon its initial release, but has since been rerated as "R." More recently, *The Best of Times* was rated "R" at first, but was rerated "PG-13" shortly after release. This revised edition of *Rating the Movies* contains the MPAA's most current ratings.

Academy Awards. In most cases, the fact that a film or those who took part in making it won or received nominations for Academy Awards is a significant argument in favor of the film's value. Therefore we've included Academy Awards and nominations in major categories. Note that some descriptions of categories—such as cinematography and writing—have changed slightly over the years. When relevant, some mention is made if a film won or was nominated in a lesser category—the costumes in a historical drama, for example, or the special effects in a science-fiction film, or the music in a musical comedy.

Running time. At the end of each review, we list the running time of the film's theatrical release. Keep in mind that the running time of a film may vary by a few minutes for any number of reasons. A film on videotape may be slightly shorter because the film-to-tape transferring process compresses a typical film by about three minutes. Also, certain scenes may be added or deleted on the videotape version of the film. In addition, films that appear on network television are edited—sometimes very heavily—to appeal to a broad audience and to fit certain time slots. Finally, because most recent movies are in color, this fact is not noted after the running time; however, black-and-white movies are designated "b&w" immediately after the running time, and those few films that contain scenes in both black and white and color are designated "b&w/color."

A

ABBOTT AND COSTELLO MEET CAPTAIN KIDD (1952)

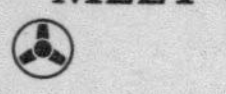

★★

Bud Abbott
Lou Costello

Routine Abbott and Costello farce with the boys competing with the venerable pirate for buried treasure. Abbott and Costello are really not up to par here. Charles Laughton as Captain Kidd is on board having a high time in a role beneath his stature. **Director**—Charles Lamont. *70 minutes*

ABBOTT AND COSTELLO MEET FRANKENSTEIN (1948)

★★★1/2

Bud Abbott
Lou Costello

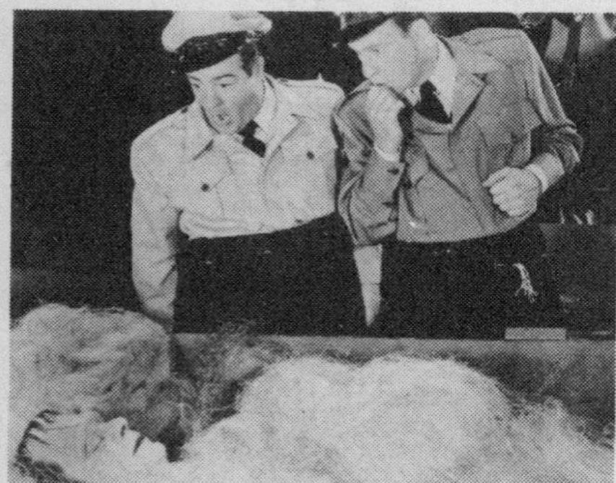

Laughs and shocks when Abbott and Costello Meet Frankenstein.

Abbott and Costello are at their funniest in this knockabout spoof of horror films. Costello's brain is slated for the monster. Dracula and the Wolf Man get in a few licks, too. It's an inspired blend of laughs and scares, with Bela Lugosi and Lon Chaney, Jr., lending their talents to the merriment. **Director**—Charles T. Barton. *83 minutes b&w*

ABE LINCOLN IN ILLINOIS (1948)

★★★

Raymond Massey
Ruth Gordon
Gene Lockhart

Massey *was* Abraham Lincoln for a generation of moviegoers, who probably would have recognized the actor as our great President sooner than they would have identified a likeness of Honest Abe himself. This reverential adaptation of Robert Sherwood's Pulitzer Prize-winning play seems a bit plodding today, but it's still earnest and literate, and the subject matter remains fascinating. The great James Wong Howe received an Academy Award nomination for photographing this portrayal of Lincoln, the shopkeeper and suitor, lawyer and legislator—a troubled idealist debating his way toward the White House. **Director**—John Cromwell. **Academy Award Nomination**—Massey, best actor.

110 minutes b&w

THE ABOMINABLE SNOWMAN (1957)

★★1/2

Peter Cushing
Forrest Tucker

Tucker and Cushing lead an expedition to high altitudes in this horror outing about the elusive and mysterious monster of the Himalayas. Effective scripting and acting help flesh out the characters. The suspense, however, lags somewhat. Maureen Connell and Richard Wattis costar. **Director**—Val Guest. **Alternate Title**—*The Abominable Snowman of the Himalayas.* *85 minutes b&w*

ABOUT LAST NIGHT . . . (1986)

★★1/2

Rob Lowe
Demi Moore

Rob Lowe and Demi Moore look for romance in About Last Night . . . .

A simplistic romantic comedy about two young singles who fail to connect with one another either as friends or lovers. This loose adaptation by Tim Kazurinsky and Denise DeClue of David Mamet's play *Sexual Perversity in Chicago* suffers from Lowe's colorless performance and too little human chemistry. Costars Jim Belushi and Elizabeth Perkins are memorable as the respective best friends of Lowe and Moore. **Director**—Edward Zwick. **(R)** *113 minutes*

ABOVE THE LAW (1988)

★★1/2 ®

Steven Seagal
Pam Grier

This slam-bang action film stars newcomer Seagal as a police detective out to annihilate Chicago drug dealers. International politics and CIA dirty tricks complicate the dedicated cop's efforts to bring in a sadistic drug smuggler. Seagal is effective in a role familiar to Clint Eastwood and Chuck Norris, but the violence and brutality of the character may be unnerving to some viewers. Grier, well known for her roles in the action-oriented blaxploitation films of the 1970s, costars as his female sidekick. Chicago's South Side provides some gritty locations, adding an authentic touch to this otherwise overblown police thriller. **Director**—Andrew Davis. **(R)** *97 minutes*

ABRAHAM LINCOLN (1930)

★★★

Walter Huston
Una Merkel
Henry B. Walthall

D. W. Griffith, the director who virtually "created" the feature film with his 1915 Civil War epic, *The Birth of a Nation*, returns to the Civil War era with this, his first sound film. It's a fine, artfully made motion picture, covering the life of the Great Emancipator from his youth and romance with Ann Rutledge to his Presidency and assassination in Ford's Theater. After two decades of feverish activity, Griffith's career was coming to a tragic end. He was able to make only one film after *Abraham Lincoln* during the remaining 18 years of his life. Huston turns in an effective, restrained performance. Stephen Vincent Benét wrote the script.

97 minutes b&w

ABSENCE OF MALICE (1981)

★★★★

Sally Field
Paul Newman

® *This movie available with closed captions for the hearing impaired.*

Sally Field is the reporter, Paul Newman her subject in Absence of Malice.

A brisk, intelligent drama that takes a penetrating look at the ethics of journalism and the quest for truth and justice. Field stars as an overeager newspaper reporter, who is duped into writing misleading and damaging stories about an investigation of a mobster's son, played by Newman. Actually, he is guilty of nothing more than having unsavory relatives. Newman is magnificent as the innocent and outraged victim, and he extracts revenge in a clever climax. Sydney Pollack's direction is crisp and pointed. Superb supporting performances strengthen the production. **(PG) Academy Award Nominations**—Newman, best actor; Melinda Dillon, best supporting actress; Kurt Luedtke, best screenplay written directly for the screen. *116 minutes*

THE ABSENT-MINDED PROFESSOR (1961)

 ★★★

Fred MacMurray
Tommy Kirk
Keenan Wynn

Weird science: Fred MacMurray in The Absent-Minded Professor.

A better-than-average Disney comedy about a scientist who invents flubber, a rubbery substance that overcomes gravity. First-rate special effects enhance the fun. MacMurray, in the title role, is in top form piloting his flubber-powered Model T through the skies. The story involves the pursuit of spies, led by Keenan Wynn, who want to steal the amazing material. Cast includes Nancy Olson and Ed Wynn. **Director**—Robert Stevenson. **(G)** *97 minutes b&w*

ABSOLUTE BEGINNERS (1986)

★★

Eddie O'Connell
Patsy Kensit
David Bowie

Highly stylized rock musical that celebrates teen culture in late-1950s London. The hard-to-follow story combines a mishmash of pop fashions with political and racial overtones. There are ample energetic song-and-dance numbers, at times reminiscent of *West Side Story.* But these extravagant musical sequences don't mix well with the violent confrontations. **Director**—Julien Temple. **(PG-13)** *107 minutes*

THE ABYSS (1989)

★★1/2

Ed Harris
Mary Elizabeth Mastrantonio
Michael Biehn

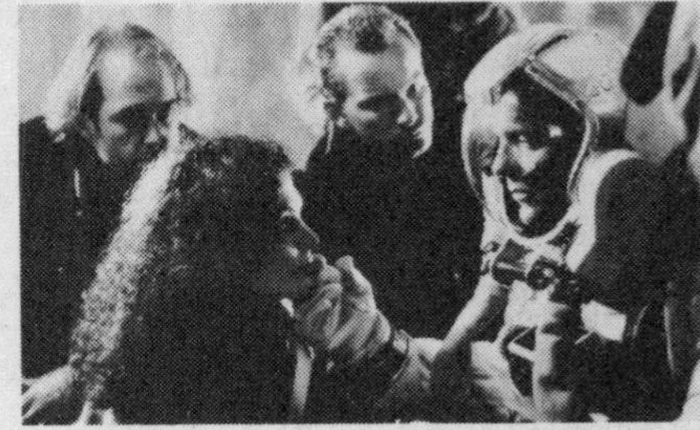

Mary Elizabeth Mastrantonio and Ed Harris during the filming of The Abyss.

This exhausting underwater epic features spectacular deep-sea special effects and elaborate high-tech hardware. Most of the film was actually shot underwater in two huge tanks that had been built for a nuclear plant that was never completed. Advanced technology was developed for the direct recording of underwater dialogue. The actors did most of their own underwater stuntwork, adding a level of tension to their performance not found in other deep-sea adventures. Unfortunately, the film's mixture of action-adventure and science fiction makes for a complicated storyline involving a doomed submarine, a nuclear warhead, a deranged naval officer, and alien invaders. A crew from an underwater oil-drilling rig faces each of these crises with wit and determination, but none of the adventures blend into a meaningful whole. Science-fiction fans will appreciate the visual effects from Industrial Light and Magic as well as the offbeat cast of supporting players, including Todd Graff, Leo Burmester, and Chris Elliott. Directed by James Cameron *(The Terminator; Aliens).* **(PG-13) Academy Award**—John Bruno, Dennis Muren, Hoyt Yeatman, and Dennis Skotak, visual effects. **Nominations**—Leslie Dilley and Anne Kuljian, art direction; Mikael Salomon, cinematography; Don Bassman, Kevin F. Cleary, Richard Overton, and Lee Orloff, sound. *140 minutes*

ACCIDENT (1967)

 ★★★

Dirk Bogarde
Stanley Baker
Jacqueline Sassard

The sometimes convoluted subtleties of Harold Pinter are often best dealt with onstage, but he is in good hands here with director Joseph Losey. Bogarde plays an Oxford professor who appears to be a happily married man—but is he really? He pines after an elusive Australian student who pines for someone else—but does she really? Needless to say, all the true drama is between the lines, and it's delicately, and often affectingly, drawn out by a fine cast that includes Delphine Seyrig, Alexander Knox, Vivien Merchant, and Michael York in his first major film role. *105 minutes*

THE ACCIDENTAL TOURIST (1988)

 ★★★1/2 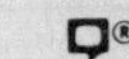

William Hurt
Geena Davis
Kathleen Turner

Hurt stars as an introverted travel writer who faces emotional difficulties following the death of his young son and separation from his wife (Turner). But a new relationship with an extroverted pet trainer (Davis) points his life in an upbeat direction. Director Law-

(Continued)

Geena Davis gets closer to William Hurt, who is The Accidental Tourist.

(Continued)
rence Kasdan's version of Anne Tyler's best-selling novel is more successful in its whimsical humor than in its heavy drama. Davis sparkles in many bright moments. **(PG) Academy Awards**—Davis, best supporting actress. **Nominations**—best picture; Kasdan, Frank Galati, best screenplay adaptation. *122 minutes*

THE ACCUSED (1988)

 ★★★

Jodi Foster
Kelly McGillis

Foster delivers a memorable performance as a gang-rape victim who demands conviction of her assailants and those who cheered them on. The story unfolds with gripping determination from the assault in a neighborhood bar to the climactic courtroom battle. The actual rape episode, carried out on a back-room pinball machine, is recounted in flashback. The provocative drama directly addresses the plight of the rape victim; indirectly it hints at the tension between the working- and middle-class worlds. McGillis costars as the DA who prosecutes the case. **Director**—Jonathan Kaplan. **(R) Academy Awards**—Foster, best actress. *110 minutes*

ACE IN THE HOLE

See The Big Carnival

ACROSS THE PACIFIC (1942)

★★★

Humphrey Bogart
Mary Astor
Sydney Greenstreet

Bogart, Greenstreet, and Astor are reteamed for this sleek World War II spy caper. Bogey tracks down enemy agents in Panama, keeps a menacing Greenstreet at bay, and falls in love with Astor. The trio is as effective as it was in *The Maltese Falcon*. Cast includes Keye Luke and Richard Loo. **Director**—John Huston. *97 minutes b&w*

ACROSS THE WIDE MISSOURI (1951)

★★

Clark Gable
Ricardo Montalban

Despite proficient acting by Gable and Montalban, this period western doesn't catch hold. Gable plays a stalwart fur trapper who marries an Indian girl. Gable's talents are not fully realized here. Cast includes John Hodiak, J. Carrol Naish, and Adolphe Menjou. **Director**—William Wellman. *78 minutes*

ACTION JACKSON (1988)

 ★★

Carl Weathers
Craig T. Nelson
Vanity

As a tough Detroit police detective, Weathers tries hard to live up to the title role. He engages in plenty of shootings, explosions, and car chases in the pursuit of Nelson, a power-hungry auto executive who is behind the murders of union leaders. Spectacular stunts dominate the picture, which is not surprising considering director Craig R. Baxley is a former stuntman. Unfortunately, the acting and dialogue take a back seat to all the action. Weathers, who was effective as Apollo Creed in the *Rocky* films, is too low-key in this lead role and lacks the anger and hard edge necessary for an action hero. Vanity adds a few sparks as Nelson's slinky mistress. **(R)** *94 minutes*

ADAM'S RIB (1949)

★★★★

Spencer Tracy
Katharine Hepburn
Judy Holliday

A perfect teaming of Tracy and Hepburn, who play husband and wife—and attorneys on opposite sides of a court case involving attempted murder. The case concerns a question of women's rights and the justice system: Did Holliday's character have the right to shoot her two-timing husband (Tom Ewell), whom she caught in the act? And, if it had been a man who had shot his wife for cheating, would he have been let off easy? The rib-tickling comedy is expertly written and directed to bring out the special chemistry between the incomparable Tracy and Hepburn. Ewell and David Wayne contribute fine performances in supporting roles. **Director**—George Cukor. **Academy Award Nomination**—Ruth Gordon and Garson Kanin, story and screenplay. *101 minutes b&w*

Adam's Rib *showcases matchless performances from Hepburn and Tracy.*

ADVENTURES IN BABYSITTING (1987)

★★

Elizabeth Shue
Anthony Rapp

In this overworked teen comedy, a babysitter leaves the suburbs with her young charges to rescue a friend stuck in the inner city. The frantic heroine and her kids then fall into a variety of improbable misadventures. They accept a ride from a psychotic truckdriver, get chased by car thieves, scale a skyscraper, and wind up at a fraternity beer blast—all in one night. One terrific scene stands out: The group lands onstage at a Chicago blues club and wails the "Babysitting Blues." Also with Maia Brewton and Keith Coogan. **Director**—Chris Columbus. **PG–13** *99 minutes*

THE ADVENTURES OF BARON MUNCHAUSEN (1989)

★★½

John Neville

Technical wizardry and fantastic, surreal sets are the high points of this lav-

® *This movie available with closed captions for the hearing impaired.*

ish comic fantasy by director Terry Gilliam. But the convoluted and uninteresting story makes this spectacular production utterly exhausting. John Neville stars as a bombastic 18th-century nobleman who embarks on an awesome expedition to save a city under siege. Robin Williams, not listed in the credits, has an appealing cameo role. **(PG) Academy Award Nominations**—Dante Ferretti and Francesca Lo Schiavo, art direction; Gabriella Pescucci, costume design; Maggie Weston and Fabrizio Storza, makeup; Richard Conway and Kent Houston, visual effects. *126 minutes*

THE ADVENTURES OF BUCKAROO BANZAI

See Buckaroo Banzai

THE ADVENTURES OF DON JUAN (1948)

 ★★1/2

Errol Flynn
Viveca Lindfors

Dashing Flynn romances Lindfors, who plays the Queen, and a number of maidens in this good-looking, tongue-in-cheek swashbuckler. This is one of the later Flynn adventure films, and some self-mockery is evident. Cast includes Raymond Burr, Alan Hale, and Ann Rutherford. **Director**—Vincent Sherman. *110 minutes*

THE ADVENTURES OF FORD FAIRLANE (1990)

Andrew Dice Clay
Priscilla Presley
Wayne Newton

Clay's character in this lowbrow comedy is an extension of his controversial stand up persona, which was manufactured in the first place to attract the attention of Hollywood. Clay stars as the "rock 'n' roll detective," whose beat is the Los Angeles music scene. The storyline follows Clay's adventures as he solves the murders of a heavy-metal singer, played by Vince Neil of Mötley Crüe, and a disgusting radio personality, played by comedian Gilbert Gottfried. True to his stand up persona, Clay swaggers, spouts rude insults, and expresses himself through a barrage of profanity. The film, which was aimed at white, juvenile male audiences, may attract those who have not yet seen Clay's act on cable. Others will be offended and not particularly amused. The eye-catching costumes by Marilyn Vance-Straker and the colorful supporting performances—including those by musical stars Newton, Morris Day, Tone Lōc, and Sheila E.—are wasted. Also with Ed O'Neill of TV's *Married with Children* and Robert Englund, who stars as Freddy Kruger in the *Nightmare on Elm Street* series. **Director**—Renny Harlin. **(R)** *100 minutes*

THE ADVENTURES OF MARCO POLO (1938)

★★1/2

Gary Cooper
Sigrid Gurie
Basil Rathbone

A slow journey that takes longer to get anywhere than did the multimillion dollar TV miniseries about Marco, produced more than four decades later. It's a lighthearted treatment, though you'd never know it, and Cooper looks anxious to escape on a horse. Samuel Goldwyn props up his historical romance with lush production values. **Director**—Archie Mayo. *100 minutes b&w*

THE ADVENTURES OF MARK TWAIN (1944)

Fredric March
Alexis Smith

This is a straightforward biography of the renowned writer and humorist. March turns in a memorable performance in the title role. Smith plays Twain's wife. The film follows Twain's life from steamboat pilot to acclaimed literary figure. The effort, however, doesn't match such great film biographies as *The Story of Louis Pasteur* or *The Life of Emile Zola.* Cast includes John Carradine, Donald Crisp, and C. Aubrey Smith. **Director**—Irving Rapper. *130 minutes b&w*

THE ADVENTURES OF ROBIN HOOD (1938)

Errol Flynn
Olivia de Havilland
Basil Rathbone
Claude Rains

Excellent acting, brilliant photography, and an exciting story make this one of the finest adventure films of all time. After contemporary blood-and-guts action movies, the outlaw hero of Sherwood Forest, played by Flynn to swashbuckling perfection, seems downright wholesome. **Directors**—William Keighley and Michael Curtiz. **Academy Award Nomination**—best picture. *105 minutes*

ADVENTURES OF SHERLOCK HOLMES (1939)

★★★ 

Basil Rathbone
Nigel Bruce
Ida Lupino

Nigel Bruce and Basil Rathbone search for clues in Adventures of Sherlock Holmes.

A strong contender as the best of the films featuring Sir Arthur Conan Doyle's ingenious sleuth of Baker Street. Here, archfiend Professor Moriarty (George Zucco), who has eluded Holmes for 11 years, plots the crime of the century. His target is the Tower of London's prize jewel, the Star of Delhi; his diversionary tactic is murder. The shocks and twists may be heady stuff for Watson (Bruce) and Lupino, as well as for us, but it's ultimately elementary for the man in the deerstalker cap. A fogbound, atmospheric Edwardian England is effectively captured, and Rathbone pulls off a most amusing interpretation of the role. From the play by William Gillette. **Director**—Alfred L. Werker. *85 minutes b&w*

THE ADVENTURES OF SHERLOCK HOLMES' SMARTER BROTHER (1975)

 ★★

Gene Wilder

Maybe this title should have been *The Adventures of Sherlock Holmes' Silly*

(Continued)

(Continued)
Brother. Wilder, who apprenticed at the Mel Brooks comedy school, wrote, directed, and stars in this spoof about the famous fictional sleuth. However, the film isn't the clever, zany romp expected from a member of the Brooks family. It is, rather, adolescent foolishness with only a smattering of true comic situations. Marty Feldman, Madeline Kahn, and Dom DeLuise—all members of the Brooks company of stock actors—are on board for this slapstick workout, which is merely elementary. **(PG)**
91 minutes

ADVENTURES OF THE WILDERNESS FAMILY (1975)

★★★

Robert Logan
Susan Shaw

Children should enjoy this adventure of a latter-day Swiss Family Robinson who, fed up with the din and smog of Los Angeles, hightail it to the mountain wilderness and set up housekeeping. They build a log cabin, befriend orphaned bear cubs, and face a menacing grizzly and wolves. Lots of striking mountain scenery. **Director**—Stewart Raffill. **(G)** *101 minutes*

ADVISE AND CONSENT (1962)

★★★

Don Murray
Charles Laughton
Henry Fonda
Walter Pidgeon

Fascinating screen adaptation of Allen Drury's novel of political maneuvering in Washington. Fine acting by a champagne cast heightens the drama surrounding the President's appointment of a controversial secretary of state. This was Laughton's last film. Other cast members include Gene Tierney, Franchot Tone, Lew Ayres, Burgess Meredith, Betty White and Peter Lawford. **Director**—Otto Preminger.
139 minutes b&w

AFFAIR IN TRINIDAD (1952)

★★

Rita Hayworth
Glenn Ford

Hayworth stands out in this sleek but routine tale of murder, espionage, and romance in the tropics. Hayworth, as a nightclub performer, seeks the murderer of her husband with the help of Ford, who plays her brother-in-law. Hayworth also does some notable dancing. The film is fun to watch on a double bill with *Gilda*, which also starred Hayworth and Ford. **Director**—Vincent Sherman. *98 minutes b&w*

AN AFFAIR TO REMEMBER (1957)

★★★ ®

Cary Grant
Deborah Kerr

Grant and Kerr star in this syrupy remake of *Love Affair*, which featured Charles Boyer and Irene Dunne. Grant, a debonair bachelor, romances former café singer Kerr aboard an ocean liner. The film begins as a comedy, turns into a tearjerker, and—of course—ends happily. Also includes Cathleen Nesbitt, Richard Denning, and Neva Patterson. **Director**—Leo McCarey. *115 minutes*

THE AFRICAN QUEEN (1951)

★★★★

Humphrey Bogart
Katharine Hepburn

Hepburn and Bogart are thrown together in The African Queen.

Hepburn is a prim missionary and Bogart is a booze-soaked boat skipper. The odd couple find romance and danger on the Congo River during World War I. A triumph of acting and direction leads to a surprising achievement of wry comedy and adventure. Cast includes Theodore Bikel, Peter Bull, and Robert Morley. **Director**—John Huston. **Academy Award**—Bogart, best actor. **Nominations**—Huston, best director; Hepburn, best actress; James Agee and Huston, screenplay. *106 minutes*

AFTER HOURS (1985)

★★★ ®

Griffin Dunne
Rosanna Arquette
Teri Garr

Waitress Teri Garr looks for commitment and romance After Hours.

Director Martin Scorsese returns to his favorite territory, the streets of New York City, for this cultish, low-budget black comedy. Dunne is a nerdy computer programmer who winds up in Manhattan's far-out SoHo district one night and encounters kinky characters and strange experiences. Acting is consistently good and the stylized photography and menacing atmosphere are equally effective. Verna Bloom and Cheech and Chong are also in the cast. **(R)** *96 minutes*

AFTER THE FOX (1966)

★★

Peter Sellers
Victor Mature
Britt Ekland

A rather forgettable Sellers comedy about an ingenious criminal who becomes a movie director as a front to pull off a gold heist. Mature, however, steals some scenes as a pompous has-been actor. The movie never gets off the ground despite Neil Simon's satirical

® *This movie available with closed captions for the hearing impaired.*

script. Cast includes Lilia Brazzi, Akim Tamiroff, and Martin Balsam. **Director**—Vittorio De Sica. *103 minutes*

AFTER THE THIN MAN (1936)

★★★

William Powell
Myrna Loy
James Stewart

A creditable sequel to Dashiell Hammett's *The Thin Man* and the first of several made between 1936 and 1947. Powell and Loy (joined by canine Asta) are back as Nick and Nora Charles, amateur detectives extraordinaire. This time it appears that a killer is circulating among Nora's blue-blooded San Francisco family. A young Stewart (this was only his second year in movies), Elissa Landi, Sam Levene, Joseph Calleia, and George Zucco add to the frothy and suspenseful fun. **Director**—W.S. Van Dyke. **Academy Award Nomination**—Frances Goodrich and Albert Hackett, screenplay. *113 minutes b&w*

AGAINST ALL FLAGS (1952)

★★

Errol Flynn
Maureen O'Hara
Anthony Quinn

Routine Flynn swashbuckler with Flynn as a dashing British officer challenging Caribbean pirate Quinn and romancing O'Hara. This is one of the last of Flynn's escapades, and he appears to wilt somewhat. With Mildred Natwick. **Director**—George Sherman. *85 minutes*

AGAINST ALL ODDS (1984)

★★1/2

Jeff Bridges
Rachel Ward

Jeff Bridges and Rachel Ward pursue romance Against All Odds.

A thick, incoherent plot trips up this steamy melodrama about a football player (Bridges) sent to track down the runaway mistress (Ward) of a big-time bookie. The story ranges from a torrid love affair in Mexico, to corruption, murder, and double crosses in Los Angeles. What worked brilliantly as a modestly produced 1940s *film noir* (*Out of the Past*) now looks overblown. Not a good bet. James Woods and Jane Greer costar. **Director**—Taylor Hackford. **(R)** *125 minutes*

AGATHA (1979)

★★1/2

Dustin Hoffman
Vanessa Redgrave

Mystery writer Agatha Christie disappeared for 11 days in 1926. This pointless film gives a fictional account of what happened during her absence. Redgrave turns in a crisp portrayal of the famous author. Hoffman provides a measure of humor in his role as an American journalist who traces Mrs. Christie to a health spa. But there's nothing to arouse much interest in the affair. Perhaps the real Agatha Christie would have come up with an exciting story. **Director**—Michael Apted. **(PG)** *98 minutes*

AGNES OF GOD (1985)

★★★

Meg Tilly
Jane Fonda
Anne Bancroft

Meg Tilly is the innocent young nun in Agnes of God.

Engrossing film adaptation of John Pielmeier's powerful Broadway play. It gleams with mystery, suspense, and above all, superb acting. Tilly is memorable as the angelic young nun accused of strangling the baby to whom she had secretly given birth in a convent. Fonda is the troubled court-appointed psychiatrist who tangles with a crusty mother superior (Bancroft) over concepts involving religious belief and scientific logic. **Director**—Norman Jewison. **(PG-13) Academy Award Nominations**—Bancroft, best actress; Tilly, best supporting actress. *98 minutes*

THE AGONY AND THE ECSTACY (1965)

★★1/2

Charlton Heston
Rex Harrison

Handsome but plodding story of Michelangelo's troubles while painting the Sistine Chapel at the urging of Pope Julius II. There are also some tiresome biographical references to the great artist's life and career. Unfortunately, there's more agony than ecstacy. Heston plays Michelangelo. Harrison plays the pontiff. With Diane Cilento and Harry Andrews. **Director**—Carol Reed. *140 minutes*

AIR FORCE (1943)

★★★

John Garfield
Gig Young
Arthur Kennedy

An effective and often exciting World War II bomber-crew saga despite its propaganda and flag-waving. Garfield, Young, and Kennedy are among the flyboys who fight the Japanese from Manila to the Coral Sea. Characterizations of the flyers are colorfully portrayed. Also stars Faye Emerson, Harry Carey, and Charles Drake. **Director**—Howard Hawks. *124 minutes b&w*

AIRPLANE! (1980)

★★★1/2

Robert Hays
Julie Hagerty
Peter Graves
Lloyd Bridges

Mel Brooks and Woody Allen have stiff competition from Jim Abrahams, David Zucker, and Jerry Zucker, who wrote and directed this laugh-a-minute broad-

(Continued)

(Continued)
side spoof of airplane dramas. Their first film was the unpolished comedy *Kentucky Fried Movie*. But this time they unleashed a torrent of effective gags with style and finesse. So fasten your seat belts, observe the "no smoking" sign, and settle back for hilarity galore. **(PG)** *88 minutes*

AIRPLANE II: THE SEQUEL (1982)

★★½

Robert Hays
Lloyd Bridges
William Shatner

This follow-up chapter, set in outer space, offers much of the good-natured charm and fun that enlivened the original spoof of disaster movies. Once again, we are on an ill-fated flight with an oddball assortment of passengers, crew, and ground controllers. The perky sight gags and wisecracks are a bit too familiar, but they still deliver an abundance of laughs. Julie Hagerty and Peter Graves are also on board to help the stars cope with incipient calamity. **Director**—Ken Finkleman. **(PG)** *85 minutes*

AIRPORT (1970)

★★★

Burt Lancaster
Dean Martin
Jean Seberg
Helen Hayes
Van Heflin

Dean Martin, the pilot, during a tense moment in Airport.

Slick, gripping melodrama based on Arthur Hailey's popular novel about a busy Midwest airport on a snowy night. Lancaster is the unflappable airport manager who keeps things in order during the efforts to land a damaged plane safely. Hayes stands out as the habitual and unlikely stowaway. There are also entertaining performances from George Kennedy and Martin. The cast also includes Jacqueline Bisset, Maureen Stapleton, Lloyd Nolan, and Barry Nelson. **Director**—George Seaton. **(G) Academy Award**—Hayes, best supporting actress. **Nominations**—best picture; Ernest Laszlo, cinematography; Seaton, best screenplay based on material from another medium. *137 minutes*

AIRPORT '77 (1977)

★★

Jack Lemmon
Lee Grant
Brenda Vaccaro
George Kennedy
James Stewart

The *Airport* theme is thoroughly exhausted in this third and mediocre all-star disaster film inspired by the Hailey novel. This time it's a private 747 jumbo jet, outfitted like a flying Holiday Inn, that crashes in the Atlantic Ocean and sinks in 100 feet of water. All sorts of standard harrowing episodes take place while waiting for the inevitable rescue by the U.S. Navy. Lemmon is out of place as the pilot. Darren McGavin, Olivia de Havilland, and Joseph Cotten also star. **Director**—Jerry Jameson. **(PG)** *113 minutes*

AIRPORT '79

See The Concorde—Airport '79

THE ALAMO (1960)

★★ ⓒ®

John Wayne
Richard Widmark
Laurence Harvey
Richard Boone

John Wayne as Col. Davy Crockett leads the futile defense of the famous fort against the onslaught of the Mexican army. The drawn-out film is often sidetracked with cliché-strewn subplots, and it seems to take forever to reach the spectacular final attack, which is the only exciting part of the film. Originally released at 199 minutes. With Frankie Avalon, Patrick Wayne, and Linda Cristal. **Director**—Wayne. **Academy Award Nominations**—best picture; Chill Wills, best supporting actor. *190 minutes*

ALAMO BAY (1985)

★★½ ⓒ®

Ed Harris
Amy Madigan

In Alamo Bay, *Amy Madigan is accused by Ed Harris of siding with the Vietnamese.*

Shallow, misguided, socially conscious film, by French director Louis Malle, about a bitter conflict between redneck Anglo shrimp fishermen and hard-working Vietnamese immigrants. The melodramatic story is based on actual events that took place in the late 1970s. An uneasy love story between a bitter and resentful fisherman and his old flame intrudes on the essential real-life situations. Ho Nguyen plays a young Vietnamese who stands up to his tormentors. **(R)** *105 minutes*

AL CAPONE (1959)

★★★

Rod Steiger
Fay Spain
Martin Balsam

Rod Steiger portrays the famous gangster in Al Capone.

Steiger is ideally cast as the ruthless gangster chieftain in this better-than-average biography. Steiger's excellent, energetic performance is enhanced by

ⓒ® *This movie available with closed captions for the hearing impaired.*

fine support from Spain and Balsam. The documentary-like account follows Capone's Prohibition days in Chicago up to his imprisonment for income-tax evasion. Also with Murvyn Vye, Nehemiah Persoff, and James Gregory. **Director**—Richard Wilson.

105 minutes b&w

ALEXANDER NEVSKY (1938)

★★★★

Nikolai Cherkassov
Nicolai Okhlopkov

A masterpiece by director Sergei Eisenstein, this historical epic is one of the greatest Russian films of all time. The Soviets had found in Eisenstein an impassioned artist and film theorist whose works, which often posed the Russian masses as hero, were powerful both emotionally and as propaganda. Although he had fallen into disfavor with the government in the 1930s, he was summoned to serve his country when the Nazis loomed as a great threat in the years preceding World War II. In *Nevsky,* Cherkassov portrays a 13th-century Russian prince who unifies the nation to stave off Teutonic invaders. Features a breathtaking battle on the ice, Sergei Prokofiev's original score, and superb photography by Edward Tisse. Different prints may vary in length. *112 minutes b&w*

ALEX AND THE GYPSY (1976)

★

Jack Lemmon
Geneviève Bujold

Lemmon looks tired and unappealing in this cynical and grubby film about the torturous relationship between a bailbondsman and a gypsy woman. Bujold, as the gypsy, isn't much help either. They scream a lot, fight a lot, and roam about the countryside. It's all a rather numbing experience. Also with James Woods. **Director**—John Korty. **(R)**

99 minutes

ALFIE (1966)

★★★1/2

Michael Caine
Vivien Merchant
Shelley Winters

Caine's career got a big boost from his superb performance as a carefree, womanizing cockney. The film, based on Bill Naughton's play, also is noted for its frank treatment of sex. Winters and Merchant heighten the interest with no-nonsense performances as the objects of Alfie's affections. Alas, Alfie is shaken from his fancy-free lifestyle by a near-crisis. Also with Millicent Martin, Shirley Anne Field, and Denholm Elliott. **Director**—Lewis Gilbert. **Academy Award Nominations**—best picture; Caine, best actor; Merchant, best supporting actress; Naughton, best screenplay based on material from another medium. *114 minutes*

ALGIERS (1938)

★★★

Charles Boyer
Sigrid Gurie
Hedy Lamarr

Welcome to the Casbah—the twisting alleyways through which criminals and love affairs pass like fleeting shadows. This Hollywood amalgam of foreign intrigue and foreign players (French-born Boyer; Viennese Lamarr, making her American film debut; and Gurie, the Brooklyn-born, Norway-reared "Siren of the Fjords," launching in 1938 a still-born career) was a surprisingly successful remake of the French sensation *Pépé Le Moko*, produced only one year earlier. The starring role of the amorous crook who plays cat-and-mouse games with North African police solidified Boyer's career as a romantic star in much the same way it served Jean Gabin in the original version. Still eminently entertaining. The great cinematographer James Wong Howe received an Academy Award nomination for his work on this picture. **Director**—John Cromwell. **Academy Award Nominations**—Boyer, best actor; Gene Lockhart, best supporting actor.

95 minutes b&w

ALIAS JESSE JAMES (1959)

★★★

Bob Hope
Rhonda Fleming
Jim Davis

Only Hope could sell an insurance policy to the notorious outlaw, and he claims a lot of laughs in the process. It's a typically funny vehicle for him as a lot of gags hit the mark. Fleming plays a pretty lass who does a pleasant singing number with Hope. There's an uproariously funny ending with cameos by many famous Hollywood cowboys. **Director**—Norman McLeod.

92 minutes

ALIAS NICK BEAL (1949)

★★★

Ray Milland
Thomas Mitchell

An upstanding politician almost sells his soul to the Devil in this on-target, latter-day version of Faust. Satisfying performances from sinister Milland as the Devil's disciple promising money and power, and Mitchell as the vulnerable district attorney who nearly accepts the deal. Efficient direction helps to bring the fantasy into sharp focus. Other good performances by Audrey Totter and George Macready. **Director**—John Farrow. *93 minutes b&w*

ALICE ADAMS (1935)

★★★

Katharine Hepburn
Fred MacMurray
Fred Stone

Based on a lovely piece of Americana by Booth Tarkington, the film was a big hit for Hepburn, whose career was starting to flounder, and a major step up in prestige for director George Stevens. A small-town adolescent, yearning to be accepted by her blue-blooded peers, pines over her family's lack of means and her father's lack of ambition. It's a successful blend of humor, tears, and insight, best represented by the famous dinner scene, in which Alice invites her beau over, and everything seems to go wrong. Evelyn Venable, Charles Grapewin, Ann Shoemaker, Hedda Hopper, and Hattie McDaniel are among the fine supporting players. **Academy Award Nominations**—best picture; Hepburn, best actress.

99 minutes b&w

ALICE DOESN'T LIVE HERE ANYMORE (1974)

★★★★

Ellen Burstyn
Alfred Lutter
Kris Kristofferson

Burstyn won an Oscar for her warm, funny, and energetic portrayal of a poor widow who learns to survive by her wits. She's broke, she has to care for her

(Continued)

Diane Ladd and Ellen Burstyn in Alice Doesn't Live Here Anymore.

(Continued)

young son, and she wants to be a singer. Kristofferson also performs well as the new man in her life. The slice-of-life theme is somewhat of a cliché, but director Martin Scorsese adds vivid dimensions with a poignant reflection of contemporary America. With Jodie Foster. **(PG) Academy Award**—Burstyn, best actress. **Nominations**—Diane Ladd, best supporting actress; Robert Getchell, best original screenplay.

113 minutes

ALICE'S RESTAURANT (1969)

★★★

Arlo Guthrie
Pat Quinn

Folksinger Guthrie's popular song inspired this satirical melodrama about the freewheeling lifestyle of the 1960s. The theme is rather flimsy, but director Arthur Penn succeeds in wringing charm, energy, and comedy from the material. Guthrie, who does quite well in his film debut, is especially funny in a scene where he is briefly inducted into the U.S. Army. With James Broderick and Michael McClanathan. **(PG) Academy Award Nomination**—Penn, best director. *111 minutes*

ALIEN (1979)

★★★1/2

Tom Skerritt
Sigourney Weaver
John Hurt

The crew of a cargo-carrying spaceship, on a return voyage to Earth, encounters a terrible monster. It's an effective horror film with impressive and scary special effects that should send you away with your knees knocking. But it's familiar stuff, with elements of *Star Wars, The Exorcist,* and *Jaws* blended into the script, which dangles many loose ends. The small cast does a good job, especially Weaver. Also with Ian Holm, Harry Dean Stanton, and Yaphet Kotto. **Director**—Ridley Scott. **(R)**

117 minutes

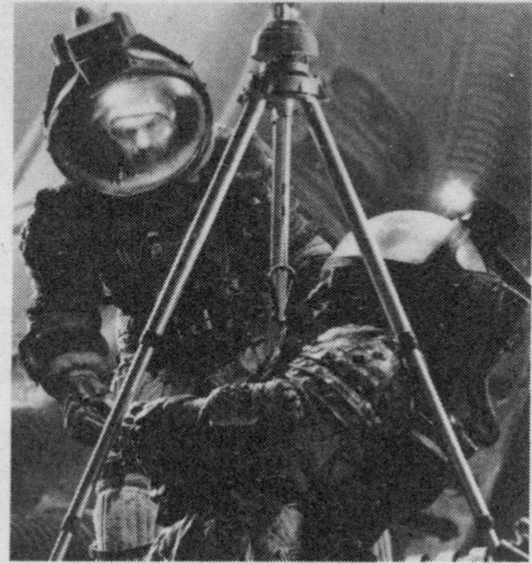

Tom Skerritt watches as John Hurt goes into an underground chamber in Alien.

ALIEN NATION (1988)

★★1/2

James Caan
Mandy Patinkin

This clever sci-fi idea revolves around two policemen: One (Caan) is an American, the other (Patinkin) is an alien. The story deals with the issue of racial equality, among other themes. The film does not live up to its initial intriguing intentions and lapses into a standard cop/buddy action-thriller with strong doses of violence and gunplay. Also with Terence Stamp. **Director**—Graham Baker. **(R)** *96 minutes*

ALIENS (1986)

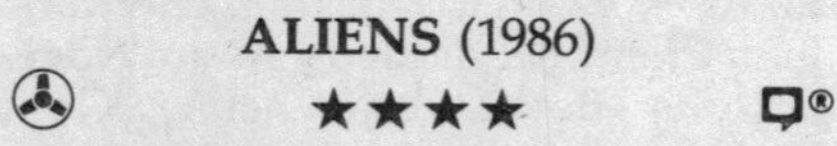

★★★★

Sigourney Weaver
Michael Biehn
Carrie Henn

Breathtaking sequel to Ridley Scott's stylish 1979 horror/science-fiction tale. Here director James Cameron *(The Terminator)* approaches the film as a sci-fi adventure, emphasizing nonstop action over the atmosphere and visual splendor of the original. Weaver returns as Warrant Officer Ripley—the only human survivor of the events of *Alien*—who has been adrift in space for over 50 years. After she is found, she is recruited to return to the planet that hosts the aliens—now colonized—to discover why all radio contact has been lost with the settlement. With her are a group of rough Marines and a representative of the company whose workers settled the planet. As in Cameron's *The Terminator,* it is again a woman—Ripley—who emerges as the ultimate hero. Excellent craftsmanship and state-of-the-art special and mechanical effects enhance the storyline to produce one of cinema's most relentlessly tense and exciting science-fiction films. Also with Paul Reiser, Lance Henricksen, Jenette Goldstein, and Bill Paxton. **(R) Academy Awards**—Robert Skotak, Stan Winston, John Richardson, and Suzanne Benson, best visual effects; Don Sharpe, best sound effects editing. **Nominations**—Weaver, best actress; Ray Lovejoy, best editing; Peter Lamont, art direction. *138 minutes*

ALL ABOUT EVE (1950)

★★★★

Bette Davis
George Sanders
Anne Baxter

This biting backstage comedy/drama about a fading actress, played by Davis, brims generously with entertainment values: a witty screenplay, top performances by a marvelous cast, and nononsense direction. Davis gives a memorable, bitchy performance as the aging Broadway star who is menaced by an overreaching younger actress played by Baxter. One of the best films ever made about the legitimate theater. **Director**—Joseph L. Mankiewicz. **Academy Awards**—best picture; Mankiewicz, best director and screenplay; Sanders, best supporting actor. **Nominations**—Baxter and Davis, best actress; Celeste Holm and Thelma Ritter, best supporting actress. *138 minutes b&w*

ALLAN QUATERMAIN AND THE LOST CITY OF GOLD (1987)

★

Richard Chamberlain
James Earl Jones
Sharon Stone

A bargain-basement clone of Steven Spielberg's *Indiana Jones and the Temple of Doom* that is filled to the brim with traps, snakes, and spear-carrying natives. The plot is as familiar and shabby as the special effects: The stalwart title character (Chamberlain) and his entourage crash through the jungle to find his missing brother, stumbling over the

This movie available with closed captions for the hearing impaired.

dumb dialogue en route to the legendary city. A filmed tour of Disneyland would have been more interesting. **Director**—Gary Nelson. **(PG)**
103 minutes

ALL FALL DOWN (1962)

★★½

Warren Beatty
Brandon De Wilde
Angela Lansbury

Eva Marie Saint and Warren Beatty in All Fall Down.

A generally well acted-drama about a spirited young man, played by Beatty, who falls in love with an older woman—Eva Marie Saint—and then causes her death. Unfortunately, the screenplay is rather farfetched and isn't redeemed by the good performances. The cast includes Karl Malden. **Director**—John Frankenheimer.
110 minutes b&w

ALLIGATOR (1980)

★★★

Robert Forster
Robin Riker

A baby pet alligator is flushed into a city sewer system and emerges 12 years later to devour some local citizens. At the outset, the film smacks of just another absurd horror picture, but director Lewis Teague quickly lays on the style and excitement. There are polished special effects, a clever script by John Sayles, and capable performances from Forster and Riker. This reptile isn't a match for the shark in *Jaws*, but it does have plenty of bite. Also with Henry Silva, Jack Carter, and Dean Jagger in small roles. **(R)** *95 minutes*

ALL DOGS GO TO HEAVEN (1989)

★★½

Not much bark or bite exists in this animated feature produced and directed by Don Bluth, who scored a hit in 1986 with *An American Tail*. Charlie, a junkyard dog with a criminal past, is killed by his greedy employer, Carface. Charlie goes to heaven but returns to Earth to retrieve the pocket watch that controls his life. Along the way, he and his canine cronies help an orphaned girl. Burt Reynolds provides the voice of Charlie and even sings several songs, though not too well. The story, which is a variation of *Little Miss Marker*, was criticized heavily by reviewers at the time of release for being clumsy and ragged. Though adults may be disappointed in the story, the forgettable songs, and the inconsistent quality of the animation, children will enjoy the colorful characters whose voices are provided by Dom DeLuise, Judith Barsi, Vic Tayback, Ken Page, Melba Moore, and Charles Nelson Reilly. **(G)** *85 minutes*

ALL MY SONS (1948)

★★★

Edward G. Robinson
Burt Lancaster

This film version of Arthur Miller's play about family conflicts is generally compelling, although it occasionally lacks conviction. A young man is shaken when he discovers that his wealthy father sold defective equipment to the military during World War II. Fine performances from Robinson, Lancaster, and Howard Duff. **Director**—Irving Reis. *94 minutes b&w*

THE ALLNIGHTER (1987)

★

Susanna Hoffs
Joan Cusack
Dedee Pfeiffer

Rock singer Susanna Hoffs of the Bangles stars in this trite romantic comedy about a college coed looking for that one "significant romance." The night before graduation, she makes a last-ditch effort to land the man of her dreams. Pfeiffer and Cusack costar as Hoff's two wacky roommates in this dreary attempt to cash in on Hoffs' youthful appeal. The film combines a college backdrop with the conventions of a beach movie, resulting in some out-of-place surfing scenes and ridiculous characters. Directed by Hoffs' mother, Tamar Simon Hoffs. **(PG–13)**
95 minutes

ALL NIGHT LONG (1981)

★½

Barbra Streisand
Gene Hackman

A futile attempt at contemporary comedy that awkwardly deals with the numbing side effects of corporate life. Superstar Streisand, as a seductive housewife, takes second billing. She is sadly miscast without a song or the verve to carry off a zany portrayal. Only Hackman, who plays a deflated chain-store executive, breathes some life into this shallow and silly story. Originally released at 88 minutes. **Director**—Jean-Claude Tramont. **(R)** *100 minutes*

ALL OF ME (1984)

★★★

Steve Martin
Lily Tomlin

Martin and Tomlin are an engaging team in this wacky frolic that harks back to the screwball comedies of the 1930s. Martin plays a frustrated lawyer whose body is inadvertently inhabited by the soul of an abrasive and wealthy spinster (Tomlin). This frustrating state of affairs leads to genuinely funny shenanigans, although Martin's physical gags are occasionally awkward. The film is graced with delightful supporting players, including Richard Libertini and Jason Bernard. **Director**—Carl Reiner. **(PG)** *93 minutes*

ALL QUIET ON THE WESTERN FRONT (1930)

★★★★

Lew Ayres
Louis Wolheim
Slim Summerville

Despite dated moments, this powerful film about young German soldiers fighting in the trenches on the Western Front during World War I remains a classic. Director Lewis Milestone presents the pacifist novel of Erich Maria Remarque in a vivid and realistic

(Continued)

(Continued)
manner. Originally released at 140 minutes. **Academy Awards**—best picture; Milestone, best director. **Nomination**—George Abbott, Maxwell Anderson, and Dell Andrews, screenplay.
103 minutes b&w

ALL THAT HEAVEN ALLOWS (1955)

Jane Wyman
Rock Hudson

Wyman and Hudson star in this slack and predictable soap opera about a widow who becomes involved with a younger man and is ostracized by her friends. Although the film reunites the stars of *Magnificent Obsession* and has a similar style, it doesn't work as well as the earlier film. Agnes Moorehead, Virginia Grey, and Conrad Nagel costar. **Director**—Douglas Sirk. *89 minutes*

ALL THAT JAZZ (1979)

 ★★★

Roy Scheider
Jessica Lange
Ann Reinking

Director Bob Fosse's autobiographical movie is the ultimate backstage drama—a masterpiece of dance, ego, and soul. It's the story of a self-destructive Broadway director/choreographer (Scheider) and his loves, obsession with work, and ultimate disintegration. Despite the adolescent shallowness of the central character, the overall production is completely absorbing. Fosse's breathtaking dance numbers are brilliantly staged, and Scheider's performance is outstanding. Leland Palmer, Cliff Gorman, and Ben Vereen costar. **(R) Academy Award Nominations**—best picture; Fosse, best director; Scheider, best actor; Robert Alan Aurthur and Fosse, best screenplay written directly for the screen. *123 minutes*

ALL THE BROTHERS WERE VALIANT (1953)

Stewart Granger
Robert Taylor

Granger and Taylor star in this soggy adventure, which is based on Ben Ames Williams' novel of sibling rivalry between two stubborn whaling sailors. Trouble ensues when one brother decides to shun blubber and hunt for treasure. There's lots of action, but the acting is below par. Ann Blyth costars as the wife of one brother, and she adds to the tension on board ship. **Director**—Richard Thorpe. *101 minutes*

ALL THE KING'S MEN (1949)

Broderick Crawford
John Ireland
Mercedes McCambridge
Joanne Dru

Mercedes McCambridge, John Ireland, and Broderick Crawford in All the King's Men.

A gripping, high-powered drama about political corruption in Louisiana, based on the career of Huey Long. The film is fleshed out with colorful detail and background. Most notable is the electrifying portrayal by Crawford as the honest small-town politician who is elected governor and is eventually overwhelmed by power. Commanding support from McCambridge, Ireland, and Dru. **Director**—Robert Rossen. **Academy Awards**—best picture; Crawford, best actor; McCambridge, best supporting actress. **Nominations**—Rossen, best director and screenplay; Ireland, best supporting actor. *109 minutes b&w*

...ALL THE MARBLES (1981)

 ★★½

Peter Falk

Director Robert Aldrich serves up pure and delectable Hollywood schmaltz with this rousing action/comedy about female wrestlers. Falk is excellent as the hustling manager of "The California Dolls," two young combatants, played by Vicki Frederick and Laurene Landon, who progress from tank-town matches to a championship bout in Reno's MGM Grand Hotel. The film offers good comic dialogue, appealing characterizations, a thrilling finale, and the "Dolls"—two gorgeous ladies who can act as well as wrestle. **(R)**
112 minutes

ALL THE PRESIDENT'S MEN (1976)

Robert Redford
Dustin Hoffman
Jason Robards

The Watergate scandal comes into sharp focus and takes on a new dimension in this spellbinding film adaptation of Carl Bernstein's and Bob Woodward's best-selling book. It's a thriller from beginning to end and breathlessly entertaining. The exciting day-by-day account of how the two young *Washington Post* reporters conducted their investigation is portrayed in fast-paced, true-to-life documentary style through the direction of Alan Pakula. Acting by the entire cast is spectacular. Redford as Woodward and Hoffman as Bernstein perform with perfection. Robards gives what may be his finest performance as *Post* editor Ben Bradlee. Cast includes Hal Holbrook, Jack Warden, and Martin Balsam. **(PG) Academy Awards**—Robards, best supporting actor; William Goldman, best screenplay adaptation. **Nominations**—best picture; Pakula, best director; Jane Alexander, best supporting actress. *138 minutes*

ALL THE RIGHT MOVES (1983)

  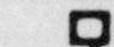

Tom Cruise

Cruise stars as an ambitious high-school football star who longs to escape life in an economically depressed mill town (à la *Flashdance*) by winning an athletic scholarship. The dank, depressing atmosphere of the dying community is realistically portrayed. Yet characters and their situations are not sufficiently compelling or convincing. A few wrong moves deflate the story's appeal. Also with Craig T. Nelson and Lea Thompson. **Director**—Michael Chapman. **(R)** *91 minutes*

ALL THE YOUNG MEN (1960)

Alan Ladd
Sidney Poitier

Standard war yarn about a Marine unit in Korea that has to deal with internal

® This movie available with closed captions for the hearing impaired.

tension as well as the enemy. Among the stereotypical situations is the problem of a black who is challenged because of his race when he takes command. Other clichés and platitudes abound. Also with Glenn Corbett, Ingemar Johansson, James Darren, and Mort Sahl. **Director**—Hall Bartlett.

87 minutes b&w

ALL THINGS BRIGHT AND BEAUTIFUL (1979)

★★★

John Alderton
Lisa Harrow
Colin Blakely

A gentle, mildly amusing family film based on the best-selling memoirs of Dr. James Herriott, the Yorkshire veterinarian. Alderton plays the young vet with likable charm; Harrow plays his wife. Alderton tends to a variety of animal illnesses and the anxieties of the animal owners. The story isn't very dramatic, except for a short graphic scene of the birth of a calf; but it should appeal to most. Blakely is fine as a cantankerous older veterinarian who takes Herriott as a partner. **Director**—Eric Till. **(G)** *94 minutes*

ALL THIS AND HEAVEN TOO (1940)

Charles Boyer
Bette Davis

Bette Davis is loved by a murderer in All This and Heaven Too.

Boyer and Davis star in this somewhat stretched but well-made period melodrama, based on the Rachel Field novel, about a French nobleman who murders his wife after he falls in love with his children's governess. The elaborate story, set in the 19th century, is rather on the weepy side, but the acting has style and class. Barbara O'Neil, Virginia Weidler, and Jeffrey Lynn costar. **Director**—Anatole Litvak. **Academy Award Nominations**—best picture; O'Neil, best supporting actress.

143 minutes b&w

ALL THROUGH THE NIGHT (1942)

★★★

Humphrey Bogart
Peter Lorre
Conrad Veidt

Bogart and Lorre team up in this entertaining spy caper set in New York City during World War II. Bogey's underworld gang helps the Feds nail some enemy agents. There are shades of wartime propaganda, but it's good fun nevertheless, with just the right touch of comedy. A young Jackie Gleason and Phil Silvers are among the cast. **Director**—Vincent Sherman.

107 minutes b&w

ALOHA SUMMER (1988)

★★

Chris Makepeace
Yuji Okumoto
Don Michael Paul

A listless sand-and-surf movie set against the lush backdrop of Hawaii in the summer of 1959. Six young men of various ethnic backgrounds become instant friends and, predictably, chase girls, ride the waves, and fight with their parents. Some interracial incidents add tension to the unimaginative story, but it's not enough to sustain momentum. The film's highlight is a demonstration of the martial art of kendo, a form of sword fighting, choreographed by Sho Kosugi. Kosugi, star of many ninja warrior films, also appears as the father of one of the boys. **Director**—Tommy Lee Wallace. **(PG)**

97 minutes

AN ALMOST PERFECT AFFAIR (1979)

Keith Carradine
Monica Vitti

The Cannes Film Festival is the backdrop to this satirical romance between a young American filmmaker, played by Carradine, and the wife of an Italian movie mogul, played by Vitti. Director Michael Ritchie handles the hoopla of the film festival with style and imagination, but the love story is essentially farfetched and rather uninteresting. There are some spirited performances, though, by the entire cast, which also includes Raf Vallone and Dick Anthony Williams. **(PG)** *93 minutes*

ALONE IN THE DARK (1982)

★★

Jack Palance
Donald Pleasence

Erland Van Lidth in the suspense thriller Alone in the Dark.

Under cover of a power blackout, homicidal maniacs break out of a mental hospital to terrorize the family of the institution's newly hired psychiatrist. The film is a cut above the typical horror schlock, and the suspense builds to an effective crescendo. Despite the fact that the story works well, the film is eventually undermined by excessive and ghastly bloodletting. Palance stars as the leading lunatic, and Pleasence plays the head psychiatrist (who appears to be as crazy as his patients). **Director**—Jack Sholder. **(R)**

92 minutes

ALONG CAME JONES (1945)

★★★

Gary Cooper
Loretta Young
Dan Duryea

Cooper turned producer to let screenwriter Nunnally Johnson have fun with the star's straight-shooting image. The result is a sweet and winsome comedy/western about a milquetoast who's mis-

(Continued)

(Continued)
taken for a wanted outlaw and grows to like the quaking respect he earns as a presumed bad guy. Along the way, he mixes it up with a trigger-happy cowgirl and the dreaded villain he's impersonating. Also with William Frawley and Melody Jones. **Director**—Stuart Heisler. *90 minutes b&w*

ALONG THE GREAT DIVIDE (1951)

Kirk Douglas
Virginia Mayo

Walter Brennan, Virginia Mayo, and Kirk Douglas in Along the Great Divide.

Lawman Douglas saves an innocent man from the noose and nabs the real criminal despite a desert storm in this so-so western/drama. The film has some spectacular scenery. John Agar, Ray Teal, and Walter Brennan round out the cast. **Director**—Raoul Walsh. *88 minutes b&w*

ALPHA BETA (1973)

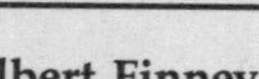

Albert Finney
Rachel Roberts

Moving and searing performances by Finney and Roberts in this filmed play about a failed, English working-class marriage. The entire cast is from the original London stage company. The film is divided into three acts to dramatically emphasize the stages of the breakup and the accumulation of the agony. The experience may be too morose and exhausting for some, but an experience it is indeed. **Director**—Anthony Page. **(No MPAA rating)** *67 minutes*

ALPHABET CITY (1984)

Vincent Spano
Kate Vernon
Michael Winslow

Spano rises above the thin material of this crime melodrama. He's an up-and-coming gangster operating amid the illicit drug community of New York City's Lower East Side. The film manages some artistic attempts at revealing the mean streets and inner-city background, but the script is as shabby as the story's environment. **Director**—Amos Poe. **(R)** *98 minutes*

ALPHAVILLE (1965)

★★★

Eddie Constantine
Anna Karina
Akim Tamiroff

The French New Wave was still new and full of exciting promise, and the career of director Jean-Luc Godard, perhaps its foremost representative, was in high gear when he made this heady piece of existential science fiction. It's partly about a private eye who travels to a futurist society where emotions are banned and who teaches the meaning of love to the daughter of a renegade scientist. It's also about moviemaking, contemporary society, and struggles between the brain and the heart. Constantine, an expatriate American who was popular in France as pulp-film detective Lemmy Caution, stars in that role and Karina, the former Mrs. Godard, plays the soulless, soulful-eyed heroine. Originally filmed in French. *100 minutes b&w*

ALTERED STATES (1980)

★★1/2

William Hurt
Blair Brown

Director Ken Russell's mind-blowing, psychedelic monster-movie begins with mystery and exhilaration and ends as mere preposterous mumbo jumbo. Hurt is cast as a young psychophysiologist who alters his consciousness to the point of changing himself temporarily into an apelike creature. Russell lays on dazzling visual displays to create an outrageous hallucinogenic effect. Then the film falls apart when it urges viewers to accept as reality what can only be taken as visionary. Also with Charles Haid. **(R)** *102 minutes*

ALWAYS (1989)

★★★

Richard Dreyfuss
Holly Hunter
John Goodman
Audrey Hepburn

In Always, *Holly Hunter falls in love with the young pilot, Brad Johnson.*

Steven Spielberg based this romantic fantasy on the 1943 drama *A Guy Named Joe*, which starred Spencer Tracy and Van Johnson. The story has been transformed from World War II to modern times, with fire-fighting pilots replacing bomber fliers as the principal characters. Dreyfuss stars in the Tracy role as an experienced pilot who dies in a crash while trying to save his best friend, played by Goodman. He returns to Earth to pass on his expertise to a novice pilot and to help girlfriend Hunter get on with her life. Dreyfuss finds it difficult to let go of his feelings as he witnesses Hunter and the young pilot fall in love. Spielberg's attempt at an adult drama resulted in mixed reviews at the time of its release, but word of mouth turned the slow-paced romance into a moderate box-office success. Though a simple story on the surface, the film makes excellent use of lighting and set design to convey mood and enhance meaning. Hepburn returns to the screen in a small role as Dreyfuss' guardian angel. Also with Brad Johnson. **(PG)** *121 minutes*

ALWAYS LEAVE THEM LAUGHING (1949)

Milton Berle
Bert Lahr

This movie available with closed captions for the hearing impaired.

Berle plays himself as a stand-up comedian on the rocky road to success. Berle, along with Lahr, hams it up delightfully for a few yuks, but the film falters somewhat when it dwells on sentimental stuff. At times, Lahr upstages the cocky Berle. You'll laugh—but not always. Virginia Mayo, Ruth Roman, and Alan Hale costar. **Director**—Roy Del Ruth. *116 minutes b&w*

AMADEUS (1984)

★★★★

Tom Hulce
F. Murray Abraham

Opulent, magnificent adaptation of Peter Shaffer's play featuring Mozart as a vulgar, clownish musical prodigy (Hulce) who arouses envy in the mediocre 18th-century composer Antonio Salieri (Abraham). The stunning film shines in all departments: inspired acting, detailed period settings, Milos Forman's brilliant direction, and the soaring score of Mozart's great music. A grand celebration of genius. The film won eight Oscars out of 11 nominations. **(PG) Academy Awards**—best picture; Forman, best director; Abraham, best actor; Peter Shaffer, best screenplay based on material from another medium. **Nomination**—Hulce, best actor. *158 minutes*

AMARCORD (1974)

★★★★

Magali Noel
Bruno Zanin

Amarcord presents a nostalgic view of Italian life in the 1930s.

Famed Italian director Federico Fellini takes a nostalgic stroll to the Italy of his youth. At times the movie may seem slow, but the beautiful photography and the poignant scenes of the lifestyles in 1930s Italy as Fellini confronts Italian fascism make this worthwhile viewing. Solid acting performances reflect Fellini's directing skills. Originally filmed in Italian. **(No MPAA rating) Academy Award**—best foreign-language film. *127 minutes*

THE AMATEUR (1982)

★★★

John Savage
Christopher Plummer
Marthe Keller

The thick plot of this international spy thriller strains credibility, but it never loses its grip. Savage portrays a CIA code expert who seeks revenge on the terrorists who killed his girlfriend. Excitement, intrigue, double crosses, and sinister encounters heighten the flavor of the exotic tale. Handsome cinematography contributes to the film's professional flair. **Director**—Charles Jarrott. **(R)** *111 minutes*

AMAZING GRACE AND CHUCK (1987)

★★

Joshua Zuehlke
Jamie Lee Curtis

Chuck, a star Little League pitcher, gives up baseball as a protest against nuclear arms. He is joined in his efforts by Boston Celtics star Amazing Grace Smith and other professional athletes, resulting in a sort of athletes' strike for peace. Though obviously well intentioned, the film soon turns silly and preposterous, especially when the President and the Soviet Premier rush to Montana to deal with Chuck's incredible powers of persuasion. An effective cast, including Denver Nuggets star Alex English as Amazing Grace, adds some interest but can't overcome the naive storyline. Also with Gregory Peck and William L. Petersen. **Director**—Mike Newell. **(PG)** *115 minutes*

AMAZON WOMEN ON THE MOON (1987)

★★

Rosanna Arquette
Ralph Bellamy
Griffin Dunne

This anthology of bawdy blackout sketches satirizes the type of programming found on off-hours TV. Among the targets are bad science-fiction movies, telethons, the contemporary dating scene, and TV advertising. Assembled much like John Landis' *Kentucky Fried Movie*, this frantic comedy involves the efforts of five directors, including Landis. Some of the gags are clever and inspired but the majority fall flat, perhaps because actual television programming is often so outrageous as to be beyond parody. Also with Henny Youngman, Steve Allen, Angel Tompkins, and Russ Meyer. **Directors**—Joe Dante, Carl Gottlieb, Peter Horton, Robert K. Weiss, and Landis. **(R)** *85 minutes*

AMBUSH (1949)

★★

Robert Taylor
John Hodiak
Arlene Dahl

A routine western with the U.S. Cavalry led by an army scout looking for an Apache chief who has kidnapped a white woman. There's some rousing action, helped along by the talents of Taylor, Hodiak, and Dahl. This was the last film by director Sam Wood, a competent but unappreciated craftsman. *89 minutes b&w*

AMERICAN ANTHEM (1986)

★★

Mitch Gaylord
Janet Jones
Michelle Phillips

Janet Jones and Mitch Gaylord flex to the American Anthem.

Champion gymnast Gaylord stars in this sports drama about a striving ath-

(Continued)

(Continued)
lete who overcomes his personal problems with his father. The formula scenario, about a talented rising star unable to gain the respect of his father, is all too familiar by now. Directed by Albert Magnoli, this tedious drama features virtually the same plot as Magnoli's earlier film *Purple Rain,* but without the exciting music or the magnetism of a performer such as Prince. There could be some appeal here for fans of gymnasts, as the stars go through a number of well-choreographed workouts, but for others, all the tumbling and twisting set against an earsplitting rock score will be overbearing. **(PG–13)** *100 minutes*

AMERICAN DREAMER (1984)

 ★★ ®

JoBeth Williams
Tom Conti
Giancarlo Giannini

JoBeth Williams and Tom Conti are kept hanging in American Dreamer.

Slightly bored American housewife (Williams) wins a trip to Paris in a mystery-writing contest. She soon finds herself embroiled in adventure and intrigue under similar circumstances as her fictional heroine. It begins like *Romancing the Stone,* but it becomes rather tame with the direction and script stumbling about. The thriller/farce bogs down in corny slapstick situations that sabotage the effervescent efforts of Williams. **Director**—Rick Rosenthal. **(PG)** *104 minutes*

AMERICAN FLYERS (1985)

 ★★ ®

Kevin Costner
David Grant

Pretentious sports-action film about bicycle-racing competition and family conflicts. The story involves two brothers, played by Costner and Grant, who participate in a grueling bike race in the Rocky Mountains. Their adequate performances cannot overcome the contrived action scenes or the strained presentation of sibling rivalry. Also with Rae Dawn Chong and Alexandra Paul. **Director**—John Badham. **(PG–13)** *114 minutes*

David Grant and Kevin Costner are the hard-pedaling American Flyers.

THE AMERICAN FRIEND (1977)

★★★★

Dennis Hopper
Bruno Ganz
Lisa Kreuzer

This stylish psychological thriller by German director Wim Wenders packs tension that's typical of an Alfred Hitchcock film. Hopper, in the title role, plays a rogue who persuades a man, who is convinced he's dying from a rare disease, to become a paid killer. There is high-level acting by a colorful cast. Also with Nicholas Ray. Action was filmed in Hamburg, Paris, and New York City. Originally filmed in German, French, and English. **(No MPAA rating)** *127 minutes*

AMERICAN GIGOLO (1980)

 ★★1/2

Richard Gere
Lauren Hutton

This melodrama about a high-class male prostitute is a film dressed up in fancy duds for a trip to the corner drugstore. The atmosphere is sleek and plush, but the story needs some zip. Gere in the title role is impressive as a hustler who takes a cynical, businesslike attitude toward the older women he services. However, we never know what really makes him tick. Director Paul Schrader, who wrote and directed *Hardcore,* continues with this film to pursue his obsession with exposing moral degradation. **(R)** *117 minutes*

AMERICAN GRAFFITI (1973)

★★★★

Richard Dreyfuss
Ron Howard
Paul Le Mat

Cindy Williams and Ron Howard are typical '60s teenagers in American Graffiti.

An accurate and moving portrait of American youth culture shown through the experiences of some high-school seniors on the eve of leaving for college or military service in the early 1960s. The plot is episodic in structure, and this landmark film sparkles with nostalgic atmosphere and hilarious dialogue. The story involves a memorable night of chasing girls, racing cars, harassing the cops, and hanging out at the local drive-in restaurant. The production enhanced the career of director George Lucas. Cast also includes Cindy Williams, Charles Martin Smith, and Candy Clark. You should also spot Harrison Ford and Suzanne Somers. **(PG) Academy Award Nominations**—best picture; Lucas, best director; Clark, best supporting actress; Lucas, Gloria Katz, and Willard Huyck, best story and screenplay based on factual material or material not previously published. *110 minutes*

AMERICAN HOT WAX (1978)

★★1/2

Tim McIntire
Fran Drescher

® *This movie available with closed captions for the hearing impaired.*

Rock 'n' roll music of the 1950s pours forth at full volume in this nostalgic film that depicts the rise and fall of disc jockey Alan Freed. But the plot comes on at a whisper, with no point of view and little insight into that period of youthful defiance. Fans of Chuck Berry, Jerry Lee Lewis, *et al.* may find this film of interest. Also with Jay Leno, Laraine Newman, and John Lehne. **Director**—Floyd Mutrux. **(PG)** *91 minutes*

AN AMERICAN IN PARIS (1951)

★★★★

Gene Kelly
Leslie Caron
Oscar Levant
Nina Foch

A vivacious, glittering musical blessed with the amazing choreography of Kelly and based on the music of George and Ira Gershwin. There's a simple romantic plot about an ex-GI, played by Kelly, who settles in Paris to be an artist and falls for a gamine, played by Caron. But it's really the showstopping dance and music sequences that make the film a fabulous hit. It's one of the best musicals of this golden era. **Director**—Vincente Minnelli. **Academy Awards**—best picture; Alan Jay Lerner, story and screenplay. **Nomination**—Minnelli, best director. *113 minutes*

THE AMERICANIZATION OF EMILY (1964)

 ★★★

Julie Andrews
James Garner

Garner and Andrews star in this unusual black comedy about an American naval officer who procures luxuries for the top brass. Paddy Chayefsky's poignant screenplay, based on William Bradford Huie's novel, is effective in its antiwar point of view. Andrews is excellent as a British war widow who perceives the officer's cowardice but falls in love with him just the same. Includes Melvyn Douglas, James Coburn, and Joyce Grenfell. **Director**—Arthur Hiller. *117 minutes b&w*

AMERICAN JUSTICE (1986)

 ★★

Jameson Parker
Gerald McRaney
Jack Lucarelli

This routine and predictable police melodrama, set along the American-Mexican border, pits honest cops against corrupt cops who are exploiting illegal aliens. The story drips with clichés, stock characters, and pedestrian dialogue that seem more at home in a soon-to-be-cancelled TV series—which is not surprising since stars Parker and McRaney gained recognition on the series *Simon and Simon.* Countless shoot-outs and eyeball-to-eyeball confrontations are used to jazz up the pace, but the results are shallow and uninvolving. **Director**—Gary Grillo. **(R)** *96 minutes*

AMERICAN POP (1981)

Director/animator Ralph Bakshi (*Fritz the Cat; Heavy Traffic*) takes us down popular music's memory lane, from early burlesque to rock. This innovative cartoon feature is embellished with newsreel footage, still photographs, and rousing music spanning more than 80 years. Although Bakshi's style is fresh and vigorous, he tries to pack in too much historical detail, a problem that leads to awkwardness and confusion. **(R)** *95 minutes*

AN AMERICAN TAIL (1986)

  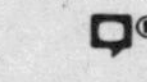

In An American Tail, *Tanya and Fievel are told there are no cats in America.*

From producer Steven Spielberg and former Disney animator Don Bluth comes this endearing cartoon feature about a family of mice who migrate from czarist Russia to the promised land of America. The story follows the harrowing adventures of young Fievel Mousekewitz and his parents and sister who believe America's streets are paved with cheese and there are no cats. The characters are pleasing, though the plot lacks the intricacies of many of the Disney cartoon features. Dom DeLuise, Phillip Glasser, and Madeline Kahn supply some of the voices. **Director**—Bluth. **(G)** *83 minutes*

AN AMERICAN TRAGEDY (1931)

Phillips Holmes
Sylvia Sidney

Sergei Eisenstein was once in the running to direct this caustic work of Theodore Dreiser, but the job went to Josef von Sternberg, who was almost Eisenstein's polar opposite. A great filmmaker brings a great novelist to the screen, and despite the occasional aesthetic clashes, it's strong material. The story of a man torn between his poor girlfriend and a wealthy beauty was remade in 1951 as *A Place in the Sun.* *95 minutes b&w*

AN AMERICAN WEREWOLF IN LONDON (1981)

David Naughton
Griffin Dunne

John Landis, who directed *Animal House,* applies his brand of comedy to the werewolf legend, and the result is a smoothly integrated mixture of humor and horror. Two American students touring England are attacked by a mysterious beast, and the survivor, Naughton, turns into a marauding werewolf at full moon. The grisly special effects are impressive, and the horror is very real, but the film is oddly touching and funny. The year this film was released was the year the Academy of Motion Picture Arts and Sciences established a makeup award, which this film won. **(R)** *97 minutes*

AMERICATHON (1979)

 ★½

Harvey Korman
John Ritter

It's 1998 and the United States is broke. Gasoline is so scarce that most people use bicycles to get around. The President is a clown who presides from the California White House. There's enough here for a minor sitcom, but the comedy never really builds momentum. Korman stars as the host of a ridiculous telethon to raise money to save

(Continued)

(Continued)
the country. With Fred Willard and Nancy Morgan. **Director**—Neil Israel. **(PG)** *90 minutes*

AMIN—THE RISE AND FALL (1982)

Joseph Olita

The viciousness of the former Ugandan despot is exploited for all it's worth in this semidocumentary account, which was filmed in Kenya. The brutal Amin is shown eating human flesh, cutting up his wife's corpse, and preserving the heads of his enemies in the refrigerator, but the film sorely neglects to examine the reasons behind such barbarity. Olita, in the title role, is amazingly similar in appearance to the real Amin. Direction and acting, however, are merely marginal. **Director**—Sharad Patel. **(R)** *101 minutes*

THE AMITYVILLE HORROR (1979)

James Brolin
Margot Kidder

This film would be just another haunted-house story were it not for plenty of effective hair-raising moments: Toilets ooze black goo, the front door is mysteriously ripped from its hinges, a rocking chair rocks with no one in it. Brolin and Kidder give adequate performances as the newlywed couple who finally flee this strange Long Island home where the previous family had been murdered. The screenplay is based on Jay Anson's supposedly factual book. Cast includes Rod Steiger and Don Stroud. **Director**—Stuart Rosenberg. **(R)** *117 minutes*

AMITYVILLE II: THE POSSESSION (1982)

Burt Young
James Olson
Jack Magner

A patchy, somewhat tiresome reworking of the same haunted-house theme that was used in the original *Amityville Horror.* Yet another middle-class family encounters strange phenomena and evil spirits at work in the white frame colonial dwelling at the water's edge. There are some effectively chilling moments, but the story does not hold up. The conclusion fails to satisfy. **Director**—Damiano Damiani. **(R)** *104 minutes*

AMITYVILLE 3-D (1983)

Tony Roberts
Tess Harper

This trashy second rehash of the famed haunted-house tale has worn out the welcome mat. Now we have magazine reporter Tony Roberts setting up shop in the eerie dwelling by the shore. He initially pooh-poohs the existence of evil spirits until a few poorly conceived horror effects set him straight. The pacing is sluggish and the 3-D effect may have you reaching for the aspirin bottle. Candy Clark costars. **Director**—Richard Fleischer. **(PG) Alternate Title**—*Amityville 3: The Demon.* *93 minutes*

THE AMOROUS ADVENTURES OF MOLL FLANDERS (1965)

Kim Novak
Richard Johnson
Angela Lansbury
George Sanders

This ambitious attempt to make a female version of *Tom Jones* doesn't quite make it. Novak, who is awkward in the title role, is part of the problem. She plays a servant girl who cavorts with rich men. There are some bawdy bedroom romps in 18th-century England, but nothing too exciting. Costumes and period settings are nice. The film is based on Daniel Defoe's novel. Cast includes Lilli Palmer, Leo McKern, and Vittorio De Sica. **Director**—Terence Young. *126 minutes*

THE AMSTERDAM KILL (1978)

Robert Mitchum
Bradford Dillman
Richard Egan

Droopy-eyed Mitchum plays a narcotics agent who smashes an international drug-smuggling ring that operates in Hong Kong, Amsterdam, and London. Mitchum's performance is effective, but at times he seems too old to be slugging it out as the hero. Robert Clouse directs this caper with a knack for fast-paced action. However, he overdoes the gunplay, and the body count climbs with each passing scene. Also with Leslie Nielsen and Keye Luke. **(R)** *90 minutes*

AMY (1981)

★★★

Jenny Agutter
Barry Newman
Nanette Fabray

A sentimental, feel-good movie from the Disney studios about a woman who leaves her stuffy lawyer-husband to teach deaf children to speak. The title role is winningly portrayed by Agutter. There's stalwart support from Newman and Fabray. But the film is most convincing because of the impressive performances of students from the California School for the Deaf. The format is rather old-fashioned, but it's executed with ample warmth and appeal. **Director**—Vincent McEveety. **(G)** *100 minutes*

ANASTASIA (1956)

Ingrid Bergman
Yul Brynner
Helen Hayes

Ingrid Bergman convincingly impersonates Russian royalty in Anastasia.

A charming drama set in Paris in 1928, about an amnesiac young woman, played by Bergman, who is recruited by exiled Russians to impersonate the daughter of the late czar. Bergman's gra-

This movie available with closed captions for the hearing impaired.

cious and award-winning performance heightens the entertainment to grand style. Hayes, as the grand duchess, also makes a magnificent acting contribution as she strives to determine Bergman's credentials. Also with Akim Tamiroff and Martita Hunt. **Director**—Anatole Litvak. **Academy Award**—Bergman, best actress. *105 minutes*

ANATOMY OF A MURDER (1959)

★★★★

James Stewart
Ben Gazzara
Lee Remick

James Stewart takes counsel from Arthur O'Connell in Anatomy of a Murder.

A long but engrossing courtroom drama, adapted from Robert Traver's best-selling novel, about a small-town lawyer in Michigan who defends an Army officer accused of murdering a bartender. Stewart is superb as the crafty defense attorney, and George C. Scott makes his mark as the prosecutor. The explicit dialogue caused a stir when the film was released. Also stars Eve Arden and Arthur O'Connell; Duke Ellington wrote the musical score. **Director**—Otto Preminger. **Academy Award Nominations**—best picture; Stewart, best actor; O'Connell and Scott, best supporting actor; Wendell Mayes, best screenplay based on material from another medium. *160 minutes b&w*

ANCHORS AWEIGH (1945)

 ★★★

Frank Sinatra
Gene Kelly
Kathryn Grayson

A light and lively musical about two sailors on liberty in Los Angeles who befriend a small boy yearning to join the Navy. The cast, led by Kelly, Sinatra, and Grayson, perform energetically. The film is notable for Kelly's dance sequence with a cartoon mouse. There's support from José Iturbi, Dean Stockwell, and Pamela Britton. **Director**—George Sidney. **Academy Award Nominations**—best picture; Kelly, best actor. *140 minutes*

THE ANDERSON TAPES (1972)

★★★

Sean Connery
Martin Balsam
Dyan Cannon

Stylish and lively crime drama about an ex-con's plan to stage a robbery at an apartment building, but the police are aware of the heist because of electronic surveillance. Connery is convincing as the thief, and the unusual climax is rather thrilling. However, a few plot holes mar the script. Also stars Alan King and Ralph Meeker. **Director**—Sidney Lumet. **(PG)** *98 minutes*

AND GOD CREATED WOMAN (1988)

 ★★

Rebecca DeMornay
Vincent Spano

For this romantic melodrama, French director Roger Vadim recycled the title of his notorious 1957 classic, which had launched the career of Brigitte Bardot. This film, however, is too far removed from the original to be called a remake. DeMornay stars as a prison inmate who marries a hard-working carpenter, played by Spano, to secure her parole. After her release, she selfishly pursues a career as a rock singer. This updated version suffers from a farfetched plot and unbelievable characters. Also with Frank Langella, Judith Chapman, and Thelma Houston. **(R)** *94 minutes*

...AND JUSTICE FOR ALL (1979)

 ★★★

Al Pacino
Jack Warden
John Forsythe

Pacino stars as a scruffy, idealistic lawyer who tangles with a tyrannical judge played by Forsythe. The film smartly indicts the legal profession much in the same spirit that *Hospital* took on medicine. This is a fascinating and compelling movie, featuring unforgettable performances and Norman Jewison's well-paced direction. Pacino generates so much power and feeling in this role that he must be regarded as one of America's foremost actors. Cast includes Lee Strasberg. **(R) Academy Award Nominations**—Pacino, best actor; Valerie Curtin and Barry Levinson, best screenplay written directly for the screen. *120 minutes*

AND NOW FOR SOMETHING COMPLETELY DIFFERENT (1972)

 ★★★½

John Cleese
Graham Chapman
Terry Gilliam
Eric Idle
Michael Palin
Terry Jones

The zany stars of "Monty Python's Flying Circus," Britain's latter-day version of the Marx Brothers, present a series of rip-roaring, rib-tickling sketches (drawn from their television show). The production is somewhat uneven, but there's loads of sidesplitting comedy throughout. **Director**—Ian McNaughton. **(PG)** *89 minutes*

ANDROCLES AND THE LION (1952)

 ★★

Alan Young
Jean Simmons
Robert Newton
Victor Mature

George Bernard Shaw's satiric fable set in the time of ancient Rome is marred by a lackluster production, although some good performances perk things up at times. The story concerns a Christian who removes a thorn from the paw of a lion. When the two meet later in the arena, the lion remembers the kindness and refuses to eat the man. Young plays the Christian. Cast includes Reginald Gardiner, Alan Mowbray, Maurice Evans, and Elsa Lanchester. **Director**—Chester Erskine. *98 minutes*

ANDROID (1984)

★★★

Klaus Kinski
Don Opper

(Continued)

This movie available on videotape and/or disc.

(Continued)
A charming, likable, low-budget science-fiction movie that features a robot with touching human characteristics. Max, the shy and sensitive robot, resides on a remote space station with obsessed scientist Kinski. Max wants to go to Earth to "be his own person," but unexpected events get in his way. Debuting director Aaron Lipstadt does the utmost with a limited budget, and the film seems slated for sleeper and cult status. **(R)** *80 minutes*

THE ANDROMEDA STRAIN (1971)

Arthur Hill
David Wayne

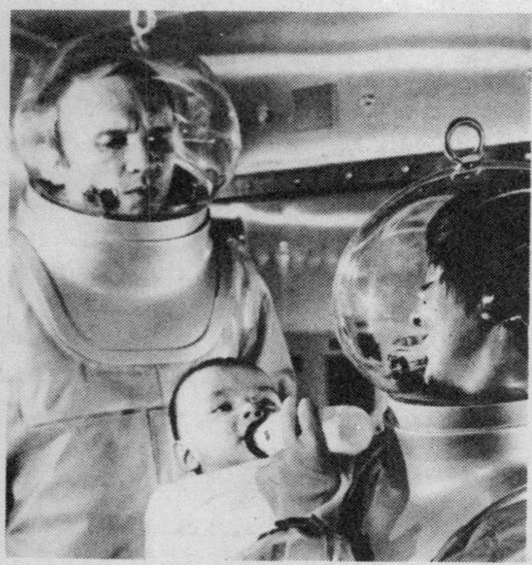

James Olson and Paula Kelly in The Andromeda Strain.

Scientists race the clock to decontaminate a remote village infected by a deadly virus from a downed satellite. The film, based on Michael Crichton's novel, is somewhat drawn out, but it packs plenty of suspense in the narrative, which concerns man's injustice to man. Also with James Olson, Kate Reid, and Paula Kelly. **Director**—Robert Wise. **(G)** *130 minutes*

AND THEN THERE WERE NONE (1945)

 ★★★

Walter Huston
Judith Anderson
Barry Fitzgerald

There have been several film versions based upon the Agatha Christie suspense novel about murder on a lonely island, but this one by director René Clair is the best by far. Excellent performances enliven the tale as ten people at a house party are murdered one by one. Because of Clair's able direction, the triteness of Christie's novel is kept to a minimum and the mystery and suspense remain strong up to the last slaying. *98 minutes b&w*

ANDY WARHOL'S BAD (1977)

 **(no stars)**

Carroll Baker
Perry King
Susan Tyrrell

This is the revolting story of a suburban housewife who operates a small-scale murder-and-mayhem contracting business staffed by strange girls. There are numerous outrageous scenes of blood and gore, which probably will make you surrender your dinner. Much of the dialogue is boring. Some of the acting is fair; the rest is awful. "Bad" it certainly is. **Director**—Jed Johnson. **(X) Alternate Title**—*Bad.* *105 minutes*

ANGEL (1984)

★1/2

Donna Wilkes

By day, she's an honor student at a swank Los Angeles prep school. At night, she's hustling tricks on Sunset Boulevard and hanging around with kooky characters. Also, she's dodging a mad-dog killer who slices up prostitutes like roast turkey. With all that, there's just enough time to knock off tomorrow's homework assignment. Wilkes is in the title role of this sleazy outing, aided and abetted by Rory Calhoun, Dick Shawn, and Cliff Gorman. Fledgling director Robert Vincent O'Neil shows his Roger Corman colors. **(R)** *93 minutes*

ANGEL AND THE BADMAN (1947)

 ★★

John Wayne
Gail Russell
Bruce Cabot

Sooner or later, every matinee idol wants to do *Hamlet,* and every horse-opera writer wants to do a morality play. Here, Wayne and writer/director James Edward Grant do penance for all the cowpokes and braves they've eagerly dispatched with six-guns. A wounded gunslinger is nursed back to health by Quaker Prudence Worth, who would have him see the folly of his ways. This was a change of pace for the studio (Republic) as well, and though it's sincere, it's also, alas, sleep-inducing. *100 minutes b&w*

ANGEL HEART (1987)

Mickey Rourke
Robert De Niro

Director Alan Parker dominates this combination private-eye and horror film with a tense, nightmarish atmosphere. Rourke stars as the seediest of Eisenhower-era gumshoes who descends into a hellish world in a quest to find a long-missing big-band crooner. The superb production design, with an emphasis on muted colors and seedy locales, enhances the exotic story, which involves murder and voodoo from Manhattan to New Orleans. A controversial love scene involving Rourke and Lisa Bonet (of TV's *The Cosby Show*) caused the film to receive an initial X-rating, which was changed after Parker reedited the scene. Both the R-version and X-version are available on video. Also with Charlotte Rampling. **(R)** *113 minutes*

ANGELO MY LOVE (1983)

Angelo Evans

Actor Robert Duvall turns director for this unusual documentary-like fiction about New York gypsies. At the heart of the story is Evans, a bright-eyed urchin who gives an appealing performance as a pint-size, streetwise con artist. Other characters, played almost without exception by real gypsies, are well defined. Unfortunately, the movie drags and lacks cohesiveness. **(No MPAA rating)** *115 minutes*

ANGEL ON MY SHOULDER (1946)

Paul Muni
Claude Rains
Anne Baxter

A light comedy/drama about a dead criminal who makes a deal with the Devil for a new lease on life. He returns to Earth as a high-minded judge and

turns the tables on Satan. The plot imitates *Here Comes Mr. Jordan,* but the film still maintains a lively entertainment level. Muni, Rains, and Baxter are excellent in starring roles. With Erskine Sanford and Hardie Albright. **Director**—Archie Mayo.
101 minutes b&w

ANGELS WITH DIRTY FACES (1938)

 ★★★½

James Cagney
Pat O'Brien
Humphrey Bogart

James Cagney helps himself to Humphrey Bogart's loot in Angels with Dirty Faces.

A top cast graces this drama about a New York hood, played by Cagney, who develops a conscience when a bunch of slum kids start looking to him as their idol. O'Brien gives a fine performance as the gangster's childhood friend who happens to be a priest. Bogart is notable as a criminal whose conscience remains unawakened. The Dead End Kids are effective as the impressionable youths. The film is a clever combination of brutality and moral comment. Also with Ann Sheridan and George Bancroft. **Director**—Michael Curtiz. **Academy Award Nominations**—best picture; Cagney, best actor; Curtiz, best director; Rowland Brown, original story. *97 minutes b&w*

ANIMAL CRACKERS (1930)

 ★★★

The Marx Brothers
Margaret Dumont

The Marx Brothers' second film brings to the screen the delirious anarchy of their Broadway hit by Morrie Ryskind and George S. Kaufman. A valuable painting has disappeared from the

In Animal Crackers, *the globe-trotting Groucho Marx considers dropping ankle.*

home of the wealthy Mrs. Rittenhouse (Dumont), and who could be better qualified to find it than big-game hunter Captain Spaulding. ("One morning I shot an elephant in my pajamas. How he got into my pajamas I'll never know.") Chico on piano, Harpo on harp, Groucho on overdrive, and Zeppo on cardboard mounting. Hooray for Captain Spaulding! **Director**—Victor Heerman. *98 minutes b&w*

ANIMAL FARM (1955)

 ★★★

On-target animation faithfully based on George Orwell's political satire. The oppressed animals free themselves from their human masters and take over management of the farm only to find themselves governed by harsh restrictions. Some of the cartoon characters are pigs, but not the "Porky Pig" variety. **Director**—John Halas.
75 minutes

ANIMAL HOUSE

See National Lampoon's Animal House

ANNA (1987)

★★★

Sally Kirkland
Paulina Porizkova

Kirkland was critically acclaimed for her performance in the title role as an over-the-hill Czech actress in New York trying to resurrect her career. Porizkova, the internationally known fashion model, costars as a young woman who befriends and then upstages the fading movie star. A low-budget, independent production, this compelling drama is a showcase of modern method acting. Also with Robert Fields. **Director**—Yurek Bogayevicz. **(PG–13) Academy Award Nomination**—Kirkland, best actress. *95 minutes*

ANNA AND THE KING OF SIAM (1946)

Irene Dunne
Rex Harrison

Impressive period drama about an English governess who takes a job in the palace in Bangkok teaching the king's many children and wins the respect of the tyrannical king. Gracefully produced with heartwarming touches. Harrison and Dunne are impressive in the key roles. The story is better known in its musical version, *The King and I.* Cast includes Linda Darnell, Gale Sondergaard, and Lee J. Cobb. **Director**—John Cromwell. **Academy Award Nominations**—Sondergaard, best supporting actress; Sally Benson and Talbot Jennings, screenplay. *128 minutes b&w*

ANNA KARENINA (1935)

 ★★★

Greta Garbo
Fredric March
Basil Rathbone

A superb performance by Garbo compensates for the flaws in bringing to the screen Leo Tolstoy's great novel about the love affair between the wife of a Russian aristocrat and a dashing cavalry officer. Although Garbo shines brightest, there are also fine performances by March as Garbo's lover, Rathbone as her husband, and Freddie Bartholomew as her son. Also with Maureen O'Sullivan, May Robson, Reginald Denny, and Reginald Owen. **Director**—Clarence Brown. *95 minutes b&w*

ANNE OF THE THOUSAND DAYS (1969)

 ★★★

Richard Burton
Geneviève Bujold

Burton gives one of his most impressive performances as Henry VIII in this somewhat inaccurate historical drama involving the king's controversial romance with Anne Boleyn, played by Bujold. It's a compelling account of a famous love affair that involved adultery. The film is based on the 1948 play by
(Continued)

This movie available on videotape and/or disc.

(Continued)
Maxwell Anderson. Lavish costumes and scenery enhance the production. With John Colicos, Irene Papas, and Anthony Quayle. **Director**—Charles Jarrott. **(PG) Academy Award Nominations**—best picture; Burton, best actor; Bujold, best actress; Quayle, best supporting actor; Richard Sokolove, best screenplay based on material from another medium. *145 minutes*

ANNIE (1982)

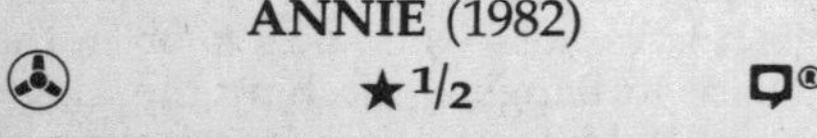

★½

Aileen Quinn

What happens when you take 40 million dollars, an obnoxious little kid with dyed red hair, choreography that looks like ball bearings in a food processor, and a director who would rather be somewhere else, and put them all together? Well, you get *Annie*, as convoluted a musical as we've seen in a long time. A mildly entertaining Broadway musical is once again mugged on its way to the screen. Quinn tries too hard in the lead role—she might have been all right in a better film. The large supporting cast, including Albert Finney, Carol Burnett, and Ann Reinking, veer back and forth between overacting and looking out-to-lunch. **Director**—John Huston. **(PG)** *128 minutes*

ANNIE GET YOUR GUN (1950)

★★★

Betty Hutton
Howard Keel

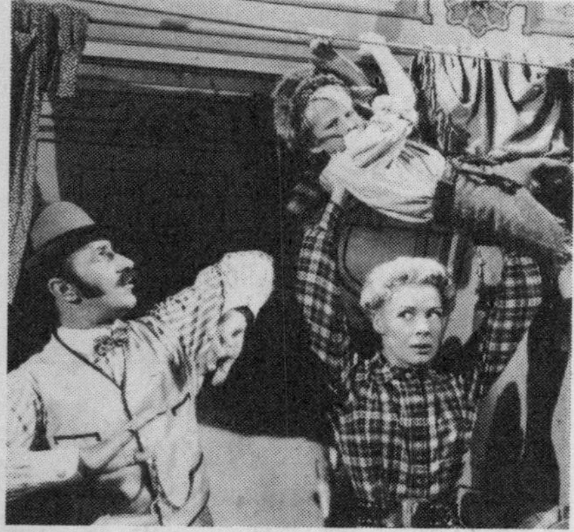

Keenan Wynn and Betty Hutton in a serene moment from Annie Get Your Gun.

Flashy film version of the Broadway hit musical about Annie Oakley, the celebrated female sharpshooter who toured with Wild West shows. Hutton and Keel belt out the lively Irving Berlin music with gusto. The direction is somewhat stilted, but the production is lavish. Edward Arnold, Keenan Wynn, Louis Calhern, and J. Carrol Naish lend support. Memorable songs include "Anything You Can Do" and "Doin' What Comes Naturally." **Director**—George Sidney. *107 minutes*

ANNIE HALL (1977)

★★★★

Woody Allen
Diane Keaton

Woody Allen, Tony Roberts, and Diane Keaton in Annie Hall.

Allen and Keaton glitter and shine in this hilarious and moving autobiographical film about their on-again, off-again romance. It's Allen's most personal film and one of his best. The familiar parade of Allen one-liners is there, but the film is also rich with emotion and introspection. He leans somewhat on Ingmar Bergman here, and this story could appropriately be named "Scenes from a Neurotic Love Affair." Cast includes Tony Roberts, Paul Simon, Shelley Duvall, Carol Kane, and Colleen Dewhurst. **Director**—Allen. **(PG) Academy Awards**—best picture; Allen, best director; Keaton, best actress; Allen and Marshall Brickman, best screenplay written directly for the screen. **Nomination**—Allen, best actor. *95 minutes*

ANNIE OAKLEY (1935)

★★

Barbara Stanwyck
Preston Foster
Melvyn Douglas

Fictionalized biography of the late-19th-century sharpshooter who toured with Buffalo Bill's Wild West Show and her peppery on-and-off romance with a fellow entertainer. Scrappy Stanwyck is in fine fettle; the film was one of the high points of her early career. But time hasn't been kind to this backstage comedy/drama, much of which falls flat today. **Director**—George Stevens. *88 minutes b&w*

THE ANNIVERSARY (1968)

Bette Davis
Jack Hedley
James Cossins

Davis, bitchy as ever and wearing an eye patch, stars as an overbearing mother who dominates her grown sons. She gathers her clan together on the anniversary of her husband's death. This black comedy/horror outing, based on the Bill MacIlwraith play, affords an opportunity to see Davis ham it up to the hilt. Otherwise, the film is routine. Also with Sheila Hancock and Elaine Taylor. **Director**—Roy Ward Baker. *95 minutes*

ANOTHER COUNTRY (1984)

★★★

Rupert Everett
Colin Firth

Revealing, well-acted melodrama that probes the confining atmosphere of an elite English boarding school. Based on Julian Mitchell's popular stage play, the story follows the experiences of several students who depart from the traditional expectations and become Russian spies. Everett is impressive as an ambitious upper-crust youth who engages in homosexual affairs and Marxist politics. Firth also is outstanding as a student with similar leanings. **Director**—Marek Kanievska. **(PG)** *90 minutes*

ANOTHER 48 HOURS (1990)

★★

Eddie Murphy
Nick Nolte

In 1982, Walter Hill's *48 Hrs.* sparked a new sub-genre, the buddy movie, in which two widely divergent characters team up to solve a crime. This disappointing sequel is only a routine example. This time around, newly released convict Murphy and rumpled detective Nolte are reunited to track down a drug dealer and his henchmen. Hill and his scriptwriters were careful to duplicate the famous sequences that made the

This movie available with closed captions for the hearing impaired.

first film a success: A scene occurs in a rowdy bar; numerous verbal insults and physical blows are exchanged between Murphy and Nolte; and Murphy belts out "Roxanne" on occasion. The film's bloodbath conclusion attempts to top those in other action movies, making for gratuitous violence and a high body count. In addition to its repetitious script and numbing violence, the film lacks the sparkle of the original. Murphy's cocky banter and hip style have been reduced to a formula. The supporting cast includes Kevin Tighe, Brion James, Bernie Casey, and Ed O'Ross. **(R)** *98 minutes*

ANOTHER MAN, ANOTHER CHANCE (1977)

★★

James Caan
Geneviève Bujold

French director Claude Lelouch (*A Man and a Woman*) gives us his version of America's frontier days, which looks like a western soap opera with a French accent. The complex plot concerns a veterinarian widower, played by Caan, who falls in love with a widowed photographer, played by Bujold, while both reside in a dusty frontier town. This film certainly isn't your typical western, but it cries out for some typical drama, action, and some three-dimensional characters. **(PG)** *128 minutes*

ANOTHER MAN'S POISON (1952)

Bette Davis
Anthony Steel
Gary Merrill

A murky melodrama about a woman writer who poisons her husband and is subsequently blackmailed. Davis isn't up to par as the hysterical authoress in this low-budget film. The material is mediocre as well. Emlyn Williams, Barbara Murray, and Reginald Beckwith costar. **Director**—Irving Rapper. *89 minutes b&w*

ANOTHER TIME, ANOTHER PLACE (1958)

 ★★

Lana Turner
Barry Sullivan

Tearful soap-opera movie with Turner as an American newspaperwoman during World War II who is involved in an affair with a British war correspondent. Turner goes to pieces when her lover is killed. An early film for Sean Connery and one that established him as an actor worth watching. Also with Glynis Johns and Sidney James. **Director**—Lewis Allen. *98 minutes b&w*

ANOTHER TIME, ANOTHER PLACE (1984)

 ★★

Phyllis Logan

Dour, slow-moving melodrama about a bored Scottish woman who engages in a secret love affair with an Italian prisoner of war. The emotionally charged story, set in a small Scottish community during World War II, highlights the cultural differences and tensions between the local farmers and the captive soldiers. But a constant bleakness pervades the production and limits its impact. Logan gives an impressive portrayal as the farmer's wife who succumbs to passion. **Director**—Michael Radford. **(R)** *101 minutes*

ANOTHER WOMAN (1988)

Gena Rowlands
Gene Hackman
Mia Farrow
Sandy Dennis

An introspective moment for Gena Rowlands in Another Woman.

Woody Allen, as director and writer, is off the mark with this overwrought melodrama about a middle-age woman philosophy professor who is forced to reflect back on her life honestly. Inspired by Bergman's *Wild Strawberries*, the film fails because it is totally humorless—as dry as the life of its central character. The stellar cast—Rowlands, Hackman, Farrow, and Dennis—are wasted in this stilted drama. Also with Ian Holm, Blythe Danner, Martha Plimpton, and John Houseman in his final performance. **(PG)** *87 minutes*

ANY NUMBER CAN PLAY (1949)

★★★

Clark Gable
Alexis Smith
Mary Astor

Skillful acting by Gable, Smith, and Astor perk up this otherwise routine drama about a gambler beset with numerous problems. Gable, who plays a casino operator, is estranged from his family, but the situation turns around when health problems prompt his retirement. Also with Wendell Corey, Audrey Totter, Marjorie Rambeau, and Lewis Stone. **Director**—Mervyn LeRoy. *112 minutes b&w*

ANY WEDNESDAY (1966)

Jane Fonda
Dean Jones
Jason Robards

A business executive, played by Robards, visits his mistress once a week, but tension develops when a company subordinate discovers the affair. This somewhat stretched-out sex farce is based on the Broadway comedy. Fonda's spritely performance as the kept girl, however, helps maintain interest. Cast includes Rosemary Murphy and Ann Prentiss. **Director**—Robert Miller. *109 minutes*

ANY WHICH WAY YOU CAN (1980)

Clint Eastwood
Sondra Locke

This funny, rollicking sequel to *Every Which Way But Loose* is better than the original. Eastwood once again teams up with Clyde the orangutan for more nonstop monkeyshines and two-fisted

(Continued)

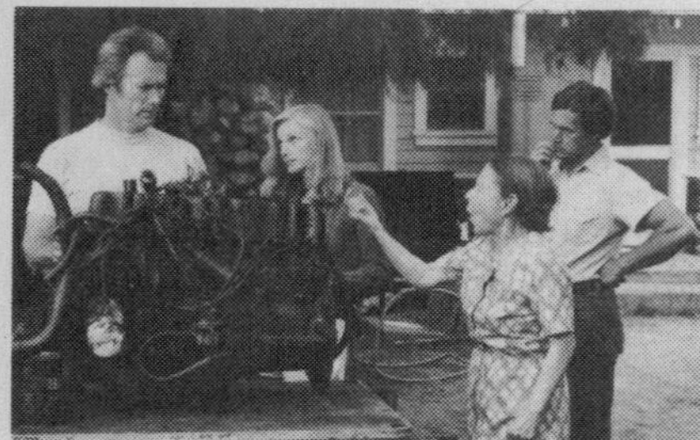

Eastwood, Locke, Ruth Gordon, and Geoffrey Lewis in Any Which Way You Can.

(Continued)
farcical mayhem. It's an undisguised comic/action vehicle for Eastwood, who has the good sense not to take himself too seriously. Locke again is pleasant as Eastwood's romantic interest. **Director**—Buddy Van Horn. **(PG)**
115 minutes

ANZIO (1968)

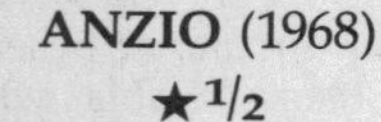

Robert Mitchum
Peter Falk
Arthur Kennedy

Trumped-up World War II drama about preparation for the 1944 invasion of the Italian peninsula. The flimsy film wastes the good cast seen struggling with their roles. Mitchum plays a war correspondent in on the action. Earl Holliman, Anthony Steel, and Robert Ryan also star. **Director**—Edward Dmytryk. *117 minutes*

APACHE (1954)

Burt Lancaster
Jean Peters

Lancaster stars as an angry Indian warrior who boldly crusades for justice for his tribe and then settles down. There are some good action scenes, but the unlikely story is sluggish in spots. Peters fills in the background as Lancaster's supportive wife. John McIntire and Charles Bronson appear in supporting roles. **Director**—Robert Aldrich.
91 minutes

THE APARTMENT (1960)

Jack Lemmon
Shirley MacLaine

Witty, bittersweet comedy/drama about a lonely, vulnerable young office worker, played by Lemmon, who lends his apartment to his superiors for their extramarital affairs. Lemmon and MacLaine turn in classic performances that are unforgettable. Billy Wilder's direction has just the right blend of cynicism, pathos, and laughs. Fred MacMurray is superb as Lemmon's philandering boss. **Academy Awards**—best picture; Wilder, best director; Wilder and I.A.L. Diamond, best story and screenplay written directly for the screen. **Nominations**—Lemmon, best actor; MacLaine, best actress; Jack Kruschen, best supporting actor.
125 minutes b&w

APARTMENT ZERO (1989)

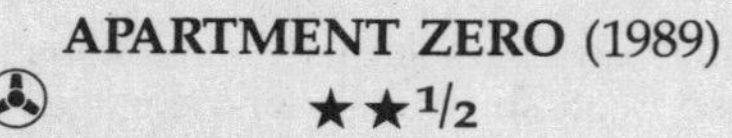

Hart Bochner
Colin Firth

In this peculiar mystery, a lonely cinephile named Adrian LeDuc (Firth) whiles away his hours at the movies or in his apartment in Buenos Aires. Unable to respond to real people, Adrian relates only to a celluloid world. When a dark stranger (Bochner) comes along to rent his spare room, Adrian is attracted to the stranger's James Dean-like persona. But, is he or isn't he a former death squad operative involved in local murders? Is he connected to the C.I.A.? The stranger succeeds in seducing most of the seedy residents of the apartment building by pretending to be what each of them desires. The eerie premise propels the film past its weaker moments, and the suggestive score adds much to the heavy atmosphere. Not rated by the MPAA at the time of release, but rated **R** for the video version, which runs 114 minutes. **Director**—Martin Donovan. *120 minutes*

APOCALYPSE NOW (1979)

Marlon Brando
Martin Sheen
Robert Duvall

Francis Coppola's unforgettable masterpiece about the Vietnam War throbs with energy, horror, irony, and grandeur. It's a cinematic work of art; an involving adventure yarn, based on Joseph Conrad's *Heart of Darkness*. All the acting is first class, but Duvall stands out as a gung-ho, pompous air-cavalry colonel who stages a brutal helicopter raid on a Viet Cong village. Top-billed Brando is finally seen in the

Marlon Brando explains his philosophy to Martin Sheen in Apocalypse Now.

last quarter of the film. He plays the shadowy Colonel Kurtz, who has gone mad in the jungle and is slated for execution by an intelligence officer, played by Sheen. Originally released at 150 minutes. Also with Frederic Forrest, Albert Hall, Dennis Hopper, and Sam Bottoms. **(R) Academy Award Nominations**—best picture; Coppola, best director; Duvall, best supporting actor; Coppola and John Milius, best screenplay based on material from another medium. *139 minutes*

APPOINTMENT WITH DEATH (1988)

Peter Ustinov
Lauren Bacall
John Gielgud

Even avid Agatha Christie fans will be sorely disappointed with this lame film adaptation of another one of her mystery novels. Ustinov returns to chew the scenery once again as the intrepid Belgian sleuth Hercule Poirot, who here solves a murder among a group of tourists in Palestine during a 1937 cruise. The period atmosphere is portrayed with care, but the film is utterly devoid of suspense, clever dialogue, or colorful characters. An all-star cast, which also includes Carrie Fisher, Piper Laurie, Hayley Mills, and David Soul, wades through the sluggish material as best they can. **Director**—Michael Winner. **(PG)** *100 minutes*

THE APPRENTICESHIP OF DUDDY KRAVITZ (1974)

★★★

Richard Dreyfuss
Micheline Lanctot
Jack Warden

This movie available with closed captions for the hearing impaired.

Poignant and amusing comedy/drama set in the 1940s about a young Jewish man from Montreal trying to make it big in the world. Excellent scenes are brought to life from Mordecai Richler's bright screenplay adapted from his novel. Dreyfuss is superb as the ambitious teenager. Also with Randy Quaid, Denholm Elliott, and Joseph Wiseman. **Director**—Ted Kotcheff. **(PG) Academy Award Nomination**—Richler and Lionel Chetwynd, best screenplay adapted from other material.
121 minutes

APPRENTICE TO MURDER (1987)

★★

Donald Sutherland
Chad Lowe
Mia Sara

Sutherland's brooding performance as a country faith healer provides some interest to this offbeat mystery tale set in Pennsylvania in the 1920s. Lowe costars as the son of a drunkard who becomes Sutherland's apprentice after the healer turns his father into an upright citizen. Sara vies for Lowe's attentions, which forces him to choose between Sutherland's magic and Sara's affections. Filmed in Norway, this unusual story is a parable of good and evil and contains several theological analogies. Unfortunately, it borrows too many devices and special effects from the horror genre to sustain the eerie quality that makes the story appealing. Also with Tiger Haynes, Rutanya Alda, Knut Husebo, and Eddie Jones. **Director**—R.L. Thomas. **(PG–13)** *94 minutes*

THE APRIL FOOLS (1969)

 ★★

Jack Lemmon
Catherine Deneuve

In The April Fools, *Catherine Deneuve flies to Paris with Jack Lemmon.*

Strained comedy/drama made as a star vehicle for Lemmon, but it doesn't work too well. Lemmon is a restless business executive who runs off to Paris with the wife of his boss. All sorts of complications ensue, but everything is straightened out for the happy ending. Myrna Loy, Sally Kellerman, Charles Boyer, Jack Weston, Harvey Korman, and Peter Lawford are in supporting roles. **Director**—Stuart Rosenberg. **(PG)** *95 minutes*

APRIL FOOL'S DAY (1986)

★★

Deborah Foreman
Jay Baker
Deborah Goodrich

A *Friday the 13th* plot formula is applied to this hokey slasher picture. It's the same old gore parade but with a satirical twist at the end. College students get together on a deserted island and one by one they are eliminated by a homicidal maniac. A youthful cast labors with the absurd material. **Director**—Fred Walton. **(R)** *90 minutes*

APRIL IN PARIS (1952)

★★

Doris Day
Ray Bolger

Claude Dauphin paints a verbal picture for Ray Bolger in April in Paris.

Lackluster, silly musical with a flimsy plot about a chorus girl, played by Day, who is mistakenly sent to Paris, where she charms an awkward state department official. Songs and dances for Day and Bolger are all pretty much forgettable. The cast includes Claude Dauphin, Eve Miller, and George Givot. **Director**—David Butler. *100 minutes*

ARABESQUE (1966)

★★½

Gregory Peck
Sophia Loren

Peck and Loren star in this handsome spy thriller with a disappointing, empty plot. Peck plays a language professor who finds himself involved with espionage while on assignment for some Arabian oil men. Some amusing moments are lost amid the lavish settings. With Alan Badel, Kieron Moore, and Carl Duering. **Director**—Stanley Donen. *105 minutes*

ARABIAN ADVENTURE (1979)

Christopher Lee
Milo O'Shea
Oliver Tobias
Puneet Sira

Flying magic carpets, genies, assorted villains, and a clever orphan boy will keep the kiddies amused for an hour and a half. This colorful Ali Baba-like adventure offers continuous action and intriguing special effects. Lee plays an evil ruler, Tobias is a handsome prince, and Mickey Rooney is the custodian of a secret cave. **Director**—Kevin Connor. **(G)** *98 minutes*

ARACHNOPHOBIA (1990)

Jeff Daniels
John Goodman

(Continued)

John Goodman is the zealous insect exterminator in Arachnophobia.

(Continued)
Borrowing many of the plot elements from *Jaws,* this glossy, playful horror film tells the tale of a large, vampiric spider that plagues a small resort town in California. Daniels, as the local doctor with a morbid fear of spiders, becomes concerned when he attributes some mysterious deaths to the mean-tempered creature. He seeks aid from both the academic community, in the form of Julian Sands as a spider specialist, and from an earthy exterminator, played by Goodman. Despite its resemblance to Spielberg's classic thriller, the film (directed by Spielberg crony Frank Marshall) manages to be effective, primarily through its combination of comedy and horror. Also with Harley Jane Kozak, Stuart Pankin, and Brian McNamara. **(PG-13)** *103 minutes*

ARCH OF TRIUMPH (1948)

★★

Ingrid Bergman
Charles Boyer
Charles Laughton

This ambitious melodrama with a first-class cast—Bergman, Boyer, Laughton—fails to catch hold despite expensive commitment from its producers. Boyer plays a refugee in Paris who has a tragic love affair with a troubled girl, played by Bergman. A depressing set of circumstances, indeed, and hardly a triumph. Louis Calhern is also in the cast. **Director**—Lewis Milestone. *120 minutes b&w*

THE ARISTOCATS (1970)

★★★

An inventive cartoon feature by the Walt Disney studios about a cat and her kittens who are abandoned in the country and then rescued by the other animals there. Fine characterizations enhanced by the voices of Eva Gabor, Phil Harris, and Sterling Holloway. The deft influence of Walt Disney is noticeably missing, yet it's still a nice lollipop for the kids. **Director**—Wolfgang Reitherman. **(G)** *78 minutes*

ARMED AND DANGEROUS (1986)

★

John Candy
Eugene Levy

Armed and Dangerous: *law-enforcement blues with Eugene Levy and John Candy.*

Former SCTV cast members Candy and Levy bumble through this witless slapstick comedy as inept security guards who expose racketeers within their company. This labored effort, under the lackluster direction of Mark Lester, relies on ridiculous situations, foolish outfits, and various vehicle smashups for comic effect. The emphasis on violence to get laughs and guns as instruments of humor is disturbing. The result is merely an exercise in bad taste. Also with Robert Loggia and Kenneth McMillan. **(PG–13)** *88 minutes*

AROUND THE WORLD IN EIGHTY DAYS (1956)

★★★

David Niven
Cantinflas
Shirley MacLaine
Robert Newton

A splendid, charming film version of Jules Verne's magnificent travelogue, with spectacular scenery from various parts of the world and scores of cameos from an all-star cast. Niven plays the British gentleman who, in 1872, honored a bet that he could circle the globe within 80 days. The lavish production, with its Academy Award-winning cinematography, works best on the large screen and unfortunately loses impact on television. **Director**—Michael Anderson. **Academy Awards**—best picture; James Poe, John Farrow, and S. J. Perelman, best adapted screenplay. **Nomination**—Anderson, best director. *170 minutes*

THE ARRANGEMENT (1969)

★½

Kirk Douglas
Faye Dunaway
Deborah Kerr

An unfocused melodrama about an advertising executive who becomes fed up with his job, bungles a suicide attempt, and then analyzes the meaning of his life. Elia Kazan, who directed from his own novel, provides rich detail about the stress of contemporary life, but the characters involved are colorless. Douglas, Dunaway, and Kerr are wasted. Also with Richard Boone and Hume Cronyn. **(R)** *127 minutes*

ARROWSMITH (1931)

★★★

Ronald Colman
Helen Hayes
Myrna Loy

Director John Ford fashioned a moving film from the Sinclair Lewis novel about a medical researcher (Colman) who loses his wife and nearly strays from his calling when temptation comes his way. Sidney Howard provided the intelligent script. **Academy Award Nominations**—best picture; Howard, adaptation. *108 minutes b&w*

ARSENIC AND OLD LACE (1942)

★★★

Cary Grant
Josephine Hull
Jean Adair

Amusing and charming film adaptation of the Broadway play about two old ladies who poison gentlemen visitors in their Brooklyn home and then bury them in the cellar. It's a lot of fun despite the concentration on corpses. Director Frank Capra pulls out all stops to induce energy and hilarity from the excellent cast, which also includes Raymond Massey, Priscilla Lane, Peter Lorre, Edward Everett Horton, and James Gleason. *118 minutes b&w*

ARTHUR (1981)

★★★

Dudley Moore
Liza Minnelli
John Gielgud

In this lively screwball comedy, Moore has the title role as an often-inebriated, poor little rich man who falls in love with a waitress, played by Minnelli. Moore tosses off a succession of zingy, clever one-liners, but it's Gielgud as Ar-

® This movie available with closed captions for the hearing impaired.

thur's snobbish valet and conscience who provides the real comic chemistry. He steals scenes with undisguised relish. Minnelli is charming, but her role gives her little to work with. **Director**—Steve Gordon. **(PG) Academy Award**—Gielgud, best supporting actor. **Nominations**—Moore, best actor; Gordon, best screenplay written directly for the screen. *97 minutes*

ARTHUR 2: ON THE ROCKS (1988)

 ★½

Dudley Moore
Liza Minnelli

Dudley Moore and Liza Minnelli live it up in Arthur 2: On the Rocks.

This bungled sequel to the effervescent 1981 romantic comedy about the tipsy millionaire playboy is a major disappointment. This time, Arthur (Moore) has lost his fabulous inheritance and must seek work. This setup only leads to boring situations that sag under the strain of crude jokes. John Gielgud, who was so crucial in the original as the wise and witty butler, makes only a brief appearance here. Also with Geraldine Fitzgerald, Cynthia Sykes, and Jack Gilford. **Director**—Bud Yorkin. **(PG)** *110 minutes*

ARTISTS AND MODELS (1955)

★★★

Dean Martin
Jerry Lewis

Lewis has nightmares that inspire the grist for comic strips drawn by Martin in this colorful comedy that represents the best of the Martin and Lewis films directed by Frank Tashlin. The subject matter—a cartoonist's imagination and inspiration—is perfectly suited to Tashlin's visually surreal style, no doubt inspired by his early career as part of the animation department at Disney studios. An excellent example of Tashlin's work, which frequently deals with the popular arts. Also with Shirley MacLaine, Dorothy Malone, Eddie Mayehoff, and Eva Gabor. *109 minutes*

THE ASPHALT JUNGLE (1950)

 ★★★★

Sterling Hayden
Sam Jaffe
Louis Calhern

Compelling crime drama, astutely directed by John Huston, about a gang of criminals who try to commit the perfect crime. The film evolves as more of a character study than a mystery. Excellent, gritty performances by Hayden, Jaffe, and James Whitmore. Marilyn Monroe has a small part that she handles well. **Academy Award Nominations**—Huston, best director; Ben Maddow and Huston, screenplay. *112 minutes b&w*

ASSASSINATION (1987)

 ★★

Charles Bronson
Jill Ireland

Bronson stars as a top Secret Service agent assigned to protect the First Lady, an arrogant and spoiled millionairess played by Ireland, who is the target of assassins. The contrived plot is laced with explosions and shoot-'em-up sequences interrupted periodically by absurd romantic interludes. Based on the novel *My Affair with the President's Wife* by Richard Sale, the film is merely another formulaic action vehicle for Bronson, who is too old to be effective in such roles. **Director**—Peter Hunt. **(PG–13)** *88 minutes*

THE ASSAULT (1986)

 ★★★

Derek de Lint

A grim drama from acclaimed Dutch director Fons Rademakers about a young man haunted by an incident from his childhood. During World War II, the man's family was murdered by the Nazis after being accused of slaying a local collaborator. The film follows the effect of this tragedy on the poor man as he matures, goes to college, marries, etc. This compelling story of one individual's suffering symbolizes the impact and long-term effect the Nazi occupation of the Netherlands had on the country as a whole. Also starring Monique van de Ven. Originally filmed in Dutch. **(PG) Academy Award**—best foreign-language film. *150 minutes*

ASSAULT FORCE

See ffolkes

ASSAULT ON A QUEEN (1966)

★½

Frank Sinatra
Virna Lisi

A group of disreputable characters get their hands on a German submarine and set out to pirate a luxury liner. A rather unlikely crime caper that fails at many levels: The acting is stilted, the special effects are unconvincing, and Rod Serling's screenplay falters. Also with Tony Franciosa, Richard Conte, and Alf Kjellin. **Director**—Jack Donohue. *106 minutes*

AT CLOSE RANGE (1986)

 ★★½

Sean Penn
Christopher Walken
Christopher Penn

Christopher Walken, Sean Penn, and Christopher Penn in At Close Range.

Walken stars as the head of an organized band of professional thieves in the farmlands of Pennsylvania, who introduces his son (Sean Penn) to a life of crime. Based on a true incident, the film unfolds from the boy's point of view, as he sees his father first as an escape route from his poor environs and then as the cutthroat murderer he really is. Unfortunately, the fascinating story, which combines the timeless theme of the corruption of youth with social commentary on the lack of opportunity for the rural poor, is undermined by director James Foley's ultraslick direction

(Continued)

(Continued)
and quick editing technique. Though the glossy style is at odds with the content, the film is notable for the performances and the script by Nicholas Kazan. Also with Millie Perkins and Mary Stuart Masterson. **(R)**
115 minutes

ATLANTIC CITY (1981)

★★★½

Burt Lancaster
Susan Sarandon
Kate Reid

Susan Sarandon is a hopeful, faintly disreputable resident of Atlantic City.

French director Louis Malle has come up with a real charmer in this unusual romantic melodrama. It's crowded with colorful people who pursue their private dreams against the backdrop of this resort city. The most engaging character is Lou, played by Lancaster, an elderly petty criminal who at last achieves a delightful moment of glory and thus regains his self-respect. Lancaster's gentle and touching portrayal is carried off with superb finesse. There are also polished performances from Sarandon, as a girl determined to have a brighter future than she can look forward to in Atlantic City, and Reid, as a widow mourning her girlhood from the safety of her bedroom. **(R) Academy Award Nominations**—best picture; Lancaster, best actor; Sarandon, best actress; Malle, best director; John Guare, best screenplay written directly for the screen. *104 minutes*

ATTACK (1956)

★★★½

Jack Palance
Eddie Albert
Lee Marvin

Gripping and intelligent drama about American soldiers involved in the Battle of the Bulge and led by a cowardly commander. The slick production is far above the routine war movie thanks to excellent acting, a finely tuned script, and impressive direction by Robert Aldrich. The theme touches on an antiwar sentiment. Also with Buddy Ebsen, Robert Strauss, and Richard Jaeckel.
107 minutes b&w

AT WAR WITH THE ARMY (1950)

Dean Martin
Jerry Lewis

Martin and Lewis demonstrate their comic chemistry together in this routine service comedy based loosely on a play by James Allardice. There are a few clever gags, but it's not all that funny. Martin and Lewis are song-and-dance men with girl trouble. Polly Bergen and Jimmie Dundee costar. **Director**—Hal Walker. *93 minutes b&w*

AUDREY ROSE (1977)

Marsha Mason
John Beck
Anthony Hopkins

Take a slice of *The Exorcist*, a measure of *The Omen*, a dash of *Rosemary's Baby*, and add plenty of water. The result is this tepid tale of an 11-year-old girl who is the reincarnation of another girl killed in a crash. The padded script contains a lot of mumbo jumbo about Indian mysticism. Mason, Beck, and Hopkins act their parts as if they have difficulty keeping a straight face. Also with Susan Swift, Norman Lloyd, and John Hillerman. **Director**—Robert Wise. **(PG)** *113 minutes*

AUNTIE MAME (1958)

 ★★★

Rosalind Russell
Forrest Tucker

Russell's *tour-de-force* portrayal of the eccentric aunt who takes her young orphaned nephew under her wing graces this entertaining film rendition of Patrick Dennis' novel. Some priceless moments spark hilarity galore as Roz plays the colorful character to the hilt. Mame believes life is a banquet, and she proves it. Peggy Cass is memorable for her "Miss Gooch" characterization. Coral Browne and Fred Clark also star. **Director**—Morton Da Costa. **Academy Award Nominations**—best picture; Russell, best actress; Cass, best supporting actress. *143 minutes*

AU REVOIR LES ENFANTS (1988)

Gaspard Manesse
Raphael Fejto

Au Revoir Les Enfants *is a poignant study of boyhood in France during World War II.*

An exceptionally moving recollection of childhood by director Louis Malle. At a Catholic school in occupied France during World War II, a pre-adolescent boy becomes friends with one of the new Jewish students. With careful restraint, Malle carefully builds up to the heartbreaking climax in which the Gestapo takes away the Jewish classmates despite the efforts of a heroic priest who tries to shield them. The title implies the young boy's farewell to innocence as he realizes that there is much violence and prejudice in the world. Originally filmed in French. **(PG) Academy Award Nominations**—best foreign-language film; Malle, best screenplay written for the screen. *103 minutes*

AUTHOR! AUTHOR! (1982)

 ★★½

Al Pacino

® *This movie available with closed captions for the hearing impaired.*

Pacino effectively portrays a struggling New York playwright who's gallantly trying to support five children from various marriages. This look at modern family life is not as compelling as that presented in *Kramer vs. Kramer,* which this film occasionally resembles. Bear with it, however, because this comedy/drama ends with a charming display of warmth and sympathy between Pacino and his kids—who survive in spite of their home life. Tuesday Weld and Dyan Cannon are wasted in their brief roles. **Director**—Arthur Hiller. **(PG)**
110 minutes

AUTUMN SONATA (1978)

★★★

Ingrid Bergman
Liv Ullmann

Ingmar Bergman directs Ingrid Bergman for the first time in this film about a mother-and-daughter love-hate relationship. Ingrid Bergman is a successful concert pianist, and Ullmann is her middle-aged daughter. They turn in dynamic and inspired performances. Ingmar Bergman is on familiar territory, relentlessly exposing complex human relationships and emotions. Originally filmed in Swedish. **(No MPAA rating) Academy Award Nominations**—Ingrid Bergman, best actress; Ingmar Bergman, best screenplay written directly for the screen. *97 minutes*

AVALANCHE EXPRESS (1979)

★½

Lee Marvin
Robert Shaw
Linda Evans

Shaw, Marvin, Joe Namath, and a few other familiar players fumble through this languid melodrama about Soviet and American agents aboard a train traveling through Europe. The action stumbles along with much banal dialogue and clumsy direction. About midway, an avalanche is set off in an attempt to eliminate a defected Russian, played by Shaw. From then on, the film continues to slide downhill. **Director**—Mark Robson. **(PG)** *88 minutes*

AVANTI (1972)

Jack Lemmon
Juliet Mills

Lemmon stars in this black comedy about a wealthy young man who falls in love with the daughter of his father's mistress. The film is drawn out, yet plenty of wit and style in the script and classy acting by a good cast sustain interest. Director Billy Wilder isn't at his top form, but his execution is satisfactory. **(R)** *144 minutes*

AVENGING FORCE (1986)

Michael Dudikoff

An ex-government agent (Dudikoff) comes to the aid of a liberal black politician who is being harassed by a group of right-wing terrorists from the Louisiana bayous. Violent shoot-outs dominate the film at the expense of characterization and plot. John P. Ryan has a colorful role as a villainous industrialist with sharp, menacing teeth. **Director**—Sam Firstenberg. **(R)**
104 minutes

THE AWAKENING (1980)

★★

Charlton Heston
Stephanie Zimbalist

Heston plays an archaeologist who invades the secret tomb of Egypt's Queen Kara and unleashes her nasty spirit on the world. The film, based on Bram Stoker's novel, starts off with intrigue and suspense as Heston uncovers the ancient crypt with its splendors. But with the mummy's curse on the loose, the atmosphere deteriorates to hokey horror fare with accentuated violence. Zimbalist does a fair job as Heston's daughter who is possessed by Kara's cruel spirit. **Director**—Mike Newell. **(R)**
105 minutes

AWAY ALL BOATS (1956)

Jeff Chandler
George Nader
Julie Adams

Routine World War II action/adventure with overwrought heroic displays dominating the film. Story revolves around a transport ship involved in the Pacific campaign. Chandler leads the troops into battle. There are supporting roles by Nader, Adams, Lex Barker, and Richard Boone. **Director**—Joseph Pevney.
114 minutes

THE AWFUL TRUTH (1937)

★★★

Cary Grant
Irene Dunne
Ralph Bellamy

Irene Dunne tries to win back Cary Grant in The Awful Truth.

Dunne, Grant, and Bellamy sparkle in this typical 1930s-style sophisticated comedy about a divorced couple who realize they still love each other. The script seems silly at times, but the actors are wise enough not to take themselves or the plot too seriously. Remade in 1953 as the musical "Let's Do It Again." **Director**—Leo McCarey. **Academy Award**—McCarey, best director. **Nominations**—best picture; Dunne, best actress; Bellamy, best supporting actor; Vina Delmar, screenplay.
90 minutes b&w

B

BABAR: THE MOVIE (1989)

★★

The adventures of Babar, the heroic elephant, which were originally detailed in the popular book series from France, comes to the screen in animated form. However, this cartoon feature lacks the gentle lyricism of the printed tales, which were rendered in pastel colors and soft outlines. The storyline explains how Babar became king of Elephantland. Along the way, Babar saves his beloved Celeste's village from the ravages of terrifying rhinos. He then learns some lessons from friendly jungle creatures. The original design of the characters, created by Jean de Brunhoff in 1931, does not lend itself to animation very well, and the feature suffers from a jerkiness reminiscent of the worst Saturday-morning cartoon fare.
(Continued)

This movie available on videotape and/or disc.

(Continued)
Still, small children should enjoy Babar's adventures. Gordon Pinsent supplies the voice of Babar, while Elizabeth Hanna is the voice of Celeste. **Director**—Alan Bruce. **(G)** *75 minutes*

THE BABE RUTH STORY (1948)

★★½ Q®

William Bendix
Claire Trevor

Bendix is convincing as the "Sultan of Swat," but an unpolished script hamstrings this film biography. Events are presented in an overly sentimental fashion. However, the Babe's image remains intact. Charles Bickford and William Frawley play supporting roles. **Director**—Roy Del Ruth. *107 minutes b&w*

BABES IN ARMS (1939)

★★★

Mickey Rooney
Judy Garland

If energy alone could make masterpieces, this MGM musical would blow off the roof. Rooney is the driving force, determined to stage a fund-raiser with his pals to save their parents, ex-vaudeville stars, from bankruptcy. He sings and dances up a storm and impersonates Clark Gable and FDR—all of which helped him become the most popular movie star of the year. You may or may not care for such an assault of irrepressibility, but it *is* vintage Rooney. It's also the first of the successful Rooney and Garland costarring vehicles and the best known of the "Let's put on a show!" musicals. Oddly, most of the songs from the original Rodgers and Hart show are gone (though "The Lady Is a Tramp" is spared), and Busby Berkeley's directing is at a low ebb. **Academy Award Nomination**—Rooney, best actor. *96 minutes b&w*

BABES IN TOYLAND (1934)

★★★

Stan Laurel
Oliver Hardy
Charlotte Henry

A Christmas gift that's a year-round pleasure, especially for kids. Producer Hal Roach's rendition of the Victor Herbert operetta has Laurel and Hardy playing Stanley Dum and Oliver Dee, assistants to a toymaker. They misinterpret an order from Santa Claus and create a set of giant soldiers, who come in handy when the Bogeymen invade Toyland. Brooklyn-born Henry, a popular child star of the early 1930s, and the star of the 1933 *Alice in Wonderland,* plays Bo Peep. **Directors**—Gus Meins and Charles R. Rogers. **Alternate Title**—*March of the Wooden Soldiers.* *73 minutes b&w*

BABETTE'S FEAST (1988)

★★★

Stephane Audran
Birgitte Federspiel
Bodil Kjer

This delightful Danish film, based on an Isak Dinesen story, is set in a remote fishing village in Denmark during the late 19th century. Audran stars as Babette, a French woman who works as a housekeeper for two elderly sisters. The village residents are members of a strict Lutheran sect, which does not allow for excessive pleasures of any type. After Babette wins the French Lottery, she prepares a sumptuous meal of mouth-watering delights for the entire village, much to their chagrin. This modest but handsome period piece serves as a lighthearted parable for a modern age obsessed with diet and exercise. Originally filmed in Danish and French. **Director**—Gabriel Axel. **(G) Academy Award**—best foreign-language film. *102 minutes*

BABY (1985)

★½

William Katt
Sean Young
Patrick McGoohan

William Katt and Sean Young with their prehistoric pet in Baby.

A contemporary jungle adventure featuring an infant brontosaurus as the object of frantic concern by a young American couple. They discover the prehistoric toddler in the African rain forest and try to protect it from an evil paleontologist (McGoohan). This tedious fantasy wants to present the baby brontosaurus as cute and sympathetic as Bambi. But the 10-foot-long rubber and plastic "hatchling" is not so convincing. **Director**—B.W.L. Norton. **(PG) Alternate Title**—*Baby. . . Secret of the Lost Legend.* *95 minutes*

BABY BLUE MARINE (1976)

★★ Q®

Jan-Michael Vincent
Glynnis O'Connor

Vincent plays a World War II bootcamp washout who pretends to be a Marine Ranger and is hailed as a hero in a small community. It's an overly sentimental story lacking significant impact to carry it through. There are warm and touching moments here and there, but the overall complexion is akin to a TV soap opera. Vincent and O'Connor, the girl who falls in love with him, are appealing and make the most of their parts. **Director**—John Hancock. **(PG)** *90 minutes*

BABY BOOM (1987)

★★½

Diane Keaton
Sam Shepard

Executive Diane Keaton takes on extra responsibility in Baby Boom.

Keaton stars in this uneven yuppie comedy as a high-powered business executive married to her job with the six-figure salary. When she unexpectedly inherits a baby girl, her motherly instincts sidetrack her climb up the corporate ladder. The first half of the film, which features Keaton's attempts to juggle her role as mother with that of ruthless executive, provides the most

Q® *This movie available with closed captions for the hearing impaired.*

humor. After she moves to the Vermont countryside to live a less hectic existence, the film turns into a sweet comic fantasy with a predictable outcome. Shepard is wasted in a throwaway role as a country vet who keeps Keaton company in Vermont. Also with Harold Ramis, James Spader, and Kristina and Michelle Kennedy. **Director**—Charles Shyer. **(PG)** *103 minutes*

BABY DOLL (1956)

★★★

Karl Malden
Eli Wallach
Carroll Baker

An engrossing screen adaptation of Tennessee Williams' moody comedy of depravity among poor people in the Deep South. The typical Williams plot is enhanced by the incisive direction of Elia Kazan. Baker is impressive as the child bride who is seduced by her husband's acquaintance. Wallach and Malden perform well in striking roles. Also with Mildred Dunnock and Rip Torn. **Academy Award Nominations**—Baker, best actress; Dunnock, best supporting actress; Williams, best adapted screenplay. *116 minutes b&w*

BABY FACE NELSON (1957)

★★★

Mickey Rooney
Cedric Hardwicke
Carolyn Jones

Rooney's energetic and colorful performance in the title role graces this low-budget film about the notorious gangster of the Depression era. A great deal of action involving bank heists, prison breaks, and shootings highlights the film. The production looks good despite the skimpy budget. Also with Jack Elam, Chris Dark, Ted De Corsia, and Leo Gordon. **Director**—Don Siegel. *85 minutes b&w*

BABY, IT'S YOU (1983)

★★★

Rosanna Arquette
Vincent Spano

An absorbing, highly charged teenage romance by writer/director John Sayles *(Return of the Secaucus 7)*. The emotional story of star-crossed young lovers stumbles over occasional holes in the plot, yet the material is consistently compel-

Rosanna Arquette is courted by Vincent Spano in Baby, It's You.

ling. Above all, the film works as a dazzling showcase for some hip performances by talented newcomers. Arquette gives a convincing performance as the bright Jewish physician's daughter who is courted by the brash, Italian working-class youth, played by Spano. **(R)** *105 minutes*

BABY, THE RAIN MUST FALL (1965)

★★

Steve McQueen
Lee Remick

An ex-con returns home to his wife and daughter, tries to mend his ways, but reverts to violence. His behavior leads to reseparation. McQueen and Remick give it a good shot but can't rescue the sentimental and pretentious material, which smacks of Tennessee Williams fare. The film is adapted from Horton Foote's play *The Traveling Lady.* Cast includes Don Murray, Paul Fix, Josephine Hutchinson, and Ruth White. **Director**—Robert Mulligan. *100 minutes b&w*

THE BACHELOR AND THE BOBBY-SOXER (1947)

★★★

Cary Grant
Myrna Loy
Shirley Temple

Ideal comedy vehicle for Grant, who plays a dashing playboy pursued by an impressionable teenager, played by Temple. Uncomplicated script paves the way for Grant's buoyant and breezy performance. It's pleasant entertainment from every angle despite the triteness of the material. Also with Rudy Vallee, Ray Collins, and Harry Davenport. **Director**—Irving Reis. **Academy Award**—Sidney Sheldon, original screenplay. *95 minutes b&w*

BACHELOR MOTHER (1939)

★★★

Ginger Rogers
David Niven
Charles Coburn

David Niven and Ginger Rogers take a stab at parenthood in Bachelor Mother.

Heard the one about the woman who finds an abandoned baby, and everyone thinks it's really hers, and although she insists it isn't, she decides to adopt it anyway? Though this was a familiar story even way back in 1939, the film is still freshly played and crisply written and directed. It turned out to be one of the surprise comedy hits of the year, firmly establishing its director, Garson Kanin, and helping Rogers begin a solo career without Fred Astaire. Niven plays the Good Samaritan son of Ginger's boss, whose innocent efforts to help the new mama place him under plenty of suspicion. **Academy Award Nomination**—Felix Jackson, original story. *81 minutes b&w*

THE BACHELOR PARTY (1957)

★★★

Don Murray
E.G. Marshall
Jack Warden

Paddy Chayefsky's TV play is expanded for the screen, and the result is an on-target social commentary graced by fine performances. A group of New York bookkeepers throw a party for a colleague prior to his wedding. The event

(Continued)

(Continued)
emphasizes the emotional problems of the guests. The superb cast includes Carolyn Jones, Philip Abbott, and Patricia Smith. **Director**—Delbert Mann. **Academy Award Nomination**—Jones, best supporting actress.
93 minutes b&w

BACHELOR PARTY (1984)

★1/2

Tom Hanks
Tawny Kitaen
Adrian Zmed

Tom Hanks and friends prepare for the rowdy fun of a Bachelor Party.

Patchy, sophomoric comedy built around a wild party for a soon-to-be-married young man, played with moderate charm by Hanks. Aside from Hanks' likable presence, the film features an array of sleazy characters who instigate various vulgar sex escapades laced with the usual assortment of scatological jokes. There's a bit of high-minded philosophizing amidst the degenerate shenanigans: Will the recipient of this bash remain pure and faithful to his bride? **Director**—Neal Israel. **(R)** *106 minutes*

BACK ROADS (1981)

★★

Sally Field
Tommy Lee Jones

Field stars as a likable hooker who falls in love with a drifter-boxer, played by Jones, as they hitchhike from Alabama to California. Both portray cheerful, gritty characters, but the pedestrian screenplay quickly runs out of energy, and the film winds up on a dead-end street. It's difficult to perceive perky Field as a washed-up streetwalker. **Director**—Martin Ritt. **(R)** *94 minutes*

BACK TO BATAAN (1945)

★★★

John Wayne
Anthony Quinn

Wayne plays a Marine colonel who leads guerrilla troops on the road to victory in the Philippines against the Japanese. It's a routine war adventure, but there is substantial action and excitement, especially for fans of the Duke. Wayne is at his macho best and is helped out nicely by Beulah Bondi, Richard Loo, and Leonard Strong. **Director**—Edward Dmytryk.
97 minutes b&w

BACK TO SCHOOL (1986)

★★★

Rodney Dangerfield
Sally Kellerman
Keith Gordon

Sally Kellerman teaches Rodney Dangerfield in Back to School.

Comedian Rodney Dangerfield stars in this vehicle tailored to his style of humor, which includes fast-paced one-liners and broad, unsophisticated physical comedy. Here, his character is more likable than in his previous films, *Caddyshack* and *Easy Money*. He plays a self-made millionaire who attends college with his son (Gordon) to help bolster the young man's self-esteem. Dangerfield attempts to buy his way through college, but eventually learns that earning it the hard way is more rewarding. Kellerman plays an English literature professor whom Dangerfield falls for. The rest of the characters, including a money-grubbing dean and a stuffy economics professor, are stereotypes and foils for Dangerfield's jokes. A highly entertaining comedy, particularly for Dangerfield's fans. Also with Burt Young, Robert Downey, Jr., Paxton Whitehead, M. Emmet Walsh, Adrienne Barbeau, and Ned Beatty. **Director**—Alan Metter. **(PG-13)**
96 minutes

BACK TO THE BEACH (1987)

★★★

Frankie Avalon
Annette Funicello

Frankie and Annette are reunited for this clever parody of the old beach party movies, which made the pair an unforgettable part of Americana. The film opens with the now-married Frankie and Annette residing in suburban Ohio with their teenage son—a wisecracking punk rocker who is constantly flicking his switchblade. When they return to Malibu to visit their daughter, they are shocked to lean that she is living with a surfer. While there, the pair bump into some of the old gang, including flirtatious Connie Stevens, who tries to steal Frankie from Annette. An assortment of cameo appearances by former TV stars and a surprise visit from Pee-Wee Herman add to the fun. Though satirical in tone, this stylish and colorful comedy is never mean-spirited. Also with Lori Loughlin and Tommy Hinkley. **Director**—Lyndall Hobbs. **(PG)** *94 minutes*

BACK TO THE FUTURE (1985)

★★★

Michael J. Fox

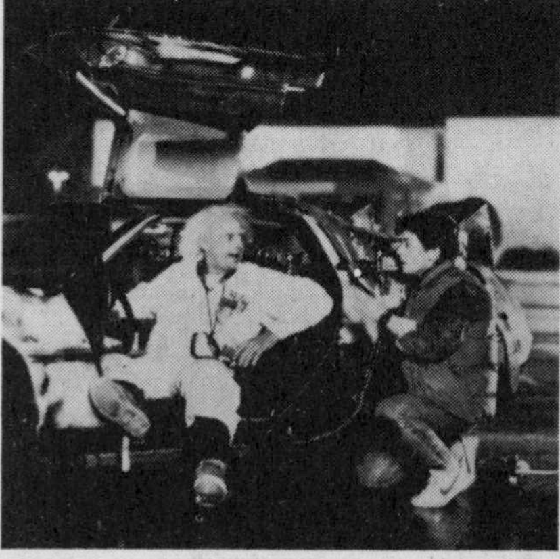

Christopher Lloyd shows Michael J. Fox his time machine in Back to the Future.

Whimsical sci-fi comedy with Fox as a crafty teenager who is transported to the "primitive" 1950s where he encounters his parents as youngsters. Some wit and warmth here, but the film depends upon cheering for the youth of one generation over the dumb bullies and bunnies of an earlier one. Judging from the box-office reaction, that's just fine with everyone. Also with Christopher Lloyd, Lea Thompson, and Crispin Glover. **Director**—Robert Zemeckis. **(PG) Academy Award Nomination**—best original screenplay. *114 minutes*

BACK TO THE FUTURE, PART II (1990)

★★½

Michael J. Fox
Christopher Lloyd
Lea Thompson
Thomas F. Wilson

Doc Brown's time machine works its magic once more in this popular but confusing sequel. Fox returns as hapless Marty McFly, who makes a worthy sidekick for the eccentric Doc, played by Lloyd. The two travel forward and backward in time to the years 2015 and 1955 in attempts to ward off various dark destinies. As the second in the series, the film suffers from an inconclusive ending, made more noticeable by the convoluted script. Viewers who have not seen the original will be lost. Also, some of the plot twists and characters are quite grim, casting a pall over what are supposed to be comic antics. Robert Zemeckis directs with a breakneck pace, which has become his trademark after the original *Back to the Future* and *Who Framed Roger Rabbit*. Thompson and Wilson reprise their original roles. Also with Harry Waters, Jr. **(PG) Academy Award Nomination**—Ken Ralston, Michael Lantieri, John Bell, and Steve Gawley, visual effects.
110 minutes

BACK TO THE FUTURE, PART III (1990)

★★★

Michael J. Fox
Christopher Lloyd
Mary Steenburgen
Thomas F. Wilson

The final chapter in the series follows Marty McFly (Fox) and Doc Brown (Lloyd) on a time-travel adventure to the Old West. Marty must save the eccentric scientist from death by tinkering with history and battling a vicious gunslinger—the ancestor of arch-

Christopher Lloyd and Michael J. Fox return in Back to the Future, Part III.

nemesis Biff Tannen. Doc is humanized somewhat by a romance with Steenburgen's character. Unlike the chaotic action and confusing time-travel logic of the second film, this last adventure settles down to one pace, making for an elaborate spoof on the western genre and its conventions. Clever references to various characters from previous episodes as well as a running send-up of Clint Eastwood's Italian westerns works well. Cameo appearances by old-time western sidekicks Harry Carey, Jr., Pat Buttram, and Dub Taylor will delight film buffs. Also with Lea Thompson and Elisabeth Shue. **Director**—Robert Zemeckis. **(PG)** *118 minutes*

THE BAD AND THE BEAUTIFUL (1952)

★★★★

Kirk Douglas
Walter Pidgeon
Lana Turner
Dick Powell

A clever drama about ambitious Hollywood types, related as an inside story. Douglas is superb as a ruthless producer who influences the lives and careers of people within his grasp. Other memorable performances come from Gloria Grahame, who plays a southern belle, and Turner, who plays an actress. Also with Barry Sullivan, Gilbert Roland, and Leo G. Carroll. Robert Surtees' Academy Award-winning cinematography is a striking example of how black-and-white photography can set an overall mood that enhances the story. **Director**—Vincente Minnelli. **Academy Awards**—Grahame, best supporting actress; Charles Schnee, screenplay. **Nomination**—Douglas, best actor. *118 minutes b&w*

BAD BOYS (1983)

★★½

Sean Penn

Penn stands out with a convincing portrayal of a moody, hard-boiled teenager who lands in a foul reform school where he has to fight for survival. Otherwise, this tense, atmospheric film is routine in narrative and fails to develop believable characters. Director Richard Rosenthal *(Halloween II)* employs various manipulative tactics that dwell too long on brutal confrontations. Eric Gurry steals scenes as Penn's crafty cellmate. **(R)** *123 minutes*

BAD COMPANY (1972)

★★★

Barry Brown
Jeff Bridges
John Savage

David Newman and Robert Benton were the hot new writers on the Hollywood scene when their first film, *Bonnie and Clyde,* became a 1967 sensation. Five years later, the team showed the same sensitivity in a story about young men turned criminals in *Bad Company,* which was Benton's first film as a director. It's a poignant account of alienated and homeless kids robbing their way to the West during the Civil War. Told from the point of view of a well-raised draft dodger, it paints an affecting picture of how easily circumstances can lead the young and the unprotected into an irreversible life of crime. **(PG)**
93 minutes

BAD DAY AT BLACK ROCK (1954)

★★★★

Spencer Tracy
Robert Ryan
Dean Jagger

A crackling suspense drama about a one-armed stranger, played by Tracy, who encounters hostility in a small western town, and then discovers the community has something to hide. Director John Sturges expertly builds tension to a smashing climax. There are fine performances from the cast, which also includes Walter Brennan, Ernest Borgnine, and Lee Marvin. **Academy Award Nominations**—Sturges, best director; Tracy, best actor; Millard Kaufman, screenplay. *81 minutes*

This movie available on videotape and/or disc.

BAD DREAMS (1988)

★★

Jennifer Rubin
Bruce Abbott
Richard Lynch

In this gory horror film, reminiscent of *A Nightmare on Elm Street*, a young girl survives a suicide ritual, lapses into a coma, and awakens 13 years later in a psychiatric hospital. With the help of the staff psychiatrist, she tries to adjust to the 1980s but can't escape the terrifying memories of the traumatic event. Rubin fares well as the besieged woman, but the low-budget production emphasizes grisly effects over a tightly constructed storyline. Also with Dean Cameron and Harris Yulin. **Director**—Andrew Fleming. **(R)** *85 minutes*

BAD INFLUENCE (1990)

★★★

Rob Lowe
James Spader
Lisa Zane

Lisa Zane is captivated by Rob Lowe in Bad Influence.

Spader stars as an innocent yuppie whose life is transformed for the worse when he accidentally meets a mysterious charmer, played by Lowe. Despite a somewhat slow start, this thriller effectively builds to a suspenseful if predictable conclusion. The film's publicity took advantage of Lowe's real-life scandal to construct an image for him of the handsome man who looks perfect on the outside but is flawed inside. The taut, moody screenplay with its clever plot twists and unnerving psychological elements owes much to Hitchcock's *Strangers on a Train*. Lowe's character is a metaphor for the dark impulses that attract all of us, making for a tantalizing if slightly uncomfortable movie-going experience. Most of the lesser characters sustain interest. Also with Christian Clemenson, Kathleen Wilhoite, Tony Maggio, Marcia Cross, and Grand Bush. **Director**—Curtis Hanson. **(R)** *99 minutes*

BADLANDS (1973)

★★★½

Martin Sheen
Sissy Spacek

A teenage misfit and her older boyfriend cross the country murdering people along the way. This skillfully perceived drama, which eventually became a cult film, is based on the actual killing spree of Charles Starkweather and Carol Fugate in the 1950s. Sheen and Spacek are impressive in the lead roles. And it's a successful debut for director Terrence Malick, who also wrote the script. Warren Oates and Ramon Bieri are in supporting roles. **(PG)** *94 minutes*

BAD MEDICINE (1985)

★★

Steve Guttenberg
Alan Arkin
Julie Hagerty

An uneven comedy about the misadventures of aspiring American physicians studying at a dilapidated Central American medical school. A few decent laughs surface, but the film strains too much with the thin material. Ultimately, the movie lives up to its title. Guttenberg stars as the not-too-bright young man who is pressured into medical school to uphold family tradition. Arkin plays the school administrator, another in his long series of wacky and eccentric characters. **Director**—Harvey Miller. **(PG-13)** *96 minutes*

THE BAD NEWS BEARS (1976)

★★★

Walter Matthau
Tatum O'Neal

A carefree and touching comedy about a down-in-the-mouth Little League baseball team—The Bears—that is rescued by a cigar-chomping, beer-guzzling coach, played by Matthau. O'Neal, in her first film since *Paper Moon*, is the ace pitcher who helps save the day. Director Michael Ritchie *(Smile; The Candidate)* continues to dwell on his favorite social theme of competition and concocts the right mixture of warmth and emotion. Matthau is at his best, and the child actors are appealing. Although this film is about kids, it is aimed primarily at adults. *Bad News* is good news. Also with Vic Morrow and Joyce Van Patten. **(PG)** *102 minutes*

THE BAD SEED (1956)

★★★

Nancy Kelly
Patty McCormack

Nancy Kelly can't believe that daughter Patty McCormack is The Bad Seed.

An intriguing story about an innocent-looking eight-year-old girl who maliciously murders various people, including some of her playmates. The film version faithfully recalls the stage play with Kelly repeating her role as the distraught mother. McCormack is convincing in the title role as the child who inherited evilness. Henry Jones and Eileen Heckart are in supporting roles. **Director**—Mervyn LeRoy. **Academy Award Nominations**—Kelly, best actress; McCormack and Heckart, best supporting actress. *129 minutes b&w*

BAD TIMING: A SENSUAL OBSESSION (1980)

★★★½

Art Garfunkel
Theresa Russell
Harvey Keitel

Expatriate Americans in Vienna—a colorless psychiatrist (Garfunkel) and an amoral beauty (Russell)—begin a dangerously passionate sexual relationship. Although Garfunkel is an interestingly aloof presence, it's Russell's show all the way. The script has few surprises (we can guess that the relationship is headed for a violent conclusion); the story's raw emotional intensity and Russell's remarkably affecting portrait

® This movie available with closed captions for the hearing impaired.

of self-destructive promiscuity are what make the film a riveting experience. The only noticeable drawback is the ludicrous miscasting of the very American Keitel as a Viennese police inspector. Directed by Nicolas Roeg with characteristic vigor and narrative inventiveness. Also with Daniel Massey and Denholm Elliott. **(R)** *123 minutes*

LA BALANCE (1982)

★★★

Philippe Leotard
Nathalie Baye

Stylish, action-packed police thriller played out amid the back alleys of the Paris underworld. A streetwise brigade of detectives painstakingly cultivates a network of informers to bring criminals to justice. The acting, pacing, and character development are accomplished with a skill that rivals the best of American gangster films. Leotard, Baye, and Richard Berry turn in credible performances. Originally filmed in French. **Director**—Bob Swain. **(R)**
102 minutes

BALL OF FIRE (1941)

★★★★

Gary Cooper
Barbara Stanwyck

Cooper's brilliant comedy talent and Howard Hawks' skillful direction make this story of a burlesque dancer (Stanwyck) who seeks shelter with seven professors a delight. The comic situations are keyed to contrast one of the professors (Cooper), who is preparing a book about slang in the English language, with the dancer and her gangster friends, who use slang as their first and only language. Also with Dana Andrews, Dan Duryea, and Gene Krupa. **Academy Award Nominations**—Stanwyck, best actress; Thomas Monroe and Billy Wilder, original story.
111 minutes b&w

LA BAMBA (1987)

★★★

Lou Diamond Phillips
Esai Morales

A heartfelt film biography of 1950s rock 'n' roll singer Ritchie Valens, who died in the same plane crash that killed Buddy Holly. As written and directed by Luis Valdez, however, the film is more than a biography. In Valdez' film, Valens uses his natural talents to lift himself out of the abject poverty he was born into, but along the way he alienates his brother and sacrifices some of his Hispanic identity. Much of the drama centers on Valens' relationship with his brother, who accuses the talented performer of turning his back on his Mexican-American background in order to sing rock 'n' roll. Excellently acted by a relatively unknown cast, the film also features a delghtful score, which was arranged and performed by Los Lobos. Also with Rosana De Soto, Elizabeth Pena, Danielle von Zerneck, and Joe Pantoliano. **(PG-13)**
108 minutes

BAMBI (1942)

★★★★

This is one of Walt Disney's best cartoon features. It is the story of a fawn that grows to be a magnificent stag. The film, based on the book by Felix Salten, is sometimes overly sentimental, yet the animal characters are heartwarming and memorable. Thumper the rabbit is unforgettable. It's a remarkable achievement from a most skillful crew of animators. *72 minutes*

BANANAS (1971)

★★★

Woody Allen
Louise Lasser

Allen plays a meek factory worker who runs off to South America, where he leads a revolution and becomes a hero. It's a typical offering of Allen's humor and unusual comic ideas, with a generous dose of sight gags. Many jokes are hilarious, but a few miss the mark. Carlos Montalban and Howard Cosell have supporting parts, and Sylvester Stallone has a minor part as a gangster. **Director**—Allen. **(PG)** *82 minutes*

BAND OF THE HAND (1986)

★★

Stephen Lang
Michael Carmine

A hyped-up action/adventure tale set among Miami's illicit drug community. Some youthful criminals learn survival tactics, adopt self-discipline, discover confidence and then return to their urban environment. These reformed punks then wage war on the bad guys. The frantic film, which features the usual heaping ration of overstated violence, was produced by Michael Mann who created the TV series *Miami Vice.* The influence of the series can be seen in the visual style of the film. **Director**—Paul Michael Glaser. **(R)**
109 minutes

THE BAND WAGON (1953)

★★★★

Fred Astaire
Cyd Charisse
Jack Buchanan

Nanette Fabray in a number from The Band Wagon.

Toe-tapping musical with the incomparable Astaire in splendid form. The standard simple plot, pegged on problems of producing a Broadway show, makes way for numerous delightful song-and-dance numbers, including "Shine on My Shoes," "Dancing in the Dark," "I Guess I'll Have to Change My Plan," and "Louisiana Hayride." Oscar Levant and Nanette Fabray are also in the cast. **Director**—Vincente Minnelli. **Academy Award Nomination**—Betty Comden and Adolph Green, story and screenplay. *112 minutes*

BANG THE DRUM SLOWLY (1973)

★★★

Michael Moriarty
Robert De Niro

De Niro and Moriarty stand out in this film version of Mark Harris' novel about a baseball player stricken with leukemia who wants to play another season before he dies. The story is somewhat cliché-strewn, but doesn't become overly sentimental. Also with Vincent Gardenia and Phil Foster. **Director**—
(Continued)

This movie available on videotape and/or disc.

(Continued)
John Hancock. **(PG) Academy Award Nomination**—Gardenia, best supporting actor. *98 minutes*

THE BANK DICK (1940)

★★★★

W.C. Fields

Yes indeed. The great Fields is at his funniest. As Egbert Sousé, a sort of nonentity, Fields foils a bank heist. As a reward he's hired as a bank guard. All sorts of hilarious high jinks take place. It's classic humor in the Fields tradition. And there's fine support from Franklin Pangborn and Shemp Howard. **Director**—Eddie Cline.
73 minutes b&w

BARBARELLA (1968)

★★

Jane Fonda
John Phillip Law

Fonda stars as an attractive 41st-century astronaut in this French-Italian sci-fi film based on a French comic strip. Razzle-dazzle special effects perk things up here and there, but the script is nonsense. There are supporting roles by Marcel Marceau, Anita Pallenberg, David Hemmings, and Ugo Tognazzi. **Director**—Roger Vadim. *98 minutes*

BARBAROSA (1982)

★★★

Gary Busey
Willie Nelson

Australian director Fred Schepisi *(The Chant of Jimmie Blacksmith)* makes his first American film—an intriguing, scrappy, and offbeat western. Even though the genre is somewhat dated, this romantic tale of a legendary desperado (Nelson) and his younger sidekick (Busey) offers a full dose of fresh charm. Nelson and Busey work well side by side. Schepisi has approached an old Hollywood theme from a new angle. **(PG)** *90 minutes*

BARBARY COAST (1935)

★★★

Edward G. Robinson
Miriam Hopkins
Joel McCrea

Sturdy, two-fisted drama that also has heart and complexity. During the San Francisco gold rush days, a drifter (McCrea) and the town tyrant (Robinson), who also runs the ever-packed gambling casino, clash over a dance hall queen (Hopkins). Stylishly written by Ben Hecht and Charles MacArthur, tightly directed by Howard Hawks, and evocatively performed by the stars and supporting players Walter Brennan, Brian Donlevy, Frank Craven, Harry Carey, and Donald Meek.
91 minutes b&w

THE BAREFOOT CONTESSA (1954)

★★★

Humphrey Bogart
Ava Gardner
Edmond O'Brien

Bogart, Gardner, and O'Brien star in this handsome tale about the rise and fall of an actress. The film holds ample fascination, yet it is somewhat long-winded. The actors fare well with some clever dialogue. O'Brien stands out as a brassy press agent. **Director**—Joseph L. Mankiewicz. **Academy Award**—O'Brien, best supporting actor. **Nomination**—Mankiewicz, story and screenplay.
128 minutes

BAREFOOT IN THE PARK (1967)

★★★

Robert Redford
Jane Fonda

Neil Simon's Broadway comedy about newlyweds coping with life in New York City holds up nicely on the screen with plenty of one-liners intact. Redford and Fonda are the charming couple who reside in a cramped Manhattan walk-up. Mildred Natwick plays the bride's mother. Charles Boyer and Herb Edelman are also in the cast. **Director**—Gene Saks. **Academy Award Nomination**—Natwick, best supporting actress. *109 minutes*

BARFLY (1987)

★★½ ®

Mickey Rourke
Faye Dunaway

Charles Bukowski adapted to the screen this autobiographical account of a talented but booze-soaked writer.

Love is where you find it: Faye Dunaway and Mickey Rourke in Barfly.

Rourke stars as the central character who, like Bukowski himself, is an alcoholic poet and novelist living on Los Angeles' Skid Row. Dunaway costars in a critically acclaimed performance as his companion in an endless series of lost weekends. Tension arises when a beautiful literary agent becomes interested in Rourke's writing—and in Rourke. This unusual drama features some fine performances and poetic dialog, but the storyline is minimal, even slight. Some may find the squalid atmosphere and Rourke's satisfaction with his grungy lifestyle to be too grim. Also with Alice Krige, Frank Stallone, and J.C. Quinn. **Director**—Barbet Schroeder. **(R)** *100 minutes*

THE BARKLEYS OF BROADWAY (1949)

★★★

Fred Astaire
Ginger Rogers

Astaire and Rogers star as a bickering song-and-dance couple who split and then make up. She wants to be a serious actress. Their dancing is delightful, and some of the memorable songs include "They Can't Take That Away From Me" and "You'd Be Hard to Replace." Oscar Levant, Billie Burke, and Jacques François play supporting roles. **Director**—Charles Walters.
109 minutes

THE BARRETTS OF WIMPOLE STREET (1934)

★★★

Norma Shearer
Fredric March
Charles Laughton

This was the sort of prestige movie that many people believed at least partly exonerated Hollywood for its frequent tawdriness. Adapted from a literate play about literary people (Elizabeth Barrett and Robert Browning), it is a drama

® *This movie available with closed captions for the hearing impaired.*

about emotions—the poets' mutual love and Browning's attempt to free the invalid Barrett from her father's spiritual stranglehold. It was meticulously produced by MGM's boy wonder Irving Thalberg and intelligently directed by Sidney Franklin. By current standards, much of the film looks stodgy and predictable, but the stars still attract and its antique veneer still shines. **Academy Award Nominations**—best picture; Shearer, best actress.

110 minutes b&w

BARRY LYNDON (1975)

★★★

Ryan O'Neal
Marisa Berenson
Patrick Magee

Master director Stanley Kubrick turns to the 18th-century W.M. Thackeray novel for this ponderous costume drama about an Irish rogue who climbs to the top of English aristocratic society. It's technically well made and beautifully photographed. But the energy is slowed to a creep, and emotion is sorely lacking. It's more like taking a stroll through a wax museum than watching a movie. Most moviegoers would probably walk out of this three-hour ordeal more dazed than entertained. O'Neal plays Lyndon, and Berenson plays the beautiful, sad, and wealthy countess he marries. Also with Hardy Krüger, Steven Berkoff, and Gay Hamilton. The production is set against the music of Bach, Handel, Schubert, Mozart, and Vivaldi. **(PG) Academy Award**—John Alcott, cinematography. **Nominations**—best picture; Kubrick, best director and best screenplay adapted from another medium. *185 minutes*

BATAAN (1943)

Robert Taylor
George Murphy
Lloyd Nolan

A rousing World War II drama about American soldiers who defend a bridge on a Pacific island against the Japanese. The film smacks somewhat of propaganda with cardboard characters, but combat action and suspense are handled nicely. Plot is reminiscent of *The Lost Patrol*. The excellent cast includes Desi Arnaz, Robert Walker, Thomas Mitchell, Lee Bowman, and Barry Nelson. **Director**—Tay Garnett.

114 minutes b&w

BATMAN (1989)

★★★

Jack Nicholson
Michael Keaton
Kim Basinger

Batman *comes to life on the screen with Michael Keaton.*

This intense, brooding adventure based on the highly respected comic book series from the 1930s is a far cry from the 1960s TV show. Keaton, a controversial choice for the title role, carefully underplays his character, which is in sharp contrast to Nicholson's entertaining tour-de-force as the Joker. Gotham City is wrapped in a striking *film-noir* production design, which enhances the meaning of the film. The dark, dank city streets not only represent the corruption of Gotham City but also connote the dark recesses of Batman's troubled mind. Rock singer Prince provides part of the soundtrack. Also with Robert Wuhl, Billy Dee Williams, Jerry Hall, and Pat Hingle. **Director**—Tim Burton. **(PG-13) Academy Award**—Anton Furst and Peter Young, art direction. *126 minutes*

*BATTERIES NOT INCLUDED (1987)

★★½

Hume Cronyn
Jessica Tandy

Toylike flying saucers are the real stars of this children's fantasy, produced by Steven Spielberg. These pint-sized visitors from space come to the rescue of

Jessica Tandy and Hume Cronyn star in *batteries not included.

some inner-city residents about to be evicted from their ancient Manhattan apartment building. The amazing miniature saucers speed through the air, swoop down from above, and purr like kittens. Designed by Industrial Light & Magic, they add a touch of whimsy to the sometimes syrupy story. Also with Frank McRae, Elizabeth Pena, Michael Carmine, Dennis Boutsikaris, and Tom Aldredge. **Director**—Matthew Robbins. **(PG)** *106 minutes*

BATTLE BEYOND THE STARS (1980)

★★½

Richard Thomas
Robert Vaughn

Science-fiction fans may find this obvious rip-off of *Star Wars* superior to that film in some respects. It is more genuinely funny, for example, and the film never takes itself seriously. The plot involves a peaceful planet threatened by invasion. Mercenaries are recruited by Thomas to repel the bad guys. The half sci-fi, half comic-book adventure is replete with strange characters, including five clones wrapped in a beach towel, and the special effects are sometimes so cheap as to be hilarious (as with the spacecraft combat that seems lifted from a video arcade). George Peppard, John Saxon, and Darlanne Fluegel are featured in supporting roles. **Director**—Jimmy T. Murakami. **(PG)** *104 minutes*

BATTLE CRY (1954)

★★★

Van Heflin
Aldo Ray
Tab Hunter
Mona Freeman

(Continued)

(Continued)
Some good performances enhance this screen treatment of Leon Uris' World War II adventure of Marines on their way to war in the Pacific. Romantic subplots are woven in with some action scenes. Dorothy Malone is memorable as an older woman who falls for one of the young warriors. The cast also includes Raymond Massey, Nancy Olson, and James Whitmore. **Director**—Raoul Walsh. *148 minutes*

BATTLEGROUND (1949)

★★★★

Van Johnson
John Hodiak
Ricardo Montalban

This drama about a group of American infantrymen involved in the Battle of the Bulge is a cut above the routine World War II action film. Excellent characterizations, inspired acting, and a compelling script complement the exciting and suspenseful action sequences. Johnson, Hodiak, Montalban, and James Whitmore are fine in memorable roles. William Wellman's efficient direction hits the mark. **Academy Award**—Robert Pirosh, story and screenplay. **Nominations**—best picture; Wellman, best director; Whitmore, best supporting actor. *118 minutes b&w*

BATTLE OF THE BULGE (1965)

★★½

Henry Fonda
Robert Shaw
Robert Ryan
Dana Andrews
George Montgomery

Henry Fonda and Robert Ryan fight the Battle of the Bulge.

An overblown World War II action drama concerning the bloody and anxious confrontation with Nazi Panzers in the Ardennes, with Allied troops narrowly escaping defeat. Emphasis is on the action and the booming battle scenes. Script, acting, and character development take a back seat. The cast also includes Pier Angeli, Telly Savalas, Ty Hardin, Charles Bronson, and James MacArthur. Videotape versions may be shorter. **Director**—Ken Annakin. *167 minutes*

BATTLESTAR GALACTICA (1979)

Richard Hatch
Dirk Benedict
Lorne Greene

This feature film is made up of episodes from a short-lived TV sci-fi series that wasn't so hot to begin with. There's really not much improvement in this venture. Survivors of interplanetary warfare embark on a space journey to Earth to establish a new life there. Lavish special effects are notable, but the ragged story holds scant interest. The *Star Wars* format is mimicked right and left, but without its imagination and mysticism. Also with Ray Milland, Lew Ayres, Jane Seymour, and Laurette Spang. **Director**—Richard A. Colla. **(PG)** *125 minutes*

BATTLE STRIPE

See The Men

BAT 21 (1988)

★★★

Gene Hackman
Danny Glover

Gene Hackman and Danny Glover in the Vietnam War story Bat 21.

Hackman plays a high-ranking reconnaissance officer shot down in Vietnam. While a friendship develops between the downed airman and a spotter pilot (Glover) who aids in his rescue, the drama, based on a true story, runs deeper. The stranded American, who previously dealt with the war at a safe distance, now experiences disgust when he views the horror close up. It's a far cry from *Rambo*. Also with Jerry Reed, David Marshall Grant, Clayton Rohner, and Erich Anderson. **Director**—Peter Markle. **(R)** *105 minutes*

BEACHES (1988)

★★½ 

Bette Midler
Barbara Hershey

Barbara Hershey and Bette Midler are the best of friends in Beaches.

Midler plays a brassy singer from the Bronx, while Hershey is a pampered WASP from San Francisco. Their enduring friendship across the continent results in a predictable tearjerker broken up only occasionally by a few laughs. Midler's saucy personality overtakes her character, particularly when she is belting out the musical numbers. Unfortunately, her vivacious energy cannot save this lukewarm, meandering, and often confusing melodrama. **Director**—Garry Marshall. **(PG-13)** **Academy Award Nomination**—Albert Brenner and Garrett Lewis, art direction. *120 minutes*

BEACH PARTY (1963)

Frankie Avalon
Annette Funicello
Bob Cummings

Who could have dreamed when *Beach Party* first surfed into neighborhood theaters two decades ago that it would one day be screened at the Museum of Modern Art? Art it's not, but it is interesting as a sociological phenomenon—a typical, modestly produced American International Pictures production that struck gold in the youth market and spawned sequels. Cummings plays an

® This movie available with closed captions for the hearing impaired.

anthropology professor studying the sexual mores of California youth. Take a dip for the fun of it, though you may not want to stay in very long. Also with Dorothy Malone, Morey Amsterdam, and Harvey Lembeck. **Director**—William Asher. *101 minutes*

THE BEAR (1989)

★★★

The Bear *confronts Tcheky Karyo, one of the hunters who has wounded him.*

A stirring animal adventure, this amazing film is told from the point of view of the animals. The film is not a documentary but a narrative in which a bear cub and a full-grown grizzly pair up for a series of adventures that span approximately one year. As directed by French filmmaker Jean-Jacques Annaud *(Quest for Fire; The Name of the Rose)*, the story emphasizes the violence of nature rather than the cute antics such as those expected from a Disney animal adventure. Except for a few lines spoken by a pair of hunters, there is virtually no dialogue in the film. Meaning is conveyed primarily through editing. The human hunters are played by Jack Wallace and Tcheky Karyo. **(PG) Academy Award Nomination**—Noëlle Boisson, editing. *93 minutes*

THE BEAST (1988)

★★

George Dzundza
Jason Patric
Steven Bauer

"The Beast" is a Soviet tank that gets lost in Afghan enemy territory. The crew must deal with the wrath of their brutal commander as well as some vengeful Afghans. Director Kevin Reynolds, a protege of Steven Spielberg, has fashioned a peculiar film that is violent, well-paced, and fascinating. Interestingly, the Russian characters speak English while the Afghani characters speak in a subtitled Afghan dialect. This reinforces the idea that the film is a metaphor for the U.S. involvement in Vietnam. A cast of young unknowns attacks the material with confidence. Also with Stephen Baldwin, Erick Avari, and Dan Harvey. **(R)** *109 minutes*

THE BEASTMASTER (1982)

★★

Marc Singer
Tanya Roberts

A lively but absurd fantasy/adventure starring muscular Singer as a sort of medieval Tarzan who rescues a pretty slave girl (Roberts) from the clutches of barbarians. Singer pulls off countless heroic deeds with the help of his animal friends, which include two mischievous ferrets and an old tiger dyed black to look like a panther. Much silly dialogue accompanies the nonstop excitement. Rip Torn gets into the action as a sinister priest with a yen for sacrificing babies and virgins. **Director**—Don Coscarelli. **(PG)** *120 minutes*

BEAT STREET (1984)

★★

Guy Davis
Robert Taylor
Rae Dawn Chong

Harry Belafonte coproduced and cowrote the music for this celebration of three young New York ghetto friends who pursue recognition as a break dancer, graffiti artist, and disco DJ. The film is largely an extended talent show, with some exhilarating dance numbers and appealing kids. With so little drama or characterization, however, it can't sustain much emotional involvement. Not enough joy spills off the screen. **Director**—Stan Lathan. **(PG)** *104 minutes*

BEAT THE DEVIL (1954)

★★★½

Humphrey Bogart
Jennifer Jones
Gina Lollobrigida
Peter Lorre

In the history of off-the-wall cinema, *Beat the Devil* holds a very special place. It's an anarchic, tongue-in-cheek spoof of caper movies, scripted by Truman Capote and director John Huston, about a bunch of misfits scrambling after some uranium. But if you're not quickly won over, you may find its kookiness coy and cloying. The spirited cast also includes Robert Morley. *92 minutes b&w*

BEAU BRUMMELL (1954)

★★

Stewart Granger
Elizabeth Taylor
Peter Ustinov
Robert Morley

Granger plays a foppish and colorful Englishman who befriends the Prince of Wales, played by Ustinov. This historical production is lavish and exquisitely photographed, but the stilted story is hard to believe. Regardless, the cast—including Taylor, at the height of her beauty—does an admirable job in the costume epic. Morley plays George III. **Director**—Curtis Bernhardt. *111 minutes*

BEAU GESTE (1939)

★★★½

Gary Cooper
Ray Milland
Robert Preston

No braver brothers ever defended God, country, and family more than the three brothers Geste. Almost as venerable as the Three Musketeers, the Geste boys go on contending with desert varmints and Foreign Legion tyrant Sgt. Markoff (Brain Donlevy) in rerun after revival after replay. Also with Susan Hayward, J. Carrol Naish, Albert Dekker, Broderick Crawford, and Donald O'Connor. **Director**—William Wellman. **Academy Award Nomination**—Donlevy, best supporting actor. *120 minutes b&w*

LE BEAU MARIAGE (1982)

★★

Beatrice Romand
André Dussollier

Eric Rohmer presents a mildly amusing romantic comedy about a young art student (Romand) who chucks her liberated woman's lifestyle and embarks on a quest to marry "Mr. Right." Rohmer's observations of traditional values are interesting, but the film neglects any significant character development and often lapses into routine talkativeness. The sweet humor produces a few smiles, but some genuine laughter would be welcome. Originally filmed in French. **(PG)** *97 minutes*

THE BEAUTIFUL BLONDE FROM BASHFUL BEND (1949)

★★

Betty Grable
Cesar Romero

Preston Sturges made this tongue-in-cheek western about a tough saloon singer, played by Grable, who becomes a schoolteacher in a small town after she mistakenly shoots a sheriff. Nothing bashful about Grable, who seems right for the role, but Sturges doesn't execute the direction with a firm hand, and the film turns out to be rather silly. Hugh Herbert is funny as a doctor with eye problems. Rudy Vallee and Sterling Holloway are also in the cast.

77 minutes

BEAUTY AND THE BEAST (1946)

★★★★

Jean Marais
Josette Day
Marcel André

Jean Marais plays the ugly captor in Beauty and the Beast.

There's enchantment to spare in this adult retelling of the fairy tale about a hostage who is treated so kindly by her monstrous captor that she falls in love with him. The adult in this case is poet/painter/writer/filmmaker Jean Cocteau, who had a way with fanciful cinema. Exquisitely photographed at the Raray palace and park, the richness of it all may get too thick for some tastes, but it's certainly worth seeing. Georges Auric wrote the moody music, and the charismatic cast has the necessary panache. Originally filmed in French. **Director**—Cocteau.

90 minutes b&w

BECKET (1964)

★★★

Richard Burton
Peter O'Toole
John Gielgud

Richard Burton is the Archbishop and Peter O'Toole is Henry II in Becket.

Sumptuous medieval spectacle that's rich with historical drama about the Archbishop of Canterbury, Thomas à Becket, and his relationship with King Henry II. Burton and O'Toole are superb in the key roles and seem to thoroughly enjoy their acting assignments. Some of the energy, however, is drained away by a too-long and, at times, tedious script. The film is based rather faithfully on Jean Anouilh's stage play. Fine supporting performances are given by Gielgud, Donald Wolfit, and Pamela Brown. **Director**—Peter Glenville. **Academy Award**—Edward Anhalt, best screenplay based on material from another medium. **Nominations**—best picture; Glenville, best director; Burton and O'Toole, best actor; Gielgud, best supporting actor.

149 minutes

BEDAZZLED (1967)

★★★

Dudley Moore
Peter Cook
Raquel Welch

Moore and Cook wrote this pre-Monty Python comic madness in which Moore plays a modern-day Faust, a short short-order cook who is granted seven sinful wishes by a modern-day Satan (Cook) in exchange for his soul. Some of the sinful escapades (as with Welch playing Lillian Lust) are disappointing, but most sparkle with an irreverent wit. Stanley Donen's direction is fast-paced, easily accommodating the verbal and visual gags. *107 minutes*

THE BEDFORD INCIDENT (1965)

★★★

Richard Widmark
Sidney Poitier

A suspenseful Cold War drama about a gung ho skipper of an American destroyer, played by Widmark, who accidentally fires an atomic weapon while stalking a Soviet submarine in the North Atlantic. Widmark's portrayal of the obsessed naval officer is superb. There's also excellent acting from Poitier, who plays a reporter on board, as well as James MacArthur and Martin Balsam. Tension swirls aboard ship in the manner of *The Caine Mutiny.* **Director**—James B. Harris.

102 minutes b&w

BEDKNOBS AND BROOMSTICKS (1971)

★★

Angela Lansbury

Angela Lansbury and Roddy McDowall in Bedknobs and Broomsticks.

Below-par Walt Disney musical about a good-natured witch, played by Lansbury, and some children who help the British war effort in the early 1940s. The film seems disorganized, despite the elaborate production. It's rather pale compared with the popular *Mary Poppins,* which it tries to imitate. Special effects and some of the cartoon sequences are handled well. The visual effects won an Academy Award. It also stars David Tomlinson, Sam Jaffe, and Roddy McDowall. **Director**—Robert Stevenson. **(G)** *117 minutes*

This movie available with closed captions for the hearing impaired.

BEDLAM (1946)

★★★

Boris Karloff

Excellent atmospheric effects enhance this chilling Val Lewton horror story about the infamous London insane asylum that flourished in the 18th century. Anna Lee plays a sane woman who is confined in an effort to expose the miserable conditions. The venerable Karloff is the head of the institution. Also with Billy House, Richard Fraser, and Ian Wolfe. **Director**—Mark Robson.

79 minutes b&w

THE BEDROOM WINDOW (1987)

Steve Guttenberg
Isabelle Huppert
Elizabeth McGovern

An uneven mystery thriller patterned on the style of director Alfred Hitchcock, but far removed from the master's subtle skill. Guttenberg stars as a young man who pretends to be a witness to an attempted murder to protect his lover (Huppert), who actually saw the crime. This bending of the truth leads to complications, which, unfortunately for the viewer, evolve as preposterous rather than intriguing. A mediocre film made weaker by the lack of chemistry between the stars. **Director**—Curtis Hanson. **(R)** *112 minutes*

BEDTIME FOR BONZO (1951)

★★

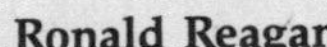

Ronald Reagan

In Bedtime for Bonzo, *Ronald Reagan tucks in his favorite chimp.*

Nonsensical comedy with Reagan as a professor rearing a chimpanzee to prove that environment affects personality. The silly monkeyshines seem to have an appeal for grownups as well as kids. The film did well enough to spawn a sequel, *Bonzo Goes to College*. It should have some added interest since Reagan served as President. Diana Lynn and Walter Slezak costar. **Director**—Frederick De Cordova.

83 minutes b&w

BEETLEJUICE (1988)

Geena Davis
Alec Baldwin
Michael Keaton

Michael Keaton is a fanciful demon in Beetlejuice.

Davis and Baldwin play a young couple who have settled down in a quaint Victorian home in New England. After they are killed in an auto accident, they return to their beloved house to haunt the far-out New Yorkers who have just moved in. Unfortunately, their amateurish efforts are ineffective so they call upon "Betelgeuse," a strange demon played by Keaton in a scene-stealing performance, to drive the outsiders away. The surrealistic set design, grotesque makeup, and surprising mechanical effects highlight this horror comedy, which was directed by Tim Burton—the man who brought us *Pee-Wee's Big Adventure*. Sylvia Sydney, a long-time star of stage and screen, is excellent as an afterlife case worker. Also with Jeffrey Jones, Catherine O'Hara, Winona Ryder, and Dick Cavett. **(PG)** **Academy Award**—Ve Neill, Steve LaPorte, and Robert Short, makeup.

92 minutes

THE BEGUILED (1971)

★★★

Clint Eastwood
Geraldine Page
Elizabeth Hartman

Eastwood stars in this odd Civil War drama about a wounded Union soldier who is brought to a girls' school in the South to receive nursing care. Eastwood's presence creates a sexual tension among the women, isolated from the outside world. An unusual role for Eastwood, but one that reveals his talents as an actor. Jo Ann Harris and Darleen Carr costar. **Director**—Don Siegel. **(R)** *109 minutes*

BEHOLD A PALE HORSE (1964)

★★

Gregory Peck
Omar Sharif
Anthony Quinn

Peck stars in this slow-paced drama about a Spanish renegade who goes into hiding and then returns to trap and kill a sadistic police chief. The film seems to have some class about it, but it eventually loses its way in a web of talky dialogue. Peck and others try their best but can't save the film. Behold a pale movie. **Director**—Fred Zinnemann. *118 minutes b&w*

BEING THERE (1979)

Peter Sellers
Shirley MacLaine
Melvyn Douglas

Peter Sellers plays a naive, sheltered gardener in Being There.

A droll comic fable about an innocent simpleton, played by Sellers, who is

(Continued)

This movie available on videotape and/or disc.

(Continued)
suddenly thrust into the world of wealth and power politics. Sellers sets aside his familiar slapstick style, plays it straight-faced, and achieves a remarkably inspired, funny performance. It's an insightful and intelligent adaptation of Jerzy Kosinski's novel. Hal Ashby's direction is capable, but the film is too long and overworks its wisdom-of-innocence theme. **(PG) Academy Award**—Douglas, best supporting actor. **Nomination**—Sellers, best actor.

130 minutes

THE BELIEVERS (1987)

 ★★

Martin Sheen
Helen Shaver

Despite the presence of several grisly animal and human sacrifices, this occult thriller remains routine and predictable. Sheen stars as a police psychologist whose young son becomes the target of Santeria worshippers. Similar in practice to voodoo, Santeria also involves ritual sacrifice. The excellent use of New York City locations, where even the most ordinary settings seem to blend with exotic practices, plus an experienced supporting cast, makes the film worthwhile viewing for fans of the occult. Also with Robert Loggia, Harley Cross, Jimmy Smits, Richard Masur, and Carla Pinta. **Director**—John Schlesinger. **(R)**

114 minutes

BELIZAIRE THE CAJUN (1986)

Armand Assante
Gail Youngs
Michael Schoeffling

Southern comfort with Gail Youngs and Armand Assante in Belizaire the Cajun.

A well-intentioned but flawed period piece about the persecution of Cajuns in Louisiana shortly before the Civil War. Assante stars in the title role as a Cajun herbal doctor who tangles with local vigilantes after his cousin is accused of murder. The thick accents of the characters and slow pacing may deter some viewers, but the authentic detail and fascinating subject make for out-of-the-ordinary viewing. Writer/director Glen Pitre is a Cajun himself, which accounts for the authenticity. Robert Duvall appears in a small part. **(PG)**

101 minutes

BELL, BOOK AND CANDLE (1958)

 ★★½

James Stewart
Kim Novak
Jack Lemmon

Screen version of John Van Druten's play ends up as a routine comedy with Novak miscast as a witch who falls in love with a book publisher, played by Stewart. However, the top cast manages to squeeze some engaging moments from the sentimental material. Ernie Kovacs, Hermione Gingold, and Elsa Lanchester contribute their fine talents. **Director**—Richard Quine.

103 minutes

THE BELLBOY (1960)

 ★★★

Jerry Lewis

Typical Lewis shenanigans with the comedian causing a ruckus at a swank Miami Beach hotel. There's no plot to speak of, just a series of blackout sketches with the usual line of gags. Worthwhile for those who appreciate Lewis. There are cameos from Milton Berle and Walter Winchell. Alex Gerry and Bob Clayton costar. **Director**—Lewis.

72 minutes b&w

THE BELLE OF NEW YORK (1952)

Fred Astaire
Vera-Ellen

Astaire walks on air here, and that seems to be the high point in this so-so musical set in New York City during the Gay Nineties. The middling plot has Fred as a playboy who flips for a Salvation Army girl, played by Vera-Ellen. There are some comic moments along with the dancing. "Let a Little Love Come In" is included among the songs. Marjorie Main, Keenan Wynn, and Alice Pearce are also in the cast. **Director**—Charles Walters.

82 minutes

A BELL FOR ADANO (1945)

★★★

John Hodiak
Gene Tierney

Charming and moving film, based on the John Hersey novel, about American occupation soldiers who earn the respect of citizens in a small Italian town by replacing the local bell. Director Henry King creates a pleasant mood and presents warm characterizations. Hodiak is fine as the American officer in charge of the town. Tierney plays the local female attraction. William Bendix, Richard Conte, and Henry Morgan also star.

103 minutes b&w

THE BELL JAR (1979)

 ★★

Marilyn Hassett
Julie Harris

The film is based on the haunting novel by Sylvia Plath, the extraordinary poet who committed suicide at 30. The screenplay faithfully follows the events of the book, but the movie fails to explore the mystery and the stress that led to the heroine's nervous breakdown. Drama and clarity are badly needed in place of the stifling flatness of Larry Peerce's direction. Anne Jackson, Barbara Barrie, and Robert Klein also star. **(R)**

107 minutes

BELLS ARE RINGING (1960)

 ★★★

Judy Holliday
Dean Martin

Holliday is at her best in this adaptation of the Broadway musical. She plays an answering service operator who listens in on conversations and can't help getting emotionally involved with clients' problems. Martin portrays an anxious playwright who becomes the object of Holliday's affections. Songs by Jule Styne include "Just in Time" and "The Party's Over." Cast includes Fred Clark, Eddie Foy, Jr., and Jean Stapleton. This

This movie available with closed captions for the hearing impaired.

was Holliday's last film. **Director**—Vincente Minnelli. *126 minutes*

THE BELLS OF ST. MARY'S (1945)

 ★★★

Bing Crosby
Ingrid Bergman

Crosby and Bergman star in this worthy follow-up to *Going My Way.* Bing is a priest at a Catholic school, and Ingrid is a nun there. The two launch a clever strategy to raise money for a school addition. It's highly entertaining in a sentimental way, with the leads in top form. There's support from Henry Travers, William Gargan, and Ruth Donnelly. **Director**—Leo McCarey. **Academy Award Nominations**—best picture; McCarey, best director; Crosby, best actor; Bergman, best actress. *126 minutes b&w*

THE BELLY OF AN ARCHITECT (1987)

★★1/2

Brian Dennehy
Chloe Webb

Dennehy stars in the title role as an American architect visiting Rome for an exhibition in honor of a little-known French architect. Against this background of classic art, Dennehy's contemporary character is plagued with a stomach ailment and a wife who is having an affair. The film is laden with comparisons of ancient craftsmanship and the frailties of modern man. The use of art as metaphor and the clash of nationalities and classes may remind viewers of director Peter Greenaway's later, more controversial film, *The Cook, The Thief, His Wife and Her Lover.* Beautiful cinematography by Sacha Vierny. Also with Lambert Wilson and Sergio Fantoni. **(R)** *108 minutes*

BELOVED INFIDEL (1959)

Gregory Peck
Deborah Kerr

This true story of F. Scott Fitzgerald's turbulent romance with Hollywood columnist Sheilah Graham lapses into soap-opera sentimentality. Peck is miscast as the famous novelist. Kerr fares better as Graham, who tries to cure Fitzgerald of alcoholism. The film mainly covers Fitzgerald's days in Hollywood in the late 1930s. It may satisfy someone looking for a good cry. Also with Eddie Albert and Philip Ober. **Director**—Henry King. *123 minutes*

BEN HUR (1959)

★★★1/2

Charlton Heston
Stephen Boyd
Jack Hawkins

A spectacular and lavish rendition of Lew Wallace's historical novel about an aristocratic Jew, played by Heston, who is persecuted by the Romans and eventually follows Christ. Heston as Ben Hur is superb in the title role, and the film, which won 11 Academy Awards, offers spectacular action sequences and magnificent cinematography. The tone, however, reverts to that of a good guy-bad guy western at times. A high point is the chariot race, with Ben Hur competing against Messala, played convincingly by Boyd. The outcome is predictable. Other cast members include Haya Harareet, Hugh Griffith, Martha Scott, and Sam Jaffe. **Directors**—William Wyler and Andrew Marton. **Academy Awards**—best picture; Wyler, best director; Heston, best actor; Griffith, best supporting actor; cinematography. **Nomination**—Karl Tunberg, best screenplay based on material from another medium. *217 minutes*

BENJI (1974)

★★1/2

Higgins (the dog)
Peter Breck
Edgar Buchanan

Young children should enjoy this film about a dog who saves two children from kidnappers and winds up as a member of their family. An improbable story but the film has lovable animal characterization. Also with Terry Carter and Christopher Connelly. **Director**—Joe Camp. **(G)** *89 minutes*

BENJI THE HUNTED (1987)

 ★★1/2

Red Steagall

Benji returns in an appealing outdoor adventure, which finds the lovable pup caring for a litter of orphaned cougar cubs. In this unique children's film, the animals are endowed with human val-

Everybody's favorite pooch (with feline friend) in Benji the Hunted.

ues and characteristics. This anthropomorphism works for the most part, except in a few offbeat scenes in which Benji recalls parts of his past via flashbacks. Human actors and dialogue are scarce, but the film features some amazing stunts from the remarkable dog and the other animals. The kids will enjoy this adventure tale especially tailored to their tastes. **Director**—Joe Camp. **(G)** *88 minutes*

THE BENNY GOODMAN STORY (1955)

 ★★1/2

Steve Allen
Donna Reed

Allen portrays the famous clarinetist in this sentimental biography that's typical of Hollywood productions. The story traces Goodman's life from his upbringing in Chicago to celebrity status in the world of swing music. Allen is fairly convincing in the title role. And the film is enhanced significantly by the clarinet playing of the real Goodman and guest appearances by big-band luminaries Gene Krupa and Harry James. Sammy Davis, Sr., and Martha Tilton lend support. **Director**—Valentine Davies. *117 minutes*

BERLIN ALEXANDERPLATZ (1983)

 ★★★★

Gunter Lamprecht
Hanna Schygulla
Barbara Sukowa

Monumental, ambitious film adaptation of Alfred Doblin's epic 1929 novel of post-World War I Berlin. Director Rainer Werner Fassbinder initially slated it as a television series. However, it was first exhibited in America in the-

(Continued)

This movie available on videotape and/or disc.

(Continued)
aters. The film is over 15 hours long, and getting through it is as exhausting as climbing to the top of the Statue of Liberty, but probably more rewarding. The sweeping story centers on an ex-convict who wants to be decent, but whose efforts are sabotaged by his miserable, depressing environment. Originally filmed in German. **(No MPAA rating)**

15 hours 21 minutes

BERT RIGBY, YOU'RE A FOOL (1989)

  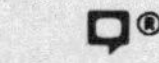

Robert Lindsay
Anne Bancroft
Corbin Bernsen

Robert Lindsay cavorts with Brenda Lee in Bert Rigby, You're a Fool.

Lindsay, in the title role, plays a jaunty British coal miner with song-and-dance talent who gets a crack at show biz and eventually Hollywood. Director and writer Carl Reiner presents such classic Hollywood songs as "The Continental" and "Singin' in the Rain." This peculiar film rambles aimlessly, and the songs have no grace or joy. **(R)** *92 minutes*

BEST BOY (1979)

 ★★★★

This is a documentary film about Philly Wohl, a 52-year-old mentally retarded man who progresses toward self-reliance. But don't be put off by the subject. It's a thrilling, uplifting, intelligent story about love, devotion, and the texture of family life. The style of director Ira Wohl—Philly's cousin—is direct and unembellished without being sentimental. Undoubtedly, this is one of the most extraordinary documentaries ever made. **(No MPAA rating) Academy Award**—Ira Wohl, feature documentary.

104 minutes

BEST DEFENSE (1984)

★1/2 

Dudley Moore
Eddie Murphy

Moore and Murphy bruise their acting careers in this dreadful slapstick comedy that spoofs weapons contractors. The effort could use some droll humor and sophistication. Yet we only get a lot of noise and some corny jokes that lead to confusion. Moore is a bumbling engineer who designs a faulty gyro for tank guidance systems. Murphy plays an Army lieutenant who must use the unworkable hardware. **Director**—Willard Huyck. **(R)** *94 minutes*

BEST FRIENDS (1982)

Burt Reynolds
Goldie Hawn

Reynolds and Hawn make a likable pair in this engaging romantic comedy. They are Hollywood screenwriters who finally marry after five years of living together. The low-key humor evolves when the couple visit their in-laws and their relationship starts feeling the strain. Savory moments of charm and honesty abound, but the story is rather thin. Jessica Tandy and Barnard Hughes costar. **Director**—Norman Jewison. **(PG)** *116 minutes*

THE BEST LITTLE WHOREHOUSE IN TEXAS (1982)

★★

Burt Reynolds
Dolly Parton

Dolly Parton and Burt Reynolds in The Best Little Whorehouse in Texas.

A film version of the hit Broadway musical about a legendary bordello known as The Chicken Ranch. Most of the song-and-dance numbers could use more bounce. There are effective performances from Reynolds as the beleaguered sheriff and Parton as the golden-hearted madam. Charles Durning, as the issue-dodging governor, has a sensational dance routine. Dom DeLuise and Jim Nabors also star. **Director**—Colin Higgins. **(R) Academy Award Nomination**—Durning, best supporting actor. *114 minutes*

THE BEST MAN (1964)

★★★1/2

Henry Fonda
Cliff Robertson
Lee Tracy

Two presidential aspirants vie for nomination and seek the blessing of the dying ex-president. Rivals Fonda and Robertson are in top form in this engrossing film version of Gore Vidal's topical play, which gives a perceptive view of the political process. Tracy stands out as the dying former chief executive. Margaret Leighton, Edie Adams, Shelley Berman, Ann Sothern, Richard Arlen, and Mahalia Jackson are in supporting roles. **Director**—Franklin Schaffner. **Academy Award Nomination**—Tracy, best supporting actor.

102 minutes b&w

THE BEST OF THE BEST (1989)

★1/2

Eric Roberts
James Earl Jones

This drab, cliché-filled sports drama follows the trials and triumphs of an American karate team competing in a South Korean match. All the formula elements are shamelessly copied here—the grizzled coach with a heart of gold, the rigorous training schedule, the victory over personal problems, and the ruthless competitors. Roberts, Jones, Sally Kirkland, Christopher Penn, and Louise Fletcher squander their talents on this trite film. **Director**—Bob Radler. **(PG-13)** *95 minutes*

THE BEST OF TIMES (1986)

  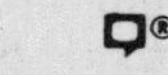

Robin Williams
Kurt Russell

This movie available with closed captions for the hearing impaired.

Paunchy, middle-aged, former high-school football players stage a rematch with their gridiron rivals of yesteryear. This comedy only works at the end when the big game is played. For most of the way, director Roger Spottiswoode fumbles with the pacing, while the plot never really develops. Williams and Russell strain at their roles as over-the-hill jocks. Pamela Reed and Holly Palance costar as frustrated wives. **(PG-13)** *105 minutes*

BEST SELLER (1987)

James Woods
Brian Dennehy

James Woods and Brian Dennehy collaborate in Best Seller.

A violent crime drama about two men on opposite sides of the law who join forces to expose the murderous ways of a corporate executive. Dennehy stars as a Los Angeles detective who writes books à la Joseph Wambaugh, and Woods plays a sleazy hit man who wants Dennehy to tell his story. The two actors are an appealing team: Their contrasting physiques and personalities seem to reflect their characters' opposing views on law and order. Unfortunately, the storyline contains far too many holes to be believable and Woods' inclination to bump people off at the drop of a hat is unsettling. The screenplay by Larry Cohen (writer/director of *It's Alive* and *The Stuff*) reflects his manic, lurid style. Also with Victoria Tennant, Paul Shenar, and Allison Balson. **Director**—John Flynn. **(R)** *95 minutes*

THE BEST THINGS IN LIFE ARE FREE (1956)

Ernest Borgnine
Gordon MacRae
Dan Dailey
Sheree North

The careers of songwriters DeSylva, Brown, and Henderson, who flourished in the 1920s, are the basis for this routine Hollywood musical. MacRae, Dailey, and Borgnine portray the Tin Pan Alley trio responsible for such hits as "Good News," "Sonny Boy," and "The Birth of the Blues." As to be expected, there's not much plot but the music is enjoyable. Norman Brooks and Murvyn Vye are also in the cast. **Director**—Michael Curtiz. *103 minutes*

THE BEST YEARS OF OUR LIVES (1946)

Fredric March
Myrna Loy
Teresa Wright
Dana Andrews

A powerful, provocative film about three GIs who return from World War II to a small American town and face difficulties adjusting to civilian life. Filmmaking quality prevails throughout with superior acting, no-nonsense direction, and perfect pacing. There are many touching moments—some amusing, some sad—that capture the mood of post-World War II America. Harold Russell, Virginia Mayo, Cathy O'Donnell, Hoagy Carmichael, Gladys George, and Ray Collins also star. **Director**—William Wyler. **Academy Awards**—best picture; Wyler, best director; March, best actor; Russell, best supporting actor; Robert E. Sherwood, screenplay. *172 minutes b&w*

BETRAYAL (1983)

 ★★★

Ben Kingsley
Jeremy Irons
Patricia Hodge

This is Harold Pinter's film version of his intriguing play about infidelity. It's loaded with subtleties, revealing observations, and beautiful moments of acting. The absorbing tale, set in London, unfolds in reverse time to expose a trail of deceptions. Despite its poignancy, the production cannot fully overcome its stagy aspects. Kingsley is remarkable as the husband whose response to adultery is unique and ultimately effective. Irons and Hodge also are superb as the adulterous lovers. **Director**—David Jones. **(R) Academy Award Nomination**—Pinter, best screenplay based on material from another medium. *95 minutes*

BETRAYED (1988)

 ★★★ 

Tom Berenger
Debra Winger

A gripping, provocative but flawed political thriller from director Constantin Costa-Gavras. Right-wing terrorists are operating in America's heartland. Undercover FBI agent Winger falls in love with Berenger, unaware that he is a member of the white-supremacist organization she is infiltrating. Many of the plot elements—especially the ending—are implausible, but the explosive story packs a punch and makes a compelling statement on racism. Also with John Heard, John Mahoney, Betsy Blair, and Ted Levine. **(R)** *123 minutes*

THE BETSY (1978)

 ★★

Laurence Olivier
Robert Duvall
Katharine Ross
Tommy Lee Jones

This melodramatic saga of intrigue, sex, and power among the upper crust of the auto industry is like a 1960 Cadillac—plush, but too much flash and too hard to handle. The classy cast, which also includes Jane Alexander and Lesley-Anne Down, turns out some neat performances. The unwieldy storyline, based on the Harold Robbins novel, is a problem with too many twists and a lot of frivolous gloss. The dialogue is loaded with howlers. **Director**—Daniel Petrie. **(R)** *125 minutes*

BETSY'S WEDDING (1990)

Alan Alda
Madeline Kahn
Molly Ringwald

The exasperation and expense a family must endure when a daughter gets married provides the subject of this uninspired comedy starring Alda as the harassed father of the bride. Ringwald costars as the offbeat daughter who is marrying the son of a prominent Manhattan family. A conflict of class and cultures ensues. Within the main storyline of the wedding, a number of subplots emerge, including one involving a romance between cop Ally Sheedy and Mafioso Anthony LaPaglia. The large

(Continued)

(Continued)
cast also features Joe Pesci, Joey Bishop, Catherine O'Hara, Burt Young, and Dylan Walsh. Each struggles with the clichéd gags and weak lines. Only newcomer LaPaglia is interesting, as the awkward Mafia prince. Alda also wrote and directed. **(R)** *97 minutes*

BETTER OFF DEAD (1985)

★★

John Cusack
David Ogden Stiers
Kim Darby

John Cusack (left) caught in another labor-management dispute in Better Off Dead.

This uneven comedy about a lovesick teenage boy offers a few moments of wit, but most of it is unfocused and in bad taste. Cusack tries hard as the nerdy high-school lad who goes to pieces when his girlfriend dumps him. His performance is usually ahead of the dopey material that ribs contemporary lifestyles. Diane Franklin costars. **Director**—Savage Steve Holland. **(PG)** *98 minutes*

BETTY BLUE (1986)

★★

Beatrice Dalle
Jean-Hughes Anglade

This curious French film by Jean-Jacques Beineix is marred by the plot's unbelievable, often outrageous events and by the exaggerated emotions of the characters. The story concerns a hot-tempered young woman whose violent actions stem from the frustrations of her existence. As she and her lover—whom she pushes to be a writer—move from town to town to escape the consequences of her destructive acts, their relationship begins to disintegrate and she descends into insanity. This third effort by Beineix lies somewhere between his highly acclaimed *Diva* and his critically ridiculed *Moon in the Gutter;* though the plot is not as incomprehensible as the latter's, the film lacks the insight and compassion for the characters of *Diva*. Originally filmed in French. **(No MPAA rating) Academy Award Nomination**—best foreign-language film. *117 minutes*

BEVERLY HILLS COP (1984)

★★★

Eddie Murphy

Murphy, as a brash, streetwise Detroit detective, shakes up posh Beverly Hills in his quest to find the killer of a friend. Murphy engagingly turns on his cool charm, pulls off numerous impersonations, and teaches the local by-the-book cops some effective police tactics. The bloody ending is heavy-handed, but there are ample laughs and thrills for thorough enjoyment—Murphy style. **Director**—Martin Brest. **(R) Academy Award Nomination**—Daniel Petrie, Jr., best screenplay written directly for the screen. *105 minutes*

BEVERLY HILLS COP II (1987)

★★

Eddie Murphy
Judge Reinhold
Brigitte Nielsen

Eddie Murphy is back for more action in Beverly Hills Cop II.

Murphy returns as Detective Axel Foley in this second installment of the adventures of the hip Detroit cop. Unfortunately, this comedy parallels the original so closely that it comes off as a copy rather than a sequel. The paper-thin plot finds Foley returning to the community of money and status to avenge a brutal attack on his friend, a sergeant on the Beverly Hills police force. Together with Reinhold and John Ashton—the two bumbling police officers of the first film—Foley uncovers the perpetrators, who are operating a sophisticated robbery ring in the area. Though much of Murphy's obviously improvised dialogue is funny, the feeble storyline is merely an excuse to showcase Murphy's comic bits. The depiction of women is particularly offensive as Foley is either oogling half-clad girls or outsmarting them with his streetwise banter. A waste of Murphy's considerable talents. Also with Ronnie Cox, Jürgen Prochnow, Dean Stockwell, Allen Garfield, and Paul Reiser. **Director**—Tony Scott. **(R)** *103 minutes*

BEYOND A REASONABLE DOUBT (1956)

★★★

Dana Andrews
Joan Fontaine
Sidney Blackmer

Just supposing someone wanted to prove the injustice of capital punishment. And supposing he had himself framed for a murder he didn't commit, to prove he could be wrongly condemned to death? That's the intriguing premise of *Beyond a Reasonable Doubt*, skillfully developed on the screen by director Fritz Lang. The low budget shows and not every plot twist works, but this last film made by Lang in America is still haunting. *80 minutes b&w*

BEYOND REASONABLE DOUBT (1980)

David Hemmings

From New Zealand, a somewhat rickety courtroom drama involving the complicated trial of a man accused of a double killing. Much of the plot, based on an actual murder case, centers on a gung ho detective who goes overboard to solve the case. Acting and direction are mainly humdrum, although Hemmings is impressive as the zealous police inspector. Also with John Hargreaves and Tony Barry. Originally released at 127 minutes. **Director**—John Laing. **(No MPAA rating)** *117 minutes*

BEYOND THE FOREST (1949)

Bette Davis
Joseph Cotten

An absurd, hysterical murder mystery with Davis overacting and adding to the muddle of the screenplay. Davis, who plays the wife of a small-town doctor, has an affair with her wealthy neighbor and then bungles a suicide attempt after murdering a witness. The rest of the cast is regrettably lost in the woods. Cotten plays the doctor; David Brian is the neighbor. Ruth Roman, Minor Watson, and Dona Drake also star. **Director**—King Vidor. *96 minutes b&w*

BEYOND THE LIMIT (1983)

★½

Richard Gere
Michael Caine

Richard Gere (right) experiences revolution first-hand in Beyond the Limit.

Much creative talent is wasted in this unfocused drama set in Paraguay about British doctor Gere having an affair with an ex-prostitute (Elpidia Carrillo), who is the wife of British consul Caine. The rambling plot also has Gere searching for his long-lost father and mixed up with political rebels. The whole enterprise does no justice to Graham Greene's novel, *The Honorary Consul.* Gere looks utterly puzzled throughout as the film tries to be torrid, but only manages to be horrid. **Director**—John Mackenzie. **(R)** *103 minutes*

BEYOND THE POSEIDON ADVENTURE (1979)

★½

Michael Caine
Sally Field
Telly Savalas
Peter Boyle

Irwin Allen takes us back to the overturned S.S. *Poseidon* for Chapter II of this disaster story. Here we find an all-star cast rummaging around the inside of the upside-down ocean liner looking for loot, dodging bullets, and mumbling idiotic dialogue. Caine, Field, Savalas, and other familiar performers have their acting reputations soaked to the skin. The audience may want to escape long before the players make it to the surface. Also with Jack Warden, Shirley Knight, Slim Pickens, Shirley Jones, and Karl Malden. **Director**—Allen. **(PG)** *122 minutes*

BEYOND THERAPY (1987)

★★

Jeff Goldblum
Julie Hagerty
Glenda Jackson
Tom Conti

Both psychiatrists and neurotics get a thorough roasting in Robert Altman's film version of Christopher Durang's play. While some of the one-liners are amusing, overall this scrambled farce is complicated to the point of frustration. Goldblum stars as a bisexual New York yuppie who meets Hagerty, a flighty young woman, through a magazine personal ad. Jackson and Conti costar as the oddball analysts. **(R)** *93 minutes*

BHOWANI JUNCTION (1956)

★★★

Ava Gardner
Stewart Granger

A fairly faithful rendering of John Masters' novel about a beautiful Anglo-Indian girl involved in romance and intrigue during the waning days of British rule in India. Gardner is convincing as the half-caste beauty who is torn between her love for an Englishman, played by Granger, and loyalty to her family. Impressive photography of the Pakistani locations enhances the drama. Bill Travers and Francis Matthews also star. **Director**—George Cukor. *110 minutes*

BIG (1988)

★★★

Tom Hanks
Elizabeth Perkins

In this lighthearted comedy, Hanks' natural charm adds much to the role of Josh Baskin, an adolescent who wakes up one morning as a young man. Thrust into the adult world, young Josh accidentally stumbles onto a job in a toy company, where his instinctive understanding of games and toys lands him a

Robert Loggia and Tom Hanks tickle the ivories in Big.

position as vice president. Though the emphasis is on laughs, the film suggests that the cutthroat competitiveness and stiffness of corporate life dulls the senses and stifles the imagination. This colorful comedy is the best of several films, popular in the late 1980s, which were dependent for their humor on the reversal of roles between a young man and an adolescent boy. Cowritten by Anne Spielberg, who is Steven Spielberg's sister. Also with Robert Loggia and John Heard. **Director**—Penny Marshall. **Academy Award Nominations**—Hanks, best actor; Gary Ross and Spielberg, best original screenplay. **(PG)** *102 minutes*

THE BIG BLUE (1988)

★½

Jean-Marc Barr
Jean Reno
Rosanna Arquette

Free-diving competition (going under water without breathing equipment) provides the basis for this romantic adventure that moves unsteadily about the globe. A French boy (Barr) and an Italian youngster (Reno) vie for the world championship. They also become involved with a young American woman (Arquette). The background scenery and underwater footage are spectacular, but the story is sketchy and ultimately uninteresting. **Director**—Luc Besson. **(PG)** *119 minutes*

THE BIG BRAWL (1980)

★★½

Jackie Chan

This martial-arts film is a step above the usual; it has a blend of humor, a decent script, and well-executed kung fu action. Chan, in his first American movie, plays the son of a Chicago res-

(Continued)

(Continued)
taurateur who subdues some local gangster bullies and then wins a free-for-all in Texas. The spunky and charming Chan trains hard for the big contest and finally wins the day in a flurry of kicks and chops against men three times his size. **Director**—Robert Clouse. **(R)** *95 minutes*

BIG BUSINESS (1988)

★★

Bette Midler
Lily Tomlin

Seeing double: Bette Midler and Lily Tomlin in Big Business.

Two sets of identical twins, mixed up and separated at birth, have an unexpected, calamitous reunion when they clash over a greedy corporation's plan to strip-mine a small town. The old identical-twin gambit worked for such comics as Laurel and Hardy and the Three Stooges (who interpreted it as three sets of identical triplets). This time, the twins are female and the basic premise seems exhausted. When both of the Midler/Tomlin pairs take rooms at New York's Plaza Hotel, you anticipate a clever good time, but the film never rises above hackneyed gags: dumbfounded waiters, astonished bums, confused suitors. Midler is annoyingly manic and Tomlin seems subdued and lost. Big laughs you won't find. Also with Fred Ward, Edward Herrmann, Michele Placido. **Director**—Jim Abrahams. **(PG)** *94 minutes*

THE BIG CARNIVAL (1951)

★★★★

Kirk Douglas
Jan Sterling

Powerful drama about a reporter, played by Douglas, who tries to promote his career by delaying the rescue of a man trapped in a cave. Splendid performances by Douglas and Sterling. Masterful direction adds to the hard-hitting impact. The film is unrelenting in its portrayal of cruelty and grim irony. **Director**—Billy Wilder. **Academy Award Nomination**—Wilder, Lesser Samuels, and Walter Newman, story and screenplay. **Alternate Title**—*Ace in the Hole.* *112 minutes b&w*

THE BIG CHILL (1983)

★★★

William Hurt
Kevin Kline
Glenn Close

Former college idealists of the 1960s, now complacent and middle-class, gather to unload upon one another at the funeral of a comrade who has inexplicably committed suicide. The ensemble acting by Hurt, Kline, Close, and the others is consistently admirable. Yet the episodic story may put off those accustomed to traditional narratives. The ultraslick production values bring the film perilously close to glibness. Tom Berenger, Mary Kay Place, Jeff Goldblum, Meg Tilly, and JoBeth Williams give support. **Director**—Lawrence Kasdan. **(R) Academy Award Nominations**—best picture; Close, best supporting actress; Kasdan and Barbara Benedek, best screenplay written directly for the screen. *103 minutes*

THE BIG CLOCK (1947)

★★★

Ray Milland
Charles Laughton

A ruthless pulp magazine publisher, played by Laughton, murders his mistress. His top crime reporter, Milland, is assigned to solve the case. It's a suspenseful drama with ace talent. Laughton isn't quite up to par, but Milland is convincing as the writer with a sticky task on hand. Maureen O'Sullivan, Rita Johnson, and Elsa Lanchester round out the cast. **Director**—John Farrow. *95 minutes b&w*

THE BIG COUNTRY (1958)

★★★

Gregory Peck
Jean Simmons
Charlton Heston

Director William Wyler's overblown but entertaining western spectacle features a lively cast at top form. Peck plays a sailor who returns to settle down on the land and winds up in the middle of a bitter feud over water rights. Heston stands out as a mean-spirited cattle foreman, and Burl Ives is impeccably cast as a gruff patriarch of one of the feuding families. There are subtle references to the Cold War. Carroll Baker, Charles Bickford, and Chuck Connors have supporting roles. Jerome Moross' score is quite memorable. **Academy Award**—Ives, best supporting actor. *166 minutes*

THE BIG EASY (1987)

★★★

Dennis Quaid
Ellen Barkin

Dennis Quaid goes overboard for Ellen Barkin in The Big Easy.

A charming New Orleans police detective and a beautiful assistant district attorney clash over police corruption. Their initial investigation leads to more serious matters both on an official and a personal level. This romantic *film noir* with a Cajun flavor is populated with colorful characters and good performances, particulary by Quaid, whose sensuous conquest of Barkin provides the film with its best scenes. The steamy New Orleans setting provides an appropriate backdrop for their smoldering affair. Nonetheless, the film's ending, with the familiar shoot-out, is too pat and predictable. Also with Ned Beatty, Lisa Jane Persky, and Charles Ludlam. **Director**—Jim McBride. **(R)** *108 minutes*

THE BIG FIX (1978)

★★★

Richard Dreyfuss
Susan Anspach

This movie available with closed captions for the hearing impaired.

Dreyfuss is perfectly cast as a small-time, contemporary gumshoe with a background in 1960s radical politics in this engaging comedy/thriller. The film takes an interesting and intelligent stand on the tumultuous decade. The plot, unfortunately, is so complex you may need the services of a detective to figure it out. Dreyfuss' performance is more subdued than usual, and his unorthodox private-eye character is memorable. There's fine support from Anspach, Bonnie Bedelia, John Lithgow, and F. Murray Abraham. **Director**—Jeremy Paul Kagan. **(PG)** *108 minutes*

BIGGER THAN LIFE (1956)

★★★

James Mason
Barbara Rush
Walter Matthau

A film that should be seen in a theater in its original wide-screen ratio (utilized so effectively by director Nicholas Ray). But this adaptation of a story by Berton Roueche about a man hooked on cortisone, still packs a wallop and represents one of the first films to ponder the dark side of miracle drugs. Mason, who also served as producer, sensitively portrays the tormented schoolteacher, whose overdoses lead to unpredicatable and violent mood swings that threaten his family and himself. *95 minutes*

THE BIG HEAT (1953)

★★★½

Glenn Ford
Gloria Grahame
Lee Marvin

Ex-cop seeks to avenge the murder of his wife by the mob. Ford has fine acting support from Grahame, who plays the bad girl who decides to help fight the mob. Marvin as a sadistic killer adds to the harsh realism of the film, and when the movie was released some critics objected to the violent scene in which boiling coffee is hurled into Grahame's face. **Director**—Fritz Lang. *90 minutes b&w*

THE BIG LAND (1957)

★★½

Alan Ladd
Virginia Mayo
Edmond O'Brien

Cattlemen and wheat farmers join to promote the building of a rail link to Texas. It's a somewhat ho-hum western with good production values. The cast, headed by Ladd, Mayo, and O'Brien, performs well enough despite the hackneyed material. The film is based on the novel *Buffalo Grass* by Frank Gruber. **Director**—Gordon Douglas. *92 minutes*

THE BIG PICTURE (1989)

★★★

Kevin Bacon
J.T. Walsh
Michael McKean

Kevin Bacon is captivated by ambitious starlet Teri Hatcher in The Big Picture.

Though somewhat uneven, this satire about the sobering education of an award-winning student filmmaker (Bacon) who gradually loses his ideals when courted by Hollywood should amuse regular filmgoers. Directed by Christopher Guest, the film purports that Hollywood is an asylum where the inmates (i.e. executive producers) run the show, and those with true talent are at the mercy of the producers' whims. An interesting cast, including Martin Short in an unbilled tour de force as a self-involved talent agent, helps to overcome the film's narrative weaknesses. **(PG-13)** *100 minutes*

BIG RED (1962)

★★

Walter Pidgeon
Gilles Payant

Run-of-the-mill boy-and-dog story from the Disney studios that is reminiscent of the Lassie film series in terms of sentimentality. Payant is the lad who becomes attached to an Irish setter owned by a wealthy man, played by Pidgeon. The dog eventually saves Pidgeon from an attacking mountain lion. Nice diversion for the kids; nothing special for adults. The film was photographed in the magnificent outdoors of Quebec. **Director**—Norman Tokar. *89 minutes*

THE BIG RED ONE (1980)

★★★½

Lee Marvin
Mark Hamill

This episodic story of soldiers who fought in the legendary First Infantry Division during World War II represents a comeback for action-film director Samuel Fuller after an absence of 15 years. Marvin provides the focal point as he leads an infantry squad, which includes Hamill and Robert Carradine, from the North African deserts to Czechoslovakia. The "big red one" of the title refers to the red patch on the arms of the soldiers who are part of the First Infantry. Fuller's vision of World War II is not romantic or heroic, but his subtle symbolism and use of metaphor make the film a unique addition to the genre. **(PG)** *113 minutes*

BIG SHOTS (1987)

★★

Ricky Busker
Darius McCrary

A white boy from the Chicago suburbs befriends a streetwise black kid from the inner city, and the pair take off on some daring escapades. This buddy comedy is much like a latter-day Tom Sawyer/Huck Finn adventure, beginning in Chicago and concluding in the Deep South. The young actors are appealing—especially McCrary as the sassy urchin who wants to locate his father—but the film features too many conventional car chases and familiar action scenes. Also with Robert Joy, Jerzy Skolimowski, Joe Seneca, and Paul Winfield. **Director**—Robert Mandel. **(PG-13)** *90 minutes*

THE BIG SKY (1952)

★★★

Kirk Douglas
Arthur Hunnicutt
Elizabeth Threatt

Douglas is a Kentucky fur trapper who leads an expedition to establish a trad-

(Continued)

This movie available on videotape and/or disc.

(Continued)
ing post on the Missouri River in 1830. All sorts of trouble ensues along the way as the party encounters Indians. The cast performs well, but the overloaded melodrama lapses after a while. The film is faithfully adapted from a historical novel by A.B. Guthrie, Jr. Dewey Martin and Buddy Baer also star. **Director**—Howard Hawks. **Academy Award Nomination**—Hunnicutt, best supporting actor.

122 minutes b&w

THE BIG SLEEP (1946)

Humphrey Bogart
Lauren Bacall

Humphrey Bogart and Lauren Bacall play telephone games in The Big Sleep.

Bogart and Bacall make the sparks fly in this saucy private-eye drama based on Raymond Chandler's novel. The plot is complex, but Bogey and Bacall make things click with crisp acting, spicy dialogue, and generous doses of suspense and excitement. Bogart is gumshoe Philip Marlowe, who's hired to keep tabs on the freewheeling daughter of a wealthy man. Before long, he's confronted with several mysterious murders. Lots of smoky atmosphere along the way. Also with Dorothy Malone, Martha Vickers, Regis Toomey, and Elisha Cook, Jr. **Director**—Howard Hawks. *114 minutes b&w*

THE BIG SLEEP (1978)

Robert Mitchum
Sarah Miles

This lukewarm remake of the *film noir* classic starring Bogart and Bacall transplants Chandler's detective novel to contemporary London, where it loses its nostalgic atmosphere of Los Angeles in the 1940s. This time Mitchum is private eye Philip Marlowe, but he's no match for Bogart. Miles, who costars, is no Lauren Bacall either. The Bogey version of this caper remains the undisputed legend. Also stars Candy Clark, Richard Boone, James Stewart, John Mills, and Joan Collins. **Director**—Michael Winner. **(R)**

100 minutes

BIG TOP PEE-WEE (1988)

Paul Reubens
Penelope Ann Miller
Valeria Golino

"Prolonged silliness" is the appropriate description of this Pee-Wee Herman adventure. The man-child in the tight gray suit stars as a farmer with some peculiar methods of husbandry. Pee-Wee (Reubens) loves his schoolteacher fiancee (Miller), but when the circus comes to town, he loses his heart to a trapeze star (Golino). This mushy romantic comedy is aimed at Pee-Wee's fans, who appreciate his unique, self-conscious humor. Others may want to be more selective in their viewing. This vehicle for Reuben's popular alter-ego lacks the sophistication that made the first Pee-Wee film (*Pee-Wee's Big Adventure*) appealing to a mainstream audience. Also with Kris Kristofferson. **Director**—Randal Kleiser. **(PG)** *82 minutes*

THE BIG TOWN (1987)

★★½

Matt Dillon
Tommy Lee Jones
Diane Lane

Matt Dillon and Diane Lane find love and danger in The Big Town.

Some effective performances by a cast of talented actors can't overcome the weak script in this melodrama about a young craps shooter from the sticks trying to hit it big in Chicago. Dillon stars as the youthful gambler while Jones, Bruce Dern, and Tom Skerritt costar as sleazy veterans of the game who try to take advantage of Dillon one way or another. Lane plays a stripper who vies for Dillon's affections along with good girl Suzy Amis. Set on the back streets of Chicago in the 1950s, the film captures the seedy atmosphere of the smoke-filled bars and strip joints. Unfortunately, the clichéd story delivers no impact. Also with Lee Grant and Del Close. **Director**—Ben Bolt. **(R)**

110 minutes

BIG TROUBLE (1986)

Alan Arkin
Peter Falk

Arkin and Falk, who were successfully teamed in *The In-Laws,* are reunited here for this frivolous comedy. Though the two comic actors again strike a good chemistry, the lightweight script lets them down. This farce owes much to the plot of Billy Wilder's *Double Indemnity*: Insurance salesman Arkin plots the death of Falk with the help of the intended victim's wife (Beverly D'Angelo). The actors are a joy to watch but the overworked antics produce only a few smiles. **Director**—John Cassavetes. **(R)** *93 minutes*

BIG TROUBLE IN LITTLE CHINA (1986)

Kurt Russell
Kim Cattrall
Dennis Dun

A slam-bang, off-the-wall action comedy set in an imaginary world beneath San Francisco's Chinatown. If that description puts you out of breath, so will this energetic movie, which is a good-natured send-up of *Indiana Jones and the Temple of Doom.* Russell stars as a bumbling truck driver swept up in a strange adventure involving the rescue of two damsels (Cattrall and Suzee Pai) from a Chinese sorcerer. Incredible special effects and stunts highlight the film, which depends on its colorful and exotic sets to convey an appropriately mysterious atmosphere. **Director**—John Carpenter. **(PG-13)** *99 minutes*

® This movie available with closed captions for the hearing impaired.

BIG WEDNESDAY (1978)

★½

Jan-Michael Vincent
William Katt
Gary Busey

John Milius' ambitious tribute to surfing turned out all wet. The limp script follows the lives of three California surfers from 1962 to 1974. Vincent, Katt, and Busey play the beach buddy roles with unusual stiffness. The tone throughout is one of muddled and uneventful seriousness. Also with Lee Purcell, Patti D'Arbanville, and Barbara Hale. **Director**—Milius. **(PG)** *120 minutes*

BILL AND TED'S EXCELLENT ADVENTURE (1989)

★★½

Alex Winter
Keanu Reeves

An Excellent Adventure *for bodacious time-travelers Alex Winter and Keanu Reeves.*

This teen comedy/adventure relies on a fast pace and an exploitable gimmick. Two high-school boys, somewhat deficient in their history lessons, discover a time machine that offers them a chance to meet such luminaries as Socrates, Sigmund Freud, and Abraham Lincoln. Winter and Reeves utter a lot of adolescent jargon but manage to capture the essence of two "dudes" from Southern California. George Carlin plays their adviser from the future. **Director**—Stephen Herek. **(PG)** *90 minutes*

BILLY BUDD (1962)

★★★

Peter Ustinov
Robert Ryan
Terence Stamp
Melvyn Douglas

Ustinov directed and stars in this handsome film version of the Herman Melville classic allegory of good and evil, set in the 18th century. Young Billy goes to sea aboard a British man-of-war, where he kills a cruel officer and then faces execution for the deed. Ustinov stands out as a sympathetic captain, and Ryan is excellent as the evil master-at-arms. The screenplay, however, is dull. Also with Paul Rogers, David McCallum, and John Neville. **Academy Award Nomination**—Stamp, best supporting actor. *112 minutes b&w*

BILLY JACK (1971)

★★

Tom Laughlin
Delores Taylor

Tom Laughlin's paean to the hippie spirit was a major event in its day—*Billy Jack* wasn't just seen, it was *experienced.* Nearly 20 years later, the film seems more simpleminded than uplifting. Laughlin is ploddingly resolute as the title character, an Arizona half-breed who uses karate to pummel bullyboys who threaten a "freedom school" even as he preaches peace and love. Young audiences cheered in 1971, but contemporary viewers will probably resent the script's shameless emotional manipulation. Directed by Laughlin under the pseudonym T.C. Frank. Also with Bert Freed, Clark Howat, and Julie Webb. **(PG)** *113 minutes*

BILLY LIAR (1963)

★★★

Tom Courtenay
Julie Christie

Courtenay has some fun as an employee of a funeral parlor who daydreams himself into a more glamorous existence. The film's success extended the cinematic British invasion by advancing the careers of Courtenay, Christie, and director John Schlesinger. Both its exuberance and social commentary seem to have lost a bit of their edge, but the film is still a sparkling good time. *96 minutes b&w*

BILOXI BLUES (1988)

★★½

Matthew Broderick
Christopher Walken

Neil Simon's hit autobiographical stage play about basic training in the Army during World War II makes for a generally agreeable screen comedy. However, it lacks the bite and wit of the Broadway production despite the heavy dose of peppery one-liners. Broderick recreates his stage role as the recruit who suffers the expected indignities, loses his virginity, and crosses the threshold to manhood. Walken costars as the crazed drill sergeant. Typically slick Neil Simon film fare, directed with skill by Mike Nichols. Also with Penelope Ann Miller, Matt Mulhern, and Corey Parker. **(PG-13)** *109 minutes*

THE BINGO LONG TRAVELING ALL-STARS AND MOTOR KINGS (1976)

★★★

Billy Dee Williams
James Earl Jones
Richard Pryor

A high-spirited and highly entertaining comedy about a renegade black baseball team that barnstorms through mid-America in 1939, when black ballplayers were barred from the white-controlled leagues. The film also has its dramatic and touching moments. The almost-all-black cast is superb. It's headed by Williams and Jones, who play a pair of razzle-dazzle ballplayers. However, character development is weak in some cases. There is a clear portrayal of how the All-Stars must resort to clowning as a means of survival in those pre-Jackie Robinson days. **Director**—John Badham. **(PG)** *110 minutes*

BIRD (1988)

★★★

Forest Whitaker

Clint Eastwood, wearing his director's hat, presents a remarkable film tribute to the short, tormented life of legendary jazz great Charlie "Bird" Parker. Although the story sometimes rambles, Eastwood captures the moody jazz club atmosphere of the 1940s and 1950s. While the picture brims with Bird's glo-

(Continued)

This movie available on videotape and/or disc.

Sam Wright and Forest Whitaker making music in Bird.

(Continued)
rious music and self-destruction, we also see the tragic drug abuse that led to the musician's untimely death. The music heard in the film is truly Parker's. His music was digitally stripped from old recordings and mixed with newly recorded rhythm tracks—a painstaking process that garnered the film an Oscar nomination for sound. Also with Diane Venora, Keith David, Michael Zolniker, and Samuel E. Wright. **(R)**

163 minutes

BIRDMAN OF ALCATRAZ (1962)

★★★★

Burt Lancaster
Karl Malden
Thelma Ritter
Edmond O'Brien

Lancaster is at his best in the title role of this engrossing biography of Robert Stroud, the celebrated convict who became a world authority on birds. Lancaster's measured delivery and John Frankenheimer's efficient direction perfectly illuminate Stroud's perplexing personality. The film also expertly explores the harshness and monotony of prison life. Malden stands out as the warden. Originally released at 143 minutes. Also with Telly Savalas, Betty Field, Neville Brand, and Hugh Marlowe. **Academy Award Nominations**—Lancaster, best actor; Savalas, best supporting actor; Ritter, best supporting actress; Burnett Guffey, cinematography. *148 minutes b&w*

BIRD ON A WIRE (1990)

★★½

Mel Gibson
Goldie Hawn

Mel Gibson and Goldie Hawn on the move in Bird on a Wire.

Gibson and Hawn star as old flames who meet again after a 15-year separation. Gibson's character has been hiding out in the federal witness protection program but must rely on Hawn's help after his cover is blown. The minimal plot serves only to propel the characters from one action sequence to the next, which becomes tedious by the middle of the movie. The relentless formulaic chase scenes detract from the chemistry between Hawn and Gibson. The film is obviously a vehicle for Hawn's talents and personality: Those who enjoy Hawn's bubbly persona will like this uninspired but high-energy comedy, while others may want to be more selective. Bill Duke and David Carradine costar as the stereotypical villains. **Director**—John Badham. **(PG-13)**

113 minutes

THE BIRDS (1963)

★★★½

Rod Taylor
Tippi Hedren
Suzanne Pleshette
Jessica Tandy

Director Alfred Hitchcock, the wizard of suspense, digs into his bag of tricks for this gripping thriller about a small California coastal town that comes under attack by thousands of birds. Taylor, Hedren, and Pleshette are adequate in the principal roles, but they fade into the background when upstaged by the onslaught of Academy Award-winning special effects and offbeat shock tactics devised by the master. *119 minutes*

BIRDY (1984)

★★★½

Matthew Modine
Nicolas Cage

Sensitive, intriguing film adaptation of William Wharton's offbeat psychological novel. It's played to perfection by Modine and Cage as two working-class youths growing up in South Philadelphia. Modine, in the title role, skillfully portrays the eccentric teenager whose obsession with birds serves as an escape from his squalid environment. Cage also is impressive as Birdy's loyal friend. Director Alan Parker succeeds with challenging material. **(R)**

120 minutes

BIRTH OF THE BLUES (1941)

★★★

Bing Crosby
Brian Donlevy

Crosby stars as a trumpet player who establishes a jazz band in New Orleans. The trivial plot is upheld by plenty of good jazz music, which makes the film worthwhile. Some of the classic tunes include "St. Louis Blues," "St. James Infirmary," and "Melancholy Baby." Bing gets support from Donlevy, Carolyn Lee, Eddie "Rochester" Anderson, Mary Martin, and jazz great Jack Teagarden. **Director**—Victor Schertzinger. *85 minutes b&w*

THE BISHOP'S WIFE (1947)

★★★

Cary Grant
David Niven
Loretta Young

A warm, thoroughly diverting Christmas fantasy from Robert Nathan, author of *Portrait of Jennie.* Niven plays a bishop who's so obsessed with the building of a new cathedral that he neglects his wife (Young) and daughter. He prays for guidance—and gets a debonair angel named Dudley (Grant), who tries to set everything straight. This best picture Oscar-nominee is richly photographed by the great Gregg Toland and winningly played by the three stars and a sparkling supporting cast, including Edmund Gwenn, Monty Woolley, James Gleason, and Elsa Lanchester. **Director**—Henry Koster. **Academy Award Nominations**—best picture; Koster, best director.

108 minutes b&w

BITE THE BULLET (1975)

★★

Gene Hackman
Candice Bergen
James Coburn

® *This movie available with closed captions for the hearing impaired.*

Who will win the long-distance horse race through the desert and other treacherous terrain of the Southwest? There's plenty of breathtaking scenery, but the story is loaded with platitudes and clichés. Also with Ben Johnson, Ian Bannen, Jan-Michael Vincent, and Paul Stewart. **Director**—Richard Brooks. **(PG)** *131 minutes*

BLACK AND WHITE IN COLOR (1976)

 ★★★★

Jean Carmet
Jacques Dufilho
Catherine Rouvel

A witty, intelligent satire attacking the arrogant human condition that leads to war. Droll and subtle performances by an excellent cast complement a moving screenplay about a bored group of Frenchmen in colonial West Africa, who fight a miniwar against a neighboring German garrison. The film was shot entirely on the Ivory Coast. Originally filmed in French. **Director**—Jean-Jacques Annaud. **(PG) Academy Award**—best foreign-language film.
90 minutes

BLACKBEARD'S GHOST (1967)

★★

Peter Ustinov
Dean Jones
Suzanne Pleshette

Ustinov stars in this slapstick Walt Disney comedy as the ghost of the infamous pirate who returns to prevent a hotel from being converted into a gambling casino. The film is overbearing, but the cast works hard to bring forth a few engaging moments. Elsa Lanchester and Richard Deacon costar. **Director**—Robert Stevenson.
107 minutes

THE BLACK BIRD (1975)

 ★★

George Segal
Stephane Audran
Lee Patrick
Elisha Cook, Jr.

The 1941 Bogart classic *The Maltese Falcon* is back as a supposedly comic sequel. Segal plays Sam Spade, Jr., who's stuck with his father's private-eye business and involved in another struggle over the mysterious falcon statuette he finds stashed away in a file drawer. There are a few bright moments at the beginning, but the wobbly and narrow plot fails to develop. Characters are left milling about and aimlessly bumping into one another. Also stars Lionel Stander, John Abbott, and Signe Hasso; includes Patrick and Cook, who were in the original film. **Director**—David Giler. **(PG)** *98 minutes*

THE BLACKBOARD JUNGLE (1955)

★★★½

Glenn Ford
Anne Francis
Louis Calhern

Ford gives a credible and engaging performance as a young teacher who gets through to some tough kids in a New York City high school. The poignant film, adapted from Evan Hunter's novel, is an honest and straightforward portrayal of urban education. Sidney Poitier is outstanding as a rebellious student with repressed talent and sensitivity. Bill Haley and the Comets fill in the background with "Rock Around the Clock." The film is biting, penetrating entertainment, with Academy Award-nominated photography by Russell Harlan. Also with Richard Kiley and Vic Morrow. **Director**—Richard Brooks. **Academy Award Nominations**—Brooks, best screenplay.
101 minutes b&w

THE BLACK CAT (1934)

★★★

Boris Karloff
Bela Lugosi

A dark, evil force: Boris Karloff in The Black Cat.

Lugosi, in a more sympathetic role than usual, plays a doctor seeking revenge against devil-worshipping architect Karloff. An air of dark and perverse menace pervades the film as exhibited through the Expressionistic set designs and the unsavory, yet fascinating, sexual undertones of the narrative. A minor horror masterpiece from director Edgar Ulmer, who managed to give a unique European sensibility to his low-budget films. *65 minutes b&w*

THE BLACK CAULDRON (1985)

★★★

This $25 million Disney "Cauldron" may not be the pot of gold that Walt's original classics were, but it's still a captivating animated spectacular. The wide-screen wonders include a couple of medieval youngsters (who try to stop an evil king from getting at a cauldron with terrible powers), a clairvoyant pig, a manic evil dwarf, and the scene-stealing furball called Gurgi. Kids old enough not to be too scared may want to see it thrice. **Directors**—Ted Berman and Richard Rich. **(PG)** *80 minutes*

THE BLACK HOLE (1979)

 ★★

Maximilian Schell
Anthony Perkins
Robert Forster
Joseph Bottoms

The Disney studios joined Hollywood's space race with this $20 million sci-fi adventure. The comic-book plot has Schell as a mad scientist who commands a renegade spaceship on the edge of a mysterious black hole—the doorway to eternity. Two friendly robots, which resemble floating fireplugs, have the best lines and upstage the human characters. There's so little imagination here that it's hard to believe this is a Disney project, though the film was nominated for Academy Awards for its cinematography and special effects. Also with Yvette Mimieux and Ernest Borgnine. **Director**—Gary Nelson. **(G)**
97 minutes

THE BLACK MARBLE (1980)

 ★★

Robert Foxworth
Paula Prentiss

(Continued)

(Continued)
Joseph Wambaugh *(The Onion Field)* works with his favorite subject again in this screenplay about police and crime, written from his own novel. It's a crude comic romance about two cops, played by Foxworth and Prentiss, who pursue a dognapper. There are some grisly details of animal mutilation and some offbeat humor that never goes over. A few moments of wit emerge, but it's a crime the way director Harold Becker finally drives the film into the ground. **(PG)**
113 minutes

BLACK MOON RISING (1986)

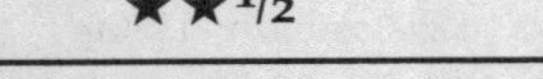

Tommy Lee Jones

Rickety, high-tech, car-chase movie that leaves all credibility behind in a trail of noise, confusion, and violence. Jones plays a small-time car thief hired by the feds to steal a company's tax records. Jones, at times, is above the material, which gradually sinks into absurdity. Black Moon is the name of the supercar in which the crucial records have been hidden. Linda Hamilton, Robert Vaughn, and Keenan Wynn are in supporting roles. **Director**—Harley Cokliss. **(R)**
100 minutes

BLACK NARCISSUS (1946)

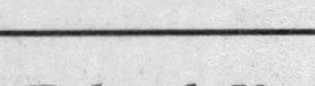

Deborah Kerr
Flora Robson
Kathleen Byron

Sex appeal, Himalayan style: Jean Simmons in Black Narcissus.

Kerr shines as a nun who deals with the tormenting problems of isolation and a harsh climate in an effort to maintain a mission in the Himalayas. The film, based on Rumer Godden's novel, packs an emotional wallop and is exquisitely photographed by Jack Cardiff, who won an Oscar for his efforts. Sabu and Jean Simmons are excellent in supporting roles. American prints of the film were originally released at 91 minutes, excluding scenes in which Kerr's character revealed her past. Those scenes have been restored to most prints. **Directors**—Michael Powell and Emeric Pressburger.
100 minutes

BLACK ORPHEUS (1959)

Marpessa Dawn
Breno Mello
Adhemar da Silva

The myth of tragic lovers Orpheus and Eurydice is set against the pulsating background of Rio at Carnival time. The swirls of color, bright costumes and locales, and, most especially, the samba beat of Luis Bonfa and Antonio Carlos Jobim's music running throughout the film generate considerable excitement. Originally filmed in Portuguese. **Director**—Marcel Camus. **Academy Award**—best foreign-language film.
98 minutes

BLACK RAIN (1989)

 ★★1/2

Michael Douglas
Ken Takakura
Andy Garcia

Stunning visual elements dominate this conventional police thriller set in Japan. So integrated is the visual design to the storyline that casual viewers will miss those details of plot and character conveyed through setting and lighting. Douglas and Garcia play New York City detectives who pursue a Japanese gangster through a garish Osaka cityscape. Douglas' unsavory character may be disconcerting to some viewers because he is prone to corruption and violence. The Japanese actors are impressive, particularly Takakura (Japan's biggest box-office star) as an honor-bound Osaka detective and Yusaku Matsuda as the object of the chase. Stylishly directed by Ridley Scott *(Alien; Blade Runner)*. Also with Kate Capshaw. **(R)**
125 minutes

THE BLACK ROSE (1950)

Tyrone Power
Cecile Aubry

Opulent but ponderous costume adventure, set in the 13th century, about an Englishman—played by Power—who travels to the Orient and triumphs over tyrannical rulers. Nothing new here, but there is some interesting action en route. Aubry, the French actress, costars in her first Hollywood film, which became her last when she failed the popularity test with American audiences. Orson Welles, Jack Hawkins, Michael Rennie, Herbert Lom, and Laurence Harvey have supporting roles. **Director**—Henry Hathaway.
120 minutes

THE BLACK STALLION (1979)

 ★★★★

Kelly Reno
Mickey Rooney

Boy meets horse, tames him, and races him in this splendidly photographed adventure fantasy that will please all age groups. Reno turns in a strong performance as the boy who develops a spiritual relationship with the wild Arabian stallion that saves his life in a shipwreck. Rooney is excellent as the trainer. But it's Cass-ole, a magnificent animal, who practically steals the film. Also with Teri Garr, Clarence Muse, and Hoyt Axton. **Director**—Carroll Ballard. **(G) Academy Award Nomination**—Rooney, best supporting actor.
119 minutes

THE BLACK STALLION RETURNS (1983)

Kelly Reno

This sequel to *The Black Stallion* is likely to please children, but not the adults who were charmed by the original film. There is plenty of action as Arab tribesmen kidnap the powerful steed and bring him to the Sahara. Alec Ramsay (Reno) follows, and encounters intrigue, danger, and friendship—all of it quite predictable. Reno is consistently pleasing as the spunky young hero, and Vincent Spano and Woody Strode are fine in supporting roles. But the film lacks the unique imagery and vision that director Carroll Ballard gave to its predecessor. **Director**—Robert Dalva. **(PG)** *103 minutes*

BLACK SUNDAY (1977)

 ★★★

Robert Shaw
Bruce Dern
Marthe Keller

Meticulous direction and superb acting elevate an otherwise routine disaster film into a slick action adventure. Shaw, who skillfully plays a hardened Israeli government agent, races against time to thwart a Palestinian terrorist plot to drop a dart-spewing bomb from the Goodyear blimp onto 80,000 Super Bowl spectators. There's a powerful and extraordinary screen performance by Dern as the jangled and half-crazed blimp pilot who collaborates with the terrorists. Also with Fritz Weaver and Steven Keats. **Director**—John Frankenheimer. **(R)** *143 minutes*

THE BLACK SWAN (1942)

Tyrone Power
Maureen O'Hara

Rootin'-tootin' swashbuckler, with Power as a dashing pirate chasing some scruffy buccaneers at a fast clip through the Caribbean. The adventure has just the right amount of hokey humor to enhance the entertainment value without spoiling its spirit. O'Hara is charming as a damsel in need of rescuing from some villains, played convincingly by Anthony Quinn and George Sanders. The screenplay is based on the novel by Rafael Sabatini. Laird Cregar and Thomas Mitchell also star. **Director**—Henry King. **Academy Award**—Leon Shamroy, cinematography. *85 minutes*

BLACK WIDOW (1987)

 ★★★

Debra Winger
Theresa Russell

Russell stars as the title character, a sultry seductress who marries wealthy men and then cleverly kills them for the inheritance. Debra Winger costars as a special investigator for the Justice Department who unravels this intriguing caper after taking a leave of absence and immersing herself in the pursuit. The plot strains credibility at times, but capable acting and the cat-and-mouse interplay between the women account for a classy thriller with many tantalizing surprises. Also with Sami Frey, Dennis Hopper, and Nicol Williamson. **Director**—Bob Rafelson. **(R)** *103 minutes*

BLADE RUNNER (1982)

 ★★★

Harrison Ford

Ford stars as a hard-boiled, Philip Marlowe-style detective in a futuristic Los Angeles. His assignment is to track down sinister "replicants" (humanlike robots). The stylish, high-tech special effects were nominated for an Academy Award; photographic effects master Douglas Trumbull *(Close Encounters; Star Trek)* and his staff created a garish, chilling cityscape of sleaze and clutter. Unfortunately, the story is sometimes muddled and the film lacks dramatic momentum. Rutger Hauer and Sean Young also star. **Director**—Ridley Scott. **(R)** *118 minutes*

BLAME IT ON RIO (1984)

 ★★

Michael Caine

Caine looks embarrassed most of the way through this contrived romantic comedy set against the backdrop of swinging, exotic Rio de Janeiro. He's seduced by his best friend's nubile teenage daughter (Michelle Johnson), who appears topless a lot. Attempts to keep this absurd love affair secret provoke a few laughs, but the crude story mainly comes off as offensive. Blame it on director and screenwriter Stanley Donen, who has done better. Joseph Bologna and Valerie Harper also star. **(R)** *109 minutes*

BLAZE (1989)

★★★1/2

Paul Newman
Lolita Davidovich

Newman's exaggerated performance vigorously embraces the colorful character of governor Earl K. Long, the rambunctious and somewhat loony Louisiana politician. The film is partially based on the scandalous affair between the governor and the lusty stripper, Blaze Starr. Yet the comedy/drama is as much an account of the South's changing political climate as it is

Paul Newman as Louisiana's Governor Earl K. Long in Blaze.

the story of these two historical personages. Ron Shelton's well-crafted screenplay and stylish direction make for one of the best of films of that year, though it was underappreciated at the time of release. Shelton, whose first effort was the popular *Bull Durham*, has a good feel for Southern culture. Davidovich is exceptional in the title role. Also with Jerry Hardin, Garland Bunting, Robert Wuhl, and Gailard Sartain. **(R) Academy Award Nomination**—Haskell Wexler, cinematography. *120 minutes*

BLAZING SADDLES (1974)

 ★★★

Cleavon Little
Gene Wilder
Slim Pickens
Harvey Korman
Madeline Kahn

Mel Brooks' howling comedy spoofs western movies and racial prejudice in a nonstop barrage of riotous skits and sight gags. Some of the comedy misfires, but there's still an onslaught of belly laughs, including a generous dose of scatological humor. Little is great as a black railroad worker who's elected sheriff of a western town. Brooks is hilarious in several small roles, including that of a Yiddish-speaking Indian chief. Kahn is a riot in a Marlene Dietrich takeoff. Korman, Wilder, and Pickens also pitch in with the lunacy. **Director**—Brooks. **(R) Academy Award Nomination**—Kahn, best supporting actress. *93 minutes*

BLIND DATE (1987)

★★1/2

Bruce Willis
Kim Basinger

Willis, star of the TV series *Moonlighting*, debuts on the big screen in this

(Continued)

This movie available on videotape and/or disc.

(Continued)
romantic farce about a young executive on the way up whose blind date with Basinger ruins his career and almost his life after one drink makes her lose control. Director Blake Edwards exploits the situation for all its comic worth, relying mostly on physical comedy and sight gags. Unfortunately, the film falters when its already thin premise is stretched beyond believability to accommodate gag after gag. Also with John Larroquette and William Daniels. **(PG–13)** *95 minutes*

THE BLOB (1958)

★★½

Steve McQueen
Aneta Corseaut

Slimy goo from outer space invades a small town, and a young McQueen comes to the rescue. This puffed-up sci-fi nonsense is primarily aimed at adolescent audiences. There are, however, a few scary scenes scattered here and there, and McQueen makes the most of the situation. Also with Olin Howlin and Earl Rowe. The film spawned a 1972 sequel called *Beware! The Blob,* also known as *Son of Blob.* **Director**—Irwin S. Yeaworth, Jr. *83 minutes*

THE BLOB (1988)

★★½

Shawnee Smith
Kevin Dillon
Donovan Leitch

This remake of the 1958 B-movie screamer, which originally starred a young Steve McQueen, is an entertaining thriller that lacks the charm of the earlier film. Despite special effects technology that gives us a new, improved Blob, the story doesn't quite work the second time around. Once again, the slimy mess gobbles some residents of a small all-American town before facing off against a group of plucky teenagers. **Director**—Chuck Russell. **(R)** *90 minutes*

BLONDE VENUS (1932)

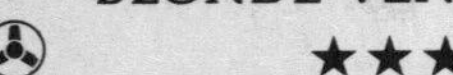

Marlene Dietrich
Cary Grant
Herbert Marshall

Passion is both the greatest curse and the greatest gift in the cinematic *tour de force* of director Josef von Sternberg, and there's plenty of it here: mother love, illicit love, the love for a dying husband. Dietrich is the impassioned heroine; Marshall plays her scientist husband afflicted by radium poisoning; Grant is the wealthy playboy who has an affair with her; and Dickie Moore is the son she almost loses. The number in which cafe singer Marlene makes her entrance in a gorilla suit (parts of which she seductively peels off) while singing "Hot Voodoo" is one of the director's most often-cited scenes. *97 minutes b&w*

BLOOD ALLEY (1955)

John Wayne
Lauren Bacall

Wayne and Bacall flee down a river from China to Hong Kong, with Chinese Communists hot on their tails. A routine anti-Red adventure, with Wayne as a bigger-than-life hero taking on the enemy single-handedly. The name cast and the slick production can't seem to overcome the threadbare script. Anita Ekberg has a minor role as a burlap-clad refugee. Also with Paul Fix, Joy Kim, Barry Kroger, and Mike Mazurki. **Director**—William Wellman. *115 minutes*

BLOOD AND SAND (1941)

Tyrone Power
Linda Darnell
Rita Hayworth

Tyrone Power is a colorful bullfighter in Blood and Sand.

If only for auld lang syne, this romantic chestnut is worth a look. Power stars as the lady-killer toreador whose meteoric success in the bullring leads him to prefer society girl Hayworth over sweetheart Darnell. Though Power lacks the animal magnetism Valentino brought to the 1922 silent film of the Vincente Blasco Ibanez scorcher, this version offers lush color. In fact, as directed by pictorialist Rouben Mamoulian, the film is a series of ravishing compositions, visually dynamic but dramatically inert. Cast includes Anthony Quinn, Nazimova, J. Carrol Naish, John Carradine, Laird Cregar, and Spanish guitarist Vicente Gomez. *123 minutes*

BLOODBROTHERS (1978)

 ★★

Richard Gere
Paul Sorvino
Tony Lo Bianco

A high-pitched emotional story about an Italian-American family living in the Bronx. Gere plays a rebellious teenage son and nephew of construction-worker brothers who brawl, booze, and chase women. Good performances, but the characters are stereotypes, and the director goes overboard in exploiting emotions. Reedited to 98 minutes by the director for cable-TV release. **Director**—Robert Mulligan. **(R) Academy Award Nomination**—Walter Newman, best screenplay based on material from another medium. *116 minutes*

BLOODHOUNDS OF BROADWAY (1989)

Madonna
Matt Dillon
Anita Morris
Rutger Hauer

The action is set entirely on New Year's Eve 1928 in this slow-moving blend of four Damon Runyon short stories. Though a number of colorful characters are introduced, they are lost amid the sluggish screenplay and dull dialogue. The period detail is impressive, and a large ensemble cast does its utmost, but the world of hot dice and fast dames has lost its luster in this updated version of Runyon's Broadway underworld. Also with Randy Quaid, Julie Hagerty, Esai Morales, and Jennifer Grey. **Director**—Howard Brookner. **(PG)** *93 minutes*

® *This movie available with closed captions for the hearing impaired.*

BLOODLINE (1979)

 ★★

Audrey Hepburn
Ben Gazzara
James Mason

High-gloss intrigue with Audrey Hepburn in Bloodline.

Hepburn stars as the head of an international pharmaceutical empire in this tepid murder mystery, based on Sidney Sheldon's popular novel. Gazzara, Mason, Omar Sharif, and other well-known players appear as suspects in the murder of the company's patriarch. What little suspense there is quickly evaporates amid the complicated and ponderous plot. Hepburn looks rather weary much of the time, which seems to be in keeping with the pace of the film. Also with Michelle Phillips and Romy Schneider. **Director**—Terence Young. **(R) Alternate Title**—*Sidney Sheldon's Bloodline.* *116 minutes*

THE BLOOD OF HEROES (1990)

★★

Rutger Hauer
Joan Chen

In this grisly, post-apocalyptic action-adventure tale, scarred gladiators amuse the general populace with a brutal jousting game called jugging. Hauer stars as a veteran player who takes on a young female apprentice in the hopes of winning the final match. Obviously influenced by George Miller's *Mad Max* films, this grim effort lacks the style, pacing, and ingenuity of Miller's influential series. The film features several fierce action scenes, but the editing is lackluster and the constant combat eventually becomes monotonous. **Director**—David Peoples. **(R)** *90 minutes*

BLOOD SIMPLE (1985)

 ★★★★

M. Emmet Walsh
Frances McDormand

A gothic thriller supreme, made on a shoestring budget, but rich in wit, intrigue, style, moodiness, and suspense. The plot is deliciously complex and rife with edgy misunderstandings: A Texas bar owner, his bored wife, her bartender lover, and a sleazy private detective are entangled in a hair-raising web of murder and double cross. The brothers Joel (director) and Ethan (producer) Coen make it all happen in an astonishing filmmaking debut. Also stars John Getz and Dan Hedaya. **(R)** *96 minutes*

BLOW OUT (1981)

 ★★★

John Travolta
Nancy Allen

Director Brian De Palma fashions a stylish, electrifying drama about a movie sound man, played by Travolta, who stumbles upon a political assassination. The film bears some similarity to Antonioni's *Blow-Up,* and De Palma also cleverly weaves in subtle references to Chappaquiddick, Nelson Rockefeller's death, and the Watergate plumbers. Travolta finally gets his teeth into an appealing, intelligent adult role, and sheds his hotshot teenage image. **(R)** *108 minutes*

BLOW-UP (1966)

★★★★

David Hemmings
Sarah Miles
Vanessa Redgrave

A fascinating and thought-provoking drama involving a London photographer who believes he has witnessed a murder. Hemmings is effective as the baffled young man, and there is a stylish performance from Redgrave. The film brims with psychological twists and complex symbolism; much is accomplished with scant plot and undeveloped characters in the trendy twilight world of London's fashion business. Models Jill Kennington and Verushka are also featured. **Director**—Michelangelo Antonioni. **Academy Award Nominations**—Antonioni, best director; Antonioni, Tonino Guerra, and Edward Bond, best story and screenplay written directly for the screen. *110 minutes*

THE BLUE BIRD (1940)

 ★★

Shirley Temple
Spring Byington

Temple and Byington star in this classic fairy tale about two children who search for the bluebird of happiness, only to find true happiness at home. The film is based on Maurice Maeterlinck's fantasy, but the plot seems similar to *The Wizard of Oz.* The production is impressive, but it pales in contrast to the popular *Oz* film, which was released about the same time. Johnny Russell, Nigel Bruce, Gale Sondergaard, and Eddie Collins also star. **Director**—Walter Lang. *88 minutes*

THE BLUE BIRD (1976)

★$^{1}/_{2}$

Elizabeth Taylor
Jane Fonda
Ava Gardner

Détente comes to the movies, but the result is a disappointment. The first major Soviet-American coproduction, filmed in Leningrad, is the classic fable about two children who search for the bluebird of happiness; the audience will find the pigeon of boredom. Taylor, Fonda, Gardner, and Cicely Tyson appear briefly in cameo roles. The film is plagued with technical problems, dull dialogue, and lackluster sets. Also with Patsy Kensit, Todd Lookinland, Will Geer, Robert Morley, and Harry Andrews. Directed by George Cukor, who should have known better. **(G)** *99 minutes*

BLUE CITY (1986)

 ★★ 

Judd Nelson
Ally Sheedy

A young man (Nelson) returns to his Florida hometown to find the killer of his father, turning the town upside down in the process. All this contrived sleuthing and revenge is carried out with much brutality. The film is based on a best-selling novel by Ross MacDonald, features an original music

(Continued)

(Continued)
score by Ry Cooder, and was coproduced by action director Walter Hill. Despite the impressive talent behind the scenes, the film fails because of the badly written script and colorless acting by the leads. Also with Paul Winfield. **Director**—Michelle Manning. **(R)** *83 minutes*

BLUE COLLAR (1978)

★★★½

Richard Pryor
Harvey Keitel
Yaphet Kotto

Paul Schrader, who wrote the script for *Taxi Driver,* directs this powerful and gritty film about frustrated automobile factory workers who are pushed around by their union and management. This fast-paced comedy/drama is awkward at times, but even so, Schrader scores with his colorful profile of believable contemporary characters. Pryor, Keitel, and Kotto are the heroes of the assembly line. Also with Ed Begley, Jr., and Harry Bellaver. **(R)** *114 minutes*

THE BLUE DAHLIA (1946)

★★★½

Alan Ladd
Veronica Lake
William Bendix

Ladd plays an ex-GI, home from the war, who discovers his wife has been unfaithful. After she's murdered, he becomes the prime suspect. The Raymond Chandler script, the only one he wrote directly for the screen, packs excitement and suspense, with the cast turning in sharp performances. Also with Howard Da Silva and Hugh Beaumont. **Director**—George Marshall. **Academy Award Nomination**—Chandler, original screenplay. *99 minutes b&w*

THE BLUE IGUANA (1988)

★½ ®

Dylan McDermott

This strained parody of Italian westerns and *films noir* fails to effectively spoof either. McDermott is merely ridiculous in the role of a bounty hunter assigned to recover $50 million stashed in a Central American bank. Some of the minor players are amusing in sending up stock character types, but the humor runs out of gas long before the cash is withdrawn. Jessica Harper, Tovah Feldshuh, Dean Stockwell, and James Russo appear in supporting roles. **Director**—John Lafia. **(R)** *90 minutes*

THE BLUE LAGOON (1949)

★★½

Jean Simmons
Donald Houston

A syrupy romantic adventure about a boy and a girl, stranded on a tropical island, who mature, fall in love, and then try to return to civilization. The lush island setting can't redeem the listless material, based on the novel by Henry de Vere Stacpoole. There is a bit of suspense when the couple is threatened by smugglers. Also with Noel Purcell, Cyril Cusack, and James Hayter. **Director**—Frank Launder. *103 minutes*

THE BLUE LAGOON (1980)

★½

Brooke Shields
Christopher Atkins

Brooke Shields and Christopher Atkins discover romance in The Blue Lagoon.

Emmeline (Shields) and Richard (Atkins) are two shipwrecked children on a tropical island who grow up to be lovers. Everything is picture-postcard pretty in cinematography by Nestor Almendros, who was nominated for an Oscar for his work on this film. But excitement and drama are nowhere to be found. The story somewhat unrealistically and awkwardly emphasizes innocent sexual awakening. The 1949 version with Jean Simmons worked better as a Hollywood-style fantasy. Also with Leo McKern and William Daniels. **Director**—Randal Kleiser. **(R)** *102 minutes*

THE BLUE MAX (1966)

★★

George Peppard
James Mason
Ursula Andress

Spectacular photography of World War I aerial dogfights is the only worthwhile virtue of this tepid drama involving German military pilots. Peppard plays an ambitious German flyer who woos the wife of his commander; Mason portrays a stereotypical German officer; and Andress is Peppard's love interest. Performances are fair but not too convincing. Also with Jeremy Kemp and Karl Michael Vogler. **Director**—John Guillermin. *156 minutes*

THE BLUES BROTHERS (1980)

★★★

John Belushi
Dan Aykroyd

Fancy footwork by Dan Aykroyd and John Belushi in The Blues Brothers.

Belushi and Aykroyd star in this musical action comedy as improbable bandleaders who try to raise $5,000 for an orphanage and cause $50 million in property damage in the process. It's a rollicking smorgasboard of soul music, auto crashes, explosions, and crazy fun. But it's really the spirited musical numbers that glue this madcap mess together. Delightful cameo performances by James Brown, Aretha Franklin, Ray Charles, and Cab Calloway add to the froth and frolic. **Director**—John Landis. **(R)** *130 minutes*

BLUE SKIES (1946)

★★★

Fred Astaire
Bing Crosby
Joan Caulfield

® *This movie available with closed captions for the hearing impaired.*

Crosby and Astaire star in this sunny musical loaded with Irving Berlin tunes. The threadbare, corny plot concerns a drawn-out rivalry for the attention of a girl. But that's incidental to the music and dancing. Bing sings the title song, and Fred dances to "Putting On the Ritz." What more do you need? Caulfield, Billy De Wolfe, and Olga San Juan are fine in supporting roles. **Director**—Stuart Heisler. *104 minutes*

BLUE STEEL (1990)

★★★

Jamie Lee Curtis
Ron Silver
Clancy Brown

Curtis stars as a rookie on the New York City police force who is stalked by a deranged serial murderer. Though the police thriller is a genre usually reserved for male actors and directors, this taut action film with a feminist twist features a strong female character in the leading role and stylish direction by a woman filmmaker. The first half is relentlessly suspenseful, while the second half explodes with bloody violence reminiscent of the late Sam Peckinpah. Silver is chilling as the killer, though the plot dynamics involving his initial connection with Curtis are too coincidental. Brown, who usually plays a villain, is effective as Curtis' superior. Also with Elizabeth Peña, Louise Fletcher, and Philip Bosco. **Director**—Kathryn Bigelow. **(R)** *103 minutes*

BLUE THUNDER (1983)

★★★

Roy Scheider

Roy Scheider and Daniel Stern survey the sky over L.A. in Blue Thunder.

A super-duper, high-tech helicopter is the centerpiece for this fast-paced action yarn, which plays out in the skies of Los Angeles. Scheider is effective as a maverick cop/pilot, who deals with an underhanded operation to subvert civil liberties. The plot has suspense, but it's too far off the wall to be plausible. The breathtaking aerial maneuvers, though, help suspend disbelief in the storyline. Malcolm McDowell and Warren Oates costar. **Director**—John Badham. **(R)** *110 minutes*

BLUE VELVET (1986)

★★★

Kyle MacLachlan
Isabella Rossellini
Dennis Hopper

Kyle MacLachlan and Isabella Rossellini in Blue Velvet.

The distinctive style of writer/director David Lynch—with its disturbing imagery and concentration on the grotesque—dominates this brooding, bizarre, and thoroughly original mystery, which explores the frightening underside of a quiet American town. A college student (MacLachlan) investigates some criminal activity and his curiosity leads to a hellhole of murder, drugs, kidnapping, and sadistic sex. The film unfolds with a sledgehammer intensity that's totally engrossing. Also with Dean Stockwell and Laura Dern. **(R) Academy Award Nomination**—Lynch, best director. *120 minutes*

BLUME IN LOVE (1973)

★★★

George Segal
Susan Anspach
Kris Kristofferson

Writer/director Paul Mazursky takes on middle-class marriage and divorce in this droll comedy/drama about a lawyer, played by Segal, who longs for his ex-wife, played by Anspach, and wants to win her back. Segal and Anspach are both affecting as sympathetic characters. The film is blessed with sparkling supporting performances including Shelley Winters as a woman whose husband left her for a stewardess, and Kristofferson as Anspach's bedmate of the moment. Also with Marsha Mason. **(R)** *116 minutes*

THE BOAT (DAS BOOT) (1981)

★★★½

Jürgen Prochnow

Gripping, finely detailed German production about U-boat life during World War II. The atmosphere of a sweaty, close-quarters existence is meticulously depicted and the ever-present sense of danger adds suspense. In contrast to typical Hollywood war movies, the German submariners are portrayed here as real people rather than stereotyped characters. Originally filmed in German. **Director**—Wolfgang Petersen. **(PG) Academy Award Nominations**—Petersen, best director; Petersen, best screenplay based on material from another medium; Jost Vacano, cinematography. *150 minutes*

BOAT PEOPLE (1983)

★★★

Lam Chi-Cheung
Cora Miao

Ann Hui's blistering account of postwar life in Vietnam reveals appalling conditions under the Communist regime as witnessed by a Japanese photographer who is able to circumvent the official government views. Yet the film, shot in China, is somewhat propagandist in itself. Nevertheless, Hui's sensitive and affecting portrayal of the continuing Vietnamese tragedy is difficult to refute. Originally filmed in Chinese. **(No MPAA rating)** *106 minutes*

BOB & CAROL & TED & ALICE (1969)

★★★

Natalie Wood
Robert Culp
Elliott Gould
Dyan Cannon

An old-fashioned romantic comedy loaded with all sorts of trendy situations: wife-swapping, psychotherapy, pot smoking, and so on. A so-called modern couple envy what seems to be

(Continued)

(Continued)
their friends' ideal marriage, and they almost end up swapping partners. Gould and Cannon are exceptional as Ted and Alice—the nervous experimenters. Wood and Culp are the chic Carol and Bob. The wacky screenplay and smart dialogue keep the situations moving along, but the ending is somewhat absurd. **Director**—Paul Mazursky. **(R)**. **Academy Award Nominations**—Gould, best supporting actor; Cannon, best supporting actress; Mazursky and Larry Tucker, best story and screenplay based on material not previously published or produced. *105 minutes*

BOBBY DEERFIELD (1977)

 ★½

Al Pacino
Marthe Keller

Pacino, in his first romantic role, plays an emotionally drained race-car driver who falls in love with a dying European beauty, played by Keller. Both are miscast in this flat-footed European version of *Love Story.* Alvin Sargent's superficial script has the two leads blabbing endlessly without generating any pathos. The beautiful Anny Duperey stands out as Bobby's enduring mistress of convenience. Also with Walter McGinn and Romolo Valli. Reedited to 99 minutes for cable-TV release. **Director**—Sydney Pollack. **(PG)** *124 minutes*

BOB LE FLAMBEUR (1955)

Roger Duchesne

This is French director Jean-Pierre Melville's version of the American gangster movie. The result is haunting and occasionally leans toward parody. Duchesne has some good moments in the title role, playing a middle-aged gambler and former bank robber who engineers one last glorious heist—the safe at a swank Deauville casino. The murky black-and-white photography enhances the somber mood. Isabel Corey costars. *102 minutes b&w*

BODY AND SOUL (1947)

 ★★★★

John Garfield
Lilli Palmer

Garfield stars as a young man from a poor family who becomes a top prizefighter by fair and foul means. It's a rough-and-tough drama that's perhaps a boxing film cliché. However, this study is compelling, exciting, and laced with impressive fight sequences. Garfield is perfect as the determined slugger, and Palmer stands out as the female lead. There's support from Hazel Brooks, William Conrad, Anne Revere, and Canada Lee. **Director**—Robert Rossen. **Academy Award Nominations**—Garfield, best actor; Abraham Polonsky, original screenplay. *104 minutes b&w*

Lilli Palmer and John Garfield in Body and Soul.

BODY AND SOUL (1981)

 ★★

Leon Isaac Kennedy

Kennedy stars as an earnest boxer who shelves a promising medical career in an effort to win big bucks by vying for the championship. This uninspired remake of the 1947 John Garfield classic lacks vitality and comes across in an undramatic way. Muhammad Ali is in the film as the aspiring champ's advisor, and adds some levity by merely playing himself. Jayne Kennedy and Peter Lawford also star. **Director**—George Bowers. **(R)** *100 minutes*

BODY DOUBLE (1984)

 ★★ ®

Craig Wasson
Gregg Henry
Melanie Griffith

Director Brian De Palma leans heavily on Hitchcock's *Rear Window* and *Vertigo* in this sleazy murder mystery that explores voyeurism and the world of porno movies. Wasson is an unemployed actor who watches a beautiful woman through a telescope and then becomes involved with her murder. De Palma creates some startling, suspenseful moments with his sophisticated camera work, but the ridiculous story makes no sense. **(R)** *114 minutes*

BODY HEAT (1981)

★★★

William Hurt
Kathleen Turner

Lawrence Kasdan triumphantly debuts as director of this sultry movie, which smacks of such 1940s *films noirs* as *Double Indemnity.* It drips with steamy atmospherics and lavishly dwells on passion and treachery. Hurt stars as an affable, second-rate lawyer who is lured into killing the well-heeled husband of a seductive woman, played by Turner. Again, Hurt demonstrates his fine acting ability. Also with Richard Crenna, Mickey Rourke, and Ted Danson. **(R)** *113 minutes*

THE BODY SNATCHER (1945)

Henry Daniell
Boris Karloff
Bela Lugosi

A blood-chilling story about a doctor in 19th-century Scotland who experiments with bodies supplied by graverobbers. Lots of good creepy atmosphere in this Val Lewton thriller, with Karloff and Lugosi at their sinister best. The film is based on a familiar story by Robert Lewis Stevenson and is executed in an inventive manner. Edith Atwater and Russel Wade are also in the cast. **Director**—Robert Wise. *77 minutes b&w*

BOLERO (1984)

★

Bo Derek

A dreary, soft-core porn film made as a vehicle to display Derek's physical charms. And opportunities to see Bo in the buff are rather limited indeed. The audience must suffer through a silly plot, dumb dialogue, and bad acting while waiting for Bo's brief sex scenes with a sheik and a bullfighter. These trysts are played more for laughs than eroticism. George Kennedy and Andrea Occhipinti are in supporting roles. **Director**—John Derek. **(X)** *105 minutes*

® *This movie available with closed captions for the hearing impaired.*

BONJOUR TRISTESSE (1958)

★★★

David Niven
Deborah Kerr
Jean Seberg

An elegant-looking film based on the Françoise Sagan novel about a teenage girl who resents her philandering father's mistress. Tragedy results when the daughter tries to break up the romance. The film is set against the lavish background of the French Riviera. The script is a little melodramatic but entertaining nevertheless. Kerr is outstanding, with help from Niven and Seberg. Mylene Demongeot, Geoffrey Horne, Juliette Greco, and Martita Hunt are also in the cast. **Director**—Otto Preminger. *94 minutes*

BONNIE AND CLYDE (1967)

 ★★★★

Warren Beatty
Faye Dunaway
Michael J. Pollard

A vivid, penetrating, and stylish film biography of the notorious bank robbers who terrorized mid-America at the depth of the Great Depression. The exciting production seems to have a bit of everything—grim drama, comedy at the right moments, social commentary, and suspense. Stunning direction by Arthur Penn is complemented by the brilliant acting of Beatty and Dunaway in the title roles. The film was a huge box-office success and a pacesetter of modern gangster movies. Pollard, Gene Hackman, Estelle Parsons, Gene Wilder, and Denver Pyle are excellent in supporting roles. **Academy Awards**—Parsons, best supporting actress; Burnett Guffey, cinematography. **Nominations**—best picture; Penn, best director; Beatty, best actor; Dunaway, best actress; Hackman and Pollard, best supporting actor; David Newman and Robert Benton, best story and screenplay written directly for the screen. *111 minutes*

BOOMERANG (1947)

★★★★

Dana Andrews
Jane Wyatt
Lee J. Cobb

A priest in a New England community is murdered, and a determined prosecuting attorney saves an innocent man from false conviction. The actual guilty person isn't apprehended although the audience knows who did it. This brilliant and fascinating drama is based on a true story and produced in semidocumentary form. First-class entertainment, with stylish direction and outstanding acting. Arthur Kennedy, Sam Levene, and Ed Begley also star. **Director**—Elia Kazan. **Academy Award Nomination**—Richard Murphy, screenplay. *88 minutes b&w*

BOOM TOWN (1940)

★★★

Clark Gable
Spencer Tracy
Claudette Colbert
Hedy Lamarr

A big-name cast livens up this action-packed drama of oil drillers who bring in black gold. Entertainment and excitement run high in a slick blending of romance, comedy, and suspense. Harold Rosson won an Oscar nomination for his black-and-white cinematography. Frank Morgan, Chill Wills, and Lionel Atwill lend a hand. **Director**—Jack Conway. *116 minutes b&w*

THE BOOST (1988)

 ★★1/2

James Woods
Sean Young

Life in the fast lane: James Woods and Sean Young in The Boost.

The theme of *Days of Wine and Roses* is updated here, with cocaine as the substance that wrecks the lives of an ambitious couple. Woods and Young star as a happily married couple who find brief prosperity in Southern California. When Woods' deals go sour, the couple turns to cocaine. The rest is obvious. Despite the predictable script, Woods' intense acting style is always fascinating to watch. Also with John Kapelos and Stephen Hill. **Director**—Harold Becker. **(R)** *95 minutes*

THE BORDER (1982)

★★★1/2

Jack Nicholson

Elpidia Carrillo encounters border patrol officer Jack Nicholson in The Border.

Nicholson brings considerable richness to his working-stiff characterization of a border patrol officer involved with corruption. The movie intelligently details the plight of illegal Mexican workers with sharp contrasts between their condition and the materialistic lifestyle of some Americans. Valerie Perrine and Harvey Keitel are excellent in supporting roles. Also with Warren Oates and Elpidia Carrillo. **Director**—Tony Richardson. **(R)** *107 minutes*

BORDERLINE (1980)

  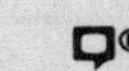

Charles Bronson

Bronson plays a border patrol officer on the trail of illegal aliens from Mexico. There's potential for some socially significant moviemaking, but the film only halfheartedly examines the sorry plight of exploited Mexicans. Most of the time, the film is just another action vehicle, with Bronson seeking revenge for the killing of a fellow officer. Bronson does his usual credible job, but his inspiration seems merely borderline. **Director**—Jerrold Freedman. **(PG)** *105 minutes*

This movie available on videotape and/or disc.

BORN FREE (1966)

 ★★★

Virginia McKenna
Bill Travers
Geoffrey Keen

Pleasant family film based on Joy Adamson's best-selling book about the lioness Elsa, who was raised as a pet and then returned to the jungle. Photography of the animals, and especially of the lioness's efforts to adapt to the wilds of Kenya, is impressive. Travers and McKenna star as the game warden and his wife who managed the retraining of Elsa. **Director**—James Hill. **Academy Awards**—best song ("Born Free," John Barry and Don Black); Barry, best original score. *95 minutes.*

BORN IN EAST L.A. (1987)

★★

Cheech Marin

In his first solo effort, Marin of Cheech and Chong fame wrote and directed this low-brow comedy. He also appears in the starring role as a hapless Mexican-American who is mistaken for an illegal alien and shipped South of the Border. There he becomes involved with a variety of jobs and silly adventures in his attempt to re-enter the U.S. Though played for laughs, the film points up the real-life problems aliens encounter on both sides of the border. Unfortunately, the comic antics are too overblown to be effective. Also with Daniel Stern, Paul Rodriguez, and Jan-Michael Vincent. **(R)** *85 minutes*

BORN ON THE FOURTH OF JULY (1989)

★★★1/2

Tom Cruise
Willem Dafoe

An intense Tom Cruise in Born on the Fourth of July.

Oliver Stone's powerhouse movie about a paralyzed Vietnam vet contains grueling, emotional scenes that are hard to forget. The story is based on the life of Ron Kovic, an all-American youth who lost faith in his country, his religion, and his family after sustaining serious injuries in the Vietnam War. Filled with rage and pain, the film serves as a swift kick in the stomach. Stone's episodic film, with its strange mixture of sweeping epic and dark irony, lacks the tautness of his award-winning *Platoon*, but Cruise's skillful, passionate performance as the central character holds the film together. Also with Kyra Sedgwick, Raymond J. Barry, and Jerry Levine. Nominated for eight Academy Awards. **(R) Academy Awards**—Stone, best director; David Brenner and Joe Hutshing, editing. **Nominations**—best picture; Cruise, best actor; Stone and Kovic, best screenplay adaptation; Robert Richardson, cinematography; John Williams, original score; Michael Minkler, Gregory H. Watkins, Wylie Stateman, Tod A. Maitland, sound. *144 minutes*

BORN YESTERDAY (1950)

★★★★

Judy Holliday
Broderick Crawford
William Holden

Holliday is sensational in this screen adaptation of Garson Kanin's hit Broadway play with a *Pygmalion* theme. She plays a dumb blonde, the girlfriend of a wealthy scrap dealer played by Crawford. Crawford wants her to be educated and sophisticated, but she falls in love with her tutor, played by Holden. The film brims with subtle humor and witty dialogue; the top cast turns in hilarious performances. Howard St. John also stars. **Director**—George Cukor. **Academy Award**—Holliday, best actress. **Nominations**—best picture; Cukor, best director; Albert Mannheimer, screenplay. *103 minutes b&w*

THE BOSTONIANS (1984)

★★★★

Vanessa Redgrave
Madeline Potter
Christopher Reeve

An exquisite film rendition of Henry James' psychological novel that explores the suffrage movement against the backdrop of 19th-century Boston. It's one of the finest period pieces to appear in some time, rich in detail, and capped with a glistening performance by Redgrave. She plays a passionate feminist who objects to the romance between her protégée, Potter, and a southern gentleman, played by Reeve. Jessica Tandy and Linda Hunt are part of the sterling-silver supporting cast. **Director**—James Ivory. **(PG) Academy Award Nomination**—Redgrave, best actress. *120 minutes*

THE BOSTON STRANGLER (1968)

★★★

Tony Curtis
Henry Fonda
Mike Kellin

Curtis gives an effective performance as the maniac who murdered several women in Boston in the mid 1960s. The semidocumentary film drags at times, but it remains a startling rendition of Gerold Frank's book about the brutal sex killings allegedly committed by Albert de Salvo, a deranged plumber. The compelling account follows the criminal's grisly deeds, his arrest, and his trial. George Kennedy and Sally Kellerman also star. **Director**—Richard Fleischer. *118 minutes*

BOULEVARD NIGHTS (1979)

★★

Richard Yniguez
Marta Du Bois
Danny De La Paz

Mexican-American youths of East Los Angeles cruise the neon-lit streets and wage gang warfare. The film tries so hard to be the Chicano version of *West Side Story* or *Saturday Night Fever* that it loses sight of its characters. The cast of unknowns does only a fair acting job. Flash and gloss seem to be more important here than story development. **Director**—Michael Pressman. **(R)** *102 minutes*

BOUND FOR GLORY (1976)

★★★

David Carradine
Ronny Cox

The great folksinger Woody Guthrie is played with slow and heartfelt perfection by Carradine. And director Hal Ashby carefully provides a stunning, detailed portrait of the Great Depression of the 1930s. The story follows Guthrie's separation from his poverty-stricken family, his experience with political activism among California's migrant laborers, and his initial radio career. The two-and-a-half hour film doesn't build dramatically and rambles too often, yet Guthrie's social consciousness shines through. (Shorter prints of the film do exist.) There's fine support from Melinda Dillon, Gail Strickland, John Lehne, and Ji-Tu-Cumbuka. **(PG) Academy Award**—Haskell Wexler, cinematography. **Nominations**—best picture; Robert Getchell, best screenplay based on material from another medium.

147 minutes

THE BOUNTY (1984)

★★★

Anthony Hopkins
Mel Gibson

Mel Gibson's dashing interpretation of Fletcher Christian in The Bounty.

This lavish third film voyage of the classic high-seas adventure is perhaps closest to the truth of the 1787 mutiny aboard the British naval ship. Lt. William Bligh, played with gripping intensity by Hopkins, is perceived as a multidimensional, somewhat heroic character. The retelling is as engrossing as ever, but the initial 1935 Charles Laughton-Clark Gable version is more enjoyable. **Director**—Roger Donaldson. **(PG)** *132 minutes*

A BOY AND HIS DOG (1975)

★★½

Don Johnson
Susanne Benton
Jason Robards
Tiger (the dog)

A mixed breed of a film set in the 21st century when the Earth's surface has been reduced to a wasteland after World War IV. A young man and his telepathic dog, played by Tiger with the voice of Tim McIntire, prowl about looking for food and sex. The man, played smartly by Johnson, is lured into a weird subterranean city ruled by dictator Robards. Director L.Q. Jones is still in the puppy stage with this one, which is at times stimulating and at times mildly revolting. From a Harlan Ellison novella. Also with Alvy Moore and Charles McGraw. **(R)** *87 minutes*

THE BOY IN BLUE (1986)

★

Nicolas Cage

Cage stars as 19th-century Canadian rowing champion Ned Hanlon in this predictable biography. The drama of the story is supposed to derive from Hanlon's clash with calculating opportunists and his hopes for a romance with an unlikely girlfriend, but the whole film lacks dramatic momentum. The lackluster acting is in keeping with the film's tedious script. Cynthia Dale and Christopher Plummer appear in supporting roles. **Director**—Charles Jarrott. **(R)** *98 minutes*

THE BOYS FROM BRAZIL (1978)

★★½

Gregory Peck
Laurence Olivier
James Mason

Laurence Olivier and Gregory Peck in a struggle from The Boys from Brazil.

Peck and Olivier star in this weird drama that exploits popular fears concerning cloning and its potential for being used for evil purposes. In this case, Dr. Josef Mengele, who conducted sadistic human experiments in Nazi death camps, is on the loose in South America with a scheme to produce 94 copies of Adolf Hitler. Mengele is played by Peck; Olivier plays a Jewish Nazi-hunter. There are moments of suspense here and there, but the shaky story, based on Ira Levin's best-selling novel, lapses into silliness. Also with Lilli Palmer, Uta Hagen, Denholm Elliott, and Steven Guttenberg. **Director**—Franklin Schaffner. **(R) Academy Award Nomination**—Olivier, best actor

123 minutes

THE BOYS IN COMPANY C (1978)

★★½

Stan Shaw
Andrew Stevens
James Canning

This drama about Marine warfare in Vietnam starts off on the right foot with an authentic account of boot-camp training. When the scene shifts to Southeast Asia, however, the story falls apart. The characters, played by an unfamiliar cast, are World War II stereotypes who mostly shout and screech at one another. The climax concerns an absurd soccer match that looks like a cheap rip-off of the football game from *M*A*S*H*. Lee Ermey, an ex-Marine drill instructor originally hired as a consultant, came up with the best acting job—playing his former real-life role. Also with Michael Lembeck and Craig Wasson. **Director**—Sidney J. Furie. **(R)**

127 minutes

THE BOYS IN THE BAND (1970)

★★★

Frederick Combs
Leonard Frey
Cliff Gorman

This impressive film version of Mart Crowley's successful Broadway play about homosexuality is full of emotion, an honest exposure of feelings, and the right touch of humor. The rather confined production concerns a homosexual birthday party to which a heterosexual is inadvertently invited. Fine acting and efficient direction keep the story moving until the stunning ending. Also with Laurence Luckinbill, Kenneth Nelson, and Reuben Greene. **Director**—William Friedkin. **(R)**

120 minutes

THE BOYS NEXT DOOR (1985)

★★

Maxwell Caulfield
Charlie Sheen

Looks can be deceiving: Maxwell Caulfield and Charlie Sheen in The Boys Next Door.

Pretentious piece of social commentary about two disenchanted teenage boys who embark on a killing spree. Initially, the film seems bent on serious examination of youthful alienation, but the outcome is merely shallow exploitation with crude acting, dreadful direction, and uneven timing. Caulfield and Sheen portray the young psychopaths. **Director**—Penelope Spheeris. **(R)**

90 minutes

BOYS TOWN (1938)

★★★

Spencer Tracy
Mickey Rooney
Henry Hull

"There's no such thing as a bad boy." So speaketh Father Flanagan (played here by Tracy), who is almost made to eat his words when tough punk Rooney is dumped into Flanagan's community for wayward boys outside Omaha. Art it's not, but it is pretty compelling sentimental drama, oozing with star chemistry (Tracy took an Oscar, and Rooney has a field day). Gene Reynolds and Tommy Noonan costar. **Director**—Norman Taurog. **Academy Awards**—Tracy, best actor; Eleanor Griffin and Dore Schary, original story. **Nominations**—best picture; Taurog, best director; John Meehan, Schary, screenplay.

96 minutes

THE BOY WHO COULD FLY (1986)

★★★

Lucy Deakins
Jay Underwood

A somber yet gently affecting fantasy that deals sympathetically with the personal problems that often afflict teenagers. Deakins stars as a young girl whose father committed suicide. She establishes an understanding and supportive relationship with an autistic boy (Underwood) who is able to fly above the treetops. The excellent performances by the young actors are ably supported by those of Bonnie Bedelia, Colleen Dewhurst, and Fred Savage. **Director**—Nick Castle. **(PG)**

120 minutes

THE BOY WITH GREEN HAIR (1948)

★★★

Dean Stockwell
Pat O'Brien

A captivating drama with a social message that emphasizes the senselessness of war. After an air raid takes the lives of his parents, a boy's hair turns green. The boy, played by Stockwell, becomes an outcast, but he wins the sympathy of other war orphans. Fine acting overcomes some of the muddle in the plot. O'Brien stands out as a likable grandfather. Also with Robert Ryan and Barbara Hale. **Director**—Joseph Losey.

82 minutes

BRADDOCK: MISSING IN ACTION III (1988)

★★

Chuck Norris

Chuck Norris is reunited with his son in Braddock: Missing in Action III.

Having rescued American war prisoners in previous outings, Norris, as Col. Jim Braddock, returns to Vietnam to retrieve his Vietnamese wife and Amerasian son. He also brings out a group of Amerasian orphans, saving them from a life of poverty and despair. In expected one-man-army fashion, poker-faced Norris wipes out Vietnamese soldiers by the regiment. This predictable action/adventure features the customary stiff dialogue and second-rate acting but, at least, some of the Asian characters are depicted with less stereotyping. Slightly better than *Missing in Action 2*, mostly because Braddock is allowed to express some emotion. Also with Aki Aleong and Roland Harrah III. **Director**—Aaron Norris. **(R)**

103 minutes

BRAINSTORM (1983)

★★½

Natalie Wood
Christopher Walken
Louise Fletcher

Louise Fletcher, Cliff Robertson, and Natalie Wood in Brainstorm.

Wood's last film, completed haphazardly after her death, concerns scientists who devise a spectacular headpiece that enables the transfer of thoughts, sensations, and emotions. The stars of this high-tech but confusing story are the blazing special effects from director Douglas Trumbull depicting the consequences of such brainwave sharing. Fletcher is outstanding as a workaholic researcher while Walken is convincing as her colleague. Wood, as Walken's wife, never had a chance to develop her role properly. **(PG)**

106 minutes

BRANNIGAN (1975)

★★

John Wayne
Richard Attenborough
Judy Geeson

This movie available with closed captions for the hearing impaired.

Wayne stars as Brannigan, a Chicago cop who goes to London to retrieve a criminal. The plot is a bit overdrawn and familiar, but the London setting is a nice change of pace for Wayne. You can expect the macho action typical of the Duke, even though he seems old for this role. Attenborough does well as a Scotland Yard detective whose style is at odds with the American's. Also with Mel Ferrer, Ralph Meeker, and John Vernon. **Director**—Douglas Hickox. **(PG)**

111 minutes

THE BRAVADOS (1958)

 ★★ Q®

Gregory Peck
Joan Collins
Stephen Boyd

After four brutes rape and kill a man's wife, the widower embarks on a manhunt to avenge the crime. Peck stars in this downtrodden western as the seeker of justice. But he becomes as despicable as the killers in his zeal for success. The production is handsome, but the execution of the story is uneven and plodding at times. Also with Albert Salmi, Henry Silva, and Lee Van Cleef. **Director**—Henry King. *98 minutes*

BRAZIL (1985)

★★★1/2 Q®

Jonathan Pryce

A controversial, offbeat black comedy set in post-Orwellian society from Terry Gilliam of Monty Python's Flying Circus. Pryce plays a hapless technocrat, smothered by the overwhelming bureaucracy. The Oscar-nominated production design is remarkable and original, though the noisy and convoluted plot is hard to follow. Heavy going most of the way, but worthwhile viewing for the imagery. Original version released at 142 minutes. Michael Palin, Robert De Niro, Katherine Helmond, Ian Holm, and Kim Greist costar. **(R)**

131 minutes

BREAD AND CHOCOLATE (1978)

★★★

Nino Manfredi
Anna Karina

Italian director Franco Brusati's bittersweet satire takes a hard look at the plight of migrant workers. The story, told with pathos and humor, concerns a disorganized Italian waiter, played by Manfredi, who painfully tries to fit in among the stuffy and orderly Swiss. Our hero, at times, resembles Charlie Chaplin's woeful tramp. Brusati illustrates the agony of the outsider with force and intelligence. Originally filmed in Italian. **(No MPAA rating)**

108 minutes

BREAKER MORANT (1979)

 ★★★★

Edward Woodward
Jack Thompson
John Waters

This film from Australia is a stirring courtroom drama set during the Boer War. Three officers tragically become scapegoats of a hypocritical British military. There are obvious parallels to Vietnam and references to the ambiguities of warfare ("We were only following orders."). The film shines with strongly developed characters. There's a powerhouse performance by Woodward in the title role, and Bruce Beresford's crisp direction is on target. Also with Charles Tingwell. **(PG) Academy Award Nomination**—Jonathan Hardy, David Stevens, and Beresford, best screenplay adapted from another medium. *106 minutes*

BREAKFAST AT TIFFANY'S (1961)

 ★★★★

Audrey Hepburn
George Peppard

A stylish and witty film version of Truman Capote's cosmopolitan story about a New York writer, played by Peppard, who has some kooky neighbors, including a daffy playgirl. The lively production is graced with hilarious scenes, memorable performances, and colorful characterizations. There's a madcap party sequence that is unforgettable. Hepburn is charming and funny as the modish Holly Golightly. Henry Mancini wrote the score, which includes the award-winning "Moon River." Also with Patricia Neal, Martin Balsam, John McGiver, Buddy Ebsen, and Mickey Rooney. **Director**—Blake Edwards. **Academy Award**—Mancini, best song. **Nominations**—Hepburn, best actress; George Axelrod, best screenplay based on material from another medium.

115 minutes

THE BREAKFAST CLUB (1985)

★★★ Q®

Emilio Estevez
Molly Ringwald
Ally Sheedy
Judd Nelson
Anthony Michael Hall

The talented young cast of John Hughes' refreshing The Breakfast Club.

A comedy/drama concerning five high-school students who bare their emotions during a nine-hour detention period in the school library. The confined situation unfolds like a drawn-out group therapy session. It is propelled mostly by caustic dialogue which becomes annoying at times. The ensemble acting by a talented young cast is commendable. **Director**—John Hughes. **(R)** *95 minutes*

BREAKHEART PASS (1976)

★★★ Q®

Charles Bronson
Ben Johnson
Richard Crenna

The film is mainly set on an old wood-burning steam train chugging through picturesque mountain country. Bronson is on board as a federal agent in disguise trying to track down a stolen arms shipment. The train is crawling with villains, corpses, and mystery. Shades of *Murder on the Orient Express*. Only in this case, the setting is the West in the 1870s. There's an intricate plot, but the film is a solidly entertaining whodunit packed with suspense and action. It's based on Alistair MacLean's book. Also with Jill Ireland, Charles Durning, and Archie Moore. **Director**—Tom Gries. **(PG)** *95 minutes*

BREAKIN' (1984)

★★

Lucinda Dickey
Adolfo Quinones
Michael Chambers

Break-dancing—lots of it—dominates this low-budget production filmed in the streets of Los Angeles. The faint plot serves primarily to introduce various dance sequences where some slick dudes show off their fancy footwork. Dickey heads the youthful cast as a waitress who wants to become a professional dancer. **Director**—Joel Silberg. **(PG)** *90 minutes*

BREAKIN' 2: ELECTRIC BOOGALOO (1984)

★★

Lucinda Dickey
Adolfo Quinones
Michael Chambers

If you gotta dance, let it be break dancing. And the kids in this sequel dance up a storm. The simple plot, of course, is merely incidental to all the popping and spinning. The youngsters put on a fund-raising show to save their community club from the ravages of greedy developers. **Director**—Sam Firstenberg. **(PG)** *94 minutes*

BREAKING AWAY (1979)

★★★$^1/_2$

Dennis Christopher
Dennis Quaid
Daniel Stern
Jackie Earle Haley

Jackie Earle Haley, Daniel Stern, Dennis Quaid, and Dennis Christopher in Breaking Away.

A simple, charming little comedy with a big heart and a gentle touch. It's about four working-class boys in Bloomington, Indiana, who challenge the college stuffed shirts in a grueling bike race. The cast is unknown, but director Peter Yates obtains sparkling performances all around. Christopher is especially delightful as a first-class rider who idolizes Italian bike champs. The climactic yet predictable big race will leave you elated and cheering. Also with Barbara Barrie and Paul Dooley. **(PG) Academy Award**—Steve Tesich, best screenplay written directly for the screen. **Nominations**—best picture; Yates, best director; Barrie, best supporting actress.

100 minutes

BREAKING IN (1989)

★★★ (closed captions)

Burt Reynolds
Casey Siemaszko

Reynolds gives a charming, well-executed performance in this gentle, eccentric comedy about an aging burglar who takes a younger man (Siemaszko) under his wing. Together, the pair pull off a variety of capers, though the story is really secondary. It is the friendship between the eccentric characters and director Bill Forsyth's appealing, low-key style that carry the film. Forsyth's trademark casualness and slow rhythms are less evident here, but he still manages to make the most of small gestures and slight expressions that reveal the personalities of his characters. Writer/director John Sayles' script is full of details about the mechanics of breaking and entering. Also with Sheila Kelley, Lorraine Toussaint, Albert Salmi, and Harry Carey, Jr. **(R)** *94 minutes*

THE BREAKING POINT (1950)

★★

John Garfield
Patricia Neal

Garfield portrays a desperate charter-boat skipper who falls in with criminals and transports some illicit cargo. The script, based on Ernest Hemingway's *To Have and Have Not*, is slightly tedious, but the film is partially salvaged by the superb performances of Garfield and Juano Hernandez, who plays Garfield's first mate. **Director**—Michael Curtiz.

97 minutes b&w

BREAKING THE SOUND BARRIER (1952)

★★★

A fine British drama about the development of jet planes, as impressive as its credits (produced and directed by David Lean; script by Terence Rattigan; music by Malcolm Arnold; and a cast that includes Ralph Richardson, Ann Todd, and Nigel Patrick). A young woman finds herself at odds with her father, whose obsession with developing planes that will fly faster than the speed of sound leads to the deaths of her husband and brother. The aerial scenes still soar; by comparison to the aviation dramas that proliferated in the 1930s, you may feel this to be far more intelligent or too stiff-upper-lip. **Academy Award Nomination**—Rattigan, story and screenplay.

115 minutes b&w

BREATHLESS (1959)

★★★★

Jean-Paul Belmondo
Jean Seberg

Wild youth: Jean-Paul Belmondo and Jean Seberg in Breathless.

Something of a turning point in modern film—one of the first and most influential films of the French New Wave, directed by Jean-Luc Godard (his first feature); François Truffaut was one of the screenwriters; the production was supervised by Claude Chabrol. Each of the three had been critics for the French film magazine *Cahiers du cinéma;* each went on to become a major director. Belmondo and Seberg are charismatic as a small-time hood (who idolizes Bogey) and his American expatriate girlfriend. Their lives, their love affair, and the film's style are redolent with doubt and agitation. There is an intensely felt anarchy in the film that is both exciting and loaded with impending doom. Originally filmed in French. *89 minutes b&w*

BREATHLESS (1983)

★★$^1/_2$

Richard Gere
Valerie Kaprisky

(closed captions symbol) This movie available with closed captions for the hearing impaired.

An uneven remake of the 1959 Jean-Luc Godard classic, set against a contemporary, pop-culture Los Angeles backdrop. Gere stands out as the crazy, petty criminal hurrying toward his doom. Newcomer Kaprisky is the "nice girl" college student who falls in love with this desperate drifter. Her awkward acting weakens their peculiar romantic relationship. **Director**—Jim McBride. **(R)** *105 minutes*

BREWSTER McCLOUD (1970)

★★★

Bud Cort
Sally Kellerman

This is a far-out, allegorical comedy as only director Robert Altman can create one. Brewster is an oddball character who wants to fly—with man-made wings—inside the Houston Astrodome. When he tries, he kills himself. Altman sets up many striking scenes—some of them are bizarre, some of them are funny, and some of them are funny and bizarre. Cort, in the title role, is effectively kooky. Also with Michael Murphy, William Windom, Shelley Duvall, and Stacy Keach. **(R)** *105 minutes*

BREWSTER'S MILLIONS (1945)

★★

Dennis O'Keefe

A familiar comedy, adequately done, about a young man, played by O'Keefe, who inherits a million dollars and knocks himself out trying to spend it in two months so he can inherit even more. Bright, fast-paced mirth with a fine cast helping out with the spending spree. It should happen to you. Also with Helen Walker, Eddie "Rochester" Anderson, and June Havoc. **Director**—Allan Dwan. *79 minutes b&w*

BREWSTER'S MILLIONS (1985)

★★

Richard Pryor

Pryor is in the title role of this remake as a man who must squander $30 million in 30 days to inherit $300 million. The well-worn screwball-comedy plot finds the frantic spendthrift blowing millions on an outrageous New York City mayoral campaign and an elaborate exhibition baseball game. Despite the uneven script, Pryor and supporting players generate a few laughs. The 1945 version required spending only $1 million. That's the upshot of inflation. Also with John Candy and Lonette McKee. **Director**—Walter Hill. **(PG)** *97 minutes*

THE BRIBE (1949)

Robert Taylor
Ava Gardner

Taylor plays a G-man who pursues some criminals in Latin America and falls in love with sultry Gardner, the wife of one of the bad guys. A glossy melodrama that is only moderately entertaining. The usually competent players aren't at their best although the crooks are impressively menacing. Also with Charles Laughton, Vincent Price, and John Hodiak. **Director**—Robert Z. Leonard. *98 minutes b&w*

THE BRIDE (1985)

★★

Sting
Jennifer Beals

Sting with Jennifer Beals, his beautiful creation, in The Bride.

Peculiar reworking of the classic thriller *Bride of Frankenstein*, with oddball casting of critical characters. Sting plays the venerable Baron who creates a splendid woman for his dreaded monster. Yet, this time, a Pygmalion theme enters in as the doctor falls in love with his female creature. The Sting/Beals relationship fails to click and the unscary film unfolds at a flat pace. **Director**—Frank Roddam. **(PG-13)** *119 minutes*

THE BRIDE CAME C.O.D. (1941)

★★★

Bette Davis
James Cagney

Davis and Cagney star in this workable comedy in which the talent salvages a cornball script. Cagney is a charter pilot who must deliver runaway bride Davis, but the plane crashes. Guess who falls in love with whom? This was Davis' first comedy role. Supporting players include Harry Davenport, Jack Carson, and Stuart Erwin. **Director**—William Keighley. *92 minutes b&w*

THE BRIDE OF FRANKENSTEIN (1935)

★★★★

Boris Karloff
Elsa Lanchester

Baron Frankenstein is coerced into reviving the monster and constructing a mate. This classic horror film, a sequel to *Frankenstein*, is better than the first film in many respects. It is expertly laced with wit, black comedy, pathos, and thrills galore. Karloff is back in his striking monster getup, and Lanchester is superb in dual roles; she plays the macabre mate of the monster and Mary Shelley. Also with Colin Clive, Valerie Hobson, and Ernest Thesiger. **Director**—James Whale. *80 minutes b&w*

THE BRIDGE OF SAN LUIS REY (1944)

Lynn Bari
Alla Nazimova
Louis Calhern

Painful, plodding film, based on Thornton Wilder's novel, about five people who are killed when a flimsy bridge in Peru collapses. A priest investigates the cause of the mishap and the reasons why the people were on the bridge at the moment of collapse. It's a hard pull for the cast and the director. The players also include Francis Lederer, Akim Tamiroff, and Donald Woods. **Director**—Rowland V. Lee. *85 minutes b&w*

THE BRIDGE ON THE RIVER KWAI (1957)

Alec Guinness
Jack Hawkins
William Holden
Sessue Hayakawa

A superb war drama distinguished by magnificent acting and direction and an

(Continued)

(Continued)
out-of-the-ordinary approach to its subject. Guinness stands out as a determined British commanding officer captured by the Japanese. He spurs his men to construct a railway bridge in Burma for their captors to maintain morale and demonstrate British engineering superiority; then he can't bear to see his creation blown up by his own side. The film is blessed with gripping action, suspense, and a compelling script that bristles with ironies. The film is based on Pierre Boulle's novel. **Director**—David Lean. **Academy Awards**—best picture; Lean, best director; Guinness, best actor; Boulle, best screenplay based on material from another medium; Jack Hildyard, cinematography. **Nomination**—Hayakawa, best supporting actor. *161 minutes*

THE BRIDGES AT TOKO-RI (1954)

 ★★★

William Holden
Grace Kelly
Mickey Rooney

A powerful film about the adventures of a pilot during the Korean conflict and the impact of the separation on his family. The action-packed thriller, based on James E. Michener's novel, is a cut above the usual war drama, with some impressive statements about fighting, comradeship, and family. The film won an Oscar for its special effects. Fine performances from Holden, Rooney, and Kelly. Also with Fredric March, Robert Strauss, and Charles McGraw. **Director**—Mark Robson.
104 minutes

A BRIDGE TOO FAR (1977)

 ★★1/2

Dirk Bogarde
James Caan
Michael Caine
Sean Connery

It seems as if an entire regiment of movie notables appears in this $26-million epic based on Cornelius Ryan's best-seller about a disastrous Allied offensive during World War II. However, the Joseph E. Levine production is just another massive war movie mired in noise and confusion. Hardly any of the big American or British stars are onscreen long enough to establish audience involvement. At an almost three-hour length, *A Bridge Too Far* is a movie too long. Also with Robert Redford, Elliott Gould, Laurence Olivier, and Ryan O'Neal. **Director**—Richard Attenborough. **(PG)** *175 minutes*

BRIEF ENCOUNTER (1946)

Celia Johnson
Trevor Howard

A touching and sensitive love story that works surprisingly well in light of its familiar theme. A middle-class housewife (Johnson) and a married local doctor (Howard) fall in love, but agree to stop seeing each other when he takes a job in another country. Outstanding craftsmanship in all quarters has produced a classic romantic drama, with memorable love scenes that are a pleasure to watch. Also with Stanley Holloway and Joyce Carey. The film is based on Noel Coward's play. **Director**—David Lean. **Academy Award Nominations**—Lean, best director; Johnson, best actress; Anthony Havelock-Allan, Lean, and Ronald Neame, screenplay.
86 minutes b&w

BRIGADOON (1954)

Gene Kelly
Cyd Charisse
Van Johnson

Gene Kelly and Van Johnson discover a magical Scottish village in Brigadoon.

Pleasant and charming film version of the Alan Jay Lerner and Frederick Loewe Broadway musical about two Americans—Kelly and Johnson—who discover a magical Scottish village that comes to life for a day every 100 years. Kelly and Charisse handle the dancing with grace and style, and the music is invigorating. The sets look artificial, which suits the whimsical storyline. Jimmy Thompson, Elaine Stewart, and Barry Jones have supporting roles. **Director**—Vincente Minnelli.
108 minutes

BRIGHT LIGHTS, BIG CITY (1988)

Michael J. Fox
Kiefer Sutherland

Jay McInerney's popular novel about a self-destructive young man on a downward spiral of drugs and nightlife limps onto the screen with little or no impact. Fox portrays the central character, a would-be writer in New York City consumed by self-pity and bent on ruining his health and career. Despite Fox's best efforts and some solid supporting work by Sutherland, Jason Robards, and Swoosie Kurtz, the story emerges as dull and vacant. Also with Frances Sternhagen, Phoebe Cates, and John Houseman. **Director**—James Bridges, **(R)** *110 minutes*

BRIGHTON BEACH MEMOIRS (1986)

★★1/2

Jonathan Silverman
Blythe Danner

A warm and nostalgic film portrait of a teenage boy growing up in Brooklyn in 1937. Excellent ensemble performances by Danner as a fretting Jewish mother and Judith Ivey as a widowed aunt bring life to the charming scenes of close family life. However, this adaptation of Neil Simon's successful autobiographical play does not translate well to the screen. The action is claustrophobic and stagebound, the direction bland, and Silverman in the lead role is weak. Also with Bob Dishy and Lisa Waltz. **Director**—Gene Saks. **(PG–13)**
108 minutes

BRIMSTONE AND TREACLE (1982)

★1/2

Sting

Bizarre, unsavory psychological thriller starring rock musician Sting. He convincingly portrays a sinister young

This movie available with closed captions for the hearing impaired.

drifter who cons his way into the home of a middle-class English couple and there molests their paralyzed daughter. The film is handsomely mounted and decently acted, but the weird scenario leaves a sour aftertaste. Forthright supporting work from Denholm Elliott and Joan Plowright as the perplexed husband and wife. **Director**—Richard Loncraine. **(R)**

87 minutes

BRINGING UP BABY (1938)

★★★★

Cary Grant
Katharine Hepburn
Charlie Ruggles

Cary Grant is bewildered by Katharine Hepburn in Bringing Up Baby.

The ultimate screwball comedy is a deliriously manic film about manic lives. Paleontologist Grant loses a dinosaur bone, and in trying to find it, gets mixed up with a fast-talking heiress (Hepburn), a leopard on the loose (named Baby), an explorer (Ruggles) who can imitate the cry of the loon, and other lunacy-engendering types (played by Barry Fitzgerald, May Robson, Walter Catlett, and others). In his dramatic films, director Howard Hawks conveyed a deeply felt acceptance of life's chaos; that powerful, implicit attitude made his comedies all the more compelling—and all the more hysterical. A classic today, the film was a financial flop when first released.

102 minutes b&w

BRING ME THE HEAD OF ALFREDO GARCIA (1974)

★★

Warren Oates
Gig Young

A blood-and-gore drama about a Mexican seeking revenge on the person who seduced his daughter. Director Sam Peckinpah serves up his usual spread of violence garnished with plenty of gruesome details. However, the action is somewhat slow for this sort of outing. Isela Vega, Robert Webber, Emilio Fernandez, Helmut Dantine, and Kris Kristofferson are also in the cast. **(R)**

112 minutes

THE BRINK'S JOB (1978)

★★½

Peter Falk
Peter Boyle

The $2.7-million Brink's stickup in Boston was called "the crime of the century," but in this flippant account, the celebrated 1950 caper comes off as petty theft. William Friedkin, who gave us the exciting *French Connection*, directs here with scant energy or spirit. After sitting through this movie, you may feel that you've been robbed, too. Also with Allen Goorwitz (Garfield), Warren Oates, and Gena Rowlands. **(PG)**

103 minutes

BRITANNIA HOSPITAL (1982)

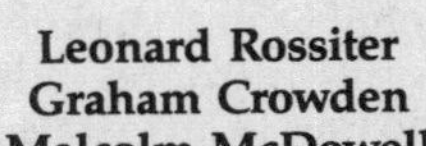

★★

Leonard Rossiter
Graham Crowden
Malcolm McDowell

A boisterous, contemporary British satire that often takes itself too seriously. The farcical story centers on a modern hospital embroiled in a labor dispute. Various noisy incidents are loosely strung together and moments of bad taste surface when a doctor carries out bloody human transplant experiments. The film ends with shrill sermonizing. A sequel of sorts to director Lindsay Anderson's *If. . .* and *O Lucky Man!* **(R)**

115 minutes

BROADCAST NEWS (1987)

★★★

Holly Hunter
William Hurt
Albert Brooks

This winning comedy/drama, set in a television station in Washington, D.C., presents an inside view, albeit a cynical one, of those people who bring us the news. The highly entertaining story involves the manic lives of three journalists: Hunter stars as a savvy producer; Hurt plays an anchorman whose career is based on his handsome looks; and Albert Brooks costars as a brilliant reporter with no camera appeal. Their lives intertwine on both a professional and a personal level, which propels the film forward. Unfortunately, James Brooks' uneven direction and a half-baked ending hamper the generally well-written script. The first half is a fast-paced satire bristling with smart dialogue, while the second half bogs down in the romantic triangle. Also with Robert Prosky, Lois Chiles, Joan Cusack, and Jack Nicholson (in an unbilled performance). **(R) Academy Award Nominations**—best picture; Hurt, best actor; Hunter, best actress; Albert Brooks, best supporting actor; James Brooks, best original screenplay.

131 minutes

BROADWAY (1942)

★★★

George Raft
Pat O'Brien

Raft takes us down memory lane to the Prohibition era when he danced in nightclubs. Gangsters, bootleggers, chorus girls, and speakeasies are the elements of this colorful drama, which involves a murder. Raft plays himself and does some dancing. O'Brien plays a cop, and Broderick Crawford is effective as a tough gangster. Also with S.Z. Sakall and Janet Blair. **Director**—William A. Seiter. *90 minutes b&w*

BROADWAY DANNY ROSE (1984)

★★★½

Woody Allen
Mia Farrow
Nick Apollo Forte

Allen is again in comfortable comic shoes with this Runyonesque fable about a good-hearted, second-rate theatrical manager. He's the familiar schlemiel, spouting wry one-liners as he makes frantic efforts to revive the career of an over-the-hill singer, played with exceptional pizzazz by Forte. Farrow is outstanding and almost unrecognizable as a bleached-blonde tootsie in dark glasses. Everything works: Woody's hilarious script and deft direction, Gordon Willis' dazzling cinematography—even Forte's self-composed lounge act. Watch for Milton Berle and a host of

(Continued)

(Continued)
other comedians playing themselves and having a ball. **(PG) Academy Award Nominations**—Allen, best director and best screenplay written directly for the screen. *84 minutes b&w*

BROKEN ARROW (1950)

★★★½

James Stewart
Jeff Chandler
Debra Paget

A serious western, with Stewart as an Army scout sympathetic to the Indians and trying to promote peace and understanding between the Apaches and the whites. The film is interesting because it doesn't present the Indians as cardboard characters; Chandler is impressive as Cochise, and Paget does well as Stewart's Indian wife. A few brisk action scenes perk up the narrative. Will Geer and Jay Silverheels costar. **Director**—Delmer Daves. **Academy Award Nominations**—Chandler, best supporting actor; Michael Blankfort, screenplay; Ernest Palmer, cinematography. *92 minutes*

BRONCO BILLY (1980)

★★★

Clint Eastwood
Sondra Locke

Clint Eastwood is owner of a traveling Wild West show in Bronco Billy.

A sweet-natured, low-key comedy with Eastwood as star and owner of a rickety Wild West show. The predictable plot is sentimental, but Eastwood has fashioned a warmhearted character and keeps the film at a respectable comic level. Eastwood's "Billy" is a big kid, living in a fantasy world, who is concerned about his likable ragtag troupe and his small-fry fans. Eastwood, who has played his Dirty Harry character to the hilt, is a charming "Mr. Clean." **Director**—Eastwood. **(PG)** *119 minutes*

THE BROOD (1979)

★★½

Oliver Reed
Samantha Eggar

An effective yet overly grotesque Canadian-made horror film, written and directed by David Cronenberg, who borrowed freely from such shockers as *Night of the Living Dead.* Eggar plays a mental patient under the care of a bizarre doctor, played by Reed. She gives birth to strange children, who murder a number of people, including her mother and father. Cronenberg builds adequate suspense, but there's plenty of plodding amid the gore. **(R)** *90 minutes*

THE BROTHER FROM ANOTHER PLANET (1984)

★★★

Joe Morton

Director John Sayles *(Return of the Secaucus Seven)* explores ghetto life through the eyes of an extraterrestrial in this low-budget comedy. Morton stars as an astonished black man from another planet who winds up in Harlem and becomes involved with various colorful characters. Sayles' peppy dialogue is salted with plenty of street lingo. Darryl Edwards and Steve James costar. **(No MPAA rating)** *110 minutes*

BROTHERS (1977)

★★★

Bernie Casey
Vonetta McGee

A dramatized semidocumentary, based on the love affair between black activist Angela Davis and George Jackson, one of the famed Soledad Brothers. The script is oversimplified and loaded in favor of the Jackson-Davis cause. Still, the film is an effective and jolting statement against racism, injustice, and the indignities of prison life. Casey in the Jackson role and McGee in the part of Davis display forceful and convincing characterizations. The film is a sober and refreshing departure from such black exploitation vehicles as *Superfly.* **Director**—Arthur Barron. **(R)** *104 minutes*

THE BROTHERS KARAMAZOV (1958)

★★½

Yul Brynner
Lee J. Cobb
Richard Basehart
Maria Schell

Typical 1950s adaptation of a literary classic: high-calorie, low-nutrition. Not that director/writer Richard Brooks didn't try to deliver more than a high-gloss pictorialization of the Feodor Dostoevski novel; he simply failed to beat the odds that were stacked against him. If you don't think about the source, this is a sometimes engrossing drama of a family torn apart by lust, money, and murder, played by Brynner, Cobb (as the domineering patriarch), Basehart, William Shatner, Albert Salmi, David Opatoshu, and Schell (in a role reportedly coveted by Marilyn Monroe). **Academy Award Nomination**—Lee J. Cobb, best supporting actor. *146 minutes*

BRUBAKER (1980)

★★

Robert Redford
Yaphet Kotto
Murray Hamilton

Redford stars as a reform-minded prison warden, who halts corruption and torture only to be dismissed by the political establishment. Redford starts out as a prisoner to secretly witness the brutality. But when he reveals his identity, the film loses impact; the grim drama ends and sentimental sermonizing begins. **Director**—Stuart Rosenberg. **(R) Academy Award Nomination**—best screenplay written directly for the screen. *131 minutes*

BRUTE FORCE (1947)

★★★★

Burt Lancaster
Charles Bickford

Exceptional big-house melodrama that lives up to its title with a graphic depiction of prison environment. Six desperate convicts plan to break out, getting revenge against a sadistic guard captain

This movie available with closed captions for the hearing impaired.

along the way. Tough, savage action leads up to a smashing climax. The fine cast also features Hume Cronyn, Ella Raines, Yvonne De Carlo, Ann Blyth, Howard Duff, and Sam Levene. **Director**—Jules Dassin. *96 minutes b&w*

BUCKAROO BANZAI (1984)

Peter Weller
John Lithgow

Wacky, jumbled, sci-fi comedy with a confusing, off-the-wall plot that contains enough elements for 10 movies. Weller is in the title role as a neurosurgeon/rock singer/race-car driver who battles aliens from Planet 10. Most of the cast doesn't act; they merely walk around in a daze. Only Lithgow, as a mad scientist, seems at all interesting. **Director**—W.D. Richter. **(PG) Alternate Title**—*The Adventures of Buckaroo Banzai.* *100 minutes*

BUCK PRIVATES (1941)

 ★★★

Bud Abbott
Lou Costello

Abbott and Costello join the Army, and after a series of energetic escapades, they accidentally become heroes. This is typical service-comedy corn with some romantic subplots thrown in, but it works for Abbott and Costello. The film was one of their first starring vehicles, and its success won them promotions as the top sergeants of movie comedy. Lee Bowman, Alan Curtis, Jane Frazee, Nat Pendleton, and the Andrews Sisters round out the cast. **Director**—Arthur Lubin.

84 minutes b&w

BUCK PRIVATES COME HOME (1946)

★★½

Bud Abbott
Lou Costello

Abbott and Costello muster out of the Army and care for a European war orphan. This is a rather flimsy slapstick comedy and certainly not at the level of *Buck Privates.* However, the film perks up considerably with a chase sequence at the finale. Beverly Simmons, Tom Brown, and Nat Pendleton costar. **Director**—Charles T. Barton.

77 minutes b&w

BUCK ROGERS IN THE 25TH CENTURY (1979)

Ⓥ 

Gil Gerard
Pamela Hensley
Erin Gray

This is a film based on the sci-fi comic strip character, but there's more inspiration from *Star Wars.* You'll see space hardware galore, a climactic shoot-out among rocket ships, and a pixie robot similar to R2-D2. The film looks dazzling most of the time thanks to the snappy direction of Daniel Haller. Children should be able to handle the simple good-guy/bad-guy plot and take delight in the wisecracks of Gerard, who plays the title role. **(PG)**

89 minutes

BUDDY BUDDY (1981)

 ★½

Jack Lemmon
Walter Matthau

What an idea: Billy Wilder directing Matthau and Lemmon in this farce about a hit man trying to bump off a stool pigeon while a suicidal schnook keeps interfering with the assassination plan. Matthau plays the hood, and Lemmon is the schnook—and what a disappointment. The comedy material is consistently off stride and only manages to generate a few smiles. It's all sadly trite and strained, not what anyone would expect from the folks responsible for hits like *The Fortune Cookie.* Paula Prentiss and Klaus Kinski costar. **(R)** *96 minutes*

THE BUDDY HOLLY STORY (1978)

 ★★★½

Gary Busey
Don Stroud
Charles Martin Smith

Gary Busey stars as the pioneer rock 'n' roll star in The Buddy Holly Story.

A first-rate, realistic film biography of the talented rockabilly composer/musician who introduced such 1950s hits as "Peggy Sue" and "That'll Be the Day." Lanky, toothy Busey, in the title role, lights up the screen with his energetic musical and dramatic performance. The story follows Holly's career from his beginnings as a roller rink musician in Texas to his death at 22 in a plane crash. Best of all is the way the film captures the joy and enthusiasm of early rock 'n' roll and its effect on young people. Busey, Stroud, and Smith do their own singing and playing. **Director**—Steve Rash. **(PG) Academy Award Nomination**—Busey, best actor.

114 minutes

THE BUDDY SYSTEM (1984)

  ▢®

Richard Dreyfuss
Susan Sarandon

Richard Dreyfuss, Wil Wheaton, and Susan Sarandon in The Buddy System.

A sparse, boy-meets-girl romantic comedy with a few tender moments amid the generally dry material. Dreyfuss is a sometime novelist/inventor who strikes up a shaky relationship with an insecure single mother played by Sarandon. The affair is eagerly engineered by the mother's precocious young son. After the couple maneuvers through various pat complications, true love predictably triumphs. Also with Wil Wheaton. **Director**—Glenn Jordon. **(PG)**

111 minutes

BUFFALO BILL AND THE INDIANS, OR SITTING BULL'S HISTORY LESSON (1976)

 ★★★

Paul Newman
Burt Lancaster

Robert Altman's intelligent and penetrating study of the legendary show-biz

(Continued)

(Continued)
hero of the late 1800s shows Buffalo Bill as an egotistical, inflated product of publicity. The film is also about genocide committed against the Indians. Newman gives a keen and often amusing performance in the title role. Lancaster is low-key but effective as Ned Buntline, the showman who turned Buffalo Bill's life into mythology. Frank Kaquitts plays an impressive, silent, and dignified Sitting Bull, who was signed to appear in Buffalo Bill's Wild West Show. There are some uneven and dreary moments, which lessen the film's impact. But it succeeds in its creativity and its reexamination of history. Also with Kevin McCarthy and Geraldine Chaplin. Longer versions of the film are in existence. **(PG)**
120 minutes

THE BUGS BUNNY/ROAD RUNNER MOVIE (1979)

 ★★★

Now you can really indulge yourself in an hour and a half of nonstop fun with Bugs, Daffy, Wile E. Coyote, and other stars from the Warner Brothers cartoon stable. Animator Chuck Jones has compiled scenes from numerous cartoons and has included several complete short features. There's about 20 minutes of new animation with Bugs as narrator. It's a nostalgic, colorful parade of great animated comedy—that's what's up, Doc! Cable versions run 78 minutes, while network television versions are 48 minutes. **(G)** *92 minutes*

BUGS BUNNY'S 3RD MOVIE: 1001 RABBIT TALES (1982)

Yosemite Sam meets our hero in Bugs Bunny's 3rd Movie: 1001 Rabbit Tales.

Those colorful Warner Brothers cartoons are back with Bugs, Tweety Bird, Yosemite Sam, Daffy Duck, and other favorite characters up to their usual cute tricks. Essentially, it's the same stuff that shows up on Saturday morning TV, but it's more enjoyable here without the commercial interruptions. Many old sketches are recycled, and there's some new material. The versatile Mel Blanc provides most of the voice characterizations. **Directors**—David Detiege, Art Davis, and Bill Perez. **(G)**
74 minutes

BUGSY MALONE (1976)

 ★★★

Scott Baio
Florrie Dugger
Jodie Foster

An ingeniously conceived and lavish 1920s gangster movie played entirely by kids whose average age is 12. Most of the youngsters perform well, dressed in pinstriped double-breasted suits and flapper outfits. The tommy guns splatter their victims with whipped cream. Veteran actress Foster (age 14) is outstanding as a brassy showgirl. The film is made with care and affection, yet its momentum is lost toward the end. The musical score was written by Paul Williams. Also with John Cassisi and Martin Lev. **Director**—Alan Parker. **(G)** *93 minutes*

BULL DURHAM (1988)

Kevin Costner
Susan Sarandon
Tim Robbins

Kevin Costner and Susan Sarandon star in Bull Durham.

A well-written comedy centered around a minor-league baseball team in Durham, North Carolina. Sarandon stars as the ultimate baseball fan, who each season chooses the most promising member of the Durham Bulls and teaches him how the game of baseball is related to the game of love. Her plans go awry one season when both rookie pitcher Robbins and aging catcher Costner vie for her attentions. The way these three characters affect each other and the team provides the heart of the story. The cast is excellent, particularly Costner as the minor league veteran brought in to provide experience for Robbins. An aura of melancholy surrounds Costner's character as he realizes he will never make it to "the show" (the major leagues). Much of the humor in this offbeat comedy occurs during the baseball games as the viewer is allowed to see first hand exactly what goes on out there on the field. Also with Trey Wilson, Robert Wuhl, and William O'Leary. **Director**—Ron Shelton. **Academy Award Nomination**—Shelton, best original screenplay. **(R)** *108 minutes*

THE BULLFIGHTER AND THE LADY (1951)

Robert Stack

One of the best of the screen's bullfighting movies, appropriately directed by genuine sportsman and action-film director Budd Boetticher (who, in 1972, filmed a documentary on the life of bullfighter Carlos Arruza). Stack stars as an American in Mexico who wants to master the sport, and unintentionally gets a matador killed in the course of his education. He faces an uphill struggle to win back the approval of the spectators and his own self-respect. Scripted by James Edward Grant (the original story was nominated for an Oscar), with solid performances by Gilbert Roland, Joy Page, Katy Jurado, and Virginia Grey. **Academy Award Nomination**—Budd Boetticher and Ray Nazzaro, motion picture story.
87 minutes b&w

BULLITT (1968)

★★★½

Steve McQueen
Jacqueline Bisset
Robert Vaughn

® *This movie available with closed captions for the hearing impaired.*

Steve McQueen stalks the killers in the thriller Bullitt.

Stylish, stirring detective thriller with McQueen smartly cast as a San Francisco cop trying to put the lid on underworld activity. A key witness in McQueen's charge is killed, and he tracks down the murderers. The action-packed drama, graced by efficient direction, ends in a classic car chase that is well above the ordinary. The editing by Frank Keller won an Academy Award. The fine supporting cast includes Don Gordon, Robert Duvall, and Simon Oakland. **Director**—Peter Yates. **(PG)**
113 minutes

BUNNY LAKE IS MISSING (1965)

★★★★

Carol Lynley
Keir Dullea
Laurence Olivier
Noel Coward

Director Otto Preminger was a master of mysteries in the 1940s, then largely left the genre for adaptations of blockbuster literary and dramatic properties. This film marked his return to the genre in 1965, and it's a triumphant return, though the visual impact of his brilliant use of wide screen is lost on television. Lynley stars as Ann Lake, a newly arrived American in London who turns desperately to a Scotland Yard inspector (Olivier) when her four-year-old daughter, Bunny, disappears. It turns out that no one but her brother (Dullea) has actually seen the child. When the police learn that Ann had an imaginary playmate whom she called Bunny, Ann fears that they're ready to abandon the search, suspecting that the girl is only a figment of the mother's imagination. Stylish, chilling, and well acted by a cast that also includes Finlay Currie and Martita Hunt.
107 minutes b&w

THE 'BURBS (1989)

★½

Tom Hanks
Bruce Dern
Carrie Fisher

Director Joe Dante's bedraggled comedy desperately searches for laughs and finds none. Hanks tarnishes his acting reputation in a throwaway role as a suburbanite who becomes paranoid over his weird new neighbors. The film is too dark to be zany and too trite to be a black comedy. A cast of oddball supporting players, including Brother Theodore, Henry Gibson, Corey Feldman, and Rick Ducommen, provides some color. **(PG)** *102 minutes*

BURGLAR (1987)

★

Whoopi Goldberg
Bob Goldthwait

A loud and boorish comedy/mystery that wastes the talent of Goldberg, who stars in the title role. Goldberg plays a sometime cat burglar who attempts to solve a murder that she witnessed during a break-in. The film is saddled with hopeless dialogue, witless gags, and formula situations, while Goldberg's character is unnecessarily crude. Goldthwait, as her wacko sidekick, manages some amusing scenes, but his screeching delivery is annoying. Directed by Hugh Wilson, the man responsible for the first *Police Academy* comedy, which undoubtedly accounts for the weaknesses in this film.
102 minutes

BURNING SECRET (1989)

★★½

Klaus Maria Brandauer
Faye Dunaway

Faye Dunaway is pursued by Klaus Maria Brandauer in Burning Secret.

Flat, ponderous drama set in post-World War I Austria about an affection-starved woman (Dunaway) who is seduced by a nobleman (Brandauer). The awkward screenplay and slow pacing sabotage the handsome production values and competent acting. Brandauer's charming war-hero character is well-drawn, but Dunaway is weak as the refined lady who is won over by the baron's dubious friendship with her overprotected young son. **Director**—Andrew Birkin. **(PG)** *107 minutes*

BURNT OFFERINGS (1976)

★★★

Karen Black
Oliver Reed

Skillful direction from Dan Curtis produces a lot of chills and tension in this thriller about a family who rents a creepy old mansion for the summer. There are solid performances, too, from Black, Reed, Lee Montgomery, and Bette Davis. Clichés are sprinkled throughout the plot, and the ending is predictable. But the eerie goings-on at that rambling murderous house and the mystery behind the locked door on the top floor will keep moviegoers on the edges of their seats. Also with Burgess Meredith and Eileen Heckart. **(PG)**
115 minutes

BUS STOP (1956)

★★★½

Marilyn Monroe
Don Murray

Marilyn Monroe as the singer and Don Murray as the cowboy in Bus Stop.

Monroe displays competent acting talent as well as her familiar sex appeal in this comedy/drama. She plays a volup-
(Continued)

This movie available on videotape and/or disc.

(Continued)
tuous cafe singer who unintentionally entices a naive cowboy, played by Murray, while his friends urge him not to get involved. The film, based on William Inge's play, offers an entertaining mixture of sensitive drama and comic moments. Betty Field stands out as a waitress. Eileen Heckart, Arthur O'Connell, Hope Lange, and Hans Conried costar. **Director**—Joshua Logan. **Academy Award Nomination**—Murray, best supporting actor.
96 minutes

BUSTER (1988)

★★½

Phil Collins
Julie Walters

Pop singer Collins stars in the title role as a small-time thief who makes a big strike by participating in Britain's infamous Great Train Robbery of 1963. Collins is exceptionally good in this breezy comedy that finds the newly rich criminal and his family on the lam in Mexico. Walters co-stars as the jaunty wife who longs to return to London. Despite the appeal of the characters, the movie seems shallow and uncompelling. Also with Larry Lamb, Stephanie Lawrence, and Ellen Beaven. The film's theme song, "Two Heart," was Oscar-nominated. **Director**—David Green. **(R)** *93 minutes*

BUSTIN' LOOSE (1981)

★★

Richard Pryor
Cicely Tyson

Pryor stars as a small-time thief who shepherds some rascally children to the West Coast in a rickety bus. Pryor fans will love some of his funny skits. His self-parodying style has great charm, but as the script gains sentimentality, his talents are undermined; the tone becomes domesticated and even tacky. The kids are precocious. Tyson plays a social worker and the unlikely romantic interest of Pryor. **Director**—Oz Scott. **(R)** *94 minutes*

BUTCH AND SUNDANCE: THE EARLY DAYS (1979)

 ★★

William Katt
Tom Berenger

This prequel to *Butch Cassidy and the Sundance Kid* explores how the two outlaws met and some of their preliminary escapades. Berenger and Katt are in the title roles, but there's no special chemistry between them as there was with Paul Newman and Robert Redford in the original, which was made 10 years earlier. The prequel also lacks spirit and style, and the script is hollow. It seems their early days were dreary days. **Director**—Richard Lester. **(PG)**
110 minutes

BUTCH CASSIDY AND THE SUNDANCE KID (1969)

★★★★

Paul Newman
Robert Redford
Katharine Ross

A winning team: Paul Newman and Robert Redford in Butch Cassidy and the Sundance Kid.

This humorous and cheerful western offers a full complement of film excellence: superb direction, winning performances, effective comedy, and the memorable tune "Raindrops Keep Fallin' on My Head." Newman and Redford strike up perfect chemistry together as clownish outlaws with a sheriff's posse always one step behind. The appealing movie begins energetically and never flags. There is enthusiastic support from Ross, Strother Martin, Jeff Corey, and Cloris Leachman. **Director**—George Roy Hill. **(PG) Academy Awards**—William Goldman, best story and screenplay based on material not previously published or produced; Conrad Hall, cinematography. **Nominations**—best picture; Hill, best director. *110 minutes*

BUTTERFIELD 8 (1960)

★★½

Elizabeth Taylor
Laurence Harvey

The only thing going for this routine melodrama is a slick performance by Taylor as a high-priced call girl who longs to get out of the profession. The film, based on John O'Hara's novel, starts off awkwardly and never really picks up steam. Harvey is impressive as Taylor's Mr. Right. There's adequate support, too, from Dina Merrill, Eddie Fisher, Mildred Dunnock, and Betty Field. **Director**—Daniel Mann. **Academy Award**—Taylor, best actress.
108 minutes

BUTTERFLIES ARE FREE (1972)

★★★

Goldie Hawn
Edward Albert

Goldie Hawn, Eileen Heckart, and Edward Albert in Butterflies are Free.

Hawn stars in this lighthearted film as a flighty actress who falls in love with a blind young man next door. Then she has to deal with his overprotective mother. Based on Leonard Gershe's Broadway play, the film adaptation is somewhat confined, but good acting by the cast overcomes the drawback. Hawn is perfectly cast, and Eileen Heckart is brilliant as the possessive mother. Albert plays the blind man. **Director**—Milton Katselas. **(PG) Academy Award**—Heckart, best supporting actress. *109 minutes*

BYE BYE BIRDIE (1963)

★★★

Janet Leigh
Dick Van Dyke
Ann-Margret

A teenage singing sensation gives his final TV-show performance before leaving for military service. This frothy musical is based on the Broadway show

This movie available with closed captions for the hearing impaired.

and features some pleasant numbers, including "Put on a Happy Face." Van Dyke is good as a songwriter, and Paul Lynde and Maureen Stapleton are impressive as frantic parents. The film should have special appeal for younger audiences. Also with Bobby Rydell and Ed Sullivan. **Director**—George Sidney.
112 minutes

C

CABARET (1972)

★★★★

Liza Minnelli
Joel Grey
Michael York

Liza Minnelli in decadent prewar Berlin in Cabaret.

Smashing, masterful musical with the showstopping performance of Minnelli as Sally Bowles, an American singer working in Berlin on the eve of World War II. The multitalented Minnelli proves to be a fantastic actress as well as a singer/dancer, and she's complemented nicely by Bob Fosse's stylish direction and choreography. The film loosely follows the Broadway musical, based on Christopher Isherwood's stories, but the script is also influenced by both the play and film *I Am a Camera.* Hitler's Germany makes for a chilling backdrop. Also with Helmut Griem, Fritz Wepper, and Marisa Berenson. **(PG) Academy Awards**—Fosse, best director; Minnelli, best actress; Grey, best supporting actor; Geoffrey Unsworth, cinematography. **Nominations**—best picture; Jay Allen, best screenplay based on material from another medium.
123 minutes

CABIN IN THE SKY (1943)

★★★

Eddie "Rochester" Anderson
Ethel Waters
Lena Horne

God and the Devil compete for the soul of a gambling man in this delightful musical, which features an all-black cast. The film doesn't quite live up to the play, but it's energetic and engrossing nevertheless. The superb cast also includes Cab Calloway and Louis Armstrong. With such giants of entertainment on board, it's watchable indeed. **Director**—Vincente Minnelli.
99 minutes b&w

CACTUS FLOWER (1969)

★★½

Ingrid Bergman
Walter Matthau
Goldie Hawn

Despite the fine cast, this film version of the Broadway comedy doesn't hold up. Matthau plays a dentist, and Bergman costars as the nurse who secretly loves him. Bergman is miscast for this sort of part, and the starchy dialogue is a noticeable drawback throughout the film. But Hawn shines as the dentist's mistress, who is eventually forsaken for the nurse. Also with Jack Weston, Vito Scotti, and Irene Hervey. **Director**—Gene Saks. **(PG) Academy Award**—Hawn, best supporting actress.
103 minutes

CADILLAC MAN (1990)

★★½

Robin Williams
Tim Robbins

Williams stars as a stereotypical car salesman faced with the selling job of his life in this vehicle designed to showcase the comic's manic humor. As in other Williams vehicles, this film works best when his character is off by himself—when he is in a situation that duplicates the isolation so essential to a stand up comic's routine. To that end, the film employs direct-to-the-camera address as well as comic asides. Unfortunately, Williams' talents cannot overcome the script's weaknesses, which makes the second half of the film entirely different from the first half in terms of pacing and plot. Also with Pamela Reed, Fran Drescher, Annabella Sciorra, and Zack Norman. **Director**—Roger Donaldson. **(R)**
95 minutes

THE CADDY (1953)

★★

Dean Martin
Jerry Lewis

Martin and Lewis star in this film about golf. The production is organized into a series of vignettes, with Lewis as a golf enthusiast trying to build up Martin's game. This is certainly not the best the pair has to offer, but there are some good moments, and Martin sings "That's Amore." Donna Reed, Fred Clark, and Barbara Bates costar. **Director**—Norman Taurog.
95 minutes b&w

CADDYSHACK (1980)

★★½

Chevy Chase
Ted Knight
Rodney Dangerfield
Bill Murray

Comedy on the golf course: Rodney Dangerfield and Chevy Chase in Caddyshack.

There are silly high jinks on the golf links with Chase, Knight, Dangerfield, and Murray participating in crude jokes that mostly misfire. There's only a ghost of a plot—something about a poor caddy trying to wheedle help for a college scholarship from an influential club member. Generally, the film is a series of throwaway vignettes that poke fun at the WASPy country-club set. **Director**—Harold Ramis. **(R)**
98 minutes

This movie available on videotape and/or disc.

CADDYSHACK II (1988)

★½

Jackie Mason
Chevy Chase
Dan Aykroyd

Dan Aykroyd has a few things to say to Chevy Chase in Caddyshack II.

A dreary follow-up to the 1980 comedy that starred Rodney Dangerfield. This time Mason steps into the central role as a flashy self-made millionaire who attempts to join a snooty country club, only to be snubbed by some snobbish members. Don't expect the biting humor of Mason's Broadway stand-up routine. The jokes fall flat, the plot is a repeat of the original, and the production is shoddy. The stellar cast wastes its time and talents. Also with Robert Stack, Dyan Cannon, Randy Quaid, and Dina Merrill. **Director**—Allan Arkush. **(PG)** *103 minutes*

LA CAGE AUX FOLLES (1978)

★★★★

Ugo Tognazzi
Michel Serrault
Michel Galabru

What do you do when you're in love with a beautiful, respectable girl, and your father is a homosexual who lives with a drag queen? Bring her folks over to meet your folks, of course. And that's when all the outrageous fun begins in this brilliant farce, which won France's version of the Oscar. Skilled performances and keen comic timing by Tognazzi and Serrault as the gay duo make this film a great comedy. Originally filmed in French. **Director**—Édouard Molinaro. **(R) Academy Award Nominations**—Molinaro, best director; Francis Veber, Molinaro, Marcello Danon, and Jean Poiret, best screenplay adapted from another medium. *91 minutes*

LA CAGE AUX FOLLES II (1981)

★★

Ugo Tognazzi
Michel Serrault

Serrault, as the temperamental drag queen, and Tognazzi, as his lover, return in this so-so sequel to the successful French comedy. This time, the duo is mixed up in a drab and predictable secret-agent melodrama with missing microfilm and several corpses. Serrault and Tognazzi generate some funny moments, but it's formula stuff without the clever ingredients that made the first film a hit. Originally filmed in French. **Director**—Édouard Molinaro. **(R)** *100 minutes*

LA CAGE AUX FOLLES 3: THE WEDDING (1986)

★★

Ugo Tognazzi
Michel Serrault

This third installment about the French odd couple finds Albin (Serrault) facing a terrible dilemma: He must marry a woman and father a child to inherit a fortune. What was funny and clever initially has now lapsed into a silly and trite reworking of their routine. An obvious disappointment despite the efforts of five screenwriters. Tognazzi once again plays the straight man. Originally filmed in French. **Director**—Georges Lautner. **(PG-13)** *88 minutes*

THE CAINE MUTINY (1954)

★★★★

Humphrey Bogart
José Ferrer
Van Johnson

Incompetent: Humphrey Bogart as the troubled Captain Queeg in The Caine Mutiny.

A powerful adaptation of Herman Wouk's gripping Pulitzer Prize-winning novel of Navy officers who rebel against the neurotic captain of a destroyer escort during World War II. The film offers exciting action and first-class performances, which graphically portray the frustrations and character traits of the subjects. Bogart is especially memorable as the unhinged skipper. The film ends in a smashing court-martial climax with the resolution of justice under question. Also with Fred MacMurray, E.G. Marshall, and Lee Marvin. **Director**—Edward Dmytryk. **Academy Award Nominations**—best picture; Bogart, best actor; Tully, best supporting actor; Stanley Roberts, screenplay. *125 minutes*

CAL (1984)

★★★

John Lynch
Helen Mirren

Somber, tragic story of the numbing violence in Northern Ireland as seen through the experience of an unemployed Catholic youth. The performances are adequate, but events are slow moving and loosely connected. A depressing atmosphere pervades the film as if to illustrate the climate of endless terror. Lynch is in the title role, and Mirren is the older woman to whom he reaches out for love. **Director**—Pat O'Connor. **(R)** *102 minutes*

CALAMITY JANE (1953)

★★★

Doris Day
Howard Keel

A pleasant, energetic musical that's just the right vehicle for Day, who stars in the title role. Doris plays the rough-and-ready frontier girl with plenty of vigor. She's tamed by Keel, who costars as Wild Bill Hickok. The film is a little on the order of *Annie Get Your Gun.* It has a pleasant score, including the Oscar-winning song "Secret Love." Phil Carey, Allyn McLerie, Dick Wesson, and Paul Harvey lend support. **Director**—David Butler. *101 minutes*

CALIFORNIA SPLIT (1974)

Elliott Gould
George Segal

This movie available with closed captions for the hearing impaired.

Uneven but entertaining comedy especially suited for those who like director Robert Altman's unique style. Gould and Segal are compulsive gamblers who become fast friends and go on a spree together. Altman manages to present these oddball characters in a way that's touching and amusing. Ann Prentiss and Gwen Welles are effective as a couple of amateur hookers. Also with Joseph Walsh and Bert Remsen. **(R)** *109 minutes*

CALIFORNIA SUITE (1978)

 ★★1/2

Jane Fonda
Alan Alda
Maggie Smith
Michael Caine
Walter Matthau
Elaine May
Richard Pryor
Bill Cosby

Walter Matthau and Denise Galik in California Suite.

A bevy of top film stars talk, talk, talk in this Neil Simon comedy, set in the Beverly Hills Hotel. This movie version of the Broadway stage production is changed from four separate playlets to a cohesive story, but the effect is a labored, ragged barrage of wisecracks. There's top-notch acting, but even the good performances wear thin from the tiresome dialogue, which sounds like incessant bickering after a while. **Director**—Herbert Ross. **(PG) Academy Award**—Smith, best supporting actress. **Nomination**—Simon, best screenplay based on material from another medium. *103 minutes*

CALIGULA (1980)

(no stars)

Malcolm McDowell
Peter O'Toole
John Gielgud

Penthouse magazine publisher Bob Guccione produced this vulgar $17-million porno spectacle set in 1st-century Rome. It's a lengthy smorgasbord of explicit sex, mixed with assorted horrors, such as disembowelment, castration, decapitation, and strangulation. After the principal shooting was completed and the actors were finished with their roles, Guccione shot much of the X-rated footage using stand-ins. This accounts for the appearances of several noteworthy actors in such a vile film. Originally released at 156 minutes, including six minutes of fairly hard-core footage. A much toned-down R-rated version also exists at 105 minutes. **Director**—Giovanni Tinto. **(No MPAA rating)**

150 minutes

CALL ME (1988)

Patricia Charbonneau
Patti D'Arbanville

Sam Freed and Patricia Charbonneau in a tense moment from Call Me.

This mean-spirited crime thriller stars Charbonneau as a restless single woman, dissatisfied with her job as a columnist as well as her relationship with her boyfriend. An obscene phone call rouses her interest but ultimately leads her into a trap involving theft and murder. The film's sleazy settings and characters make for a bleak atmosphere, while Charbonneau's character seems too naive to be believable—especially for a New Yorker. Also with Sam Freed, Boyd Gaines, Stephen McHattie, and Steve Buscemi. **Director**—Sollace Mitchell. **(R)** *97 minutes*

CALL ME BWANA (1962)

Bob Hope
Anita Ekberg

Hope goes to Africa to find a lost space capsule and tries to elude foreign agents. This farce contains some effective jokes, but not enough to sustain the movie. Ekberg and Edie Adams are Hope's female foils. Golf great Arnold Palmer makes a cameo appearance. Lionel Jeffries, Percy Herbert, and Paul Carpenter are also in the cast. **Director**—Gordon Douglas. *103 minutes*

CALL ME MADAM (1953)

Ethel Merman
Donald O'Connor
George Sanders
Vera-Ellen

Merman belts out Irving Berlin songs with her typical gusto in this lively and colorful film version of the Broadway musical based on the life of Perle Mesta. She plays an energetic Washington party-giver ("the hostess with the mostess"), who is appointed U.S. Ambassador to Lichtenberg. Merman is supported by a splendid cast. Some of the political jokes, however, are out-of-date. Also with Billy De Wolfe, Helmut Dantine, and Walter Slezak. **Director**—Walter Lang. *117 minutes*

CALL NORTHSIDE 777 (1948)

James Stewart
Lee J. Cobb
Helen Walker

Stewart plays a determined Chicago reporter. He painstakingly uncovers evidence to free a man who was convicted of murder 11 years earlier. The compelling semidocumentary thriller, based on a true story, is executed with impressive atmosphere and excellent acting. Stewart's step-by-step assembly of the facts is handled with pacing that builds suspense toward a satisfying climax. Also with E.G. Marshall, Kazia Orzazewski, and Richard Conte. **Director**—Henry Hathaway. *111 minutes b&w*

CAMELOT (1967)

 ★★1/2

Richard Harris
Vanessa Redgrave

An overblown, overstuffed version of the successful Lerner and Loewe

(Continued)

(Continued)

Broadway musical, which strains for style and charm, but never makes it. Harris and Redgrave star in the classic story of King Arthur and his gallant knights. The acting is fine, but no one does justice to the memorable songs. Joshua Logan's glossy direction is filled with needless close-ups and lacks cohesiveness. David Hemmings, Lionel Jeffries, and Franco Nero are also in the cast. John Truscott's costumes won an Academy Award. The videotape version runs 150 minutes. **Academy Award Nomination**—Richard H. Kline, cinematography. *178 minutes*

CAMILLE (1936)

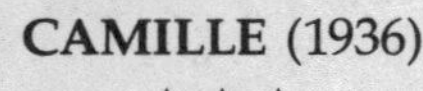

★★★

Greta Garbo
Robert Taylor

Tragic romance with Robert Taylor and Greta Garbo in Camille.

Garbo brings life and vitality to this screen version of Alexandre Dumas' novel about a dying prostitute who falls in love with an innocent young man, played by Taylor. Although Taylor is adequate, Garbo steals the show. Lionel Barrymore, Elizabeth Allen, and Laura Hope Crews also star. **Director**—George Cukor. **Academy Award Nomination**—Garbo, best actress. *108 minutes b&w*

CAN-CAN (1960)

★★½

Frank Sinatra
Shirley MacLaine

This shallow version of the Cole Porter musical stars Sinatra as a 19th-century Parisian lawyer, who defends a nightclub entertainer, played by MacLaine, for performing the can-can, an allegedly lewd dance. Sinatra doesn't seem to be with it, and MacLaine is miscast. Maurice Chevalier and Louis Jourdan add charm, but it's not enough to prop up the sagging script. Some memorable songs are featured throughout, including "C'est Magnifique," "I Love Paris," and "Just One of Those Things." Also with Juliet Prowse and Leon Belasco. **Director**—Walter Lang. *131 minutes*

THE CANDIDATE (1972)

★★★

Robert Redford
Peter Boyle

Redford plays a liberal lawyer from California, who runs for senator and discovers there are more than issues and ideals at stake. Redford seems right at home in this probing and honest political satire that captures the flavor of the campaign trail. The film maintains its vibrant energy to the very end. Don Porter and Melvyn Douglas are effective in supporting roles. **Director**—Michael Ritchie. **(PG) Academy Award**—Jeremy Larner, best story and screenplay based on factual material or material not previously published. *109 minutes*

CANDLESHOE (1977)

★★

Jodie Foster
Helen Hayes
David Niven

A charming sugarplum from Walt Disney. Foster is a streetwise orphan who poses as a lost heiress in the estate of Hayes to find a hidden family treasure. Niven plays the butler and three other characters with obvious relish. With such a first-rate cast and the Disney formula of wholesome comedy and suspense, it's fun and merriment for the family. Of course, there's a happy ending. Also with Leo McKern, Veronica Quilligan, and Ian Sharrock. **Director**—Norman Tokar. **(G)** *101 minutes*

CANNERY ROW (1982)

★★

Nick Nolte
Debra Winger

Whimsical and set-bound adaptation of John Steinbeck's novellas *Cannery Row* and *Sweet Thursday,* about several characters living on Monterey's dilapidated waterfront. These stories are, perhaps, among the lesser of Steinbeck's works, and under the guidance of writer/director David Ward (*The Sting*), they evolve into a lesser movie. Nolte and Winger perform adequately as unlikely lovers (he's a marine biologist; she's a floozie), but they don't have sufficient material at their command. **(PG)** *120 minutes*

CANNONBALL (1976)

★

David Carradine
Bill McKinney

Another car-wreck saga with special appeal to the crash crowd. This orgy of screeching tires and bashed fenders involves a race from Los Angeles to New York with $100,000 for the winner. Carradine and McKinney lead the convoy across the continent, leaving a wake of flaming wrecks. Directed by Paul Bartel, who got his start in the business by working on vehicles such as this for New World Films. Also with Veronica Hamel, Judy Canova, and Gerrit Graham. **(PG)** *93 minutes*

THE CANNONBALL RUN (1981)

★★

Burt Reynolds

Reynolds and many of his pals star in yet another reckless-driving movie on the order of *Smokey and the Bandit.* The story concerns a coast-to-coast car race that defies the country's speed laws. But this theme is so worn by now that the film runs out of steam long before the cars can cross the finish line. A steady stream of cornball gags accompanies the crashes and breakdowns. The good breezy fun of the *Smokey* outings is sorely missing. **Director**—Hal Needham. **(PG)** *95 minutes*

CANNONBALL RUN II (1984)

★

Burt Reynolds

Reynolds and a huge cast of celebrities embark on a familiar cross-country car chase that seems to wind up where it starts. The shopworn gags come off as tired and frazzled as the many cameo players who populate this silly sequel. Dean Martin, Sammy Davis, Jr., Frank

® *This movie available with closed captions for the hearing impaired.*

Sinatra, Shirley MacLaine, Telly Savalas, etc., etc., tarnish their careers among the bent fenders. **Director**—Hal Needham. **(PG)** *108 minutes*

CAN SHE BAKE A CHERRY PIE? (1983)

★★

Karen Black

Black chatters like a magpie, and sings some too, as a neurotic New Yorker seeking love in the big city. She finds her man (Michael Emil), whose orderly lifestyle seems to make up for her flightiness. This spontaneous comedy paints some amusing characters, but the plot lacks structure. The film may run longer on videotape versions. **Director**—Henry Jaglom. **(PG)**
90 minutes

CAN'T BUY ME LOVE (1987)

★½

Patrick Dempsey
Amanda Peterson

Patrick Dempsey and Amanda Peterson have a business relationship in Can't Buy Me Love.

A socially inept high-school boy pays a popular cheerleader to be his girlfriend for a month as a key to instant acceptance by his peers. The scheme works too well, however, and he is transformed into a shallow snob, turning his back on his old friends and losing interest in his studies. The obvious message of this simplistic comedy is to always be yourself. However, the teenagers in this low-grade teen film are so unappealing and materialistic that any message is undercut by their shallow values. Also with Courtney Gains, Seth Green, and Sharon Farrell. **Director**—Steve Rash. **(PG–13)** *94 minutes*

CAPE FEAR (1962)

★★★

Gregory Peck
Robert Mitchum
Polly Bergen

A grim thriller with moderate suspense about an ex-convict who seeks revenge on the lawyer he believes responsible for his prison sentence. Mitchum plays the sadistic criminal who threatens to rape the wife of lawyer Peck. The wife is played by Bergen. The performances are convincing. The film, based on a John D. MacDonald novel, is set in the bayous of the Deep South. Martin Balsam, Jack Kruschen, Lori Nelson, and Telly Savalas also star. **Director**—J. Lee Thompson. *106 minutes b&w*

CAPRICORN ONE (1978)

★★½

Elliott Gould
James Brolin
Karen Black
Telly Savalas

James Brolin, O.J. Simpson, and Sam Waterston in Capricorn One.

NASA tries to pull off a fake landing on Mars in this action melodrama starring Gould and Brolin. The plot is farfetched, and whenever the suspense and excitement start to build (which is often), the mood is broken by the wooden dialogue of director/writer Peter Hyams. One high point is a chase sequence with two helicopters and a crop-dusting plane piloted by Savalas, which seems reminiscent of a similar encounter in Hitchcock's *North by Northwest*. Also with Sam Waterston, Brenda Vaccaro, O.J. Simpson, and Hal Holbrook. **(PG)** *124 minutes*

CAPTAIN BLOOD (1935)

★★★½

Errol Flynn
Olivia de Havilland
Basil Rathbone

Swashbuckling superstar: the immortal Errol Flynn as Captain Blood.

The classic swashbuckler that made Flynn a superstar and established him as king of the genre (the role of Captain Blood was originally Robert Donat's, but he supposedly gave it up during a contract dispute). Adapted from Rafael Sabatini's novel, the film depicts the adventures of a young British surgeon who turns pirate after he is wrongly persecuted for participating in the Monmouth uprising. He plies the Caribbean, romances de Havilland, and duels archfoe Rathbone (a worthy antagonist for Flynn, also pitted against him in *The Adventures of Robin Hood*). Despite its relatively low budget, the high-seas adventure looks lush. Lionel Atwill, Guy Kibbee, and Donald Meek costar. Originally released at 119 minutes. **Director**—Michael Curtiz. **Academy Award Nomination**—best picture.
99 minutes b&w

CAPTAIN HORATIO HORNBLOWER (1951)

★★★

Gregory Peck
Virginia Mayo

Peck plays Hornblower, the 19th-century English naval hero who outmaneuvers the Spanish and the French during the Napoleonic wars. Peck sweats and strains in this sprawling sea epic, but he manages to look valiant. The colorful film, based on the C.S.

(Continued)

This movie available on videotape and/or disc.

(Continued)

Forester novels, also features Robert Beatty, James Robertson Justice, and Denis O'Dea in supporting roles. **Director**—Raoul Walsh. *117 minutes*

CAPTAINS COURAGEOUS (1937)

Spencer Tracy
Freddie Bartholomew

A typical MGM prestige picture of the 1930s and a popular literary adaptation (from Kipling) that became a children's classic. Tracy won his first Oscar as the simple Portuguese fisherman who rescues a boy who has fallen from an ocean liner. He teaches the boy a thing or two about life, labor, and courage during the three months the boy is on board his fishing vessel. Impressive work by the entire cast (including Lionel Barrymore, Melvyn Douglas, Charley Grapewin, John Carradine, Leo G. Carroll, and Mickey Rooney), director Victor Fleming *(Gone With the Wind; The Wizard of Oz)*, and cinematographer Hal Rossen. **Academy Award**—Tracy, best actor. **Nominations**—best picture; Marc Connolly, John Lee Mahin, and Dale Van Every, screenplay. *116 minutes b&w*

THE CAPTAIN'S PARADISE (1953)

Alec Guinness
Yvonne De Carlo
Celia Johnson

A fine droll comedy starring Guinness as a ferryboat skipper who has a wife at each end of his route. Guinness expertly fills the role with his usual measure of dry wit played with a straight face. De Carlo and Johnson are perfectly cast as the unsuspecting wives, who accommodate the contrasting aspects of the captain's personality. It's a great sophisticated romp. Bill Fraser and Charles Goldner also star. **Director**—Anthony Kimmins. **Academy Award Nomination**—Alec Coppel, motion picture story. *80 minutes b&w*

CARBON COPY (1981)

George Segal
Susan Saint James

Segal stars as a successful businessman who had an affair with a black woman long ago, and now his black son comes knocking on his door. This silly comedy confronts racial prejudice in an absurd manner as Segal faces numerous problems because of his son. However, the cliché-strewn film ends on a happy note. Also with Jack Warden, Denzel Washington, and Paul Winfield. **Director**—Michael Schultz. **(PG)** *92 minutes*

THE CARE BEARS ADVENTURE IN WONDERLAND! (1987)

That old gang o' mine: The Care Bears' Adventure in Wonderland!

This third animated feature with the Care Bears involves the search for a princess kidnapped by an evil wizard. This time the sugary plot is laced with various characters from Lewis Carroll's *Alice's Adventures in Wonderland*. The story involves minimal imagination and the animation quality is below par. Tiny tots should love the cuddly characters and nonviolent action, but adults will be bored. Features the voice of Colin Fox; all others uncredited. **Director**—Raymond Jafelice. **(G)** *75 minutes*

THE CARE BEARS MOVIE (1985)

  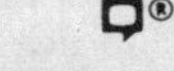

A sweet-natured cartoon feature rendered in pastel shades for children ages three to six. The cuddly bears of the title have names such as Tenderheart, Cheer, and Love-a-Lot. They rescue a boy magician who comes under the spell of an evil spirit that wants everyone to stop caring. Mickey Rooney handles the narration appropriately. **Director**—Arna Selznick. **(G)** *75 minutes*

CARE BEARS MOVIE II: A NEW GENERATION (1986)

For tiny tots, an unoriginal, syrupy animated story filled with plugs for stuffed animals based on the title characters. The warmed-over plot concerns efforts of the cuddly creatures—with names such as True Heart Bear and Noble Heart Horse—to teach the values of love and sharing at a summer camp. Adults may become restless with all this goo long before the youngsters exhaust their attention span. Maxine Miller and Pam Hyatt supply the voices for the main characters. **Director**—Dale Schott. **(G)** *77 minutes*

CAREFREE (1938)

Fred Astaire
Ginger Rogers

And delightfully entertaining, too: Fred Astaire and Ginger Rogers are Carefree.

This frothy musical comedy about a psychiatrist who falls in love with his patient is one of the last teamings of Astaire and Rogers. The plot is limp and the dialogue fails to sparkle, but the dancing and the excellent Irving Berlin songs such as "Change Partners" and "I Used to Be Color Blind" make the production a joy. Astaire and Rogers are ably supported by Jack Carson and Ralph Bellamy. **Director**—Mark Sandrich. *85 minutes b&w*

CAREFUL, HE MIGHT HEAR YOU (1984)

Nicholas Gledhill
Wendy Hughes
Robyn Nevin
John Hargreaves

An exceptionally moving psychological drama set in Australia in the Depression era. The story involves the emotional experience of a seven-year-old boy (Gledhill) who is used as a pawn by his rival aunts. Young Gledhill performs admirably and convincingly. Director Carl Schultz has a firm hold on the material and manages precise performances from a professional cast. **(PG)** *116 minutes*

CARMEN JONES (1954)

★★★

Dorothy Dandridge
Harry Belafonte

Otto Preminger brought to the screen Oscar Hammerstein II's 1943 Broadway hit, which set Bizet's *Carmen* in the South during World War II. Both the play and the film feature an all-black cast. Dandridge, in her most charismatic film performance, plays a sultry worker in a parachute factory who beguiles a soldier (Belafonte) about to go to flying school but is unfaithful to him. If not a total success, it is ambitious and full of electricity, with maximum impact when seen in its original wide-screen format. Interestingly, the singing voices of the stars are dubbed; Marilyn Horne sings for Dandridge and Le Vern Hutcherson for Belafonte. The strong supporting cast includes Pearl Bailey, who sings her own songs, Diahann Carroll, and Brock Peters. **Academy Award Nomination**—Dandridge, best actress. *105 minutes*

CARNAL KNOWLEDGE (1971)

⊛ ★★★½

Jack Nicholson
Art Garfunkel
Candice Bergen
Ann-Margret

Jack Nicholson is the arrogant male in Carnal Knowledge.

Writer Jules Feiffer and director Mike Nichols team up to explore the sexual attitudes and problems of the American male as seen through the experiences of two men from college to middle age. Nicholson and Garfunkel do well as the main subjects in this uneven comedy/drama that strikes out in new directions. Ann-Margret deserves applause for her shining role as Nicholson's coquettish mistress. Also with Rita Moreno, Cynthia O'Neal, and Carol Kane. **(R) Academy Award Nomination**—Ann-Margret, best supporting actress. *97 minutes*

CARNY (1980)

⊛ ★★½

Jodie Foster
Gary Busey
Robbie Robertson

In Carny, *Jodie Foster works the strip show to stay in the carnival.*

A brassy, semidocumentary look at carnival life, with perceptive performances by Foster, Busey, and Robertson. Director Robert Kaylor captures the grimy atmosphere of carny life. Unfortunately, a feeble script fritters away the talents of the energetic cast. Busey is fascinating as a dunk-tank bozo, and Foster is good in her role as a bored teenager who joins the show. But the film bogs down in an unfocused romantic triangle and finally ends on an unsatisfying note. Robertson, of the rock group the Band, also produced and cowrote the film. The supporting cast includes Kenneth McMillan, John Lehne, Elisha Cook, Jr., and Bert Remson. **(R)** *106 minutes*

CAROUSEL (1956)

★★★

Gordon MacRae
Shirley Jones

A handsome film musical based on Ferenc Molnár's play *Liliom*, with the memorable Rodgers and Hammerstein music pleasantly adapted. MacRae plays a gruff carnival barker who wants a better way of life when he marries a modest girl, played by Jones. Tragedy, however, gets in the way of his ambition. MacRae and Jones sing beautifully, and the photography is stunning. Songs include "If I Loved You" and "You'll Never Walk Alone." Also with Cameron Mitchell, Robert Rounseville, and Gene Lockhart. **Director**—Henry King. *128 minutes*

THE CARPETBAGGERS (1964)

⊛ ★★½

George Peppard
Carroll Baker
Alan Ladd

A brash young man takes over an aircraft manufacturing business and then pyramids his fortune into other ventures, including moviemaking. This film version of the Harold Robbins novel, which parallels the career of Howard Hughes, is made in a garish fashion, but it's entertaining nevertheless. Peppard portrays the eccentric industrialist. This was Ladd's last film. Also with Martin Balsam, Bob Cummings, Elizabeth Ashley, Lew Ayres, and Archie Moore. **Director**—Edward Dmytryk. *150 minutes*

CARRIE (1976)

⊛ ★★★

Sissy Spacek
Piper Laurie

Sissy Spacek doesn't like the prize awarded to the prom queen in Carrie.

A horror tale about a repressed girl who is tormented by her high-school class-

(Continued)

⊛ *This movie available on videotape and/or disc.*

(Continued)
mates. In the end she uses her telekinetic powers to get revenge. Based on a novel by Stephen King and directed by shock master Brian De Palma, the critically acclaimed film represents a turning point in both their careers. King's popularity soared after its success, and De Palma graduated to larger budgets and more freedom to indulge in his excesses. Also with William Katt, John Travolta, and Amy Irving. **(R) Academy Award Nominations**—Spacek, best actress; Laurie, best supporting actress.
97 minutes

CAR WASH (1976)

★★½

Richard Pryor
Irwin Corey
Franklyn Ajaye
George Carlin

Zany characters jive, work in rhythm, and play jokes on one another in this noisy film about a day at a Los Angeles car wash. The comedy is a hip mixture of scatological jokes, physical gags, and humor oriented to black audiences. Though the episodic narrative may seem formless at first glance, the film's style ultimately becomes more important than the content. The cast consists of comedians and character actors familiar to blacks. Critics at the time were harsh on the film, reflecting a lack of understanding on their part of films aimed at a subaudience. Directed by Michael Schultz, who was responsible for *Cooley High*. **(PG)** *97 minutes*

CASABLANCA (1942)

★★★★

Humphrey Bogart
Ingrid Bergman
Claude Rains
Paul Henreid

Paul Heinreid, Ingrid Bergman, and Humphrey Bogart in Casablanca.

Crackling intrigue, tingling romance, and a superb moody atmosphere make this taut melodrama one of the best World War II films. Bogart, in a memorable performance, is in top form as the owner of a Casablanca nightclub. He helps an old flame (Bergman) and her husband, an underground leader (Henreid), escape the Nazis. This classic, witty thriller seems to earn more appreciation as time goes by. Also with Conrad Veidt, S.Z. Sakall, Peter Lorre, Dooley Wilson, and Sydney Greenstreet. **Director**—Michael Curtiz. **Academy Awards**—best picture; Curtiz, best director; Julius J. Epstein, Philip G. Epstein, and Howard Koch, screenplay. **Nominations**—Bogart, best actor; Rains, best supporting actor; Arthur Edeson, cinematography.
102 minutes b&w

CASANOVA'S BIG NIGHT (1954)

★★

Bob Hope
Joan Fontaine

Hope plays a tailor's apprentice who masquerades as the great Italian lover and winds up in some intriguing comic situations. The urbane Vincent Price appears as the real Casanova. This film is the last of Hope's lavish costume farces, and it generally wastes his talents. However, just his presence is good for some laughs. The film plods haphazardly despite the supporting efforts of Basil Rathbone and Raymond Burr. **Director**—Norman McLeod.
86 minutes

THE CASSANDRA CROSSING (1977)

★½

Sophia Loren
Burt Lancaster
Richard Harris
Ava Gardner

This tedious film, directed by George Pan Cosmatos and produced by Carlo Ponti, is another all-star disaster epic filled with strained and hokey situations. It's mainly about 1,000 disease-exposed passengers trapped on board an express train heading for a rickety bridge somewhere in Poland. Loren, Harris, Lancaster, and others are hopelessly miscast. The cardboard script is loaded with dreary interpersonal problems. Half the train hurtles to destruction in a final special-effects gimmick. As for the deadly germs, they mutate to something like an annoying cold, which is similar to sitting through this movie. Also with Martin Sheen, O.J. Simpson, and John Phillip Law. **(PG)**
127 minutes

CASS TIMBERLANE (1947)

★★★

Spencer Tracy
Lana Turner

Tracy plays a judge in a midwestern community who marries a young working-class girl, played by Turner, and strives to keep up with her youthful ways. This nicely mounted drama, based on the Sinclair Lewis novel, offers Tracy an ideal, sympathetic role. Although the story is not among Lewis' best, it is played out well on the screen. The fine cast also includes Zachary Scott, Tom Drake, Mary Astor, and Albert Dekker. **Director**—George Sidney.
119 minutes b&w

CAST A GIANT SHADOW (1966)

★★

Kirk Douglas

This action-accented portrayal of Israel's struggle to become an independent state centers around New York's Mickey Marcus (Douglas), a former colonel and military lawyer who helps whip Israel's nascent army into fighting shape. It seems to go on forever, and substitutes colorful location shooting and a colorful cast (Angie Dickinson, Senta Berger, Topol, Luther Adler, Gary Merrill; cameos include John Wayne, Frank Sinatra, and Yul Brynner, among others) for a script that has no color, no light, and no shadow. **Director**—Melville Shavelson. *142 minutes*

CASUAL SEX? (1988)

★★

Lea Thompson
Victoria Jackson

A lightweight comedy about a pair of single women seeking Mr. Right after the sexual revolution has long since been over and AIDS has everyone more than a little scared. In true sitcom fashion, the two attend a health spa, believing everyone there will have a healthy and safe attitude toward sex just as they do toward their bodies. Some imagina-

® This movie available with closed captions for the hearing impaired.

tive dream sequences prove quite humorous, but much of the film is trite and dull. Despite the provocative title, this adaptation of an offbeat stage revue turns out to be merely a variation of *Where the Boys Are*. Stephen Shellen and Andrew Dice Clay costar as two of the hunks at the spa. **Director**—Genevieve Robert. **(R)** *90 minutes*

CASUALTIES OF WAR (1989)

Michael J. Fox
Sean Penn

Sean Penn and Michael J. Fox are in a moral battle in Casualties of War.

A haunting and moving morality story involving the gang rape and murder of a young Vietnamese woman by American soldiers during the Vietnam War. Fox is remarkable as a conscious-stricken G.I. who refuses to participate in the brutality and later brings charges against his comrades. The film attempts to metaphorically interpret America's involvement in Vietnam while defining, in general, the moral complexities of military combat. The storyline is derived from journalist Daniel Lang's well-known *New Yorker* article, which chillingly recounted the actual atrocity. Director Brian De Palma's penchant for violence has been mitigated here, but some viewers may still be disturbed by the brutal acts. Penn, always interesting to watch, gives a memorable performance as the callous sergeant. Also with Don Harvey, John C. Reilly, Thuy Thu Le, and Sam Robards. **(R)**
120 minutes

CAT BALLOU (1965)

★★★

Jane Fonda
Lee Marvin

Marvin is marvelous as a whiskey-soaked, over-the-hill gunslinger, who is hired to eliminate a vicious killer. He plays the role of the killer, too. This unusual western spoof features Fonda in the title role, as a young outlaw who employs the gunslinger. The smart screenplay contributes to the mirth and the direction is on the money. Michael Callan, Nat King Cole, Stubby Kaye, Dwayne Hickman, and Reginald Denny are in supporting roles. **Director**—Elliot Silverstein. **Academy Award**—Marvin, best actor. **Nomination**—Walter Newman and Frank R. Pierson, best screenplay based on material from another medium.
96 minutes

CATCH-22 (1970)

★★★½

Alan Arkin
Martin Balsam
Richard Benjamin
Art Garfunkel

Alan Arkin as Yossarian, the perplexed soldier whose life is ruled by Catch-22.

This wry black comedy, based on Joseph Heller's popular novel, is one of the best antiwar films. This story concerns a medium-bomber group in the Mediterranean during World War II. One by one, officers are killed in various ways. Arkin leads the gallery of outsized characters with his portrayal of Yossarian, a desperate and logical flyer who strives to be classified insane so he can avoid going on bombing missions. Buck Henry, who appears in a minor role, also wrote the script. Other fine performances are given by Jack Gilford, Bob Newhart, Paula Prentiss, Anthony Perkins, Jon Voight, Martin Sheen, and Orson Welles. **Director**—Mike Nichols. **(R)** *122 minutes*

THE CAT FROM OUTER SPACE (1978)

★★

Ken Berry
Sandy Duncan
McLean Stevenson

Walt Disney Productions joins the movie space race with this film about a cat from another planet, who makes an emergency landing on Earth. The handsome feline—named Jake—encounters adventure and excitement as he attempts to return to the planet of the pussycats with the help of space scientists Berry and Duncan. The plot is predictable, but the special effects and fast pacing should delight youngsters. Also with Harry Morgan, Roddy McDowall, and Ronnie Schell. **Director**—Norman Tokar. **(G)** *104 minutes*

CAT ON A HOT TIN ROOF (1958)

★★★★

Elizabeth Taylor
Paul Newman
Burl Ives

This film version of Tennessee Williams' powerful play about a patriarchal Southern family is somewhat stagebound but is entertaining on many levels. Taylor is excellent as the wife of a frustrated young man, played by Newman, who refuses his wife's attentions and takes to alcohol. Ives is convincing as "Big Daddy," the overwhelming plantation owner, and the rest of the cast turns in credible performances. The homosexuality and more blatant sexual references of the play have been omitted here, but the drama is still intense. Also with Jack Carson, Judith Anderson, and Madeleine Sherwood. **Director**—Richard Brooks. **Academy Award Nominations**—best picture; Brooks, best director; Newman, best actor; Taylor, best actress; Brooks and James Poe, best screenplay based on material from another medium; William Daniels, cinematography. *108 minutes*

CAT PEOPLE (1942)

★★★

Simone Simon
Kent Smith

A man marries a beautiful woman who believes she is the surviving member of a race of people who can turn into panthers in this well-plotted and engrossing horror film. The acting of Simon as the panther-girl and Smith as her lover is superior to most performances in such movies. This was the first of producer Val Lewton's horror films and was noteworthy at the time because the feline monster barely appears on-

(Continued)

This movie available on videotape and/or disc.

(Continued)

screen. The horror is effectively suggested through sound effects, camera angles, and an eerie atmosphere. **Director**—Jacques Tourneur.

73 minutes b&w

CAT PEOPLE (1982)

★★½

Nastassja Kinski

Director Paul Schrader revamps the 1942 horror classic with cold and flashy graphic effects that do small justice to the imaginative and haunting mood of the original. Kinski is captivating as the mysterious woman who turns into a vicious black leopard; Malcolm McDowell and John Heard also turn in strong performances. But the screenplay is thin and the style uneven. **(R)**

118 minutes

CAT'S EYE (1985)

 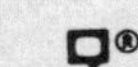

Drew Barrymore

Drew Barrymore finds her parents don't believe her in Cat's Eye.

Three short stories by Stephen King are adapted for the screen with mediocre results. The segments, connected by the presence of a cat, concern a bizarre stop-smoking facility, a gambler who torments a tennis player, and a little girl harassed by a noisy gremlin. Only the second vignette offers adequate tension. Here, a man bets his wife's lover he can walk around the outside of a tall building. Also stars Kenneth McMillan and Alan King. **Director**—Lewis Teague. **(PG-13)** *94 minutes*

CATTLE ANNIE AND LITTLE BRITCHES (1980)

Burt Lancaster
Rod Steiger
Amanda Plummer
Diane Lane

The western gets a comic kick in the pants with this lighthearted tale of two teenage girls who try to inject some spirit into the fading Doolin-Dalton gang. The cast is impeccable. Lancaster is magnificent as the aging outlaw boss. Steiger is brittle and eloquent as the U.S. marshal. And watch out for Plummer as Annie; this young actress, making her screen debut, gives class and dazzle to the spunky character. **Director**—Lamont Johnson. **(PG)**

95 minutes

CAUGHT IN THE DRAFT (1941)

★★★

Bob Hope
Dorothy Lamour

One of Hope's earlier films and one of his better comedies. There are plenty of well-timed gags and nice support from a good cast. Bob appears as a movie star who resists joining the Army, but he accidentally enters the service at last. A sprightly, funny service comedy also starring Lynne Overman, Clarence Kolb, and Eddie Bracken. **Director**—David Butler. *82 minutes b&w*

CAVEMAN (1981)

Ringo Starr
Dennis Quaid
Barbara Bach

A feeble spoof of our prehistoric ancestors, who defend themselves against dinosaurs and discover fire, the slingshot, love, and jealousy. The broad slapstick comedy is sort of a primitive version of Mel Brooks' *Silent Movie,* with some campy special effects tossed in. The tribesmen are cartoon characters who don't actually speak; they grunt bits of strange dialogue, which becomes tiresome before long. The Flintstones are funnier and more colorful. Also with Shelley Long, Jack Gilford, and John Matuszak. **Director**—Carl Gottlieb. **(PG)** *91 minutes*

THE CHALLENGE (1982)

 ★★★

Scott Glenn
Toshiro Mifune

John Frankenheimer *(Birdman of Alcatraz)* directed this martial-arts feature set in Japan. Good acting and Frankenheimer's direction invest the film with a touch of class. Glenn stars as an American low-life who agrees to retrieve a ceremonial sword for a Japanese family involved in a feud. The American chooses sides in the conflict, and attempts to train himself in the grueling samurai ethic. The final battle, set in a high-security, ultramodern office building, is a symbolic clash of opposing forces—the East against the West; the ancient ways against new ones; machine guns against swords. The script is by director John Sayles *(Brother from Another Planet).* **(R)** *112 minutes*

THE CHAMP (1979)

 ★½

Jon Voight
Faye Dunaway
Ricky Schroder

Jon Voight on the comeback trail as The Champ.

The tear-drenched Wallace Beery-Jackie Cooper tale of 1931 returns to the screen, with Voight as the has-been boxer and moppet Schroder as his adoring son. Along comes the boy's mother, played by Dunaway, after a seven-year absence to claim her child. What follows is such unrestrained pa-

This movie available with closed captions for the hearing impaired.

thos that any honest drama is drowned in its wake. Director Franco Zeffirelli doesn't spare a single gimmick to wrench tears from the viewer, but under the slick veneer is a distinct staleness. Also with Jack Warden, Arthur Hill, Strother Martin, Joan Blondell, and Elisha Cook, Jr. **(PG)** *121 minutes*

CHAMPION (1949)

★★★½

Kirk Douglas
Arthur Kennedy
Lola Albright

A stylish, rousing fight film based on the Ring Lardner short story. Douglas is in the title role as a determined boxer who bulldozes his way to the top, alienating friends and relatives along the way. Obviously, the story is a cliché by now, but it's nicely handled and acted with much energy. A good role for Douglas and effective backup from Kennedy, Albright, Marilyn Maxwell, and Ruth Roman. **Director**—Mark Robson. **Academy Award Nominations**—Douglas, best actor; Kennedy, best supporting actor; Carl Foreman, screenplay. *99 minutes b&w*

CHAMPIONS (1983)

★★★

John Hurt
Gregory Jones
Mike Dillon

This true story follows the career of English steeplechase jockey Bob Champion, played by Hurt, who overcame cancer and went on to win the Grand National. The well-worn theme (somewhat reminiscent of *Chariots of Fire*) unfolds with such cinematic and acting skill that it transcends a rather weak and clinical script. The grueling horse race finale is predictable but spirited nonetheless. **Director**—John Irvin. **(PG)** *115 minutes*

CHANCES ARE (1989)

★★

Cybill Shepherd
Robert Downey, Jr.
Mary Stuart Masterson

A juvenile romantic comedy centered around reincarnation. A young Washington lawyer dies, goes to heaven, and returns 23 years later as the boyfriend (Downey) of his own daughter (Masterson). The gimmick involves Downey's attempts to romance his widowed wife (Shepherd), now a generation older. Absurd complications ruin any efforts at effective satire. Also with Ryan O'Neal. The film's theme song, "After All," was Oscar-nominated. **Director**—Emille Ardolino. **(PG)** *108 minutes*

THE CHANGELING (1979)

★★★

George C. Scott
Trish Van Devere
Melvyn Douglas

A haunted Victorian mansion. Strange noises in the night. A piano plays by itself. An eerie seance. The dusty room in the attic. Déjà vu? Perhaps. But director Peter Medak adds stylish and chilling dimensions to this stock material that would frighten Dracula's mother. Scott, who rents the spooky old house, unravels a 70-year-old murder mystery with the help of a vengeful spirit. Scott and Douglas contribute strong performances to make this a truly suspenseful story. Also with John Colicos and Jean Marsh. **(R)** *113 minutes*

A CHANGE OF SEASONS (1980)

★★

Shirley MacLaine
Anthony Hopkins
Bo Derek

MacLaine, Hopkins, and Derek star in this complex comedy about the sexual revolution. When professor Anthony has an affair with fetching student Bo, wife Shirley fights back by having an affair with the young campus carpenter. The plot gets even more involved, and what's supposed to be satire becomes just absurd. MacLaine turns in a fine performance; as for Bo, she's still only a sex symbol. Also with Michael Brandon and Mary Beth Hurt. **Director**—Richard Lang. **(R)** *102 minutes*

THE CHANT OF JIMMIE BLACKSMITH (1978)

★★★

Tommy Lewis

This handsome, compelling Australian film explores racism through the experience of an earnest half-caste young man, who violently rebels after being exploited by white employers. The film bulges with excessive detail and plot. Nevertheless, director Fred Schepisi effectively conveys a sense of helplessness and rage at the upshot of the encroachment of European culture on the Aborigines. Lewis is effective in the title role. Most American prints are 108 minutes. **(No MPAA rating)** *122 minutes*

CHAPTER TWO (1979)

★★

James Caan
Marsha Mason
Valerie Harper

Seriocomic romance with James Caan and Marsha Mason in Chapter Two.

Neil Simon brings this semiautobiographical Broadway play to the screen. It's the story of a successful writer, played by Caan, who remarries shortly after his first wife's death, but guilt plagues his efforts to settle into an earnest romance. Simon's glib lines undercut the serious scenes. Caan is miscast, but Mason, as his second wife, grabs the full flavor of her role. As well she might, because she was the second Mrs. Simon. Also with Joseph Bologna. **Director**—Robert Moore. **(PG) Academy Award Nomination**—Mason, best actress. *124 minutes*

CHARADE (1963)

★★★½

Cary Grant
Audrey Hepburn

Grant is suave as usual in this romantic comedy set in glittering Paris. Hepburn plays a widow whose late husband

(Continued)

This movie available on videotape and/or disc.

(Continued)
stashed away a fortune. Some bad guys want the money, and they believe Audrey knows where it's hidden. Along comes handsome Grant offering help and sympathy, but is he really on her side? Lightweight fare patterned after Hitchcock's style. The excellent supporting cast includes Walter Matthau, James Coburn, and George Kennedy. The title song by Henry Mancini was nominated for an Academy Award. **Director**—Stanley Donen. *113 minutes*

THE CHARGE OF THE LIGHT BRIGADE (1968)

★★ 

Trevor Howard
John Gielgud
David Hemmings

This handsome drama is well acted but fails to come across. It's based on the events at the time of the 1854 battle at Balaclava, Turkey, during the Crimean War, when the British were defeated by the Russians. The film makes an antiwar statement and offers an impressive battle scene, but it stumbles into plot potholes too often. Richard Williams' special animated portions help a little. The cast includes Vanessa Redgrave and Jill Bennett. **Director**—Tony Richardson. **(PG)** *141 minutes*

CHARIOTS OF FIRE (1981)

★★★1/2

Ben Cross
Ian Charleson

Ben Cross runs for personal reasons in the uplifting Chariots of Fire.

A handsome, well-made drama based on the true story of two English champion runners who compete in the 1924 Paris Olympics. Hugh Hudson, directing his first theatrical film, magnificently assembles a film that's full of finely detailed characterizations. His command of the atmosphere of the period is remarkable. Cross is genuinely compelling as running ace Harold Abrahams, who competes to compensate for religious bigotry. Charleson gives a more subtle but equally satisfying performance as Eric Liddell, who runs for the glory of God. It's an interesting exercise to examine the different circumstances that motivate these two athletes—or to contrast their dedication with the megabucks mentality that's often apparent on the contemporary sports scene. **(PG) Academy Awards**—best picture; Colin Welland, best screenplay written directly for the screen. **Nominations**—Hudson, best director; Ian Holm, best supporting actor. *123 minutes*

CHARLEY AND THE ANGEL (1973)

★★

Fred MacMurray
Cloris Leachman
Harry Morgan

A typical Walt Disney sentimental piece about a small-town merchant, played by MacMurray, who mellows his attitude toward his family when he finds out he has only a short time to live. Morgan plays the angel. There are some amusing moments and a predictably happy ending, but the expected Disney warmth seems trumped up. The plot partially follows the events of *On Borrowed Time.* Also with Kurt Russell, Kathleen Cody, and Vincent Van Patten. **Director**—Vincent McEveety. **(G)** *93 minutes*

CHARLEY'S AUNT (1941)

★★★

Jack Benny
Kay Francis
Reginald Owen

Benny hams it up with glee in this familiar Victorian farce about the Oxford student who impersonates a rich maiden aunt to help out a roommate. The comedy is strained at times, but it's a good opportunity to observe the great Benny at work. Other cast members are also in top form, including James Ellison, Anne Baxter, Laird Cregar, and Edmund Gwenn. **Director**—Archie Mayo. *81 minutes b&w*

CHARLIE BUBBLES (1968)

★★★

Albert Finney
Billie Whitelaw
Liza Minnelli

Finney directs and stars in this clever fantasy about a young man who suddenly becomes very wealthy, only to find boredom with the emptiness of an artificial environment. The film is sometimes slow and uneven, but it offers a fascinating character sketch and some effective scenes of a man inundated by pointless electronic gadgets. Minnelli turns in a good acting job as Finney's secretary. The ending, however, when Finney tries to return to his original lifestyle, is a letdown. Colin Blakely, Timothy Garland, and Alan Lake are also in the cast. **(R)** *91 minutes*

CHARLY (1968)

★★★

Cliff Robertson
Claire Bloom
Lilia Skala

Robertson's stellar performance dominates this tale of a mentally retarded baker's assistant who becomes a genius after submitting to a new surgical technique. It's based on Daniel Keyes' *Flowers for Algernon.* The screenplay, however, is overly sentimental and somewhat unconvincing—especially during a romantic interlude between Charly and an intelligent woman, played by Bloom, after the operation has taken effect. Also with Leon Janney and Dick Van Patten. **Director**—Ralph Nelson. **(PG) Academy Award**—Robertson, best actor. *106 minutes*

CHATTAHOOCHEE (1990)

★★

Dennis Hopper
Gary Oldman

A relentlessly grim account of conditions at a real-life state mental hospital as experienced by a Korean War veteran who was a patient there. Oldman stars as Emmett Foley, who suffered a nervous breakdown and was confined to a Florida state facility for many years. Eventually, his protests over the brutal treatment of the inmates led to major

This movie available with closed captions for the hearing impaired.

reforms. Hopper costars as a criminal convict who is thrown in among the mental patients. Despite the film's noble intentions, the recounting of the atrocious conditions is surprisingly flat and uninvolving. Also with Pamela Reed, Frances McDormand, Ned Beatty, and M. Emmett Walsh. **Director**—Mick Jackson. **(R)** *96 minutes*

THE CHEAP DETECTIVE (1978)

Peter Falk
Ann-Margret
Sid Caesar
Louise Fletcher

Eileen Brennan, James Coco, and Peter Falk in The Cheap Detective.

Writer Neil Simon fondly parodies a slew of Humphrey Bogart melodramas of the 1940s with wit, humor, and a good-natured elbow-poke to the ribs. The timing doesn't always work well and the plot tries to cover too much ground, but the Simon dialogue, loaded with stalwart one-liners, goes down easily. The blue-ribbon cast has a fine time carving up *The Maltese Falcon, Casablanca,* and *The Big Sleep.* Falk leads the pack with a priceless imitation of Bogart. Also with Madeline Kahn, Nicol Williamson, Eileen Brennan, Stockard Channing, Dom DeLuise, James Coco, and many other stars. **Director**—Robert Moore. **(PG)** *92 minutes*

CHEAPER BY THE DOZEN (1950)

Clifton Webb
Myrna Loy

Webb is perfectly cast as Frank Gilbreth, the patriarch who runs his large family with the same discipline and efficiency that he applies to motion and time study methods for industry. The lilting comedy, set in the 1920s, is based on the popular book by two of the 12 Gilbreth children. This is definitely one of Webb's best performances, set in a somewhat corny but funny framework. Loy is exceptionally good, too, as the stalwart mother of the family. Other cast members include Jeanne Crain, Edgar Buchanan, Barbara Bates, and Mildred Natwick. **Director**—Walter Lang. *86 minutes*

CHECKING OUT (1989)

 ★½

Jeff Daniels
Melanie Mayron

Daniels plays a hysterical hypochondriac in this lame comedy. He drives his physicians and family up the wall by submitting to a battery of medical tests and constantly checking his pulse. Despite such feverish activity, this one-joke movie is dull and lacks the pacing and satirical bite usually found in such dark comedies. Also with Ann Magnuson. **Director**—David Leland. **(R)** *98 minutes*

CHEECH AND CHONG'S NEXT MOVIE (1980)

 ★

Cheech Marin
Thomas Chong

Another chapter in the silly misadventures of Cheech and Chong of counterculture comedy fame. The scroungy, pot-smoking duo carry their inane antics to a welfare office, a massage parlor, the home of a wealthy family, and finally into space, all the while mumbling their repetitious and dopey dialogue. It's a sort of stoned version of a Marx Brothers comedy that wouldn't work even if they were acting sober. Unfortunately, this wasn't their last movie. **Director**—Chong. **(R)** *99 minutes*

CHEECH AND CHONG'S NICE DREAMS (1981)

 ★★

Cheech Marin
Thomas Chong

A third round of spaced-out high jinks from "Los Guys." This time the maestros of the marijuana set peddle their wares from an ice cream truck and engage in a variety of disjointed situations. The film is short on plot, and many skits are merely silly. But this outing is executed with the typically unflagging, hazy humor that will surely appeal to the turned-on set. **Director**—Chong. **(R)** *110 minutes*

CHEECH AND CHONG'S THE CORSICAN BROTHERS (1984)

Cheech Marin
Thomas Chong

The boys depart from their dreamy, freewheeling routine and portray brothers in France involved with chaotic events on the eve of the Revolution. Big surprise—they do not smoke pot. And big disappointment—the film is a dreary succession of crude comic routines, all so loosely connected it seems like three movies are going on at once. One gag is tediously repeated: When one brother is hit, the other feels the pain. Roy Dotrice and Shelby Fiddis costar. **Director**—Chong. **(PG)** *90 minutes*

CHEETAH (1989)

Keith Coogan
Lucy Deakins

A wild animal crosses Africa to return home in Cheetah.

A California family leaves the safe suburbs for the wilds of Kenya in this animal adventure from the Disney studios. The story begins when the children discover a cheetah cub whose mother has been killed by poachers. When the cat matures, the teens make a dangerous trek across the African wilderness to release her in the wild. Though the storyline amounts to little more than predictable family fare, the film emphasizes respect for animals and nature—something Disney's live-action animal movies have always stressed. Also, the G rating makes the film suitable viewing for the entire family. **Director**—Jeff Blyth. **(G)** *83 minutes*

This movie available on videotape and/or disc.

CHEYENNE AUTUMN (1964)

 ★★★

Richard Widmark
Carroll Baker
Dolores Del Rio

Carroll Baker and Richard Widmark in John Ford's epic, Cheyenne Autumn.

Director John Ford's sprawling epic western tells the harrowing story of starving Indians trekking from their barren Oklahoma reservation to their original home, 1,500 miles away in Wyoming. The Indians also have to fight the U.S. Cavalry, which wants them to stay put. The handsome production features fine acting by Widmark, Baker, and Karl Malden. Also with Ricardo Montalban, Gilbert Roland, Sal Mineo, and Victor Jory. There are nice cameos, too, from James Stewart and Edward G. Robinson. However, the historical drama may seem ponderous after a while. **Academy Award Nomination**—William Clothier, cinematography.
160 minutes

THE CHEYENNE SOCIAL CLUB (1970)

 ★★

James Stewart
Henry Fonda
Shirley Jones

Stewart and Fonda running a brothel on the Western frontier? That's good for some laughs, but there aren't enough of them in this comedy, which offers too many clichés and too much adolescent humor. A shoot-out at the end perks things up, but what is really needed are some bawdy girls and some bawdy jokes that work. Jones plays the madam of the house. Also with Sue Ane Langdon, Robert Middleton, and Arch Johnson. **Director**—Gene Kelly. **(PG)** *102 minutes*

CHIEF CRAZY HORSE (1955)

 ★★

Victor Mature
Suzan Ball
John Lund

Mature is in the title role as the famous Indian chief who leads his braves at the Little Bighorn and defeats General Custer. The clichéd western, which is seen from the side of the Indians, involves the chief's dealings with an Army officer. Also with Keith Larsen and Ray Danton. **Director**—George Sherman.
86 minutes

CHILDREN OF A LESSER GOD (1986)

 ★★★ 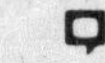

William Hurt
Marlee Matlin

Marlee Matlin forms an understanding with William Hurt in Children of a Lesser God.

Mark Medoff's award-winning play translates to the screen with some difficulty but remains compelling viewing. The story concerns a romance between a teacher of the deaf (Hurt) and a deaf student (Matlin) who refuses to learn to use her voice, communicating only in sign language. Hurt is superb as the idealistic instructor who breaks through the young woman's cynical shell and falls in love. Matlin, herself hearing-impaired, matches Hurt's acting skill with hardly a spoken word. Also with Piper Laurie and Philip Bosco. **Director**—Randa Haines. **(R) Academy Award**—Matlin, best actress. **Nominations**—best picture; Hurt, best actor; Laurie, best supporting actress; Hesper Anderson and Medoff, best screenplay based on material from another medium. *119 minutes*

CHILDREN OF THE CORN (1984)

  ★

Peter Horton
Linda Hamilton

In a small Nebraska town, children have slaughtered the adults and set up a sinister religious cult. Young physician Horton and his girlfriend Hamilton stumble into this terrifying community and encounter a variety of supernatural episodes. Based on Stephen King's short story, the film is trite, poorly acted, and filled with mumbo-jumbo dialogue. **Director**—Fritz Kiersch. **(R)** *93 minutes*

THE CHILDREN'S HOUR (1962)

  ★★★

Audrey Hepburn
Shirley MacLaine

MacLaine and Hepburn star in this touching drama about a malicious schoolgirl. She alleges that her teachers are lesbians, causing them untold grief. The film, based on Lillian Hellman's play, was originally filmed as *These Three.* The explicit treatment of lesbianism was somewhat daring at the time of release, but the interpretation has lost impact. Yet the movie is compelling, and Hepburn and MacLaine are exceptional as the maligned teachers. There is good support from James Garner, Miriam Hopkins, and Fay Bainter. **Director**—William Wyler. **Academy Award Nomination**—Bainter, best supporting actress. *108 minutes b&w*

CHILD'S PLAY (1988)

  ★½ 

Catherine Hicks
Chris Sarandon

A child's doll is possessed by evil magic and goes on a murderous spree. Hicks stars as a single mother whose young son is caught up in the web of terror. The frightening premise—a sinister doll that comes to life—is a familiar one in the horror genre and not much new is added here. However horror fans will appreciate the fast pace and simple but competent technical effects. Predictable but with some chilling moments. Also with Alex Vincent, Brad Dourif, Dinah Manoff, and Tommy Swerdlow. **Director**—Tom Holland. **(R)** *88 minutes*

® *This movie available with closed captions for the hearing impaired.*

CHINA GIRL (1987)

★★½

James Russo
Sari Chang
Richard Panebianco

A teenage boy from Little Italy, played by newcomer Panebianco, falls in love with a girl from Chinatown, played by Chang, in this contemporary version of *Romeo and Juliet*. The innocent but star-crossed romance touches off a wave of hatred and violence among the couple's relatives and friends. The familiar plot is offset by some well-directed action sequences and a feel for the gritty Lower Manhattan milieu. Strong supporting performances by David Caruso and Russell Wong help sustain the film's energy. **Director**—Abel Ferrara. **(R)** *89 minutes*

CHINA SEAS (1935)

★★★

Clark Gable
Jean Harlow

The cast's the attraction here: Gable, Harlow, Wallace Beery, and Rosalind Russell (not to mention Robert Benchley and C. Aubrey Smith). The high-seas adventure about passengers on a boat from Hong Kong to Singapore who run into a vicious twister and even more vicious Chinese pirates packed them in, largely because of the stellar leads. Screenwriter Jules Furthman wrote classier material for Howard Hawks and Josef von Sternberg, but this remains a moderately entertaining package. **Director**—Tay Garnett. *89 minutes b&w*

THE CHINA SYNDROME (1979)

★★★★

Jane Fonda
Jack Lemmon
Michael Douglas

Michael Douglas and Jane Fonda break a terrifying story in The China Syndrome.

A nuclear power plant goes on the fritz and touches off a dangerous confrontation. Fonda gives a super performance as an ambitious "Brenda Starr" TV newswoman. Lemmon performs convincingly as the plant engineer with a nagging conscience. Director James Bridges maintains relentless tension from the start right up to the hair-raising climax. It's classic entertainment that makes a vivid social observation. Also with Scott Brady, James Hampton, Peter Donat, and Wilford Brimley. **(PG) Academy Award Nominations**—Lemmon, best actor; Fonda, best actress; Mike Gray, T. S. Cook, and Bridges, best screenplay written directly for the screen. *123 minutes*

CHINATOWN (1974)

★★★★

Jack Nicholson
Faye Dunaway
John Huston

Compelling and suspenseful private-eye yarn filled with all sorts of goodies in the spirit of Hammett-Chandler mysteries. Nicholson is excellent as the Los Angeles gumshoe who becomes involved over his head in an intricate web of murder and political corruption concerning a fortune in land and water rights. He's led into this complex situation by the beautiful Dunaway as *femme fatale extraordinaire.* Director Roman Polanski handles the 1930s atmosphere with exceptional skill. Also with Perry Lopez and Burt Young. **(R) Academy Award**—Robert Towne, best original screenplay. **Nominations**—best picture; Polanski, best director; Nicholson, best actor; Dunaway, best actress; John A. Alonzo, cinematography. *131 minutes*

THE CHIPMUNK ADVENTURE (1987)

★★½

Alvin, Simon, and Theodore—the Three Chipmunks of television cartoon fame—appear in their own animated feature. The frolicsome Chipmunks team up with their female counterparts, the Chipettes, for a balloon race around the world. Very young kids should find the adventure exciting enough, and the Chipmunks are more appealing than the more saccharine Care Bears, but the animation is of low quality. **Director**—Janice Karman. **(G)** *76 minutes*

CHITTY CHITTY BANG BANG (1968)

★★½

Dick Van Dyke
Sally Ann Howes

Van Dyke and the rest of the cast mainly waste their time with this flimsy children's fantasy/musical about an inventor who produces a flying car. Nothing seems to click, including the special effects and a score that features many forgettable songs. There are a few scenes for the kids to laugh at, but it's tame material. The script is based on a book by Ian Fleming. Anna Quayle, Gert Frobe, Lionel Jeffries, Benny Hill, and James Robertson Justice also star. **Director**—Ken Hughes. **(G)** *142 minutes*

CHLOE IN THE AFTERNOON (1972)

★★★

Zouzou
Bernard Verley

Zouzou tempts Bernard Verley into love in Chloe in the Afternoon.

An engrossing French drama about a married man who wants to remain faithful but finds himself constantly tempted by other women—especially by an old acquaintance named Chloe. It is amazing how much suspense director Eric Rohmer can build around a basically talky "Moral Tale" (the last of six in his series) that seems to deliver an exclamation point after every expression and gesture. Unlike other films about infidelity, this drama's emotional ramifications aren't as important as its ethical issues; yet this film has a greater impact than most commercial ventures with this theme. Also with Françoise Verley, François Fabian, and Beatrice Romand. Originally filmed in French. **(No MPAA rating)** *97 minutes*

This movie available on videotape and/or disc.

THE CHOIRBOYS (1977)

★

Perry King
Don Stroud
James Woods

A vulgar, cheap-looking black comedy based on one of Joseph Wambaugh's best-selling novels about Los Angeles cops. The inept production is a series of rambling vignettes sprinkled with adolescent sex jokes and coarse cutups. The direction by Robert Aldrich is chaotic, and the acting is amateurish. Also with Charles Durning, Lou Gossett, Jr., and Tim McIntire. **(R)** *119 minutes*

CHOKE CANYON (1986)

★½

Stephen Collins
Janet Julian

Stephen Collins gets his own way as the maverick physicist in Choke Canyon.

A sci-fi/western burdened with ridiculous dialogue and an outrageous plot. Our cowboy hero of the nuclear age is a horse-riding physicist (Collins) who gallantly protects his territory from insidious industrial polluters. The action scenes, involving explosions, helicopter chases, and various shoot-'em-up episodes, overwhelm the storyline. It's hard to tell if this film is a comedy or a drama because of the silliness, which may or may not be intentional. Bo Svenson also stars. **Director**—Chuck Bail. **(PG)** *94 minutes*

A CHORUS LINE (1985)

★★

Michael Douglas
Alyson Reed
Vicki Frederick

The long-running stage sensation has been transformed into a mildly entertaining but disappointing movie. The play's innovative structure involving several dancers who reveal their dreams and backgrounds while auditioning for a Broadway chorus line is mishandled here, so that each character's segment comes off as a self-indulgent confession, rather than a revelation. Douglas as Zack and Reed as Cassie are miscast and overbearing. The fault lies with director Richard Attenborough, who has no feel for the complexities of the musical genre. The film's only saving grace are a few of the song-and-dance numbers. Also with Audrey Landers, Yamil Borges, Cameron English, Nicole Fosse, and Gregg Burge. **(PG-13)** *117 minutes*

THE CHOSEN (1981)

★★★

Rod Steiger
Maximilian Schell
Robby Benson
Barry Miller

A struggle with religious beliefs: Robby Benson in The Chosen.

Friendship between two young Jewish men is the subject of this film set in Brooklyn at the close of World War II. Their relationship, however, is affected by the divergent religious views of their strong-willed fathers. The story, adapted from Chaim Potok's novel, is moving and brilliantly captures the atmosphere of the period. **Director**—Jeremy Paul Kagan. **(PG)** *108 minutes*

CHRISTIANE F (1981)

★★

Natja Brunkhorst

This overwrought account of drug addiction among German teenagers is based on a true story and contains relentless graphic details of the wretched condition. There are so many sordid scenes of youngsters injecting themselves with heroin or vomiting amid filthy surroundings, that the semidocumentary film becomes merely sensational. Brunkhorst, in the title role, is convincing as the young girl with the golden arm who swiftly descends into a life of horror and degradation. **Director**—Ulrich Edel. **(R)** *124 minutes*

CHRISTINE (1983)

★★½

Keith Gordon

Keith Gordon and Alexandra Paul are stunned by the damage done to Christine.

A blood-red 1958 Plymouth Fury, restored in 1978 by mild-mannered high-school student Gordon, is an automobile possessed by demons. The born-again jalopy reveals a nasty disposition and even takes bloody revenge on Gordon's schoolmates, who have been tormenting him. The car is the star, and although much of this occult vehicle remains pedestrian, director John Carpenter gets some extra mileage with his imaginative treatment. Also with Harry Dean Stanton and John Stockwell. **(R)** *110 minutes*

CHRISTMAS IN CONNECTICUT (1945)

★★★

Barbara Stanwyck
Dennis Morgan
Sydney Greenstreet

® This movie available with closed captions for the hearing impaired.

Stanwyck stars in this lightweight but delightful farce. She's a newspaper columnist who invites a war hero, played by Morgan, to her home for Christmas to impress her editor, played by Greenstreet. Since she has no family, she must assemble one for the occasion, and the excellent cast succeeds in making the most of this premise. A fine holiday film with many funny lines and a warm spirit. Also with Reginald Gardiner, S.Z. Sakall, and Robert Shayne. **Director**—Peter Godfrey.

110 minutes b&w

CHRISTMAS IN JULY (1940)

★★★

Dick Powell
Ellen Drew

It's "The Oldest Story in the World No. 4,574"—but in the hands of master comedy writer/director Preston Sturges, it works. Powell stars as a clerk who believes he's won big bucks in a contest and goes on a no-holds-barred buying spree. Drew plays his girl, and the wonderful supporting cast of comic actors includes William Demarest, Franklin Pangborn, and Ernest Truex. Sturges had just turned director the year this film came out, and the film has the wit, energy, and insight that characterized the amazing string of hits he turned out in only four years (between 1940 and 1944). *70 minutes b&w*

A CHRISTMAS STORY (1983)

★★★

Melinda Dillon
Darren McGavin
Peter Billingsley

A Thirties family celebrates A Christmas Story.

You'll be delighted by this hilarious tale of childhood and yuletide greed adapted by humorist Jean Shepherd from his sidesplitting memoir. Young Ralphie (Billingsley) is willing to put up with the day-to-day indignities of life in the Depression-era Midwest as long as Mom and Dad come through with a Red Ryder air rifle at Christmas. Ralphie's childish dreams of glory and his desperate schemes to manipulate his parents to his way of thinking provide plenty of solid laughs. Billingsley is a marvel and Dillon is quietly amusing as his long-suffering mother, while McGavin turns in a terrific comic performance as Ralphie's volatile, faintly eccentric father. Narrated by Shepherd, with witty direction by Bob Clark. **(PG)**

98 minutes

CHUCK BERRY HAIL! HAIL! ROCK 'N' ROLL! (1987)

★★★

The master struts his stuff in Chuck Berry Hail! Hail! Rock 'n' Roll!

A jubilant and sometimes candid documentary celebrating the contributions of Chuck Berry to the history of rock 'n' roll. The two-hour valentine features numerous interviews with such rock luminaries as Bruce Springsteen, Little Richard, and Keith Richards, as well as some revealing insights by family members and old friends. These interviews provide the core of the film, presenting Berry as an engimatic figure, happy-go-lucky on the one hand but guarded and shrewd on the other. The film ends with a rousing concert, filmed in Berry's hometown of St. Louis, in celebration of his 60th birthday. Several popular rock performers, including Julian Lennon, Robert Cray, Eric Clapton, and Linda Ronstadt, join Berry onstage. Berry's back-up band for that night was led by Richards, who produced the music for the film. **Director**—Taylor Hackford. **(PG)** *120 minutes*

C.H.U.D (1984)

★★

John Heard
Kim Greist
Daniel Stern

This low-budget horror tale has its moments of tension, but most often it chugs along in anticipation of a monster or two to prey on the next victim. The menacing creatures reside in New York City's underground passageways. They exist because some bad federal government guys dumped nuclear waste where they weren't supposed to. A photographer (Heard), his model girlfriend (Greist), a courageous cop (Christopher Curry), and other public-spirited citizens help return the Big Apple to normalcy. **Director**—Douglas Cheek. **(R)** *88 minutes*

THE CINCINNATI KID (1965)

★★★

Steve McQueen
Edward G. Robinson
Ann-Margret
Tuesday Weld

McQueen does well in the title role, as a roving poker player who likes big games with big stakes. It's sort of *The Hustler* of card games. A big card game at the finale adds a dimension to the adventure. However, the romantic interludes don't fare as well. This film version of Richard Jessup's novel is set in the late 1930s in New Orleans. There's nice support from the talented cast, which also includes Karl Malden, Joan Blondell, Rip Torn, Jack Weston, and Cab Calloway. **Director**—Norman Jewison. *113 minutes*

CINDERELLA (1950)

★★★1/2

The Charles Perrault fairy tale gets an overhaul Disney-style in this feature-length animated cartoon. Here, the beautiful but unfortunate young woman, who is forced to wait on her wicked stepmother and stepsisters, is befriended by a bevy of animal bud-

(Continued)

(Continued)
dies, who provide the humor and heart of this lively version. Enhanced by gorgeous Technicolor, amusing tunes, and the animated style of Disney's original group of artists (the "eight old men"), this cartoon feature is one of the studio's best. With the voices of Ilene Woods, William Phipps, Eleanor Audley, Rhoda Williams, Lucille Bliss, and Verna Felton. **Directors**—Wilfred Jackson, Hamilton Luske, and Clyde Geronimi. **(G)** *74 minutes*

CINDERFELLA (1960)

★★

Jerry Lewis
Ed Wynn
Judith Anderson

Lewis puts his comic twist on the classic fairy tale, and the whole film turns into a pumpkin. The production is lavish, but Lewis' jokes are ordinary. There's lots of talk between gags, and the musical sequences are uninspired. There may be some enjoyment if you're a big Lewis fan; otherwise, there's not much to laugh at. Also with Anna Maria Alberghetti and Count Basie. **Director**—Frank Tashlin. *91 minutes*

CITIZEN KANE (1941)

★★★★

Orson Welles
Joseph Cotten
Everett Sloane

Citizen Kane *(Orson Welles) at the height of his power.*

Welles' masterpiece about a tyrannical newspaper publisher who built a vast empire. Every moment of the story, which parallels the career of William Randolph Hearst, is filled with intelligence, excitement, and pure entertainment. Welles cowrote, directed, and starred in this magnificent production, which broke new ground in cinematic craftsmanship. Seeing it today is still a remarkable experience, and it surely will remain a gem among Hollywood's offerings. Also stars George Coulouris, Dorothy Comingore, Ruth Warrick, Paul Stewart, and Agnes Moorehead. **Academy Award**—Herman J. Mankiewicz and Welles, original screenplay. **Nominations**—best picture; Welles, best director; Welles, best actor; Gregg Toland, cinematography. *119 minutes b&w*

CITIZENS BAND (1977)

★★

Paul LeMat
Candy Clark

This slaphappy comedy revolves around the Citizens Band radio craze from a few years back. The film borrows much of its style from *American Graffiti*, but does not have the expert direction of that classic hit. Here the numerous subplots bog down the main storyline, which involves the problems of a bigamous trucker and a lad who tries to enforce the regulations governing CB radio operation. Also with Ann Wedgeworth and Marcia Rodd. **Director**—Jonathan Demme. **(PG) Alternate Title**—*Handle with Care.* *98 minutes*

CITY HEAT (1984)

★★

Burt Reynolds
Clint Eastwood

Superstars Reynolds and Eastwood team up in this spoof of 1930s private-eye movies and their own reputations. Burt is a dapper but broke gumshoe and Clint is a stone-faced police lieutenant—both friends once, but now bantering rivals. Unfortunately, a muddled plot and some excessive violence cool off the breeziness of this tongue-in-cheek affair. However, Burt and Clint work well together. Likable cast also includes Jane Alexander, Madeline Kahn, and Rip Torn. **Director**—Richard Benjamin. **(PG)** *94 minutes*

CITY OF WOMEN (1981)

★★★

Marcello Mastroianni
Ettore Manni
Anna Prucnal

Director Federico Fellini takes on women's lib as only Fellini can, with bombastic dream sequences that parade onward with exuberance and extravagance. Mastroianni is ideally cast as the maestro's alter ego, who stumbles on a feminist convention. Here, he's attacked as a spy and at last rescued by a macho man. Despite the usual Fellini flamboyance, the film is devoid of drama. However, serious Fellini fans may still rejoice. Also with Katren Gebelein and Donatella Damiani. Originally filmed in Italian. **(No MPAA rating)** *140 minutes*

CLAIRE'S KNEE (1970)

★★★

Jean-Claude Brialy
Beatrice Romand

The fifth of French director Eric Rohmer's "Moral Tales," a series of surprisingly spellbinding films that are short on narrative and long on ethical quandaries. A man who's soon to be married vacations separately from his fiancée at the Swiss border. There he's drawn to an attractive young woman with one of the most gorgeous knees he's ever seen on a leg. Will his mounting romantic obsession lead him to stray from premarital fidelity, or can he keep himself faithful through the torrid summer month? Rohmer makes us care. Originally filmed in French. **(No MPAA rating)** *103 minutes*

THE CLAN OF THE CAVE BEAR (1986)

★

Daryl Hannah

Daryl Hannah is out for some target practice in The Clan of the Cave Bear.

This movie available with closed captions for the hearing impaired.

Tedious caveman movie based on Jean M. Auel's best-selling novel. The film does no justice to the book as events unfold haphazardly at a plodding pace. Blonde, blue-eyed Hannah is unconvincing as a prehistoric feminist who learns to wield a deadly slingshot, thereby arousing the hostility of some tribesmen. Apparently, even Neanderthals suffered from neurosis. Dialogue amounts to grunts and gibberish, which are translated into English subtitles. Also with Pamela Reed and Thomas G. Waites. **Director**—Michael Chapman. **(R) Academy Award Nomination**—Michael G. Westmore and Michael Burke, best makeup.
100 minutes

CLARA'S HEART (1988)

★★1/2

Whoopi Goldberg
Neil Patrick Harris

Whoopi Goldberg gives Neil Patrick Harris much-needed comfort in Clara's Heart.

Goldberg is fantastic as a wise, sympathetic Jamaican housekeeper who strongly influences the life of a wealthy white boy. Harris is also impressive as the lad who craves understanding in the face of his parents' divorce. There are some lapses into sentimentality, which some viewers *may* find excessive. Also with Michael Ontkean and Kathleen Quinlan. **Director**—Robert Mulligan. **(PG-13)** *108 minutes*

CLASH OF THE TITANS (1981)

★★★

Harry Hamlin
Judi Bowker
Burgess Meredith

Greek mythology is the basis for this spirited, romantic adventure, featuring many glorious monsters created by special-effects wiz Ray Harryhausen. Square-jawed Hamlin plays Perseus, who engages in assorted daring feats to save his lady love (Bowker) from being sacrificed to the huge sea monster, the Kraken. Perseus gets around with the help of Pegasus, the flying horse. He valiantly battles a two-headed wolf, a giant vulture, and a woman whose stare can kill. **Director**—Desmond Davis. **(PG)** *120 minutes*

CLASS (1983)

★

Jacqueline Bisset
Cliff Robertson
Rob Lowe
Andrew McCarthy

A crudely made adolescent fantasy about a prep school boy who unwittingly has an affair with his roommate's mother, played by Bisset. This awkward takeoff of *The Graduate* is preposterous from start to finish. The entire cast strains with the garbled script and undeveloped characters. Robertson is wasted as the domineering, wealthy husband/father. It's hard to understand why director Lewis John Carlino, with *The Great Santini* under his belt, would bother with this second-class idea. **(R)** *98 minutes*

THE CLASS OF MISS MACMICHAEL (1978)

Glenda Jackson
Oliver Reed

Jackson, projecting her very proper British manner, plays a dedicated teacher who struggles with a roomful of unruly teenagers. It's her and the kids against the world and an authoritative principal, overplayed by Reed. This theme has been worn thin on the screen and on TV, and the situations are predictable. Jackson and most cast members do a serviceable job. Also with Michael Murphy and Rosalind Cash. **Director**—Silvio Narizzano. **(R)** *99 minutes*

CLASS OF 1984 (1982)

★★1/2

Roddy McDowall
Perry King

Another variation of *The Blackboard Jungle* theme with much violence woven into the fabric. The setting is an urban high school where a punk-rock gang intimidates students and teachers at will. The story is engrossing for a while, but the film finally deteriorates in an implausible, horror-filled climax. The acting is a mixed bag: McDowall does well as a cynical biology teacher, while King awkwardly portrays a mild-mannered music instructor who obtains brutal revenge. **Director**—Mark Lester. **(R)**
93 minutes

The Class of 1984 *is out looking for a few thrills.*

CLASS OF 1999 (1990)

Bradley Gregg
Traci Lind
Malcolm McDowell

In this futuristic *Blackboard Jungle,* students check their submachine guns at the high-school door, and teachers are androids who impose draconian discipline. Though some of the tongue-in-cheek humor is effective and the special effects are noteworthy, this hard-boiled film eventually deteriorates into a mindless orgy of violence, explosions, and shootings. Gregg stars as the student hero, but the adult cast is most interesting: They include McDowell, Stacy Keach, and Pam Grier. Directed by Mark Lester as a follow-up to his 1981 film *Class of 1984.* **(R)** *98 minutes*

CLASS OF NUKE 'EM HIGH (1986)

★

Gilbert Brenton
Janelle Brady

This low-budget exploitation horror/comedy treads the same territory as *Toxic Avenger,* which is not a surprise considering both are from the same production company, Troma Inc. A leaky nuclear power plant has polluted the high school's water supply, bringing out the worst behavior in the stu-

(Continued)

(Continued)
dents. The usual portions of disgusting special effects are featured along with many boring scenes and some atrocious dialogue. **Directors**—Richard W. Haines and Samuel Weil. **(R)** *81 minutes*

CLEAN AND SOBER (1988)

★★★

Michael Keaton
Kathy Baker
Morgan Freeman

Michael Keaton faces some difficult choices in Clean and Sober.

A grim drama about cocaine addicts and alcoholics struggling to shake their dependencies. The subject is depressing, but director Glenn Gordon Caron steers clear of sentimentality and preachiness. Keaton gives an impressive, controlled performance as a recovering addict. He gets excellent support from Baker as a young woman with similar problems. **(R)** *125 minutes*

CLEAN SLATE

See Coup de Torchon

CLEOPATRA (1963)

★★

Elizabeth Taylor
Richard Burton
Rex Harrison

Much heralded prior to its release, this historical drama is a horrendous disappointment. Despite its tremendous expense and length, there's perhaps an hour's worth of decent entertainment. Taylor, in the title role, is lovely to look at, but that's it. Harrison is good as Caesar, but Burton as Anthony turns in an uneven performance. Also with Pamela Brown, Roddy McDowall, Martin Landau, and Michael Hordern. Released for television at 194 minutes. **Director**—Joseph L. Mankiewicz. **Academy Award**—Leon Shamroy, cinematography. **Nominations**—best picture; Harrison, best actor. *243 minutes*

CLOAK & DAGGER (1984)

★★

Henry Thomas
Dabney Coleman

Uneasy mixture of Hardy Boys adventure, Hitchcock-style spy melodrama, and computer-game fantasy. A young tyke, played confidently by Thomas (*E.T.*), gets tangled up with a mysterious spy and murder caper. Only the adults don't believe him because his overactive imagination is stimulated by too much exposure to video games. This gimmicky plot is occasionally appealing, but the action turns unbelievable and unnecessarily brutal. **Director**—Richard Franklin. **(PG)** *101 minutes*

THE CLOCK (1945)

★★★

Judy Garland
Robert Walker

Garland stars in this frothy romantic drama as a New York City secretary. She meets a soldier, played by Walker, and marries him before his 24-hour leave is up. During their whirlwind courtship, the lovebirds meet an assortment of pleasant characters. Garland is as charming as ever, but she doesn't sing. James Gleason, Lucille Gleason, Keenan Wynn, and Marshall Thompson are also in the cast. **Director**—Vincente Minnelli. *90 minutes b&w*

CLOCKWISE (1986)

★★

John Cleese

A gifted star and a funny idea fail to produce a winning comedy in this case. Cleese plays the rigid, time-obsessed headmaster of a British school. When he must scramble to arrive on time for the most important business meeting of his career, he only succeeds in piling mishap on mishap. There's some occasional lunacy, but the pacing is too sluggish to inspire many laughs. **Director**—Christopher Morahan. **(PG)** *95 minutes*

A CLOCKWORK ORANGE (1971)

★★★★

Malcolm McDowell
Patrick Magee
Michael Bates

Stanley Kubrick's perceptive, dark satire about the future was adapted from Anthony Burgess' novel. The scene is 21st-century England, where gangs of young hoodlums run rampant, and ordinary citizens are afraid to venture out. A young murderer returns to society after being brainwashed by the authorities in a prison experiment and finds that the violent nature of society has increased. The film is generously laced with stark images and a chilling political message about the future. Also with Adrienne Corri, Aubrey Morris, and James Marcus. **(R) Academy Award Nominations**—best picture; Kubrick, best director and best screenplay based on material from another medium. *136 minutes*

CLOSE ENCOUNTERS OF THE THIRD KIND (1977)

★★★★

Richard Dreyfuss
François Truffaut
Melinda Dillon

Steven Spielberg's $19-million epic about UFOs begins somewhat incoherently. The film then lapses a little more toward the middle. But the final portion—when earthlings and extraterrestrial beings rendezvous on a Wyoming mountain—suddenly flares to a dazzling climax. The special effects by Douglas Trumbull are stunning, and Spielberg's awesome imaginative effort comes into full focus. Also with Teri Garr, Cary Guffey, and Bob Balaban. Reedited by Spielberg in 1980 and reissued at 132 minutes as *The Special Edition*. For television showings more footage was added, which is the version available on videotape. **(PG) Academy Award**—Vilmos Zsigmond, cinematography. **Nominations**—Spielberg, best director; Dillon, best supporting actress. *135 minutes*

THE CLOWN (1953)

Red Skelton
Jane Greer

This movie available with closed captions for the hearing impaired.

Skelton has a rare dramatic role in this sentimental version of *The Champ.* He plays a has-been comic who is urged by his son to make a comeback. Skelton handles the part well, but he's better off working with comedy. There's adequate support from Tim Considine and Loring Smith. Look for Charles Bronson in the scene with the dice game. **Director**—Robert Z. Leonard.

92 minutes b&w

CLUB LIFE (1987)

★

Tony Curtis
Michael Parks

Curtis compromises his career to appear in this dreary drama about a seedy Los Angeles disco. He plays a nightclub owner who must contend with a mob murder, an attempted takeover by gangsters, and a funeral conducted on the dance floor. Other characters in this sordid affair include an aspiring actor who works as a bouncer, a washed-up singer, and a small-town girl turned prostitute. The acting is as unappealing as the disco's surroundings. Tom Parsekian and Dee Wallace costar. **Director**—Norman Thaddeus Vane. **(R)**

92 minutes

CLUB PARADISE (1986)

★★

Robin Williams
Peter O'Toole
Twiggy

Robin Williams, as an ex-firefighter, meets a new flame, Twiggy, in Club Paradise.

Several notches above *National Lampoon's* slapstick comedies, this farce about a dilapidated Caribbean resort offers some witty dialogue. But the comedy ultimately loses its tropical steam. Williams strains in his role as a former Chicago fireman who tries to revive the seedy hotel while battling local corruption and international wheeler-dealers. O'Toole and Twiggy, in supporting roles, try in vain to pump life into the faltering parody. Also with Rick Moranis, Andrea Martin, Brian Doyle-Murray, Adolph Caesar, and reggae singer Jimmy Cliff. **Director**—Harold Ramis. **(PG–13)** *96 minutes*

CLUE (1985)

★★1/2

Madeline Kahn
Eileen Brennan
Tim Curry
Leslie Ann Warren
Christopher Lloyd

Miss Peacock (Eileen Brennan) with the knife in the film version of Clue.

An unusual mystery/suspense film in that it is an adaptation of a popular board game. Someone is making corpses out of the mysteriously assembled guests at a New England mansion. Is it Miss Peacock? Professor Plum? Even if we wanted to tell you who did it, we couldn't: The mystery has three endings. Three versions of the film, each with a different ending, were released to the theaters. The culprit's identity was different in each version. **Director**—Jonathan Lynn. **(PG)**

96 minutes

COAL MINER'S DAUGHTER (1980)

★★★★

Sissy Spacek
Tommy Lee Jones

Spacek gives a stunning, virtuoso performance in the title role of this rags-to-riches biography of Loretta Lynn, the country singer superstar. First-rate support from Jones, as Lynn's everlovin' manager/husband, also moves the film along, even when the screenplay seems to lose some energy. Director Michael Apted captures the authentic detail of Appalachia in a careful documentary style. It's a winning film, filled with plenty of heart, hope, and some surprisingly good singing from Spacek. Also with Beverly D'Angelo, Levon Helm (of the Band), and Phyllis Boyens. **(PG) Academy Award**—Spacek, best actress. **Nominations**—best picture; Tom Rickman, best screenplay based on material from another medium. *124 minutes*

COAST TO COAST (1980)

★★

Dyan Cannon
Robert Blake

Blake and Cannon barrel across the country in a huge trailer truck while various enemies intercept them along the way. This action/comedy is nothing more than another routine variation of such cat-and-mouse chase films as *Smokey and the Bandit.* Blake and Cannon, who seem to be imitating Burt Reynolds and Sally Field, ham it up with gusto. But it's a forgettable trip. Also with Quinn Redeker. **Director**—Joseph Sargent. **(PG)** *95 minutes*

COBRA (1986)

★★

Sylvester Stallone
Brigitte Nielsen
Reni Santoni

Slickly produced police procedural tale starring Stallone as Marion Cobretti, nicknamed "Cobra," a member of the L.A.P.D.'s "zombie squad." The squad is assigned nearly impossible tasks no other cops will do. Here Cobra and his partner (Santoni) track down a serial killer, who belongs to a dangerous gang of fanatics bent on starting a new terrorist society. Cobra must also protect a beautiful model—played by Stallone's real-life wife, Nielsen—who is the only witness to the gang's activities. Though well crafted with impressive cinematography by Ric Waite, the film's not-so-subtle message suggesting that hardened criminals do not deserve any

(Continued)

(Continued)
civil rights is reactionary. Cobretti's only solution to any problem is a violent one—a disturbing trend in action films of the mid-1980s. Also with Andrew Robinson, Lee Garlington, Val Avery, and Brian Thompson. **Director**—George Cosmatos. **(R)** *87 minutes*

COCKTAIL (1988)

★★

Tom Cruise
Bryan Brown

Tom Cruise learns all the tricks of the Cocktail *trade.*

Cruise is trapped in a ludicrous role as a materialistic, opportunistic bartender. Brown fares better as Cruise's mentor in mixing drinks and hustling women. Slick production values, exotic locations, and a contemporary musical score make for a glossy but shallow film. The story is another in a series starring Cruise as a talented but naive man who falls under the wing of a father figure. Elisabeth Shue and Lisa Barnes also star. **Director**—Roger Donaldson. **(R)** *100 minutes*

COCOANUTS (1929)

★★★

The Marx Brothers
Margaret Dumont

The Marx Brothers' first film. If that isn't reason enough for you to watch it, you should probably stay away. It's a pretty static, clunky version of the stage hit by George S. Kaufman and Morrie Ryskind, all about a hotel manager eager to cash in on the Florida real-estate boom. When the boys are on the screen, doing their "Why a duck?" routine for example, you're watching the kind of epochal—and still hilarious—material on which careers are launched. When they leave the scene, you should too. Dumont and Kay Francis costar, and there's music by Irving Berlin. **Directors**—Joseph Santley and Robert Florey. *96 minutes b&w*

COCOON (1985)

★★★

Steve Guttenberg
Tahnee Welch
Brian Dennehy

Extraterrestrials, who visit Earth to recover some colleagues, offer new leases on life to elderly folks residing in a Florida retirement community. This sweet, sci-fi fantasy can be regarded as a cross between *Close Encounters of the Third Kind* and *On Golden Pond*. Hume Cronyn, Don Ameche, and Wilford Brimley are excellent as old codgers who find the fountain of youth. **Director**—Ron Howard. **(PG) Academy Awards**—Ameche, best supporting actor; Ken Ralston and Mitch Suskin, visual effects. *118 minutes*

COCOON: THE RETURN (1988)

★★½

Don Ameche
Wilford Brimly
Hume Cronyn

Don Ameche and Hume Cronyn think it's great to be alive in Cocoon: The Return.

Director Daniel Petrie turns out a listless sequel to the sweet original. The sprightly senior citizens venture back to Earth for a visit, but they should have stayed on the utopian planet Antarea. The fine veteran actors of the first episode reprise their roles with charm and spirit, but it is not enough to redeem this trite science-fiction fantasy. Also stars Jack Gilford, Maureen Stapleton, Jessica Tandy, Gwen Verdon, Steve Guttenberg, Courteney Cox, and Tahnee Welch. **(PG)** *116 minutes*

CODE OF SILENCE (1985)

★★★

Chuck Norris

Norris, as a Chicago police sergeant and one-man army, mops up a powerful drug ring. The blaze of violence is exceptionally bloodthirsty, with an unusually high body count. Norris displays his martial-arts ability, but the real thrust is on elaborate stunts, car chases, and conventional mayhem. In this slick actioner, Norris graduates to the hallowed territory of Clint Eastwood and Charles Bronson. But his acting ability continues to lack style. **Director**—Andy Davis. **(R)** *102 minutes*

COLD FEET (1984)

★★

Griffin Dunne
Marissa Chibas

A slow-moving comedy about a man and a woman, previously stung by unhappy relationships, who now are cautiously trying to rekindle romance. The central characters are appealing enough, but the material tends to be overly talky and unfunny. Director/writer Bruce van Dusen makes some sharp observations on contemporary lifestyles. Too bad the film can't stand up for the full count. **(PG)** *96 minutes*

THE COLLECTOR (1965)

★★★

Terence Stamp
Samantha Eggar

Terence Stamp pursues an unusual hobby, Samantha Eggar, in The Collector.

® *This movie available with closed captions for the hearing impaired.*

An unusual story about a strange young man who collects butterflies and decides to add a beautiful art student, played by Eggar, to his collection. Stamp is convincing as the disturbed youth who kidnaps Eggar and keeps her in his basement. The suspense builds nicely under the fine direction of William Wyler. The chilling drama is based on John Fowles' popular novel. Maurice Dallimore and Mona Washbourne have supporting roles. **Academy Award Nominations—**Wyler, best director; Eggar, best actress; Stanley Mann and John Kohn, best screenplay based on material from another medium. *119 minutes*

THE COLOR OF MONEY (1986)

★★★

Paul Newman
Tom Cruise
Mary Elizabeth Mastrantonio
Helen Shaver

Powerhouse acting and distinctly drawn characters propel this follow-up to the 1961 drama *The Hustler.* Newman reprises his role as former pool hustler Fast Eddie Felson, who becomes a mentor to a young, flamboyant, but inexperienced pool player (Cruise). They take to the road together in quest of glory and money. Directed by Martin Scorsese, the film conveys the gritty world of pool halls and its hustlers in authentic detail. Unfortunately, the visual style, including the beautifully edited scenes of the games, overwhelms the weak script by newcomer Richard Price. **Academy Award**—Newman, best actor. **Nominations**—Mastrantonio, best supporting actress; Price, best screenplay based on material from another medium. **(R)** *119 minutes*

THE COLOR PURPLE (1985)

★★★½

Whoopi Goldberg
Oprah Winfrey
Margaret Avery

Director Steven Spielberg, the master of teenage adventure epics, succeeds wonderfully with this serious material. And a hearty hooray for Goldberg in her second film role as the initially timid, abused young woman of Alice Walker's prize-winning story of poor blacks in rural Georgia. Goldberg is magnificent and triumphant as a person who slowly develops an awareness of her own worth. Supporting performances by Winfrey, Avery, Danny Glover, and Adolphe Caesar are uniformly fine in this rich and poignant film with poetic texture. **(PG-13) Academy Award Nominations—**best picture; Goldberg, best actress; Avery and Winfrey, best supporting actress; Menno Meyjes, best screenplay based on material from another medium. *155 minutes*

COLORS (1988)

★★★

Robert Duvall
Sean Penn

A contemporary account of vicious street gangs, who chew up the ghettos of Los Angeles with the latest weapons while dealing drugs to inner-city residents. Duvall and Penn play a pair of cops assigned to the L.A.P.D.'s woefully undermanned gang unit. Aside from the stress related to their beat, the two conflict over how to deal with gang members. Directed by Dennis Hopper, the film's power is its inside look at gang culture, which is often violent and sometimes deadly. Haskell Wexler's cinematography captures the gritty urban environment as does Ice-T's hard-edged rap song, which serves as the film's theme. The film was criticized at the time of its release for inciting gang violence and for its negative portrayal of minorities. Also with Maria Conchita Alonso, Randy Brooks, Grand Bush, and Trinidad Silva. **(R)** *120 minutes*

COMA (1978)

★★★

Geneviève Bujold
Michael Douglas

When the full moon rose in the sky and Count Dracula and the Wolf Man prowled about, it scared the daylights out of you. This horror story, which takes place in a Boston hospital, is scary enough, too, but the fun and satisfaction are absent. Bujold is a resident surgeon, who unravels a sinister plot to send healthy patients into irreversible comas and then steal their organs for transplants. The mystery unfolds amid the antiseptic glare of modern institutions with little style, imagination, or humor. Also with Elizabeth Ashley, Rip Torn, and Richard Widmark. Michael Crichton directed this film, which is based on Robin Cook's novel. **(PG)** *113 minutes*

THE COMANCHEROS (1961)

★★★

John Wayne
Stuart Whitman

Wayne is right at home in this rough, tough western as a Texas Ranger who is determined to rid the territory of a gang supplying guns and whiskey to the Indians. Whitman plays a gambler/prisoner forced to tag along with Wayne. The Duke gets involved with some lively gunplay, yet there's just the right amount of levity mixed in with the action. Wayne and the rest of the cast seem to be having an enjoyable time with the material. Also with Lee Marvin, Bruce Cabot, Nehemiah Persoff, and Ina Balin. The last film by veteran Hollywood director Michael Curtiz *(Casablanca; Mildred Pierce; White Christmas).* *107 minutes*

COME AND GET IT (1936)

★★★

Edward Arnold
Frances Farmer
Joel McCrea
Walter Brennan

Walter Brennan, Frances Farmer, and Edward Arnold in Come and Get It.

Howard Hawks directed most of this rich and vigorous adaptation of Edna Ferber's novel. Top-notch performances are given by Arnold as a 19th-century lumber tycoon who lets nothing stand in his way for success; by Farmer, as both a cabaret singer (whom Arnold spurns) and her daughter (whom Arnold, advancing in years, unsuccessfully woos); and by Brennan, who won an Oscar as the trusty sidekick. Producer Sam Goldwyn replaced Hawks with William Wyler toward the end of the shooting, but the last-minute directorial change didn't hurt the film. Lushly photographed by Gregg Toland and Rudolph Maté. Andrea Leeds and Frank Shields costar. **Academy Award—**Brennan, best supporting actor. *99 minutes b&w*

COME BACK, LITTLE SHEBA (1952)

★★★★

Shirley Booth
Burt Lancaster

Top-notch performances propel this emotionally charged drama about a slovenly housewife trying to cope with her alcoholic husband. The film, based on the William Inge play, is somewhat stagebound, but effective nevertheless. Booth is splendid as the wife, and Lancaster is superb as the husband. Terry Moore and Richard Jaeckel are fine in supporting roles. **Director**—Daniel Mann. **Academy Award**—Booth, best actress. **Nomination**—Moore, best supporting actress. *99 minutes b&w*

COME BACK TO THE FIVE AND DIME JIMMY DEAN, JIMMY DEAN (1982)

 ★★

Sandy Dennis
Cher
Karen Black

Robert Altman's low-budget screen version of the Broadway play bogs down in its overbearing staginess. The confined setting is a seedy Texas dime store where a group of women are holding a 20-year reunion of their James Dean fan club. Superb ensemble acting captures the various kooky characters who here reveal their strange secrets and frailties. Yet those Altmanesque observations are often obscured by a confusing script. **(PG)** *109 minutes*

COME BLOW YOUR HORN (1963)

★★★

Frank Sinatra
Tony Bill
Lee J. Cobb
Molly Picon

Sinatra plays a swinging bachelor with a stable of girls, who teaches his younger brother the ways of the world. The Neil Simon play is successfully transposed to the screen, with the funny characters and funny lines firmly intact. Sinatra is well cast as the bachelor, and Bill plays the awestruck kid brother with conviction. Cobb and Picon are good as anxious parents. Sinatra sings the title song. Jill St. John, Barbara Rush, and Dan Blocker have supporting roles. **Director**—Bud Yorkin. *112 minutes*

THE COMEDIANS (1967)

Richard Burton
Elizabeth Taylor
Alec Guinness
Peter Ustinov

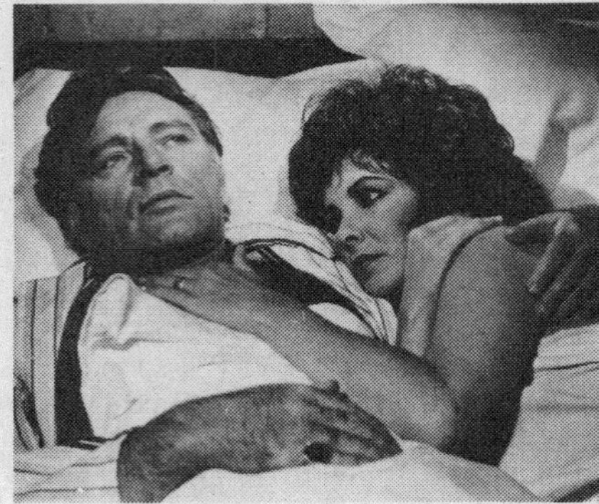

Love, Haitian-style: Richard Burton and Elizabeth Taylor in The Comedians.

A champagne cast can't do much with this labored and awkward film version of Graham Greene's novel about politics and violence in Haiti under the rule of Papa Doc Duvalier. Burton and Taylor play odd characters involved with intrigue. The clumsy, cliché-heavy script seems to overwhelm the acting, and the direction lacks inspiration. Supporting players include Lillian Gish, Paul Ford, Roscoe Lee Browne, Raymond St. Jacques, James Earl Jones, and Cicely Tyson. **Director**—Peter Glenville. *160 minutes*

THE COMEDY OF TERRORS (1963)

Vincent Price
Peter Lorre
Boris Karloff
Basil Rathbone

This spoof of the macabre features a quartet of horror-film greats. Although there are a few effective scenes, this film falls short of expectations. Price plays a sinister undertaker who schemes to increase his business by hastening the demise of prospective clients. They should have buried the script instead. Joe E. Brown and Joyce Jameson are also in the cast. **Director**—Jacques Tourneur. *84 minutes*

COME FILL THE CUP (1951)

James Cagney
Phyllis Thaxter

A solid performance by Cagney graces this melodrama. Cagney plays an ex-newspaperman trying to cure himself of alcoholism and get his life back together. He also tries to help the son of his boss, who has ties to gangsters. There's fine support from Gig Young, who plays the son—a tipsy playboy. Raymond Massey and James Gleason are also in the cast. **Director**—Gordon Douglas. **Academy Award Nomination**—Young, best supporting actor. *113 minutes b&w*

COMES A HORSEMAN (1978)

 ★★

Jane Fonda
James Caan
Jason Robards

Young, struggling ranchers stand up to a cattle baron and oil industrialists. It's a version of a theme used in countless westerns of yesteryear, and it is used again here with middling results. Only this time, some sensitivity is blended in with a dash of modern feminism. The film walks most of the time when it should gallop, despite the strong performances by the cast. Fonda plays a rancher, Caan is the rescuer, and Robards plays the cattle baron. Also with George Grizzard, Richard Farnsworth, and Jim Davis. **Director**—Alan J. Pakula. **(PG) Academy Award Nomination**—Farnsworth, best supporting actor. *118 minutes*

COME TO THE STABLE (1949)

Loretta Young
Celeste Holm

A charming, heartwarming film about two French nuns who seek support to build a children's hospital in a New England town. Young and Holm are perfectly suited for their parts, and they exude considerable grace and sweetness in this tasteful production. Henry Koster directs with simplicity and efficiency. Also with Hugh Marlowe, Elsa Lanchester, Mike Mazurki, and Regis Toomey. **Academy Award Nominations**—Young, best actress; Holm and Lanchester, best supporting actress;

® This movie available with closed captions for the hearing impaired.

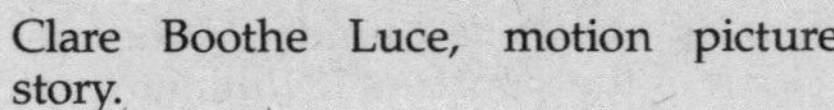

Clare Boothe Luce, motion picture story.

94 minutes b&w

COMFORT AND JOY (1984)

★★½

Bill Paterson

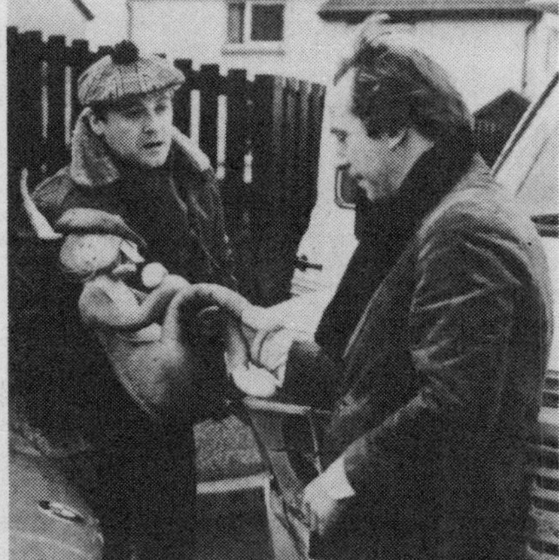

Bill Paterson (right) meets Alex Norton's mascot in Comfort and Joy.

Scottish director Bill Forsyth *(Gregory's Girl)* offers a subdued, offbeat comedy that does not quite live up to his earlier film projects. The frothy story centers on the career turning point of a Glasgow disk jockey (Paterson) who wants to break into news reporting. He's also trying to resolve the abrupt departure of his eccentric girlfriend. Interesting characters could compensate for such loose plotting, but Paterson does not come through in that category. **(PG)**

106 minutes

COMING HOME (1978)

★★★½

Jon Voight
Jane Fonda
Bruce Dern

Fonda was the motivating force behind the production of this post-Vietnam melodrama, which concentrates on the effects of the war at home. The main storyline involves a Marine captain's wife (Fonda) who has an affair with a paraplegic vet (Voight). The subject matter of the Vietnam experience is an emotional and powerful one, and was particularly so at the time of the film's release; and the filmmakers seem to be so concerned with not offending anyone that their point is one-dimensional, while their position and attitudes are foggy. Still, the performances are strong and the attempt to put together some sort of perspective for the populace on such a controversial and heartbreaking war is an admirable one. Also with Robert Carradine, Penelope Milford, and Robert Ginty. **Director**—Hal Ashby. **(R)** **Academy Awards**—Voight, best actor; Fonda, best actress; Nancy Dowd, Waldo Salt, and Robert Jones, best screenplay written directly for the screen. **Nominations**—best picture; Ashby, best director; Dern, best supporting actor. *127 minutes*

COMING TO AMERICA (1988)

★★½

Eddie Murphy
Arsenio Hall
Shari Headley

Glossy production values and Murphy are the main selling points in this predictable farce about a naive African prince who journeys to Queens, New York, to find a bride. Despite the nudity and street language, the story has its basis in comedies from as far back as the 1940s. Murphy is appealingly subdued, and Hall has some good moments as the prince's long-suffering friend. Also with James Earl Jones, John Amos, and Madge Sinclair. **Director**—John Landis. **(R)** *115 minutes*

COMMAND DECISION (1948)

★★★

Clark Gable
Walter Pidgeon
Van Johnson

This gripping World War II drama focuses on the top brass who must make the distressing decisions that will send many men to their deaths. Gable is the general who huddles with his staff to discuss the strategy for bombing missions over Nazi Germany. This straightforward adaptation of William Haines' Broadway play also features Brian Donlevy, John Hodiak, Edward Arnold, and Charles Bickford. **Director**—Sam Wood. *112 minutes b&w*

COMMANDO (1985)

★★

Arnold Schwarzenegger

Schwarzenegger stars as a former elite army colonel pressed back into action when his daughter is kidnapped by murderous guerrillas. He goes to work with machine guns, knives, and axes to accomplish his vengeful, violent mission. This super-firepower, high-body-count actioner merely follows the bloody pattern of the genre. Only this number contains a bit of suspense and improved acting from Schwarzenegger. Rae Dawn Chong costars. **Director**—Mark Lester. **(R)** *90 minutes*

COMMUNION (1989)

★½

Christopher Walken
Lindsay Crouse

Despite a colorful performance by Walken, this tale of a writer's contact with extraterrestrials is simply silly. Walken plays real-life author Whitley Strieber, who claims to have been abducted by aliens and then returned to his country home. The script earnestly follows Streiber's best-selling book, to the point where the film is as self-important and banal as the book. The special effects, including the aliens, appear too artificial compared to the casual, almost mundane depiction of everyday urban life. This movie will appeal only to those who believe what they read in supermarket tabloids. Also with Frances Sternhagen. **Director**—Philippe Mora. **(R)** *103 minutes*

THE COMPANY OF WOLVES (1985)

★★★

Angela Lansbury

What big eyes you have, Granny! Angela Lansbury in The Company of Wolves.

(Continued)

(Continued)
Intriguing and imaginative variation on the Little Red Riding Hood fable, adorned with psychological symbols and contemporary horror elements. The convoluted plot centers on an adolescent girl's nightmares, which are filled with murky images dominated by wolves. In the climactic sequences, a young girl meets up with a man at Granny's cottage who changes into a snarling wolf. Lansbury hams it up as the tale-telling Granny. Also with David Warner and Sarah Patterson. **Director**—Neil Jordan. **(R)** *95 minutes*

LES COMPÈRES (1984)

 ★★★

Gérard Depardieu
Pierre Richard

Pierre Richard (left) and Gérard Depardieu mount a comic search in Les Compères.

French writer/director Francis Veber *(La Cage aux Folles)* serves up a delicious, playful farce based on an odd-couple routine. Depardieu is a tough, aggressive news reporter. Richard is a meek, depressive character. Both are duped into searching for a teenager whom each believes is his son.Originally filmed in French. **(No MPAA rating)** *98 minutes*

THE COMPETITION (1980)

 ★★

Richard Dreyfuss
Amy Irving

He (Dreyfuss) is a brilliant young classical pianist. She (Irving) is also a musical prodigy. They fall in love while vying for top honors in a piano competition. Beethoven and Prokofiev get a workout at the keyboards, but this overlong love story is drab and predictable. Half-baked subplots contribute to the film's awkwardness. Dreyfuss and Irving are convincing as dedicated musicians, but they don't seem to hit the right notes as young lovers. Also with Lee Remick and Sam Wanamaker. **Director**—Joel Oliansky. **(PG)** *129 minutes*

COMPROMISING POSITIONS (1985)

Susan Sarandon
Judith Ivey

Sarandon is perky and charming as a restless housewife turned Nancy Drew reporter to solve the murder of a philandering dentist. This crisp, entertaining comedy/mystery is full of effective performances and smart dialogue offering loads of breezy, playful humor and whodunit suspense. Ivey steals a few scenes as a wisecracking neighbor. Based on Susan Isaacs' novel, the film offers a spicy view of suburbia. Also with Raul Julia and Edward Herrmann. **Director**—Frank Petty. **(R)** *98 minutes*

COMPULSION (1959)

Dean Stockwell
Bradford Dillman

A fictionalized account of the infamous Leopold-Loeb murder case of the 1920s is brought to the screen with solid performances and impressive direction. The plot mainly concerns the murder trial of the two brilliant but twisted Chicago students. The students, played by Stockwell and Dillman, are put on trial for killing a young boy for thrills. Orson Welles stands out as a character based on defense lawyer Clarence Darrow. And there are fine performances, too, from Diane Varsi, E.G. Marshall, and Martin Milner. **Director**—Richard Fleischer. *103 minutes b&w*

CONAN THE BARBARIAN (1982)

 ★★

Arnold Schwarzenegger
Sandahl Bergman
James Earl Jones

This overblown sword-and-sorcery saga based on the comic-book hero serves as a showcase for the magnificent muscles of Schwarzenegger, who hulks about chopping off heads and flexing his biceps until he finally triumphs over the villainous, snakeworshipping Thulsa Doom (Jones). The production design by Ron Cobb steals Schwarzenegger's thunder. Other versions of the film run 129 minutes and 123 minutes. **Director**—John Milius. **(R)** *115 minutes*

CONAN THE DESTROYER (1984)

★1/2

Arnold Schwarzenegger
Grace Jones
Wilt Chamberlain

Arnold Schwarzenegger teams with Sarah Douglas in Conan the Destroyer.

Schwarzenegger, in the title role, muscles through another sword-and-sorcery, comic-book adventure, flexing his biceps to the maximum and mumbling dialogue to the minimum. Some scenery is striking, but the sword-swinging action is as pedestrian as ever. This time, our hero must recover a magnificent stone and protect the virginity of a young princess. **Director**—Richard Fleischer. **(PG)** *103 minutes*

THE CONCORDE—AIRPORT '79 (1979)

★★

Alain Delon
Susan Blakely
Robert Wagner
Sylvia Kristel

The *Airport* saga continues. This time it's the supersonic Concorde jet that encounters assorted hair-raising mishaps. The special effects are praiseworthy, but the plot, which mainly concerns an arms sale scandal, is rather déjà vu. The usual gallery of oddball characters is on board for the globe-trotting flight. The large cast also includes George Kennedy, Eddie Albert, Bibi Andersson, and Martha Raye. **Director**—David Lowell Rich. **(PG)** **Alternate Title**—*Airport '79.* *123 minutes*

CONDUCT UNBECOMING (1975)

★★★

Michael York
Richard Attenborough
Trevor Howard

This magnificent British film, taken from the successful play by Barry England, smartly explodes myths about duty, valor, and honor in Victorian India. The suspenseful drama deals with the kangaroo trial of a young, aristocratic lieutenant, who is accused of attacking the widow of an officer. Excellent cinematography enhances the rich atmosphere. Also with Stacy Keach, Susannah York, Christopher Plummer, James Faulkner, and James Donald. **Director**—Michael Anderson. **(PG)** *107 minutes*

CONEY ISLAND (1943)

★★★

Betty Grable
Cesar Romero
George Montgomery

Grable struts and sings in this glossy, lighthearted period musical set at the turn of the century. She's a saloon songstress; Montgomery and Romero—two showmen—vie for her attention. Later remade by Grable as *Wabash Avenue.* Also with Phil Silvers and Matt Briggs. **Director**—Walter Lang. *96 minutes*

CONFIDENTIALLY YOURS (1983)

★★★

Jean-Louis Trintignant
Fanny Ardant

François Truffaut's romantic detective story, shot in black and white, is an homage to 1940s *film noir* thrillers. Small-town businessman Trintignant is suspected of murdering his wife and her lover. Quick to the rescue is his beautiful girl Friday, played with exquisite charm and style by Ardant. The movie successfully straddles a fence between satire and seriousness. Originally filmed in French. **Director**—Truffaut. **(PG)**
111 minutes b&w

THE CONFORMIST (1971)

★★★

Jean-Louis Trintignant
Gastone Moschin

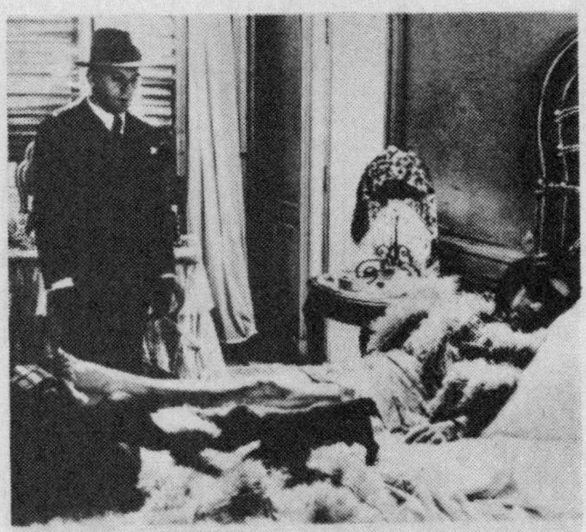

Rich-looking images of the 1930s fill the screen in The Conformist.

Trintignant stars in the title role as a man desperate to be accepted into respectable, middle-class Italian society in the 1930s, while repressing homosexual impulses. His pursuit of conformity results in his joining the secret police and participating in the assassination of an anti-Mussolini politician who was once his philosophy professor. Director Bernardo Bertolucci, a one-time poet and enfant terrible, made this free-form film of the Alberto Moravia novel at age 30, and it's a flashy piece of moviemaking, full of arresting images and provocative social commentary. The able and highly photogenic cast includes Dominique Sanda, Stefania Sandrelli, and Pierre Clementi. **(R)** **Academy Award Nomination**—Bertolucci, best screenplay based on material from another medium. *115 minutes*

A CONNECTICUT YANKEE IN KING ARTHUR'S COURT (1949)

★★★

Bing Crosby
Rhonda Fleming
William Bendix

Crosby is an engaging Sir Boss in this jazzed-up musical version of the classic Mark Twain comedy. Bing is a blacksmith who's transported back in time to Camelot, where Merlin declares him a wizard. Bing sings some forgettable tunes, yet he handles the acting chores with aplomb. Also with Cedric Hardwicke and Murvyn Vye. **Director**—Tay Garnett. *107 minutes*

THE CONQUEROR (1956)

★★

John Wayne
Susan Hayward

Yep, it's John Wayne as Genghis Khan, in what has become one of the most beloved examples of lunatic casting in the history of Hollywood. On the other hand, this was never exactly intended as fare for intellectuals; as exotic and expensive horse opera, it does deliver the goods. Hayward plays Genghis' tempestuous captive, and Pedro Armendariz, Agnes Moorehead, Thomas Gomez, Lee Van Cleef, and William Conrad are among the colorful Mongols and Tartars blustering across the screen. Howard Hughes produced and Dick Powell directed. *112 minutes*

THE CONSTANT NYMPH (1943)

Joan Fontaine
Charles Boyer

Fontaine is in top form as a young girl in love with a sophisticated musician, played by Boyer. Top-notch performances by other cast members enhance this well-produced drama. Also with Alexis Smith, Brenda Marshall, Charles Coburn, Dame May Whitty, and Peter Lorre. **Director**—Edmund Goulding. **Academy Award Nomination**—Fontaine, best actress. *112 minutes b&w*

CONTINENTAL DIVIDE (1981)

★★

John Belushi
Blair Brown

Belushi plays a gruff Chicago newspaper columnist. Brown plays a brainy, reclusive ornithologist, working to save the bald eagle. They meet high in the Rocky Mountains; they argue; they fall in love; they part; they find each other again. This romantic comedy setup is similar to those that Tracy and Hepburn handled so nicely. Belushi and Brown play interesting characters, but they're too diverse to be believable. The film strains too often to be witty. Also with Allen Goorwitz (Garfield), Carlin Glynn, and Tony Ganois. Lawrence Kasdan, later the director of *Body Heat* and *The Big Chill,* wrote the script while Steven Spielberg served as executive producer. **Director**—Michael Apted. **(PG)** *103 minutes*

This movie available on videotape and/or disc.

THE CONVERSATION (1974)

★★★★

Gene Hackman
John Cazale
Frederic Forrest
Cindy Williams

Elizabeth McRae and Gene Hackman share a dance in The Conversation.

Compelling, fresh mystery/drama about a determined wiretap expert, played by Hackman, who finally is bugged by his own conscience when he goes too far. Director Francis Coppola, who also wrote the screenplay, made a huge impact with this film, released shortly after the Watergate scandal. The plot involves murder, but the theme also focuses on the loss of privacy and the erosion of democracy as new technologies are misused. Hackman digs into his role with straight-faced discipline. Also with Allen Garfield, Teri Garr, and Harrison Ford. **(PG) Academy Award Nominations**—best picture; Coppola, best original screenplay. *113 minutes*

CONVOY (1978)

★★

Kris Kristofferson
Ali MacGraw
Ernest Borgnine

Scores of huge trailer trucks barrel across the screen to the tune of C.W. McCall's trucker ballad. Director Sam Peckinpah romanticizes the freewheeling, cowboy image of these drivers and, as expected, pours on the violent action. Logic and good taste are often left stranded by the roadside. Also with Burt Young, Madge Sinclair, and Franklyn Ajaye. **(R)** *110 minutes*

COOGAN'S BLUFF (1968)

★★★

Clint Eastwood
Lee J. Cobb
Susan Clark

Clint Eastwood teaches a city boy some manners in Coogan's Bluff.

Big, bad Eastwood plays an Arizona deputy sheriff who comes to New York City and tries to retrieve an escaped murderer, played by Don Stroud. After the thug slips away from him, Eastwood resorts to western-style methods, much to the chagrin of the city cops, to recapture his man. Cobb plays a city detective. The contrast between Cobb's urban cop and Eastwood's western lawman plus the evocation of the western myth give the film its appeal. Also with Tisha Sterling, Betty Field, and Tom Tully. **Director**—Don Siegel. **(PG)** *100 minutes*

THE COOK, THE THIEF, HIS WIFE & HER LOVER (1990)

★★★

Richard Bohringer
Michael Gambon
Helen Mirren
Alan Howard

British filmmaker Peter Greenaway fashions a controversial film with a strong political statement in this unusual drama. Gambon stars as a sadistic, lower-class criminal who takes horrible revenge on his wife's lover, a learned intellectual. The existence of several repulsive scenes, including those involving excrement, brutality, and cannibalism, makes for a harrowing viewing experience, and some viewers may be offended. Yet the characters act as metaphors for contemporary British society, and their actions and the plot should be interpreted as parables. Every aspect of the film is meant to be symbolic or metaphoric. Even the sets and costumes are coded in terms of color to add meaning to the storyline. Rather than submit to an X-rating, which the MPAA was sure to give this film, the production company chose to release the film theatrically with no rating. For video, both an uncut version and an R-rated version were released. About 25 minutes were cut to meet the criteria for an R-rated version. **(No MPAA rating)** *120 minutes*

COOKIE (1989)

★★½ ®

Peter Falk
Emily Lloyd
Dianne Wiest

Peter Falk and Emily Lloyd play the mob against the law in Cookie.

This satire of organized crime revolves around a quirky father-daughter relationship. British actress Lloyd stars in the title role as an undisciplined teenager who goes to work for her gangster father, played by Falk. Just released from prison, Falk's character must deal with rival mobsters as well as federal authorities, who want him back behind bars. As directed by Susan Seidelman *(Desperately Seeking Susan)*, the film features interesting details of urban life and lingers on colorful shots of the city. Yet this languid style of direction is inappropriate for the material, which needs a tighter structure. Also with Michael V. Gazzo, Brenda Vaccaro, Adrian Pasdar, Lionel Stander, Jerry Lewis, and Ricki Lake. **(R)** *93 minutes*

® *This movie available with closed captions for the hearing impaired.*

COOLEY HIGH (1975)

★★★

Glynn Turman
Lawrence-Hilton Jacobs
Garrett Morris

The film is a bit like *American Graffiti*, but this time it's the story of black adolescents on Chicago's Near North Side in 1964. Instead of cruising the main drag in flashy automobiles, they get together under elevated trains and hitch free rides on the backs of buses. Impressively written and directed, the film is blessed with the exceptional talents of Turman, Jacobs, and Morris. Also with Cynthia Davis, Corin Rogers, and Maurice Leon Havis. **Director**—Michael Schultz. **(PG)**

107 minutes

COOL HAND LUKE (1967)

★★★★

Paul Newman
George Kennedy

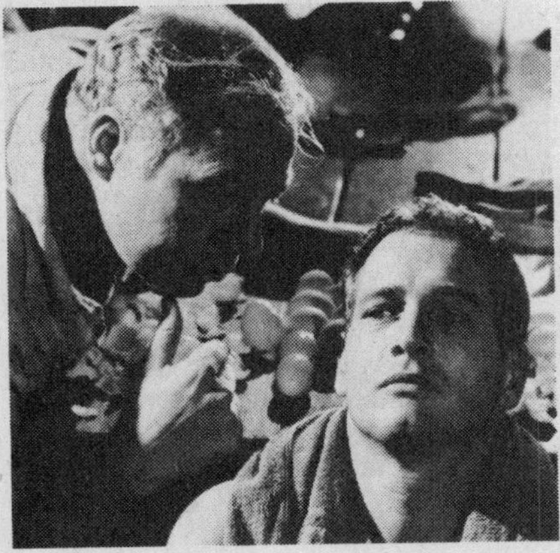

Paul Newman plays the title role in Cool Hand Luke; *George Kennedy eggs him on.*

Forthright, gripping drama about a chain-gang prisoner, played by Newman, who has a burning determination to maintain his individualism despite his compromising situation. Newman's portrayal is stunning, and he's backed with an award-winning performance by Kennedy. The character of Luke, particularly the way he becomes a sacrificial symbol to his fellow prisoners, is presented as a Christ figure, giving the role a deeper significance. Also with Jo Van Fleet, J.D. Cannon, Lou Antonio, Robert Drivas, and Strother Martin. **Director**—Stuart Rosenberg. **(PG) Academy Award**—Kennedy, best supporting actor. **Nominations**—Newman, best actor; Donn Pearce and Frank R. Pierson, best screenplay based on material from another medium.

126 minutes

COONSKIN (1975)

★★½

This movie is a blend of live action and animation from director Ralph Bakshi, who produced the X-rated feature cartoons *Heavy Traffic* and *Fritz the Cat*. *Coonskin* is about three black characters who leave the South for Harlem and try to take over the rackets. Though Bakshi intended to make a statement against racism, the film has provoked denunciations from the Congress of Racial Equality and other black organizations for portraying blacks as stereotypes. The voices of Barry White, Scatman Crothers, and Charles Gordone are used. **(R)** *83 minutes*

COP (1988)

★★

James Woods
Lesley Ann Warren

Woods stars as a stressed-out Los Angeles police detective obsessed with capturing a serial killer. His neurotic state causes him to make several mistakes in judgment, which do not escape the notice of his superiors. Despite the presence of Woods, who once again demonstrates his skill at portraying edgy, hard-boiled characters, this police tale is convoluted and unbelievable. The film concludes with a one-on-one showdown between Woods and the killer, which could have been plucked from a hundred other cop thrillers. Supporting performers include Charles Durning, Raymond J. Barry and Charles Haid. **Director**—James B. Harris. **(R)**

110 minutes

CORNBREAD, EARL AND ME (1975)

★★★

Moses Gunn
Bernie Casey
Rosalind Cash

A sensitive story about a college-bound black basketball star, who is accidentally killed by the police. This urban tragedy and courtroom drama is a far cry from the typical black exploitation film. However, it's flawed by uneven directing. Also with Madge Sinclair, Keith Wilkes, and Tierre Turner. **Director**—Joe Manduke. **(PG)** *95 minutes*

CORVETTE SUMMER (1978)

★★

Mark Hamill
Annie Potts
Eugene Roche

Hamill of *Star Wars* fame plays a naive high-school boy in love with a flashy car and an equally flashy would-be hooker, played by Potts. This unusual, breezy, and innocuous film is primarily aimed at teen audiences. Director Matthew Robbins keeps the action moving along, but the picture often stumbles over too much silliness. Also with Kim Milford and Richard McKenzie. **(PG)**

105 minutes

THE COTTON CLUB (1984)

★★★

Richard Gere
Gregory Hines

A lavish, slick blend of a 1930s gangster saga and Hollywood musical that lacks a traditional straightforward narrative. This uneven period piece revolves around the popular Harlem nightclub that featured famous black entertainers onstage but admitted only whites as patrons. A $47 million budget provides dazzling sets and lively dance numbers. The look is impressive, but its self-conscious attempt to comment on myth and movies will be lost on the average viewer. The blend of actual historical persons with fictional characters (à la novelist E.L. Doctorow) is intriguing. Gere, as a trumpet player, and Diane Lane, as a gangster's moll, are miscast; but James Remar as Dutch Schultz, Bob Hoskins as Owney Madden, and Hines as an ambitious dancer are excellent. **Director**—Francis Coppola. **(R)**

127 minutes

THE COUCH TRIP (1988)

★★

Dan Aykroyd
Walter Matthau

A few entertaining sight gags enliven this otherwise dull farce about a mental patient who becomes a hit radio therapist in Beverly Hills. Aykroyd is well cast as the air waves shrink whose

(Continued)

(Continued)

frank and outrageous advice sends the ratings soaring. Matthau costars as a loony hustler who is on to Aykroyd's true identity. Not particularly well written or clever, the film quickly becomes bogged down in clumsy slapstick gags and too many broadly sketched characters. Also with Charles Grodin, Donna Dixon, Mary Gross, and Arye Gross. **Director**—Michael Ritchie. **(R)** *98 minutes*

COUNTRY (1984)

★★★

Jessica Lange
Sam Shepard

Sam Shepard and Jessica Lange fight to save their home in Country.

An embattled Iowa farm family fights a faceless government bureaucracy to save their land. The powerful and poignant story emphasizes the courage, integrity, and grit of rural Americans. And it carries a strong political message. Lange and Shepard provide believable and forceful performances as farmer and farm wife whose way of life is on the brink of bankruptcy. Also with Wilford Brimley and Matt Clark. **Director**—Richard Pearce. **(PG) Academy Award Nomination**—Lange, best actress. *108 minutes*

THE COUNTRY GIRL (1954)

★★★★

Bing Crosby
Grace Kelly

Fantastic performances by Crosby and Kelly enhance this absorbing drama about an alcoholic singer trying to make a comeback. When Crosby, formerly feeling sorry for himself, is stimulated to get back on his feet, wife Kelly demonstrates her support. The film, which is adapted from the play by Clifford Odets, features some songs by Ira Gershwin and Harold Arlen. Also with William Holden, Anthony Ross, and Gene Reynolds. **Director**—George Seaton. **Academy Awards**—Kelly, best actress; Seaton, screenplay. **Nominations**—best picture; Seaton, best director; Crosby, best actor; John F. Warren, cinematography. *104 minutes b&w*

COUP DE TORCHON (1981)

★★

Philippe Noiret
Isabelle Huppert
Stephane Audran

Philippe Noiret and Isabelle Huppert in Coup de Torchon.

Bertrand Tavernier's uneven account of French colonists in Africa just prior to World War II partly intrigues but mostly confuses. The strange, meandering story centers on a timid, sloppy village police chief (Noiret) who suddenly rebels by bumping off various unsavory citizens. Noiret's character is clearly colorful, but the haphazard progress of events rarely keeps him in proper focus. Originally filmed in French. Available on videotape under its English-language title *Clean Slate.* **(No MPAA rating)** *128 minutes*

COUPE DE VILLE (1990)

★★ ®

Daniel Stern
Arye Gross
Patrick Dempsey

Three feuding brothers drive a powder-blue 1954 Cadillac from Detroit to Miami at their father's request. By the trip's end, they have established a meaningful relationship based on mutual love and respect. As in most road movies, the characters embark on an emotional journey to maturity as well as a physical journey to a specific destination. The familiar symbolism of the road as well as the predictable outcome make this film a trite reworking of conventional material. Set in 1963, the film uses nostalgia to make the story more precious than it really is. Serious filmgoers will appreciate director Joe Roth's use of the wide-screen format, which effectively places all three brothers in the same frame at once to better depict their interaction. Also with Annabeth Gish, Rita Taggart, Alan Arkin, and Joseph Bologna. **(PG-13)** *99 minutes*

COURAGE MOUNTAIN (1990)

★★ ®

Juliette Caton
Charlie Sheen
Leslie Caron

This small, low-key film features the further adventures of Heidi (Caton), the spunky Alpine heroine. The story takes place during World War I, when Heidi's education in Italy is interrupted by the war. Heidi is depicted as more mature in this film than in previous adventures, and the storyline involves an action-filled plot. The real adventure begins when the Swiss lass and her friends are confined to a terrible orphanage and rescued by her stalwart boyfriend (Sheen). Though the Heidi saga has been updated for later generations, the material remains pedestrian throughout. A considerable waste of Caron's talents and Sheen's attractive presence. **Director**—Christopher Leitch. **(PG)** *92 minutes*

THE COURT JESTER (1956)

★★★★

Danny Kaye
Glynis Johns
Basil Rathbone

Kaye is a knockout in this superb, made-to-order comedy set in medieval times. The delightful romp, which spoofs costume movies, has Kaye posing as a jester to infiltrate a plot against the king. There are all sorts of effective comic situations, decorated with delightful tunes and well-staged action. The fine supporting cast includes Angela Lansbury, Mildred Natwick, Cecil Parker, Edward Ashley, and Ro-

® *This movie available with closed captions for the hearing impaired.*

bert Middleton. **Directors**—Norman Panama and Melvin Frank.
101 minutes

THE COURT MARTIAL OF BILLY MITCHELL (1955)

Gary Cooper
Rod Steiger
Ralph Bellamy

Straightforward but slow-paced account of the prophetic American general who accused his superiors of being unprepared for invasion and was subsequently court-martialed. His warning came almost two decades prior to the sneak attack on Pearl Harbor. Cooper is convincing in the title role. The film concludes effectively in a stirring courtroom sequence. Also with Charles Bickford, Elizabeth Montgomery, Fred Clark, and Darren McGavin. **Director**—Otto Preminger. **Academy Award Nomination**—Milton Spirling and Emmett Lavery, story and screenplay.
100 minutes

THE COURTSHIP OF EDDIE'S FATHER (1963)

Glenn Ford
Ronny Howard
Shirley Jones

Ronny Howard and Glenn Ford in The Courtship of Eddie's Father.

A cute, teary-eyed comedy that is handled well for this sort of material. Ford plays the title role of a man who loses his wife. His young son plays cupid so that the family can have a new mom. There's just the right measure of humor and sentimentality to maintain the film's charming aspects most of the way through. Other cast members include Stella Stevens and Dina Merrill. **Director**—Vincente Minnelli. *117 minutes*

COUSIN, COUSINE (1975)

Marie-Christine Barrault
Victor Lanoux

This pleasant romantic comedy about French social mores, directed by Jean-Charles Tàcchella, stops a step or two short of turning into a farce. Barrault and Lanoux turn in brilliant performances as cousins—by marriage—who first become friends and eventually fall in love. They finally have an affair when all their friends and relatives assume they are doing just that. Also with Marie-France Pisier, Guy Marchand, Ginette Garcin, and Sybil Maas. Originally filmed in French. **(No MPAA rating) Academy Award Nominations**—Barrault, best actress; Tacchella and Daniele Thompson, best screenplay written directly for the screen.
95 minutes

COUSINS (1989)

Isabella Rossellini
Ted Danson
Sean Young
William Petersen

Americanized version of the popular 1976 French comedy *Cousin, Cousine.* This tale of adultery among two married couples fails to capture the buoyant spirit of the initial French effort. Instead, there's dull dialogue and a contrived screenplay. Danson (of TV's *Cheers*) and Rossellini star as the most noticeable pair of illicit lovers, while Young and Petersen carry on their own affair. Structured around a series of family events, the film's episodic nature makes for a pleasant, fluid pace. Also with Lloyd Bridges, Keith Coogan, and Norma Aleandro. **Director**—Joel Schumacher. **(PG-13)** *111 minutes*

COVER GIRL (1944)

 ★★★

Rita Hayworth
Gene Kelly

A lively, toe-tapping musical with the spectacular dancing of Kelly and the memorable music of Jerome Kern. Hayworth stars as a chorus girl, who breaks out of the chorus line to become a magazine cover model. That's it for the simple plot. The strengths here are Kelly's solo numbers and a fine supporting role by Eve Arden as a wisecracking secretary. The score includes "Long Ago and Far Away." Also with Phil Silvers, Lee Bowman, Jinx Falkenburg, Otto Kruger, and Ed Brophy. **Director**—Charles Vidor. *107 minutes*

COWBOY (1958)

Jack Lemmon
Glenn Ford

Generally pleasant western yarn, based on *On the Trail,* the autobiography of Frank Harris. It concerns a lad who becomes a cowboy and then discovers it's not the glamorous life he envisioned. Lemmon plays Harris, and Ford stars as his trail boss. Also with Anna Kashfi, Brian Donlevy, Dick York, Richard Jaeckel, and King Donovan. **Director**—Delmer Daves. *92 minutes*

THE COWBOYS (1972)

 ★★1/2

John Wayne
Roscoe Lee Browne

Wayne stars in this unorthodox and violent western, as a cattleman who is forced to recruit 11 schoolboys for his roundup after his regular drovers quit. The youngsters become killers to revenge the death of their boss. Wayne is a commanding presence as always, but he has fared better with this genre. Also with Bruce Dern, Colleen Dewhurst, and Slim Pickens. **Director**—Mark Rydell. **(PG)** *128 minutes*

CRACKERS (1984)

Donald Sutherland
Sean Penn

Sean Penn, Larry Riley, and Donald Sutherland are safecrackers in Crackers.

(Continued)

(Continued)

An occasionally amusing caper comedy by director Louis Malle *(Atlantic City)* based on the Italian classic *Big Deal on Madonna Street*. Sutherland plays an unemployed electrician who leads a group of misfits to burglarize a seedy San Francisco pawn shop. A few characters stand out, but Malle fails to sustain sufficient energy and the film concludes on an innocuous, stale note. Also stars Larry Riley and Jack Warden. **(PG)**

92 minutes

CRAZY PEOPLE (1990)

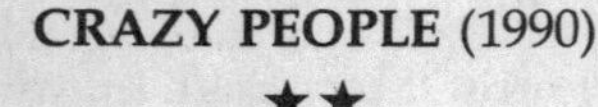

★★

Dudley Moore
Daryl Hannah

In this dull satire of the high-powered world of advertising, the premise has potential, but the execution falters. When a burned-out copywriter (Moore) cooks up several painfully honest ad campaigns (United Airlines: "Most of our passengers get there alive"), he's packed off to a mental hospital. There, he falls in love with a sweet, shy patient (Hannah) and settles down to a calmer existence. When his advertising slogans are accidentally released, they prove to be wildly successful with the public. While the parody of advertising provides some wicked moments of humor, the saccharine romance undermines the satirical tone and slows the film down. Also with Paul Reiser, Mercedes Ruehl, J.T. Walsh, Dick Cusack, and Alan North. **Director**—Tony Bill. **(R)**

92 minutes

CREATOR (1985)

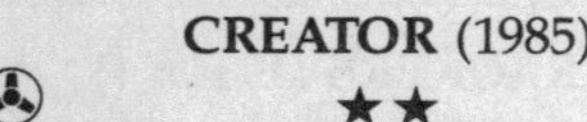

★★

Peter O'Toole

Peter O'Toole tries an experiment with Mariel Hemingway in Creator.

O'Toole is likable as an eccentric biology professor obsessed with cloning his wife who died some 30 years ago. But this peculiar film is hardly as pleasing when it abruptly shifts gears to a love story and then to a tearjerker. All these meandering elements appear out of sync and lead to frustration. Vincent Spano, Mariel Hemingway, and Virginia Madsen costar. **Director**—Ivan Passer. **(R)** *107 minutes*

THE CREATURE FROM THE BLACK LAGOON (1954)

★★★

Richard Carlson
Julie Adams
Richard Denning

Surprisingly effective sci-fi thriller—originally a 3-D movie—about some explorers who discover a half-man/half-fish monster, which emerges from a lagoon adjacent to the Amazon River. This B-movie is rife with clichés and hokey horror gimmicks, but it delivers plenty of chills. Sequels include *Revenge of the Creature* and *The Creature Walks Among Us.* Also with Antonio Moreno, Nestor Paiva, and Ricou Browning. **Director**—Jack Arnold. **(G)**

79 minutes b&w

CREEPSHOW (1982)

★★

Hal Holbrook
Leslie Nielsen
E.G. Marshall

Director George Romero *(Night of the Living Dead)* and screenwriter Stephen King *(The Shining)* present a mixed bag of five horror vignettes. An intriguing moment surfaces occasionally, but for the most part the proceedings creep along, and there's an underlying tone of mild humor. Perhaps the best tale of the lot concerns a nasty patriarch, murdered by his relatives, who returns from a moldy grave to claim his piece of Father's Day cake. **(R)** *129 minutes*

CREEPSHOW 2 (1987)

★1/2

Lois Chiles
George Kennedy
Dorothy Lamour

This anthology of three Stephen King horror stories is patterned after the original *Creepshow.* Unfortunately, neither film has enough horrifying moments to live up to the title. This time only one of the vignettes is at all effective: A deadly oil slick is on the loose devouring teenagers. Other tales include that of a cigar-store Indian who seeks revenge for murder; the final story features a hitchhiker who is struck down by a frantic woman driver but returns to settle the score. Despite the script by veteran horror director George Romero, the stories are juvenile and flat. Page Hannah, Domenick John, and makeup artist Tom Savini are also in the cast. King makes a cameo appearance as a truck driver. **Director**—Michael Gornick. **(R)** *89 minutes*

CRIES AND WHISPERS (1972)

★★★

Liv Ullmann
Ingrid Thulin
Harriet Andersson
Kari Sylwan

Ingmar Bergman's highly charged drama about a turn-of-the-century young woman (Andersson) who's dying of cancer, and the sisters (Thulin, Ullmann) and servant (Sylwan) who attend the painful death vigil. Needless to say, this is heavy material, from the master of serious, meaningful drama, and the New York Film Critics voted it the year's best picture. Others may prefer Bergman's earlier, somewhat less harrowing works; those who could live without Bergman altogether will probably find this interminable, indulgent masochism. Whatever your view, plenty is attempted here, and it's certainly worth a look. Sven Nykvist's cinematography won an Oscar. Erland Josephson costars. Music by Chopin and Bach. Originally filmed in Swedish. **Academy Award Nominations**—best picture; Bergman, best director and best story and screenplay based on factual material not previously published. **(R)** *94 minutes*

CRIMES AND MISDEMEANORS (1989)

★★★1/2

Martin Landau
Anjelica Huston
Woody Allen
Mia Farrow
Alan Alda

Allen deftly combines tragedy and comedy to make his observations about

Joanna Gleason and Alan Alda in Crimes and Misdemeanors.

life's moral choices in this well-crafted film. The serious storyline involves a prominent ophthalmologist (Landau) who arranges the murder of his mistress (Huston) after she threatens to expose their affair to his wife. The lighter side involves Allen as a serious documentary filmmaker who competes with a shallow but wealthy television producer for the affections of a production assistant (Farrow). Though the two stories are separate, the lives of the characters intertwine at various social functions. An impressive ensemble cast effectively handles the somber, thought-provoking material. Allen wrote, directed, and starred in this dark tale in which nobody gets what they want or deserve. Also with Jerry Orbach, Joanna Gleason, Jenny Nichols, Sam Waterston, Claire Bloom, and Caroline Aaron. **(PG-13) Academy Award Nominations**—Allen, best director and best original screenplay; Landau, best supporting actor. *104 minutes*

CRIMES OF PASSION (1984)

★½

Kathleen Turner
Anthony Perkins

It looks like a sex exploitation film trying hard to be brutally incisive. It's merely awful. Turner plays a streetwalker who is a career woman during the day. She's stalked by a minister (Perkins) who is really a lunatic. There is something here to repel everyone: sledgehammer obscenities and enough embarrassing moral posturing to put voyeurs to sleep. An X-rated version is available on videotape. **Director**—Ken Russell. **(R)** *102 minutes*

CRIMES OF THE HEART (1986)

★★½

Sissy Spacek
Diane Keaton
Jessica Lange

Keaton, Lange, and Spacek knock themselves out in this distorted screen version of Beth Henley's Pulitzer Prize-winning play. The story involves the comic yet tragic events in the lives of three eccentric sisters from an oddball Southern family. Though the actresses interpret their roles with the right combination of quirky mannerisms and sensitivity, the lack of a climactic event or revelation dissipates the drama. This Southern Gothic story, with its emphasis on scandal and hidden family secrets, nevertheless has an optimistic conclusion. Tess Harper steals a few scenes as a busybody cousin who lives next door. Also with Sam Shepard and Hurd Hatfield. **Director**—Bruce Beresford. **(PG–13) Academy Award Nominations**—Spacek, best actress; Harper, best supporting actress; Henley, best screenplay based on material from another medium. *105 minutes*

THE CRIMINAL CODE (1931)

★★★

Walter Huston
Boris Karloff

Constance Cummings and Walter Huston in The Criminal Code.

Good, tough prison picture, with especially fine work by director Howard Hawks and star Huston. Huston plays a district attorney turned warden, who's not exactly Mr. Popularity, running a prison filled with many inmates he had helped send up. He's gutsy, though, and well meaning; he walks unarmed among a crowd of prisoners on the verge of rioting and he tries to help a convict who's been unjustly sentenced. The film also marked the first major success for Karloff (as a prisoner), who catapulted to stardom later that year in *Frankenstein*. Phillips Holmes and Constance Cummings costar. **Academy Award Nomination**—Seton Miller and Fred Niblo, Jr., adaptation.
97 minutes b&w

CRIMINAL LAW (1989)

 ★★½

Gary Oldman
Kevin Bacon

Oldman stands out as a determined defense lawyer who successfully frees a murder suspect only to worry later that his client (Bacon) may indeed be a vicious serial killer. The drama gets off to a promising start but eventually becomes ridiculous. The plot is finally thrown off course when an anti-abortion issue surfaces. Karen Young, Joe Don Baker, and Tess Harper costar. **Director**—Martin Campbell. **(R)**
112 minutes

CRISS CROSS (1948)

 ★★★

Burt Lancaster
Yvonne De Carlo
Dan Duryea

Yvonne De Carlo and Burt Lancaster scheme their way to disaster in Criss Cross.

A brooding, suspenseful cops-and-robbers film about an armored-car guard who gets mixed up in a heist and is double-crossed by his ex-wife and friends. Lancaster does a commendable job, and Duryea plays a villain extraordinaire who is out to get Lancaster. Also with Stephen McNally, Richard Long, and Alan Napier. **Director**—Robert Siodmak. *87 minutes b&w*

CRITICAL CONDITION (1987)

 ★★

Richard Pryor
Ruben Blades

Pryor fractures a few funny bones as a small-time con artist who masquerades

(Continued)

(Continued)
as an emergency room physician. There are a few hilarious scenes in the film, as when Pryor tries to set a broken leg or when he attempts to examine a young sexy female, but most of the jokes fall flat thereafter and the story turns silly. Is there a script doctor in the house? Also with Rachel Ticotin. **Director**—Michael Apted. **(R)** *100 minutes*

CRITIC'S CHOICE (1963)

Bob Hope
Lucille Ball
Marilyn Maxwell

Hope plays a hard-nosed drama critic, whose wife, played by Ball, writes a play. Their marriage suffers after he gives the play an unflattering review. This screen adaptation of Ira Levin's Broadway play can't be saved by such talented performers, so the film comes off as an uneven vehicle. Some of the supporting players have better moments than the leads. Also with Rip Torn, Jim Backus, and Marie Windsor. **Director**—Don Weis. *100 minutes*

CRITTERS (1986)

Dee Wallace Stone
Billy Green Bush
Scott Grimes

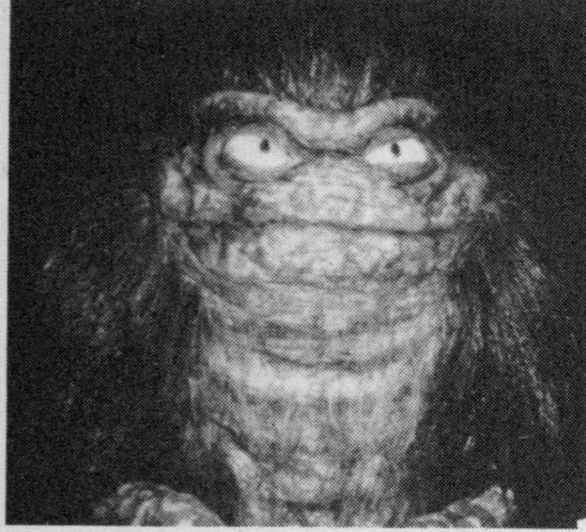

Hearty appetite: One of the Critters *thinks you look good enough to eat.*

Nasty creatures that resemble vicious porcupines drop in from outer space and harass a Kansas farming community. The sinister critters also act cute and comical on occasions—a strong resemblance to *Gremlins*. However, this film does not have the appeal of that popular feature. Script, dialogue, and direction don't measure up. **Director**—Stephen Herek. **(PG-13)** *86 minutes*

CRITTERS 2 (1988)

Scott Grimes
Liane Curtis
Don Opper

Those ravenous "space porcupines" from the original *Critters* return to the small town of Grover's Bend for more silly mischief. After eating a few unsavory people and engaging in a food fight, the furry creatures are blasted into oblivion by bounty hunters toting ray guns. Though virtually a carbon copy of the first film, this sequel does contain some darkly humorous moments satirizing small-town life. Grimes and Opper reprise their roles from the original film. Barry Corbin and Tom Hodges are also in the cast. **Director**—Mick Garris. **(PG-13)** *86 minutes*

"CROCODILE" DUNDEE (1986)

Paul Hogan
Linda Kozlowski

Australian actor Hogan, in the title role, enlivens this low-key romantic comedy with a generous blend of warmth and charm. He plays a legendary adventurer—a latter-day "natural man"—who comes to Manhattan and finds the concrete jungle as perilous as the outback. The initial portion of the film is set Down Under, with the action and humor picking up when the celebrated croc hunter takes on Gotham. Kozlowski costars as the reporter who discovers him. **Director**—Peter Faiman. **(PG–13) Academy Award Nomination**—Hogan, Ken Shadie, and John Cornell, best screenplay written directly for the screen.
102 minutes

"CROCODILE" DUNDEE II (1988)

★★½

Paul Hogan
Linda Kozlowski

Hogan reprises his role as the charming and resourceful Australian, Mick "Crocodile" Dundee, in this low-key sequel. The rugged hunter from the outback again outwits a variety of big-city types, including a vicious drug czar who kidnaps Dundee's "mate," Sue (Kozlowski). The adventure then shifts Down Under, where Dundee terrorizes the drug dealers with his native cunning. Though Hogan is an undeniably appealing personality, this sequel lacks the energy necessary for an adventure film, even a humorous one. Also, Kozlowski's role has been undermined this time, with her character reduced to that of a damsel in distress. The script was written by Hogan and his son, Brett Hogan. Also with John Meillon, Charles Dutton, and Hechter Ubarry. **Director**—John Cornell. **(PG)**
110 minutes

CROMWELL (1970)

★★

Richard Harris
Alec Guinness
Robert Morley

A good-looking, but ponderous, historical drama set at the time of Britain's 17th-century civil war and the rise to power of Oliver Cromwell, who became a revolutionary and then a dictator. The events include the execution of Charles I and some notable battle scenes. Harris handles the title role unconvincingly, while Guinness plays an acceptable King Charles. This subject may be tough to grasp in some school textbooks, but you don't expect the same treatment on the screen. Supporting players include Frank Finlay, Dorothy Tutin, and Patrick Magee. **Director**—Ken Hughes. **(G)** *140 minutes*

CROSS CREEK (1983)

★★½

Mary Steenburgen
Rip Torn
Alfre Woodard

The memoirs of author Marjorie Kinnan Rawlings *(The Yearling)*, who lived a remote life in the Florida backwoods, are set to film. Director Martin Ritt successfully touches on the courage, stamina, and humanity of the area inhabitants. Yet the syrupy, sentimental story is in dire need of drama and urgency. Steenburgen turns in a decent portrayal of the determined authoress. Torn, Woodard, and Dana Hill are effective in supporting roles. **(PG) Academy Award Nominations**—Torn, best supporting actor; Woodard, best supporting actress; Leonard Rosenman, best original score. *122 minutes*

This movie available with closed captions for the hearing impaired.

CROSSED SWORDS
See The Prince and the Pauper

CROSSFIRE (1947)
★★★½

Robert Young
Robert Mitchum
Robert Ryan

A taut, exciting melodrama about an unhinged, bigoted soldier who murders a Jew in a New York City hotel and is pursued by the police. This landmark film is one of the first to deal so directly with racial prejudice. The film was shot mostly at night, and this technique contributes to its moody atmosphere. Fine performances are given by a top cast that also includes Gloria Grahame, Paul Kelly, Sam Levene, Jacqueline White, and Steve Brodie. **Director**—Edward Dmytryk. **Academy Award Nominations**—best picture; Dmytryk, best director; Ryan, best supporting actor; Grahame, best supporting actress; John Paxton, screenplay. *86 minutes b&w*

CROSSING DELANCEY (1988)
★★★

Amy Irving
Peter Riegert

Amy Irving isn't taken in by Jeroen Krabbé's smooth-talking charm in Crossing Delancey.

Irving stars as a sophisticated single woman in New York City looking for companionship. The woman's grandmother arranges a love affair with the help of a marriage broker, and Irving ends up rejecting a smooth-talking novelist for a solid and sincere pickle merchant (Riegert). The story projects warmth, pathos, and ethnic charm. Also with Reizl Bozyk, Jeroen Krabbe, and Sylvia Miles. **Director**—Joan Micklin Silver. **(PG)** *97 minutes*

CROSS MY HEART (1987)
★★

Martin Short
Annette O'Toole

Annette O'Toole and Martin Short get cozy in Cross My Heart.

Short and O'Toole star in this leaden romantic comedy with a simplistic message that calls for honest relationships. The story revolves around the details of that all-important third date. He tries to hide his unstable financial situation, while she puts off telling him about her seven-year-old daughter. The compression of the story into the time frame of one evening is an intriguing device, but the humor gets lost in the endless arguments and cute conversations. Coscripted by veteran comedy writer Gail Parent. Also with Paul Reiser and Joanna Kerns. **Director**—Armyan Bernstein. **(R)** *96 minutes*

CROSS OF IRON (1977)
★★

James Coburn
Maximilian Schell
James Mason

German officer James Coburn leads his men through battle in Cross of Iron.

Sam Peckinpah's first World War II movie is a puffed-up cliché about a small detachment of German soldiers fighting on the Russian front. Peckinpah, as can be expected, trowels on heavy doses of gore and violence—some of it in slow motion—while he skips lightly over plot, dialogue, and acting. There are dull and uneven performances from Coburn, Schell, and Mason. The film lasts two hours, which is more than enough time to inflict battle fatigue on any audience. Also with David Warner, Senta Berger, and Klaus Lowitsch. **(R)** *120 minutes*

CROSSROADS (1986)
★★½

Ralph Macchio
Joe Seneca

A bluesy walk to the Crossroads *with Ralph Macchio.*

Interesting film odyssey about a teenager (Macchio) who travels to Mississippi with an ancient, once-famous blues singer (Seneca). The kid hopes the old man will teach him a long-lost blues tune, which he will record and thereby become famous. The film includes their adventures with a pretty runaway girl (Jami Gertz), and a subplot about the old-timer's pact with the Devil. The combination of diverse plot elements makes for an uneven narrative, and some viewers may find it difficult to relate to the characters, but Seneca's performance and the blues music by Ry Cooder make the film worth viewing. **Director**—Walter Hill. **(R)** *98 minutes*

THE CROWD ROARS (1932)
★★★

James Cagney
Joan Blondell

Few directors could capture the world of men who lead dangerous lives as

(Continued)

This movie available on videotape and/or disc.

(Continued)
well as Howard Hawks. Here that world is auto racing, with Cagney (one year after *Public Enemy*) starring as a top racer whose obsession with preventing his doting younger brother from entering the profession results in the accidental racetrack death of a buddy. After half a century in the can, it can still rev up audiences. Eric Linden, Ann Dvorak, Guy Kibbee, Frank McHugh, and Regis Toomey costar.
85 minutes b&w

THE CRUEL SEA (1953)

★★★★

Jack Hawkins
Donald Sinden
Stanley Baker

A compelling screen adaptation of Nicholas Monsarrat's best-selling novel about the rigors aboard a British corvette in the North Atlantic during World War II. The taut drama depicts the dangers of encountering convoy-hunting Nazi subs as well as dealing with harsh weather. There are strong characterizations of the officers and men, too. Also with John Stratton, Denholm Elliott, John Warner, and Bruce Seton. **Director**—Charles Frend. **Academy Award Nomination**—Eric Ambler, screenplay. *121 minutes b&w*

CRUISING (1980)

★★1/2

Al Pacino
Paul Sorvino
Karen Allen

Al Pacino enters New York's seedy night world in Cruising.

It's hard to tell what director William Friedkin *(The Exorcist; The French Connection)* is driving at in this grim tour of New York City's freaky leather bars. Pacino plays a young detective who infiltrates this bizarre fringe of the homosexual world to flush out a killer, and whose own sexual identity becomes blurred in the process. It's strong, disturbing, and ultimately confusing material, although Pacino is great in the starring role. Also with Richard Cox and Don Scardino. **(R)**
106 minutes

CRY-BABY (1990)

★★1/2

Johnny Depp
Amy Locane
Ricki Lake
Traci Lords

Kim McGuir, Darren E. Burrows, Johnny Depp, Ricki Lake, and Traci Lords in Cry-Baby.

Director John Waters, who specializes in campy cult films, parodies the 1950s era in this oddball musical comedy. Depp, the teen heartthrob from television's *21 Jump Street,* satirizes his own image in his role as a delinquent in pursuit of a square high-school sweetie, played by Locane. Waters fashions some fabulous, highly stylized rock 'n' roll song-and-dance routines, which echo the era without duplicating it. He seems to be as interested in America's nostalgic longing for this time period as he is the era itself. As is typical for Waters' films, the offbeat cast includes everyone from Patty Hearst to David Nelson. **(PG-13)** *85 minutes*

CRY FREEDOM (1987)

★★★

Denzel Washington
Kevin Kline

Director Richard Attenborough offers a powerful statement in this epic drama about the injustices and brutality of South Africa's apartheid. The film focuses on the true story of the charismatic black activist, Stephen Biko, who died in police custody. The drama is told through the eyes of Donald Woods, a liberal white editor who smuggled the details of Biko's struggle and subsequent murder out of South Africa. The film's flaw is its emphasis on Woods' story during the last hour of the film at the expense of Biko's. Washington is moving as the martyred black leader and Kline fares well as the courageous editor. The film's African-flavored musical score by George Fenton and Jonas Gwangwa received an Oscar nomination. Also with Penelope Wilton, Kevin McNally, John Thaw, and Timothy West. **(PG) Academy Award Nomination**—Washington, best supporting actor. *155 minutes*

CRY IN THE DARK (1988)

★★★1/2

Meryl Streep
Sam Neill

Meryl Streep with a nine-week-old daughter in Cry in the Dark.

A sensational Australian murder case is recounted in vivid detail under Fred Schepisi's brilliant direction. Based on a true story, this searing drama emerges as a strong indictment of hysterical public perceptions, bloodthirsty media, and sloppy forensic investigation. Streep, speaking with a convincing Aussie accent, is superb as the mother whose infant is found missing and presumed killed by a dingo (wild dog). Her tragedy is compounded when she is charged with murder. Also with Charles Tinqwell, Bruce Myles, and Dennis

Miller. **(PG-13) Academy Award Nomination**—Streep, best actress. *121 minutes*

CRY TERROR (1958)

★★★

James Mason
Rod Steiger
Inger Stevens

Mason and Steiger are good in this taut drama about a tricky extortion scheme, which involves a kidnapping. Steiger stars as a crafty criminal who forces Mason, an electronics expert, to aid in the caper. Stevens plays Mason's wife. New York City locations add to the tense atmosphere. Also with Angie Dickinson, Jack Klugman, Neville Brand, and Jack Kruschen. **Director**—Andrew Stone. *96 minutes b&w*

CRY, THE BELOVED COUNTRY (1951)

★★★

Canada Lee
Sidney Poitier

Crisp drama and tense moments highlight this screen version of Alan Paton's novel about apartheid in South Africa. A black preacher travels to the city, where he finds the black population living in dreadful poverty. This vivid account of the conditions separating the races is treated with candor and intelligence. The fine cast also includes Charles Carson, Geoffrey Keen, Charles McRae, and Joyce Carey. Some television prints are cut to 96 minutes. **Director**—Zoltan Korda. *111 minutes b&w*

CUBA (1979)

✇ ★★★

Sean Connery
Brooke Adams
Chris Sarandon

On the eve of Fidel Castro's seizure of power from the corrupt Batista regime, a British mercenery (Connery) travels to Cuba to advise the faltering government troops. His rapid disillusionment with his employers is complicated by his renewed involvement with an old flame (Adams), whose family is part of the spoiled ruling class that the insurgents have vowed to overthrow. Connery is effectively thoughtful and subdued; Sarandon is notable as Adams' hopelessly self-centered husband. The film's deceptively pastel imagery and preoccupation with the diseased hearts and minds of the wealthy is fascinating. The solid supporting cast includes Hector Elizondo, Denholm Elliott, Jack Weston, and Martin Balsam. **Director**—Richard Lester. **(R)** *121 minutes*

CUJO (1983)

✇ ★½

Dee Wallace
Daniel Hugh Kelly

Manipulative, high-pitched horror yarn, based on Stephen King's novel about a gentle St. Bernard who becomes rabid and viciously attacks humans. The uninspired plot involves a middle-class couple, and more than half the film dwells on their dull domestic problems. Finally, the snarling dog goes into action. He traps the mother and her child in their stalled car, and the suspense picks up. But Cujo's whipped-cream makeup is more likely to leave you laughing than gasping. **Director**—Lewis Teague. **(R)** *97 minutes*

CUL-DE-SAC (1966)

★★★

Lionel Stander
Donald Pleasence
Jack MacGowran

Roman Polanski's terse direction propels this black comedy, which is set on a lonely island. Two fugitive gangsters hide out in a rambling castle and terrorize the inhabitants, a fey middle-aged man and his gorgeous wife. There are some bland moments, but the film works well overall. Also with Françoise Dorleac, Willliam Franklyn, and Jacqueline Bissett. *111 minutes b&w*

THE CURSE OF FRANKENSTEIN (1957)

✇ ★★½

Peter Cushing
Christopher Lee

Another chapter in the tale of the famous monster, with Cushing and Lee in the key roles. This version is more gory than earlier depictions, thus sacrificing some wit and stylish atmosphere. This is the first of Hammer Films' groundbreaking series of horror films, however, and is noteworthy for breathing new life into the Frankenstein tale. Also with Hazel Court, Robert Urquhart, and Valerie Gaunt. **Director**—Terence Fisher. *83 minutes*

THE CURSE OF THE PINK PANTHER (1983)

✇ ★★

Ted Wass
Herbert Lom

Ted Wass shows off his best gal in The Curse of the Pink Panther.

A Pink Panther film without the great Peter Sellers is cursed, indeed. Wass plays the world's worst detective, from New York City, recruited to find the long lost Inspector Clouseau. Blake Edwards' direction and script offer funny situations, but Wass is no match for the legend. In fact, he's hardly a comic actor at all. As usual, Chief Inspector Dreyfus (Lom) gets his drubbing. Also with Robert Wagner and David Niven in his final film role. **(PG)** *110 minutes*

CUTTER'S WAY (1981)

✇ ★★

Jeff Bridges
John Heard

Bridges and Heard star in this peculiar murder mystery, which expends considerable energy and ends up nowhere. Bridges is Bone, a young freewheeling southern Californian, who is falsely accused of murdering a high-school girl. Heard plays Cutter, a slightly loony Vietnam vet, who works up an absurd scheme to clear Bone. The entire screenplay and dialogue are absurd as well, and the film bogs down in utter confusion. Also with Lisa Eichhorn, Ann Dusenberry, and Stephen Elliott. **Director**—Ivan Passer. **(R)** *109 minutes*

CYBORG (1989)

★1/2

Jean Claude Van Damme

A confusing, futuristic action-adventure inspired by the *Mad Max* series. Martial arts expert Jean Claude Van Damme helps a beautiful female cyborg save a devastated planet. The usual carnage takes place in an alternatively grim and silly atmosphere. Van Damme's performance is sluggish, and the direction and dialogue are thin. Deborah Richter and Vincent Klyn also star. **Director**—Albert Pyun. **(R)**

96 minutes

CYRANO DE BERGERAC (1950)

★★★★

José Ferrer
Mala Powers

An exceptional and moving performance by Ferrer in the title role says it all, in this film version of Edmond Rostand's classic love story, which is set in the 17th century. Cyrano is the poet with the long nose who writes tender love letters to a beautiful lady for his friend. However, Cyrano genuinely loves the woman, too. Powers plays the Lady Roxanne. Also with William Prince and Morris Carnovsky. **Director**—Michael Gordon. **Academy Award**—Ferrer, best actor.

112 minutes b&w

D

DAD (1989)

★★

Jack Lemmon
Ted Danson
Olympia Dukakis

Ted Danson shows Jack Lemmon how to do household chores in Dad.

Lemmon's power as an actor is stifled in this emotionally manipulative comedy/drama in which he plays an octogenarian who patches up a relationship with his son, played by Danson of television's *Cheers*. The excessively sentimental film, which was heavily influenced by *On Golden Pond*, lapses into a series of trite events involving various family crises. Director Gary David Goldberg, more at home with TV sitcoms, fails to relate the material to the big screen. Steven Speilberg served as executive producer on the film, continuing his fixation on stories about father figures. Also with Kathy Baker, Kevin Spacey, Ethan Hawke, Zakes Mokae, and J.T. Walsh. **(PG) Academy Award Nomination**—Ken Diaz, Dick Smith, and Greg Nelson, makeup.

117 minutes

DADDY LONG LEGS (1955)

★★

Fred Astaire
Leslie Caron

The energetic dancing of Astaire and Caron tops this romantic musical about a French orphan girl who is secretly supported by a rich playboy. Fred's the playboy and Leslie's the waif. The production, however, is too long and occasionally awkward. The film, based on Jean Webster's popular novel, has sly references to the classic *Cinderella* story. Also with Fred Clark, Thelma Ritter, Terry Moore, and Larry Keating. **Director**—Jean Negulesco.

126 minutes

DAKOTA (1988)

★★

Lou Diamond Phillips
DeeDee Norton

In Dakota, *Lou Diamond Phillips learns to cope with a conflict in his past.*

Phillips stars in the title role of this sentimental melodrama that carries a message about decency and responsibility. Unfortunately, it does not make much of an impact. Phillips is a troubled teen who works on a Texas ranch. He romances the owner's daughter (Norton) and displays compassion toward her handicapped brother. Mostly flat with a few touching scenes. Also with Herta Ware, Jordan Burton, and Eli Cummins. **Director**—Fred Holmes. **PG**

96 minutes

THE DAM BUSTERS (1954)

★★★★

Michael Redgrave
Richard Todd

Michael Redgrave and Richard Todd check their engineering in The Dam Busters.

Gripping, straightforward World War II account of the development of the RAF's skip-bombing technique, which was used to blow up the Ruhr dams in 1943 to cripple some vital German industries. An intense climate of suspense and danger builds as the British execute their plan step by step. Fine acting and impressive, Oscar-nominated special effects enhance the production. Also with Ursula Jeans, Derek Farr, Patrick Ban, and Basil Sydney. **Director**—Michael Anderson.

102 minutes b&w

DAMIEN—OMEN II (1978)

★★

William Holden
Lee Grant
Jonathan Scott-Taylor

Damien, that little demon from *The Omen*, is now 13 and living with his rich uncle in Chicago. About a dozen victims are murdered this time around in the most grisly fashion. The movie has

® This movie available with closed captions for the hearing impaired.

a slick look and a good cast, led by Holden and Grant, but it is burdened with tedious dialogue. Director Don Taylor took over for Michael Hodges, who helped with the screenplay. Another sequel, *The Final Conflict*, was released three years later. Also with Lew Ayres, Sylvia Sidney, and Robert Foxworth. **(R)** *107 minutes*

THE DAMNED (1969)

 ★★★

Dirk Bogarde
Ingrid Thulin
Helmut Berger
Charlotte Rampling

Decadence is the order of the day in this dark family epic about munitions makers during the rise of the Nazis from 1933 to 1934. The perversions of power and internal conflict that destroy the Von Essenbecks reflect the Nazis' own seeds of self-destruction. Italian director Luchino Visconti often reveals a florid, excessive style (he's staged a number of operas), and he has a field day with this material. For some tastes, "excessive" may even seem a euphemism as applied to this film (originally released with an X rating); but it's ambitious, bold, and worth watching. **(R) Academy Award Nomination**—Nicola Badalucco, Enrico Medioli, and Visconti, story and screenplay based on material not previously published or produced. *155 minutes*

DAMN YANKEES (1958)

 ★★★

Gwen Verdon
Tab Hunter

In Damn Yankees, *Gwen Verdon shows Tab Hunter that whatever Lola wants, Lola gets.*

This is a competent film version of the hit Broadway musical about a baseball fan who becomes a star player with the help of the Devil. Verdon tops the cast lineup as the temptress Lola, with lively dancing and singing. She especially upstages Hunter, who plays the critical role of the spectacular athlete. Tab strikes out when it comes to the footwork and the songs, but Ray Walston is an amusing Devil. Famous songs include "(You Got to Have) Heart" and "Whatever Lola Wants." Bob Fosse did the choreography. Also with Russ Brown and Shannon Bolin. **Directors**—George Abbott and Stanley Donen. *110 minutes*

DANCE WITH A STRANGER (1985)

 ★★★

Miranda Richardson

A sizzling performance by debuting actress Richardson dominates and uplifts this otherwise drab British melodrama, set in the mid-1950s. Richardson dynamically portrays a flashy nightclub hostess caught up in a tormented relationship that ends with her killing her playboy lover. Many undefined characters and baffling events are shrouded in the foggy London atmosphere. Based on the true story of Ruth Ellis, the last woman to receive the death penalty in England. **Director**—Mike Newell. **(R)** *102 minutes*

DANCING IN THE DARK (1986)

★★

Martha Henry
Neil Munro
Rosemary Dunsmore

The complacent, orderly world of a dedicated wife shatters when she discovers her "perfect" husband is having an affair. Henry is convincing as the housewife who resorts to desperate action when faced with her spouse's infidelity. But this neatly constructed film unfolds at a plodding pace with a noticeable lack of drama and suffers from a dull voice-over. **Director**—Leon Marr. **(PG–13)** *98 minutes*

DANGEROUS LIAISONS (1989)

 ★★★

Glenn Close
John Malkovich
Michelle Pfeiffer

Scheming leads to Dangerous Liaisons *for Glenn Close and John Malkovich.*

The period detail is exquisite and the costumes are sumptuous, but this comedy/drama based on Christopher Hampton's play about decadent 18th-century French aristocrats plays as an elaborate soap opera. Close stars as the icy marquise who engineers some battles of the boudoir. Malkovich co-stars as a rake bent on seducing women merely for the challenge. Also with Uma Thurman, Keanu Reeves, Mildred Natwick, and Swoosie Kurtz. **Director**—Stephen Frears. **(R) Academy Award**—Christopher Hampton, best screenplay adaptation. **Nominations**—best picture; Close, best actress; Pfeiffer, best supporting actress. *118 minutes*

DANGEROUSLY CLOSE (1986)

★

John Stockwell
Carey Lowell

High-school vigilantes, who closely resemble young neo-Nazis, get out of control in this drab teen film that follows a rigid commercial formula. As with similar exploitation outings, adults are portrayed as bunglers while the kids seem to have extraordinary power. The youthful cast, saddled with a threadbare script, plods through the dreary scenes with robotlike stiffness. **Director**—Albert Pyun. **(R)** *95 minutes*

DANIEL (1983)

★★

Timothy Hutton
Lindsay Crouse
Ed Asner

Intense, often confusing fictionalization about the agony-plagued children of Ju-

(Continued)

(Continued)

lius and Ethel Rosenberg, the American couple executed in 1953 for stealing atomic secrets. Director Sidney Lumet, working with a screen version of E.L. Doctorow's novel, never succeeds in bringing the harrowing events and emotions into proper focus. Apparently, Lumet is more interested in preaching than enlightening. Also with Amanda Plummer, Mandy Patinkin, Ellen Barkin, and John Rubenstein. **(R)**

129 minutes

DANTON (1982)

★★★★

Gérard Depardieu

Cheers after a rousing speech to Gérard Depardieu as Danton.

From Polish director Andrzej Wajda (*Man of Iron*), an engrossing historical account of the incipient despotism that followed in the wake of the French Revolution. Depardieu is outstanding in the title role as a patriot fighting vociferously for democratic ideals. Although the film is a period piece, it parallels modern Poland in that there are obvious similarities between Danton and Lech Walesa. Originally filmed in French. **(PG)** *136 minutes*

DARBY O'GILL AND THE LITTLE PEOPLE (1959)

★★★

Sean Connery
Albert Sharpe
Janet Munro

A breezy Walt Disney fantasy based on an Irish folktale. Darby, played by Sharpe, is a caretaker who tells tall tales and becomes involved with leprechauns. The Disney special effects are outstanding, and there's a lively script to keep the kids anchored to their seats. The fine cast also includes Jimmy O'Dea and Jack MacGowran. **Director**—Robert Stevenson. **(G)**

93 minutes

DARBY'S RANGERS (1958)

★★

James Garner
Etchika Choureau
Jack Warden

Garner plays Maj. William Darby, the heroic commander who led assaults in North Africa and Italy during World War II. The troops experience frontline action and romantic interludes. An uneven film with some adequate moments. Also with Edward Byrnes, Venetia Stevenson, and David Janssen. **Director**—William Wellman.

121 minutes b&w

THE DARK AT THE TOP OF THE STAIRS (1960)

★★★

Robert Preston
Dorothy McGuire

William Inge's play about family life in a small Oklahoma town in the 1920s is expertly produced for the screen with much of the emotions unfettered. Preston stars as the father, and McGuire plays the wife with proper stateliness. Eve Arden, Angela Lansbury, and Shirley Knight stand out in supporting roles. **Director**—Delbert Mann. **Academy Award Nomination**—Knight, best supporting actress. *124 minutes*

DARK EYES (1987)

★★½

Marcello Mastroianni
Silvana Mangano

Marcello Mastroianni enjoys life to the fullest in Dark Eyes.

Russian director Nikita Mikhalkov fashions a lush, elegant film based on the stories of Chekhov. Mastroianni was nominated for an Oscar for his role as an aging Italian who pursues the love of his life into Russia. The 19th-century setting is beautifully captured in Franco di Giacomo's cinematography and the excellent acting throughout makes the film worthwhile viewing. The storyline, however, is too convoluted, with the many twists and turns of fate eventually becoming contrived and difficult to follow. Marthe Keller and Elena Sofonova also star. Originally filmed in Italian. **(No MPAA rating) Academy Award Nomination**—Mastroianni, best actor. *118 minutes*

THE DARK MIRROR (1946)

★★★

Olivia de Havilland
Lew Ayres

A taut, clever whodunit about identical twins, one of whom is a murderess. De Havilland is excellent playing the roles of the twins. Ayres plays a doctor who is faced with the challenge of identifying the killer. An excellent example of *film noir* from an era in which that genre flourished. Also with Thomas Mitchell, Richard Long, Charles Evans, and Gary Owen. **Director**—Robert Siodmak. **Academy Award Nomination**—Vladimir Pozner, original story.

85 minutes b&w

DARK PASSAGE (1947)

★★★

Humphrey Bogart
Lauren Bacall

Bogart plays a man who escapes from the big house and then tries to prove he didn't kill his wife. He masks his identity with plastic surgery and hides out with Bacall. Not one of the best Bogey-Bacall films, it entertains only because of the stars' professionalism and their magnetic appeal. The plot, however, is rather farfetched. There are good performances from Agnes Moorehead, Tom D'Andrea, Bruce Bennett, and Houseley Stevenson. **Director**—Delmer Daves. *106 minutes b&w*

DARK VICTORY (1939)

★★★

Bette Davis
George Brent
Humphrey Bogart
Geraldine Fitzgerald

The classic tearjerker about which Jack L. Warner, in the preproduction stages,

George Brent reads Bette Davis' palm in Dark Victory. He predicts an Oscar.

is reported to have said: "Who wants to see a dame go blind?" The film, however, went on to become one of Davis' most enduring hits. She stars as a Long Island socialite who discovers that she is dying of a brain tumor—and going blind in the process. Brent plays the surgeon who is treating her, and who falls in love with her; Fitzgerald plays her close friend; and the excellent supporting cast includes Ronald Reagan, Cora Witherspoon, and Henry Travers. As a show on Broadway with Tallulah Bankhead, *Dark Victory* didn't have much of a run; as a screen vehicle, it earned Oscar nominations for Davis and the film in a year when *Gone With the Wind* swept the awards. **Director**—Edmund Goulding. **Academy Award Nominations**—best picture; Davis, best actress. *106 minutes b&w*

DARLING (1965)

★★★★

Julie Christie
Dirk Bogarde

A slick, stylish, and cynical drama about an ambitious London model who succeeds socially by having a series of affairs. Quite a perceptive and honest approach to contemporary morals, all graced with the brilliant performance of Christie, the efficient direction of John Schlesinger, and plenty of smart dialogue. Also with Laurence Harvey and Alex Scott. **Academy Awards**—Christie, best actress; Frederic Raphael, best story and screenplay written directly for the screen. **Nominations**—best picture; Schlesinger, best director. *122 minutes b&w*

D.A.R.Y.L. (1985)

★★

Barret Oliver

Moderately absurd, bland adventure about a superkid (Oliver) with a microchip brain and conventional human emotions. His foster parents want to keep him, but some military officials declare he must be "terminated." That conflict leads to some chase action and suspense. But the film takes itself too seriously for this sort of fantasy. Such stories were more fun when the boy hero came from the planet Krypton. Mary Beth Hurt and Michael McKean also star. **Director**—Simon Wincer. **(PG)** *99 minutes*

DATE WITH AN ANGEL (1987)

★

Michael E. Knight
Phoebe Cates
Emmanuelle Beart

A ridiculous romantic comedy about a mysterious angel, played by French actress Beart, who comes to earth and interferes with a young man's impending marriage. Knight, a popular soap-opera actor, stars as the engaged man who must contend with his fiancee's growing jealousy over the angel's attentions. There is no life in this mindless fantasy, which relies too heavily on broad supporting characters for humor and unbridled sentimentality for warmth. Also with David Dukes, Bibi Besch, and Vinny Argiro. **Director**—Tom McLoughlin. **(PG)** *105 minutes*

DAVID AND BATHSHEBA (1951)

★★

Gregory Peck
Susan Hayward

A routine Bible epic that's top-heavy with impressive sets and gorgeous costumes. However, someone neglected to work diligently on the script, so the film drags in spots and lacks effective dialogue. Peck and Hayward, who lead the cast, don't seem to have their hearts in the project. The familiar plot has to do with King David's love for the wife of one of his soldiers. His Majesty, played by Peck, conspires to have the man killed in battle. Hayward plays Bathsheba. The film was nominated for Oscars in several technical categories, including cinematography, art direction, and costume design. Also with Raymond Massey, Jayne Meadows, and Francis X. Bushman. **Director**—Henry King. **Academy Award Nomination**—Philip Dunne, story and screenplay. *116 minutes*

DAVID AND LISA (1962)

★★★1/2

Keir Dullea
Janet Margolin

An earnest and touching low-budget film that works beautifully because of its poignant script, efficient direction, and fine acting by a novice cast. The plot concerns two mentally ill teenagers at a private institution who share a bond of mutual understanding. Dullea and Margolin are exceptionally good as the troubled youngsters. Howard Da Silva stands out as an understanding doctor. Neva Patterson, Clifton James, and Richard McMurray round out the cast. **Director**—Frank Perry. **Academy Award Nomination**—Perry, best director; Eleanor Perry, best screenplay based on material from another medium. *94 minutes b&w*

DAVID COPPERFIELD (1935)

★★★★

Freddie Bartholomew
W.C. Fields
Lionel Barrymore
Edna May Oliver

W.C. Fields as Mr. Micawber and Freddie Bartholomew as David Copperfield.

Grand vintage Hollywood adaptation of Charles Dickens' classic novel. It's a richly textured, densely packed array of

(Continued)

This movie available on videotape and/or disc.

(Continued)
colorful characters encountered by young David (played by Bartholomew as a boy, Frank Lawton as a young man) as he grows into adulthood in 19th-century England. Fields is marvelous as the penurious but philosophical Mr. Micawber; Roland Young and Basil Rathbone are the villainous Uriah Heep and Mr. Murdstone; Oliver and Barrymore are the humane Aunt Betsy and Dan Peggotty; Maureen O'Sullivan and Madge Evans are both luminous as Dora and Agnes. Master director George Cukor pulls it all together and makes the whole film a harmonious, emotionally rewarding blend of diverse moods and personalities. Lushly produced for MGM by David O. Selznick. **Academy Award Nominations**—best picture; Joseph Newman, assistant director. *133 minutes b&w*

DAWN OF THE DEAD (1979)

★★★

Gaylen Ross
Ken Foree

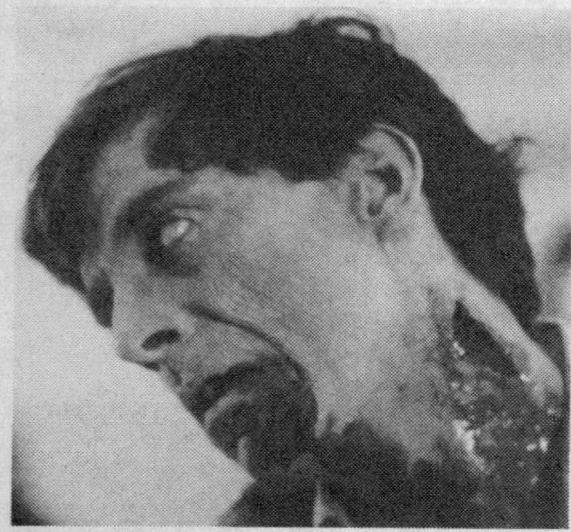

Is there a dermatologist in the house? An unhappy zombie in Dawn of the Dead.

Director George Romero whips up the horror and gore again in this sequel to his 1968 *Night of the Living Dead*. This film, however, lacks the gritty authenticity of its predecessor. Romero outdoes himself with grisly images, such as flesh being torn apart, severed heads, and spurting blood. An army of cannibalistic zombies invade a suburban shopping mall where our heroes slaughter them in an orgy of mayhem. The mall setting serves to satirize America's consumer culture, while the comic-book color exaggerates the more gruesome aspects of the film. Also with Scott Reiniger and David Emge. Nontheatrical prints are 140 minutes. **(R)** *125 minutes*

THE DAWN PATROL (1930)

★★★★

Douglas Fairbanks, Jr.
Richard Barthelmess

Director Howard Hawks' first sound film remains one of the finest aerial dramas. The fliers of a squadron in World War I France go stoically into combat, and often to their deaths, accepting whatever destiny brings them. A terse and beautifully visualized tribute to courage and loyalty, with thrilling dogfight scenes and expressive performances by Barthelmess, Fairbanks, and Neil Hamilton. **Academy Award**—John Monk Saunders, original story. *82 minutes b&w*

A DAY AT THE RACES (1937)

★★★

The Marx Brothers
Margaret Dumont
Maureen O'Sullivan

The Marx Brothers and an unsuspecting patient in A Day at the Races.

Dr. Hugo Hackenbush (Groucho) may only be a horse doctor, but as far as Mrs. Upjohn (Dumont) is concerned, he's the man to run the sanitarium she's financing. He runs off to the races, Chico sells tutti-frutti ice cream, and it's fast and sweet Marx Brothers fun. The whole is a bit less than its most inspired parts (the Brothers tested their gags in nationwide live performances before making the film), but so what? Groucho cited Hackenbush as his favorite role. With Allan Jones and Sig Ruman. **Director**—Sam Wood. *111 minutes b&w*

DAY OF THE DEAD (1985)

★★

Richard Liberty

George A. Romero, the sultan of splatter, pulls out all stops to turn stomachs in this third chapter of his cultish, grisly zombie saga. Now, a handful of conventional humans struggle to survive underground as thousands of hungry "dead" flesh-eaters threaten their sanctuary. Blood and guts spill all over the screen while the humans attempt to talk themselves to death. The juxtaposition of extreme gore and long-winded speeches is somewhat jarring. With Lori Cardille and Terry Alexander. **(No MPAA rating)** *102 minutes*

THE DAY OF THE DOLPHIN (1973)

★★

George C. Scott
Trish Van Devere

George C. Scott and intelligent friend in The Day of the Dolphin.

A so-so thriller about a marine biologist, played by Scott, who trains dolphins to talk and unwittingly becomes entangled in a plot to assassinate the President. Despite the big money and top talent involved, the film fails. There's a bit of comedy and suspense here and there, but the film ends on a discouraging note. Also with Paul Sorvino, Fritz Weaver, Leslie Charleson, John Korkes, and Edward Herrmann. **Director**—Mike Nichols. **(PG)** *104 minutes*

THE DAY OF THE JACKAL (1973)

★★★

Edward Fox
Cyril Cusack

Frederick Forsyth's suspenseful novel about an OAS attempt to assassinate

® *This movie available with closed captions for the hearing impaired.*

Charles de Gaulle is adapted for the screen with all the thrills neatly intact. Fox plays the role of the professional killer who is hired by some conspiring French generals for the dastardly deed. Tension mounts as the police step up their manhunt while the assassin prepares for his strike. Good supporting acting, excellent pacing, and impressive European locations add to the professional production. TV commercials, however, can ruin the pace. Michel Lonsdale, Eric Porter, Delphine Seyrig, and Alan Badel also star. **Director**—Fred Zinnemann. **(PG)** *142 minutes*

THE DAY OF THE LOCUST (1975)

 ★★★½

Donald Sutherland
William Atherton
Karen Black
Burgess Meredith

A naive young art director (Atherton) takes a job at a Hollywood studio in the 1930s and sinks into a bleak nightmare of crushed hopes and failed dreams. Nathanael West's brilliant Depression-era novel reaches the screen with none of its impact diminished. Sutherland's performance as a simple midwesterner who falls in love with a venal bit player (Black) is astonishingly good; you've never seen decency so terribly wronged. Meredith scores as a sick-at-heart ex-vaudevillian who struggles to make a living as a door-to-door salesman. A disturbing but fascinating film, brilliantly photographed by Conrad Hall and keenly directed by John Schlesinger. Also with Geraldine Page, Richard Dysart, and Bo Hopkins. **(R)** *140 minutes*

DAYS OF HEAVEN (1978)

 ★★★

Richard Gere
Brooke Adams

Writer/director Terrence Malick's spectacular art film is a technical achievement of exquisite photography and beautiful images. The story, set in 1916, is about three poverty-stricken vagabonds who become involved with a wealthy Texas wheat farmer. But the plot is secondary to both the visuals and the narration by Linda Manz, which sets a mood of nostalgia and sadness. Some viewers will not appreciate the film despite its visual power, and will miss a more coherent and complex storyline. The visuals will be lost on a small screen. Also with Sam Shepard and Robert Wilke. **(PG) Academy Award**—Nestor Almendros, cinematography. *95 minutes*

DAYS OF THUNDER (1990)

Tom Cruise
Robert Duvall

Nicole Kidman and Tom Cruise in Days of Thunder.

Cruise stars as a rookie stock-car racer who competes with rivals both on and off the track. He falls under the wing of a fatherly crew chief, skillfully acted by Duvall, and clashes often with a veteran driver, played by Michael Rooker *(Henry: Portrait of a Serial Killer)*. Eventually, he pulls himself together to beat the odds and win the big race at Daytona. He matures via his experiences on the track and through his relationship with a serious-minded doctor, played by Australian actress Nicole Kidman. The film was obviously patterned after Cruise's smash hit *Top Gun*, and the same producers and director who fashioned that blockbuster reteamed for this one—a resemblance that did not escape the critics. Yet, *Days* offers a more accessible milieu than the military setting of *Top Gun* and is greatly enhanced by Duvall's subtle but moving performance. Interestingly, the film represents another in the series of Cruise roles in which he plays an inexperienced young man who seeks guidance from a substitute father figure. Also with Cary Elwes, Randy Quaid, John C. Reilly, Fred Dalton Thompson, and Don Simpson (one of the producers) in a small role. **Director**—Tony Scott. **(PG-13)** *105 minutes*

DAYS OF WINE AND ROSES (1962)

 ★★★★

Jack Lemmon
Lee Remick

A brilliant, uncompromising drama about a public relations man, played by Lemmon, who becomes disillusioned with his work, turns to drink, and leads his wife, played by Remick, down the alcoholic path. Lemmon and Remick are at their acting best, and there's excellent work from all quarters—direction, script, and supporting roles. Charles Bickford, Jack Klugman, Alan Hewitt, Tom Palmer, and Jack Albertson costar. **Director**—Blake Edwards. **Academy Award Nominations**—Lemmon, best actor; Remick, best actress. *117 minutes b&w*

THE DAY THE WORLD ENDED (1956)

★★½

Richard Denning
Lori Nelson
Touch (Mike) Connors

This early example of the still-topical "day after" school of science fiction is the first of many sci-fi thrillers directed by the prolific Roger Corman. Following atomic war, a ragged group of survivors straggle to a well-stocked house that has been shielded from radiation. Squabbles and violence soon erupt, but a greater danger lurks in the surrounding hills, where a hideous mutant forages for food. Undeniably cheesy, the film works up a misty ambience that is simultaneously amusing and disturbing. Be prepared for some surprisingly effective scare sequences, and a wild monster created by unheralded makeup designer Paul Blaisdell. *80 minutes b&w*

D.C. CAB (1983)

★★

Mr. T
Gary Busey

The title refers to a broken-down Washington, D.C., taxi company that consists of dilapidated cars and wacky drivers. For all the zaniness and rampant energy, this film's off-the-wall humor may be too broad for some. The plot, what there is of it, starts late and

(Continued)

(Continued)
the actors seem to be improvising at times. The venerable Mr. T plays a glowering cabbie and Busey stars as an extroverted driver hung up on rock 'n' roll. The large cast also includes Adam Baldwin, Charlie Barnett, Max Gail, and Whitman Mayo. **Director**—Joel Schumacher. **(R)** *104 minutes*

D-DAY, THE SIXTH OF JUNE (1956)

★★★

Robert Taylor
Richard Todd
Dana Wynter
Edmond O'Brien

Two officers—one an American, the other British—fall in love with the same girl during World War II about the time of the Normandy invasion. Taylor and Todd are the rivals; Wynter is the girl. The film is highlighted by impressive action scenes, while the romantic plot is too familiar. **Director**—Henry Koster. *106 minutes*

THE DEAD (1987)

★★½

Anjelica Huston
Donal McCann

Donal McCann and Anjelica Huston at a family gathering in The Dead.

Director John Huston's last completed film is based on James Joyce's final short story in his collection entitled *The Dubliners.* The elegant mood piece is set in 1904 Dublin at a family gathering, where many disturbing memories are uncovered and secrets of lost love revealed. Both Joyce's story and Huston's execution of it are quite dense, and many viewers may find the slow pace and melancholy atmosphere oppressive. Huston's last effort was truly a family affair: Daughter Angelica is part of the superb ensemble case, while son Tony expertly adapted the script from Joyce's novella. Also with Helena Carroll, Cathleen Delaney, Donal Donnelly, and Dan O'Herlihy. **(PG) Academy Award Nomination**—Tony Huston, best screenplay based on material from another medium. *83 minutes*

DEAD-BANG (1989)

★★½

Don Johnson
Penelope Ann Miller

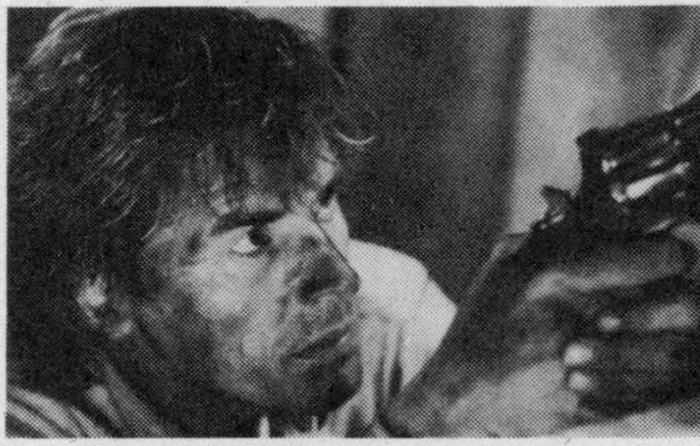

Don Johnson uncovers a band of bizarre killers in Dead-Bang.

Johnson, of TV's *Miami Vice,* stars as a homicide detective in this conventional police thriller by John Frankenheimer. This anemic action/drama has Johnson on the case of a neo-Nazi conspiracy. The characterizations are too familiar, while the violent action involving the white supremacists seems culled from standard TV fare. Also with William Forsythe, Bob Balaban, and Frank Military. **(R)** *109 minutes*

DEAD CALM (1989)

★★½

Sam Neill
Nicole Kidman
Billy Zane

Sam Neill and Nicole Kidman are stranded at sea in Dead Calm.

A moderate amount of suspense surfaces in this tightly wound, moody thriller. But the plot is predictable, and the three-character scenario at sea creates an annoyingly confined atmosphere. A yachtsman (Neill) and his wife (Kidman) pick up a survivor (Zane) from a nearby stricken vessel, and the situation turns unexpectedly menacing. Australian director Phillip Noyce offers few surprises in this psychological workout, though fans of the genre may appreciate the skilled presentation of familiar conventions. **(R)** *95 minutes*

DEAD END (1937)

★★★½

Humphrey Bogart
Joel McCrea
Sylvia Sydney

Beautifully directed film that preserves the stage setting of Sidney Kingsley's Broadway play. The drama shows the harsh reality of New York City slum life, contrasting tenements with adjacent luxury apartment houses along the East River. There are fine performances by McCrea and Sydney as young lovers struggling against the odds. Bogart and Claire Trevor as the gangster and "fallen woman" highlight the social realism. The film is also notable for introducing the Dead End Kids. **Director**—William Wyler. **Academy Award Nominations**—best picture; Trevor, best actress; Gregg Toland, cinematography. *93 minutes b&w*

DEAD HEAT (1988)

★½

Joe Piscopo
Treat Williams

Zombie cops chase zombie criminals in this dreadful film, which falls under a variety of genres—science fiction, horror, comedy, and police thriller. Unfortunately, it isn't a good film under any classification. Williams and Piscopo are teamed as detective partners working on a case involving criminals who have been resurrected from the dead. When Williams is killed, Piscopo returns him to life via a resurrection machine. Together they track down the villains responsible for such grisly mayhem. The mixture of genres leaves the film without clear direction: The filmmakers are undecided as to whether their creation is a dark parody or an action-packed adventure. The makeup and special ef-

® *This movie available with closed captions for the hearing impaired.*

fects are particularly effective or tasteless, depending on your point of view. Also with Darren McGavin, Vincent Price, Lidsay Frost, and Clare Kirkconnell. **Director**—Mark Goldblatt. **(R)**
86 minutes

DEADLINE, USA (1952)

★★★

Humphrey Bogart
Kim Hunter
Ethel Barrymore

Bogart stars in this terse drama as a courageous newspaper editor who publishes stories about an influential criminal and then must struggle to prevent his superiors from bending to intimidation. Bogey is enjoyable, and there are good dramatic scenes with him and Barrymore, who plays the publisher. Hunter plays Bogey's ex-wife. Some newspaper clichés here and there, but not enough to spoil the fun. Also with Ed Begley, Paul Stewart, Warren Stevens, Martin Gabel, and Jim Backus. **Director**—Richard Brooks.
87 minutes b&w

THE DEADLY AFFAIR (1967)

★★★

James Mason
Simone Signoret

A gripping whodunit, with Mason as a British agent investigating the apparent suicide of a colleague and uncovering a nest of spies. The film is well plotted, with the suspense building at an even pace. The story is based on the John Le Carré novel *Call for the Dead*. Mason is convincing, and he's backed up nicely with good acting by Signoret, Maximilian Schell, Lynn Redgrave, and Max Adrian. **Director**—Sidney Lumet.
106 minutes

DEADLY BLESSING (1981)

 ★1/2

Maren Jensen
Ernest Borgnine

This is a strange horror story about some mysterious deaths among a religious sect called the Hittites. A farmer is run over by his own tractor, and others are murdered with knives, snakes, and spiders. It's not certain who does the killing in this illogical film, yet there are many suspects for the perpetrator, referred to as "the incubus" by the Hittites. Borgnine is interesting as the fanatical religious leader. **Director**—Wes Craven. **(R)** *102 minutes*

DEADLY FORCE (1983)

 ★

Wings Hauser

Routine car chases and gunfights fill a preposterous and predictable action melodrama that resembles countless TV police series. Hauser plays a tough Los Angeles ex-cop who returns to his old territory to nab a madman killer. The task is even more difficult since he is persona non grata with most of his former associates. Lame acting by an unfamiliar cast adds to the many other drawbacks of this exercise in tedium. Also with Joyce Ingalls. **Director**—Paul Aaron. **(R)** *95 minutes*

DEADLY FRIEND (1986)

 ★★

Matthew Laborteaux
Kristy Swanson

A preposterous teen horror movie about a 15-year-old high-school boy who specializes in brain research. Credibility is strained when Laborteaux, as the adolescent Dr. Frankenstein, implants a computer-chip brain in the skull of his dead girlfriend (Swanson), who had been killed by her abusive father. The girl miraculously springs to life and seeks revenge on her tormentors. Mediocre fare from Wes Craven, the director of *A Nightmare on Elm Street*. **(R)** *91 minutes*

DEAD MEN DON'T WEAR PLAID (1982)

 ★★★

Steve Martin
Rachel Ward

A wonderful, witty parody of 1940s detective movies, with gumshoe Martin cleverly interacting with actual clips from those marvelous classic melodramas. Carl Reiner wrote and directed this hilarious gem with affection and skill. The delightful gimmick places Martin into the old scenes and involves him in conversations with such film greats as Humphrey Bogart, Alan Ladd, and Barbara Stanwyck. An engaging, comic romp and irresistible fun, especially for movie buffs. **(PG)**
89 minutes b&w

DEAD OF NIGHT (1946)

★★★

Mervyn Johns
Roland Culver

A superior, bone-chilling thriller about a man who has strange dreams that appear to interconnect with the dreams of other people. The film is composed of five stories of the supernatural, which are blended well for the utmost in eerie atmosphere and suspenseful thrills. It's all topped off with fine acting. Also stars Michael Redgrave, Googie Withers, Anthony Baird, Judy Kelly, and Sally Ann Howes. **Directors**—Alberto Cavalcanti, Basil Dearden, Robert Hamer, and Charles Crichton.
104 minutes b&w

DEAD OF WINTER (1987)

 ★★★

Mary Steenburgen
Roddy McDowall
Jan Rubes

An eerie, isolated Gothic mansion, a raging snowstorm, and a disappearing corpse set the stage for this atmospheric thriller that will send chills up your spine. Steenburgen stars as an unsuspecting young actress lured into a nightmarish trap who turns to her acting skills to escape the horror. McDowall and Rubes are deliciously diabolic as nasty blackmailers in control of this sinister scheme that unfolds with hair-raising surprises and suspense. **Director**—Arthur Penn. **(R)**
100 minutes

DEAD POETS SOCIETY (1989)

★★★1/2

Robin Williams

Williams turns in a stirring performance as a latter-day Socrates who instills in his students a passion for literature and for life itself. Set in a rigid prep school in 1959, this captivating drama illuminates the contrast between the prestigious institution's starchy atmosphere and the students' striving for creativity and individuality. The courageous spirit of this unconventional teacher is inspiring. Also with Robert Sean Leonard, Ethan Hawke, Josh Charles, and Gale Hansen. **Director**—Peter Weir. **(PG) Academy Award**—Tom Schulman, best original screenplay.

(Continued)

This movie available on videotape and/or disc.

(Continued)
Nominations—best picture; Williams best actor; Weir, best director.

124 minutes

THE DEAD POOL (1988)

★★★

Clint Eastwood
Liam Neeson

This time Clint Eastwood has to protect himself from falling in The Dead Pool.

Eastwood's trigger finger is as itchy as ever in this fifth Dirty Harry action thriller. In this lively but predictable outing, the cynical Harry blows away various bad guys at precise intervals while solving a series of murders involving local celebrities. Harry's own name is also on the hit list. Some comic touches—notably a wonderfully inventive car chase—and good technical flourishes surface among the growing pile of corpses. Costars Patricia Clarkson, Evan Kim, and David Hunt. **Director**—Buddy Van Horn. **(R)**

91 minutes

DEAD RECKONING (1947)

★★★

Humphrey Bogart
Lizabeth Scott

Bogart plays a World War II veteran who investigates the murder of his friend during a trip to Washington to receive a medal. Standard *film noir* fare, but it's enhanced by some good acting, especially Bogart's reliable performance as a tough character. Also with Morris Carnovsky, William Prince, and Wallace Ford. **Director**—John Cromwell.

100 minute b&w

DEAD RINGERS (1988)

★★★1/2

Jeremy Irons
Geneviève Bujold

A fascinating, unnerving, and formidable psychological thriller loosely based on the bizarre circumstances of the Marcus brothers. These renowned twin gynecologists were found dead in their Manhattan apartment, apparently of suicide. The physicians' medical skill as well as their strange interdependency, drug addiction, and abuse of their patients are presented with power and iciness. Irons delivers a sleek, splendid performance in the dual role. An elegant horror tale that gathers strength as it unfolds. From Canadian director David Cronenberg, known for his fascination with morbid subjects and grotesque imagery. Also with Heidi von Palleske, Barbara Gordon, and Stephen Lack. **(R)**

115 minutes

THE DEAD ZONE (1983)

★★★

Christopher Walken
Martin Sheen

Christopher Walken has a terrifying glimpse of the future in The Dead Zone.

Stephen King's suspenseful novel has been adapted into an intermittently engrossing and eerie film. Walken plays an auto accident victim who emerges from a five-year coma with the power of second sight. His dark visions—a child in a fire, a trigger-happy U.S. President—are numbing. Then he discovers he can use his clairvoyant powers to alter such catastrophes. Under David Cronenberg's subtle direction, the drama comes alive. Also with Brooke Adams and Colleen Dewhurst. **(R)**

102 minutes

DEAL OF THE CENTURY (1983)

★★

Chevy Chase
Sigourney Weaver

Gregory Hines, Chevy Chase, and Sigourney Weaver in Deal of the Century.

The weapons industry is a juicy target for satirization, but director William Friedkin misses the mark in this uneven send-up. Chase stars as a sleazy arms salesman who peddles bazookas and machine guns to pip-squeak Third World dictators and revolutionaries. He finally graduates to high-tech military machinery while most of the gags fizzle out. Gregory Hines costars and delivers a few much-needed laughs. **(PG)**

98 minutes

DEAR AMERICA: LETTERS HOME FROM VIETNAM (1988)

★★★★

An eloquent, powerful, and heartbreaking statement about the Vietnam War presented through the straightforward, honest words of the men and women who fought there. Letters are read by scores of actors and actresses, including such stars as Robert De Niro, Martin Sheen, Kathleen Turner, and Sean Penn, while director Bill Couturie dramatically illustrates the narration with newsreel footage, home movies, and music from the period. To watch this extraordinary documentary is an unforgettable experience. **(PG-13)**

90 minutes

DEATH BEFORE DISHONOR (1987)

★

Fred Dryer
Brian Keith

® *This movie available with closed captions for the hearing impaired.*

A flag-waving, hopelessly shallow military actioner involving terrorists in a fictional Arab country. Dryer, from the TV series *Hunter,* comes to the rescue when his commanding officer (Keith) is kidnapped. He pursues the "filthy scum" with a vengeance. Cardboard characters, clichés, and ridiculous dialogue abound in this hackneyed film, obviously inspired by the right-wing patriotism of *Delta Force* and *Rambo.* Also with Paul Winfield and Joanna Pacula. **Director**—Terry J. Leonard. **(R)**

95 minutes

DEATH HUNT (1981)

★★★

Charles Bronson
Lee Marvin

Granite-hard Bronson and grizzled, rawhide-tough Marvin are matched in this action-packed adventure filmed in northern Canada. Marvin is a whiskey-soaked Mountie on the brink of retirement, who reluctantly pursues a quiet trapper, played by Bronson, who is wrongly accused of murder. Both stars portray larger-than-life adversaries who gradually develop respect for one another. It's an old-fashioned story, set in the 1930s amid perilous terrain, with heroes worth cheering. **Director**—Peter Hunt. **(R)** *96 minutes*

DEATH OF A SALESMAN (1951)

★★★★

Fredric March
Kevin McCarthy
Mildred Dunnock
Cameron Mitchell

Cameron Mitchell, Fredric March, and Kevin McCarthy in Death of a Salesman.

Arthur Miller's powerful and heartfelt drama is brought to the screen with all the emotion and pathos of the magnificent Broadway play. March has never been better than as the indelible Willy Loman, the over-the-hill traveling salesman who confronts the disappointment of his career. Flashbacks are cleverly used to bring out an extra dimension of this great American classic tragedy. Dunnock plays his wife; McCarthy and Mitchell play his sons. Also with Howard Smith, Royal Beal, and Jesse White. **Director**—Laslo Benedek. **Academy Award Nominations**—March, best actor; McCarthy, best supporting actor; Dunnock, best supporting actress; Frank Planer, cinematography.

112 minutes b&w

DEATH ON THE NILE (1978)

★★★

Peter Ustinov
Bette Davis
David Niven
Mia Farrow
Angela Lansbury
George Kennedy
Maggie Smith

Celebrated Belgian sleuth Hercule Poirot, played by Ustinov, encounters suspects galore as he unravels a murder mystery on a Nile River cruise as only Dame Agatha Christie could tell it. A big, first-rate cast, elegant settings, and lively acting add up to a charming, old-fashioned movie whodunit. Anthony Powell won an Oscar for his detailed period costumes. Old pros Davis and Lansbury ham it up and steal a number of scenes on the way to an intriguing ending, where the droll Monsieur Poirot unmasks the killer of a beautiful heiress. **Director**—John Guillermin. **(PG)** *140 minutes*

DEATHTRAP (1982)

★★★

Michael Caine
Christopher Reeve
Dyan Cannon

Clever plot twists, plenty of smart dialogue, and superb acting overcome the staginess in this stylish film version of Ira Levin's Broadway mystery play. Caine is in best form as a has-been playwright with murder on his mind. And there are exceptional performances, too, from Reeve and Cannon. The direction and screenplay could have allowed for more humor, but there are enough surprises in this thriller to maintain enjoyment. **Director**—Sidney Lumet. **(PG)**

116 minutes

DEATH WEEKEND

See The House by the Lake

DEATH WISH (1974)

★★★

Charles Bronson
Hope Lange

In New York City, muggers brutally rape the wife and daughter of a placid businessman, who then launches a one-man vigilante crusade against numerous thugs he encounters on the streets. The script is farfetched, but chilling and cathartic. Bronson is at his best as the stone-faced citizen out for revenge. Also with Vincent Gardenia, Stuart Margolin, and Stephen Keats. **Director**—Michael Winner. **(R)**

94 minutes

DEATH WISH II (1982)

★

Charles Bronson
Jill Ireland

Once more vigilante justice is dished out with unblinking determination in this retread of the 1974 melodrama. The setting, this time, is Los Angeles, and the story is just as preposterous as before: Stern-faced Bronson blazes away at the replusive thugs who raped and killed his daughter and housekeeper, while the cops remain helpless and confused. Though the original film combined a hard edge with a touch of melancholy to raise the level of the story above most action fare, the remainder of the series merely exploits violence for the sake of violence. **Director**—Michael Winner. **(R)**

89 minutes

DEATH WISH 3 (1985)

★★

Charles Bronson
Deborah Raffin
Martin Balsam

Bronson is the determined vigilante once again. This time he avenges the death of an army buddy and other victims of New York City gang members. As in previous chapters, this outing takes an exaggerated view of urban crime and the failure of police protection. The film begins with some wit, but lapses into chaos at the end when

(Continued)

(Continued)
Bronson mows down scores of punks with various weapons, from a machine gun to a rocket launcher. **Director**—Michael Winner. **(R)** *100 minutes*

DEATH WISH 4: THE CRACKDOWN (1987)

Charles Bronson
Kay Lenz

More vigilante justice from Bronson, the man primarily associated with this type of formula action vehicle. This time he pursues the dirty drug dealers responsible for the death of his girlfriend's daughter. Numerous punks and villains are blown away with some heavy artillery, including submachine guns and even a grenade launcher. Bronson's dialogue is typically sparse: His weapons do most of the talking. Not surprisingly, the story is very predictable, though the well-paced direction in this sequel is handled by veteran action director J. Lee Thompson. Also with John P. Ryan and Perry Lopez. **(R)** *99 minutes*

THE DECEIVERS (1988)

 ★★½

Pierce Brosnan
Saeed Jaffrey
Helena Mitchell

A British officer (Brosnan) in 19th-century India infiltrates a vicious criminal cult whose members plunder and murder travelers. This historical drama nicely develops the color and feel of the period, but the plot is often confusing. The history of this barbaric group, known as "Thuggees" and supposedly responsible for some two million killings, is insufficiently developed. Also with Keith Michell and Shashi Kapoor. **Director**—Nicholas Meyer. **(PG-13)** *103 minutes*

DECEPTION (1946)

 ★★★

Bette Davis
Claude Rains

Davis and Rains shine in this stylish but sloshy melodrama, set in the world of classical music. Rains is a wealthy pianist who loves Davis, but she weds her former boyfriend, played by Paul Henreid. That makes Claude jealous, indeed. Good acting all around, but Henreid is upstaged by the dynamic performances of Davis and Rains. Also with John Abbott and Benson Fong. **Director**—Irving Rapper. *112 minutes b&w*

THE DECLINE OF THE AMERICAN EMPIRE (1986)

Dominique Michel
Pierre Curzi
Dorothee Berryman

Several friends who teach at a Montreal university and their spouses get together for a dinner party, where they discuss sex and sexual relations at length. Because the film covers a short period of time—24 hours in the lives of the characters—and because the private lives of these characters are never shown but only talked about, this low-key drama is reminiscent of *My Dinner with Andre.* But the cynical point of view, about the illusions of romantic love and the loss of passion that sometimes accompanies intellectual pursuits, is harsh and pessimistic. Also with Louise Portal, Remy Girard, and Gabriel Arcand. Originally filmed in French. **Director**—Denys Arcand. **(R)** **Academy Award Nomination**—best foreign-language film. *101 minutes*

THE DEEP (1977)

 ★★

Robert Shaw
Jacqueline Bisset
Nick Nolte

Peter Benchley wrote this underwater adventure, but it lacks the suspense and thrills of his earlier novel *Jaws* and its film adaptation. Spectacular underwater photography is the only virtue in this rather shallow production, which concerns a scramble for sunken treasure off the Bermuda coast. So-so acting jobs by Nolte and Bisset; a realistic performance from Shaw. Also with Lou Gossett, Jr., and Eli Wallach. **Director**—Peter Yates. **(PG)** *123 minutes*

DEEPSTAR SIX (1989)

 ★★

Taurean Blacque
Nancy Everhard

This horror film resembles *Alien,* only the action takes place six miles under the surface of the sea. A diverse crew of Navy technicians accidentally disturbs a prehistoric monster. The story suffers from a lack of suspense, while the dialogue consists mainly of terse techno-jargon shouted over a noisy background. There's only one glimpse of the rubbery-looking creature near the end. **Director**—Sean S. Cunningham. **(R)** *99 minutes*

THE DEER HUNTER (1978)

Robert De Niro
John Cazale
John Savage
Meryl Streep
Christopher Walken

Good friends celebrate a final time before leaving for Vietnam in The Deer Hunter.

Director Michael Cimino's protracted film about the Vietnam experience is extraordinarily powerful and original. Cimino uncorks a fascinating multitude of emotions and insights about war and violence. Essentially, the story deals with three young steelworkers from a Pennsylvania steel town who are devastated by the horror of the war. Superb performances by De Niro, Walken, and Streep. Also with George Dzundza and Chuck Aspegren. **(R)** **Academy Awards**—best picture; Cimino, best director; Walken, best supporting actor. **Nominations**—De Niro, best actor; Streep, best supporting actress; Cimino, Louis Garfinkle, Quinn K. Redeker, and Deric Washburn, best screenplay written directly for the screen. *183 minutes*

THE DEFIANT ONES (1958)

Tony Curtis
Sidney Poitier

This movie available with closed captions for the hearing impaired.

An inspired racial drama, with Curtis and Poitier as escaped convicts who are chained together and attempt to flee a police dragnet. This is excellent material that deals squarely with hatred. There are some excellent performances and well-paced action directed by Stanley Kramer. Theodore Bikel, Cara Williams, and Lon Chaney, Jr., turn in fine supporting performances. **Academy Award**—Nathan Douglas and Harold Jacob Smith, best story and screenplay written directly for the screen. **Nominations**—best picture; Kramer, best director; Curtis and Poitier, best actor; Bikel, best supporting actor; Williams, best supporting actress.
97 minutes b&w

DELIVERANCE (1972)

Burt Reynolds
Jon Voight
Ned Beatty

Burt Reynolds and his friends fight for survival in Deliverance.

Four well-to-do young men embark on a canoe trip down a swift Georgia river, but their weekend outing turns into a nightmare when they're set upon by some sadistic mountain men. This engrossing film, adapted by James Dickey from his novel, offers lucid contrasts between the haves and have-nots, and it brims with suspense and terror. Superb direction and tight editing enhance the thrilling and terrifying adventure. Exceptionally good acting from Voight, Reynolds, Beatty, Ronny Cox, Bill McKinney, and Herbert Coward. **Director**—John Boorman. **(R) Academy Award Nominations**—best picture; Boorman, best director; Tom Priestley, film editing. *109 minutes*

DELTA FORCE (1986)

Chuck Norris
Lee Marvin

A hurray-for-our-side action/adventure tale loosely based on the 1985 TWA jet hijacking by Palestinian terrorists. The first half of the film pokes along while an all-star cast of hostages confronts their captors in midair. The pace picks up when the American commando force goes to work in Beirut with machine guns, rockets, and bombs. Scores of villains bite the dust. **Director**—Menahem Golan. **(R)** *126 minutes*

DEMETRIUS AND THE GLADIATORS (1954)

  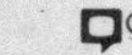

Victor Mature
Susan Hayward
Michael Rennie

Humdrum sequel to *The Robe,* with Mature hamming it up as a slave in possession of Christ's garment. Emperor Caligula, played by Jay Robinson, wants it. The hokey script dwells on heroics rather than religiousness. There is some worthwhile action in the arena with the gladiators battling away. The costumes and sets—probably left over from *The Robe*—are impressive. Also with Debra Paget, Anne Bancroft, Richard Egan, Ernest Borgnine, and Barry Jones. **Director**—Delmer Daves. *101 minutes*

DEMON SEED (1977)

Julie Christie
Fritz Weaver

Proteus IV is an ultrasophisticated computer capable of philosophical decisions and creativity. It wants to perpetuate itself in the flesh by impregnating a human female. Just how this feat is accomplished evolves into a bizarre and intriguing science-fiction tale that's sort of a cross between *Rosemary's Baby* and *2001: A Space Odyssey.* Christie is excellent as the reluctant object of the electronic brain's affections. The story is preposterous, but it's smartly executed with effective direction by Donald Cammell, top-notch special effects, and a haunting climax. Also with Gerrit Graham, Berry Kroeger, and Lisa Lu. **(R)**
94 minutes

DESERT BLOOM (1986)

Jon Voight
Annabeth Gish

Some solid acting rises above this small, flimsy family drama set in Las Vegas against the backdrop of early atomic-bomb testing. Voight is especially moving as the unstable, boozing service-station owner who abuses his family. The story is told via the experiences of his 13-year-old stepdaughter, played by Gish. Yet the film never realizes its full potential. Also with JoBeth Williams and Ellen Barkin. **Director**—Eugene Corr. **(PG)** *106 minutes*

THE DESERT FOX (1951)

James Mason
Jessica Tandy
Cedric Hardwicke

Mason is fantastic as German Field Marshal Erwin Rommel in this film biography, which follows his defeat in North Africa and his disillusionment on his return to Nazi Germany. The engrossing drama features some stunning desert location scenes. Mason followed up his Rommel role in *The Desert Rats.* Also with Luther Adler, Everett Sloane, Leo G. Carroll, George Macready, and Richard Boone. **Director**—Henry Hathaway. *88 minutes b&w*

THE DESERT RATS (1953)

Richard Burton
James Mason

A well-made follow-up to *The Desert Fox,* with Mason once again portraying German Field Marshal Erwin Rommel. This exciting war drama is seen from the Allied side, with Burton leading Australian troops against Nazi armor in the siege of Tobruk. There are impressive battle scenes, with good support from Robert Newton as a soldier who was a professor in civilian life. Also with Robert Douglas, Torin Thatcher, and Chips Rafferty. **Director**—Robert Wise. **Academy Award Nomination**—Richard Murphy, story and screenplay.
88 minutes b&w

THE DESERT SONG (1933)

★★½

Gordon MacRae
Kathryn Grayson

A third film version of Sigmund Romberg's operetta with MacRae and Gray-

(Continued)

(Continued)

son acceptably singing and acting in the key roles. The score offers "The Riff Song" and "One Alone." The setting is Africa, and MacRae plays the leader of the Riffs, who fight some evil tribesmen. Steve Cochran, Raymond Massey, and William Conrad are also in the cast. **Director**—H. Bruce Humberstone. *110 minutes*

DESIGN FOR LIVING (1933)

Miriam Hopkins
Fredric March
Gary Cooper

A story about "three people who love each other very much" (Noel Coward's description of his play upon which the film is based). Ben Hecht's screenplay unfortunately does not recapture the wit and style of the play. Hopkins is well cast, but March and Cooper as her live-in lovers, despite their physical charms, are no match for Alfred Lunt and Coward, who starred on Broadway. Ernst Lubitsch's touch as director adds the only real entertainment value. *90 minutes b&w*

DESIRE UNDER THE ELMS (1958)

 ★★½

Sophia Loren
Anthony Perkins
Burl Ives

Slow-paced and stagy screen version of Eugene O'Neill's play about the conflicts of a New England farm family in the 19th century. Loren is out of her element as an elderly farmer's young wife who falls in love with her stepson. There are a few minor moments of visible drama, but most of the film is murky. Perkins plays the young stepson; Ives is the father. Frank Overton, Pernell Roberts, and Anne Seymour also star. **Director**—Delbert Mann. *111 minutes b&w*

DESK SET (1957)

 ★★★ ▢®

Spencer Tracy
Katharine Hepburn

Tracy and Hepburn highlight this adult comedy, which is based on William Marchant's play. Hepburn's character runs a broadcast company's reference section. Tracy plays an efficiency expert who wants to improve the operation. Though enemies at first, the two eventually fall in love. Plenty of good dialogue and laughs along the way. Supporting roles are played by Joan Blondell, Gig Young, and Dina Merrill. **Director**—Walter Lang. *103 minutes*

THE DESPERATE HOURS (1955)

Humphrey Bogart
Fredric March
Arthur Kennedy

Three escaped convicts hide out in the home of a respected family and hold them hostage. A suspenseful battle of wits ensues, with Bogart playing one of the cons. Fine performances, too, from Martha Scott, Dewey Martin, and Gig Young. Based on the Joseph Hayes novel and play. **Director**—William Wyler. *112 minutes b&w*

DESPERATELY SEEKING SUSAN (1985)

Rosanna Arquette
Madonna

Too hip: Rosanna Arquette and Madonna in Desperately Seeking Susan.

Arquette plays a bored suburban housewife who exchanges identities with a freewheeling New Wave woman (Madonna). This hip romp has elements of a Preston Sturges screwball comedy set in the funky world of lower Manhattan. The excessive complications aren't as funny as they're meant to be, but the style and panache of the likable cast pull it off. Ultramodern and old-fashioned at the same time. Also stars Aidan Quinn, Mark Blum, and Robert Joy. **Director**—Susan Seidelman. **(PG–13)** *104 minutes*

DESPERATE SIEGE

See Rawhide

DESTINATION TOKYO (1943)

Cary Grant
John Garfield
Alan Hale

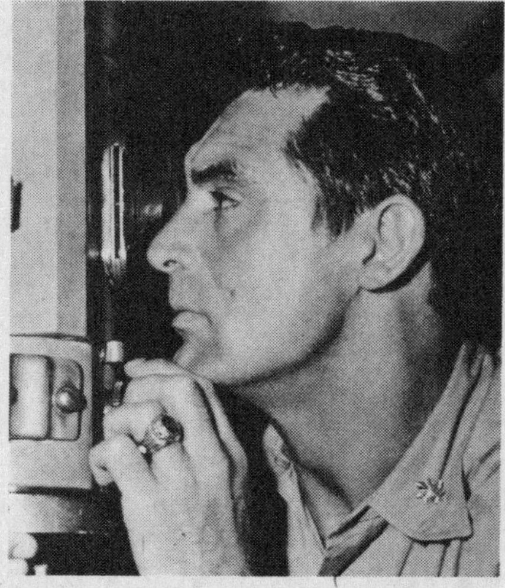

Cary Grant is skipper of a U.S. submarine in Destination Tokyo.

Taut World War II action/adventure, with Grant the skipper of a submarine that slips into Tokyo Bay. Suspense as well as good acting heighten this enjoyable wartime drama. There is fine interplay among the crew members as tension mounts. Garfield and Dane Clark come across as colorful submariners. Faye Emerson and John Forsythe are also in the cast. **Director**—Delmer Daves. **Academy Award Nomination**—Steve Fisher, original story. *135 minutes b&w*

DESTROYER (1943)

Edward G. Robinson
Glenn Ford

Robinson plays an old salt who ships out on a destroyer and clashes with the young sailors. A routine and predictable flag-waving film with below-par production values. Ford is on board as a novice seaman with his own methods of doing things, but Robinson emerges as the real pro. Marguerite Chapman, Edgar Buchanan, and Leo Gorcey contribute support. **Director**—William A. Seiter. *99 minutes b&w*

▢® *This movie available with closed captions for the hearing impaired.*

DESTRY RIDES AGAIN (1939)

★★★★

James Stewart
Marlene Dietrich
Brian Donlevy

Marlene Dietrich vamps James Stewart in Destry Rides Again.

A classic western, loaded with rousing action, suspense, satire, pathos, and even some fine musical numbers. Stewart is superb as a polite sheriff who gets fed up with local rowdiness and corruption and decides to clean up the town. Dietrich is great as a saloon dancer who sings "See What the Boys in the Back Room Will Have." This Hollywood gem spawned several imitators, but this version is the best. Lively acting from Charles Winninger, Samuel S. Hinds, and Jack Carson. **Director**—George Marshall. *94 minutes b&w*

DETECTIVE (1985)

★★

Nathalie Baye
Johnny Halliday
Claude Brasseur

New Wave filmmaker Jean-Luc Godard dishes up a thick stew of obscure characters, confusing dialogue, and murky plot in this comic homage to *films noirs.* Various men and women wander around a Paris hotel seeking love, money, and contentment. It takes some detective work on the audience's part to sort out the course of events. Originally filmed in French. **Director**—Godard. **(No MPAA rating)** *95 minutes*

THE DETECTIVE (1968)

★★★

Frank Sinatra
Lee Remick
Ralph Meeker

Sinatra makes the most of the sleazy material as he plays a tough New York City detective assigned to a case involving the murder of a homosexual. The film is based on a best-selling novel by Roderick Thorp, but the script and smart dialogue by Abby Mann are typical of Mann's moralistic and socially relevant style. The film was criticized at the time of release for being particularly brutal, but it can now be seen as a forerunner to the hard-edged, more violent detective thrillers of today. Jacqueline Bisset, Jack Klugman, William Windom, Tony Musante, and Al Freeman play supporting roles. **Director**—Gordon Douglas. *114 minutes*

DETECTIVE STORY (1951)

★★★½

Kirk Douglas
Eleanor Parker
William Bendix

Douglas is excellent as a tough city detective whose sense of morality and honesty erodes after extensive contact with criminals and a shocking revelation about his wife's past. The action occurs for the most part during a day in a New York City police station. The film, adapted from Sidney Kingsley's fine Broadway play, retains much of its impact on the screen. Lee Grant makes her screen debut as a shoplifter, Bendix turns in a fine performance as a police sergeant, and Parker is magnificent as Douglas' neglected wife. Also with Cathy O'Donnell, George Macready, and Horace MacMahon. **Director**—William Wyler. **Academy Award Nominations**—Wyler, best director; Parker, best actress; Grant, best supporting actress; Philip Yordan and Robert Wyler, screenplay. *103 minute b&w*

THE DEVIL AND MAX DEVLIN (1981)

★★

Elliott Gould
Bill Cosby

Gould plays Max Devlin, a grumpy Los Angeles landlord who escapes eternal damnation by conning three innocents into signing their souls over to Satan. Cosby plays the Devil. The plot is familiar (*Heaven Can Wait; Angel on My Shoulder*), and the ending is predictable. But this Disney production is executed with warmth and a decent amount of suspense. There are endearing performances, too—especially from Gould, who works like the devil to secure the confidence of his young victims. **Director**—Steven Stern. **(PG)** *96 minutes*

THE DEVIL AND MISS JONES (1941)

★★★

Jean Arthur
Charles Coburn

A delightful comedy filled with captivating moments and social awareness. Coburn is exceptionally effective as a department-store owner who masquerades as a clerk in his own establishment to solve problems among his employees. The humor is old-fashioned, but it retains its impact. Robert Cummings, Spring Byington, S.Z. Sakall, and William Demarest also star. **Director**—Sam Wood. **Academy Award Nominations**—Coburn, best supporting actor; Norman Krasna, original screenplay. *92 minutes b&w*

THE DEVIL'S PLAYGROUND (1976)

★★

Simon Burke
Arthur Dignam
Nick Tate
Charles McCallum

This Australian film by director Fred Schepisi is filled with good intentions, but it isn't particularly moving. The somewhat autobiographical story, set in a Catholic seminary, involves the sexual awakening of a 13-year-old boy, played by Burke, who is studying for the priesthood. He's caught between temptations of the flesh and controls imposed by the brothers, who are also tormented by such restrictions. The performances are decent, with Dignam, Tate, and McCallum standing out. **(No MPAA rating)** *107 minutes*

DIABOLIQUE (1955)

★★★★

Simone Signoret
Charles Vanel

Signoret's masterful acting and Henri-Georges Clouzot's superb directing turn this thriller into a film gem. The wife and mistress of a schoolmaster work together to murder him, only to discover they might have bungled the job. The tension builds slowly and de-

(Continued)

(Continued)
liberately to a high pitch. Also with Vera Clouzot and Paul Meurisse. Originally filmed in French. *107 minutes b&w*

DIAL M FOR MURDER (1954)

★★★

Ray Milland
Grace Kelly
Robert Cummings
John Williams

Robert Cummings and Grace Kelly in Dial M for Murder.

Alfred Hitchcock adapted Frederick Knott's Broadway mystery/drama for the screen with interesting results, but this isn't among Hitchcock's greatest efforts. A man (Milland) plots his wife's death to inherit money, but the scheme goes awry when the wife kills the hired assassin in self-defense. Kelly plays the wife; Williams is the police inspector. Also with Anthony Dawson. Originally filmed in 3-D. The 3-D version was rereleased in 1980 with a PG rating. *105 minutes*

DIAMOND HEAD (1962)

★★

Charlton Heston
Yvette Mimieux

Heston stars as an overbearing Hawaiian plantation owner whose stubbornness makes things difficult for his family. The film, based on Peter Gilman's novel, comes off as a dazzling soap opera, with the cardboard characters involved in run-on conflicts. The tropical settings are easy on the eyes, but the script is predictable and labored. Supporting players also include France Nuyen, James Darren, Aline MacMahon, and Richard Loo. **Director**—Guy Green. *107 minutes*

DIAMOND HORSESHOE (1945)

★★★

Betty Grable
Dick Haymes

A lavish musical with some old pros performing their acts in Billy Rose's famous night spot. The routine plot has Grable playing a nightclub singer who chucks fame and fortune to marry a struggling medical student, played by Haymes. "The More I See You" is among the musical numbers. William Gaxton, Phil Silvers, Beatrice Kay, Carmen Cavallaro, and Margaret Dumont also participate in the frolic. **Director**—George Seaton. *104 minutes*

DIAMOND JIM (1935)

★★★

Edward Arnold
Jean Arthur
Binnie Barnes

Film biography of Diamond Jim Brady, the turn-of-the-century millionaire with a grand appetite for food, money, and Lillian Russell. Brady's questionable business ethics reflect the Gay Nineties lifestyle in this light period drama. Glittering costumes and sets and strong performances by Arthur, Barnes, Cesar Romero, and Eric Blore add to the entertainment. Arnold made the title role his own and seemed to literally and figuratively grow with it. **Director**—A. Edward Sutherland. *94 minutes b&w*

DIAMONDS ARE FOREVER (1971)

★★★

Sean Connery

Sean Connery and Lana Wood go for broke in Diamonds Are Forever.

Connery returns to the role of James Bond in the eighth of this popular series. Set in Las Vegas, the film boasts more gimmicks and stunts than its predecessors, often at the expense of the storyline. But 007 fans will be happy to see their hero pitted once more against a villain bent on ruling the world. Jill St. John, Bruce Cabot, Charles Gray, Lana Wood, and Bernard Lee are among the supporting cast who keep the entertainment value high. **Director**—Guy Hamilton. **(PG)** *119 minutes*

DIARY OF A MAD HOUSEWIFE (1970)

★★★★

Carrie Snodgress
Richard Benjamin

Thoroughly enjoyable satire of a bored housewife who has an affair with an arrogant writer, played convincingly by Frank Langella. Snodgress gives an excellent performance as the wife. Smart dialogue, snappy direction, and fine performances are everywhere in this insightful look at a deteriorating contemporary marriage. Benjamin is on target as the self-centered, overreaching husband whose law career founders. Lorraine Cullen and Frannie Michel appear in supporting roles. **Director**—Frank Perry. **(R) Academy Award Nomination**—Snodgress, best actress. *95 minutes*

THE DIARY OF ANNE FRANK (1959)

★★★★

Millie Perkins
Joseph Schildkraut
Shelley Winters
Ed Wynn

Moving and gripping account of a family of Dutch Jews who hide from the Nazis in a factory loft for two years. The film faithfully follows the Broadway play, based on the meticulous and touching diary of the young girl who eventually died in a Nazi concentration camp. Perkins, in the title role, looks a lot like the real Anne, but her performance isn't up to the role. Excellent acting from the supporting cast and good direction, however, make up for this minor weakness. Also with Lou Jacobi, Richard Beymer, and Diane Baker. Some versions of the film on videotape run 150 minutes. **Director**—George Stevens. **Academy Awards**—Winters, best supporting actress; William C. Mellor, cinematography. **Nominations**—best picture; Stevens, best director; Wynn, best supporting actor.

170 minutes b&w

DICK TRACY (1990)

★★★½

Warren Beatty
Al Pacino
Madonna

Out of the comic pages and onto the screen comes this ultra-stylish and inventive film about the square-jawed crimebuster. Beatty, in the title role, plays straight man to a cast of grotesquely made up villains in a setting that was inspired by the colorful pages of the Sunday comics. The makeup and set design are foregrounded to such a degree that the film's few critics complained that these production elements got in the way of the story. Yet, the visual elements *are* the story in that the villainy of a character is denoted by the heavy makeup, while the primary-color production design implies a simple world where the line between good and evil is clear-cut. The viewer comprehends a good portion of the narrative as soon as he sees the visuals. A number of big-name stars and character actors make cameo appearances as the villains, including Dustin Hoffman as Mumbles, William Forsythe as Flattop, Mandy Patinkin as 88 Keys, Paul Sorvino as Lips, and R.G. Armstrong as Pruneface; but it is Pacino, as the notorious Big Boy Caprice, who almost steals the movie. Madonna was born to play Breathless Mahoney, the vampy saloon singer, while Glenne Headly makes the most of her dull role of Tess Trueheart. A fantastic celebration of pop culture. **Director**—Beatty. **(PG)**

103 minutes

DIE HARD (1988)

★★★½

Bruce Willis
Alan Rickman
Reginald VelJohnson

John McTierman directs an exciting action thriller packed with clever (though often violent) surprises. The setting is a Los Angeles high-rise office building, and a visiting New York cop (Willis) takes on some sophisticated terrorists holding hostages who were attending a Christmas Eve party. Rickman, who plays the terrorist leader, and VelJohnson, as an L.A. policeman, provide fine supporting work. Willis' working-class hero, John McClane, is tough and resourceful, but he is irreverent and physically vulnerable, too. Willis gives a star-making performance that offers fans everything they expect, while gently spoofing the conventions of the genre. **(R)** *127 minutes*

Bruce Willis works up a sweat tackling the bad guys in Die Hard.

DIE HARD 2: DIE HARDER (1990)

★★½

Bruce Willis
Bonnie Bedelia
William Sadler

A band of American terrorists, determined to free a Manuel Noriega–like foreign dictator, seizes control of Dulles airport on Christmas Eve. Maverick detective John McClane, again played by the affable Willis, just happens to be there awaiting the arrival of wife Bedelia. Once again, McClane gets entrapped into subduing the terrorists and rescuing his wife. This highly touted sequel matches the original in terms of the frenetic pace, daring stunts, large-scale mechanical and special effects (though a couple of effects do misfire), and riveting suspense. But this time around, little effort was made to dig into McClane's character. Without the buddy relationship with the sympathetic beat cop from the first film, this follow-up has no device with which McClane can reveal his thoughts and feelings. He merely leaps from one improbable stunt to another, losing some of the working-class, everyman quality that made the character so appealing the first time out. Also with Franco Nero, William Atherton, John Amos, Reginald VelJohnson, Art Evans, Fred Dalton Thompson, and Dennis Franz. **Director**—Renny Harlin. **(R)**

124 minutes

DILLINGER (1945)

★★★

Lawrence Tierney
Edmund Lowe
Eduardo Ciannelli

Tierney stars as John Dillinger, the infamous bank robber whose career ended abruptly in front of the Biograph Theater in Chicago, when he was gunned down by the police in 1934 after a well-documented manhunt. Elisha Cook, Jr., Marc Lawrence, and Anne Jeffries turn in strong supporting performances in this taut and well-paced thriller. Less violent than John Milius' 1973 version of *Dillinger* (though still a shocker in its time), this film says more with less and keeps our attention with the well-written script by Philip Yordan and tight direction by Max Nosseck.

89 minutes b&w

DILLINGER (1973)

★★★

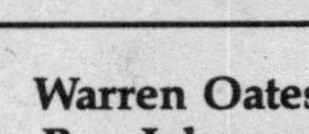

Warren Oates
Ben Johnson
Michelle Phillips
Richard Dreyfuss

Oates is perfectly cast in director John Milius' explosively violent look at the criminal career of one of the Depression era's most notorious badmen, the clever and cocky John Dillinger. Also on hand are Baby Face Nelson (Dreyfuss), Pretty Boy Floyd (Steve Kanaly), and a host of other tough guys. Johnson is appropriately single-minded as G-man Melvin Purvis, who won't rest until Dillinger is brought to justice. The period flavor is impeccable, and the film has a sardonic sense of humor, but the highlights are the brilliantly staged gun battles, which erupt with the fury of Vesuvius. Rough stuff, but terrific entertainment for those who can take it. Solid support by Harry Dean Stanton, Cloris Leachman, and Geoffrey Lewis. **(R)** *96 minutes*

DINER (1982)

★★★½

Kevin Bacon
Mickey Rourke
Ellen Barkin

Screenwriter Barry Levinson debuts as a director with this comedy. The action, set in the late 1950s, converges on a local hangout/eatery. The plot involves

(Continued)

(Continued)
five male friends trying to cope with early adult life. Although the film is heavy going at times, it's an authentic portrayal of the period. The characters are so fully realized you can even look into their futures—which don't appear too promising. There's laughter and high spirits throughout, which sometimes mask the film's darker side. This movie gains much of its impact from the sharp, funny screenplay and the fine acting of several very talented new performers. **(R) Academy Award Nomination**—Levinson, best original screenplay. *110 minutes*

DIRTY DANCING (1987)

★★★

Patrick Swayze
Jennifer Grey

Patrick Swayze and Jennifer Grey fall in love in Dirty Dancing.

An appealing love story set in a Catskills resort hotel in 1963 against a backdrop of early rock music and modern dance. Grey stars as the teenage daughter of a prominent doctor; Swayze costars as the working-class dance instructor she falls in love with. The *Romeo and Juliet* plot may be familiar, but the execution of the dance sequences is stylish and energetic. "Dirty dancing" becomes a metaphor in the film for the sexual awakening of Grey's character as well as for the introduction of working class culture, via rock music and free-form dancing, into the mainstream. The film gave Swayze, formerly a dancer with Eliot Feld's company, his first opportunity to display his dancing skills on the big screen. A surprise box-office smash at the time of release. Also with Jerry Orbach, Cynthia Rhodes, and Jack Weston, with a special appearance by tap-dancing great Honie Coles. **Director**—Emile Ardolino. **(PG–13) Academy Award**—Franke Previte, John DeNicola, and Donald Markowitz, best song ("I've Had the Time of My Life"). *100 minutes*

THE DIRTY DOZEN (1967)

★★★½

Lee Marvin
Jim Brown
Ernest Borgnine
John Cassavetes
Robert Ryan
Charles Bronson

Slam-bang, overly violent World War II adventure with an intriguing angle on combat. Twelve convicts, most of them murderers, get out of prison in exchange for their services in a military commando unit, where they're trained to kill for the army. It's professionally done, with lots of tough, he-man action scenes. Director Robert Aldrich doesn't neglect character development, and he offers some insights into the personalities of these unusual recruits. Marvin and Cassavetes stand out among the cast, which also includes Donald Sutherland, Trini Lopez, Clint Walker, Ralph Meeker, George Kennedy, and Richard Jaeckel. **Academy Award Nomination**—Cassavetes, best supporting actor. *150 minutes*

DIRTY HARRY (1971)

★★★½

Clint Eastwood
Harry Guardino

Clint Eastwood dispenses his own brand of law and order in Dirty Harry.

Eastwood stars as a San Francisco supercop who stops at nothing to bring in a crazy sniper who calls himself Scorpio. Eastwood is at his steely-eyed best, and whether or not you agree with the notions of vigilante justice put forth here, you have to admire the force with which they're presented. Director Don Siegel's lightning-fast pace makes this first Harry Callahan film superior to such sequels as *Magnum Force, The Enforcer,* and *Sudden Impact*. The cast also includes Reni Santoni, John Vernon, and Andy Robinson. **(R)** *103 minutes*

DIRTY ROTTEN SCOUNDRELS (1988)

★★★

Michael Caine
Steve Martin

Steve Martin and Michael Caine have a common interest in Dirty Rotten Scoundrels.

Caine and Martin are delightful as competing conmen in the business of relieving wealthy women of their money. Set on the French Riviera, this breezy remake of the 1964 comedy *Bedtime Story* offers some inspired moments with Caine as the suave aristocrat and Martin as the klutz. The script falters occasionally, but there are enough goofy escapades as well as good star chemistry to keep the film entertaining. Glenne Headly costars as an inviting target for the swindlers. **Director**—Frank Oz. **(PG)** *110 minutes*

DISORDERLIES (1987)

★½

The Fat Boys
Ralph Bellamy

The Fat Boys, three hefty rap music stars, play bumbling medical aides in this raucous but hopelessly inept farce. Bellamy costars as an ailing Palm Beach millionaire to whom the Boys administer their far-out brand of medical care. Hired by Bellamy's scheming nephew in the hopes of worsening the old man's condition, the Boys actually cure him of his mostly psychosomatic illnesses. The slapstick antics here are corny, awkward, and gross—especially scenes showing the Boys stuffing their mouths with food or slapping each other

This movie available with closed captions for the hearing impaired.

The Fat Boys take care of millionaire Ralph Bellamy in The Disorderlies.

around. The Fat Boys (Mark Morales, Damon Wimbley, and Darren Robinson) try hard to capture the Three Stooges' style, but Larry, Curly, and Moe can rest peacefully. Also with Anthony Geary. **Director**—Michael Schultz. **(PG)** *96 minutes.*

DISORGANIZED CRIME (1989)

★★

Corbin Bernsen
Ruben Blades
Lou Diamond Phillips
Fred Gwynne

This comedy about a group of inept bank robbers follows the formula of a few dozen previous heist pictures; only the faces are different. Bernsen, Blades, Gwynne, and Phillips play bumbling criminals bent on holding up a Montana bank. They generate some energy, but with a minimum of humor and suspense. **Director**—Jim Kouf. **(R)**

98 minutes

A DISPATCH FROM REUTERS (1940)

★★★

Edward G. Robinson
Edna Best
Eddie Albert

An interesting and informative film biography about the man who founded Europe's first news service. Robinson does a fine acting job as Reuter, and production details are first-class. Also with Gene Lockhart, Otto Kruger, Nigel Bruce, and Albert Basserman. **Director**—William Dieterle.

90 minute b&w

DISRAELI (1929)

★★★

George Arliss
Joan Bennett
Anthony Bushell

Arliss steals this one as the brilliant British Prime Minister and wily statesman who inspired the building of the Suez Canal. Arliss won an Oscar for his authoritative portrayal of the great man in this glamorized historical drama, after having played the same role in a silent version in 1921. A light touch is added when Arliss serves as matchmaker to Bennett and Bushell. The script by Julian Josephson gently depicts this man of many facets. **Director**—Alfred E. Green. **Academy Award**—Arliss, best actor. **Nominations**—best picture; Josephson, writing achievement. *89 minutes b&w*

DISTANT THUNDER (1975)

★★★★

This vivid and powerful film by Indian director Satyajit Ray is about a famine that took the lives of five million people in 1943. The story, set in a remote Bengali village, focuses on the impact among the villagers as their rice supply is slowly depleted. The crisis prompts the social awakening of a pompous village Brahmin. Richly photographed, and exquisitely performed and directed. Originally filmed in Bengali. **(No MPAA rating)**

100 minutes

DISTANT THUNDER (1988)

★★

John Lithgow
Ralph Macchio

Lithgow stars as a Vietnam veteran who never got over the anguish of his war experience. He seeks reconciliation with his 18-year-old son (Macchio), whom he hasn't seen since the boy was an infant. Their burgeoning relationship may be the vet's best hope to return to reality. Despite good intentions, this crude melodrama is riddled with clichés and unnecessary violence. The fine actors do their best with the amateurish script. Also with Kerrie Kean, Reb Brown, and Janet Margolin. **Director**—Dick Rosenthal. **(R)**

114 minutes

DIVA (1982)

★★★

Frédéric Andrei
Wilhelmenia Fernandez

French director Jean-Jacques Beineix is off to an impressive start with this remarkable, fast-moving mystery/thriller set in Paris. The churning plot involves a young messenger who becomes the prey of sinister characters after he secretly tapes the performance of an opera soprano. Even though the story at times does not make much sense, the film's flamboyant energy and delicious imagery are always fascinating. Originally filmed in French. **(R)**

123 minutes

DIVINE MADNESS (1980)

★★½

Bette Midler

Midler belts out an assortment of musical numbers, struts about in wild costumes, and tells raunchy jokes in this concert film that displays her extraordinary talents. The Divine Miss M demonstrates amazing energy and showmanship that should please her fans. Some of the songs are unappealing, however, and the pacing is often uneven. The result is a mixture of Midler's magical madness and many irritating lapses in her performance. **Director**—Michael Ritchie. **(R)** *94 minutes*

DIVORCE AMERICAN STYLE (1967)

★★★

Dick Van Dyke
Debbie Reynolds

The great talents of writer/producer Norman Lear and director Bud Yorkin combine for this stinging and stylish satire on suburban marriage and family problems. Van Dyke and Reynolds star as the upper-middle-class Los Angeles couple who are on the verge of splitting, but conclude they're in for more trouble if they divorce. This is a highly entertaining film with good performances all around. Others in the cast are Jason Robards, Jean Simmons, Van Johnson, Joe Flynn, Shelley Berman, Lee Grant, and Tom Bosley. **Academy Award Nomination**—Robert Kaufman and Lear, best story and screenplay written directly for the screen.

109 minutes

This movie available on videotape and/or disc.

DIVORCE—ITALIAN STYLE (1962)

★★★★

Marcello Mastroianni

Excellent satirical comedy on modern Italian morals and lifestyles. Mastroianni gives a fine performance as a Sicilian nobleman who, driven by archaic laws prohibiting divorce, manages to get rid of his wife by having her seduced and later eliminated by a jealous lover. With superb direction by Pietro Germi, this black comedy was the prototype for a series of lesser films that tried to imitate it but never captured its wit and sheer comic brilliance. **Academy Award**—Ennio de Concini, Alfredo Giannetti, and Germi, best story and screenplay written directly for the screen. **Nominations**—Germi, best director; Mastroianni, best actor.

104 minutes b&w

D.O.A. (1988)

★★★

Dennis Quaid
Meg Ryan
Daniel Stern

Quaid stars as an English professor who discovers he is fatally poisoned in this stylish mystery thriller. He desperately tries to find his own assassin during the final hours of his life. This inventive mystery is an effective reworking of the 1949 *film noir* thriller that starred Edmond O'Brien. The film relies a great deal on its visual style—distorted perspectives, dark settings puncuated with lurid colors, and brisk pacing—to create an atmosphere suitable for the dark human emotions and despair of the storyline. The supporting cast includes Charlotte Rampling, Jane Kaczmarek, and Rob Knepper. **Directors**—Rocky Morton and Annabel Jankel. **(R)**

100 minutes

THE DOCTOR AND THE DEVILS (1985)

★★★

Timothy Dalton
Jonathan Pryce
Twiggy

A tense, striking Gothic horror film loosely based on the careers of two 19th-century English graverobbers and murderers who supplied a respected doctor with fresh corpses. Some scenes

Jonathan Pryce, Twiggy, and Stephen Rea in The Doctor and the Devils.

are exceptionally graphic and grisly. But the vivid production design also expertly depicts English society of the period. Acting and characterizations are first-rate. **Director**—Freddie Francis. **(R)**

92 minutes

DOCTOR DETROIT (1983)

★½

Dan Aykroyd
Howard Hesseman
Kate Murtagh

Aykroyd hams it up here as a square college professor who masquerades as a big-time pimp. Such shifts in personality have been the subject of many a movie comedy, but Aykroyd pursues this well-worn theme on leaden feet. This is labored, sloppy filmmaking, heavy on confusion and short on good jokes. **Director**—Michael Pressman. **(R)**

89 minutes

DR. DOOLITTLE (1967)

★★

Rex Harrison
Anthony Newley
Samantha Eggar

Overlong fantasy/musical based on the novels of Hugh Lofting, about the magnificent veterinary doctor who can talk to animals. Some animals may get a kick out of this one, but for Homo sapiens, it's a charmless, plodding affair. The songs are forgettable; the acting is lackluster. Harrison is in the title role with support from Newley, Eggar, Richard Attenborough, and Peter Bull. Some prints run 144 minutes. **Director**—Richard Fleischer. **Academy Award Nominations**—best picture; Robert Surtees, cinematography.

152 minutes

DR. JEKYLL AND MR. HYDE (1932)

★★★★

Fredric March
Miriam Hopkins

Of the several cinematic versions of the Robert Louis Stevenson classic, this one is most noted for its innovative use of makeup and camera tricks that highlight the transformation from good doctor to evil monster. March won an Oscar for his performance as the tormented scientist who discovers the formula that isolates and unlocks the evil in his soul. Hopkins performs beautifully as the temptress Ivy. The pace is exciting and the interpretation imaginative under the creative and skillful direction of Rouben Mamoulian. **Academy Award**—March, best actor. **Nomination**—Percy Heath and Samuel Hoffenstein, adaptation.

82 minutes b&w

DR. NO (1962)

★★★★

Sean Connery
Ursula Andress
Jack Lord

This first in the popular James Bond superspy thriller series is one of the best. Connery plays British secret agent 007, who tries to save the world from a powerful fiend operating from a base in Jamaica. The film sparkles with fabulous tongue-in-cheek humor, snappy action, gorgeous girls, exotic hardware, and beautiful locales. After this success, Ian Fleming's indestructible hero just kept coming back to the screen for more adventures. Also with Joseph Wiseman, Bernard Lee, John Kitzmiller, Lois Maxwell, and Anthony Dawson. **Director**—Terence Young.

111 minutes

DR. STRANGELOVE: OR, HOW I LEARNED TO STOP WORRYING AND LOVE THE BOMB (1964)

★★★★

Peter Sellers
George C. Scott
Peter Bull
Sterling Hayden

Director Stanley Kubrick's towering black comedy seems to become more poignant and pertinent as time marches on. The plot concerns a fanati-

® *This movie available with closed captions for the hearing impaired.*

cal U.S. general who launches a nuclear attack on Russia. And when a bomber cannot be recalled, the U.S. sadly awaits devastating retaliation. Sellers, in the best acting job of his career, is magnificent in three memorable roles—the U.S. President, a British officer, and a creepy nuclear scientist. Other fabulous portrayals abound, with Hayden, Scott, Keenan Wynn, and Slim Pickens leading the way. Kubrick's perceptive view of our fragile security in the nuclear age is presented with biting humor and suspense. It's remarkable, classic moviemaking. Also with James Earl Jones and Tracy Reed. **Academy Award Nominations**—best picture; Kubrick, best director; Sellers, best actor; Kubrick, Peter George, and Terry Southern, best screenplay based on material from another medium. **(PG)**

93 minutes b&w

DOCTOR ZHIVAGO (1965)

 ★★★★

Omar Sharif
Julie Christie
Rod Steiger
Alec Guinness

Julie Christie comforts revolutionary Tom Courtenay in Doctor Zhivago.

An exquisite historical film with spectacular production detail, based on Boris Pasternak's novel about Russia at the time of the Revolution. The movie seems overextended at times, yet it offers some engrossing moments and fine performances by a good cast. The plot involves a number of characters whose lives intertwine over the course of the film. Most memorable is Sharif as a Russian doctor who's forced into the army; Christie and Geraldine Chaplin play the women in his life. The big-name cast also includes Tom Courtenay, Rita Tushingham, and Ralph Richardson. **Director**—David Lean. **(PG) Academy Awards**—Robert Bolt, best screenplay based on material from another medium; Freddie Young, cinematography. **Nominations**—best picture; Lean, best director; Courtenay, best supporting actor. *197 minutes*

DODSWORTH (1936)

★★★★

Walter Huston
Ruth Chatterton
Mary Astor
Maria Ouspenskaya

A cinematic classic based on the Sinclair Lewis novel of a self-made American businessman and his wife, whose lives are irrevocably altered when they confront European society's morals and values. The entire cast is superb, with Huston in the title role and Chatterton as the frivolous wife who cannot face growing old gracefully. Brilliant performances are also turned in by Astor as the world-weary American divorcée who knows the real value of Dodsworth, and by Ouspenskaya as a European dowager who puts Chatterton in her place. William Wyler's direction is intelligent and sensitive. **Academy Award Nominations**—best picture; Wyler, best director; Huston, best actor; Sidney Howard, screenplay.

101 minutes b&w

DOG DAY AFTERNOON (1975)

★★★★

Al Pacino
John Cazale
Charles Durning

In Dog Day Afternoon, *John Cazale and Al Pacino try to rob a bank but bungle the job.*

A true story based on a bungled bank heist in Brooklyn on a hot summer day. It's a thrilling, energetic mixture of comedy and tension. Brilliant acting by Pacino as the bisexual robber out to get money for a sex-change operation for his boyfriend, played by Chris Sarandon. There are other shining characterizations by a large supporting cast, which includes Sully Boyar and James Broderick. **Director**—Sidney Lumet. **(R) Academy Award**—Frank Pierson, best original screenplay. **Nominations**—best picture; Lumet, best director; Pacino, best actor; Sarandon, best supporting actor. *130 minutes*

THE DOGS OF WAR (1980)

★★★

Christopher Walken
Colin Blakely
Tom Berenger

Steely-eyed, mysterious Jamie Shannon, played by Walken, runs a dial-a-mercenary service from his seedy New York City apartment. He and his pals are dispatched to overthrow an Idi Amin-type dictatorship. The final combat scenes are executed with stunning shoot-'em-up flourish. The film, based on the Frederick Forsyth novel, never fully explores the psychology of soldiers of fortune. But director John Irvin, in his first narrative movie, puts together a taut and intelligent action/adventure, with smashing performances by Walken, Blakely, and Berenger. British prints are 118 minutes. **(R)**

102 minutes

LA DOLCE VITA (1960)

 ★★★★

Marcello Mastroianni
Anita Ekberg

Epic satire of contemporary Roman society seen through the eyes of a gossip columnist. This lengthy but brilliant panorama of Italy's upper classes is effectively shown in a series of connected episodes, each more visually stunning than the previous; and each more devastating as it reveals a frivolous and valueless lifestyle without moral consequence. Director Federico Fellini creates a masterpiece for his time and sets the stage for a decade of cinematic inventiveness among his peers. The excellent, star-studded cast also includes Anouk Aimée, Alain Cuny, Yvonne Furneaux, Magali Noel, Nadia Gray,

(Continued)

This movie available on videotape and/or disc.

(Continued)
and Lex Barker. Originally filmed in Italian. **Academy Award Nominations**—Fellini, best director; Fellini, Tullio Pinelli, Ennio Flaiano, and Brunello Rondi, best story and screenplay written directly for the screen.
175 minutes b&w

A DOLL'S HOUSE (1973)

★★★

Claire Bloom
Anthony Hopkins

Ibsen's 19th-century play about women's rights is handled with efficient direction and good acting. Bloom and Hopkins do well in the key roles; Bloom is Nora, the mousy wife who declares her independence when her husband approaches death. Supporting roles are performed by Ralph Richardson, Denholm Elliott, Anna Massey, and Edith Evans. **Director**—Patrick Garland. **(G)** *95 minutes*

A DOLL'S HOUSE (1973)

★★

Jane Fonda
Trevor Howard

Fonda takes a shot at playing Nora, the shy 19th-century housewife who strikes out for liberation from her overbearing husband. This role would seem to be well-suited for Fonda, but she handles the Ibsen character rather unevenly. Howard, however, does better as Dr. Rank. The movie's statement on behalf of women's liberation is muddled, but this version of the play is the most cinematic, featuring location shooting and an attempt to accurately depict the Scandinavian environs. Also stars David Warner and Edward Fox. **Director**—Joseph Losey. **(No MPAA rating)** *103 minutes*

DOMINICK AND EUGENE (1988)

★★1/2 ®

Tom Hulce
Ray Liotta

Brotherly love provides the core of this heartwarming drama, which unfolds without undue sentimentality. Eugene (Liotta), an ambitious medical student, takes care of his twin brother Dominick (Hulce), a mentally handicapped garbage man. Dominick's labors help pay for his brother's education. Their close bond is threatened when Eugene gets an opportunity to finish his medical studies across the country at Stanford. The poignant story is highlighted by excellent performances, particularly by Hulce as the vulnerable and kindhearted sibling. **Director**—Robert M. Young. **(PG–13)** *111 minutes*

THE DOMINO PRINCIPLE (1977)

★

Gene Hackman
Candice Bergen
Richard Widmark

Hackman plays a convict who's sprung from prison by a powerful intelligence organization that wants his assistance in an assassination job. It's never explained in this incoherent and humdrum movie who the victim is, what the conspiracy is about, who is behind this nameless secret agency, or why we should even care. Also with Mickey Rooney, Edward Albert, and Eli Wallach. A bad mark for director Stanley Kramer, who is known for better filmmaking. **(R)** *97 minutes*

DONOVAN'S REEF (1963)

★★★

John Wayne
Lee Marvin
Jack Warden

There's fun and frolic with this broad comedy about some war veterans who reside on a Pacific island. Their carefree life is interrupted when a daughter of one of the men pays them a visit. Everyone has a fine time with the bouncy comedy and spirited action. Also in the cast are Dorothy Lamour, Elizabeth Allen, Cesar Romero, and Mike Mazurki. **Director**—John Ford. *108 minutes*

DON'T BOTHER TO KNOCK (1952)

★★1/2

Marilyn Monroe
Richard Widmark

Monroe stars as a disturbed girl hired as a babysitter in a hotel, who threatens to harm the youngster in her care. A tough act for Monroe at the outset of her career because of the lackluster script. Veteran actor Widmark fares only slightly better, as a tough but nice guy who comes to the rescue. Anne Bancroft costars as a singer who works in the hotel. Jeanne Cagney, Donna Corcoran, Elisha Cook, Jr., Gloria Blondell, and Jim Backus also star. **Director**—Roy Baker.
76 minutes b&w

Marilyn Monroe meets her little charge, Donna Corcoran, in Don't Bother to Knock.

DON'T GO NEAR THE WATER (1957)

★★

Glenn Ford
Fred Clark
Gia Scala

An adolescent service comedy about a World War II public-relations operation on an exotic South Pacific island. The uneven farce offers moments of amusement with equal amounts of boredom. The film is based on William Brinkley's novel. Also with Anne Francis, Eva Gabor, Romney Brent, Mickey Shaughnessy, and Keenan Wynn. **Director**—Charles Walters.
107 minutes

DON'T LOOK NOW (1973)

★★★1/2

Donald Sutherland
Julie Christie

Daphne du Maurier's suspense story is handled with eerie style and a bit of artiness by director Nicolas Roeg, who filmed against the spooky background of Venice in winter. A young British woman tries to contact her daughter, killed in an accident, through a medium. The husband refuses to believe it is possible. The attempt only leads to further tragedy. Fine performances by Sutherland and Christie, with support from Hilary Mason, Clelia Matania, and Massimo Serato. **(R)** *110 minutes*

® *This movie available with closed captions for the hearing impaired.*

DO THE RIGHT THING (1989)

★★★½

Danny Aiello
Spike Lee
Ossie Davis
Ruby Dee

Provocative filmmaking from the talented Lee, who wrote, directed, and starred in this portrait of racial tension in a predominantly black Brooklyn neighborhood. The complexities of inner-city frustrations and racial disharmony are intelligently presented, and no facile, easy-to-digest conclusion (as in *Driving Miss Daisy*) is reached. The story concerns an Italian restaurant owner at odds with some of his black clientele. The strength of the film lies in Lee's efforts to present many black voices, instead of assuming that all have the same position. Some are militant, some are resigned to their lot in life, and some are practical in their approach to race relations. Though some scenes are uncomfortable to watch, Lee succeeds in forcing the viewer to think and confront the issues addressed in the film. In addition to the meaningful subject, Lee's visual style is strikingly bold and colorful. Also with Joie Lee (Spike's sister), Giancarlo Esposito, Bill Nunn, and John Turturro. **(R) Academy Award Nominations**—Aiello, best supporting actor; Lee, best original screenplay. *120 minutes*

DOUBLE INDEMNITY (1944)

Fred MacMurray
Barbara Stanwyck
Edward G. Robinson

Barbara Stanwyck and Fred MacMurray plot to kill in Double Indemnity.

This is one of the best *films noirs* of the 1940s. The Raymond Chandler script is based on the James M. Cain novel of conspiracy and murder. MacMurray plays an insurance salesman conned into killing the husband of a fetching beauty, played by Stanwyck, to collect the insurance money. Director Billy Wilder coaxes dynamite performances from the entire cast, and John Seitz's Oscar-nominated cinematography effectively captures the seedy surroundings associated with the plot. Robinson also stands out as MacMurray's boss, who cracks the case. There's double suspense and triple excitement. Also with Tom Powers, Porter Hall, and Jean Heather. **Academy Award Nominations**—best picture; Wilder, best director; Stanwyck, best actress; Chandler and Wilder, screenplay; John Seitz, cinematography. *107 minutes b&w*

A DOUBLE LIFE (1947)

★★★★

Ronald Colman
Shelley Winters

Colman gives one of the best performances of his career as a Shakespearean actor whose offstage life imitates his theater role. Colman, who is playing the role of Othello, kills a woman he believes to be Desdemona. The electrifying melodrama is laced with effective suspense and crackling dialogue. Fine support from Winters, Signe Hasso, Edmond O'Brien, and Millard Mitchell. **Director**—George Cukor. **Academy Award**—Colman, best actor. **Nominations**—Cukor, best director; Ruth Gordon and Garson Kanin, original screenplay. *103 minutes b&w*

DOWN AND OUT IN BEVERLY HILLS (1986)

★★★

Nick Nolte
Bette Midler
Richard Dreyfuss

Wonderfully acted social satire that gently exposes the failings of the upwardly mobile. An outrageously rich couple (Dreyfuss and Midler) "adopt" one of their community's homeless (a charismatic Nolte). They spruce up his appearance, and give him a taste for *la dolce vita*. He seems to have a knack for solving the family's emotional problems, but ultimately his presence proves disturbing. Director Paul Mazursky has translated a 1932 Jean Renoir film classic, *Boudu Saved from Drowning*, into an American story for the 1980s with surprising élan and bountiful belly laughs. **(R)** *97 minutes*

DOWN BY LAW (1986)

★★½

Tom Waits
John Lurie
Roberto Benigni

Independent director Jim Jarmusch's follow-up to his critically acclaimed *Strangers in Paradise* features the same quirky humor and distinctive visual style. Three prisoners—two disillusioned Americans and one naive Italian—escape from a Louisiana jail, making their way through the bayous to civilization. The contrast between the two glum Americans and their cheerful and optimistic Italian companion (similar to the Hungarian tourist character in *Strangers in Paradise*) provides most of the thought-provoking comedy. Unfortunately, the parallels between Jarmusch's first film and this one are often too close, resulting in predictability. The beautifully eerie cinematography of Germany's Robby Muller enhances the film considerably. Also with Ellen Barkin, Nicoletta Braschi, and Billie Neal. **(R)** *96 minutes b&w*

DOWNTOWN (1990)

★★

Forest Whitaker
Anthony Edwards

A forgettable buddy-cop movie, which was obviously inspired by *Lethal Weapon*. Edwards stars as a suburban policeman, who is transferred from his plush environment to the volatile inner city. He is teamed with a maverick, streetwise officer played by Whitaker. The partners investigate the murder of a fellow officer, which is tied to a stolen-car ring. Aside from the too-familiar formula involving a pair of very different cops teaming to solve a case, this movie is poorly paced and lacks a coherent structure. Scenes are episodic, never coalescing into a whole. Sloppiness pervades throughout: Though supposedly set in Philadelphia, mountains are clearly seen in the background of some scenes. Only Whitaker, who starred as Charlie "Bird" Parker in *Bird*, stands out. Also with Penelope Ann Miller, Joe Pantoliano, and David Clennon. **Director**—Richard Benjamin. **(R)** *97 minutes*

This movie available on videotape and/or disc.

DRACULA (1931)

★★★★

Bela Lugosi
David Manners
Helen Chandler

Bela Lugosi is the classic representation of the Transylvanian vampire Dracula.

This classic screen adaptation of Bram Stoker's haunting novel remains the granddaddy of horror films. Lugosi is fantastic as the Transylvanian vampire who travels to London looking for blood. The strange, misty atmosphere drives home the chills. Actually, the film is somewhat slow and uneven. Yet, for some uncanny reason, this version continues to cast its spell. Many sequels and imitations have gone in its wake. A 75-minute version also exists. Also with Dwight Frye and Edward Van Sloan. **Director**—Tod Browning.
84 minutes b&w

DRACULA (1979)

★★★

Frank Langella
Laurence Olivier
Donald Pleasence

The evil count from Transylvania is on the prowl for more blood in this lavish, moody, and scary film based on the successful Broadway production of the late 1970s. Langella plays the Count as a sensual being, and the film is ripe with sexual overtones. However, it does lack the tongue-in-cheek approach that made the modern production of the play a hit. Also with Kate Nelligan, Trevor Eve, and Janine Duvitski. **Director**—John Badham. **(R)** *109 minutes*

DRAGNET (1987)

★★½ ®

Dan Aykroyd
Tom Hanks

Dan Aykroyd as Joe Friday's nephew and Tom Hanks as his partner in Dragnet.

A strained send-up of Jack Webb's famous television series. Aykroyd is well-suited to the role of the straight-arrow nephew of the late Sgt. Friday, and Hanks is likable as Friday's hip partner, though the slight script lets both of them down. The story involves Friday's efforts to bring to justice a sinister gang bent on dominating the pornography business, but it really exists only to support Aykroyd's feature-length impression of Jack Webb. Too many car chases further detract from an already weak plot. Aykroyd coscripted this problematic parody with director Tom Mankiewicz and Alan Zweibel. The film features a colorful supporting cast, including Dabney Coleman, Elizabeth Ashley, Harry Morgan (reprising his role from the second incarnation of the *Dragnet* TV show), Christopher Plummer, and Alexandra Paul. **(PG–13)**
107 minutes

DRAGON SEED (1944)

★★

Katharine Hepburn
Walter Huston

This unsuccessful film version of Pearl Buck's novel may have had good intentions, but the results are patronizing and occasionally offensive. Peasants in a Chinese village battle Japanese invaders, while the effects of war on a simple Chinese family are explored. The all-white cast portraying the Asians is distracting, even given the time frame of the film's release. Also with Turhan Bey, Agnes Moorehead, Akim Tamiroff, J. Carrol Naish, and Aline MacMahon. **Directors**—Jack Conway and Harold S. Bucquet. **Academy Award Nomination**—MacMahon, best supporting actress. *144 minutes b&w*

DRAGONSLAYER (1981)

★★½

Peter MacNicol
Ralph Richardson

A Dark Ages fairy tale that's partly flawed by mediocre acting and a tedious script. Young MacNicol plays a sorcerer's apprentice who is called upon to slay a fearsome flying dragon; it seems that the citizens are fed up with appeasing the beast by sacrificing virgins. The super special effects, which were nominated for an Oscar, are the real stars. When that huge fire-breathing dragon goes into action, the story comes alive. But that's rather late in the film. **Director**—Matthew Robbins. **(PG)**
108 minutes

DREAM A LITTLE DREAM (1989)

★ ®

Corey Feldman
Jason Robards
Meredith Salenger

This worn-out comedy about an exchange of personalities centers on an adolescent love affair. Feldman is the teen boy who mysteriously acquires the personality of an adult (Robards)—all the better to pursue the affections of Salenger. The flimsy script, coupled with unsteady direction, fails to spark much interest. Also with Harry Dean Stanton. Cable versions of the film run 113 minutes. **Director**—Marc Rocco. **(PG-13)** *99 minutes*

DREAMER (1979)

★★

Tim Matheson
Susan Blakely
Jack Warden

Tim Matheson and Susan Blakely are very much in love in Dreamer.

® *This movie available with closed captions for the hearing impaired.*

Remember Paul Newman shooting a wicked game of pool in *The Hustler?* And *Rocky,* where an unknown contender struggles to win the big fight? Well, here Hollywood has given this treatment to bowling, without much style or depth. There's some authentic detail about kegling and the Americana that surrounds it, yet the story lacks real dramatic tension or credible moral conflict to give the characters stature. Also with Richard B. Schull, Barbara Stuart, and Pedro Gonzalez-Gonzalez. **Director**—Noel Nosseck. **(PG)** *86 minutes*

DREAM LOVER (1986)

Kristy McNichol
Ben Masters

Sleep disorders provide the subject of this muddled psychological thriller that's likely to have viewers dozing off midway through the film. McNichol turns in a halfhearted performance as a young New York jazz flutist who partakes in dream research following a traumatic experience with an intruder. But these experiments, by a well-meaning scientist (Masters), are unsuccessful and the film plods on to an unexciting conclusion. **Director**—Alan J. Pakula. **(R)** *104 minutes*

DREAMSCAPE (1984)

 ★★1/2

Dennis Quaid
Max Von Sydow
Christopher Plummer

An uneven, sci-fi thriller that involves a government research project whereby a "dreamlinker" can manipulate another's dreams. Even the President of the United States participates in the experiment. As long as the script is slightly whimsical, the story remains entertaining. But the film eventually bogs down in unconvincing suspense gimmicks, a hokey romance, and confusing political intrigue. **Director**—Joseph Ruben. **(PG–13)** *98 minutes*

THE DREAM TEAM (1989)

Michael Keaton
Christopher Lloyd
Peter Boyle

Laughter, suspense, and a bit of pathos are effectively combined in Howard Zieff's breezy comedy. Four mental patients on their way to a Yankees baseball game become separated from their doctor and must cope with the perils of New York City. Snappy dialogue, well-drawn characters, and brisk direction propel the comic misadventures. Keaton, Lloyd, and Boyle are at their best. Also with Stephen Furst. **(PG-13)** *113 minutes*

Christopher Lloyd, Peter Boyle, Stephen Furst, and Michael Keaton in The Dream Team.

DRESSED TO KILL (1980)

Michael Caine
Angie Dickinson
Nancy Allen

Director Brian De Palma liberally borrows from Alfred Hitchcock's *Psycho* and other classics for this slick but shallow suspense movie about a transvestite who attacks women with a straight razor. De Palma sets up several impressive sequences and displays dazzling camera technique. But the characters are vague and uninteresting, despite decent performances by Caine, Dickinson, and Allen. The film offers style but no substance. **(R)** *105 minutes*

THE DRESSER (1983)

 ★★★1/2

Albert Finney
Tom Courtenay

Finney and Courtenay pour out a torrent of eloquent acting skill in this magnificent film adaptation of the prize-winning play. Finney howls and roars as the temperamental veteran Shakespearean actor who musters his strength for yet another performance as England buckles under the Nazi blitz. And Courtenay is dead on-target in the pivotal title role as the effeminate, mother-hen valet who prods the great man onto the stage. A double-barreled *tour de force.* **Director**—Peter Yates. **(PG)** **Academy Award Nominations**—best picture; Finney and Courtenay, best actor; Ronald Harwood, best screenplay based on another medium. *118 minutes*

DRIVE-IN (1976)

Lisa Lemole
Glen Morshower
Gary Cavagnaro

This easygoing, low-budget production focuses on youths at a drive-in theater in a rural Texas town. Much of the plot is composed of bits stolen from *American Graffiti* and *The Last Picture Show,* but the results are appealing. A bumbling stickup, a gang rumble, and troubled romance are confronted at the drive-in location. Meanwhile, the big screen features its own version of catastrophe in *Disaster '76,* which is a blend of *Jaws, The Towering Inferno,* and *The Poseidon Adventure.* A lot of fresh and unknown faces make up the lively cast. Also with Billy Milliken, Lee Newsom, and Regan Kee. **Director**—Rod Amateau. **(PG)** *96 minutes*

THE DRIVER (1978)

Ryan O'Neal
Bruce Dern
Isabelle Adjani

Bruce Dern is the detective in pursuit in The Driver.

This pretentious film glorifies the driver of a getaway car. It's filled with squeal-

(Continued)

(Continued)
ing tires, preposterous smash-'em-up car chases, and dialogue so absurd that it's unintentionally funny. O'Neal is The Driver, Dern is The Detective who pursues him, and Adjani is The Player, a mysterious gambler who serves as an alibi for O'Neal. Their acting careers suffer as many dents as the wrecked cars. Also with Ronee Blakley, Matt Clark, and Felice Orlandi. **Director**—Walter Hill. **(R)** *90 minutes*

DRIVING MISS DAISY (1989)

★★★½

Jessica Tandy
Morgan Freeman
Dan Aykroyd

Jessica Tandy and her chauffeur, Morgan Freeman, in Driving Miss Daisy.

Freeman and Tandy invoke grace and dignity with their well-drawn roles in this sensitive treatment of race relations and old age. Freeman stars as a gentle, wise black chauffeur in the service of a spunky Jewish widow, played by Tandy. As the years pass, their relationship evolves into a remarkable friendship despite their diverse backgrounds. The film, skillfully adapted from the prize-winning play, unfolds against the backdrop of civil rights changes in the South. Perhaps too simple to be a strong statement about race relations, it works better as an essay on aging with dignity. Freeman, who won an Obie for his performance in the play, has emerged as one of America's most powerful actors. Australian director Bruce Beresford uses a languid pacing, which effectively evokes the South of years past. Also with Patti Lapone and Esther Rolle. **(PG) Academy Awards**—best picture; Tandy, best actress; Alfred Uhry, best screenplay adaptation; Manlio Rocchetti, makeup. **Nominations**—Freeman, best actor; Aykroyd, best supporting actor; Mark Warner, editing; Bruno Rubeo and Crispian Sallis, art direction; Elizabeth McBride, costume. *99 minutes*

THE DROWNING POOL (1975)

★★

Paul Newman
Joanne Woodward
Tony Franciosa

Newman appears for the second time as Lew Harper, the 1950s-era private eye. It's a listless drama set against the backdrop of some colorful surroundings in New Orleans and its bayou countryside. The talented cast, however, can't rescue the film. Also with Murray Hamilton, Melanie Griffith, and Richard Jaeckel. **Director**—Stuart Rosenberg. **(PG)** *108 minutes*

DRUGSTORE COWBOY (1989)

★★★½

Matt Dillon
Kelly Lynch

An unusually honest inside account of drug users, based on the unpublished novel of addict James Fogle, currently serving a prison sentence. Dillon excels as the young leader of a small gang that burglarizes drugstores in search of narcotics. Set in Portland, Oregon, during the 1970s, the film follows the self-assured but unglamorous characters from one theft to another. Eventually Dillon's character decides to dry out, though his decision is made with no moralizing. He simply applies the same zeal to staying clean as he had previously to getting high. Director Gus Van Sant, Jr., details the seedy milieu of the 1970s drug culture without romanticizing it. Beat poet William Burroughs appears briefly as an aging addict who offers an interesting commentary on contemporary attitudes toward drugs. James Le Gros, Heather Graham, and James Remar costar. **(R)** *100 minutes*

DRUMS ALONG THE MOHAWK (1939)

★★★

Claudette Colbert
Henry Fonda
Edna May Oliver

Fine action drama of pre-Revolutionary colonists who fight to survive Indian attacks and the harshness of primitive farming conditions in Upstate New York. A rich, warm story that mingles bravery with love and humor, deftly handled in characteristic style by director John Ford. Colbert as the frightened wife who learns to cope and Fonda as her stern but loving husband are sympathetic and totally believable. Oliver is especially fine in a key supporting role. **Academy Award Nomination**—Oliver, best supporting actress. *103 minutes*

A DRY WHITE SEASON (1989)

★★★

Donald Sutherland
Janet Suzman
Zakes Mokae
Marlon Brando

Marlon Brando and Donald Sutherland in A Dry White Season.

A blunt, stirring antiapartheid drama about the moral and political awakening of a complacent white history teacher during the 1976 Soweto uprising. Sutherland appears in the starring role, giving one of his best performances in recent years. Brando is a powerful presence in an extended cameo as a cynical liberal lawyer who is weary of battling the brutality inflicted by the South African minority government. Cowritten and directed by black female filmmaker Euzhan Palcy. Also with Jurgen Prochnow, Susan Sarandon, and Winston Ntshona. **(R)** *105 minutes*

THE DUCHESS AND THE DIRTWATER FOX (1976)

★

George Segal
Goldie Hawn

® This movie available with closed captions for the hearing impaired.

A period western strung together with corny gags that lead nowhere. Hawn plays a dance-hall hooker who teams up with Segal, a bumbling card shark. Segal is trying to escape from a gang of bank robbers from whom he has stolen $40,000. Hawn and Segal seem to work well together at times, but such moments are too few. This film would have been better as a 15-minute animated cartoon. Also with Conrad Janis, Thayer David, and Roy Jenson. **Director**—Melvin Frank. **(PG)** *103 minutes*

DUCK SOUP (1933)

★★★★

The Marx Brothers
Margaret Dumont

Chico Marx awaits Groucho's next pronouncement in Duck Soup.

A wild offering of one-liners plus the famous mirror sequence put this comic romp in the Marx Brothers Hall of Fame. Groucho plays Rufus T. Firefly, the president of Freedonia, and ineptly instigates war against a neighboring country. Some critics find meaning and satire in this farce, and they may be right, but viewers will enjoy the comedy at face value. The last appearance on film by Zeppo with the other Marx Brothers. Also with Edgar Kennedy. **Director**—Leo McCarey. *70 minutes b&w*

DUEL IN THE SUN (1946)

★★★½

Jennifer Jones
Joseph Cotten
Gregory Peck
Lionel Barrymore
Lillian Gish

Big, sprawling epic western with the influence of writer/producer David O. Selznick very much in evidence. The plot centers on a half-breed Indian girl, played by Jones, who sparks rivalry between two brothers—Cotten and Peck—when she comes to reside in the home of a powerful cattle rancher. The film boasts some great romantic scenes and rousing action—especially a bizarre gun battle in the finale. Barrymore and Gish are exceptional in supporting roles. Also with Walter Huston, Herbert Marshall, Charles Bickford, and Otto Kruger. Based on Niven Busch's novel. **Director**—King Vidor. **Academy Award Nominations**—Jones, best actress; Gish, best supporting actress. *138 minutes*

THE DUELLISTS (1977)

★★

Keith Carradine
Harvey Keitel
Albert Finney

Screen adaptation of the Joseph Conrad short story about two Hussar officers, played by Carradine and Keitel, who fight a protracted series of duels during the Napoleonic wars. Director Ridley Scott has taken meticulous care in reconstructing the period. The lavish production abounds with elegant settings and breathtaking vistas. But the film comes up tragically short with a dull script and stiff dialogue. The principal characters seem rather awkward and unconvincing. Also with Edward Fox, Cristina Raines, and Robert Stephen. **(PG)** *101 minutes*

DUET FOR ONE (1987)

★★

Julie Andrews
Alan Bates
Max Von Sydow

Alan Bates and Julie Andrews share the memory of sweet romance in Duet for One.

Despite a winning cast, this elegant but dour drama about a classical musician strikes discordant notes. Andrews portrays a virtuoso violinist who goes to pieces when stricken with multiple sclerosis. As the central character becomes more despondent, resulting in bizarre behavior, the story loses credibility and impact. Based on Tom Kempinski's two-person stage play. **Director**—Andrei Konchalovsky. **(R)** *107 minutes*

DUMBO (1941)

★★★★

Lovable circus elephant Dumbo *yearns for a new friend.*

Memorable and touching Walt Disney cartoon feature, about the baby circus elephant with ears so big that he can use them as wings and fly. This project represents the studio at the peak of its creative years. Unforgettable scenes include the crows' song and the drunken nightmare. Voices include Sterling Holloway, Edward Brophy, and Verna Felton. **Director**—Ben Sharpsteen. *64 minutes*

DUNE (1984)

★★

Kyle MacLachlan
Richard Jordan

Ponderous, overblown, and failed attempt to make sense of author Frank Herbert's 1965 sci-fi epic. Director David Lynch packs in too many details and adorns the affair with outlandish, ornate sets. The film also sags under the weight of incomprehensible gobbledygook dialogue. The plot, for what it's worth, concerns a battle in the year 10191 for possession of a powerful, mind-blowing spice found on the title

(Continued)

(Continued)
planet. Rock musician Sting, formerly of the Police, appears in a supporting role. Francesca Annis, José Ferrer, Linda Hunt, Kenneth McMillan, and Max Von Sydow top the cast. **(PG–13)**
140 minutes

DUST (1986)

★

Jane Birkin
Trevor Howard
John Matshikiza
Natine Uwampa

Birkin stars as a lonely, sexually frustrated young woman trying to cope with her isolated existence on a South African sheep farm. The film, based on J.M. Coetzee's novel *In the Heart of the Country,* effectively underscores the barren life of this desperate spinster. Yet, the story is hardly compelling, and the film is tedious and difficult to view. **Director**—Marion Hansel. **(No MPAA rating)** *88 minutes*

E

THE EAGLE HAS LANDED (1977)

★★★

Michael Caine
Donald Sutherland
Robert Duvall

Caine, Sutherland, and Duvall deliver first-rate performances in director John Sturges' film about a Nazi plot to kidnap Winston Churchill. There's a fair amount of suspense, drama, and battle action to overcome occasional plot potholes. The well-paced screenplay is based on Jack Higgins' novel. The photography is spectacular, especially the scenes of the beautiful Norfolk coast of England. Original release time was 134 minutes. Also with Jenny Agutter, Donald Pleasence, Larry Hagman, and Anthony Quayle. **(PG)** *123 minutes*

EARTH GIRLS ARE EASY (1989)

★★★ ⧠®

Geena Davis
Jeff Goldblum
Julie Brown

A colorful, fun-loving musical comedy that celebrates contemporary pop culture. Davis, a ditsy valley girl, latches on to three sex-starved space aliens whose rocket ship lands in her swimming pool. The film features glitzy backdrops and splashy colors, while the dialogue is peppered with phrases familiar from TV commercials. Some of the musical numbers (particularly Brown's celebration of blondeness) display energy, but the overall production is uneven. Costars Charles Rocket, Damon Wayans, and Jim Carrey. **Director**—Julien Temple. **(PG)**
100 minutes

THE EARTHLING (1981)

★

William Holden
Ricky Schroder

Schroder plays a recently orphaned city boy who learns to survive in the Australian wilderness with the help of Holden, a cantankerous old man who returns to his birthplace to die. This muddled, cliché-strewn film pretends to be sentimental, but it can't fool anyone. However, there's no denying the appealing photography of the Australian bush country, with kangaroos and wallabies romping over the outback's unique landscape. Also with Jack Thompson and Olivia Hamnett. **Director**—Peter Collinson. **(PG)**
97 minutes

EARTHQUAKE (1974)

★★

Charlton Heston
Ava Gardner
Lorne Greene
Marjoe Gortner
George Kennedy

Charleston Heston tries to forestall disaster in Earthquake.

This disaster film has a dumb script and lackluster acting, but great visual and aural effects. There are disasters galore as a massive earthquake strikes Los Angeles. Also with Richard Roundtree, Geneviève Bujold, Lloyd Nolan, Walter Matthau, and Sensurround. The film won an Academy Award for special achievement in visual effects. **Director**—Mark Robson. **(PG)**
129 minutes

EASTER PARADE (1948)

★★★★

Judy Garland
Fred Astaire
Peter Lawford
Ann Miller

Fred Astaire and Judy Garland meet high society in Easter Parade.

MGM's golden age of musicals was at its peak with this delightfully entertaining film, brimming with Irving Berlin's fabulous songs. The trivial plot has Miller leaving dance partner Astaire. To prove to Miller he doesn't need her, Astaire vows to make a star out of an unknown, played by Garland. Astaire and Garland's version of "We're a Couple of Swells" is now considered a classic bit from the film. Also with Jules Munshin. **Director**—Charles Walters.
109 minutes

EAST OF EDEN (1955)

★★★★

Raymond Massey
James Dean
Julie Harris

A splendid film version of John Steinbeck's novel, focusing on a teenager's torment over the lack of love from his father. Dean proves his superb acting

⧠® *This movie available with closed captions for the hearing impaired.*

ability in his starring debut as the rebellious adolescent. Jo Van Fleet is also magnificent as the boy's mother, who operates a brothel. Director Elia Kazan, at the height of his career, directs method actor Dean and character star Massey with equal aplomb. Also with Richard Davalos, Burl Ives, and Albert Dekker. **Academy Award**—Van Fleet, best supporting actress. **Nominations**—Kazan, best director; Dean, best actor; Paul Osborn, screenplay. *115 minutes*

EAST SIDE, WEST SIDE (1949)

James Mason
Barbara Stanwyck
Van Heflin
Ava Gardner

Slick soap opera, set among New York City's upper crust. Mason and Stanwyck are a wealthy couple with marital problems involving Gardner and Heflin. There's some entertainment value thanks to the stylish treatment and a professional cast. But the story, based on Marcia Davenport's novel, is superficial. Also with Gale Sondergaard, Cyd Charisse, Nancy Davis, and William Conrad. **Director**—Mervyn LeRoy. *108 minutes b&w*

EASY MONEY (1983)

 ★½

Rodney Dangerfield
Joe Pesci

Dangerfield waves his arms a lot, pops his eyes, and tosses out one-liners galore in this vulgar comedy about a baby photographer. But where are the laughs? He plays a bumbling slob who must give up a variety of bad habits to inherit $10 million from his snooty mother-in-law. He and most of the cast strain with the flimsy comic material. Sorry, Rodney. Still no respect for you or this idiotic movie. Geraldine Fitzgerald costars. **Director**—James Signorelli. **(R)** *95 minutes*

EASY RIDER (1969)

 ★★★★

Peter Fonda
Dennis Hopper
Jack Nicholson

A trendsetting movie about two hippies who cross the Southwest on motorcycles and meet disaster at the hands of trigger-happy rednecks. This remarkable and unusual film symbolizes its era, with its casual statements on hatred and a society that for some is too structured and too organized. Hopper and Fonda are exceptionally good as the freewheeling bikers, but Nicholson steals the film as a tipsy small-town lawyer who goes along for the ride. Versions on videotape run 88 minutes. Also with Luana Anders, Robert Walker, Jr., and Karen Black. **Director**—Hopper. **(R) Academy Award Nominations**—Nicholson, best supporting actor; Fonda, Hopper, and Terry Southern, best story and screenplay based on material not previously published or produced. *94 minutes*

Easy Rider, *the angry counterculture statement that became a smash hit.*

EATING RAOUL (1982)

 ★★★

Paul Bartel
Mary Woronov

A wry, fairly sophisticated black comedy by Bartel that satirizes swinging lifestyles and middle-class values. Told in a matter-of-fact and amusing tone, the story concerns a prissy, middle-aged couple who concoct an outrageous scheme to lure "sexual perverts" to their apartment and murder them for their money. The farce steers clear of slapstick. **Director**—Bartel. **(R)** *83 minutes*

EAT MY DUST! (1976)

 ★★★

Ron Howard
Christopher Norris

Teenagers should enjoy this car-chase comedy starring Howard and Norris. The teenage son of a small-town California sheriff swipes a stock car and takes a blonde for a joyride; the sheriff recruits a bumbling posse of cars to chase the madcap pair. The result is a demolition derby with no injuries. The wrecks and stunts are well done, and the photography is attractive. Also with Warren Kemmerling, Dave Madden, and Rance Howard. Directed and written by Charles Griffith. **(PG)** *90 minutes*

ECHO PARK (1986)

 ★★

Susan Dey
Tom Hulce

Three young people, residing in a rundown Los Angeles neighborhood, dream of making it big in show biz. This portrait of the hopeful oddballs has only fleeting moments of interest. Mainly, the film lacks direction and wanders aimlessly from scene to scene. Like the characters involved, it never lives up to expectations. Dey stars as an aspiring actress who settles for a job as a "strippergram." Hulce plays a pizza delivery boy—quite a comedown from *Amadeus,* which was shot after, but released before, this film. **Director**—Robert Dornhelm. **(R)** *93 minutes*

EDDIE AND THE CRUISERS (1983)

Michael Paré

Rock 'n' roll nostalgia with a touch of mystery is the theme of this uneven film that looks at an up-and-coming rock group from the early 1960s. Paré portrays the young singer who supposedly committed suicide at the height of his career. Or did Eddie purposefully go into hiding, taking with him some sensational unreleased tapes? There are compelling moments. Yet the story goes astray too often, lapsing into silliness and outright confusion. Tom Berenger and Ellen Barkin also star. **Director**—Martin Davidson. **(PG)** *94 minutes*

EDDIE AND THE CRUISERS II: EDDIE LIVES (1989)

 ★½

Michael Paré
Marina Orsini

Credibility is seriously strained in this flimsy sequel concerning the fate of fic-

(Continued)

This movie available on videotape and/or disc.

(Continued)

tional rock legend Eddie Wilson. According to this second installment, Eddie didn't drown when his car careened off a bridge into the river. Instead, he hid his true identity while working construction in Montreal. Now he wants to tackle the comeback trail, belting out rock songs in the style of Bruce Springsteen. Paré returns in the title role, lip-syncing the ample rock songs by John Cafferty and the Beaver Brown Band. Orsini plays Eddie's love interest. Also with Matthew Laurence, Bernie Coulson, and Michael Rhoades. **Director**—Jean-Claude Lord.
(PG-13) *100 minutes*

EDDIE MURPHY RAW (1988)

★★1/2

Eddie Murphy

This film version of Murphy's stand-up comedy act features the comedian in a rapid-fire monologue filled with profanity, scatological jokes, and some astute impressions of Bill Cosby, Richard Pryor, and other performers. The way in which individual viewers respond to Murphy's controversial and abrasive stand-up humor will determine how much they will enjoy this filmed concert. Those offended by intense profanity and frank discussions of sex should not even consider seeing this; Murphy's fans will appreciate his attempts to push stand-up comedy to the extremes in terms of language. Some bits of his routine, including his comments on gays and women, were criticized when the film opened. Initially given an X rating by the MPAA, the film was trimmed by the director before release. **Director**—Robert Townsend.
(R) *91 minutes*

EDGE OF SANITY (1989)

★★

Anthony Perkins
Glynis Barber

Perkins, a familiar contributor to the horror genre, does a contemporary rendition of the classic *Dr. Jekyll and Mr. Hyde.* In this version, Mr. Hyde's hostile behavior can be blamed on freebased cocaine. Kinky sex, gory makeup effects, and a sly reference to Jack the Ripper as Hyde sadistically carves up some London prostitutes are also thrown in. Too grisly to be effective. Barber plays the perplexed Mrs. Jekyll. **Director**—Gerard Kikoine. **(R)** *86 minutes*

EDGE OF THE CITY (1957)

★★★1/2

Sidney Poitier
John Cassavetes
Jack Warden

An exciting, gripping melodrama, filmed on the docks of New York City much in the style of *On the Waterfront.* Poitier and Cassavetes play longshoremen who confront a brutal and bigoted union boss, portrayed convincingly by Warden. The film, which has something significant to say about racial integration, is based on Robert Alan Aurthur's TV play, *A Man Is Ten Feet Tall.* Also with Kathleen Maguire, Ruby Dee, and Robert Simon. **Director**—Martin Ritt. *85 minutes b&w*

EDISON, THE MAN (1940)

★★★

Spencer Tracy
Rita Johnson

Straightforward and slightly sentimental film biography of America's most famous inventor, made as a sequel to *Young Tom Edison.* The script traces Edison's life from his obscure years in poverty to his emergence as the scientific genius who invented the lightbulb and the phonograph. Good casting of Tracy in the title role. There's earnest support from Charles Coburn, Gene Lockhart, and Lynne Overman. **Director**—Clarence Brown. **Academy Award Nomination**—Hugo Butler and Dore Schary, original story.
107 minutes b&w

EDUCATING RITA (1983)

★★★

Michael Caine
Julie Walters

Julie Walters shows Michael Caine her skills in Educating Rita.

A predictable, but fun, latter-day version of *Pygmalion* with Caine and Walters in perfect form as teacher and student. He's a disillusioned, drunken professor whose life is turned around when he tutors plucky hairdresser Walters, who has an honest hunger for classic literature. The plot is threadbare and the direction somewhat stagy (the film is based on a play), but this is an actor's picture, and it's a pleasure to watch Caine and Walters together. **Director**—Lewis Gilbert. **(PG) Academy Award Nominations**—Caine, best actor; Walters, best actress; Willy Russell, best screenplay based on material from another medium. *110 minutes*

EDWARD, MY SON (1949)

★★

Spencer Tracy
Deborah Kerr

An overbearing and somewhat artificial screen adaptation of a compelling play about a wealthy man's unbecoming conduct toward his son. Tracy, as the unscrupulous father, seems ill at ease in an unsuitable role. Kerr plays his distraught wife, and there is support from Ian Hunter, James Donald, Leueen McGrath, and Mervyn Johns. **Director**—George Cukor. *112 minutes b&w*

THE EFFECT OF GAMMA RAYS ON MAN-IN-THE-MOON MARIGOLDS (1972)

Joanne Woodward

Fine adaptation of the Pulitzer Prize-winning play by Paul Zindel. Woodward deserves acting honors for her portrayal of the middle-aged, self-deluding loser who never loses hope that she and her daughters will achieve a measure of greatness. Director Paul Newman deftly handles the translation from stage to screen and brings a new dimension to the story. Nell Potts, Roberta Wallach, and Judith Lowry are all excellent in the supporting cast. **(PG)**
101 minutes

THE EGG AND I (1947)

★★★

Claudette Colbert
Fred MacMurray

Colbert and MacMurray are effective in this warm comedy about a city couple

This movie available with closed captions for the hearing impaired.

who buy a chicken farm and struggle with numerous problems. The film is notable for introducing Marjorie Main and Percy Kilbride as Ma and Pa Kettle. The script is based on Betty McDonald's popular book. Also with Louise Allbritton, Richard Long, and Billy House. **Director**—Chester Erskine. **Academy Award Nomination**—Main, best supporting actress.

108 minutes b&w

THE EIGER SANCTION (1975)

★★

Clint Eastwood
George Kennedy

Jonathan Hemlock, played by Eastwood, is hired to assassinate the killers of an American agent. Though most of the year Hemlock teaches art, while he is on vacation he's a secret agent who works for a government organization. He uses the money he earns from his missions to buy works of art. Generally, it's a dreary film, with all the clichés of suspense thrillers thrown in. The film, based on one of Trevanian's popular novels, is set in the Swiss Alps; the Eiger is a Swiss peak. Some vitality and humor from the supporting cast, which includes Vonetta McGee, Jack Cassidy, and Heidi Bruhl. **Director**—Eastwood. **(R)** *128 minutes*

8½ (1963)

★★★★

Marcello Mastroianni
Claudia Cardinale
Anouk Aimée
Sandra Milo
Barbara Steele

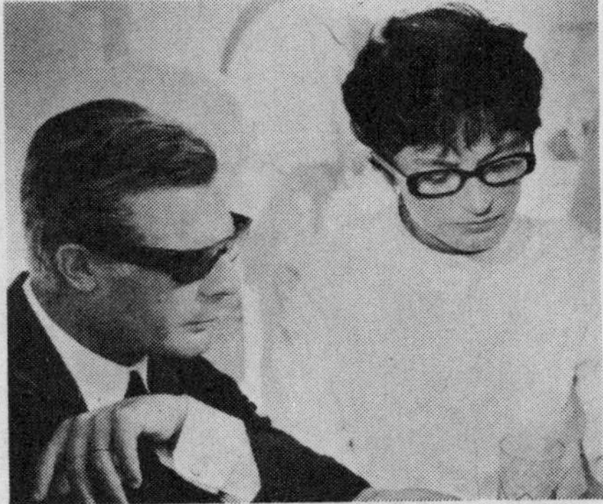

Marcello Mastroianni and Anouk Aimée in Fellini's fascinating 8½.

In this archetypal Fellini film, a movie director (Mastroianni), spiritually paralyzed by a midlife crisis, loses himself in fantasy and reminiscences. His introspections spin around sexual, religious, and sociological themes in a free-form style that can be taken as cinematic poetry, self-analysis, or self-indulgence. From the moment the protagonist floats out of a traffic jam in the opening scene, the cinema of the 1960s began opening out as well, to a much more self-consciously stylized approach. Fellini's autobiographical *tour de force* was film number 8½ (counting each of three shorts as half a film) in his career. Originally filmed in Italian. **Academy Awards**—best foreign-language film; Piero Gherardi, costume design. **Nominations**—Fellini, best director; Fellini, Ennio Flaiano, Tullio Pinelli, and Brunello Rondi, best story and screenplay written directly for the screen.

135 minutes b&w

18 AGAIN (1988)

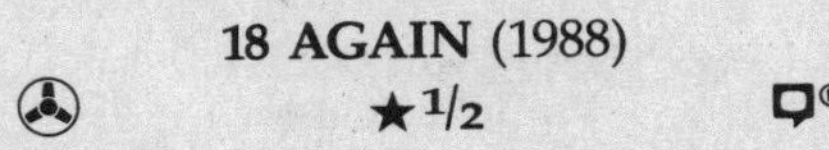

★½

George Burns
Charlie Schlatter

Burns plays a swinging grandfather who, after a mysterious car accident, switches bodies with his introverted grandson, played by newcomer Schlatter. The old man's personality inhabits the young man's body and vice versa. Despite top billing, Burns is not onscreen very much, and the trite comedy is almost totally dependent on Schlatter's impression of a teenaged Burns. Schlatter's attempt to take on Burns' mannerisms becomes grating quite quickly, and the rest of the characters are too flat to take up the slack. Also with Tony Roberts, Anita Morris, and Red Buttons. **Director**—Paul Flaherty. **(PG)** *99 minutes*

EIGHT MEN OUT (1988)

★★★½

John Cusack
D.B. Sweeney

A moving, historical account of the Chicago "Black Sox" scandal, when eight Chicago White Sox players threw the 1919 World Series. John Sayles (who also plays writer Ring Lardner) directs an excellent cast while deftly re-creating the elements of greed, manipulation, and frustration that led to the conspiracy. Though based on the book by Eliot Asinof, Sayles uses the story as a parable about the dark side of capitalism. The low-key lighting and exquisite period detail suggest the innocence of an era long gone. Also with Charlie Sheen, Christopher Lloyd, Clifton James, Michael Lerner, John Mahoney, David Strathairn, Don Harvey, Michael Rooker, James Read, Perry Lang, and Studs Turkel. **(PG)** *120 minutes*

D.B. Sweeney ("Shoeless" Joe) and Charlie Sheen in Eight Men Out.

8 MILLION WAYS TO DIE (1986)

★★

Jeff Bridges
Rosanna Arquette

A frantic crime thriller loaded with numerous shrieking and shouting confrontations that become irritating all too quickly. Bridges stars as a Los Angeles narcotics cop involved with cocaine dealers and prostitutes. The script most often seems to be vamping for time in anticipation of the climactic shoot-out, which is accomplished with minimal imagination. In terms of setting and visual detail, the style recalls that of *films noirs* of the 1940s. Also with Alexandra Paul. **Director**—Hal Ashby. **(R)**

115 minutes

84 CHARING CROSS ROAD (1987)

★★

Anne Bancroft
Anthony Hopkins

Bancroft's marvelous performance as a lonely New York bookworm and TV scriptwriter occasionally brightens this difficult and dowdy drama. The film is about the iconoclastic spinster's 20 years of correspondence with a London bookstore in her quest for hard-to-find English literature. Her flood of letters sparks a curious transatlantic romance with the store's stuffy manager

(Continued)

(Continued)
(Hopkins). Though warmhearted and based on a true story, the film suffers from pretentious direction (the characters sometimes turn to the camera and express their thoughts directly to the viewer) and a superficial sentimentality. **Director**—David Jones. **(PG)**
88 minutes

84 CHARLIE MOPIC (1989)

★★★½

Richard Brooks

Byron Thames, Richard Brooks, and Jonathan Emerson in 84 Charlie MoPic.

Unique, fictional account of Vietnam combat presented from the viewpoint of an Army cameraman making a training film. The drama follows a six-man platoon into enemy-infested jungle, drawing out a tense and moving portrait of the men's mission, comradery, and hope for survival. Writer/director Patrick Duncan, a Vietnam veteran, avoids falling into trite psychological soul-searching. Brooks is especially effective as the resourceful platoon sergeant. Features a talented cast of unknowns, including Jonathan Emerson, Christopher Burgard, Nicholas Cascone, and Byron Thomas. **(R)**
95 minutes

EL CID (1961)

★★★

Charlton Heston
Sophia Loren
Raf Vallone

Sprawling, opulent period epic with Heston portraying the legendary hero who rid Spain of the Moors in the 11th century. The magnificent spectacle features an eyeful of flashy costumes, impressive settings, and big battle scenes. The script, however, doesn't live up to the visual splendor. The cast also includes Geneviève Page, Hurd Hatfield, Gary Raymond, Herbert Lom, and John Fraser. **Director**—Anthony Mann.
184 minutes

EL DORADO (1967)

★★★

John Wayne
Robert Mitchum

Big John straps on his shootin' irons and helps his friend, a drunken sheriff played by Mitchum, fight a crooked cattle baron. Director Howard Hawks whips together this funny, action-packed, old-fashioned western, based loosely on his own *Rio Bravo.* Not the best of Hawks' westerns, but it's likable. James Caan, Charlene Holt, Michele Carey, and Ed Asner are also in the cast. *126 minutes*

ELECTRIC DREAMS (1984)

★★

Lenny Von Dohlen
Virginia Madsen

Virginia Madsen and Lenny Von Dohlen in Electric Dreams.

A high-tech romantic comedy involving a young San Francisco architect and his almost-human computer, both competing for the affection of a young female concert cellist. The story aspires to be cute and hip, but it merely becomes silly and preposterous. For music fans, though, there are generous portions of classical and rock numbers woven in among the electronic gadgets and jargon. **Director**—Steve Barron. **(PG)**
96 minutes

THE ELECTRIC HORSEMAN (1979)

★★★

Robert Redford
Jane Fonda

Redford and Fonda generate the right chemistry together in this winning film that roasts conglomerates and consumer manipulation. Redford is a hard-drinking ex-rodeo star, who sells out to a giant company to promote breakfast cereal. Outraged at the abuse of a multimillion-dollar racehorse, he dramatically kidnaps the animal. Fonda, as a TV news reporter, pursues him through the picturesque Rocky Mountains. Also with Valerie Perrine, Willie Nelson, and John Saxon. **Director**—Sydney Pollack. **(PG)** *120 minutes*

ELENI (1985)

★★

Kate Nelligan
John Malkovich

Flat, disappointing film based on Nicholas Gage's best-selling book about his mother, who was tortured and executed by Greek Communists in the late 1940s. The movie, unfortunately, drains away the passion of Gage's story because of Steve Tesich's unbalanced screenplay and Peter Yate's drab direction. The casting is wrong as well: Nelligan appears too highbrow in the title role and Malkovich is out of touch as Gage. **(PG)** *120 minutes*

THE ELEPHANT MAN (1980)

★★★½

Anthony Hopkins
John Hurt
Anne Bancroft
John Gielgud

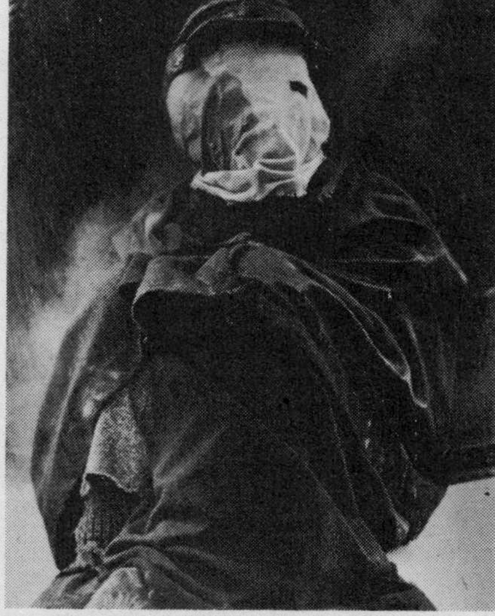

The Elephant Man *(John Hurt) undertakes a tortuous journey to dignity.*

This is the story of John Merrick, the turn-of-the-century man who suffered from numerous disorders that left him hideously deformed. Director David Lynch enhances the drama with a graceful dreamlike texture. But it's the magnificent performance by Hurt in a most difficult title role that really expresses the humanity and gentleness of this grotesque-looking young man. Also with Wendy Hiller. **(PG) Academy Award Nominations**—best picture; Hurt, best actor; Lynch, best director; Christopher DeVore, Eric Bergren, and Lynch, best screenplay based on material from another medium.

125 minutes b&w

ELEPHANT WALK (1954)

Elizabeth Taylor
Peter Finch

Taylor stars as the new wife of a Ceylon tea plantation owner who has difficulty adjusting to her new environment. Liz looks beautiful, and there's an impressive elephant stampede finale; otherwise, the film is merely a puffed-up soap opera with a confusing script. Finch plays the wealthy tea planter. Also with Dana Andrews and Abraham Sofaer. **Director**—William Dieterle.

103 minutes

ELMER GANTRY (1960)

 ★★★★

Burt Lancaster
Jean Simmons
Arthur Kennedy
Shirley Jones

In Elmer Gantry, *Shirley Jones and Burt Lancaster share a past.*

Lancaster is fantastic as the hypocritical evangelist in this exciting and absorbing screen version of the Sinclair Lewis novel. The film brims with first-class performances, including Simmons as an ambitious lady preacher, Kennedy as a sharp newspaper reporter, and Jones as Gantry's former girlfriend turned prostitute. Also with Dean Jagger, Edward Andrews, and Patti Page. **Director**—Richard Brooks. **Academy Awards**—Lancaster, best actor; Jones, best supporting actress; Brooks, best screenplay based on material from another medium. **Nomination**—best picture.

146 minutes

ELVIRA MADIGAN (1967)

 ★★★½

Pia Degermark
Thommy Berggren

A feast for the eyes and ears, this romantic tragedy is a triumph for writer, director, and editor Bo Widerberg. The film is based on a true story of a Swedish army officer and a circus performer who commit suicide rather than part from each other. Cinematographer Jorgen Person's lush color and muted tones create visual beauty; Motzart's music makes an effective background. The performances by Degermark and Berggren are adequate but take a back seat to the production. Originally filmed in Swedish. **(PG)** *89 minutes*

ELVIRA, MISTRESS OF THE DARK (1988)

Cassandra Peterson

A tame, silly spoof of horror films and small-town prudishness with TV movie host Peterson in the title role. The flimsy plot concerns Elvira's clash with uptight townsfolk when she arrives to claim an inheritance, part of which includes recipes to create monsters. The picture mainly focuses its gags on Elvira's scanty costume, which reveals an abundance of cleavage. Also with W. Morgan Sheppard, Jeff Conaway, and Edie McClurg. **Director**—James Signorelli. **(PG-13)** *96 minutes*

EMBRYO (1976)

Rock Hudson
Diane Ladd

An absurd variation of the Frankenstein theme, with Hudson as a doctor who injects a human fetus with a growth hormone. A little more than a week later, there's a full-grown, beautiful woman who can play chess. Of course, Hudson falls in love with her, but then things turn sour just as they did with Frankenstein's monster. Also with Barbara Carrera, Roddy McDowall, and Anne Schedeen. **Director**—Ralph Nelson. **(PG)** *104 minutes*

THE EMERALD FOREST (1985)

★★★

Powers Boothe
Meg Foster
Charley Boorman

Director John Boorman is the true star of this suspenseful, exotic Amazon jungle adventure. The film concerns a father's search for his son who had been captured by primitive Indians years earlier. Although the plot becomes complicated, Boorman emphasizes the near-mystical themes to advantage. He details the Indians' tribal life and makes a striking contrast with modern civilization. First-rate performances from Boothe, Foster, and Charley Boorman (John's son) as the child of both cultures. **(R)** *115 minutes*

THE EMPEROR WALTZ (1948)

Bing Crosby
Joan Fontaine

Crosby stars as a phonograph salesman trying to get an order from Emperor Franz Joseph of Austria. This oddball operetta is pleasant, but it carries scant impact. Also, director Billy Wilder is out of place with this fluffy material. The script is merely routine, and the music is forgettable. Others in the cast include Roland Culver and Richard Haydn.

106 minutes

EMPIRE OF THE SUN (1987)

Christian Bale
John Malkovich

Steven Spielberg directed this epic drama about the experiences of Jim Graham, a privileged 11-year-old English boy who survives internment in a Japanese prison camp during World

(Continued)

Christian Bale, Emily Richard, and Rupert Frazer in Empire of the Sun.

(Continued)

War II. The demanding role is carried impressively by young Bale, who appears in almost every scene. Malkovich costars as fellow prisoner Basie, a cynical adventurer who hustles precious commodities in the camp. The film is well crafted in Spielberg's dreamy style, particularly in terms of its spectacular set pieces, beautiful cinematography, and haunting images. The narrative, however, suffers from Spielberg's attempts to be profound. **Academy Award Nominations**—John Williams, music score; Allen Daviau, cinematography; Norman Reynolds and Harry Cordwell, art direction; Bob Ringwood, costume design; Michael Kahn, editing. **(PG)** *152 minutes*

THE EMPIRE STRIKES BACK (1980)

Mark Hamill
Harrison Ford
Carrie Fisher
Billy Dee Williams

Mentor Yoda with Mark Hamill in The Empire Strikes Back.

Space-opera maestro George Lucas, creator of *Star Wars,* scores again with another breathtaking fantasy adventure in a galaxy far, far away. It's a worthy and sumptuous sequel, with action galore and imaginative special effects that are special indeed. Old friends are back—Luke Skywalker, Han Solo, Chewbacca, R2-D2, C-3P0—gallantly defending the Rebel Forces from the evil Emperor. And there's a startling plot twist involving archvillain Darth Vader. Also with Alec Guinness, David Prowse, Frank Oz, and Anthony Daniels. The film won an Academy Award for special achievement in visual effects. **Director**—Irvin Kershner. **(PG)** *124 minutes*

THE ENCHANTED COTTAGE (1945)

Dorothy McGuire
Robert Young

An agreeable romantic fantasy that works well despite a syrupy and sentimental script. Young is a disfigured war veteran, and McGuire is a plain young girl. They discover beauty and love in each other, or is it only the enchantment of the New England cottage where they meet? Sensitive direction by John Cromwell pulls it off. Herbert Marshall, Mildred Natwick, Hillary Brooke, and Spring Byington also star. *91 minutes b&w*

THE END (1978)

★★

Burt Reynolds
Sally Field
Dom DeLuise

How can a story about a man about to die be something to laugh about? Reynolds strains hard in this endeavor, but doesn't succeed. DeLuise steals many a scene, but the film is an embarrassing attempt at gallows humor. The end doesn't come soon enough. Also with Joanne Woodward, Kristy McNichol, Robby Benson, David Steinberg, Norman Fell, and Carl Reiner. **Director**—Reynolds. **(R)** *100 minutes*

ENDANGERED SPECIES (1982)

★1/2

Robert Urich
JoBeth Williams

Hyped-up melodrama about mysterious cattle mutilations investigated by a tough ex-cop from New York (Urich) and a spunky Colorado sheriff (Williams). The film has adequate production values, but plays like supermarket-tabloid journalism. Contrivances and clichés are mixed in with the suspense. Urich of TV fame makes an impressive theatrical film debut, but the character he portrays is hardly believable. **Director**—Alan Rudolph. **(R)** *97 minutes*

ENDLESS LOVE (1981)

Brooke Shields
Martin Hewitt

This syrupy soap-opera movie, based on Scott Spencer's sultry novel, stars Shields and Hewitt as obsessive, ill-fated teenage lovers. The screenplay, which begins with passionate puppy love, shifts midway to tragedy, embroiling the youngsters and their families in unbearable distress. Shields and Hewitt are impressively pretty, but there is hardly any acting talent between them. The erratic direction of Franco Zeffirelli merely emphasizes the film's triteness. Endless nonsense. **(R)** *115 minutes*

ENDLESS SUMMER (1966)

Two young surfers travel around the world in search of the perfect wave. The concept was unique, and it made for an entertaining and visually attractive documentary. Bruce Brown as writer, director, and cinematographer did much to popularize the sport and simultaneously provide refreshing comments on almost all of the locations visited. You don't need to be a surfing fan to enjoy this gem. *95 minutes*

END OF THE LINE (1988)

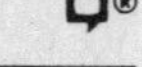

Wilford Brimley
Levon Helm

This well-meaning story about the decline of America's railroads starts out as an interesting slice-of-life tale but rapidly turns into a familiar road comedy. Brimley and Helm play dedicated railroad workers who steal a locomotive and take it from Arkansas to Chicago in the hopes of persuading company brass not to close the local railyard. The early

® This movie available with closed captions for the hearing impaired.

Kevin Bacon in the railroad story End of the Line.

scenes, which detail the everyday lives of the residents of small-town Arkansas, are remarkably fresh and natural. Unfortunately, after Helm and Brimley begin their quest, the events become comically overblown and predictable. The notable cast, including Holly Hunter in an early role, does much with the slight script. Also with Kevin Bacon, Mary Steenburgen, Barbara Barrie, and Bob Balaban. **Director**—Jay Russell. **(PG)** *105 minutes*

ENEMIES, A LOVE STORY (1990)

★★★

Anjelica Huston
Ron Silver
Lena Olin

Silver stars as a Holocaust survivor who is married to one woman while having an affair with another, when his first wife, believed dead, suddenly appears. He attempts to race from one borough of New York to another to spend time with each spouse. Silver's character is a man whose experiences have left him with a faltering sense of morals and a shifting identity. Based on the novel by Isaac Bashevis Singer, this unusual drama also features some biting humor. As directed by Paul Mazursky, the film is rich in period detail—it is set in 1949—but lacks a coherent visual style. Excellent acting by the entire cast makes up for any weaknesses. Also with Margaret Sophie Stein, Alan King, and Anna King. **(R) Academy Award Nominations**—Huston and Olin, best supporting actress; Roger L. Simon and Mazursky, best screenplay adaptation. *119 minutes*

THE ENEMY BELOW (1957)

★★★

Robert Mitchum
Curt Jurgens
Theodore Bikel

An absorbing World War II action drama. An American destroyer and a German U-boat stalk one another in the South Atlantic. Interest is maintained throughout, thanks to gripping underwater action, notable photography, and impressive special effects. Lots of tense moments heighten the suspense. Also with David Hedison, Russell Collins, and Doug McClure. The film won an Academy Award for its special effects. **Director**—Dick Powell. *98 minutes*

ENEMY MINE (1985)

★★

Dennis Quaid
Lou Gosset, Jr.

Quaid, a 21st-century space pilot from Earth, and Gosset, an alien pilot from a strange world, are marooned together on a desolate planet. Initially, a state of distrust exists. But eventually, they learn mutual respect and even affection. This familiar scenario, derived from countless B-movie plots, disintegrates into banality. It's all too manipulative and hardly entertaining. Gosset, who plays a lizardlike creature, is unrecognizable in his scaly costume. Directed by Wolfgang Petersen, whose film *Das Boot* was an international hit. **(PG-13)** *108 minutes*

THE ENFORCER (1976)

★★

Clint Eastwood
Tyne Daly
Harry Guardino

Eastwood, in this third Dirty Harry Callahan film, takes on a gang of San Francisco political terrorists. Here Harry is partnered with policewoman Daly, presented as unglamorous, yet efficient and caring. The use of a female partner for Harry, and his attitude toward her, emphasizes Harry's old-fashioned and out-of-date ways. However, the film upholds Harry's brutal methods as the only solution to the terrorists' tactics, which accounts for the accusations by some critics that the film is reactionary. This is the least interesting of the Dirty Harry films because the script, by Stirling Silliphant and Dean Reisner, is too predictable and Eastwood's character lacks the ambiguity that makes him so intriguing in the other films. Here he merely comes off as self-righteous. Also with Bradford Dillman, John Mitchum, and DeVeren Bookwalter. **Director**—James Fargo. **(R)** *96 minutes*

ENIGMA (1983)

★★

Martin Sheen
Sam Neill
Brigitte Fossey

A routine Cold War spy caper swarming with red herrings and double crosses. Sheen is the secret agent who penetrates East Berlin security; his mission is to nab a mysterious code scrambler in hopes of preventing the assassinations of Soviet dissidents. The globe-hopping plot unwinds at such breakneck speed that characters and storyline are lost amid the chaos. **Director**—Jeannot Szwarc. **(PG)** *101 minutes*

THE ENTERTAINER (1960)

★★★★

Laurence Olivier

The magnificent Olivier is at his best in the role of a second-rate music-hall comedian with a bloated ego, in the twilight of his career. This screen version of John Osborne's play is obviously stagy, but Olivier's triumphant performance overcomes any obstacle. He brilliantly portrays the tragedy of this man with large expectations but little talent to achieve them. The atmosphere of a seedy seaside resort adds to the characterization. The fine supporting cast includes Roger Livesey, Brenda de Banzie, Alan Bates, Joan Plowright, and Albert Finney. **Director**—Tony Richardson. **Academy Award Nomination**—Olivier, best actor. *96 minutes b&w*

ENTER THE DRAGON (1973)

★★★½

Bruce Lee
John Saxon

A surprisingly good martial-arts action film, with kung fu expert Lee kicking up a storm. He's hired by British agents to infiltrate a remote fortress and smash a drug-smuggling operation. Forget

(Continued)

This movie available on videotape and/or disc.

(Continued)

about any logical script; it's the action that counts here. Also with Yang Tse, Jim Kelly, and Bob Wall. **Director**—Robert Clouse. **(R)** *97 minutes*

THE ENTITY (1983)

Barbara Hershey
Ron Silver
George Coe

Hershey turns in a decent performance as a young woman possessed by an invisible spirit. But this documentary-like horror film never builds momentum, mystery, or suspense. Predictably, psychiatrists and parapsychologists are called in to explain the phenomenon. Frank DeFelitta wrote the screenplay from his own novel, which supposedly is based on the actual case of a California woman. **Director**—Sidney Furie. **(R)** *116 minutes*

ENTRE NOUS (1983)

Isabelle Huppert
Miou-Miou

Diane Kurys' poignant and observant account of two women who become intimate friends and eventually shuck their dull marriages for newly found liberation. Set in France during the 1950s, the film also deals sympathetically with the subtle pain and humiliation suffered by the abandoned husbands. The acting is superb, and the story builds to a startling climax. Originally filmed in French, and released as *Coup de Foudre.* **Director**—Kurys. **(PG) Academy Award Nomination**—best foreign-language film. *110 minutes*

EQUUS (1977)

Richard Burton
Peter Firth

Peter Shaffer's prizewinning play about psychological trauma loses much of its emotional impact and imagination in the transfer from stage to screen. Director Sidney Lumet's realistic treatment of the subject matter, the relationship between a psychiatrist and a troubled stable boy who blinds six horses, is less effective than the allegorical approach of the play. The performances, however, are excellent all around. Burton plays

Richard Burton and his troubled patient, Peter Firth, in Equus.

the psychiatrist with steady fortitude; Firth brings depth to his role as the boy. Also with Colin Blakely, Joan Plowright, and Harry Andrews. **(R) Academy Award Nominations**—Burton, best actor; Firth, best supporting actor; Shaffer, best screenplay based on material from another medium. *138 minutes*

ERASERHEAD (1977)

 ★★★★

John Nance

David Lynch, who directed the award-winning *The Elephant Man,* launched his career with this strange shocker that has found its way to the midnight-movie theater circuit. The nightmarish story explores the relationship of man and monster, but it's the visual imagery and atmosphere that are the keys to this film. Nance plays the title role of the weird character with a peculiar, elongated head and hair that stands on end. His girlfriend gives birth to a hideous, premature baby. This film—six years in the making—is now a cult classic. Also stars Charlotte Stewart and Jeanne Bates. **(No MPAA rating)** *90 minutes b&w*

ERNEST GOES TO JAIL (1990)

★1/2

Jim Varney

In his third film, Ernest P. Worrell ends up in the slammer because of mistaken identity. Eventually, he survives the electric chair, becomes magnetized, tangles with a runaway floor polisher, and impersonates James Cagney. Featured in a dual role this time out, the rubbery-faced Varney plays the evil criminal, Mr. Nash, in addition to sweet-natured Ernest. Though such lowbrow slapstick is aimed at children, this third installment is fairly amusing. Obviously made on a low budget, the director has still managed to fashion a stylish vehicle. This one is the best of the cartoonish series of films starring the annoying but inoffensive character. Also with Gailard Sartain, Bill Byrge, Barbara Bush, Randall "Tex" Cobb, and Charles Napier. **Director**—John Cherry. **(PG)** *81 minutes*

ERNEST SAVES CHRISTMAS (1988)

Jim Varney
Douglas Seale

Jim Varney spreads holiday cheer in Ernest Saves Christmas.

Varney hams it up in this mildly silly children's comedy set in Florida. The current Santa (Seale) wants to retire, and he's in Orlando to seek a successor to take over his reins. Varney is a local cab driver who helps St. Nick in his mission. Most of the humor is physical and the sight gags are predictable, but the kids should find it inoffensive. Also with Gailard Sartain and Billie Bird. **Director**—John Cherry. **(PG)** *89 minutes*

THE ERRAND BOY (1961)

 ★★1/2

Jerry Lewis
Brian Donlevy

Typical Lewis silliness, with the comedian playing a bumbling paperhanger on the rampage in a Hollywood studio. There are sight gags galore—a few effec-

This movie available with closed captions for the hearing impaired.

tive ones but many others that fall flat. Fans of Lewis will appreciate this more than others. Sig Ruman, Fritz Feld, and Doodles Weaver are also involved with the nonsense. **Director**—Lewis.
92 minutes b&w

THE ESCAPE ARTIST (1982)

 ★★

Griffin O'Neal
Raul Julia
Desi Arnaz

Griffin O'Neal (son of Ryan, brother of Tatum) is fresh and appealing as a precocious teenage magician who takes on the adult world. But, alas, he's trapped in a fantasy film so muddled that interest is never sustained. The story, based on David Wagoner's novel, would seem to promise an intriguing movie, but the project is mishandled by director Caleb Deschanel, the talented cinematographer of *The Black Stallion*. Veteran actors Arnaz, Gabriel Dell, Huntz Hall, and Jackie Coogan are featured in character roles. **(PG)** *96 minutes*

ESCAPE FROM ALCATRAZ (1979)

 ★★★

Clint Eastwood
Patrick McGoohan

Eastwood, looking mean and lean, stars in this tough and realistic prison film, which ranks with such classics as *White Heat* and *Brute Force*. Producer/director Don Siegel is in top form, masterfully mixing tension with the grim mood of prison life. There's fine supporting work from McGoohan as the cold-hearted warden. Richard Tuggle's efficient screenplay is based on the actual breakout of three prisoners from "the Rock" in 1962. Also with Roberts Blossom and Jack Thibeau. **(PG)**
112 minutes

ESCAPE FROM FORT BRAVO (1953)

William Holden
Eleanor Parker
John Forsythe

Better-than-average western, starring Holden as the commanding officer of a Union fort in Arizona during the Civil War. Some Confederates try to escape, but they're attacked by Indians who don't distinguish between white men of the North and those from the South. The climactic ambush sequence is the film's highlight. Also with William Demarest and Polly Bergen. **Director**—John Sturges. *98 minutes*

ESCAPE FROM NEW YORK (1981)

★★½

Kurt Russell
Ernest Borgnine

It's 1997, and New York City is a walled-in, escape-proof prison, populated by thousands of criminals and loonies. John Carpenter (*Halloween; The Fog*) dreamed up this mindless melodrama, which features characters and action of exceptional viciousness and violence. In the midst of this ominous hellhole, the President's plane crash-lands, and a cunning criminal, played by Russell, masterminds the rescue in trade for his freedom. Also with Isaac Hayes, Lee Van Cleef, Harry Dean Stanton, and Adrienne Barbeau. **(R)** *99 minutes*

E.T.—THE EXTRATERRESTRIAL (1982)

 ★★★★

Henry Thomas
Drew Barrymore
Robert MacNaughton
Dee Wallace

Drew Barrymore gives a tender kiss to her new friend, E.T.—The Extraterrestrial.

While most sci-fi pictures dwell on spectacular hardware, this extraordinary extraterrestrial adventure by director Steven Spielberg concentrates on character, feelings, and friendship. It's a wonderful, magical story about an ungainly little space creature stranded on Earth who is befriended and protected by some California youngsters. Thomas never hits a false note as the ordinary boy who gets involved in an unusual friendship. But the real star is E.T., the lovable, frightened, and homesick alien creature. **(PG) Academy Awards**—John Williams, best original score; Carlo Rambaldi, Dennis Muren, and Kenneth F. Smith, visual effects. **Nominations**—best picture; Spielberg, best director; Melissa Mathison, best screenplay written directly for the screen; Allen Daviau, cinematography. *115 minutes*

EUREKA (1985)

★★

Gene Hackman

A prospector (Hackman) strikes gold, becomes the richest man in the world, and eventually one of the unhappiest. Director Nicolas Roeg hypes up this film with outrageous scenes including a voodoo ceremony, a grisly suicide and murder, and sexual workouts. The absurd dialogue generates much unintended laughter. Such misspent energy is not so much boring as it is confusing. Theresa Russell, Rutger Hauer, and Mickey Rourke are in supporting roles. **(R)** *130 minutes*

THE EUROPEANS (1979)

 ★★★

Lee Remick
Robin Ellis

Henry James' novel, which contrasts American and European cultures, is tastefully adapted to the screen as a literate comedy of manners. Remick and Ellis are the sophisticated Europeans—a brother and sister—who move in with their staid New England cousins. Remick is lovely and plays the Baroness Munster with grace. The New England autumn countryside is photographed in full glory, and the 1850 time period is meticulously recreated. Also with Wesley Addy, Tim Choate, and Lisa Eichhorn. **Director**—James Ivory. **(G)**
90 minutes

EVERYBODY'S ALL-AMERICAN (1988)

★★½

Dennis Quaid
Jessica Lange

Slick performances by Quaid and Lange highlight this otherwise hollow

(Continued)

This movie available on videotape and/or disc.

Jessica Lange and Dennis Quaid in Everybody's All-American.

(Continued)

account of the gradual downfall of a one-time football hero. The story spans about 25 years—beginning with Quaid's stint as a star quarterback and Lange's bid as the campus beauty queen. Eventually, the two marry. As the drama progresses, it drifts into a series of clichés and superficial incidents about middle-age perplexities. Timothy Hutton and John Goodman costar. **Director**—Taylor Hackford. **(R)** *127 minutes*

EVERYBODY WINS (1990)

Debra Winger
Nick Nolte

Debra Winger and Nick Nolte try to free an innocent man in Everybody Wins.

Though Arthur Miller wrote the screenplay (his first since *The Misfits*), and Winger and Nolte top the cast, this mystery tale is mired in lofty intentions, bizarre details, and lackluster direction. Nolte plays a private detective; Winger costars as a sometime hooker. They collaborate in an attempt to free an innocent man from prison. The characters are uninteresting and unconvincing, and the tedious story evolves into a state of confusion. Director Karel Reisz attempts a *film-noir* look, which may appeal to film buffs. Also with Will Patton, Judith Ivey, Kathleen Wilhoite, Jack Warden, and Frank Converse. **(R)** *97 minutes*

EVERY MAN FOR HIMSELF AND GOD AGAINST ALL

See The Mystery of Kaspar Hauser

EVERYTHING YOU ALWAYS WANTED TO KNOW ABOUT SEX (BUT WERE AFRAID TO ASK) (1972)

Woody Allen
Lynn Redgrave
Anthony Quayle
John Carradine
Lou Jacobi

Director Allen lampoons sex in a series of inventive comic sketches; some of them work, some fizzle. But those that succeed are a howl. Segments include a giant female breast, Gene Wilder as a doctor attracted to a sheep, Redgrave modeling a chastity belt, and a tour of the male body with Woody portraying a sperm. Others in the cast are Louise Lasser, Tony Randall, and Burt Reynolds. **(R)** *87 minutes*

EVERY TIME WE SAY GOODBYE (1986)

Tom Hanks
Cristina Marsillach

Hanks is miscast as an American volunteer RAF pilot who falls in love with a gentle Jewish beauty (Marsillach) in Jerusalem during WWII. The two struggle to overcome the obstacles created by their diverse cultures. Some effective lyrical moments surface, but the film suffers from meager substance and a too-leisurely pace. **Director**—Moshe Mizrahi. **(PG–13)** *97 minutes*

EVERY WHICH WAY BUT LOOSE (1978)

Clint Eastwood
Sondra Locke

Eastwood, in contrast to his *Dirty Harry* character, tries to latch on to Burt Reynolds' good-ol'-boy routine in this dimwitted comedy. Eastwood earns money in pickup fistfights, travels with a cute orangutan, and is chased by mean cops and a gang of motorcycle toughs. The orangutan upstages the actors, which says it all about this film. Also with Geoffrey Lewis, Beverly D'Angelo, and Ruth Gordon. The sequel, *Any Which Way You Can*, is a better film. **Director**—James Fargo. **(R)** *119 minutes*

THE EVIL DEAD (1983)

Bruce Campbell
Ellen Sandweiss

Vacationing teens discover the Sumerian Book of the Dead in a Tennessee cabin and are forced to do battle with the bloodthirsty spirits who want to possess them. Although low-budget and frequently ragged, this exuberant thriller has enough shocks and raw energy for a dozen such films. Young director Sam Raimi, who was barely in his twenties at the time, shows an uncannily clever sense of camera movement and visual composition. The film's final ten minutes—a wildly bloody mélange of gore, weird sound effects, even stop-motion animation—will leave you limp from screaming and laughing. Also stars Betsy Baker. **(No MPAA rating)** *85 minutes*

EVIL DEAD 2: DEAD BY DAWN (1987)

Sarah Berry
Bruce Campbell

A grisly, violent screamer with a touch of self-conscious humor from director Sam Raimi. The film returns to the setting of the original *The Evil Dead*—a cabin in the woods where demons possess several hapless victims. The thinnest of plots is merely an excuse to let loose with chainsaws, axes, a decapitation with a shovel, and a torrent of blood. This campy horror picture, brimming with special effects, is reminiscent

® *This movie available with closed captions for the hearing impaired.*

of the manic style of the Three Stooges. The film's strength lies in the fact that it is not so much about the supernatural as it is about horror films. Just when you think you are likely to be sick, you laugh. **(No MPAA rating)** *85 minutes*

THE EVIL OF FRANKENSTEIN (1964)

Peter Cushing
Peter Woodthorpe

Another episode in the notorious monster series; this one lacks the style and impact of Boris Karloff's portrayals. Cushing plays Dr. Frankenstein, who returns to his laboratory where he finds the monster, played by Kiwi Kingston, frozen in ice. Terror ensues when the monster thaws out and rampages through the community. The television print differs from the theatrical version in that some scenes were cut, while new footage was added. TV prints run 97 minutes. Also with Sandor Eles, Duncan Lamont, and Katy Wild. **Director**—Freddie Francis. *87 minutes*

THE EVIL THAT MEN DO (1984)

★★

Charles Bronson
Joseph Maher

Bronson stars in another formula revenge film. This time the action occurs in Central America and Bronson is pitted against a vile assassin (Maher) and his henchmen. The unflappable Bronson is lured out of retirement after viewing videotapes of torture victims. He's soon at work eliminating the bad guys with an assortment of weapons and clever tactics. The film is heavy with scenes of brutality, blood, and mayhem. **Director**—J. Lee Thompson. **(R)** *89 minutes*

EVIL UNDER THE SUN (1982)

★★½

Peter Ustinov
Maggie Smith
James Mason
Diana Rigg

A nice-looking but rather dried-out film version of Agatha Christie's whodunit, set on a Mediterranean resort island. In typically droll fashion the indomitable Belgian sleuth Hercule Poirot (Ustinov) points out the murderer during the inevitable drawing-room showdown. But the events leading to the solution and the introduction of too many stuffy characters have all happened at too monotonous a pace to sustain interest. **Director**—Guy Hamilton. **(PG)** *102 minutes*

EXCALIBUR (1981)

 ★★★

Nigel Terry
Nicol Williamson

Nicol Williamson is the wizard Merlin in Excalibur.

The Arthurian legend is retold by director John Boorman in a visually fascinating style that enhances the mythic quality of the story. The narrative begins with Arthur's father, Uther Pendragon, and his feuds with other lords and landowners; continues with Arthur's union of small territories into the kingdom of Britain; and concludes with Arthur's battle against his evil son, Mordred. The presence of the magician Merlin (Williamson) ties the incredibly eventful story together. There is much bloodletting and violence in the tale as well as some overtly sexual scenes. The excellent production values, Academy Award-nominated cinematography by Alex Thompson, and erotic overtones make this an adult version of the popular legend. Also with Helen Mirren, Nicholas Clay, and Cherie Lunghi. **(R)** *140 minutes*

EXECUTIVE SUITE (1954)

 ★★★

Fredric March
William Holden
June Allyson
Barbara Stanwyck
Walter Pidgeon

Effective screen treatment of Cameron Hawley's book about wheeling and dealing in the boardroom of a big company. When the president dies, the vice-presidents vie for control, and tension mounts. The story also explores some domestic matters, but the thrust of the movie is corporate power. A big-name cast in effective performances. Also with Shelley Winters, Paul Douglas, Louis Calhern, Dean Jagger, and Nina Foch. **Director**—Robert Wise. **Academy Award Nomination**—Foch, best supporting actress. *104 minutes b&w*

EXODUS (1960)

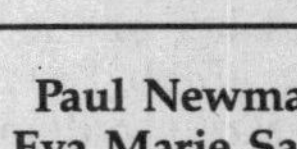

★★★

Paul Newman
Eva Marie Saint
Ralph Richardson
Peter Lawford
Lee J. Cobb
Sal Mineo

This sprawling epic, based on Leon Uris' chronicle of the formation of the state of Israel, offers some exciting moments with the struggling settlers. However, the direction is often heavy-handed, with some wooden performances distracting from the drama. A shorter version might have worked better; after three hours it ends on a tiresome note. Yet it's a well-intentioned historical film. Some versions on videotape are slightly shorter. The cast also includes John Derek, Hugh Griffith, David Opatoshu, and Martin Milner. **Director**—Otto Preminger. **Academy Award Nominations**—Mineo, best supporting actor; Sam Leavitt, cinematography. *213 minutes*

THE EXORCIST (1973)

 ★★★½

Ellen Burstyn
Max Von Sydow
Jason Miller
Linda Blair

A highly commercial and extremely effective horror film, based on William Peter Blatty's best-selling novel, about a young girl possessed by demons. Director William Friedkin goes to extremes to keep you on the edge of your seat from beginning to end. The film's compelling aspects are derived from sensational tricks as well as chilling suspense. Blair is good as the bedeviled child, and Miller is memorable as the priest who

(Continued)

This movie available on videotape and/or disc.

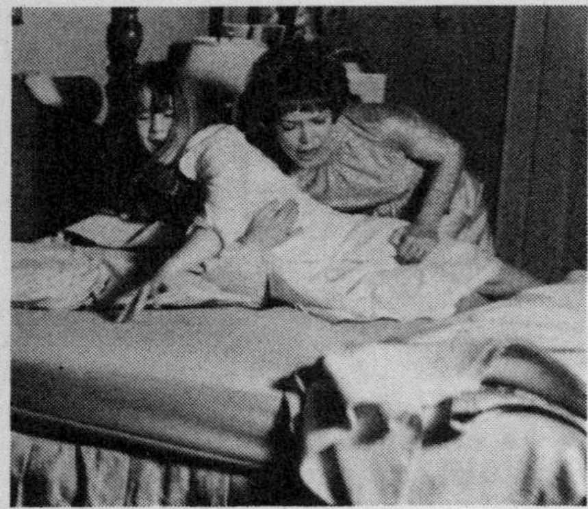

Ellen Burstyn struggles with daughter Linda Blair in The Exorcist.

(Continued)

attempts to rid her of the evil spirits. Also with Lee J. Cobb, Kitty Winn, and Jack MacGowran. **Academy Award**—Blatty, best screenplay based on material from another medium. **Nominations**—best picture; Friedkin, best director; Burstyn, best actress; Miller, best supporting actor; Blair, best supporting actress; Owen Roizman, cinematography. **(R)** *117 minutes*

EXORCIST II: THE HERETIC (1977)

Richard Burton
Linda Blair
Louise Fletcher

This overstuffed sequel isn't up to the scary effectiveness of the original. It's just so much warmed-over, supernatural mumbo jumbo inspired by the initial story. The angelic-faced Blair is now four years older and still bothered by a demon. Burton plays a priest assigned to wrestle with it. He seems very busy chasing the Devil to all parts of the globe, but actually there's not much happening. Reduced from 117 minutes after initial release. Also stars Max Von Sydow, Kitty Winn, James Earl Jones, and Ned Beatty. **Director**—John Boorman. **(R)** *110 minutes*

EXPERIENCE PREFERRED... BUT NOT ESSENTIAL (1983)

Elizabeth Edmonds

Charming, warm, and typically British comedy bubbling with various oddball characters. The centerpiece of this breezy concoction is innocent student Edmonds, who takes a summer job as waitress in a seaside hotel where she attempts to acquire some romantic experience. Director Peter Duffell skillfully coaxes fine ensemble acting from the competent cast, which also includes Sue Wallace and Ron Bain. **(PG)** *80 minutes*

EXPERIMENT IN TERROR (1962)

 ★★★

Glenn Ford
Lee Remick
Ross Martin

Ford and Remick head the cast of this gripping thriller set in San Francisco. Ford is convincing as an FBI agent fast on the trail of a criminal who terrorizes a bank teller, played by Remick, and kidnaps her sister as part of a robbery scheme. Martin is the villain; Stefanie Powers plays the sister. Lots of meticulous detail and suspense are used effectively by director Blake Edwards. Also with Ned Glass and Roy Poole. *123 minutes b&w*

EXPLORERS (1985)

Ethan Hawke
River Phoenix
Jason Presson
Amanda Peterson

Three youngsters blast off into space where they encounter aliens who learned about life on Earth by intercepting American TV signals. The slimy, green creatures spout pop-culture clichés—from Groucho Marx one-liners to soap commercials. This eccentric sci-fi/comedy, with its cornucopia of special effects and technical illusions, should delight kids. Adults, though, may find it drawn out. **Director**—Joe Dante. **(PG)** *110 minutes*

EXPOSED (1983)

★$^1/_2$

Nastassja Kinski
Rudolf Nureyev
Harvey Keitel

Kinski stars as a farm girl, college student, waitress, pianist, and high-fashion model in this unfocused political thriller. She eventually becomes tangled in an international terrorist plot as the upshot of a fleeting romance with a screwball violinist (Nureyev). The Russian ballet dancer's graceless mangling of his dialogue is unintentionally funny. **Director**—James Toback. **(R)** *99 minutes*

EXTREME PREJUDICE (1987)

 ★★★

Nick Nolte
Powers Boothe
Maria Conchita Alonso

A hard-boiled, modern western, set on the Tex-Mex border, involving a drug smuggler (Boothe) who is the target of a covert group of military operatives. Nolte plays a squinty-eyed Texas Ranger caught in the middle between the military commander and the drug kingpin, a former friend. Director Walter Hill, known for bringing a sophisticated visual styling to action genres (*The Warriers; The Long Riders*), concentrates on weaponry and shoot-outs here, contrasting the ultramodern hardware of the military with the old-fashioned six-gun of the Texas Ranger. Though the film contains as much violence as most action dramas, the depth of character and attention to theme make for more satisfying viewing. Alonso costars as Nolte's current girlfriend, who was once Booth's lover. Also with Rip Torn. **(R)** *105 minutes*

EXTREMITIES (1986)

 ★★

Farrah Fawcett
James Russo

Fawcett repeats her off-Broadway role as an intended rape victim who turns the tables on her attacker in this screen version of the stage production. Unfortunately, the film retains the staginess of the play and the story loses impact. The acting tends to be overwrought and the preachy dialogue becomes irritating. Russo also re-creates his stage role as the cagey rapist. Diana Scarwid and Alfre Woodard appear in supporting roles. **Director**—Robert M. Young. **(R)** *89 minutes*

AN EYE FOR AN EYE (1981)

Chuck Norris

Martial-arts champ Norris takes on scores of bad guys packing guns and knives in his quest for revenge on the killer of his pals. But even as martial-arts films go, this one is uninspired and

® This movie available with closed captions for the hearing impaired.

rather subdued. The routine plot features Norris as a San Francisco cop on the trail of murderous drug peddlers. He single-handedly faces a platoon of foes and is challenged by an Oriental thug twice his size, but the outcome is predictable. **Director**—Steve Carver. **(R)** *106 minutes*

EYE OF THE NEEDLE (1981)

★★★½

Donald Sutherland
Kate Nelligan

Donald Sutherland and Kate Nelligan enjoy a seaside stroll in Eye of the Needle.

This absorbing, suspenseful World War II spy thriller, based on Ken Follett's popular novel, combines a balanced working of romance and intrigue in war-torn England. Sutherland plays a master Nazi spy, who strives to smuggle out secrets of the impending Allied invasion of Europe. But he's thwarted in a breathtaking climax by beautiful Nelligan, who plays the wife of a crippled British pilot. Nelligan gives extraordinary warmth, intelligence, and excitement to her part. **Director**—Richard Marquand. **(R)** *111 minutes*

EYES OF LAURA MARS (1978)

★★★

Faye Dunaway
Tommy Lee Jones

The world of chic fashion photography is the setting for this classy whodunit. There are suspects galore to keep the audience guessing right up to the moment of the clever ending. Dunaway, in the title role, puts it all together as the trendy photographer who has horrifying premonitions of murder. Director Irvin Kershner's evenhanded direction, effective eerie backdrops, and superb casting also contribute to this sharp-edged thriller. Also with Brad Dourif. **(R)** *103 minutes*

EYEWITNESS (1981)

★★½

William Hurt
Sigourney Weaver

Director Peter Yates and writer Steve Tesich, conceivers of the hit *Breaking Away,* collaborate again with this romantic mystery. But this time, their effort is flawed by a farfetched plot that's loaded with red herrings. Yet there are charming performances by the principal actors. Hurt portrays a softspoken janitor who discovers a murder victim and woos the beautiful, sophisticated TV reporter covering the crime story; Weaver plays the reporter. Also with Christopher Plummer, James Woods, Irene Worth, and Steven Hill. **(R)** *102 minutes*

F

THE FABULOUS BAKER BOYS (1989)

★★★

Jeff Bridges
Michelle Pfeiffer
Beau Bridges

Jeff Bridges plays while Michelle Pfeiffer sings in The Fabulous Baker Boys.

The brothers Bridges star in a film together for the first time, as dual piano players working local lounges. Pfeiffer costars as the free spirit who revives their fading act. Under the helm of debuting director Steve Kloves, the film takes advantage of a smoky atmosphere and late-night settings to convey a sultry mood, which represents the underlying sexual tension between Jeff Bridges and Pfeiffer. Their melancholy romance leads to major changes for all three characters. Pfeiffer, who belts out a number of pop standards in a husky, sensual voice, is excellent as Susie Diamond, while the Bridges brothers effortlessly convey both the rapport and rivalry necessary for the storyline. Veteran director Sydney Pollack served as executive producer. Jennifer Tilly stands out as one of the girls who auditions for the act. **(R) Academy Award Nominations**—Pfeiffer, best actress; Michael Ballhaus, cinematography; William Steinkamp, editing; David Grusin, original score. *114 minutes.*

A FACE IN THE CROWD (1957)

★★★★

Andy Griffith
Lee Remick
Walter Matthau
Patricia Neal

Unscrupulous singer Andy Griffith tastes success in A Face in the Crowd.

Griffith is outstanding as a small-town country boy who becomes a celebrated TV wit after a manipulating reporter, played by Neal, discovers him and promotes his career. Budd Schulberg's script is on target in its perception of the entertainment business. Griffith's convincing performance plus fine supporting work by a top-notch cast adds dimension to the fascinating melodrama. Also with Anthony Franciosa, Percy Waram, and Kay Medford. **Director**—Elia Kazan. *126 minutes b&w*

FACE TO FACE (1976)

★★★★

Liv Ullmann

An Ingmar Bergman masterpiece about a psychiatrist going through a nervous breakdown. The intimacy with which

(Continued)

(Continued)
the camera reveals the drama gives the viewer a perspective rarely encountered in film. Ullmann gives one of her greatest performances as the doctor who records her own crack-up on film. Erland Josephson is also excellent. As usual, Bergman wrote the screenplay as well as directed this somber, troubling story. Originally filmed in Swedish. **(No MPAA rating) Academy Award Nominations**—Bergman, best director; Ullmann, best actress. *136 minutes*

THE FACTS OF LIFE (1960)

★★★

Bob Hope
Lucille Ball

Bob Hope tries a mid-life fling in The Facts of Life.

Comic pros Hope and Ball team up in this romantic comedy as middle-aged suburbanites who have a brief extramarital fling. It's an effective poke at American middle-class values, done with finesse and only a small amount of slapstick. Hope and Ball are supported expertly by Ruth Hussey, Don Defore, Louis Nye, and Philip Ober. **Director**—Melvin Frank. **Academy Award Nomination**—Norman Panama and Frank, best story and screenplay written directly for the screen. *103 minutes b&w*

FADE TO BLACK (1980)

Dennis Christopher
Linda Kerridge

Christopher, who played the young biker in *Breaking Away,* stars as a weird young man whose obsession with movies leads him to a spree of killings. He dresses up as Dracula, Hopalong Cassidy, and other movie immortals to carry out his revenge on various enemies. He most often imagines himself to be James Cagney playing Cody Jarrett in *White Heat.* But unlike such classics, this film is uneven, with mediocre acting. It's touted as a thriller but is more often silly than scary. **Director**—Vernon Zimmerman. **(R)** *100 minutes*

FAHRENHEIT 451 (1966)

★★★★

Oskar Werner
Julie Christie

Sci-fi drama from the Ray Bradbury novel about a future civilization that bans the written word, burns all books, and punishes readers. The film is a curiously touching and visually haunting masterpiece (lushly photographed by Nicolas Roeg), with an excellent musical score by Bernard Herrmann. Werner and Christie are the lovers who attempt to preserve a part of history by memorizing whole novels. In a dual role, Christie also plays the ignorant wife who collaborates with the authorities. The final scene of the recitation of *David Copperfield* in snow-covered woods will linger in the viewer's mind for a long time. Director François Truffaut's first film in English. *112 minutes*

FAIL-SAFE (1964)

★★★★

Henry Fonda
Walter Matthau
Dan O'Herlihy

An earnest and sober drama about the impending horrors and terrible decisions to be made after an American bomber is accidentally ordered to drop atomic bombs on Moscow. The theme is similar to the black comedy *Dr. Strangelove,* but here the point is made with gripping seriousness. First-rate performances all around. Also with Frank Overton, Fritz Weaver, Sorrell Booke, and Larry Hagman. **Director**—Sidney Lumet. *111 minutes b&w*

THE FALCON AND THE SNOWMAN (1985)

Sean Penn
Timothy Hutton

Compelling drama about two young men from affluent California families who sell government secrets to the Russians and are convicted of espionage. Director John Schlesinger relates the details of this true crime story with persistent energy. Yet, various unanswered questions concerning the spies' motives leave the film in a muddled state. Hutton and Penn give dynamic performances as the two chums turned traitors. **(R)** *131 minutes*

Timothy Hutton and Sean Penn sell secrets in The Falcon and the Snowman.

THE FALLEN IDOL (1948)

Ralph Richardson
Michele Morgan
Bobby Henrey

Graham Greene's short story is turned into a terse and stylish film that works on many levels. The plot involves a young ambassador's son who respects the family butler. When the servant's bitchy wife dies accidentally, the boy innocently focuses suspicion on his friend. The film offers an intelligent depiction of human emotions, with the story told mainly from the child's point of view. The fine cast also includes Sonia Dresdel and Jack Hawkins. **Director**—Carol Reed. **Academy Award Nominations**—Reed, best director; Greene, screenplay. *94 minutes b&w*

FALLING IN LOVE (1984)

Robert De Niro
Meryl Streep

Despite the powerhouse talents of De Niro and Streep, this thin, sudsy romance offers meager passion and drama, and almost no star chemistry. They portray married suburbanites who strike up a love relationship after they meet on a commuter train and

® This movie available with closed captions for the hearing impaired.

then agonize over continued temptations. The film, which bears resemblance to *Brief Encounter*, primarily serves as a showcase for the two superstars. **Director**—Ulu Grosbard. **(PG–13)** *106 minutes*

FAME (1980)

★★★

Eddie Barth
Irene Cara
Gene Anthony Ray

An extraordinary film about students at New York's High School for the Performing Arts. Structured in semidocumentary vignettes, the film virtually overflows with joy, emotion, comedy, energy, and inspiration as it follows the budding performers from initial auditions to graduation. The cast is mostly young unknowns who display incredible talent. Director Alan Parker (*Midnight Express*) deserves credit for the film's amazing charm and zest. The film won Academy Awards for its score and title song. **(R) Academy Award Nomination**—Christopher Gore, best screenplay written directly for the screen. *133 minutes*

FAMILY BUSINESS (1989)

★★1/2

Sean Connery
Dustin Hoffman
Matthew Broderick

Matthew Broderick, Sean Connery, and Dustin Hoffman in Family Business.

A family of thieves—featuring Connery as the wily grandfather, Hoffman as his cautious son, and Broderick as the brainy grandson—team up to burglarize a genetic research laboratory. The uneasy partnership-in-crime not only provides the grist for a humorous caper comedy, but it is also used as a device to explore the value of family ties. The script is sometimes strained, but the performances overcome the weaknesses in the narrative. Director Sidney Lumet makes excellent use of the New York City locations, giving an insider's view of the city. Also with Rosana DeSoto, Janet Carroll, and Victoria Jackson. **(R)** *115 minutes*

FAMILY PLOT (1976)

★★1/2

Karen Black
Bruce Dern
Barbara Harris
William Devane

Alfred Hitchcock's last completed film is this tongue-in-cheek comedy involving kidnapping, murder, and spiritualism. Playing against Devane's image as a steadfast hero based on the actor's portrayals of John Kennedy, Hitchcock here cast Devane as the cold-hearted villain; similarly, he cast perennial psychotic Dern as the everyman who solves the mystery. The film abounds in clever bits and exciting, but amusing, chase scenes. Considered lightweight Hitchcock at the time of its release, the film has been better appreciated since the death of the great director. The script is by Ernest Lehman. Also with Ed Lauter, Cathleen Nesbitt, and Katherine Helmond. **(PG)** *120 minutes*

THE FAN (1981)

★★

Lauren Bacall
James Garner

Solid acting by Bacall is the only high point of this routine thriller. As a Broadway star who is terrorized by an embittered fan, Bacall enlivens the part with the style that has marked her career from the beginning. The story is a notch above the usual horror fare, but much appeal is frittered away by awkward handling of the psychotic young man who turns to murder after he is rejected by Bacall. Garner is wasted in a secondary role. Also features Maureen Stapleton, Michael Biehn, and Hector Elizondo. **Director**—Edward Bianchi. **(R)** *95 minutes*

FANCY PANTS (1950)

★★★

Bob Hope
Lucille Ball

Hope is all dressed up as a butler to bring proper manners to a frontier town in this western farce. With Ball on board, fun and laughs galore are guaranteed in this remake of *Ruggles of Red Gap.* There are a few slow moments now and then, but the stars shine in one of their better vehicles. Bruce Cabot, Eric Blore, and Jack Kirkwood help with supporting roles. **Director**—George Marshall. *92 minutes*

FANDANGO (1985)

★★

Kevin Costner
Sam Robards
Judd Nelson

Silly, familiar coming-of-age movie laced with the usual allotment of adolescent humor. Set in 1971, five recent college graduates take an adventurous trip across Texas before facing military service or civilian jobs. A few sight gags provoke laughter, but excess sentimentality intrudes on the comedy. It's ultimately forgettable. **Director**—Kevin Reynolds. **(PG)** *91 minutes*

FANNY (1961)

★★★

Charles Boyer
Maurice Chevalier
Leslie Caron

This standard version of Marcel Pagnol's trilogy of films, about a girl in Marseilles involved with a sailor, is effectively carried along by the charm of a marvelous cast and beautiful photography. Boyer and Chevalier give colorful performances, and they are aided by the beautiful Caron. The songs from the Broadway musical version are used here only as backdrop music. Also with Horst Buchholz, Georgette Anys, and Lionel Jeffries. **Director**—Joshua Logan. **Academy Award Nominations**—best picture; Boyer, best actor; Jack Cardiff, cinematography. *133 minutes*

FANTASIA (1940)

★★★★

A rare, innovative animated feature from Walt Disney that combines classical music with cartoons. The music of Bach, Tchaikovsky, Stravinsky, Beethoven, Mussorgsky, and other masters is presented under the direction of Leopold Stokowski and the Philadel-

(Continued)

This movie available on videotape and/or disc.

Mickey's foolishness leads to a water problem in Fantasia.

(Continued)
phia Orchestra. The cartoon interpretations are especially inspiring. And this brilliant production serves as a wonderful introduction—especially for children—to the world of classical music. **Supervisor**—Ben Sharpsteen. **(G) Academy Awards**—special awards to Walt Disney, William Garity, John N. A. Hawkins, Stokowski, and RCA.
135 minutes

FANTASTIC VOYAGE (1966)

★★★

Stephen Boyd
Raquel Welch
Edmond O'Brien
Donald Pleasence

Here's a truly unusual science-fiction feature that's entertaining and informative. A scientist needs delicate brain surgery after an assassination attempt, so a medical team is shrunk to the size of bacteria and enters his bloodstream to perform the vital work. The photography, editing, and sound effects were Oscar-nominated, while the special effects did receive the Academy Award. It's a fantastic trip, indeed. Also with Arthur Kennedy, Arthur O'Connell, and William Redfield. **Director**—Richard Fleischer. *100 minutes*

THE FAR COUNTRY (1955)

★★★

James Stewart
Walter Brennan

Cattleman Stewart, looking stoic and tall in the saddle, drives his herd to Alaska and finds trouble along the way. It's a solid adventure story, set handsomely against the Alaskan mining country. Stewart is effective, and there's an excellent supporting performance by Brennan. Also with Ruth Roman, Jay C. Flippen, Corinne Calvet, and Harry Morgan. **Director**—Anthony Mann.
97 minutes

FAREWELL, MY LOVELY (1975)

★★★

Robert Mitchum
Charlotte Rampling

Mitchum stars as the quintessential Philip Marlowe in this third film version of Raymond Chandler's archetypal hard-boiled detective novel. The story revolves around Marlowe's search for the long-lost girlfriend of an ex-con, a task that leads to murder, blackmail, and larceny. Mitchum, known for his roles in many *films noirs* made in the 1950s, is the real force behind this film and his presence evokes the nostalgia and melancholy inherent in the genre. Though set during the 1940s, this *film noir* was made in 1975, making Mitchum's Marlowe much older than earlier interpretations of the role. This adds a sense of weariness to his character as his lined face reveals the hard knocks and disillusionment caused from a lifetime of dealing with the corrupt side of civilization. The period production design by Dean Tavoularis enhances the prevailing mood of melancholy. Also with John Ireland, Sylvia Miles, Harry Dean Stanton, and Jack O'Halloran. **Director**—Dick Richards. **(R) Academy Award Nomination**—Miles, best supporting actress.
97 minutes

A FAREWELL TO ARMS (1932)

★★★

Gary Cooper
Helen Hayes

Wounded American ambulance driver Cooper falls in love with nurse Hayes in a romantic adaptation of the Ernest Hemingway novel. Although the book was more vivid and realistic, the screen version is salvaged by Hayes' brilliant performance in one of her few film efforts. Also with Adolphe Menjou. **Director**—Frank Borzage. **Academy Award**—Charles Bryant Lang, Jr., cinematography. **Nomination**—best picture.
78 minutes b&w

FAREWELL TO THE KING (1989)

★★ ®

Nick Nolte
Nigel Havers
Frank McRae
James Fox

Nick Nolte, a jungle monarch in Farewell to the King.

A shaggy-haired Nolte is unconvincing as a World War II Army deserter who becomes king of a Borneo jungle tribe. This unfocused, hackneyed adventure is reminiscent of *Lord Jim* and *The Man Who Would Be King*. Unfortunately, any classic pretensions are quickly derailed when the film lapses into comic-book action sequences played out with stock characters. A segment involving General Douglas MacArthur comes off as unintentionally laughable. **Director**—John Milius. **(PG-13)** *117 minutes*

FAR FROM THE MADDING CROWD (1967)

★★

Julie Christie
Peter Finch
Alan Bates
Terence Stamp

An overlong and somewhat plodding screen treatment of Thomas Hardy's novel about a beautiful English farm girl who affects the lives of three men. Christie is out of step as the headstrong beauty, although Finch and Bates perform well as objects of her desire. The film boasts exceptional production values with exquisite photography and a stirring score. Also with Prunella Ransome. **Director**—John Schlesinger. **(PG)**
169 minutes

® *This movie available with closed captions for the hearing impaired.*

THE FARMER'S DAUGHTER (1947)

★★★½

Loretta Young
Joseph Cotten

A smartly made comedy/drama about a willful servant girl, played by Young, who runs for the congressional seat occupied by her boss. It's an effective treatment of the Cinderella theme, with a top cast providing excellent performances. Also with Ethel Barrymore, Charles Bickford, and Harry Davenport. **Director**—H.C. Potter. **Academy Award**—Young, best actress. **Nomination**—Bickford, best supporting actor.

97 minutes b&w

FAR NORTH (1988)

★★

Charles Durning
Jessica Lange
Tess Harper

Way up in the Far North, *Jessica Lange must deal with her crotchety father.*

Playwright Sam Shepard, in his initial film-directing effort, can't get this muddled comedy off the ground. The cast makes an earnest effort, but the story proceeds lamely. Durning portrays a cranky farmer residing in northern Minnesota who sees his traditional male role disintegrate amid changes in family values. Lange plays his urban, career-oriented daughter, who must cope with the old geezer's eccentricities. Also with Ann Wedgeworth and Patricia Arquette. **(PG-13)** *90 minutes*

FAST FORWARD (1985)

★★

Don Franklin

Eight eager, bright-eyed youths from Sandusky, Ohio, descend on New York City to make it big as a hotshot dance team. After a round of rejections, they dance up a storm on the streets, at a posh hotel, and in a disco, and then win the big dance contest—all in two weeks' time. Miracle of miracles. Even the folks in Sandusky might consider such a feat preposterous. Shades of *Flashdance* and *Fame* are everywhere. With John Scott Clough and Tamara Mark. **Director**—Sidney Poitier. **(PG)** *110 minutes*

FAST TIMES AT RIDGEMONT HIGH (1982)

★★★

Sean Penn
Jennifer Jason Leigh
Phoebe Cates

An episodic account of teenage life based on the observations of a young writer who posed as a high-school student. Sex, drugs, rock 'n' roll, and holding down their part-time jobs are forever on the minds of these youngsters. The uneven film manages to be warm and appealing. The production introduces some fresh and likable new performers. Penn's comic portrayal of the drugged-out surfer startled and amused audiences and critics alike. **Director**—Amy Heckerling. **(R)**

92 minutes

FATAL ATTRACTION (1987)

★★★

Michael Douglas
Glenn Close
Anne Archer

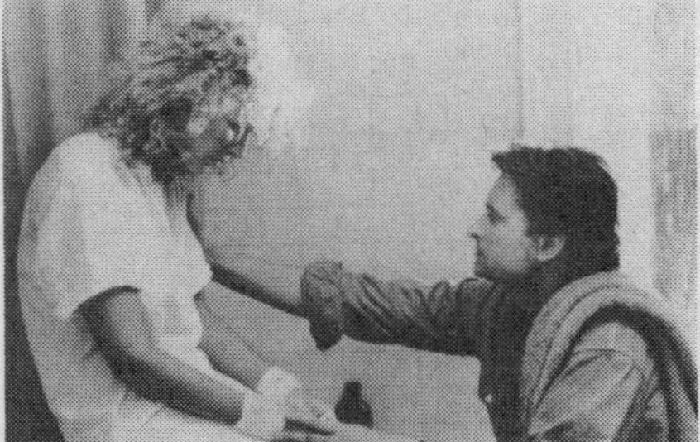

Michael Douglas' Fatal Attraction *for Glenn Close mushrooms out of control.*

One of the most talked-about films of the last decade, this psychological thriller cleverly taps into society's current fears about sexually promiscuous behavior. Douglas stars as a happily married, upscale lawyer who has a weekend fling with a beautiful, intelligent career woman, played by Close. She refuses to let the brief encounter come to an end, and the relationship becomes awkward and eventually life threatening. The tightly constructed script and well-paced editing propel the film forward, while the believable characters and excellent performances draw the viewer into the narrative. A slickly produced moral fable for our times. **Director**—Adrian Lyne. **(R) Academy Award Nominations**—best film; Close, best actress; Archer, best supporting actress; Lyne, best director; James Dearden, best screenplay based on material adapted from another medium; Michael Kahn and Peter E. Berger, best editing. *120 minutes*

FATAL BEAUTY (1987)

Whoopi Goldberg
Sam Elliott

Goldberg wastes her comic talent in this violent police thriller about the hunt for tainted cocaine. She plays a tough-talking Los Angeles cop along the lines of Eddie Murphy's character in *Beverly Hills Cop.* The humorous wisecracks, however, are undercut by a torrent of violent shootings, beatings, and other comic-book mayhem, which makes the film implausible and absurd. The close relationship between the verbal humor and the intense violence, in which a character makes a witty remark before blasting someone to pieces, is unsettling to watch. Elliott's role seems ill defined as well. Viewers are led to expect a romantic liaison between Elliott and Goldberg, but this never occurs. Also with Ruben Blades, Harris Yulin, Brad Dourif, and Cheech Marin. **Director**—Tom Holland. **(R)**

103 minutes

FAT CITY (1972)

★★★

Stacy Keach
Jeff Bridges
Susan Tyrrell

Keach brilliantly portrays an over-the-hill boxer trying to get back on his feet in this touching film adapted from Leonard Gardner's novel. The setting is a small California town, and the story incisively explores the frustrations and

(Continued)

(Continued)
heartbreaks of the poor. Fine supporting work by Bridges and Tyrrell builds interest in the characters. John Huston's direction is among his best efforts. Also with Candy Clark and Nicholas Colasanto. **(PG) Academy Award Nomination**—Tyrrell, best supporting actress.
96 minutes

FATHER GOOSE (1964)

★★★

Cary Grant
Leslie Caron
Trevor Howard

This ordinary, half-baked farce is salvaged mainly because of the special charms of Grant, who stars as a South Seas beach bum during World War II. Grant's part-time mission is to spot aircraft for the Australian navy, but then a beautiful French schoolteacher (Caron) and her pupils arrive, and the fun begins. **Director**—Ralph Nelson. **Academy Award**—S.H. Barnett, Peter Stone, and Frank Tarloff, best story and screenplay written directly for the screen.
115 minutes

FATHER OF THE BRIDE (1950)

★★★½

Spencer Tracy
Joan Bennett
Elizabeth Taylor

Spencer Tracy and Joan Bennett are among the stars in Father of the Bride.

A fantastic comedy, graced with a champagne cast and a witty script. Tracy is in top form as the happy but frustrated father faced with organizing and financing his daughter's wedding. And the bride is Taylor at her loveliest. Also with Don Taylor, Billie Burke, Leo G. Carroll, and Russ Tamblyn. **Director**—Vincente Minnelli. **Academy Award Nominations**—best picture; Tracy, best actor; Francis Goodrich and Albert Hackett, screenplay.
93 minutes b&w

FAT MAN AND LITTLE BOY (1989)

Paul Newman
Dwight Schultz
Bonnie Bedelia

The development of the atomic bomb during World War II is explored in this historical drama from English director Roland Joffe. Joffe, who specializes in stories about personal relationships set against a wider sociopolitical context *(The Killing Fields; The Mission)* misses the mark here. His predilection for an epic style seems out of place in a film in which the characters are engaged in such a destructive mission, and the casting of Newman and Schultz is a mistake. Schultz, one of the stars of television's *The A-Team,* is no match for Newman onscreen. While Newman is appropriately gruff and commanding as Gen. Leslie R. Grovers, the coordinator of the Manhattan Project, Schultz is lackluster and dull as J. Robert Oppenheimer, the brilliant physicist who headed the creative team. Also, the moral complexities and shifting motivations behind the building of the atomic bomb are not adequately conveyed, perhaps because a number of subplots get in the way. Also with John Cusack, Laura Dern, Ron Frazier, John C. McGinley, and Natasha Richardson. **(PG-13)** *126 minutes*

FATSO (1980)

★

Dom DeLuise
Anne Bancroft

Anne Bancroft and Dom DeLuise confront the horrors of food in Fatso.

This flabby satire, about a fat man who struggles in vain to stop eating, may make you hungry, but there's not enough comic nourishment for honest entertainment. DeLuise is often funny and appealing as the overweight protagonist. Yet he cannot overcome the thin script by Bancroft, who debuts as writer and director. She fails to maintain the proper balance between humor and pathos. **(PG)** *94 minutes*

FEDORA (1978)

William Holden
Marthe Keller

Director Billy Wilder's romantic melodrama is about a Garbo-like screen goddess, played by Keller, who retires at the height of her fame and beauty to live in seclusion on a remote Greek island with her "secret." The film is reminiscent of the director's 1950 success, *Sunset Boulevard.* Even Holden stars again to narrate the tragic tale in the same ironic tone. Wilder's satiric observations and comic touches can still be entertaining, but they've lost their bite over the years. Also with Hildegarde Neff, José Ferrer, Frances Sternhagen, Henry Fonda, and Michael York. **(PG)**
114 minutes

FEDS (1989)

Rebecca DeMornay
Mary Gross

Mary Gross and Rebecca DeMornay as FBI agent trainees in Feds.

A buddy-cop movie with a twist—this time the buddies are *female* FBI trainees. Though inspired by the *Police Academy* series, this romp unfortunately doesn't have as much going for it. DeMornay and Gross play the prospective federal cops with spunk despite the creaky slapstick routines and silly dialogue. **Director**—Dan Goldberg. **(PG-13)** *83 minutes*

FELLINI'S CASANOVA (1976)

★★

Donald Sutherland
Tina Aumont
Cicely Browne

Director Federico Fellini's 2½-hour epic about the fabled 18th-century Venetian is a ponderous essay that reflects the director's own alienation from his subject. The film is strung together with repetitive and joyless scenes of a man who makes love like a robot. An eye-popping production design adds a measure of dazzle to this otherwise chilly spectacle. Sutherland, his face grotesquely rearranged, has the title role. Some versions of the film run slightly longer. Also with John Karlsen. **(R) Academy Award**—Danilo Donati, best costume design. **Nomination**—Fellini and Bernadino Zapponi, best screenplay based on material from another medium. *158 minutes*

FERRIS BUELLER'S DAY OFF (1986)

★★

Matthew Broderick
Alan Ruck
Mia Sara

Ferris Bueller (Broderick) goes to elaborate lengths to fool his parents and his high-school principal into believing he is sick so he can play hooky one more time. He, his girlfriend, and his best friend (Ruck) borrow a cherished antique Ferrari owned by Ruck's father and head for downtown Chicago for a day of rest and relaxation. The trio visits some of the city's recognizable sites—the Sears Tower, Wrigley Field—but nothing particularly amusing or spectacular happens to them. Written, directed, and produced by John Hughes, the lightweight comedy uses certain elements familiar from other Hughes films, such as the rock music soundtrack, the gentle rebelliousness of the teens, the cleverness of the youths as compared to the adults, etc. However, Ferris' easygoing philosophy of life and the lack of any real conflict make for a frivolous film. The young actors rise above the slight material. Also with Jeffrey Jones, Jennifer Grey, Charlie Sheen, and Del Close. **(PG–13)** *103 minutes*

FEVER PITCH (1985)

★

Ryan O'Neal

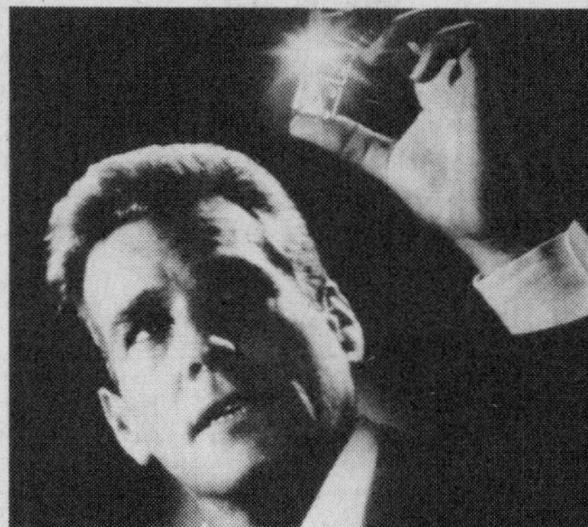

Ryan O'Neal discovers the glitter of gambling in Fever Pitch.

The multibillion-dollar gambling business is explored in this hard-nosed message movie that finally goes soft on credibility. O'Neal delivers a flat performance as a well-known sports columnist who writes an exposé on gamblers. In the process, he develops a gambling problem of his own. This film by Richard Brooks probably would have played better as a straight documentary. Catherine Hicks and Giancarlo Giannini also star. **(R)** *95 minutes*

FFOLKES (1980)

★★★

Roger Moore
James Mason
Anthony Perkins

Hijackers threaten to blow up a North Sea oil-drilling rig and a billion-dollar production platform. Moore, as an eccentric underwater commando, outsmarts the terrorists and saves the British Empire from untold humiliation; he's delightful as an adventurer who loves cats and distrusts women. He undertakes his daring assignment with unblinking cockiness. Suspense is relentless as the hours tick off toward the impending disaster. Mason and Perkins are credible in supporting roles. Also with Michael Parks and David Hedison. **Director**—Andrew V. McLaglen. **(PG)** *99 minutes*

F FOR FAKE (1977)

★★★

Director Orson Welles conducts a playful and cynical tour of the world of fakery, forgery, and impostors in this semidocumentary that may itself be a put-on. Master of ceremonies Welles concentrates on the deceptions of literary forger Clifford Irving and art forger Elmyr de Hory. Welles suggests that the signature on a piece of art isn't as important as the work itself. The film is engrossing and clever. **(No MPAA rating)** *85 minutes*

FIDDLER ON THE ROOF (1971)

★★★

Topol
Norma Crane
Leonard Frey
Molly Picon

A worthy screen version of the long-running Broadway musical, with the rousing songs intact. Topol plays Tevye, the Jewish dairyman in the small Russian village who deals with family problems and the strain of persecution by the authorities. He's not quite as good as Zero Mostel, but he's convincing, and his version of the popular "If I Were a Rich Man" comes off quite well. Also with Paul Mann, Rosalind Harris, and Michele Marsh. The rooftop fiddling is by Isaac Stern. **Director**—Norman Jewison. **(G) Academy Award**—Oswald Morris, cinematography. **Nominations**—best picture; Jewison, best director; Topol, best actor; Frey, best supporting actor. *180 minutes*

FIELD OF DREAMS (1989)

★★★½

Kevin Costner
Amy Madigan
Burt Lancaster
James Earl Jones

A superb movie fantasy reminiscent of the films of Frank Capra. Costner plays an Iowa farmer who builds a baseball diamond in his cornfield so the legendary Shoeless Joe Jackson will return from the dead and play there. Overtly sentimental, this whimsical tale is about faith and redemption. Director Phil Alden Robinson also wrote this screen adaptation of W.P. Kinsella's book, *Shoeless Joe.* Also with Ray Liotta, Timothy Busfield, Gaby Hoffman, and Frank Whaley. **(PG) Academy Award Nominations**—best picture; Robinson, best screenplay adaptation; James Horner, original score. *106 minutes*

THE FIENDISH PLOT OF DR. FU MANCHU (1980)

Peter Sellers

The last film starring the late, great Sellers is a weak and disappointing attempt at comedy. It's obviously not the fault of the beloved comedian, who once more plays multiple roles with his usual versatile skill. *The Fiendish Plot* has a flat, no-laugh plot that concerns the efforts of master-criminal Dr. Fu Manchu to steal one of England's crown jewels. The direction and script aren't up to par for one of the movie industry's most prolific comic talents. **Director**—Piers Haggard. **(PG)**

108 minutes

52 PICK-UP (1986)

 ★★★

Roy Scheider
Ann-Margret
John Glover

Roy Scheider and Ann-Margret are victimized by blackmailers in 52 Pick-up.

Elmore Leonard's clever screenplay, based on his own novel, and John Frankenheimer's staccato direction highlight this chilling crime drama featuring colorful heroes and villains. Scheider plays an industrialist who is blackmailed by three ruthless, cold-blooded thugs. How he manipulates the blackmailers by using their greed and cruelty against them propels this dark melodrama. Ann-Margret costars as his ambitious wife who is thrust in the middle of her husband's problems through no fault of her own. Glover is chilling as the sly leader of the extortionists. Also with Clarence Williams III, Lonny Chapman, Vanity, and Robert Trebor. **(R)** *114 minutes*

FIGHTER SQUADRON (1948)

Edmond O'Brien
Robert Stack

Standard World War II action story with some good air combat sequences. O'Brien plays a gung ho pilot who takes unusual risks. The script is loaded with clichés. Also with John Rodney, Henry Hull, Walter Reed, and Rock Hudson (in his first film). **Director**—Raoul Walsh. *96 minutes*

FIGHTING BACK (1982)

Tom Skerritt
Michael Sarrazin
Patti LuPone

Tom Skerritt runs into a little trouble in Fighting Back.

Another look at vigilante justice that delves briefly into the social aspects of the situation but winds up being just as preposterous as *Death Wish.* The brisk story offers some thought-provoking ideas, but too much of the film is devoted to intense, violent confrontations. Skerritt stars as a hotheaded Philadelphia store owner who organizes a citizen's anticrime patrol after members of his family are brutalized by local thugs. **Director**—Lewis Teague. **(R)**

98 minutes

THE FIGHTING KENTUCKIAN (1949)

John Wayne
Vera Ralston

A frontiersman battles greedy villains planning to steal land from French settlers in Kentucky during the early 19th century. In the process he courts a French general's daughter. A typical western vehicle for Wayne with plenty of action and little else. The storyline is minimal and predictably banal. Oliver Hardy is featured in an unusual role without Stan Laurel. **Director**—George Waggner. *100 minutes b&w*

FIGHTING MAD (1976)

Peter Fonda

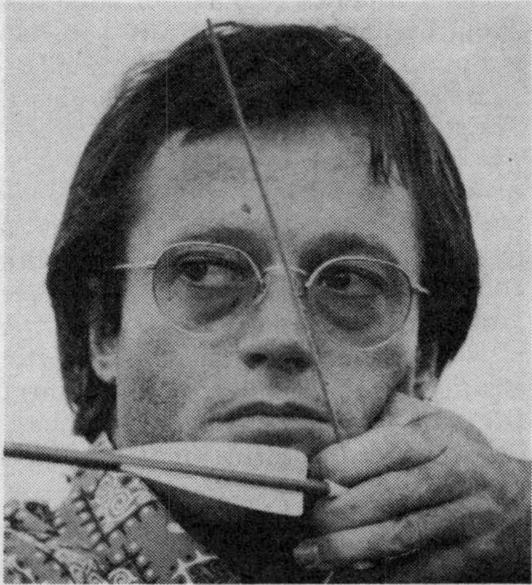

Strip miners, beware: Peter Fonda knows who you are, and he's Fighting Mad.

The familiar vengeance plot, which originated in *Death Wish* and *Walking Tall,* is effectively used in this action drama set in rural Arkansas. Fonda plays a young man who returns to the family ranch and wages a one-man battle against crooked strip-mining operators. The script is filled with holes, but there's plenty of emotion and nonstop violent action to satisfy audiences who relish such fare. Also with Lynn Lowry, John Doucette, and Philip Carey. Written and directed by Jonathan Demme. **(R)** *90 minutes*

THE FIGHTING O'FLYNN (1949)

Douglas Fairbanks, Jr.
Helene Carter

Fairbanks plays the title role with robust energy. He's a poor Irish swashbuckler who interferes with Napoleon's invasion scheme. But all in all, it's a low-level adventure, with the rest of the cast not up to Fairbanks' high spirits. The film is based on Justin McCarthy's novel. Also with Richard Greene, Patricia Medina, and Arthur Shields. **Director**—Arthur Pierson.

94 minutes b&w

This movie available with closed captions for the hearing impaired.

THE FIGHTING SEABEES (1944)

★★★

John Wayne
Susan Hayward
Dennis O'Keefe

Wayne is involved with the Navy's construction battalion, busy repairing installations and fighting the Japanese during World War II. There's plenty of action for Wayne fans, with a romantic subplot occasionally breaking the pace. The good cast also includes William Frawley, Duncan Renaldo, and Addison Richards. **Director**—Edward Ludwig.
100 minutes b&w

THE FIGHTING 69th (1940)

James Cagney
Pat O'Brien

A sentimental World War I film, with Cagney hamming it up as a tough Irish trooper who becomes a hero. The tale packs plenty of spirit, some rough-and-tumble comedy, and ripsnorting battle scenes. It's pure Hollywood-style entertainment. Also with George Brent, Jeffrey Lynn, Alan Hale, and Dennis Morgan. **Director**—William Keighley.
90 minutes b&w

FINAL CHAPTER—WALKING TALL (1977)

Bo Svenson

Svenson continues as the heroic Tennessee sheriff in this third screen installment on the life of Buford Pusser. This chapter covers crusading sheriff Pusser's success in selling his life's story to a Hollywood producer and his efforts to wipe out a gambling joint owned by the local crime boss. As usual, the violence is overdone. Also with Margaret Blye, Forrest Tucker, and Lurene Tuttle. **Director**—Jack Starrett. **(R)**
112 minutes

THE FINAL CONFLICT (1981)

Sam Neill

Neill plays Damien, the Antichrist, in this third installment of the *Omen* series. This time, Damien is head of an international conglomerate; he attempts to track down Jesus Christ, who he believes has been reborn. There are the standard violent gore sequences and more of the preposterous plot that's rather shopworn by now. This film concludes the trilogy; Hollywood has decided to give the Devil a rest and the rest of us a break from such nonsense. **Director**—Graham Baker. **(R)**
100 minutes

THE FINAL COUNTDOWN (1980)

Kirk Douglas
Martin Sheen
Katharine Ross
James Farentino

The USS *Nimitz,* the nuclear-powered aircraft carrier, is thrown back in time and confronts the fateful Japanese attack on Pearl Harbor. This plot idea generates rousing drama and excitement—for a few minutes. Not even the excellent cast can disguise the fact that this is like a half-hour *Twilight Zone* plot posing as as a feature film. The technical details are authentic, and Douglas is outstanding as the skipper of the *Nimitz;* but the enterprise as a whole sinks nonetheless. **Director**—Don Taylor. **(PG)** *103 minutes*

THE FINAL OPTION (1982)

Judy Davis
Richard Widmark

Gung ho drama about British commandos who rescue American embassy officials from leftist terrorists. A political message, decrying radical elements of the peace movement, underlies this rickety film, which is short on credibility. The acting isn't any better than the trumped-up material. Davis is a machine-gun-toting terrorist and Lewis Collins is the suave military officer who infiltrates her group. **Director**—Ian Sharp. **(R)** *125 minutes*

FINDERS KEEPERS (1984)

Michael O'Keefe
Beverly D'Angelo

This uneven, madcap farce about the pursuit of a stolen $5 million in cash begins sluggishly but builds a fair head of steam toward the end. Much action takes place aboard a transcontinental train headed for New York with an assortment of oddball characters staking claim to the loot. Some gags misfire, but more often they find their mark. O'Keefe plays an erstwhile roller skating team manager. D'Angelo is funny as the dizziest of blondes. Also with Lou Gossett, Jr., Ed Lauter, David Wayne, and Brian Dennehy. **Director**—Richard Lester. **(R)** *92 minutes*

A FINE MESS (1986)

Ted Danson
Howie Mandel

Ted Danson and Howie Mandel are pals who find themselves in A Fine Mess.

There are pratfalls, car chases and crashes, and much screeching in this desperate slapstick comedy by Blake Edwards. A few laughs come through despite the ill-conceived routines based on the physical comedy of such old-time comedians as Laurel and Hardy and the Three Stooges. The rickety plot follows the efforts of two Hollywood goof-offs (Danson and Mandel) to avoid a gang of equally bumbling crooks. Also with Richard Mulligan and Stuart Margolin. **(PG)** *100 minutes*

FINGERS (1978)

Harvey Keitel
Jim Brown
Michael V. Gazzo

Obsessive, fascinating oddity about a brooding young neurotic (Keitel) who struggles to reconcile the wildly divergent influences of his father, an amoral New York City mobster, and his
(Continued)

This movie available on videotape and/or disc.

(Continued)
mother, a mentally ill classical musician. Perennially underrated Keitel creates a compelling portrait of the would-be concert pianist who makes violent strong-arm collections for his father. Brown is terrific in his best role ever, as a quietly brutal lover of women. The savage, purgative climax will knock you into next week. Directorial debut of writer/director James Toback. Also with Tisa Farrow. **(R)** *91 minutes*

FINIAN'S RAINBOW (1968)

★★★

Fred Astaire
Petula Clark

Uneven and overdone film version of the Broadway musical, which combines social statements with Irish fantasy. The pacing and dialogue seem out of kilter, yet this colorful wide-screen production still offers plenty of entertainment with the memorable music and the great talent of Astaire, who plays a key role. Also with Tommy Steele, Keenan Wynn, Barbara Hancock, Al Freeman, Jr., and Don Francks. **Director**—Francis Ford Coppola. *145 minutes*

FIRE AND ICE (1983)

★★

The mysterious Darkwolf battles against the Ice Lord Nekron in Fire and Ice.

A sword-and-sorcery animated feature, directed by Ralph Bakshi in the same style as his *Lord of the Rings.* The film dwells too much on violent, sinister situations, and is populated with stock heroes, villains, and fearsome monsters. A ho-hum struggle between good and evil characters takes place among glaciers, steamy swamps, and belching volcanoes. Fantasy artist Frank Frazetta contributed his skills to the production. **(PG)** *81 minutes*

FIRE BIRDS (1990)

★★

Tommy Lee Jones
Nicolas Cage
Sean Young

High-tech attack helicopters are the centerpiece of this flag-waving adventure, which is more like an army recruiting film than a Hollywood feature. Cage stars as a gung-ho chopper pilot who wages war on South American drug smugglers—Hollywood's latest candidate for all-purpose archvillains of the American people. Jones, the only worthwhile part of the film, costars as a no-nonsense flight instructor who sees himself in Cage. Young plays the hero's romantic interest who also flies helicopters. The formulaic script and trite, ultrapatriotic dialogue are a half-baked rehash of *Top Gun* and *Iron Eagle*. **Director**—David Green. **(PG-13)** *85 minutes*

FIREFOX (1982)

★★

Clint Eastwood
Freddie Jones
David Huffman

James Bond apparently went on a working vacation, so Hollywood called in stone-faced Eastwood for this high-flying spy adventure involving the abduction of a secret Russian superplane. Eastwood is miscast as a Vietnam veteran ace pilot who sneaks into the Soviet Union on this "mission impossible." Several other problems mar this tedious production, including the poor special effects and the holes in the script. **Director**—Eastwood. **(PG)** *136 minutes*

FIREPOWER (1979)

★

Sophia Loren
James Coburn
O.J. Simpson

Producer/director Michael Winner put together this action/adventure with a heavy dose of explosions, fires, and shootings. All the hubbub seems to be about the tracking down of a Howard Hughes-type tycoon, who is hiding out in the Caribbean. The violent episodes drown out the plot, and the film lapses into confusion. Also with Eli Wallach, Anthony Franciosa, and George Grizzard. **(R)** *104 minutes*

FIRESTARTER (1984)

★★★

Drew Barrymore

Drew Barrymore has a terrifying talent in Firestarter.

The telekinesis storyline has been overused by Hollywood films of the 1980s. But this version, based on a Stephen King novel, is deliciously campy and moves briskly with the proper mixture of suspense and special effects. Barrymore (*E.T.*) is excellent as a charming 8-year-old who turns the bad guys into flaming shish kebab by thinking mean thoughts. David Keith, George C. Scott, Martin Sheen, Art Carney, and Louise Fletcher are delightful in supporting roles. **Director**—Mark Lester. **(R)** *116 minutes*

FIREWALKER (1986)

★

Lou Gossett, Jr.
Chuck Norris

A flimsy rip-off of such recent adventure films as *Indiana Jones and the Temple of Doom* and *Romancing the Stone.* Norris and Gossett star as mercenaries operating in a South American jungle. The film is billed as Norris' first comedy although audiences will be hard pressed to find anything amusing. The film bulges with clichés, cardboard villains, and ridiculous dialogue. The paper-thin plot involves the search for Aztec treasure. Also with Melody Anderson and Will Sampson. **Director**—J. Lee Thompson. **(PG)** *107 minutes*

FIRE WITH FIRE (1986)

★

Craig Sheffer
Virginia Madsen

® This movie available with closed captions for the hearing impaired.

What happens when a young convict at a detention camp falls in love with a student at a nearby Catholic girls' school? It's really not worth the time to find out in this soggy teenage *Romeo and Juliet* story. Many of the romantic encounters, as well as the couple's escape from authority, are contrived and predictable. And the performances of Sheffer and Madsen, as the young lovers, hardly live up to the picture's title. **Director**—Duncan Gibbons. **(PG-13)** *90 minutes*

FIRST BLOOD (1982)

★★½

Sylvester Stallone
Richard Crenna

Sylvester Stallone is a one-man war machine in First Blood.

Stallone stars as a brooding ex-Green Beret soldier provoked by small-town redneck police into fighting a grueling guerrilla war. Plenty of violent macho action propels the film along. But the one-man-against-the-world screenplay is hardly impressive or original. Stallone's physical presence dominates the proceedings, but he's given little opportunity to act. **Director**—Ted Kotcheff. **(R)** *97 minutes*

FIRST BORN (1984)

★★★

Teri Garr
Peter Weller
Christopher Collet

A compelling domestic drama that features a teenage boy as a heroic, responsible person. Collet is the young son who rescues his divorced mother (Garr) from a disastrous relationship with her scoundrel boyfriend (Weller). Adult shortcomings are viewed through the eyes of the perceptive youngster, who rises to the occasion with exceptional maturity and courage. Crisp direction and solid performances contribute to this first-class topical film. **Director**—Michael Apted. **(PG-13)** *104 minutes*

THE FIRST DEADLY SIN (1980)

★★½

Frank Sinatra
Faye Dunaway

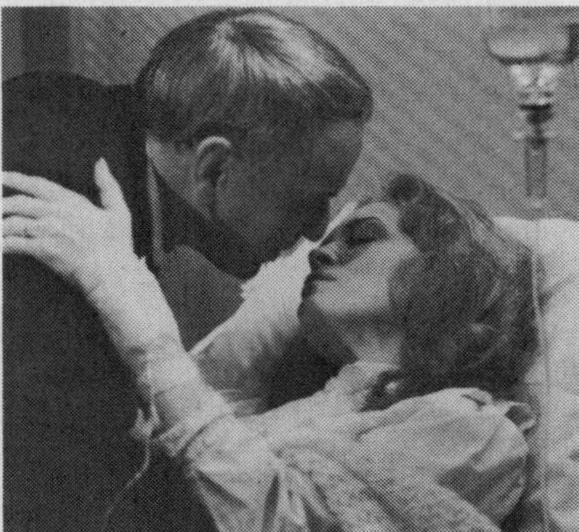

Frank Sinatra comforts his dying wife in The First Deadly Sin.

Sinatra, ending a long pause from theatrical films, plays a detective in this dull and disappointing outing. Sinatra departs somewhat from his tough Tony Rome character to portray a mellow cop who is close to retirement—a role appropriate to his age. Dunaway is wasted as Sinatra's dying wife, but David Dukes is chilling as the psychotic killer. **Director**—Brian Hutton. **(R)** *112 minutes*

FIRST MONDAY IN OCTOBER (1981)

★★

Walter Matthau
Jill Clayburgh

Matthau and Clayburgh star in this talky comedy, based on the stage play, about the first woman appointed to the United States Supreme Court. Although Clayburgh is the center of attention as a conservative appointee from California, it's Matthau who steals the film as a wisecracking liberal associate justice, on the order of the late William O. Douglas. The film received a great deal of publicity at the time of release because Sandra Day O'Connor had just been appointed to the Supreme Court. **Director**—Ronald Neame. **(R)** *98 minutes*

THE FIRST NUDIE MUSICAL (1976)

★★

Bruce Kimmel
Cindy Williams
Stephen Nathan

This naughty parody of porno movies and 1930s musicals is silly and amateurish, but does include some eager young talent and hilarious musical numbers that make up for some of the deficiencies. There's some nudity, but the overall effect is not offensive. Kimmel wrote the screenplay and music, codirected with Mark Haggard, and has a leading part. Also with Diana Canova and Leslie Ackerman. **(R)** *100 minutes*

THE FIRST POWER (1990)

★★

Lou Diamond Phillips
Tracy Griffith
Jeff Kober

The spirit of a serial killer who died in the gas chamber takes over the bodies of the living to murder again. Though embellished here with a few interesting special effects, this familiar theme has worn thin by now and the dialogue is merely typical horror-film mumbo-jumbo. Debuting director Robert Resnikoff fails to provide an appropriately eerie atmosphere, which would have done much to mask the script's all-too-familiar conventions. Phillips stars as the youthful Los Angeles detective on the case, who supposedly specializes in serial killers. Kober, an intense actor who is featured on television's *China Beach*, is riveting as the fiend who refuses to die. Fans of horror films may be more interested than the average viewer because of the recent wave of films with similar storylines *(Shocker; The Horror Show)*. **(R)** *98 minutes*

A FISH CALLED WANDA (1988)

★★★

John Cleese
Jamie Lee Curtis
Kevin Kline
Michael Palin

An offbeat English comedy written by Monty Python veteran John Cleese and directed by Charles Crichton, the man responsible for the famed Ealing Studio comedies of the 1950s. The complex

(Continued)

Jamie Lee Curtis practices her wiles on John Cleese in A Fish Called Wanda.

(Continued)
plot involves the frantic efforts of a jewel thief (Curtis) to seduce an uptight barrister, played by Cleese. Her romantic advances are meant to gain information about the location of some hidden gems. With its emphasis on eccentric criminals, the storyline follows the tradition of Crichton's earlier films. Quirky and with obtuse characters, the film represents the best attributes of English comedy. **(R) Academy Award**—Kline, best supporting actor. **Nominations**—Crichton, best director; Cleese and Crichton, best original screenplay. *107 minutes*

THE FISH THAT SAVED PITTSBURGH (1979)

Julius Erving
James Bond III
Stockard Channing
Jonathan Winters
Meadowlark Lemon

A basketball team is on the skids, and it can only be saved by astrology in this lowbrow, farfetched spoof. The team is then reorganized with a wacky bunch of players, all born under the astrological sign of Pisces (The Fish). Channing is the astrologer who draws their horoscopes and coaches them to a championship. Basketball greats Erving and Lemon turn in some fancy courtwork while Winters adds some humorous moments. **Director**—Gilbert Moses. **(PG)** *102 minutes*

F.I.S.T. (1978)

 ★★★

Sylvester Stallone
Rod Steiger
Peter Boyle

An ambitious, handsome melodrama, about a truckers' union, beginning in idealism and ending in corruption. Stallone is effective as a two-fisted Jimmy Hoffa-like character, but the charm of his Rocky character is missing. Director Norman Jewison's style evokes those early Warner Bros. social dramas. The entire cast is excellent. Also with Melinda Dillon, Tony Lo Bianco, and David Huffman. **(PG)** *145 minutes*

FITZCARRALDO (1982)

 ★★★

Klaus Kinski
Claudia Cardinale

From German director Werner Herzog comes this bold, imaginative film about adventurers and entrepreneurs operating in the Amazon basin at the turn of the century. Kinski is magnificent in the title role as an eccentric and incorrigible dreamer who hatches a wild scheme to open a rubber plantation in a remote part of the jungle. Some impact is diminished by the film's extraordinary length and patchy construction, but its outrageousness and exquisite detail make up for the flaws. Originally filmed in German. **(PG)** *157 minutes*

FIVE CARD STUD (1968)

Dean Martin
Robert Mitchum
Inger Stevens

So-so western with a hint of mystery in the storyline. Martin stars as a gambler in a poker game. One by one, the game's participants are killed. The predictable film also features Roddy McDowall, Katherine Justice, John Anderson, and Yaphet Kotto. They're all dealt bad hands by director Henry Hathaway. *103 minutes*

FIVE CORNERS (1988)

Jodie Foster
Tim Robbins
Todd Graff
John Turturro

Newcomer Robbins stands out in this urban tragicomedy, which follows the lives of several characters over a three-day period. Set in 1964, the film focuses on the members of a working-class community in the Bronx. The multilayered story is the work of John Patrick Shanley, who won an Oscar for his screenplay for *Moonstruck*. Foster plays a young woman who had been terrorized as a teenager by Turturro, a psychotic character who is released from jail as the film opens. She seeks protection from Robbins in case Turturro attempts revenge. The combination of some outrageously eccentric characters and the intense dramatic action makes for a darkly humorous tale. **Director**—Tony Bill. **(R)** *92 minutes*

FIVE DAYS ONE SUMMER (1982)

Sean Connery
Betsy Brantley

Sean Connery as the doctor who finds romance in Five Days One Summer.

Majestic Swiss Alpine scenery in this elegant Fred Zinnemann film upstages a plodding romantic story. The plot, set in 1932, stars Connery as a middle-aged Scottish doctor who romances his young niece (Brantley) while on a mountain-climbing holiday. Some suspense is generated on the icy slopes, but the bizarre love affair is uneventful, moody, and leaves the viewer rather cold. **(PG)** *108 minutes*

FIVE EASY PIECES (1970)

Jack Nicholson
Karen Black
Susan Anspach

Nicholson is at his best in this inspired film that vividly observes middle-class values. He plays a gifted musician from a wealthy, neurotic family, who drops out to work in oil fields and drift about the country. The story seems influenced by *Easy Rider,* but it has memorable moments that are most original. There are winning supporting parts all around, with Black, Anspach, and Helena Kallianiotes outstanding. Also with Lois Smith, Billy Green Bush, and Fannie Flagg. Bob Rafelson's direction packs a wallop. **(R) Academy Award Nominations**—best picture; Nicholson, best actor; Black, best supporting actress; Rafelson and Adrien Joyce, best story and screenplay based on factual material or material not previously published.

98 minutes

FIVE FINGERS (1952)

★★★★

James Mason
Danielle Darrieux
Michael Rennie

Mason stands out in this gripping espionage thriller set in Turkey during World War II. He plays a British diplomat's butler who peddles military information to the Germans. The compelling story is brought off in convincing semidocumentary style, and it's loaded with suspense. Based on the book *Operation Cicero,* a true story. Excellent acting from the supporting cast, which includes Walter Hampden, Michael Pate, and Richard Loo. **Director**—Joseph L. Mankiewicz. **Academy Award Nominations**—Mankiewicz, best director; Michael Wilson, screenplay.

108 minutes b&w

FIVE GRAVES TO CAIRO (1943)

★★★

Erich von Stroheim
Anne Baxter
Akim Tamiroff
Franchot Tone

In this spy melodrama set in a Sahara Desert hotel during World War II, British spies try to destroy Rommel's supply dumps. The cast is generally excellent, with von Stroheim doing a caricatural interpretation of the role of Rommel. Baxter and Tamiroff play the hotel-keepers, and Tone stars as the hero. The script by Charles Brackett and director Billy Wilder is intelligent and suspenseful. Beautifully photographed by John Seitz, who received an Academy Award nomination for his work. *96 minutes b&w*

FIVE WEEKS IN A BALLOON (1962)

★★

Cedric Hardwicke
Peter Lorre
Red Buttons
Barbara Eden

A pedestrian and strained comedy adventure, based on the Jules Verne story about a balloon expedition to claim territory in Africa in 1862. The comedy situations fall flat, and the script is rife with clichés. However, the film is occasionally kept aloft by the cast. Also with Fabian, Richard Haydn, and Billy Gilbert. **Director**—Irwin Allen.

101 minutes

THE FIXER (1968)

Alan Bates
Dirk Bogarde

This adaptation of Bernard Malamud's prizewinning novel is too ponderous. However, it does offer some fine acting. Bates performs extraordinarily well as a poor Jewish handyman in czarist Russia, who is imprisoned on trumped-up charges and humiliated relentlessly. Bogarde plays a sympathetic defense attorney. Also with Georgia Brown, Elizabeth Hartman, David Warner, Carol White, and Hugh Griffith. **Director**—John Frankenheimer. **Academy Award Nomination**—Bates, best actor.

132 minutes

THE FLAME AND THE ARROW (1950)

★★★

Burt Lancaster
Virginia Mayo

Burt Lancaster trains some youthful archers in The Flame and the Arrow.

A colorful costume drama set in medieval Italy. Lancaster, who is energetic in his role as a lusty rebel leading a campaign against evil forces, performs some of his best gymnastics. Mayo is his leading lady. Robert Douglas, Aline MacMahon, and Nick Cravat are also in the cast. **Director**—Jacques Tourneur.

88 minutes

FLAME OF THE BARBARY COAST (1945)

Ann Dvorak
John Wayne

An adequate western/comedy set in San Francisco at the time of the 1906 earthquake. Wayne plays a gambling hall owner who falls in love with a saloon singer, played by Dvorak. This film may be interesting for Wayne fans, but the low-key action doesn't exactly set the screen on fire. Also with Joseph Schildkraut. **Director**—Joseph Kane.

91 minutes b&w

THE FLAMINGO KID (1984)

Matt Dillon
Richard Crenna

Matt Dillon opts for the easy road to success in The Flamingo Kid.

Amusing coming-of-age comedy about a 1960s Brooklyn teenager (Dillon) who is seduced by the easy living at a posh beach club. Working there as a cabana boy, he falls under the influence of a smooth-talking car dealer (Crenna) who convinces him he would be better off selling Porsches than going to college. Ace TV director Garry Marshall

(Continued)

This movie available on videotape and/or disc.

(Continued)
scores well with comic charm and fine performances by the entire cast. Also with Hector Elizondo and Fisher Stevens. **(PG–13)** *100 minutes*

FLAMINGO ROAD (1949)

Joan Crawford
Zachary Scott
Sydney Greenstreet

The storyline is farfetched in this film version of Robert Wilder's novel about a carnival dancer involved with politicians in a small town. However, Crawford, as the tough entertainer, does well in this role, which suits her image. Greenstreet plays a crooked politician. Also with David Brian, Gertrude Michael, and Gladys George. **Director**—Michael Curtiz.
94 minutes b&w

FLASHBACK (1990)

 ★1/2 

Dennis Hopper
Kiefer Sutherland
Carol Kane

A mild comic send-up of the radical 1960s, which contrasts the liberal lifestyle and values of that era with the straight-laced conservatism of the 1980s. Hopper virtually parodies his own 1960s persona in his role as an ageless, Abbie Hoffman–like political radical who is being brought to justice by a young, uptight FBI agent, played by Sutherland. Eventually, and predictably, the odd couple learn they have much in common. Unfortunately, the comedy isn't biting enough to be effective satire and lampooning or waxing nostalgic for an era that was so turbulent seems inappropriate. Perhaps the producers should not have selected Franco Amurri, an Italian director making his American film debut, to helm this feature. Also with Paul Dooley, Cliff DeYoung, Richard Masur, and Michael McKean. **(R)** *108 minutes*

FLASHDANCE (1983)

Jennifer Beals
Belinda Bauer
Michael Nouri

Beautiful Beals plays a welder by day and a trendy dancer by night (the actual dancing is done by Marine Jahan). The music and dancing, in a sort of high-tech rock 'n' roll setting, are what really count here, but the film falls flat when it comes to script and characterization. Director Adrian Lyne (*Foxes*) aspired to make a youth movie akin to *Saturday Night Fever*, but *Flashdance* is merely a flash in the pan. **(R) Academy Award Nomination**—Don Petermen, cinematography. *96 minutes*

Blue-collar dreams with Michael Nouri and Jennifer Beals in Flashdance.

FLASH GORDON (1980)

 ★★

Sam Jones
Max Von Sydow
Melody Anderson

An overblown, over-budgeted extravaganza, based on those heroic space-opera serials of the 1930s. For all the glitter and lavish special effects, this puffed-up version isn't as much fun as the B-movie matinee cliffhangers. Platinum blond pretty-boy Jones is in the title role, but he has no screen presence. Only Von Sydow, as the menacing Emperor Ming, carries off his role with aplomb. Also with Topol and Ornella Muti. **Director**—Mike Hodges. **(PG)**
110 minutes

A FLASH OF GREEN (1984)

★★★

Ed Harris
Blair Brown
Richard Jordan

Excellent performances by the entire cast and skillful direction mark this drama, based on the novel by John D. MacDonald, about conflicts between greedy land developers and conservationists in a small Florida community. Harris stars as a local newspaper reporter, with a foot in both camps, who eventually strives to preserve the natural environment. The sultry atmosphere of the southern town is expertly delineated. Also with John Glover, George Coe, and Helen Stenborg. **Director**—Victor Nuñez. **(No MPAA rating)** *131 minutes*

FLASHPOINT (1984)

 ★★★

Kris Kristofferson
Treat Williams

Kristofferson and Williams play border-patrol officers who stumble on $800,000 in cash that was buried in the Texas desert some 20 years ago. Their startling discovery leads to mystery, conspiracy, and murder. The ending, though somewhat contrived, packs a wallop nevertheless. Kristofferson and Williams are believable as civil servants up against events beyond their comprehension. Kurtwood Smith and Rip Torn are good in supporting roles. **Director**—William Tannen. **(R)** *93 minutes*

FLESHBURN (1984)

 ★★

Steve Kanaly
Karen Carlson
Macon McCalman

Four psychiatrists are kidnapped and stranded in the Arizona desert by a revengeful Vietnam veteran. This desperate situation is supposed to generate tension, but it's as gripping as trying to cope with mild sunburn. The three men and one woman encounter unbearable heat, a lack of food and water, personal injuries, dangerous animals, and a script that is as dry as the desert terrain. **Director**—George Gage. **(R)**
90 minutes

FLETCH (1985)

★★1/2

Chevy Chase

Patchy comedy/mystery with Chase as a hotshot investigative reporter on the trail of drug dealers. The film, based on Gregory MacDonald's novel, is primarily a showcase for Chase, who tosses off throwaway wisecracks and dons silly disguises with abandon. Some breezy action occasionally heightens interest, but too much witless dialogue eventually takes the wind out of Chevy's comic sails. Dana Wheeler-Nicholson and Tim Matheson are in supporting roles. **Director**—Michael Ritchie. **(PG)**
98 minutes

® This movie available with closed captions for the hearing impaired.

FLETCH LIVES (1989)

★★

Chevy Chase
Hal Holbrook
Julianne Phillips

Chase returns as the wisecracking investigative reporter from Los Angeles. Clichés abound in this flimsy sequel set in Louisiana. He encounters Ku Klux Klan members, sleazy televangelists, a southern belle, and other stereotypes. Chase doesn't put much vigor into this vehicle, which finally dies of exhaustion. Also with Cleavon Little, Randall "Tex" Cobb, R. Lee Ermey, and Richard Belzer. **Director**—Michael Ritchie. **(PG)** *95 minutes*

THE FLIGHT OF THE EAGLE (1982)

★★★

Max Von Sydow

Long yet intensely fascinating semidocumentary of a doomed three-man Swedish expedition bound for the North Pole. Director/cinematographer Jan Troell has captured magnificent vistas of the frozen wasteland, and some startling photos found in the cameras of the dead explorers also appear on screen. Von Sydow is capable as the brooding leader of the adventure. Goran Stangertz and Sverre Anker Ousdal play his comrades. Versions on tape are cut by 30 minutes. Originally filmed in Swedish. **(No MPAA rating)** *141 minutes*

FLIGHT OF THE NAVIGATOR (1986)

★★★

Joey Cramer

A commendable family film about a boy who falls into a ravine and awakens eight years later to find he hasn't aged a day. He attempts to find his way back to his own time and place with the help of an extraterrestrial robot. This *E.T.* in reverse results in a colorful adventure despite its lack of originality. Sparkling special effects and lively performances add to the film's appeal—especially for youngsters. Veronica Cartwright and Cliff De Young costar as the boy's parents. Pee-Wee Herman (Paul Reubens, credited as Paul Mall) provides the voice of the robot. **Director**—Randal Kleiser. **(PG)** *89 minutes*

THE FLIGHT OF THE PHOENIX (1965)

★★★

James Stewart
Richard Attenborough
Hardy Kruger
Peter Finch

James Stewart seeks a way to survive in The Flight of the Phoenix.

A plane carrying an oil-drilling crew crash-lands in the Arabian desert, and the survivors use their wits and primitive skills to rebuild the plane and fly to safety. Tension mounts dramatically, and there are fine character studies of the desperate men. Stewart is right at home as the pilot, and there are other sterling performances by the cast, which also includes Dan Duryea, Ernest Borgnine, Ian Bannen, and George Kennedy. Director Robert Aldrich puts it all together in grand style. **Academy Award Nomination**—Bannen, best supporting actor. *149 minutes*

THE FLIM FLAM MAN (1967)

★★½

George C. Scott
Michael Sarrazin
Sue Lyon

This lightweight comedy is bolstered by the lively performance of Scott, who plays a rascally con man working small towns. Scott gives it his best shot, but the storyline falters after a while. Sarrazin also does well as a young military deserter who joins Scott and learns that too much honesty gets in the way. Also with Harry Morgan, Jack Albertson, Alice Ghostley, and Albert Salmi. **Director**—Irvin Kershner. *104 minutes*

FLIPPER (1963)

★★

Chuck Connors
Luke Halpin

Routine animal adventure about a boy in Florida who rescues a wounded dolphin; they soon become great friends. Halpin is fine as the plucky lad. Nice fluff for the kids, but adults will probably find it tiresome. This film led to two sequels and a TV series. Also with Kathleen Maguire and Connie Scott. **Director**—James B. Clark. *90 minutes*

FLOWER DRUM SONG (1961)

★★½

Nancy Kwan
James Shigeta

A mildly entertaining screen version of the Rodgers and Hammerstein Broadway musical about life and love in San Francisco's Chinatown. The staging is colorful, the choreography is adequate, and the songs are good, but nothing is memorable. The film's major flaw is its length. Also with Juanita Hall, Benson Fong, Miyoshi Umeki, James Soo, and Sen Yung. **Director**—Henry Koster. *133 minutes*

FLOWERS IN THE ATTIC (1987)

★

Louise Fletcher
Victoria Tennant

Louise Fletcher is the sadistic grandmother in Flowers in the Attic.

A dreary horror film, based on V.C. Andrews' best-selling novel, about four

(Continued)

(Continued)
children who are kept in an attic so as not offend their dying grandfather. Fletcher makes the most of her role as the sadistic grandmother, while Tennant seems ill at ease as the misguided mother of the confused youngsters. Some key scenes from Andrews' book were not included here, making for a bland film adaptation. Also with Kristy Swanson, Jeb Stuart Adams, Ben Ganger, and Lindsay Parker. **Director**—Jeffrey Bloom. **(PG–13)** *95 minutes*

THE FLY (1958)

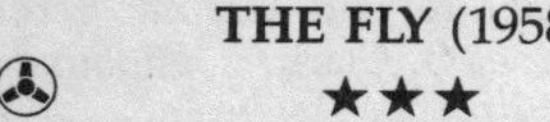

★★★

Al (David) Hedison
Vincent Price
Patricia Owens
Herbert Marshall

A brilliant young scientist (Hedison) steps into his matter-transmission device, unaware that a housefly has buzzed into the chamber with him. When he emerges, the scientist has the man-sized head and claw of the fly, while the fly . . . well, suffice it to say that the household begins a frantic search for the "strange fly with the funny white head." Although not up to the hysterical energy level of David Cronenberg's 1986 remake, the film is great fun, thanks to vivid color cinematography by ace Karl Struss and a solid cast that plays it straight. Based on George Langelaan's celebrated short story, the screenplay was written by James *(Shogun)* Clavell. No one who has witnessed the picture's final sequence will ever forget it. Help mee! **Director**—Kurt Neumann. *94 minutes*

THE FLY (1986)

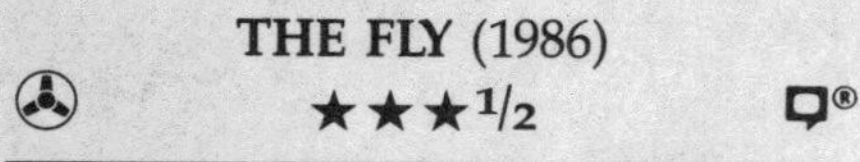

★★★½

Jeff Goldblum
Geena Davis

Jeff Goldblum's scientific experiments backfire in The Fly.

Goldblum is excellent as the scientist who discovers how to merge human genes with those of an insect in this remake of the 1958 chiller. When he tries the technique, his atoms accidentally scramble with those of a housefly. The result is grisly indeed. Some viewers may be disturbed by director David Cronenberg's shocking visual details, but the clever plot twists build momentum and the dialogue is ripe with humor. An effective blend of horror and pathos. Also with John Getz. **(R) Academy Award**—Chris Walas and Stephen Dupuis, best makeup. *95 minutes*

THE FLY II (1989)

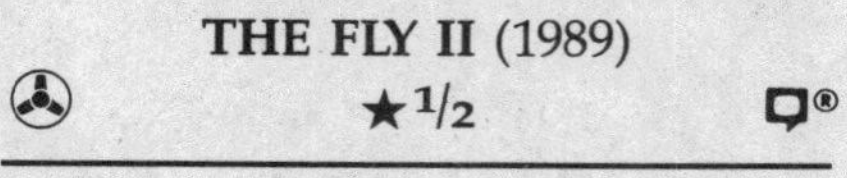

★½

Eric Stoltz
Daphne Zuniga

Will Daphne Zuniga continue to date Eric Stoltz as he changes into The Fly II?

This sequel to 1986's *The Fly* has the scientist's offspring (Stoltz) carrying the same mutation, which eventually turns him into a huge housefly bent on destruction and revenge. Unfortunately, this continuation unfolds without the wit and fascination of its predecessor. Director Chris Walas merely marks time until the climactic transformation, which relies on standard slime and ooze special effects. Bring your fly swatter for this one. **(R)** *104 minutes*

FLYING DOWN TO RIO (1933)

★★★

Fred Astaire
Ginger Rogers
Gene Raymond

Rogers and Astaire get together for the first time in this musical about a beautiful woman who has to select between two men down in Rio. Without the dancing of the dazzling duo, this corny movie would crash into the ocean. The musical number in which women dance on the wings of moving airplanes is the film's most memorable sequence. Also with Dolores Del Rio and Franklin Pangborn. **Director**—Thornton Freeland. *89 minutes b&w*

FLYING LEATHERNECKS (1951)

★★

John Wayne
Robert Ryan

Wayne takes to the skies as a martinet Marine officer in World War II. There are some striking battle scenes against Japanese forces, but a poor script keeps most of the drama grounded. A standard macho performance by the Duke, with support from Ryan, Janis Carter, Don Taylor, and Jay C. Flippen. **Director**—Nicholas Ray. *102 minutes*

FLYING TIGERS (1942)

★★★

John Wayne
John Carroll

Wayne and company join the famous Flying Tiger squadron in China to fight the Japanese. Lots of good aerial combat scenes, with some time off for Wayne to romance an attractive nurse. The standard World War II clichés and heroics abound in this wartime movie, but it's exciting nonetheless. Also with Anna Lee, Paul Kelly, and Mae Clarke. **Director**—David Miller.
102 minutes b&w

FM (1978)

★★

Michael Brandon
Eileen Brennan
Alex Karras
Martin Mull

A silly youth film, about the tribulations of a popular rock radio station. The DJs and their loyal fans go on a rampage against the men in the business office who try to wring extra profits from the good vibes. The hollow plot doesn't hold up too well, but the rock music—including some impressive numbers by Linda Ronstadt—brightens things up. Also with Cassie Yates and Norman Lloyd. **Director**—John A. Alonzo. **(PG)** *105 minutes*

® This movie available with closed captions for the hearing impaired.

THE FOG (1980)

★★½

Adrienne Barbeau
Hal Holbrook
Janet Leigh
Jamie Lee Curtis

Director John Carpenter *(Halloween)* strikes again with this traditional yet effective chiller. Carpenter is no Hitchcock, but he can certainly spin a scary tale. Leigh, Curtis, and Holbrook are residents of a seaside town in California, where a supernatural fog carries ashore ghosts from a century-old shipwreck to wreak revenge. Also with John Houseman. **(R)** *91 minutes*

FOLLOW THAT BIRD (1985)

★★★

First-class, likable kiddie comedy with Big Bird of TV fame making his feature film debut. The somewhat klutzy, 8-foot fowl is lured from the comfort of his Sesame Street home. His Muppet friends charge to the rescue. There's loads of lively humor and ample togetherness philosophy to put smiles on the faces of youngsters as well as their parents. John Candy, Chevy Chase, and Joe Flaherty join in the jolly adventure. **Director**—Ken Kwapis. **(G)**
88 minutes

FOLLOW THE FLEET (1936)

★★★

Fred Astaire
Ginger Rogers

Splendid Irving Berlin songs bring out the best in Astaire and Rogers. Astaire and Randolph Scott portray sailors who romance sisters Rogers and Harriet Hilliard (later Harriet Nelson) in this delightful musical. The songs include "Let's Face the Music and Dance," "Let Yourself Go," and "We Saw the Sea." Lucille Ball and Betty Grable appear in small roles. **Director**—Mark Sandrich.
110 minutes b&w

FOOL FOR LOVE (1986)

★★½

Sam Shepard
Kim Basinger

Shepard stars in the film version of his own play about a bizarre, intense love affair between a latter-day cowboy and a sex kitten. Director Robert Altman attempts to expand the stage drama for the screen, yet the production contains too much talk and symbolism. Shepard shines as the ornery rodeo star who tangles with the tempting Basinger. Typically offbeat Altman fare. **(R)**
106 minutes

FOOLIN' AROUND (1980)

★★

Gary Busey
Annette O'Toole

Down-to-earth farm boy, played by Busey, courts and wins a well-heeled coed, played by O'Toole, after showing up the girl's snooty fiancé. The entire cast, which includes Cloris Leachman, Eddie Albert, and Tony Randall, performs with enthusiasm. But this predictable romantic plot has been exhaustively run through the Hollywood mill. Videotape versions of the film are ten minutes shorter. **Director**—Richard T. Heffron. **(PG)**
111 minutes

FOOTLIGHT PARADE (1933)

★★★

James Cagney
Joan Blondell
Ruby Keeler
Dick Powell

One of the best Warner Bros./Busby Berkeley musicals, with an all-star cast. Cagney plays the producer of lavish Broadway shows trying to stage a bigger and better one in the face of impossible odds and insurmountable problems. Naturally, the show goes on. Three of the best Berkeley numbers provide a truly spectacular finish: "Honeymoon Hotel," "By a Waterfall," and "Shanghai Lil." **Director**—Lloyd Bacon. *104 minutes b&w*

FOOTLOOSE (1984)

★★★

Kevin Bacon
John Lithgow

A toe-tapping, finger-snapping youth musical inspired by the success of *Flashdance*. Bacon stars as the new boy in town who has trouble adjusting to the stuffy community's law against dancing. Surprisingly, the film is sympathetic to adults, especially a troubled fire-and-brimstone minister, played by Lithgow, whose daughter Bacon romances. The film boasts infectious music, exuberant dancing, and likable performances. Also with Lori Singer, Christopher Penn, and Dianne Wiest. **Director**—Herbert Ross. **(PG)**
107 minutes

FORBIDDEN PLANET (1956)

★★★★

Walter Pidgeon
Anne Francis
Leslie Nielsen

Walter Pidgeon (center) explains the awesome secrets of Altair-IV, the Forbidden Planet.

An excellent sci-fi adventure, stylishly executed with imagination and just the right touch of humor. The plot is loosely based on Shakespeare's *The Tempest*. A team of scientists visits a remote planet to make contact with previous explorers and finds a sinister one-man empire in control. Pidgeon is the reclusive survivor of the pioneering explorers; Francis plays his daughter. Pidgeon's mechanical aide, Robby the Robot, is as personable as any human in the cast. Excellent performances by Pidgeon, Francis, and Nielsen in the key roles. The cast also includes Warren Stevens, Jack Kelly, Richard Anderson, and Earl Holliman. The viewer should be aware of 95-minute prints, which exclude footage that reveals the film's monster. **Director**—Fred McLeod Wilcox. **(G)** *98 minutes*

FORCED VENGEANCE (1982)

★★

Chuck Norris

Karate ace Norris, who talks softly and wields a big kick, takes on some Hong Kong mobsters who are trying to muscle in on a small gambling casino. The stale and creaky plot is occasionally re-

(Continued)

(Continued)
lieved by the martial-arts action. Norris routinely puts away scores of bad guys who seemingly leap through the windows and pop out of the woodwork. The majestic Hong Kong cityscape contributes a modest amount of atmosphere. **Director**—James Fargo. **(R)**
103 minutes

FORCE OF EVIL (1948)

★★★

John Garfield
Thomas Gomez

A striking crime drama about the numbers racket, vividly filmed against the background of New York City. Garfield is excellent, portraying an involved man desperately trying to break away from crime. Expertly directed, with a moody atmosphere and smart dialogue. Beatrice Pearson, Roy Roberts, and Marie Windsor also star. **Director**—Abraham Polonsky. *78 minutes b&w*

FORCE 10 FROM NAVARONE (1978)

Robert Shaw
Harrison Ford

Familiar war adventure billed as a continuation of—not a sequel to—*The Guns of Navarone.* Lots of action for fans, including narrow escapes, the spectacular destruction of a dam and a bridge, and other impressive special effects. The heroes are a mixed bag of Allied commandos assigned to harass the Nazis in Yugoslavia. Shaw is good as an American major. Some appealing humor is offset by stretched credibility. Also with Edward Fox, Franco Nero, Barbara Bach, and Richard Kiel. **Director**—Guy Hamilton. **(PG)** *118 minutes*

FOREIGN BODY (1986)

★★★

Trevor Howard
Victor Banerjee
Warren Mitchell

A flavorful British comedy about a poor Calcutta refugee who sets up a phony medical practice in London catering to the wealthy. Banerjee plays the fake doctor with aplomb, maneuvering through various misadventures. Mitchell, a notable star of English television, portrays the immigrant's scheming relative. Geraldine McEwan appears in a supporting role. **Director**—Ronald Neame. **(PG-13)**
108 minutes

FOREIGN CORRESPONDENT (1940)

Joel McCrea
Laraine Day
Herbert Marshall

Joel McCrea hunts for spies in Hitchcock's Foreign Correspondent.

Alfred Hitchcock is at his best with this gripping tale of an American reporter in Europe who's hot on the trail of spies. The master builds suspense to a glorious crescendo and spices the film with an effective atmosphere. Some of the memorable scenes include a murder attempt in Westminster Cathedral and a plane crash. McCrea is excellent in the title role, and there's fine supporting work from Day, Marshall, Albert Basserman, Edmund Gwenn, George Sanders, Robert Benchley, and Harry Davenport. **Academy Award Nominations**—best picture; Basserman, best supporting actor; Charles Bennett and Joan Harrison, original screenplay; Rudolph Maté, cinematography.
120 minutes b&w

FOREVER AMBER (1947)

Linda Darnell
Cornel Wilde
George Sanders

Kathleen Windsor's steamy novel about an ambitious woman in 17th-century England gets a mediocre treatment on the screen. The production is handsome, but the script plods along, occasionally perking up with some lively scenes. The players seem unenthusiastic most of the time. Also with Richard Greene, Richard Haydn, Jessica Tandy, Robert Coote, and Leo G. Carroll. **Director**—Otto Preminger. *138 minutes*

FOREVER, LULU (1987)

Hanna Schygulla
Deborah Harry
Alec Baldwin

Despite an interesting cast, this silly action comedy is merely a pale imitation of *Desperately Seeking Susan*. Schygulla, one of Germany's top actresses, struggles dismally with the foolish material. She plays a New York writer whose misadventures begin when she stumbles onto some misplaced drugs and cash. Throughout the course of this complicated and absurd film, she seeks the elusive title character, played by rock singer Harry, who utters only two lines of dialogue. Also with Annie Golden, Dr. Ruth Westheimer, and Paul Gleason. **Director**—Amos Kollek. **(R)**
85 minutes

FOR KEEPS (1988)

★★

Molly Ringwald
Randall Batinkoff

A memorable prom night for Molly Ringwald and Randall Batinkoff in For Keeps.

This melodramatic teen movie misses an opportunity to send a serious message about teenage pregnancy and motherhood. Ringwald stars as a popular and bright high-school student who unexpectedly becomes pregnant. She and her unbelievably true-blue boyfriend opt to keep the child and get married, despite their plans for ambitious careers. John Avildsen's direction is too heavy-handed and any light touches in the film are deadened by his sledgehammer approach. Though Ringwald is a natural charmer, Batinkoff is merely bland beefcake. Also with Kenneth Mars, Conchata Farrell, and Mariam Flynn. **(PG–13)** *98 minutes*

FOR LOVE OF IVY (1968)

Sidney Poitier
Abbey Lincoln

An ill-conceived, although well-intentioned, romance concerning a black maid and her bid to better her condition. When Ivy, played by Lincoln, decides to quit her job to go to secretarial school, the family pressures a congenial black man, played by Poitier, to be her boyfriend in the hopes that she will remain their maid. Also with Beau Bridges, Carroll O'Connor, Nan Martin, and Laurie Peters. **Director**—Daniel Mann. **(PG)** *100 minutes*

FOR ME AND MY GAL (1942)

Judy Garland
Gene Kelly
George Murphy

This is a marvelously entertaining, old-fashioned musical with a star-studded cast. The routine plot, set prior to World War I, features two vaudeville hoofers trying to make the big time while grappling with romantic problems. Look for great songs and dancing from Garland, Murphy, and Kelly (in his first film). Horace (Stephen) McNally, Keenan Wynn, and Ben Blue also grace the cast. **Director**—Busby Berkeley. *104 minutes b&w*

THE FORMULA (1980)

George C. Scott
Marlon Brando
Marthe Keller

Scott plays a police detective who pursues an intricate trail of clues and murders that leads to the inner sanctum of the big oil companies, and a secret formula for producing synthetic fuel. Scott's investigation also leads to a tense confrontation with an oil tycoon, played by Brando, who magnificently steals the few scenes in which he appears. But alas, Steve Shagan's cumbersome screenplay, adapted from his best-selling novel, is as complicated as the piping at an oil refinery. James Crabe's cinematography was nominated for an Academy Award. Also with Beatrice Straight, John Gielgud, and G.D. Spradlin. **Director**—John G. Avildsen. **(R)** *117 minutes*

FOR QUEEN AND COUNTRY (1989)

Denzel Washington

Director Martin Stellman makes a broad political statement about social conditions in England under the Thatcher government. Washington performs magnificently in this grim drama as an army veteran who struggles to adapt to civilian life. He confronts blatant racism, crime, and injustice, and his homecoming turns out to be as unpleasant as his combat experiences. A compelling portrait of survival in a hostile atmosphere. Also with Dorian Healey, Amanda Redman, and Sea Chapman. **(R)** *106 minutes*

FORT APACHE (1948)

 ★★★

Henry Fonda
John Wayne
Shirley Temple

John Wayne and Henry Fonda powwow en route to Fort Apache.

A handsome and thoughtful epic western, which pays more attention to character than to action. Fonda excels as a gung ho Army colonel whose stubbornness irritates his troops and prompts trouble with the Indians. Wayne plays a practical-minded officer under Fonda's command. Based on a short story entitled "Massacre," by James Warner Bellah, the film is the first in director John Ford's so-called cavalry trilogy. The cast also includes Ward Bond, Pedro Armendariz, John Agar, Anna Lee, and Victor McLaglen. *127 minutes b&w*

FORT APACHE, THE BRONX (1981)

Paul Newman
Edward Asner

A powerful, realistically depicted drama involving an embattled police station house in one of New York's most poverty-stricken and crime-ridden boroughs. The film is more than a routine cops-and-bad-guys story; it offers a moving and impressive view of the urban decay and the people intimately affected. Newman gives a first-rate performance as a veteran cop who struggles with his thankless assignments and his conscience. Also with Kathleen Beller, Pam Grier, Ken Wahl, and Rachel Ticotin. **Director**—Daniel Petrie. **(R)** *125 minutes*

THE FORTUNE (1975)

Jack Nicholson
Warren Beatty
Stockard Channing

A funny tale about two con men who covet the fortune of a dim-witted New York heiress. Mike Nichols directs an excellent cast, which includes a slick, pencil-mustached Beatty, seedy sidekick Nicholson, and filthy-rich heiress Channing. The film is set in the 1920s in southern California. Channing scores as a refreshing and accomplished comic actress. Also with Florence Stanley, Richard B. Shull, and John Fiedler. **(PG)** *88 minutes*

THE FORTUNE COOKIE (1966)

★★★1/2

Walter Matthau
Jack Lemmon

This insightful Billy Wilder comedy effectively satirizes middle-class values and the pursuit of success. Lemmon is perfectly cast as a TV cameraman who's slightly injured during a football game. But it's Matthau who really ties the film

(Continued)

(Continued)
together. He delivers a superb, memorable performance as "Whiplash Willie," the shyster-lawyer brother-in-law who schemes to collect outrageous personal-injury claims from the insurance company. Ron Rich costars as the guilt-stricken football player who knocked Lemmon down during the game. Cliff Osmond, Judi West, and Lurene Tuttle perform in supporting roles. **Academy Award**—Matthau, best supporting actor. **Nomination**—Wilder and I.A.L. Diamond, best story and screenplay written directly for the screen. *125 minutes b&w*

48 HRS. (1982)

★★★

Nick Nolte
Eddie Murphy

Eddie Murphy and Nick Nolte are hilarious as unlikely partners in 48 Hrs.

Murphy steals scene after scene as a wisecracking convict on a two-day furlough to help nab a pair of San Francisco cop-killers. He teams up with a sullen detective (Nolte) for some slam-bang violent action, which is laced with riotously comic episodes. Murphy's film debut is impressive, indeed. He's cool and funny. The film falters only when it dwells on destructive car chases and brutal gun fights. **Director**—Walter Hill. **(R)** *96 minutes*

42nd STREET (1933)

★★★

Ginger Rogers
Ruby Keeler

This zesty production is one of the few musicals that provides good music and dance numbers *and* a believable plot. Although some parts of the movie have aged, the Busby Berkeley musical numbers are still memorable, and the splendid cast, including Rogers, Keeler, Warner Baxter, Bebe Daniels, and Ned Sparks, creates the authentic backstage atmosphere that makes the show so entertaining. Top songs include "Young and Healthy," "You're Getting to Be a Habit with Me," "Shuffle Off to Buffalo," and the title tune. Also with Dick Powell and Una Merkel. **Director**—Lloyd Bacon. **Academy Award Nomination**—best picture. *90 minutes b&w*

FOR WHOM THE BELL TOLLS (1943)

★★★★

Gary Cooper
Ingrid Bergman

Ingrid Bergman and Gary Cooper in For Whom the Bell Tolls.

Ernest Hemingway's classic adventure of the Spanish Civil War is presented with high drama and mounting suspense. Cooper is at his best as an American mercenary who helps a band of peasants blow up a bridge. Bergman is the object of Cooper's affections. Effectively directed, with first-rate supporting performances by Katina Paxinou, Akim Tamiroff, Arturo de Cordova, and Joseph Calleia. Some versions of the film run 130 minutes. **Director**—Sam Wood. **Academy Award**—Paxinou, best supporting actress. **Nominations**—best picture; Cooper, best actor; Bergman, best actress; Tamiroff, best supporting actor. *170 minutes*

FOR YOUR EYES ONLY (1981)

★★★

Roger Moore

Once again, British secret agent James Bond, played by Moore, saves the world—this time outrunning and outfoxing his enemies on ski slopes, under water, and on the face of a vertical cliff. This 12th adventure in the popular series isn't the most exuberant; the film returns to a simplified plot with less gadgetry and space-age gimmicks. But there are still plenty of hair-raising thrills with the usual chase sequences. Moore exhibits a hard edge to the Bond character in this film, which adds dimension to the role. **Director**—John Glen. **(PG)** *127 minutes*

FOUL PLAY (1978)

★★

Goldie Hawn
Chevy Chase

Detective Chevy Chase is at a temporary disadvantage in Foul Play.

Saucer-eyed Hawn is the best thing going for this mystery/comedy set in San Francisco. Her warm and mature performance as an innocent librarian caught up in a scheme to assassinate the Pope overshadows the entire movie. Chase plays a detective. The plot steals from a half-dozen Hitchcock films and ends with an all-too-familiar car chase. Also with Burgess Meredith, Dudley Moore, and Rachel Roberts. **Director**—Colin Higgins. **(PG)** *116 minutes*

THE FOUNTAINHEAD (1949)

★★★

Gary Cooper
Patricia Neal
Raymond Massey

Ayn Rand's ponderous but fascinating novel of aggressive individualism reaches the screen as a quirky mix of passionate melodrama and deco-modern set design. Cooper is appealing (if miscast) as a brilliant architect who would rather destroy his own work than see it corrupted by inferior talents. Neal is the strong-willed beauty who champions his cause. This is movie-

® This movie available with closed captions for the hearing impaired.

making done in big, bold strokes—a film in which mere glances speak volumes and small emotions do not exist. The preachiness of Rand's screenplay nearly becomes self-spoofing, but the film's kitschy energy is irresistible. Directed with ferocious style by King Vidor. *114 minutes b&w*

FOUR FRIENDS (1981)

★★1/2

Craig Wasson
Jodi Thelen
Michael Huddleston
Jim Metzler

Screenwriter Steven Tesich, who gave us the exhilarating *Breaking Away,* misses the mark with this grand tour of the turbulent 1960s, as seen through the experiences of a young man from East Chicago, Indiana, played by Wasson. Tesich's partly autobiographical story is somewhat perceptive, but his script packs in too many incoherent episodes; the pieces never come together, and many of the characters lack focus. Also with Lois Smith and Reed Birney. **Director**—Arthur Penn. **(R)** *115 minutes*

THE FOUR HORSEMEN OF THE APOCALYPSE (1961)

★★

Glenn Ford
Ingrid Thulin
Charles Boyer

Overblown and awkward updating of the 1921 silent film, which starred Rudolph Valentino. This version concerns an Argentine family's involvement in World War II, with members fighting on both sides. The script and the direction are no help to the actors, who approach their assignments with little enthusiasm. The cast also includes Paul Henreid, Lee J. Cobb, Paul Lukas, and Yvette Mimieux. **Director**—Vincente Minnelli. *153 minutes*

THE FOUR MUSKETEERS (1975)

★★★

Michael York
Oliver Reed
Frank Finlay
Richard Chamberlain
Raquel Welch
Faye Dunaway
Charlton Heston

Steely: Christopher Lee is Rochefort in The Four Musketeers.

This sequel to *The Three Musketeers* has the same swashbuckling cast as the original. It is, however, funnier and less burdensome than the first film. Both were filmed simultaneously. Also stars Christopher Lee, Simon Ward, and Geraldine Chaplin. **Director**—Richard Lester. **(PG)** *108 minutes*

THE FOUR POSTER (1952)

Rex Harrison
Lilli Palmer

Excellent performances by then-married Harrison and Palmer liven up this comic story of a married couple's life, with the scenes played about their bed. The script is pleasingly adapted from the successful Broadway play by Jan de Hartog. The use of animated cartoons to connect the scenes provides a nice touch. **Director**—Irving Reis. *103 minutes b&w*

THE FOUR SEASONS (1981)

★★★

Alan Alda
Carol Burnett
Sandy Dennis
Rita Moreno
Jack Weston

Alda wrote, directed, and stars in this warm and friendly salute to the middle-aged and the middle class. The low-key comedy involves three couples who vacation together at various locales. Alda depends too much on the dialogue; the result is a rather stagy production. But a game cast injects ample humor and appeal in this good-natured slice of ordinary life. **(PG)** *107 minutes*

THE FOURTH PROTOCOL (1987)

Michael Caine
Pierce Brosnan

A well-paced British spy drama based on Frederick Forsyth's novel about a KGB plot to detonate a small atomic bomb near an American air base in England. Caine stars as the resolute and iconoclastic British agent who learns of the scheme but does not know exactly who the perpetrators will be. Brosnan fares well as the icy Russian operative who assembles the nuclear device. Though the plot seems convoluted at times, the various twists and turns are cleverly tied up at the end. Also with Joanna Cassidy and Ned Beatty. **Director**—John Mackenzie. **(R)** *120 minutes*

THE FOURTH WAR (1990)

★★1/2

Roy Scheider
Jurgen Prochnow

The Czechoslovak–West German border is the setting for a dangerous and personal feud between a hot-headed American colonel (Scheider) and a Soviet colonel who mirrors his temperament and attitudes (Prochnow). In an era of *glasnost,* these two remain unreformed and unrepentant. Their private battle provides a metaphor for the absurd cold-war mentality of past decades. Veteran director John Frankenheimer provides some exciting moments, but the film lacks an effective sense of place and the overbearing tension of other cold-war dramas. Tim Reid fares well as an officer beneath Scheider in rank who does not condone his actions. Also with Lara Harris, Harry Dean Stanton, Dale Dye, and Bill MacDonald. **(R)** *95 minutes*

THE FOX AND THE HOUND (1981)

A new generation of Walt Disney animators made this $12-million cartoon about the deteriorating friendship of two animals. The film is full of Disney playfulness and sentimentality. Yet the tone is often heavy-handed and overly serious, especially in dealing with a parable on race relations. Somehow, that special Disney magic hasn't been

(Continued)

(Continued)
fully realized by the new generation. Voices include those of Mickey Rooney, Kurt Russell, Pearl Bailey, and Jack Albertson. **Director**—Art Stevens. **(G)** *83 minutes*

FOXES (1980)

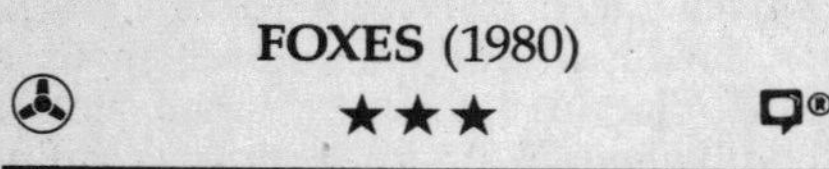

★★★

Sally Kellerman
Jodie Foster

A moving and highly realistic story about the social and emotional problems of four teenage girls growing up in Los Angeles. Foster and Kellerman head a cast of mostly unknowns, but every performance is convincing. The film succeeds in depicting the adolescent world beset by the inadequacies of home and school. This portrait is the dark side of *American Graffiti*. **Director**—Adrian Lyne. **(R)** *106 minutes*

FRANCES (1982)

★★

Jessica Lange
Sam Shepard
Kim Stanley

Disturbing, controversial film biography of 1930s Hollywood golden girl Frances Farmer, whose rebellious behavior led to her tragic confinement in various hellhole mental institutions. The story is burdened with ugly scenes, including shock treatments and a frontal lobotomy. Such depictions tend to disgust rather than convince, but Lange's spirited performance in the title role stands out from the bad taste. Stanley costars as the actress' ambitious mother. **Director**—Graeme Clifford. **(R)** **Academy Award Nominations**—Lange, best actress; Stanley, best supporting actress. *139 minutes*

FRANKENSTEIN (1931)

★★★★

Boris Karloff
Colin Clive
Mae Clarke

This is the granddaddy of horror films and still one of the most haunting and effective around. With somber mood and misty background, the film, based on Mary Shelley's fascinating novel, tells the tale of the determined scientist who recreates human life in the form of a monster assembled from corpses.

The Monster (Boris Karloff) menaces the bride (Mae Clarke) of his creator in Frankenstein.

Karloff is impressive as the mistreated monster who terrorizes the local community. And there are other fine performances by Clive, Clarke, and Edward Van Sloan. This film spawned a slew of sequels and launched its stars and director on their way to further fame. **Director**—James Whale. *71 minutes b&w*

FRANKENSTEIN MEETS THE WOLF MAN (1943)

★★★

Lon Chaney, Jr.
Ilona Massey
Bela Lugosi

The Wolf Man, alias Lawrence Talbot, takes a trip to find a cure for his moon madness, but all he finds is Frankenstein's monster on the loose. Chaney and Lugosi team up for the horror high jinks, and it's all done with stylish art direction. However, Lugosi isn't too convincing as the monster. Also with Patric Knowles, Maria Ouspenskaya, and Lionel Atwill. **Director**—Roy Neill. *73 minutes b&w*

FRANTIC (1988)

★★1/2

Harrison Ford
Emmanuelle Seigner
Betty Buckley

Roman Polanski's skill as a director of suspense tales is evident in this absorbing thriller set in Paris. Ford stars as a physician whose wife mysteriously disappears from their hotel room. His desperate efforts to find her lead to a web of intrigue that unfolds slowly and deliberately. As a man caught up in frantic pursuit, Ford handles the part with exceptional authority. Despite Polanski's experience with this genre, however, the editing here is slack and imprecise. Some scenes seem to go on far too long, while others serve no purpose but to bog the film down. **(R)** *115 minutes*

FRATERNITY ROW (1977)

★★★

Peter Fox
Gregory Harrison
Scott Newman

The script for this sobering drama began as a student filmmaking project and evolved into an intelligent movie aimed at exposing the excesses and hypocrisy of college fraternity life. The film is set in the mid-1950s at a small Eastern college. The young novice cast does rather well—especially Newman, as a sadistic frat brother, and Harrison, as an idealistic pledge who suffers under the hazing system. Also with Nancy Morgan and Robert Emhardt. There's sensitive direction from Thomas J. Tobin. **(PG)** *101 minutes*

FRATERNITY VACATION (1985)

★

Stephen Geoffreys
Sheree J. Wilson
Cameron Dye

So-so, thoroughly familiar sex farce set among the posh accommodations of Palm Springs. Three college boys from the Midwest abandon the winter cold to chase girls in the warm sunshine. There is nothing on board that is terribly offensive and there is not much that is funny. **Director**—James Frawley. **(R)** *95 minutes*

FREAKY FRIDAY (1977)

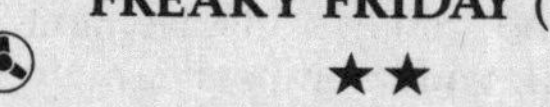

★★

Barbara Harris
Jodie Foster

Harris and Foster play a frustrated 35-year-old mother and a tomboy teenage daughter who mysteriously switch places for a day. This Disney family comedy is chock full of formula slapstick and Freudian undertones. Harris and Foster turn on their talent and charm to salvage several scenes that would otherwise misfire because of the repetitive screenplay. As with most latter-day Disney fare, it's harmless fun with a few laughs here and there—if you stay alert to catch them. Also with John Astin, Patsy Kelly, Dick Van Patten, and Sorrell Booke. **Director**—Gary Nelson. **(G)** *95 minutes*

This movie available with closed captions for the hearing impaired.

THE FRENCH CONNECTION (1971)

★★★★

Gene Hackman
Roy Scheider

The violent side of life in the drug trade, as seen in The French Connection.

Slam-bang cops-and-smugglers film, filled with exciting action, mounting suspense, and colorful characterizations. The semidocumentary story is based on the experiences of New York City detectives who broke up a lucrative narcotics operation. Featured is one of the screen's most exciting and nerve-jangling chases, with a car pursuing a subway train. Hackman, Scheider, and Fernando Rey are excellent. Also with Tony Lo Bianco and Marcel Bozzuffi. **Director**—William Friedkin. **(R) Academy Awards**—best picture; Friedkin, best director; Hackman, best actor; Ernest Tidyman, best screenplay based on material from another medium. **Nominations**—Scheider, best supporting actor; Owen Roizman, cinematography. *104 minutes*

FRENCH CONNECTION II (1975)

 ★★★ 🗨®

Gene Hackman
Fernando Rey

Hackman again plays detective Popeye Doyle, on leave from the New York City Police Department to battle the French police and the underworld. He takes Marseilles by storm, while on the trail of his old dope-dealing enemy. This sequel has its own distinct style and more concentration on mood and the supercharged character of Popeye. Also with Bernard Fresson and Jean-Pierre Castaldi. **Director**—John Frankenheimer. **(R)** *104 minutes*

THE FRENCH LIEUTENANT'S WOMAN (1981)

 ★★★

Meryl Streep
Jeremy Irons

A handsomely mounted period drama, based on John Fowles' romantic Victorian novel. The novel uses asides to make its comments on society; the film uses a story-within-a-story structure, about a filmmaking company whose players duplicate their onscreen involvements when they're off the screen. Streep, in the title role, plays a young woman of doubtful reputation, and Irons is the wealthy Englishman who is fascinated by her. It's an intelligent, inventive production, yet it leans toward the pretentious. **Director**—Karel Reisz. **(R) Academy Award Nominations**—Streep, best actress; Harold Pinter, best screenplay based on material from another medium. *123 minutes*

FRENCH POSTCARDS (1979)

 ★★★

Miles Chapin
Blanche Baker
Mandy Patinkin
Debra Winger

Gloria Katz and Willard Huyck, the screenwriters for *American Graffiti*, brings us this sunny and likable tale of American students in Paris. The film gets a lot of its zing from the talents of some eager young newcomers; Chapin is especially pleasing as a shy American who gets an ego boost from a charming French girl, played by Valerie Quennessen. There are a few problems with plot and too many characters, but the film ends on a refreshing note. Also with David Marshall Grant and Marie-France Pisier. **Director**—Huyck. **(PG)** *92 minutes*

FRENZY (1972)

 ★★★1/2

Jon Finch
Alec McCowen
Barry Foster

Director Alfred Hitchcock does it again with this gripping tale about an innocent man tagged as the London Strangler because of circumstantial evidence. The plot is déjà vu, but Hitchcock adds his unique touches and comes up with a good thriller. Virtuoso camera movements and some biting black humor set this film above other suspense yarns. A cast of unknowns delivers the goods with style; Foster plays the strangler, and Finch plays the innocent man. Anthony Shaffer's taut screenplay is based on Arthur La Bern's novel *Goodby Piccadilly, Farewell Leicester Square.* Also with Vivien Merchant, Barbara Leigh-Hunt, and Anna Massey. **(R)** *116 minutes*

FRESH HORSES (1988)

 ★★ 🗨®

Molly Ringwald
Andrew McCarthy

Andrew McCarthy gets a different perspective on life from Molly Ringwald in Fresh Horses.

Dreary romantic drama about a college senior (McCarthy) who dumps his upper-crust fiancée for a mysterious high school dropout (Ringwald). The dull script lets down Ringwald. Good use of location shooting adds atmosphere, but not enough to overcome the film's weaknesses. Also with Patti D'Arbanville, Molly Hagan, and Doug Hutchison. **Director**—David Anspaugh. **(PG-13)** *105 minutes*

THE FRESHMAN (1990)

 ★★★

Marlon Brando
Matthew Broderick
Bruno Kirby

Brando steals the film in a role that parodies his unforgettable performance in *The Godfather*. Here, the legendary star plays Carmine Sabatini with all of the mannerisms and vocal inflections of Don Corleone. Sabatini, supposedly an importer of exotic animals, convinces a

(Continued)

(Continued)
naive college freshman, played by Broderick, to take a high-paying but menial job as a delivery boy. Other references to classic films abound; director Andrew Bergman has more in mind than the plot. Brando's return to the big screen at the end of the 1980s (see *A Dry White Season*) is a reminder of his talent and influence as America's premier actor. Bert Parks makes a memorably funny cameo appearance. Also with Penelope Ann Miller, Frank Whaley, Jon Polito, Paul Benedict, and Maximilian Schell. **(PG)** *102 minutes*

FREUD (1962)

Montgomery Clift
Larry Parks
Susannah York

Straightforward, intelligent film biography of the founder of psychoanalysis. The story dwells on the treatment of a boy with a mother-fixation and Freud's early efforts to find acceptance for his revolutionary methods. Clift gives a sensitive performance in the title role. Originally released at 139 minutes. Others in the cast include Eileen Herlie, David McCallum, and Susan Kohner. **Director**—John Huston. **Academy Award Nomination**—Charles Kaufman and Wolfgang Reinhardt, best story and screenplay written directly for the screen. *120 minutes b&w*

FRIDAY THE 13TH (1980)

Betsy Palmer
Adrienne King
Harry Crosby

A diabolical murderer stalks a summer camp, dispatching several young counselors in various bloody methods, all within a day's time. Director Sean Cunningham offers a few suspenseful moments, but most of the story is unconvincing. The novice players act out their parts with appeal despite the wooden dialogue. **(R)** *95 minutes*

FRIDAY THE 13TH, PART 2 (1981)

Amy Steel
John Furey
Adrienne King

Summer camp turns into a bloodbath in Friday the 13th, Part 2.

This sequel to the commercially successful horror movie revisits the New Jersey summer camp for more grisly slaughter. There are a few romantic interludes among the young counselors; then it's time for assembly-line murder by the hooded killer with a mother-fixation. He systematically dispatches his victims with a garrote, an ax to the head, and other horrifying means aimed at increasing the shock effect. This film was the first of several sequels, all financially successful. **Director**—Steve Miner. **(R)** *87 minutes*

FRIDAY THE 13TH, PART 3 (1982)

 **(no stars)**

Tracie Savage
Dana Kimmell

The third in this series is an exceptionally vile horror-screamer that reworks the same plot as its predecessors. The terrible-tempered Jason again prowls Crystal Lake hacking, skewering, and slicing the teenagers with robot-like proficiency. Acting, direction, and logic are minimal, while the blood and gore—filmed in 3-D—are overwhelming. One young girl (Kimmell) survives the slaughter, thus leaving the door open for Part IV. **Director**—Steve Miner. **(R)** *96 minutes*

FRIDAY THE 13TH—THE FINAL CHAPTER (1984)

 **(no stars)**

Kimberly Beck
Corey Feldman
Crispin Glover

The vicious Jason is at work again, hacking, stabbing, and slicing dozens of victims in mechanical fashion. This blood-drenched film is no more than a rehash of the formula horror plot that served the previous outings. Only this time, the masked killer is stopped by a boy who wields a mean machete. And despite the title's final tone, the door is left ajar again for another round of grisly mayhem. **Director**—Joseph Zito. **(R)** *91 minutes*

FRIDAY THE 13TH—A NEW BEGINNING (1985)

 **(no stars)** 

John Shepherd
Melanie Kinnaman

Despite its title, this fifth chapter in the horrible slasher series is merely more of the same old formula. This time, however, it's the boy who stopped Jason in *The Final Chapter* who becomes the masked killer. Armed with a machete, he hacks up numerous teenagers until only a few are left to deal with the fiend's demise. **Director**—Danny Steinmann. **(R)** *92 minutes*

FRIDAY THE 13TH, PART VI: JASON LIVES (1986)

 **(no stars)** 

Thom Mathews
Jennifer Cooke

The body count continues in this sixth chapter of the formula slasher series, hitting an all-time high of about one brutal killing every five minutes. The thin plot finds some kids digging up the bloodthirsty Jason's grave to make sure he's dead. The outcome of such curiosity is obvious. Minimal logic and dreadful acting accompany the usual brutal rampage. **Director**—Tom McLoughlin. **(R)** *87 minutes*

FRIDAY THE 13TH, PART VII—THE NEW BLOOD (1988)

(no stars)

Jennifer Banko
Lar Park Lincoln

Again, the indestructible Jason dispatches teen victims right and left at blood-soaked Crystal Lake. This time the mad murderer in the hockey mask is disposed of by a young girl, played by Lincoln, who has telekinetic abilities. It's a sort of "Carrie" meets "Jason" plot. The usual stabbings, drownings, spikings, and batterings occur, so fans

This movie available with closed captions for the hearing impaired.

of the series won't be disappointed. The series has degenerated so badly at this point that each entry is barely worth mentioning. **Director**—John Carl Buechler. **(R)** *90 minutes*

FRIDAY THE 13TH, PART VIII—JASON TAKES MANHATTAN (1989)

(no stars)

Jensen Daggett
Scott Reeves
Kane Hodder

In another bloody rampage, Jason the hockey-masked murderer (Hodder) dispatches high-school students on a cruise ship en route to New York. Ax-slashing, harpooning, electrocution, and decapitation are some of the methods employed, though at this point Jason is beginning to repeat himself. The Manhattan setting, which is actually Vancouver, doesn't appear until the picture is almost over. The body count, for those keeping track, is about 17. At this point, these films are so poor and repetitive that they are only worth mentioning to keep the series up to date. Also with a supporting cast of teen actors you'll never hear from again. **Director**—Rob Hedden. **(R)** *100 minutes*

FRIENDLY PERSUASION (1956)

★★★★

Gary Cooper
Dorothy McGuire
Anthony Perkins

Anthony Perkins is counseled by peace-loving Gary Cooper in Friendly Persuasion.

A beautiful and sensitive story of a peace-loving Quaker family in Indiana whose lives are disrupted by the Civil War. Cooper and McGuire do well as the mother and father, but there's an especially winning performance by Perkins as their son. Based on the stories of Jessamyn West, the film is sentimental but well directed, with beautiful production values. Also with Marjorie Main, Richard Eyer, and Robert Middleton. **Director**—William Wyler. **Academy Award Nominations**—best picture; Wyler, best director; Perkins, best supporting actor. *139 minutes*

FRIGHT NIGHT (1985)

★★★

William Ragsdale
Chris Sarandon
Roddy McDowall

Latter-day vampire yarn cleverly put together by debuting director Tom Holland. Ragsdale plays a bright-eyed teenager who discovers his new next-door neighbor (Sarandon) only comes out at night, and when he does, he abruptly grows fangs. Trouble is, no one believes the youngster's claim that a vampire prowls the community. Though Bela Lugosi can rest safely in his coffin, this tale has enough going to please horror fans. **(R)** *105 minutes*

THE FRISCO KID (1979)

★★

Gene Wilder
Harrison Ford

Wilder plays a befuddled Polish rabbi who sets off across the United States on horseback in 1850 to head a congregation in San Francisco. Wilder occasionally does well with this overdrawn ethnic joke, but the story is jagged and uneven. Part of the problem seems to be director Robert Aldrich, who is more at home with action westerns than with this sort of comedy. Also with William Smith, Ramon Bieri, and Penny Peyser. **(PG)** *122 minutes*

FRITZ THE CAT (1972)

★★★

Biting, satirical animated feature that irreverently attacks the mores, standards, and styles of the 1960s. Writer/director/animator Ralph Bakshi spares no one in his vitriolic and witty near-masterpiece cartoon. Based on Robert Crumb's underground comic strip, it is probably the first cartoon to achieve an X rating. The overwhelmingly downbeat nature and violence may cause some viewers to wince, but the overall sophistication of its insights will please still more. **(X)** *78 minutes*

FROM BEYOND (1986)

★★

Jeffrey Combs
Barbara Crampton

This campy horror film, based on an H.P. Lovecraft short story, revolves around a strange machine that allows humans to make contact with horrifying creatures from an unknown world. The thin plot, which primarily concerns the murder of a scientist, is overshadowed by the special effects, particularly the slimy monsters, which are more technically awesome than scary. Directed by Stuart Gordon, whose previous effort, *Re-animator,* was similar in style and approach. **(R)** *88 minutes*

FROM HERE TO ETERNITY (1953)

★★★★

Burt Lancaster
Deborah Kerr
Montgomery Clift
Frank Sinatra
Donna Reed

Burt Lancaster and Deborah Kerr savor forbidden romance in From Here to Eternity.

First-rate, compelling drama about Army life in Hawaii on the eve of World War II. This screen version of James Jones' best-selling novel comes across with power and passion, thanks to sterling performances and taut direction. Clift, Lancaster, and Kerr head the cast, but the supporting performances of Sinatra and Reed highlight the film. Also with Ernest Borgnine, Philip Ober, and Mickey Shaughnessy. **Director**—Fred Zinnemann. **Academy Awards**—best picture; Zinnemann, best director;

(Continued)

(Continued)
Sinatra, best supporting actor; Reed, best supporting actress; Daniel Taradash, screenplay; Burnett Guffey, cinematography. **Nominations**—Clift and Lancaster, best actor; Kerr, best actress. *118 minutes b&w*

FROM NOON TIL THREE (1976)

★★

Charles Bronson
Jill Ireland

Director Frank Gilroy's comic western stars Bronson in an unconventional, satirical role; he plays a two-bit bandit who holes up in a plush Victorian mansion belonging to an attractive and kooky widow, played by Ireland. The story is cheerful, mildly funny, and intelligent, although it takes a long time to make its point. **(PG)** *100 minutes*

FROM RUSSIA WITH LOVE (1963)

 ★★★★

Sean Connery
Robert Shaw

More rollicking spy adventures in this second James Bond film caper. This time secret agent 007 is on the hit list of a Russian agent, played by Shaw, who also wants possession of a Russian coding machine. Connery has always been the best Bond, and this film is one of the highlights of the whole series. Veteran stage actress Lotte Lenya plays a vicious spy out for his blood. It's all accomplished with tongue-in-cheek humor against the exotic backgrounds of Istanbul and Venice. Also with Pedro Armendariz, Daniela Bianchi, Bernard Lee, Eunice Gayson, and Lois Maxwell. **Director**—Terence Young. **(PG)** *118 minutes*

FROM THE HIP (1987)

 ★★½ ®

Judd Nelson
John Hurt

Disorder in the court is the focal point of this energetic comedy about an overly eager young lawyer from a prestigious Boston firm (Nelson) who resorts to outrageous antics to win his cases. His brashness pays off when he takes on a difficult murder case. Hurt practically steals the movie as an arrogant English professor accused of killing a prostitute. The film is marred by a few implausible scenes and colorless direction by Bob Clark *(Porky's)*. Also with Elizabeth Perkins and Darren McGavin. **(PG)** *111 minutes*

FROM THE TERRACE (1960)

 ★★

Paul Newman
Joanne Woodward
Myrna Loy

Good-looking but leaden treatment of John O'Hara's novel, about family problems among the upper crust in Pennsylvania. Newman, Woodward, and Loy give adequate performances, but the film goes on too long, and the characters aren't interesting. Also in the cast are Ina Balin, Leon Ames, George Grizzard, Patrick O'Neal, and Elizabeth Allen. **Director**—Mark Robson. *144 minutes*

THE FRONT (1976)

 ★★★

Woody Allen
Zero Mostel
Herschel Bernardi

Here's a bold, entertaining, and moving comedy/drama about the entertainment industry's painful experience involving the political witch-hunts of the 1950s. Allen is outstanding as a goggle-eyed, politically naive chump who fronts for blacklisted TV writers by submitting their scripts under his name. Many involved with this film—director Martin Ritt, screenwriter Walter Bernstein, and performers Mostel, Bernardi, Joshua Shelley, and Lloyd Gough—had been blacklisted themselves. This uncompromising look at that tragic period is handled with intelligence, feeling, and humor. Also with Michael Murphy, Andrea Marcovicci, and Remak Ramsay. **(PG) Academy Award Nomination**—Bernstein, best screenplay written directly for the screen. *94 minutes*

THE FRONT PAGE (1931)

 ★★★★

Pat O'Brien
Adolphe Menjou
Mae Clarke

Fast-paced, snappy drama from the stage play by Ben Hecht and Charles MacArthur, who also wrote the screenplay. O'Brien portrays the star reporter who wants to leave the hectic Chicago newspaper scene and marry. His editor (Menjou) talks him into covering one more story, a prison execution that misfires. The action is lively and rapid, with excellent direction from Lewis Milestone. Although an early talkie, this landmark film still stands out for its fast cutting and cinematic style. Mary Brian plays the fiancée O'Brien forgets. Edward Everett Horton, Frank McHugh, and George E. Stone also turn in good backup performances. **Academy Award Nominations**—best picture; Milestone, best director; Menjou, best actor. *101 minutes b&w*

THE FUGITIVE KIND (1959)

 ★★

Marlon Brando
Anna Magnani
Joanne Woodward

A gloomy Tennessee Williams drama, based on his play *Orpheus Descending*. Brando stars as a footloose young man who becomes involved with women in a strange southern town; Magnani and Woodward are the objects of his desires. Even with such heavyweights in the cast, the film is not a successful interpretation of the material. Victor Jory and Maureen Stapleton also star. **Director**—Sidney Lumet. *135 minutes b&w*

THE FULLER BRUSH GIRL (1950)

★★

Lucille Ball
Eddie Albert

Lucille Ball sells cosmetics to the ladies in The Fuller Brush Girl.

® *This movie available with closed captions for the hearing impaired.*

Ball stars in the title role, as an enthusiastic cosmetics saleslady who gets tangled up with murderers and thieves. Typical slapstick material, with Lucy delightful as always. It's worthwhile if you love Lucy; otherwise, forget it. Scripted by Frank Tashlin, who later directed the classic Jerry Lewis/Dean Martin comedies. Supporting cast also includes Carl Benton Reid, Gale Robbins, Lee Patrick, Jeff Donnell, and Jerome Cowan. **Director**—Lloyd Bacon. *85 minutes b&w*

THE FULLER BRUSH MAN (1948)

 ★★

Red Skelton
Janet Blair

Skelton dishes up the slapstick as an eager door-to-door salesman who becomes involved in murder. A predictable storyline, with some meandering, but it's well suited for Skelton's comedic style. Lots of fun if you enjoy this sort of comedy. Don McGuire and Adele Jergens costar. **Director**—S. Sylvan Simon. *93 minutes b&w*

FULL METAL JACKET (1987)

 ★★★★

Matthew Modine
Adam Baldwin
Vincent D'Onofrio

Adam Baldwin experiences the pressures of war in Full Metal Jacket.

From Stanley Kubrick comes this thought-provoking account of the Vietnam War, brimming with black humor, irony, and shocking plot twists. Essentially structured into two parts, the film is based on Gustav Hasford's brutal novel *The Short-Timers*. The first act involves a gut-wrenching depiction of the harshness of Marine Corps boot camp, which is joltingly transformed to the realities of Vietnam combat in the second part via a shocking act of violence. Splendid performances abound, especially that of Lee Ermey—a former Marine sergeant—who portrays the bellowing drill instructor. Also with Dorian Harewood, Arliss Howard, and Kevin Major Howard. **(R) Academy Award Nomination**—Kubrick, Michael Herr, and Gustav Hasford, best screenplay adapted from material from another medium. *118 minutes*

FULL MOON IN BLUE WATER (1988)

 ★★ 

Gene Hackman
Teri Garr

Burgess Meredith, Gene Hackman, and Teri Garr in Full Moon in Blue Water.

This mediocre comedy stars Hackman as a down-in-the-dumps bar owner facing personal problems in a backwater Texas town. His wife is missing and presumed dead. His business is about to be seized for back taxes. Real estate sharks want to cash in on his misfortune. And a woman friend (Garr) wants to ignite a love affair. There's more, but none of it creates much interest or humor. Also with Burgess Meredith and Elias Koteas. **Director**—Peter Masterson. **(R)** *98 minutes*

THE FUNHOUSE (1981)

 ★★

Elizabeth Berridge
Cooper Huckabee
Miles Chapin

Director Tobe Hooper, who established his cult film credentials with the frightful *Texas Chainsaw Massacre*, serves up another ration of gore, but this time there's too much nonsense mixed in with the terror. Four teenagers spend the night in an elaborate carnival funhouse where they are terrorized by a vile monster. Before the sun comes up, dead bodies are strewn all over the place. Hooper puts his imagination and bizarre style into full force, but the film is deflated by amateurish performances. Also with Sylvia Miles and Kevin Conway. **(R)** *95 minutes*

FUNNY FACE (1957)

★★★★

Fred Astaire
Audrey Hepburn

This is among the best of the Astaire musicals, with the dean of dancing turning in some fancy footwork to the beat of great Gershwin tunes. Astaire plays a fashion photographer who meets a rather colorless bookstore clerk (Hepburn) and turns her into a glamorous fashion model. Sparkling Parisian locations enhance the stylish production. Kay Thompson, Michel Auclair, and Suzy Parker perform well in supporting roles. **Director**—Stanley Donen. **Academy Award Nomination**—Leonard Gershe, best story and screenplay written directly for the screen. *103 minutes*

FUNNY FARM (1988)

★★

Chevy Chase
Madolyn Smith

Chevy Chase and Madolyn Smith abandon the city for Funny Farm.

A hollow comedy, which contains very few laughs and has nothing to do with

(Continued)

(Continued)

farming. Chase and Smith play a city couple who move to a small town in the country so that he can write that first big novel. The country is not the idyllic respite they expected, however, as they experience a variety of misadventures and encounter a number of eccentric townfolk. This type of premise was handled much better in such comedy classics as *Mr. Blandings Builds His Dream House*; this trite update only proves disappointing. George Roy Hill (*The Sting; Butch Cassidy and the Sundance Kid*) directed this predictable material with an unsure hand. Also with Kevin O'Morrison, Joseph Maher, Mike Starr, Jack Gilpin, and Caris Corfman. **(PG)**
98 minutes

FUNNY GIRL (1968)

★★★★

Barbra Streisand
Omar Sharif
Walter Pidgeon

Streisand is perfectly cast as comedienne Fanny Brice in this glittering musical. She gives it her best shot, belting out a slew of showstopping tunes with exceptional gusto. The Jule Styne/Bob Merrill score is first-rate; "Don't Rain on My Parade" and "People" are memorable. This was Streisand's film debut, and she proves that she is a powerhouse performer. The fine supporting cast also includes Kay Medford and Anne Francis. **Director**—William Wyler. **(G) Academy Award**—Barbra Streisand, best actress. **Nominations**—best picture; Medford, best supporting actress; Harry Stradling, cinematography.
155 minutes

FUNNY LADY (1975)

★★

Barbra Streisand
James Caan
Omar Sharif
Ben Vereen

This sequel to *Funny Girl* involves the further adventures of Fanny Brice, again portrayed by Streisand. There are a few comic moments, and the film is occasionally shored up by the shining talents of the great Streisand. But when she stops singing, the picture limps along amid phoney Hollywood-type romantic suffering and unconvincing characterizations. The great cinematographer James Wong Howe was nominated for an Academy Award for his work on this film. Also with Roddy McDowall and Larry Gates. **Director**—Herbert Ross. **(PG)** *137 minutes*

A FUNNY THING HAPPENED ON THE WAY TO THE FORUM (1966)

★★★

Zero Mostel
Phil Silvers

Mostel is fabulous in this musical comedy set in ancient Rome. Zero plays a scheming slave in the home of a wealthy family; he's trying hard to gain his freedom. Richard Lester directs with plenty of style and pep, and there's no shortage of good laughs. Most of the supporting roles are also performed excellently, with Silvers, Michael Crawford, Jack Gilford, Michael Hordern, and Beatrix Lehmann in top form. The film is adapted from the Broadway production, with the score by Stephen Sondheim mostly intact.
99 minutes

FUN WITH DICK AND JANE (1977)

★★★

Jane Fonda
George Segal

Segal and Fonda are cheerful and funny in this social comedy about a middle-class couple who turn to crime when the husband loses his job as an aerospace engineer. Both perform resourcefully and work hard to keep the laughter flowing in their perky slapstick routines. The story is as contemporary as the latest recession, and it points out some vulgar aspects of middle-class values. The supporting cast is excellent, especially Ed McMahon, who plays Segal's former employer. Also with Dick Gautier, John Dehner, and Allan Miller. **Director**—Ted Kotcheff. **(PG)**
95 minutes

FURY (1936)

★★★

Spencer Tracy
Sylvia Sidney

Devastating social drama of small-town America where an innocent man is lynched by a crazed mob for a murder he didn't commit. Director Fritz Lang in his first American film vividly portrays the danger of mob rule and the ease with which the innocent can be corrupted. Tracy escapes the mob through a fluke but becomes a bitter, hardened man seeking revenge on his tormentors. Sidney is the girl he loses as his obsession grows. Excellent performances by Bruce Cabot, Walter Abel, and Walter Brennan. The second half of the film does not live up to the lynching, but this still remains forceful filmmaking. **Academy Award Nomination**—Norman Krasna, original story.
94 minutes b&w

THE FURY (1978)

★★

Kirk Douglas
John Cassavetes
Carrie Snodgress

Brian De Palma, who directed *Carrie*, uses the psychokinetic gimmick again in this gruesome, blood-drenched chiller. The sometimes confusing script concerns a teenager (Andrew Stevens) with telekinetic power—the ability to move objects by will—who is kidnapped by a super-secret government agency. De Palma stresses form over content in this visually fascinating film, which may not emphasize plot and characters enough for the average viewer. Also with Amy Irving and Charles Durning. **(R)** *118 minutes*

F/X (1986)

★★★ ®

Bryan Brown
Brian Dennehy

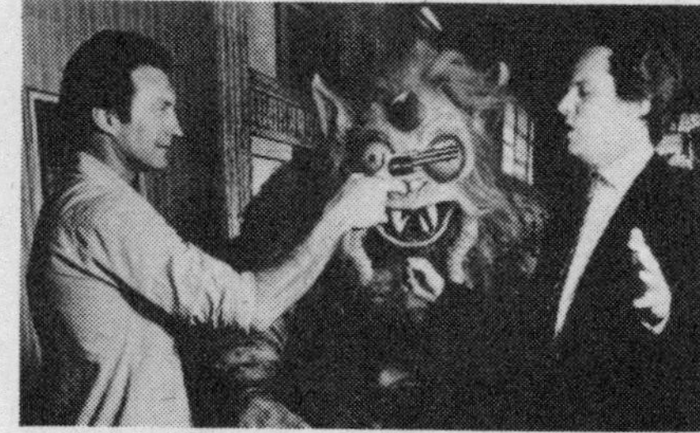

Effects man Bryan Brown surprises government agent Cliff De Young in F/X.

An entertaining thriller packed with fast action, clever twists and turns, and creative special effects. In fact, an ace movie special-effects man (Brown) is the centerpiece of the plot. He is hired to stage a phoney rub-out of a mobster and subsequently becomes the victim of double and triple crosses. He uses his special-effects skills to outmaneuver

® *This movie available with closed captions for the hearing impaired.*

his pursuers. Preposterous elements are overcome by good acting and suspenseful pacing. Also with Diane Venora, Cliff De Young, and Mason Adams. **Director**—Robert Mandel. **(R)**
106 minutes

G

GABY (1956)

★★

Leslie Caron
John Kerr

Caron and Kerr star in this tepid remake of *Waterloo Bridge*. It's the romantic story of a ballerina (Caron) who's in love with a søldier (Kerr) about to be sent into battle in World War II. The film is too melodramatic to be as effective as the 1940 version starring Vivien Leigh and Robert Taylor. Also with Cedric Hardwicke, Taina Elg, and Margalo Gillmore. **Director**—Curtis Bernhardt.
97 minutes

GABY—A TRUE STORY (1987)

★★★

Rachel Levin
Norma Aleandro
Liv Ullmann

An extraordinary and powerful account of writer Gabriela Brimmer, who overcame cerebral palsy to become an accomplished poet. Unable to move most of her body, Gaby was taught to write and study by her devoted nurse, played by Aleandro in an Oscar-nominated performance. Though occasionally poignant and painfully touching, the story is never overly sentimental. Stage actress Levin, who recently recovered from her own paralysis due to Guillain-Barre syndrome, stars in the title role. **Director**—Luis Mandoki. **(R) Academy Award Nomination**—Aleandro, best supporting actress. *110 minutes*

GAILY, GAILY (1969)

★★★

Brian Keith
Beau Bridges
Melina Mercouri

The reminiscences of Chicago journalist Ben Hecht provide the basis for this colorful tale of a cub reporter in the big city during the early 1900s. The film's script is somewhat uneven, but the recreation of the period is impressive, and the production is executed with just the right amount of humor. Bridges gives an appealing performance as the determined cub reporter, assisted nicely by Keith as the older journalist who takes Bridges under his wing. Also with George Kennedy, Hume Cronyn, Margot Kidder, Melodie Johnson, and Wilfrid Hyde-White. **Director**—Norman Jewison. **(PG)** *117 minutes*

GALAXINA (1981)

★

Dorothy R. Stratten

A flimsy, adolescent spoof of galactic films, with a surplus of silly dialogue and a critical shortage of laughs. The late Dorothy R. Stratten, a former *Playboy* Playmate, is in the title role, as a gorgeous robot who pilots a spacecraft. Wooden performances and cardboard characters prevail amid the gleaming space hardware, and the action never reaches orbit. **Director**—William Sachs. **(R)** *95 minutes*

GALAXY OF TERROR (1982)

★

Edward Albert
Erin Moran
Ray Walston

This thinly plotted sci-fi adventure follows a group of astronauts who attempt to rescue a spaceship on a strange planet and are attacked by reptilelike monsters. The script, much on the order of *Alien*, is absurd, and the characters are strictly cardboard. In one tasteless sequence, a female astronaut is raped by a giant worm. **Director**—B.D. Clark. **(R) Alternate Titles**—*Mindwarp: An Infinity of Terror* and *Planet of Horrors.* *80 minutes*

GALLIPOLI (1981)

★★★

Mark Lee
Bill Kerr
Mel Gibson

Australian director Peter Weir fashions a handsome and intimate historical film that deals intelligently with the exploitations of youthful zeal, ambition, and innocence. Lee and Gibson are convincing as two athletic young men who enlist in the Australian army and fight in the disastrous World War I battle of Gallipoli. Weir concentrates primarily on personal relationships at the expense of drama and urgency. Nevertheless, his provocative statement is most memorable. Also with Robert Grubb, Tim McKenzie, Bill Hunter, and John Morris. **(PG)** *110 minutes*

GAMBIT (1966)

★★★

Michael Caine
Shirley MacLaine

A nifty crime caper, with Caine as a determined but inept thief out to steal a valuable statue from a wealthy man. He has the help of MacLaine, cast effectively as a mysterious Eurasian woman he hires to participate in the heist. The script is spotty but clever. Also with Herbert Lom, Roger C. Carmel, and John Abbott. **Director**—Ronald Neame.
109 minutes

GANDHI (1982)

★★★★

Ben Kingsley

Ben Kingsley plays Gandhi, *spiritual leader and liberator of India.*

Richard Attenborough's magnificent, sweeping, inspirational biography of India's architect of nonviolent action, who led his country to freedom from British oppression and occupation. At the center of this epic undertaking is Kingsley, the Anglo-Indian actor, as the saintly Mahatma (great soul). His towering portrayal is amazingly convincing and vivid. Although the film is more
(Continued)

(Continued)
than three hours long, it never loses its power and passion. An unforgettable movie. Excellent support from Edward Fox, John Gielgud, and Rohini Hattangandy. **(PG) Academy Awards**—best picture; Attenborough, best director; Kingsley, best actor; John Briley, best screenplay written directly for the screen; Billy Williams and Ronnie Taylor, cinematography. *188 minutes*

GARBAGE PAIL KIDS (1987)

(no stars)

Anthony Newley
Mackenzie Astin

A feature-length film based on the disgusting bubble gum cards currently collected by children. In this live-action version, the Kids are played by midgets. The tacky characters have such names as Messy Tessie, Valerie Vommit, Foul Phil, and Windy Winston, and each behaves in the manner that his or her name implies. Newley, in a new career low, plays an antique dealer who accidentally lets the Kids out of their garbage pail home. The film's message is that beauty is only skin deep, but it's hard to get the point across with such tasteless antics. The video version runs 87 minutes. **Director**—Rod Amateau. **(PG)** *100 minutes*

GARBO TALKS (1984)

★★★

Anne Bancroft
Ron Silver
Carrie Fisher

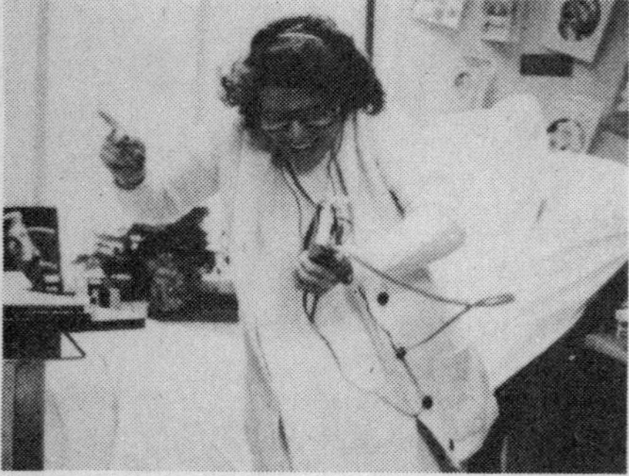

Anne Bancroft brings some gaiety to her life in Garbo Talks.

Bancroft is amusing as an eccentric woman stricken with cancer, whose last wish is to meet the great movie star Greta Garbo. Her son (Silver) tries to locate the reclusive screen legend. This warm, breezy comedy is also about New York City's inhabitants and the spirit with which they face urban life. Howard Da Silva, Dorothy Loudon, Harvey Fierstein, and Hermione Gingold are outstanding in their portrayals of colorful characters. **Director**—Sidney Lumet. **(PG-13)** *105 minutes*

THE GARDEN OF THE FINZI-CONTINIS (1971)

★★★★

Dominique Sanda
Helmut Berger

Beautifully photographed drama about a patrician Jewish family in Fascist Italy in 1938. The well-bred Finzi-Continis live in their own naive dreamworld enclosed by a brick-walled garden, unaware and choosing to ignore the political changes going on around them. Sanda is riveting as the daughter, and Berger is superb as her fragile brother. Vittorio De Sica's masterful direction slowly tracks the family to its inevitable downfall. A harrowing portrayal of Jews being stripped of possessions, dignity, and freedom in a world whose physical beauty mocks its distorted spirit. Originally filmed in Italian. **(R) Academy Award**—best foreign-language film. **Nomination**—Ugo Pirro and Vittorio Bonicelli, best screenplay based on material from another medium. *95 minutes*

GARDENS OF STONE (1987)

★★★

James Caan
James Earl Jones
Anjelica Huston

James Caan, D.B. Sweeney, and James Earl Jones in Gardens of Stone.

Francis Coppola once again turns to Vietnam for his subject matter in this heartrending drama about the effects of the war at home. Caan, making a screen comeback after a decade of unsuccessful films, stars as a career army officer who, after several years in Vietnam, believes the war to be a mistake. Currently a part of the Old Guard, the company that services Arlington Cemetery, Caan becomes a surrogate father to an ambitious young recruit who desperately wants to fight in Vietnam. An overwhelming sense of sadness and loss pervades the film as repeated scenes of burials point to the inevitable conclusion. Coppola offers no clear-cut statement on the trauma that was Vietnam, but instead captures the confusion of the people at home, whose loyalties and beliefs were divided. Jones excels in a supporting role as Caan's army buddy. Also with D.B. Sweeney, Lonette McKee, Mary Stuart Masterson, and Dean Stockwell. **(R)** *112 minutes*

GASLIGHT (1944)

★★★

Charles Boyer
Ingrid Bergman

Charles Boyer plots to drive wife Ingrid Bergman mad in Gaslight.

Dated but still entertaining drama about a man attempting to drive his wife mad. A top cast in stylish performances, in addition to the effective visuals, helps bring out the suspense. The screenplay is based on Patrick Hamilton's play. Also with Joseph Cotten, Dame May Whitty, and Angela Lansbury. **Director**—George Cukor. **Academy Award**—Bergman, best actress. **Nominations**—best picture; Boyer, best actor; Lansbury, best supporting actress; John L. Balderston, Walter Reisch, and John Van Druten, best screenplay; Joseph Ruttenberg, cinematography.

114 minutes b&w

This movie available with closed captions for the hearing impaired.

GATOR (1976)

★★

Burt Reynolds
Jack Weston
Lauren Hutton

Reynolds is mischievous moonshiner Gator McClusky in this choppy follow-up to the more lucrative *White Lightning*. This time, Gator is recruited to infiltrate the organization of a backwater crime boss. Reynolds also serves as the director, but handles the job in an uneven manner. There are moments of excitement and drama interlaced with unsophisticated humor, contrived action sequences, and lethargic romantic scenes. There are, however, interesting character portrayals by Weston, Hutton, and Jerry Reed. Also with Alice Ghostley, Mike Douglas, and Dub Taylor. **(PG)** *116 minutes*

THE GAUNTLET (1978)

★★★

Clint Eastwood
Sondra Locke

Clint Eastwood and Sondra Locke on an important journey in The Gauntlet.

Eastwood is both the director and star of this caper about a hard-drinking detective who risks all to bring a Las Vegas hooker, played by Locke, to Phoenix to testify against the mob. Eastwood's character is a slight departure from his familiar *Dirty Harry* routine. The film's action and scenes of choreographed violence are adequate, and include narrow escapes in assorted vehicles such as a motorcycle and an armored bus. The film is much like a violent, good-natured comic book, but Eastwood's stylish direction is credible. Also with Pat Hingle, William Prince, and Bill McKinney. **(R)** *109 minutes*

THE GAY DIVORCÉE (1934)

★★★

Fred Astaire
Ginger Rogers
Betty Grable

Ginger Rogers and Fred Astaire enjoy post-marital bliss in The Gay Divorcée.

Astaire plays an infatuated dancer who mopes about until the woman he loves agrees to marry him. Despite the dated material, the star-studded cast, including Erik Rhodes, Edward Everett Horton, Eric Blore, and Alice Brady, is still fresh and contemporary. Top songs include Cole Porter's "Night and Day" and the Oscar-winning "Continental" by Con Conrad and Herb Magidson. **Director**—Mark Sandrich. **Academy Award Nomination**—best picture. *107 minutes b&w*

THE GEISHA BOY (1958)

★★

Jerry Lewis

Lewis plays a bumbling magician traveling with a USO troupe in the Far East. Typical Lewis high jinks prevail, with a number of effective sight gags generating some laughs—but not enough to sustain interest. Lewis strains a little too much, and at times the film lapses into sentimentality. Also with Marie McDonald, Sessue Hayakawa, Barton MacLane, and Suzanne Pleshette. **Director**—Frank Tashlin. *98 minutes*

GENEVIEVE (1953)

★★★★

Dinah Sheridan
John Gregson
Kay Kendall
Kenneth More

A warm British comedy done with exceptional skill and care. It involves a good-natured cross-country race between two couples in vintage cars. Along the way, there are many charming and memorable moments, brilliantly executed by a delightful cast. Kendall stands out in some saucy comedy scenes. And there are other delicious performances from Sheridan, Gregson, More, Geoffrey Keen, Joyce Grenfell, Reginald Beckwith, and Arthur Wontner. **Director**—Henry Cornelius. **Academy Award Nomination**—William Rose, story and screenplay. *86 minutes*

GENTLEMAN JIM (1942)

★★★½

Errol Flynn
Alan Hale

Flynn plays the title role in this highly entertaining film biography of famous 1890s boxer Jim Corbett. Flynn's portrayal of this colorful hero offers just the right amount of dash and comedy. A romanticized depiction of an era when the sport was prohibited in some areas. Jack Carson, Alexis Smith, and Ward Bond are among the costars. **Director**—Raoul Walsh. *104 minutes b&w*

GENTLEMAN'S AGREEMENT (1947)

★★★★

Gregory Peck
Dorothy McGuire
John Garfield

Dorothy McGuire and Gregory Peck fight anti-Semitism in Gentleman's Agreement.

A fascinating and powerful story about a journalist, played by Peck, who poses as a Jew and encounters much hatred. The film, based on Laura Hobson's intelligent novel, was rather startling at the time of its release, and it's still com-

(Continued)

This movie available on videotape and/or disc.

(Continued)
pelling. Fine acting all around, with Celeste Holm outstanding as a lonely fashion editor. Cast also includes Anne Revere, June Havoc, Albert Dekker, Jane Wyatt, and Dean Stockwell. **Director**—Elia Kazan. **Academy Awards**—best picture; Kazan, best director; Holm, best supporting actress. **Nominations**—Peck, best actor; McGuire, best actress; Moss Hart, screenplay.
118 minutes b&w

GENTLEMEN PREFER BLONDES (1953)

 ★★★

Jane Russell
Marilyn Monroe

Jane Russell, Marilyn Monroe, and Tommy Noonan in Gentlemen Prefer Blondes.

Monroe and Russell are right at home in this agreeable musical comedy about a couple of entertainers off to Paris on a luxury ocean liner. The plot is incidental to the musical numbers, which include the classic "Diamonds Are a Girl's Best Friend." Charles Coburn adds a touch of comedy to the splashy proceedings. Based on the Broadway musical of the 1920s. Also with Tommy Noonan and George Winslow. **Director**—Howard Hawks. *91 minutes*

GEORGY GIRL (1966)

 ★★★★

Lynn Redgrave
James Mason

Redgrave is marvelous in the role of an awkward young girl who chucks her bizarre lifestyle and marries a wealthy widower, played by Mason, who is old enough to be her father. The charming comedy/drama examines contemporary attitudes and develops entertaining characterizations along the way. The entire cast performs splendidly, with an exceptional supporting role by Charlotte Rampling as Redgrave's freewheeling roommate. Alan Bates and Bill Owen also star. **Director**—Silvio Narizzano. **Academy Award Nominations**—Redgrave, best actress; Mason, best supporting actor; Ken Higgins, cinematography. *100 minutes b&w*

GET CRAZY (1983)

 ★★

Malcolm McDowell
Daniel Stern
Ed Begley, Jr.
Gail Edwards

Director Allan Arkush, who gave us *Rock 'n' Roll High School,* sprinkles energetic high jinks and lively musical numbers throughout this mixed-bag send-up of a gala rock concert. Yet most of the gags fall flat and the proceedings are crowded with too many fleeting characters who become lost in the confusion. McDowell is convincing as a strutting rock superstar and Lori Eastside is impressive as the leader of an all-female punk-rock act. Many of the other backstage portrayals are forgettable, but watch for Lou Reed. Also with Allan Goorwitz (Garfield), Miles Chapin, Franklin Ajaye, Fabian Forte, and Bobby Sherman. **(R)** *92 minutes*

GET OUT YOUR HANDKERCHIEFS (1978)

 ★★★★

Gérard Depardieu
Patrick Dewaere
Carole Laure

Gérard Depardieu explores the feminine mystique in Get Out Your Handkerchiefs.

An exhilarating, audacious comedy by French director Bertrand Blier. Depardieu and Dewaere are two bumbling pals who can't understand why Depardieu's beautiful wife is down in the dumps, but a precocious 13-year-old boy knows what the woman wants. Blier's observation of the feminine mystique has never been so funny. The subject of this film could have been offensive, but it's carried off with cool intelligence. Also with Michel Serrault and Eleonore Hirt. Originally filmed in French. **(R) Academy Award**—best foreign-language film. *109 minutes*

GETTING STRAIGHT (1970)

 ★★

Elliott Gould
Candice Bergen

A dated and only occasionally interesting comedy/drama about political radicalism of the 1960s. Gould plays a veteran who returns to college as a student and is torn between idealism and the conventional attitude of the administration. An on-campus confrontation between the students and the police results in meaningless violence. Also with Jeff Corey, Cecil Kellaway, John Rubinstein, Jeanne Berlin, Max Julien, and Robert F. Lyons. **Director**—Richard Rush. **(R)** *125 minutes*

GHOST (1990)

Patrick Swayze
Demi Moore
Whoopi Goldberg

Demi Moore gets protection from Patrick Swayze in Ghost.

Swayze stars in the title role of this engaging romantic mystery with a supernatural twist. Killed in what appears to be a street robbery, he returns from the dead to protect his fiancée from his murderers. Moore costars as the long-suffering girlfriend. The two communicate through Goldberg, a phoney psychic who is surprised to discover

she has some true powers. Excellent performances, beautiful cinematography, a poignant romance, and some comic turns from Goldberg made this film an unexpected summer hit upon its initial release. Also with Tony Goldwyn, Rick Aviles, and Gail Boggs. **Director**—Jerry Zucker. **(PG-13)**
128 minutes

THE GHOST AND MRS. MUIR (1947)

★★★

Gene Tierney
Rex Harrison

An engaging and charming comedy about a widow, played by Tierney, who lives by the sea and strikes up a romance with the ghost of a sea captain, played by Harrison. It's a handsomely produced fantasy, with the proper measure of sentimentality included. Also with George Sanders, Edna Best, Vanessa Brown, Robert Coote, Anna Lee, and Natalie Wood. **Director**—Joseph L. Mankiewicz.
104 minutes b&w

GHOSTBUSTERS (1984)

★★★

Bill Murray
Dan Aykroyd

Bill Murray and Dan Aykroyd nab a bothersome bit of ectoplasm in Ghostbusters.

Elaborate slapstick satire starring *Saturday Night Live* alumni Murray and Aykroyd as fly-by-night parapsychologists who chase around New York City zapping demons. Although the broad, physical humor may not appeal to all, the talented Murray, an impressive array of special effects, and a hit theme song made this film a top money-maker in 1984. Also with Sigourney Weaver, Ernie Hudson, Rick Moranis, and Harold Ramis. **Director**—Ivan Reitman. **(PG)** *105 minutes*

GHOSTBUSTERS II (1989)

★1/2

Bill Murray
Dan Aykroyd
Sigourney Weaver

Manhattan is menaced by a river of slime. A sinister spirit wants to take over a baby's body and rule the world. Even the Titanic returns from its watery grave. Who ya gonna call? Murray, Aykroyd, and the others return from the original 1984 comedy for this sequel, which lacks the snappy pace of the first film. Without the adult-oriented dialogue, the film lapses into children's fare. Also with Ernie Hudson, Harold Ramis, Rick Moranis, Annie Potts, and Peter MacNicol. **Director**—Ivan Reitman. **(PG)** *102 minutes*

GHOST DAD (1990)

★

Bill Cosby

Salim Grant, Brooke Fontaine, Bill Cosby, and Kimberly Russell in Ghost Dad.

Cosby, who became a household name because of his highly successful television series, fails on the big screen once again in this poorly executed farce that would scarcely suffice as TV sitcom fare. He plays the title role of a widower who has no time for his three children. When he dies unexpectedly in a taxi accident, he returns to Earth to make amends. Cosby flies through the air and passes through walls with the aid of some creaky special effects, but his tendency to play comic scenes too broadly makes this a grating, unfunny film. Perhaps the cinema is just not Cosby's forte. Directed by actor Sidney Poitier, who has made far better comedies in the past. Also with Kimberly Russell, Denise Nicholas, Ian Bannen, and Christine Ebersole. **(PG)**
84 minutes

GHOST STORY (1981)

★★

John Houseman
Fred Astaire
Melvyn Douglas
Douglas Fairbanks, Jr.

Four elderly men are suddenly haunted by a ghastly deed they committed 50 years ago, while a mysterious woman, effectively portrayed by Alice Krige, appears in their small New England town to seek revenge. The novel by Peter Straub, on which the film was based, was quite menacing, but here the narrative quickly bogs down in trite fright effects, unimpressive atmospherics, and other failed attempts to scare. Houseman, Astaire, Douglas, and Fairbanks try to give the production some class, but they waste their talents. Craig Wasson also appears. **Director**—John Irvin. **(R)** *110 minutes*

GIANT (1956)

★★★★

Elizabeth Taylor
Rock Hudson
James Dean
Carroll Baker

This sprawling epic, based on the novel by Edna Ferber, is about a Texas family involved in cattle ranching. The film is rendered with style and fine acting by a good cast. Hudson and Dean are excellent as two opposing men in love with the beautiful Taylor. Director George Stevens expertly develops a feeling for the period and the lives of the characters who achieved success from the land. There's fine supporting work, too, from Baker, Sal Mineo, Mercedes McCambridge, Chill Wills, Dennis Hopper, and Rod Taylor. This was Dean's last picture. **(G) Academy Award**—Stevens, best director. **Nominations**—best picture; Dean and Hudson, best actor; McCambridge, best supporting actress; Fred Guiol and Ivan Moffat, best adapted screenplay. *197 minutes*

GIDGET (1959)

★★

Sandra Dee
Cliff Robertson
James Darren

Fluffy teenage comedy/adventure has Dee in the title role, making goo-goo
(Continued)

(Continued)
eyes at a surfer, played by Darren; but mom and dad are skeptical of the romance. Robertson plays a beach bum. This original feature led to several *Gidget* sequels. Also with Doug McClure, Joby Baker, Arthur O'Connell, and Yvonne Craig. **Director**—Paul Wendkos. *95 minutes*

GIGI (1958)

★★★★

Leslie Caron
Louis Jourdan
Maurice Chevalier

Colorful and delightful Lerner and Loewe musical, graced with memorable songs and fine acting. Caron is ideal in the part of a young French girl who becomes a stunning woman and charms a handsome rake, played by Jourdan. The film, however, is best remembered for the performance of Chevalier as Jourdan's uncle; he sings "Thank Heaven for Little Girls." The Oscar-winning costumes and turn-of-the-century Paris settings are wonderful. Costars Hermione Gingold, Jacques Bergerac, Eva Gabor, and John Abbot. Winner of nine Academy Awards. **Director**—Vincente Minnelli. **(G) Academy Awards**—best picture; Minnelli, best director; Alan Jay Lerner, best screenplay based on material from another medium; Joseph Ruttenberg, cinematography. *116 minutes*

GILDA (1946)

★★★½ ®

Rita Hayworth
Glenn Ford
George Macready

A moody drama set in South America, starring Ford as a gambling man involved with the wife of his boss, a casino owner played by Macready. Hayworth, in her most alluring role, portrays the seductive wife. Her provocative rendition of "Put the Blame on Mame" created a controversy at the time because it is performed in the manner of a striptease, though she actually takes off only one glove and her jewelry. The atmosphere, setting, and storyline are typical of most *films noirs,* but the sexual undertones are more overt than usual and slightly perverse, making this Hollywood classic a bit notorious. Also with Steve Geray and Joseph Calleia. **Director**—Charles Vidor. *110 minutes b&w*

GINGER AND FRED (1986)

★★

Marcello Mastroianni
Giulietta Masina

Italian director Federico Fellini gives television a swift kick in the pants with this often irritating satire. The dour message is conveyed through the nostalgic reunion of two former imitators of the Fred Astaire and Ginger Rogers dance team who appear on a grotesque TV variety show. Masina and Mastroianni portray the over-the-hill hoofers with style and skill. Their final dance sequence is marvelous. But most of the film is burdened with tiresome dialogue against a background of Fellini's typically eccentric characters. Originally filmed in Italian. **(PG-13)** *130 minutes*

THE GIRL CAN'T HELP IT (1956)

★★★

Jayne Mansfield
Tom Ewell
Edmond O'Brien

Jayne Mansfield displays her obvious assets in The Girl Can't Help It.

Mansfield stars as the dumb-blonde girlfriend of mobster O'Brien in this entertaining comedy by Frank Tashlin. She is reluctantly promoted for singing stardom by press agent Ewell. There are many sight gags, including comic pokes at Jayne's famous figure, as well as a subtle satire of the entertainment industry. A number of rock 'n' roll stars, including Little Richard, Fats Domino, Eddie Cochran, and Gene Vincent, are featured. Also with Julie London and Ray Anthony. *97 minutes*

GIRL CRAZY (1943)

★★★

Judy Garland
Mickey Rooney

Garland and Rooney belt out some fabulous Gershwin numbers in this romantic musical. Rooney plays a rich young man from the East, who is sent to a remote southwestern school to take his mind off girls. But Garland is there and the fun begins. Other fine talent includes Guy Kibbee, Gil Stratton, Rags Ragland, June Allyson, Nancy Walker, and Tommy Dorsey and his orchestra. **Director**—Norman Taurog. *99 minutes b&w*

GIRLFRIENDS (1978)

★★

Melanie Mayron
Eli Wallach
Bob Balaban
Anita Skinner

Producer/director Claudia Weill's first feature film is an amateurish and overly emotional study of loneliness in the big city. This familiar theme is presented this time from a feminist point of view. The low-budget look of the film allows for authentic-looking locales but has lost its freshness with the passage of time. The material is dated as well. Mayron stars as a young, neurotic photographer who is shaken when her roommate leaves to be married. Also with Christopher Guest and Viveca Lindfors. **(PG)** *86 minutes*

GIRLS JUST WANT TO HAVE FUN (1985)

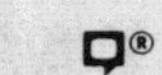

Sarah Jessica Parker
Lee Montgomery

Energetic dance numbers, featuring hundreds of teenagers dressed in funky attire, propel this trendy youth film. Parker plays an attractive youngster who overcomes the objections of her strict father and participates in a TV rock-music dance show. There, she is paired with a handsome partner (Montgomery) and they fall in love. Inspired by the Cyndi Lauper song, the film features production numbers edited in the style of *Flashdance.* The young cast is highly professional, but the storyline is routine and predictable. **Director**—Alan Metter. **(PG)** *87 minutes*

® *This movie available with closed captions for the hearing impaired.*

GIVE MY REGARDS TO BROAD STREET (1984)

★★

Paul McCartney

Tracey Ullman says thanks to Paul McCartney in Give My Regards to Broad Street.

A number of rock songs enliven this loosely structured romp starring McCartney of Beatles fame. The music alone is a treat for Beatles fans, though the flimsy plot—something to do with Paul's search for a missing master recording tape—comes off as excess baggage. A few new songs are introduced along with some reworkings of old tunes. Ringo Starr, Barbara Bach, Bryan Brown, Ralph Richardson, and Linda McCartney add their talents to the frolic. **Director**—Peter Webb. **(PG)** *108 minutes*

GIVE MY REGARDS TO BROADWAY (1948)

Dan Dailey
Charles Winninger

A flimsy musical about a veteran vaudeville hoofer, played by Winninger, trying to make a comeback even though his type of entertainment is on the wane. The creaky plot involves a lot of sentimentality about the love affairs of the vaudevillian's children. A few familiar songs are featured; otherwise it's only routine. Also included in the cast are Fay Bainter, Charles Ruggles, and Nancy Guild. **Director**—Lloyd Bacon. *89 minutes*

GIZMO (1977)

★★★

Harebrained inventions have a field day in this zany and cheerful documentary compiled by *Village Voice* columnist Howard Smith. Film clips show goggles with windshield wipers, an electric fork for turning spaghetti, rickety flying machines that go kerplunk, a commuter airplane that ejects passengers at their destinations, and so on. Perhaps these loony schemes didn't bring fame and fortune to their inventors, but displayed here, they leave us with a laugh or two. **(G)** *77 minutes b&w/color*

THE GLASS MENAGERIE (1950)

Gertrude Lawrence
Jane Wyman
Kirk Douglas
Arthur Kennedy

A sincere film rendition of Tennessee Williams' thoughtful stage play. The drama is about a lonely crippled girl and her strained relationship with her mother, who is an aging southern belle. Both women, as well as the girl's idealistic brother, live in their own fantasy world. There are many touching moments brought out by a top cast. Efficiently directed by Irving Rapper. *107 minutes b&w*

THE GLASS MENAGERIE (1987)

★★★

Joanne Woodward
Karen Allen

Karen Allen and Joanne Woodward are fragile dreamers in The Glass Menagerie.

With careful fidelity, Paul Newman directed this film version of Tennessee Williams' semi-autobiographical play. Woodward stars as the domineering mother who presides over the lives of her family in a dark, dank apartment in St. Louis. Allen portrays the shy, fragile daughter victimized by her mother's possessiveness. Though Newman follows the action of the play closely and the claustrophobic sets recall the confines of a stage setting, the film still works as a piece of cinematic art. The acting is toned down to accomodate the big screen and the cinematography by Michael Ballhaus evokes a haunting atmosphere. An excellent performance by Allen highlights the classic drama. Also with James Naughton and John Malkovich. **(PG)** *135 minutes*

GLEAMING THE CUBE (1989)

★$^{1}/_{2}$

Christian Slater
Steven Bauer

Skateboarding is the main mode of transportation in this ludicrous murder mystery. A California teenager (Slater) plays the whiz on wheels who investigates the murder of his adopted Vietnamese brother. The trail leads to some Vietnamese villains, who are merely two-dimensional, cardboard characters. A few skateboard stunts might perk up the youngsters; otherwise the story is unremarkable. Also with Ed Lauter, Micole Mercurio, and Le Tuan. **Director**—Graeme Clifford. **(PG-13)** *104 minutes*

THE GLENN MILLER STORY (1954)

★★★

James Stewart
June Allyson

A sentimental, romantic film biography of the popular big-band leader of the 1930s and 1940s. Stewart is exceptionally convincing in the title role, and Allyson is fine as Miller's wife. However, it's Miller's fabulous music that really carries the film. Worthwhile if you love the Miller sound; there's plenty of it here. Also with Harry Morgan, Frances Langford, Charles Drake, Louis Armstrong, and Gene Krupa. **Director**—Anthony Mann. **(G)** **Academy Award Nomination**—Valentine Davies and Oscar Brodney, story and screenplay. *116 minutes*

GLORIA (1980)

★★★

Gena Rowlands
John Adames

Rowlands, in the title role, plays a tough-talking ex-gun-moll who is

(Continued)

Gena Rowlands is a resourceful gun moll out to beat the mob in Gloria.

(Continued)
forced to protect an eight-year-old Puerto Rican boy marked for assassination by gangsters, even though she says she doesn't like the kid. Rowlands' performance is credible and appealing as the hard-bitten dame who suddenly discovers her mothering instincts, and director John Cassavetes' screenplay is cheerfully contrived. However, the desperate chase around New York City does eventually become tiresome. Also with Buck Henry and Julie Carmen. **(PG) Academy Award Nomination**—Rowlands, best actress. *123 minutes*

GLORY (1989)

★★★½

Morgan Freeman
Denzel Washington
Matthew Broderick

A glorious tribute to the little-known legions of black soldiers who bravely fought for the Union in the Civil War. The story focuses on the struggle of the 54th Regiment of Massachusetts Volunteer Infantry for recognition as worthy fighting men as well as for their valor under fire. Unlike recent attempts to depict racial issues in South Africa, the story of the white characters does not overpower that of the black characters. Director Edward Zwick, with the script contributions of Freeman and Washington, presents a balanced interpretation of the formation of the 54th Regiment, the first unit of black soldiers. Shot on a small budget, the film depended on the cooperation of Civil War buffs who allowed him to film their battlefield recreations for no compensation. Despite the budgetary constraints, the sweeping battle scenes are both epic in scope and effective in conveying the horror of war. Also with Cary Elwes, Jihmi Kennedy, Andre Braugher, John Finn, Alan North, and Cliff DeYoung. Jane Alexander and Raymond St. Jacques appear in unbilled roles. **(R) Academy Awards**—Washington, best supporting actor; Freddie Francis, cinematography; Donald O. Mitchell, Gregg C. Rudloff, Elliot Tyson, Russell Williams 2nd, sound. **Nominations**—Norman Garwood and Garrett Lewis, art direction; Steven Rosenblum, editing.
122 minutes

THE GO-BETWEEN (1971)

★★★

Alan Bates
Julie Christie
Dominic Guard

A beautiful and moody movie, set in turn-of-the-century England, involving a boy who passes love letters between an aristocratic woman and a farmer. Harold Pinter's screenplay is touching, and the production is mounted handsomely. Christie and Bates play the unlikely lovers with tenderness; Guard plays the boy. A most unusual and richly rewarding film. The cast also includes Michael Redgrave, Michael Gough, Margaret Leighton, and Edward Fox. **Director**—Joseph Losey. **(PG) Academy Award Nomination**—Leighton, best supporting actress.
116 minutes

THE GODDESS (1958)

★★★★

Kim Stanley
Lloyd Bridges

Kim Stanley and Lloyd Bridges meet the press in The Goddess.

Stanley is exceptionally appealing as a beauty from a small town who seeks fame as a Hollywood sex symbol, but finds heartache instead. Paddy Chayefsky's biting and intelligent script is partially based on the career of Marilyn Monroe. Parts of the film are slightly overwrought, but it's held together by Stanley's brilliant portrayal and fine performances by the rest of the cast. Also with Steven Hill and Betty Lou Holland. **Director**—John Cromwell. **Academy Award Nomination**—Chayefsky, best story and screenplay written directly for the screen.
105 minutes b&w

THE GODFATHER (1972)

★★★★

Marlon Brando
Al Pacino
Robert Duvall
James Caan

The Godfather, *Marlon Brando, confers with his son, Al Pacino.*

A brilliant and exciting epic crime drama, masterfully fashioned by director Francis Coppola from Mario Puzo's best-selling novel. The engrossing plot follows the career of a Mafia leader and the struggle for power between his family and rival family organizations. The drama, suspense, and character development are of the highest order. The film is more than just a compelling gangster saga; it's also a fascinating study of the struggle for achievement and success in America. Exceptional performances by Brando, Pacino, Duvall, Caan, John Cazale, Richard Castellano, and Diane Keaton. **(R) Academy Awards**—best picture; Brando, best actor; Puzo and Coppola, best screenplay based on material from another medium. **Nominations**—Coppola, best director; Caan, Duvall, and Pacino, best supporting actor.
175 minutes

® *This movie available with closed captions for the hearing impaired.*

THE GODFATHER, PART II
(1974)

★★★★

Al Pacino
Robert Duvall
Diane Keaton
Robert De Niro
John Cazale

Al Pacino tastes the bitter fruit of power in The Godfather, Part II.

A worthy sequel to the first film. This continuation of the epic saga fills in the early life of family patriarch Don Corleone and then picks up the story after his death, with young Michael (Pacino) taking control and expanding the crime empire. Engrossing scenes and sensational acting abound. Pacino is excellent, and De Niro, underplaying his part, is outstanding as young Don Vito, establishing his family and power at the turn of the century. Duvall, Keaton, Cazale, Talia Shire, Lee Strasberg, and Michael Gazzo are terrific in supporting roles. **Director**—Francis Coppola. **(R) Academy Awards**—best picture; Coppola, best director; De Niro, best supporting actor; Coppola and Mario Puzo, best screenplay adapted from other material. **Nominations**—Pacino, best actor; Gazzo and Strasberg, best supporting actor; Shire, best supporting actress. *200 minutes*

GOD IS MY CO-PILOT (1945)

★★★

Dennis Morgan
Dane Clark
Raymond Massey

A better-than-average air-combat film about the Flying Tigers, the famed air squadron that fought in the Pacific during World War II. There are some predictable moments, but the action scenes are well done. Also with Alan Hale, Andrea King, Donald Woods, John Ridgely, and Stanley Ridges. **Director**—Robert Florey. *89 minutes b&w*

GOD'S LITTLE ACRE (1958)

★★

Robert Ryan
Aldo Ray
Tina Louise
Buddy Hackett

This watered-down version of Erskine Caldwell's novel, has some good acting and characterizations. Ryan is effective as the patriarch of a family of poor Georgia farmers. He brings even more misery to the family in his desperate and unproductive search for gold on his land. Louise is fetching and convincing as a cheating wife. Also with Jack Lord, Fay Spain, and Vic Morrow. **Director**—Anthony Mann. **(PG)** *110 minutes b&w*

THE GODS MUST BE CRAZY
(1984)

★★1/2

Marius Weyers
Sandra Prinsloo

A wobbly farce, set in Botswana, Africa, that contrasts the uncomplicated life of nomadic tribesmen with the frenzied existence of modern urban dwellers. The film is on solid ground as long as it concentrates on the affairs of the Bushmen in the Kalahari Desert. Enter "civilized" people, and the story turns to tiresome slapstick. **Director**—Jamie Uys. **(PG)** *109 minutes*

THE GODS MUST BE CRAZY II
(1990)

★★

N!xau
Lena Farugia
Hans Strydom

The continued adventures of good-natured N!xau finds the African bushman searching for his lost children, which brings him in touch with peculiar "civilized" white people. Jamie Uys, the South African filmmaker who directed the original, fashions a weak sequel that patronizes N!xau and native Africans as gentle, spritely beings who are content to commune with nature. After insulting native tribesmen, Uys proceeds to insult women by introducing a female character (Farugia) who shrieks, darts about, and is constantly shown with her dress pulled over her head. Strydom costars as her male counterpart, who turns into a "Crocodile Dundee" figure by the end. Uys' idea of comedy is to shoot his slapstick gags in fast motion—an outdated device that becomes tedious quite quickly. Fans of the first film may enjoy this sequel; others will want to be more selective. **(PG)** *98 minutes*

GODSPELL (1973)

★★

Victor Garber
David Haskell
Jerry Sroka

The life of Jesus is here staged as a rock musical in contemporary New York. Though performed with much pep and enthusiasm, the film lacks a compelling narrative. A band of hippie disciples follow their leader to the beat of numerous musical numbers, composed by Stephen Schwartz. The young cast sings and dances well, but the production overall is hollow. Also with Robin Lamont and Lynne Thigpen. **Director**—David Greene. **(G)** *102 minutes*

GODZILLA 1985 (1985)

★★

Raymond Burr

After a decade-long vacation, that humongous monster is astir again, and menacing Tokyo once more. However, this updated, Japanese production seems too colorful and slick to sustain the campy effect of the black-and-white versions. Nevertheless, when the giant lizard is on, the film perks up. Not even flat acting and ridiculous dialogue can stop the lumbering creature from munching power plants and knocking over skyscrapers. Burr reprises his role as reporter Steve Martin from the 1956 version of the film. Keiju Kobayashi and Ken Tanaka are also in the cast. **Directors**—Koji Hashimoto and R.J. Kizer. **(PG)** *91 minutes*

GODZILLA VS. MEGALON
(1976)

★★

Katsuhiko Sasaki
Hiroyuki Kawase

This imaginative, comic-book film from Japan has the good monster Godzilla

(Continued)

(Continued)
defending Tokyo from the ravages of similar prehistoric monsters. The film's storyline is appealing, the technical effects are superb, and the violence is low-key. Lots of fun for the kiddies, and for adults who know not to take it seriously. Also with Yutaka Hayashi and Robert Dunham. **Director**—Jun Fukuda. **(G)** *80 minutes*

GO FOR BROKE! (1951)

 ★★★

Van Johnson
Lane Nakano
George Miki

Johnson plays the commander of Nisei troops—Americans of Japanese ancestry—fighting in Europe during World War II. Good acting and interesting characterizations highlight this unusual war movie. Also with Akira Fukunaga, Warner Anderson, and Gianna Canale. **Director**—Robert Pirosh. **Academy Award Nomination**—Pirosh, story and screenplay. *93 minutes b&w*

GOING BERSERK (1983)

 ★

John Candy

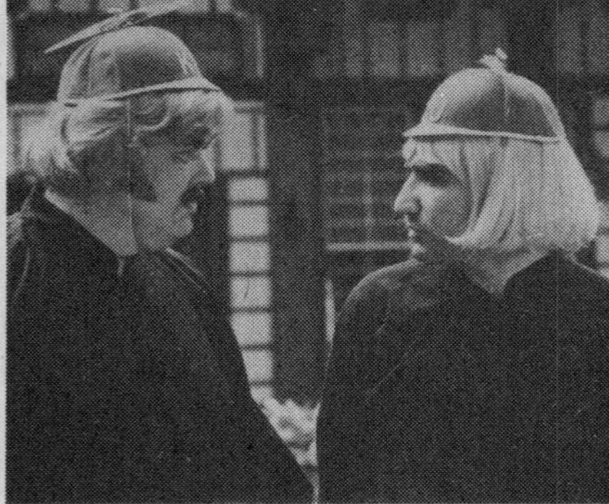

School daze with John Candy and Eugene Levy in Going Berserk.

Candy, Joe Flaherty, and Eugene Levy rib religious cults, politics, and fad exercise regimens. The corpulent Candy manages to put over a few gags as a limo driver who is convinced he must assassinate his future father-in-law. Yet most of the situations are merely blasé, not berserk. Director David Steinberg is a lot funnier in front of the camera than behind it. Another tame comedy from some highly talented SCTV graduates who haven't all reached their potential on film yet. **(R)** *85 minutes*

GOING IN STYLE (1979)

★★

George Burns
Art Carney
Lee Strasberg

George Burns, Art Carney, and Lee Strasberg: clever codgers in Going In Style.

Three senior citizens, frustrated with idleness and the limits of Social Security, plan and execute a bank robbery. Burns, Carney, and Strasberg play the aged robbers. The film comments on the problems of the aging, and the three old pros turn in appealing performances, but limp direction by Martin Brest makes the movie itself appear caught in the aging process. More drama and more comic energy are badly needed. Also with Charles Hallahan and Pamela Payton-Wright. **(PG)** *96 minutes*

GOING MY WAY (1944)

 ★★★★

Bing Crosby
Barry Fitzgerald

Crosby is perfectly cast in this sentimental comedy as a young priest in a New York slum parish. Fitzgerald had the role of his career as the elderly pastor who is finally charmed by the personable newcomer after Crosby teaches a gang of street kids responsibility and respect. Crosby, perhaps at the top of his film career, sings "Swinging on a Star" and "Too-ra-Loo-ra-Loo-ra." Interestingly, Fitzgerald was nominated for Oscars in both the best actor and best supporting actor categories, and won the award as best supporting actor. Afterward, the Academy changed its rules so that this could not occur again. Good supporting work is provided by Frank McHugh, Gene Lockhart, and Porter Hall. **Director**—Leo McCarey. **Academy Awards**—best picture; McCarey, best director; Crosby, best actor; Fitzgerald, best supporting actor; McCarey, original story. **Nominations**—Fitzgerald, best actor; Lionel Lincoln, cinematography. *126 minutes b&w*

GOIN' SOUTH (1978)

 ★★

Jack Nicholson
Mary Steenburgen

A thin, uneven comedy/western with Nicholson in the saddle as a scruffy outlaw who escapes the gallows by marrying a prim spinster, played by Steenburgen in her screen debut. Nicholson, who also directed, hams it up, wasting his remarkable talent on hokey material. The film begins with promise, but never gets going. John Belushi, Christopher Lloyd, and Veronica Cartwright also star. **(PG)** *109 minutes*

THE GOLDEN CHILD (1986)

 ★★ ®

Eddie Murphy
Charlotte Lewis
Randall "Tex" Cobb

Charlotte Lewis and Eddie Murphy paddling in Tibet in The Golden Child.

Murphy stars in this wobbly hybrid of *Beverly Hills Cop* and *Indiana Jones and the Temple of Doom* as a Los Angeles investigator who searches for missing children. He is coerced by a beautiful Tibetan woman (Lewis) into tracking down the missing "Golden Child," who is part of her mystical Eastern religion. The child has special powers that can bring either peace or destruction to the world. The film suffers from too many special effects and colorful Eastern locales and sets, which distract from Murphy's street-smart humor. Eventually the overblown production and many chase sequences become tedious. The film was a financial success despite its shortcomings, attesting to Murphy's

® *This movie available with closed captions for the hearing impaired.*

overwhelming popularity. **Director**—Michael Ritchie. **(PG–13)** *92 minutes*

THE GOLDEN SEAL (1983)

★★

Steve Railsback

Slow-paced, sentimental boy-and-his-seal movie, set on a remote Aleutian island. Puppies or black stallions are not to be found in this outpost, so young Eric (Torquil Campbell) befriends a legendary golden seal that he protects from sinister adults who want to kill it. Predictably, the youngster learns about nature and the realities of the adult world. The outdoor photography is striking, and the animals often upstage the human performers. **Director**—Frank Zuniga. **(PG)** *95 minutes*

THE GOLDEN VOYAGE OF SINBAD (1974)

★★★

John Phillip Law
Caroline Monroe

Lively reworking of the Sinbad story, with the adventurer dueling with a magician. The fantasy progresses in grand style, and it's beautifully enhanced by Ray Harryhausen's magnificent trick photography, which brings to life the figurehead of a ship and other inanimate objects. Also with Tom Baker, Douglas Wilmer, and John Garfield, Jr. **Director**—Gordon Hessler. **(G)** *105 minutes*

GOLDFINGER (1964)

★★★★

Sean Connery
Honor Blackman
Gert Frobe

Among the best of the James Bond adventures, with agent 007, played by Connery, stopping a sinister gold smuggler from plundering Fort Knox. Frobe plays the title role. The slick production brims with the expected spread of gadgetry, beautiful women, menacing villains, and lots of tongue-in-cheek humor. The indestructible Bond ties it up smartly in a spectacular climax. Harold (Oddjob) Sakata, Bernard Lee, Shirley Eaton, and Lois Maxwell join in the fun. The film won an Academy Award for its sound effects. **Director**—Guy Hamilton. **(PG)** *112 minutes*

GONE WITH THE WIND (1939)

★★★★

Clark Gable
Vivien Leigh
Olivia de Havilland
Leslie Howard

Clark Gable consoles Vivien Leigh in Gone With the Wind.

This stirring romantic spectacle is among the best and most memorable of all Hollywood productions. Based on Margaret Mitchell's compelling novel of the South during the Civil War, the epic tells the story of an aristocratic plantation family and its involvement with the war. Leigh is magnificent as Scarlett O'Hara, the spoiled beauty, and Gable is at his best as the dashing Rhett Butler. Many other sterling performances abound. Producer David O. Selznick provided film audiences with one of the greatest examples of storytelling ever to be made on film. This masterpiece, which won eight Academy Awards out of 13 nominations, will be with us forever. Also with Thomas Mitchell, Barbara O'Neil, Hattie McDaniel, Butterfly McQueen, Ward Bond, Evelyn Keyes, Laura Hope Crewes, Jane Darwell, George Reeves, Victory Jory, and Ona Munson. **Director**—Victor Fleming. **(G)** **Academy Awards**—best picture; Fleming, best director; Leigh, best actress; McDaniel, best supporting actress; Sidney Howard, screenplay; Ernest Haller and Ray Rennahan, cinematography. **Nominations**—Gable, best actor; de Havilland, best supporting actress. *231 minutes*

GOODBYE, COLUMBUS (1969)

★★★

Richard Benjamin
Ali MacGraw

An on-target screen version of Philip Roth's insightful look at a status-seeking Jewish family in suburban New York. The biting drama centers on a young librarian from the Bronx who falls for a spoiled college girl from a *nouveau riche* family. Benjamin is superb in his film debut as the librarian, and MacGraw is excellent as the snobbish young woman with whom he becomes disillusioned. An opulent wedding sequence—for the girl's brother—is a gem. First-class supporting performances from Jack Klugman, Nan Martin, Michael Meyers, and Lori Shelle. **Director**—Larry Peerce. **(PG) Academy Award Nomination**—Arnold Schulman, best screenplay based on material from another medium. *105 minutes*

THE GOODBYE GIRL (1977)

★★★

Richard Dreyfuss
Marsha Mason
Quinn Cummings

Neil Simon's romantic comedy focuses on an over-the-hill dancer and a struggling actor who share a New York apartment. This wrinkle in the odd-couple theme is loaded with cornball wisecracks and verbal sparring. To no one's surprise, the boy, played by Dreyfuss, finally gets the girl, played by Mason. **Director**—Herbert Ross. **(PG)** **Academy Award**—Dreyfuss, best actor. **Nominations**—best picture; Mason, best actress; Cummings, best supporting actress; Simon, best screenplay written directly for the screen. *110 minutes*

GOODBYE, MR. CHIPS (1939)

★★★★

Robert Donat
Greer Garson

Donat is perfectly cast in this story, based upon the James Hilton novel, about a shy English schoolmaster. Some critics feel the film has aged; though it might be a bit slow-moving, the solid production values prevail. Garson gives a skilled performance as the only person who gets the schoolmaster to overcome his shyness. There is good support from Paul Henreid (billed here as Paul von Hernreid), Judith Furse, Austin Trevor, John Mills, and Terry Kilburn. **Director**—Sam Wood. **Academy Award**—Donat, best actor. **Nominations**—best picture; Wood, best director; Garson, best actress; Eric Maschwitz, R.C. Sheriff, and Claudine West, screenplay. *114 minutes b&w*

GOODBYE, NEW YORK (1985)

 ★

Julie Hagerty
David Topaz

Awkward, amateurish Israeli production that leans heavily on Goldie Hawn's *Private Benjamin* character. The film is badly acted and fraught with failed humor. Hagerty plays a frustrated urban New York career woman. She travels to Israel where she becomes involved in numerous comic misadventures—some satiric, some slapstick, but none genuinely amusing. Writer/director/costar Amos Kollek (the son of Jerusalem's mayor at the time the film was shot) demonstrates an appallingly crude style of moviemaking. **(R)**
90 minutes

THE GOOD EARTH (1937)

★★★

Paul Muni
Luise Rainer

Paul Muni and Luise Rainer eke out a living in The Good Earth.

A prestigious production of the Pearl Buck novel set in Hollywood's China. The film contains beautiful performances by Muni and Rainer as the peasant farm couple who battle the elements to survive, only to be defeated by Muni's greed for money. A visually splendid film with breathtaking photography and some extraordinary technical effects, including the locust invasion. The film, however, suffers under its own weight and becomes tedious as it progresses. Still worthwhile for the acting and visual beauty. The good supporting cast includes Walter Connolly, Tilly Losch, Jessie Ralph, Charley Grapewin, Keye Luke, and Harold Huber. Some prints are in sepia. **Director**—Sidney Franklin. **Academy Awards**—Rainer, best actress; Karl Freund, cinematography. **Nominations**—best picture; Franklin, best director. *138 minutes b&w*

GOOD GUYS WEAR BLACK (1978)

 ★

Chuck Norris

A dull martial-arts adventure based on commando operations in Vietnam. Karate champ Norris handles most of the heavy action, but he really doesn't get warmed up until the film is more than half over. The scripting and character development are at low levels. Anne Archer, James Franciscus, Jim Backus, and Dana Andrews, veteran of many crime dramas of the 1940s and 1950s, are also in the cast. **Director**—Ted Post. **(PG)** *96 minutes*

GOOD MORNING, BABYLON (1987)

 ★★½

Vincent Spano
Joaquim de Almeida
Greta Scacchi

A lavish account of two Italian stonecutters who become set builders for legendary director D.W. Griffith during Hollywood's silent era. The film is visually stunning, featuring moments of lyrical beauty as well as some impressive scenes depicting the monumental sets for Griffith's masterpiece *Intolerance.* However, this offbeat drama represents Paolo and Vittorio Taviani's first English-language film, and sometimes the dialogue is awkward and unconvincing. Charles Dance plays the enigmatic Griffith. Also with Desiree Becker. **(PG–13)** *115 minutes*

GOOD MORNING, VIETNAM (1987)

 ★★★ 

Robin Williams
Forest Whitaker
Bruno Kirby

Williams lets loose in a role tailored to suit his manic talent. Based on the true story of Adrian Cronauer, this film biography follows the story of an iconoclastic Armed Forces disc jockey broadcasting from Saigon in 1965. Cronauer's antimilitary humor, his playlist of hot rock 'n' roll records, and his attempts to transmit uncensored news repeatedly get him in trouble with the military brass. While on the air, the character is a rush of energy, and William's stand-up humor and fast-paced delivery are perfect in that capacity. However, the film's weakness is the depiction of the Cronauer character off the air as a sensitive and gentle soul. It is simply too contradictory to his on-air persona. An excellent supporting cast includes Whitaker as Cronauer's best ally, J.T. Walsh, Noble Willingham, and Robert Wuhl. **Director**—Barry Levinson. **(R) Academy Award Nomination**—Williams, best actor.
120 minutes

Irreverent deejay Robin Williams greets the troops in Good Morning, Vietnam.

THE GOOD MOTHER (1988)

 ★★ ®

Diane Keaton
Liam Neeson
James Naughton

Asia Vieira with Diane Keaton in The Good Mother.

Unsatisfying version of Sue Miller's controversial novel, with Keaton star-

® *This movie available with closed captions for the hearing impaired.*

ring in the title role. A single mother has an affair with a bohemian artist (Neeson), and her ex-husband (Naughton) seizes upon this sexual activity to bring a child-custody suit. The drama is stripped of emotion under Leonard Nimoy's unsure direction. A final courtroom sequence is almost clinical in approach. Also with Jason Robards, Ralph Bellamy, Teresa Wright, Joe Morton, and Katey Sagal. **(R)**
104 minutes

GOOD NEIGHBOR SAM (1964)

Jack Lemmon

Lemmon stars in this drawn-out comedy as an advertising man pretending to be the husband of a gorgeous divorcée living next door. Romy Schneider plays the divorcée. Good comic opportunities are frittered away by an unworkable script and gags that seem repetitious. Lemmon has some funny moments, but there's not enough substance to develop a satisfying film. Edward G. Robinson appears in a cameo role. Also with Mike Connors, Edward Andrews, Dorothy Provine, Louis Nye, and Joyce Jameson. **Director**—David Swift. *130 minutes*

GOOD NEWS (1947)

June Allyson
Peter Lawford

A lively, toe-tapping college musical, based on the popular Broadway hit of the 1930s, with a professional cast giving it their best shot. The minor plot concerns a football game intermingled with various campus romances. But the music is the highlight of the film, and there are plenty of snappy tunes, such as "Varsity Drag" and "The French Lesson." Allyson is fantastic at belting out the numbers. Also with Patricia Marshall, Joan McCracken, and Mel Torme. **Director**—Charles Walters.
95 minutes

THE GOOD, THE BAD, AND THE UGLY (1966)

Clint Eastwood

A brutal and violent but oddly compelling story about the search by three gunmen for stolen loot belonging to the Confederate government during the U.S. Civil War. This is the third in a trilogy of Italian westerns directed by Sergio Leone starring Eastwood as the Man with No Name. The series made Eastwood a star and greatly influenced the conventions of the western genre. Director Leone's exaggerated dramatic style is just right for the material. Eli Wallach and Lee Van Cleef round out the cast. *161 minutes*

THE GOOD WIFE (1987)

Rachel Ward
Bryan Brown
Sam Neill

A repressed housewife (Ward) living in the harsh and lonely Australian countryside of the 1930s seeks sexual release not only with her husband, but also with her loutish brother-in-law and the dashing new bartender in the nearby town. Though the acting, character development, and period detail are consistently good, this solemn account of the young woman's obsessions is never emotionally satisfying. **Director**—Ken Cameron. **(R)** *97 minutes*

THE GOONIES (1985)

Sean Astin
Josh Brolin
Jeff Cohen

Steven Spielberg's inspired, tumble-bumble children's adventure resembles a thrilling but toned-down variation of *Indiana Jones and the Temple of Doom.* Some spirited urchins search for a pirate's treasure in a spooky, obstacle-strewn cavern. Babbling dialogue and some sentimental teenage romance are occasionally annoying. But there are oodles of kid-pleasing special effects and zany characters to maintain the fun. Also with Kerri Green, Joe Pantoliano, Martha Plimpton, Ke Huy-Quan, and Corey Feldman. **Director**—Richard Donner. **(PG)** *111 minutes*

GORILLAS IN THE MIST (1988)

★★★1/2

Sigourney Weaver

American-born naturalist Dian Fossey spent some 20 years in central Africa studying and protecting endangered mountain gorillas. This moving drama

Sigourney Weaver with a friendly gorilla in Gorillas in the Mist.

is a magnificent tribute to the dedication and courage of this obsessed and heroic woman. Weaver is sensational as Fossey; her scenes with the gentle primates are vivid and touching. Bryan Brown costars as Fossey's sometime lover, but the vulnerable apes (some designed by makeup whiz Rick Baker) are the real stars. **Director**—Michael Apted. **(PG-13) Academy Award Nominations**—Weaver, best actress; Anna Hamilton Phelan and Tab Murphy, best screenplay adaptation. *129 minutes*

GORKY PARK (1983)

William Hurt
Lee Marvin

Joanna Pacula and William Hurt investigate gruesome murders in Gorky Park.

Hurt plays a world-weary Russian police detective trying to unravel a complex triple murder, while tangling with

(Continued)

(Continued)
cynical American businessman Marvin. The film captures most of the intricate plot and characters of Martin Cruz Smith's best-seller, but little of the texture of Soviet daily life that made the book so fascinating. Still, it's an effective thriller, set against the bleak, cold backdrop of a Moscow (actually Helsinki) winter. Brian Dennehy and Joanna Pacula costar. **Director**—Michael Apted. **(R)** *128 minutes*

GOSPEL ACCORDING TO VIC (1986)

★★

Tom Conti
Helen Mirren

Conti stars in this whimsical Scottish comedy about a nonreligious man who teaches at the Blessed Edith Semple school. When he survives a rooftop fall without injury, he finds himself in the ironic position of being the beneficiary of a miraculous act. School officials attempt to use this "miracle" to elevate the school's namesake, Edith Semple, to sainthood, much to Conti's chagrin. This low-key film is quietly charming, with Conti giving an uncharacteristically restrained performance. **Director**—Charles Gormley. **(PG–13)** *92 minutes*

GOTCHA! (1985)

★★

Anthony Edwards
Linda Fiorentino

A college student (Edwards) vacations in Europe, where he gets tangled in an espionage plot involving Russian agents and CIA operatives. This teenage comedy version of a Hitchcock spy thriller has intriguing moments, but primarily it is pretentious and silly. The title refers to a campus game where players hunt one another with paint-pellet guns. This fantasy pastime is soon translated into real guns and bullets. Costars Nick Corri. **Director**—Jeff Kanew. **(PG-13)** *97 minutes*

GO TELL THE SPARTANS (1978)

★★

Burt Lancaster

Lancaster plays an Army major who commands a detachment of military advisors, futilely defending an outpost in South Vietnam. Lancaster and the novice supporting cast make an earnest effort, but the story seems incompatible with postwar moods. Overall, the movie plods along under the burden of heavy-handed symbolism and irony. Also with Craig Wasson, Marc Singer, Jonathan Goldsmith, and Joe Unger. **Director**—Ted Post. **(R)** *114 minutes*

GOTHIC (1987)

★

Gabriel Byrne
Julian Sands
Natasha Richardson

Lord Byron, Percy Bysshe Shelley, Mary Godwin Shelley, and other literary luminaries gather at a Geneva villa one night in 1816 to engage in eerie seances, orgies galore, and mind-blowing hallucinations. Director Ken Russell, renowned for his baroque biographies of famous artists *(Lisztomania; Valentino)* and subject matter that is provocative and shocking *(Crimes of Passion)*, dominates the film with garish and surreal images. Unfortunately, Russell once again goes beyond the tastes of mainstream audiences, wallowing in his own excesses. Richardson, daughter of actress Vanessa Redgrave and director Tony Richardson, appears in her first major screen role. **(R)** *90 minutes*

GO WEST (1940)

★★

The Marx Brothers

Groucho, Harpo, and Chico hit the trail and take on the villains out West. A rather uneven comedy most of the way through until the smashing finale. Then it's the Marx Brothers in all their glory as they disassemble a moving train. It's certainly worth the trip. John Carroll, Diana Lewis, and Robert Barrat costar. **Director**—Edward Buzzell. *82 minutes b&w*

GRACE QUIGLEY (1984)

★

Katharine Hepburn
Nick Nolte

Ill-conceived black comedy starring Hepburn in the title role as an enterprising elderly woman. She teams up with a dim-witted hit man (Nolte) to kill off old people who no longer want to live. This peculiar, abrasive farce tries to make a social statement on the plight of some elderly folks who suffer from loneliness and neglect. But here the subject is neither enlightening nor funny. Despite such drawbacks, Hepburn performs with her expected charm and authority. Some video versions run 102 minutes. **Director**—Anthony Harvey. **(PG)** *87 minutes*

THE GRADUATE (1967)

★★★★

Anne Bancroft
Dustin Hoffman
Katharine Ross

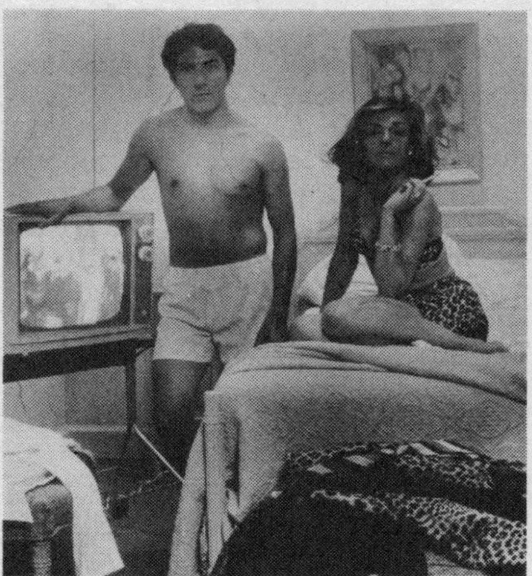

Dustin Hoffman has a chilly affair with Anne Bancroft in The Graduate.

A milestone masterpiece about a young college graduate who has an affair with the wife of his father's partner. Underneath it all, the story intelligently reveals the youth's inner feelings—that his success in college was primarily for the benefit of his wealthy, status-seeking parents. Despite his illicit affair, he attempts to establish his own set of values. The film entertains on many levels, with great moments of charm, humor, suspense, and drama. Hoffman began a brilliant acting career with this role as the young graduate. Bancroft plays the seductive older woman; Ross plays her daughter, with whom Hoffman falls in love. Also with Murray Hamilton and William Daniels. Mike Nichols' direction is a triumph. **(PG)** **Academy Award**—Nichols, best director. **Nominations**—best picture; Hoffman, best actor; Bancroft, best actress; Ross, best supporting actress; Calder Willingham and Buck Henry, best screenplay based on material from another medium; Robert Surtees, cinematography. *105 minutes*

® This movie available with closed captions for the hearing impaired.

GRAND ILLUSION (1937)

★★★★

Erich von Stroheim
Pierre Fresnay
Jean Gabin

Brilliant acting, an intelligent script, and superior direction create a masterpiece of filmmaking. The story is about a group of French prisoners during World War I and the German commandant who shapes their destiny. Director Jean Renoir, one of France's most influential filmmakers, focuses on the bonds that bring men together, particularly those bonds of class. Von Stroheim and Fresnay are excellent in their roles as members of the aristocracy who are on opposing sides of the war but drawn together by their social status. Gabin plays a working-class mechanic and Marcel Dalio plays a Jew; they are two of the handful to survive the experience, emphasizing Renoir's point that the aristocracy is a doomed class. Originally filmed in French, with German and English actors speaking in their own languages. **Academy Award Nomination**—best picture.

111 minutes b&w

GRANDVIEW, U.S.A. (1984)

★★

Jamie Lee Curtis
C. Thomas Howell

Small-town life with Jamie Lee Curtis and C. Thomas Howell in Grandview, U.S.A.

Innocuous piece of Americana, overpopulated with uninteresting characters trying to sort out personal problems in a backwater midwestern town. Curtis is a tomboyish woman who operates a demolition-derby racetrack. Howell plays a high-school senior who dreams of being a marine biologist. And Patrick Swayze portrays a frantic construction worker with a floozy wife, who is fooling around with a dishwasher salesman (Troy Donahue). Call it "bland view of the U.S.A." **Director**—Randal Kleiser. **(R)**

98 minutes

THE GRAPES OF WRATH (1940)

★★★★

Henry Fonda
Jane Darwell
John Carradine

A magnificent film, based on John Steinbeck's moving account of poor Oklahoma farmers migrating from the Dust Bowl to California during the Depression to reestablish their lives. The film, which brims with unforgettable moments of drama and poignant characterizations, reveals considerable compassion for poor, honest people struggling for dignity against seemingly insurmountable odds. Also with Charley Grapewin, Dorris Bowdon, and Russell Simpson. **Director**—John Ford. **Academy Awards**—Ford, best director; Darwell, best supporting actress. **Nominations**—best picture; Fonda, best actor; Nunnally Johnson, screenplay.

128 minutes b&w

THE GRASS IS GREENER (1960)

★★★

Cary Grant
Deborah Kerr
Robert Mitchum

Stylish comedy of manners with an air of slow-paced staginess about it, yet enlivened by good performances. Grant and Kerr play a noble English couple. Their marriage is upset when an American millionaire, played by Mitchum, enters the picture. Based on a play by Hugh and Margaret Williams. Also with Jean Simmons and Moray Watson. **Director**—Stanley Donen.

105 minutes

GRAY LADY DOWN (1978)

★★

Charlton Heston
David Carradine
Stacy Keach

What happens when an American nuclear sub is rammed by a freighter and sinks off the coast of Connecticut? The U.S. Navy comes to the official rescue with all sorts of wonderful gadgets, stiff upper lips, and disaster-movie clichés. Heston, who has seen better days riding chariots, plays the fearless sub skipper; Keach is one of his officers. Carradine plays a nonconformist officer and a designer of a diving craft who saves the day just before the sub's oxygen supply—and the audience's patience—wears out. Also with Ned Beatty and Ronny Cox. **Director**—David Greene. **(PG)** *111 minutes*

GREASE (1978)

★★★

John Travolta
Olivia Newton-John
Stockard Channing

A zesty musical based on the long-running Broadway hit show about a 1950s high-school class. Travolta and Newton-John star as the sentimental teenage sweethearts. Both do well in terms of dancing, singing, and acting. The excellent musical numbers are well staged and high-spirited. The talented supporting cast does an impressive job. Channing, as the tough girl with a heart of gold, steals a few scenes. Also with Jeff Conaway, Didi Conn, Eve Arden, and Sid Caesar. **Director**—Randal Kleiser. **(PG)** *110 minutes*

GREASE 2 (1982)

★★

Maxwell Caulfield
Michelle Pfeiffer

Maxwell Caulfield and Michelle Pfeiffer are a cute—but stale—couple in Grease 2.

Aside from some buoyant song-and-dance numbers, this sequel to one of Hollywood's most successful musicals drags and sags. The trite script and

(Continued)

(Continued)
foolish dialogue might have been conceived with less than half a mind, and Caulfield and Pfeiffer hardly fill the leather outfits of John Travolta and Olivia Newton-John. This time the story reverses the original roles, with Caulfield as the clean-cut student at Rydell High trying to win the attention of tough, foxy Pfeiffer. Directed by Patricia Birch, who did the choreography in the first film. **(PG)** *115 minutes*

GREASED LIGHTNING (1977)

★★★

Richard Pryor
Beau Bridges

Pryor gives a cool and subtle performance in this action-filled biography of Wendell Scott, the first black stock-car racing champion. The zesty pace is captured nicely by director Michael Schultz. Bridges contributes effective support as a local driver who joins Scott's crew. The film might have been better with more emphasis on character; however, it's still good entertainment with a significant social message. Also with Pam Grier, Cleavon Little, and Vincent Gardenia. **(PG)**
94 minutes

GREAT BALLS OF FIRE (1989)

★★★ CC

Dennis Quaid
Winona Ryder

Dennis Quaid stars as legendary rock-'n'-roller Jerry Lee Lewis in Great Balls of Fire.

Director Jim McBride fashions an interesting statement on American rock 'n' roll culture via the controversial career of the legendary rockabilly singer Jerry Lee Lewis. Unfairly criticized at the time of release for not being faithful to Lewis' real life, the film was not intended as a straightforward biography. Instead Lewis serves as a metaphor for the vitality of American culture, particularly the notorious nature of rock 'n' roll and the American predilection for walking on the wild side. To this end, Quaid emphasizes Lewis' egocentric mannerisms, and he attacks both the role and the music with gusto. "The Killer" himself provides the vocals. The film is seen through the eyes of Lewis' child bride, Myra, who is played by Ryder. The viewer identifies with Myra: We are attracted to how far Lewis will go but we are afraid to take the ride with him. Alec Baldwin costars as Lewis' evangelist cousin, Jimmy Swaggart; Trey Wilson plays the legendary Sam Phillips; and Michael St. Gerard, who starred as Elvis Presley in the short-lived television series *Elvis,* plays the King of Rock 'n' Roll. **(PG-13)**
102 minutes

THE GREAT BANK HOAX (1978)

★

Richard Basehart
Burgess Meredith
Ned Beatty

Bumbling bank officers in a small town try to cover up an embezzlement by staging a robbery. It's supposed to be comedy, but you'll probably find more laughs in a life insurance policy. Basehart, Beatty, and Meredith play stereotyped characters who come close to the style of the Three Stooges. Such antics may have gone over in the early days of filmmaking; now, it's just so much silliness. Also with Paul Sand and Michael Murphy. **Director**—Joseph Jacoby. **(PG)** **Alternate Title**—*Shenanigans.*
89 minutes

THE GREAT CARUSO (1951)

★★★

Mario Lanza
Ann Blyth

Lanza plays the famous Italian tenor in this handsome but slightly embellished film biography. The production lacks sufficient drama, and the dialogue is somewhat stiff; yet the settings are colorful, and Lanza sings a wide variety of opera numbers. He's not as great as Caruso, but he does an adequate job. Also with Dorothy Kirsten, Jarmilia Novotna, and Carl Benton Reid. **Director**—Richard Thorpe. **(G)**
109 minutes

THE GREAT DICTATOR (1940)

★★★

Charles Chaplin
Paulette Goddard
Jack Oakie

Effective spoof of Adolf Hitler with Chaplin in a dual role; he plays a Jewish barber as well as Adenoid Hynkel, the dictator of Tomania. Oakie is also outstanding as Benzino Napaloni, the ruler of the rival country of Bacteria. Chaplin's unique satire focuses on humanity by way of his familiar slapstick routine. Chaplin's first full talking feature. Also with Reginald Gardiner, Henry Daniell, Billy Gilbert, and Maurice Moscovich. **Director**—Chaplin. **(G)** **Academy Award Nominations**—best picture; Chaplin, best actor and original screenplay; Oakie, best supporting actor. *129 minutes b&w*

THE GREAT ESCAPE (1963)

★★★★ CC

James Garner
Steve McQueen
Richard Attenborough
James Donald
Charles Bronson

Slam-bang action adventure, about Allied prisoners attempting to bust out of a German POW camp during World War II. The film is based on a true story. A top cast keeps the excitement building despite the film's length. There's an especially daring sequence with McQueen on a motorcycle, trying to reach freedom. The film was nominated for an Academy Award for its excellent editing. Also with Donald Pleasence, Gordon Jackson, James Coburn, and David McCallum. **Director**—John Sturges. **(PG)** *168 minutes*

THE GREATEST (1977)

★★★

Muhammad Ali
Ernest Borgnine
Robert Duvall

Boxing great Ali plays himself as no one else could in this charming movie biography, which recounts his life story from his beginnings as Cassius Clay of Louisville to the high point of his career

This movie available with closed captions for the hearing impaired.

as the bombastic world heavyweight champion of the 1970s. Ali proves he can be a good actor; his performance matches those of the fine supporting cast. It's an old-fashioned, upbeat movie, with Ali's colorful personality dominating scene after scene. Also with John Marley, James Earl Jones, Roger E. Mosley, Ben Johnson, and Paul Winfield. **Director**—Tom Gries. **(PG)**
101 minutes

THE GREATEST SHOW ON EARTH (1952)

★★★

Betty Hutton
Cornel Wilde
James Stewart
Charlton Heston

Director Cecil B. De Mille takes us to the circus and uncorks some thrilling excitement and drama in this slick, expensive production. The film brims with amusing cameos, especially Stewart dressed up as a clown. However, the climax, featuring a train wreck, is a bit of a letdown. Also with Dorothy Lamour, Gloria Grahame, Lyle Bettger, Henry Wilcoxon, Emmett Kelly, and John Ringling North. **Academy Awards**—best picture; Frederic M. Frank, Theodore St. John, and Frank Cavett, motion picture story. **Nomination**—De Mille, best director.
153 minutes

THE GREATEST STORY EVER TOLD (1965)

Max Von Sydow
Dorothy McGuire
Claude Rains
José Ferrer
David McCallum
Charlton Heston

Overlong and unwieldy telling of the story of Christ. Von Sydow does an earnest job in the role of Jesus, but much of this plodding epic is taken up with many unworkable bit parts. For example, there's John Wayne as a Roman officer involved with the details of the Crucifixion. The elaborate settings look too perfect, too unreal—sort of like a series of Christmas cards. It's hardly the greatest picture ever made. Other versions with different running times are also available, including one at 225 minutes, one at 190 minutes, and one at 141 minutes. Also with Sidney Poitier, Donald Pleasence, Roddy McDowall, Carroll Baker, Van Heflin, Shelley Winters, Ed Wynn, Telly Savalas, and Angela Lansbury. The film was nominated for several Academy Awards in the areas of production. **Director**—George Stevens. **(G)** *260 minutes*

GREAT EXPECTATIONS (1946)

★★★★

John Mills
Bernard Miles
Finlay Currie
Martita Hunt
Valerie Hobson

Pip (John Mills, left) becomes a gentleman in Great Expectations.

A first-class screen adaptation of the beloved Charles Dickens classic. All the interesting characters, faithfully portrayed by a top cast, are brought brilliantly to life under the superb guidance of director David Lean. The film also boasts detailed settings and fine photography. There have been other attempts to film this story of the poor orphan boy who becomes a gentleman thanks to the help of a mysterious escaped convict, but this version is tops. Superb performances are given by Mills, Hobson, Currie, Hunt, Alec Guinness, and Jean Simmons. **Academy Award**—Guy Green, cinematography. **Nominations**—best picture; Lean, best director; Lean, Ronald Neame, and Anthony Havelock-Allan, screenplay.
118 minutes b&w

THE GREAT GATSBY (1974)

★★

Robert Redford
Mia Farrow
Karen Black

Mia Farrow and Robert Redford in The Great Gatsby.

This third rendition of F. Scott Fitzgerald's novel of the Roaring Twenties is lavishly mounted, but the narrative and characters as they are depicted here are not compelling. Redford, in the title role, is the hustling bootlegger who has everything except the woman he loves. He does an adequate job, but his performance is forgettable. The script was adapted by Francis Coppola. Also with Scott Wilson, Bruce Dern, Sam Waterston, and Lois Chiles. **Director**—Jack Clayton. **(PG)** *146 minutes*

THE GREAT IMPOSTOR (1960)

★★★

Tony Curtis
Raymond Massey
Karl Malden

Curtis stars in the title role as the incredible con artist Ferdinand Waldo Demara, who successfully posed as a naval doctor, a prison warden, and a teacher. Curtis is right at home in this striking but episodic tale, and the film maintains interest throughout. Also with Edmond O'Brien, Arthur O'Connell, Gary Merrill, and Frank Gorshin. **Director**—Robert Mulligan.
112 minutes b&w

THE GREAT LIE (1941)

★★★★

Bette Davis
Mary Astor
George Brent

This complex and talky soap opera is spruced up by the supreme, bitchy performances of Davis and Astor. Davis marries the man (Brent) who used to be married to Astor. Astor, meanwhile, is

(Continued)

(Continued)
pregnant, and when Brent dies in a plane crash, Davis rears the child as her own. Soap fans should have fun sorting out this one. The film is set against a background of classical music. Lucile Watson, Hattie McDaniel, and Grant Mitchell also star. **Director**—Edmund Goulding. **Academy Award**—Astor, best supporting actress.
107 minutes b&w

THE GREAT McGINTY (1940)

★★★★

Brian Donlevy
Akim Tamiroff

Smashing debut for writer/director Preston Sturges, who fashioned this biting political satire. Donlevy plays a bum who gains political power and then lets it slip away. This inventive film gets its point across with unusual efficiency and a liberal amount of snappy dialogue. **Academy Award**—Sturges, original screenplay. *81 minutes b&w*

THE GREAT MOUSE DETECTIVE (1986)

★★★

A delightfully witty animated feature from Walt Disney Pictures featuring just the right tart flavor to please both kids and adults. The detective of the title is none other than a mouse version of Sherlock Holmes, here called Basil of Baker Street. He employs the full force of his intellect to save the British Empire from an evil genius. The voice of Vincent Price makes the villain, Ratigan, delectably diabolical. A winning combination of colorful characters and skillful animation. **Directors**—John Musker, Ron Clements, Dave Michener, and Burny Mattinson. **(G)** *73 minutes*

THE GREAT MUPPET CAPER (1981)

Miss Piggy, Kermit the Frog, Fozzi Bear, and other adorable Muppet characters prevent a London jewel heist in this cheerful musical/melodrama. The incomparable Miss Piggy steals scenes as the star of an Esther Williams water ballet and in a Busby Berkeley nightclub production. The film is rather uncertain as to its intended audience; some of the humor is childish, but many gags are aimed at adults. The puppet characters perform with a live cast, including Charles Grodin and Diana Rigg. **Director**—Jim Henson. **(G)** *95 minutes*

THE GREAT OUTDOORS (1988)

★½

John Candy
Dan Aykroyd

A rancid summer vacation movie with Candy and Aykroyd as disagreeable brothers-in-law who share a woodsy cabin along with their families. The slapstick gags usually generate groans rather than laughs. Most of the focus is on Candy, who takes on water skiing, horseback riding, and an unwelcome bear. None of these routines work, and the movie is a waste of the stars' time and talent. Also with Stephanie Faracy, Annette Bening, Robert Prosky, and Chris Young. **Director**—Howard Deutch. **(PG-13)** *90 minutes*

THE GREAT RACE (1965)

★★½

Jack Lemmon
Tony Curtis
Peter Falk
Natalie Wood

The first New York-to-Paris automobile race, set in the early 1900s, is the centerpiece of this tongue-in-cheek comedy. Though uneven and strained, it manages to offer a few funny moments. Some gimmicky slapstick is notable—a barroom brawl and a climactic pie-throwing melee, for example. After a while, however, it becomes tiresome. Lemmon plays Professor Fate, a dastardly villain; Curtis is the Great Leslie, a dashing hero in a white suit. Also with Ross Martin, Vivian Vance, Keenan Wynn, and Larry Storch. **Director**—Blake Edwards. *150 minutes*

THE GREAT SANTINI (1980)

Robert Duvall
Blythe Danner
Michael O'Keefe

An affecting, modest movie about a gung ho Marine fighter pilot who presides over his family with the same pile-driving authority he uses on his squadron. The setting is peacetime in the early 1960s, and the focus is on family stress and a father/son conflict.

Robert Duvall gives his son, Michael O'Keefe, a hard time in The Great Santini.

Duvall plays the title role with a dynamic, overwhelming performance that makes this perplexing character totally believable and worthy of sympathy. O'Keefe plays his son. **Director**—Lewis John Carlino. **(PG) Academy Award Nominations**—Duvall, best actor; O'Keefe, best supporting actor.
115 minutes

THE GREAT SCOUT AND CATHOUSE THURSDAY (1976)

★½

Lee Marvin
Oliver Reed
Kay Lenz

Marvin stars as a legendary vagabond scout out to collect $60,000 from a wealthy ex-friend in Colorado in the year 1908. The slapstick western/comedy tries to emulate the successful *Cat Ballou*, but falls flat on its face. The film is loaded down with hokey situation gags and a tedious plot. Marvin, however, does a fair enough job as the aging brawler. Also with Robert Culp, Elizabeth Ashley, and Strother Martin. **Director**—Don Taylor. **(PG)**
102 minutes

THE GREAT TRAIN ROBBERY (1979)

★★★

Sean Connery
Donald Sutherland
Lesley-Anne Down

Connery plays the charming rascal who pulled off England's first recorded moving-train heist in 1855. Writer/director Michael Crichton, working from his own best-selling novel, serves up dazzling excitement and spicy wit, wrapped in the elegant detail of early Victorian England. Sutherland is an

® *This movie available with closed captions for the hearing impaired.*

Sean Connery perfects his timing for The Great Train Robbery.

amusing accomplice, as is Down, who radiates sex appeal and beauty to rival Marilyn Monroe. It's great movie entertainment, alive with classy action and spine-tingling suspense. Also with Alan Webb, Malcolm Terris, and Robert Lang. **(PG)** *111 minutes*

THE GREAT WALDO PEPPER (1975)

★★★

Robert Redford
Bo Svenson
Bo Brundin
Susan Sarandon

Robert Redford modestly acknowledges that he is The Great Waldo Pepper.

A former World War I pilot (Redford) dreams of air combat against a German ace he never fought during the war. He realizes his dream at last when he gets a stunt-flying job in Hollywood and meets the German—also a stunt pilot. The flying sequences highlight the film, which was not well received at the time of release. Well worth a look. Redford stars as the pilot. Also with Margot Kidder and Geoffrey Lewis. George Roy Hill directed and produced. **(PG)** *107 minutes*

THE GREAT WHITE HOPE (1970)

★★★★

James Earl Jones
Jane Alexander

A high-voltage film based on the life of Jack Johnson, the black heavyweight boxing great who won the world title in 1908. Jones and Alexander repeat their Broadway roles onscreen. The film is faithful to the play, and details much of the pain and humiliation the central character, here called Jefferson, suffers because of his affair with a white woman, played by Alexander. Jones is magnificent in the central role. Lou Gilbert, Beah Richards, Joel Fluellen, Chester Morris, Robert Webber, and Hal Holbrook costar in supporting roles. **Director**—Martin Ritt. **(PG) Academy Award Nominations**—Jones, best actor; Alexander, best actress. *101 minutes*

THE GREEK TYCOON (1978)

★★

Anthony Quinn
Jacqueline Bisset

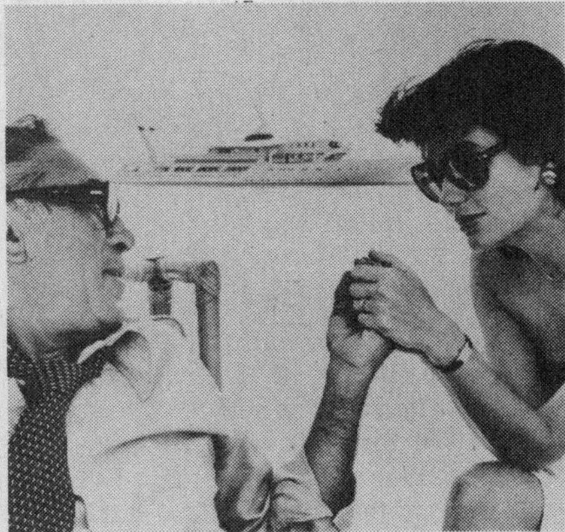

Anthony Quinn and Jacqueline Bisset provoke déjà vu in The Greek Tycoon.

This trashy film blatantly exploits the headlines and gossip columns about Jackie and Aristotle Onassis. The producers obviously spent a fortune on lush settings and fancy clothes, but apparently pinched pennies on a dull script. Quinn and Bisset plod through their roles as the world's most glamorous couple. The supporting cast, including Raf Vallone and Edward Albert, adds to the tedium. **Director**—J. Lee Thompson. **(R)** *106 minutes*

THE GREEN BERETS (1968)

★

John Wayne
David Janssen
Jim Hutton

John Wayne leads his troops in The Green Berets.

This overblown and undernourished war movie, made at the height of the Vietnam War, is nothing more than flag-waving mumbo jumbo at its worst. Wayne plays a Special Forces colonel, with all his gung ho flourishes, leading troops against the enemy. It's a very shallow treatment of an extremely complex situation. Also with Aldo Ray, Raymond St. Jacques, Jack Soo, and Bruce Cabot. **Director**—Wayne. **(G)** *141 minutes*

GREEN DOLPHIN STREET (1947)

★★

Lana Turner
Van Heflin
Donna Reed

Slick but humdrum romantic drama set in New Zealand in the 19th century. Turner and Reed play sisters who want to marry the same man. The situation sets off all sorts of absurd complications. The tedium is relieved by a climactic earthquake. Also with Edmund Gwenn and Richard Hart. **Director**—Victor Saville. *141 minutes b&w*

GREEN FOR DANGER (1946)

★★★★

Alastair Sim
Sally Gray
Trevor Howard

Smartly made whodunit, set in an English hospital during World War II, that

(Continued)

This movie available on videotape and/or disc.

(Continued)
neatly mixes mystery and comedy. Sim is at his witty best as a determined detective who nails an operating-table murderer after some careful sleuthing. There's some effective humor at the right moments. The top cast also includes Rosamund John, Leo Genn, Megs Jenkins, and Judy Campbell. **Director**—Sidney Gilliat.
93 minutes b&w

GREEN MANSIONS (1959)

Anthony Perkins
Audrey Hepburn
Lee J. Cobb

W.H. Hudson's intriguing romantic fantasy doesn't adapt comfortably to the screen. Perkins plays a young adventurer who enters a South American rain forest, where he encounters a mysterious nature girl and falls in love with her. Hepburn isn't up to the role of Rima, a beautiful nymph dedicated to protecting the jungle wildlife. However, some scenes do effectively depict the theme and mood of the novel. Also with Sessue Hayakawa and Henry Silva. **Director**—Mel Ferrer.
101 minutes

GREGORY'S GIRL (1982)

 ★★★

Gordon John Sinclair
Dee Hepburn

From Scotland, a warm and engaging film about adolescent love. Gangling, cheerful Sinclair is just right for the part of the awkward high-school youth who giddily falls for an athletic beauty (Hepburn). Although the pace is choppy, the well-observed story abounds with charm and the characters are engaging. The all-Scottish cast is exceptionally good, and director Bill Forsyth displays an impressively deft style. **(PG)**
91 minutes

GREMLINS (1984)

Zach Galligan
Phoebe Cates

Dad brings home an exotic Christmas gift—a cute, furry animal that suddenly multiplies into an army of repulsive creatures—and all hell breaks loose. Although they are nasty and vicious, the creatures carry out their mischievous work with appealing glee: They get drunk, foul up traffic signals, tear up a movie theater. Their disgraceful and wild antics produce a delicious mixture of comedy and horror. Produced by Steven Spielberg, whose influence on the film is obvious. **Director**—Joe Dante. **(PG)** *105 minutes*

GREMLINS 2: THE NEW BATCH (1990)

Zach Galligan
Phoebe Cates

Zach Galligan with friend in Gremlins 2: The New Batch.

This entertaining follow-up is an exception to the axiom that sequels are never as good as the original. Some critics actually preferred this second installment of the gremlin saga over the first. Here the creatures wreak havoc in a Manhattan skyscraper owned by a Donald Trump–like billionaire in an obvious send-up of corporate America. More emphasis is placed on humor than fright this time around so that the film can be enjoyed by family audiences. Director Joe Dante returns to helm for this second outing, emphasizing fast-paced sight gags and physical comedy throughout. Modern architecture, cable TV, cartoons and even the original *Gremlins* take a share of the ribbing. Galligan and Cates reprise their roles as the cute young couple, who have migrated from small-town America to the city. Also with John Glover, Haviland Morris, Robert Prosky, and Christopher Lee. **(PG-13)** *108 minutes*

THE GREY FOX (1983)

 ★★★

Richard Farnsworth

A low-key and offbeat western based on the life of bandit Bill Miner, who allegedly originated the phrase, "Hands up." Former stuntman Farnsworth is impressive as the gentlemanly and grandfatherly stagecoach bandit who turns to robbing trains upon his release from a 30-year prison stretch. The film paints a sympathetic and heroic picture of a man who finds more dignity as a bandit than in working as a common laborer. The photography of the Canadian Pacific Northwest is exquisite, as is the soundtrack by the Chieftains, a traditional Irish group. Also with Jackie Burroughs and Wayne Robson. **Director**—Philip Borsos. **(PG)** *92 minutes*

GREYSTOKE: THE LEGEND OF TARZAN, LORD OF THE APES (1984)

Ralph Richardson
Andie McDowell
Christopher Lambert

This lavish production is closer to the original Edgar Rice Burroughs story than its B-movie predecessors. It's also surprisingly fresh and compelling. In 1886, the orphaned son of Scottish aristocrats is reared by apes in Africa and then brought to Europe. This moving film contrasts the exhilaration of jungle life with the suffocating constrictions of Edwardian "civilization." Interestingly, the voice of McDowell was dubbed by Glenn Close. **Director**—Hugh Hudson. **(PG) Academy Award Nominations**—Richardson, best supporting actor; Robert Towne and Michael Austin (under pseudonym P.H. Vazak), best screenplay based on material from another medium. *129 minutes*

GROSS ANATOMY (1989)

Matthew Modine
Daphne Zuniga
Christine Lahti

An uneven romantic comedy that tells of the rigors of first-year medical students. Modine stars as a laid-back student who refuses to let the relentless pressure get to him. Zuniga costars as his lab partner, with whom he strikes up

Matthew Modine and Daphne Zuniga are lab partners in Gross Anatomy.

a romance as they dissect a corpse. This effort lacks the depth of *Paper Chase,* a similar film about law students. Lahti plays an anatomy professor who both inspires and provokes Modine. The derivative material combined with familiar characters makes for a routine viewing experience. Also with Todd Field, Robert Desiderio, Zakes Mokae, J.C. Quinn, and Rutyana Alda. **Director**—Thom Eberhardt. **(PG-13)**

107 minutes

GROUND ZERO (1988)

★★½

Colin Friels
Jack Thompson
Donald Pleasence

A taut, lively political thriller about the aftermath of nuclear testing by the British government in the Australian outback. Friels is excellent as a man who investigates his father's mysterious death. He becomes entangled in intrigue involving a possible cover-up of deaths as a result of the atomic blasts. It's an entertaining drama with a message, but the plot is too convoluted to follow. Excellent supporting performances by Thompson as a slippery government agent and Pleasence as a desert hermit. **Directors**—Michael Pattinson and Bruce Myles. **(PG-13)**

90 minutes

THE GROUP (1966)

★★★

Joanna Pettet
Candice Bergen
Jessica Walter
Joan Hackett

A decent adaptation of Mary McCarthy's novel that overcomes much of the soap-opera aspects of the story. The plot follows the lives of eight women who were graduated from Vassar in 1933. An earnest effort is made to flesh out the characters. Fascinating performances from Pettet, Hackett, Walter, Shirley Knight, and Kathleen Widdoes. Also with Elizabeth Hartman, Larry Hagman, and Hal Holbrook. **Director**—Sidney Lumet. *150 minutes*

GUADALCANAL DIARY (1943)

★★★

Preston Foster
Lloyd Nolan
William Bendix

A top World War II action/adventure, with the Marines slugging it out to capture a strategic base in the Pacific. It's a bit heavy on the heroics and flag-waving, but that's to be expected from this wartime film, based on Richard Tregaskis' book. The fine cast also includes Anthony Quinn. **Director**—Lewis Seiler. *93 minutes b&w*

THE GUARDIAN (1990)

★½

Jenny Seagrove
Dwier Brown
Carey Lowell

A young yuppie couple hire a British nanny (Seagrove) who turns out to be a satanic Druid. She sacrifices babies to a sinister tree as part of her evil custom. The couple finally realize something is amiss when the young woman's references do not check out. Directed by William Friedkin, the film represents a return to the supernatural material of Friedkin's hit *The Exorcist.* Yet this meager horror film is a failure from the beginning—trite material, poor writing, and poor acting sink the film quite quickly. A killer tree is just not credible or sinister, even within the context of this absurd story. Also with Brad Hall, Miguel Ferrer, and Natalia Nogulich. **(R)** *93 minutes*

GUESS WHO'S COMING TO DINNER? (1967)

★★★ ®

Spencer Tracy
Katharine Hepburn
Sidney Poitier
Katharine Houghton

A wealthy San Francisco white woman (Houghton) becomes engaged to a

Poitier, Tracy, and Hepburn: Liberalism put to the test in Guess Who's Coming to Dinner?

black man (Poitier), and announces their plans to her parents, who are considered very liberal-minded—but are they? The film is confined and overly cautious with its touchy subject. However, the picture succeeds primarily because of the adroit performances of Hepburn and Tracy, in their last appearance together, as the perplexed elders. Also with Cecil Kellaway, Beah Richards, and Roy E. Glenn, Sr. **Director**—Stanley Kramer. **Academy Awards**—Hepburn, best actress; William Rose, best story and screenplay written directly for the screen. **Nominations**—best picture; Kramer, best director; Tracy, best actor; Kellaway, best supporting actor; Richards, best supporting actress. *112 minutes*

THE GUMBALL RALLY (1976)

★½

Michael Sarrazin
Normann Burten
Gary Busey

Kooky characters from every walk of life race their souped-up vehicles from New York to California in defiance of the 55-mile-an-hour speed limit. The skimpy plot and the adolescent comic situations quickly run out of gas while the autos noisily roar on, leaving a trail of contrived smashups. There's a limit to what can be done with scenes of passing cars, and after a while, the film becomes as tedious as a rush-hour traffic jam. **Director**—Chuck Bail. **(PG)**

107 minutes

GUNFIGHT AT THE O.K. CORRAL (1957)

★★★

Burt Lancaster
Kirk Douglas

Doc Holliday (Douglas) and Wyatt Earp (Lancaster) team up to take on the

(Continued)

(Continued)

Clanton gang. A slick, action-packed western that's a bit overwrought, but shows a sharp sense of style. Fine performances by a first-class cast heighten the interest. The editing, which contributes to the suspense, was nominated for an Academy Award. Also with Rhonda Fleming, Jo Van Fleet, John Ireland, and Lee Van Cleef. **Director**—John Sturges. *122 minutes*

THE GUNFIGHTER (1950)

★★★

Gregory Peck
Helen Westcott

Peck is outstanding in this inventive western. He plays an aging gunfighter who would like to quit, but his past keeps catching up with him. The finely crafted screenplay is quite suspenseful as the action is confined to one space and occurs in the span of only a few hours. A dark and brooding western that was widely imitated. Also with Karl Malden, Skip Homeier, Millard Mitchell, and Jean Parker. **Director**—Henry King. **Academy Award Nomination**—William Bowers and André De Toth, motion picture story. *84 minutes b&w*

GUNGA DIN (1939)

Cary Grant
Victor McLaglen
Douglas Fairbanks, Jr.
Sam Jaffe

Rudyard Kipling's memorable poem becomes a splendid action/adventure with just the right amount of comic touches. Grant, Fairbanks, and McLaglen are comrades-in-arms in India, fighting a native revolt. The film brims with sweeping battle scenes, swashbuckling derring-do, and a cheerful, fun-filled outlook. Director George Stevens coaxes great performances from the entire cast; Jaffe is particularly memorable as the smiling, loyal water boy. Also with Joan Fontaine, Robert Coote, and Eduardo Ciannelli. *117 minutes b&w*

GUNG HO (1986)

Michael Keaton
Gedde Watanabe

What happens when an uptight, efficiency-minded Japanese company takes over an American auto factory? The results are some good laughs and insights into the contrasts between Eastern and Western cultures. Yet this breezy situation comedy does have its share of defects. Perhaps the scriptwriters should have worked some overtime. Performances are generally good with the affable Keaton heading the cast as the American factory foreman caught between strict management and the hang-loose workers. **Director**—Ron Howard. **(PG-13)** *120 minutes*

THE GUNS OF NAVARONE (1961)

Gregory Peck
David Niven
Stanley Baker
Anthony Quinn

The underground fighters prepare for their assault on The Guns of Navarone.

A high-powered World War II action yarn, based on an Alistair MacLean novel. Allied commandos embark on a do-or-die mission to silence big German guns perched high on a cliff-top fortress along the Aegean Sea. Suspense builds at a near-perfect pace leading to an explosive climax. Also with Anthony Quayle, James Darren, Gia Scala, and James Robertson Justice. **Director**—J. Lee Thompson. **Academy Award Nominations**—best picture; Thompson, best director; Carl Foreman, best screenplay based on material from another medium. *159 minutes*

GUYS AND DOLLS (1955)

Frank Sinatra
Marlon Brando
Jean Simmons
Vivian Blaine

An entertaining musical comedy, based on Damon Runyon's story about a gambler who takes a sucker bet that he can date a prudish Salvation Army girl, played by Simmons. Brando is miscast as the determined Romeo. However, the film succeeds marvelously because of the saucy, Runyonesque characters, played by perfectly cast supporting actors. Sinatra is outstanding as the proprietor of "the oldest established, permanent floating crap game in New York." Also with Stubby Kaye, Sheldon Leonard, B.S. Pully, Robert Keith, and George E. Stone. **Director**—Joseph L. Mankiewicz. *149 minutes*

GYMKATA (1985)

Kurt Thomas

Former Olympic star Kurt Thomas adds his formidable gymnastic skills to karate workouts in this noisy, routine adventure tale. Such embellishments do not compensate for the abysmal acting and the anemic plot. Thomas portrays a gymnast who embarks on a diplomatic mission to a far-off country. There, he encounters hordes of cutthroats and then dispatches them with predictable aplomb. **Director**—Robert Clouse. **(R)** *90 minutes*

GYPSY (1962)

★★½

Rosalind Russell
Natalie Wood

Undernourished musical taken from the Broadway production about the career of Gypsy Rose Lee and her energetic stage mother. The main problem is Wood in the title role; she's an unlikely stripteaser. The Jule Styne/Stephen Sondheim score is appealing, but it sounded better on the stage. Russell is okay as the mother, but the part was made for Ethel Merman, who brought the character to life on Broadway. Also with Karl Malden and Parley Baer. **Director**—Mervyn LeRoy. *149 minutes*

H

HAIL THE CONQUERING HERO (1944)

Eddie Bracken
Ella Raines
William Demarest

® *This movie available with closed captions for the hearing impaired.*

A rip-roaring satire, starring Bracken as a military reject who is thought to be a war hero when he returns to his small-town home. This hearty comedy offers some serious points to ponder as well. The films of writer/director Preston Sturges are known for their well-timed verbal and visual humor aimed at aspects of American society; Sturges here subtly satirizes patriotism and hero worship, a risky endeavor considering the film was shot during the height of World War II. There are effective supporting performances from Demarest, Raines, Franklin Pangborn, Raymond Walburn, and Alan Bridge. **Academy Award Nomination**—Sturges, original screenplay. *101 minutes b&w*

HAIR (1979)

★★★

John Savage
Treat Williams
Beverly D'Angelo

Director Milos Forman reworks the 1960s "tribal love-rock musical" with effective screen results. The film has a more straightforward narrative than the play, and follows the adventures of a naive midwestern farmer's son as he becomes involved with a band of hippies on the eve of his induction into the Army. The choreography by Twyla Tharp is energetic and impressive, and the film contains some showstopping song-and-dance numbers, particularly in the sequence where the flower children crash a high-society party. Also with Annie Golden (formerly with the rock band the Shirts), Don Dacus (formerly with the group Chicago), and Dorsey Wright. **(PG)** *121 minutes*

HAIRSPRAY (1988)

★★★

Divine
Ricki Lake

Divine irons for the neighbors until her daughter becomes a local TV star in Hairspray.

John Waters, director of such notorious cult films as *Pink Flamingos* and *Lust in the Dust*, cleans up his act in this entertaining burlesque of teen lifestyles of the 1960s. As the writer/director of this camp comedy, he presents a typically offbeat cast in a wacky plot about an overweight teen who dreams of joining the youthful regulars on a local TV dance program á la *American Bandstand*. Lake stars as the portly lass who finally manages to upstage the slim but snobby star of the show. The colorful cast also includes Divine in a dual role, rock singer Deborah Harry, Sonny Bono, Jerry Stiller, and Pia Zadora. **(PG)** *89 minutes*

HALF MOON STREET (1986)

★★

Michael Caine
Sigourney Weaver

Sigourney Weaver is not just another brilliant mind in Half Moon Street.

Slack energy and a lack of credibility characterize this political melodrama based on Paul Theroux's novel, *Dr. Slaughter.* Weaver stars as Dr. Lenore Slaughter, who holds a Ph.D. from Harvard and is living in London on a fellowship in Middle Eastern studies. In what is perhaps the film's most unconvincing plot device, this intelligent woman turns out to be moonlighting as a call girl. Caine costars as a British diplomat who falls in love with her. Though the performances are worth watching, the material is badly handled and without depth. **Director**—Bob Swaim. **(R)** *90 minutes*

HALLOWEEN (1978)

★★★

Donald Pleasence
Jamie Lee Curtis

A maniac escapes from a mental hospital to stalk and kill young women on Halloween night. The silly script offers minimal logic, but there are scares and suspense galore. Director John Carpenter builds the terrifying atmosphere with deft skill. His use of subjective camerawork to indicate the killer's point of view heightens the suspense, and has since become a standard cinematic device in slasher films. The cast is mainly composed of novice actors. Curtis, daughter of Tony Curtis and Janet Leigh, is effective as an intended victim. This low-budget but infamous horror film is the forerunner of the "teen screams" so prevalent in the 1980s. Also with Nancy Loomis and P.J. Soles. **(R)** *93 minutes*

HALLOWEEN II (1981)

★

Donald Pleasence
Jamie Lee Curtis

Jamie Lee Curtis frantically searches for somewhere to hide in Halloween II.

More corpses pile up in this illogical sequel, as Michael, the zombielike maniac, prowls the corridors of a small hospital and performs gruesome, unauthorized surgery on the staff. Plenty of inventive tricks heighten suspense and induce scares, but the excessively violent film drips with unnecessary gore and features a mechanical style of dispatching victims. Once again, scream-queen Curtis is pursued and terrorized, and narrowly escapes. Pleasence costars as a beleaguered psychiatrist. **Director**—Rick Rosenthal. **(R)** *92 minutes*

This movie available on videotape and/or disc.

H

HALLOWEEN III: SEASON OF THE WITCH (1982)

★★

Tom Atkins
Stacey Nelkin

A deadly mask becomes a savage trick in Halloween III: Season of the Witch.

Tommy Lee Wallace directed this third chapter in the *Halloween* horror series begun by John Carpenter and associates. Instead of the familiar maniac in a mask on the loose, the central villain is a madman toymaker (Dan O'Herlihy) who makes booby-trapped Halloween masks programmed to harm thousands of innocent children. The usual disgusting repertoire of gruesome effects is prominently featured, but the fiendish premise is executed with occasional flair. **(R)** *98 minutes*

HALLOWEEN 4: THE RETURN OF MICHAEL MYERS (1988)

★1/2

Danielle Harris
Donald Pleasence

This fourth episode in the horror series finds the terrifying madman on the loose from a mental hospital once again. The bloody hacker from Haddonfield is after his young niece (Harris). Pleasence returns as the venerable doctor determined to kill the monster. Dwight Little takes over directorial duties from John Carpenter, but he fails to build much excitement, although ample portions of mayhem fill the screen. Also with Ellie Cornell, George P. Winmont, and Beau Starr. **(R)** *88 minutes*

HALLS OF MONTEZUMA (1950)

★★

Richard Widmark
Jack Palance

The Marines hit the beaches in the Pacific during World War II and defeat the enemy in a blaze of heroics. The film is recruiting-poster material, with lots of comic-book-type action and characterizations to match. It's all done to the beat of the Marine Corps Hymn. Widmark and Palance head the competent cast, which also includes Reginald Gardiner, Robert Wagner, Karl Malden, Richard Boone, Skip Homeier, and Jack Webb. **Director**—Lewis Milestone. *113 minutes*

HAMBURGER HILL (1987)

★★1/2

Anthony Barrile
Michael Patrick Boatman
Dylan McDermott

Tim Quill, M.A. Nickles, and Anthony Barrile in Hamburger Hill.

In this rugged entry in the recent crop of Vietnam War films, American troops engage in a bloody conflict to take a strategic hill. Based on a real-life battle, the film focuses on the struggle of a squad of soldiers caught up in the horror. Ultimately, the mission is abandoned but not before the lives of many men are lost. The futility of this battle becomes a metaphor for the futility of that war. Despite the noble message, the production is more physically graphic than emotionally compelling. The effective youthful cast also includes Don Cheadle, Michael Dolan, Courtney Vance, and Don James. **Director**—John Irvin. **(R)** *110 minutes*

HAMBURGER...THE MOTION PICTURE (1986)

★

Leigh McCloskey
Randi Brooks

Dopey, slapdash comedy about the misadventures of a goof-off college student who eventually winds up at a school for hamburger franchisers. The performances by the group of unknown actors are broad and uncontrolled, and the offensive humor runs the familiar course of jokes about food, sex, blacks, and religion. It's about as much fun as standing in a long line at a fast-food restaurant. **Director**—Mike Marvin. **(R)** *90 minutes*

HAMLET (1948)

★★★★

Laurence Olivier
Eileen Herlie
Basil Sydney
Jean Simmons

Even if you find Shakespeare heavy going, you'll probably appreciate this absorbing screen version of his magnificent play. Olivier stars as the melancholy Dane in a controversial performance that interprets Hamlet as being indecisive and wavering. The direction, also by Olivier, emphasizes pace and atmosphere. Much of the play has been discarded for this film version, but the award-winning acting is compelling. Also with Felix Aylmer and Norman Wooland. **Academy Awards**—best picture; Olivier, best actor. **Nominations**—Olivier, best director; Simmons, best supporting actress. *153 minutes b&w*

HAMMETT (1983)

★★1/2

Frederic Forrest

German director Wim Wenders offers this fictitious account of hard-boiled detective writer Dashiell Hammett, who alternates between his typewriter and a search for a missing prostitute in San Francisco's Chinatown. The stylish production oozes *film noir* atmosphere, yet the story suffocates under excessive twists and triple crosses that are hard to track. Apparently the focus got lost during Wenders' fight with producer Francis Coppola over what direction the film should take. Peter Boyle, Elisha

Cook, Marilu Henner, Sylvia Sidney, and former Hollywood director Sam Fuller costar. **(PG)** *97 minutes*

THE HAND (1981)

★★

Michael Caine

Psychological thriller about a cartoonist, played by Caine, whose severed hand becomes a symbol of uncontrolled rage and frustration. The disembodied hand, lost in an auto accident, follows Caine from location to location, perpetrating a chain of murderous events. The film is heavily laced with Freudian clichés, yet it's an impressive showcase for Caine's solid, unwavering performance. An early directorial effort by Oliver Stone (*Platoon*). **(R)** *104 minutes*

A HANDFUL OF DUST (1988)

★★★1/2

James Wilby
Kristin Scott Thomas
Rupert Graves

James Wilby and Kristin Scott Thomas share a happy moment in A Handful of Dust.

A handsome adaptation of Evelyn Waugh's piercing novel exposing the unsavory lifestyle of some of the British aristocracy. Thomas plays the heartless, bored wife of an English nobleman (Wilby). She runs off to London and engages in an affair with a good-looking parasite (Graves). The good performances bring out the sharp wit of Waugh's insights. There are also some top-notch supporting performances from Anjelica Huston, Alec Guinness, and Judi Dench. **Director**—Charles Sturridge. **(PG)** *117 minutes*

HANDLE WITH CARE

See Citizens Band

THE HANDMAID'S TALE (1990)

★★

Natasha Richardson
Faye Dunaway
Aidan Quinn
Robert Duvall

A grim science-fiction tale about a bleak future society in which women are subservient pawns and some—the "handmaids"—are relegated to breeding duties. Based on the acclaimed novel by Margaret Atwood, the film was adapted for the screen by veteran scriptwriter Harold Pinter and directed by Volker Schlondorff, who is known for his film versions of literary classics (*The Tin Drum; Swann in Love*). Though most science fiction stories serve as a warning or criticism of contemporary society, this tale is so didactic as to be preachy and self-righteous. Richardson's character is supposed to be the symbolic everywoman, but without any individualizing characteristics, she remains flat throughout. As a military commander and his wife, Duvall and Dunaway turn in the best performances. This feminist version of *1984* lacks the depth and credibility of the novel. Also with Elizabeth McGovern and Victoria Tennant. **(R)** *109 minutes*

HANG 'EM HIGH (1968)

★★1/2

Clint Eastwood
Inger Stevens
Ed Begley

Eastwood stars as a victim of a lynching party who survives the noose and then sets out for revenge on the nine men who tried to kill him. The film offers a double dose of brutality, much in the manner of an Italian western. The slick production moves along fairly well, and features a bit role by veteran cowboy star Bob Steele. Also with Pat Hingle, Ben Johnson, James MacArthur, Arlene Golonka, Bruce Dern, and Dennis Hopper. **Director**—Ted Post. **(PG)** *114 minutes*

THE HANGING TREE (1959)

★★★

Gary Cooper
Maria Schell

A doctor who murdered his philandering wife tries to get his life back on track in a frontier mining town in Montana. Along the way, the doctor, impressively played by Cooper, helps a blind girl, played by Schell. An intelligent western/drama, enhanced by fine photography and realistic background detail. Also with George C. Scott, Karl Malden, and Ben Piazza. **Director**—Delmer Daves. *106 minutes*

HANKY PANKY (1982)

★★

Gene Wilder
Gilda Radner

Wilder stars in this strained and muddled comedy/adventure as an unsuspecting architect caught up in a sinister plot to steal top military secrets. He's aided by Radner, who sadly wastes her talents in a throwaway romantic part that neglects her comic abilities. A few laughs surface here and there, but most of the film is taken up with repetitive and exhausting chase scenes. Richard Widmark costars in a typical role as a heavy. **Director**—Sidney Poitier. **(PG)** *110 minutes*

HANNAH AND HER SISTERS (1986)

★★★1/2

Woody Allen
Mia Farrow
Dianne Wiest
Barbara Hershey
Michael Caine

Allen's glowing romantic comedy about contemporary New Yorkers is a masterpiece of keen insight and clear observation. He exquisitely balances clever comic turns with astute psychology to portray the foibles of three sisters and their men during a two-year period. This exhilarating film represents America's neurotic laureate at his best. The film was nominated for seven Academy Awards. **(PG-13) Academy Awards**—Caine, best supporting actor; Wiest, best supporting actress; Allen, best screenplay written directly for the screen. **Nominations**—best picture; Allen, best director. *107 minutes*

HANNA K. (1983)

★★

Jill Clayburgh

Costa-Gavras directed this political drama with his usual radical slant but

(Continued)

This movie available on videotape and/or disc.

(Continued)
without his expected powerhouse punch. The ill-conceived film confronts the Israeli-Palestinian controversy and stars Clayburgh in the title role. She's an American lawyer in Jerusalem who defends and then falls in love with an Arab who wants to reclaim his Left Bank homeland. The story, which seems to side with the Palestinians, is hampered by a soap-opera approach. Also with Gabriel Byrne and Mohammed Bakri. **(R)** *108 minutes*

HANNA'S WAR (1988)

★★½

Maruschka Detmers
Donald Pleasence
Ellen Burstyn

Maruschka Detmers portrays a woman of indomitable courage in Hanna's War.

The true story of Jewish heroine and martyr Hanna Senesh, who served as a British-trained commando during World War II. Director Menahem Golan chronicles Senesh's torture and subsequent execution by her fellow Hungarians. She was captured after parachuting into her homeland to organize escape routes for downed RAF pilots. With Detmers starring as Hanna, the international cast gives this compelling account a strong emotional impact, though Golan's direction is misguided and rambling. Also with Anthony Andrews, David Warner, and Denholm Elliott. **(PG-13)** *150 minutes*

THE HANOI HILTON (1987)

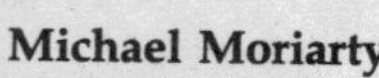

★★

Michael Moriarty
Paul LeMat

A dramatic retelling of the tortuous existence of American POWs in North Vietnam's Hoa Lo prison, ironically nicknamed the Hanoi Hilton. Though the story is well meaning and an effective reminder of the suffering experienced by some U.S. servicemen, the lack of dramatic development and a series of verbal and dramatized attacks on noted opponents of the war limit the impact of this exasperating and lengthy film. An ensemble cast, including Moriarty, LeMat, Jeffrey Jones, David Soul, and John Diehl, turn in good performances. **Director**—Lionel Chetwynd. **(R)** *123 minutes*

HANOVER STREET (1979)

★

Harrison Ford
Lesley-Anne Down

Harrison Ford and Lesley-Anne Down survive an air raid in Hanover Street.

An American bomber pilot has a secret love affair with a married British nurse amid the London blitz of 1943. Ford stars as the pilot; Down plays the nurse. More tears and war-film clichés fall than enemy bombs in this unbelievable turkey. Such contrived sentimentality may have worked during the frantic World War II years, but now this sort of material is hopelessly dated. The acting doesn't help the limp screenplay by writer/director Peter Hyams. **(PG)** *105 minutes*

HANS CHRISTIAN ANDERSEN (1952)

★★★

Danny Kaye

Kaye is ideally suited to the title role in this appealing children's fantasy, about a poor shoemaker and storyteller who makes dancing slippers for a ballerina and then falls in love with her. The colorful production comes across with a thick coating of sugar, yet the score is appealing. Danny sings such favorites as the Oscar-nominated "Thumbelina" and "Ugly Duckling." The film was also nominated for an Academy Award for Harry Stradling's cinematography. Zizi Jeanmaire, Farley Granger, and John Qualen costar. **Director**—Charles Vidor. *120 minutes*

THE HAPPIEST DAYS OF YOUR LIFE (1950)

★★★★

Alastair Sim
Margaret Rutherford
Joyce Grenfell

A great cast of British character players has a field day with this energetic comedy about a group of schoolgirls who are mistakenly quartered at a boys' boarding school. A first-rate, effective screen adaptation of John Dighton's popular postwar play. Also with Richard Wattis, Guy Middleton, Muriel Aked, and Edward Rigby. **Director**—Frank Launder. *81 minutes b&w*

THE HAPPY HOOKER (1975)

★★

Lynn Redgrave
Jean-Pierre Aumont

This story about Xaviera Hollander, distinguished by Lynn Redgrave's excellent characterization, is a comedy about greed and lust with an amusing but sanitized look at the kinky world of hookers. Also with Lovelady Powell and Nicholas Pryor. **Director**—Nicholas Sgarro. **(R)** *96 minutes*

THE HAPPY TIME (1952)

★★★

Charles Boyer
Louis Jourdan

Charles Boyer and Linda Christian in The Happy Time.

This movie available with closed captions for the hearing impaired.

A pleasant situation comedy concerning the day-to-day lives of a French Canadian family in the 1920s. Boyer is appealing as the father of this oddball group, who are involved in various comic interpersonal relationships. Jourdan plays an uncle. It's smartly directed by Richard Fleischer, with effective performances all around. Others in the cast include Bobby Driscoll, Linda Christian, and Marsha Hunt.

94 minutes b&w

HARDBODIES (1984)

★

Mark Griffiths
Gary Wood
Grant Cramer
Teal Roberts

Trite, silly beach-party comedy that serves mainly as an excuse to display numerous bare-breasted young women. The foolish story involves three middle-aged men experiencing second childhood. While frolicking at the shore, they hire a slick young Romeo to teach them the latest techniques in attracting girls. **Director**—Mark Griffiths. **(R)** *88 minutes*

HARD CHOICES (1986)

★★

Margaret Klenck
Gary McCleery

A social worker (Klenck) falls in love with her client (McCleery), a 15-year-old prisoner, and engineers his escape from jail. This low-budget film succeeds as social commentary but fails as compelling drama mostly because the relationship between the older woman and the adolescent is not believable. The supporting cast, featuring John Seitz and John Sayles, fares well in an otherwise flawed effort. **Director**—Rick King. **(No MPAA rating)** *90 minutes*

HARDCORE (1979)

★★★

George C. Scott
Peter Boyle

A religious businessman (Scott) from Grand Rapids, Michigan, searches for his teenage daughter, who has fallen in with pornographic filmmakers. Boyle plays a hard-boiled detective who helps in the search. Writer/director Paul Schrader gives us a hard-hitting, vivid tour of the sleazy, sex-for-sale underworld. He also presents a chilling contrast between complacent Middle American culture and the seamy big-city jungle. Boyle and Scott are convincing in this violent but intelligent drama, which contains some heartrending moments. Also with Season Hubley, Dick Sargent, and Leonard Gaines. **(R)**

108 minutes

A HARD DAY'S NIGHT (1964)

★★★★

The Beatles

The Beatles—George, Paul, John, and Ringo—star in this sensational comedy, which revolves around their hectic schedule during a trip to London. The mop tops demonstrate that they can excel at clowning as well as singing, and the madcap affair comes off with enormous energy and good humor. There's also plenty of favorite Beatle songs in the Oscar-nominated score. Wilfred Brambell and Victor Spinetti costar. The film was rated by the MPAA when it was reissued in 1982 with a short prologue. **Director**—Richard Lester. **(G)** **Academy Award Nomination**—Alun Owen, best story and screenplay written directly for the screen.

85 minutes b&w

THE HARDER THEY FALL (1956)

★★★

Humphrey Bogart
Rod Steiger

Bogart is good as a press agent who blows the whistle on unethical dealings in the prizefight business. The searing drama, based on Budd Schulberg's novel, is sympathetic to athletes who are controlled by selfish managers. Steiger gives an excellent performance as Bogart's antagonistic employer. This is Bogey's last feature film. Also stars Jan Sterling, Mike Lane, and real-life boxer Max Baer. **Director**—Mark Robson. *109 minutes b&w*

HARDLY WORKING (1981)

★★

Jerry Lewis

Lewis brings back his familiar style of slapstick comedy in this story of a circus clown who loses his job and then bungles his way through a variety of other occupations. There are a few amusing episodes, but much of the humor is repetitious and even desperate. Some of the gags are recycled from his earlier movies, and many of the new routines are uninspired. Scattered throughout are some serious moments that don't seem to fit in this confusing and uneven movie. **Director**—Lewis. **(PG)** *91 minutes*

HARD TIMES (1975)

★★★

Charles Bronson
James Coburn

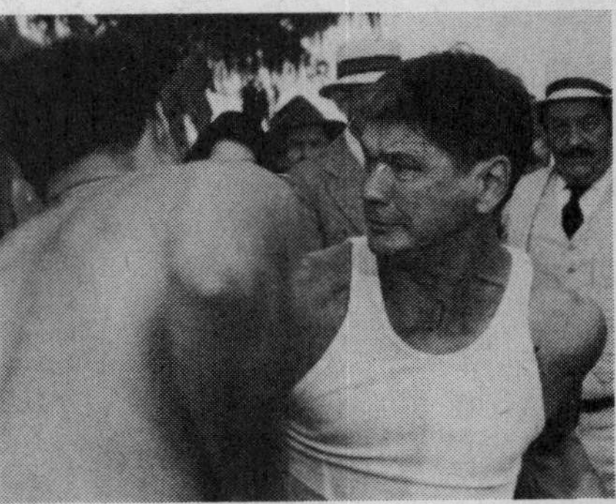

Charles Bronson is a bare-knuckle prizefighter in Hard Times.

The setting adds much to this film, which takes place in the midst of the Depression in colorful New Orleans. Bronson plays a moody, silent loner who earns a living by illegal bare-knuckle prizefighting. It's a gripping and exciting action drama that's also frequently funny. Coburn does well as the shifty fight manager. Also with Jill Ireland and Strother Martin. A winning debut by director Walter Hill. **(PG)**

97 minutes

HARD TO HOLD (1984)

★

Rick Springfield
Janet Eilber

Only the rock music is worthwhile in this otherwise tedious vehicle custom-fitted for pop idol Springfield. The cliché-strewn soap-opera plot essentially explores a heartrending proposition: Can a self-indulgent rock superstar find happiness in the arms of a cultured teacher of retarded children? Too much silly dialogue and poor acting make it difficult to care. Also with Patti Hansen, Bill Mumy, and Albert Salmi. **Director**—Larry Peerce. **(PG)**

93 minutes

This movie available on videotape and/or disc.

HARD TO KILL (1990)

★★½

Steven Seagal
Kelly Le Brock

Steven Seagal seeks revenge for the murders of his wife and child in Hard to Kill.

Seven years in a coma didn't cool the resolve and martial-arts skills of Los Angeles detective Mason Storm, played by Seagal. After awakening in the hospital, Storm seeks revenge against the syndicated crime mob and the dirty politicians who put him there. Like most athletes-turned-actors, Seagal is at his best when he allows his body and physical presence to do most of the acting. When he is involved in an extended dialogue scene, he simply lacks the conviction and intensity needed for his tough-guy role. Still, several sequences of bone-breaking action propel the film forward at a rapid pace, and action fans will not be disappointed. Le Brock, Seagal's real-life wife, plays the doctor who nurses him back to consciousness. Also with William Sadler and Frederick Coffin. **Director**—Bruce Malmouth. **(R)** *96 minutes*

HARLAN COUNTY, U.S.A. (1977)

★★★★

This powerful, passionate documentary about a strike by coal miners has as much excitement as any fictional drama. It's a pro-miner film that revolves around a brutal confrontation in Brookside, Kentucky, in 1973. The film also illuminates a broader portrait of perilous mining conditions over the years and the corruption of some elements of organized labor and some managements. It's an impressive debut for Barbara Kopple, who directed the project over a three-year period. **(PG)** **Academy Award**—documentary feature. *103 minutes*

HARLEM NIGHTS (1989)

★★

Eddie Murphy
Richard Pryor
Redd Foxx

Murphy wrote, directed, and starred in this awkward period comedy about black gangsters in Harlem, circa 1938. The sparse storyline involves a sting on a white mobster who wants to muscle in on a nightclub run by Pryor and his friends. Though criticized at the time of release for the profanity-laden dialogue, the film suffers less from the dialogue's profanity than from its crudeness—that is, its lack of rhythm, its repetitiveness, and Murphy's own penchant for ad-libbing while others muddle through the lines as written. Some of the comic setups seem mean-spirited and needlessly violent compared to the sparse plot and lackadaisical performances by Pryor and Murphy. The offhanded way Murphy tosses his lines around makes his character seem more distracting than funny. To say that Murphy took on more than he could handle with this film is an understatement, but Murphy's fans may find this ambitious—if unsuccessful—undertaking of interest. Della Reese, Jasmine Guy, Arsenio Hall, Michael Lerner, Danny Aiello, and Stan Shaw also star. **(R)** **Academy Award Nomination**—Joe I. Tompkins, costume design. *118 minutes*

HAROLD AND MAUDE (1972)

★★★

Bud Cort
Ruth Gordon

A nutty black comedy that has evolved into a cult film. Cort plays a strange young man who often contemplates death. He pals around with an equally odd 79-year-old adventurous woman, hilariously portrayed by Gordon. The two fall in love; she shows him a picture of herself and it's a sunflower; she commits suicide but shows him how to live. Weird as it is, this campy outing is done with style, wit, and spirit, thanks to an inventive screenplay by Colin Higgins and perceptive direction by Hal Ashby. Also with Vivian Pickles, Cyril Cusack, Charles Tyner, and Ellen Geer. **(PG)** *92 minutes*

HARPER (1966)

★★★

Paul Newman
Lauren Bacall

A fast-paced detective yarn similar to the hard-boiled detective capers of the 1940s. Director Jack Smight strains to capture the *film noir* flavor, but doesn't quite succeed; however, the fine cast compensates. Newman is Lew Harper, a private eye hired to track down the missing husband of a rich California woman, played by Bacall. He's a slick bird dog who gets himself into a variety of scrapes along the way. Based on Ross MacDonald's novel *The Moving Target*. Other players include Julie Harris, Shelley Winters, Janet Leigh, Robert Wagner, and Arthur Hill. *121 minutes*

HARPER VALLEY P.T.A. (1979)

★★

Barbara Eden
Ronny Cox
Nanette Fabray

Inspired by the 1960s country tune of the same name, this flat comedy pokes fun at snootiness and hypocrisy. Eden plays the sexy mom in miniskirts who wreaks revenge on some stuffy P.T.A. board members in Harper Valley, Ohio. Most of the gags are juvenile. Also with Pat Paulsen, Susan Swift, Louis Nye, and John Fiedler. **Director**—Richard Bennett. **(PG)** *93 minutes*

HARRY AND SON (1984)

★

Paul Newman
Robby Benson

A big disappointment from Newman, who wrote, directed, and stars in this syrupy film. He plays a widowed construction worker trying to cope with Benson, who is badly miscast as his 21-year-old son, a would-be writer. The strained, unfocused story meanders through irritating situations without drawing any meaningful conclusions. Newman, as the callous father, mopes a lot and intermittently explodes at his sweet-tempered offspring, who works at menial jobs. Also with Ellen Barkin and Joanne Woodward. **(PG)** *118 minutes*

® *This movie available with closed captions for the hearing impaired.*

HARRY AND THE HENDERSONS (1987)

 ★★

John Lithgow
Melinda Dillon
Don Ameche

This overly sentimental comedy follows the misadventures of a middle-class family who briefly adopts a huge but gentle creature that may be the legendary Bigfoot. Meanwhile, the authorities and the terrified community want the beast hunted down and destroyed. This manipulative film, produced by Steven Spielberg's Amblin Entertainment, borrows many of the plot elements of *E.T.*, but features none of that classic's charm or imagination. Children will enjoy this shaggy dog story, but adults may find it trite and derivative. Also with Kevin Peter Hall, Joshua Rudoy, Margaret Langrick, and Lainie Kazan. **Director**—William Dear. **(PG) Academy Award**—Rick Baker, makeup design.
110 minutes

HARRY AND TONTO (1974)

  ★★★

Art Carney
Ellen Burstyn

Harry (Art Carney) takes Tonto on a cross-country journey in Harry and Tonto.

After being evicted, a New York senior citizen and his cat, Tonto, take a sentimental journey across the country. A variety of funny and sad episodes occur along the way. Carney, as Harry, makes the character come alive with affection and pathos. There's good support from Burstyn, Chief Dan George, Geraldine Fitzgerald, and Larry Hagman. **Director**—Paul Mazursky. **(R) Academy Award**—Carney, best actor. **Nomination**—Mazursky and John Greenfeld, best original screenplay. *115 minutes*

HARRY AND WALTER GO TO NEW YORK (1976)

 ★

James Caan
Elliott Gould

Caan and Gould play a couple of talentless vaudeville entertainers who go to New York to organize the heist of a Massachusetts bank. What's supposed to be funny turns out pathetic and embarrassing; Caan and Gould scream, jump, pull each other's ears, and strain their professional reputations. Clumsily directed by Mark Rydell. New York is in enough trouble; Harry and Walter should have stayed home. Also with Michael Caine, Diane Keaton, Lesley Ann Warren, and Charles Durning. **(PG)** *123 minutes*

HARVEY (1950)

★★★★

James Stewart
Josephine Hull

James Stewart happily regards the image of his invisible friend, Harvey.

Mary Chase's touching play about a middle-aged tippler with an imaginary huge white rabbit as his companion comes to the screen with all the wonderful dialogue and memorable moments firmly in place. Stewart is wonderful as the gentle Elwood P. Dowd, under pressure by his relatives to enter a mental hospital. Hull also stands out as the perplexed sister who is constantly apologizing for Dowd's nutty behavior. The engrossing story wisely questions the definition of "normal." There are other good performances from Victoria Horne, Peggy Dow, Cecil Kellaway, and Jesse White. **Director**—Henry Koster. **Academy Award**—Hull, best supporting actress. **Nomination**—Stewart, best actor.
104 minutes b&w

THE HARVEY GIRLS (1946)

 ★★★

Judy Garland
Ray Bolger

A delightful musical about young women who go West to be waitresses for a 19th-century restaurant chain operating in frontier communities. Much of the script is nonsense, but this drawback is redeemed by good performances and a memorable score, including the popular song "Atchison, Topeka, and the Santa Fe." Garland and Bolger head the fine cast, which also includes John Hodiak, Preston Foster, Angela Lansbury, and Marjorie Main. **Director**—George Sidney. *101 minutes*

THE HASTY HEART (1949)

 ★★★

Richard Todd
Patricia Neal

A touching story about an overbearing Scottish soldier who's brought to an army hospital in Burma. The attitudes toward him drastically change when it's discovered that he will soon die. Todd is especially convincing as the young trooper. The film is based on John Patrick's play, which worked slightly better on the stage. Other cast members include Ronald Reagan and Orlando Martins. **Director**—Vincent Sherman. **Academy Award Nomination**—Todd, best actor. *99 minutes b&w*

A HATFUL OF RAIN (1957)

★★★

Eva Marie Saint
Don Murray

A powerful story about a young man, played by Murray, who becomes addicted to drugs, and how his deteriorating condition affects his family and friends. Fine acting by a competent cast highlights this searing drama, which was one of the first to examine addiction with intelligence and understanding. Based on Michael V. Gazzo's Broadway play. Also with Anthony Franciosa, Lloyd Nolan, and Howard Da Silva. **Director**—Fred Zinnemann. **Academy Award Nomination**—Franciosa, best actor. *109 minutes b&w*

HAUNTED HONEYMOON (1986)

★★

Gene Wilder
Gilda Radner
Dom DeLuise

Boo! Gilda Radner, Gene Wilder, and Dom DeLuise in Haunted Honeymoon.

A creaky comedy/horror film with few scares and even fewer laughs. Wilder heads the cast as a radio star who honeymoons with his bride (Radner) at a haunted mansion, where his family members are plotting his demise. Most of the gags and routines are as musty as the old family estate. Only DeLuise, in drag as the venerable old aunt, manages some delightful comic scenes. Also with Jonathan Pryce. **Director**—Wilder. **(PG)** *82 minutes*

HAUNTED SUMMER (1988)

★★1/2

Eric Stoltz
Alice Krige
Alex Winter
Phillip Anglim
Laura Dern

A slow-moving tale about the summer of 1816, when several English literary luminaries gathered in Switzerland to experiment with drugs and sex as well as to engage in intellectual conversation. Percy Shelley (Stoltz), Lord Byron (Anglim), Mary Godwin (Krige), and John Polidori (Winter) are the writers involved. Their unusual summer holiday gave inspiration to Mary Godwin Shelley's *Frankenstein* and Polidori's *Vampyre.* Viewers familiar with these literary legends will find this film adaptation of interest, while others may not understand the significance of the characters' actions. Directed by Ivan Passer, whose work includes a number of engaging if not highly successful films. Based on Anne Edwards' novel. The video version, which runs about 106 minutes, is rated **R. (No MPAA rating)** *115 minutes*

HAWAII (1966)

★★★

Max Von Sydow
Julie Andrews
Richard Harris

Jocelyn Lagarde punches out Max Von Sydow in Hawaii.

Mammoth film epic based on portions of James Michener's ambitious historical novel, about the intrusion of western culture on native Hawaiians in the early 1800s. The narrative flow is handled in a choppy fashion, but the acting is adequate, and the production is presented with lavish care. Von Sydow stars in the key role of a young missionary who tries to impose his religious dogma on the islanders. Also with Jocelyn Lagarde, Carroll O'Connor, and Gene Hackman. The film also exists in a 171-minute and a 151-minute version. **Director**—George Roy Hill. **Academy Award Nominations**—Lagarde, best supporting actress; Russell Harlan, cinematography. *186 minutes*

THE HAWAIIANS (1970)

Charlton Heston
Tina Chen
Geraldine Chaplin

This continuation of James Michener's chronicle brings the story up to the 1900s. However, this sequel doesn't work mainly because the spectacular production takes in too many episodes in one bite. Heston stars as a businessman who comes to the islands and encounters a mixture of good fortune, disease, revolution, destruction, and anguish over morality. The huge cast also includes John Phillip Law, Mako, Alec McCowen, and Ann Knight. **Director**—Tom Gries. **(PG)** *132 minutes*

HEAD OFFICE (1986)

★★

Judge Reinhold
Eddie Albert
Danny DeVito

A patchy send-up of multinational big business. There are some good moments, especially when the film skewers the overreaching corporate climber, but the script and direction do not pack enough punch to sustain the entire film. Reinhold heads the competent cast as a young public relations executive who often is skeptical of official company policy. Lori-Nan Engler costars. **Director**—Ken Finkleman. **(PG-13)** *90 minutes*

HEALTH (1979)

Glenda Jackson
Carol Burnett
James Garner
Lauren Bacall
Dick Cavett
Henry Gibson

Director Robert Altman uses a health-food convention in Florida as an opportunity to satirize national politics in his highly individual style. The top-name cast has a field day with this rambling and shapeless material, and some splendid characterizations emerge. The film often appears flat and thin, but this is Altman engaging in the techniques that made him famous, and many glorious moments shine through. Also with Alfre Woodard, Paul Dooley, and Donald Moffat. **(PG)** *102 minutes*

THE HEARSE (1980)

★★

Trish Van Devere
Joseph Cotten

Van Devere plays a daring divorcée who moves into an old house, and before long she's up to her neck in wicked ghosts from the past. Among the evil demons who pursue her is the chauffeur of the vehicle from the film's title. Cotten is effective as a grumpy lawyer

This movie available with closed captions for the hearing impaired.

who presents obstacles to Van Devere's taking legal possession of the house. The film offers enough frightening moments, but it's really just another routine twist to the haunted-house movie. Also with Perry Lang. **Director**—George Bowers. **(PG)** *95 minutes*

HEARTACHES (1982)

 ★★

Margot Kidder
Annie Potts

Mushy, romantic comedy set in Toronto about two female roommates trying to sort out their precarious love affairs. Kidder is believable as the brassy, free-spirited mattress factory worker who falls for the boss' suave nephew. She's slightly ahead of the material, which plays too much like a soap opera. Potts portrays an insecure waif who's afraid to tell her adolescent husband that he is not the father of her expected baby. Also with Robert Carradine, Winston Rekert, and George Touliatos. **Director**—Donald Shebib. **(R)** *90 minutes*

HEART BEAT (1980)

 ★★1/2

Nick Nolte
Sissy Spacek
John Heard

The 1950s beat generation is explored rather timidly in this biographical film about novelist Jack Kerouac *(On the Road)* and his friends Neal and Carolyn Cassady. The story is engaging and stylish at times, as it delves into the nonconformist lifestyles of the characters. But too often the loosely constructed movie wanders off the road and fritters away dramatic impact. Nolte, as the freewheeling Neal Cassady, turns in a sizzling performance that provides some much-needed energy. Spacek plays Carolyn, and Heard plays Kerouac. Also with Ray Sharkey, Tony Bill, Steve Allen, and Anne Dusenberry. **Director**—John Byrum. **(R)** *109 minutes*

HEARTBEEPS (1981)

 ★1/2

Andy Kaufman
Bernadette Peters

A romantic comedy about robots that seems to have been written by a computer and could only be appreciated by someone with a mechanical brain. Kaufman and Peters play amorous robots who meet at a repair facility and venture into the wide world where they encounter similar creatures. One of them, called "Catskill," spouts Henny Youngman one-liners; another is "Crimebusters," which looks like a tank. Part of the film's problems stemmed from the fact that it was taken out of the hands of director Allan Arkush and reedited. Those interested in more than just superficial entertainment may want to check out the Oscar-nominated makeup by Stan Winston. **(PG)** *88 minutes*

HEARTBREAKERS (1985)

 ★★

Peter Coyote
Nick Mancuso

Bobby Roth's ponderous but thoughtful film explores the fragile male friendship between a struggling artist (Coyote) and a clothing firm executive (Mancuso). This candid, contemporary story delves much deeper into emotions and competitiveness than the standard buddy movie. Though these two middle-aged, mixed-up bachelors never quite resolve their status, they seem more real for their failure. Coyote's portrayal is exceptional. **(R)** *95 minutes*

HEARTBREAK HOTEL (1988)

  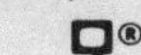

David Keith
Tuesday Weld

It's every Elvis Presley fan's dream: The King himself is a houseguest. In this glitzy and likable fantasy, some youngsters kidnap Elvis and bring him home to perk up poor mom (Weld), an ardent Presley worshiper. Keith portrays the rock 'n' roll idol with plenty of vigor and charm. Also with Charlie Schlatter, Chris Mulkey, and Karen Landry. **Director**—Chris Columbus. **(PG-13)** *102 minutes*

THE HEARTBREAK KID (1972)

Charles Grodin
Cybill Shepherd
Jeannie Berlin

Neil Simon's compelling screenplay, based on Bruce Jay Friedman's play, is alternately funny and sad—but either way, it cuts to the bone. Grodin plays a cocky young man on his honeymoon, who abruptly abandons his bride to pursue a seemingly more attractive girl. Though the situation is outrageous, the film is intelligent and insightful. Berlin, daughter of director Elaine May, is effective as the ditched newlywed, and Shepherd is fine as the new love interest. Eddie Albert and Audra Lindley have supporting roles. **(PG) Academy Award Nominations**—Albert, best supporting actor; Berlin, best supporting actress. *106 minutes*

Eddie Albert, Charles Grodin, and Cybill Shepherd in The Heartbreak Kid.

HEARTBREAK RIDGE (1987)

 ★★1/2 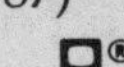

Clint Eastwood
Mario Van Peebles
Marsha Mason

Marsha Mason is reunited with Clint Eastwood in Heartbreak Ridge.

Eastwood directed and stars in this action/drama about a brawling, combat-scarred Marine sergeant who tries to whip a platoon of new recruits into fighting shape. Though Eastwood gives the film a modern touch by using dia-

(Continued)

(Continued)

logue heavily laced with four-letter words, the plot and his crusty character are all too familiar from countless other war movies. Lackluster direction and mediocre performances from supporting actors do not make up for this lack of originality. The film's conclusion focuses on the American invasion of Grenada during the early 1980s, an event that is only a footnote in American history, but here is recast as a heroic triumph for the Marines. Nevertheless, Eastwood is always interesting to watch even in this flawed effort, which did well at the box office. The film was nominated for an Oscar for best sound. Also with Arlen Dean Snyder and Eileen Heckart. **(R)** *130 minutes*

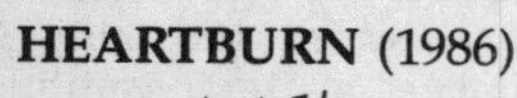

HEARTBURN (1986)

★★½

Meryl Streep
Jack Nicholson

Sophisticated comedy based on Nora Ephron's best-selling novel, which is a fictionalized account of her marriage to *Washington Post* reporter Carl Bernstein. Streep stars as a cookbook editor who meets and falls in love with a newspaper columnist, played by Nicholson. The film is handsomely directed by Mike Nichols but is slow moving, a result of Nichols' directorial style involving long takes with little emphasis on editing. Though Ephron's book had a great deal of humor and color, her screenplay for this film excises much of what made the book interesting. Here, the couple's professional lives are seldom referred to, and the trappings of their middle-class lifestyle are emphasized over any personal revelations about the characters. As a result, Streep's and Nicholson's characters seem incomplete and hollow. Streep's portrayal especially suffers, as the story is told from her point of view, yet the audience is not given enough information to be sympathetic toward her character. Also with Jeff Daniels, Maureen Stapleton, Milos Forman, Stockard Channing, Richard Masur, and Catherine O'Hara. **(R)** *108 minutes*

HEART CONDITION (1990)

★★

Bob Hoskins
Denzel Washington

A slovenly, racist policeman (Hoskins) receives the transplanted heart of a

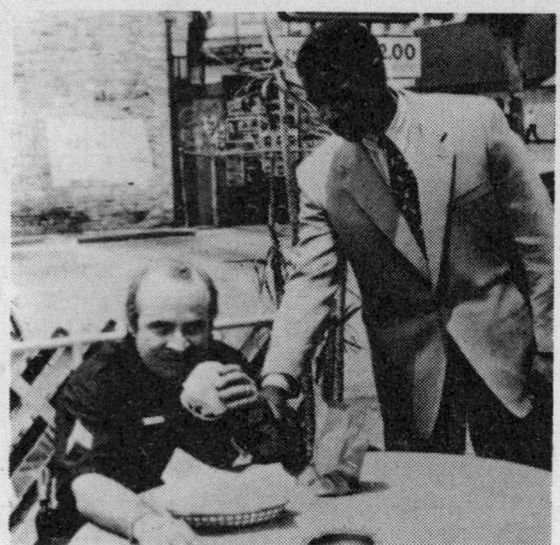

Bob Hoskins gets more than a heart from Denzel Washington in Heart Condition.

dapper black lawyer (Washington) killed in a suspicious car accident. The cop and the lawyer's ghost then collaborate to solve the lawyer's murder in this far-fetched buddy movie. Obviously, the film attempts to use comedy to comment on racial prejudice, though the racial slurs and insults that fly out of the mouth of Hoskins' character sabotage that intent. Hoskins overacts considerably, which seems in keeping with the picture's hysterical tone. Also with Chloe Webb, Roger E. Mosley, and Alan Rachins. **Director**—James D. Parriott. **(R)** *96 minutes*

THE HEART IS A LONELY HUNTER (1968)

★★★

Alan Arkin
Sondra Locke

Arkin gives a moving performance as a kindhearted deaf-mute who resides in a small southern town. Based on the compelling novel by Carson McCullers, the film sensitively touches on isolation and cruelty. Locke plays a girl who befriends Arkin. Nicely acted by a capable cast that also includes Stacy Keach, Cicely Tyson, and Laurinda Barrett. **Director**—Robert Ellis Miller. **(G) Academy Award Nominations**—Arkin, best actor; Locke, best supporting actress. *125 minutes*

HEARTLAND (1981)

★★★

Conchata Ferrell
Rip Torn

The plucky spirit of American pioneer life is richly portrayed in this low-budget but handsomely made film set in 1910. The unpretentious story concerns a poor young widow, played by Ferrell, who signs on as a housekeeper for a stoic Wyoming rancher, played by Torn, and eventually marries him. Megan Folson plays Ferrell's daughter. Richard Pearce, in his directorial debut, beautifully captures the challenges and hardships of frontier life without being overly sentimental. Also with Barry Primus and Lilia Skala. **(PG)** *93 minutes*

HEART LIKE A WHEEL (1983)

★★★

Bonnie Bedelia
Beau Bridges

Beau Bridges and Bonnie Bedelia on the drag strip in Heart Like a Wheel.

An entertaining and winning film based on the life of Shirley ("Cha-Cha") Muldowney, a champion drag-strip racer. Director Jonathan Kaplan brings this piece of Americana to life with vivid detail and excitement. The heart of this slight but realistic-looking production is Bedelia's performance as the spunky woman racing ace who triumphs on the track but wrecks her family life. Excellent support from Leo Rossi and Hoyt Axton. **(PG)** *113 minutes*

HEART OF DIXIE (1989)

★★½

Ally Sheedy
Virginia Madsen
Phoebe Cates

A Southern college coed breaks with tradition and becomes active in the civil rights movement, circa 1957. Sheedy stars as the pretty Alabama sorority sister who awakens to the racial injustices

® *This movie available with closed captions for the hearing impaired.*

around her. Madsen is notable as her friend, a typical Southern belle whose sole existence revolves around being crowned Honeysuckle Queen. Unfortunately, Cates' character, a beatnik who yearns to live in Greenwich Village, lacks definition. Most of her part seems to have ended up on the cutting-room floor. Treat Williams, in a secondary role, plays a reporter who pushes Sheedy to do the right thing. Though filled with good intentions, the film trivializes a turbulent era of American history by mixing politics and romance. Michael St. Gerard makes a cameo appearance as Elvis Presley: A few months later, he landed the same role in the short-lived television series *Elvis*. Also with Don Michael Paul, Kyle Secor, Lisa Zane, and Francesca Roberts. **Director**—Martin Davidson. **(PG)**
96 minutes

HEARTS OF THE WEST (1975)

★★★

Jeff Bridges
Alan Arkin
Andy Griffith

A warm, merry movie about an Iowa farm boy who goes to Hollywood in the 1930s to become a cowboy actor and write western movies. Bridges plays the hero with style and charm, and there are other excellent performances by Arkin and Griffith. The film is artistically directed by Howard Zieff, who has a keen appreciation of moviemaking of that era. In all, it's a well-blended mixture of color, romance, suspense, nostalgia, and comedy. Also with Blythe Danner, Donald Pleasence, and Richard B. Shull. **(PG)** *102 minutes*

HEAT (1987)

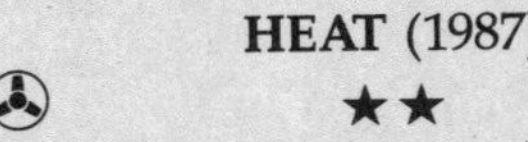

★★

Burt Reynolds
Peter MacNicol

A patchy, underdeveloped drama set in Las Vegas featuring Reynolds in a suitable role as a compulsive gambler and good-hearted tough guy. Reynolds plays this colorful character with typical aplomb, but the film unfolds in fits and starts. Other characters appear and fade too quickly and the story ends with an exhausting, violent showdown. Despite some good performances, the picture will leave you cold. Karen Young, Diana Scarwid, and Neill Barry appear in supporting roles. **Director**—R.M. Richards. **(R)** *101 minutes*

HEAT AND DUST (1983)

★★

Julie Christie
Greta Scacchi

Drab, cluttered saga of mysterious India's effect on two English women separated by six decades. The film irritates as it oscillates from colonial India to the 1980s, making it difficult to sort out characters and events. Christie handles the contemporary role with finesse, and Scacchi is equally competent as the young woman of the 1920s. Lavishly photographed and brimming with details of India now and then, but without a meaningful story. **Director**—James Ivory. **(R)** *130 minutes*

HEATHERS (1989)

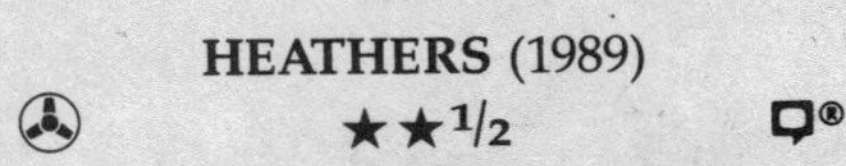

★★½

Winona Ryder
Christian Slater

Christian Slater is one of the student killers in Heathers.

Teen suicide and student social competition are keenly observed in this audacious and mean-spirited satire. Various popular youths are murdered by two students who disguise their crimes as suicides. Though the film is an effective black comedy, the perpetrators are so flippant that some viewers may be offended. Ryder and Slater do a good job portraying the two youthful killers. Also with Shannen Doherty, Lisanne Falk, Kim Walker, and Penelope Milford. **Director**—Michael Lehmann. **(R)** *102 minutes*

HEAVEN (1987)

★★

Actress Diane Keaton directed this pointless documentary about the "average" person's conception of the afterlife. She interviews the devoutly religious, the young, the elderly, some kooks, and even boxing promoter Don King. The answers are hardly surprising or enlightening. Laced among the interviews are scenes of Hollywood's version of heaven from such movies as *The Green Pastures* and *The Horn Blows at Midnight*. Though occasionally amusing, the film suffers from a smug and condescending attitude toward the people interviewed. **(PG–13)**
80 minutes b&w/color

HEAVEN CAN WAIT (1978)

★★★★

Warren Beatty
Julie Christie
Jack Warden
Dyan Cannon

Beatty's remake of the 1941 comedy/drama *Here Comes Mr. Jordan* is a cheerful gem of a movie, brimming with priceless moments and inspired dialogue. It's about an enthusiastic football quarterback who dies prematurely and returns to earth as a powerful industrialist. Beatty is sensational in the leading role and works harmoniously with the marvelous cast. Although the film is a retread, it's contemporary in most respects and shines with its own madcap personality. Also with Charles Grodin, James Mason, Buck Henry, and Vincent Gardenia. **Directors**—Beatty and Henry. **(PG) Academy Award Nominations**—best picture; Beatty and Henry, best director; Beatty, best actor; Warden, best supporting actor; Cannon, best supporting actress; Elaine May and Beatty, best screenplay adaptation; William Fraker, cinematography.
100 minutes

HEAVEN HELP US (1985)

★★

Andrew McCarthy
Kevin Dillon

Poignant but predictable coming-of-age comedy, set in a Brooklyn Catholic school, follows the misadventures of several teenage boys who pull off various pranks and suffer brutal consequences. The cast of young players is appealing and they provide a striking picture of their strict religious-school experience. Also with Philip Bosco, Jeannie Dundas, Donald Sutherland, and Kate Reid. **Director**—Michael Dinner. **(PG)** *104 minutes*

This movie available on videotape and/or disc.

HEAVEN KNOWS, MR. ALLISON (1957)

★★★

Robert Mitchum
Deborah Kerr

Mitchum and Kerr perform well together in this mildly preposterous but predictable film. Mitchum plays a gruff Marine corporal who is stranded on a Japanese-controlled South Pacific island at the height of World War II. He must depend on his only companion, a nun played by Kerr, to help him outfox the Japanese to get them to safety. John Huston directs with style and skill. **Academy Award Nominations**—Kerr, best actress; John Lee Mahin and Huston, best screenplay based on material from another medium. *105 minutes*

HEAVENLY BODIES (1985)

★

Cynthia Dale
Patricia Idlette
Richard Rebiere

Dreary, predictable rip-off of *Flashdance* set in the pulsating world of a dancercise club. Aerobic dancing, involving scores of young, good-looking participants, is the centerpiece of the film, which unfolds with sparse dialogue. A half-baked plot concerns a rickety romance between the club's female owner and a pro-football player. Dale, Idlette, and Rebiere head the cast of unknowns. **Director**—Lawrence Dane. **(R)** *89 minutes*

THE HEAVENLY KID (1985)

★★

Jason Gedrick
Lewis Smith

Lewis Smith gives Jason Gedrick advice in The Heavenly Kid.

This guardian angel movie starts awkwardly but has an upbeat ending. Smith plays a young man of the 1960s, killed in a car crash, who returns to bolster the ego of a wimpy teenager of the 1980s (Gedrick). Much of the storyline is derived from such classics as *Here Comes Mr. Jordan, It's a Wonderful Life,* and *Rebel Without a Cause.* **Director**—Cary Medoway. **(PG-13)** *92 minutes*

HEAVEN'S GATE (1980)

★★

Kris Kristofferson
Isabelle Huppert
Christopher Walken
John Hurt

Kris Kristofferson sides with the poor settlers in Heaven's Gate.

Michael Cimino's $40-million epic western about the 1890 Johnson County, Wyoming, cattle wars is still muddled and overblown despite improvements in the editing and voice-over narration. Kristofferson stars as a Harvard educated federal marshal who sides with poor settlers marked for extermination by wealthy landowners. His role, as well as those of the other actors, is ill-defined and mostly incoherent. It seems as if Cimino's theme of the corrupting influence of money and power corrupted the movie itself. However, the film's Oscar-nominated art direction, in addition to Vilmos Zsigmond's cinematography, makes this notorious western worthwhile viewing. A 149-minute version also exists. **(R)** *219 minutes*

HEAVY METAL (1981)

★½

A brash, crude, animated anthology, based on the grotesque fantasy magazine of the same name. The various segments deal with sword-and-sorcery, violence, sex, science fiction, drugs, and mysticism—all tied together with ear-blasting rock music. The cartoon fantasies are bridged by a luminous green ball that represents evil. It's a heavy trip that begins with a bang but gradually runs out of energy. **Director**—Gerald Potterton. **(R)** *90 minutes*

HEDDA (1975)

★★

Glenda Jackson

The talented Jackson dominates this film version of Ibsen's *Hedda Gabler* with a steely and intelligent performance, playing the bored and impatient woman who wrecked the lives of the men who pursued her. It's a first-class acting job, but the movie itself is stale and unmoving. Trevor Nunn directed and wrote the screenplay, based on the Royal Shakespeare production. The transferal from stage presentation to screen is strained. Also with Peter Eyre and Jennie Linden. **(PG) Academy Award Nomination**—Jackson, best actress. *104 minutes*

THE HEIRESS (1949)

★★★★

Olivia de Havilland
Montgomery Clift

Olivia de Havilland is The Heiress, *a guileless woman seduced by a fortune hunter.*

De Havilland is brilliant as a plain, lonely, but rich spinster who is wooed by a sly, charming fortune-seeker, played by Clift. The smartly styled film, set in turn-of-the-century New York, is based on Henry James' play *Washington Square*. All parts are portrayed effectively, with Ralph Richardson, Miriam

Hopkins, Vanessa Brown, Mona Freeman, and Ray Collins in supporting roles. **Director**—William Wyler. **Academy Award**—de Havilland, best actress. **Nominations**—best picture; Wyler, best director; Richardson, best supporting actor; Leo Tover, cinematography. *115 minutes b&w*

HELLBOUND: HELLRAISER II (1988)

Ashley Laurence
Clare Higgins
Kenneth Cranham

One of the monsters from Hellbound: Hellraiser II.

In this sequel to 1987's *Hellraiser,* the heroine (Laurence) is now in a psychiatric hospital, where she encounters more grotesque creatures. The screenplay is confusing, serving mainly as a vehicle to present a cavalcade of obnoxious monsters. Many are minus their skin. Lacks the coherence of the first film, though it is equally as gruesome. **Director**—Tony Randel. **(R)** *98 minutes*

HELLFIGHTERS (1969)

John Wayne
Jim Hutton
Katharine Ross

This sophomoric action yarn about rough-tough men who battle oil-well fires is upgraded a half-notch by the presence of Wayne. Wayne leads his crew against the flames and finds time to deal with his ex-wife, too. Some action scenes are notable. Also with Vera Miles, Bruce Cabot, Jay C. Flippen, and Barbara Stuart. **Director**—Andrew V. McLaglen. **(G)** *121 minutes*

HELL NIGHT (1981)

★

Linda Blair

This film is more teenage sex-and-terror fare, cranked off the Hollywood horror assembly line with a minimum of inspiration and talent. Some fraternity pledges spend their initiation night at a haunted house where survivors of a family murdered 12 years ago take their revenge on the youths. The usual head-choppings and other gory deaths go on until most of the kids are eliminated. Blair is the only familiar player, and she escapes the massacre. **Director**—Tom DeSimone. **(R)** *101 minutes*

HELLO AGAIN (1987)

 ★★ 

Shelley Long
Judith Ivey
Corbin Bernsen

In this gimmicky comedy, Long stars as a suburban housewife who dies unexpectedly but returns from the grave a year later. Her arrival is less than joyful for her social-climbing husband who has remarried in the meantime. This sort of fantasy only succeeds if there is delicate direction, a clever and unsentimental script, and irresistible performances. Unfortunately, this film is short on all counts. Long manages to pull off a few bright moments despite the mediocre material, but the bulk of the film is dull and predictable. **Director**—Frank Perry. **(PG)** *96 minutes*

HELLO, DOLLY! (1969)

★★★

Barbra Streisand
Walter Matthau
Michael Crawford

Barbra Streisand (center) plays matchmaker in Hello, Dolly!

Big, brassy musical, based on the Broadway success about a New York matchmaker in the early 1900s who ends up getting married herself. Streisand plays the title role in her usual powerhouse style, but she's obviously too young for the part. However, all is forgiven when she belts out some enjoyable songs with exceptional gusto. Louis Armstrong adds immeasurably to the frolic. Armstrong and Streisand team up to sing the title song. The film is based on Thornton Wilder's play *The Matchmaker*. Other cast members include E.J. Peaker and Marianne McAndrew. Some prints have been edited to 118 minutes. **Director**—Gene Kelly. **(G)** **Academy Award Nominations**—best picture; Harry Stradling, cinematography. *146 minutes*

HELLRAISER (1987)

 ★★½

Andrew Robinson
Clare Higgins

Horror writer Clive Barker wrote and directed this fiendishly imaginative horror thriller about an amoral hedonist who suffers the pleasures—and torments—of the damned after using a mysterious box to enter another dimension. His flesh literally flayed from his body, the victim must depend on his unscrupulous sister-in-law to lure men to her home so that he can steal their skin. Complication: the horrifying demons who want their box returned to them. This is gruesome, hard-core horror that is definitely not for the squeamish, but hardy viewers will find it an irresistible thrill ride. **(R)** *95 minutes*

HELLS ANGELS FOREVER (1983)

The Hells Angels
Bo Diddley
Willie Nelson

A murky-looking documentary that attempts to glorify and apologize for the notorious motorcycle gang. Much footage apparently was shot by the Angels themselves, and the scenes have a home-movie quality as well as a certain perverse fascination. We see the scruffy-looking bikers riding their motorcycles, partying on a boat, attending a wedding ceremony, discussing their peculiar freewheeling philosophy, and engaging in fistfights. Also, there's

(Continued)

(Continued)
much self-righteous comment about attempts by government agencies to destroy the organization. **Director**—Richard Chase. **(R)** *92 minutes*

HELLZAPOPPIN (1941)

Ole Olsen
Chic Johnson

Olsen and Johnson present a screen version of their madcap Broadway burlesque show, and the results are highly entertaining. The zany duo decides to make a movie, and they cook up their own plot as they progress. A few gags misfire, but most of them are amusing. The supporting cast also features Hugh Herbert, Martha Raye, and Mischa Auer. **Director**—H.C. Potter. *84 minutes b&w*

HENRY: PORTRAIT OF A SERIAL KILLER (1989)

Michael Rooker

Rooker, who costarred with Tom Cruise in *Days of Thunder,* appears in the title role of this relentlessly grim horror tale. Henry is a pathological liar and serial killer who murders almost everyone with whom he comes in contact. Filmmaker John McNaughton is surgically precise in presenting the grotesque crimes, but he passes no judgments and shows no justice. This approach is sure to offend many conservative viewers, while more seasoned moviegoers will be fascinated by Rooker's performance and the lengths to which McNaughton takes the events. Based on a true story; some comfort is offered by the knowledge that the real-life Henry was captured and convicted. To avoid an X rating, both the theatrically released version and the video version were not rated by the MPAA, so younger viewers should not be allowed to watch this film. Also with Tom Towles and Tracy Arnold. Produced and directed by McNaughton with Steve Jones. **(No MPAA rating)** *90 minutes*

HENRY V (1945)

★★★★

Laurence Olivier
Robert Newton

No one does Shakespeare like Olivier, and he triumphs here as both director and lead actor. The production is presented as an example of a play at the Globe Theatre in the early 1600s, and then it brilliantly evolves as a contemporary screen rendition. Olivier's acting is magnificent, and the film offers many glorious moments; the battle scenes, splendidly photographed in color, are engrossing. Also with Leslie Banks, Esmond Knight, Leo Genn, Renée Asherson, and Ralph Truman. **Academy Award Nominations**—best picture; Olivier, best actor. *137 minutes*

HENRY V (1989)

★★★

Kenneth Branagh

Branagh gives a brilliant performance in the title role as Shakespeare's 15th-century warrior king. The production rivals Laurence Olivier's 1945 version, though it utilizes a grittier setting, emphasizes a dirty realism in the fighting sequences, and concentrates on Henry's inner conflicts. As such, Branagh, who also directed the film, owes much to Orson Welles' dark screen interpretations of *Macbeth* and *Chimes at Midnight.* Several eminent British actors, including Derek Jacobi, Ian Holm, Brian Blessed, Robert Stephens, Christian Bale, and Judi Dench, complement Branagh in supporting roles. **(PG)** **Academy Award**—Phyllis Dalton, costume design. **Nominations**—Branagh, best actor and best director. *135 minutes*

HER ALIBI (1989)

★★ ®

Tom Selleck
Paulina Porizkova

Tom Selleck tries to learn Paulina Porizkova's secret in Her Alibi.

A boring romantic comedy starring Selleck and model-turned-actress Porizkova, who fail to ignite any sparks. He's a celebrated mystery novelist. She's a suspect in a murder case. The limp connection? If she writes about the case for him, he'll be her alibi. Director Bruce Beresford, more at home with serious drama, falters with the silly slapstick and worn-out clichés. A weak, lamebrained script adds to the overall ineptness. Also with William Daniels, James Farentino, and Patrick Wayne. **(PG)** *95 minutes*

HERCULES (1983)

★ ®

Lou Ferrigno
Sybil Danning

Hulking muscleman Ferrigno, grunting and flexing his bulbous biceps, is in the title role of this ridiculous epic adventure. Clad in skimpy gladiator skivvies to show off his overgrown physique, Ferrigno battles various villains and monsters in his quest to rescue a princess. The absurd screenplay makes a shambles of Greek mythology, and the film is rife with flashy effects more suited to sci-fi extravaganzas. Mirella D'Angelo and Brad Harris costar. **Director**—Lewis Coates (Luigi Cozzi). **(PG)** *98 minutes*

HERE COMES MR. JORDAN (1941)

★★★★

Robert Montgomery
Evelyn Keyes

Robert Montgomery and Edward Everett Horton in Here Comes Mr. Jordan.

This is an inventive comedy/fantasy about a boxer who dies in a plane crash by mistake, and is sent to Earth to occupy someone else's body. Montgom-

® *This movie available with closed captions for the hearing impaired.*

ery plays the prizefighter who dies before his time. The film's novel twist about heaven and death works on many levels and sustains interest and comic vitality to the end; the theme has been reused in many subsequent movies. Also with Claude Rains, Rita Johnson, Edward Everett Horton, James Gleason, and Donald MacBride. **Director**—Alexander Hall. **Academy Awards**—Harry Segall, original story; Sidney Buchman and Seton I. Miller, screenplay. **Nominations**—best picture; Hall, best director; Montgomery, best actor; Gleason, best supporting actor; Joseph Walker, cinematography.
93 minutes b&w

HERE COME THE WAVES (1944)

★★★

Bing Crosby
Betty Hutton

Bouncy World War II musical morale-builder, with Crosby in the Navy and romancing identical twin Waves. Hutton plays the twins. As expected, there's not much plot, but there are plenty of good songs. Bing sings "Accent-tchu-ate the Positive" and more. Sonny Tufts costars in his first singing role. Also with Ann Doran and Gwen Crawford. **Director**—Mark Sandrich.
98 minutes b&w

A HERO AIN'T NOTHIN' BUT A SANDWICH (1978)

★★

Cicely Tyson

Paul Winfield
Larry B. Scott

This frank family film concerns a 13-year-old-boy who grapples with a drug problem. Tyson and Winfield give decent performances, but they're often upstaged by Scott, 16, as the intelligent but troubled youth. The movie, for the most part, is preachy and pedantic. Also with Helen Martin and Glynn Turman. **Director**—Ralph Nelson. **(PG)**
105 minutes

HERO AND THE TERROR (1988)

★★

Chuck Norris
Jack O'Halloran

Norris stars as a heroic Los Angeles detective who subdues a vicious serial

Chuck Norris tracks down a psychopath in Hero and the Terror.

killer. There's a slight twist for the karate champ in this cop action thriller: He shows his emotional side when he faces the prospect of fatherhood as his girlfriend bears their child. Despite such newfound domesticity, Norris still manages the usual quota of kicks and chops. The climactic showdown takes place in a large movie theater where the psychopath (O'Halloran) has stored his victims' corpses. Also with Brynn Thayer, Steve W. James, Ron O'Neal, and Billy Drago. **Director**—William Tannen. **(R)**
96 minutes

HERO AT LARGE (1980)

★★1/2

John Ritter
Anne Archer
Bert Convy

Ritter of TV's *Three's Company* plays a struggling actor in New York City. He becomes an instant hero when he foils a robbery attempt while clad as a comic-book hero for a movie promotion. Ritter is at his easygoing best as the young man in the superhero suit who can save the world. But midway, the script runs out of steam, and what charm there is deteriorates into excessive sentimentality. Unfortunately, a good idea gets pushed too far. Archer plays the girl next door. Also with Kevin McCarthy. **Director**—Martin Davidson. **(PG)**
98 minutes

HEROES (1977)

★

Henry Winkler
Sally Field

Winkler and Field costar in this erratic and poorly written story about the escapades of a troubled Vietnam veteran. Winkler, in his first effort as leading

Henry Winkler and Sally Field in a happy moment from Heroes.

man, has trouble shaking off his television image of "The Fonz" and adapting to the big screen. Field, however, evokes energy and charm in her role as Winkler's companion. The film too often resembles a conventional television drama, and ultimately fails to be effective. Harrison Ford excels in a small role as one of Winkler's war buddies. **Director**—Jeremy Kagan. **(PG)**
113 minutes

HESTER STREET (1975)

★★★

Steven Keats
Carol Kane

Joan Micklin Silver wrote and directed this compassionate movie about Jewish immigrants struggling to adapt to the New World at the turn of the century. The story concerns a young immigrant, played by Keats, who is charmed with the ways of his new country. His wife, played by Kane, arrives later with their son and finds assimilation painful. The plot is predictable, but the performances are keen and extraordinary. Also with Mel Howard, Dorrie Kavanaugh, and Doris Roberts. Mostly in Yiddish with English titles. **(PG) Academy Award Nomination**—Kane, best actress.
92 minutes b&w

HEY BABU RIBA (1987)

★★★

Gaala Videnovic
Nebojsa Bakocevic

From Yugoslavia comes this bittersweet account of a group of young people growing up under the influence of the Communist bureaucracy of the early 1950s and longing for a freer lifestyle. Their desires attract them to the images

(Continued)

This movie available on videotape and/or disc.

(Continued)
and sounds of American pop culture, including rock 'n' roll. Colorful performances highlight the drama, which is told in flashback. The political overtones of the film do not detract from the story. Also with Relja Bacic, Dragan Bjelogrlic, Srdjan Todorovic, and Milan Strljic. Originally filmed in Serbo-Croatian. **Director**—Jovan Acin. **(R)**
109 minutes

THE HIDDEN (1987)

★★★

Michael Nouri
Kyle MacLachlan

Michael Nouri and Kyle MacLachlan pursue an unearthly criminal in The Hidden.

An alien creature inhabits the bodies of various earthlings and then embarks on a killing spree. The film initially appears to be a routine science-fiction tale, but elements of the police thriller are included, resulting in an entertaining hybrid of two popular genres. Nouri stars as a the overworked homicide detective baffled by the strange case. MacLachlan as an eerily subdued FBI agent is the perfect partner for the excitable Nouri. Cleverly scripted, with plenty of action and unexpected moments of tenderness. Also with Ed O'Ross, Clu Gulager, and Claudia Christian. **Director**—Jack Sholder. **(R)** *98 minutes*

HIDE IN PLAIN SIGHT (1980)

★★$^1/_2$

James Caan
Jill Eikenberry

Caan directed and stars in this restrained drama about a divorced factory worker's frustrating efforts to locate his children, who are in hiding under the government's Witness Relocation Program, which is designed to protect witnesses from criminal retaliation. This is Caan's directorial debut, and he handles the assignment at a sluggish pace. The film, based on a true story, needs a shot of adrenaline. But the supporting cast is especially good, and the film manages to depict ordinary people with authenticity. Also with Robert Viharo, Kenneth McMillan, and Danny Aiello. **(PG)** *98 minutes*

HIDING OUT (1987)

Jon Cryer
Annabeth Gish

Cryer, who gained some critical respect for his performance as "Ducky" in *Pretty in Pink,* stars as a yuppie stockbroker who is called as a witness in an insider trading case. After one of the other witnesses is shot, Cryer flees the city for a small town where he hides out by disguising himself as a teen and enrolling in high school. He runs for class president and also falls for teenager Gish. The high-school scenes are pleasant enough, with the fish-out-of-water theme resulting in some humorous segments. However, the combination of teen comedy and mystery thriller is not an effective one, and the hectic chases that begin and the end the film seem from another movie altogether. **Director**—Bob Giraldi. **(PG–13)** *98 minutes*

THE HIDING PLACE (1975)

★

Julie Harris
Eileen Heckart
Arthur O'Connell

This film, elaborately produced by the Billy Graham Association, is based on a true account of a Dutch Christian family who led an underground operation in Holland to assist Jews during World War II. Here is a splendid opportunity to develop an exciting and moving movie; instead, the film plods along in the manner of an overlong sermon. The action hardly moves in situations that must have been suspenseful. Also with Jeanette Clift and Robert Rietty. Filmed in the Netherlands and Great Britain. **Director**—James F. Collier. **(PG)**
145 minutes

THE HIGH AND THE MIGHTY (1954)

★★★

John Wayne
Robert Newton
Robert Stack

A gripping drama about a crippled airliner trying to reach safety during a long flight over the Pacific. The nervous passengers, contemplating a crash landing in the ocean, reveal their emotions. Wayne is effective as a copilot who keeps his cool. See *Airplane!* for a terrific parody of this pioneer *Airport* film. Also with Doe Avedon, Claire Trevor, Laraine Day, Jan Sterling, Phil Harris, Sidney Blackmer, and David Brian. **Director**—William Wellman. **Academy Award Nominations**—Wellman, best director; Trevor and Sterling, best supporting actress. *147 minutes*

HIGH ANXIETY (1977)

★★

Mel Brooks
Madeline Kahn
Cloris Leachman
Harvey Korman

Mel Brooks spoofs suspense thrillers in High Anxiety.

Another parody from Brooks, who seems to be running out of ideas. This time he's very specific, making the films of Alfred Hitchcock his target. Brooks seems convinced that merely making a visual reference to any well-known scene in a Hitchcock film constitutes a joke. Those who agree with him may find this romp funny. Those who prefer development or wit or original slapstick will be disappointed, though Brooks' usual performing company tries hard. Brooks also directed, produced, and

® *This movie available with closed captions for the hearing impaired.*

even wrote a song for this one. Dick Van Patten, Ron Carey, and Howard Morris costar. **(PG)** *94 minutes*

HIGH–BALLIN' (1978)

  ★★

Peter Fonda
Jerry Reed

Fonda and Reed are good guys who fight a gang of hijackers trying to put the squeeze on independent truckers. This action/adventure tale sends 18-wheelers careening through snowstorms in some daring chase scenes. The dialogue is pat and the storyline isn't original, but there's lots of flashy action along with some decent performances. Also with Helen Shaver and Chris Wiggins. Filmed in Canada. **Director**—Peter Carter. **(PG)**

100 minutes

HIGH HOPES (1988)

★★★1/2

Philip Davis
Ruth Sheen

Director Mike Leigh's sharp-edged comedy deftly skewers Margaret Thatcher's England. The slice-of-life sketches look closely at the British working class and contrast their gritty world with that of the more privileged classes. The top-notch cast does a splendid job of portraying the colorful characters, mainly through improvisation. Davis and Sheen are remarkable as the working couple who elicit the most sympathy. Also with Edna Dore, Philip Jackson, Heather Tobias, and Lesley Manville. **(No MPAA rating)**

110 minutes

HIGHLANDER (1986)

   ★★

Christopher Lambert
Clancy Brown
Sean Connery

Ancient enemies from 16th-century Scotland, who are immortal, appear on the streets of New York City to battle with broadswords. This situation, not surprisingly, confounds the authorities. After the third head is chopped off, the film becomes tiresome despite the flashy banging and clanging of the relentless duels. The film is all too noisy, overblown, and senseless. **Director**—Russell Mulcahy. **(R)** *111 minutes*

HIGH NOON (1952)

 ★★★★

Gary Cooper
Grace Kelly

One of the best westerns of the 1950s, with tight-lipped Cooper doing a sensational job as a determined lawman who bravely faces the villains alone because the town's citizens are too afraid to help him. Kelly stars as his young Quaker wife whose stand against violence tears the just-married couple apart. The script by Carl Foreman is well known for its psychological insights into the characters and their motivations. Fred Zinnemann's direction is tight, with a keen sense of suspense aided by the fact that the action of the film occurs in real time. (The story begins at 10:40 A.M. and concludes at noon, which equals the running time of the film's narrative.) Thomas Mitchell, Lloyd Bridges, Otto Kruger, Lon Chaney, Katy Jurado, and Henry Morgan appear in supporting roles. **Academy Award**—Cooper, best actor. **Nominations**—best picture; Zinnemann, best director; Foreman, screenplay. *85 minutes b&w*

HIGH PLAINS DRIFTER (1973)

 ★★★

Clint Eastwood
Verna Bloom

Eastwood directs and stars in this violent western influenced in narrative and style by the films of Sergio Leone. He plays a mysterious drifter who comes to a small town, terrorizes the people, but then stays on to save the inhabitants from a group of escaped convicts. The theme of the stranger who rides in from the wilderness to defend the community is a common one in westerns (*Shane*), but the hint of the supernatural in this plotline makes the film a bit offbeat. And, in terms of story and mood, it can be considered a forerunner of Eastwood's *Pale Rider* (1985). Also with Mariana Hill, Mitchell Ryan, Jack Ging, and Stefan Gierasch. **(PG)**

105 minutes

HIGH RISK (1981)

 ★★★

James Brolin
Bruce Davison
Chick Vennera
Cleavon Little

A clever, lighthearted adventure about four "nice guys" who steal $5 million from a Colombian drug kingpin, and then encounter unexpected obstacles during their escape. Writer/director Stewart Raffill offers an efficient script with a proper portion of humor amid the action. The film is nicely cast, with Brolin, Davison, Vennera, and Little as the unlikely heroes, and James Coburn, Ernest Borgnine, and Anthony Quinn in effective cameo roles. **(R)**

94 minutes

HIGH ROAD TO CHINA (1983)

★★

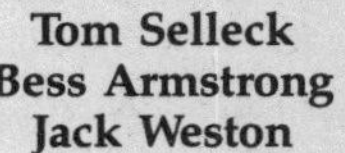

Tom Selleck
Bess Armstrong
Jack Weston

Tom Selleck and Bess Armstrong find adventure in High Road to China.

Selleck, star of TV's *Magnum, P.I.* series, makes his movie star debut in this derring-do actioner set just after World War I. He manages to work up some charm and dazzle as a boozing daredevil pilot who escorts a beautiful heiress (Armstrong) on a dangerous mission to find her father in China. But the screenplay—a second cousin to *Raiders of the Lost Ark*—often takes the low road of strained credibility, which ruins the entire production. **Director**—Brian G. Hutton. **(PG)** *105 minutes*

HIGH SCHOOL CONFIDENTIAL! (1958)

 ★★1/2

Russ Tamblyn
Jan Sterling
Mamie Van Doren

A young undercover agent (Tamblyn) poses as a new student so that he can infiltrate a high-school narcotics ring. Though obviously made for exploita-

(Continued)

(Continued)
tion purposes, this low-budget melodrama does capture the raw energy and high spirits associated with the rock 'n' roll culture of the 1950s, which the film was simultaneously condemning and exploiting. Van Doren, the Marilyn Monroe of B-movies, seethes with sexuality as Tamblyn's seductive aunt. The rest of the supporting cast features an interesting group of actors who were either has-beens at the time of the film's release or never made it big in the first place—Jackie Coogan, John Drew Barrymore, and Sydney Chaplin (Charlie's son). Rocker Jerry Lee Lewis sings the title song while playing the piano on the back of a flatbed truck. That scene alone makes the film worthwhile viewing. **Director**—Jack Arnold.
85 minutes b&w

HIGH SIERRA (1941)

★★★

Humphrey Bogart
Ida Lupino

Humphrey Bogart gathers his gang and lays down the law in High Sierra.

A forceful crime drama about a veteran gangster, played by Bogart, operating in the California mountain country. The film's success is due to Bogey's fine performance as Mad Dog Earle, a ruthless killer who nevertheless is capable of some moments of kindness. Lupino plays the tough but decent woman who stays with Earle despite his aloofness. Also with Joan Leslie, Alan Curtis, Arthur Kennedy, Henry Hull, and Henry Travers. **Director**—Raoul Walsh.
100 minutes b&w

HIGH SOCIETY (1956)

★★★

Bing Crosby
Grace Kelly
Frank Sinatra
Celeste Holm

This musical version of *The Philadelphia Story* is entertaining, but lacks the pointed humor of the original. Crosby stars as a man of means who tries to stop his ex-wife, played by Kelly, from marrying again. Sinatra and Holm play reporters sent to cover the wedding. Cole Porter's score adds pleasure to the proceedings. Kelly's final screen role. Also stars Louis Armstrong, Louis Calhern, John Lund, and Sidney Blackmer. **Director**—Charles Walters.
107 minutes

HIGH SPIRITS (1988)

★★ ®

Peter O'Toole
Daryl Hannah
Steve Guttenberg

Peter O'Toole, Daryl Hannah, and Steve Guttenberg in High Spirits.

In this clumsy slapstick comedy, O'Toole stars as a strapped descendant of Irish aristocrats. He tries to retain the family castle by pretending the place is haunted, thus luring paying tourists. But lo and behold, it really is haunted. The bright cast manages some good moments but doesn't have a chance with this trite treatment of a promising premise. Also with Beverly D'Angelo, Liam Neeson, Peter Gallagher, Jennifer Tilly, and Connie Booth. **Director**—Neil Jordan. **(PG-13)** *96 minutes*

HIGH TIDE (1988)

★★1/2

Judy Davis
Jan Adele

Davis portrays an interesting but irresponsible woman who tries to renew a relationship with the daughter she abandoned many years ago. As a backup singer for an Elvis Presley impersonator, Davis decides her life is going nowhere and that she needs to settle down in the real world. Despite the promising beginning, this Australian-made film soon lapses into familiar melodrama, focusing on the tenuous bond between Davis and her teenage daughter. Director Gillian Armstrong, who worked with Davis on *My Brilliant Career,* coaxes some excellent performances from her cast. Claudia Karvan costars as the teenage daughter.
(PG–13) *103 minutes*

THE HINDENBURG (1976)

★★

George C. Scott
Anne Bancroft
Burgess Meredith

A disaster movie about the German dirigible that exploded while docking at Lakehurst, New Jersey, in 1937. The Academy Award-winning visual effects are impressive, and for some this alone may prove worthwhile, but the script moves along slowly, and the suspense is lighter than air. Scott stars as a Nazi security agent on board to identify a possible saboteur. Also with William Atherton, Roy Thinnes, Charles Durning, and Gig Young. **Director**—Robert Wise. **(PG)** *125 minutes*

HIROSHIMA, MON AMOUR (1959)

★★★★

Emmanuele Riva
Eiji Okada

Alain Resnais catapulted into the front rank of the world's directors with this movie about the love story of French actress Riva and Japanese architect Okada. Resnais brilliantly contrasts the love affair against the grim and stark scenes of destruction caused by the bombing at Hiroshima. The low-key acting enhances the melancholy mood created by Resnais. Also with Pierre Barband and Stella Dassas. Originally filmed in French. **Academy Award Nomination**—Marguerite Duras, best story and screenplay written directly for the screen. *88 minutes b&w*

HIS GIRL FRIDAY (1940)

★★★★

Rosalind Russell
Cary Grant

A howlingly funny version of *The Front Page,* brought off at a fast clip by director

® *This movie available with closed captions for the hearing impaired.*

Howard Hawks, and featuring a cast of pros giving it their all. Grant stars as a scheming newspaper editor; Russell plays Hildy Johnson, the prima donna reporter. As Hildy is about to marry a mild-mannered businessman, played by Ralph Bellamy, a hot murder scoop tempts her back into the business for one last story. Lots of live-wire supporting players add to the fun. Also with Gene Lockhart, Porter Hall, Ernest Truex, Clarence Kolb, Roscoe Karns, and Billy Gilbert. *92 minutes b&w*

HIS MAJESTY O'KEEFE (1953)

★★

Burt Lancaster

Lancaster swashbuckles around the South Seas islands helping the natives fend off pirates. Adequate action and a bit of romance make up this adventure film, but Lancaster fares better in *The Crimson Pirate.* Also with Joan Rice, André Morell, Benson Fong, Philip Ahn, and Grant Taylor. **Director**—Byron Haskin. *92 minutes*

HISTORY OF THE WORLD—PART I (1981)

★★

Mel Brooks
Dom DeLuise
Madeline Kahn
Harvey Korman

Funnyman Brooks rewrites history with comic pokes at the Stone Age, the Roman Empire, the Spanish Inquisition, and the French Revolution. Brooks stars in various roles and generates a fair portion of belly laughs and inspired comic situations. However, many skits are undermined by excessive crudeness. The comedy is uneven despite the appearances of several comic actors, including Cloris Leachman, Ron Carey, Sid Caesar, Howard Morris, and Spike Milligan. **Director**—Brooks. **(R)** *92 minutes*

THE HITCHER (1986)

★★½

Rutger Hauer
C. Thomas Howell

Hauer stars as a hitchhiking psychopath who leaves a trail of mayhem and dismembered corpses throughout the lonely Texas landscape. This above-average slasher film packs plenty of terror and tension, but the manipulative

C. Thomas Howell regrets picking up Rutger Hauer, who is The Hitcher.

story raises many questions left unanswered and the vicious slaughterings finally become tiresome. Viewers may emerge confused as well as frightened. Howell costars as the hapless youth who becomes embroiled in the mysterious killer's web. **Director**—Robert Harmon. **(R)** *97 minutes*

HITLER (1961)

★★

Richard Basehart

Basehart stars in the title role as the bloodthirsty Nazi führer. The film traces Hitler's career from his early adult life to his defeat and suicide in his Berlin bunker. This film biography treads rather lightly on a subject that deserves more insight, and Basehart isn't all that convincing as the mad dictator. Others in the cast include Maria Emo, Martin Kosleck, and John Banner. **Director**—Stuart Heisler. *107 minutes b&w*

HOBSON'S CHOICE (1954)

★★★

Charles Laughton
Brenda de Banzie
John Mills

Laughton sparkles in this family comedy, based on a play by Harold Brighouse, as a strong-willed bootsmith in the 1890s who tries to control the lives of his daughters. Well-directed example of droll British humor, enhanced by excellent performances. Also with Richard Wattis and Daphne Anderson. **Director**—David Lean. *107 minutes b&w*

HOLD BACK THE DAWN (1941)

★★★

Charles Boyer
Olivia de Havilland

Gigolo Charles Boyer marries Olivia de Havilland in Hold Back the Dawn.

Boyer is in top form as a refugee from Nazi Germany who marries a schoolteacher in Mexico, played by de Havilland, merely to gain entrance to the United States. It's a moving wartime melodrama, stylishly produced and heightened by fine acting and direction. The cast also includes Paulette Goddard, Victor Francen, Walter Abel, and Rosemary DeCamp. **Director**—Mitchell Leisen. **Academy Award Nominations**—best picture; de Havilland, best actress; Charles Brackett and Billy Wilder, screenplay; Leo Tover, cinematography. *115 minutes b&w*

HOLIDAY (1930)

★★★

Ann Harding
Mary Astor
Edward Everett Horton

Bright, witty comedy (from the successful Broadway play by Philip Barry) of two wealthy sisters, one a nonconformist, the other a prig, who love the same man. This early talkie is almost as good as the more popular 1938 version and deserves attention. Excellent cast also includes Hedda Hopper, Monroe Owsley, and Robert Ames. Sophisticated fun for all. **Director**—Edward H. Griffith. **Academy Award Nominations**—Harding, best actress; Horace Jackson, adaptation. *96 minutes b&w*

HOLIDAY INN (1942)

★★★★

Bing Crosby
Fred Astaire

Crosby sings and Astaire dances in this colorful musical. The routine romantic plot concerns competition for the atten-

(Continued)

Bing Crosby, Virginia Dale, and Fred Astaire in Holiday Inn.

tion of a woman between former show-biz partners. However, the magnificent Irving Berlin score is the real cause for interest here, with Crosby crooning "White Christmas." Also with Walter Abel, Marjorie Reynolds, Virginia Dale, and Louise Beavers. **Director**—Mark Sandrich. **Academy Award Nomination**—Berlin, original story.
101 minutes b&w

HOLLYWOOD BOULEVARD (1976)

★★1/2

Candice Rialson
Dick Miller

Here's a B-movie from the Roger Corman studios that's a spoof of B-movies. Rialson stars as an aspiring actress who breaks into low-budget films and becomes involved with a number of perilous situations, including some bizarre murders. Shots from other Corman films are woven into the story representing the movies Rialson is supposedly starring in. Also with Mary Woronov and Rita George. **Directors**—Joe Dante and Allan Arkush. **(R)**
83 minutes

HOLLYWOOD CANTEEN (1944)

★★

Joan Leslie
Robert Hutton
Dane Clark
Janis Paige

A galaxy of Hollywood stars make guest appearances in this review of the entertainment community's supporting efforts during World War II. Some of the music is pleasant, but the story goes nowhere. It's about a soldier hankering for a date with a pretty girl. Other luminaries include Joan Crawford, Bette Davis, the Andrews Sisters, Jack Benny, Eddie Cantor, Roy Rogers, Sidney Greenstreet, Peter Lorre, and Barbara Stanwyck. **Director**—Delmer Daves.
123 minutes b&w

THE HOLLYWOOD KNIGHTS (1980)

Fran Drescher
Stuart Pankin
Tony Danza

California teenagers pull off some outrageous monkeyshines on Halloween night in 1965 to protest the closing of their favorite drive-in restaurant. Most of the pranks are aimed at harassing authoritative adults. A few jokes go over, but much of the movie, which looks like a combination of *American Graffiti* and *Animal House,* is merely ill-conceived silliness. Also with Robert Wuhl and Michelle Pfeiffer. **Director**—Floyd Mutrux. **(R)** *91 minutes*

HOLLYWOOD SHUFFLE (1987)

★★★

Robert Townsend

Townsend wrote, directed, and stars in this low-budget but likable comedy about the frustrations of a struggling black actor in Hollywood. The film, structured as a series of vignettes, is based on Townsend's personal experiences as an actor. Although the skits are loosely constructed, the satire effectively conveys Townsend's message about the stereotyping of blacks by Hollywood. Also with Anne-Marie Johnson and Starletta Dupois. **(R)**
82 minutes

HOMBRE (1967)

★★★

Paul Newman
Diane Cilento
Fredric March

Paul Newman is the moralistic rebel called Hombre.

An engrossing western drama, starring Newman as a young white man brought up by Indians. The action begins when Newman boards a stagecoach and helps the passengers in an encounter with outlaws. An intelligent script and interesting characterizations mix well with suspense and action. Moral dilemmas involving the relationship of Newman's character to the Indians add some depth to an otherwise ordinary western. Also with Richard Boone, Martin Balsam, Barbara Rush, and Cameron Mitchell. **Director**—Martin Ritt. *111 minutes*

HOME OF THE BRAVE (1949)

★★★

James Edwards
Lloyd Bridges

A compelling drama set during World War II, about a black soldier who suffers from the intolerance of his white comrades-in-arms. The film had more impact at the time of its release, but it's still watchable. Based on the play by Arthur Laurents. Also with Frank Lovejoy, Jeff Corey, and Steve Brodie. **Director**—Mark Robson. *86 minutes b&w*

HOMEWORK (1982)

Michael Morgan
Joan Collins

This silly, soft-core teen-sex comedy involves an awkward affair between an adolescent boy (Morgan) and his girlfriend's mother (Collins). Along the way, the film meanders through numerous confused subplots. The few gags fizzle (most are in poor taste), and the serious moments seem to have wound up in the wrong film. Various nude scenes are featured in an apparently desperate effort to keep the viewer's mind on the movie. Also with Carrie Snodgress. **Director**—James Beshears. **(R)** *90 minutes*

HONDO (1953)

John Wayne
Geraldine Page

An out-of-the-ordinary western about a cavalry soldier (Wayne), who discovers a widow and her son living in an isolated part of Texas and stays to defend them against an Indian attack. The vio-

This movie available with closed captions for the hearing impaired.

lence is toned down and the warm characterizations are played up in this interesting story, which is similar to *Shane,* produced in the same year. Page is excellent in her role as the plucky widow. Ward Bond, James Arness, and Michael Pate also star. Originally a 3-D film. **Director**—John Farrow. **Academy Award Nomination**—Page, best supporting actress. *84 minutes*

HONEY, I SHRUNK THE KIDS (1989)

Rick Moranis
Matt Frewer
Marcia Strassman

Engaging special effects highlight this clever children's adventure about four kids who are accidentally reduced in size by a shrinking machine. The 1/4-inch-high youngsters face perils in the form of monster bees and a backyard lawn that has more hazards than a jungle. Moranis stars as the goofy scientist, with Jared Rushton, Amy O'Neill, Thomas Brown, and Robert Oliveri as the unfortunate kids. An entertaining romp for the whole family. **Director**—Joe Johnston. **(PG)** *93 minutes*

HONEYSUCKLE ROSE (1980)

Willie Nelson
Dyan Cannon
Amy Irving
Slim Pickens

Nelson picks a mean guitar and sings rousing country-western songs in this low-key film. But, when the music stops, there's only a wisp of a plot—mostly borrowed from *Intermezzo*—about Nelson's infidelity while on the road. Cannon plays the long-suffering wife and sings a country song with style and gusto. **Director**—Jerry Schatzberg. **(PG)** *119 minutes*

HONKY TONK FREEWAY (1981)

Beau Bridges
William Devane
Beverly D'Angelo
Geraldine Page

Director John Schlesinger (*Midnight Cowboy*) can't bring together this uneven, silly, and meandering comedy. The flimsy story concerns efforts of citizens to secure a highway off-ramp at their small Florida town. Meanwhile, the film detours all over the country collecting some uninteresting people—and some animals—who eventually converge on this community. Everyone has a few gags to play with, but most fall flat. **(PG)** *107 minutes*

HONKYTONK MAN (1982)

 ★★½

Clint Eastwood

Director/actor Eastwood shifts into low gear with this mildly appealing 1930s tale of a hard-drinking country music singer. Eastwood, in the title role, has hopes of performing at the Grand Ole Opry. His 14-year-old nephew (played by Eastwood's son, Kyle) is along for some predictable rites-of-passage episodes. The story gradually peters out for lack of drama. Country music legend Marty Robbins appears in a touching scene; ironically, Robbins died just days before the film was released. **(PG)** *122 minutes*

HOOPER (1978)

Burt Reynolds
Jan-Michael Vincent
Sally Field

Reynolds stars in the title role as the greatest Hollywood stuntman of his time. He is challenged in his craft by a younger man, played by Vincent, until they team up at the end to perform a particularly dangerous stunt. This movie-within-a-movie should please most fans of Reynolds, who plays up his raucous, wise-guy character. There's a variety of well-executed stunts—car crashes, a chariot race, and a helicopter jump—as well as the behind-the-scenes look at moviemaking, which provide the interest in this lighthearted film. Also with Brian Keith, Robert Klein, Adam West, James Best, and John Marley. **Director**—Hal Needham. **(PG)** *100 minutes*

HOOSIERS (1986)

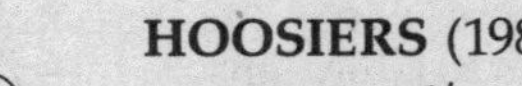

Gene Hackman
Dennis Hopper
Barbara Hershey

The storyline is familiar and even predictable: A basketball coach with a

Basketball coach Gene Hackman finds new hope in Hoosiers.

clouded past comes to a small Indiana town and inspires the underdog team to the state championship. However, the realistic characters and the poetic direction, which visually conveys the strength of the characters via long, steady shots of the beautiful and solid landscape, lift the film above the ordinary. Excellent performances by Hackman as the coach and Hopper as the town drunk highlight the film. It's a small movie with a big heart. **Director**—David Anspaugh. **(PG) Academy Award Nominations**—Hopper, best supporting actor; Jerry Goldsmith, best original score. *114 minutes*

HOPE AND GLORY (1987)

Sarah Miles
Sebastian Rice Edwards

Writer/director John Boorman presents an affectionate and fascinating autobiographical tale of World War II London as seen through the experiences of a young boy. Boorman expertly captures the flavor of these desperate but invigorating times as he dwells on the events of the boy's everyday life—collecting shrapnel, playing around the bombed houses, finding a wayward barrage balloon. This comedy/drama is not a standard war film based on the experiences of a few brave soldiers. Instead, it centers on the ordinary lives of the women and children left at home to pick up the pieces. Episodic in structure, the film moves forward slowly and deliberately, revealing the characters to be every bit as heroic as those soldiers on the front. Also with Geraldine Muir, David Hayman, Sammi Davis, and Ian Bannen. **(PG-13) Academy Award Nomi-**

(Continued)

(Continued)
nations—best picture; Boorman, best director and best original screenplay written directly for the screen; Philippe Rousselot, cinematography; Anthony Pratt and Joan Woollard, art direction. *118 minutes*

HOPSCOTCH (1980)

 ★★

Walter Matthau
Glenda Jackson

Glenda Jackson and Walter Matthau share romance and danger in Hopscotch.

Matthau stars as a disillusioned CIA agent who writes an embarrassing exposé about his bumbling colleagues and then leads them on a cat-and-mouse chase. The ever-appealing Matthau gives it his rumpled best, with Jackson adding a touch of class as his wily accomplice. The film can't seem to make up its mind whether it's a comedy or a drama. At times, the mood is straightforward, but then the movie lapses into silly slapstick. Also with Ned Beatty. **Director**—Ronald Neame. **(R)** *104 minutes*

THE HORN BLOWS AT MIDNIGHT (1945)

Jack Benny
Alexis Smith

Benny stars in this slapstick farce as an angel assigned to destroy Earth with blasts from Gabriel's horn. Benny took delight in panning this film, but it's a lot better than he made it out to be. The plot leans heavily on *Here Comes Mr. Jordan*. Also with Franklin Pangborn, Guy Kibbee, Dolores Moran, Reginald Gardiner, and Margaret Dumont. **Director**—Raoul Walsh. *78 minutes b&w*

HORROR SHOW (1989)

 ★½

Brion James
Lance Henriksen

Standard slasher fare about a cleaver-wielding murderer (James) who returns from the dead. The only inspired aspect of this nonsense is the killer's difficult execution in the electric chair, where the current energizes his evil spirit. The monster harasses the detective (Henriksen) responsible for his capture before the story lapses into the expected slice-and-dice clichés. Similar in storyline to *Shocker* and *The First Power,* which were made at about the same time. **Director**—James Isaac. **(R)** *94 minutes*

HORSE FEATHERS (1932)

 ★★★★

The Marx Brothers

A hilarious and zany Marx Brothers comedy set on a college campus. Groucho as president of Huxley College tries to lead the school to football stardom to keep the place financially afloat. The routines and gags, most of which have become classics, are fast and furious, and if you can't keep track of the silly plot it won't matter because you'll be too busy laughing. Groucho, Harpo, Chico, and Zeppo star with Thelma Todd and Nat Pendleton. **Director**—Norman Z. McLeod. *69 minutes*

THE HORSE'S MOUTH (1958)

 ★★★★

Alec Guinness

Brilliantly witty and sparkling social satire from the Joyce Cary novel about a nonconformist painter who thumbs his nose at the world and goes his own way. Guinness wrote the screenplay and also stars as Gully Jimson, the gruff social outcast. In his quest for new surfaces on which to paint delightful "feet," Gully covers walls and sidewalks, invades apartments, and applies paint to anything else he can reach. The entire cast is splendid, including Kay Walsh as his girlfriend and watchdog, Renee Houston as his former wife, Robert Coote, Michael Gough, and Ernest Thesiger. **Director**—Ronald Neame. **Academy Award Nomination**—Guinness, best screenplay based on material from another medium. *93 minutes*

THE HORSE SOLDIERS (1959)

★★

John Wayne
William Holden

This Civil War drama about a Union officer sent into Confederate territory to hasten the war's end by destroying a supply depot ultimately loses momentum and falters. John Ford's direction lacks its usual control and permits the elaborate storyline to sprawl and go afield. A solid cast will please some fans but most will lose interest due to too much talk and too little action. Constance Towers, Althea Gibson, Anna Lee, Strother Martin, Ken Curtis, and Hoot Gibson also appear. *119 minutes*

THE HOSPITAL (1971)

 ★★★

George C. Scott
Diana Rigg

A biting black comedy that firmly skewers incompetence and mismanagement within the medical profession as seen at a large city hospital. Paddy Chayefsky's award-winning screenplay digs into its subject with the force of a jackhammer, as a series of mishaps cause chaos and death. Scott is magnificent as a disillusioned chief doctor, and he gets plenty of support from Barnard Hughes, Richard Dysart, and Nancy Marchand. **Director**—Arthur Hiller. **(PG) Academy Award**—Chayefsky, best story and screenplay based on factual material or material not previously published. **Nomination**—Scott, best actor. *101 minutes*

HOT DOG...THE MOVIE (1984)

★★

David Naughton
Patrick Houser
Tracy Smith

This *Animal House* on skis features competition on California's Squaw Valley slopes by day and partying and sexual cavorting at night. Among the youthful high times are some splashing around in hot tubs, a wet T-shirt contest, and

This movie available with closed captions for the hearing impaired.

lots of booze consumption. Though the acrobatic skiing is quite spectacular, the dialogue, acting, character development, and infantile humor are painful to watch. **Director**—Peter Markle. **(R)** *96 minutes*

THE HOTEL NEW HAMPSHIRE (1984)

Nastassja Kinski
Jodie Foster
Beau Bridges
Rob Lowe

A rambling, offensive movie based on John Irving's best-seller about a weird family engaged in several hotel enterprises. The frantic plot involves various unsavory events, including gang rape, incest, terrorism, and suicide. This bizarre concoction attempts to be coy and humorous, while making a desperate statement about survival. **Director**—Tony Richardson. **(R)** *110 minutes*

HOTEL TERMINUS: THE LIFE AND TIMES OF KLAUS BARBIE (1988)

Documentarian Marcel Ophuls *(The Sorrow and the Pity)* presents a powerful and provocative account of Klaus Barbie, the brutal World War II gestapo commander responsible for numerous atrocities in France. Fascinating but very long, the film also hammers away at the current indifference to the horrors of that era. Ophuls relentlessly interviews people involved with or aware of the "Butcher of Lyon," uncovering a lack of outrage at such barbaric acts. **(No MPAA rating)** *267 minutes*

HOT LEAD AND COLD FEET (1978)

Jim Dale
Darren McGavin
Karen Valentine

This comedy/western by the Disney studio plods along trying to amuse the kids and adults, but fails with both audiences. British comic actor Dale plays three characters, a cantankerous old land dealer and his two sons, who compete for their inheritance. Don Knotts and Jack Elam are on board with top billing, but actually they're assigned to cameo roles. **Director**—Robert Butler. **(G)** *90 minutes*

HOT PURSUIT (1987)

★1/2

John Cusack
Wendy Gazelle

A sluggish and predictable comedy/adventure starring Cusack as a lovesick youth who struggles to rendezvous with the gorgeous Gazelle at sea in the Caribbean. His efforts lead to a series of silly mishaps typical of many second-rate teen comedies. Cusack barely manages with the absurd material, while the rest of the cast merely goes through the motions. Also with Robert Loggia, Jerry Stiller, Monte Markham, and Shelley Fabares. **Director**—Steven Lisberger. **(PG–13)** *93 minutes*

HOT STUFF (1979)

 ★★★

Dom DeLuise
Suzanne Pleshette
Jerry Reed

DeLuise directs and stars in this good-natured screwball comedy about some Miami cops who catch petty thieves through a sting operation involving stolen goods. The script is silly and predictable, but DeLuise has assembled a fine cast of character actors to help him keep the fun and laughter perking from start to finish. It's the style of visual slapstick in which DeLuise excels, and he often steals the show. Pleshette and Reed do well as his partners in the undercover setup. Also with Luis Avalos and Ossie Davis. **(PG)** *87 minutes*

HOT TO TROT (1988)

Bob Goldthwait
Dabney Coleman

TV's *Mr. Ed* was obviously the inspiration for this lame talking-horse comedy. The shrieking Goldthwait stars as a dim-witted stockbroker. The horse, with the voice of John Candy, gives tips on stock trading. Coleman is the conniving stepfather who competes with Goldthwait. A few genuinely funny moments, but the horse often upstages the human players. Also with Cindy Pickett, Jim Metzler, Tim Kazurinsky, and Gilbert Gottfried. **Director**—Michael Dinner. **(PG)** *83 minutes*

THE HOUND OF THE BASKERVILLES (1939)

Basil Rathbone
Nigel Bruce

Basil Rathbone creates the role of Sherlock Holmes in The Hound of the Baskervilles.

Rathbone, in his first appearance as Sherlock Holmes, solves the mystery of a supernatural canine from the underworld that threatens the life of a man who has inherited an estate from his uncle. Rathbone receives solid acting support from Bruce as Dr. Watson. The suspense is greatly enhanced by the film's visuals, which emphasize eerie, fogbound locales and shadowy interiors. Also with Lionel Atwill, Wendy Barrie, Mary Gordon, and John Carradine. **Director**—Sidney Lanfield. *80 minutes b&w*

HOUSE (1986)

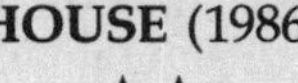 

William Katt
George Wendt
Kay Lenz

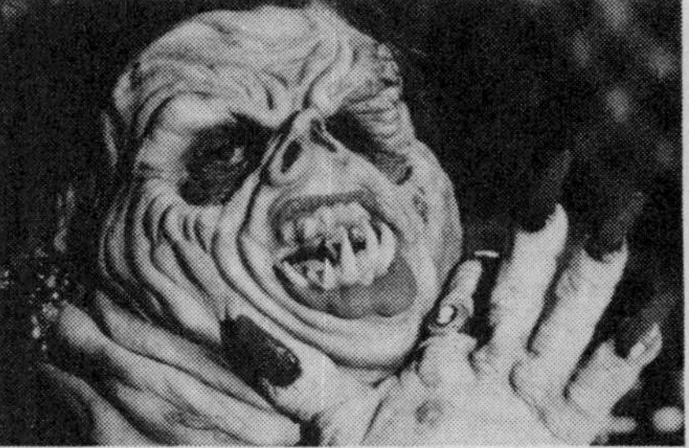

One of the pretty faces in the spook film House.

A haunted-house film that fails to present a consistent story or spooky events with adequate impact. Steve

(Continued)

This movie available on videotape and/or disc.

(Continued)
Miner, who directed a few of the *Friday the 13th* films, seems to be reaching for a higher level that is never attained. The acting, though, is ahead of the questionable material. Katt does well as a horror-story writer who moves into the mysterious gothic dwelling. **(R)** *93 minutes*

HOUSE II: THE SECOND STORY (1987)

 ★½ ®

Arye Gross
Jonathan Stark

An absurd tale of haunted house antics, which bears little resemblance to the original *House.* Two buddies return to the old mansion where one of the young men meets the ghost of his great great grandfather. The feisty old spirit conjures up many creatures from the past, including a baby pterodactyl! The plot is ridiculous and the action gets sillier as the film progresses. **Director**—Ethan Wiley. **(PG)** *88 minutes*

HOUSEBOAT (1958)

 ★★★

Cary Grant
Sophia Loren

Grant and Loren make the sparks fly in this predictable but charming comedy. He's a widower residing in a houseboat with three children. She comes on board as a maid and provides some motherly love for the kids. Unbeknownst to Grant, however, she's really a woman with social standing. A good role for Loren, whose talents as a comedienne have gone largely unnoticed. Martha Hyer, Eduardo Ciannelli, and Harry Guardino perform well in supporting roles. **Director**—Melville Shavelson. **Academy Award Nomination**—Jack Rose and Shavelson, best story and screenplay written directly for the screen. *110 minutes*

THE HOUSE BY THE LAKE (1977)

Brenda Vaccaro
Don Stroud

A grisly suspense drama about four sadistic punks who terrorize a playboy dentist and his girlfriend at a remote hideaway in Ontario, Canada. This mindless exploitation of bloody violence depicts a rape and deaths by drowning, fire, and shotgun. The cast is convincing, especially Stroud as the leader of the hoodlums and Vaccaro as the rape victim who eventually gets revenge. But there's too much emphasis on wanton terror as a form of entertainment. Also with Chuck Shamata and Richard Ayres. Written and directed by William Fruet. **(R) Alternate Title**—*Death Weekend.* *89 minutes*

HOUSE CALLS (1978)

★★★

Walter Matthau
Glenda Jackson
Art Carney
Richard Benjamin

Walter Matthau reacts with exasperation in House Calls.

A lightweight romantic comedy that plays off the charm of Matthau and the steely demeanor of Jackson. Matthau is good as a middle-aged, swinging surgeon—recently widowed—who falls for strong-minded Jackson—recently divorced. The uneven script has a moderate case of the clichés, but the one-liners and laughs roll along with ease. Carney gets some mileage out of his part as the senile chief of surgery. Also with Candice Azzara and Dick O'Neill. **Director**—Howard Zieff. **(PG)** *98 minutes*

HOUSEKEEPING (1987)

★★★ ®

Christine Lahti
Sara Walker
Andrea Burchill

All peculiar on the home front: Christine Lahti in Housekeeping.

Scottish director Bill Forsyth (*Gregory's Girl; Local Hero*) comes up with a modest but endearing comedy in his first American effort. Lahti gives a flavorful performance as a screwball aunt who cares for her sister's two orphaned daughters in a small Northwestern town during the 1950s. Based on Marilynne Robinson's novel, Forsyth's film glorifies those who march to a different drummer. Walker and Burchill are also excellent as the teenage nieces. **(PG–13)** *117 minutes*

HOUSE OF FRANKENSTEIN (1944)

Boris Karloff
John Carradine
Lon Chaney, Jr.

Universal Pictures once more rallies its monsters for sinister work. Karloff stars as an evil scientist and manager of a freak show who rejuvenates Frankenstein's creation and the Wolf Man, and sets out to pay back those who crossed him. A regular cast of horror heavies give it their best shot. Also with George Zucco, J. Carrol Naish, and Lionel Atwill. **Director**—Erle C. Kenton. *71 minutes b&w*

HOUSE OF GAMES (1987)

★★★½ ®

Lindsay Crouse
Joe Mantegna

Playwright David Mamet makes an impressive directing debut with this witty, offbeat tale about the murky underworld of con artists. Crouse (Mamet's wife) stars as a renowned psychiatrist who gets caught up with these crooked gamblers. Stage actor Mantegna gives an excellent performance as the ringleader of the con men who frequent the

® *This movie available with closed captions for the hearing impaired.*

House of Games, a hang-out for swindlers, gamblers, and other assorted thieves. Mamet, who also wrote the screenplay, craftily sets up a series of fascinating twists and turns for the characters in the plot, which neatly represent some universal moral dilemmas we all face. An appropriate allegory for our times. Also with Mike Nussbaum, Lilia Skala, J.T. Walsh, and Steve Goldstein. **(R)** *102 minutes*

HOUSE OF USHER (1960)

★★★

Vincent Price

Effective horror tale based on the classic Edgar Allan Poe chiller. Price heads the cast as a member of Usher, the family involved in various forms of madness and terror. When a young man arrives at the House of Usher to ask permission to marry a family member, the terror is released. Director Roger Corman, who went on to make seven other Poe adaptations, puts it together with impressive style. Some versions run 85 minutes. Also with Myrna Fahey, Mark Damon, and Harry Ellerbe. *79 minutes*

HOUSE OF WAX (1953)

★★½

Vincent Price
Carolyn Jones

Adequate remake of *The Mystery of the Wax Museum,* with Price striking terror into the hearts of the innocent as the owner of a wax museum. After it's destroyed in a fire, he rebuilds his exhibits using dead bodies. The film was initially shot in 3-D, and many of the gimmicks are designed for this process. Also with Phyllis Kirk, Frank Lovejoy, Paul Picerni, and Charles Buchinski (Bronson). **Director**—André De Toth. *88 minutes*

THE HOUSE ON CARROLL STREET (1988)

★★½

Kelly McGillis
Jeff Daniels

A taut, smartly paced thriller set during the McCarthy era when anticommunist hearings had all liberals, intellectuals, and artists terrified of false accusations and misleading innuendoes. McGillis stars as an idealistic photo editor, blacklisted from her job, who exposes a conspiracy to sneak Nazi war criminals into the United States. The plot unfolds briskly with straightforward suspense and ironic twists. Period details are expertly captured and the intelligent script is well handled by once-blacklisted writer Walter Bernstein. Also with Mandy Patinkin and Jessica Tandy. **Director**—Peter Yates. **(PG)** *100 minutes*

THE HOUSE ON 92nd STREET (1945)

★★★★

William Eythe
Lloyd Nolan
Signe Hasso

A fast-paced spy thriller set in New York City during World War II, with the FBI bearing down on Nazi agents seeking to steal atomic bomb secrets. This is a smartly styled production that effectively uses a combination of documentary technique and exciting drama. It set the trend for subsequent "realistic" films such as *The Naked City.* Also with Gene Lockhart and Leo G. Carroll. **Director**—Henry Hathaway. **Academy Award**—Charles G. Booth, original story. *88 minutes b&w*

HOUSE PARTY (1990)

★★½

Christopher Reid
Christopher Martin
Robin Harris

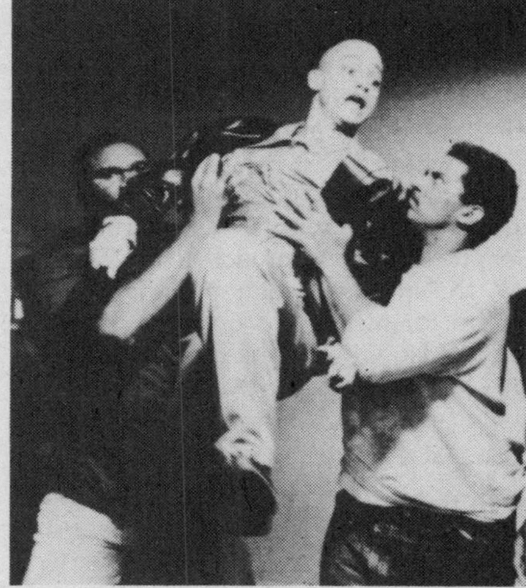

Christopher Reid gets into a bad situation in House Party.

The culture of hip black youths provides the centerpiece of this energetic but disjointed musical comedy. Reid stars as the young hero with the tall haircut whose goal is to attend a party thrown by his peers while avoiding his restrictive father and some local toughs. However, the plot is an excuse to emphasize popular fashion, rap music, street slang, and raucous antics. Harris, the late stand-up comic whose career was just about to take off when he died unexpectedly, makes one of his last public appearances. Also with Tisha Campbell and A.J. Johnson. **Director**—Reginald Hudlin. **(R)** *105 minutes*

THE HOUSE WHERE EVIL DWELLS (1982)

 ★★

Edward Albert
Susan George

This is a standard haunted-house story transplanted to Japan. An American family rents a home that was the site of murders committed over a century ago. Predictably, the ghosts of the victims are still hanging around to cause bloody mischief and reenact the initial tragedy. The Japanese scenery offers some picturesque and exotic atmosphere—an unusual twist for this sort of nonsense. **Director**—Kevin Connor. **(R)** *88 minutes*

HOWARD THE DUCK (1986)

 ★★ 

Lea Thompson
Jeffrey Jones
Ed Gale

A disappointing comic fantasy based on the adventures of Steve Gerber's comic-book character, Howard the Duck. George Lucas served as executive producer on the film, which is hampered by an overkill of special effects and the ill-timed direction of William Huyck. There are so many explosions and annihilations that the final battle is anticlimactic. The storyline involves a talking duck with other human characteristics who is blasted to Earth from an alien planet when a laser gun backfires. Also blown from the planet is the power-hungry Dark Lord of the Universe, whose evil machinations Howard must stop. Thompson plays Beverly Switzler, the rock 'n' roll singer Howard falls for. Howard is portrayed by Gale in a latex rubber suit covered with feathers. The script by Huyck and wife Gloria Katz (*American Graffiti*)

(Continued)

lacks definition and sufficient suspense. Also with Tim Robbins and Chip Zien. **(PG)** *111 minutes*

HOW GREEN WAS MY VALLEY (1941)

★★★★

Walter Pidgeon
Maureen O'Hara
Roddy McDowall
Donald Crisp

Touching and heartwarming drama of life in a Welsh coal-mining town. Memorable and moving moments abound. Much effort was lavished on exquisite production detail, giving eloquent class to the film, which is based on Richard Llewellyn's novel. Cast also includes Barry Fitzgerald, Sara Allgood, Anna Lee, and John Loder. **Director**—John Ford. **Academy Awards**—best picture; Ford, best director; Crisp, best supporting actor; Arthur Miller, cinematography. **Nominations**—Allgood, best supporting actress; Philip Dunne, screenplay. *118 minutes b&w*

HOW I GOT INTO COLLEGE (1989)

★$^1/_2$

Corey Parker
Lara Flynn Boyle

This adolescent comedy unsuccessfully spoofs the college admissions ritual. Parker plays a not-too-bright student who strives to be admitted to a certain college because a girl he admires (Boyle) is slated to go there. The unfunny satire is hampered by a weak script, much predictability, and childish comic situations. Also with Anthony Edwards, Charles Rocket, and Brian Doyle-Murray. **Director**—Savage Steve Holland. **(PG-13)** *86 minutes*

THE HOWLING (1981)

★★★

Dee Wallace

A stylish, tongue-in-cheek horror film in which the entire cast turns into werewolves. Wallace plays an attractive TV reporter who goes to a secluded Esalen-like spa to unwind. Before long, she's face-to-face with monstrous werewolves who want her to join their pack. The production team for this horror tale was first-rate. The wolf transformation special effects by Rob Bottin are truly ambitious and terrifying. The script by John Sayles (*Brother from Another Planet*) is full of his usual film-buff jokes and hip humor. Director Joe Dante moves the film along with his flair for wildly skewed irony. **(R)** *90 minutes*

HOWLING II . . . YOUR SISTER IS A WEREWOLF (1984)

★

Christopher Lee
Reb Brown
Sybil Danning

A poor sequel to the surprisingly stylish *The Howling*. This follow-up picks up where the original left off, with Brown determined to uncover and destroy the colony of werewolves that made his sister one of their own. Horror veteran Lee costars as a professor who shows Brown the wolves' sacred temple in Transylvania. Danning plays the "Leader of the Pack," but even her usually entertaining presence can't save this low-low-budget horror film. Beware of the video version: The film-to-tape transfer was handled badly, resulting in some very dark sequences. Also with Marsha A. Hunt and Annie McEnroe. **(R)** *91 minutes*

HOWLING III (1987)

★

Barry Otto
Imogen Annesley

This third entry in the popular werewolf series is done slightly tongue-in-cheek, though that does little to keep the film from being dull and predictable. The action is set primarily in Australia, where a part-marsupial girl and a Russian ballerina grow hair and fangs and fall in love with a pair of humans. Despite a light approach to the material, the humor is far too strained and the horror scenes are surprisingly subdued. Also with Dasha Blahova. **Director**—Philippe Mora. **(PG–13)** *94 minutes*

HOW THE WEST WAS WON (1963)

★★$^1/_2$

Debbie Reynolds
George Peppard
Carroll Baker
Lee J. Cobb

George Peppard is ready for action in How the West Was Won.

An overlong epic that follows the pioneering efforts of several generations of an adventurous farming family from New England across the continent. The trail is strewn with clichés and underdeveloped episodes. The production, however, is done lavishly, which will lose impact on TV screens. Cast also includes Karl Malden, Carolyn Jones, Gregory Peck, Henry Fonda, James Stewart, and John Wayne. Spencer Tracy narrates. **Directors**—Henry Hathaway, John Ford, and George Marshall. **Academy Award**—James R. Webb, best story and screenplay written directly for the screen. **Nominations**—best picture; William H. Daniels, Milton Krasner, Charles Lang, Jr., and Joseph LaShelle, cinematography. *155 minutes*

HOW TO BEAT THE HIGH COST OF LIVING (1980)

★★

Susan Saint James
Jessica Lange
Jane Curtin

Three seemingly respectable young women burglarize a shopping mall because inflation has deflated their lifestyles. This listless comedy is a variation of *Fun with Dick and Jane,* but hardly as funny. Rising prices are no laughing matter, especially in this film. Saint James, Curtin, and Lange play the bungling, thieving threesome who pull off the caper. Also with Richard Benjamin and Eddie Albert. **Director**—Robert Scheerer. **(PG)** *110 minutes*

® *This movie available with closed captions for the hearing impaired.*

HOW TO GET AHEAD IN ADVERTISING (1989)

★★½

Richard E. Grant
Rachel Ward

Grant is dazzling as a London advertising executive who becomes cynical about the hard-sell tactics of his profession. The centerpiece of this biting satire is a mysterious boil that gradually grows—like Pinocchio's nose—on the adman's neck. It talks, grows a mustache, and engages in arguments. Unfortunately, the film eventually becomes too heavy-handed and the humor forced and desperate. **Director**—Bruce Robinson. **(R)** *95 minutes*

HOW TO MARRY A MILLIONAIRE (1953)

★★★

Lauren Bacall
Marilyn Monroe
Betty Grable
William Powell

Fun-filled comedy with Bacall, Monroe, and Grable perfectly cast as schemers out to trap wealthy men as husbands. The stars lend sparkle to the amicable proceedings, set in New York City, and there are plenty of lavish settings to heighten the frolic. In the end, the girls get more than they intended. Also with Cameron Mitchell, David Wayne, and Rory Calhoun. **Director**—Jean Negulesco. *96 minutes*

HOW TO MURDER YOUR WIFE (1965)

★★★

Jack Lemmon
Virna Lisi
Terry-Thomas

Smart, sophisticated comedy with wry comic situations that move along at a fast pace. Lemmon is great as a bachelor comic-strip writer who wakes up one morning after a wild party to find himself unexpectedly married to beautiful Lisi. He thinks of ways to get rid of her. And when she vanishes, the police believe he murdered her. A top supporting cast contributes to the fun. Eddie Mayehoff plays a lawyer friend, and Terry-Thomas is a wisecracking butler. Sidney Blackmer and Claire Trevor also star. **Director**—Richard Quine. *118 minutes*

HOW TO SUCCEED IN BUSINESS WITHOUT REALLY TRYING (1967)

★★★

Robert Morse
Rudy Vallee
Michelle Lee

Robert Morse learns How to Succeed in Business Without Really Trying.

Morse superbly repeats his Broadway role as an ambitious window-washer who gets to be president of a large corporation through cunning rather than energy and talent. Many of the delights from the stage musical, based on Shepard Mead's book, are kept intact. Frank Loesser's songs are appealing, and include "I Believe in You" and "Brotherhood of Man." Modern audiences may find the material a bit dated. Also with Anthony Teague and Maureen Arthur. **Director**—David Swift. *119 minutes*

THE HUCKSTERS (1947)

Clark Gable
Deborah Kerr
Ava Gardner

The advertising business is skewered in this impressive film drama based on Frederic Wakeman's insightful novel. Gable does well as an advertising executive who becomes frustrated by questionable methods of the profession; Sydney Greenstreet is well cast as a tyrannical soap company president. Also with Adolphe Menjou, Keenan Wynn, and Edward Arnold. **Director**—Jack Conway. *115 minutes b&w*

HUD (1963)

★★★★

Paul Newman
Patricia Neal
Melvyn Douglas

The cynical new West: Paul Newman and Patricia Neal in Hud.

Newman gives an excellent character portrayal as the irresponsible son of a hardworking Texas rancher. The powerful film takes a hard look at interpersonal family relationships and the deterioration of moral values. Neal stands out as the wise housekeeper who readily perceives the complex problems; Douglas is also good as the harassed father. Martin Ritt's direction and James Wong Howe's handsome black-and-white cinematography are exceptional. Also with Brandon De Wilde and John Ashley. **Academy Awards**—Neal, best actress; Douglas, best supporting actor; Howe, cinematography. **Nominations**—Ritt, best director; Newman, best actor; Irving Ravetch and Harriet Frank, Jr., best screenplay based on material from another medium. *112 minutes b&w*

THE HUMAN COMEDY (1943)

★★★½

Mickey Rooney
Frank Morgan
James Craig

This screen adaptation of William Saroyan's novel is moving although occasionally too sentimental. Touching characterizations are simply portrayed in this slice of life in small-town America during World War II. Rooney heads the cast that also includes Marsha Hunt, Fay Bainter, Van Johnson, and Donna Reed. **Director**—Clarence Brown. **Academy Award**—Saroyan, original story. **Nominations**—best picture; Brown, best director; Rooney, best actor; Harry Stradling, cinematography. *117 minutes b&w*

This movie available on videotape and/or disc.

THE HUMAN FACTOR (1975)

 ★★

George Kennedy
John Mills

An American computer expert, working with NATO in Italy, stalks and kills a group of radicals who assassinated his family. It's a poor reworking of the vigilante angle of *Death Wish*. The film suffers from limp direction, unmoving performances, and a wobbly script. Kennedy's talent is wasted in the leading role. Costars Raf Vallone, Barry Sullivan, and Rita Tushingham. **Director**—Edward Dmytryk. **(R)**

96 minutes

THE HUMAN FACTOR (1980)

 ★★★

Richard Attenborough
Derek Jacobi
Nicol Williamson

Espionage is, in all likelihood, a routine job carried out by drab civil servants. If such is the case, this Otto Preminger film of Graham Greene's topical novel is authentic. Williamson plays a mild-mannered double agent who leaks secrets to the Russians. The story is intelligent, and the cast of fine British actors is impressive. Also with Robert Morley, John Gielgud, and Ann Todd. **(R)** *115 minutes*

HUMANOIDS FROM THE DEEP (1980)

 ★★½

Doug McClure
Vic Morrow
Ann Turkel
Cindy Weintraub

Libidinous amphibians spawned by mutated DNA invade a fishing village, where they kill the men and have their way with the women. A schizoid mix of science fiction, ecological allegory, and male rape fantasy, sprinkled with equal doses of female nudity and self-mocking humor. Director Barbara Peeters even throws in a "liberated" female scientist (Turkel) who talks tough but looks like she stepped off the cover of *Vogue*. Some moody moments along the way, but our favorite scene is at a carnival, where one of the monsters gamely pursues a victim by riding a merry-go-round! **(R)** *80 minutes*

HUMORESQUE (1946)

★★★

Joan Crawford
John Garfield

Crawford stars as a wealthy patron of the arts who sponsors a promising violinist, played by Garfield. Though Crawford is married, the two fall in love, threatening her social position. Crawford excelled at this type of melodrama, prevalent during the 1940s, in which she usually played the suffering heroine. Here, the exquisite setting and superb acting make this "weepie," or women's picture, a classic example of the genre. A classical music backdrop and some funny antics from Oscar Levant add to the quality. Also with J. Carrol Naish, Craig Stevens, and Ruth Nelson. **Director**—Jean Negulesco. *125 minutes b&w*

THE HUNCHBACK OF NOTRE DAME (1939)

 ★★★½

Charles Laughton
Cedric Hardwicke
Maureen O'Hara
Edmond O'Brien

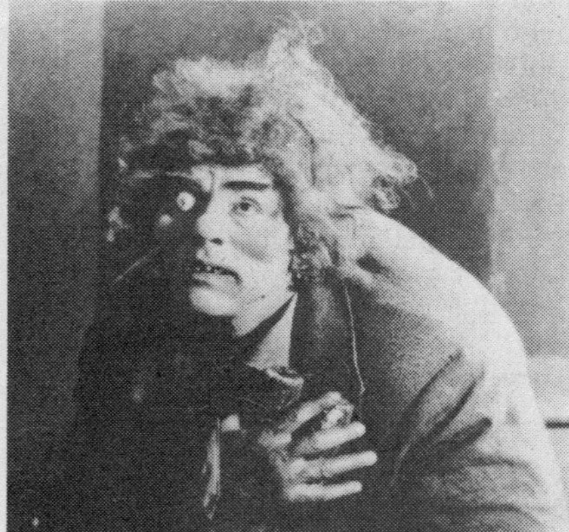

The Hunchback of Notre Dame *stars Charles Laughton in the title role.*

The classic Victor Hugo story receives superior screen treatment with impressive sets, costumes, and direction, aimed at recreating the mood of medieval Paris. And there's great acting to match, with Laughton as the deformed bell-ringer who rescues a gypsy girl from the clutches of a mob. It's a worthy remake of the silent version with Lon Chaney. Also with Thomas Mitchell and Harry Davenport. **Director**—William Dieterle. *117 minutes b&w*

THE HUNGER (1983)

 ★★

Catherine Deneuve
David Bowie
Susan Sarandon
Ann Magnuson

Catherine Deneuve and David Bowie share an evil love in The Hunger.

A chic, flashy, latter-day vampire yarn with Deneuve and Bowie as Manhattan townhouse dwellers who haunt New Wave bars for victims. When Bowie begins to show his true age (200 years), Deneuve moves on to an affair with Sarandon. All its kinky touches and glossy settings can't compensate for a script that is bloodless to the point of anemia. **Director**—Tony Scott. **(R)**

98 minutes

THE HUNTER (1980)

 ★★

Steve McQueen
LeVar Burton
Eli Wallach

McQueen plays a modern-day bounty hunter who risks his neck tracking down bail-jumpers. It's a dirty job that only someone desperate for money would undertake, and McQueen sloshes through this film as if he's desperate for a paycheck. A jumbled script, based on the real-life story of bounty hunter Ralph Thorson, and too many undeveloped characters keep things at a low boil, though the story perks up during some spectacular chase scenes. However, there's not enough originality or style to prevent McQueen's star image from being tarnished. Also with Kathryn Harrold and Ben Johnson. **Director**—Buzz Kulik. **(PG)** *97 minutes*

THE HUNT FOR RED OCTOBER (1990)

★★★

Sean Connery
Alec Baldwin
Scott Glenn

Sean Connery is the Soviet captain in The Hunt for Red October.

A well-acted and well-directed thriller based on Tom Clancy's best-selling novel. A runaway Russian nuclear submarine approaches the U.S. mainland. Is the captain a madman planning to launch a nuclear strike on the U.S.; or, is he a defector, trying to escape the Soviet Union with their most advanced submarine? Slickly packaged, the film bristles with riveting tension, smart dialogue, and excellent performances. Connery is commanding as the assertive Russian captain with nerves of steel, while Baldwin complements him as the gentle, nervous CIA analyst. Director John McTiernan *(Die Hard)* makes efficient use of the wide-screen and maintains a quick pace throughout. Also with Sam Neill, James Earl Jones, Joss Ackland, Richard Jordan, Peter Firth, Tim Curry, Jeffrey Jones, and Fred Dalton Thompson. **(PG)** *135 minutes*

HURRICANE (1979)

 ★★

Jason Robards
Mia Farrow
Max Von Sydow
Trevor Howard

Dino De Laurentiis' $20-million romantic epic, filmed in Bora Bora, is boring, boring. The script is based on the engaging Nordhoff and Hall novel about ill-fated lovers. But here the story plods along, the characters are one-dimensional, and the silly dialogue makes the actors appear foolish. The storm is impressive, but the rest is just tedious nonsense. Also with Dayton Ka'ne. **Director**—Jan Troell. **(PG)** *119 minutes*

HURRY SUNDOWN (1967)

Jane Fonda
Michael Caine
Rex Ingram
Diahann Carroll

Director Otto Preminger butchers this melodrama, based on a best-selling novel by K.B. Gilden. Although the murky production boasts a superior cast and some lavish settings, it lapses into absurdity only a few minutes into the film. The story concerns racial problems in a small Georgia community. Cast also includes Burgess Meredith, Faye Dunaway, John Phillip Law, Robert Hooks, Beah Richards, and George Kennedy. *142 minutes*

HUSH...HUSH SWEET CHARLOTTE (1965)

 ★★★

Bette Davis
Olivia de Havilland
Joseph Cotten

A stylish chiller about a lonely woman, played by Davis. She's set upon by her cousin and her romantic suitor, who both want her property. The plot borrows liberally from *What Ever Happened to Baby Jane?*, but it's watchable to the end. The acting by a pro cast is reliably good, and Robert Aldrich's direction achieves the desired macabre effect. Also with Cecil Kellaway, Mary Astor, Victor Buono, and Agnes Moorehead. **Academy Award Nominations**—Moorehead, best supporting actress; Joseph Biroc, cinematography; Michael Luciano, editing. *133 minutes b&w*

HUSTLE (1975)

★★$^1/_2$

Burt Reynolds
Catherine Deneuve

An intriguing, fast-moving, but disjointed cop movie about the investigation of the death of a teenage girl from a middle-class family. Reynolds plays a tough and suave detective who discovers that the dead woman has been exploited by a corrupt and powerful lawyer. The plot hopscotches confusingly from one situation to another; only at the end, and too late, does it all seem to make sense. Deneuve plays a high-class prostitute romantically attached to Reynolds. With Ben Johnson, Eddie Albert, Paul Winfield, Eileen Brennan, and Ernest Borgnine. **Director**—Robert Aldrich. **(R)** *120 minutes*

THE HUSTLER (1961)

 ★★★★

Paul Newman
Jackie Gleason
George C. Scott

Jackie Gleason plays Minnesota Fats in The Hustler.

Newman gives a terrific character portrayal of hustling pool shark Fast Eddie Felson, whose game is spoiled when he meets the woman he loves, played by Piper Laurie. The film offers impressive atmosphere of the world of seedy pool halls, and there's effective suspense during the pool games. Watch for an excellent dramatic performance by Gleason as the venerable Minnesota Fats. The cast also includes Myron McCormick and Murray Hamilton. Newman reprised his role as Felson in the 1986 sequel *The Color of Money.* **Director**—Robert Rossen. **Academy Award**—Eugene Shuftan, cinematography. **Nominations**—best picture; Rossen, best director; Newman, best actor; Laurie, best actress; Gleason and Scott, best supporting actor; Sidney Carroll and Rossen, best screenplay based on material from another medium. *135 minutes b&w*

I

I AM A CAMERA (1955)

★★★

Julie Harris
Laurence Harvey

Harris and Harvey star as young adventurers in Berlin just prior to World War II. Harris is excellent as a freewheeling English girl; Harvey, who plays an English author recording events in the German capital, matches her performance. This romantic comedy is an intelligent adaptation of Christopher Isherwood's stories about prewar Berlin. The plot is also the basis for the Broadway musical and film *Cabaret*. Also with Shelley Winters, Ron Randell, and Patrick McGoohan. **Director**—Henry Cornelius. *98 minutes b&w*

I AM A FUGITIVE FROM A CHAIN GANG (1932)

★★★★

Paul Muni

A gripping and powerful drama about the injustices of southern penal institutions, based on an autobiographical story by Robert E. Burns. Muni brilliantly portrays an innocent man who is convicted and sentenced to a chain gang. He is brutalized by the system and ultimately driven to real criminal activity. The last shot of his haunted face will sear itself into your memory. Director Mervyn LeRoy uses shock value to convey a strong social message but never loses artistic control. The film influenced the style of all socially conscious films to come out of Hollywood from the 1930s through the 1950s. Excellent support by Glenda Farrell, Helen Vinson, Preston Foster, Allen Jenkins, and Edward Ellis. **Academy Award Nominations**—best picture; Muni, best actor. *90 minutes b&w*

ICE CASTLES (1979)

★★

Lynn-Holly Johnson
Robby Benson

A pretty girl from a small town in Iowa gets a chance at an Olympic skating medal, but is accidentally blinded on the brink of success. She learns to skate despite her handicap with the encouragement of the boy she left behind. Johnson plays Alexis, the blinded skater; Benson is her sympathetic boyfriend. This sentimental story is aimed right at the tear ducts, so bring along a *big* handkerchief. The characters, however, are superficial, and the film lacks suspense at crucial moments. Johnson's figure skating does make the film worthwhile viewing. Also with Colleen Dewhurst, Tom Skerritt, and Jennifer Warren. **Director**—Donald Wrye. **(PG)** *109 minutes*

Pathos on ice: Lynn-Holly Johnson and Robby Benson in Ice Castles.

ICEMAN (1984)

★★★

John Lone
Timothy Hutton
Lindsay Crouse

Scientists bring back to life a Neanderthal man frozen in the Arctic wastes for 40,000 years. This unusual story is not a monster thriller, but an exhilarating drama about a sympathetic and complex human being grappling with a strange environment. Lone gives a critically acclaimed performance in the title role. Hutton stars as the anthropologist who is the only one who doesn't treat him like a lab specimen. **Director**—Fred Schepisi. **(PG)** *101 minutes.*

THE ICE PIRATES (1984)

★★

Robert Urich
Mary Crosby

A jumbled sci-fi adventure that combines a space-opera plot with swashbuckling action. The madhouse events whiz by so fast it's hard to keep track of the story and characters—not that they matter much here. The plot has something to do with hijacking spaceships that supply ice to a water-starved galaxy. Urich, Crosby, and a platoon of robots head the cast, which also includes Anjelica Huston and John Matuszak. **Director**—Stewart Raffill. **(PG)** *95 minutes*

ICE STATION ZEBRA (1968)

★★★

Rock Hudson
Patrick McGoohan

Submarine spy adventure set at the North Pole. The story, from an Alistair MacLean novel, is filled with cold-war intrigue, treachery, and the threat of an international incident of monumental proportions. The Oscar-nominated photography by Daniel Haller is spectacular and the all-male cast is of star caliber. Hudson plays the captain of the sub, and McGoohan is a British agent who searches for a Russian spy. Ernest Borgnine, Tony Bill, Jim Brown, and Lloyd Nolan round out the cast. The film is notorious as Howard Hughes' favorite movie, which he viewed repeatedly. **Director**—John Sturges. *148 minutes*

I CONFESS (1953)

★★★

Montgomery Clift
Anne Baxter

A murderer confesses his crime to a priest, played by Clift, who upholds the sanctity of the confessional even though he becomes a suspect in the murder case. This Alfred Hitchcock mystery, filmed mostly in Canada, isn't among his best, yet it's interesting because of the moody atmosphere set against the background of Quebec. Also with Brian Aherne, Karl Malden, and Dolly Haas. *94 minutes b&w*

THE IDOLMAKER (1980)

★★★

Ray Sharkey
Peter Gallagher
Paul Land

An energetic and compelling drama about a hard-driving promoter of rock singers during the late 1950s. Sharkey is superb in the title role, which is loosely

Ray Sharkey (left) is The Idolmaker, *who grooms Paul Land for rock stardom.*

based on the life of Bob Marcucci, the manager of Frankie Avalon and Fabian. The film presents the rock 'n' roll era in colorful detail. Gallagher and Land are well cast as pop singers whose looks are more vital to their stardom than their musical abilities. **Director**—Taylor Hackford. **(PG)** *119 minutes*

I DOOD IT! (1943)

Red Skelton
Eleanor Powell

In this sophomoric slapstick comedy, Skelton plays a tailor who romances a movie star, played by Powell. The film offers too much strained humor, but there are some memorable musical numbers, including "Take a Chance on Love." Skelton is known for better work. Also with Butterfly McQueen, Lena Horne, and Jimmy Dorsey. **Director**—Vincente Minnelli. *102 minutes b&w*

IF . . . (1969)

★★★★

Malcolm McDowell
David Wood

Searing, intelligent drama set in an English boarding school, where students rebel against harsh discipline. Director Lindsay Anderson cleverly portrays this school setting as an allegory for the oppression of the individual by authority. The story is not presented as a straightforward narrative, but is interrupted by surrealistic images, the use of both black-and-white and color cinematography, and title cards. The use of such cinematic devices makes the audience aware of the techniques of filmmaking, and requires the complete attention of the viewer in order to understand what is going on. Also with Richard Warwick, Peter Jeffrey, Christine Noonan, and Robert Swann. **(R)** *111 minutes b&w/color*

IF IT'S TUESDAY, THIS MUST BE BELGIUM (1969)

Suzanne Pleshette
Ian McShane
Mildred Natwick
Norman Fell

Fast-paced comedy about American vacationers on a whirlwind tour of seven European countries in 18 days. All sorts of hilarious adventures occur along the route, including some unexpected romantic situations. Apparently, this group didn't leave home without their sense of humor. Also with Murray Hamilton, Michael Constantine, Sandy Baron, Peggy Cass, and Marty Ingels. **Director**—Mel Stuart. **(G)** *98 minutes*

I'LL BE SEEING YOU (1944)

Ginger Rogers
Joseph Cotten

Rogers plays a convicted killer allowed to go home for the Christmas holidays. She meets and falls in love with a shell-shocked soldier, played by Cotten. A good cast can't overcome the maudlin script, which was based on a radio drama. Also with Shirley Temple, Spring Byington, Tom Tully, and Chill Wills. **Director**—William Dieterle. *85 minutes b&w*

I'LL CRY TOMORROW (1955)

★★★½

Susan Hayward
Richard Conte
Eddie Albert
Jo Van Fleet

This is a powerful film biography of Lillian Roth, recounting her marital problems and her battle with alcoholism. Hayward's superb portrayal of the 1930s stage and film star is authentic, and she gets excellent support from Van Fleet as Roth's despondent mother. Roth's husbands are played by Conte, Albert, and Don Taylor. **Director**—Daniel Mann. **Academy Award Nominations**—Hayward, best actress; Arthur Arling, cinematography. *117 minutes b&w*

I LOVE YOU, ALICE B. TOKLAS (1968)

Peter Sellers
Jo Van Fleet
Leigh Taylor-Young

Peter Sellers (left) and friends in I Love You, Alice B. Toklas.

Sellers stars as a Los Angeles lawyer with an overbearing mother, played by Van Fleet. When he decides to chuck it all to join the dropped-out generation, he thinks he finds truth and happiness with a young hippie, played by Taylor-Young. There are many excellent comic moments and even a subtle message in the film, which was written by Paul Mazursky and Larry Tucker. Also with Joyce Van Patten, David Arkin, and Herb Edelman. **Director**—Hy Averback. *93 minutes*

I LOVE YOU TO DEATH (1990)

Kevin Kline
Tracey Ullman
William Hurt
Keanu Reeves

This tedious black comedy is based on the true account of a philandering pizza parlor owner who was targeted for murder by his exasperated wife. Director Lawrence Kasdan allows his actors free reign in the interpretation of their characters, and the result is mixed at best. Kline *(A Fish Called Wanda)*, trying to advance his career with another high-profile comic role, merely appears foolish as the womanizing husband. Ullman portrays the wife as a colorless hausfrau, but her approach backfires; her character is dull in comparison to the rest of the oddball cast. Hurt and

(Continued)

(Continued)
Reeves squander their talent as bumbling, drugged-out hit men. The scenes involving the foiled murder attempts unfold in a plodding, awkward fashion. Also with Joan Plowright, River Phoenix, James Gammon, Victoria Jackson, Miriam Margolyes, Phoebe Cates, and Kathleen York. **(R)** *96 minutes*

IMAGINE: JOHN LENNON (1988)

Imagine: John Lennon *is a remembrance of the rock musician (here with his son, Sean).*

Director Andrew Solt *(This Is Elvis)* put together this treat for Beatles fans—a vivid documentary of the late rock musician that uses footage gleaned from some 200 hours of tape, supplied mostly by his widow, Yoko Ono. Although the portrait is complimentary to Lennon, the film is frank and spontaneous. Lennon's voice, derived from his many interviews, often provides the narration. The footage covers his childhood and years with the Beatles, but most of the account concerns his time with Ono. **(R)** *103 minutes*

I'M ALL RIGHT, JACK (1960)

★★★★

Ian Carmichael
Peter Sellers
Terry-Thomas
Richard Attenborough

Spirited satire about labor/management conflicts, set in England in the 1950s. The film touches on the questionable practices of both sides. A youthful bumbler, played by Carmichael, gets a factory job, provokes a strike, and is caught up in a controversy between the workers and the bosses. Sellers is memorable as an oafish labor official. Also with Dennis Price and Margaret Rutherford. **Directors**—John Boulting and Roy Boulting. *104 minutes b&w*

I'M DANCING AS FAST AS I CAN (1982)

Jill Clayburgh
Nicol Williamson

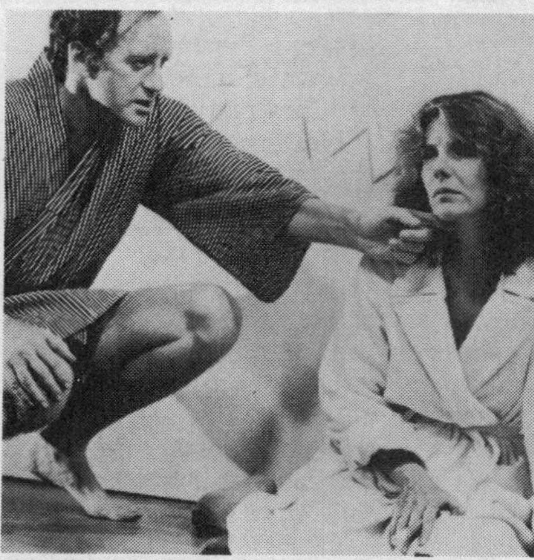

Nicol Williamson comforts a drugged-out Jill Clayburgh in I'm Dancing as Fast as I Can.

This uneven film takes a serious look at Valium addiction, much in the way that alcohol and heroin abuse have been studied in earlier movies. Clayburgh overplays the part of award-winning TV producer Barbara Gordon, who actually was hooked on tranquilizers but recovered after treatment in a mental hospital. Novice director Jack Hofsiss doesn't present the intense material well, and the screenplay never adequately explores the underlying causes of such dependency. **(R)** *107 minutes*

I'M GONNA GIT YOU SUCKA (1989)

Keenen Ivory Wayans

Wayans (of television's *In Living Color*) directed and stars in this lively parody of black stereotypes and the blaxploitation films that were popular in the 1970s. He plays a dude who seeks to even the score with a white gangster. The film hums with energy and offers the clever, appealing casting of Bernie Casey, Isaac Hayes, and Jim Brown as crotchety, middle-aged black superheroes. Also with Antonio Fargas, Steve James, Ja'net Dubois, Dawnn Lewis, and John Vernon. **(R)** *90 minutes*

IMITATION OF LIFE (1959)

★★★

Lana Turner
Juanita Moore

Slick reworking of the Fannie Hurst tearjerker. Turner plays the beauty who becomes a successful actress only to find disappointment in her personal relationships; Moore is the black housekeeper who shares her problems with Turner. Moore's troubles concern her daughter, played by Susan Kohner, who wants to pass for white. This racial aspect, however, gets shoved aside while the romantic entanglements of the women are emphasized. The 1934 version, starring Claudette Colbert, was better. Also with John Gavin, Sandra Dee, and Robert Alda. **Director**—Douglas Sirk. **Academy Award Nominations**—Moore and Kohner, best supporting actress. *124 minutes*

IMMEDIATE FAMILY (1989)

 ★★½

Glenn Close
James Woods
Mary Stuart Masterson

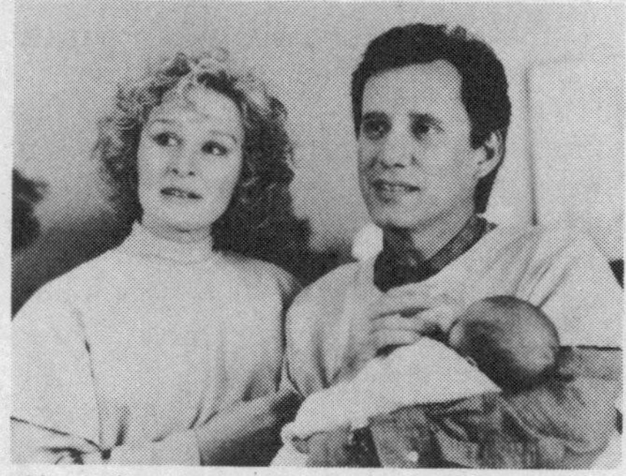

Glenn Close and James Woods with their new baby in Immediate Family.

A wrenching, bittersweet account of an unwed mother who agrees to give up her baby to a childless couple desperate to adopt. Close and Woods (in a conventional role compared to the manics, alcoholics, and losers he has played in the past) provide solid performances as the well-to-do future parents. Masterson is convincing as the young pregnant girl faced with a weighty decision. The straightforward tearjerker is emotionally manipulative, but it is also well acted considering the predictable material. Those who like sentimental tales of family and sacrifice will enjoy this benign tale; others may want to be more selective. Also with Kevin Dillon, Jane Greer, Mimi Kennedy, and Linda Darlow. **Director**—Jonathan Kaplan. **(PG-13)** *95 minutes*

IMPULSE (1984)

★★

Meg Tilly
Tim Matheson

Residents of a small town start to act irrational and hostile in this eerie thriller that eventually loses its credibility. A young woman (Tilly) and her physician boyfriend (Matheson) arrive on the scene and try to get at the source of such bizarre and dangerous behavior. While a few sinister incidents create some tension, the film ends in unsatisfying confusion. Hume Cronyn and John Karlen costar. **Director**—Graham Baker. **(R)** *91 minutes*

IMPULSE (1990)

★★★

Theresa Russell
Jeff Fahey
George Dzundza

Theresa Russell is an undercover detective in Impulse.

A typical cop thriller that closely follows the conventions of the genre, except that the main character is a woman. Russell stars as the female undercover detective involved with vice and drug cases who suffers from stress and burnout. In addition to the pressure of her job, she is edgy because of the unwanted advances of her superior and a string of destructive romantic relationships with other cops. Regrettably, the plot is filled with unbelievable coincidences, which weakens the film considerably. Director Sondra Locke uses the dark, moody tones of the *film noir* style to suggest the ambiguous morality of the characters and the tension beneath the surface of the action. **(R)** *108 minutes*

IN A LONELY PLACE (1950)

★★★

Humphrey Bogart
Gloria Grahame

This atmospheric and brooding melodrama with a Hollywood setting has an intelligent script and solid performances. Bogart stars as a hard-bitten screenwriter accused of murder, but cleared when neighbor Grahame provides an alibi. She begins to doubt his innocence when he attacks her in a jealous rage. Director Nicholas Ray paints a cynical picture of behind-the-scenes Hollywood. Also stars Frank Lovejoy, Carl Benton Reid, Jeff Donnell, and Art Smith. *93 minutes b&w*

INCHON (1982)

★★

Laurence Olivier
Jacqueline Bisset
Ben Gazzara

An absurd epic telling of the landing at Inchon during the Korean War. The film had one of the largest budgets of any film ever, reportedly almost $50 million. The Reverend Sun Myung Moon of the Unification Church was involved with the production, which may account for its flag-waving, quasi-religious flavor. The venerable General Douglas MacArthur is played, with an attitude of winking mockery, by the great Olivier. Much attention is devoted to spectacular shoot-'em-up battle scenes, which provide some diversion from the ridiculous dialogue. Originally released at 140 minutes. Also with Richard Roundtree, David Janssen, and Toshiro Mifune. **Director**—Terence Young. **(PG)** *105 minutes*

IN COLD BLOOD (1967)

★★★★

Robert Blake
Scott Wilson

First-class film rendition of Truman Capote's book about two young ex-convicts who brutally kill a Kansas farm family. The semidocumentary account digs deep into motives, characterizations, and the stark contrasts between the lifestyles of the killers and the victims. The horrible murders, life on the run, capture, and execution are handled in taut step-by-step fashion for the maximum realistic effect. Blake and Wilson are excellent as the desperate killers. Also with John Forsythe, Paul Stewart, Gerald S. O'Loughlin, and Jeff Corey. **Director**—Richard Brooks. **Academy Award Nominations**—Brooks, best director and best screenplay based on material from another medium; Conrad Hall, cinematography. *134 minutes b&w*

IN COUNTRY (1989)

★★½

Bruce Willis
Emily Lloyd

Bruce Willis, Peggy Rea, and Emily Lloyd in In Country.

A moving drama about the lingering psychological scars of the Vietnam War, as experienced by the inhabitants of a small Kentucky town. In trying to understand the war that took her father's life, a teenage girl turns to her uncle, who is a Vietnam vet with problems. Willis gives a fair if not compelling performance in his first serious dramatic role, while English actress Lloyd deftly handles her role—Southern accent and all. A loose, episodic structure weakens the film's cumulative effect. Based on Bobbie Ann Mason's novel. Also with Joan Allen, Kevin Anderson, John Terry, Peggy Rea, Judith Ivey, and Richard Hamilton. **Director**—Norman Jewison. **(R)** *120 minutes*

THE INCREDIBLE SARAH (1976)

★

Glenda Jackson

Jackson, who plays the remarkable and eccentric actress Sarah Bernhardt in this film, goes through some 40 cos-

(Continued)

This movie available on videotape and/or disc.

(Continued)
tume changes and almost as many temper tantrums. Despite such lavishness and energy, this attempt at biography is no more than a series of humdrum vignettes, which fail to illuminate the legendary showmanship of the French actress. The costumes by Anthony Mendleson were nominated for an Academy Award. Also with Daniel Massey and Douglas Wilmer. **Director**—Richard Fleischer. **(PG)**
106 minutes

THE INCREDIBLE SHRINKING MAN (1957)

Grant Williams

A superior sci-fi thriller despite its modest budget. Williams plays a scientist exposed to a radioactive fog, who then shrinks to a minute size, where he views the world from a new perspective. Inventive trick photography provides interest and adds to the suspense. A thought-provoking script by Richard Matheson heightens the proceedings. A science-fiction classic that is still relevant. Also stars Randy Stuart, April Kent, William Schallert, and Paul Langton. **Director**—Jack Arnold.
81 minutes b&w

THE INCREDIBLE SHRINKING WOMAN (1981)

Lily Tomlin
Charles Grodin

Lily Tomlin finds fun and adventure in The Incredible Shrinking Woman.

Tomlin plays a modern-day housewife who shrinks to Barbie Doll proportions because of an intolerance to chemical additives in household products. Grodin is her bewildered husband. Tomlin is a first-rate comedienne, but her talents are subdued by a half-baked script that doesn't reach its potential as social satire on American consumerism. Makeup genius Rick Baker appears as Sidney, the gorilla. Cast also includes Ned Beatty. **Director**—Joel Schumacher. **(PG)**
88 minutes

THE INCUBUS (1982)

 ★★

John Cassavetes

A so-so horror film about the supernatural that features rape amid the violence inflicted by a mysterious demon. Several characters in the story suffer nightmares that are connected to brutal attacks on various women in a small Wisconsin community. This confused and uneven Canadian production is occasionally engrossing, but ultimately unsatisfying. Cassavetes heads the cast, which also includes John Ireland, Kerrie Keane, and Erin Flannery. **Director**—John Hough. **(R)**
92 minutes

INDEPENDENCE DAY (1983)

Kathleen Quinlan
David Keith
Dianne Wiest

Kathleen Quinlan is attracted to David Keith in Independence Day.

Family crises in a small southwestern town are fitfully dramatized in this predictable film. Quinlan tries hard as a young woman who longs to pursue a photography career in the big city. Meanwhile, she's romantically involved with a local auto mechanic (Keith), who wants to be the town's best drag racer. The picture's central theme is upstaged by a subplot involving Wiest as a battered wife. Also with Cliff DeYoung, Richard Farnsworth, and Frances Sternhagen. **Director**—Robert Mandel. **(R)**
110 minutes

INDIANA JONES AND THE LAST CRUSADE (1989)

Harrison Ford
Sean Connery
Alison Doody

Director Steven Spielberg maintains the bold action and breathless pace in this third, and perhaps last, installment involving the two-fisted archaeologist. Ford stars again in the title role. This time Indy is joined by his father, played by Connery. We also catch a glimpse of Indy as a boy (played by River Phoenix). Ford and Connery bravely search for the Holy Grail while sinister Nazis snap at their heels. Also with Denholm Elliott, John Rhys-Davies, Julian Glover, and Alex Hyde-White. **(PG-13) Academy Award**—Ben Burtt, and Richard Hymns, sound effects editing. **Nominations**—John Williams, original score; Burtt, Gary Summers, Shawn Murphy, and Tony Dawe, sound. *125 minutes*

INDIANA JONES AND THE TEMPLE OF DOOM (1984)

Harrison Ford
Kate Capshaw

A tense moment with Harrison Ford in Indiana Jones and the Temple of Doom.

All stops are out in this second installment of the adventures of the two-fisted archaeologist. A relentless cavalcade of thrilling cliff-hangers will leave you exhausted as Ford deals with some nasty characters in India and rescues enslaved children. There's just the right dose of tongue-in-cheek humor, although some scenes are too intense for young children. Nevertheless, it's another well-crafted action tale from director Steven Spielberg. Capshaw is the

® *This movie available with closed captions for the hearing impaired.*

weak link as the wimpy heroine. **(PG) Academy Award**—Dennis Muren, Michael McAlister, Lorne Peterson, and George Gibbs, special visual effects. *118 minutes*

INDISCREET (1958)

★★★

Cary Grant
Ingrid Bergman

Charming upper-crust comedy about a dashing American diplomat romancing a beautiful actress in London. Grant and Bergman are the perfect couple for this sort of ritzy, sophisticated production, enhanced with lush sets. The film is based on Norman Krasna's play *Kind Sir;* Krasna also wrote the screenplay. Also with Phyllis Calvert, Cecil Parker, David Kossoff, and Megs Jenkins. **Director**—Stanley Donen. *100 minutes*

I NEVER PROMISED YOU A ROSE GARDEN (1977)

★★★

Bibi Andersson
Kathleen Quinlan

This sincere story, set in a psychiatric hospital, is about a young girl's fight against madness. The film has good intentions, but is excessively grim. There are impressive performances by Quinlan as the disturbed girl and Andersson as her faithful psychiatrist. It's an exhausting movie, one more likely to be admired than enjoyed. Adapted from Hannah Green's 1964 best-selling novel. Also with Reni Santoni, Susan Tyrrell, and Signe Hasso. **Director**—Anthony Page. **(R) Academy Award Nomination**—Gavin Lambert and Lewis John Carlino, best screenplay based on material from another medium. *96 minutes*

I NEVER SANG FOR MY FATHER (1970)

★★★

Melvyn Douglas
Gene Hackman

Douglas and Hackman make a powerful acting duo in this moving film version of Robert Anderson's play. Hackman is a middle-aged man who tries to cope with his aging but strong-willed father, played by Douglas. There are intelligent and profound character studies all around. Also features Dorothy Stickney and Estelle Parsons. **Director**—Gilbert Cates. **(PG) Academy Award Nominations**—Douglas, best actor; Hackman, best supporting actor; Anderson, best screenplay based on material from another medium. *92 minutes*

THE INFORMER (1935)

★★★★

Victor McLaglen
Preston Foster
Una O'Connor
Joseph Sawyer

A brilliant portrait of a traitor who is hounded by his own conscience. McLaglen is captivating as the IRA rogue who betrays his leader to collect a reward during Ireland's Sinn Fein rebellion. The direction by John Ford superbly creates an eerie and tense atmosphere, enhanced by the foggy and grimy depiction of the Irish landscape. Max Steiner's musical score creates the proper dramatic pace. Also with Heather Angel, Margot Grahame, Donald Meek, and Wallace Ford. **Academy Awards**—Ford, best director; McLaglen, best actor; Dudley Nichols, screenplay. **Nomination**—best picture. *91 minutes b&w*

IN GOD WE TRU$T (1980)

★

Marty Feldman
Peter Boyle
Louise Lasser
Richard Pryor

Strained comedy with banjo-eyed Feldman as a Trappist monk on the prowl for some fast cash to pay the monastery's debts. Out in the wicked world—Los Angeles—innocent Marty encounters a blustering television evangelist and a kindhearted prostitute. He also meets "God"—played by Pryor—in the form of a big computer in the sky. Feldman also cowrote and directed this humorless comedy. *97 minutes*

INHERIT THE WIND (1960)

★★★★

Spencer Tracy
Fredric March

A fascinating episode in American history is brought brilliantly to the screen in an adaptation of the Jerome Lawrence and Robert E. Lee play, about the

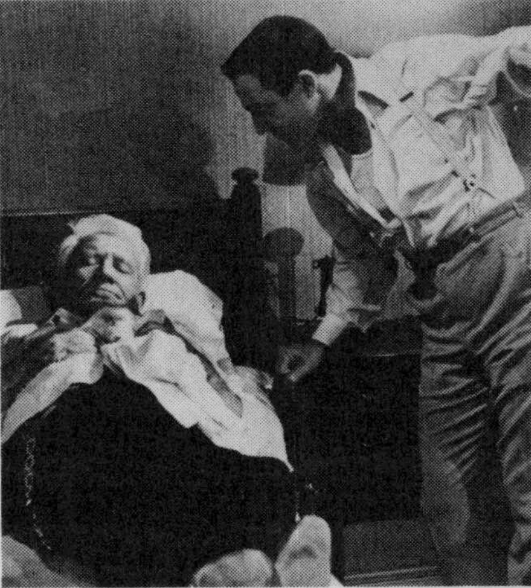

Spencer Tracy and Gene Kelly are unlikely allies in Inherit the Wind.

famous 1925 Scopes "monkey trial" in Tennessee. Tracy and March are superb as the defense lawyer and prosecutor in the case, who are based on Clarence Darrow and William Jennings Bryan, the real-life attorneys in the actual trial. They argue the merits of Darwin's theory of evolution passionately. The sultry atmosphere of a small-town courtroom in midsummer adds to the authenticity. An excellent supporting cast includes Dick York, Gene Kelly, Florence Eldridge, Elliot Reid, and Harry Morgan. **Director**—Stanley Kramer. **Academy Award Nominations**—Tracy, best actor; Nathan E. Douglas and Harold Jacob Smith, best screenplay based on material from another medium; Ernest Laszlo, cinematography. *127 minutes b&w*

THE IN-LAWS (1979)

★★★

Peter Falk
Alan Arkin

Falk and Arkin team up in this wacky and hilarious comedy about a New York dentist who unwittingly becomes involved with his daughter's future in-law, who claims to be a CIA agent. Arkin plays the dentist; Falk plays the CIA man. Andrew Bergman, who collaborated with Mel Brooks in *Blazing Saddles,* has come up with a gem of a comic script; it falters occasionally, but at the right moments provokes side-splitting laughter. Falk and Arkin make an effective and funny twosome. Also with Richard Libertini, Nancy Dussault, Penny Peyser, and Arlene Golonka. **Director**—Arthur Hiller. **(PG)** *103 minutes*

This movie available on videotape and/or disc.

INNERSPACE (1987)

★★★

Dennis Quaid
Martin Short
Meg Ryan

Joe Dante directed this ambitious comedy with a frenzy that most action directors would envy. The complicated plot, which recalls the 1966 science-fiction classic *Fantastic Voyage,* involves a miniaturized test pilot who is accidentally injected into the body of a meek grocery clerk. With the courageous pilot inside his brain and body, the mild-mannered clerk is transformed into a heroic, self-confident figure who saves the day. Quaid, with his boyish good looks and dashing demeanor, is well suited to the character of the test pilot. His swaggering personality helps overcome the limitations of his role, which do not allow him much physical movement. Comedian Short, who has not been effective in his few film appearances, finds his best part to date as the hapless grocery clerk. The fast-paced editing and far-out storyline make for entertaining escapist fare. Produced by Steven Spielberg. Also with Kevin McCarthy, Fiona Lewis, Vernon Wells, and Robert Picardo. **(PG) Academy Award**—Dennis Muren, William George, Harley Jessup, and Kennith Smith, visual effects. *120 minutes*

AN INNOCENT MAN (1989)

★★

Tom Selleck
F. Murray Abraham

Tom Selleck is caught in a trap in An Innocent Man.

A violent prison picture starring Selleck as a happily married airline mechanic who is framed for drug dealing by crooked cops. In the brutal prison environment, the innocent convict is driven to kill to survive. An interesting idea for a vehicle for Selleck is botched by a contrived set-up, an unbelievable ending, and Selleck's own colorless acting. As it plays, the film merely posits violence as the answer to the moral and emotional dilemmas brought up in the story. Also with Laila Robins, David Rasche, Richard Young, Badja Djola, and Todd Graff. **Director**—Peter Yates. **(R)** *113 minutes*

THE INN OF THE SIXTH HAPPINESS (1958)

★★★

Ingrid Bergman
Curt Jurgens
Robert Donat

Engrossing drama, based on a true story, set in China just prior to World War II. Bergman stars as an English missionary in the Far East who bravely shepherds children through enemy territory. Jurgens costars as her romantic love interest. Donat, in his last film, is notable in the role of a mandarin. An exciting climactic scene effectively ends the film. Other performers are Athene Seyler, Ronald Squire, and Richard Wattis. **Director**—Mark Robson. **Academy Award Nomination**—Robson, best director. *158 minutes*

IN PRAISE OF OLDER WOMEN (1979)

★

Tom Berenger
Karen Black
Susan Strasberg
Alexandra Stewart

An awkward soft-core porn film, set in Hungary and Canada, about a boy's sexual experiences with older women. Berenger, as the lad who strikes out with girls his own age, doesn't light any fires. He merely carries on with some married women played by Black, Strasberg, and Stewart, who appear seminude through most of the film. Most of the sex scenes are embarrassing rather than erotic. Also with Helen Shaver and Marilyn Lightstone. **Director**—George Kaczender. **(R)** *108 minutes*

INSERTS (1976)

★

Richard Dreyfuss
Jessica Harper

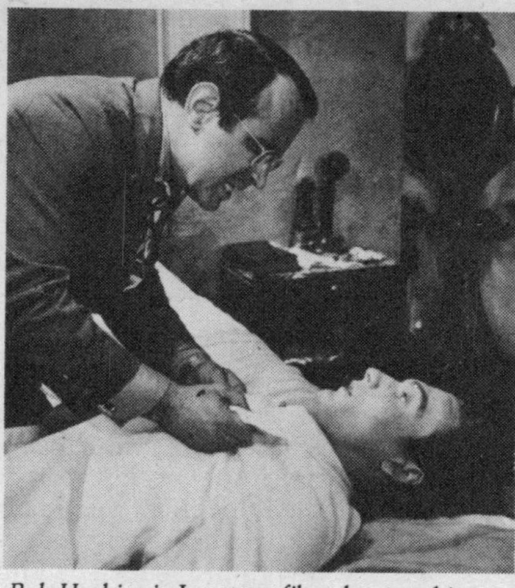

Bob Hoskins in Inserts, *a film about making pornographic films in the 1930s.*

Despite its MPAA rating, this film is hardly pornographic; as might be expected, it's hardly a movie either. The plot concerns the making of pornographic movies in the 1930s. Dreyfuss stars as a has-been director who, in desperation, resorts to shooting skin flicks in his living room. The film never leaves this setting, and it tediously drones on for almost two hours. Harper plays a woman who tries to cure Dreyfuss' withdrawal from life. Also with Bob Hoskins and Veronica Cartwright. **Director**—John Byrum. **(X)** *117 minutes*

INSIDE DAISY CLOVER (1965)

★★

Natalie Wood
Robert Redford

Wood plays the title role in this half-baked story of a young movie star's Hollywood career in the 1930s. Redford plays a troubled matinee idol who marries her. Many of the characters are wet cardboard—Wood included. Only Christopher Plummer does well as a bombastic studio boss. The film is mostly style and little substance. Also with Ruth Gordon and Roddy McDowall. **Director**—Robert Mulligan. **Academy Award Nomination**—Gordon, best supporting actress. *128 minutes*

INSIDE MOVES (1980)

★★

John Savage
David Morse

A moving drama about regulars at a neighborhood bar who are all afflicted with some sort of physical ailment. Savage plays a crippled man who helps his bartending buddy (Morse) obtain a knee operation, which opens the door to a successful basketball career. Though the film is well intentioned, the plot at times is too sentimental and loosely constructed—a situation that detracts from the film's compassion for its characters. Interestingly, Harold Russell, who won an Oscar as the handicapped war veteran in *The Best Years of Our Lives* (1946), appears here for the first time since that film. Also with Diana Scarwid and Amy Wright. **Director**—Richard Donner. **(PG) Academy Award Nomination**—Scarwid, best supporting actress. *113 minutes*

INSIDE OUT (1986)

★

Elliott Gould
Howard Hesseman
Jennifer Tilly

Gould stars as a wealthy man afflicted with agoraphobia—a neurotic state in which the victim is afraid to leave home. Despite this handicap, Gould is able to live quite nicely, because various electronic gizmos help him maintain his apartment, he has all of his necessities delivered, and he relies on an escort service for female companionship. Even his barber makes house calls. It is only after he meets the affectionate and unassuming Tilly that he realizes his life is amiss. Gould is convincing as the frantic recluse whose condition worsens as the movie progresses, but the script is stilted and the dialogue flat. Robert Taicher's direction is so heavy-handed that the emotions of each scene are telegraphed far in advance. Another failure in Gould's floundering career. Also with Beah Richards and Dana Elcar. **(R)** *87 minutes*

THE INSPECTOR GENERAL (1949)

★★★

Danny Kaye

Top-of-the-line star vehicle for Kaye, who masquerades as an important official in 19th-century Russia. Kaye turns on the charm and the energy in this good-looking comedy of errors, tarnished only by a few plodding moments. Costars Walter Slezak, Barbara Bates, Elsa Lanchester, and Gene Lockhart. **Director**—Henry Koster. *101 minutes*

INTERIORS (1978)

★★★

Diane Keaton
Geraldine Page
Kristin Griffith
Mary Beth Hurt

Woody Allen's first serious drama as writer/director is surprisingly effective, considering its overall gloominess. The style reflects Allen's admiration for Ingmar Bergman, but the story is not unlike the plays of Arthur Miller. The plot involves a series of intense emotional crises in a wealthy New York family, whose members all strive for achievement and creativity but appear unhappy whether or not they get what they want. Excellent acting by Page, Keaton, Maureen Stapleton, E.G. Marshall, and Sam Waterston. **(PG) Academy Award Nominations**—Page, best actress; Stapleton, best supporting actress; Allen, best screenplay. *99 minutes*

INTERMEZZO (1939)

★★★

Ingrid Bergman
Leslie Howard

Married violinist Leslie Howard can't resist Ingrid Bergman in Intermezzo.

A well-done love story about a famous married violinist, played by Howard, who falls hopelessly in love with a young pianist, played by Bergman. The movie offers some fine moments of charm and sentimentality, and Bergman is impressive in her English-speaking debut. Others in the cast include John Halliday, Edna Best, and Cecil Kellaway. **Director**—Gregory Ratoff. *69 minutes b&w*

INTERNAL AFFAIRS (1990)

★★★

Richard Gere
Andy Garcia

A beautifully photographed cop thriller starring Gere as a menacing police detective under investigation by internal affairs. Garcia costars as the temperamental honest cop who investigates his vicious colleague. The storyline is convoluted and some of Gere's actions don't make sense in the end, but simple plot mechanics are not what makes this film worthwhile. It is Gere's gripping performance and director Mike Figgis' stylish and intense interpretation of specific scenes that are memorable. Figgis, as he did in his moody *Stormy Monday,* mixes working-class characters with ultra-chic arty folk, which results in a interesting subplot involving Garcia and his wife, played by Nancy Travis. Also with Laurie Metcalf, Richard Bradford, and William Baldwin. **(R)** *115 minutes*

INTERNATIONAL VELVET (1978)

★★1/2

Tatum O'Neal
Christopher Plummer
Nanette Newman

O'Neal stars in this handsome sequel to *National Velvet,* the 1944 girl-meets-horse movie that featured young Elizabeth Taylor. Velvet, now grown up and played in this film by Newman, resides in the picturesque English countryside. O'Neal, who plays her orphaned niece, follows in the footsteps of her famous aunt, and wins a gold medal in the exciting Olympic equestrian competition. Also with Anthony Hopkins and Dinsdale Landen. **Director**—Bryan Forbes. **(PG)** *127 minutes*

IN THE HEAT OF THE NIGHT (1967)

★★★★

Sidney Poitier
Rod Steiger

Poitier plays a highly professional, big-city homicide detective on a visit to a backwater Mississippi town. A murder is committed, and he joins forces with a bigoted police chief to solve the case. Steiger is exceptional as the pompous

(Continued)

(Continued)
sheriff who learns some professional crime-solving methods from the black cop. Director Norman Jewison brings out their personality clash with amazing skill, and the film, an insightful study of prejudices and lifestyles in the South, is enhanced by the top supporting work from Lee Grant, Warren Oates, Quentin Dean, William Schallert, and Scott Wilson. **Academy Awards**—best picture; Steiger, best actor; Stirling Silliphant, best screenplay based on material from another medium. **Nomination**—Jewison, best director. *110 minutes*

IN THE MOOD (1987)

★★★

Patrick Dempsey
Beverly D'Angelo
Talia Balsam

Patrick Dempsey and Beverly D'Angelo in In the Mood.

Based on the true story of Sonny Wisecarver, this affectionate but modest screwball comedy captures the look and the spirit of World War II America. Known as the Woo Woo Kid, Wisecarver made headlines in the 1940s when, at age 14, he eloped with a 21-year-old mother of two. Shortly thereafter, he eloped with the wife of a Marine. The film uses the Wisecarver story as a means to nostalgically view a variety of topics. The performances are delightful, particularly D'Angelo, who effectively slings the slang of the period. Best line: As Sonny elopes for the first time, he exclaims, "Oh, this is so much better than the ninth grade." **Director**—Phil Alden Robinson. **(PG–13)** *98 minutes*

IN THE SPIRIT (1990)

★★

Elaine May
Peter Falk
Marlo Thomas

A goofy screwball comedy featuring the talented May in a much-welcomed comic role. However, the film offers little else of interest. May plays a wealthy woman who connects with a New Age companion, played by Thomas. The storyline evolves into a female odd-couple adventure when the girls are pursued by a murderer. Creaky direction and much extraneous dialogue contribute to the film's weaknesses. Also with Melanie Griffith, Jeannie Berlin, and Olympia Dukakis, who seems unable to follow her Oscar-winning performance in *Moonstruck* with a significant role in a decent film. **Director**—Sandra Secat. **(R)** *93 minutes*

INTO THE NIGHT (1985)

★★1/2

Jeff Goldblum
Michelle Pfeiffer

Michelle Pfeiffer is a spunky woman of mystery in Into the Night.

Goldblum stars as an insomniac who finds himself mixed up with an attractive emerald smuggler (Pfeiffer). She is being pursued by desperados from all nations. The thriller/comedy, set in Los Angeles, has an evocative opening shot and an interesting airport climax; in between there's scarcely a chuckle or a chill. Also, the in-jokes involving the film industry are too distracting. Performers also include Richard Farnsworth, Irene Papas, Kathryn Harrold, David Bowie, and Dan Aykroyd. **Director**—John Landis. **(R)** *115 minutes*

INTRUDER IN THE DUST (1949)

★★★★

Juano Hernandez
Elizabeth Patterson
David Brian

A gripping drama, enhanced by indelible characterizations, about a black man who is wrongfully accused of murder. He's rescued from a lynch mob by a boy and an old woman, who find the real killer. Hernandez is the accused black, and Brian and Patterson are his rescuers. The film, based on William Faulkner's novel, works as a mystery as well as straightforward social observation. There's top-notch acting with well-paced direction. Also with Claude Jarman, Jr., Porter Hall, and Will Geer. **Director**—Clarence Brown. *87 minutes b&w*

INVADERS FROM MARS (1986)

★★

Karen Black
Hunter Carson

Director Tobe Hooper's remake of the 1953 sci-fi thriller is overproduced and too lavish for what is essentially a B-movie. The story of aliens who control the minds of small-town residents is all too familiar by now, and Hooper brings no new ideas to the film, nor is there even any interesting dialogue in the screenplay. The film emphasizes clichés of the genre and movie-related in-jokes, yet it is difficult to tell if the film is really intended as a spoof. A dull and lackluster effort. Black, Carson, and Timothy Bottoms do what they can with the script. Also with Louise Fletcher, Bud Cort, Laraine Newman, and James Karen. **(PG)** *100 minutes*

INVASION OF THE BODY SNATCHERS (1956)

★★★★

Kevin McCarthy
Dana Wynter
Carolyn Jones
King Donovan

The humans defend themselves against the Invasion of the Body Snatchers.

This movie available with closed captions for the hearing impaired.

A classic science-fiction thriller made on a small budget, with a relatively unknown cast and no special effects. A small American town is invaded by strange pods from outer space, and the residents are replaced by soulless duplicates of themselves, which are hatched from the pods. McCarthy, in one of his few roles as a leading man, stars as a doctor who tries to stop the silent invasion. The film's direction by Don Siegel is simple but effective: The sense of suspense and doom, for example, is created not by visual effects or elaborate settings, but by consistently placing McCarthy where he has to hide in smaller and smaller and darker and darker places. At the end, when McCarthy finally does break away from his claustrophobic hiding places, he bursts forth onto the freeway to warn the rest of the world before it's too late—one of the most famous moments in cinema history. Originally the film was to end there, but studio heads demanded a less depressing conclusion, and a more conventional finale was added. The film has frequently been cited as an allegory for McCarthyism, but can be enjoyed at face value as an excellent example of 1950s science fiction.

80 minutes b&w

INVASION OF THE BODY SNATCHERS (1978)

 ★★★1/2

Donald Sutherland
Brooke Adams

Donald Sutherland in the remake of Invasion of the Body Snatchers.

The 1956 sci-fi classic gets a coat of gloss and some flashy new thrills in this remake by director Philip Kaufman. Aliens arrive on earth in the form of strange seedpods to replace humans, but this time the setting is San Francisco instead of a small town. Sutherland stands out as a beleaguered public health officer who tries to unscramble the mystery. The film slows down a bit about midway, but there are enough scary scenes to keep the chills flowing to the end. Kevin McCarthy, who played the Sutherland role in the original film, and Don Siegel, the director of the 1956 version, both appear in cameo roles. Also look for Robert Duvall in a bit part. Jeff Goldblum, Veronica Cartwright, and Leonard Nimoy costar. **(PG)**

115 minutes

INVASION U.S.A. (1985)

 ★★

Chuck Norris

Machine guns, bazookas, and dynamite charges explode all over the screen in this vile, preposterous exploitation film aimed at fans of military action tales. A small army of terrorists, led by people with Russian-sounding names, invades the Florida shore and touches off chaos. Only a former intelligence agent, played by stone-faced Chuck Norris, can stop this menace. At times, Norris takes on an enemy that seems to pack more firepower than the D-Day landing force. What nonsense. **Director**—Joseph Zito. **(R)**

108 minutes

THE INVISIBLE KID (1988)

(no stars)

Jay Underwood
Karen Black
Chynna Phillips

This sophomoric teen comedy depends on that overworked gimmick in which a character ingests a mysterious substance that renders him invisible. Underwood plays an unpopular high-school nerd who swallows a compound that makes him invisible for limited time spans. The character takes advantage of these brief episodes to partake in such familiar antics as peeping into the girls' locker room. This trite film, which had only a limited theatrical release, is worse than most teen comedies. Phillips is the daughter of actress/singer Michelle Phillips. **Director**—Avery Crounse. **(PG)**

95 minutes

THE INVISIBLE MAN (1933)

 ★★★★

Claude Rains
Gloria Stuart

Rains became a star in this role as a mad scientist who discovers how to make himself invisible with a special elixir. Excellent trick photography and a solid plot, based on the H.G. Wells novel, result in a superior sci-fi film, as Rains runs amok and vows to use his power to rule the world. E.E. Clive, Una O'Connor, Henry Travers, Dudley Digges, and William Harrigan perform admirably. James Whale (*Frankenstein*) provides suitably atmospheric direction.

80 minutes b&w

INVITATION TO A GUNFIGHTER (1964)

 ★★

Yul Brynner
George Segal

There's more talk than action in this tepid western about a community that recruits a gunman to do some dirty work. The characterizations come off as too pat despite the efforts of a decent cast. Also with Janice Rule, Brad Dexter, and Pat Hingle. **Director**—Richard Wilson.

92 minutes

IN WHICH WE SERVE (1942)

 ★★★★

Noel Coward

Stirring British World War II drama tells the personal stories of the surviving crew of a torpedoed destroyer. Writer/codirector/composer/star Coward does a superb job in all categories and creates a poignant and moving story of patriotism, heroism, and honor without an iota of cloying sentiment. The excellent cast includes Bernard Miles, John Mills, Richard Attenborough, Celia Johnson, Kay Walsh, Joyce Carey, Michael Wilding, and James Donald. The production has withstood the test of time. **Directors**—Coward and David Lean. **Academy Award Nominations**—best picture; Coward, original screenplay.

114 minutes b&w

I OUGHT TO BE IN PICTURES (1982)

 ★★

Walter Matthau
Dinah Manoff
Ann-Margret

Matthau's delivery of cantankerous wisecracks adds some spice to this oth-

(Continued)

(Continued)
erwise blasé film based on Neil Simon's Broadway play. Matthau plays a down-and-out Hollywood screenwriter who is reunited with his teenage daughter (Manoff) after a 16-year separation. A lot of sarcastic sparring ensues, in typical Simon manner. But the relentless recriminations and sentimental gushings never develop beyond the banal. **Director**—Herbert Ross. **(PG)** *108 minutes*

THE IPCRESS FILE (1965)

★★★

Michael Caine
Nigel Green

Taut, relentlessly absorbing espionage caper, based on Len Deighton's novel, with Caine perfectly cast as Harry Palmer, a low-key secret agent who tracks a missing scientist behind the Iron Curtain and discovers one of his superiors is a spy. Sidney J. Furie's efficient direction upholds the tension throughout the film, and the script is plotted for maximum suspense. The film led to two sequels. Also stars Guy Doleman, Sue Lloyd, and Gordon Jackson. *108 minutes*

IPHIGENIA (1977)

★★★

Tatiana Papamoskou
Irene Papas

This Euripides drama transforms well to the screen, illuminating the power and passion of the classic Greek tragedy. It's the story of King Agamemnon, who is forced to sacrifice his daughter, Iphigenia, to appease the gods and assure favorable passage for his fleet to Troy. Fourteen-year-old Papamoskou is magnificent as the martyred daughter. Also with Costa Kazakos. Classy direction by Michael (*Zorba the Greek*) Cacoyannis. Originally filmed in Greek. **Academy Award Nomination**—best foreign-language film. *127 minutes*

I REMEMBER MAMA (1948)

★★★★

Irene Dunne
Barbara Bel Geddes

A nice bit of nostalgia as a novelist remembers growing up with her stout-hearted Norwegian family, struggling to attain the American dream in San Francisco. Dunne is wonderful as the

In I Remember Mama, *Barbara Bel Geddes recalls growing up in a caring family.*

energetic mother whose devotion and fortitude keep the family on an even keel; Bel Geddes plays the novelist. The film is filled with rich details of turn-of-the-century San Francisco. Other good performances include those by Oscar Homolka, Edgar Bergen, Philip Dorn, Ellen Corby, and Cedric Hardwicke. **Director**—George Stevens. **Academy Award Nominations**—Dunne, best actress; Homolka, best supporting actor; Bel Geddes and Corby, best supporting actress; Nicholas Musuraca, cinematography. *134 minutes b&w*

IRMA LA DOUCE (1963)

★★★

Shirley MacLaine
Jack Lemmon

The delightful film, a nonmusical version of the Broadway play, is executed with style and flavor. Writer/director Billy Wilder succeeds with this comic romp about a Paris cop, played by Lemmon, who falls in love with a prostitute, played by MacLaine. Lemmon is in top form, and he's matched by the spirited performance of MacLaine as the sweet, good-natured trollop. Nonstop fun, especially for adult audiences. Costars Lou Jacobi, Herschel Bernardi, Joan Shawlee, and Bruce Yarnell. **Academy Award Nominations**—MacLaine, best actress; Joseph LaShelle, cinematography. *146 minutes*

IRON EAGLE (1986)

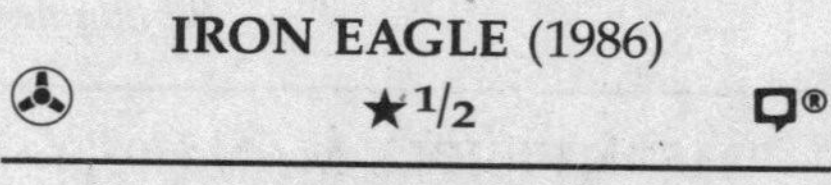

★½

Jason Gedrick
Lou Gossett, Jr.

A *Rambo*-style plot is applied to this movie involving teenage heroics, resulting in preposterous situations. Gedrick stars as the son of a military pilot shot down over an unfriendly Middle East country resembling Libya. With the help of a retired colonel (Gossett), the youth becomes a one-man air force as he streaks off in an F-17 fighter to rescue his father. This unlikely dream of glory is little more than an unbelievable and manipulative comic-strip film that insults the intelligence. **Director**—Sidney J. Furie. **(PG-13)** *116 minutes*

IRON EAGLE II (1988)

★★

Louis Gossett, Jr.
Mark Humphrey

Louis Gossett, Jr., and Mark Humphrey in Iron Eagle II.

This action/drama sequel is just as mediocre as the 1986 original. Gossett, recreating his role as a hotshot fighter pilot, is called out of retirement to destroy a cache of nuclear weapons in a Middle Eastern country. This time the Americans team up with Russians for the daring mission. Some of the aerial action is spectacular, but the storyline is predictable and the drama is virtually nonexistent. **Director**—Sidney J. Furie. **(PG)** *100 minutes*

THE IRON TRIANGLE (1989)

★★

Beau Bridges
Liem Whatley

A Viet Cong soldier's diary was rumored to be the basis for the screenplay of this war drama that presents a different twist on the Vietnam War. An American officer (Bridges) and his young Viet Cong captor (Whatley) develop respect for one another. Unfortunately, the picture is hampered by weak acting, script, and direction. This alternative view generally portrays the Viet Cong and North Vietnamese in a better

® *This movie available with closed captions for the hearing impaired.*

light than the South Vietnamese, who are shown as corrupt and sadistic. Also with Dr. Haing S. Ngor. **Director**—Eric Weston. **(R)** *91 minutes*

IRONWEED (1987)

★★½

Jack Nicholson
Meryl Streep

Good times? Meryl Streep, Jack Nicholson, and Fred Gwynne in Ironweed.

Despite Nicholson's sturdy performance as a derelict haunted by ghosts of the past, this film adaptation of William Kennedy's Pulitzer-Prize-winning novel never comes to life on the screen. At fault seems to be Kennedy's screenplay, which does not include the interior monologues that made the book so powerful, and Hector Babenco's direction, which dwells on dour scenes of Depression-era Albany, New York. The result is a hopelessly static and relentlessly depressing drama about human failure. The storyline basically follows the return of Nicholson's character to Albany to see the family he abandoned 22 years earlier. Streep costars in a secondary role as a failed concert pianist who is also on the skids. Also with Carroll Baker, Michael O'Keefe, Diane Venora, Tom Waits, and Fred Gwynne. **(R) Academy Award Nominations**—Nicholson, best actor; Streep, best actress. *145 minutes*

IRRECONCILABLE DIFFERENCES (1984)

★★

Ryan O'Neal
Shelley Long
Drew Barrymore

This satiric comedy opens with a cute 10-year-old girl (Barrymore) seeking a divorce from her neglectful, ever-bickering parents. But the clever scenario is merely a setup for the story of an ambitious Hollywood couple (O'Neal and Long) told mostly in flashbacks. He's a film director and she's a writer, both suffering from their own bloated egos brought about by quick success. **Director**—Charles Shyer. **(PG)** *112 minutes*

ISADORA (1969)

★★★

Vanessa Redgrave

A film biography of modernist dancer and freethinker Isadora Duncan told in curious flashback and flash-forward sequences. Redgrave becomes Isadora in an inspired performance that gives the film an exciting aura. Though overly long, despite a cut from its original 168 minutes, and occasionally confusing, the very drama of this tempestuous woman's life is spellbinding. Redgrave is ably supported by Jason Robards and James Fox. **Director**—Karel Reisz. **Academy Award Nomination**—Redgrave, best actress. *138 minutes*

ISHTAR (1987)

★★½

Warren Beatty
Dustin Hoffman
Isabelle Adjani

Dustin Hoffman and Warren Beatty find themselves stranded in Ishtar.

Elaine May directed this almost $40 million comedy starring Beatty and Hoffman as two down-and-out singer/songwriters who are booked into a nightclub in the mythical country of Ishtar. The two are soon caught up in Middle Eastern intrigue as they both try to aid a beautiful revolutionary, played by Adjani, who wants to help her backward country. The film, much like a Bob Hope-Bing Crosby *Road* movie, is structured into a series of comic bits that feature Beatty and Hoffman doing their shtick as the worst singers imaginable, crooning songs that are equally as bad. As a result, the storyline lacks momentum, falters midway through the film, and finally fizzles out. The relationship between Beatty and Hoffman, however, provides the heart of the film, and their desperate need to become a part of show business is both humorous and touching. Negative press about production problems and behind-the-scenes turmoil provoked critics into writing scathing reviews at the time of release. Though the film is flawed, it did not deserve its reputation and is worth watching. Also with Charles Grodin, Jack Weston, Tess Harper, and Carol Kane. **(PG–13)** *105 minutes*

THE ISLAND OF DR. MOREAU (1977)

★★

Burt Lancaster
Michael York

In 1933, the filmed version of this H.G. Wells horror fantasy was called *The Island of Lost Souls.* In that film, Charles Laughton starred as a sinister scientist who tries to breed animals into humans and vice versa. This $6 million remake is a nice try with Lancaster in the title role, but alas, the strange critters aren't as creepy, and the atmosphere is hardly ghoulish. Also with Barbara Carrera. **Director**—Don Taylor. **(PG)** *104 minutes*

ISLANDS IN THE STREAM (1977)

★★

George C. Scott
David Hemmings
Claire Bloom

This introspective movie version of Ernest Hemingway's novel begins well, but fails to gain any momentum. Scott plays the artist-hero—a self-exiled sculptor whose marriages have failed—with gruff macho spirit. But the film doesn't do justice to the Hemingway prose, and the story drifts along with no point of view. Also with Susan Tyrrell, Michael-James Wixted, and Gilbert Roland. **Director**—Franklin J. Schaffner. **(PG)** *105 minutes*

This movie available on videotape and/or disc.

IS PARIS BURNING? (1966)

★★

Leslie Caron
Kirk Douglas
Charles Boyer
Jean-Paul Belmondo
Orson Welles

Meandering and overblown all-star epic account of the efforts to prevent the destruction of Paris by the retreating Germans in World War II. The story is put together as a succession of vignettes, and the film is loaded with half-baked cameos that only provoke annoyance and lead to dreariness. Also with Alain Delon, Jean-Pierre Cassel, Gert Frobe, Glenn Ford, and Robert Stack. **Director**—René Clément. *173 minutes b&w*

IT CAME FROM HOLLYWOOD (1983)

★★½

A compilation of filmdom's schlocky moments with notable snippets from such potboilers as *The Slime People* and *Attack of the 50-Foot Woman*. Fans of outrageous B-movies may find something to chuckle about, but the material is haphazardly assembled and this cavalcade of the ridiculous eventually becomes tiresome. Segments are introduced by Dan Aykroyd, Gilda Radner, Cheech and Chong, and John Candy. Their presence adds little to the proceedings. **Director**—Malcolm Leo. **(PG)** *76 minutes*

IT HAPPENED ONE NIGHT (1934)

★★★★

Clark Gable
Claudette Colbert

Clark Gable and Claudette Colbert in the classic It Happened One Night.

A spoiled rich girl (Colbert) runs away from her daddy and sets off to marry her gigolo boyfriend. She is accompanied on this crazy odyssey by a story-hungry reporter (Gable). She wants to use him to help her get away, he wants to use her to get a good story, and of course they fall in love. This delightful romance was a forerunner to all the great screwball comedies of the 1930s, and remains one of the best comedies of all time. Gable and Colbert make the ideal bickering couple, but there is a sensuality between them that adds warmth to the witty dialogue and funny situations. A rare combination of talents. **Director**—Frank Capra. **Academy Awards**—best picture; Capra, best director; Gable, best actor; Colbert, best actress; Robert Riskin, adaptation. *105 minutes b&w*

IT HAPPENED ONE SUMMER

See State Fair

IT HAPPENS EVERY SPRING (1949)

★★★

Ray Milland
Jean Peters

A chemistry professor, played by Milland, becomes an unlikely pitching ace after he discovers a formula that makes baseballs repel wood, including baseball bats. Milland handles the part with skill and coaxes plenty of smiles from the buoyant material. Also stars Paul Douglas, Ed Begley, Ted De Corsia, and Ray Collins. **Director**—Lloyd Bacon. **Academy Award Nomination**—Shirley W. Smith and Valentine Davies, motion picture story. *80 minutes b&w*

I, THE JURY (1982)

★★

Armand Assante
Barbara Carrera
Paul Sorvino

Blazing nonstop action, laced with sex and violence, characterizes this reworking of Mickey Spillane's famous private-eye adventure tale. The complex, supercharged plot includes new twists such as CIA operatives, a sex clinic, mind control, and big-shot gangsters. Assante overplays the hard-boiled gumshoe, Mike Hammer. Also with Alan King and Laurene Landon. **Director**—Richard T. Heffron. **(R)** *109 minutes*

IT'S ALIVE! (1974)

★½

John Ryan
Sharon Farrell

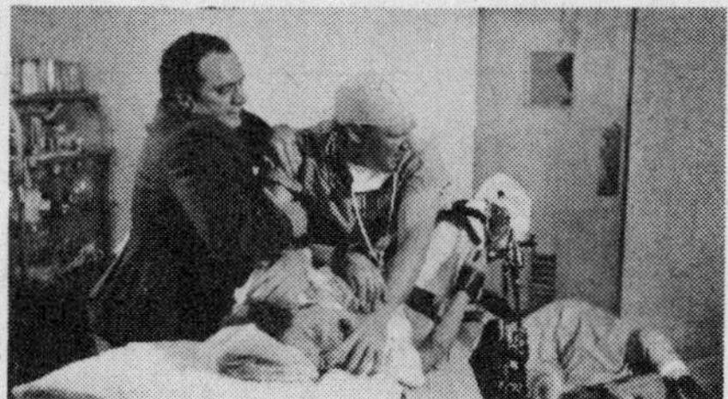

John Ryan (left) and Sharon Farrell get a nasty surprise in It's Alive!

This nonsensical movie concerns a weird newborn baby with long fangs that goes on a killing spree, beginning with the doctors and nurses in the delivery room. The acting is awful, the dialogue silly. However, director/producer/writer Larry Cohen manages a few moments of suspense and a mild comment on the overuse of drugs. The film has a cult following, but is not for everyone. Also with Andrew Duggan and Guy Stockwell. **(PG)** *91 minutes*

IT'S A MAD MAD MAD MAD WORLD (1963)

★★★

Spencer Tracy
Jimmy Durante
Milton Berle
Sid Caesar
Ethel Merman

A full-frontal assault on the funnybone, with virtually every Hollywood comedian getting in their licks. The two-and-a-half-hour romp is about a mad scramble to recover hidden loot from a robbery. Tracy plays a detective trying to recover the booty. All sorts of wild chases and slapstick antics abound. The large cast also includes Buddy Hackett, Mickey Rooney, Dick Shawn, Jack Benny, Jerry Lewis, Terry-Thomas, Phil Silvers, Edie Adams, Jonathan Winters, and many more. **Director**—Stanley Kramer. *154 minutes*

IT'S A WONDERFUL LIFE (1946)

★★★★

James Stewart
Henry Travers
Donna Reed

® This movie available with closed captions for the hea ring impaired.

Family values and the decency of the human spirit are celebrated in It's a Wonderful Life.

This is perhaps Frank Capra's best film; it shows his uniquely warm and charming brand of humor. Stewart is superb as a small-town businessman who dedicates himself to the welfare of others for most of his life. When he decides to end it all because he thinks he's a failure, a guardian angel, played by Travers, comes to Earth to show him what tragedies would have happened had he not been born. Reed plays Stewart's wife. It is film sentimentality done to perfection and displayed with a silver lining. A Christmas favorite. Also with Lionel Barrymore, Thomas Mitchell, Ward Bond, and Gloria Grahame. **Academy Award Nominations**—best picture; Capra, best director; Stewart, best actor. *129 minutes b&w*

IT'S MY TURN (1980)

 ★★

Jill Clayburgh
Michael Douglas
Charles Grodin

Clayburgh plays a successful math professor, trying to resolve her career and her love life in this vague comedy/drama. The performances are engaging, but Eleanor Bergstein's muddled screenplay keeps the film on the level of a soap opera. The movie eventually stops in its tracks, dangling all sorts of unanswered questions. Douglas and Grodin costar as Clayburgh's lovers of the moment—one in New York, the other in Chicago. Also with Beverly Garland. **Director**—Claudia Weill. **(PG)** *91 minutes*

IVANHOE (1952)

★★★

Robert Taylor
Joan Fontaine
Elizabeth Taylor

A splendid costume adventure, based on Sir Walter Scott's colorful tale of brave knights and fair damsels in medieval England. Robert Taylor plays the title role, galloping off on daring assignments and romancing Taylor and Fontaine. The production values stand out with lavish sets and striking photography. The script, however, lacks excitement. Also stars Emlyn Williams, George Sanders, Robert Douglas, and Sebastian Cabot. **Director**—Richard Thorpe. **Academy Award Nominations**—best picture; F.A. Young, cinematography. *106 minutes*

I WALKED WITH A ZOMBIE (1943)

Frances Dee
Tom Conway
James Ellison

A nurse visits a Caribbean island to take care of the zombielike wife of a planter and discovers skeletons and voodoo rituals lurking about. There is enough style and spooky atmosphere to maintain interest throughout in this early effort by director Jacques Tourneur. The film represents the second effort in a series of low-budget horror films that teamed director Tourneur with producer Val Lewton. The films, rich in eerie settings and fascinating storylines, are now considered minor classics. Also with James Bell and Theresa Harris. *69 minutes b&w*

I WANNA HOLD YOUR HAND (1978)

★★★ 

Nancy Allen
Bobby DiCiccio
Mark McClure

A group of teenagers try to crash the Beatles' New York hotel suite when the famous mop tops pay their first visit to America to appear on *The Ed Sullivan Show* in 1964. Sparkling performances by a young cast add to the film's charm. Allen is particularly effective as an innocent girl who learns the real meaning of romance after experiencing the magic of the Beatles. First-time director Robert Zemeckis had obviously been influenced by the freewheeling spirit of *American Graffiti*. **(PG)** *104 minutes*

I WANT TO LIVE! (1958)

★★★★

Susan Hayward
Simon Oakland

Smashing crime drama, based on the case of Barbara Graham, who was executed in the gas chamber for murder amid debate about the severity of her punishment. Hayward gives a *tour-de-force* performance as the tough prostitute, and the production is neatly assembled for maximum impact by director Robert Wise. Especially compelling are the details of the execution. The film offers a moving plea for the abolition of capital punishment. Good supporting efforts by Oakland, Virginia Vincent, Theodore Bikel, and Philip Coolidge. **Academy Award**—Hayward, best actress. **Nominations**—Wise, best director; Nelson Gidding and Don Mankiewicz, best screenplay based on material from another medium; Lionel Linden, cinematography. *120 minutes b&w*

I WAS A MALE WAR BRIDE (1949)

Cary Grant
Ann Sheridan

The title may sound absurd, but this energetic comedy is highly entertaining. Grant plays a World War II French army officer who gets dressed up in women's clothing as part of a scheme to join Sheridan, his American WAC wife, on a return trip to the United States. Grant and Sheridan are hilarious, and they have a funny script to work with. Also with Marion Marshall and Randy Stuart. **Director**—Howard Hawks. *105 minutes b&w*

I WAS A TEENAGE WEREWOLF (1957)

Michael Landon
Whit Bissell

A low-budget monster movie that has unexpected style. A doctor uses a delinquent youth as a guinea pig for some

(Continued)

(Continued)
experiments in regression. Unfortunately, the young man, played by Landon, becomes a werewolf. It's an interesting mixture of horror and humor. And who can forget that crazy title? Also with Yvonne Lime and Guy Williams. **Director**—Gene Fowler, Jr.
76 minutes b&w

I WILL, I WILL...FOR NOW (1976)

★

Elliott Gould
Diane Keaton
Victoria Principal

A stale and wretched sex farce starring Gould and Keaton as a rich, hip New York couple who get involved with a sex clinic, a contract marriage, and extramarital affairs. The film is full of adolescent gags that consistently fall flat. Norman Panama, who wrote and directed comedies in the 1940s, directed this one and collaborated on the script. The film is hopelessly dated, and Panama seems out of touch with the modern world. Also with Paul Sorvino and Robert Alda. **(R)** *96 minutes.*

I WONDER WHO'S KISSING HER NOW (1947)

★★★

Mark Stevens
June Haver

This pleasant film biography of 1890s songwriter Joseph E. Howard works mainly because of its great music. The plot, embellished with some fiction, is merely routine. A talented cast, however, helps bring it along. Also stars Martha Stewart, Reginald Gardiner, Lenore Aubert, William Frawley, and Gene Nelson. **Director**—Lloyd Bacon. *104 minutes*

J

JABBERWOCKY (1977)

★★

Michael Palin
Max Wall

A shabby-looking medieval farce; a second cousin to *Monty Python and the Holy Grail,* but hardly achieving its quality. Occasional flashes of humor are quickly drowned in a confused outpouring of adolescent slapstick and bad taste. The wobbly script involves knights, a king, grubby peasants, a bumbling hero, and a vile monster—the Jabberwock. Also with Deborah Fallender. Written and directed by Terry Gilliam. **(PG)** *100 minutes*

JACKNIFE (1989)

★★★ 

Robert De Niro
Ed Harris
Kathy Baker

Superb acting electrifies this compelling psychological drama about three believable people trying to cope with various troubles in their lives. De Niro plays a gruff Vietnam vet who tries to perk up his alcoholic buddy (Harris). De Niro eventually falls in love with his friend's plain sister (Baker). The often stagy film works best as a charming and heart-tugging love story. Stephen McNally adapted the screenplay from his play *Strange Snow.* **Director**—David Jones. **(R)** *120 minutes*

THE JACKPOT (1950)

★★★

James Stewart
Barbara Hale

An ordinary guy wins a large sum of money on a radio quiz show. After he attains notoriety, his life changes drastically. A low-key comedy starring Stewart as the winner, who gets a fair share of headaches along with extra income. Others in the cast include James Gleason, Fred Clark, Alan Mowbray, and Natalie Wood. **Director**—Walter Lang. *85 minutes b&w*

JAGGED EDGE (1985)

★★★

Jeff Bridges
Glenn Close

A slick, suspenseful murder-mystery about a charming, wealthy newspaper publisher (Bridges) accused of brutally killing his socialite wife. There are plenty of thrilling twists and turns as the intriguing melodrama unfolds at a steady pace. The unexpected ending took some viewers by surprise, but those carefully watching for the clues will figure it out. Close stars as the reluctant defense attorney who becomes

Defense attorney Glenn Close and the accused, Jeff Bridges, in Jagged Edge.

romantically involved with her client. Peter Coyote and Robert Loggia stand out in fine supporting roles. **Director**—Richard Marquand. **(R) Academy Award Nomination**—Loggia, best supporting actor. *108 minutes*

JAILHOUSE ROCK (1957)

★★★

Elvis Presley
Judy Tyler
Mickey Shaughnessy

Elvis' most famous film, if not his most popular. Presley cashes in on the notorious side of his image as he plays a young man with a chip on his shoulder who is accused of manslaughter and sent to prison. There he learns to play guitar from a has-been country/western singer. After his release, he embarks on a singing career, and as it turns out, he has an exciting new sound. Tyler costars as a record producer who helps him achieve success, and eventually that success leads him to Hollywood. As is obvious, particularly to fans, the plot parallels Presley's own career. The title-song sequence, which was choreographed by Elvis himself, is now a classic. Sadly, Elvis was unable to bring himself to watch this film because Tyler was killed in a car accident shortly after its release. The music and Elvis' performing style transcend the predictable material. Also with Dean Jones and Vaughn Taylor. **Director**—Richard Thorpe. *96 minutes b&w*

JAKE SPEED (1986)

★★

Wayne Crawford
Dennis Christopher
Karen Kopins

Borrowing heavily from *Romancing the Stone,* this overblown action/adventure

This movie available with closed captions for the hearing impaired.

tale involves a woman who hires a legendary adventurer to rescue her sister from white slavers. Narrow escapes abound, but most of this derring-do is too hyped and misdirected to be effective even as fantasy. Video versions run 93 minutes. Also with John Hurt and Monte Markham. **Director**—Andrew Lane. **(PG)** *100 minutes*

JAMAICA INN (1939)

★★★

Charles Laughton
Maureen O'Hara

Taut and exciting melodrama by Alfred Hitchcock set during the Victorian era in the country around Cornwall. O'Hara, an innocent orphan, is taken in by a country squire, Laughton, who secretly heads a band of British pirates. A faithful adaptation of the Daphne du Maurier novel, the film has a rich atmosphere and a gothic quality. A good thriller with fine performances. The supporting players include Leslie Banks, Robert Newton, and Emlyn Williams. *107 minutes b&w*

JANE EYRE (1944)

★★★

Joan Fontaine
Orson Welles

Charlotte Brontë's classic romantic story, set in Victorian times, is faithfully adapted for the screen. The gothic elements of the novel are successfully translated to the screen via a brooding atmosphere and bleak-looking settings. Fontaine heads the cast as an unfortunate orphan girl who becomes a governess for the daughter of a wealthy Englishman and gets involved with mystery and romance. Also with Margaret O'Brien, Henry Daniell, John Sutton, Agnes Moorehead, and Elizabeth Taylor. **Director**—Robert Stevenson. *96 minutes b&w*

THE JANUARY MAN (1989)

★★

Kevin Kline
Mary Elizabeth Mastrantonio
Rod Steiger
Susan Sarandon

Screenwriter John Patrick Shanley, who fared so well with *Moonstruck*, disappoints with this semi-comic police mystery set in New York City. The plot is illogical, the dialogue is choppy and crude, and the story lacks suspense. The characters and casting don't work at all. Kline is miscast as a quirky former detective called back to the force to stop a serial strangler. Steiger rants and raves as the mayor, and Mastrantonio costars as Steiger's daughter—who merely exists to provide Kline with a romance. Also with Harvey Keitel and Danny Aiello. **Director**—Pat O'Connor. **(R)** *97 minutes*

Mary Elizabeth Mastrantonio and Kevin Kline in The January Man.

JAWS (1975)

★★★★

Robert Shaw
Roy Scheider
Richard Dreyfuss

A man-eating shark comes to dine at a Long Island summer resort. The film was designed to scare the hell out of you and has since become a modern horror classic. Shaw plays an experienced shark hunter, Dreyfuss is an ichthyologist, and Scheider is the area's police chief, but the great white shark—a 25-foot mechanical marvel—is the film's real star. The direction by 27-year-old Steven Spielberg is excellent, but the film's shocking effect depends on the Oscar-winning editing by Verna Fields. The film's much-emulated musical score by John Williams and its innovative sound also won Oscars. Adapted from the novel by Peter Benchley. Also with Lorraine Gary, Murray Hamilton, and Carl Gottlieb. **Academy Award Nomination**—best picture. **(PG)** *124 minutes*

JAWS 2 (1978)

★★½

Roy Scheider
Lorraine Gary

This sequel to the big, money-making shark movie offers a moderate ration of excitement when the huge mechanical man-eater swallows some skin divers or chomps on some sailboating teenagers. But this time it's all done without the imagination and slick style that director Steven Spielberg lavished on the original film. The plot, which is mostly a threadbare rehash of the initial *Jaws* theme, never quite builds to a satisfying climax. Scheider again plays the resort community's embattled police chief. Also with Murray Hamilton, Joseph Mascolo, and Jeffrey Kramer. **Director**—Jeannot Szwarc. **(PG)** *117 minutes*

JAWS 3-D (1983)

★★

Dennis Quaid
Bess Armstrong
Lou Gossett, Jr.

The shark returns: Dennis Quaid and Bess Armstrong in Jaws 3-D.

This third, and uneven, installment of the shark saga finds the great white creating havoc at a Florida water park not unlike Sea World, where the film was shot. There are some tense moments, but by now we're so familiar with the antisocial habits of the mammoth predator that its attacks on tourists and employees at the aquarium park are about as scary as feeding time at the zoo. The 3-D process is more of a distraction than an enhancement. Also with Simon MacCorkindale and Lea Thompson. **Director**—Joe Alves. **(PG)** *97 minutes*

JAWS—THE REVENGE (1987)

★

Lorraine Gary
Michael Caine
Lance Guest
Mario Van Peebles

(Continued)

The great white shark surfaces yet again in Jaws—The Revenge.

(Continued)

The great white has definitely lost its bite in this fourth installment of the Brody family's encounters with the menacing man-eater. Gary reprises her role as Ellen Brody, the wife of Roy Scheider's character in the first two films. In this sequel, she is a widow who visits her oldest son in the Bahamas after her youngest son is attacked by a great white in Amity. Viewers are supposed to believe that the big shark follows her to the Caribbean seeking revenge on the remaining members of the Brody family. The asinine storyline concludes with Gary sailing alone into the ocean to sacrifice herself to the shark in order to stop the killing. Caine, in an embarrassing role as a jaunty pilot, costars as Gary's love interest. After a miserable theatrical showing in the U.S., the film was given a new ending for its European release, but to no avail. **Director**—Joseph Sargent. **(PG–13)**

90 minutes

THE JAZZ SINGER (1980)

★★

Neil Diamond
Laurence Olivier
Lucie Arnaz

Neil Diamond and Lucie Arnaz in The Jazz Singer.

Pop singer Diamond stars as the cantor's son who pursues a show-business career in this cliché-filled remake of the 1927 original melodrama that featured Al Jolson. Instead of singing "Mammy," Diamond belts out "Love on the Rocks" and other pop tunes; he's obviously a better singer than actor. But there are energetic performances from Olivier, as the heartbroken father, and from Arnaz, as the young woman who promotes Diamond's career. Also with Catlin Adams. **Director**—Richard Fleischer. **(PG)** *115 minutes*

J.D.'s REVENGE (1976)

★★

Glynn Turman
Lou Gossett, Jr.

Gore and violence dominate this thriller aimed at a black audience about a young law student possessed by the spirit of a slain hoodlum. Turman works hard in the lead role, and there's good support from Gossett as a revivalist minister. Professional direction from Arthur Marks and a tight script also help keep the film moving, but much of the material is too far out to be taken seriously. Also with Joan Pringle, David McKnight, and Carl Crudup. **(R)**

95 minutes

JEAN DE FLORETTE (1986)

★★★★

Gérard Depardieu
Yves Montand

Gérard Depardieu and Daniel Auteuil in Jean de Florette.

The attempts of two farmers to deceive and ruin their neighbor is the subject of this unforgettable melodrama set in rural France during the 1920s. Powerful and vivid performances shape the rich narrative, which unfolds slowly but deliberately. Depardieu stars in the title role as a romantic city dweller who is ecstatic to inherit some farmland and move to the country. His pitiful struggle at farming has disastrous results because of the greedy machinations of his neighbors, played by Montand and Daniel Auteuil. The story is continued in the excellent sequel *Manon of the Spring*. Originally filmed in French. **Director**—Claude Berri. **(PG)**

121 minutes

THE JERK (1979)

★★1/2

Steve Martin
Bernadette Peters

Wild and crazy Martin, in his first starring feature film, lives up to his title role; but he's a silly jerk instead of a funny jerk. In this harmless story, Steve—the son of a poor, black sharecropper—leaves home at age 35 to take a series of odd jobs, becomes wealthy, and finally loses his fortune. If you're alert, you can catch a few good gags, but most of the humor is predictable. Also with Catlin Adams, Mabel King, and Richard Ward. **Director**—Carl Reiner. **(R)** *94 minutes*

JESUS CHRIST, SUPERSTAR (1973)

★★

Ted Neeley
Carl Anderson

An uneven screen version of the Broadway rock opera, filmed on location in the Holy Land. The story of Christ is enacted to the beat of rock music written by Tim Rice and Andrew Lloyd Webber, and with some contemporary trappings. It's an inventive adaptation of the Scriptures. The cast performs well and the music is invigorating, but the interpretation of the material will not be appreciated by everyone. Also with Yvonne Elliman and Barry Dennen. **Director**—Norman Jewison. **(G)**

103 minutes

JESUS OF MONTREAL (1989)

★★★1/2

Lothaire Bluteau
Catherine Wilkening

A fascinating allegory of the life of Christ set among some thespians who perform the Passion Play at a basilica in Montreal. In a life-imitates-art sequence, they begin to adopt the quali-

® This movie available with closed captions for the hearing impaired.

ties of the characters they portray. Bluteau stars as the main actor and director of the Passion Play, who thoroughly researches the life of Jesus Christ while putting together the production. His interpretation emphasizes the subversiveness of Christ's teachings, which upsets the hypocritical Catholic hierarchy in Montreal. Aside from positing Christ in a different light than do the teachings of conventional Christianity, the film criticizes crass commercialism as well as pretentious bourgeois art patrons. Director Denys Arcand *(The Decline of the American Empire)* deftly combines theology with drama without being heavy-handed. Originally filmed in French. Also with Johanne-Marie Tremblay, Remy Girard, Robert Lepage, Gilles Palletier, and Yves Jacques. **(R)** *119 minutes*

JETSONS: THE MOVIE (1990)

★★1/2

The Jetson family comes to the big screen in Jetsons: The Movie.

This feature-length theatrical version of the 1960s television series may be disappointing for fans of the original show, because not much was done to update and upgrade the characters or the animation. Drawn in the minimal style of the Hanna-Barbera animation studios, the production is aimed at younger viewers, who will enjoy it simply because it is a colorful cartoon. George Jetson is the same perplexed father who, in this episode, gets transferred to an asteroid where he manages a mining operation. Jane, Judy, Elroy, and their dog, Astro, are on hand to provide the familiar domestic escapades. Pop singer Tiffany provides the music as well as the voice of Judy Jetson. The late George O'Hanlon and the late Mel Blanc supply some of the voices. Other voices are provided by Penny Singleton (from the old *Blondie* movie series), Ronnie Schell, Patti Deutsch, Dana Hill, and Rick Dees. **Directors**—William Hanna and Joseph Barbera. **(G)** *82 minutes*

THE JEWEL OF THE NILE (1985)

★★★

Kathleen Turner
Michael Douglas
Danny DeVito

This brisk sequel to the spirited *Romancing the Stone* packs in plenty of action and cliff-hangers for a satisfying adventure. Yet much of the novelty and wit of the initial spunky romp is absent here. Turner, as pulp fiction writer Joan Wilder, is in the clutches of a scheming Arab potentate. Her macho adventurer (Douglas) attempts to pull off a daring rescue while DeVito provides some comic relief. **Director**—Lewis Teague. **(PG)** *105 minutes*

JEZEBEL (1938)

★★★★

Bette Davis
Henry Fonda

Davis is sensational in this excellent melodrama about a southern belle with a knack for manipulating the men in her life. Fonda plays her fiancé. The film is also known for its smart script, stylish direction, and superb photography. Its dramatic power derives, for the most part, from Davis' Academy Award-winning performance. An excellent supporting cast includes George Brent, Margaret Lindsay, Donald Crisp, Fay Bainter, Spring Byington, and Eddie Anderson. **Director**—William Wyler. **Academy Awards**—Davis, best actress; Bainter, best supporting actress. **Nominations**—best picture; Ernest Haller, cinematography. *104 minutes b&w*

THE JIGSAW MAN (1984)

★★

Michael Caine
Laurence Olivier

This complex spy thriller, which pits the Russian KGB against British Intelligence, reaches new levels of confusion as the story progresses. Caine stars as a British agent who had defected to the Soviets. He returns to England where he's caught up in a web of intrigue. Olivier is consistently entertaining as the cranky British Secret Service chief. Unfortunately, Caine doesn't fare as well. The film itself is like a jigsaw puzzle, with some of the pieces missing. **Director**—Terence Young. **(PG)** *96 minutes*

JINXED (1982)

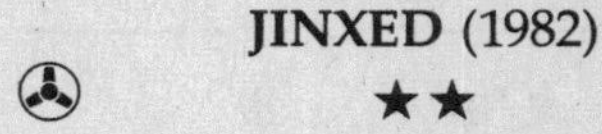

★★

Bette Midler
Ken Wahl
Rip Torn

The black cat discovers that Bette Midler is bad luck in Jinxed.

Midler's energetic talents are misused in this foolish, half-baked comedy/drama set in Nevada's gambling communities. She's a struggling lounge singer who conspires with a young blackjack dealer (Wahl) to murder her nasty gambler boyfriend (Torn). The Divine Miss M only gets a few cracks at some brassy musical numbers. Most of the time she's lost in uncomfortable dramatic situations in a story that vaguely resembles *Double Indemnity.* **Director**—Don Siegel. **(R)** *103 minutes*

JOAN OF ARC (1948)

★★

Ingrid Bergman
José Ferrer

Mediocre treatment based on Maxwell Anderson's play, with a general feeling of pretentiousness throughout the lavish production. Bergman stars as Joan, the French peasant girl who led military campaigns against British forces and was eventually burned as a heretic. Bergman and the rest of the cast seem to be suffering from a bout of tired blood. Also with George Coulouris, Francis L. Sullivan, Gene Lockhart, Ward Bond, John Ireland, and J. Carrol Naish. Some versions of the film run

(Continued)

(Continued)
100 minutes. **Director**—Victor Fleming. **Academy Award**—Joseph Valentine, William V. Skall, and Winton Hoch, cinematography. **Nominations**—Bergman, best actress; Ferrer, best supporting actor. *145 minutes*

JOE (1970)

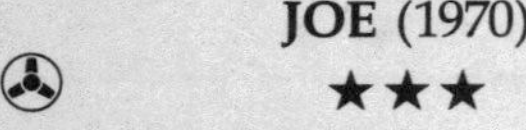

Peter Boyle
Dennis Patrick

A haunting film about a loudmouthed foundry worker and a well-heeled advertising executive who become unlikely friends and end up killing some hippies. Boyle gives a vivid performance as the raging reactionary, and Patrick is convincing as the smooth adman. The compelling story makes a strong social statement about hatred and bigotry, and the message is hammered home by the similarities and the stark contrasts in the two characters. The film, which is humorous in some respects, ends on a shocking note. Ragged-looking production values detract from the serious content. Also stars Audrey Caire and Susan Sarandon. **Director**—John G. Avildsen. **(R)** **Academy Award Nomination**—Norman Wexler, best story and screenplay based on factual material or material not previously published. *107 minutes*

JOE VERSUS THE VOLCANO (1990)

★★1/2

Tom Hanks
Meg Ryan

Tom Hanks and Meg Ryan (in one of her three roles) in Joe Versus the Volcano.

Despite the large budget, colorful sets, and top-name cast, this romantic comedy is disappointing. Obviously, the studio-made sets are supposed to be part of the humor, but the scenes never take full advantage of the props or sets. The exception is the opening sequence, in which the dark, dreary set design defines Hanks' dullard character and illustrates his hopeless situation. Hanks plays a pathetically dull hypochondriac who is tricked into traveling to a remote island where he must appease the natives by jumping into a volcano. Ryan costars in a trio of roles, two of which are merely exaggerated caricatures. Director John Patrick Shanley, the writer who scored a hit with his screenplay for *Moonstruck,* has the imagination but not the technical skill to make a film. Lloyd Bridges, Robert Stack, Ossie Davis, and Abe Vigoda have small supporting parts. **(PG)** *99 minutes*

JOHNNY BE GOOD (1988)

★

Anthony Michael Hall
Robert Downey, Jr.

This botched teen comedy is loaded with misfired gags and embarrassing moments for the cast. Hall stars as a high-school quarterback courted by unscrupulous college athletic recruiters. They lure him with cash, alcohol, sex, and the prospect of easy courses. Though the story is timely, it relies on such slapstick bits as flying food and exploding fire extinguishers for its humor. Chicago Bears quarterback Jim McMahon appears as himself in a scene that includes his entire 30-second commercial for Adidas athletic shoes. In a film that is supposedly criticizing the commercialization of sports, this seems hypocritical to say the least. Also with Paul Gleason. **Director**—Bud Smith. **(PG–13)** *85 minutes*

JOHNNY BELINDA (1948)

★★★

Jane Wyman
Lew Ayres

Wyman gives a magnificent performance as a deaf-mute who is raped; Ayres is effective as a doctor involved with the young girl. This film is dramatic and touching, with the authentic-looking setting of a Nova Scotian fishing village adding much to the film's believability. Wyman does a magnificent job of acting without the benefit of speech. Also with Charles Bickford, Agnes Moorehead, Stephen McNally, and Jan Sterling. **Director**—Jean Negulesco. **Academy Award**—Wyman, best actress. **Nominations**—best picture; Negulesco, best director; Ayres, best actor; Bickford, best supporting actor; Moorehead, best supporting actress; Irmgard Von Cube and Allen Vincent, screenplay; Ted McCord, cinematography. *103 minutes b&w*

JOHNNY DANGEROUSLY (1984)

★★

Michael Keaton
Marilu Henner
Joe Piscopo

An uneven spoof of 1930s gangster movies, with Michael Keaton in the title role doing a parody of the types of characters often played by James Cagney. The trite screenplay bogs down too often with crude gags. The cliché-strewn plot has Johnny turning to crime to pay for his poor mother's various operations. He's finally brought to heel by his younger brother, a crusading district attorney. **Director**—Amy Heckerling. **(PG–13)** *90 minutes*

JOHNNY HANDSOME (1989)

★★★

Mickey Rourke
Ellen Barkin
Morgan Freeman

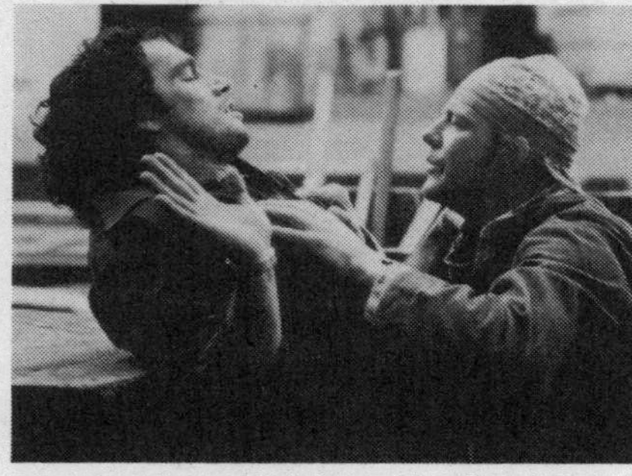

Mickey Rourke chooses to seek revenge for his fate in Johnny Handsome.

Rourke stars as a two-bit New Orleans criminal with a facial deformity in this violent *film noir* by director Walter Hill. While Rourke's character is in prison, a kindly plastic surgeon remakes his face in the hopes that his new face will change his disposition. But as an archetypal *film noir* antihero, Rourke's character is doomed to despair: Faced with the moral choice of leading a straight life with a decent woman (Elizabeth McGovern) or seeking revenge against the people who put him in jail, Rourke seals his fate when he chooses the lat-

This movie available with closed captions for the hearing impaired.

ter. The music by Ry Cooder and cinematography by Matthew F. Leonetti convey the necessary atmosphere for such a pessimistic tale. The supporting cast of unsavory characters includes Barkin, Lance Henriksen, and Scott Wilson. Freeman plays the police lieutenant who knows Rourke will never change. **(R)** *96 minutes*

JOJO DANCER, YOUR LIFE IS CALLING (1986)

★★1/2

Richard Pryor
Carmen McRae
Debbie Allen

Debbie Allen and Richard Pryor in Jojo Dancer, Your Life Is Calling.

Pryor's semi-autobiographical film is an uneven self-analysis of the pitfalls of his own career. Pryor stars as JoJo Dancer, an incarnation of Pryor himself. Dancer's story is clumsily constructed in a series of flashbacks, from childhood, through his rise to stardom, to his near-fatal experience with freebasing cocaine. The low-budget, amateurish look of the production is bothersome at first, but it suits the emotional aspects of the material and Pryor's broad portrayal of Dancer. A fine supporting cast, including McRae, Allen, Paula Kelly, and Billy Eckstine, often upstages Pryor. **Director**—Pryor. **(R)** *97 minutes*

A JOKE OF DESTINY (1984)

★★

Ugo Tognazzi
Piera Degli Esposti
Gastone Moschin

Director Lina Wertmuller's satire on unmanageable technology and political hypocrisy is as clumsy as the inept bureaucrats it wants to lampoon. A chain of mishaps evolves when the Italian Minister of Interior becomes trapped in his electronically sophisticated, computer-controlled limousine. Unfortunately, the uninspired comedy stalls along with the disabled automobile. Originally filmed in Italian. **(PG) Alternate Title**—*A Joke of Destiny Lying in Wait Around the Corner Like a Bandit.* *105 minutes*

THE JOKER IS WILD (1957)

★★★

Frank Sinatra
Mitzi Gaynor

Sinatra portrays nightclub comic Joe E. Lewis, who began his long career in the Roaring Twenties.Originally a singer, his musical career was cut short after Chicago gangsters slit his throat when he refused to continue performing in their nightclub. This atmospheric film biography is carried off with adequate energy, and it offers Sinatra an opportunity to sing favorite tunes, including the Academy Award-winning "All the Way." Gaynor and Jeanne Crain are well cast as objects of Sinatra's affections. Also with Eddie Albert, Beverly Garland, and Jackie Coogan. **Director**—Charles Vidor. *123 minutes b&w*

THE JOLSON STORY (1946)

★★★

Larry Parks
William Demarest

A highly successful film biography of the 1920s superstar who might have been a cantor, but became one of the greatest entertainers of the century. Parks superbly portrays the great performer, with the real Jolson dubbing his voice for a slew of popular songs, including "Swanee" and "April Showers." It's a first-class depiction of the subject of show business. Also with Evelyn Keyes, Ludwig Donath, Tamara Shayne, and Scotty Beckett. **Director**—Alfred Green. **Academy Award Nominations**—Parks, best actor; Demarest, best supporting actor; Joseph Walker, cinematography. *128 minutes*

JONAH—WHO WILL BE 25 IN THE YEAR 2000 (1976)

★★★

Jean-Luc Bideau
Myriam Boyer

A jaunty Swiss comedy about eight friends who were active in political disturbances of the late 1960s, and who still hold idealistic views. The film, rich with irony, may be too talky for some viewers. Set in Geneva, with a superb cast. Also with Jacques Denis, Rufus, and Miou-Miou. Originally filmed in French. **Director**—Alain Tanner. **(No MPAA rating)** *110 minutes*

JOSEPH ANDREWS (1977)

★

Ann-Margret
Peter Firth

Director Tony Richardson, who gave us the delightful *Tom Jones,* falls flat on his face with this similar 18th-century costume tale. It's about a young footman, played by Firth, who is the object of the lustful desires of Lady Booby, his employer; she's played by Ann-Margret. Firth's title character is fairly uninteresting, and the film is mostly a noisy jumble of tasteless arguing and brawling. Although well-photographed, it is too tedious to be enjoyed. Also with Michael Hordern and Beryl Reid. **(R)** *103 minutes*

JOSHUA THEN AND NOW (1985)

★★

James Woods
Gabrielle Lazure

James Woods, Gabrielle Lazure, and Alan Arkin in Joshua Then and Now.

A crude, loosely constructed comedy that follows the life and times of a Jewish writer and TV personality from Canada. Woods, in the title role, is not especially convincing, nor is Lazure, who plays his blonde, gentile wife from an upper-class background. The story also consists of a series of flashbacks

(Continued)

(Continued)

that include Joshua's childhood and his days as a leftist writer in London. Also with Alan Arkin and Michael Sarrazin. **Director**—Ted Kotcheff. **(R)**

118 minutes

JOURNEY INTO FEAR (1942)

★★★★

Orson Welles
Joseph Cotten
Dolores Del Rio

This gripping spy chapter, based on the Eric Ambler novel, is ablaze with a keen atmosphere and embellishments as only Orson Welles could construct. The story concerns cat-and-mouse espionage during World War II, with an American munitions expert trying to escape from the clutches of enemy agents in Turkey. There are spine-tingling pursuits and tense confrontations, all expertly concocted for maximum shock. Welles and Cotten are credited with the script; Welles also worked on the direction, but received no screen credit for it. Also with Jack Moss, Agnes Moorehead, and Ruth Warrick. **Director**—Norman Foster.

71 minutes b&w

THE JOURNEY OF NATTY GANN (1985)

★★★

Meredith Salenger
John Cusack

Elements of *The Grapes of Wrath* are found in this sentimental, Depression-era road movie. Salenger stars as the plucky tomboy who treks from Chicago to Seattle, accompanied by a friendly wolf, in search of her father. While there are moments of adventure, the journey at times is too episodic and slow-paced. Period details are impressive, though, and the authentic-looking costumes won an Academy Award nomination. Lainie Kazan, Scatman Crothers, Barry Miller, and Ray Wise costar. **Director**—Jeremy Kagan. **(PG)**

101 minutes

JOURNEY TO THE CENTER OF THE EARTH (1959)

James Mason
Arlene Dahl
Pat Boone

James Mason and Pat Boone go on a Journey to the Center of the Earth.

Outlandish but enjoyable sci-fi nonsense, based on the Jules Verne fantasy about a Scottish professor and colleagues who enter a nonactive volcano in Iceland and travel to the Earth's core. The special effects are emphasized here, with some good performances and a modest touch of humor. Also with Peter Ronson, Diane Baker, and Thayer David. **Director**—Henry Levin.

132 minutes

JUAREZ (1939)

★★★

Paul Muni
Bette Davis
Brian Aherne
Claude Rains

Dramatically effective and prestigious historical biography of the Mexican revolutionary hero who brought about the defeat of Emperor Maximillian, though at times it all appears too weighted by its own pretensions. John Garfield as General Diaz is excellent in an unusual role and joins a large and competent cast including Donald Crisp, Gale Sondergaard, Joseph Calleia, Gilbert Roland, Pedro de Cordova, Montagu Love, and Harry Davenport. John Huston contributed to the highly literate script. Videotape versions run 122 minutes. **Director**—William Dieterle. **Academy Award Nomination**—Aherne, best supporting actor. *132 minutes b&w*

JUDGMENT AT NUREMBERG (1961)

★★★½

Spencer Tracy
Marlene Dietrich
Burt Lancaster
Richard Widmark
Maximilian Schell

A distinguished film treatment of the famous 1948 trial of Nazi officers accused by the Allies of terrible crimes against humanity. It's intelligently done in semidocumentary style and graced with powerful performances. Primarily, the film confronts that nagging rationalization for such outrageous behavior: "We were only following orders." Schell is outstanding as a defense attorney, and Tracy is effective as the court's presiding judge. Also with Judy Garland, Montgomery Clift, William Shatner, Edward Binns, and Werner Klemperer. **Director**—Stanley Kramer. **Academy Awards**—Schell, best actor; Abby Mann, best screenplay based on material from another medium. **Nominations**—best picture; Kramer, best director; Tracy, best actor; Clift, best supporting actor; Garland, best supporting actress; Ernest Laszlo, cinematography. *178 minutes b&w*

JULES AND JIM (1961)

★★★★

Jeanne Moreau
Oskar Werner
Henri Serre

Continental delight: Jeanne Moreau and Oskar Werner in Jules and Jim.

François Truffaut's celebration of love and cinema is both playful and tragic, and consistently full of energy. It rode in on the crest of France's New Wave, and will probably remain the film with which star Moreau is most often linked. Two friends—a Frenchman and an Austrian—fall for the same beguiling woman in pre-World War I Paris. Their relationship is chronicled into the postwar years. Georges Delerue wrote the haunting musical score. This film was the basis for the American film *Willie & Phil.* Also stars Marie Dubois. Originally filmed in French.

104 minutes b&w

This movie available with closed captions for the hearing impaired.

JULIA (1977)

★★★

Jane Fonda
Vanessa Redgrave

Vanessa Redgrave as Julia, *the unusual friend of Lillian Hellman.*

Fred Zinnemann (*High Noon*) directed this handsome period film, based on Lillian Hellman's memoir of a friendship between two brilliant and strong-willed young women. Keen and subtle performances by Fonda, Redgrave, and the fine supporting cast are short-circuited by a lack of passion, drama, and suspense in the screenplay, but the film, set on the eve of World War II, still has much appeal. Also with Jason Robards, Maximilian Schell, and Hal Holbrook. **(PG) Academy Awards**—Robards, best supporting actor; Redgrave, best supporting actress; Alvin Sargent, best screenplay based on material from another medium. **Nominations**—best picture; Zinnemann, best director; Fonda, best actress; Schell, best supporting actor. *118 minutes*

JULIA & JULIA (1988)

★★½

Kathleen Turner
Gabriel Byrne
Sting

Turner, who starred in the time-travel fantasy *Peggy Sue Got Married*, appears in a dramatic interpretation of similar events in this surreal melodrama shot in Italy. Turner plays a young wife whose husband (Byrne) is killed in a car crash on their wedding day. Six years later, she suddenly finds herself in an eerie world where not only is her husband alive but they also have a young son. To complicate matters, Sting turns up as her mysterious lover. Though the acting by the mostly European cast is quite good, the story is slow-going and confusing. The film offers no explanation for Turner's parallel lives, which may frustrate some viewers. Of interest to film buffs: This is the first feature shot in high-definition television (HDTV) and then transferred to film, an experiment in cost-cutting for feature production. **Director**—Peter Del Monte. **(R)** *96 minutes*

JULIET OF THE SPIRITS (1965)

★★★

Giulietta Masina

Another surrealistic fantasy from director Federico Fellini, this time exploring the psyche and spirit of a middle-aged woman whose husband is unfaithful. Masina, Fellini's real-life wife, plays the semi-autobiographical heroine who explores her own sensuality through a series of dreamlike sequences, each providing further titillation and satiric comment. This is not Fellini at his best, and as a counterpart to *8½*, it is a poor comparison, but the illusions are pictorially splendid (it was Fellini's first color film) and the concept is valid. The cast includes Mario Pisu, Sandra Milo, Valentina Cortese, and Sylva Koscina. Originally filmed in Italian. *145 minutes*

JULIUS CAESAR (1953)

★★★★

John Gielgud
James Mason
Marlon Brando

Casca (Edmond O'Brien) strikes the first blow against Julius Caesar.

Excellent acting by a top-name cast and a sumptuous production do justice to Shakespeare's compelling tragedy about conspiracy and revenge in the Roman Empire. Joseph L. Mankiewicz's direction captures the mood of this moment in history as imagined by the great bard. Mason, as Brutus, and Gielgud, as Cassius, stand out in key roles. Brando plays Marc Antony, and Louis Calhern is Julius Caesar. Also with Greer Garson, Deborah Kerr, Edmond O'Brien, and George Macready. **Academy Award Nominations**—best picture; Brando, best actor; Joseph Ruttenberg, cinematography. *121 minutes b&w*

JUMPING JACKS (1952)

★★★

Dean Martin
Jerry Lewis

Martin and Lewis join the Army and sign up for paratrooper duty. Plenty of funny sight gags roll along at a fast pace in this predictable but enjoyable comedy. As usual, Lewis plays the hyper misfit, and Martin is the straight man to Lewis' antics. Costars Mona Freeman, Robert Strauss, and Don Defore. **Director**—Norman Taurog. *96 minutes b&w*

JUMPIN' JACK FLASH (1986)

★★

Whoopi Goldberg
Stephen Collins

Goldberg tries desperately to perk up this lame spy comedy, but her energetic efforts are in vain. She plays a lonely, bored computer operator who becomes involved in an espionage caper when a British agent, trapped behind the Iron Curtain, pleads for help via her video terminal. Director Penny Marshall (Laverne of *Laverne and Shirley*) fails to generate suspense or laughs, and the film ends up a flash in the pan. John Wood, Annie Potts, Roscoe Lee Browne, Jonathan Pryce, Jim Belushi, and Carol Kane costar. **(R)** *100 minutes*

THE JUNGLE BOOK (1942)

★★★

Sabu
Joseph Calleia
John Qualen

This children's story by Rudyard Kipling is produced for the screen with lavish detail. Sabu stars as the lad who befriends animals in the Indian jungle and learns their ways. Also with Frank

(Continued)

This movie available on videotape and/or disc.

(Continued)
Puglia and Rosemary DeCamp. **Director**—Zoltan Korda. *109 minutes*

JUST A GIGOLO (1978)

★★

David Bowie
Kim Novak
Curt Jurgens
Marlene Dietrich

Bowie, Novak, Jurgens, and Dietrich star in this bizarre, baroque comedy set in the decadent society of post-World War I Berlin. The story centers on Bowie, an aristocratic Prussian War veteran who drifts in an out of menial jobs before becoming a gigolo. The performances are impressive, but the material is so uneven and loosely constructed that there's scant satisfaction from such notable talent. Dietrich, looking somewhat sad and uneasy, sing-talks the title song. Directed by British actor David Hemmings. **(R)** *105 minutes*

JUST BETWEEN FRIENDS (1986)

★★★

Mary Tyler Moore
Christine Lahti
Ted Danson

Moore is a modest, mousy housewife, and Lahti plays a wisecracking, independent career woman. They are the "friends" in this romantic comedy of two women in love with the same man. Although the approach is that of a highly polished sitcom, the script is marked by witty, satirical comments on modern lifestyles and delightfully comic dialogue. Despite a tragic turn, the story remains buoyant. **Director**—Allan Burns. **(PG–13)** *120 minutes*

JUST ONE OF THE GUYS (1985)

★★

Joyce Hyser

Deborah Goodrich, Clayton Rohner, and Joyce Hyser in Just One of the Guys.

Poor Terry. Her teachers don't take her journalistic talents seriously. So she crops her hair, masquerades as a boy, and attends another high school where she writes about a girl's experience pretending to be a boy. Though the script is uneven, Hyser is refreshing in her role as the ambitious teenage reporter who sacrifices her female identity for a good story. Also with Clayton Rohner and Billy Jacoby. **Director**—Lisa Gottlieb. **(PG–13)** *100 minutes*

JUST TELL ME WHAT YOU WANT (1980)

★★

Ali MacGraw
Alan King

King plays Max Herschel, a pushy tycoon who's as childish as he is shrewd, in this mean-spirited romantic comedy. Despite all the trappings of elegance surrounding his character, King still comes off as a stand-up nightclub comedian. The meager plot involves an attempt by Max's mistress, played by MacGraw, to break away from his domination. Sidney Lumet directs with determined frenzy. There are a few funny moments, but all the shouting and bullying becomes tiresome. Also with Peter Weller, Myrna Loy, Dina Merrill, and Keenan Wynn. **(R)** *112 minutes*

JUST THE WAY YOU ARE (1984)

★★

Kristy McNichol
Michael Ontkean
Robert Carradine

Michael Ontkean and Kristy McNichol in Just the Way You Are.

A romantic comedy about a lame young woman (McNichol) who overcomes her handicap and finds love. Director Édouard Molinaro (*La Cage aux Folles*), in his first English-language feature, can't overcome the predictable material or the sappy dialogue. Some impressive background scenery of the French Alps is the film's only appeal. **(PG)** *95 minutes*

JUST YOU AND ME, KID (1979)

★★

George Burns
Brooke Shields

Lovable Burns plays a retired vaudeville performer who befriends a pretty 14-year-old orphan, played by Shields. As long as Burns does what comes naturally—ticking off one-liners and doing the old soft shoe—there's some appeal. Aside from that, it's a half-baked, lethargic comedy. Shields' stiff performance pales against the warm glow of the venerable old trouper. Also with Lorraine Gary, Nicholas Coster, Burl Ives, and Ray Bolger. **Director**—Leonard Stern. **(PG)** *95 minutes*

K

THE KARATE KID (1984)

★★★

Ralph Macchio
Noriyuki "Pat" Morita

Director John G. Avildsen (*Rocky*) applies his root-for-the-underdog formula to this teenage drama and comes up with heartwarming, satisfying fare. Macchio plays the scrawny lad who is tormented by bullies until he learns the spiritual and physical disciplines of karate from an elderly master, played by Morita. The outcome is predictable but uplifting. The surrogate father-son relationship is a high point of the story, with Morita the effective scene-stealer. **(PG)** *126 minutes*

THE KARATE KID PART II (1986)

Ralph Macchio
Noriyuki "Pat" Morita

Macchio and Morita reprise their roles from *The Karate Kid* in this predictable sequel. This time karate master Miyagi (Morita) and pupil Daniel (Macchio) journey to Japan to confront Miyagi's past. As a young man he had left his

® *This movie available with closed captions for the hearing impaired*

Ralph Macchio and Noriyuki "Pat" Morita team up again in The Karate Kid Part II.

native land because he had fallen in love with a woman already betrothed to someone else via an arranged marriage. Miyagi's rival, Sato, also a karate expert, never forgave him for leaving Japan instead of fighting for the woman in a karate match. Now that Miyagi has returned, Sato expects to finally settle the dispute. Miyagi's dialogue is spiced with the same wise, old platitudes that characterized the first film, and Daniel is again forced into another karate duel at the climax of the film. The formula that worked so well in *The Karate Kid* is repeated, but the lack of originality mars this sequel. John G. Avildsen, who directed the first film, returned to execute this one, but to no avail. Also with Nobu McCarthy, Danny Kamekona, Yuji Okumato, and Tamlym Tomita. **(PG) Academy Award Nomination**—Peter Cetera, David Foster, and Diane Nini, best song ("Glory of Love"). *113 minutes.*

THE KARATE KID, PART III (1989)

★★

Ralph Macchio
Noriyuki "Pat" Morita

The third installment of this series is merely a rehash of previous episodes. The formula is intact, but the surprise is gone. The Kid of the title, played again by Macchio, has neither matured as a person nor evolved emotionally. This time, he is bullied and tricked into defending his crown by a rich villain (Thomas Ian Griffith). As expected, the wise Mr. Miyagi (Morita) keeps the youngster on the proper path until the inevitable showdown. Macchio is much too old for the role that he originated six years earlier, and Morita's platitudes are so trite as to be unintentionally funny. The shallowness of the two sequels gives the original film—a warm-hearted comedy/drama—a bad name. Also with Robyn Lively and Martin L. Kove. **Director**—John G. Avildsen. **(PG)** *111 minutes*

THE KEEP (1983)

★

Scott Glenn

A rickety, pretentious horror film, overburdened with outlandish special effects. The gothic tale takes place during World War II in a mysterious Rumanian castle where German soldiers accidentally set loose a monster. The silly, trumped-up plot is utter confusion embellished with an ear-shattering soundtrack. The dialogue is mere mumbo jumbo. Glenn, Ian McKellen, and Jurgen Prochnow (the U-boat skipper in *Das Boot*) merely stumble through this nonsense. **Director**—Michael Mann. **(R)** *97 minutes*

THE KENTUCKIAN (1955)

★★★

Burt Lancaster

A frontier adventure set in the early 1800s with Lancaster, a Kentucky backwoodsman, braving the elements to establish a new home in Texas. The film offers some interesting moments of rugged action, romance, and even a bit of humor. Some decent acting contributes to the interesting tale. Walter Matthau makes his film debut in a small role. Supporting players include Dianne Foster, Diana Lynn, Una Merkel, and John Carradine. **Director**—Lancaster. *104 minutes*

KENTUCKY FRIED MOVIE (1977)

Evan Kim
Master Bong Soo Han

A mixed bag of youth-oriented, satirical sketches on the order of *The Groove Tube* and *Tunnelvision.* The film, divided into 22 segments, takes on TV newscasts, martial-arts and porno movies, and commercials. Some of the skits are clever and funny, but frequent doses of bad taste spoil the fun. The project is the outgrowth of the Kentucky Fried Theater, a satirical group formed at the University of Wisconsin whose most talented members—Jim Abrahams, David Zucker, and Jerry Zucker—went on to write and direct *Airplane!* There are cameos by Bill Bixby, Henry Gibson, Donald Sutherland, and George Lazenby. Videotape versions include a few more comic segments. **Director**—John Landis. **(R)** *78 minutes*

KEY LARGO (1948)

★★★½

Humphrey Bogart
Edward G. Robinson
Lauren Bacall
Claire Trevor

Humphrey Bogart and Claire Trevor battle personal demons in Key Largo.

Tense, electrifying gangster yarn set in the Florida Keys, starring Bogart and Robinson as harsh adversaries. Robinson plays a sinister criminal who holds a group of people captive at a remote hotel during a violent coastal storm; Trevor plays his moll. Bogey is an ex-GI who stands up to Robinson's intimidation. Director John Huston precisely captures the dramatic mood and coaxes excellent performances from the cast. He and cowriter Richard Brooks adapted their script from the play by Maxwell Anderson. Also with Lionel Barrymore and Thomas Gomez. **Academy Award**—Trevor, best supporting actress. *101 minutes b&w*

KHARTOUM (1966)

Charlton Heston
Laurence Olivier

This slice of history, about England's involvement with Arab nations in the late 19th century, is highlighted with some well-staged battle scenes, but it gets bogged down by pompous dialogue. Heston stars as General Charles "Chinese" Gordon, who meets his match in

(Continued)

(Continued)
the Arab warriors led by the Mahdi, played by Olivier. There's good acting by these two principals, but their characters lack depth. Also with Richard Johnson, Ralph Richardson, Hugh Williams, Nigel Green, and Johnny Sekka. **Director**—Basil Dearden. **Academy Award Nomination**—Robert Ardrey, best story and screenplay written directly for the screen. *134 minutes*

KICKBOXER (1989)

 ★★

Jean-Claude Van Damme

An action-filled B-movie starring kickboxing champion Van Damme as a rookie who journeys to Thailand for a revenge bout with the world champion kickboxer. Owing much to the formula established by the *Rocky* series, the film features our hero strenuously training for the big showdown under the tutelage of a wise master (Dennis Chan). The fight scenes will impress fans of this little-known sport, which became popular during the 1980s, but the acting and the direction are amateurish. **Directors**—Mark Di Salle and David Worth. **(R)** *97 minutes*

THE KIDNAPPING OF THE PRESIDENT (1980)

 ★★

William Shatner
Hal Holbrook
Van Johnson
Ava Gardner

Third-world terrorists abduct the President of the United States during a visit to Toronto and hold him captive in an explosive-filled armored car. This Canadian-made movie stirs up moderate suspense as authorities press their rescue plans, but the improbable plot is riddled with clichés and dumb dialogue. Shatner plays the man in charge of rescuing the President. Holbrook plays the President with conviction, and there are stylish performances from Johnson as the Vice President and Gardner as Holbrook's wife. **Director**—George Mendeluk. **(R)** *113 minutes*

THE KILLER ELITE (1975)

 ★★

James Caan
Robert Duvall

A farfetched action drama about Japanese terrorists who try to kill a Chinese anti-Communist leader. The confusing plot also involves the CIA. Caan and Duvall star as a team of gun-toting operatives who eventually wind up on opposite sides. There's a smorgasbord of violence with handguns, machine guns, karate, swords, and kung fu. Also with Gig Young, Arthur Hill, and Bo Hopkins. **Director**—Sam Peckinpah. **(PG)** *122 minutes*

KILLER FORCE (1975)

★★★

Peter Fonda
Telly Savalas

A fairly entertaining action drama about desperados out to steal several million dollars worth of diamonds from a South American diamond syndicate. Fonda plays a double agent in the plan to rob the company. Savalas, menacing and coldhearted, is the company's security boss. The desert dunes bristle with security gadgets and armed patrols, which the thieves must penetrate to reach the diamonds. The plot is hardly convincing, but the fast-paced action makes up for such drawbacks. Also with Hugh O'Brian, Christopher Lee, Maud Adams, and O. J. Simpson. **Director**—Val Guest. **(R)** *101 minutes*

THE KILLERS (1946)

★★★½

Burt Lancaster
Edmond O'Brien

A high-voltage crime drama that is smartly directed and professionally acted. A prizefighter (Lancaster, in his film debut) is killed in a small town, and an insurance investigator finds out why. The script, by Anthony Veiller and an uncredited John Huston, is taut and suspenseful, and enhanced by the visual style of *film noir.* Based on a short story by Ernest Hemingway. Also with Ava Gardner, Albert Dekker, Sam Levene, and William Conrad. **Director**—Robert Siodmak. **Academy Award Nominations**—Siodmak, best director; Veiller, screenplay. *105 minutes b&w*

THE KILLING FIELDS (1984)

 ★★★½

Sam Waterston
Dr. Haing S. Ngor

Sam Waterston is a correspondent in Cambodia in The Killing Fields.

Detailed, wrenching account of the fall and brutal devastation of Cambodia, based on *New York Times* correspondent Sydney Schanberg's magazine article. The story focuses on the friendship between Schanberg (Waterston) and his loyal Cambodian guide/translator Dith Pran (Ngor), and Pran's experiences in the hands of the despicable Khmer Rouge. Unfortunately, the beautiful, Oscar-nominated cinematography by Chris Menges often contradicts the harrowing events of the war. Yet the film ultimately emerges as a gripping panorama of the Cambodian holocaust. The film's well-paced editing emphasizes the grueling episodes of Pran's experiences, making the viewer empathize with the character. Also with John Malkovich, Julian Sands, and Craig T. Nelson. **Director**—Roland Joffe. **(R)** **Academy Award**—Ngor, best supporting actor. **Nominations**—best picture; Joffe, best director; Waterston, best actor; Bruce Robinson, best screenplay based on material from another medium. *139 minutes*

KILLING HEAT (1984)

★★

Karen Black
John Thaw
John Kani

A 30-year-old city woman (Black) fails to adapt to farm life in southern Africa. She gradually lapses into hopeless depression, which leads to a tragic ending. This brooding, intense picture of rural Africa is based on Doris Lessing's novel *The Grass Is Singing.* It's intelligent and well-meaning, yet too overwrought, uneven, and bleak to be entertaining. **Director**—Michael Raeburn. **(R)** *104 minutes*

® *This movie available with closed captions for the hearing impaired.*

THE KILLING OF A CHINESE BOOKIE (1976)

Ben Gazzara

John Cassavetes, who scored with *A Woman Under the Influence,* fizzles in directing this pointless tale about the sleazy world of nightclub entertainers. Cosmo Vitelli, played by Gazzara, is the owner of a Hollywood strip joint who pays off a gambling debt to the mob by bumping off a Chinese bookie. Gazzara's performance as the hit man is shallow, and the story fails to generate much interest. Also with Timothy Agoglia Carey and Seymour Cassel. **(R)**
136 minutes

THE KILLING TIME (1987)

 ★★

Beau Bridges
Kiefer Sutherland

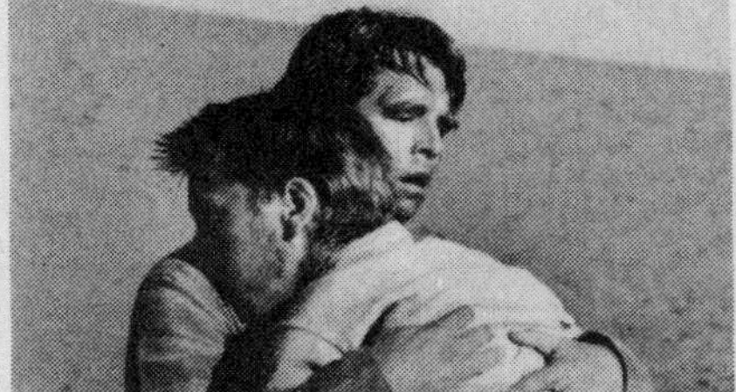

Beau Bridges welcomes Kiefer Sutherland with open arms in The Killing Time.

A drab thriller set in a small California coastal town where the local sheriff's office is involved with various schemes and double crosses. Cast against type, the affable Bridges stars as an unscrupulous deputy sheriff involved in a plot to murder his lover's husband. Sutherland plays a rookie deputy, who may end up taking the blame for the killing. Despite such complications, the film offers little suspense and doesn't quite capture the dark atmosphere needed to suggest that such events could occur in this sleepy little town. Wayne Rogers, Joe Don Baker, and Camelia Kath appear in supporting roles. **Director**—Rick King. **(R)**
95 minutes

KIM (1951)

 ★★★

Errol Flynn
Dean Stockwell

Rudyard Kipling's tale of the English lad reared in 19th-century India among the Hindus is energetic and colorful. Stockwell plays the title role of the young adventurer who becomes involved with intrigue and uprisings. Flynn costars, with assists from Paul Lukas, Robert Douglas, Thomas Gomez, Laurette Luez, and Cecil Kellaway. **Director**—Victor Saville.
112 minutes

KIND HEARTS AND CORONETS (1949)

 ★★★★

Alec Guinness
Dennis Price

Dennis Price tries to eliminate his competition in Kind Hearts and Coronets.

Guinness has a field day playing eight roles in this stylish black comedy set in Edwardian England. A scheming young man, played by Price, decides that the family fortune belongs to him, and he attempts to achieve his goal by knocking off the competing heirs. Guinness plays the other members of the family. This film represents one of the best of a series of comedies released by Britain's Ealing Studios. Under the guidance of Sir Michael Balcon, the studio gained a reputation for producing sophisticated, irreverent comedies characterized by a dry and subtle wit. Also with Valerie Hobson, Joan Greenwood, and Miles Malleson. **Director**—Robert Hamer. *104 minutes b&w*

THE KINDRED (1987)

Kim Hunter
David Allen Brooks

Splashy special effects and a slimy, slithering monster are the centerpieces of this draggy horror film, made even worse by a weak plot and stiff acting. Seems Mom (Hunter), a scientist, has concocted a horrible creature through genetic engineering. After she dies, her son (Brooks) must destroy this hideous being, which just might be his brother. Rod Steiger appears in a cameo role as an evil scientist who wants to help the monster. Also with Amanda Pays. **Directors**—Jeffrey Obrow and Stephen Carpenter. **(R)** *93 minutes*

THE KING AND I (1956)

 ★★★

Deborah Kerr
Yul Brynner

A lavish musical, based on the Broadway musical, which in turn was based on the play *Anna and the King of Siam.* Good acting and the Rodgers and Hammerstein music add up to pleasant entertainment; but the film doesn't achieve the high spirits of the stage version. Kerr does well as the perplexed young widow hired to teach the children of the stubborn Siamese monarch. Brynner gives a powerful performance as the mighty ruler with whom Kerr eventually falls in love. There are also several classic songs, including "Hello, Young Lovers" and "Getting to Know You." The film won several Oscars in the areas of production. Also stars Rita Moreno, Martin Benson, Alan Mowbray, and Terry Saunders. **Director**—Walter Lang. **Academy Award**—Brynner, best actor. **Nominations**—best picture; Lang, best director; Kerr, best actress; Leon Shamroy, cinematography.
133 minutes

KING DAVID (1985)

 ★★ 

Richard Gere
Alice Krige

And Paramount said: "Let there be *David.*" And there was David...and Saul, and Bathsheba, and all the other Old Testament figures. Gere, in the title role, is unconvincing mostly because his contemporary acting style clashes with the epic material, and the initially compelling narrative weakens after David attains his crown. Occasionally, however, the script, in director Bruce Beresford's (*Tender Mercies*) hands, does capture some of the more complex issues of the Bible. Best among the supporting actors is Edward Woodward as Saul. **(PG-13)** *114 minutes*

This movie available on videotape and/or disc.

KING KONG (1933)

★★★★

Robert Armstrong
Fay Wray
Bruce Cabot

Fay Wray in the clutches of King Kong *as the monster terrorizes New York.*

A thrill-packed monster movie that has achieved screen-classic status, thanks to the imaginative and skillful use of special effects and well-paced direction. A giant ape is brought from the jungle to New York, where it escapes and causes havoc in the city; the memorable climax on the Empire State Building is a masterpiece. Wray stars as the beauty the beast finds irresistible. Prints not shown on broadcast television may run 103 minutes. Also with Noble Johnson, Victor Wong, and Frank Reicher. **Directors**—Merian C. Cooper and Ernest Schoedsack. *100 minutes b&w*

KING KONG (1976)

★★ ®

Jeff Bridges
Jessica Lange

A $24-million retread of the 1933 classic. The lavish Dino De Laurentiis production lacks the mythic quality of the original mostly because it doesn't take itself seriously. Instead, the script and actors take a flippant approach to the material. Makeup expert Rick Baker is the man inside the gorilla suit. Lange's screen debut. Also with Charles Grodin, Ed Lauter, John Agar, and John Randolph. **Director**—John Guillermin. **(PG)** *134 minutes*

KING KONG LIVES (1986)

★★ ®

Brian Kerwin
Linda Hamilton

More monkey business from producer Dino De Laurentiis, who was responsible for the 1976 remake of *King Kong*. The giant, chest-thumping gorilla has been in a coma since his fall from the World Trade Center, but a mechanical heart transplant brings him around. He strikes up a romance with a lady Kong, only to find himself once again at the mercy of jittery humans. Routine acting and a pedestrian plot make this sequel a tiresome effort. It's time to bury this legendary ape, but Mrs. Kong gives birth and the door is left open for *Son of Kong*. Also with John Astin. **Director**—John Guillermin. **(PG–13)** *105 minutes*

THE KING OF COMEDY (1983)

★★★½

Robert De Niro
Jerry Lewis

Talk-show host Jerry Lewis with would-be comic Robert De Niro in The King of Comedy.

There are lots of laughs in director Martin Scorsese's ironic and stimulating essay on America's obsession with celebrities, but the subject of the film is serious business. De Niro is fascinating as a brash stand-up comic who achieves national exposure by kidnapping a TV talk-show host. Lewis plays the role of the host straight and smart, and he's terrific. Part of the theme concerns the media-saturated climate that can breed a Manson or a Hinckley, and that's no joke. Also with Sandra Bernhard, Diahnne Abbott, and Ed Herlihy. **(PG)** *108 minutes*

KING OF HEARTS (1966)

★★★★

Alan Bates
Geneviève Bujold

A smashing, thought-provoking antiwar movie with a satirical punch that's unforgettable. Bates plays a Scottish soldier in World War I, sent on a mission to defuse a bomb in a French town. All the inhabitants have fled except the inmates of an insane asylum, and they turn out to be more rational than those engaged in fighting the war. Bujold plays a dancer who's an asylum inmate. Directed and acted with exceptional style, the film has become a cult favorite. Costars Pierre Brasseur and Jean-Claude Brialy. Originally filmed in French. **Director**—Philippe de Broca. *102 minutes*

KING OF KINGS (1961)

★★★½

Jeffrey Hunter

Excellent biblical epic about the life of Jesus Christ, filmed in lush CinemaScope. The visual effects are stunning, and the simple, straightforward story is moving. Director Nicholas Ray does a skillful job of elevating the film above the usual hackneyed Bible sagas, and presents it as an intelligent drama. Hunter gives his best performance as a youthful, if unlikely, blue-eyed Christ, and is well supported by Siobhan McKenna, Robert Ryan, Hurd Hatfield, Viveca Lindfors, Rita Gam, and Rip Torn. *168 minutes*

THE KING OF MARVIN GARDENS (1972)

★★★

Jack Nicholson
Bruce Dern
Ellen Burstyn

An offbeat, bittersweet drama about two brothers, played by Nicholson and Dern, who long to achieve the American dream, but whose ways and means aren't enough to reach the goal. Nicholson is excellent as a radio talk-show host, and Dern is impressive as a small-time operator with big ideas. Burstyn plays an aging beauty. Overly symbolic and talky at times, the film may be too dark and depressing for some. Director Bob Rafelson, whose earlier effort was *Five Easy Pieces*, isn't up to the level of that film here. Also with Julia Anne Robinson and Scatman Crothers. **(R)** *104 minutes*

KING OF THE GYPSIES (1978)

★★

Sterling Hayden
Eric Roberts
Susan Sarandon

® *This movie available with closed captions for the hearing impaired.*

A contemporary story of a feuding gypsy family, based on Peter Maas' book. There are some fascinating moments, but the film is disorganized and unconvincing. There's an encouraging debut by Roberts as the young rebel who struggles to escape from the bizarre gypsy world, but Hayden, Shelley Winters, and Judd Hirsch are miscast in stereotyped roles. Also with Annette O'Toole and Brooke Shields. Unfortunately writer/director Frank Pierson missed the mark. **(R)**

112 minutes

KING SOLOMON'S MINES (1950)

★★★1/2

Stewart Granger
Deborah Kerr

Ripsnorting adventure in darkest Africa, with Granger and Kerr heading an exploration team to find Kerr's missing husband and lost diamond mines. The impressive-looking production, based on H. Rider Haggard's novel, is nicely paced and leads to a magnificent climax, and there's adequate excitement and suspense along the way. Also with Richard Carlson, Hugo Haas, and Lowell Gilmore. **Director**—Compton Bennett. **Academy Award**—Robert Surtees, cinematography. **Nomination**—best picture. *102 minutes*

KING SOLOMON'S MINES (1985)

★★

Richard Chamberlain
Sharon Stone

This third film version of the popular African adventure plays like a threadbare *Romancing the Stone* adorned with some Three Stooges comedy antics. Chamberlain is the determined white hunter in quest of lost treasure; Stone is at his side as the wily heroine. Together they weave through a maze of nonstop peril so unrealistic and rife with clichés and cardboard characters that the derring-do loses its impact. **Director**—J. Lee Thompson. **(PG-13)** *100 minutes*

KING'S ROW (1942)

★★★1/2

Ann Sheridan
Robert Cummings
Ronald Reagan

A penetrating look at a small, turn-of-the-century American community. The story exposes the pettiness and anxiety that are often characteristic of small-town life. The story unfolds as an early-century *Peyton Place,* with much style and high drama. Superb characterizations abound, and most of the acting is outstanding. Also with Claude Rains, Charles Coburn, and Judith Anderson. **Director**—Sam Wood. **Academy Award Nominations**—Wood, best director; James Wong Howe, cinematography.

127 minutes b&w

KINJITE: FORBIDDEN SUBJECTS (1989)

★

Charles Bronson
Peggy Lipton

This action thriller has to be the most distasteful of Bronson's formula projects. Bronson, as squinty-eyed and poker-faced as ever, plays an angry L.A. cop who wages war against a pimp exploiting vulnerable teenagers. But the film exploits the subject matter without offering a single insight or surprise. Director J. Lee Thompson has sunk pretty low since *The Guns of Navarone.* Also with Juan Fernandez, James Pax, Perry Lopez, and Kumiko Hayakawa. **(R)**

97 minutes

KISMET (1944)

Ronald Colman
Marlene Dietrich

Adequate telling of the Arabian Nights fable with a wonderful cast. The production, starring Colman and Dietrich, has a lot of polish, and there's a striking dance scene with Marlene all aglow in gold body paint. The proceedings could use a bit of levity, but it's worthwhile viewing nevertheless. Also with James Craig, Edward Arnold, Harry Davenport, and Florence Bates. **Director**—William Dieterle. *100 minutes*

KISMET (1955)

★★1/2

Howard Keel
Ann Blyth

Disappointing film version, starring Keel and Blyth, of the hit musical stage production of romance and intrigue in Old Baghdad. Alexander Borodin's music is beautiful, but the story is static. Still, fans of large-scale Hollywood musicals will not be disappointed. Also with Vic Damone, Monty Woolley, Dolores Gray, Sebastian Cabot, and Jack Elam. **Director**—Vincente Minnelli.

113 minutes

THE KISS (1988)

★1/2

Joanna Pacula
Meredith Salenger
Nicholas Kilbertus

This unappetizing mix of various horror-film elements is made worse by dreadful special effects. Pacula plays a witchy European model who comes to America, where she intends to pass on her evil powers to a close relative by way of a devastating kiss. The creaky plot is full of unanswered questions, and tacky horror tricks are introduced indiscriminately. **Director**—Pen Densham. **(R)** *100 minutes*

KISS ME DEADLY (1955)

Ralph Meeker
Albert Dekker
Cloris Leachman

It's a dark, grisly adaptation of a Mickey Spillane Mike Hammer mystery—and it may also be the ultimate *film noir.* Meeker stars as an amoral detective who finds himself caught in a web of corruption and violence, spun by hoods on the trail of radioactive material. You can take it simply as a tight, compellingly stylized melodrama, or as a haunting, nightmarish vision of an immoral world rushing toward apocalypse. Either way it's strong stuff, expressively directed by Robert Aldrich. Also with Maxine Cooper, Gaby Rodgers, Paul Stewart, Jack Elam, and Jack Lambert. *105 minutes b&w*

KISS ME GOODBYE (1982)

★★

Sally Field
James Caan
Jeff Bridges

Patchy, hollow romantic comedy loosely based on the Brazilian film *Dona Flor and Her Two Husbands.* Field plays a young widow who's about to marry a stuffy Egyptologist (Bridges) when the

(Continued)

This movie available on videotape and/or disc.

(Continued)
ghost of her late husband (Caan) appears to stir up trouble. Some of the 1930s-style comic complications come across, but the story is essentially so much hot air. The elegant production gets good supporting work from Claire Trevor as the huffy mother of the bride. **Director**—Robert Mulligan. **(PG)**
101 minutes

KISS ME KATE (1953)

 ★★★

Howard Keel
Kathryn Grayson

A perky backstage musical taken from the Broadway hit and filled with Cole Porter's delightful tunes. Keel and Grayson portray married thespians performing in Shakespeare's *Taming of the Shrew* adapted for music. The film features much energetic dancing, a touch of comedy, and such great songs as "Another Opening, Another Show," "Wunderbar," and "Brush Up Your Shakespeare." Also among the cast are Ann Miller, Keenan Wynn, Bobby Van, James Whitmore, Tommy Rall, and Bob Fosse. **Director**—George Sidney.
109 minutes

KISS OF DEATH (1947)

★★★½

Victor Mature
Richard Widmark

Richard Widmark (center) and Victor Mature (right) in Kiss of Death.

Taut, moody gangster thriller scripted by Ben Hecht and Charles Lederer, and filmed on location in New York City. A thief rats on his pals, and a ruthless hit man trails him to get revenge. There are outstanding performances by Mature and by Widmark, who is perfectly cast as the giggling, psychopathic killer. Widmark made his screen debut in this suspenseful mystery tale, which contains the notorious scene where Widmark pushes a wheelchair-bound old lady down a flight of stairs. Remade as *The Fiend Who Walked the West*. Also with Brian Donlevy, Karl Malden, Mildred Dunnock, and Colleen Gray. **Director**—Henry Hathaway. **Academy Award Nominations**—Widmark, best supporting actor; Eleazar Lipsky, original story. *98 minutes b&w*

KISS OF THE SPIDER WOMAN (1985)

 ★★★★ 

William Hurt
Raul Julia

Raul Julia pays for his political activism in Kiss of the Spider Woman.

Manuel Puig's grim novel, set in a squalid South American prison, comes across on the screen with power and originality. A remarkable performance by Hurt drives the provocative story to its sad conclusion. Hurt brilliantly portrays a drag queen who shares a cell with a brooding revolutionary, skillfully acted by Julia. The two prisoners eventually experience a remarkable friendship, and are influenced by each other's personal beliefs. Director Hector Babenco weaves the material together for maximum impact. **(R) Academy Award**—Hurt, best actor. **Nominations**—best picture; Babenco, best director; Leonard Schrader, best screenplay based on material from another medium. *159 minutes*

KISS TOMORROW GOODBYE (1950)

 ★★★

James Cagney
Barbara Payton

Cagney plays his typical gangster character in this violent drama that's worthwhile mainly because of the star's performance. The film, however, isn't up to the level of Cagney's *White Heat*. Here, the tough guy plays an ecaped convict who embarks on a series of bloody holdups. William Cagney, Jimmy's brother, produced the film and appears as his brother. Also with Ward Bond, Luther Adler, Steve Brodie, and Helena Carter. **Director**—Gordon Douglas. *102 minutes b&w*

KITTY (1945)

★★★

Paulette Goddard
Ray Milland

Another version of the *Pygmalion* story. Set in 18th-century London, the film stars Goddard as a poor girl who becomes a well-mannered woman with the help of an artist, played by Milland. The film is well made and there is excellent use of costumes and period detail. Goddard's performance is tops, and she's nicely assisted by Milland, Cecil Kellaway, Constance Collier, Reginald Owen, Patric Knowles, and Sara Allgood. **Director**—Mitchell Leisen.
103 minutes b&w

KITTY AND THE BAGMAN (1983)

 ★★

Liddy Clark
John Stanton
Val Lehman
Gerard McGuire

From Australia, a slick, semicomic tale of brothels, booze, gambling, and corruption during the 1920s. Clark portrays an unlikely rackets boss, but does not do justice to this difficult role. Period details are impressive, but the chain of frantic events that make up the plot is not. The film is billed as an homage to Warner Brothers gangster movies. The Warner folks are likely to cringe a bit. **Director**—Donald Crombie. **(R)**
95 minutes

KITTY FOYLE (1940)

Ginger Rogers

An above-average love story with a fine performance by Rogers as a working girl who has problems in her relationships. The story is weighted down with heavy moralizing and depressing

This movie available with closed captions for the hearing impaired.

events, including the death of Foyle's baby. The film is adapted from Christopher Morley's dramatic novel, and it features other good performances from Dennis Morgan, Eduardo Ciannelli, Gladys Cooper, and James Craig. **Director**—Sam Wood. **Academy Award**—Rogers, best actress. **Nominations**—best picture; Wood, best director; Dalton Trumbo, screenplay.

108 minutes b&w

KLUTE (1971)

★★★★

Jane Fonda
Donald Sutherland

Detective Donald Sutherland and call girl Jane Fonda in Klute.

Fonda gives a smashing performance as a sophisticated call girl in this gripping crime thriller. The story involves a small-town cop, played by Sutherland, who comes to New York City to locate a missing friend. During his investigation, he meets Fonda and falls in love with her. Fonda portrays her character expertly, with much credibility and colorful detail, and the film offers some insightful character studies. Also with Charles Cioffi, Roy Scheider, Jean Stapleton, and Rita Gam. **Director**—Alan J. Pakula. **(R) Academy Award**—Fonda, best actress. **Nomination**—Andy and Dave Lewis, best story and screenplay based on factual material or material not previously published.

114 minutes

KNIFE IN THE WATER (1963)

★★★★

Leon Niemczyk
Jolanta Umecka
Zygmunt Malanowicz

This brilliant cinematic debut by director Roman Polanski has all the elements of his later works: sexual undercurrents, jealousy, physical danger, and dramatic confrontation of the generations. The simple but intelligent script by Jerzy Skolimowski, Jakub Goldberg, and Polanski concerns a couple off for a weekend of sailing, who bring a younger hitchhiker into their midst. The tensions that follow grow out of the interplay of characters, which is skillfully manipulated by director Polanski. Originally filmed in Polish. **Academy Award Nomination**—best foreign-language film. *94 minutes b&w*

KNIGHTRIDERS (1981)

★★

Ed Harris
Gary Lahti

George Romero (*Night of the Living Dead*) applies the legend of King Arthur to the modern-day knights who tour the country staging jousting contests on motorcycles. Harris and Lahti star in a cast of largely unknown actors. The performances are adequate, and the motorcycle stunts are well coordinated, yet there's meager dramatic impetus as these gasoline-propelled warriors pursue honor and glory atop their Harley-Davidsons. In fact, it's rather tame in contrast to Romero's previous bloodletting horror excesses. Also with Tom Savini and Amy Ingersoll. **(R)**

145 minutes

K-9 (1989)

★★

James Belushi
Mel Harris

Narcotics detective James Belushi with his capable partner in K-9.

Belushi plays an unorthodox narcotics detective who waltzes through all the usual drug-involved crime-thriller elements before the villains are captured. There's a new wrinkle in the standard cop-buddy movie in this comedy: The mismatched partner is a German shepherd police dog. This time, though, the heroic pooch gets most of the credit. Also with Kevin Tighe and Ed O'Neill. **Director**—Rod Daniel. **(PG)**

105 minutes

KNUTE ROCKNE—ALL AMERICAN (1940)

★★★

Pat O'Brien
Gale Page
Ronald Reagan

This memorable film biography of the famous Notre Dame football coach is more intriguing since Reagan has become President. O'Brien is convincing as the determined coach, and Reagan is adequate as George Gipp, the team's star player. The story is predictable, with considerable emphasis on gridiron glory. The script contains the indelible locker room plea: "...win it for the Gipper!" Unfortunately, this scene is cut from TV prints due to legal problems. Also costars Donald Crisp and Albert Bassermann. **Director**—Lloyd Bacon. *98 minutes b&w*

KRAMER VS. KRAMER (1979)

★★★

Dustin Hoffman
Meryl Streep
Jane Alexander
Justin Henry

A love story about a father and son who really get to know each other when the wife/mother abruptly walks out on them. Hoffman plays the father, Henry is the son, and Streep is the woman trying to find herself; Alexander plays a concerned family friend. Ordinarily, such fare is grist for flimsy soap operas, but this film is blessed with insight, sensitivity, and intelligence; it also dissects a number of current social problems. Hoffman, Streep, and six-year-old Henry are in rare form. Also with Howard Duff and George Coe. **Director**—Robert Benton. **(PG) Academy Awards**—best picture; Benton, best director; Hoffman, best actor; Streep, best supporting actress; Benton, best screenplay adapted from another medium. **Nominations**—Henry, best supporting actor; Alexander, best supporting actress; Nestor Almendros, cinematography. *105 minutes*

This movie available on videotape and/or disc.

KRULL (1983)

★★

Ken Marshall
Lysette Anthony

Visually striking yet overblown sword-and-sorcery fantasy that borrows brazenly and ineptly from similar sagas, from *King Arthur* to *Star Wars*. Marshall is a prince from a strange planet who fights his way through a predictably treacherous obstacle course to rescue his princess bride (Anthony) from The Beast. Despite the slick special effects and thundering soundtrack, the derring-do adventure seems stale and monotonous. **Director**—Peter Yates. **(PG)** *126 minutes*

KRUSH GROOVE (1985)

★★

Sheila E.

Rap music, pulsating and loud, is the centerpiece of this youthful celebration of inner-city street culture. There are plenty of energetic song-and-dance numbers to satisfy fans, but the screenplay is thin and familiar, with the usual backstage anxieties and silly romances. Notable rap performers such as Run-D.M.C., the Fat Boys, and Kurtis Blow strut their stuff. **Director**—Michael Schultz. **(R)** *95 minutes*

L

LAMBADA (1990)

★

J. Eddie Peck
Melora Hardin

A ridiculous exploitation movie (if that's not redundant), which was haphazardly slapped together to take advantage of the Brazilian dance craze of the title. The laughable story involves a Beverly Hills math teacher who tutors poor Hispanic kids in the East Los Angeles barrio in his spare time. Unbeknownst to his wealthy colleagues, he is really a leather-jacketed lambada expert. The plot is merely an excuse for the dance sequences. Unfortunately, the production numbers are photographed so choppily that none of the fluid rhythm and sensual movement of the lambada is captured. **Director**—Joel Silberg. **(PG)** *104 minutes*

LA BAMBA

See Bamba, La

LABYRINTH (1986)

★★

Jennifer Connelly
David Bowie

David Bowie as Jareth, the ominous ruler of the Labyrinth.

A labored children's fantasy/adventure about a teenage girl (Connelly) who must rescue her baby brother from goblins. To accomplish her mission, she embarks on a treacherous journey through a maze to the castle of the Goblin King (Bowie), a trip that is similar in spirit to Dorothy's journey down the Yellow Brick Road in *The Wizard of Oz*. Despite the combined talents of producer George Lucas and muppeteer Jim Henson, the characters are unattractive and the story is pedestrian. However, Henson's ability to make inanimate creatures come to life and an emphasis on visual inventiveness will delight fantasy lovers. Former member of Monty Python, Terry Jones, wrote the script. Also with David Goelz and Frank Oz. **Director**—Henson. **(PG)** *101 minutes*

THE LACEMAKER (1977)

★★★

Isabelle Huppert
Yves Beneyton

Swiss director Claude Goretta's gentle and delicate film is about a tragic affair between mismatched lovers. Huppert dominates the film, with a warmly appealing performance as the sweet-natured beauty-parlor assistant who is eventually dismissed by her lover, an intellectual student played by Beneyton. Their romance could not survive the differences between the classes that the two lovers represent. Goretta's masterful touch conveys the sensitivity needed to tell the story. Originally filmed in French. **(No MPAA rating)** *108 minutes*

LADY CHATTERLEY'S LOVER (1982)

★★

Sylvia Kristel

This is a disappointing screen adaptation of D.H. Lawrence's classic, smoldering story of a woman's search for sexual satisfaction. Much of its eroticism is subdued, so the film turns the spotlight instead on the English nobility of the period and their wealthy surroundings. Despite this emphasis, the film looks cheap and colorless. Kristel brings minimal sensuality to the role of the frustrated noblewoman. Nicholas Clay costars as her gamekeeper lover, and Shane Briant is the war-wounded Lord Chatterley. **Director**—Just Jaeckin. **(R)** *101 minutes*

THE LADY EVE (1941)

★★★★

Barbara Stanwyck
Henry Fonda

Lively, witty romantic farce by director Preston Sturges. Stanwyck stars as a con artist who tries to pull a fast one on a gullible, millionaire herpetologist, played by Fonda. This is one of Sturges' best films and features his trademark fast-paced verbal and visual humor. Expert support from Charles Coburn, Eugene Pallette, William Demarest, and Eric Blore. **Academy Award Nomination**—Monckton Hoffe, original story. *97 minutes b&w*

LADYHAWKE (1985)

★★★

Rutger Hauer
Michelle Pfeiffer
Matthew Broderick

An appealing medieval romantic adventure about a pair of lovers under a curse. Hauer is a master swordsman

Rutger Hauer loves his Ladyhawke, *Michelle Pfeiffer, in the face of curses.*

who turns into a wolf by night. His beautiful lady love (Pfeiffer) is a hawk by day. They can never touch one another as humans. Despite some script drawbacks, the well-crafted film has a splendid adventurous spirit and a sophisticated sense of humor. Striking landscapes and colorful period costumes provide an authentic look. Broderick costars as the comic sidekick. **Director**—Richard Donner. **(PG–13)**
121 minutes

LADY IN A CAGE (1964)

★★

Olivia de Havilland

Overwrought suspense story about a rich woman trapped in an elevator by some young thugs who vandalize her apartment. There are some tense moments, but most of the film is pretentious and somewhat unsavory. De Havilland is wasted as the harassed and vulnerable widow. Supporting roles are played by James Caan, Ann Sothern, and Jeff Corey. **Director**—Walter Grauman. *97 minutes b&w*

LADY IN CEMENT (1968)

★★

Frank Sinatra
Raquel Welch

More adventures in the life of private eye Tony Rome. This time the film features even more flashy sex and violence than the first film, though the storyline is as predictable. Sinatra again plays the hip gumshoe, and he's on the trail of a killer after discovering a woman's corpse with its feet anchored in cement. Welch and Lainie Kazan provide the glamour, with support from Richard Conte and Dan Blocker. **Director**—Gordon Douglas. **(PG)** *93 minutes*

LADY IN THE DARK (1944)

★★★

Ginger Rogers

Ray Milland and Ginger Rogers star in Lady in the Dark.

A lavish and colorful romantic comedy about a magazine editor who suffers mental anguish over the men in her life. Rogers, in the starring role, turns on the charm as the perplexed career woman. And there are ample comic moments for the entire cast, which also features Ray Milland, Warner Baxter, Jon Hall, Mischa Auer, and Barry Sullivan. Adapted from Moss Hart's Broadway musical, but lacking many of the songs. **Director**—Mitchell Leisen.
100 minutes

LADY IN WHITE (1988)

Ⓥ ★★★ Ⓒ

Lukas Haas
Len Cariou
Katherine Helmond

Excellent production values and colorful characters highlight this effective ghost story set in a small New England town. Haas is believable and even charming as the young boy who helps unravel a mystery surrounding the murder of a little girl ten years earlier. Director Frank LaLoggia avoids the gory, violent elements of many contemporary horror films to tell a poignant tale, but one with some heartstopping moments of real terror. Alex Rocco, Renata Vanni, Angelo Bertolini, and Jason Presson are superb as members of Haas' immigrant family. **(PG–13)**
112 minutes

LADY JANE (1986)

Ⓥ ★★ Ⓒ

Helena Bonham-Carter

A solemn costume drama about the 15-year-old queen who ruled Britain for only nine days and then was beheaded. Although the 16th-century historical details are elegantly re-created, the story creaks along, even when it involves palace intrigues and adolescent romance. Bonham-Carter fares well in the title role. Also with Cary Elwes and John Wood. Trevor Nunn, who directed the lively *Nicholas Nickleby*, neglected to apply such vigor here. **(PG–13)**
142 minutes

LADY SINGS THE BLUES (1972)

Ⓥ ★★★

Diana Ross
Billy Dee Williams

The tumultuous and tragic life of singing great Billie "Lady Day" Holiday is portrayed with amazing clarity and style by Ross, a singing sensation in her own right. This film biography seems light on facts and heavy on drama, but it's high-level entertainment nevertheless, thanks to Ross' grasp of the role. She croons the songs in a convincing style, and her acting is impressive, too. Williams plays her husband. Also with Richard Pryor and Sid Melton. **Director**—Sidney J. Furie. **(R) Academy Award Nominations**—Ross, best actress; Terence McCloy, Chris Clark, and Suzanne de Passe, best story and screenplay based on factual material or material not previously published.
144 minutes

THE LADY VANISHES (1938)

Ⓥ ★★★★

Dame May Whitty
Paul Lukas
Margaret Lockwood
Michael Redgrave

Clever and witty suspense melodrama involving foreign intrigue on a train traveling through Europe. A charming old lady disappears from her compartment and is pursued by Lockwood and Redgrave through a series of unlikely but convincing incidents. A well-written script, excellent star performances, and the masterly hand of director Alfred Hitchcock make this a

(Continued)

(Continued)
classic to be seen again and again. The wonderful cast also includes Basil Radford, Naunton Wayne, Catherine Lacey, Cecil Parker, Linden Travers, Googie Withers, Mary Clare, and Margaretta Scott. *97 minutes b&w*

THE LAIR OF THE WHITE WORM (1988)

★★½

Amanda Donohoe
Hugh Grant

Amanda Donohoe is enticing in The Lair of the White Worm.

Ken Russell directs this outlandish film version of a story by Bram Stoker, author of *Dracula*. This combination of horror and droll humor involves serpent worshipers operating in the English countryside. There are plenty of bizarre characters, a variety of strange episodes, and many references to wriggling creatures, but the offbeat story is often hard to follow. Also with Catherine Oxenberg, Sammi Davis, and Peter Capaldi. **(R)** *94 minutes*

THE LAND BEFORE TIME (1988)

★★★

This is a good animated adventure that kids and their parents will enjoy. Littlefoot is a charming baby brontosaurus who seeks sanctuary in the Great Valley after his parents are killed in an earthquake. Although the circumstances are unhappy, the saga is engrossing and exciting. Director Don Bluth's colorful and detailed animation rivals the best of the golden era of Disney. The little prehistoric creatures have plenty of appeal. With the voices of Pat Hingle, Gabriel Damon, Helen Shaver, and Judith Barsi. **(G)** *73 minutes*

THE LAND THAT TIME FORGOT (1975)

★★

Doug McClure

The film, based on an Edgar Rice Burroughs novel, is about a crew of German submariners who, together with a group of survivors from a sunken British ship, discover a lost continent where prehistoric beasts roam. The script is trite and confusing, but the so-so special effects may appeal to science-fiction fans. Also with John McEnery, Susan Penhaligon, and Keith Barron. **Director**—Kevin Connor. **(PG)** *91 minutes*

LASSIE COME HOME (1943)

★★★½

Roddy McDowall
Elizabeth Taylor
Donald Crisp
Edmund Gwenn

Roddy McDowall with the real star of the film Lassie Come Home.

This sentimental tale pulls hard at the heartstrings. A poor family must sell its faithful collie, but the loyal dog makes a brave journey back to its familiar home. This is a family film of the highest order, and it spawned several sequels and a TV series. The remarkable cast also includes Dame May Whitty, Elsa Lanchester, Nigel Bruce, and, of course, Lassie. Remade as *Gypsy Colt* in 1954 and *The Magic of Lassie* in 1978. **Director**—Fred M. Wilcox. **Academy Award Nomination**—Leonard Smith, cinematography. *88 minutes*

LASSITER (1984)

★★

Tom Selleck
Jane Seymour
Lauren Hutton

Selleck, in the title role, is suave and debonair as a slick jewel thief in London on the eve of World War II. His assignment: Grab $10 million in diamonds from the Nazis before they use the fortune to buy weapons. While Selleck looks good, the film is merely predictable formula fare that finally succumbs to its own lassitude. Costars Bob Hoskins. **Director**—Roger Young. **(R)** *100 minutes*

THE LAST AMERICAN VIRGIN (1983)

Lawrence Monoson
Diane Franklin
Steve Antin

A typically inane, adolescent exploitation film about the escapades of three high-school boys in pursuit of sexual conquests. The story includes all the familiar situations: confrontations with frantic parents, stuffy teachers, awkward classmates, and lots of eager girls. There's even a locker room peephole scene on the order of *Porky's*. This mindless activity is carried on to the beat of a blaring soundtrack that features Blondie, the Cars, and the Police. **Director**—Boaz Davidson. **(R)** *90 minutes*

THE LAST ANGRY MAN (1959)

★★★★

Paul Muni

Sensitive story, adapted from Gerald Green's book, about an elderly family doctor in a poor Brooklyn neighborhood who is more concerned with the welfare of his impoverished patients than with making lots of money. The film makes a strong statement against those in the profession who are in it only for the money and status. Muni, in his last screen role, is excellent as the idealistic physician. There's good support as well from David Wayne, Betsy Palmer, and Luther Adler. **Director**—Daniel Mann. **Academy Award Nomination**—Muni, best actor. *100 minutes b&w*

THE LAST DETAIL (1973)

Jack Nicholson
Otis Young
Randy Quaid

® *This movie available with closed captions for the hearing impaired.*

A bittersweet comedy/drama about justice without mercy in the Navy. Two senior petty officers—Nicholson and Young—escort a young sailor accused of petty theft on a two-day trip to the Portsmouth, New Hampshire, brig. En route, they take pity and treat him to a last fling before imprisonment. Nicholson shines as the tough but sympathetic career man; Quaid is outstanding as the hapless sailor whose impending punishment doesn't fit the crime. And there are excellent character studies throughout. Also with Clifton James, Carol Kane, Nancy Allen, Gilda Radner, Luana Anders, and Michael Moriarty. **Director**—Hal Ashby. **(R) Academy Award Nominations**—Nicholson, best actor; Quaid, best supporting actor; Robert Towne, best screenplay based on material from another medium. *104 minutes*

THE LAST DRAGON (1985)

★★

Vanity
Taimak

Taimak stars as a young karate devotee who strives to preserve his honor when challenged by a sadist. He also must protect a gorgeous video star (Vanity) from exploitation by a sinister producer. The martial-arts action is interspersed with lots of song-and-dance video production numbers, which give the film a somewhat jumbled appearance. While events unfold at a fast clip, the story is often absurd and mean-spirited. Leo O'Brien, as the main character's brother, steals a few scenes. **Director**—Michael Schultz. **(PG–13)** *108 minutes*

THE LAST EMBRACE (1979)

★★

Roy Scheider
Janet Margolin

Janet Margolin and Roy Scheider share The Last Embrace.

Scheider stars as a worried-looking government agent who believes someone is about to kill him. Margolin plays a graduate student who mysteriously enters his life. Scheider and Margolin are excellent; their underplayed performances add to the film's suspense. But director Jonathan Demme's romantic thriller is meager, illogical, and often confusing. The movie winds up at the edge of Niagara Falls; by that time, the story seems all wet. Also with Sam Levene, John Glover, and Christopher Walken. **(R)** *102 minutes*

THE LAST EMPEROR (1987)

★★★★

John Lone
Joan Chen
Peter O'Toole

Richard Vuu is the boy who will grow up to be The Last Emperor of China.

A beautifully filmed epic about China's last imperial ruler, Pu Yi. The film follows the emperor's life from his appointment to the throne at age three to his death as an ordinary citizen in the People's Republic in 1967. Though filmmaker Bernardo Bertolucci tells a sweeping story of a man controlled by historical forces, he still manages to reveal intimate details of the ruler's personal life. The drama is engrossing and the Oscar-winning cinematography is a visual splendor. The film received nine Academy Awards, winning in every category in which it was nominated. **(PG–13) Academy Awards**—best film; Bertolucci, best director; Mark Peploe and Bertolucci, best screenplay based on material from another source; Vittorio Storaro, cinematography; Ferdinando Scarfiotti and Bruno Cesari, art direction; Gabriella Critiani, best editing; James Acheson, best costume design. *160 minutes*

LAST EXIT TO BROOKLYN (1990)

★★1/2

Jennifer Jason Leigh
Stephen Lang

The mean streets of the Brooklyn waterfront in 1952 provide a relentlessly oppressive backdrop for this somber tale. Based on the gritty novel by Hubert Selby, Jr., the film touches on brutal labor confrontations as well as the activities of various sordid characters, including a mean hooker, a drug-dependent transvestite, and combatant factory workers. The critically acclaimed performances by Lang and Leigh highlight the film, but the grotesque, shocking events and constant gloom are overwhelming. Seasoned viewers may find this film a worthy statement on social ills; others will be offended by the sordidness. Also with Peter Dobson, Jerry Orbach, Stephen Baldwin, Alexis Arquette, Zette, and Ricki Lake. **Director**—Uli Edel. **(R)** *102 minutes*

THE LAST FLIGHT OF NOAH'S ARK (1980)

Elliott Gould
Geneviève Bujold
Ricky Schroder
Tammy Lauren

Disney's modern-day version of the well-known Bible story is a pat and predictable adventure film where kids prevail over adults once more. Gould and Bujold crash-land on a Pacific island in a lumbering B-29 full of animals and a couple of stowaway kids, played by Schroder and Lauren. They all escape by converting the plane into a ship. The animals are also taken along at the youngsters' insistence. Also with Vincent Gardenia. **Director**—Charles Jarrott. **(G)** *97 minutes*

THE LAST HARD MEN (1976)

Charlton Heston
James Coburn

Vengeance is the theme of this routine western set in Arizona in the early 1900s. Coburn plays a half-breed Navajo who lures a retired lawman, played by Heston, to a slow and grue-

(Continued)

(Continued)
some death. Coburn and Heston are convincing as the hard-boiled adversaries, but Michael Parks steals the film as a reform-seeking sheriff. Too violent and tasteless to be effective. Also with Barbara Hershey and Christopher Mitchum. **Director**—Andrew V. McLaglen. **(R)** *98 minutes*

THE LAST HURRAH (1958)

★★★★

Spencer Tracy
Jeffrey Hunter

Entertaining account of big-city politics, with Tracy expertly portraying a mayor who holds power through shrewdness. Tracy is completely at ease in the role, and he receives top support from a veteran cast. Adapted from Edwin O'Connor's novel, inspired by the career of Boston Mayor James Curley. Also costars Pat O'Brien, Basil Rathbone, Donald Crisp, James Gleason, Anna Lee, Edmund Lowe, John Carradine, Jane Darwell, and Wallace Ford. **Director**—John Ford. *121 minutes b&w*

THE LAST MARRIED COUPLE IN AMERICA (1980)

★★

George Segal
Natalie Wood

George Segal and Natalie Wood are The Last Married Couple in America.

Segal and Wood are Jeff and Mari of Los Angeles, who observe their friends' marriages breaking up and wonder if they're next. The predictable TV-sitcom screenplay is only mildly amusing as it examines the despair of the sexual revolution. The acting, however, is well above the material; Wood is especially good in her comic role. And there are some classy scenes with Richard Benjamin, Dom DeLuise, and Valerie Harper. **Director**—Gilbert Cates. **(R)** *103 minutes*

THE LAST METRO (1980)

★★★

Catherine Deneuve

Director François Truffaut (*The 400 Blows; Jules and Jim*) scores again with this affecting story of backstage theater life during the Nazi occupation of Paris. Beautiful Deneuve runs a small Paris theater by proxy for her husband, a Jewish director, played by Heinz Bennent, who goes into hiding. Gérard Depardieu is splendid as a rakish actor who turns out to be quite a patriot. A fine supporting cast adds to this charming slice-of-life drama of love and heroism. Also with Jean-Louis Richard, Jean Poiret, and Sabine Haudepin. Originally filmed in French. **(No MPAA rating) Academy Award Nomination**—best foreign-language film. *130 minutes*

THE LAST OF THE FINEST (1990)

★★

Brian Dennehy
Joe Pantoliano

Ron Canada and Brian Dennehy in The Last of the Finest.

A predictable police thriller sporting the usual number of high-speed chases and shoot-outs. The acting is not particularly noteworthy, the characters are not well-drawn, and the direction is not unique. Dennehy portrays a renegade Los Angeles cop who is suspended from the force. He and his boys decide to track down, on their own terms, a drug kingpin who has connections in the police force. Some sensitive moral issues are touched upon but never settled when the vigilante cops latch onto laundered drug money. Also with Jeff Fahey, Bill Paxton, and Michael C. Gwynne. **Director**—John Mackenzie. **(R)** *106 minutes*

LAST OF THE RED HOT LOVERS (1972)

★★

Alan Arkin

So-so film version of Neil Simon's stage comedy. The title character is the owner of a seafood restaurant who attempts an extramarital fling with three women, though not all at once. Arkin manages to arouse a few smiles as the klutzy Don Juan, but there isn't enough comic energy to sustain the film. Also with Paula Prentiss, Sally Kellerman, and Renée Taylor. **Director**—Gene Saks. **(PG)** *98 minutes*

THE LAST PICTURE SHOW (1971)

Timothy Bottoms
Jeff Bridges
Cybill Shepherd
Ben Johnson

A nostalgic but melancholy look at life in a small Texas town in the early 1950s, as seen through the experiences of high-school students. The events that unfold result in the death of innocence for those involved, which is visually reflected in the desolate townscape and the flat black-and-white photography by Robert Surtees. Based on a novel by Larry McMurtry. First-class performances by Bottoms, Bridges, Shepherd, Johnson, Cloris Leachman, and Ellen Burstyn. **Director**—Peter Bogdanovich. **(R) Academy Awards**—Johnson, best supporting actor; Leachman, best supporting actress. **Nominations**—best picture; Bogdanovich, best director; Bridges, best supporting actor; Burstyn, best supporting actress; McMurtry and Bogdanovich, best screenplay based on material from another medium; Surtees, cinematography. *114 minutes b&w*

THE LAST REMAKE OF BEAU GESTE (1977)

Marty Feldman
Ann-Margret
Michael York
Peter Ustinov

Marty Feldman and Ann-Margret in The Last Remake of Beau Geste.

Pop-eyed Feldman strikes out on his own as star, director, and writer of this parody of Foreign Legion films. The uneven picture is funny at times, but is often too strained. Feldman borrows generously from his mentor, Mel Brooks, but his execution is heavy-handed and reckless. Some of the barren stretches are shored up by a first-rate cast, which also includes Trevor Howard, James Earl Jones, Terry-Thomas, and Henry Gibson. **(PG)**
83 minutes

LAST RESORT (1986)

Charles Grodin

A noisy, threadbare excuse for a comedy about the misadventures of a family on an economy vacation at a Caribbean island resort. Grodin is lost in the shuffle of bad jokes as the father of the unfortunate family, whose members experience a number of indignities during their stay. But the greatest indignity is to the audience who endures this tasteless, unfunny movie. Robin Pearson Rose costars as the hapless wife. **Director**—Zane Busby. **(R)**
84 minutes

LAST RITES (1988)

  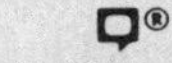

Tom Berenger
Daphne Zuniga
Dane Clark

This laughably contrived thriller pairs a handsome priest (Berenger) with a young woman (Zuniga) who's fleeing from the Mafia after witnessing a gangland murder. Zuniga develops feelings of trust and affection for Berenger, unaware that he's the son of a mob chieftain. Shadowy cinematography and stylized violence are not enough to overcome the implausibility of the storyline. Also with Anne Twomey, Paul Dooley, and Chick Vennera. **Director**—Donald P. Bellisario. **(R)**
103 minutes

THE LAST STARFIGHTER (1984)

★★½

Robert Preston
Lance Guest

Lance Guest teams up with an alien, Dan O'Herlihy, in The Last Starfighter.

A delectable, intergalactic tale about a bored teenager (Guest) who is visited by a fast-talking extraterrestrial (Preston). The alien decides the youth has just the right stuff to defend an embattled star league against rebel invaders. So he whisks the lad off to a distant planet to challenge evil forces. The film lacks the style and budget of the genre's finest, but its tongue-in-cheek approach is entertaining, and the sci-fi creatures and effects are impressive. **Director**—Nick Castle. **(PG)** *100 minutes*

LAST SUMMER (1969)

 ★★★

Barbara Hershey
Cathy Burns
Bruce Davison
Richard Thomas

Sensitive, well-acted drama of the rites of passage of four teenagers during a summer on Fire Island. The excellent script by Eleanor Perry from the novel by Evan Hunter traces the romantic interplay and sexual stirrings of its characters and captures the cruelties that blossom as well. Director Frank Perry restrains the production, which makes a shattering climax even more chilling. All of the performances are first-rate, with Burns exceptional in her role. **(R)** **Academy Award Nomination**—Burns, best supporting actress. *97 minutes*

LAST TANGO IN PARIS (1973)

★★★

Marlon Brando
Maria Schneider

Loveless: Maria Schneider and Marlon Brando in Last Tango in Paris.

A controversial film by Italian director Bernardo Bertolucci, starring Brando as a middle-aged American widower who embarks on a passionate but loveless affair with a young French girl, played by Schneider. Brando's character is suffering from pain and guilt over the loss of his wife, who committed suicide over their stormy marriage. He takes out his anger and frustration through the brutal and aggressive sexual acts performed with Schneider. Brando was allowed much freedom in improvising his role and interpreting his character, and his performance is considered one of his best. The film exists in both an R-rated and an X-rated version, with the latter containing a number of explicit sex scenes not suited for family viewing. The film costars Jean-Pierre Léaud, well known for his roles in François Truffaut's Antoine Doinel series. **(X)** **Academy Award Nominations**—Bertolucci, best director; Brando, best actor. *129 minutes*

THE LAST TEMPTATION OF CHRIST (1988)

 ★★★½

Willem Dafoe

A profound and powerful interpretation of the life of Jesus, based on Nikos Kazantzakis's passionate novel. Jesus (Dafoe) is presented in very human terms. Tormented by doubt, weakness, lust, and guilt, he finally gathers the

(Continued)

(Continued)
tremendous courage needed to carry out his act of love and faith. Director Martin Scorsese's challenging, controversial film is a far cry from lavish, artificial Cecil B. De Mille pageantry. Also stars Harvey Keitel, Barbara Hershey, Harry Dean Stanton, David Bowie, Verna Bloom, Andre Gregory, Irvin Kershner, Nehemiah Persott, and Barry Miller. **(R) Academy Award Nomination**—Scorsese, best director.
160 minutes

THE LAST TYCOON (1976)

★★

Robert De Niro
Tony Curtis
Robert Mitchum
Jack Nicholson

Lethargy pervades this screen version of F. Scott Fitzgerald's unfinished novel about the flourishing Hollywood of the 1930s. De Niro plays the film producer who's working himself to death. The all-star cast, including De Niro, Curtis, Mitchum, and Nicholson, is wasted in ill-defined roles. The meandering story has no real climax. Harold Pinter wrote the screenplay. Also with Ingrid Boulting, Donald Pleasence, Jeanne Moreau, and Ray Milland. **Director**—Elia Kazan. **(PG)** *125 minutes*

THE LAST UNICORN (1982)

★★★

Children will adore this enchanting and magical animated feature. Adults may be charmed as well. Mia Farrow is the voice behind the title character, a lovely lady unicorn who strikes out on a dangerous journey to find her lost companions. The animation style lacks the depth and rich color of Disney, but is pleasant nonetheless. The plot is sometimes reminiscent of events in *The Wizard of Oz.* Tammy Grimes, Angela Lansbury and Alan Arkin supply some of the other voices. **Director**—Arthur Rankin, Jr. **(G)** *88 minutes*

THE LAST WALTZ (1978)

★★★

The Band
Bob Dylan
Neil Young

Martin Scorsese directed this rock-music documentary, focusing on the farewell concert by the Band in 1976 in San Francisco. Interviews with the group's members are interspersed among the musical numbers, which come on full blast in Dolby stereo. Dylan, Young, Joni Mitchell, Neil Diamond, Muddy Waters, and Eric Clapton, among others, join in with some rousing songs. **(PG)** *117 minutes*

THE LAST WINTER (1984)

★★

Yona Elian
Kathleen Quinlan

The 1973 Yom Kippur War is the backdrop for this awkward film concerning two women anxiously awaiting the return of their husbands, who are Israeli soldiers. To build suspense, the plot relies on a gimmick in which each woman identifies the same man, seen in a blurry newsreel of prisoners, as her spouse. The acting is mundane and the emotional relationship between the women is unimpressive. **Director**—Riki Shelach. **(R)** *90 minutes*

THE LATE SHOW (1977)

★★★

Art Carney
Lily Tomlin

Writer/director Robert Benton creates a group of rich and unforgettable characters in this latter-day version of the 1940s private-eye movie. Carney is sensational as an over-the-hill gumshoe who pursues the killer of an old colleague. He's matched by Tomlin's winning performance as his loony sidekick who dabbles in show biz, astrology, and Eastern religions. The complex plot is difficult to unravel, but the decaying milieu reflects an appropriate atmosphere of melancholy, much like that of classic *films noirs.* Also with Bill Macy, Eugene Roche, Joanna Cassidy, John Considine, and Howard Duff. **(PG) Academy Award Nomination**—Benton, best screenplay written directly for the screen. *94 minutes*

LAURA (1944)

★★★★

Dana Andrews
Clifton Webb
Gene Tierney

A gripping murder mystery based on a novel by Vera Caspary. Andrews stars as a police detective who investigates the murder of a young woman, played by Tierney. As he questions the victim's circle of smug, intellectual friends, and becomes preoccupied with details of her past, he begins to fall in love with her. The film, a classic example of *film noir,* was an early directorial effort by Otto Preminger. The mood and atmosphere of the film enhance the suspense of the storyline. The acting is generally above average, with Webb outstanding as a cynical columnist. Also with Judith Anderson, Vincent Price, Dorothy Adams, and Grant Mitchell. **Academy Award**—Joseph LaShelle, cinematography. **Nominations**—Preminger, best director; Webb, best supporting actor.
85 minutes b&w

Gene Tierney piques the interest of Vincent Price in Laura.

THE LAVENDER HILL MOB (1951)

★★★★

Alec Guinness
Stanley Holloway

A lively, droll comedy full of sharp wit and smart dialogue. Guinness triumphs as a mild-mannered bank clerk who engineers a clever scheme to steal a fortune in gold bullion from an armored car. In this case, crime doesn't pay, but there's a big reward in the laughter. See if you can spot Audrey Hepburn in a bit part. Also costars Sidney James, Alfie Bass, Marjorie Fielding, and John Gregson. **Director**—Charles Crichton. **Academy Award**—T.E.B. Clarke, story and screenplay. **Nomination**—Guinness, best actor.
82 minutes b&w

LAWMAN (1970)

★★★

Burt Lancaster
Robert Ryan
Lee J. Cobb

This movie available with closed captions for the hearing impaired.

A top cast helps this grim western story about a showdown between a marshal determined to arrest some lawbreakers and the local citizens who resist his efforts. Lancaster is good as the duty-bound lawman, and Cobb is convincing as the cattleman whose hired hands are involved with the killing of an old man. Also with Sheree North, Robert Duvall, Joseph Wiseman, Albert Salmi, John McGiver, and J.D. Cannon. **Director**—Michael Winner. **(PG)** *99 minutes*

LAWRENCE OF ARABIA (1962)

★★★★

Peter O'Toole
Omar Sharif
Arthur Kennedy

Peter O'Toole plays the great British adventurer in Lawrence of Arabia.

Grandiose epic about the exploits of enigmatic British adventurer T.E. Lawrence in the Middle East during World War I. The film features stunning photography, excellent performances, and an intelligent script; however, it offers little insight into Lawrence, a complex and mysterious character. O'Toole is outstanding in the title role, which made him a star, and there's impressive supporting work from Sharif, Kennedy, Claude Rains, Donald Wolfit, Anthony Quinn, Anthony Quayle, Alec Guinness, and José Ferrer. Originally 222 minutes in length, the film was cut by 20 minutes after its initial release. In 1989, the 70mm version was restored and rereleased to theaters with most of its footage intact, a few additional shots edited by Lean. The 70mm print runs 216 minutes and is available on video in the letter-box format. **Director**—David Lean. **Academy Awards**—best picture; Lean, best director; Fred A. Young, cinematography. **Nominations**—O'Toole, best actor; Sharif, best supporting actor; Robert Bolt, best screenplay based on material from another medium. *222 minutes*

LEADBELLY (1976)

Roger E. Mosley

An engaging biography of black bluesman Huddie "Leadbelly" Ledbetter, who's best known for his songs "Goodnight Irene," "The Rock Island Line," and "The Midnight Special." Mosley plays the title role convincingly, although he occasionally seems too polished; the real Leadbelly spent much of his chaotic life serving time on prison chain gangs and singing in brothels. The film, however, is beautifully photographed and captures much of the atmosphere of the old Deep South. Gordon Parks directs with much feeling and focuses on Leadbelly's music, which is sung by HiTide Harris. Also with James E. Brodhead and John McDonald. **(PG)** *126 minutes*

LEAN ON ME (1989)

Morgan Freeman
Robert Guillaume

Jermaine Hopkins gets a lecture from Morgan Freeman in Lean on Me.

Freeman is electrifying as Joe Clark, the controversial New Jersey principal who used bullying methods to clean the drugs and crime out of a chaotic high school. A simplistic treatment of a complex story is carried out in typical Hollywood fashion by director John G. Avildsen *(Rocky)*, who chooses to manipulate rather than challenge the audience. Despite the flaws, the drama succeeds admirably as compelling entertainment and character portrayal. Also with Alan North, Beverly Todd, Lynne Thigpen, and Robin Bartlett. **(PG-13)** *108 minutes*

LEAVE HER TO HEAVEN (1945)

Gene Tierney
Cornel Wilde

Lushly photographed romantic melodrama about a psychotic woman who destroys everyone around her and eventually herself as well. Tierney is perfectly cast as the beautiful but deadly woman who carries her amorality to its most evil conclusions, letting nothing stand in her way. The script, from a best-seller by Ben Ames Williams, has all the characteristics of a good soap opera. The fine cast also includes Jeanne Crain, Vincent Price, Mary Phillips, Ray Collins, Gene Lockhart, Reed Hadley, and Chill Wills. **Director**—John M. Stahl. **Academy Award**—Leon Shamroy, cinematography. **Nomination**—Tierney, best actress. *111 minutes*

THE LEFT HAND OF GOD (1955)

Humphrey Bogart
Gene Tierney
Lee J. Cobb

Bogart stars as an American pilot posing as a Catholic priest in China just after World War II. He gets involved with a renegade warlord, played by Cobb, who is immersed in conflict. The drama is slow moving, but the film watchable because of the cast, which is much better than the material. Also costars E.G. Marshall, Agnes Moorehead, and Benson Fong. **Director**—Edward Dmytryk. *87 minutes*

THE LEGACY (1979)

Katharine Ross
Sam Elliott
John Standing

Ross and Elliott travel from Los Angeles to England, where Ross is told she is one of the heirs of the estate of wealthy Standing. Elliott, an architect, tags along to study Standing's stately mansion. Much to their surprise, the man-

(Continued)

(Continued)
sion is inhabited by followers of Satan, and the dying Standing wants to devolve his power as leader on to Ross. In this dreary horror film, numerous gruesome deaths are offered to heighten the shock effect: a man is burned to a crisp, another has his throat brutally slashed, and someone else chokes to death. All this is sickening—not scary. Also with Ian Hogg, Roger Daltrey, Charles Gray, and Margaret Tyzack. **Director**—Richard Marquand. **(R)** *100 minutes*

LEGAL EAGLES (1986)

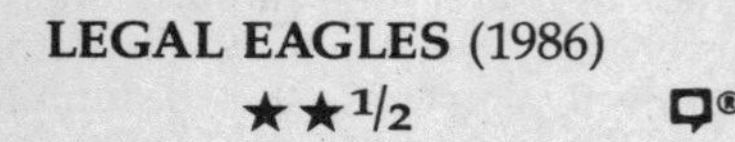

★★½

Robert Redford
Debra Winger
Daryl Hannah

Attorneys Debra Winger and Robert Redford examine the evidence in Legal Eagles.

An uneven but charming romantic comedy starring Redford as a well-respected prosecutor assigned to bring to justice the daughter of a famous artist. Hannah plays the spaced-out young woman—a performance artist—who is charged with attempting to steal one of her dead father's paintings. Winger costars as an unconventional defense attorney who helps Hannah. Eventually, Redford begins to believe that Hannah is innocent and that a cover-up has been perpetrated involving her father's estate. Winger and Redford work together to free Hannah and soon find themselves attracted to each other. Though the storyline is muddled with too many pieces to the puzzle, Winger and Redford have enough chemistry together to make this lightweight comedy enjoyable. Also with Brian Dennehy, Terence Stamp, Steven Hill, and Roscoe Lee Brown. **Director**—Ivan Reitman. **(PG)** *114 minutes*

LEGEND (1986)

★★½

Tom Cruise
Tim Curry
Mia Sara

Tom Cruise is on a mission to rescue Mia Sara in Legend.

This visually striking fantasy/adventure is burdened with a weak script. Essentially, the story is a drab mixture of J.R.R. Tolkien, "Jack and the Beanstalk," and the Old Testament. A young hermit (Cruise) is pitted against the Dark Lord (Curry) in an attempt to rescue a princess (Sara). However, the beautiful forest setting and magnificent lair of the Dark Lord are stunning achievements in terms of set design; likewise, the cinematography by Ridley Scott (also the director) makes the film worthwhile viewing. But those viewers unable to accept the fairy-tale approach of the film should stay away. The film was nominated for an Oscar for its makeup design by Rob Bottin and Peter Robb-King. **(PG)** *89 minutes*

THE LEGEND OF BILLIE JEAN (1985)

★★

Helen Slater

A teenage girl and her male companion become media heroes and cult figures when they demand justice from bullies who ruined a motor scooter. The trite incident is blown up into a sort of martyrdom of the youths, with even a reference to Joan of Arc. The film gains a momentum from the trumped-up events in the storyline, which tend to emotionally manipulate the audience. Ultimately, however, the film evolves as a preposterous and foolish action/adventure tale. Keith Gordon and Christian Slater (no relation to Helen) costar. **Director**—Matthew Robbins. **(PG–13)** *96 minutes*

THE LEGEND OF THE LONE RANGER (1981)

★

Klinton Spilsbury
Michael Horse

The legend is better off dormant if this bland version is the best that can be done with it. This straight-faced western tells the story of the well-known champion of justice—why he put on a mask and chose to fight crime. But the film is so out of kilter and so innocuous that some of the serious dialogue provokes unintentional laughter. Clean-cut Spilsbury plays the title role; Horse plays Tonto. Neither makes much impact. Also with Jason Robards and Christopher Lloyd. **Director**—William A. Fraker. **(PG)** *98 minutes*

THE LEMON DROP KID (1951)

★★★

Bob Hope
Marilyn Maxwell

Many laughs and much sentiment characterize this well-made film, based on a Damon Runyon story. Hope plays a racetrack tout who's in hock to the mob, and he must pay or face the consequences. Hope's style of comedy, emphasizing a quick wit and one-liners, is well suited to his role as the fast-talking tout. A colorful vehicle set in New York City during the Christmas season. "Silver Bells" is the memorable song. Remade from a 1934 film starring Lee Tracy. Also with Lloyd Nolan, Jane Darwell, Andrea King, Fred Clark, and Jay C. Flippen. **Director**—Sidney Lanfield. *91 minutes b&w*

LENNY (1974)

★★★★

Dustin Hoffman
Valerie Perrine

Hoffman gives a powerhouse performance as the controversial nightclub performer Lenny Bruce, best known for his monologues laced with obscene and scatological humor. The biographical film follows Lenny's rocky career, from his meager beginning to his many arrests on charges of obscenity, and finally to his death from an overdose of

® This movie available with closed captions for the hearing impaired.

The tragedy of a comic: Valerie Perrine and Dustin Hoffman in Lenny.

drugs. Perrine is convincing as his faithful wife, stripper Honey Harlowe, who suffers as much as her husband. Bob Fosse directs, using a documentary-like style that heightens the reality of the story, making the tragedies depicted in the film all the more heartbreaking. Jan Miner, Stanley Beck, and Gary Morton also star. **(R) Academy Award Nominations**—best picture; Fosse, best director; Hoffman, best actor; Perrine, best actress; Julian Barry, best screenplay adapted from other material; Bruce Surtees, cinematography.

111 minutes b&w

LEONARD PART 6 (1987)

★1/2

Bill Cosby
Tom Courtenay

Cosby temporarily lost his magic touch with this innocuous spy spoof intended for family audiences. He stars in the title role as a retired secret agent called back into action to stop a maniacal villainess from taking over the world. Her scheme includes training domestic animals to attack the general populace so that the viewer is bombarded with scenes of amphibians, lobsters, and other animals pouncing on innocent bystanders. Aside from the banal plot, the action is static and the gags telegraphed well in advance. Cosby is credited with the idea for the story. Joe Don Baker, Moses Gunn, Gloria Foster, and George Kirby appear in supporting roles. **Director**—Paul Weiland. **(PG)**

85 minutes

LESS THAN ZERO (1987)

★★1/2

Andrew McCarthy
Jami Gertz
Robert Downey, Jr.

Bret Easton Ellis' popular novel about the alienated youth of Beverly Hills has been altered somewhat for the screen, but the book's somber tone and atmosphere of cool decadence remain intact. McCarthy stars as a college freshman who returns home at Christmas to find his friends burned out by an endless stream of parties and cocaine. In the film's best performance, Downey plays a former high-school friend who has been disowned by his family for his drug use and irresponsible behavior. Ironically, despite the plot's antidrug message, the slick style of the film almost glamorizes the shallow, reckless world that these characters inhabit. Also with James Spader and Tony Bill. **Director**—Marek Kanievska. **(R)**

96 minutes

LETHAL WEAPON (1987)

★★★1/2

Mel Gibson
Danny Glover
Gary Busey

Danny Glover and Mel Gibson are hard-hitting cops in Lethal Weapon.

An exhilarating, action-packed police drama about a spaced-out, suicidal detective (Gibson), who is partnered with a cautious, older homicide cop (Glover). The relentless pace plus scene after scene of shoot-outs, explosions, violent confrontations, and brutal torture does much to mask the complicated and unbelievable plot involving high-class drug smugglers. Gibson and Glover create an appealing chemistry despite the opposing natures of their characters, and Busey is menacing as the most ruthless of the smugglers. The excellent editing by Stuart Baird and well-choreographed action hurl the film forward at a lightning pace, accentuating the edge of danger that surrounds Gibson's character while overcoming any flaws in the plot. Also with Darlene Love, Mitchell Ryan, Tom Atkins, and Traci Wolfe. **Director**—Richard Donner. **(R)**

107 minutes

LETHAL WEAPON 2 (1989)

★★1/2

Mel Gibson
Danny Glover

Back in action: Mel Gibson and Danny Glover in Lethal Weapon 2.

This highly popular sequel features even more action sequences than the original. Unfortunately, it glosses over Gibson's over-the-edge character. It posits the death of his wife as the superficial reason for Gibson's behavior, eliminating the Vietnam subplot of the original and discounting burnout as the root of his tense personality. Thus the road is paved for more laughs at the expense of character and drama. Gibson and Glover return as the odd couple who, this time, battle a ring of South African drug smugglers. Their special rapport is entertaining, but trying for superficial laughs on top of violent action scenes is often disturbing. Joe Pesci stands out as an ingratiating federal witness under the care of the two detectives. Also with Derrick O'Connor, Joss Ackland, Darlene Love, and Patsy Kensit. **Director**—Richard Donner. **(R) Academy Award Nomination**—Robert Henderson and Alan Robert Murray, sound effects editing.

111 minutes

LET IT RIDE (1989)

★1/2

Richard Dreyfuss
David Johansen
Teri Garr

Dreyfuss stars as a habitual gambler who risks his marriage to the under-

(Continued)

This movie available on videotape and/or disc.

(Continued)

standing Garr for one more big win at the race track. That is literally all there is to this lightweight comedy, which tries so hard to be zany that it groans. Dreyfuss' career, which had been revived by his roles in *Down and Out in Beverly Hills, Tin Men,* and *Stakeout,* will surely lose ground because of this straight-to-video production. The supporting cast, including Allen Garfield, Jennifer Tilly, Robbie Coltrane, Mary Woronov, and Michelle Phillips, adds some much-needed color but not enough to make the film worthwhile viewing. The movie was filmed mostly at Florida's Hialeah racetrack. **Director**—Joe Pytka. **(PG-13)** *90 minutes*

LET'S DO IT AGAIN (1975)

★★★

Sidney Poitier
Bill Cosby

Two lodge brothers—Poitier and Cosby—raise money for a new temple by fixing a prizefight and pulling a scam on the mob. This entertaining comedy is a follow-up to the less successful *Uptown Saturday Night,* and in terms of narrative is reminiscent of *The Sting.* Cosby is a howl, and Poitier makes an effective straight man. The two later teamed up for *A Piece of the Action.* A fine supporting cast includes Calvin Lockhart, Jimmie Walker, Ossie Davis, and Denise Nicholas. **Director**—Poitier. **(PG)** *112 minutes*

LET'S SCARE JESSICA TO DEATH (1971)

Zohra Lampert
Barton Heyman

Routine horror tale about a woman who recuperates from a nervous breakdown in an old country home where she hears strange sounds and sees creepy visions. There's enough here to generate a few screams, but nothing remarkable. Also with Kevin O'Connor and Mari-Claire Costello. **Director**—John Hancock. **(PG)** *89 minutes*

THE LETTER (1940)

★★★★

Bette Davis
Herbert Marshall

Gale Sondergaard and Bette Davis in the tense drama The Letter.

Davis stars in one of the most critically acclaimed roles of her career as a woman who kills her lover when he threatens to leave her. Based on a Somerset Maugham story, the film is set in Malaya, where the white ruling class maintains control of the social system by covering up for each other. Tension mounts when Davis is set free by reason of self-defense. Davis' portrayal of a passionate woman who represses her desires because of her social standing, and William Wyler's tight, well-paced direction make this melodrama a classic. Also with James Stephenson, Sen Yung, Frieda Inescort, and Gale Sondergaard. **Academy Award Nominations**—best picture; Wyler, best director; Davis, best actress; Stephenson, best supporting actor; Gaetano Gaudio, cinematography. *95 minutes b&w*

LETTER FROM AN UNKNOWN WOMAN (1948)

★★★★

Joan Fontaine
Louis Jourdan

A superior tearjerker about a woman madly in love with a suave, callow pianist, who doesn't sincerely return her affection. The film features stunning production values and is set in 19th-century Vienna. The setting greatly enhances the predictable material. Fontaine plays the woman, and Jourdan is the dashing musician. Also with Mady Christians, Art Smith, and Marcel Journet. **Director**—Max Ophuls. *89 minutes b&w*

LETTER TO BREZHNEV (1986)

★★★★

Alexandra Pigg
Margi Clark
Peter Firth

A masterful comedy/romance, set in the slums of grimy Liverpool, about a love affair that blossoms in one night between a Russian sailor (Firth) and a lonely working-class girl (Pigg). When Pigg decides to join her Russian beau in his homeland, only her best friend (Clark) supports her decision. Frank Clarke's script, which is rich in sentiment without being maudlin, beautifully captures the friendship between the two women, who come from the same environment but are so different. Also with Alfred Molina. **Director**—Chris Bernard. **(R)** *94 minutes*

A LETTER TO THREE WIVES (1949)

★★★1/2

Jeanne Crain
Ann Sothern
Linda Darnell

Linda Darnell, Ann Sothern, and Jeanne Crain read A Letter to Three Wives.

Three women receive a letter from a mutual acquaintance that says she has run off with one of their husbands, but doesn't reveal which one. The wives react by reexamining their marriages in a series of flashbacks. There are several ironic revelations, which account for much of the dramatic conflict. Also with Kirk Douglas and Paul Douglas. A superior achievement from writer/director Joseph L. Mankiewicz. **Academy Awards**—Mankiewicz, best director and screenplay. **Nomination**—best picture. *102 minutes b&w*

LEVIATHAN (1989)

★★1/2

Peter Weller
Richard Crenna

Another slimy creature adventure that follows in the footsteps of *Alien* and

® *This movie available with closed captions for the hearing impaired.*

Deepstar Six. Crewmembers of an underwater mining operation stumble upon a failed genetic experiment, setting loose a menacing mutant monster. The pace is brisk and the cast, with Weller as the dauntless captain and Crenna as the doctor with a clouded past, tries hard. Unfortunately, the story is too familiar. Also with Amanda Pays, Daniel Stern, Ernie Hudson, Hector Elizondo, and Lisa Eilbacher. **Director**—George Pan Cosmatos. **(R)** *130 minutes*

LIANNA (1983)

★★★

Linda Griffiths
Jon DeVries

Writer/director John Sayles presents a sensitive tale of a young wife who falls in love with another woman when her marriage to an arrogant college professor collapses. The film is an intelligent treatment of family emotions, and Griffiths is convincing in the title role. DeVries is also good as the insensitive husband. The film was made independently of the Hollywood system, and its low-key style is less slick-looking than most Hollywood productions. **(R)** *110 minutes*

LICENSE TO DRIVE (1988)

★½

Corey Haim
Corey Feldman
Carol Kane

Corey Haim, Heather Graham, and Corey Feldman in License to Drive.

A shallow comedy/adventure about a teenage boy (Haim) who longs for the freedom, power, and excitement of driving a car. A situation involving the youngster's license examination is hilarious, though most of the plot is predictable adolescent fare. A too-casual attitude in the film toward drinking and driving may upset some viewers. **Director**—Greg Beeman. **(PG-13)** *90 minutes*

LICENCE TO KILL (1989)

★★★

Timothy Dalton
Robert Davi

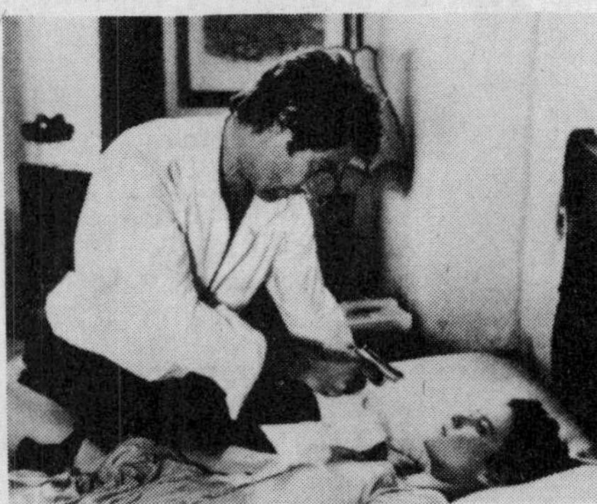

Does Timothy Dalton have a License to Kill *Carey Lowell?*

This 16th James Bond adventure continues the series with all of the conventions intact—the slick action, hearty villains, beautiful women, and a suave 007, played by Dalton. In this adventure, Dalton portrays Bond with a moody demeanor as he seeks revenge against a Central American drug king, played by Davi. The approach is a welcome change after the years of cartoonish behavior by predecessor Roger Moore. Director John Glen, who has filmed a number of Bond adventures, quickens the pace here and dispenses with the science-fiction hardware that marred the series in recent years. The weakest elements in this episode are the leading female characters, played by Carey Lowell and Talisa Soto: Neither is a strong enough actress to make her role memorable. The Bond series remains the champagne of spy thrillers. Also with Wayne Newton, Frank McRae, Everett McGill, Desmond Llewlyn, David Hedison, and Anthony Zerbe. **(PG-13)** *135 minutes*

LIES MY FATHER TOLD ME (1975)

★★★

Yossi Yadin
Len Birman
Jeffrey Lynas

A warm, colorful story about the close relationship between a six-year-old Jewish boy and his grandfather, a junk dealer, in Montreal during the 1920s. The boy's father is an unsuccessful inventor who constantly seeks financial help from the deeply religious grandfather. There's sensitive direction by Jan Kadar and appealing performances from Lynas, Birman, and Yadin. Also with Marilyn Lightstone. **(PG) Academy Award Nomination**—Ted Allan, best original screenplay. *102 minutes*

THE LIFE AND TIMES OF GRIZZLY ADAMS (1976)

★★

Dan Haggerty

This is the story of James Adams, a 19th-century trapper and mountaineer exiled in the wilderness, who befriended the animals, including a big bear. Disney-type sentimentality abounds, but it's hardly a believable tale. A bearded Haggerty makes an impressive denizen of the forest. Filmed in Utah's Wasatch Mountains, this was the basis for a television series. Also with Don Shanks, Lisa Jones, and Marjorie Harper. **Director**—Richard Friedenberg. **(G)** *93 minutes*

LIFE AT THE TOP (1965)

★★

Laurence Harvey
Jean Simmons

This sequel to the well-made *Room at the Top* is routine and predictable at best, although there are a few worthwhile scenes. The story continues ten years later, with Joe Lampton, played by Harvey, married to the daughter of his boss. He's financially secure, but restless and unhappy, and involved in an affair. Harvey's performance is adequate, and he gets worthy support from Simmons as his unhappy wife. Also with Honor Blackman, Michael Craig, Margaret Johnston, Donald Wolfit, and Robert Morley. **Director**—Ted Kotcheff. *117 minutes b&w*

LIFEBOAT (1944)

★★★

Tallulah Bankhead
Walter Slezak

Searing drama about survivors of a passenger ship sunk by a German submarine during World War II. A group of

(Continued)

(Continued)

passengers, including the commander of the attacking U-boat, are adrift together at sea and lay their emotions bare. Director Alfred Hitchcock handles the confined and stressful situation with amazing skill, and extracts excellent performances from an interesting cast. Bankhead is outstanding as a wealthy journalist, and Slezak is convincing as the Nazi skipper. Jo Swerling and novelist John Steinbeck collaborated on the script. Also with Henry Hull, John Hodiak, Canada Lee, Hume Cronyn, Heather Angel, Mary Anderson, and William Bendix. **Academy Award Nominations**—Hitchcock, best director; John Steinbeck, original story; Glen MacWilliams, cinematography.

96 minutes b&w

LIFEFORCE (1985)

Steve Railsback
Peter Firth

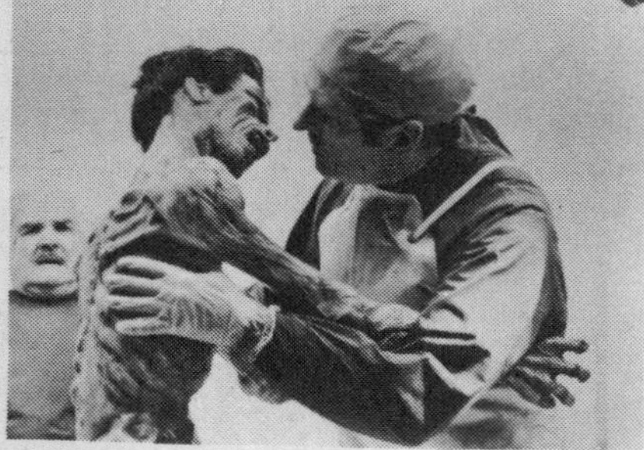

This extraterrestrial creature will drain the Lifeforce *from the unsuspecting doctor.*

A noisy, hyped-up sci-fi fantasy about extraterrestrial vampires who cause havoc among the earth's population with life-draining kisses of death. Director Tobe Hooper (*Poltergeist*) crams the film with various shrill and glitzy special effects that overwhelm the film and produce minimal results. The foolish dialogue provokes unintentional laughter in many scenes. Also with Mathilda May and Frank Finlay. **(R)**

100 minutes

LIFEGUARD (1976)

★★½

Sam Elliott
Anne Archer
Kathleen Quinlan

This is a rather somber sociological study of an aging southern California beach boy who exists as a perennial adolescent through his job as a lifeguard. Ron Koslow's lucid screenplay adroitly explores a series of personal conflicts, but without sufficient passion or energy. Elliott does well in the title role. Also with Stephen Young, Steve Burns, and Parker Stevenson. **Director**—Daniel Petrie. **(PG)**

96 minutes

THE LIFE OF BRIAN (1979)

Graham Chapman
John Cleese
Terry Gilliam
Eric Idle
Terry Jones
Michael Palin

England's most notorious comic troupe, Monty Python's Flying Circus, parodies the story of Christ in this outrageous and hilarious comedy that stops at nothing in taking apart various biblical legends. Chapman plays Brian of Nazareth, a ne'er-do-well Judean, who is reluctantly chosen as the messiah. Many routines are masterpieces of satire and burlesque. **Director**—Jones. **(R)**

93 minutes

THE LIFE OF EMILE ZOLA (1937)

Paul Muni
Joseph Schildkraut

Paul Muni as the famed French writer in The Life of Emile Zola.

Honest and dignified biography of 19th-century French writer Emile Zola, who sprang to the defense of Captain Alfred Dreyfus, a Jewish officer wrongly accused of treason. The lavish production is painstakingly faithful to the facts but, as with many of Hollywood's prestigious efforts, it is a bit too impressed with itself. The acting is notable, especially Muni as Zola and Schildkraut as the wrongly accused Dreyfus. The solid cast also includes Gale Sondergaard, Donald Crisp, Dickie Moore, and Louis Calhern. **Director**—William Dieterle. **Academy Awards**—best picture; Schildkraut, best supporting actor; Heinz Herald, Geza Herczeg, and Norman Reilly Raine, screenplay. **Nominations**—Dieterle, best director; Muni, best actor.

116 minutes b&w

LIFE WITH FATHER (1947)

★★★½

William Powell
Irene Dunne

Charming and handsomely mounted screen version of the hit Broadway play about a turn-of-the-century New York family under the influence of an eccentric patriarch. Powell is outstanding as the irascible head of the family, and Dunne does well as his long-suffering wife. The film is based on Clarence Day's book and the Lindsay and Crouse stage production. Others in the cast include Edmund Gwenn, Zasu Pitts, Martin Milner, Jimmy London, and Elizabeth Taylor. **Director**—Michael Curtiz. **Academy Award Nominations**—Powell, best actor; Peverell Marley and William V. Skall, cinematography.

118 minutes

THE LIGHTHORSEMEN (1988)

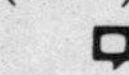

John Walton
Tim McKenzie

Cannon to the right of them, cannon to the left of them, as 800 mounted Australian troops bear down on a German desert stronghold during World War I. This spectacular charge of the light brigade is the climactic highlight of an otherwise pedestrian war adventure, which involves the familiar experiences of some rugged but good-natured soldiers. The well-crafted film features some spectacularly beautiful scenes of horses in motion, but is otherwise sluggish and uncompelling. Also with Peter Phelps. **Director**—Simon Wincer. **(PG)**

115 minutes

® *This movie available with closed captions for the hearing impaired.*

LIGHT OF DAY (1987)

★★1/2

Michael J. Fox
Joan Jett
Gena Rowlands

Fox, costar of television's *Family Ties*, and real-life rock 'n' roll singer Jett are the drawing cards in this fierce family drama set in a blue-collar neighborhood of Cleveland. Fox stars as a young man who works in a factory by day and plays music by night in his sister's rock band, while she feuds with their devoutly religious mother (Rowlands). Jett, in her film debut, is excellent as Fox's rebellious and talented sister. The attempt at gritty but sensitive realism frequently lapses into clichés, but the two charismatic young stars bring life to both their dramatic and musical scenes. Bruce Springsteen wrote the title song especially for the film. Also with Michael McKean and Jason Miller. **Director**—Paul Schrader. **(PG–13)** *107 minutes*

THE LIGHTSHIP (1986)

★★

Robert Duvall
Klaus Maria Brandauer

Duvall stars as the cunning, foppish leader of a trio of criminals who overtake a lightship navigated by Brandauer. Duvall and Brandauer then engage in a tense battle of wits aboard the stationary vessel. This psychological thriller bears a vague resemblance to *Key Largo*, but John Huston's 1948 melodrama is more accessible and suspenseful. The expert peformances of the two leads propel this minor effort directed by Jerzy Skolimowski, whose film *Moonlighting* (with Jeremy Irons) won critical acclaim. **(PG–13)** *90 minutes*

LIKE FATHER, LIKE SON (1987)

★★

Dudley Moore
Kirk Cameron

A prominent surgeon and his teenage son accidentally swallow a serum that temporarily traps the mind of the father in the body of the son and vice versa. The plot is reminiscent of an old Disney comedy called *Freaky Friday*, but, ironically enough, this stale retread actually set off a number of films with similar storylines in the late 1980s. Moore's attempts to portray a teenager are insulting, while TV heartthrob Cameron hasn't the range to play a mature adult. Strictly for younger audiences. **Director**—Rod Daniel. **(PG–13)** *97 minutes*

Kirk Cameron and Dudley Moore live each other's lives in Like Father, Like Son.

LI'L ABNER (1959)

★★★

Peter Palmer
Leslie Parrish
Stubby Kaye

Al Capp's wonderful cartoon characters come to life on the screen with plenty of energy and color. Based on the Broadway musical, the comedy is strictly corn pone, but the music and dance numbers are done with extraordinary vigor. Palmer is well suited to the title role, Parrish is fetching as Daisy Mae, and Kaye is charming as Marryin' Sam. Other denizens of Dogpatch include Howard St. John, Julie Newmar, Stella Stevens, Robert Strauss, and Billie Hayes. **Director**—Melvin Frank. *113 minutes*

LILIES OF THE FIELD (1963)

★★★★

Sidney Poitier
Lilia Skala

Charming, sentimental drama starring Poitier as a jack-of-all-trades who helps a group of German nuns, led by Skala, build a chapel in New Mexico. The film is done on a small scale, but offers much human insight and an Academy Award-winning performance by Poitier. Ralph Nelson's direction is nicely paced. Also with Lisa Mann, Isa Crino, and Stanley Adams. **Academy Award**—Poitier, best actor. **Nominations**—best picture; Skala, best supporting actress; James Poe, best screenplay based on material from another medium; Ernest Haller, cinematography. *94 minutes b&w*

LIMELIGHT (1952)

★★★★

Charles Chaplin
Claire Bloom

The wonderful directorial and acting skills of Chaplin are in full evidence in this touching love story set in London. Chaplin is charming and sentimental as a broken-down music-hall clown who prevents the suicide of a ballerina, played by Bloom. There are many tender and compassionate scenes as only Chaplin could envision them. Bloom's brilliant performance complements the heartwarming production. Buster Keaton appears in a small role as a fellow entertainer who performs onstage with Chaplin's character in a brief scene, marking the first and only time the two great comedians worked together. The film won a belated Oscar for best original dramatic score (composed by Chaplin, Raymond Rasch, and Larry Russell) in 1972 upon its rerelease. Sydney Chaplin and Nigel Bruce also star. *144 minutes b&w*

THE LION IN WINTER (1968)

★★★★

Katharine Hepburn
Peter O'Toole

Fantastic acting by O'Toole and Hepburn adorns this splendid drama set in medieval England. O'Toole is a magnificent Henry II, and Hepburn is tremendous as Eleanor of Aquitaine. They square off on Christmas Eve as the fate of the throne is debated. There are some dry moments, but many high-powered scenes dominate the film. Also with Jane Merrow, John Castle, and Anthony Hopkins. **Director**—Anthony Harvey. **(PG) Academy Awards**—Hepburn, best actress; James Goldman, best screenplay based on material from another medium. **Nominations**—best picture; Harvey, best director; O'Toole, best actor. *134 minutes*

A LION IS IN THE STREETS (1953)

★★★

James Cagney

Cagney gives a striking portrayal of a power-hungry politician with humble roots in this intense drama, which is similar to *All the King's Men*. The plot

(Continued)

This movie available on videotape and/or disc.

(Continued)

goes astray now and then, but there's enough energy in the production to sustain interest. It's a striking portrait of ambition and corruption featuring Cagney in one of his best roles. Also with Barbara Hale, Anne Francis, Warner Anderson, Jeanne Cagney, and Lon Chaney, Jr. **Director**—Raoul Walsh.

88 minutes

LION OF THE DESERT (1981)

★★★

Anthony Quinn
Oliver Reed

Quinn plays a wise and majestic Bedouin warrior who wages a relentless and effective guerrilla campaign against the Italian occupiers of Libya from 1912 to 1931. Reportedly costing more than $30 million, the film is of epic proportions, with sweeping battle scenes of the determined Bedouins at times humiliating the well-equipped Fascist troops. A thread of propaganda runs through the spectacle, but this doesn't detract from its superb vigor and style. Rod Steiger appears as Benito Mussolini. Also with John Gielgud, Irene Papas, Raf Vallone, and Gastone Moschin. **Director**—Moustapha Akkad. **(PG)**

160 minutes

LIPSTICK (1976)

★

Margaux Hemingway
Chris Sarandon

Margaux Hemingway is an unwilling victim in Lipstick.

This disappointing film about rape undercut the acting career of Margaux Hemingway before it began. A beautiful photographer's model, played by Margaux, is raped by a shy music teacher. After the rapist goes free and attacks her younger sister, she arms herself with a rifle and seeks revenge. Mariel Hemingway, Margaux's then 14-year-old sister, also plays her sister in the film, and delivers a surprisingly impressive performance. Also with Anne Bancroft, Perry King, and Robin Gammell. **Director**—Lamont Johnson. **(R)**

89 minutes

LIQUID SKY (1983)

★★½

Anne Carlisle

An oddball, stylishly photographed sci-fi tragicomedy that should find a comfortable following on the midnight-movie circuit. The somewhat absurd storyline concerns aliens who visit Manhattan in search of drugs. They murder by remote control while their victims are having sex and extract drugs from their bodies. Soviet emigré Slava Tsukerman directed this curiosity, which delves surrealistically into the new-wave drug/rock scene. With Paula Sheppard. **(R)** *112 minutes*

LISTEN TO ME (1989)

★★

Kirk Cameron
Jamie Gertz
Roy Scheider

Kirk Cameron watches as Monica Tomanski "eats her words" in Listen to Me.

Cameron and Gertz star as two college students who are members of debating teams. The story attempts to present debate competition as a high-minded activity that stirs up as much enthusiasm as the homecoming football game. Instead, the melodrama betrays its intellectual pretensions, coming off as shallow and manipulative instead—especially when it addresses the issue of abortion. Scheider plays the Knute Rockne of debate coaching. Cameron's on-again, off-again Oklahoma accent seriously undermines his character's credibility. **Director**—Douglas Day Stewart. **(PG-13)** *107 minutes*

THE LIST OF ADRIAN MESSENGER (1963)

★★★

George C. Scott

Director John Huston directs this mystery thriller about an intelligence officer out to capture a murderer. Scott is well cast as the officer tracking a killer who appears in several clever disguises; it's a who-is-it rather than a who-done-it gimmick. Four "mystery" guest stars—Robert Mitchum, Frank Sinatra, Burt Lancaster, and Tony Curtis—also appear heavily made up and costumed. It's good fun guessing which character which actor is, and the murder plot itself is solidly constructed. The star-studded cast also includes Kirk Douglas, Dana Wynter, Clive Brook, Herbert Marshall, and Gladys Cooper.

98 minutes b&w

LISZTOMANIA (1975)

★★

Roger Daltrey

Ken Russell wrote and directed this glittering and noisy movie, which portrays Franz Liszt and Richard Wagner as the pop stars of their time. At first, it's amusing, but quickly becomes overblown and garish. Daltrey, who starred in *Tommy,* plays Liszt. Ringo Starr portrays the Pope. Also with Sara Kestelman, Paul Nicholas, Fiona Lewis, and John Justin. **(R)** *105 minutes*

LITTLE BIG MAN (1970)

★★★★

Dustin Hoffman

Episodic western tale seen through the experiences of 121-year-old Jack Crabb (Hoffman), the sole survivor of Custer's Last Stand. The compelling film, based on the novel by Thomas Berger, offers a grand tour of a portion of American history with liberal doses of satire and pathos. Made during the Vietnam War, this is a milestone film because it subtly criticizes America's imperialist policies by using this country's treatment of the American Indian as a metaphor for aggressive action in Vietnam. The film is

® *This movie available with closed captions for the hearing impaired.*

told from the Indians' point of view. The complex story climaxes with Custer's defeat at the Little Bighorn. Also stars Martin Balsam, Faye Dunaway, Chief Dan George, and Richard Mulligan. Directed with extraordinary skill by Arthur Penn. Dick Smith's makeup for Hoffman as the 121-year-old Crabb is outstanding. **(PG) Academy Award Nomination**—George, best supporting actor. *157 minutes*

LITTLE CAESAR (1930)

★★★★

Edward G. Robinson

Edward G. Robinson is the amoral Enrico Bandello, better known as Little Caesar.

More than 50 years later, this classic gangster movie is still fascinating. Robinson is magnificent as Enrico Bandello, the ruthless killer who takes over a gang of criminals and then is gunned down by the cops. The pace is fast, the story is exciting, and it even features a special style of sly humor. A young-looking Robinson did such a convincing job with the role that he became identified with the character throughout his career. The film, based on a novel by W.R. Burnett, is a prototype for the gangster genre. Also with Douglas Fairbanks, Jr., Glenda Farrell, William Collier, Jr., Stanley Fields, and Sidney Blackmer. **Director**—Mervyn LeRoy. **Academy Award Nomination**—Francis Faragoh and Robert N. Lee, adaptation. *77 minutes b&w*

LITTLE DARLINGS (1980)

★★

Kristy McNichol
Tatum O'Neal
Matt Dillon

In this disappointing movie, teenagers McNichol and O'Neal race to see which one will be the first to lose her virginity. The youngsters are appealing, and they are certainly better than the simple-minded script. Despite the sexual titillation and exploitation, the ending is socially redeeming; yet the film leaves a bad aftertaste. Also with Kris Erickson and Armand Assante. **Director**—Ronald Maxwell. **(R)** *92 minutes*

LITTLE DORRIT (1988)

★★★

Sarah Pickering
Alec Guinness
Derek Jacobi
Cyril Cusack

Sarah Pickering and Derek Jacobi in the Dickens classic Little Dorrit.

Elegant film adaptation of the Charles Dickens classic. Set in Victorian England, the drama centers on a young girl who leaves debtor's prison for a life of luxury. The full-bodied story touches on the wide range of mean-spirited, unusual, and amusing characters typical of Dickens' satire: callous businessmen, inept politicians, pampered social climbers, and various money-grubbers. The picture is six hours long, but director Christine Edzard makes it consistently earnest and poignant. First-rate acting is offered by an all-pro cast, with Pickering in the title role. This slow-moving adaptation is not for everyone's taste. **(G) Academy Award Nominations**—Guinness, best supporting actor; Edzard, best screenplay adaptation. *360 minutes*

THE LITTLE DRUMMER GIRL (1984)

★★

Diane Keaton

Overly complicated, implausible film adaptation of John Le Carré's best-selling spy yarn that is itself rather complex. Keaton, as an actress recruited by Israeli agents to trap a Palestinian terrorist, is lost in the convoluted shuffle. There's little room to develop sympathetic, fleshed-out characters in this lavish, overplotted story that marches out of step. Yorgo Voyagis and Klaus Kinski costar. **Director**—George Roy Hill. **(R)** *130 minutes*

THE LITTLE FOXES (1941)

★★★★

Bette Davis
Herbert Marshall
Teresa Wright

High drama with sharp characterizations about a greedy southern family involved in corrupt business schemes. Davis is excellent as the formidable head of the clan. The film is expertly adapted from Lillian Hellman's play about the passing of an era, when 19th-century landowners and robber barons were faced with the perplexities of the 20th century. Other fine performances by Marshall, Wright, Dan Duryea, Charles Dingle, and Patricia Collinge. **Director**—William Wyler. **Academy Award Nominations**—best picture; Wyler, best director; Davis, best actress; Collinge and Wright, best supporting actress; Hellman, screenplay. *116 minutes b&w*

THE LITTLE GIRL WHO LIVES DOWN THE LANE (1976)

★★★

Jodie Foster
Martin Sheen
Alexis Smith

Foster gives a first-rate performance in this provocative thriller. She plays a composed and independent 13-year-old who dispatches a few nasty adults with aplomb. The script is flawed in part, but the suspense compensates, and there's a poignant relationship between Foster and Scott Jacoby, who supports her endeavors. Also with Mort Shuman. **Director**—Nicolas Gessner. **(PG)** *94 minutes*

This movie available on videotape and/or disc.

THE LITTLE MERMAID (1989)

★★★

The Little Mermaid *longs for love and the life above water.*

A charming and lively animated feature from the Disney studios, which should take its place alongside such classics as *Cinderella* and *Snow White*. Based on a Hans Christian Andersen fairy tale, the story involves a rebellious undersea mermaid who longs for the surface world and her handsome prince. Though Andersen's tale has been reworked Disney-style, thereby losing some of its emotional impact, it provides enough fodder for the Disney storytellers to produce one of their best cartoons in recent years. The best Disney animated features usually include a menacing but campy villain and a series of show-stopping songs that help advance the story. Here the former is in evidence in the form of Ursula the sea witch, while the latter includes the Oscar-winning tune "Under the Sea." With the voices of Jodi Benson, Pat Carroll, Samuel E. Wright, Kenneth Mars, Buddy Hackett, and Rene Auberjonois. **Directors**—John Musker and Ron Clements. **(G) Academy Awards**—Alan Menken and Howard Ashman for "Under the Sea," best song; Menken, original score. **Nomination**—Menken and Ashman for "Kiss the Girl," best song. *82 minutes*

LITTLE MISS MARKER (1934)

★★★

Shirley Temple
Adolphe Menjou

This tear-jerking star vehicle for Temple has enough energy and vigor to make it appealing. The winning combination of young Temple at her sweetest and a Damon Runyon story about a racetrack gambler reformed by the young tyke, who was left with him as collateral for an IOU, made this a hit at the box office. Menjou is ideal as the cynical, fast-talking horseplayer who is won over and ultimately saved by Temple. The colorful cast also includes Dorothy Dell, Charles Bickford, Lynne Overman, Frank McGlynn, and Willie Best. **Director**—Alexander Hall. *80 minutes b&w*

LITTLE MISS MARKER (1980)

★★★

Walter Matthau
Julie Andrews
Tony Curtis

Matthau is excellent as the grumpy gambler Sorrowful Jones in this fourth version of Damon Runyon's sentimental tale. Originally, it starred Shirley Temple. In this film, newcomer Sara Stimson plays the cute kid left in the care of Sorrowful as an IOU (or marker) for a gambling debt. Matthau's special style of sour, cynical humor saves the unlikely story. Andrews plays a once-wealthy socialite, and Curtis is a gangster. Also with Lee Grant, Brian Dennehy, and Bob Newhart. **Director**—Walter Bernstein. **(PG)** *112 minutes*

A LITTLE NIGHT MUSIC (1978)

★★

Elizabeth Taylor
Diana Rigg

This film version of the hit Broadway musical doesn't transfer successfully to the screen. The production looks elegant, but it's uneven, slow, and flat-footed. Even Taylor, somewhat plump and matronly, isn't that effective as the seductive Desiree Armfeldt. Stephen Sondheim's enchanting music and lyrics highlight the film. Also with Len Cariou, Hermione Gingold, and Lesley-Anne Down. **Director**—Harold Prince. **(PG)**

124 minutes

LITTLE NIKITA (1988)

★★½

Sidney Poitier
River Phoenix

Poitier returns to the big screen after a 13-year absence in this espionage thriller, which does not do justice to his talents. Poitier stars as an FBI agent investigating Russian spies. He enlists the aid of a San Diego teenager, played by Phoenix, who traumatically learns his parents work for the KGB. The complex story features a clever premise and an effective cast but suffers from a chaotic

River Phoenix is comforted by Sidney Poitier in Little Nikita.

conclusion with several loose ends. Directed by actor Richard Benjamin. Also with Richard Jenkins, Caroline Kava, Richard Bradford, and Lucy Deakins. **(PG)** *98 minutes*

THE LITTLE PRINCE (1974)

★★

Richard Kiley
Steven Warner

Disappointing musical version of the classic Antoine de St. Exupery children's story about a boy from another planet who visits Earth. Kiley plays the aviator who takes the prince on a tour of our world and introduces him to our ways of living and loving. The musical score by Frederick Loewe and Alan Jay Lerner is a low ebb for these talented composers. The cast tries hard and some good performances are delivered by Gene Wilder and especially Bob Fosse, but the cutesy, pretentious production doesn't work. **Director**—Stanley Donen. **(G)** *89 minutes*

A LITTLE ROMANCE (1979)

★★

Laurence Olivier
Arthur Hill
Sally Kellerman

Director George Roy Hill's comedy of puppy love in Paris is too cute and often trite. Two teenagers, one the son of a taxi driver and the other the daughter of a wealthy American actress, run off to Venice to kiss under the Bridge of Sighs. The kids are played by Thelonious Bernard and Diane Lane. The couple is helped on their romantic esca-

This movie available with closed captions for the hearing impaired.

pade by a softhearted pickpocket, played by Olivier. The kids are winsome while the great Olivier, in a Maurice Chevalier role, hams it up shamelessly. Kellerman and Hill are wasted as Lane's concerned parents. Also with Broderick Crawford. **(PG) Academy Award Nomination**—Allan Burns, best screenplay based on material from another medium.

108 minutes

A LITTLE SEX (1982)

★★

Tim Matheson
Kate Capshaw

Tim Matheson and Kate Capshaw in the comedy A Little Sex.

Matheson stars in this trite, meandering comedy about marital infidelity. There are a few amusing moments as Matheson chases just about every skirt in Manhattan, but the film is primarily talkative sitcom stuff with a predictable ending. The theme of the philanderer is familiar grist for the movie mill and by now it needs a little more originality than it's given here. **Director**—Bruce Paltrow. **(R)** *94 minutes*

THE LITTLE SHOP OF HORRORS (1960)

★★★

Jonathan Haze
Jackie Joseph
Mel Welles
Dick Miller

An eccentric young man who works in a skid-row flower shop develops a talking plant that also has an insatiable appetite for human flesh. After accidentally killing a number of people, the young horticulturalist disposes of the bodies by feeding them to the voracious weed. Things go from bad to worse in this mad, incredibly low-budget horror/comedy, which almost single-handedly inspired the cult that surrounds director Roger Corman. Watch for a young Jack Nicholson as a masochistic undertaker who gets his kicks in a dentist's chair. Corman shot this film in less than a week, but it provides a year's worth of solid laughs.

70 minutes b&w

LITTLE SHOP OF HORRORS (1986)

★★★½

Rick Moranis
Ellen Greene

Rick Moranis has a chat with his plant in Little Shop of Horrors.

A thoroughly enjoyable, fun-filled musical comedy that evolved from an off-Broadway production (1980), which, in turn, was inspired by Roger Corman's infamous low-budget horror film from 1960. The implausible plot involves a shabby flower shop, a boy-girl romance, and a man-eating, jive-talking plant that changes everyone's lives. Moranis and Greene are delightful as the innocent lovers. Some excellent cameos, including Steve Martin as a sadistic dentist, enhance the outrageous antics. Leroy Stubbs of the singing group the Four Tops provides the voice of the plant. Also with Jim Belushi, Bill Murray, and Vincent Gardenia. **Director**—Frank Oz. **(PG–13) Academy Award Nominations**—Alan Menken and Howard Ashman, best original song ("Mean Green Mother from Outer Space"); Lyle Conway, Brian Ferren, and Martin Gutteridge, best visual effects.

90 minutes

THE LITTLEST HORSE THIEVES (1977)

★★★

Alastair Sim
Peter Barkworth

A trio of charming children come to the rescue of pit ponies slated for the glue factory when new machinery is introduced in a small English mining town. The pleasant Walt Disney adventure, set in picturesque Yorkshire, is rather bland, but the story will appeal to children as it adequately depicts their feelings toward animals. The film also makes a modest statement about the working conditions of miners. The children—Andrew Harrison, Benjie Bolgar, and Chloe Franks—handle their parts with sentimental appeal. Also with Maurice Colbourne and Susan Tebbs. **Director**—Charles Jarrott **(G)**

104 minutes

THE LITTLE THIEF (1989)

★★½

Charlotte Gainsbourg
Didier Bezace

François Truffaut began this project before he died in 1984, and it has been taken to a successful conclusion by his producer, Claude Berri, and his faithful assistant, Claude Miller. Gainsbourg gives a sharp and spirited portrayal of a complex, unloved French girl. She becomes a petty thief to gain attention and then falls in with a young male criminal (Simon de la Brosse) who elevates her self-esteem. Echoes of Truffaut's acclaimed *400 Blows* are evident in this astonishing characterization, though Miller's direction is not as capable as Truffaut's. Originally filmed in French. The film was unrated in its initial theatrical release but rated **R** for video. **(No MPAA rating)** *108 minutes*

LITTLE WOMEN (1933)

★★★★

Katharine Hepburn
Joan Bennett
Frances Dee
Jean Parker

Tasteful adaptation of the American classic by Louisa May Alcott about a family's sorrows and joys during the harsh years of the Civil War. The excellent script by Victor Heerman and Sarah Y. Mason evokes sympathy without being mawkish, and the restraint imposed by director George Cukor permits all of the vitality and honesty of the book to shine through without cheap sentimentality. The fine cast also includes Paul Lukas, Spring Byington, Edna May Oliver, Douglass Montgom-

(Continued)

(Continued)
ery, and Henry Stephenson. **Academy Award**—Heerman and Mason, adaptation. **Nominations**—best picture; Cukor, best director. *115 minutes b&w*

LIVE AND LET DIE (1973)

★★★1/2

Roger Moore
Yaphet Kotto
Jane Seymour

Moore stars for the first time as superspy James Bond in this eighth 007 film, with the usual doses of tongue-in-cheek humor, wonderful gadgets, and sexy women. This time, our hero is after a formidable drug dealer, operating out of exotic Caribbean territory. The title song was a hit for Paul McCartney. Also with Clifton James, Bernard Lee, Lois Maxwell, David Hedison, and Geoffrey Holder. **Director**—Guy Hamilton. **(PG)** *121 minutes*

LIVES OF A BENGAL LANCER (1935)

★★★★

Gary Cooper
Franchot Tone

Good sweat-and-leather action drama about men at war in the famed Bengal Lancer division of the colonial British army on the Northwest frontier of India. The skill of director Henry Hathaway is never more evident than in this classic story of loyalty, camaraderie, and trust among soldiers. As a picturesque spectacle, it was considered a superproduction in its time. Tone and Cooper are likable and effective as staunch, fearless soldiers who take protective care of Richard Cromwell as the Commander's naive son. The excellent cast also includes C. Aubrey Smith, Sir Guy Standing, and Monte Blue. **Academy Award**—Clem Beauchamp and Paul Wing, assistant directors (award no longer given). **Nominations**—best picture; Hathaway, best director; Achmed Abdullah, John L. Balderston, Grover Jones, William Slavens McNutt, and Waldemar Young, screenplay. *109 minutes b&w*

THE LIVING DAYLIGHTS (1987)

★★★

Timothy Dalton
Maryam d'Abo
Jeroen Krabbe

The new James Bond: Timothy Dalton in The Living Daylights.

Dalton takes over the role of Ian Fleming's superspy James Bond with the proper mixture of wit and debonair machismo. In this adventure, Agent 007 settles the score with a gang of sinister arms and drug dealers, who are involved with not only the KGB but also a dangerous American renegade. Though this 16th Bond feature packs plenty of exciting high-tech action and globe-trotting excitement, there is something different this time out. Here Bond becomes involved with only one woman, played by d'Abo, adding a romantic dimension often missing from other 007 films. Also with Joe Don Baker, John Rhys-Davies, Art Malik, Desmond Llewelyn, Caroline Bliss, and Robert Brown. **(PG)** *130 minutes*

LOCAL HERO (1983)

★★★★

Peter Riegert
Burt Lancaster

Houston oil men want to buy up a picturesque Scottish fishing village to construct a refinery. Eager young company man Riegert is dispatched to make the deal. The townsfolk are only too willing to sell and pocket all those American dollars. The film provides a great setup for social commentary in addition to detailing the clash of two cultures, at once criticizing and admiring both sides. The movie treads this tricky path with total confidence, pointing up the idiosyncrasies of both cultures with affection and accuracy. There's a wonderful performance from Lancaster as the oil company's head honcho. Bill Forsyth (*Gregory's Girl*) directed this understated, wry comedy with great attention to detail. The supporting cast, including Jenny Seagrove, Fulton MacKay, and Denis Lawson, is a delight. **(PG)** *110 minutes*

LOCK UP (1989)

★★1/2

Sylvester Stallone
Donald Sutherland

Sylvester Stallone is a man searching for justice in Lock Up.

Stallone appears in another vehicle to showcase his image as the tough guy with a heart of gold. In this gritty big-house adventure, he plays a model prisoner doing hard time on trumped-up charges. The guards are sadistic and the mean-spirited warden, overplayed by Sutherland, is vengeful, but Stallone's character gathers his strength and resolve to overcome such brutality. The film concludes according to the formula. Stallone's dialogue is typically minimal, which works in his favor. He accomplishes much with body language. Sadly, the film's direction, which could have added so much to such formulaic material, is merely competent at best. A good supporting cast, including John Amos, Sonny Landham, Tom Sizemore, Frank McRae, Darlanne Fluegel, and Larry Romano, does a great deal with mediocre material. **Director**—John Flynn. **(R)** *106 minutes*

LODZ GHETTO (1989)

★★★1/2

Powerful, heart-wrenching account of the horrors inflicted by the Nazis on a Polish Jewish community during World War II. The chilling documentary makes skillful use of hundreds of photographs taken by victims, as well as some German newsreels. Much of the

This movie available with closed captions for the hearing impaired.

narration is taken from the writings of the doomed inhabitants themselves. Mordechai Rumkowski, the Nazi-appointed ghetto leader, is portrayed as a tragic figure who served as an effective pawn. Voice-overs by Jerzy Kosinski and Theodore Bikel. **Directors**—Kathryn Taverna and Alan Adelson.
(no MPAA rating) *103 minutes*

LOGAN'S RUN (1976)

Michael York
Richard Jordan
Jenny Agutter

A science-fiction adventure set in the 23rd century. In this depiction of the future, people reside in an elaborate, dome-enclosed city and aren't allowed to live past their 30th birthday. Those who try to avoid "renewal" and escape to the outside are chased and killed by special policemen. The elaborate production seems typical of many sci-fi films, with artificial sets that look as if they were borrowed from Disneyland. York gives an unmoving performance as a policeman who realizes that "renewal" is actually extermination, and makes it to the outside world. Also with Roscoe Lee Browne, Farrah Fawcett-Majors, and Peter Ustinov. **Director**—Michael Anderson. **(PG)**
120 minutes

LOLA (1982)

★★★

Barbara Sukowa

This film by the late German director Rainer Werner Fassbinder—one of his last—examines moral corruption against the background of West Germany's amazing period of reconstruction in the 1950s. The film is populated with intriguing characters, expertly portrayed by a fine cast. Sukowa plays Lola, a bewitching cabaret singer with powerful connections in business and politics. Originally filmed in German.
(R) *114 minutes*

LOLITA (1962)

 ★★★

James Mason
Shelley Winters
Sue Lyon

This screen version of Vladimir Nabokov's sensational, intellectually ambitious novel is watered down, but it's still effective. Mason performs well as the professor who's infatuated with a 14-year-old temptress, played by Lyon. To be near her, he marries her mother, played by Winters. The film offers notable moments of satire and drama, and is as fascinating as the book. First-class performances from Winters and Peter Sellers. **Director**—Stanley Kubrick.
152 minutes b&w

THE LONELINESS OF THE LONG DISTANCE RUNNER (1962)

Tom Courtenay
Michael Redgrave

An exceptional story of a delinquent youth in a reform school who attains recognition by competing in track contests. Courtenay stars as the rebellious youth, and Redgrave plays the school headmaster. Magnificent direction by Tony Richardson makes this film one of the best of the starkly realistic, socially conscious films from Britain's "angry young man" generation. The film, which is brilliantly photographed and exquisitely produced, ends with a rousing race sequence. Also with James Fox, Avis Bunnage, and Alec McCowen.
103 minutes b&w

LONELY ARE THE BRAVE (1962)

★★★½

Kirk Douglas

Kirk Douglas is pursued by a modern posse in Lonely Are the Brave.

A melancholy, modern-day western starring Douglas as a middle-aged cowboy who breaks out of jail, hoping to escape to Mexico. He attempts to flee by horseback and is pursued by a posse utilizing modern methods of transportation and contemporary means of communication. The film is an obvious metaphor for the passing of the Old West and the rugged individualism that characterized it, a theme emphasized by David Miller's direction, which juxtaposes images of the Old West with those of the new. Dalton Trumbo's script is poignant and thought-provoking. The supporting cast includes Walter Matthau, Gena Rowlands, Carroll O'Connor, and George Kennedy. *107 minutes b&w*

THE LONELY GUY (1984)

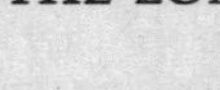

Steve Martin
Charles Grodin

Some free time for Steve Martin and Charles Grodin in Lonely Guy.

An uneven, schmaltzy comedy loosely based on Bruce Jay Friedman's *Lonely Guy's Book of Life*. Martin stars in this thinly plotted tour of the singles scene in New York City. There are a few isolated moments of genuine hilarity, but the viewer most likely will come away lonely for consistent amusement. Judith Ivey costars. **Director**—Arthur Hiller. **(R)** *93 minutes*

THE LONELY LADY (1983)

Pia Zadora

One of Harold Robbins' minor novels is adapted to the screen with minimal results. The predictable, soap-opera story involves a young, energetic writer

(Continued)

(Continued)
(Zadora) who struggles to succeed in Hollywood after marrying a famous screenwriter (Lloyd Bochner), who is old enough to be her father. Singer/actress Zadora stands out among the second-rate cast, and that really isn't saying much. **Director**—Peter Sasdy. **(R)** *92 minutes*

THE LONELY PASSION OF JUDITH HEARNE (1988)

★★1/2

Maggie Smith
Bob Hoskins

Despite the efforts of an ensemble cast of outstanding British actors, this drama based on Brian Moore's novel remains unbearably somber. Smith stars in the title role as a Dublin spinster who yearns to find a man; Hoskins costars as the Irish-American she mistakenly believes wants to marry her. The story hinges on whether either character will see the other for who he or she really is. Such heavy-handed despair is difficult to endure. Also with Wendy Hiller, Marie Kean, Ian McNeice, Alan Devlin, and Rudi Davies. **Director**—Jack Clayton. **(R)** *110 minutes*

LONE WOLF McQUADE (1983)

★★1/2

Chuck Norris
David Carradine

Martial-arts champ Norris is in the title role as a no-nonsense Texas Ranger. Macho action explodes all over the screen, and Norris confronts his enemies with an array of assorted weaponry and becomes involved in the usual quota of karate fights. There's abundant mayhem, while the plot and the acting are treated superfluously. The well-paced direction and competent editing, however, make the film worthwhile viewing. **Director**—Steve Carver. **(PG)** *105 minutes*

LONG DAY'S JOURNEY INTO NIGHT (1962)

★★★★

Ralph Richardson
Katharine Hepburn
Jason Robards

Eugene O'Neill's brilliant, autobiographical play is transferred to the screen with considerable richness, and highlighted by superb acting. The stagy but compelling production is about a Connecticut family in the early 1900s beset with emotional problems. Hepburn is fantastic as a drug-addicted wife, and Richardson is outstanding as her overbearing actor-spouse. Robards repeats his fine stage role as the eldest, alcoholic son. Sidney Lumet directed the critically acclaimed film. Also with Dean Stockwell and Jeanne Barr. Originally released at 174 minutes. **Academy Award Nomination**—Hepburn, best actress. *136 minutes b&w*

THE LONGEST DAY (1962)

★★★

John Wayne
Robert Mitchum
Henry Fonda
Robert Ryan
Rod Steiger

Sprawling, ambitious war saga about the Allied invasion of Normandy during World War II, starring an army of well-known actors. The film is impressive for its grand details of the various events of the D-day landings, but the huge cast is spread around rather thinly, thereby thwarting proper characterizations. Yet the spectacular account offers relentless fascination. The epic proportions, including the CinemaScope photography, will be lost on the small screen. Also among the huge cast are Robert Wagner, Stuart Whitman, Steve Forrest, Fabian, Richard Todd, Richard Burton, Paul Anka, Sean Connery, and Peter Lawford. **Directors**—Andrew Marton, Ken Annakin, and Bernhard Wicki. **Academy Award**—Jean Bourgoin and Walter Wottitz, cinematography. **Nomination**—best picture. *180 minutes b&w*

THE LONGEST YARD (1975)

★★★

Burt Reynolds
Eddie Albert

A prison film where the good guys are the cons and the bad guys are the guards. Reynolds plays a former professional football star who is sent to prison. Albert is the warden who sponsors a semi-pro team composed of the prison's guards. The cons put together a team, quarterbacked by Reynolds, and fight it out with the guards in a ferocious gridiron battle. A suspenseful narrative, plus some hard-edged comedy, highlights the film. Michael Luciano's skillful editing was nominated for an Academy Award. Also with Ed Lauter, Michael Conrad, and James Hampton. **Director**—Robert Aldrich. **(R)** *123 minutes*

Burt Reynolds quarterbacks a football team of jailbirds in The Longest Yard.

THE LONG GOOD FRIDAY (1980)

★★★★

Bob Hoskins
Helen Mirren
Eddie Constantine

A finely crafted British gangster movie not unlike those made in Hollywood. Hoskins is overpowering as a London mob leader struggling to keep his empire intact during a particularly eventful Good Friday. At times the violence is overwhelming, and the British accents can be a problem for American viewers, but sharp acting and energetic direction overcome the drawbacks resulting in a powerful action story. Constantine, famous in Europe as the star of a series of French mystery films during the 1950s, is excellent in a supporting role as a cold American gangster who wishes to cut a deal with the British mob. **Director**—John MacKenzie. **(R)** *114 minutes*

THE LONG GRAY LINE (1955)

★★★

Tyrone Power
Maureen O'Hara

Warmhearted drama about the long career of an athletic trainer at West Point. Power stars as an Irish immigrant who came to the military academy under humble circumstances and stayed on as a trainer for many years. O'Hara plays his wife. Director John Ford contributes a special sentimental touch. Also with Donald Crisp, Ward Bond, Betsy Palmer, Robert Francis, Phil Carey, and Patrick Wayne. *138 minutes*

THE LONG, HOT SUMMER (1958)

Orson Welles
Paul Newman
Joanne Woodward

A moody drama, expertly adapted from William Faulkner's short stories, about a wealthy family in the Deep South. Welles plays a strong-willed father with a determined daughter, played by Woodward. Sparks fly when Newman, a drifter with a bad reputation, comes to town and begins to court her. Director Martin Ritt effectively details a lazy, hazy southern atmosphere, which conflicts with the tense and quick movements of Newman's character. An anticlimactic ending is a disappointment considering the cast and storyline. The excellent cast also includes Anthony Franciosa, Lee Remick, and Angela Lansbury. *118 minutes*

LONG JOHN SILVER (1953)

★★★

Robert Newton

Entertaining continuation of the *Treasure Island* adventure, with Newton in the title role giving a hammy but lusty portrayal of the gruff buccaneer. In this film, Long John Silver and young Jim Hawkins return to the mysterious island with new clues for another attempt to recover pirates' treasure. Filmed in Australia. Also stars Kit Taylor, Connie Gilchrist, and Grant Taylor. **Director**—Byron Haskin. *109 minutes*

THE LONG RIDERS (1980)

James Keach
Stacy Keach
David Carradine
Keith Carradine
Robert Carradine
Dennis Quaid
Randy Quaid

Walter Hill's stylish interpretation of the Jesse James legend stars Stacy and James Keach as Frank and Jesse James, and features the Carradines as the Younger brothers, and the Quaids as the Miller brothers. Nicholas and Christopher Guest appear as the Fords, the two brothers responsible for shooting Jesse in the back. The clever casting gimmick serves to make the brotherly bonding of the characters in the film more believable. The script depicts the James boys as Robin Hood-type heroes, not unlike other Hollywood versions of the story, but Hill's visual style emphasizes the mythic qualities of the legend through the use of slow-motion photography, deep-focus shots of the "long riders" silently gliding across the western landscape, and such effective imagery as the gang quietly emerging from the mist to confront their enemies. The highly stylized approach also mediates the violence, which is fairly bloody. Pamela Reed is a scene stealer as Cole Younger's (David Carradine) occasional lover, Belle Starr. Ry Cooder's musical score is authentic. Also with Amy Stryker, Harry Carey, Jr., James Whitmore, Jr., and Savannah Smith. **(R)** *100 minutes*

Amy Stryker with Keith Carradine, one of the Younger brothers in The Long Riders.

LONGTIME COMPANION (1990)

Campbell Scott
Bruce Davison

A touching, honest account of the AIDS crisis as experienced by a group of upper-middle-class gay men. An ensemble cast performs well, with Davison remarkable as a wealthy, charming man who witnesses the painful death of his lover, played by Mark Lamos. The episodic story begins with a reference to the 1981 news article about the disease and then progresses through a series of scenes that suggest the gradual development of the epidemic. Though some may find the straightforward style too reminiscent of a television movie of the week, the film is one of only a few to depict gays as three-dimensional characters. Written by Craig Lucas and directed by Norman Rene, who have developed a number of theatrical plays, including Broadway's *Prelude to a Kiss.* Also with Stephen Caffrey, Patrick Cassidy, John Dossett, and Mary-Louise Parker. **(R)** *96 minutes*

THE LONG VOYAGE HOME (1940)

John Wayne

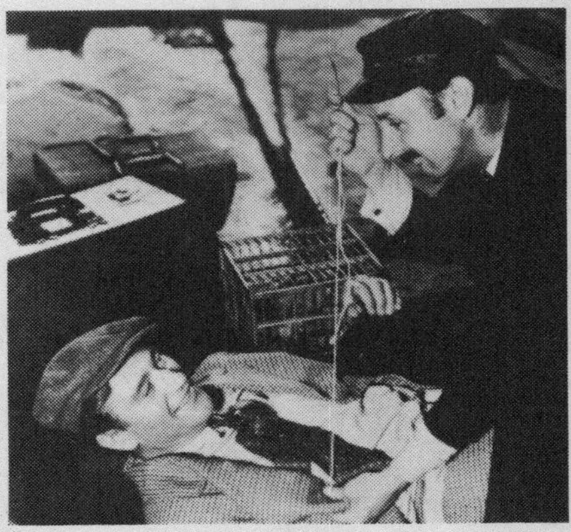

Seafaring friends John Wayne and John Qualen in The Long Voyage Home.

Superb account of the lives and loves of merchant seamen from four one-act plays by Eugene O'Neill. This excellent production boasts Gregg Toland's atmospheric photography of the picturesque docks and the ship's interior, as well as director John Ford's wonderful attention to detail. The acting is first-rate, with Wayne giving one of his better performances. Also with Thomas Mitchell, Ward Bond, Ian Hunter, and Barry Fitzgerald. Scriptwriter Dudley Nichols did a good job of weaving the four separate stories into a cohesive drama. **Academy Award Nominations**—best picture; Nichols, screenplay. *104 minutes b&w*

LOOK BACK IN ANGER (1958)

Richard Burton
Claire Bloom
Mary Ure

Burton gives a powerful performance as a rebellious young working-class merchant angry over his lot in life. He aims his anger at the establishment and takes

(Continued)

(Continued)

his frustrations out on his marriage. This engrossing screen adaptation of John Osborne's realistic play features some smart dialogue and memorable scenes reflecting the concerns of Britain's talented theater and film community in the 1950s. Also with Edith Evans, Gary Raymond, and Donald Pleasence. **Director**—Tony Richardson.

99 minutes b&w

LOOKER (1981)

★

Albert Finney
James Coburn
Susan Dey

This slick mystery/drama about computers, advertising, and murder begins with promise but quickly deteriorates into farfetched nonsense. Finney stars as a Beverly Hills plastic surgeon who traces the murders of some of his women patients to a large corporation that uses strange advertising methods. Writer/director Michael Crichton tosses in numerous absurd sci-fi gimmicks and he never explains the reasons for the murders. **(R)** *94 minutes*

LOOKING FOR MR. GOODBAR (1977)

★★★

Diane Keaton
Richard Gere

Keaton gives an extraordinary, provocative performance in this powerful film version of Judith Rossner's best-selling novel. Keaton, as the girl who teaches deaf children by day and cruises singles bars at night, is sad, funny, vulnerable, sweet, and sexy. Writer/director Richard Brooks reveals both the sordidness and compassion of her life, as the film builds to its shattering climax. Great acting from Gere, Tuesday Weld, and Alan Feinstein. Also with William Atherton, Tom Berenger, Richard Kiley, and LeVar Burton. **(R) Academy Award Nominations—**Weld, best supporting actress; William A. Fraker, cinematography. *135 minutes*

LOOKIN' TO GET OUT (1982)

★★

Jon Voight
Burt Young
Ann-Margret

Contrived, glossy, and sporadically funny buddy story about two small-time New York hustlers (Voight and Young) trying to make a big score in Las Vegas. Voight strains as the brash con artist who bamboozles his way into the posh MGM Grand Hotel as a big spender. Young goes to the other extreme and underplays the faithful sidekick. The film's energy lacks focus and eventually drains away. The filmmakers appear anxious to show off the glitter of MGM's entertainment palace. **Director**—Hal Ashby. **(R)**

104 minutes

LOOK WHO'S TALKING (1989)

★★1/2 ▢®

John Travolta
Kirstie Alley

John Travolta babysits for his little friend in Look Who's Talking.

Alley makes good use of her flair for comedy in this sleeper hit about a young single woman who becomes pregnant. Travolta enjoys his first good role in years as a jovial New York cab driver who falls in love with the unwed mom and her baby. Though a slight film that is unabashedly corny at times, this comedy became a smash hit upon its initial theatrical run. Aside from the timing of its release (after *Batman* and the other much-hyped summer blockbusters of 1989), the film's popularity owes much to its simple but effective gimmick: The baby's thoughts, from fetus to early childhood, can be heard by the viewer as the film progresses. The voice of the baby is provided by Bruce Willis, who is perfect for conveying the baby's hip, smart-alecky banter. Also with Olympia Dukakis, George Segal, Abe Vigoda, and Twink Caplan. **Director**—Amy Heckerling. **(PG-13)**

96 minutes

THE LOONEY LOONEY LOONEY BUGS BUNNY MOVIE (1981)

Animation maestro Friz Freleng presents a wonderful compilation of his best work, which represents some 50 years of cartooning. That "cwazy wabbit" and many of his sidekicks—Yosemite Sam, Daffy Duck, Porky Pig, and so on—are up to their usual high jinks, and the result is nonstop hilarity. About 20 minutes of new material is mixed in with the older stuff, for an enjoyable romp with these lovable and durable characters. **(G)** *80 minutes*

LOOSE CANNONS (1990)

★

Gene Hackman
Dan Aykroyd
Nancy Travis

Dom DeLuise, Dan Aykroyd, and Gene Hackman in Loose Cannons.

Hackman and Aykroyd are mismatched cops in this embarrassing tale directed by Bob Clark, who also brought us *Porky's* and *Rhinestone.* Not surprisingly, the film is filled with mindless violence and condom jokes. Amid the misfired gags and witless action sequences, Hackman and Aykroyd seek to recover a porno film starring Adolf Hitler. They encounter Israeli agents and neo-Nazis along the way. Part of Aykroyd's so-called comic shtick is to imitate pop culture characters such as Tweetie Pie and the Cowardly Lion whenever his character is threatened with violence. It's enough to make you cringe. Definitely a step down for Hackman after his Oscar-nominated performance in *Mississippi Burning*. Also with a familiar cast of character actors, including Dom DeLuise, Ronny Cox, Robert Prosky, and Paul Koslo. **(R)** *94 minutes*

▢® *This movie available with closed captions for the hearing impaired.*

LORD JIM (1965)

 ★★★

Peter O'Toole

Colorful screen version of Joseph Conrad's famous novel about the adventures of a British merchant seaman in the Far East during the late 1800s. The exotic tale, about a man's efforts to atone for an act of cowardice, is helped by lavish location photography in the Orient and some decent acting. The film doesn't achieve the flavor and dramatic power of the book. Also with James Mason, Eli Wallach, Paul Lukas, Jack Hawkins, Daliah Lavi, Akim Tamiroff, and Curt Jurgens. **Director**—Richard Brooks. *154 minutes*

LORD OF THE FLIES (1963)

★★★1/2

James Aubrey
Tom Chapin

Unusual account of a group of English schoolboys stranded on a lonely island after a plane crash. Eventually, they revert to savagery. The compelling film, adapted from William Golding's allegorical novel, has many tense moments. The cast of youngsters also includes Hugh Edwards, Roger Elwin, and Tom Gaman. **Director**—Peter Brook. *90 minutes b&w*

LORD OF THE FLIES (1990)

★★

Balthazar Getty
Chris Furth

Chris Furth, Balthazar Getty, and Danuel Pipoly in Lord of the Flies.

This second version of the William Golding novel about a group of boys who turn into savages when stranded on a deserted island has lost much of the impact of the book. And, it is not a worthy successor to the first film version, which was released in 1963. The production team, including English director Harry Hook, inexplicably turned the principal characters from English schoolboys into cadets from an American military school. In taking away the indirect reference to England's rigid class system, the parable loses much of its power. Hook also opted for untrained unknowns to fill all of the roles, which results in some amateurish acting. With a dark story that cries for visual stylization, Hook chooses to shoot the film in a straightforward style. Thus the production was weakened by bad choices from beginning to end. Getty, who plays the responsible, mature Ralph, is the great-grandson of the famous oil tycoon. Also with Danuel Pipoly, Badgett Dale, and Michael Greene. **(R)** *90 minutes*

LORD OF THE RINGS (1978)

★★

Ralph Bakshi, an innovator of X-rated cartoons, applies his animating skills to the work of J.R.R. Tolkien. The two-hour film is technically impressive, but if you aren't familiar with the ways of Hobbits and Middle Earth, you'll most likely be overwhelmed by the flood of information. Bakshi offers only half a ring from the cult fantasy; the movie ends abruptly without reaching the conclusion of Tolkien's trilogy. The door is left open for a sequel to the saga. **(PG)** *133 minutes*

THE LORDS OF DISCIPLINE (1983)

★★★

David Keith
Robert Prosky
G.D. Spradlin

David Keith is chastised in The Lords of Discipline.

A tense, compelling melodrama set in a southern military academy, where a secret society of cadets resorts to torture in an attempt to rid the institution of its first black student. The film often overdoes its emphasis on brutality, but the story unfolds briskly in the spirit of a slick whodunit. Keith shines as a courageous senior cadet who exposes the school's phoney code of honor. **Director**—Franc Roddam. **(R)** *103 minutes*

THE LORDS OF FLATBUSH (1974)

★★★

Martin Davidson
Perry King
Sylvester Stallone
Henry Winkler

A frisky comedy about tough high-school youths in Brooklyn in the late 1950s. The film is perhaps best remembered for displaying the budding talents of Stallone and Winkler, who play colorful members of a Flatbush gang. The movie is much in the style of *The Blackboard Jungle,* but hardly as serious. A few scenes are real standouts. Also with Paul Mace, Susan Blakely, and Renée Paris. **Directors**—Stephen F. Verona and Martin Davidson. **(PG)** *88 minutes*

LOSIN' IT (1983)

★

Tom Cruise
Jackie Earle Haley
Shelley Long

A mindless adolescent romp about four horny high-school boys who visit Tijuana with mischief in mind. Their itinerary includes a visit to a bordello. The film seems bent on nonstop foolishness, and there's little effort to develop appealing characters. You don't have to strain to figure out what the lads are losing South of the Border. **Director**—Curtis Hanson. **(R)** *104 minutes*

LOST AND FOUND (1979)

★★

George Segal
Glenda Jackson

Jackson and Segal are reunited in this film after their successful 1973 film *A Touch of Class.* But in this lackluster romantic comedy, they lose their touch.

(Continued)

(Continued)
Segal is a tweedy professor in a small-town university, and Jackson is his quarrelsome wife. Both strain at the slapstick routines, and the picture ends up a lost cause. Also with Maureen Stapleton, Hollis McLaren, and Paul Sorvino. **Director**—Melvin Frank. **(PG)**
112 minutes

LOST ANGELS (1989)

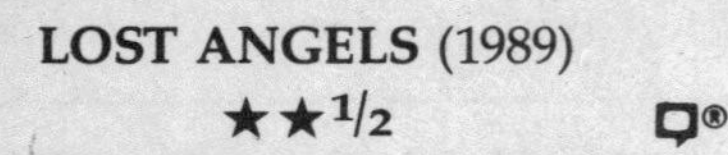
★★½

Adam Horovitz
Donald Sutherland

Donald Sutherland counsels Adam Horovitz in Lost Angels.

Horovitz, of the Beastie Boys rock group, stars as a troubled teen from a well-to-do family who is placed in a private psychiatric hospital. Sutherland plays the caring psychiatrist offering hope and help. The characters are sympathetic, but the film is shallow and unfocused. The drama ends on an upbeat note that doesn't seem honest. Also with Amy Locane, Don Bloomfield, Kevin Tighe, and Park Overall. **Director**—Hugh Hudson. **(R)**
118 minutes

THE LOST BOYS (1987)

★★½

Jason Patric
Corey Haim
Kiefer Sutherland
Dianne Wiest

A brat pack of teenage vampires disguised as a motorcycle gang is on the loose in a California seaside community. When Wiest and her two teenage sons, played by Patric and Haim, move to town, the oldest is lured into the gang by the only female member. The younger boy decides it is his responsibility to save his brother and family from destruction. What could have been an interesting update of the vam-

Keifer Sutherland (center) and his friends are The Lost Boys.

pire legend is here ruined by an anemic screenplay (no pun intended) and an overbearing rock soundtrack. Still, a good cast makes for worthwhile viewing for fans of the horror genre. Sutherland's intense presence is powerfully effective as the leader of the punkish bloodsuckers. **Director**—Joel Schumacher. **(R)** *107 minutes*

THE LOST HONOR OF KATHARINA BLUM (1975)

★★★

Angela Winkler
Dieter Laser

An emotional and compelling German film that focuses on the excesses of modern democracy and views the world in terms of good and evil. A young and reserved waitress takes home a man suspected of radical political activities. For several days, she's harassed and humiliated by the police and a ruthless reporter because of the brief association. There are realistic performances by Winkler as Katharina the waitress and Laser as the unscrupulous newsman. Adapted from a novel by Nobel Prize-winner Heinrich Böll. Written and directed by Volker Schlöndorff and his wife, Margarethe von Trotta. Originally filmed in German. **(R)**
102 minutes

LOST HORIZON (1973)

★

Peter Finch
Liv Ullmann
James Shigeta

Foolhardy remake of the 1937 classic film based on James Hilton's romantic story of paradise found. The beginning adheres to the original movie's narrative about a small group of people who are kidnapped and find themselves in a strange but serene Tibetan mountain civilization. However, the film collapses into nonsense when Shangri-La is reached and some out-of-place song-and-dance numbers are injected. Also with Sally Kellerman, Bobby Van, George Kennedy, Michael York, Olivia Hussey, John Gielgud, and Charles Boyer. **Director**—Charles Jarrott. **(G)**
143 minutes

LOST IN A HAREM (1944)

★★★

Bud Abbott
Lou Costello

Energetic Abbott and Costello high jinks, with Bud and Lou as magicians on tour in the Middle East and involved with a cunning sultan and a beautiful harem girl, played by Marilyn Maxwell. This feature, with the usual doses of slapstick and sight gags, is among the best of their films. Douglass Dumbrille costars as the sultan. Also with John Conte and Jimmy Dorsey and his orchestra. **Director**—Charles Riesner.
89 minutes b&w

LOST IN AMERICA (1985)

★★★½

Albert Brooks
Julie Hagerty

Julie Hagerty and Albert Brooks in the fast lane in Lost in America.

Brooks and Hagerty are a yuppie couple who chuck their executive jobs and hit the road in search of adventure and laughs. They find both. Brooks, who also directed and worked on the script, explores the lost dreams of freedom that the 1960s generation seems to have given up in favor of financial security. Bitingly funny, this film may be too real for some to laugh comfortably. Also with Garry Marshall and Art Frankel. **(R)** *91 minutes*

THE LOST PATROL (1934)

★★★

Victor McLaglen
Boris Karloff

Riveting action drama about a small British military unit under siege by Arab fanatics in the Mesopotamian desert. John Ford deftly handles the mounting suspense as repeated attacks diminish the colorful group of men one by one. The acting seems a bit stilted now but still conveys powerful emotion, with McLaglen starring as the leader of the patrol vainly trying to keep the spirit of his men from collapsing. The cast also includes Wallace Ford, Reginald Denny, J.M. Kerrigan, Billy Bevan, and Alan Hale. Some prints run 65 minutes.

74 minutes b&w

THE LOST WEEKEND (1945)

★★★★

Ray Milland
Jane Wyman

Ray Milland receives support from Jane Wyman in The Lost Weekend.

Stark, powerful drama about a struggling writer, played by Milland, who has become an alcoholic. Milland gives a striking performance, which effectively and sympathetically illuminates his desperate character. Billy Wilder's script (with Charles Brackett) and direction are relentless in providing the details of personal pain, dejection, and terror. Howard Da Silva is exceptional in a supporting role as a bartender. There are other good performances, too, from Wyman, Philip Terry, Doris Dowling, and Frank Faylen. **Academy Awards**—best picture; Wilder, best director; Milland, best actor; Brackett and Wilder, screenplay. **Nomination**—John F. Seitz, cinematography.

101 minutes b&w

LOVE AND BULLETS (1979)

★

Charles Bronson
Rod Steiger
Jill Ireland

Bronson plays a cop on special assignment for the FBI in this limp and predictable adventure yarn. He flies to Switzerland to retrieve a mobster's girlfriend, played by Ireland, whom the FBI hopes will supply incriminating evidence. Steiger plays the gangster. Bronson and Ireland spend considerable time observing picturesque Swiss scenery at the expense of the action and suspense. Also with Strother Martin, Bradford Dillman, and Henry Silva. **Director**—Stuart Rosenberg. **(R)**

103 minutes

LOVE AND DEATH (1975)

★★★

Woody Allen
Diane Keaton

Allen wrote, directed, and starred in this funny but sometimes obscure film about a militant coward in the land of *War and Peace.* He plays a Russian trying to avoid the draft during the Napoleonic War. Keaton plays his cousin Sonja, the girl he worships. Also with Harold Gould, Olga Georges-Picot, Frank Adu, and Alfred Lutter. **(PG)**

82 minutes

LOVE AT FIRST BITE (1979)

★★★

George Hamilton
Susan Saint James

George Hamilton needs to find a new home in Love at First Bite.

Alas, Count Dracula is evicted from his Transylvania castle. So he goes to New York City, where he raids the blood bank and falls in love with a fashion model, played by Saint James. This B-movie romantic comedy, starring Hamilton as the funny and engaging vampire, works most of the time. There are enough clever gags and high spirits to even win a smile from Bela Lugosi. The excellent supporting cast, including Richard Benjamin, Dick Shawn, Isabel Sanford, and Arte Johnson, hams it up with delight. **Director**—Stan Dragoti. **(PG)**

96 minutes

LOVE AT LARGE (1990)

★★1/2

Tom Berenger
Elizabeth Perkins
Anne Archer

Detective Tom Berenger is on the trail in Love at Large.

Thoughts of 1940s hard-boiled detective mysteries come to mind while viewing this moody, tongue-in-cheek comedy/romance. Berenger is well-cast as a gravel-voiced private eye hired to trail a mysterious woman's lover. Of course, not unlike other tales in this genre, unexpected complications turn the simple investigation into a complex moral dilemma for the detective. The film unfolds with a deliciously twisted plot, cockeyed characters, sly liaisons, and a highly artificial style. Don't expect a conventional film with a plot that means something. As directed by Alan Rudolph *(Choose Me; Trouble in Mind; The Moderns)*, the movie's individual scenes and unique characters are commets on film genres and style. Rudolph has once again assembled an offbeat ensemble of actors, which also includes Kate Capshaw, Ted Levine, Annette

(Continued)

(Continued)
O'Toole, Ann Magnuson, and Kevin J. O'Connor. Not for everyone's tastes. **(R)** *97 minutes*

THE LOVE BUG (1969)

★★★

Dean Jones
Michele Lee

A fun-filled Disney romp about a Volkswagen Beetle automobile with a distinct personality and its own ideas of where it wants to go. This heart-warming family comedy is aimed at the kids, yet it offers some well-timed slapstick and clever stunts, mostly set in the streets of San Francisco, for the adults. Several *Love Bug* sequels followed. Also with David Tomlinson, Buddy Hackett, and Joe Flynn. **Director**—Robert Stevenson. **(G)** *107 minutes*

LOVE CHILD (1982)

Amy Madigan
Beau Bridges
MacKenzie Phillips

Convict Amy Madigan wants to keep her unborn baby in Love Child.

Poignant, sympathetic prison film enhanced by a remarkable performance by Madigan in the central role. She gives a believable portrait of a young waif who becomes pregnant by a guard while she's in prison, and then has to fight for her right to keep the child. Prison life is depicted with adequate realism, although it is rather mild in comparison to some prison movies. **Director**—Larry Peerce. **(R)** *96 minutes*

THE LOVED ONE (1965)

★★★

Robert Morse
John Gielgud
Rod Steiger

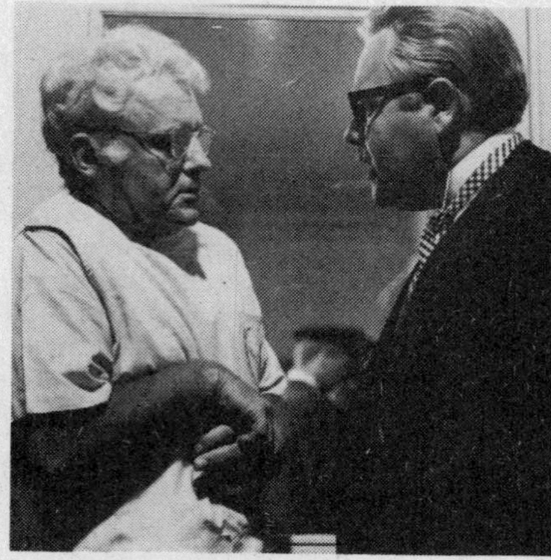

Rod Steiger and Jonathan Winters in the black comedy The Loved One.

An effective satire, based on Evelyn Waugh's novel about the funeral industry in the United States, that is both stylish and offensive. Morse stars as a young Britisher who attends his uncle's funeral in Los Angeles and gets stuck with an outrageous bill for the burial services. The black comedy is handled in a grand manner by a large professional cast that also includes Liberace, Jonathan Winters, Robert Morley, Tab Hunter, Roddy McDowall, Anjanette Comer, Dana Andrews, and Milton Berle. **Director**—Tony Richardson. *116 minutes b&w*

LOVE HAPPY (1949)

★★

The Marx Brothers

A Marx Brothers comic farce about a group of diamond thieves who get mixed up with a starving acting troupe. Harpo takes the lead in this lesser Marx Brothers vehicle, with Chico backing him up and Groucho appearing in only a few scenes. While there is no comparison between this and some of the earlier classics, devoted fans can still find a few gems, including the rooftop chase. The supporting cast includes Eric Blore, Ilona Massey, and Vera-Ellen. Marilyn Monroe appears in a brief scene with Groucho that has since become a classic. **Director**—David Miller. *85 minutes b&w*

LOVE IN THE AFTERNOON (1957)

★★★

Gary Cooper
Audrey Hepburn

This witty romantic comedy set in Paris has some sophisticated dialogue and lively moments, but director Billy Wilder is slightly off track in casting Cooper as the middle-aged American lothario who becomes involved in a May-December romance with Hepburn. She comes off better as the daughter of a private detective trying to warn Cooper of an outraged husband's plan to kill him. Maurice Chevalier is charming as the detective and gets some clever lines from the Wilder/I.A.L. Diamond script. *126 minutes b&w*

LOVE IS A MANY SPLENDORED THING (1955)

★★

Jennifer Jones
William Holden

A tear-drenched soap opera about a Eurasian woman doctor who falls in love with an American correspondent in Hong Kong during the Korean Conflict. Jones is the Eurasian, and Holden is the journalist. The plot is routine, but the film is well acted and produced. The movie is based on the autobiographical book by Han Suyin. The popular theme song gave the film added recognition. Also with Torin Thatcher, Isobel Elsom, Murray Matheson, and Richard Loo. **Director**—Henry King. **Academy Award**—Sammy Fain and Paul Francis Webster, best song ("Love Is a Many Splendored Thing"). **Nominations**—best picture; Jones, best actress; Leon Shamroy, cinematography. *102 minutes*

LOVE LETTERS (1945)

Jennifer Jones
Joseph Cotten

Contrived romantic soaper about an amnesiac whose memory is restored through love. Jones plays the fragile young woman who loses her memory during the war, and Cotten is the amorous letter-writer who disentangles the cobwebs in her mind. Despite the obvious sentimentality, a richness of style

® This movie available with closed captions for the hearing impaired.

raises the film above the banal. All done with moody, atmospheric photography by Lee Garmes and haunting music by Victor Young. A fine supporting cast includes Ann Richards, Gladys Cooper, Anita Louise, Cecil Kellaway, and Reginald Denny. **Director**—William Dieterle. **Academy Award Nomination**—Jones, best actress. *101 minutes b&w*

LOVE LETTERS (1983)

★★★½

Jamie Lee Curtis
James Keach
Amy Madigan
Bud Cort

After discovering evidence of her late mother's extramarital affair, a young woman (Curtis) becomes the mistress of a married man (Keach). The parallelism—and crucial differences—in the stories of mother and daughter are fascinating. A simple story beautifully told, with Curtis outstanding as the woman who desires love at any price. Keach is fine as her very married lover; splendid support from Madigan and Cort. Sensitively directed by Amy Jones. **(R)** *102 minutes*

LOVELY TO LOOK AT (1952)

Howard Keel
Kathryn Grayson

A tepid remake of the musical *Roberta*, set against the background of Paris fashion houses. The storyline is flimsy, but the great Jerome Kern songs, such as "Smoke Gets in Your Eyes," and the lavish settings contribute some entertainment value. Grayson and Keel handle the singing with aplomb, and Marge and Gower Champion display their dancing talents. Ann Miller and Red Skelton round out the cast. **Director**—Mervyn LeRoy. *102 minutes*

LOVE ME OR LEAVE ME (1955)

★★★

Doris Day
James Cagney

Compelling show-biz film biography about 1920s singer Ruth Etting. Day, in the lead role, shows her talent to best advantage. Cagney, however, steals many a scene as her gangster boyfriend who propels her career, but also contributes to her drinking problem. Doris belts out some fine songs of the period, including "Ten Cents a Dance" and the title tune. Also with Cameron Mitchell, Robert Keith, Tom Tully, and Richard Gaines. **Director**—Charles Vidor. **Academy Award**—Daniel Fuchs, motion picture story. **Nomination**—Cagney, best actor. *122 minutes*

James Cagney orders Doris Day to Love Me or Leave Me.

LOVE ME TENDER (1956)

★★

Elvis Presley
Debra Paget
Richard Egan

There's only one reason to see this film: It's Elvis Presley's screen debut. However ordinary this vehicle is, it has an irresistible fascination for that reason. Made at the beginning of Elvis' career, this post-Civil War western centers on a troubled Texas family. A returning soldier (Egan) finds that his younger brother (Elvis) has married his former sweetheart. The sibling rivalry is intensified by a family quarrel over newfound wealth. Elvis sings the title song, and a couple of 19th-century folk ballads. **Director**—Robert D. Webb. *89 minutes b&w*

LOVERBOY (1989)

★½

Patrick Dempsey

Dempsey stars in the title role as a young pizza delivery boy who also provides stud service to frustrated Beverly Hills wives. Our hero becomes exhausted from the overflow of sexual demands. This formula comedy handles the various seduction scenes with too much caution, and the humor turns out bland and obvious. Aside from the lack of believability, the film's flirtation with incest is tasteless. Also with Kate Jackson, Kirstie Alley, Vic Tayback, Barbara Carrera, Carrie Fisher, Rob Camilletti, and Kim Miyori. **Director**—Joan Micklin Silver. **(PG-13)** *98 minutes*

LOVER COME BACK (1961)

★★★

Doris Day
Rock Hudson

Snappy romantic comedy with a clever plot satirizing the advertising game. Day and Hudson, in one of their earliest and best pairings, compete in business while playing the mating game. Will Day get the client or will she lose her virtue? Will Hudson's wily deceptions prove the triumph of Madison Avenue cynicism or will he unwittingly find love? The elaborate but witty story twists and turns until it comes out right. The strong supporting cast is involved with numerous subplots and includes a remarkably funny Tony Randall, Edie Adams, and Jack Oakie. **Director**—Delbert Mann. **Academy Award Nomination**—Stanley Shapiro and Paul Henning, best story and screenplay written directly for the screen. *107 minutes*

LOVERS AND LIARS (1979)

★

Goldie Hawn
Giancarlo Giannini

Hawn teams up with Italy's popular movie star Giannini for this mixed-bag comedy, but the film turns out badly. She's on vacation in Rome; he's married and looking for a fast fling. They're off to Pisa for a few days of romance, but it's an ill match from the start. A shabby script and awkward direction hamper Hawn's attempts at her familiar dizzy humor. Originally released at 126 minutes. **Director**—Mario Monicelli. **(R)** *96 minutes*

LOVERS AND OTHER STRANGERS (1970)

★★★★

Bonnie Bedelia
Michael Brandon
Gig Young
Anne Jackson

A rib-tickling, sophisticated comedy about a young couple who decide to

(Continued)

Anne Meara and Harry Guardino in the comedy Lovers and Other Strangers.

(Continued)
marry after living together while away at college. Bedelia and Brandon play the engaged couple. The setting of a large American wedding provides the basis for some priceless scenes, with many good character actors having a field day with some good lines. Young is memorable as the stalwart father of the bride; Jackson plays a cast-off mistress, and Richard Castellano is good as the father of the bridegroom. Also with Beatrice Arthur, Robert Dishy, Harry Guardino, Cloris Leachman, Anne Meara, and Marion Hailey. **Director**—Cy Howard. **(PG) Academy Award Nominations**—Castellano, best supporting actor; Renée Taylor, Joseph Bologna, and David Zelag Goodman, best screenplay based on material from another medium. *104 minutes*

LOVESICK (1983)

★★

Dudley Moore
Elizabeth McGovern

A watered-down romantic comedy starring Moore as a prominent New York psychiatrist who commits the ultimate no-no—he falls in love with his beautiful patient (McGovern). Writer/director Marshall Brickman's subdued humor pokes fun at the psychiatric profession, but the satire soon becomes tiresome. Moore is okay, and McGovern projects innocent charm, but the stars are given weak material to work with. Alec Guinness and John Huston have supporting roles. **(PG)** *96 minutes*

LOVE STORY (1970)

★★½

Ali MacGraw
Ryan O'Neal

Effective film treatment of Eric Segal's sad tale of two college students. They fall in love and marry, and just when things are looking up, she dies. MacGraw and O'Neal play the star-crossed lovers. Ordinarily, this cliché-strewn film would be just another piece of sentimental Hollywood fluff. But the movie is made with above-average production values and offers some good acting along with the flood of tears. Ray Milland and John Marley have supporting roles. **Director**—Arthur Hiller. **(PG) Academy Award Nominations**—best picture; Hiller, best director; O'Neal, best actor; MacGraw, best actress; Marley, best supporting actor; Segal, best story and screenplay based on factual material or material not previously published. *100 minutes*

LOVE STREAMS (1984)

★★

John Cassavetes
Gena Rowlands

Cassavetes and Rowlands marshal their magnificent acting talents and imaginative skills in portraying eccentric, neurotic persons desperately seeking love and dignity. The film bursts with emotion and poignant character studies, but, alas, this intense psychodrama drags on too long and some scenes seem repetitive. Cassavetes is an unstable, hard-drinking, skirt-chasing writer. Rowlands is just as quirky as his sister with multiple hang-ups. **Director**—Cassavetes. **(PG–13)** *136 minutes*

LOVE WITH THE PROPER STRANGER (1963)

★★★

Steve McQueen
Natalie Wood

Natalie Wood and Steve McQueen in Love with the Proper Stranger.

Finely tuned romantic comedy/drama about an easygoing musician, played by McQueen, who falls in love with a store clerk, played by Wood. A combination of excellent acting and an authentic New York setting makes this film above the ordinary. Edie Adams is memorable in a supporting role, as are Tom Bosley and Herschel Bernardi. **Director**—Robert Mulligan. **Academy Award Nominations**—Wood, best actress; Arnold Schulman, best story and screenplay written directly for the screen; Milton Krasner, cinematography. *100 minutes b&w*

LOVING COUPLES (1980)

★★

Shirley MacLaine
James Coburn

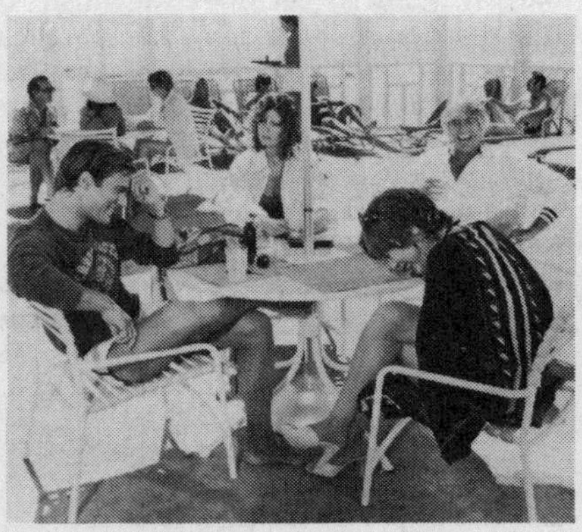

The predictable side of mate-swapping with the Loving Couples.

An overly cute and predictable romantic comedy with MacLaine and Coburn as two doctors married to each other, who take a brief fling at mate-swapping. This theme had appeal in the 1960s with *Bob & Carol & Ted & Alice,* but in light of current moral standards, such escapades seem rather uneventful. Craggy-faced Coburn flashes a lot of teeth, while MacLaine strains to appear ten years younger than she is. The film offers a few mild chuckles; the rest is just banal conversation. **Director**—Jack Smight. **(PG)** *97 minutes*

THE L-SHAPED ROOM (1963)

★★★★

Leslie Caron
Brock Peters

Top romantic drama starring Caron in an outstanding role as a poor and pregnant French girl, living in a sleazy London rooming house. There, she encounters all sorts of interesting characters, including a determined young writer who offers her love and hope. Caron is perfectly cast, and she's backed up with superb supporting performances by Tom Bell, Cicely Courtneidge, Avis Bunnage, and Emlyn Williams. Writer/director Bryan Forbes does a superb job with the material. **Academy Award Nomination**—Caron, best actress. *125 minutes b&w*

LUCAS (1986)

★★★

Corey Haim
Kerri Green

An appealing sleeper about a bright, small-framed, but gutsy 14-year-old who falls for the new girl in town. Initially, the film appears to be just another teen picture, but it is full of charming surprises and memorable moments. The story involves kids in the process of discovering their "center of gravity." And, despite a few unsteady moments, David Seltzer's film finds its own center with impressive results. Well played by Haim (in the title role) and Green. Also with Charlie Sheen. **(PG–13)** *100 minutes*

THE LUCK OF THE IRISH (1948)

★★

Tyrone Power
Cecil Kellaway

A leprechaun comes to the aid of a reporter in Ireland in this slight, whimsical romantic drama. Power stars as the handsome Irish-American newsman who acquires Kellaway as a combination conscience/guardian-angel as he tries to choose between a sweet Irish lass and the boss' daughter. A solid cast including Anne Baxter, Lee J. Cobb, James Todd, Jayne Meadows, J.M. Kerrigan, and Phil Brown contributes to raise the work above its slim story. **Director**—Henry Koster. **Academy Award Nomination**—Kellaway, best supporting actor. *99 minutes b&w*

LUCKY LADY (1975)

★

Liza Minnelli
Gene Hackman
Burt Reynolds

The film cost about $13 million; the script is by Willard Huyck and Gloria Katz, who helped write *American Graffiti;* and the stars are such heavies as Minnelli, Hackman, and Reynolds. With all that going for it, this action comedy still turned out to be a ridiculous, incoherent, and tasteless mess that's hardly funny. The stars are miscast, and all strain too hard with the material. The three play small-time bootleggers who battle rival mobsters and the U.S. Coast Guard while transporting booze from Mexico to California. Also with Michael Hordern and Geoffrey Lewis. **Director**—Stanley Donen. **(PG)** *118 minutes*

LUNA (1979)

★★

Jill Clayburgh
Matthew Barry

Matthew Barry is the troubled teenager in Luna.

Clayburgh is miscast as an American opera star, a widow, who lives in Rome with her disturbed and drug-addicted teenage son, played by Barry. As she tries to console him and relieve his addiction, they develop a morbidly erotic relationship that involves a good deal of emotional and physical involvement. Director Bernardo Bertolucci, who made *Last Tango in Paris,* directs with eloquence, but this long melodrama is unbelievable and absurd. Also with Veronica Lazar, Renato Salvatori, and Fred Gwynne. **(R)** *137 minutes*

LUST FOR LIFE (1956)

★★★

Kirk Douglas
Anthony Quinn

Vivid and colorful screen treatment of Irving Stone's biography about the stormy life of famous artist Vincent Van Gogh. Douglas provides an absorbing portrayal of the master, who encountered much anguish along with his great artistic talent. Quinn excels as Van Gogh's close friend and mentor, artist Paul Gauguin. Many superb Van Gogh masterpieces are displayed. Also stars James Donald, Pamela Brown, Everett Sloane, and Lionel Jeffries. **Director**—Vincente Minnelli. **Academy Award**—Quinn, best supporting actor. **Nominations**—Douglas, best actor; Norman Corwin, best adapted screenplay. *122 minutes*

LUST IN THE DUST (1985)

★

Divine

Limp send-up of western movies, with Divine, the notorious 300-pound transvestite, as the centerpiece of this dreadful mess. The ragtag plot has to do with the search for gold in the desert by various scroungy characters. But the film comes up short in all departments: The stale gags fizzle, there's not enough outrageousness for camp, and the acting is consistently third-rate. Tab Hunter and Lainie Kazan are also in the cast. **Director**—Paul Bartel. **(R)** *85 minutes*

M

MAC AND ME (1988)

★★

Jade Calegory

This shamelessly derivative sci-fi adventure lifts its premise and emotional tone from *E.T.—The Extraterrestrial.* An alien family lands on Earth and a young, impish member of the group befriends a wheelchair-bound lad. Some kids may find this sentimental fantasy amusing, but MAC (mysterious alien creature), despite looking suspiciously like E.T., is no substitute for the original. Also with Katrina Caspary, Lauren Stanley, and Jonathan Ward. **Director**—Stewart Raffill **(PG)** *93 minutes*

MACARONI (1985)

★★

Jack Lemmon
Marcello Mastroianni

A cranky American businessman (Lemmon) returns to Naples after 40 years and rekindles a friendship with an ec-

(Continued)

(Continued)
centric local resident (Mastroianni). Lemmon and Mastroianni ham it up in this sentimental comedy, which doesn't have enough comic situations to raise the film above a trifling level. A contrived ending doesn't help matters. Filmed in Italy by Italian director Ettore Scola. **(PG)** *104 minutes*

MacARTHUR (1977)

★★★

Gregory Peck
Ed Flanders

Gregory Peck plays the title role in the biographical film MacArthur.

Don't expect the snap and spirit of *Patton* here, but this biographical feature is an earnest and interesting account of the egocentric general's career from the beginning of World War II to his dismissal during the Korean Conflict. Peck's portrayal of the great commander is imposing and convincing. Most of the supporting characters seem lost in the background, but Flanders sparkles as President Harry S Truman. Straightforward directing by Joseph Sargent. Also with Dan O'Herlihy, Sandy Kenyon, Dick O'Neill, and Art Fleming. Originally released at 144 minutes. **(PG)** *130 minutes*

THE MACKINTOSH MAN (1973)

★★

Paul Newman
James Mason

Busy, fast-paced spy caper about a British agent, played by Newman, who is assigned to expose a Communist infiltrator. The film offers ample excitement with the usual chases and narrow escapes, but the cold-war plot is déjà vu by now. The performances, however, are generally good, and the production is well done. Mason costars as the double agent, and other supporting roles are played by Dominique Sanda, Nigel Patrick, Harry Andrews, and Ian Bannen. The screenplay is attributed to Walter Hill, later a director of action-packed genre films. Filmed in England, Ireland, and Malta. Some versions of the film run 105 minutes. **Director**—John Huston. **(PG)** *98 minutes*

MACK THE KNIFE (1989)

★★

Raul Julia
Richard Harris
Julie Walters

Raul Julia and Julia Migenes in Mack the Knife, *set in Victorian London.*

A sturdy but unexciting film version of Bertolt Brecht's and Kurt Weill's *The Threepenny Opera.* One of the world's most famous social satires, the musical is set in Victorian London's underworld, which is populated by beggars, murderers, prostitutes, and thieves. Julia reprises the role of cold-hearted thief MacHeath (Mack the Knife), which made him a Broadway star in the 1976 stage production. MacHeath swaggers about his squalid milieu until he is betrayed by the women who love him. Harris and Walters overplay their roles as Mr. and Mrs. Peachum, as does rock singer Roger Daltry in the part of the Street Singer. Though this adaptation may please some opera buffs, the low energy level, hammy acting, and dark period sets weaken the overall production. Also with Julia Migenes, Rachel Robertson, Clive Revill, and Bill Nighy. **Director**—Menahem Golan. **(PG-13)** *120 minutes*

THE MACOMBER AFFAIR (1947)

★★★

Gregory Peck
Joan Bennett
Robert Preston

Taut, well-made safari adventure, based on an Ernest Hemingway story, about the triangle that develops among a husband, his wife, and their guide on a big-game hunting expedition. Peck turns in a superb performance as the guide, as do Preston and Bennett as the couple with marital difficulties. An intelligent script contributes to the impact. Also stars Reginald Denny and Carl Harbord. **Director**—Zoltan Korda. *89 minutes b&w*

MADAME CURIE (1943)

Greer Garson
Walter Pidgeon

A lofty, well-made film biography about the woman scientist who discovered radium. Though slow-paced at times, this intelligent production offers ample historical information about the discovery of this vital element. Garson and Pidgeon, a popular team at the time because of their success the year before in *Mrs. Miniver*, are excellent as the Curies. There's notable support from Henry Travers, Albert Basserman, Robert Walker, C. Aubrey Smith, and Dame May Whitty. **Director**—Mervyn LeRoy. **Academy Award Nominations**—best picture; Pidgeon, best actor; Garson, best actress; Joseph Ruttenberg, cinematography. *124 minutes b&w*

MADAME ROSA (1977)

★★½

Simone Signoret

Signoret plays an aging former prostitute with a big heart who cares for the children of streetwalkers. Signoret offers a vivid characterization of a weary, proud woman grasping at the last threads of life. However, despite her powerful presence, this overlong French drama is muddled and overly sentimental. Also with Claude Dauphin, Samy Ben Youb, and Gabriel Jabbour. Originally filmed in French. **Director**—Moshe Mizrahi. **(PG) Academy Award**—best foreign-language film. *105 minutes*

MADAME SOUSATZKA (1988)

★★½

Shirley MacLaine
Navin Chowdhry

® This movie available with closed captions for the hearing impaired.

Shirley MacLaine plays the demanding piano teacher in Madame Sousatzka.

MacLaine stars as a stern, eccentric piano teacher living in London, who tries to impart her skills and values to a talented teenage prodigy, played by Chowdhry. MacLaine holds the audience's attention with this colorful character, but she has played better roles. The film is meandering, overlong, and tries too hard to be Academy Award material. Also starring Dame Peggy Ashcroft and Twiggy. **Director**—John Schlesinger. **(PG-13)** *122 minutes*

MAD DOG (1976)

Dennis Hopper

Hopper stars in the title role as "Mad Dog" Daniel Morgan, a 19th-century Australian outlaw who terrorized the kangaroo territory and antagonized colonial officials. The film is rife with gore and brutality, including a man choking to death on his own blood after his throat is slit. Ironically, the so-called civilized people who hunt down the pitiful and mentally disturbed Morgan are depicted as being no more moral than their quarry. Directed and written by Philippe Mora, whose efforts at social commentary fall flat. Television prints run 93 minutes. **(R) Alternate Title**—*Mad Dog Morgan.* *102 minutes*

MAD DOGS AND ENGLISHMEN (1971)

Joe Cocker

Interesting documentary of British rock musician Cocker during his American tour in 1970. While the appeal is primarily to rock fans, the film provides some good insights into the social phenomenon of rock concerts and can be enjoyed by everyone. It's a period that easily evokes nostalgia. Cocker performs many good musical numbers including "Let It Be" and "Space Captain" in his own unique style, with a strong assist from Leon Russell and Claudia Linnear. There are also appearances by Rita Coolidge, Chris Stainton, Carl Radle, Bobbie Keys, and John Price. **Director**—Pierre Adidge. **(No MPAA rating)** *119 minutes*

MADE IN HEAVEN (1987)

Kelly McGillis
Timothy Hutton

Kelly McGillis and Timothy Hutton have a love affair that's Made in Heaven.

Hutton falls in love with McGillis in heaven after he dies in a tragic car accident. The romantic pair are separated when, under the rules of heaven, McGillis must go to earth to be reborn as a new spirit. Hutton's only chance of being with her for all eternity is to meet and fall in love with her while they are both on earth. This romantic drama by Alan Rudolph (*Trouble in Mind; Choose Me*) is quirky and charming, much like his other work, though the events of this film are too episodic and loosely constructed to be wholly satisfying. Rudolph's penchant for offbeat casting is evident here as he casts Debra Winger in a small role as a *male* emissary from heaven. Maureen Stapleton, Don Murray, and Tim Daly do well in secondary roles. Appearing in bit parts are Ellen Barkin (in an unbilled performance), writer Tom Robbins, cartoonist Gary Larson, and rock singers Tom Petty, Ric Ocasek, and Neil Young. **(PG)** *102 minutes*

MADHOUSE (1990)

★½

Kirstie Alley
John Larroquette

John Larroquette and Kirstie Alley are not enjoying themselves in Madhouse.

Obnoxious relatives overextend their welcome at the once-peaceful home of an upwardly mobile couple. This comic premise is good for a few inspired laughs, but the film too closely resembles a mediocre TV sitcom—not surprising, since Larroquette and Alley are both stars of the small screen. First-time director Tom Ropelewski seems to be striving for farce with this cartoonish material but succeeds only in getting the most mundane slapstick. Also with John Diehl, Alison La Placa, Jessica Lundy, Bradley Gregg, and Dennis Miller. **(PG-13)** *90 minutes*

MADIGAN (1968)

★★★

Richard Widmark
Henry Fonda

A tough-talking, action-packed police yarn set in New York City. Widmark is well cast as a determined detective who brings in his man at all costs. Other excellent characterizations include Fonda as a hard-nosed police commissioner and Harry Guardino as Widmark's partner. The film offers some realistic details on the workings of a big-city police department. Also stars James Whitmore, Inger Stevens, Michael Dunn, Steve Inhat, Sheree North, and Susan Clark. **Director**—Don Siegel. *100 minutes*

MAD MAX (1980)

★★★

Mel Gibson

Out of an apocalyptic, post-World War III Australian outback roars one of the most violent and action-packed cycle dramas you're ever likely to see. Details of this futuristic vision are sketchy as the film focuses on the ravaging hordes

(Continued)

(Continued)

of degenerates that drive the few remaining cars and burn up the last gallons of gasoline. Good cop Max (Gibson) tries to keep the peace à la Dirty Harry until he goes on a rampage and *really* fights dirty. The film is intense but engaging, and certainly doesn't lack for excitement. Be aware of the poor dubbing. **Director**—George Miller. **(R)** *90 minutes*

MAD MAX BEYOND THUNDERDOME (1985)

★★★

Mel Gibson
Tina Turner

Mel Gibson joins forces briefly with Tina Turner in Mad Max Beyond Thunderdome.

Gibson stars in the title role once again in this third installment of the grim, post-apocalyptic adventure series. This time he's not quite as mad, and the action, as compared to the more exciting second outing, *The Road Warrior*, flags too often. But there's plenty of funky, nasty characters and weird settings on hand to maintain proper atmosphere. This time, Max fights for his life in a strange sports arena, and rescues a group of children trying to survive in the wasteland. **Directors**—George Miller and George Ogilvie. **(PG–13)** *108 minutes*

THE MADWOMAN OF CHAILLOT (1969)

★★

Katharine Hepburn

Much money and talent was squandered in this foolhardy effort to film Jean Giradoux's small-scale play about an oddball Parisian woman and her kooky friends who want to do good. The opulent treatment doesn't fit the material, and the all-star spectacle quickly lapses into tedium. Hepburn is wasted in the title role, as were some other talented actors. Also stars Yul Brynner, Danny Kaye, Edith Evans, Charles Boyer, Claude Dauphin, Paul Henreid, and Richard Chamberlain. **Director**—Bryan Forbes. **(G)** *132 minutes*

MAGIC (1978)

★★

Anthony Hopkins
Ann-Margret
Burgess Meredith

Is it Magic?—Anthony Hopkins as the ventriloquist tormented by his evil dummy.

William Goldman's horror/suspense tale about a ventriloquist controlled by his dummy is reminiscent of the classic 1946 British chiller *Dead of Night*. This screen version of the popular novel, however, never lives up to expectations, despite high-powered performances by Hopkins as the ventriloquist, and Meredith as his agent. Ann-Margret plays Hopkins' old sweetheart. Director Richard Attenborough comes up with a few interludes of eerie suspense, but he doesn't have the magic touch to maintain tension to the end. Also with Ed Lauter and Jerry Houser. **(R)** *106 minutes*

THE MAGIC FLUTE (1974)

★★★★

Ulrik Gold
Josef Kostlinger

Filming an opera is difficult, but the magic of Swedish director Ingmar Bergman has pervaded *The Magic Flute*, the Mozart opera, and the result is a sparkling, funny, and intelligent movie. The film was initially made for Swedish TV at a modest cost of $650,000, yet superb casting, quality camera-work, exceptional sound recording, and Bergman's extraordinary directorial ability have resulted in a triumphant cinematic experience. Originally filmed in Swedish. **(G)** *134 minutes*

THE MAGIC OF LASSIE (1978)

★

James Stewart
Mickey Rooney
Alice Faye

A contrived, sugary film that flagrantly manipulates children's emotions. This lackluster effort has none of the imagination or style of the original *Lassie Come Home* (1943), which starred young Elizabeth Taylor. In this bland movie, Lassie, actually a descendant of the original movie collie, experiences a series of tragic adventures leading up to the eventual happy ending. It's not magic; it's more of a cheap trick. Also with Pernell Roberts, Stephanie Zimbalist, Michael Sharrett, and Mike Mazurki. **Director**—Don Chaffey. **(G)** *100 minutes*

THE MAGNIFICENT AMBERSONS (1942)

★★★★

Joseph Cotten
Dolores Costello
Agnes Moorehead
Tim Holt

Excellent adaptation of the Booth Tarkington novel, directed by Orson Welles at the peak of his creativity. The rich period drama concerns the decline of a wealthy family, and the emotional relationship between the mother and the youngest son. Welles' innovative use of such cinematic devices as deep-focus photography, moving camera, and sharp contrast between light and shadow serves to emphasize the conflicts between the characters, but his visually exciting style was considered inappropriate by the studio. Welles' 148-minute version of the film was re-edited to 88 minutes, and a happy ending, which is incongruous to the rest of the film, was added on. Still, much of Welles' original vision remains to make this film a classic. Good performances are given by Cotten, Costello, Moorehead, Holt, Anne Baxter, and Ray Collins. **Academy Award Nominations**—best picture; Moorehead, best support-

® *This movie available with closed captions for the hearing impaired.*

ing actress; Stanley Cortez, cinematography. *88 minutes b&w*

THE MAGNIFICENT SEVEN (1960)

★★★

Yul Brynner
Steve McQueen

Gunslinger Yul Brynner prepares for action in The Magnificent Seven.

A supercharged western that closely follows the storyline of the Japanese film *The Seven Samurai*. A Mexican village is harassed by bandits, led by a greedy Eli Wallach, and the people hire seven American gunslingers to protect them. There's plenty of shoot-'em-up activity by a good cast. Elmer Bernstein was nominated for an Oscar for his score. Also with Robert Vaughn, James Coburn, Brad Dexter, Charles Bronson, and Horst Buchholz. **Director**—John Sturges. *126 minutes*

THE MAGNIFICENT YANKEE (1950)

Louis Calhern
Ann Harding

Stately and dignified film biography of Supreme Court Justice Oliver Wendell Holmes, from the play by Emmet Lavery. Director John Sturges exercises restraint over the production to present a refined if somewhat somber portrayal of the noted legal giant. Well acted by Calhern in the lead, with Harding as his devoted wife. The film also stars Eduard Franz, Philip Ober, Richard Anderson, and Edith Evanson. **Academy Award Nomination**—Calhern, best actor. *80 minutes b&w*

MAGNUM FORCE (1973)

★★½

Clint Eastwood
Hal Holbrook

More unrestrained gunfire in this diluted sequel to *Dirty Harry*. Tight-lipped Eastwood again stars as Harry Callahan, the invincible homicide cop, but this time he's after some colleagues, led by Holbrook, who do most of the killing as self-appointed executioners of underworld thugs. The violence is more brutal than in the first Dirty Harry film, and the film is directed with much less style. Written by John Milius and Michael Cimino. Also with Mitchell Ryan, David Soul, Tim Matheson, and Felton Perry. **Director**—Ted Post. **(R)** *124 minutes*

MAHOGANY (1975)

★★

Diana Ross
Billy Dee Williams
Anthony Perkins

The incomparable Ross is stunning as a poor Chicago secretary turned international model and fashion designer, but a silly and shoddy script wastes such talent. Perkins plays a photographer responsible for her success in the fashion world. Directed by Motown mogul Berry Gordy. Also with Jean-Pierre Aumont, Nina Foch, and Beah Richards. **(PG)** *110 minutes*

MAID TO ORDER (1987)

★★★

Ally Sheedy

Ally Sheedy goes from riches to rags in Maid to Order.

A small but charming comic fantasy about a spoiled rich girl who overdoses on her father's credit cards. A chain-smoking fairy godmother arranges for her to be a maid in someone else's home—sort of a Cinderella story in reverse. Sheedy, as the shallow shopper, learns humility in her new station and transforms into a worthwhile human being. This old-fashioned situation comedy is delightful schmaltz with a slight hint of a social theme. Those actors in secondary roles, including Michael Ontkean, Beverly D'Angelo, Merry Clayton, Tom Skerritt, and Dick Shawn, add a great deal of seasoning to the film. **Director**—Amy Jones. **(PG)** *93 minutes*

THE MAIN EVENT (1979)

★★½

Barbra Streisand
Ryan O'Neal

Ryan O'Neal and Barbra Streisand find romance during The Main Event.

Streisand plays a wealthy perfume manufacturer who becomes the victim of embezzlement. She loses everything except her tax-shelter contract with reluctant prizefighter O'Neal. O'Neal and Streisand attempt to repeat their success from the madcap *What's Up, Doc?* in this romantic comedy, but Howard Zieff's direction can't compare to the cleverness of Peter Bogdanovich's. The attempt to recreate the screwball comedy of the 1930s is not wholly successful. Also with Paul Sand, Patti D'Arbanville, and Whitman Mayo. **(PG)** *112 minutes*

THE MAJOR AND THE MINOR (1942)

Ginger Rogers
Ray Milland

This bright romantic comedy marks Billy Wilder's directorial debut and

(Continued)

(Continued)
shows the talented writer/director's clever way with a storyline. Rogers is a struggling young working girl who disguises herself as a 12-year-old to save train fare. En route she meets Milland, head of a military school, and nature takes its course. Cowritten with Charles Brackett, the script offers many situational bons mots and double entendres, all done with a sophisticated flair. The amusing cast includes Rita Johnson, Robert Benchley, and Diana Lynn.
100 minutes b&w

MAJOR LEAGUE (1989)

★★★ ®

Tom Berenger
Charlie Sheen
Corbin Bernsen

Though this comedy about America's favorite pastime is filled with familiar characters and predictable events, its inside jokes, unsentimental humor, and baseball references make it one of the best movies about the sport. The snooty owner of the perennially slumping Cleveland Indians hires misfit ballplayers so the team will collapse and allow her to move the club to sunny Florida. It doesn't take long to figure out how these losers will actually perform. A colorful supporting cast, including James Gammon, Wesley Snipes, and Bob Uecker, adds to the fun. **Director**—David Ward. **(R)**
105 minutes

MAKING LOVE (1982)

★★

Michael Ontkean
Kate Jackson
Harry Hamlin

Michael Ontkean and Kate Jackson are a couple with a problem in Making Love.

A slick soap opera about a young doctor, happily married to a beautiful woman for eight years, who discovers that he is latently homosexual. The story is overly sentimental, not unlike *Love Story,* also directed by Arthur Hiller. The homosexual theme is handled gingerly and with sympathy, but the story comes off as syrupy and trite. The happy ending fails to touch the heart. **(R)** *111 minutes*

MAKING MR. RIGHT (1987)

★★

John Malkovich
Ann Magnuson
Glenne Headly

"A good man is hard to find" is the theme of this awkward comedy with a clever premise. Magnuson, a performance artist in real life, plays a publicist who falls in love with an android created by a bumbling scientist. The point of the film revolves around the fact that the android is endowed with more charm and sensitivity than the publicist's male acquaintances. The comic situations and dialogue are often trite and the story is contrived, despite the comic potential of the premise. Malkovich appears in the dual role of robot and nerdy inventor. Also with Laurie Metcalf and Polly Bergen. **Director**—Susan Seidelman. **(PG-13)**
98 minutes

MAKING THE GRADE (1984)

★

Judd Nelson
Gordon Jump
Jonna Lee

We'll give this silly teen comedy a D-minus for déjà vu gags that fall flat and amateurish direction by Dorian Walker. The storyline involves a stuck-up rich teenager who hires a desperate city kid from the wrong side of town to earn his diploma at a snobby prep school. A talented ensemble cast makes the most of the limited screenplay and struggles through a string of colorless preppie jokes. **(R)** *105 minutes*

MALCOLM (1986)

★★

John Hargreaves
Lindy Davies
Colin Friels

A mildly amusing but marginally interesting tale about a trio of robbers who employ various mechanical gadgets to commit their crimes. Friels stars in the title role as a likable tinkerer who teams up with an ex-con to stage a heist by remote control. Though vaguely reminiscent of *The Lavender Hill Mob,* this odd comedy does not sustain the style or wit of that classic film. **Director**—Nadia Tass. **(PG-13)** *90 minutes*

MALONE (1987)

★★ ®

Burt Reynolds
Lauren Hutton

Burt Reynolds goes after a neo-fascist group in Malone.

An older and more interesting Reynolds stars in this melancholy thriller as a disillusioned ex-CIA operative who takes on a powerful neo-fascist organization in rural Oregon. His mysterious loner character is initially fascinating—a sort of modern-day Shane—but the film is undone by haphazard plotting. The scope and identity of this supposedly diabolical group are vague, and the viewer never really feels that they are a threat. Hutton's character has little to do but provide a brief romantic interlude for Reynolds, interrupting any tension created by the main storyline. Cliff Robertson phones in his role as the head of the neo-fascist group. Also with Cindy Gibb and Ken McMillan. **Director**—Harley Cokliss. **(R)** *92 minutes*

THE MALTESE FALCON (1941)

★★★★ ®

Humphrey Bogart
Mary Astor
Sydney Greenstreet

Director John Huston's famous detective tale, starring Bogart as hard-boiled private eye Sam Spade. Based on the character created by Dashiell Hammett,

® *This movie available with closed captions for the hearing impaired.*

Bogart, Lorre, Astor, and Greenstreet—and The Maltese Falcon.

Bogart's portrayal of Spade is hard and cynical, though he still adheres to some personal code of honor regarding his profession. Spade's world, as depicted by Huston, is a dark one, both visually and figuratively. Dark offices, shadowy and misty night scenes, and harsh shadows across the walls characterize the film, adding a moody and sinister atmosphere, and prefiguring the *film noir* style that would dominate the detective film after World War II. The storyline involves the search for a stolen statuette called the Maltese Falcon by a number of unsavory villains, who want the Falcon for their own greedy purposes. Many of the principal actors—Bogart, Astor, Greenstreet, Peter Lorre, and Elisha Cook, Jr.—created characters that became archetypes of the genre. An unsurpassed directorial debut by Huston, who also wrote the screenplay. Also with Barton MacLane, Lee Patrick, and Gladys George. **Academy Award Nominations**—best picture; Greenstreet, best supporting actor; Huston, screenplay. *101 minutes b&w*

A MAN AND A WOMAN (1966)

★★★

Anouk Aimée
Jean-Louis Trintignant

Well-acted, well-written romantic love story about a French widow and widower who meet, fall in love, and find a second chance. One of the most popular cinematic romances of its time, it is marred by excessive use of filters, dreamy images, and long shots on a wintry beach reminiscent of TV commercials, which cheapen the work. The sensitive couple are superbly played by Aimée and Trintignant, who are believable and sympathetic. The fine screenplay by Claude Lelouch and Pierre Uytterhoeven captures the essence of loneliness and desire, raising the piece far above soap-opera level. Originally filmed in French. **Director**—Lelouch. **Academy Award**—Lelouch and Uytterhoeven, story and screenplay. **Nominations**—Lelouch, best director; Aimée, best actress. *102 minutes*

A MAN AND A WOMAN: 20 YEARS LATER (1986)

Jean-Louis Trintignant
Anouk Aimée

Claude Lelouch dusted off his 1966 Oscar-winning romantic drama and updated the story to a generation later. Aimée and Trintignant, who played the lovers in the original, return for this sequel, but too many cinematic tricks and a convoluted plot make the film almost too ironic and self-reflexive to be effective. Francis Lai's robust score is used again, this time with an updated pop beat. Also with Richard Berry and Evelyne Bouix. Originally filmed in French. **(PG)** *112 minutes*

A MAN, A WOMAN AND A BANK (1979)

★

Donald Sutherland
Brooke Adams
Paul Mazursky

Paul Mazursky, Donald Sutherland, and Brooke Adams in A Man, a Woman, and a Bank.

Sutherland and Mazursky play clever con men who plan to rob a Vancouver bank by invading the sophisticated security system during construction stages of the bank building. This drawn-out caper seems to have everyone running in place. There are so many unexciting complications and dull romantic interludes along the way, one wishes the crooks would get on with the job, which isn't that exciting when they finally pull it off. Also with Allen Magicovsky. **Director**—Noel Black. **(PG)** *100 minutes*

A MAN CALLED HORSE (1970)

★★

Richard Harris

An unusual story that strives to capture the authenticity of American Indian culture and rituals, but dwells too much on excessive harshness and gore. Harris portrays a polished Englishman who is captured by the Sioux in 1825 in the Dakotas; after some brutal torture, he's converted and accepted by the tribe and eventually becomes a leader. Also with Judith Anderson, Jean Gascon, Manu Tupou, and Corinna Tsopei. The film spawned three sequels. **Director**—Elliot Silverstein. **(PG)** *114 minutes*

THE MANCHURIAN CANDIDATE (1962)

★★★★

Frank Sinatra
Janet Leigh
Laurence Harvey

Frank Sinatra begins to understand the master plot in The Manchurian Candidate.

An intelligent and brilliantly conceived spy thriller about a Korean war veteran, played by Harvey, who's brainwashed by the Communists. Under their influence, he returns to the United States and attempts to assassinate a conservative politician. The film, based on Richard Condon's novel, is eerie in mood but satirical in tone. Shot in both Korea and the U.S., the film represents an early directorial effort by John Frankenheimer, whose work at this time was characterized by the stark black-and-white photography used here. Held back for many years from television because of the subject matter, the film was re-released to the theaters in 1988. Also in the cast are Angela Lansbury, Henry Silva, and James Gregory. **Academy Award Nomination**—Lansbury, best supporting actress. *126 minutes b&w*

This movie available on videotape and/or disc.

A MAN FOR ALL SEASONS (1966)

★★★★

Paul Scofield
Wendy Hiller
Robert Shaw

Impeccable screen version of Robert Bolt's intelligent play about the clash of ideals between Sir Thomas More and King Henry VIII. Scofield plays More, Hiller is Alice More, and Shaw is the monarch. Period detail is brought out with splendor by director Fred Zinnemann, but the film's strong point is the intense attention to character development. Scofield, as the honorable religious leader, provides a rich portrayal. The talented supporting cast includes Orson Welles, Leo McKern, Susannah York, and Vanessa Redgrave. **Academy Awards**—best picture; Zinnemann, best director; Scofield, best actor; Bolt, best screenplay based on material from another medium; Ted Moore, cinematography. **Nominations**—Shaw, best supporting actor; Hiller, best supporting actress. *120 minutes*

THE MAN FROM LARAMIE (1955)

★★★

James Stewart

Stewart is excellent as a stalwart cattleman who relentlessly pursues the killers of his brother. The gripping western features moments of brutal action, some interesting characterizations, and the use of the rough western terrain to symbolize the conflicts in the story—all elements of director Anthony Mann's style. This was Stewart's sixth film with Mann. The supporting cast is excellent, and includes Arthur Kennedy, Donald Crisp, Cathy O'Donnell, Alex Nicol, Wallace Ford, and Jack Elam. *104 minutes*

THE MAN FROM SNOWY RIVER (1982)

★★★

Tom Burlinson
Kirk Douglas

A sweeping, handsome Australian western with a delightfully old-fashioned script. Against lush, panoramic vistas and heart-pounding scenes of thundering wild horses, a

Tom Burlinson romances Sigrid Thornton in Australia's The Man from Snowy River.

bright-eyed lad (Burlinson) wins his spurs as a man and woos the refined daughter of a wealthy rancher. Douglas stands out with a remarkable dual performance as the rancher and the grizzled miner who is the rancher's brother. **Director**—George Miller. **(PG)** *105 minutes*

THE MANGO TREE (1977)

★★

Christopher Pate
Geraldine Fitzgerald

This loosely constructed Australian film, set during World War I, centers on the rites of passage of a high-school student (Pate). Unfortunately, director Kevin Dobson fails to establish continuity, and the confused story unfolds haphazardly, though the handsome production splendidly captures the atmosphere of the period. There's a standout performance by veteran actress Fitzgerald as the boy's wise and feisty grandmother. **(No MPAA rating)** *93 minutes*

MANHATTAN (1979)

★★★★

Woody Allen
Diane Keaton

Director/actor Allen returns to the satiric style of *Annie Hall* with greater success in this portrait of sophisticated New Yorkers and their foibles, fancies, loves, and frustrations. Not only do he and Keaton again reveal their special brilliance for hilarious comedy, but Woody has developed a much deeper and more serious romantic spirit. His witty observations stir feelings while drawing laughter. A truly touching comic valentine to the Big Apple. Gordon Willis' beautiful wide-screen, black-and-white photography and the George Gershwin soundtrack enhance the romanticism. Also with Michael Murphy, Mariel Hemingway, Meryl Streep, and Anne Byrne. **(R) Academy Award Nominations**—Hemingway, best supporting actress; Allen and Marshall Brickman, best screenplay written directly for the screen. *96 minutes b&w*

THE MANHATTAN PROJECT (1986)

★★

Christopher Collet
Cynthia Nixon
John Lithgow
Jill Eikenberry

John Lithgow and Christopher Collet would love to disarm The Manhattan Project.

Writer/director Marshall Brickman takes on the serious subject of nuclear proliferation in this uneven comedy/drama about a high-school student who builds an atomic bomb. The film soon becomes slack and implausible after including too many conventional and contrived teen-adventure situations. It is also irresponsible in that it encourages the audience to sympathize with and root for the central character, who breaks into a laboratory and steals plutonium. **(PG–13)** *117 minutes*

MANHUNTER (1986)

★★★

William Petersen
Dennis Farina
Kim Greist

A slick, intense detective thriller from director Michael Mann, creator of tele-

® This movie available with closed captions for the hearing impaired.

Obsessive: William Petersen as the troubled FBI agent in Manhunter.

vision's *Miami Vice.* This grisly tale about the search for a serial murderer who butchers entire families, including their pets, is at once fascinating and disturbing. Petersen stars as the relentless FBI agent who stalks the madman with a skill based on simulating the killer's thoughts, though he risks psychological damage to himself in the process. Tom Noonan appears as the lunatic killer. Also with Brian Cox and Stephen Lang. **(R)** *118 minutes*

MAN IN THE GLASS BOOTH (1975)

★★

Maximilian Schell

Flawed screen adaptation of Robert Shaw's wrenching play based on Nazi criminal Adolf Eichmann's trial for war atrocities. This American Film Theater production is overblown and pompous, losing much of the play's impact primarily due to screenwriter Edward Auhatts' interpretation. Writer Shaw disowned the version and had his name removed from the titles. The acting is still potent with the always professional Schell well supported by Lois Nettleton, Luther Adler, Lawrence Pressman, Henry Brown, and Richard Rasof. **Director**—Arthur Hiller. **(PG) Academy Award Nomination**—Schell, best actor. *117 minutes*

THE MAN IN THE GRAY FLANNEL SUIT (1956)

★★★

Gregory Peck
Fredric March

First-class rendering of Sloan Wilson's poignant novel about a New York public relations executive caught in the dilemma of succeeding in his high-pressure job or maintaining his integrity. Though the production is slick and melodramatic, the story moves briskly and maintains consistent interest. Peck is well suited to the title role as the button-down Madison Avenue type. Also with Jennifer Jones, Ann Harding, Arthur O'Connell, Henry Daniell, Lee J. Cobb, Keenan Wynn, and Gene Lockhart. **Director**—Nunnally Johnson. *153 minutes*

THE MAN IN THE WHITE SUIT (1952)

 ★★★★

Alec Guinness
Joan Greenwood
Cecil Parker

Guinness is in great form as a faintly naive scientist who invents an amazing textile that apparently won't wear out and actually repels dirt. Britain's textile industry is thrown into turmoil, and clothing makers scramble to get their hands on the astonishing material. A fantastic combination of wit and social satire from Britain's famed Ealing Studios, noted for their dry but biting comedies. Also with Vida Hope, Michael Gough, and Ernest Thesiger. **Director**—Alexander Mackendrick. **Academy Award Nomination**—Roger MacDougall, John Dighton, and Mackendrick, screenplay. *81 minutes b&w*

MANNEQUIN (1987)

★

Andrew McCarthy
Kim Cattrall

He's easy to please: Andrew McCarthy finds the perfect date in Mannequin.

A plodding comedy about a young man (McCarthy) who falls in love with a department store mannequin (Cattrall), which comes to life when the couple is alone. The movie itself is lifeless, however, because of an uninspired script, poor direction, and a sexist, dated premise. *One Touch of Venus,* the 1948 film starring Ava Gardner, covered the same ground with much more enchantment. Estelle Getty and G.W. Bailey appear in supporting roles. **Director**—Michael Gottlieb. **(PG) Academy Award Nomination**—Albert Hammond and Diane Warren, best song ("Nothing's Going To Stop Us Now"). *90 minutes*

THE MAN OF A THOUSAND FACES (1957)

★★★

James Cagney
Dorothy Malone

An engaging film biography of silent-screen great Lon Chaney, who devised many intriguing characters with his amazing makeup skills. In *The Hunchback of Notre Dame,* for example, Chaney wore some 40 pounds of makeup. The plot follows Chaney's screen career and private life. There's impressive detail about this era of silent filmmaking, yet interest is sidetracked because of numerous subplots. Cagney, in the title role, gives another fantastic performance; Malone plays Chaney's first wife. Also with Jane Greer, Marjorie Rambeau, Jeanne Cagney, and Jim Backus. **Director**—Joseph Pevney. **Academy Award Nomination**—Ralph Wheelright, R. Wright Campbell, Ivan Goff, and Ben Roberts, best story and screenplay written directly for the screen. *122 minutes b&w*

MAN OF IRON (1981)

★★★

Jerzy Radziwilowicz
Krystyna Janda

Fact and fiction are excitingly interwoven in this fresh account of recent history—the workers' rebellion in Poland and the rise of the Solidarity labor movement. Polish director Andrzej Wajda made this film as a sequel to his *Man of Marble.* This continuation involves political activities during the shipyard strike in Gdansk and a worker's love affair with a woman filmmaker. Solidarity leader Lech Walesa and other union notables have theatri-

(Continued)

This movie available on videotape and/or disc.

(Continued)
cal parts and appear in newsreel inserts. Originally filmed in Polish. **(PG)** **Academy Award Nomination**—best foreign-language film. *140 minutes*

MAN OF LA MANCHA (1972)

★½

Peter O'Toole
Sophia Loren

The classic Cervantes fable about Don Quixote, produced with extraordinary power and beauty on the stage, is incomprehensible on the screen. The brilliant musical numbers come across with dreariness, and the entire endeavor plods lamely along. The settings are impressive, but it's an essentially disappointing experience. Also with James Coco, Harry Andress, and John Castle. Some prints of the film are shorter by several minutes. **Director**—Arthur Hiller. **(PG)** *140 minutes*

MANON OF THE SPRINGS (1986)

★★★

Yves Montand
Daniel Auteuil
Emmanuelle Béart

This follow-up to the magnificent French drama *Jean de Florette* is a poignant account of bittersweet revenge, and it settles many intriguing questions left unanswered in the original. Manon, played by Béart, witnessed her father's torturous destruction in the first film, which was brought about by the cruel machinations of neighbors Auteuil and Montand. Manon is now a grown beauty living as a reclusive shepherd, and she vows to make those who caused the death of her father pay for their sins. Montand turns in a powerful performance as the treacherous conniver. Originally filmed in French. **Director**—Claude Berri. **(PG)** *113 minutes*

THE MAN ON THE EIFFEL TOWER (1949)

★★★

Charles Laughton
Burgess Meredith

An intense and intriguing crime drama set against the backdrop of Paris. Police Inspector Maigret and a mad killer relentlessly match wits and nerves until the mystery is solved in a tense climax. The production, based on a Simenon novel, is enhanced by excellent acting and imaginative, almost experimental, cinematography. Also with Franchot Tone, Robert Hutton, Jean Wallace, and Wilfrid Hyde-White. **Director**—Meredith. *97 minutes*

MANPOWER (1941)

★★★

Edward G. Robinson
George Raft
Marlene Dietrich

Powerful, action-packed adventure about the men who work on high-voltage power lines. Robinson and Raft, who play two linemen, argue over nightclub hostess Dietrich. The upshot is a gripping man-to-man fistfight on a high-tension tower during a stormy night; the sparks fly in all directions. Also with Alan Hale, Frank McHugh, Eve Arden, Barton MacLane, and Ward Bond. **Director**—Raoul Walsh. *103 minutes b&w*

THE MAN WHO CAME TO DINNER (1941)

★★★★

Monty Woolley
Bette Davis

Bette Davis is secretary to egomaniac Monty Woolley in The Man Who Came to Dinner.

Woolley is exceptional in this side-splitting comedy about a bombastic celebrity who's injured while on tour and must stay with a local family to recuperate. His hosts are driven up the wall by his eccentric demands and the assorted oddball characters who come to visit him. Despite its stagy setting, the action moves quickly. Davis seems wasted as Woolley's secretary, but there are good caricatures from Jimmy Durante, Reginald Gardiner, and Ann Sheridan. The film was adapted from the successful play by Moss Hart and George S. Kaufman, who based the title character on well-known radio personality Alexander Woollcott. Also with Billie Burke, Richard Travis, and Grant Mitchell. **Director**—William Keighley. *112 minutes b&w*

THE MAN WHO FELL TO EARTH (1976)

★★★★

David Bowie

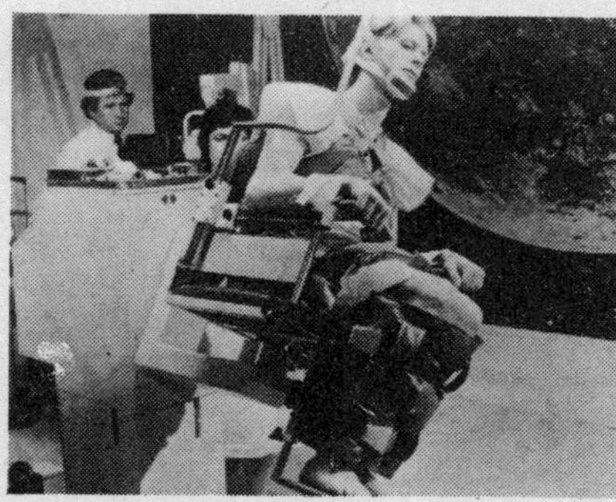

Extraterrestrial David Bowie undergoes tests in The Man Who Fell to Earth.

Nicolas Roeg's riveting and fascinating science-fiction tale, based on a novel by Walter Tevis, is about an extraterrestrial traveler who comes to Earth to find water for his dying planet. He organizes a vast scientific conglomerate, à la Howard Hughes, and becomes entangled in earthly corruption. Rock star Bowie plays the visitor from outer space with credibility. Rip Torn, Buck Henry, and Candy Clark also deliver appealing performances. The film says much about life on Earth through the eyes of a man from another world. Originally released at 118 minutes. **(R)** *140 minutes*

THE MAN WHO KNEW TOO MUCH (1934)

★★★

Leslie Banks
Edna Best

The first and less successful of two versions of an international spy melodrama by Alfred Hitchcock. Banks and Best are parents of a child who is kidnapped to ensure that they will not reveal what they have accidentally learned about an assassination plot. Several well-known scenes, including one set in a dentist's office and the fi-

This movie available with closed captions for the hearing impaired.

nale in Albert Hall, are clumsily handled and telegraphed to the audience so that the gunshot and scream on cue during the concert scene, for example, are woefully anticlimactic. Most of the acting seems overdone by today's standards, but Peter Lorre as the archvillain in sheep's clothing is an unadulterated ham. Also with Pierre Fresnay, Nova Pilbeam, and Frank Vosper.

84 minutes b&w

THE MAN WHO KNEW TOO MUCH (1956)

 ★★★½

James Stewart
Doris Day

According to Hitchcock, the first version of this work (1934) was done by a talented amateur and this one by a professional. This exciting melodrama, filled with foreign intrigue, kidnappings, assassination plots, and murders, begins innocently as an American family in Morocco is swept into a sinister net by a chance encounter on a bus. Stewart and Day are perfectly cast as the guileless victims of circumstance who use all of their resources to free their kidnapped son. A superb supporting cast, including Bernard Miles, Brenda De Banzie, Daniel Gelin, Alan Mowbray, Carolyn Jones, and Hillary Brooke, contributes to the overall effect. The song "Que Sera, Sera," introduced by Day in the film, won an Oscar.

120 minutes

THE MAN WHO LOVED CAT DANCING (1973)

 ★★

Sarah Miles
Burt Reynolds
Lee J. Cobb

Lee J. Cobb is a sympathetic Wells Fargo agent in The Man Who Loved Cat Dancing.

A sluggish western about a restless wife who is kidnapped by a gang of train robbers and falls in love with their leader. Miles stars as the unhappy wife, and Reynolds plays the desperado. Cobb leads a posse after the bandits. An impressive cast can't make much of this movie based on the novel by Marilyn Dunham. Supposedly, Reynolds injured himself doing his own stunts. Also with Jack Warden, George Hamilton, Bo Hopkins, and Jay Silverheels. **Director**—Richard C. Sarafian. **(PG)**

114 minutes

THE MAN WHO LOVED WOMEN (1977)

★★★★

Charles Denner
Leslie Caron
Brigitte Fossey

Director François Truffaut's charming tale of a Frenchman who is obsessed with women is witty and sophisticated. The cast is headed by Denner, whose gentle manner makes the title character appealing, with a mixture of comic delight and innocence. The film is fun to watch for its clever variations on a familiar theme. Also stars Geneviève Fontanel and Nelly Borgeaud. Originally filmed in French. **(No MPAA rating)**

119 minutes

THE MAN WHO LOVED WOMEN (1983)

★★ 🗨®

Burt Reynolds
Julie Andrews

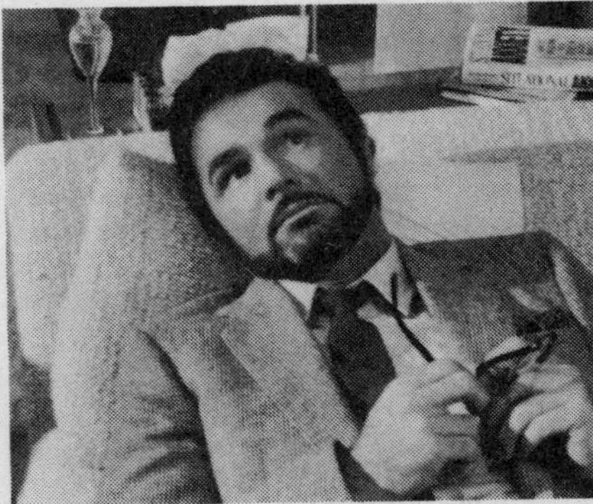

Burt Reynolds has a problem—he's The Man Who Loved Women.

Macho man Reynolds is convincing as an appealing lothario who is more helpless than heartless in his pursuit of the opposite sex. The film is part sensitive psychological drama, part slapstick farce, though it is not as compelling as its star. Director Blake Edwards' reworking of the 1977 François Truffaut comedy is frequently charming, but too slow to be engrossing. Some of the women in Reynolds' life include Andrews (as the psychiatrist who cares for him), Kim Basinger, and Marilu Henner. **(R)**

118 minutes

THE MAN WHO SHOT LIBERTY VALANCE (1962)

★★★½

James Stewart
John Wayne
Lee Marvin
Vera Miles

James Stewart and John Wayne in The Man Who Shot Liberty Valance.

A tenderfoot lawyer from the East (Stewart) arrives out West, and is terrorized, along with the residents of Shinbone, by outlaw Liberty Valance. The only man able to stand up to Valance is gunfighter Tom Doniphon (Wayne). The lawyer instigates profound changes in Shinbone, which all point to progress for the wild and woolly town. Eventually a shoot-out is forced upon the young tenderfoot by Valance, and the encounter results in unexpected and ironic twists. This late western by director John Ford is a darker vision of the West than depicted in his previous films. Gone are the beautiful Monument Valley landscapes as this film was shot on a soundstage in black and white, with much of the action occurring at night. As in most of Ford's westerns, the story here is an allegory about the taming of the Wild West. But as the gloomy setting might suggest, this tale emphasizes the negative side of the western myth: Though the tenderfoot brings civilization to the West and gets credit for ridding the territory of Va-

(Continued)

(*Continued*)
lance, it is at the expense of rugged individualists such as Doniphon, who could not adjust to a more modern society. A poignant and melancholy western, with memorable performances by Wayne, Stewart, and Marvin. Also with Edmond O'Brien, Jeannette Nolan, Andy Devine, Woody Strode, John Carradine, Strother Martin, Lee Van Cleef, and John Qualen.

122 minutes b&w

THE MAN WHO WASN'T THERE (1983)

★

Steve Guttenberg

Guttenberg stars in this uneven and farfetched 3-D comedy as a Washington bureaucrat caught up in an international plot to steal invisibility potions. The well-worn, gimmicky plot involves much chasing around, with both Russian and American agents, and even some gangsters, all trying to recover the amazing formula. The 3-D in this case stands for "Dumb, Dumb, Dumb." Lisa Langlois and Jeffrey Tambor appear in supporting roles. **Director**—Bruce Malmuth. **(R)** *111 minutes*

THE MAN WHO WOULD BE KING (1975)

★★★★

Sean Connery
Michael Caine
Christopher Plummer

Sean Connery is worshipped as a god in The Man Who Would Be King.

Connery and Caine play two soldiers turned con men who set themselves up as rulers of Kafiristan, a remote and primitive country, so they can loot the royal treasury. The film, set at the turn of the century, is based on Rudyard Kipling's romantic short story and succeeds as an exotically charming, old-fashioned adventure tale, laced with comradeship and courage. The duo's scheme falls apart when Danny Dravot, played by Connery, becomes attached to his responsibilities as god-king. Plummer gives a remarkable but brief performance as Kipling. Also with Saeed Jaffrey, Shakira Caine, and Jack May. **Director**—John Huston. **(PG)** **Academy Award Nomination**—Huston and Gladys Hill, best screenplay adapted from other material.

127 minutes

THE MAN WITH BOGART'S FACE

See Sam Marlowe, Private Eye

THE MAN WITH ONE RED SHOE (1985)

★

Tom Hanks

Jim Belushi, Lori Singer, and Tom Hanks in The Man With One Red Shoe.

Bungled attempt by director Stan Dragoti to translate a bright French spy farce (*The Tall Blond Man with One Black Shoe*) into an American comedy. In this down-at-the-heels version, Hanks stars as a hapless Washington, D.C., violinist who becomes entangled between two CIA factions competing for power. Undercover agents fall all over themselves in a series of gags that would be more at home in a TV sitcom. Also with Dabney Coleman, Lori Singer, and Jim Belushi. **(PG)** *92 minutes*

THE MAN WITH THE GOLDEN ARM (1955)

★★★

Frank Sinatra
Kim Novak

Sinatra is excellent in this stark drama, based on a Nelson Algren novel, as a drug addict who painfully kicks the habit. The film was considered sensational at the time of its release because of the subject matter, and it retains much of its power. Otto Preminger's direction, with its exaggerated style, may seem dated, however. Elmer Bernstein's jazzy, Oscar-nominated score heightens the mood. Also with Eleanor Parker, Darren McGavin, Arnold Stang, and Robert Strauss. **Academy Award Nomination**—Sinatra, best actor.

119 minutes b&w

THE MAN WITH THE GOLDEN GUN (1974)

★★

Roger Moore
Christopher Lee

One of the lesser James Bond extravaganzas set primarily in the Far East, with 007 pursuing yet another archvillain, Scaramanga, chillingly portrayed by Lee. Moore, in his second Bond role, is still a weak shadow of his predecessor, Sean Connery, but for addicts of the genre, he's adequate. The colorful cast offers Britt Ekland, Maud Adams, Herve Villechaize, and Richard Loo. But for all its gimmicks and gadgetry, the script lacks the usual satiric Bond wit. **Director**—Guy Hamilton. **(PG)**

125 minutes

THE MAN WITH TWO BRAINS (1983)

★★★

Steve Martin
Kathleen Turner
David Warner

Martin stars as a wacky brain surgeon with wife problems in this spoof of horror films, skillfully directed by Carl Reiner. Martin's wry humor works to the advantage of the witty and inspired script, and Turner handles her role of the alluring but mercenary wife with surprising finesse. The film represents the third collaboration between director Reiner and Martin. **(R)** *93 minutes*

MAN, WOMAN AND CHILD (1983)

★★

Martin Sheen
Blythe Danner

® *This movie available with closed captions for the hearing impaired.*

Dewy-eyed mush from the tear-stained pages of Erich Segal (*Love Story*). A comfortably married California college professor is suddenly confronted by his ten-year-old illegitimate son. This creates predictable family anxiety—and torrents of sentimentality. Despite the artificiality of the material, Sheen and Danner manage to come up with skillful performances as the professor and his wife. **Director**—Dick Richards. **(PG)**
99 minutes

MARATHON MAN (1976)

 ★★★

Dustin Hoffman
Laurence Olivier

Director John Schlesinger's supercharged thriller about a Columbia University graduate student who, for reasons he cannot understand, is pursued and tormented by a surviving Nazi war criminal. Hoffman stars as the student, and Olivier plays the long-dormant Nazi, who is also a former dentist. The film is paradoxical. At times, it generates tension that is nearly unbearable, and there are moments of intense excitement. It's crammed with brutal killings, bone-chilling torture, and triple crosses. Yet it's all wrapped in a murky and confusing plot that doesn't make sense at times. Hoffman, Olivier, and the rest of the cast are in fine form. The screenplay was written by William Goldman from his own novel. Also with Marthe Keller, Roy Scheider, and William Devane. **(R) Academy Award Nomination**—Olivier, best supporting actor. *125 minutes*

MARCH OF THE WOODEN SOLDIERS

See Babes in Toyland

MARCH OR DIE (1977)

Gene Hackman
Catherine Deneuve
Terence Hill

Stiff, listless French Foreign Legion adventure with beautiful location photography, but a dull and uninspired script. The complicated storyline concerns an expedition to steal Arab treasure buried in the Sahara. More footage was added for network television broadcasts. Also with Max Von Sydow and Ian Holm. **Director**—Dick Richards. **(PG)**
104 minutes

MARIANNE AND JULIANE (1982)

Jutta Lampe
Barbara Sukowa

Margarethe von Trotta, the West German writer/director, presents a grim, overwrought account of the quarrelsome relationship between two sisters caught up in the political turmoil of the 1960s and 1970s. The film touches on the girls' strict upbringing, but too much of the story is devoted to incessant arguing—much of it when Juliane (Lampe), a magazine writer, visits terrorist Marianne (Sukowa) in prison. The film was inspired by the real-life Ensslin sisters—Gudrun and Christiane. Originally filmed in German. **(No MPAA rating)** *106 minutes*

MARIE (1985)

Sissy Spacek

Uplifting drama, based on the true story of Marie Ragghianti, who bravely exposed political corruption in Tennessee's state government. Spacek stars in the title role and her performance enhances the familiar average-person-vs.-big-bureaucracy storyline. The film alternates critical events with scenes of domesticity to indicate the effect of her courageous actions on her family. Supporting performances are consistently good, with Jeff Daniels, Keith Szarabajka, and Morgan Freeman in key roles. **Director**—Roger Donaldson. **(PG–13)**
111 minutes

MARIE ANTOINETTE (1938)

Robert Morley
Norma Shearer

Historical epic of pre-revolutionary France in the court of Louis XVI. This extravagant production is best noted for its elaborate costumes and sets, which overburden an interesting story of love and personal tragedy. Some powerful performances are achieved by the all-star cast, especially Morley as a tortured king and Shearer as the ill-fated Marie; but the drama is excessively long and tedious. The resplendent cast also features Tyrone Power, John Barrymore, Anita Louise, Gladys George, and Joseph Schildkraut. **Academy Award Nominations**—Shearer, best actress; Morley, best supporting actor.
149 minutes b&w

MARJOE (1972)

★★★

Marjoe Gortner

Well-conceived and well-executed Academy Award-winning documentary of revivalist minister Gortner, who grew up in the circuit and became a "star" as a fake evangelist. The probing camera captures him manipulating hordes of gullible worshippers throughout the country, as he performs a kind of witchcraft based on personal charm and appeal. This unique documentary could only have been made with his consent as a final gesture to his questionable profession; not surprisingly, Gortner went on to become an actor. **Director**—Howard Smith and Sarah Kernochan. **(PG)** *88 minutes*

MARJORIE MORNINGSTAR (1958)

Natalie Wood
Gene Kelly

A young Jewish girl with stars in her eyes strives to make it to the big time in New York City, but winds up as an ordinary housewife. This screen adaptation of Herman Wouk's popular novel is bland and dated, although a few scenes are moving. Wood seems ill at ease in the title role as do most of the supporting players. Also with Claire Trevor, Everett Sloane, Ed Wynn, Martin Milner, Carolyn Jones, and Martin Balsam. **Director**—Irving Rapper. *123 minutes*

THE MARK OF ZORRO (1940)

Tyrone Power
Basil Rathbone

A ripsnorting, swashbuckling adventure starring Power as Diego de Vega, an aristocrat who dons a mask and routs the bad guys in California in the early 1800s. Well-staged and executed with much energy, the film offers some of the best dueling scenes in the cinema. Power is as dashing as ever. The excellent cast also includes Linda Darnell, J. Edward Bromberg, Eugene

(Continued)

(Continued)
Pallette, and Montagu Love. A remake of the 1920 silent classic starring Douglas Fairbanks, Sr. **Director**—Rouben Mamoulian. *94 minutes b&w*

MARLENE (1986)

★★★

The enigmatic movie star Marlene Dietrich is the subject of the documentary Marlene.

Assembled by internationally acclaimed actor Maximilan Schell, this unusual documentary about the legendary Marlene Dietrich attempts to explore both her image and her private self. Though Dietrich refused to be photographed for the film, she was interviewed extensively and her voice provides a cryptic commentary on the film clips and photographs that make up the image track. Unfortunately, Schell bogs the film down with his own discourse on his difficulties making the film and his views on more theoretical issues concerning film and reality, while the interviews with Dietrich are futile attempts to draw her out. Ultimately, this curious film is both an exploration of Dietrich's screen career and a tribute to her power and status as a movie star, one of Hollywood's last, who can still captivate her director and audience with only a handful of ancient film clips and her voice. **Director**—Schell. **(No MPAA rating)** *96 minutes*

MARLOWE (1969)

★★★

James Garner
Rita Moreno

Garner tries his hand at playing Philip Marlowe, Raymond Chandler's private-eye character, and the results are fairly good. A girl has lost track of her brother and hires Marlowe to find him. The thriller, based on Chandler's *The Little Sister*, is well paced, and displays some of the squalid atmosphere associated with such capers. Garner gets first-class assistance from Gayle Hunnicutt, Sharon Farrell, Carroll O'Connor, and Bruce Lee. **Director**—Paul Bogart. **(PG)** *95 minutes*

MARNIE (1964)

★★★

Tippi Hedren
Sean Connery

Sean Connery falls in love with Marnie, *the beautiful thief played by Tippi Hedron.*

Curiously fetishistic psychological drama about a beautiful but frigid woman who steals to compensate for her traumatic childhood. The film stars Connery as the rich and handsome businessman who loves, marries, and tries to save Hedren, who plays the emotionally flawed thief. Alfred Hitchcock teasingly juxtaposes the artificial with the real, using obviously painted backdrops and stage sets to heighten Hedren's dream/nightmare state of mind. While not one of his masterpieces, this overly ambitious work deserves more attention and praise than it has received. Also with Diane Baker, Alan Napier, Martin Gabel, Louise Lathem, and Bruce Dern. *130 minutes*

THE MARRIAGE OF MARIA BRAUN (1978)

★★★½

Hanna Schygulla
Klaus Lowitsch

Sultry and beautiful Schygulla plays the title role in this film about survival in postwar Germany. As Maria, she achieves success through shrewdness and energy as the country emerges into a period of miraculous prosperity. Maria and the events surrounding her life serve as a metaphor for the history of postwar Germany. Directed by one of modern Germany's most influential directors, Rainer Werner Fassbinder, the film was the first in a trilogy, which also included *Lola* and *Veronika Voss*, that provides a parable for Germany's sociopolitical situation after the war. Also with Ivan Desny and Gottried John. Originally filmed in German. **(R)** *120 minutes*

MARRIED TO THE MOB (1988)

★★★ (CC)

Michelle Pfeiffer
Matthew Modine
Dean Stockwell

Michelle Pfeiffer and Matthew Modine in Married to the Mob.

Romance and the American dream are explored with quirky good humor in this engaging comic romance, vigorously directed by Jonathan Demme. Pfeiffer stars as a fed-up Mafia wife who moves from the posh suburbs to lower Manhattan after her husband is bumped off. Gangly, unorthodox FBI agent Modine wants to use Pfeiffer to get the goods on other mobsters, and gradually falls for her sweetness and feisty charm. Together, they scramble to keep a step ahead of dim-witted but persistent mob triggermen. A delightful change-of-pace role for porcelain-pretty Pfeiffer; Stockwell is hilarious as a lecherous mob chieftain. **(R) Academy Award Nomination**—Dean Stockwell, best supporting actor. *104 minutes*

THE MARRYING KIND (1952)

★★★

Judy Holliday
Aldo Ray

An intelligent tragicomedy played with style and sensitivity by Holliday and Ray, as a couple with marital problems

(CC) *This movie available with closed captions for the hearing impaired.*

who straighten things out after analyzing their lives. Holliday does a fine job with the serious moments as well as the comic situations. Madge Kennedy and Mickey Shaughnessy also star. **Director**—George Cukor. *93 minutes b&w*

MARTY (1955)

★★★★

Ernest Borgnine
Betsy Blair

This is one of the most compassionate and touching films about the lives and problems of ordinary people ever produced. Borgnine is perfectly cast as the lonely middle-aged butcher resigned to an unmarried life, who finally falls in love with a girl in similar circumstances; Blair plays the lonely girl. Paddy Chayefsky's script was initially written as a TV play, and it gains further impact and importance as a feature film. It's a movie masterpiece, filled with subtleties, irony, and truth. Borgnine's performance is magnificent, and there's excellent support from Blair, Esther Minciotti, Joe Mantell, and Jerry Paris. **Director**—Delbert Mann. **Academy Awards**—best picture; Mann, best director; Borgnine, best actor; Chayefsky, best screenplay. **Nominations**—Mantell, best supporting actor; Blair, best supporting actress; Joseph LaShelle, cinematography.
91 minutes b&w

MARVIN AND TIGE (1983)

★★

John Cassavetes
Griban Brown

Minor-league heart-tugger about a middle-class dropout (Cassavetes) who befriends an 11-year-old homeless black boy (Brown). The syrupy sweet film is well intentioned, but the script is hampered by an overabundance of soul-searching dialogue between the leading characters. Cassavetes and Brown perform with determination despite the limited material. Also with Billy Dee Williams and Denise Nicholas-Hill. **Director**—Eric Weston. **(PG)** *104 minutes*

MARY POPPINS (1964)

★★★★

Julie Andrews
Dick Van Dyke

Dick Van Dyke and Julie Andrews in the Walt Disney fantasy Mary Poppins.

This delightful musical fantasy from Disney is about two English children under the care of a strict but wonderful nanny who has magical powers and takes them on exciting adventures. Andrews, in her film debut, is splendid in the title role, and the film exudes charm and energy. The combination of animation and live-action sequences represents the Disney studio at its best. There's also a serious message involved: Kids need love and attention, not just wealthy surroundings, to truly make them happy. Also with David Tomlinson, Glynis Johns, Ed Wynn, Elsa Lanchester, and Arthur Treacher. **Director**—Robert Stevenson. **Academy Award**—Andrews, best actress. **Nominations**—best picture; Stevenson, best director; Bill Walsh and Don DaGradi, best screenplay based on material from another medium; Edward Colman, cinematography. *139 minutes*

M*A*S*H (1970)

★★★★

Donald Sutherland
Elliott Gould
Sally Kellerman

Director Robert Altman scores big with this smart black comedy about doctors at a Mobile Army Surgical Hospital (MASH) in Korea who relieve the boredom, tension, and horror of their situation by pulling pranks and defying authority. A trendsetting film and a most unusual farce, splendidly acted by Sutherland, Gould, and Kellerman in the key roles. The film introduced Altman's innovative directorial style—with its overlapping dialogue, episodic structure, and improvised bits—to the public. The extraordinary screenplay by Ring Lardner, Jr., is based on the popular novel by Richard Hooker (a pseudonym for a real-life doctor). A great film that spawned an excellent TV show. Also stars Tom Skerritt, Robert Duvall, John Schuck, Roger Bowen, René Auberjonois, Fred Williamson, Bud Cort, Jo Ann Pflug, and Gary Burghoff. **(PG) Academy Award**—Lardner, best screenplay based on material from another medium. **Nominations**—best picture; Altman, best director; Kellerman, best supporting actress. *116 minutes*

MASK (1985)

★★★

Eric Stoltz
Cher
Sam Elliott

Uplifting, touching account of a disfigured teenage boy (Stoltz) whose positive attitude overcomes his affliction. The boy's courageous outlook is enhanced by the warm, special relationship he has with his kooky but devoted mother, played effectively by Cher. Director Peter Bogdanovich occasionally overindulges in the emotional aspects of this story, based on real-life characters, but the core of the film is compelling and genuinely moving. An Oscar-winner for its makeup design. **(PG–13)**
120 minutes

THE MASK OF DIMITRIOS (1944)

★★★

Peter Lorre
Sydney Greenstreet
Zachary Scott

Lorre and Greenstreet are right at home in this stylish tale of intrigue, based on an Eric Ambler novel. Lorre plays a Dutch writer in the Middle East, seeking out a clever criminal, played by Scott in his first film role. Plenty of smoky atmosphere enhances the story. Interesting for its time because there are no "movie stars" in the film, only character actors and unknowns. Also with Faye Emerson, Victor Francen, Steven Geray, and Florence Bates. **Director**—Jean Negulesco. *95 minutes b&w*

MASQUERADE (1988)

★★½

Rob Lowe
Meg Tilly

Greed and intrigue highlight this atmospheric romantic mystery set in the posh Hamptons of Long Island. Lowe

(Continued)

This movie available on videotape and/or disc.

Heiress Meg Tilly marries Rob Lowe in Masquerade.

is well cast as a handsome yachtsman who woos and beds the wealthy ladies of the area. He falls in love and marries a lovely but strangely passive heiress, played by Tilly. The complex story progresses with several delightful twists and turns reminiscent of the best *films noirs* of the 1940s, but the abruptly violent conclusion may leave some viewers puzzled. Kim Cattrall, Doug Savant, and John Glover are in supporting roles. **Director**—Bob Swain. **(R)**
90 minutes

MASS APPEAL (1984)

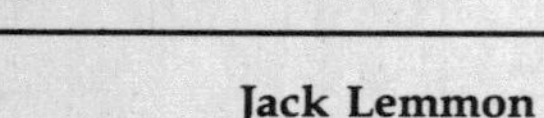

★★★

Jack Lemmon
Zeljko Ivanek
Charles Durning

Winning screen adaptation of Bill C. Davis' stage comedy about conflicting consciences in the Catholic church. Lemmon is superb as the popular, complacent priest assigned to tone down an idealistic young seminary student (Ivanek) who challenges conventional morality. The film succeeds because of the witty, bantering dialogue between the two protagonists. **Director**—Glenn Jordan. **(PG)** *99 minutes*

MASTERS OF THE UNIVERSE (1987)

★★

Dolph Lundgren
Frank Langella
Meg Foster

A comic-book-style adventure based on the popular line of toy figures. The muscle-bound Lundgren stars as He-Man squaring off against the evil Skeletor (Langella) for a planet's soul. Much laser zapping and many grotesque creatures fill the action-packed sequences, and children should be entertained by this noisy movie obviously tailored to their interests. Lundgren looks terrific, but the character he portrays is empty. Any of the film's color derives from a cast of character actors giving it their all. Also with Billy Barty, Courteney Cox, Christina Pickles, Jon Cypher, James Tolkan, and Robert Duncan McNeill. **Director**—Gary Goddard. **(PG)**
108 minutes

MATEWAN (1987)

★★★½

Chris Cooper
James Earl Jones
Kevin Tighe

Striking miners are pitted against a heartless coal company in this poignant drama set in West Virginia during the 1920s. Independent writer/director John Sayles shows the conflict from the point of view of the strikers, who eventually face a bloody showdown with company goons. The film's strength lies in its realistic depiction of a hard lifestyle and its emphasis on the heroism of the working man. Based on a true incident, this low-budget film features beautiful location cinematography and low-key, natural performances by a cast of mostly unknowns. Jones stands out as the spokesperson for the black miners. Also with Will Oldham, Ken Jenkins, and Jace Alexander. **(PG-13) Academy Award Nomination**—Haskell Wexler, cinematography. *132 minutes*

A MATTER OF TIME (1976)

★★

Liza Minnelli
Ingrid Bergman
Charles Boyer

Vincente Minnelli directs daughter Liza in this Cinderella story of a chambermaid who's transformed into a glamorous movie star. The film, set in Rome in 1949, is rich in lush scenery and glittery costumes, but the plot is unbelievable, and the dialogue is awkward. Bergman costars as an eccentric, down-and-out contessa who inspires the young peasant girl. Minnelli and Bergman perform well, but they're much too good for such mediocre material. The last film for both Boyer and Vincente Minnelli, (who later disowned the film as edited). Also with Tina Aumont and Spiros Andros. **(PG)** *99 minutes*

MAURICE (1987)

★★½

James Wilby
Hugh Grant
Rupert Graves

From the team that brought *A Room with a View* to the screen comes this less commercial drama, also based on a novel by E.M. Forster. Two aristocratic male students at Cambridge become very close friends and declare their love for each other. One sees his homosexuality as something to be overcome and breaks off the friendship to marry and go into politics. Devastated, the other begins a passionate but destructive affair with a lower-class gamekeeper. Director James Ivory and producer Ismail Merchant present their story with the same handsome production values and beautiful cinematography that made *A Room with a View* so stunning. This film's serious subject matter, however, lends itself to a somber tone that becomes oppressive by the end. Also with Denholm Elliott, Simon Callow, Billie Whitelaw, and Ben Kingsley. **(R) Academy Award Nomination**—Jenny Beavan and John Bright, best costume design.
140 minutes

MAX DUGAN RETURNS (1983)

★★

Jason Robards
Marsha Mason

Marsha Mason and Jason Robards with cash to spend in Max Dugan Returns.

Mason plays a spunky, widowed schoolteacher living on the brink of poverty in Venice, California. Along

comes her long-lost, ex-con father (Robards) with a suitcase full of cash, which he lavishes on the forlorn household. The script is by Neil Simon, who seems to have lost his comic touch here. The movie manages a few smiles, but it's mostly stale material. Also with Donald Sutherland and Matthew Broderick. **Director**—Herbert Ross. **(PG)**
98 minutes

MAXIE (1985)

★★

Glenn Close
Mandy Patinkin

Flimsy comedy about a San Francisco couple whose lives are disrupted by the ghost of a rowdy 1920s vamp. Deprived of a movie career by an early death, the flapper seeks a second chance by possessing the wife's body. Close and Patinkin are appealing but miscast as the odd trio. The film doesn't have a ghost of a chance of piercing the heart or rattling the funny bone. The late Ruth Gordon contributes some of the best scenes in her last film role. **Director**—Paul Aaron. **(PG)** *90 minutes*

MAXIMUM OVERDRIVE (1986)

★★

Emilio Estevez
Pat Hingle

Author Stephen King makes his directorial debut with this grisly, blood-splattered horror film about a passing comet that makes all the machines on earth come alive and destroy human beings. Examples include an electric knife that slices up a waitress, chainsaws and lawn mowers on a rampage, and massive 18-wheeled trucks that attempt to run down their victims. The script, as well, seems to have been written by machines and the acting is strictly mechanical. Also with Laura Harrington, Yeardley Smith, and John Short. **(R)** *97 minutes*

McCABE & MRS. MILLER (1971)

★★★1/2

Warren Beatty
Julie Christie

Robert Altman shows off his innovative directorial style in this turn-of-the-century western, about a gambler who established a bordello in a remote Northwest boom town. Beatty's performance, as the opportunistic braggart, displays just the right amount of pathos and droll humor. Christie costars as the ambitious woman who runs his establishment. Based on the novel *McCabe* by Edmund Naughton, the film makes for an offbeat western mostly due to Altman's realistic interpretation of the setting and unglamorous depiction of the western hero. Supporting roles by René Auberjonois, Hugh Millais, Shelley Duvall, John Schuck, and Keith Carradine. **(R) Academy Award Nomination**—Christie, best actress.
120 minutes

McLINTOCK! (1963)

★★★

John Wayne
Maureen O'Hara

Wayne demonstrates his ability to handle comedy in this wild and woolly western. The Duke plays a formidable cattle baron who knows how to run his business and the community, but has trouble controlling his wife. Lots of high spirits and raucous slapstick maintain steady interest in this farce that parodies Shakespeare's *The Taming of the Shrew.* O'Hara is effective as Wayne's difficult wife, and there are other good performances by Yvonne De Carlo, Patrick Wayne, Stefanie Powers, Chill Wills, and Bruce Cabot. **Director**—Andrew V. McLaglen. *127 minutes*

THE MEAN SEASON (1985)

★★1/2

Kurt Russell
Mariel Hemingway

Hardball journalism: Mariel Hemingway and Kurt Russell in The Mean Season.

A sporadically entertaining thriller about a newspaper reporter (Russell) who becomes personally involved with a serial murderer while covering a crime story. The film also probes ethical questions of media celebrity that involve both killer and reporter. The pace is interrupted with unnecessary red herrings and an overwrought, formula ending, but Russell's performance is credible. Richard Jordan, an underrated actor, is excellent in a supporting role. **Director**—Philip Borsos. **(R)**
106 minutes

MEAN STREETS (1973)

★★★1/2

Harvey Keitel
Robert De Niro

Harvey Keitel experiences the violence of the Mean Streets.

A compelling and sharply detailed story about life in New York City's Little Italy, as seen through the experiences of a group of small-time hoods. Director Martin Scorsese captures the atmosphere of the area and expertly brings out the sense of competitiveness and family life of the inhabitants. Scorsese made a name for himself with this moody and brutal portrait. Also with David Proval, Amy Robinson, Cesare Danova, and Richard Romanus. **(R)**
110 minutes

MEATBALLS (1979)

★★

Bill Murray
Harvey Atkin
Kate Lynch

This silly farce about life at summer camp seems aimed at the under-16-year-old set. A lack of fresh comic invention will make anyone with an iota of sophisticated taste restless. What's left is predictable and infantile non-
(Continued)

This movie available on videotape and/or disc.

(Continued)
sense that might tickle the funny bones of kids just old enough to go to the movies by themselves. Murray, however, is appealing as always. Also with Kristine DeBell, Chris Makepeace, Russ Banham, and Sarah Torgov. **Director**—Ivan Reitman. **(PG)** *92 minutes*

MEATBALLS PART II (1984)

★

Paul Reubens
Archie Hahn

This desperate sequel to the 1979 summer camp comedy goes out of control quickly and only gets worse as the ridiculous events progress. The tired, uninspired plot that primarily involves competition between some adolescent campers and the vicious inhabitants of a nearby military camp. Reubens would later gain fame under the name Pee-Wee Herman. Also with Richard Mulligan, John Mengatti, John Larroquette, Misty Rowe, and Hamilton Camp. **Director**—Ken Wiederhorn. **(PG)** *87 minutes*

MEDIUM COOL (1969)

★★★

Robert Forster

A remarkable and revealing semidocumentary film about the effects of television on our lifestyles and on our perceptions of violence in contemporary society. Director Haskell Wexler, also an award-winning cinematographer, sets his story in the arena of conflicts at the 1968 Democratic National Convention in Chicago, where he focuses on a TV news cameraman who mechanically goes about his duties in the midst of emotional events. The film is executed with style and intelligence and wrapped up with a thoughtful ending. In a particularly frightening scene, Wexler uses footage of the actors at the actual Convention at the point when the proceedings began to get violent. Forster plays the detached cameraman; he's supported by Verna Bloom, Peter Bonerz, and Marianna Hill. **(R)** *110 minutes*

MEET JOHN DOE (1941)

★★★★

Gary Cooper
Barbara Stanwyck
Edward Arnold

Gary Cooper causes a media stir in Meet John Doe.

Poignant social commentary of political treachery and lurking fascist tendencies in America. A naive tramp, beautifully portrayed by Cooper, becomes the unwitting tool of corrupt politician Arnold. Cooper threatens suicide as a protest against world conditions, and thousands of good citizens try to prevent his death by changing things. Director Frank Capra manages to weave some comedy, as well as a touching love affair with reporter Stanwyck, into the drama to bring off a masterpiece. The all-star cast also features Walter Brennan, James Gleason, Spring Byington, and Gene Lockhart. **Academy Award Nomination**—Richard Connell and Robert Presnell, original story. *123 minutes b&w*

MEET ME IN ST. LOUIS (1944)

★★★★

Judy Garland
Margaret O'Brien

Margaret O'Brien and Judy Garland put on a show in Meet Me in St. Louis.

A bright, charming musical in MGM's best tradition, about a family in St. Louis the year before the 1904 World's Fair. Garland tops the cast and sings most of the sentimental songs, including "The Boy Next Door" and "The Trolley Song." Leon Ames and Mary Astor costar as the parents; O'Brien plays Judy's sister. It's exceptionally romantic, nostalgic, and heartwarming. There's also fine support from June Lockhart, Harry Davenport, and Marjorie Main. O'Brien won a special miniature Oscar that year as the outstanding child actress of 1944. **Director**—Vincente Minnelli. **Academy Award Nomination**—George Folsey, cinematography. *113 minutes*

MEGAFORCE (1982)

★

Barry Bostwick
Michael Beck
Persis Khambatta

High-tech military hardware dominates this action/adventure about elite soldiers defending a small nation from invasion. An array of super-lasers, computer-guided rockets, and flying motorcycles zaps the villains. The production looks as though a movie was made out of an arcade video game. As for the dialogue, it's strictly gibberish. The cast performs woodenly against a background of smoke and noise. **Director**—Hal Needham. **(PG)** *93 minutes*

MELVIN AND HOWARD (1980)

★★★½

Paul LeMat
Jason Robards
Mary Steenburgen

A charming and often hilarious social satire taken from the much-publicized account of Melvin Dummar, the service-station attendant who claims to be a beneficiary in Howard Hughes' will. LeMat plays Melvin with a likable freshness that colorfully illuminates this good-hearted character who is eluded by the American dream. Supporting players Robards (who plays Hughes) and Steenburgen contribute excellent performances to this stylish comedy. Also with Dabney Coleman, Gloria Grahame, Michael J. Pollard, and Pamela Reed. **Director**—Jonathan Demme. **(R)** **Academy Awards**—Steenburgen, best supporting actress; Bo Goldman, best screenplay written directly for the screen. **Nomination**—Robards, best supporting actor. *95 minutes*

® This movie available with closed captions for the hearing impaired.

MEMORIES OF ME (1988)

★★1/2

Billy Crystal
Alan King

Alan King, Billy Crystal, and JoBeth Williams in Memories of Me.

Former TV star Henry Winkler directed this sentimental comedy/drama that seems influenced by the 1986 film *Nothing in Common*. Crystal stars as a young heart surgeon who tries to come to terms with his flamboyant, self-centered father, played by comedian King. The uneven film careens from funny one-liners to melodrama, but it is not too convincing as either. Also with JoBeth Williams, Janet Carroll, and David Ackroyd. **(PG-13)** *104 minutes*

MEN (1986)

★★★

Heiner Lauterbach
Uwe Ochsenknecht
Ulrike Kriener

A wry and clever comedy of the sexes by German filmmaker Doris Dörrie. An uptight advertising executive (Lauterbach) moves in with his wife's free-thinking, bohemian lover (Ochsenknecht) to discover why his wife (Kreiner) is so attracted to him. The unlikely buddies eventually exchange identities, leading to an unusual outcome. Originally filmed in German. **(No MPAA rating)** *99 minutes*

THE MEN (1950)

★★★1/2

Marlon Brando
Teresa Wright

Brando made his film debut in this absorbing drama with an impressive performance as a wounded war veteran struggling to overcome his disability. The film is a realistic and penetrating treatment of a sensitive subject. Also with Everett Sloane, Jack Webb, and Howard St. John. **Director**—Fred Zinnemann. **Academy Award Nomination**—Carl Foreman, story and screenplay. **Alternate Title**—*Battle Stripe.* *85 minutes b&w*

MEN DON'T LEAVE (1990)

★★★

Jessica Lange
Chris O'Donnell
Arliss Howard
Joan Cusack

Chris O'Donnell, Jessica Lange, and Charlie Korsmo in Men Don't Leave.

Lange stars as a newly widowed mother who struggles to adjust to the changes in her life. Suggested by the French movie *La Vie continue,* this comedy/drama sets a slow pace but offers a moving portrait of a family's devastation after the death of one of its members. Though the subject matter resembles that of a soap opera, director Paul Brickman's slow-paced style, his subtle use of imagery, and the excellent performances by the actors raise it above the level of cliché. Lange's performance here is more interesting than her Oscar-nominated performance for *The Music Box,* which was released in the same year, and Cusack is hilarious as an X-ray technician who seduces Lange's 17-year-old son. Also with Charlie Korsmo, Tom Mason, Kathy Bates, and Core Carrier. **(PG-13)** *115 minutes*

MEN OF THE FIGHTING LADY (1954)

★★★

Van Johnson
Walter Pidgeon

Above-average saga aboard a U.S. aircraft carrier during the Korean Conflict. The characters are rather wooden, but the film moves briskly, with a semidocumentary flavor enhanced by actual combat scenes. Also with Keenan Wynn, Frank Lovejoy, Dewey Martin, Robert Horton, and Louis Calhern. **Director**—Andrew Marton. *80 minutes*

THE MEN'S CLUB (1986)

★

Roy Scheider
Frank Langella
Harvey Keitel
Treat Williams

A group of men from various occupations get together and talk, talk, talk about women, themselves, and life in general in this stagy, uptight exercise in soul-searching. An interesting cast of many of this decade's best actors tackle the thin material, but with limited results. Slack direction and a feeble script indicate that most members neglected to pay their dues. Also with David Dukes, Richard Jordan, and Craig Wasson. **Director**—Peter Medak. **(R)** *100 minutes*

MERRILL'S MARAUDERS (1962)

★★★

Jeff Chandler
Ty Hardin

Rough, tough combat adventure with battle-hardened U.S. Army troops winning the hard way against enemy forces in Burma during World War II. Typical heroic storyline, with the emphasis on the limits of hardship under life-or-death conditions. The film was directed by B-movie great Samuel Fuller, whose unique visual style and affinity for action movies were well suited for such material. Decently acted by Chandler—his final film—and supporting players, including Hardin, Andrew Duggan, Peter Brown, Will Hutchins, and Claude Akins. *98 minutes*

MERRY CHRISTMAS, MR. LAWRENCE (1983)

★★1/2

David Bowie
Ryuichi Sakamoto
Tom Conti

Rock star Bowie's meticulous performance as a New Zealand officer confined to a Japanese prisoner-of-war

(Continued)

(Continued)
camp is intriguing. The film, however, is uneven and often unnecessarily harsh and gory. It tries to explore the differences and similarities of Western and Oriental cultures, a sort of intellectual version of *Bridge on the River Kwai*. But it pulls in too many directions at once and fails to achieve coherence. Takeshi and Jack Thompson costar. Sakamoto's soundtrack music is impressive. **Director**—Nagisa Oshima. **(R)**
120 minutes

THE MERRY WIDOW (1934)

★★★

Maurice Chevalier
Jeanette MacDonald

A lively, lavish Ernst Lubitsch musical with all of the charm and sparkle of the Lehar operetta combined with Lubitsch's unique style and flair. The superb cast includes Chevalier and MacDonald as the handsome pair of lovers, with excellent support from Edward Everett Horton and Una Merkel. The original musical score is still as captivating as ever and will leave you humming. *99 minutes b&w*

MESSAGE FROM SPACE (1978)

Vic Morrow
Sonny Chiba

Squadrons of spaceships race among the planets. Heroes and villains duel with laser-beam swords. There's even a cute little robot. This Japanese science-fiction film seems inspired by *Star Wars*, though it has none of the appeal of that classic. The special effects have lots of zip, but the acting and plotting are second-rate. Morrow is the only familiar face in the crowd of unknown players; he has a brief role but still gets top billing. **Director**—Kinji Fukasaku. **(PG)**
105 minutes

MESSENGER OF DEATH (1988)

★★½

Charles Bronson

Bronson sheds his tough-guy image to portray a mild-mannered reporter covering the story of a bloody multiple killing in scenic Colorado. The change of pace for Bronson doesn't enhance this unsuccessful mystery concerning a feuding Mormon family. However, the drama is graced with notable performances by veteran character players: Jeff Corey and John Ireland costar as brothers involved with a cult, and Laurence Luckinbill plays a politically ambitious police chief. **Director**—J. Lee Thompson. **(R)** *92 minutes*

METALSTORM (1983)

Jeffrey Byron
Mike Preston
Richard Moll

Jeffrey Byron is confronted with a Cyclopean God in Metalstorm.

A slow-paced, mangy-looking sci-fi adventure, shot in 3-D and overloaded with nonsense about evil forces at work in the universe. Byron heads the undistinguished cast as a heroic space ranger assigned to rescue a damsel and put an end to a villain. Also with Tim Thomerson and Kelly Preston. **Director**—Charles Band. **(PG) Alternate Title**—*Metalstorm: The Destruction of Jared-Syn.*
84 minutes

METEOR (1979)

★★

Sean Connery
Natalie Wood
Karl Malden

This is one more disaster epic for fans who can't get enough of devastation by earthquakes, tidal waves, and so on. This time it's a gigantic meteor speeding toward Earth, and the Americans and Russians combine nuclear technology to stop it. Connery, Wood, and other notables put in time at the movie factory to portray cardboard characters. Some of the special effects are interesting, such as Manhattan's destruction. Henry Fonda plays the President—again. Also with Brian Keith, Martin Landau, Trevor Howard, and Richard Dysart. **Director**—Ronald Neame. **(PG)**
103 minutes

METROPOLIS (1926)

★★★★

Brigitte Helm

Fritz Lang directed this visually impressive classic of the German silent cinema. The film is a brooding vision of life in the year 2000, and the real star is its awesome set depicting a futuristic city (said to have been based on Lang's interpretation of the New York City skyline), with expressionist lighting and compositions. The story (written by Lang's wife, Thea von Harbou) involves a female automaton who incites the dronelike workers—who live beneath the elite's elegant metropolis—to revolt against their employers. The imagery (37,000 extras moving through the geometric landscapes) is compelling. And the film's depiction of a dehumanized society is still effective. In 1984, Giorgio Moroder reconstructed the film, adding some lost scenes and a digital soundtrack featuring rock music. Both versions are available on videotape.
120 minutes b&w

MIAMI BLUES (1990)

★★★

Alec Baldwin
Jennifer Jason Leigh
Fred Ward

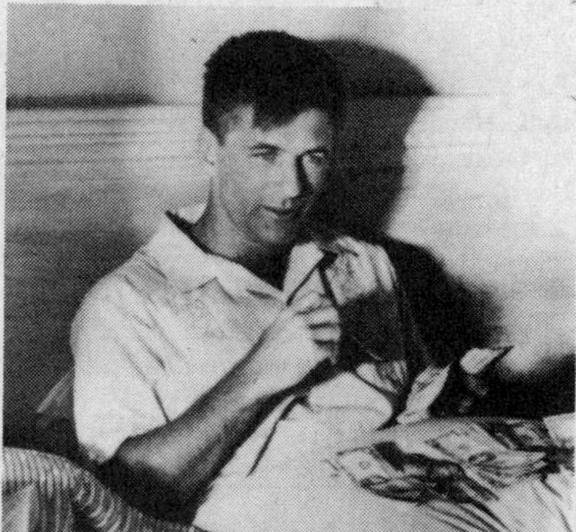

Alec Baldwin is the appealing criminal in Miami Blues.

A quirky comedy/drama involving a young, charismatic criminal, a simple-minded prostitute, and a rumpled homicide detective. The screwball characters are absorbing and individual

This movie available with closed captions for the hearing impaired.

scenes are fascinating, but the story lacks coherency. It drifts from episode to episode until the end, when a violent climax abruptly concludes the storyline. Baldwin is excellent as the slightly off-balance Junior, while Leigh brings sympathy and dimension to her role as Susie, the prostitute with a talent for baking offbeat Southern dishes. Oddly, it is Junior and Susie who strive for a conventional lifestyle—in a clean, quiet suburb of Miami—while the grizzled detective, played by Ward, resides in a grimy room in a sleazy inner-city hotel. The film does not pass judgment on its characters: Each one is charming yet vile in his or her own way. Details like these make the movie atypical and refreshing viewing. Also with Nora Dunn, Charles Napier, Jose Perez, and Paul Gleason. **Director**—George Armitage. **(R)** *97 minutes*

MICKI & MAUDE (1984)

★★★

Dudley Moore
Ann Reinking
Amy Irving

Happy bigamy with Dudley Moore and Amy Irving in Micki & Maude.

Oh, the mess Moore has on his hands: He plays a frustrated TV reporter with two wives (Reinking and Irving) who are both pregnant at the same time. This farcical setup leads to a maternity ward full of belly laughs as frantic Dudley attends to both women simultaneously while trying to maintain his secret. It's an ideal vehicle for Moore's likable charm. Blake Edwards directs from a clever script. **(PG-13)** *115 minutes*

MIDDLE AGE CRAZY (1980)

★★

Bruce Dern
Ann-Margret
Graham Jarvis

Dern stars as a successful architect with a beautiful wife (Ann-Margret) who confronts a midlife crisis. Dern gives the part ample warmth and appeal, but the tedious script is bogged down with clichés and sentimentality. The upshot is a disappointing film. This social problem has been explored time and again, and here the subject is overworked. Inspired by the country/western song by Jerry Lee Lewis. Also with Eric Christmas and Deborah Wakeman. **Director**—John Trent. **(R)** *95 minutes*

MIDDLE OF THE NIGHT (1959)

Fredric March
Kim Novak

Satisfactory film rendition of Paddy Chayefsky's teleplay about a middle-aged widower in love with a much younger girl. March is convincing as the worldly-wise businessman seeking a new experience, but Novak is nearly as good as the youthful object of his affections. This isn't among the best of Chayefsky's efforts, but the story is moving nevertheless. Glenda Farrell, Jan Norris, Lee Grant, and Martin Balsam are adequate in supporting roles. **Director**—Delbert Mann. *118 minutes b&w*

MIDNIGHT COWBOY (1969)

★★★★

Jon Voight
Dustin Hoffman

Outstanding drama about a naive young man from Texas who comes to New York City to make it as a gigolo. He ends up being hustled, and he discovers it's just as dreary and lonesome in the big city as it was in the hick town he came from. The stark chain of events is played out against the squalid backdrop of New York's decaying 42nd Street area, and the film offers some memorable character studies of desperate souls. Director John Schlesinger employs a number of formal cinematic devices, such as rapid cutting and fancy camerawork, to enhance the storyline. Voight is triumphant in the title role, and his excellent performance is matched by Hoffman as Ratso Rizzo, his disheveled friend. Sylvia Miles, John McGiver, Barnard Hughes, Ruth White, Jennifer Salt, Bob Balaban, Paul Morrissey, and Brenda Vaccaro also star. Received an X rating upon initial release. Television prints are cut drastically. **(R) Academy Awards**—best picture; Schlesinger, best director; Waldo Salt, best screenplay based on material from another medium. **Nominations**—Hoffman and Voight, best actor; Miles, best supporting actress. *113 minutes*

MIDNIGHT CROSSING (1988)

★½

Faye Dunaway
Daniel J. Travanti
Kim Cattrall

A limp plot, dreadful dialogue, and cardboard characters sink this melodrama about a group of unscrupulous people seeking to recover buried loot on an island near Cuba. Various double crosses emerge throughout the film, most of which merely confuse the plot. Dunaway tarnishes her already tenuous film career by overacting the part of a blind woman, whose husband originally buried the fortune. John Laughlin and Ned Beatty also slink about in this old-fashioned embarrassment. **Director**—Roger Holzberg. **(R)** *104 minutes*

MIDNIGHT EXPRESS (1978)

★★★½

Brad Davis
John Hurt
Randy Quaid

Mike Kellin tries to comfort imprisoned Brad Davis in Midnight Express.

Harsh, gut-wrenching portrayal of the brutality, degradation, and frustration suffered by a young American in a Turkish prison. The film is based on the true story of Billy Hayes, who was arrested in 1970 in Istanbul for trying to smuggle two kilos of hashish. Davis, playing Hayes, gives a remarkable performance. Director Alan Parker expertly

(Continued)

(Continued)
crafts the harrowing moods and sordid scenes of this latter-day version of Dante's *Inferno*. Also with Irene Miracle and Bo Hopkins. **(R) Academy Award**—Oliver Stone, best screenplay based on material from another medium. **Nominations**—best picture; Parker, best director; Hurt, best supporting actor.
121 minutes

MIDNIGHT RUN (1988)

★★★

Robert De Niro
Charles Grodin

John Ashton, Charles Grodin, and Robert De Niro in Midnight Run.

Masterful performances by De Niro and Grodin elevate this unsurprising but exceptionally entertaining action/comedy. De Niro stars as a bounty hunter assigned to return a bail-jumping accountant, played by Grodin, who embezzled $15 million from gangsters. Their rollicking cross-country trek with mobsters, the FBI, and a rival bounty hunter snapping at their heels results in both laughs and thrills. De Niro's legendary ability to transform himself into his character gives the film a depth it may not have had otherwise. De Niro and Grodin make an appealing odd couple. Also with Yaphet Kotto, John Ashton, Dennis Farina, Joe Pantoliano, Wendy Phillips, and Richard Foronjy. **Director**—Martin Brest. **(R)**
122 minutes

A MIDSUMMER NIGHT'S DREAM (1935)

★★★

James Cagney
Mickey Rooney

This early Hollywood version of the Shakespeare play is extravagantly set, costumed, and cast. As a technical production, it can't be flawed, with music by Mendelssohn, choreography by Nijinsky, and photography by Hal Mohr, Fred Jackson, Byron Haskin, and H.F. Koenekamp. The all-star cast features Cagney, Dick Powell, Jean Muir, Ross Alexander, and Olivia de Havilland; but is best remembered for its splendid characterizations by Rooney, Joe E. Brown, Hugh Herbert, Arthur Treacher, Frank McHugh, and many more. The film is a treat to the senses and its minor drawbacks are no match for its overall success. **Directors**—Max Reinhardt and William Dieterle. **Academy Awards**—Mohr, cinematography; Ralph Dawson, editing. **Nomination**—best picture.
117 minutes b&w

A MIDSUMMER NIGHT'S SEX COMEDY (1982)

★★½

Woody Allen
Mia Farrow
Josè Ferrer
Mary Steenburgen

In this picturesque but empty production, Allen presides over a romantic roundelay among three couples at a turn-of-the-century country home. Allen gets off a few wisecracks, but the film bogs down in ceaseless chatter about sexual problems. Once more, Allen seems to be rehashing someone else's movie; there are obvious references to Ingmar Bergman's *Smiles of a Summer Night*. Also with Tony Roberts and Julie Hagerty. **Director**—Allen. **(PG)**
88 minutes

MIDWAY (1976)

★½

Charlton Heston
Henry Fonda
Glenn Ford
James Coburn
Hal Holbrook
Robert Mitchum

The sea-air Battle of Midway was a turning point in the Pacific during World War II, but this plodding and cliché-strewn film version is hardly a turning point in war movies. The lame script covers well-worn territory, and it's all wrapped in the Sensurround gimmick, which is more of an earache than an emotional effect. Veteran actors, including Robert Wagner and Cliff Robertson, appear briefly to deliver a few stiff lines. Fonda has a somewhat larger part as Admiral Nimitz. Stock footage from other war films plus real war footage was used for the battle sequences. **(PG)**
132 minutes

MIGHTY JOE YOUNG (1949)

★★★

Terry Moore
Ben Johnson

A competent retread of the King Kong fable, but not as stylish as the 1933 movie. A promoter brings back a gorilla from the African jungles and uses it in a nightclub routine. The animal breaks away and terrorizes the city. Just standard monkey business, with good special effects by Ray Harryhausen and *King Kong* special-effects designer Willis O'Brien; Moore is in the Fay Wray role. Also with Robert Armstrong and Frank McHugh. Directed by Ernest B. Schoedsack, who worked as codirector on the original *King Kong*. **Academy Award**—special effects.
94 minutes b&w

THE MIGHTY QUINN (1989)

★★★ ®

Denzel Washington
Robert Townsend
James Fox

Washington is amusing and confident in this appealing mystery set on a Caribbean island. He stars in the title role as a police chief charged with investigating a grisly murder, but the probe soon becomes entangled in personal and political conflicts. The breezy, colorful tale is generously seasoned with reggae music. Also with M. Emmet Walsh, Mimi Rogers, Sheryl Lee Ralph, Art Evans, Esther Rolle, and Keye Luke. **Director**—Carl Schenkel. **(R)**
99 minutes

MIKE'S MURDER (1984)

★★½

Debra Winger

Low-key melodrama set against Los Angeles' cocaine underworld. Winger stars as a lonely bank teller who falls in love with a charming tennis player (Mark Keyloun). When he is killed because of his drug connections, she at-

® *This movie available with closed captions for the hearing impaired.*

Mark Keyloun and Debra Winger fall in love in Mike's Murder.

tempts to unravel the mystery and eventually uncovers his dismal background. The slick film plays up atmosphere, but the characters are mostly uninteresting and the pace is slow—possibly the result of writer/producer/director James Bridges biting off more than he could chew. Also with Paul Winfield and Darrell Larson. **(R)**

109 minutes

THE MILAGRO BEANFIELD WAR (1988)

★★½

Rubén Blades
Richard Bradford
Sonia Braga

A sluggish account of impoverished Chicano villagers in New Mexico who confront some typically greedy land developers. This breezy story of little people pitted against powerful capitalists should have carried more dramatic impact, but Robert Redford's unsteady direction places the emphasis on whimsical touches and quaint characters. Most of the interesting cast, including Braga of *Kiss of the Spider Woman* and Blades, a noted singer of salsa music, do a lot with the limited material. One of those Hollywood projects that took ten years to develop and two to direct, but with varying results. Also with Chick Vennera, Julie Carmen, Melanie Griffith, John Heard, Daniel Stern, and Christopher Walken. **(R) Academy Award**—Dave Grusin, music original score. *118 minutes*

MILDRED PIERCE (1945)

★★★★

Joan Crawford
Ann Blyth
Zachary Scott
Eve Arden

First-class, glossy soap opera starring Crawford as a divorced mother who works her way up from waitress to the owner of a restaurant chain. The mother-daughter relationship is the focus, with Blyth in top form as Crawford's unthankful offspring. Based on the novel by James Cain, the film is considered a classic women's picture, with Crawford in one of her finest roles. Competent supporting roles by Jack Carson and Bruce Bennett. **Director**—Michael Curtiz. **Academy Award**—Crawford, best actress. **Nominations**—best picture; Arden and Blyth, best supporting actress; Ranald MacDougall, screenplay; Ernest Haller, cinematography. *113 minutes b&w*

MILES FROM HOME (1988)

★★

Richard Gere
Kevin Anderson

Richard Gere travels Miles from Home *after he loses his farm to foreclosure.*

Gere and Anderson play brothers who are victims of the 1980s agricultural crisis. After their farm is foreclosed, they embark on a spree of bank robbery, arson, and car theft. This latter-day outlaw activity is supposed to elicit our sympathy for their economic plight, but the pair's maverick behavior seems more foolhardy than heroic. Penelope Ann Miller and Laurie Metcalf provide bright performances in small roles. Directed by actor Gary Sinise, one of the members of Chicago's Steppenwolf Theater. **(R)** *113 minutes*

MILLENNIUM (1989)

★★

Kris Kristofferson
Cheryl Ladd

A shabby science-fiction adventure that suffers from jumbled direction, wooden performances, silly dialogue, a creaky script, and flimsy special effects. Kristofferson stars as an airline crash investigator who falls in love with a woman from 1,000 years in the future, played by Ladd. She seeks to save her people from extinction by returning to the past. Also with Daniel J. Travanti and Robert Joy. **Director**—Michael Anderson. **(PG-13)**

106 minutes

MILLION DOLLAR MYSTERY (1987)

★½

Rich Hall
Eddie Deezen

A corny comedy/adventure about the frantic search for $4 million stashed away by a corrupt government official. Tom Bosley plays the man with the hidden loot who mutters some clues just before he dies after eating chili in a diner. The greedy bystanders then hightail it into the Arizona desert in search of the fortune. A series of routine car crashes and badly timed comedy pranks make up the bulk of this mediocre movie, which fails to capture the comic calamity of *It's a Mad Mad Mad Mad World*. Also with Penny Baker, Wendy Sherman, and Rick Overton. **Director**—Richard Fleischer. **(PG)**

93 minutes

MIN AND BILL (1930)

★★★

Marie Dressler
Wallace Beery

Dorothy Jordan, Marie Dressler, and Wallace Beery in Min and Bill.

Moving, sentimental waterfront saga of an aging, down-and-out couple bucking the system to maintain custody of their daughter. Dressler and Beery are memorable as the independent but socially unacceptable pair who tough out the world. The solid supporting cast in-

(Continued)

(Continued)
cludes Dorothy Jordan as the daughter, Marjorie Rambeau, Donald Dillaway, and Russell Hopton. This gentle comedy was so successful that it gave rise to *Tugboat Annie,* with the original stars playing similar roles. **Director**—George Hill. **Academy Award**—Dressler, best actress. *69 minutes b&w*

MINDWARP: AN INFINITY OF TERROR

See Galaxy of Terror

MIRACLE MILE (1989)

★★

Anthony Edwards
Mare Winningham

An oddball thriller about the few remaining hours of several Los Angeles citizens awaiting a nuclear attack. Edwards and Winningham play young lovers who frantically try to escape the big city before the attack comes. Despite being many years in the making, the film is poorly executed and lapses into chaos in its last minutes. Also with John Agar, Mykel T. Williamson, and Denise Crosby. **Director**—Steve DeJarnatt. **(R)** *87 minutes*

THE MIRACLE OF MORGAN'S CREEK (1944)

★★★★

Betty Hutton
Eddie Bracken

Eddie Bracken and Betty Hutton sparkle in The Miracle of Morgan's Creek.

A top comedy by director Preston Sturges, about the misadventures of a girl made pregnant by a soldier at a party. But which soldier? This subject would have no problem today, but the censors of that era held this film from release for over a year. Produced during World War II, the film offers a view of life on the home front different from the sentimental tales so popular at that time. Hutton is excellent as the hapless mother-to-be. William Demarest, Diana Lynn, and Brian Donlevy also star. **Academy Award Nomination**—Sturges, original screenplay. *99 minutes b&w*

MIRACLE ON 34TH STREET (1947)

★★★★

Edmund Gwenn
Natalie Wood
Maureen O'Hara
John Payne

Kris Kringle (Edmund Gwenn) sparks Natalie Wood's imagination in Miracle on 34th Street.

An amazingly cheerful, heartwarming, and uplifting fable, about an elderly gentleman, hired as a department store Santa Claus, who claims to be the real St. Nick. It's a clever and charming blend of humor and pathos with a holiday message for young and old. This film seems as enduring as Christmas itself. Gwenn is delightful as "Kris Kringle." Porter Hall, William Frawley, and Gene Lockhart are in supporting roles. **Director**—George Seaton. **Academy Awards**—Gwenn, best supporting actor; Valentine Davies, original story; George Seaton, screenplay. **Nomination**—best picture. *94 minutes b&w*

THE MIRACLE WORKER (1962)

★★★★

Anne Bancroft
Patty Duke

An absorbing account of the early life of Helen Keller and her amazing struggle to overcome the multiple handicaps of being blind, deaf, and mute. The story is as much about her determined teacher, and the role is played brilliantly by Bancroft. Duke is excellent as well, as the young Keller who finally learns to communicate. A few scenes are exceptionally moving. Also with Victor Jory, Inga Swenson, Andrew Prine, and Beah Richards. **Director**—Arthur Penn. **Academy Awards**—Bancroft, best actress; Duke, best supporting actress. **Nominations**—Penn, best director; William Gibson, best screenplay based on material from another medium. *107 minutes b&w*

MIRAGE (1965)

★★★

Gregory Peck
Diane Baker
Walter Matthau

Expertly conceived thriller, presented in much the same style as an Alfred Hitchcock film, about a man with amnesia who becomes tangled in a murder mystery. Peck plays the amnesiac, Baker is the mysterious girl who enters his life, and Matthau is a rumpled private detective. The suspense is effectively paced and developed, and the film is enhanced with striking photography of New York City locations. There's an interesting performance by Matthau. Also with Walter Abel, Kevin McCarthy, Jack Weston, Leif Erickson, and George Kennedy. **Director**—Edward Dmytryk. *109 minutes b&w*

THE MIRROR CRACK'D (1980)

★★★

Angela Lansbury
Edward Fox

Stylish, tart Agatha Christie whodunit with an all-star cast, about a series of murders on the set of an American movie being made in England. Elizabeth Taylor and Kim Novak, in their best roles in years, are delightful as rival fading movie stars. Lansbury is a convincing Miss Jane Marple, who figures out who poisoned the drink at the cocktail party. Also with Rock Hudson, Tony Curtis, and Geraldine Chaplin. **Director**—Guy Hamilton. **(PG)** *105 minutes*

MISCHIEF (1985)

★★

Doug McKeon
Kelly Preston

The mid-1950s is the setting for this nostalgic teenage comedy that over-

® This movie available with closed captions for the hearing impaired.

flows with clichés. Most characters seem borrowed from similar movies or plucked from "Archie" comics. McKeon gets the most attention as the awkward adolescent who, to his surprise, beds the hotshot high-school beauty (Preston). A wide selection of hit songs from the period fills the background. Also with Chris Nash and Catherine Mary Stewart. **Director**—Mel Damski. **(R)**

97 minutes

THE MISFITS (1961)

★★★

Clark Gable
Marilyn Monroe
Montgomery Clift

Gable and Monroe in their last completed film, The Misfits.

Arthur Miller's pensive screenplay about latter-day cowboys is alternately compelling and sullen. Monroe plays a confused divorcée involved with an aging cowboy (Gable), who sets out to round up wild horses in the desert. Clift costars as an unlucky rodeo rider who joins Monroe and her group of "misfit" friends. The rumors about the problems that plagued the production (Monroe's emotional distress, Clift's drinking, the intolerable heat) only serve to enhance the tension and sadness that are part of the film's story. The last completed film for both Gable and Monroe. Also with Eli Wallach, Thelma Ritter, and Kevin McCarthy. **Director**—John Huston. *124 minutes b&w*

MISS FIRECRACKER (1989)

★★★

Holly Hunter
Alfre Woodard
Tim Robbins
Mary Steenburgen

A film adaptation of playwright Beth Henley's hit stage production about the trials and tribulations of Carnelle Scott, who wants to win the Miss Firecracker contest in her hometown of Yazoo City, Mississippi. Carnelle lacks the looks and talent to win but is portrayed with so much spunk by Hunter that viewers are left with the idea that she has a chance. Like most of Henley's work, the film is filled with quirky characters and peculiar episodes, which work well in the colorful Southern setting. Robbins costars as wayward cousin Delmount, while Woodard skillfully portrays the most outrageous character, Popeye, the uneducated seamstress. Steenburgen makes the most of her role as Carnelle's cousin, a former Miss Firecracker herself. Not for all tastes but worth a look for the performances. Also with Trey Wilson, Ann Wedgeworth, and Scott Glenn. **Director**—Thomas Schlamme. **(PG)** *102 minutes*

MISS GRANT TAKES RICHMOND (1949)

Lucille Ball
William Holden

Ball plays a zany secretary who helps put the lid on a bookie operation. Typical slapstick shenanigans, enjoyable if you love Lucy. Holden is an effective costar. Also with Janis Carter, James Gleason, and Frank McHugh. **Director**—Lloyd Bacon. *87 minutes b&w*

MISSING (1982)

★★★★

Jack Lemmon
Sissy Spacek

Sissy Spacek and Jack Lemmon grapple with Latin American bureaucracy in Missing.

A powerful, compelling political melodrama masterfully directed by Constantin Costa-Gavras (Z) and well played by Lemmon and Spacek. The plot stars Lemmon as an American businessman involved in a frustrating search for his missing son, who's been caught up in a turbulent political situation in a South American country. The father is jolted out of his complacency when he runs into a wall of double-talk and red tape from American embassy and local government officials. Based on a true story. **(PG) Academy Award**—Costa-Gavras and Donald Stewart, best screenplay based on material from another medium. **Nominations**—best picture; Lemmon, best actor; Spacek, best actress. *122 minutes*

MISSING IN ACTION (1984)

Chuck Norris

Plenty of shoot-'em-up action propels this simpleminded adventure about the rescue of a few American war prisoners from Vietnam. Norris stars as a one-man army who blasts away with machine guns, grenades, and explosives against scores of Vietnamese soldiers. They obligingly bite the dust without showing much blood or gore. In typical B-movie fashion, the Americans are portrayed as brave and virtuous while the enemy is composed of cardboard villains. Also with M. Emmet Walsh. **Director**—Joseph Zito. **(R)**

101 minutes

MISSING IN ACTION 2 (1985)

★★

Chuck Norris

More shoot-'em-up, flag-waving adventures featuring Colonel Braddock (Norris) and his troops. This time the action takes place *during* the Vietnam War, when they were prisoners of the North Vietnamese. The first two-thirds of this prequel to *Missing in Action* establishes the Vietnamese captors as heartless, vile torturers. In the remaining portion, Norris launches an all-out escape effort with a blaze of gunfire, explosions, and karate action. Fans of such overstated heroics should relish the furious climax. Also with Soon-Teck Oh. **Director**—Lance Hool. **(R)**

94 minutes

THE MISSION (1986)

Robert De Niro
Jeremy Irons

This sweeping, epic drama set in 18th-century South America involves the

(Continued)

(Continued)
consequences of a decision by imperialist Spain and Portugal to close a jungle mission and subject the peaceful Indians to the ravages of slavery. De Niro and Irons are the Jesuits who oppose this decision, which has been sanctioned by the Vatican. Unfortunately, the film's central characters are sketchily drawn and the script contains ponderous dialogue and confusing scenes. The Oscar-winning cinematography by Chris Menges overwhelms the story, which suffers from self-righteous characters and a sanctimonious attitude. **Director**—Roland Joffe. **(PG) Academy Award Nominations**—best picture; Joffe, best director; Jim Clark, best editing; Ennio Morricone, best original score; Enrico Sabbatini, best costume design; Stuart Craig and Jack Stephens, best art direction and set decoration.
125 minutes

THE MISSIONARY (1982)

 ★★

Michael Palin
Maggie Smith
Trevor Howard

Palin, of the Monty Python comedy troupe, stars in this meandering satire on Edwardian morality. He's a missionary preacher assigned to rescue London's "fallen women," but he can't resist taking a very nonclerical interest in his charges in the process. The British production is exquisitely appointed, well acted, and quietly amusing much of the time. But it's a thin story underneath all the surface charm. **Director**—Richard Loncraine. **(R)** *90 minutes*

MISSISSIPPI BURNING (1988)

Gene Hackman
Willem Dafoe

The sentiments of Gene Hackman and Willem Dafoe differ in Mississippi Burning.

Director Alan Parker's fictionalized account of the 1964 FBI investigation of the disappearance and suspected murder of three civil-rights workers. Hackman stars as a Southern-born federal agent whose cunning tactics are more effective than the orthodox methods of his liberal Northern partner, played by Dafoe. Despite the powerful statement against racism, the film is another example of an essentially black story told from a white man's point of view. The effect is that the FBI agents were the heroes of this era, which was certainly a misrepresentation. Another historical era gets the Hollywood treatment. Also with Frances McDormand, Brad Dourif, R. Lee Ermey, Michael Rooker, Park Overall, and Gailard Sartain. **(R) Academy Award**—Peter Biziou, cinematography. **Nominations**—best picture; Parker, best director; Hackman, best actor; Frances McDormand, best supporting actress; Gerry Hambling, editing.
127 minutes

THE MISSOURI BREAKS (1976)

★★★

Marlon Brando
Jack Nicholson

Superstars Brando and Nicholson deliver delightful and dazzling performances in Arthur Penn's period western set in the majestic Montana hills in 1880. Brando plays an eccentric and sadistic hired gun commissioned by a wealthy cattle baron to wipe out a gang of horse thieves headed by Nicholson. But without these two magnificent talents, the film would be a tedious horse opera. Screenwriter Thomas McGuane merely set the clock back on the plot that served his earlier film, *Rancho Deluxe,* and added some late-20th-century philosophizing. Newcomer Kathleen Lloyd demonstrates extraordinary potential in the role of the cattleman's liberated daughter, who falls in love with the likable Nicholson. Also with Randy Quaid, Harry Dean Stanton, and Frederic Forrest. **(PG)**
126 minutes

MR. AND MRS. SMITH (1941)

Robert Montgomery
Carole Lombard
Gene Raymond
Jack Carson

Director Alfred Hitchcock demonstrated a talent for comic touches in many of his films, but this is the only one that is pure comedy. Not that there isn't mayhem: Montgomery and Lombard star as a bickering couple who discover that, as a result of a technicality involving the state line, they aren't really married. Can Mr. Smith win back the hand of Mrs. Smith? Hitchcock brings considerable style to Norman Krasna's Punch-and-Judy script, though it takes some getting used to and you may keep expecting a murder or two to thicken the plot throughout the first half. A far cry from Hitchcock's best, but it's well shot and acted. Also with Philip Merivale, Betty Compson, and Lucile Watson. *95 minutes b&w*

MR. BLANDINGS BUILDS HIS DREAM HOUSE (1948)

 ★★★★

Cary Grant
Myrna Loy
Melvyn Douglas

A rib-tickling, middlebrow comedy about a New York advertising executive who decides to build a house in the country and discovers the project is no piece of cake. There are many clever and funny moments in this slick production with the stars at their hilarious best. Grant is perfectly cast as the exasperated homeowner. Also with Reginald Denny, Louise Beavers, and Jason Robards, Sr. **Director**—H.C. Potter.
94 minutes b&w

MR. DEEDS GOES TO TOWN (1936)

Gary Cooper
Jean Arthur
George Bancroft

Excellent 1930s comedy, voted best picture of the year by The New York Film Critics, and an Oscar-winner for director Frank Capra. Cooper stars as Longfellow Deeds, the small-town Vermont greeting-verse writer who inherits $20 million from his late uncle, and finds his world turned topsy-turvy by his new fortune. Because the humble tuba player wants to give away much of his wealth, he is accused of being simpleminded by those who would prefer to manipulate his money themselves. The film is beguiling as vintage comedy and fascinating as Depression-era social consciousness. Beautifully played by Cooper, Arthur (as a New York reporter who first exploits, then loves Deeds), Bancroft, Raymond Walburn, Lionel Stander, Walter Catlett, and H.B. Warner. **Academy Award**—Capra, best director. **Nominations**—best picture; Cooper, best actor; Robert Riskin, screenplay. *118 minutes b&w*

MR. LOVE (1986)

Barry Jackson
Maurice Denham
Margaret Tyzack

Could a bashful gardener really be the legendary ladies' man of a quiet English seaside town? This small-scale romantic comedy answers the question by illuminating the extramarital affairs of the title character. However, the film too often turns sentimental at the expense of the comedy. Jackson seems well suited to the unlikely Don Juan role. **Director**—Roy Battersby. **(PG–13)** *92 minutes*

MR. LUCKY (1943)

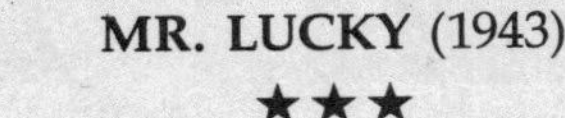

Cary Grant
Laraine Day

Grant is effectively charming and amusing as a gambling-ship owner who concocts a dubious scheme to raise cash. But love intervenes, and he goes straight. A smooth blend of comedy and drama, handled skillfully by a professional cast, which also includes Charles Bickford, Gladys Cooper, and Alan Carney. Later developed into a successful television series. **Director**—H.C. Potter. *98 minutes b&w*

MR. MOM (1983)

Michael Keaton
Teri Garr

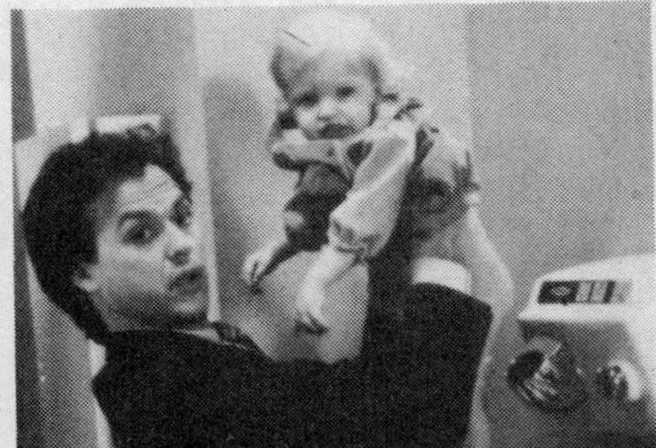

Harried Mr. Mom *(Michael Keaton) hits upon a novel quick-dry technique.*

Dad (Keaton) loses his job at the recession-plagued auto factory. He stays home to mind the kids while Mom (Garr) goes to work and becomes a successful ad-agency executive. This role reversal bit may seem familiar, but the performances are spirited and the dialogue is witty. John Hughes, who later wrote and directed *Sixteen Candles* and *The Breakfast Club,* did the script. The film establishes Keaton as one of the best comic actors around. Martin Mull and Ann Jillian costar. **Director**—Stan Dragoti. **(PG)** *91 minutes*

MR. NORTH (1988)

Anthony Edwards
Lauren Bacall
Harry Dean Stanton

A sparkling comic fable based on Thornton Wilder's final novel. Edwards takes the title role as an attractive young man who makes quite an impact on the wealthy citizens of 1926 Newport, Rhode Island. A veteran cast furnishes polished performances, though the film seems sentimental and uneven at times. The script was cowritten by John Huston. Also stars Robert Mitchum, Anjelica Huston, Mary Stuart Masterson, Virginia Madsen, and David Warner. **Director**—Danny Huston. **(PG)** *92 minutes*

MR. PEABODY AND THE MERMAID (1948)

★★½

William Powell
Ann Blyth

Mildly amusing fantasy about a middle-aged man who discovers a beautiful mermaid and takes a fresh look at his life. A few scenes work, but just as many are too silly. Powell is suited for the title role. Also with Irene Hervey, Andrea King, and Clinton Sundberg. **Director**—Irving Pichel. *89 minutes b&w*

MISTER ROBERTS (1955)

★★★½

Henry Fonda
James Cagney
William Powell
Jack Lemmon

Boredom and pettiness aboard a supply ship in the Pacific during World War II

Henry Fonda is the idealistic Navy officer in Mister Roberts.

provides the subject for this winning comedy. Fonda is great in the title role as an idealistic Navy officer who longs to be transferred to a fighting ship. There's rampant scene-stealing by Lemmon as a bumbling Ensign Pulver and Cagney as the neurotic skipper of the cargo vessel. Powell plays the ship's doctor. A superb blend of hilarity and sentiment, based on the Broadway play by Joshua Logan and author Thomas Heggen. Due to artistic differences between Fonda and director John Ford, Ford was replaced with Mervyn LeRoy. Also with Ward Bond, Betsy Palmer, and Phil Carey. **Academy Award**—Lemmon, best supporting actor. **Nomination**—best picture. *123 minutes*

MR. SKEFFINGTON (1944)

★★★

Bette Davis
Claude Rains
Walter Abel

Bette Davis gets a taste of the high life in Mr. Skeffington.

This epic melodrama chronicles some 30 years in the life of a self-centered New York siren, who marries a successful stockbroker for the comfortable life

(Continued)

(Continued)
he can provide her, but gives him little in return except grief. Only many years later, after he's gone blind and her looks have been ravaged by diphtheria, does she learn what love really means. A star vehicle for Davis, the film was highly popular in its day. Originally released at 146 minutes. **Director**—Vincent Sherman. **Academy Award Nominations**—Davis, best actress; Rains, best supporting actor. *127 minutes b&w*

MR. SMITH GOES TO WASHINGTON (1939)

★★★★

James Stewart
Claude Rains
Jean Arthur

This is among the best of director Frank Capra's comedy/dramas. Stewart gives a stirring performance as a forthright freshman senator who encounters corruption in the nation's capital. It's an inspiring portrait of how elected officials ought to behave. Stewart's naive, inarticulate, and clumsy character is an interesting contrast to Rains, who portrays a sophisticated and manipulative orator—a contrast that enhances Capra's theme of the triumph of the ordinary person over the corrupt elite. Also with Harry Carey, Thomas Mitchell, Edward Arnold, Guy Kibbee, and Beulah Bondi. **Academy Award**—Lewis R. Foster, original story. **Nominations**—best picture; Capra, best director; Stewart, best actor; Carey and Rains, best supporting actor; Sidney Buchman, screenplay. *130 minutes b&w*

MRS. MINIVER (1942)

★★★★

Greer Garson
Walter Pidgeon

A highly moving account of courageous British villagers struggling to cope with the hardships and dangers of World War II. The film is melodramatic, but it's extremely well made, and it served as an effective wartime morale booster. Fine performances throughout. Also with Teresa Wright, Henry Travers, Richard Ney, and Dame May Whitty. **Director**—William Wyler. **Academy Awards**—best picture; Wyler, best director; Garson, best actress; Wright, best supporting actress; George Froeschel, James Hilton, Claudine West, and Arthur Wimperis, screenplay; Joseph Ruttenberg, cinematography. **Nominations**—Pidgeon, best actor; Travers, best supporting actor; Whitty, best supporting actress. *134 minutes b&w*

MRS. PARKINGTON (1944)

Greer Garson
Walter Pidgeon
Edward Arnold
Agnes Moorehead

Greer Garson and Frances Rafferty in Mrs. Parkington.

Countering Warner's extravagant 1944 Bette Davis weepie *Mr. Skeffington* was MGM's big-budgeted 1944 Greer Garson marital drama *Mrs. Parkington*. Both made money. Metro was cashing in on the continuing appeal of Garson and Pidgeon, who had established themselves as the perfect screen couple in the Oscar-winning *Mrs. Miniver*. In this adaptation of a best-seller, they're an on-and-off-and-on-again couple; he is a miner who makes it big, and she is the ambitious wife who pushes him. The fine cast also includes Cecil Kellaway, Gladys Cooper, Tom Drake, Peter Lawford, Dan Duryea, and Hugh Marlowe. **Director**—Tay Garnett. **Academy Award Nominations**—Garson, best actress; Moorehead, best supporting actress. *124 minutes b&w*

MRS. SOFFEL (1984)

Diane Keaton
Mel Gibson
Matthew Modine

This potentially exciting tale has been stripped of its dramatic impact and emerges flat and subdued. Keaton adequately portrays the title character, a proper prison-warden's wife who falls in love with a condemned murderer and helps him escape. But good performances cannot overcome the plodding way the events unfold. Based on a true story set in 1901. **Director**—Gillian Armstrong. **(PG-13)** *110 minutes*

MISUNDERSTOOD (1984)

★★

Gene Hackman
Henry Thomas

Henry Thomas needs more love than Gene Hackman can give him in Misunderstood.

Drab, two-hanky, modern melodrama starring Hackman as a shipping tycoon residing in Tunisia with his family. When his wife dies, Hackman can't seem to fulfill the emotional needs of his two precocious young sons. The children are engagingly played by Thomas (*E.T.*) and Huckleberry Fox (*Terms of Endearment*). Their interrelationship is the only interesting aspect of this contrived and sappy story, which is often difficult to understand. Also with Rip Torn. **Director**—Jerry Schatzberg. **(PG)** *91 minutes*

MO' BETTER BLUES (1990)

★★★ ®

Denzel Washington
Cynda Williams
Spike Lee
Joie Lee

Writer/director Lee presents a film involving personal issues rather than social ones in this tale about a young man and his horn. Washington stars as a self-absorbed jazz musician who regards romance as a hindrance to his creativity. His aloof attitude causes friction with his women friends, who press him for a commitment. Not as gripping as

® *This movie available with closed captions for the hearing impaired.*

Do the Right Thing, the film suffers because of Washington's character, who is so cool on the surface that he has no depth. However, the secondary characters, including Giancarlo Esposito as a faltering piano player and Wesley Snipes as an ambitious sax player, make for an entertaining ensemble who recite Lee's provocative, hip dialogue with style and ease. As in most of Lee's other films, the production design and costumes are original and colorful. Though the film disappointed some critics at the time of release, Lee's less successful features are far more interesting than most Hollywood blockbusters. Also with the late Robin Harris, Bill Nunn, Dick Anthony Williams, John Turturro, Ruben Blades, and Tracy Camilla Johns. **(R)**
127 minutes

MOBY DICK (1956)

★★★

Gregory Peck
Richard Basehart

Herman Melville's classic tale of a ship captain fiercely struggling to land a great white whale is impressively produced for the screen, but the pace is erratic. Peck is ill at ease as Captain Ahab, the obsessed skipper, but there are some good moments from Basehart as Ishmael and Friedrich Ledebur as Queequeg. The beautiful photography by Oswald Morris captures the cool, wet atmosphere of the Northern seacoast. The script was written by director John Huston and novelist Ray Bradbury. Leo Genn, Harry Andrews, and Orson Welles appear in supporting roles. *116 minutes*

MODERN GIRLS (1986)

★

Daphne Zuniga
Virginia Madsen
Cynthia Gibb

Zuniga, Madsen, and Gibb are the girls of the title, but their freshness and vitality can't compensate for the ridiculous, simpleminded story about young women with routine jobs who seek excitement at Los Angeles nightclubs. The superficial characters lack intelligence, wit, and morals, and are an insult to modern women rather than a representation of them. Director Jerry Kramer concentrates on style at the expense of story. **(PG–13)**
84 minutes

MODERN PROBLEMS (1981)

★

Chevy Chase

A creaky clunker of a comedy with Chase playing a young blade who accidentally acquires telekinetic powers, which he uses to win back his former girlfriend. The production is beset with problems—stale jokes, sloppy direction, shabby performances, and an unbearable script. Chase mopes about with an amazing lack of energy and comic skill; the film is an unmitigated fiasco. Also stars Patti D'Arbanville, Mary Kay Place, Nell Carter, and Dabney Coleman. **Director**—Ken Shapiro. **(PG)**
92 minutes

MODERN ROMANCE (1981)

★★★

Albert Brooks
Kathryn Harrold

Negotiate the rocky road of romance with director/cowriter Brooks, who stars as a neurotic Hollywood film editor with a galloping insecurity that threatens to ruin his love affair with a beautiful bank officer (Harrold). Whether in full-blown sexual paranoia or merely laboring in quiet desperation, Brooks is a telling image of self-induced angst. This is a low-key, frequently hilarious movie, with added laughs spun from its behind-the-scenes look at the movie business. Best bits: Brooks' misfired date with a woman from his past, and his exercise in absurdity at a soundtrack recording studio. Also with Barry Gordon, Bruno Kirby, Bob Einstein (Brooks' real-life brother), and George Kennedy. **(R)** *93 minutes*

THE MODERNS (1988)

★★★

Keith Carradine
Linda Fiorentino
John Lone

Director Alan Rudolph fashions an intriguing film about the expatriate artists who inhabited Paris during the 1920s. Starring Keith Carradine as a painter who forges some works by the modern masters, this engimatic comedy/drama makes some interesting statements about fine art, commercial art, and even about love. Rudolph's penchant for sweeping romanticism is evident here as the characters can't seem to function when they fall hopelessly in love. Rudolph's unusual casting adds to the appeal of this offbeat tale. Wallace Shawn, Geraldine Chaplin, Geneviève Bujold, and Kevin J. O'Connor (as Ernest Hemingway) also appear in this film. **(No MPAA rating)**
126 minutes

Linda Fiorentino and Keith Carradine rekindle their past affair in The Moderns.

MODERN TIMES (1936)

★★★★

Charlie Chaplin
Paulette Goddard
Chester Conklin

Industrialization gone amok—Charlie Chaplin in Modern Times.

Chaplin wrote, directed, starred in, and scored this comedy for all seasons. It was his last "silent" film (there's music, sound effects, and limited speech), made nine years into the sound era, and was the last incarnation of the Little Tramp. His pantomimic art had reached its peak, and an age of innocence was ending forever. The film is a wonderful satire of the perils of modern life. Charlie plays a factory worker who goes berserk, tries his hand at a variety of jobs, and befriends a homeless young woman—played by his real-life

(Continued)

(Continued)
wife at that time, Goddard—who steals his heart. The humor is witty and wise, slapstick and visual. At times the film is disarmingly romantic. There's something for almost everyone to enjoy in this classic film, which becomes better with repeated viewings.
87 minutes b&w

MOGAMBO (1953)

★★★

Clark Gable
Ava Gardner
Grace Kelly

Romantic, adventure-filled white-hunter saga with plenty of colorful performances. Gable is excellent as the big-game hunter who becomes involved with two alluring women—Gardner and Kelly. A gorilla hunt highlights the jungle action. The film is a remake of *Red Dust*, with Gable repeating his role. Also with Donald Sinden, Laurence Naismith, and Denis O'Day. **Director**—John Ford. **Academy Award Nominations**—Gardner, best actress; Kelly, best supporting actress. *116 minutes*

THE MOLLY MAGUIRES (1970)

★★

Richard Harris
Sean Connery

Occasionally engrossing account of a secret society of Pennsylvania coal miners in the 1870s who use extreme measures to improve working conditions. A private detective infiltrates the group and reports on their violent activities. The serious, well-made film is based on true events. However, the story ends ambiguously. Connery is convincing as a leader of the society, and Harris performs well as the undercover Pinkerton man. Also stars Samantha Eggar, Frank Finlay, Anthony Zerbe, and Art Lund. **Director**—Martin Ritt. **(PG)**
123 minutes

MOMENT BY MOMENT (1978)

★

Lily Tomlin
John Travolta

Tedious drama about a well-heeled middle-aged woman who has an affair with a young drifter. Tomlin and Travolta play the odd couple, but have no onscreen chemistry together. The film's main trouble seems to be the humdrum script by writer/director Jane Wagner, who has worked with Tomlin for some time. With all the bad dialogue, drippy clichés, and contrived situations, the whole experience seems to drag on hour by hour. Also with Andra Akers and Bert Kramer. **(R)**
102 minutes

MOMMIE DEAREST (1981)

★★

Faye Dunaway
Diana Scarwid

Faye Dunaway as movie queen Joan Crawford in Mommie Dearest.

Dunaway plays screen idol Joan Crawford in this tacky version of the tacky book by Crawford's adopted daughter, Christina. Dunaway's characterization is lifelike, but the script is not. The dialogue is so bad that Dunaway's excellent portrayal of the hard-driving, ambitious, insecure, and occasionally raving-mad movie queen is totally wasted. Mara Hobel plays Christina as a suffering child, and Scarwid plays her as an insufferable adult. The film has since become a classic bit of camp in some circles. Also with Steve Forrest and Henry Da Silva. **Director**—Frank Perry. **(PG)** *129 minutes*

MONA LISA (1986)

★★★

Bob Hoskins
Cathy Tyson
Michael Caine

A stinging, hard-bitten *film noir* set in Soho, London's sordid district of mobsters, hookers, and drug addicts. Although the story takes some time to unwind, this bittersweet melodrama bristles with savory atmosphere and spellbinding performances. Hoskins' portrayal of a gruff, but sentimental, small-time hood who falls in love with a call girl is dynamic and riveting. Tyson (Cicely Tyson's niece) is equally as effective as the young prostitute he chauffeurs to assignments. **Director**—Neil Jordan. **(R) Academy Award Nomination**—Hoskins, best actor.
100 minutes

MONDO CANE (1961)

★★

If life hasn't already convinced you it's a dog's world, and a pretty sick one at that, this film will. A documentary of sorts, it depicts some of humankind's more bizarre habits and cruelties, from the slaughter of swine to dining on dogs. Believe it or not. Even less believable is that the film did quite well in 1961, spawning a couple of sequels as well as the ironically lyrical, Oscar-nominated theme song, "More." **Producer**—Gaultiero Jacopetti.
105 minutes

THE MONEY PIT (1986)

★★ ®

Shelley Long
Tom Hanks
Alexander Godunov

This latter-day version of *Mr. Blandings Builds His Dream House* is constructed on a weak comic foundation and soon falls apart in a torrent of ill-conceived slapstick gags. The main fault seems to be Richard Benjamin's heavy-handed direction and the script's unevenness. Hanks and Long play the yuppie couple who move into a bargain $200,000 mansion only to find the place is deteriorating around them. They recover but the film doesn't. Also with Maureen Stapleton. Steven Spielberg served as executive producer. **(PG)**
91 minutes

MONKEY BUSINESS (1952)

★★★

Cary Grant
Ginger Rogers

A madcap comedy about a scientist who discovers an amazing elixir that restores youth. Grant plays the researcher, and Rogers costars as his wife. A late screwball comedy scripted by

® *This movie available with closed captions for the hearing impaired.*

Marilyn Monroe makes another conquest in Monkey Business.

Ben Hecht and I.A.L. Diamond, and directed at a furious pace by Howard Hawks. Charles Coburn plays Grant's boss, and Marilyn Monroe plays his naive but provocative secretary who doesn't type! *97 minutes b&w*

MONKEY SHINES (1988)

★★

Jason Beghe

Jason Beghe's helpmate turns against him in Monkey Shines.

This uneven horror tale, directed by George A. Romero, begins almost as an uplifting documentary about animals who help the disabled but it ends as a sensationalized thriller. A wheelchair-bound quadriplegic (Beghe) is assisted by an amazing monkey that gradually changes from helpmate to jealous killer. The weird plot spins out of control, and the film eventually loses its credibility. Also with John Pankow and Kate McNeil. **(R)** *113 minutes*

MON ONCLE D'AMERIQUE (1980)

★★★

Gérard Depardieu
Nicole Garcia

Alain Resnais' comedy is a complex examination of human behavior. The film follows the lives of three ambitious but mixed-up characters. Resnais treats his subject with coyness, charm, and intelligence; but the various case histories aren't clearly connected, and this situation becomes an annoying distraction. Also with Roger Pierre. Originally filmed in French. **(PG) Academy Award Nomination**—Jean Gruault, best screenplay written directly for the screen. *125 minutes*

MONSIGNOR (1982)

★

Christopher Reeve
Geneviève Bujold

Christopher Reeve plays Vatican politics in Monsignor.

Cumbersome, lethargic, and ludicrous melodrama about corruption among the Catholic Church's hierarchy. Reeve delivers a wooden portrayal of a cynical, ambitious priest with Mafia connections, who ends up controlling the Vatican's finances. The awkward screenplay and dreary dialogue lead to much confusion and tedium. **Director**—Frank Perry. **(R)** *122 minutes*

MONSTER IN THE CLOSET (1986)

★½

Donald Grant
Denise DuBarry
Claude Akins

A lame spoof of 1950s horror films and the various characters who inhabit them. Grant stars as a reporter who resembles Clark Kent; DuBarry plays a beautiful scientist. Together they track down some California monsters who are jumping out of closets and killing innocent people. Film buffs and fans of old science fiction and horror movies may have some fun watching this satire; others will find little of interest. Also with Howard Duff, Stella Stevens, Henry Gibson, John Carradine, and Jesse White. **Director**—Bob Dahlin. **(PG)** *87 minutes*

THE MONSTER SQUAD (1987)

★★

Andre Gower
Robby Kriger

Count Dracula, Frankenstein's Monster, the Wolfman, and other famous scary creatures invade a small town to stir up evil. Only a gang of small fry, who call themselves the Monster Club because they have studied the habits of ghouls and monsters, can rid the community of such menace. As a feature film for youth—perhaps aiming for the same audience as *The Goonies*—this horror/comedy is not very successful. Drab humor and sentimental scenes will not appeal to older kids, while the grisly mayhem and gory violence are too disturbing for younger ones. Also with Stephen Macht, Duncan Regehr, Tom Noonan, Brent Chalem, and Ashley Bank. **Director**—Fred Dekker. **(PG–13)** *81 minutes*

MONTENEGRO (1981)

★★

Susan Anspach

Yugoslavian director Dusan Makavejev presents a loosely constructed comedy that can be recognized for its intelligence, but is not mainstream entertainment. The film, set in Sweden, centers on Anspach, the restless American wife of a wealthy Swedish industrialist. She's kidnapped, almost willingly, by some freewheeling immigrants and held at a sleazy nightclub where she experiences a spiritual awakening. Makavejev makes an interesting social statement, but his directorial style, influenced by his Eastern European background and training, will be difficult for American audiences to relate to. Also stars Erland Josephson and Per Oscarsson. **(R)** *95 minutes*

A MONTH IN THE COUNTRY
(1988)

★★½

Colin Firth
Natasha Richardson

Colin Firth, Natasha Richardson, and Kenneth Branagh in A Month in the Country.

A small English film with a strong statement about the effects of war on the human condition. Based on the novel by J.L. Carr, the screenplay involves a World War I veteran (Firth) who takes a summer job restoring a medieval church mural. The former soldier suffers from the mental scars of combat and maintains a cynical attitude toward the complacent Yorkshire villagers. The painting, which he uncovers, conveys a haunting and prophetic message. Also with Kenneth Branagh. **Director**—Pat O'Connor. **(PG)** *96 minutes*

MONTY PYTHON AND THE HOLY GRAIL (1974)

★★★½

Graham Chapman
John Cleese
Terry Gilliam
Eric Idle
Michael Palin
Terry Jones

Graham Chapman and Terry Gilliam in Monty Python and the Holy Grail.

A cheerful, comic reworking of the legend of King Arthur and the search for the Holy Grail. The quest leaves Camelot in a shambles of laughter. It's written and acted by the brilliant Monty Python troupe, made famous by British TV. Plenty of laughs, chuckles, sight gags, sick jokes, and wit in this loony satire. **Directors**—Gilliam and Jones. **(PG)** *90 minutes*

MONTY PYTHON LIVE AT THE HOLLYWOOD BOWL
(1982)

★★★

Graham Chapman
John Cleese
Eric Idle
Terry Jones
Terry Gilliam
Michael Palin

This filmed performance of the noted English comedy group is an extension of their famous TV shows, adapted for the stage and with a few new bits. A couple of skits miss the mark but most are hilarious, and the material seems as fresh as ever—especially in front of a live audience. Among the acts: a soccer match between famous philosophers, and a game show starring Marx, Lenin, Che Guevara, and Mao Tse Tung. **Director**—Terry Hughes. **(R)** *77 minutes*

MONTY PYTHON'S THE MEANING OF LIFE (1983)

★★★

Graham Chapman
John Cleese
Eric Idle
Michael Palin

John Cleese attracts his students' attention in Monty Python's The Meaning of Life.

Britain's bad boys of outrageous satire serve up a mixed grill of sketches that touch on such subjects as birth, sex, religion, death, war, and middle-class lifestyles. Much of the film is out of control and offensive, yet moments of inspired hilarity shine through. One unforgettable, repulsive scene shows a bloated patron of a posh French restaurant alternately ordering gourmet entrees and vomiting. Also with Terry Gilliam and Terry Jones, who appear less frequently in this outing than the other Monty Python members. **Director**—Jones. **(R)** *103 minutes*

THE MOON IN THE GUTTER
(1983)

★

Gérard Depardieu
Nastassja Kinski

French director Jean-Jacques Beineix, who fared well with *Diva*, falls on his face with this second effort, a suffocating and pretentious film based on the novel by David Goodis. Depardieu plays a lumbering stevedore on the prowl for the rapist of his sister. In the process, he latches on to sultry, wealthy Kinski. Both stars come off poorly as Beineix overindulges the production with a murky, listless atmosphere. Originally filmed in French. **(R)** *126 minutes*

THE MOON IS BLUE (1953)

★★

Maggie McNamara
David Niven
William Holden

This sex comedy raised eyebrows at the time of release because of the use of such then-shocking words as "virgin" and "mistress." Now the film is considered mild, with most of the gags straining to evoke a smile or two. The story involves the escapades of an attractive lass, played by McNamara, who stirs the passions of several gentlemen. Also with Tom Tully and Dawn Adams. **Director**—Otto Preminger. **Academy Award Nomination**—McNamara, best actress. *96 minutes b&w*

MOONLIGHTING (1982)

★★★★ ®

Jeremy Irons

Polish filmmaker Jerzy Skolimowski makes a weighty statement about his country's political situation. This moody film is set in England, and the subtle story involves the plight of four Polish workers who are temporarily in London to restore a townhouse for a mysterious "boss." Their English-speaking foreman (Irons) desperately tries to hide from his men the news of the military takeover back home. Also with Eugene Lipinski, Jiri Stanislav, and Eugeniusz Haczkiewicz. **(PG)**
97 minutes

MOON OVER MIAMI (1941)

★★★

Don Ameche
Betty Grable
Carole Landis

A pleasant musical, graced by a likable cast and based on the familiar theme of gorgeous girls on the prowl for rich husbands. Grable, Landis, and popular 1940s comedienne Charlotte Greenwood are the fortune hunters who find romance and more in this colorful film. Musical numbers include the title song and "You Started Something." Also with Jack Haley and Robert Cummings. **Director**—Walter Lang. *92 minutes*

MOON OVER PARADOR (1988)

★★

Richard Dreyfuss
Sonia Braga
Raul Julia

Dreyfuss stars as a New York actor who is forced to impersonate the recently deceased dictator of a fictional Latin American country in order to prevent public unrest. The comedy works on various levels: a spoof of actors and acting, political satire, and a parody of U.S. foreign policy. Good supporting performances by Julia as the scheming police chief and Braga as the dictator's sexy mistress highlight this otherwise uneven film. There are excellent cameos by Jonathan Winters, Fernando Rey, Sammy Davis Jr., and Charo. **Director**—Paul Mazursky. **(PG-13)** *105 minutes*

MOONRAKER (1979)

★

Roger Moore
Lois Chiles
Richard Kiel

In this embarrassing and vacuous entry in the James Bond series, Bond saves the world from a cunning aerospace tycoon. It's the 11th film for 007, played here by an aging Moore, and the storyline with a space motif seems to have been generated by the success of *Star Wars*. However, the Oscar-nominated special effects are empty without a decent plot or colorful cast of villains to support them. Chiles, who has a flat, bland presence, costars as Bond's romantic interest, and Kiel reappears as the towering, steel-toothed "Jaws." Though marginally funny in *The Spy Who Loved Me*, Kiel's character is profoundly unfunny a second time around. A criminal waste of a colossal budget, and a real disappointment to fans of the Bond series. Also with Michael Lonsdale, Corinne Clery, Bernard Lee, and Lois Maxwell. **Director**—Lewis Gilbert. **(PG)** *126 minutes*

MOONSTRUCK (1987)

★★★

Cher
Nicolas Cage
Vincent Gardenia
Olympia Dukakis

Nicholas Cage, Cher, and the rest of the delightful cast on Moonstruck.

A warmhearted romantic comedy involving a Brooklyn Italian-American family beset with problems of the heart. Cher won an Oscar for her performance as a 37-year-old widow who unexpectedly falls in love with her fiance's brother (Cage). Paralleling Cher's romantic turmoil is her parents' relationship, which has deteriorated because of lack of communication. The father is a none too clever philanderer and her mother exasperates herself trying to figure out why older men want to be unfaithful. Definitely an actors' movie, the action is simple and the story straightforward. A loving tribute to the importance of the family. Also with Danny Aeillo as the hapless fiance. **Director**—Norman Jewison. **(PG) Academy Awards**—Cher, best actress; Dukakis, best supporting actress; John Patrick Shanley, best original screenplay. **Nominations**—best film; Jewison, best director; Gardenia, best supporting actor. *102 minutes*

MORE AMERICAN GRAFFITI (1979)

★★

Candy Clark
Bo Hopkins
Ron Howard
Cindy Williams
Paul LeMat

This clumsy sequel to the popular 1973 hit follows the lives of the characters through the turmoil of the mid-1960s. The story is jumbled into four disjointed vignettes that range from the battlefields of Vietnam to the antiwar movement at home. Most of the original cast is back, and they're certainly appealing, but writer/director B.W.L Norton overreaches, and the lack of a cohesive storyline hurts the overall film. Also with Charles Martin Smith and Mackenzie Phillips. **(PG)**
111 minutes

THE MORE THE MERRIER (1943)

★★★½

Jean Arthur
Joel McCrea
Charles Coburn

A charming and comic tale about a girl who shares a small apartment with two men in Washington during a housing shortage in the midst of World War II. The unlikely trio includes government worker Arthur, engineer McCrea, and businessman Coburn. Coburn slyly plays cupid to get Arthur and McCrea romantically involved. **Director**—George Stevens. **Academy Award**—Coburn, best supporting actor. **Nominations**—best picture; Stevens, best director; Arthur, best actress; Frank Ross and Robert Russell, original story; Richard Flournoy, Lewis R. Foster, Frank Ross, and Robert Russell, screenplay. *104 minutes b&w*

This movie available on videotape and/or disc.

MORGAN! (1966)

★★★

David Warner
Vanessa Redgrave

Warner made the greatest impact of his acting career in this film about a talented young painter, but impossible spouse, who discovers he is losing his wife (Redgrave) to an art dealer and friend. The "gifted idiot," misanthrope, lunatic, or Everyman (depending on your point of view) loses himself in fantasies about gorillas. Very much a film of its time and place—the "swinging sixties" in mod England—it also helped establish Redgrave as a star to be reckoned with. Robert Stephens and Irene Handl are featured. **Director**—Karel Reisz. **Academy Award Nomination**—Redgrave, best actress.

97 minutes b&w

MORGAN STEWART'S COMING HOME (1987)

★½

Jon Cryer
Lynn Redgrave
Nicholas Pryor

Cryer stars in the title role as a "poor little rich kid" who returns from prep school to bolster the image of his father, a senator up for re-election. The comedy sags with predictable plot elements and the family portrait is strictly from a TV sitcom. Only Redgrave seems effective as the overbearing mother, often dressed in bright red, who seems to be a send-up of Nancy Reagan. Viveka Davis and Paul Gleason also appear. Directed by "Alan Smithee," the industry's pseudonym for anonymous or disputed direction. In this case, the real culprit behind this mediocre comedy is Paul Aaron. **(PG–13)** *96 minutes*

THE MORNING AFTER (1986)

★★

Jane Fonda
Jeff Bridges
Raul Julia

Neither the powerhouse cast nor the expertise of veteran director Sidney Lumet can save this romantic thriller from its rickety script. Fonda plays an alcoholic, washed-up actress who awakens to find her casual lover dead in bed with a knife in his chest. Bridges costars

Jeff Bridges and Jane Fonda are embroiled in murder in The Morning After.

as an ex-cop who tries to unravel the mystery, which unfolds with weak suspense and little credibility. A disappointingly passive role for Fonda, known for portraying characters of great strength and will. **Director**—Lumet. **(R) Academy Award Nomination**—Fonda, best actress.

103 minutes

MORNING GLORY (1933)

★★★

Katharine Hepburn
Douglas Fairbanks, Jr.

Hepburn won her first Oscar for this film (her third), and it's her spark that keeps this movie at the forefront of backstage dramas. Hepburn plays Eva Lovelace, the stagestruck girl from New England determined to make it on the New York stage. She has just the will to survive disappointment after disappointment, until she finally gets her big break. Though the script has lost its luster over the years, in some ways the film's more interesting in retrospect: It is Hepburn's career as well as Eva's that is really taking off with this picture. Remade in 1958 as *Stage Struck,* with Susan Strasberg in the Hepburn role. Adolphe Menjou and C. Aubrey Smith costar. **Director**—Lowell Sherman. **Academy Award**—Hepburn, best actress. *74 minutes b&w*

THE MORTAL STORM (1940)

★★★★

James Stewart
Margaret Sullavan
Frank Morgan
Robert Young

This was Hollywood's first major film to strike out against Nazism; but far more than potent propaganda, it has endured as searing drama. Morgan was never better than as the German professor who stands up against the Nazis in 1933, and is carted off to a concentration camp. His stepsons become Nazis, while his daughter (Sullavan) tries to flee Germany with her boyfriend, played by Stewart. The entire cast gives wrenching performances, under the guidance of one of MGM's greatest directors, Frank Borzage. Also starring Robert Stack, Bonita Granville, and Maria Ouspenskaya. *99 minutes b&w*

MORTUARY (1984)

★

Mary McDonough
Christopher George
Bill Paxton

Routine, uneven, stab-'em-slab-'em horror story built around young lovers and a psychotic mortician. The usual red herrings and gory murders abound. For the morbidly minded, there are graphic details of embalmers at work. Students of human nature may appreciate the psychological revelations about the unbalanced undertaker who attempts to embalm one of his victims while she is alive. Also with Lynda Day George. **Director**—Howard Avedis. **(R)**

91 minutes

MOSCOW ON THE HUDSON (1984)

★★★

Robin Williams
Maria Conchita Alonso
Cleavant Derricks

Robin Williams plays a Russian defector who loves America in Moscow on the Hudson.

Director Paul Mazursky's gentle comedy intelligently explores the differ-

This movie available with closed captions for the hearing impaired.

ences between Russian and American cultures. Although the plot is sometimes too episodic, the observations are appealing. In a remarkably restrained performance, Williams is delightful as a Russian circus musician who abruptly defects to America. His bewildered immigrant characterization offers fresh insights into the great American melting pot. **(R)** *115 minutes*

THE MOSQUITO COAST (1986)

★★½

Harrison Ford
Helen Mirren
River Phoenix

Harrison Ford tries to escape from civilization in The Mosquito Coast.

A gripping but depressing saga, based on Paul Theroux's novel, about an eccentric inventor who resettles his family in a remote jungle outpost to avoid the crass commercialization of modern life. Ford is excellent as the cranky patriarch who eventually goes insane despite the change in environment. Unfortunately, the story is overdrawn and disjointed, and the direction by Australian Peter Weir, who had teamed with Ford on *Witness*, adds nothing to the story. Also with Butterfly McQueen and Martha Plimpton. **(PG)** *117 minutes*

MOTEL HELL (1980)

★★½

Rory Calhoun
Paul Linke

Kindly farmer Vincent, played by Calhoun, is also a motel-keeper who runs a smoked-meat business on the side. His secret ingredient is human flesh blended in with the pork. Morbid laughs and a dash of suspense are mixed with the blood and gore, but don't look for logic in this unrestrained horror/comedy that plays like a fever dream. Calhoun is hilarious as farmer Vincent; you've never seen anyone as resolutely off-kilter. "Don't worry. I have a cast-iron stomach," chirps Nina Axelrod, as she innocently tours Vincent's meat-preparation building. That's a warning for the audience, too! Also with Nancy Parsons and Wolfman Jack. **Director**—Kevin Connor. **(R)** *106 minutes*

MOTHER, JUGS & SPEED (1976)

★★★

Bill Cosby
Raquel Welch
Harvey Keitel

Cosby, Welch, and Keitel star in a fast-paced black comedy about Los Angeles ambulance drivers. There are some outrageous moments, but it does entertain with a contrasting blend of farce and serious drama. Welch, in a strong role as a fetching switchboard operator, complements her physical attractiveness with a competent performance. Cosby, Keitel, and the rest of the cast give their best. Peter Yates (*Bullitt*) directs in a freewheeling style. Also with Allen Garfield and Larry Hagman. **(PG)** *95 minutes*

MOTHER TERESA (1986)

★★★

An earnest documentary honoring the life and deeds of Nobel Prize-winner Mother Teresa. The film provides a biographical portrait of this formidable yet frail-looking woman, often described as a living saint. The footage of Mother Teresa and her devoted colleagues tending the poorest of the poor is most stirring, though other sequences tend to be flatly directed. Richard Attenborough provides the narration. **Director**—Ann Petrie and Jeanette Petrie. **(No MPAA rating)** *88 minutes*

MOTHER WORE TIGHTS (1947)

★★★

Betty Grable
Dan Dailey

Excellent showcase for the talents of Grable and Dailey as a vaudeville couple involved with their colorful career and raising a family. Perhaps Grable's most popular film with the public, the production moves along smartly with charming song-and-dance numbers. Based on the book by Miriam Young. Also with Mona Freeman, Connie Marshall, Señor Wences, Vanessa Brown, and Veda Ann Borg. **Director**—Walter Lang. **Academy Award Nomination**—Harry Jackson, cinematography. *107 minutes*

MOTHRA (1961)

★★½

Franky Sakai
Hiroshi Koizumi

The caterpillar that ate Tokyo: extra-special effects in Mothra.

Japanese science-fiction film about two very unusual, miniscule twin girls (Emi and Yumi Itoh) and their special link to a gargantuan caterpillar that transforms into the biggest moth you're ever likely to see. It causes plenty of headaches in Tokyo, and even threatens to destroy the Earth (naturally). And what about the link to the thumb-sized twins? Even after seeing the movie, you may not be able to figure it out. Nice special effects. **Director**—Inoshiro Honda and Lee Kresel. *99 minutes*

MOULIN ROUGE (1952)

★★★★

José Ferrer
Zsa Zsa Gabor

Brilliant film biography of French painter Henri Toulouse-Lautrec, whose deformed legs caused him mental and physical anguish. The dramatic and colorful account details the famous artist's sad outlook on the world and its despairing effect on his love affairs. Director John Huston presents a striking view of 19th-century Montmartre and its many flavorful characters. The art di-

(Continued)

(Continued)
rection by the legendary Cedric Gibbons and set direction by Edward Carfagno won an Academy Award. A magnificent can-can sequence is a real showstopper. Also with Suzanne Flon, Katherine Kath, Colette Marchand, Eric Pohlmann, and Christopher Lee. **Academy Award Nominations**—best picture; Huston, best director; Ferrer, best actor; Marchand, best supporting actress.
123 minutes

MOUNTAIN FAMILY ROBINSON (1979)

Robert Logan
Heather Rattray
Ham Larsen

This is the third film about the sentimental adventures of the rosy-cheeked family of four who escape traffic-snarled Los Angeles to reside in a mountain log cabin. But even in this wilderness paradise, they can't avoid government bureaucracy. A cranky forest ranger tries to evict them because they're on a government-controlled mining-claim area. Once again, the forest animals and the spectacular scenery upstage the human cast. **Director**—John Cotter. **(G)** *100 minutes*

THE MOUNTAIN MEN (1980)

Charlton Heston
Brian Keith

Heston and Keith are grizzled mountaineers who fight Indians and trap beavers in this routine outdoor adventure. Heston falls in love with a beautiful Indian girl, played by Victoria Racimo. She's also claimed by an Indian chief, and this conflict leads to some spectacular hand-to-hand combat. The film offers picturesque Wyoming settings, but it's still familiar fare. The screenplay was written by Heston's son, Fraser Clark Heston. **Director**—Richard Lang. **(R)** *102 minutes*

MOUNTAINS OF THE MOON (1989)

Patrick Bergin
Iain Glen

An attractive but old-fashioned period adventure about English explorers

A search through 19th-century Africa: Mountains of the Moon.

Richard Burton and John Speke, who braved the African wilderness to chart the source of the river Nile. A great deal of attention is paid to re-creating the 19th-century African environment, including strange native customs and various hardships of the journey, but the glorifying of Britain's imperialistic attitudes of that period is a misguided perspective. When Burton and Spekes engage in a rivalry over who should get credit for the discovery, the film barely touches on the fact that native Africans knew the source of the Nile long before the two egotistical white Englishmen stumbled across it. The film presents the natives in the way Western cultures have too often viewed them—as dangerous, exotic peoples or as loyal servants who are willing to sacrifice themselves for their employers. An unenlightened rendering of a small event in British history. Also with Richard E. Grant, Fiona Shaw, Bernard Hill, Delroy Lindo, and Bheki Tonto Ngema. **Director**—Bob Rafelson. **(R)**
135 minutes

MOURNING BECOMES ELECTRA (1947)

Michael Redgrave
Rosalind Russell

A good cast gets bogged down in this heavy drama about tragedy striking a New England family during the Civil War. A wife murders her husband, and the children plot revenge. The film is based on the play by Eugene O'Neill. Also with Kirk Douglas, Katina Paxinou, and Raymond Massey. Many television prints run 105 minutes. **Director**—Dudley Nichols. **Academy Award Nominations**—Redgrave, best actor; Russell, best actress.
170 minutes b&w

THE MOUSE THAT ROARED (1959)

Peter Sellers
Jean Seberg

In The Mouse That Roared, *Peter Sellers has a novel scheme for getting foreign aid.*

A snappy topical satire about the Duchy of Grand Fenwick, a small, bankrupt country that seeks to solve its financial problems by declaring war on the United States with the intention of losing the conflict and then receiving foreign aid. Sellers has a grand time playing three roles, including that of the Grand Duchess. **Director**—Jack Arnold. *85 minutes*

MOVE OVER, DARLING (1963)

Doris Day
James Garner
Polly Bergen

Day, Garner, and Bergen seem to be having a fine time in this uneven remake of *My Favorite Wife,* although the original with Cary Grant and Irene Dunne was much better. A wife, presumed dead in a plane crash, returns home after five years and finds her husband on the threshold of remarrying. Some hilarious moments still work here, thanks to the top cast of character actors. Also with Thelma Ritter, Chuck Conners, Edgar Buchanan, and Fred Clark. **Director**—Michael Gordon.
103 minutes

MOVERS AND SHAKERS (1985)

Charles Grodin

Uneven, tired send-up of the movie-making business. The story essentially is about the frantic efforts of some studio people to develop a suitable screenplay for a film based on a popular sex manual. Ironically, this very movie is in dire need of a decent screenplay as well as forceful direction. Grodin stars as the desperate screenwriter. Walter Matthau is the studio chief. Gilda Radner and Steve Martin appear in cameos. **Director**—William Asher. **(PG)** *80 minutes*

MOVIE, MOVIE (1978)

 ★★★

George C. Scott
Trish Van Devere
Eli Wallach
Red Buttons
Barbara Harris
Art Carney

An affectionate, funny, and clever parody of Depression-era movies. The program, of course, is a double feature: first an up-from-the-slums boxing drama and then a corny backstage musical. Scott, Buttons, and Wallach have a great time twisting all those old movie clichés. The film occasionally falls flat, but all in all it's a pleasant trip down Hollywood's memory lane. Also with Harry Hamlin, Barry Bostwick, and Ann Reinking. **Director**—Stanley Donen. **(PG)** *107 minutes color/b&w*

MOVING (1988)

 ★★ ®

Richard Pryor
Beverly Todd

Pryor merely goes through the motions in this surprisingly inept comedy. He portrays a transit engineer who relocates to Idaho from New Jersey and suffers the typical annoyances that go along with moving to a new community. The mishaps do produce some laughs, but they are more in line with television antics than with big-screen comedy. *Saturday Night Live* alums Randy Quaid and Dana Carvey are in supporting roles. **Director**—Alan Metter. **(R)** *94 minutes*

MOVING VIOLATIONS (1985)

 ★ ®

John Murray

Silly, sophomoric teen comedy involving driving offenders required to attend traffic school. The series of formula shenanigans focuses on the students who defy the authority of the police-officer teachers. Murray (Bill's brother) is the ringleader of the rebellious violators who engage in various labored slapstick routines. The gags, like some of the automobiles, stall at crucial moments. Jennifer Tilly and James Keach are also in the cast. **Director**—Neal Israel. **(PG–13)** *91 minutes*

MS. 45 (1981)

★★½

Zoe Tamerlis

Gory but undeniably effective movie about an attractive, young mute girl who embarks on a revengeful killing spree after being raped twice in one day. In one particularly grisly sequence, she kills the second rapist, cuts the body into small pieces, and stows the parts in her refrigerator. Despite such horrendous scenes, Tamerlis displays impressive talent in the title role, and Abel Ferrara directs with noticeable style and pacing. Perhaps next time they'll find more restrained outlets for their skills. Also with Steve Singer, Jack Thibeau, and Peter Yellen. **(R)** *84 minutes*

THE MUMMY (1932)

★★★½

Boris Karloff
Zita Johann
David Manners

Boris Karloff is the ancient Egyptian Im-ho-tep, also known as The Mummy.

In an incredible burst of creative fervor, Universal Pictures turned out three of Hollywood's most enduring horror classics within a two-year period: *Dracula, Frankenstein,* and *The Mummy.* There's more mood than mayhem in this one, though the scenes of the mummy first coming to life (with the archaeologist who discovered him bursting into bone-chilling hysterical laughter), and the Egyptian priest Im-ho-tep (Karloff) being embalmed alive are pure horror enough for any film. Karloff is delectably creepy as the 3,700-year-old resurrected priest who covets a young woman (Johann) whom he believes to be his ancient love reincarnated. Directed by the famed German expressionist cinematographer Karl Freund. Also with Edward Van Sloan and Noble Johnson. *72 minutes b&w*

THE MUPPET MOVIE (1979)

 ★★★

The Muppets

Kermit the Frog strums his way to Hollywood in The Muppet Movie.

Jim Henson's lovable puppet characters star in their first feature film. It's a bright, cheerful musical comedy that will please children and adults. Kermit the Frog, who plans to become a star, sets off for Tinsel Town with Miss Piggy, the Great Gonzo, and other Muppet friends. Along the way they briefly encounter Mel Brooks, Steve Martin, Bob Hope, and other Hollywood notables. **Director**—James Frawley. **(G)** *94 minutes*

THE MUPPETS TAKE MANHATTAN (1984)

 ★★★ ®

The Muppets

This third feature with Jim Henson's colorful puppet brigade spoofs old-time Hollywood musicals. Kermit the Frog makes a gallant effort to launch a song-and-dance extravaganza on The Great White Way with plenty of the-show-must-go-on spirit. And the divine Miss

(Continued)

This movie available on videotape and/or disc.

(Continued)
Piggy has wedding bells on her mind as she pursues the frog of her dreams. Snappy musical numbers and lively comedy routines will delight kids and adults alike. Guest stars include Dabney Coleman, Art Carney, Joan Rivers, James Coco, Gregory Hines, and Linda Lavin. Also with Juliana Donald and Lonny Price. **Director**—Frank Oz. **(G)**
93 minutes

MURDER BY DEATH (1976)

★★½

Peter Falk
Alec Guinness
Peter Sellers
Truman Capote
David Niven

Peter Sellers is a famous Asian sleuth in Murder by Death.

An all-star cast and stylish acting shore up Neil Simon's lightweight spoof of detective fiction. Falk, Niven, Sellers, James Coco, and Elsa Lanchester play five famous fictional detectives invited to a spooky old mansion for dinner and a murder to be committed. The performances are superb, but the script makes little sense, and there aren't enough amusing lines to keep it moving briskly. Capote debuts as the host of honor—an eccentric amateur criminologist who believes he can outsmart the world's greatest sleuths. Also with Maggie Smith, Eileen Brennan, and Nancy Walker. **Director**—Robert Moore. **(PG)**
94 minutes

MURDER BY DECREE (1979)

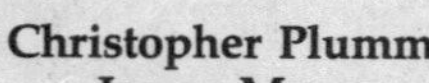

Christopher Plummer
James Mason

Plummer plays the intrepid Sherlock Holmes, and Mason is a delightful Dr. Watson. They attempt to solve the savage Jack the Ripper murders. The pro-

James Mason and Christopher Plummer are Watson and Holmes in Murder by Decree.

duction design of 19th-century London is handsomely staged, with swirling fog, flickering gaslights, and rumbling carriages; but the plot is hardly elementary, my dear fellow—it's too complicated and unsuspenseful. This is the 134th movie to feature the famous English gumshoe; Holmes made his screen debut in a 1903 one-reeler. Also with Donald Sutherland, Geneviève Bujold, David Hemmings, John Gielgud, and Susan Clark. **Director**—Bob Clark. **(PG)**
121 minutes

MURDERER'S ROW (1966)

Dean Martin
Ann-Margret

Flimsy continuation of novelist Donald Hamilton's Matt Helm character, with Martin again playing the superspy role as a spoof. This time, Helm is after a sinister international operator, played by Karl Malden, who has kidnapped a scientist. Ann-Margret is the scientist's daughter. Martin handles his part badly, and the dated material has little to offer. Set against the background of the Riviera. Also with Camilla Sparv, James Gregory, and Beverly Adams. The other two films in the series are *The Silencers* and *The Ambushers.* **Director**—Henry Levin.
108 minutes

MURDER, INC. (1960)

★★★

Stuart Whitman
May Britt
Peter Falk
Henry Morgan

An average crime melodrama elevated by a dynamite, Oscar-nominated performance by Falk as the notorious 1930s hit man Abe Reles. It's the kind of quirky, gripping performance that earmarked Falk for bigger things to come. Aside from showcasing Reles' ruthlessness, the film tells the story of a couple who are victimized by Louis Lepke's crime syndicate. With David J. Stewart and Morey Amsterdam. **Directors—**Burt Balaban and Stuart Rosenberg. **Academy Award Nomination**—Falk, best supporting actor.
103 minutes b&w

MURDER, MY SWEET (1944)

★★★★

Dick Powell
Claire Trevor

A stylish, engrossing film based on Raymond Chandler's private-eye yarn *Farewell, My Lovely.* Powell is excellent as Philip Marlowe, a battered gumshoe on the trail of a tough guy's girlfriend. Director Edward Dmytryk effectively brings out the run-down, moody atmosphere of a decaying big city. It's a remarkable *film noir* that epitomizes the genre. Chandler regarded this film as the best adaptation of any of his novels. The title was changed from the original because the studio felt audiences might take it for a musical comedy, particularly since the star was Powell, who had achieved stardom in musicals. Also with Anne Shirley, Mike Mazurki, and Otto Kruger. *95 minutes b&w*

MURDER ON THE ORIENT EXPRESS (1974)

Albert Finney
Ingrid Bergman
Lauren Bacall
Wendy Hiller
Sean Connery
Vanessa Redgrave

Lavish treatment of Agatha Christie's suspenseful whodunit, set in the 1930s aboard the well-known train bound for Calais from Istanbul. On board is Belgian sleuth Hercule Poirot, played by Finney, who must solve the murder of a passenger stabbed to death when the train hits a snowdrift. A number of colorful characters become suspects. There are many slow moments along with the thrills, but mystery fans should have a good time all the same. Included in the all-star cast are Martin Balsam, Richard Widmark, Jacqueline Bisset, Michael York, Rachel Roberts, John Gielgud, and Anthony Perkins. **Director**—Sidney Lumet. **(PG) Academy Award**—Bergman, best supporting actress.

Nominations—Finney, best actor; Paul Dehn, best screenplay adapted from other material; Geoffrey Unsworth, cinematography. *127 minutes*

MURDERS IN THE RUE MORGUE (1971)

 ★★

Jason Robards
Herbert Lom
Christine Kaufmann

Mediocre film version of Edgar Allan Poe's classic chiller, set in a Paris theater. The actors in a murder mystery become the real-life victims, and the police investigate. Lots of gory details in this fourth film version of Poe's tale. Also with Lilli Palmer, Adolfo Celi, and Michael Dunn. **Director**—Gordon Hessler. **(PG)** *86 minutes*

MURPHY'S LAW (1986)

★★

Charles Bronson
Kathleen Wilhoite
Carrie Snodgress

Outraged at murder: Charles Bronson in Murphy's Law.

Overwrought mayhem marks this Bronson action film rife with *film noir* atmosphere. Stone-faced Bronson plays a desperate Los Angeles detective pursued by a psychopath murderess, local gangsters, and fellow cops. The film still manages some interesting character and plot development despite the overwhelmingly violent scenes. **Director**—J. Lee Thompson. **(R)** *97 minutes*

MURPHY'S ROMANCE (1985)

★★★

James Garner
Sally Field
Brian Kerwin

Sally Field falls for appealing older fella James Garner in Murphy's Romance.

Winning, believable performances by Field and Garner grace this refreshing, romantic comedy that focuses on the old-fashioned value of self-reliance. Field plays a recent divorcée determined to make a new start in a small Arizona town. Garner is the local pharmacist who wins her heart; Kerwin is excellent as Field's shiftless ex-husband. Martin Ritt's direction brings out the warmth and humanity of this insightful story. Also with Corey Haim. **(PG-13) Academy Award Nomination**—Garner, best actor. *107 minutes*

MUSIC BOX (1989)

★★½

Jessica Lange
Armin Mueller-Stahl

Jessica Lange defends Armin Mueller-Stahl in Music Box.

A heavy courtroom drama about a successful Chicago lawyer (Lange) who must defend her Hungarian-born father (Mueller-Stahl) against accusations that he is a vicious Nazi war criminal. Gradually she begins to doubt her own father: Is he a victim of a conspiracy, or is he really the former "monster of Budapest"? Politically minded director Constantin Costa-Gavras (*Missing, Z*) asks some thought-provoking questions, but the drama seems ponderous while the courtroom scenes are not very gripping. The cast and director seem to be too mindful of their weighty material, as though they knew they were Oscar candidates from the beginning. Also with Frederic Forrest, Donald Moffat, Lukas Haas, and Cheryl Lynn Bruce. **(PG-13) Academy Award Nomination**—Lange, best actress. *123 minutes*

THE MUSIC MAN (1962)

★★★★

Robert Preston
Shirley Jones

A buoyant, thoroughly enjoyable romantic musical based on Meredith Wilson's hit Broadway production. Preston is fantastic as the city-slicker salesman who cons the citizens of a small Iowa town into organizing a boys' band so he can sell them musical instruments. Jones also stands out as Marian the librarian, Preston's romantic interest. The film boasts colorful, turn-of-the-century period detail and a strong statement about provincial narrow-mindedness. Many of the musical numbers are real showstoppers; they include "'Till There Was You" and "76 Trombones." There's outstanding support from Hermione Gingold, Paul Ford, and Buddy Hackett. **Director**—Morton Da Costa. **Academy Award Nomination**—best picture. *151 minutes*

THE MUSIC TEACHER (1988)

★★½

Jose van Dam
Anne Roussel

A retired opera star trains two budding singers at his isolated chateau. One is the daughter of a longtime friend and the other is a talented young tenor who was discovered picking pockets at a country fair. The story builds to a climax involving a singing contest. The picture is handsomely if conservatively staged, and it features the music of Mahler, Verdi, and Mozart. Classical music enthusiasts will appreciate this film more than other viewers, who will find the story predictable and the pacing slow. Also with Philippe Volter, Sylvie Fennec, and Patrick Bauchau. **Director**—Gerard Corbiau. **(PG) Academy Award Nomination**—best foreign film. *100 minutes*

MUTINY ON THE BOUNTY (1935)

★★★★

Charles Laughton
Clark Gable

Mutiny on the Bounty: *Rough seas with Charles Laughton and Clark Gable.*

A classic movie adventure based on Nordhoff and Hall's moving account of hardships aboard an 18th-century British man-of-war. Laughton is unforgettable as the heartless Captain Bligh, whose sadistic treatment of the crew provokes mutiny. The entire production is expertly handled. Gable excels as first mate Fletcher Christian, and there are other good performances by Franchot Tone, Herbert Mundin, Eddie Quillan, Dudley Digges, and Donald Crisp. **Director**—Frank Lloyd. **Academy Award**—best picture. **Nominations**—Lloyd, best director; Gable, Laughton, and Tone, best actor; Jules Furthman, Talbot Jennings, and Carey Wilson, screenplay. *135 minutes b&w*

MUTINY ON THE BOUNTY (1962)

★★★

Trevor Howard
Marlon Brando

This opulent, somewhat overblown remake of the 1935 film is competently done, but not as effective despite the lavish production. Howard stars as Captain Bligh, and Brando plays Fletcher Christian; they're adequate, but not as dynamic as Charles Laughton and Clark Gable in the earlier film. Brando's British accent and acting style throw the movie slightly off course. Also stars Richard Harris, Hugh Griffith, Tarita, Richard Haydn, Percy Herbert, and Noel Purcell. **Director**—Lewis Milestone. **Academy Award Nominations**—best picture; Robert L. Surtees, cinematography. *179 minutes*

MY BEAUTIFUL LAUNDRETTE (1985)

★★1/2

Gordon Warnecke
Daniel Day-Lewis

A curious social comedy about a group of ambitious Pakistanis who achieve economic success in London while the local English seethe with resentment. It's a subject with obvious possibilities and the film makes its point, yet the plot is unnecessarily complex and the characters unfocused. **Director**—Stephen Frears. **(R) Academy Award Nomination**—Hanif Kureishi, best screenplay written directly for the screen. *93 minutes*

MY BODYGUARD (1980)

★★★

Chris Makepeace
Adam Baldwin
Ruth Gordon

A sensitive comedy/drama about high-school students that depicts adolescent problems with realism and sympathy. Makepeace stars as a frail, middle-class kid who is relentlessly harassed by bullies at school. He enlists a mysterious and strong classmate to protect him, and this relationship sparks a friendship that adds warmth and intelligence to the story. Tony Bill, making his directorial debut, brings out the best in the cast of young unknowns. Also with Martin Mull, Matt Dillon, and John Houseman. **(PG)** *99 minutes*

MY BRILLIANT CAREER (1980)

★★★

Judy Davis
Sam Neill
Wendy Hughes

This remarkable and spirited Australian film concerns the struggle of an impoverished farm girl in her quest to become a writer. The movie is based on a 1901 semi-autobiographical novel by Miles Franklin, who wrote about the need for women to be independent when she was just 16 years old. The story lapses at times, but the film is skillfully directed by Gillian Armstrong. It features an energetic performance by Davis in the lead role. **(PG)** *101 minutes*

MY CHAUFFEUR (1986)

★★

Deborah Foreman
Sam Jones
E.G. Marshall

Trite romantic comedy about a poor girl who becomes involved with a young tycoon through her unlikely chauffeur's job. Foreman, in the title role, is watchable as the perky heroine. However, many of her escapades as limo driver are silly and preposterous—including the bizarre relationship with her wealthy love interest, played by Jones. Also with Howard Hesseman and new-wave magicians/comedians Penn and Teller. **Director**—David Beaird. **(R)** *94 minutes*

MY DARLING CLEMENTINE (1946)

★★★★

Henry Fonda
Victor Mature
Walter Brennan

Ward Bond and Victor Mature size up the O.K. Corral in My Darling Clementine.

Among the best of director John Ford's westerns, this is about Wyatt Earp, Doc Holliday, and their activities in Tombstone, Arizona, including the famous shoot-out at the O.K. Corral. Like many of Ford's westerns, the film is an allegory about advancing civilization and its effect on the Old West. It is appropriate that the film features "Clementine" in the title, even though the storyline involves the famous feud between the Earps and the Clantons, because, as the schoolmarm, it is she who brings civilization (in the form of education) to Tombstone. The results of her actions will eventually lead to the demise of such gunmen as the Earps and the Clantons. Mature gives one of the best performances of his career as Doc Holliday. The beautiful black-and-white photography enhances the melancholy mood. Also with Linda Darnell, Cathy Downs, Tim Holt, Ward Bond, Alan Mowbray, and John Ireland. *98 minutes b&w*

MY DEMON LOVER (1987)

 ★★

Scott Valentine
Michelle Little

A modern-day version of *The Wolf Man* with a couple of new twists to accommodate contemporary tastes. Valentine, of television's *Family Ties,* plays the title role of a scrubby but likable young man who transforms into a beast when sexually aroused. Seems he was cursed by a Romanian woman. Little costars as the daffy but cute girl who wins his affections. The cast handles the material with aplomb, but there is not that much to howl about. **Director**—Charles Loventhal. **(PG–13)** *86 minutes*

MY FAIR LADY (1964)

 ★★★★

Rex Harrison
Audrey Hepburn
Stanley Holloway

Rex Harrison has turned cockney Audrey Hepburn into My Fair Lady.

Exuberant and highly entertaining screen version of the Broadway smash musical, based on George Bernard Shaw's *Pygmalion*. Harrison is delightful as Professor Henry Higgins, who sets out to make a lady of Eliza Doolittle, a cockney flower-seller, played by Hepburn. He succeeds, of course, and then falls in love with her. The Lerner and Loewe music is firmly intact and provides much charm. The scenery, photography, and costumes are enchanting. Also with Wilfrid Hyde-White, Theodore Bikel, and Gladys Cooper. **Director**—George Cukor. **Academy Awards**—best picture; Cukor, best director; Harrison, best actor; Harry Stradling, cinematography. **Nominations**—Holloway, best supporting actor; Cooper, best supporting actress; Alan Jay Lerner, best screenplay based on material from another medium. *170 minutes*

MY FAVORITE BLONDE (1942)

★★★

Bob Hope
Madeleine Carroll

Top-notch comedy caper starring Hope as a second-rate vaudeville performer who reluctantly gets mixed up in a spy adventure with beautiful British agent Carroll. The film is well paced and features Hope's usual barrage of one-liners. Also in the cast are Gale Sondergaard, George Zucco, and Victor Varconi. **Director**—Sidney Lanfield. *78 minutes b&w*

MY FAVORITE BRUNETTE (1947)

 ★★★

Bob Hope
Dorothy Lamour

Laughs galore with Hope as a photographer masquerading as a private eye to help Lamour. Meanwhile, he's being pursued by mobsters. Peter Lorre and Lon Chaney, Jr., round out the cast of this romp, which parodies *Farewell, My Lovely*. Also with John Hoyt, Charles Dingle, and Reginald Denny. **Director**—Elliott Nugent. *87 minutes b&w*

MY FAVORITE WIFE (1940)

 ★★★★

Cary Grant
Irene Dunne

Irene Dunne and Cary Grant in the comedy My Favorite Wife.

Dunne stars as a woman, presumed lost in a shipwreck, who returns after several years to find her husband (Grant) remarried. It's a contrived and predictable situation, but the talent involved makes this screwball comedy one of the classics of the genre. Remade with Doris Day and James Garner as *Move Over, Darling*. Also with Gail Patrick, Randolph Scott, and Ann Shoemaker. **Director**—Garson Kanin. **Academy Award Nomination**—Leo McCarey, Bella Spewack, and Samuel Spewack, original story. *88 minutes b&w*

MY FAVORITE YEAR (1982)

 ★★★

Peter O'Toole
Mark Linn-Baker
Jessica Harper
Joseph Bologna

Peter O'Toole is delightful as an aging movie star who copes with TV in My Favorite Year.

Television's "Golden Age" is fondly remembered in this backstage story of a comedy program modeled after *Your Show of Shows*. The wobbly satire concerns frantic efforts to get O'Toole, as a faded, drunken Errol Flynn-like actor, to perform live on the show. O'Toole's sleek, larger-than-life performance overcomes the hectic, sentimental script. Also with Selma Diamond, Bill Macy, Lainie Kazan, Cameron Mitchell, and Lou Jacobi. **Director**—Richard Benjamin. **(PG) Academy Award Nomination**—O'Toole, best actor. *92 minutes*

MY FIRST WIFE (1984)

★★★★

John Hargreaves
Wendy Hughes

This deeply moving drama is a superb portrait of a disintegrating relationship, on par with Bergman's *Scenes from a Marriage*. Australian writer/director

(Continued)

(Continued)
Paul Cox uses the estranged couple's families, friends, and lovers to give a more rounded context in which to understand their problems. Hargreaves and Hughes are genuinely impressive and credible as the beleaguered husband and wife. An absorbing and astute psychological study of human emotions. **(No MPAA rating)**

99 minutes

MY FRIEND FLICKA (1943)

★★★

Roddy McDowall
Preston Foster

Engaging and sentimental story about a boy who befriends a maverick horse. An expertly crafted animal film enhanced with magnificent scenery. McDowall does well as the winsome lad. Rita Johnson, James Bell, and Jeff Corey are also in the cast. A sequel, *Thunderhead, Son of Flicka*, was made in 1945 with most of the same cast. **Director**—Harold Schuster. *89 minutes*

MY FRIEND IRMA (1949)

★★

Marie Wilson
John Lund

Wilson stars in the title role as a dumb blonde who becomes involved with a new singing sensation discovered at a refreshment stand. Broad, slapstick humor abounds in this wacky comedy, based loosely on the radio series. Dean Martin and Jerry Lewis made their screen debut with this movie. **Director**—George Marshall.

103 minutes b&w

MY LEFT FOOT (1989)

 ★★★ ⓒ

Daniel Day-Lewis
Brenda Fricker

Day-Lewis' remarkable and physically demanding performance elevates this moving autobiography of Irish-born Christy Brown. Brown, stricken with cerebral palsy at a young age, was an artist and author who accomplished his feats of genius with the only body part he could control—his left foot. What could have been merely sentimental melodrama evolves here as a vigorous character study, which emphasizes the man's complex personality. All supporting performances are noteworthy. A blaring soundtrack by Elmer Bernstein almost ruins the otherwise straightforward film. Also with Alison Whelan, Kirsten Sheridan, and Declan Croghan. **Director**—Jim Sheridan. **(R) Academy Awards**—Day-Lewis, best actor; Fricker, best supporting actress. **Nominations**—best picture; Sheridan, best director; Sheridan and Shane Connaughton, best screenplay adaptation.

103 minutes

MY LIFE AS A DOG (1986)

★★★

Anton Glanzelius
Tomas von Brömssen

This warmhearted and poignant comedy from Sweden proved quite successful when it was released in American theaters. A 12-year-old boy is sent to live with relatives in a small rural village during the 1950s. Feeling alienated and alone, he identifies himself with Laika, the little Russian dog shipped into space by the Soviets. He becomes fast friends with a girl who disguises herself as a boy to play on a soccer team. Both of them feel the loneliness that so often characterizes puberty. Based on an autobiographical novel by Reidal Jönsson. Also with Anki Liden, Melinda Kinnaman, and Kicki Rundgren. Originally filmed in Swedish. **Director**—Lasse Hallström. **(No MPAA rating) Academy Award Nominations**—Hallström, best director; Hallström, Jönsson, Brasse Brannstrom, and Per Berglund, best screenplay based on material from another medium.

101 minutes

MY LITTLE CHICKADEE (1940)

★★★

Mae West
W.C. Fields

Two legends: W.C. Fields and Mae West in My Little Chickadee.

Memorable pairing of West and Fields in this western/comedy. Just watching the great Fields and the voluptuous West batting the corny dialogue back and forth is supreme joy. The plot and other characters are completely irrelevant and treated as such by these two comic giants. Fields and West wrote their own dialogue. Joseph Calleia, Dick Foran, Margaret Hamilton, and Donald Meek also star. **Director**—Edward Cline. *83 minutes b&w*

MY LITTLE PONY (1986)

★★ ⓒ

A sticky-sweet, animated fantasy designed to amuse toddlers and also sell them pony toys. The familiar good vs. evil story concerns cute, playful ponies, which are threatened by a wicked witch. Eventually, they are saved by the good-hearted Grundels. Disney did this sort of animated feature with much more imagination. Danny DeVito, Tony Randall, and Madeline Kahn supply some of the voices for the characters. **Director**—Michael Joens. **(G)**

87 minutes

MY MAN GODFREY (1936)

★★★★

William Powell
Carole Lombard

Carole Lombard takes William Powell in as a butler in My Man Godfrey.

Screwball comedy—the fast, zany screen humor of the 1930s—was at its zenith with this film, as were its two deliciously droll stars. Lombard plays the wealthy daughter of a well-to-do family. She wins a scavenger hunt during a

ⓒ *This movie available with closed captions for the hearing impaired.*

party by coming back with a "forgotten man," unemployed and homeless, played by Powell. After she takes him into her home as the family butler, she makes some surprising discoveries about him—and herself. The sterling cast also includes Eugene Pallette, Alice Brady, Gail Patrick, Mischa Auer, Grady Sutton, Franklin Pangborn, Jean Dixon, and Alan Mowbray. Gregory La Cava, who had previously worked with W.C. Fields, directed. **Academy Award Nominations**—La Cava, best director; Powell, best actor; Lombard, best actress; Auer, best supporting actor; Brady, best supporting actress; Eric Hatch and Morris Ryskind, screenplay.

90 minutes b&w

MY SCIENCE PROJECT (1985)

★★

John Stockwell
Danielle Von Zerneck
Dennis Hopper

So-so teenage comedy/adventure about a high-school science assignment that transports a teacher and some students back in time. The youths encounter cavemen, prehistoric animals, and Roman gladiators. Their teacher gets a chance to relive his youth in the 1960s. The film starts cleverly, but soon runs out of steam. **Director**—Jonathan Betnel. **(PG)** *95 minutes*

MY SISTER EILEEN (1942)

★★

Rosalind Russell
Janet Blair
Brian Aherne
June Havoc

A perky story about two sisters from Ohio who get a comic dose of New York when they settle into their Greenwich Village basement apartment. Russell is the would-be writer, Ruth; Blair plays her attractive sibling Eileen, an aspiring actress. The laughs are sporadic in this adaptation of the Joseph Fields/Jerome Chodorov play, which itself was based on Ruth McKinney's *New Yorker* stories. But Russell, in one of her best-loved, Oscar-nominated roles, still shines. The play was later made into a Broadway musical called *Wonderful Town*, which in turn was adapted to film and released as *My Sister Eileen* (1955). With Allyn Joslyn, George Tobias, and Richard Quine. **Director**—Alexander Hall. **Academy Award Nomination**—Russell, best actress. *96 minutes b&w*

MY STEPMOTHER IS AN ALIEN (1988)

★★

Dan Aykroyd
Kim Basinger
Alyson Hannigan

Dan Aykroyd seems quite pleased with alien Kim Basinger in My Stepmother Is an Alien.

Aykroyd stars as a widowed scientist and who marries a voluptuous extraterrestrial in the form of Basinger. Hannigan costars as the teen daughter who is perplexed by her new mom from a far-off galaxy. Basinger's handling of some scenes is delightful, particularly those in which she encounters such earthly joys as romance and eating. But the one-joke premise is stretched thin. Also with Jon Lovitz, Seth Green, and Joseph Maher. **Director**—Richard Benjamin. **(PG-13)** *108 minutes*

THE MYSTERY OF KASPER HAUSER (1975)

 ★★★

Bruno S.

A provocative film by director Werner Herzog about a mute 15-year-old boy who mysteriously appears in the Nuremberg main square in 1828, with apparently no prior contact with civilization. His innocence clashes with his new social environment. Based on a popular story, supposedly true but enhanced to the point of legend, the film is visually exciting, but it may be too ponderous for some. Stars Bruno S., believed to be an actual schizophrenic, as Hauser. Also with Walter Ladengast and Brigitte Mira. Originally filmed in German. **(No MPAA rating) Alternate Title**—*Every Man for Himself and God Against All.* *110 minutes*

MYSTERY TRAIN (1990)

★★★

Masatoshi Nagase
Youki Kudoh
Screamin' Jay Hawkins
Cinque Lee

This offbeat comedy by filmmaker Jim Jarmusch moves slowly because his characters tend to be passive, allowing their milieu to sweep them up in events beyond their control. Yet this haunting experiment in film time and narrative space is colorful, intriguing, and, most of all, hip. The film is constructed in three independent vignettes, all centering around a seedy Memphis hotel. Though each vignette has its own plot and characters, each is connected to the others because they share a span of time. Most of Jarmusch's characters are foreigners—a Japanese couple in the first story, an Italian woman in the second, and an Englishman in the third—which allows us to look at American culture through a detached point of view. Blues and rock 'n' roll music of the 1950s adds to the funky atmosphere. Also with Joe Strummer, Nicoletta Braschi, Rick Aviles, Elizabeth Bracco, and Steve Buscemi. **(R)**

110 minutes

MYSTIC PIZZA (1988)

Julia Roberts
Annabeth Gish
Lili Taylor

Three hometown girls who work in a pizza parlor face various romantic crises and misadventures. This small-scale romantic comedy is a familiar coming-of-age story but from a female point of view. The low budget and small scale work to the film's advantage, giving the film a low-key, sweet quality. Also with Vincent D'Onofrio, William Moses, and Conchata Ferrell. **Director**—Donald Petrie. **(R)** *102 minutes*

MY SWEET LITTLE VILLAGE (1986)

★★½

Janos Ban
Marian Labuda
Rudolph Hrusinsky

Czech filmmaker Jiri Menzel directed this small, sincere comedy/drama about

(Continued)

This movie available on videotape and/or disc.

(Continued)
a group of ordinary people from an ordinary village who band together to stop a coldhearted bureaucrat from usurping the humble home of a village man and turning it into his summer cottage. Though the film contains many moments of gentle, ironic humor, its nostalgic, sentimental tones and lightweight story lack the power and pointed social criticism of Menzel's earlier work, particularly *Closely Watched Trains.* **(No MPAA rating) Academy Award Nomination**—best foreign-language film. *100 minutes*

NADINE (1987)

★★

Kim Basinger
Jeff Bridges

Texas romance with Kim Basinger and Jeff Bridges in Nadine.

Basinger, in the title role, and Bridges play a pair of offbeat but likable characters in this romantic comedy set in the 1950s. The story revolves around their shaky marriage, which gets back on track when they try to outwit a gang of swindlers and murderers. The good performances, though, can't compensate for a dim script with a convoluted exposition and slapstick routines that lead nowhere. Rip Torn costars as a deliciously sinister villain. Also with Gwen Verdon, Jerry Stiller, and Glenne Headley. **Director**—Robert Benton. **(PG)** *83 minutes*

THE NAKED AND THE DEAD (1958)

★★

Aldo Ray
Cliff Robertson

Aldo Ray (left) is at loggerheads with a fellow dogface in The Naked and the Dead.

This is a disappointing treatment of Norman Mailer's novel about a platoon of U.S. soldiers in combat in the Pacific during World War II. The story also touches on the tension between officers and the troops. Unfortunately, there's an ordinariness about the production, with its second-rate direction, superficial screenplay, and mediocre acting. Also with Raymond Massey, William Campbell, and Richard Jaeckel. **Director**—Raoul Walsh. *131 minutes*

THE NAKED CITY (1948)

★★★★

Barry Fitzgerald
Don Taylor
Howard Duff

A captivating police drama filmed on location in New York City—an innovation at the time. A girl is found brutally murdered, and cops launch a manhunt to find the killer. This documentary-like thriller offers considerable detail on police work and authentic scenes of city life, and inspired a television series with the same title. The film's tag line ("There are eight million stories in the naked city; this has been one of them") was used in the series and became a widely known phrase of the era. The excellent cast also includes Dorothy Hart, Ted De Corsia, and Adelaide Klein. **Director**—Jules Dassin. **Academy Award**—William Daniels, cinematography. **Nomination**—Marvin Wald, motion picture story. *96 minutes b&w*

THE NAKED GUN (1988)

★★★

Leslie Nielsen
George Kennedy
Priscilla Presley

Zucker, Abrahams, and Zucker, who brought us *Airplane,* have fashioned another riotously funny comedy. This goofy theatrical version of the *Police Squad* television series is packed with howling vulgar humor. Nielsen is perfect in his deadpan portrayal of a bumbling Los Angeles detective. Tucked in between all the laughs is a plot that has to do with drug smuggling and an assassination attempt on visiting Queen Elizabeth II. Also with O.J. Simpson, George Kennedy, Ricardo Montalban, and Nancy Marshand. **Director**—David Zucker. **(PG-13)** *89 minutes*

THE NAKED PREY (1966)

★★★

Cornel Wilde
Gert Van Den Berg
Ken Gampu

Is that tribal drums we hear?—or the pounding of safari leader Wilde's heart, as he flees through the jungle, naked and unarmed, pursued by savage natives bent on nabbing their human prey. Wilde also directed and coproduced this violent adventure filmed on location in Africa. It sometimes thrills, occasionally disgusts, but certainly moves. **Academy Award Nomination**—Clint Johnston and Don Peters, best story and screenplay written directly for the screen. *94 minutes*

THE NAME OF THE ROSE (1986)

★★★

Sean Connery
F. Murray Abraham

Sean Connery is a 14th-century sleuth in The Name of the Rose.

Franciscan monk William of Baskerville (Connery) visits a Benedictine Abbey to participate in a scholarly debate but becomes involved in solving a series of murders occurring at the abbey. Based on Umberto Eco's difficult but popular novel, the film is slow-moving, with an emphasis on lofty speeches and grandi-

This movie available with closed captions for the hearing impaired.

ose performances. Connery's character, however, is skillfully drawn and the authentic medieval atmosphere provides much suspense. The eerie calm of the abbey belies the horrors that occur deep inside it, while Connery's handsome face is in sharp contrast to those of the physically deformed monks who inhabit the monastery. Abraham, whose performance is exaggerated as though for the stage, is the film's only major flaw. Though a financial failure in America at the time of release, the film was highly successful in Europe. Also with Christian Slater, William Hickey, Ron Perlman, and Michael Lonsdale. **Director**—Jean-Jacques Annaud. **(R)** *128 minutes*

NASHVILLE (1975)

Ronee Blakley
Lily Tomlin

Nashville's country-and-western music scene is the setting for this panoramic reflection of America's joys, frustrations, and complacency. Director Robert Altman uses an episodic structure to present this unusual tale, seen through the eyes of 24 characters who eventually convene at a Nashville political rally. It's a masterful and free-flowing film with memorable performances and a shocking ending. The screenplay was written by Altman associate Joan Tewkesbury, though actors were encouraged to improvise and work on their own musical material. The electric cast includes Karen Black, Keith Carradine, Geraldine Chaplin, Michael Murphy, Allen Garfield, Henry Gibson, Keenan Wynn, Cristina Raines, Barbara Harris, Shelley Duvall, and Ned Beatty. **(R) Academy Award**—Carradine, best original song. **Nominations**—best picture; Altman, best director; Blakley and Tomlin, best supporting actress. *159 minutes*

NASTY HABITS (1977)

 ★★

Glenda Jackson
Melina Mercouri
Geraldine Page
Sandy Dennis

This feeble lampoon of Nixon and the Watergate mess takes place in an imaginary Philadelphia convent, with some of the ambitious nuns engaging in assorted dirty tricks to win an election. It's a funny idea, but not well executed. The vague and choppy script generates only a few minor laughs. An aristocratic Jackson plays the Nixon figure, and a bespectacled Dennis is witty as a John Dean-sort. **Director**—Michael Lindsay-Hogg. **(PG)** *96 minutes*

NATE AND HAYES (1983)

Tommy Lee Jones
Michael O'Keefe

This hyperactive buccaneer adventure, set in the 1880s, offers a grand array of sword and musket fights, boarding-party skirmishes, and narrow escapes. Jones stars as a grinning pirate who teams up with young missionary O'Keefe to rescue the latter's fiancée (Jenny Seagrove) from the clutches of a marauding scoundrel. Errol Flynn did it much better. **Director**—Ferdinand Fairfax. **(PG)** *100 minutes*

NATIONAL LAMPOON'S ANIMAL HOUSE (1978)

John Belushi
Tim Matheson
John Vernon
Verna Bloom

Stephen Furst and John Belushi in National Lampoon's Animal House.

A raunchy, uneven comedy of frat-house silliness set in a small college in 1962. The film follows the bawdy style of the famed humor magazine, and the youthful players, led by Belushi, make an earnest effort. The tasteless but funny film set the trend for a whole new style of comedy aimed at youthful audiences. Cast includes Tom Hulce, Peter Riegert, Karen Allen, Stephen Furst, Cesare Danova, and Donald Sutherland. **Director**—John Landis. **(R)** *109 minutes*

NATIONAL LAMPOON'S CHRISTMAS VACATION (1989)

 ★★½

Chevy Chase
Beverly D'Angelo
Randy Quaid

Gross humor and tacky pratfalls make up this third installment of the *Vacation* series. Chase resurrects his role as the ever-unlucky Clark Griswold, a well-meaning all-American father who never succeeds in getting things right. Christmastime finds the family at home while their oddball relatives visit for a chaotic holiday. Though the film was a box-office hit at the time of release, the film is not the best of the series. The black humor and satirical edge of the original has given way to simple slapstick this time around. Though competent direction generates some humor from these sight gags, the production team is definitely aiming at younger audiences here. Fans of the first film will enjoy Quaid's reprise of his role as Chase's flaky rural relative. Also with Diane Ladd, John Randolph, E.G. Marshall, Mae Questel, William Hickey, and Miriam Flynn. **Director**—Jeremiah Chechik. **(PG-13)** *97 minutes*

NATIONAL LAMPOON'S CLASS REUNION (1982)

Gerrit Graham
Shelley Smith

Crude, vulgar comedy that's a feeble spoof of horror films. The frantic shenanigans are set at a high-school reunion attended by assorted crazies and one vengeful madman who murders some of his classmates. A rather large cast is spread thinly, and everyone seems to be struggling with the flimsy, witless material, which is more annoying than amusing. Also with Michael Lerner, Zane Buzby, Stephen Furst, and Fred McCarren. **Director**—Michael Miller. **(R)** *85 minutes*

NATIONAL LAMPOON'S EUROPEAN VACATION (1985)

Chevy Chase

The Griswolds, that outrageous middle-class American family headed by Chase, stumble through Europe

(Continued)

Ⓐ *This movie available on videotape and/or disc.*

Ugly Americans: The Griswalds assault Paris in National Lampoon's European Vacation.

(Continued)
with less comic success than was sparked by their breezier summer tour of the United States two years earlier. This wobbly sequel contains mostly uninspired, slapstick humor as Dad, Mom, and the kids encounter various mishaps throughout England, France, Germany, and Italy. Many sight gags rely on routine car chases, no better than those on TV action dramas. Beverly D'Angelo costars with Dana Hill and Jason Lively. **Director**—Amy Heckerling. **(PG–13)** *95 minutes*

NATIONAL LAMPOON'S VACATION (1983)

 ★★★

Chevy Chase
Christie Brinkley

Chase strikes the proper note as a square, middle-class father who takes his family on a cross-country trip to a Disney-like amusement park called Wally World. The breezy comedy is worth a laugh every 100 miles as Dad, Mom, and kids get lost in the desert, encounter deadbeat relatives, and survive various tourist traps. Familiar situations are made quite funny thanks to good direction by Harold Ramis and a clever screenplay by John Hughes. Also with Beverly D'Angelo, Anthony Michael Hall, Dana Barron, Randy Quaid, Imogene Coca, and John Candy. **(R)** *100 minutes*

NATIONAL VELVET (1945)

Mickey Rooney
Elizabeth Taylor

A captivating family drama about a plucky youngster who trains a horse to win the Grand National race. Enid Bagnold's novel is adapted for the screen with much of the sentiment in place. The film is most notable for the presence of Taylor as the young horsewoman. Also with Anne Revere, Donald Crisp, Angela Lansbury, and Reginald Owen. **Director**—Clarence Brown. **(G) Academy Award**—Revere, best supporting actress. **Nominations**—Brown, best director; Leonard Smith, cinematography. *125 minutes*

NATIVE SON (1986)

Victor Love
Carroll Baker
Akosua Busia

Richard Wright's controversial novel about impoverished blacks gets short-changed in this screen version made on a modest budget. The story's hero, a young black man who accidentally kills a wealthy white woman, is inadequately defined in terms of Wright's interpretation of black anger and frustration. However, the urban poverty of the Depression era is impressively conveyed. Also with Matt Dillon, Elizabeth McGovern, Geraldine Page, and Oprah Winfrey. **Director**—Jerrold Freedman. **(PG)** *112 minutes*

THE NATURAL (1984)

Robert Redford
Robert Duvall
Glenn Close
Wilford Brimley

Robert Redford is a legendary baseball hitter in The Natural.

Redford slugs at least a triple in the title role as an aging baseball superstar of the 1930s. This arty, low-key film adaptation of Bernard Malamud's novel contains the necessary imagery of myth and legend. The story, although occasionally too sentimental, adequately relates the trials of an all-American wonder boy confronting the cynicism of big-league sports. **Director**—Barry Levinson. **(PG)** *134 minutes*

NAUGHTY MARIETTA (1935)

Nelson Eddy
Jeanette MacDonald
Frank Morgan
Elsa Lanchester

Victor Herbert's 1910 operetta paired Eddy and MacDonald on the screen for the first time. The chemistry was just right, and the two became the movies' most popular warbling duo. This is one of their more genuinely charming vehicles, still reasonably fresh (if not exactly naughty) and juiced up by droll supporting performances from Morgan and Lanchester. To avoid a forced marriage, French princess MacDonald flees to the American colonies, where she falls for stalwart Indian scout Eddy. Songs include "Ah, Sweet Mystery of Life," "Tramp, Tramp, Tramp," "The Italian Street Song," and "I'm Falling in Love." **Director**—W.S. Van Dyke. **(G) Academy Award Nomination**—best picture. *106 minutes b&w*

NAVY SEALS (1990)

Charlie Sheen
Michael Biehn

Sheen heads the cast of this unremarkable action film about the elite Navy unit known as the Navy Seals. He and Biehn play gung-ho commandos assigned to destroy American-made stinger missiles that have fallen into the hands of Middle Eastern terrorists. Despite the heavy-duty star power, the superficial script brings the film down. Fans of the genre may appreciate the star performances and the action scenes, but this style of heroics was done better in Hollywood's golden age. Joanne Whalley-Kilmer appears in a brief role as a Lebanese television reporter. Also with Cyril O'Reilly, Rick Rossovich, Bill Paxton, and Paul Sanchez. **Director**—Lewis Teague. **(R)** *113 minutes*

® *This movie available with closed captions for the hearing impaired.*

NEAR DARK (1987)

★★★

Adrian Pasdar
Lance Henriksen
Jenny Wright

This slickly produced vampire story may be violent and gory but it is also a profound statement on alienation and despair. Pasdar stars as an innocent young man who is bitten on the neck by a strange girl, played by newcomer Wright. Stumbling across a barren landscape while trying to make it home, he is suddenly swept up by a group of marauding vampires. The travels of this ragtag bunch of rebels and misfits across a burned-out Southwest resembles the outlaw escapades of a bloodthirsty Bonnie and Clyde-type gang. Their abnormal lifestyle is erotic yet sick; sad but gruesome; poignant yet meaningless. The film's narrative resembles Nicholas Ray's classic *They Live by Night*. Also with Jenette Goldstein, Bill Paxton, and Tim Thomerson. **Director**—Kathryn Bigelow. **(R)** *95 minutes*

NEIGHBORS (1981)

★★1/2

John Belushi
Dan Aykroyd
Kathryn Walker
Cathy Moriarty

A weird couple moves next door to a family of peaceful suburbanites, headed by Belushi and Walker. The new neighbors drive Belushi up the wall with their peculiar antics. This promising black comedy, based on the novel by Thomas Berger, soon turns sour, however, and eventually falls apart at the seams. Many of the boisterous gags are tasteless and crude. Aykroyd and Moriarty give strained performances as the strange new neighbors, and director John G. Avildsen is at sea with the absurd material. **(R)** *95 minutes*

NETWORK (1976)

★★★★

Faye Dunaway
William Holden
Peter Finch

Television is worked over in this provocative and outrageous satire about a network news department that will do anything to grab an audience. Paddy

Peter Finch becomes a broadcast demagogue in Network.

Chayefsky's original script is brilliant and audacious. There are excellent performances by Holden as a scrupulous news division chief, Dunaway as a cunning and predatory programming executive, and Finch as an anchorman who goes mad. The remainder of the outstanding cast includes Robert Duvall, Beatrice Straight, Wesley Addy, and Ned Beatty. Sidney Lumet, known for his socially relevant films, directed. **(R)** **Academy Awards**—Finch, best actor; Dunaway, best actress; Straight, best supporting actress; Chayefsky, best screenplay written directly for the screen. **Nominations**—best picture; Lumet, best director; Holden, best actor; Beatty, best supporting actor; Owen Roizman, cinematography. *120 minutes*

NEVER CRY WOLF (1983)

★★★

Charles Martin Smith

Charles Martin Smith is obsessed with a species of wolves in Never Cry Wolf.

An exhilarating, visually spectacular wilderness film that examines the behavior of Arctic wolves. This screen adaptation of Farley Mowat's best-selling book traces the adventures of a young biologist (Smith) assigned to determine if wolves are responsible for the decline in the caribou herd. His discovery leads to an appreciation of the often-maligned wolves. Much of the humor and feel of Mowat's book is left intact, though some of the depth is missing. The real stars are the wolves, the eloquent photography of Hiro Narita, and the direction by Carroll Ballard, who succeeds here as well as he did in *The Black Stallion*. **(PG)** *105 minutes*

THE NEVERENDING STORY (1984)

★★

Noah Hathaway
Barret Oliver

Noah Hathaway and his horse begin their quest in The Neverending Story.

Lavish, technically striking children's fantasy that quickly bogs down in complex philosophizing. The meandering screenplay follows the quest of a youthful warrior bent on saving a mythical land (Fantasia) from destruction by a strange force (The Nothing). During his mission, he encounters various strange and unappealing creatures who either help or interfere with his progress. Most kids are apt to be confused by the heavy-handed approach. **Director**—Wolfgang Petersen. **(PG)** *94 minutes*

NEVER GIVE AN INCH

See Sometimes a Great Notion

NEVER GIVE A SUCKER AN EVEN BREAK (1941)

★★★★

W.C. Fields

The great Fields is the whole show in this wacky farce; it has virtually no

(Continued)

(Continued)
plot, but plenty of hilarious scenes. Fields, three sheets to the wind, falls out of an airplane and lands in a strange country called Ruritania, where he meets an attractive girl who's never met a man. Fields relates the whole story to a movie producer in the hopes of getting some money to back a film about his exploits. The last starring role for the notorious comedian. Costars Margaret Dumont, Gloria Jean, Leon Errol, Franklin Pangborn, and Ann Miller. **Director**—Edward Cline.

70 minutes b&w

NEVER ON SUNDAY (1960)

★★★★

Melina Mercouri
Jules Dassin

Mercouri stands out in a memorable performance as a worldly-wise prostitute who resists being reformed by a stuffy tourist visiting Greece. Dassin, who directed, plays Homer, the frustrated tourist. This is Dassin's best-known film, and as in much of his other work, the theme involves an individual's responsibilities and relationship to society. The authentic musical score, featuring bouzouki music, is by Manos Hadjidakis. Also with Georges Foundas and Titos Vandis. **Academy Award Nominations**—Dassin, best director; Mercouri, best actress; Dassin, best story and screenplay written directly for the screen. *91 minutes b&w*

NEVER SAY NEVER AGAIN (1983)

★★★

Sean Connery
Klaus Maria Brandauer

After a 12-year hiatus, Connery returns to the familiar role of superspy James Bond. The excitement and intrigue are as rich as ever, and the film doesn't hesitate to gently poke fun at the outrageous Bond image. Agent 007 is pitted against a sinister villain (Brandauer) who is blackmailing the world with stolen nuclear-tipped cruise missiles. A new array of glitzy gadgets, tongue-in-cheek humor, and gorgeous women is included to keep moviegoers happily in Bondage. Also starring Kim Basinger and Barbara Carrera. Supporting players include Max Von Sydow, Bernie Casey, and Edward Fox. **Director**—Irvin Kershner. **(PG)** *137 minutes*

THE NEW ADVENTURES OF PIPPI LONGSTOCKING (1988)

★★

Tami Erin

Tami Erin in The New Adventures of Pippi Longstocking.

A flat, charmless children's adventure based on Astrid Lindgren's tales of an independent pirate girl. Erin teams up with some neighbor children and they take off for an adventure in her special flying machine. But the series of episodes is rather lifeless, and the Pippi character often comes off as bratty rather than spirited. Erin overacts in her portrayal of the pigtailed title character. Also with Eileen Brennan and Dennis Dugan. **Director**—Ken Annakin. **(G)**

100 minutes

THE NEW CENTURIONS (1972)

★★★

George C. Scott
Stacy Keach

An unusual and insightful police drama, focusing on the personal and psychological pressures of being a cop. Scott contributes considerable dignity to the proceedings as the cynical veteran officer who shows his rookie partner the ropes; Keach plays the rookie cop. Competently based on Joseph Wambaugh's novel about men on the Los Angeles police force. Top performances all around. Also with Jane Alexander, Rosalind Cash, Erik Estrada, Isabel Sanford, James B. Sikking, and Scott Wilson. **Director**—Richard Fleischer. **(R)** *103 minutes*

A NEW LIFE (1988)

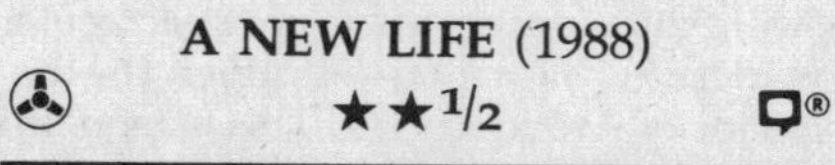

★★½

Alan Alda
Ann-Margret
Hal Linden
Veronica Hamel

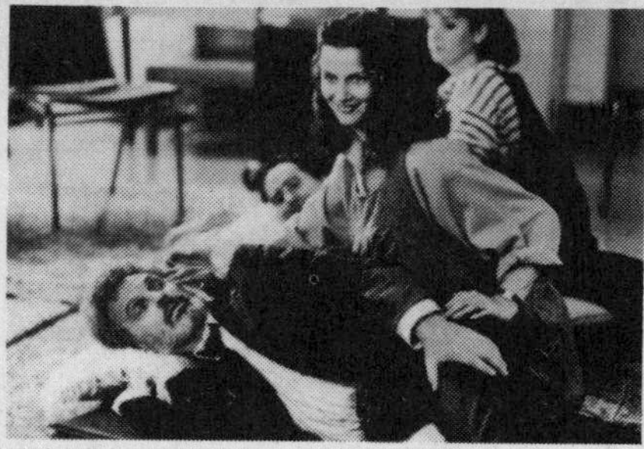

Middle age and Veronica Hamel mean changes for Alan Alda in A New Life.

An adult comedy that revolves around the exasperating problems of a middle-aged couple trying to adjust to their lives following divorce. Alda is perfect as a testy, workaholic stockbroker who must cope with the singles life after 26 years of marriage. Ann-Margret costars as the ex-wife who initiated the breakup. Although the storyline is predictable and the characters familiar, the film does feature solid performances, funny gags, and sharp dialogue. Those in minor roles are equally as splendid, including John Shea, Mary Kay Place, Beatrice Alda, and David Eisner. Alda also wrote and directed this contemporary comedy. **(PG–13)** *105 minutes*

NEWSFRONT (1978)

★★★

Bill Hunter
Chris Haywood

An intriguing Australian film that vividly portrays the theatrical newsreel business during its waning years, just prior to the advent of television. Though not a documentary, the film features actual clips of newsreel stories woven into the fictional story, which romanticizes the personal lives of the characters behind the cameras. An excellent cast, headed by Hunter and Haywood, delivers polished portrayals of those almost forgotten journalists. Also with Wendy Hughes, Gerard Kennedy, Bryan Brown, and Angela Punch. **Director**—Philip Noyce. **(PG)**

110 minutes color/b&w

NEW YORK CONFIDENTIAL (1955)

★★½

Broderick Crawford
Anne Bancroft

An undramatic yet authentic-looking account of organized crime in New

® *This movie available with closed captions for the hearing impaired.*

York. A local syndicate boss is bumped off by one of his own henchmen. A good cast, headed by Crawford and Bancroft, heightens the otherwise routine proceedings, which depict racketeers as shrewd businessmen. Also with Richard Conte, Marilyn Maxwell, and J. Carrol Naish. **Director**—Russell Rouse. *87 minutes b&w*

NEW YORK, NEW YORK (1977)

★★★

Liza Minnelli
Robert De Niro

Director Martin Scorsese's big-band-era backstage romance is a downbeat musical, but a fascinating one nonetheless. De Niro gives an outstanding performance as a selfish but talented jazz saxophonist who falls for band singer Minnelli, but eventually parts company with her. The intentional contrast between the happy swing music and this sordid emotional situation is poignant and powerful. Scorsese recaptures the feel of the great Hollywood musicals of the 1940s and 1950s (such as those by Minnelli's father, Vincente) in order to tell the kind of story seldom told in such vehicles. Also with Lionel Stander, Mary Kay Place, and Barry Primus. Originally released at 153 minutes, and rereleased in 1981 at 163 minutes. The video release restores some worthy footage. **(PG)** *137 minutes*

NEW YORK STORIES (1989)

★★★

Nick Nolte
Woody Allen
Mia Farrow
Heather McComb

Woody Allen in "Oedipus Wrecks," one of the New York Stories.

Anthology of three short films that showcases the talents of directors Martin Scorsese, Francis Coppola, and Woody Allen. Nolte is especially good in Scorsese's drama, *Life Lessons,* about a self-absorbed artist. Allen's comedy, *Oedipus Wrecks,* has priceless moments about a fiftyish lawyer who has problems with his mother. Coppola's *Life Without Zoe,* a fanciful tale of a poor-little-rich girl, ranks third in terms of effectiveness. The segments don't aspire to great heights, but they are expertly crafted by America's foremost filmmakers. Also with Rosanna Arquette, Deborah Harry, Talia Shire, and Mae Questel. **(PG)** *123 minutes*

NEXT OF KIN (1989)

★★½

Patrick Swayze
Liam Neeson
Adam Baldwin

Bill Paxton, Patrick Swayze, and Liam Neeson in Next of Kin.

Swayze stars as a Chicago police detective who originally hails from Kentucky in this action-filled cop thriller. When his younger brother is killed by the mob, Swayze's older brother arrives from back home to carry out revenge Kentucky-style. Swayze is caught in the middle between upholding society's law and siding with his family, which echoes the age-old dilemma of the Appalachian people. This well-crafted film closely follows the conventions of the action genre so that the outcome of the story is predictable from the outset. However, fans of the this type of movie will appreciate the conclusion, in which a group of hard-edged hill people fight the mob with everything from crossbows to rattlesnakes. Also with Helen Hunt, Andreas Katsulas, Bill Paxton, Ben Stiller, and Michael J. Pollard. **Director**—John Irvin. **(R)** *111 minutes*

NEXT STOP, GREENWICH VILLAGE (1976)

★★★

Lenny Baker
Shelley Winters

Director Paul Mazursky's warm and touching autobiographical film about an aspiring young comedian's life in the Village in the 1950s. Lanky newcomer Baker, playing the awkward-looking Larry Lapinsky, heads an outstanding cast that lends credibility and humanity to the story. Winters is convincing as an overbearing Jewish mother. The film is full of nostalgic memories of this period. Also with Ellen Greene, Lou Jacobi, Christopher Walken, and Mike Kellin. **(R)** *109 minutes*

NIAGARA (1953)

★★★

Marilyn Monroe
Joseph Cotten
Jean Peters

Joseph Cotton sees that Marilyn Monroe pays dearly for her scheming in Niagara.

Monroe stars in this suspenseful tale about a faithless wife who schemes to kill her husband while they are on vacation. Cotten plays the victimized husband. Cowritten by Charles Brackett, the film is one of the few to make use of the negative aspect of Monroe's provocative image. The cast also includes Don Wilson, Richard Allan, and Casey Adams. **Director**—Henry Hathaway. *89 minutes*

NICHOLAS AND ALEXANDRA (1971)

★★★

Michael Jayston
Janet Suzman
Laurence Olivier
Jack Hawkins

This interpretation of the events surrounding the Russian Revolution fo-

(Continued)

(Continued)
cuses on Russia's last Czar and Czarina, from 1904 to their execution in 1918. Though the film has a distinguished cast and pictorial splendor, as photographed by Oscar nominee Frederick A. Young, director Franklin Schaffner hasn't brought the same fire to the facts that he brought to *Patton*. Tom Baker adds some interest as Rasputin, but overall the cast is swamped by the sweeping production. **Academy Award Nominations**—best picture; Suzman, best actress; Young, cinematography. **(PG)** *189 minutes*

NICKELODEON (1976)

Ryan O'Neal
Burt Reynolds
Tatum O'Neal

Director Peter Bogdanovich's affectionate and entertaining tribute to the early pioneers of filmmaking. An excellent cast portrays the rollicking slapstick and madcap adventures of Hollywood before World War I, when America was charmed with its new plaything, the moving picture. It's uneven in places, but it's rich in feeling and educational as well. Also with Brian Keith, Stella Stevens, Harry Carey, Jr., and John Ritter. **(PG)** *121 minutes*

NIGHT AND DAY (1946)

★★★

Cary Grant
Alexis Smith
Mary Martin
Monty Woolley

The life of songwriter Cole Porter receives a fictionalized, Hollywood treatment, yet Porter's wonderful music stands out, and an excellent cast puts on a worthy show. Grant is effective as the popular composer, and even sings "You're the Top." Martin's rendition of "My Heart Belongs to Daddy" is a classic. Also with Jane Wyman, Eve Arden, and Dorothy Malone. **Director**—Michael Curtiz. *128 minutes*

A NIGHT AT THE OPERA (1935)

★★★★

The Marx Brothers

A Marx Brothers comedy classic, with Groucho, Chico, and Harpo destroying and finally saving an opera production.

Allan Jones joins Chico and Harpo Marx for A Night at the Opera.

The film contains the sequence involving the overcrowded stateroom, considered one of their best bits. Perhaps their most financially successful film, with a script written by Morrie Ryskind and playwright George S. Kaufman. Also with Margaret Dumont, Kitty Carlisle, Allan Jones, and Sig Ruman. **Director**—Sam Wood. *96 minutes b&w*

NIGHTBREED (1990)

★★

Craig Sheffer
Anne Bobby
David Cronenberg

A mediocre monster tale from director Clive Barker, who adapted the screenplay from his novel *Cabal*. Sheffer plods through his role as Boone, a young man falsely accused of murder. Boone hides out in a strange world populated by weird creatures. The ghoulish freaks are the centerpiece of this horror tale, but their rubbery masks are not that convincing or scary. However, horror fans will find intriguing the premise of an underground city inhabited by creatures who are neither dead nor alive and neither supernatural nor immortal. Famed horror director Cronenberg *(The Brood; Videodrome; Dead Ringers)* plays an evil psychiatrist. Rumor has it that the film was plagued by production problems and subsequently butchered. Also with Charles Haid, Hugh Quarshie, Hugh Ross, and Doug Bradley. **(R)** *99 minutes*

NIGHT HAS A THOUSAND EYES (1948)

Edward G. Robinson

Robinson stars as a vaudeville mentalist who discovers he actually has the ability to predict the future. The uneven drama is intriguing at times, but there are many corny moments. However, Robinson is as watchable as ever. Costars Gail Russell, John Lund, Virginia Bruce, and William Demarest. **Director**—John Farrow. *80 minutes b&w*

NIGHTHAWKS (1981)

★★★

Sylvester Stallone
Billy Dee Williams
Rutger Hauer

Sylvester Stallone and Billy Dee Williams corner a killer in Nighthawks.

Stallone steps out of his Rocky role to play a tough New York City cop who, along with Williams, tracks down a diabolical international terrorist. This standard police story is uneven in spots, but delivers excitement at a fast-paced clip. Stallone's character is an enraged man, but he remains a hero with a conscience, and he eventually triumphs over evil. Dutch actor Hauer is quite impressive as the cold-blooded fiend who is brought to bay in a heart-pounding, surprise finale. Also with Persis Khambatta, Nigel Davenport, and Lindsay Wagner. **Director**—Bruce Malmuth. **(R)** *99 minutes*

A NIGHT IN CASABLANCA (1946)

★★½

The Marx Brothers

Groucho, Chico, and Harpo check into a Casablanca hotel where they smoke out some Nazi spies. Not the best of the Marx Brothers, but there's enough sustained lunacy to please devotees. This film was perhaps the last big one for the zany trio. Costars Sig Ruman, Lisette Verea, Charles Drake, and Lois Collier. **Director**—Archie Mayo. *85 minutes b&w*

A NIGHT IN HEAVEN (1983)

★

Lesley Ann Warren
Christopher Atkins

Sleazy, dreary tale of a square high-school teacher (Warren) who has a brief affair with one of her students (Atkins) after she discovers him moonlighting as a male stripper. Events progress with the pace of a rush-hour traffic jam, and this ridiculous mess seems an embarrassment for all involved. Talented Warren, the dizzy moll in *Victor/Victoria,* is tragically wasted, and it's hard to believe John Avildsen (*Rocky*) directed such drivel. **(R)** *83 minutes*

A NIGHT IN THE LIFE OF JIMMY REARDON (1988)

  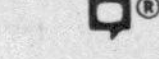

River Phoenix
Meredith Salenger
Ione Skye Leitch

River Phoenix and Matthew Perry in A Night in the Life of Jimmy Reardon.

A trite and often confusing comedy about an oversexed teenage boy residing in a Chicago suburb in the early 1960s. The screenplay, based on a novel written by director William Richert when he was 19, avoids many of the standard clichés of the teen comedy but hardly makes for inspired filmmaking. Phoenix stars in the title role as the adolescent who chases girls, is seduced by his mother's divorced friend, and frets about not being accepted into an Ivy League college. Also with Ann Magnuson, Matthew L. Perry, Louanne, Paul Koslo, and Jane Hallaren. **(R)** *92 minutes*

NIGHTMARE ALLEY (1947)

Tyrone Power
Joan Blondell

Power skillfully portrays a carnival barker who succeeds for a while as a con man until his luck runs out. This is an odd, moody, and captivating drama, filled with strange, intriguing characters. Based on the novel by William Lindsay Gresham, the film is surprisingly gritty, and Power's role is an anomaly in his career. Also with Coleen Gray, Helen Walker, Mike Mazurki, and Taylor Holmes. **Director**—Edmund Goulding. *111 minutes b&w*

A NIGHTMARE ON ELM STREET (1984)

Heather Langenkamp
Ronee Blakley
John Saxon

Freddy Krueger (Robert Englund) creates A Nightmare on Elm Street.

An entertaining and well-crafted modern horror tale involving four teenagers who experience a shared nightmare about a disfigured child-killer named Freddy, who comes back from the dead to kill them. The plot device of shared dreams, where reality and nightmare are difficult to distinguish, is a clever and frightening one. The supernatural killer threatens to kill the teens while they sleep, and the four try hard to stay awake—playing on everyone's childhood fears about falling asleep and never waking up. Blakley, who experienced some recognition as the country/western singing star in *Nashville,* appears as the alcoholic mother of one of the teens. Also with Robert Englund and Amanda Wyss. **Director**—Wes Craven. **(R)** *91 minutes*

A NIGHTMARE ON ELM STREET 2: FREDDY'S REVENGE (1985)

Mark Patton
Robert Englund
Kim Myers

Routine follow-up to the horror film about the demonic monster with long, slashing razors on his fingers, who invades the dreams and bodies of teenagers. This time, a high-school boy (Patton) is the object of Freddy's bloody mischief. The lad is singled out for such treatment when his family occupies the haunted Elm Street residence. Drab acting and familiar special effects make this screamer more forgettable than scary. Also with Hope Lange and Clu Gulager. **Director**—Jack Sholder. **(R)** *87 minutes*

A NIGHTMARE ON ELM STREET 3: DREAM WARRIORS (1987)

Robert Englund
Craig Wasson
Heather Langenkamp

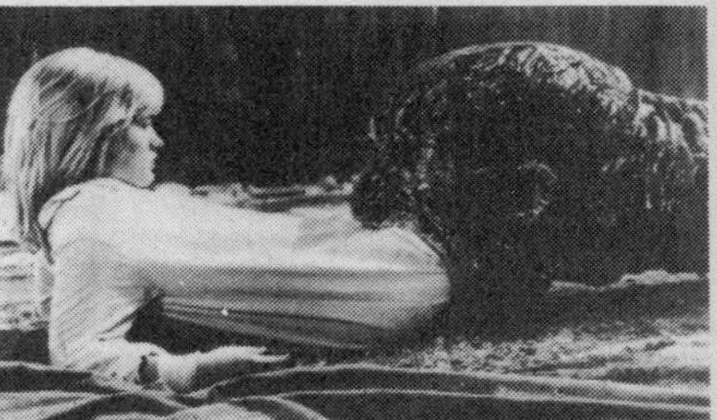

Freddy Krueger assumes a serpentine form in A Nightmare on Elm Street 3: Dream Warriors.

Freddy Krueger, the indestructible monster with the razor-blade fingernails and scar-tissue skin, seeks revenge once more in this third chapter of the well-known slasher saga. Here Freddy enters the dreams of a group of teenage psychiatric patients who are the offspring of the vigilantes who had torched him years ago. Though the gory special effects are creative, the tormented characters are colorless, evoking minimal sympathy. Also with Patricia Arquette. **Director**—Chuck Russell. **(R)** *96 minutes*

A NIGHTMARE ON ELM STREET 4: THE DREAM MASTER (1988)

Robert Englund
Rodney Eastman
Danny Hassel

Killings illustrated by innovative special-effects highlight this gore-fest,

(Continued)

(Continued)
once again featuring the vengeful monster Freddie Krueger (Englund). One young victim is turned into an insect and dies in a Roach Motel. Another drowns in his own waterbed. Although Freddie's sardonic humor is at least one redeeming quality, the plot is as predictable as ever. Also with Brooke Bundy, Andras Jones, and Tuesday Knight. **Director**—Renny Harlin. **(R)**
93 minutes

A NIGHTMARE ON ELM STREET 5: THE DREAM CHILD (1989)

★1/2 ®

Robert Englund
Lisa Wilcox

Freddy Krueger, the mass murderer with the menacing fingernails, confronts his tragic birth in this unusually tame episode with an intriguing premise. Freddy's mother, a nun, was raped by various maniacs in an asylum. (Remember her confession to the hero of *A Nightmare on Elm Street 3: Dream Warriors*?) Freddy, played again by Englund, seeks rebirth through the fetus of Alice, the young girl who bested him in *Nightmare 4*. In this latest chapter, Freddy continues his vicious killings while Alice's companions endeavor to stop him. Unfortunately, the interesting premise is never flushed out, as the producers are more concerned in cranking out the formula than in pursuing the interesting connotations of the Krueger character. New Line Cinema, the company that produces these films and owns the rights to the Freddy Krueger character, should retire the series before it becomes even more of a joke or at least bring back the series' originator, director Wes Craven. **Director**—Stephen Hopkins. **(R)**
90 minutes

'NIGHT, MOTHER (1986)

★★★ ®

Sissy Spacek
Anne Bancroft

A gripping, thought-provoking film adaptation of the Pulitzer Prize-winning stage play about suicide. Bancroft and Spacek deliver strong, virtuoso performances as a mother and daughter facing the looming crisis of the younger person's determination to kill herself. The atmosphere is grim and claustrophobic, but the characters will arouse sympathy and intense emotions. Intelligent dialogue and skillful acting make for a meaningful film experience. **Director**—Tom Moore. **(PG–13)** *97 minutes*

Anne Bancroft and Sissy Spacek try to come to terms in 'night, Mother.

NIGHT MUST FALL (1937)

★★★

Robert Montgomery
Rosalind Russell
May Whitty

A classic chiller about a likable young man (Montgomery) who is actually a psychotic killer. He cons his way into the household of a dislikable old lady (Whitty), whose niece (Russell) he enchants. Montgomery picked the perfect part in which to break from his familiar role of the urbane leading man. John Van Druten scripted, from the British stage hit by Emlyn Williams. **Director**—Richard Thorpe. **Academy Award Nominations**—Montgomery, best actor; Whitty, best supporting actress.
117 minutes b&w

NIGHT OF THE COMET (1984)

★★★ ®

Catherine Mary Stewart
Kelli Maroney

Effective tongue-in-cheek humor and some remarkable performances elevate this doomsday sci-fi fantasy. A deadly comet devastates the southern California population. Two young sisters (Stewart and Maroney) survive the deadly rays. Now they must deal with carnivorous zombies and evil scientists who want their life-giving blood. Writer/director Thom Eberhardt has the proper comic touch for such low-budget fare. Also with Mary Woronov, Robert Beltran, Sharon Farrell, and Geoffrey Lewis. **(PG–13)** *94 minutes*

NIGHT OF THE CREEPS (1986)

★★ ®

Jason Lively
Jill Whitlow

Slimy extraterrestrial creatures incubate their eggs in human brains, turning their hosts into zombies, in this uneven horror effort by first-time director Fred Dekker. Liberally borrowing from *Aliens* and *Night of the Living Dead*, the film does feature some humor and some frightening moments, but the momentum is not sustained. Lively and Whitlow head a cast of unknowns. **(R)**
89 minutes

THE NIGHT OF THE HUNTER (1955)

★★★★

Robert Mitchum
Shelley Winters

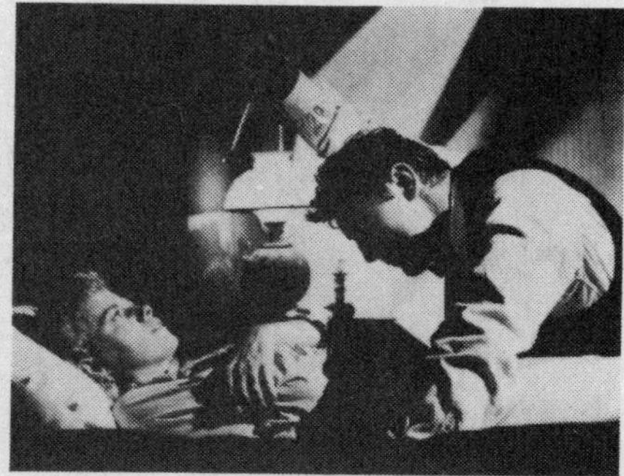

Psychotic preacher Robert Mitchum threatens Shelley Winters in The Night of the Hunter.

A sinister, brooding allegory involving a religious zealot, played by Mitchum, relentlessly pursuing hidden money. Mitchum believes the money to be in the possession of a young widow and her children. He converts the widow and eventually marries her, but the kids remain skeptical and aloof. They escape his clutches after he murders their mother, and drift downriver in a small boat, followed by Mitchum each step of the way. A moody and eerie horror tale, the film was Charles Laughton's only attempt at directing. Mitchum is excellent in the offbeat role of preacher Harry Powell, who has "love" tatooed on the fingers of one hand and "hate" on the other. A critical and financial flop in its time, the film has since been reevaluated as an innovative masterpiece. Also with Lillian Gish, James Gleason, Evelyn Varden, and Peter Graves. *93 minutes b&w*

THE NIGHT OF THE IGUANA (1964)

 ★★★

Richard Burton
Deborah Kerr
Ava Gardner

Intense, moody, and often amusing tale of a defrocked clergyman, played by Burton, struggling to reestablish his life in Mexico. There he becomes intimately involved with various women, including Kerr, a spinster, and Gardner, the sultry owner of a run-down tourist hotel. The screenplay faithfully adheres to Tennessee Williams' play and offers a vivid account of some interesting characters. Sue Lyon, Grayson Hall, and Cyril Delevanti costar. **Director**—John Huston. **Academy Award Nominations**—Hall, best supporting actress; Gabriel Figueroa, cinematography. *125 minutes b&w*

NIGHT OF THE JUGGLER (1980)

★★

James Brolin

Driven: James Brolin searches for his kidnapped daughter in Night of the Juggler.

A nonstop chase thriller, with Brolin playing an ex-cop who pursues his daughter's kidnapper through the crowded streets of New York City. The film has plenty of frantic action; dozens of cars were supposedly smashed up to achieve the breathless chase scenes. But the thin screenplay has credibility problems, and the characters aren't developed in sufficient detail. Cliff Gorman, Richard Castellano, and Julie Carmen also star. **Director**—Robert Butler. **(R)** *100 minutes*

NIGHT OF THE LIVING DEAD (1968)

 ★★★1/2

Judith O'Dea
Russell Streiner

Ghouls rise up from the cemetery to terrorize and sup on the unfortunate souls who cross their path. Not a pretty picture, but stylish and terrifying in its low-budget, graphic way. The gritty and grainy look makes the film crudely realistic and therefore more effective. The film placed director George A. Romero among the ranks of great horror directors, though it was dismissed by many critics on its initial release. It has since become one of the most popular independently made films of all time, and is to the 1960s what John Carpenter's *Halloween* is to the 1970s. Costars Karl Hardman, Keith Wayne, and Duane Jones. **(R)** *96 minutes b&w*

THE NIGHT OF THE SHOOTING STARS (1982)

 ★★★★

Omero Antonutti
Margarita Lozano

The Taviani brothers (Paolo and Vittorio) detail various crises among Tuscan villagers during the final days of World War II. Townsfolk are caught between the desperate, retreating Germans and the advancing Americans. The film recalls harrowing moments of courage, pathos, and tragedy. Originally filmed in Italian. **(R)** *106 minutes*

NIGHT PASSAGE (1957)

James Stewart
Audie Murphy

A competently made western about a railroad troubleshooter (Stewart) in charge of a train payroll that an outlaw gang plans to rob. Complications arise when it's learned that the troubleshooter and the outlaw leader (Murphy) are brothers. Sufficient action and excitement follows, and the film ends with a tense gunfight. Also with Dan Duryea, Brandon De Wilde, and Dianne Foster. **Director**—James Neilson. *90 minutes*

NIGHT PATROL (1985)

(no stars)

Murray Langston
Pat Paulsen
Linda Blair

Shabby, idiotic rip-off of *Police Academy*, propelled by a nonstop stream of desperate gags that compete for new heights in bad taste and vulgarity. Langston heads the cast as a bumbling Los Angeles cop with ambitions to be a stand-up comedian. The film consistently falls flat with a ragtag assortment of sex jokes, homosexual spoofs, toilet humor, and racial slurs. **Director**—Jackie Kong. **(R)** *82 minutes*

NIGHT SHIFT (1982)

★★★

Henry Winkler
Michael Keaton
Shelley Long

Winkler plays a timid night attendant at the city morgue, which becomes the hub of a call-girl operation after new employee Keaton arrives to spice up Winkler's life. Fast-talking Keaton made an impressive screen debut in this comedy directed by Ron Howard (*Splash*). Long plays a prostitute in love with Winkler. **(R)** *105 minutes*

THE NIGHT THE LIGHTS WENT OUT IN GEORGIA (1981)

 ★★

Dennis Quaid
Kristy McNichol
Mark Hamill

A listless story about the misadventures of a skirt-chasing country/western singer (Quaid), and his precocious teenage sister (McNichol), who serves as his manager. While traveling to Nashville, the two get sidetracked in a hick town, where Quaid runs afoul of the law and falls for a local beauty. The script, padded with much idle chatter, resembles a few TV episodes strung together. Hamill of *Star Wars* fame is hopelessly waxen as a friendly state trooper. **Director**—Ronald F. Maxwell. **(PG)** *120 minutes*

THE NIGHT THEY RAIDED MINSKY'S (1968)

Jason Robards
Britt Ekland
Elliott Gould

A colorful and captivating behind-the-scenes look at burlesque during its heyday. The story revolves around a shy Quaker girl, played by Ekland, who comes to the big city and gets a job as a

(Continued)

(Continued)
stripper in a burlesque show. She becomes romantically involved with Robards, a comic. The background detail is emphasized, with many nostalgic moments showing baggy-pants comics and the squalid atmosphere of the theater. Also with Norman Wisdom, Forrest Tucker, Joseph Wiseman, Bert Lahr, and Harry Andrews. **Director**—William Friedkin. **(PG)** *99 minutes*

A NIGHT TO REMEMBER (1942)

★★★

Loretta Young
Brian Aherne

Aherne and Young play mystery writers living in Greenwich Village. After they discover a body in their apartment, the two set out to find the murderer. It's a clever and buoyant whodunit, with amusing moments and sharp dialogue. Top performances bolster the production. Also with Jeff Donnell, William Wright, Sidney Toler, Gale Sondergaard, Donald MacBride, and Lee Patrick. **Director**—Richard Wallace. *91 minutes b&w*

A NIGHT TO REMEMBER (1958)

★★★★

Kenneth More
Honor Blackman
David McCallum

An inspired semidocumentary about the sinking of the luxury liner *Titanic* in the North Atlantic in 1912. The account, based on Walter Lord's book, features much striking detail and scores of cameo roles to describe the heroism and drama of that fateful night when the vessel struck an iceberg. Expert direction and superb performances combine for an admirable movie. Also with Michael Goodliffe, George Rose, Anthony Bushell, Jill Dixon, Alec McCowen, and Laurence Naismith. **Director**—Roy Baker. *123 minutes b&w*

NIGHT TRAIN TO MUNICH (1940)

★★★★

Rex Harrison
Margaret Lockwood

Intrigue and comedy are cleverly blended in this excellent suspense film about the efforts of British agents to keep a secret formula from the clutches of the Nazis. Skillful use of meticulous detail enhances this movie, which is similar to an Alfred Hitchcock thriller. Also with Paul Henreid, Basil Radford, and Naunton Wayne. **Director**—Carol Reed. **Academy Award Nomination**—Gordon Wellesley, original screenplay. **Alternate Titles**—*Gestapo; Night Train.* *93 minutes b&w*

NIGHTWING (1979)

Nick Mancuso
David Warner
Kathryn Harrold

Thousands of plague-infested vampire bats invade an Indian reservation in yet another Hollywood version of Mother Nature on the rampage. It's supposed to scare the daylights out of you, but nothing doing. Up close, the bats reveal big teeth; but there's little bite in the predictable screenplay, and the special effects are unimaginative. Also with Stephen Macht, Strother Martin, and George Clutesi. **Director**—Arthur Hiller. **(PG)** *105 minutes*

NIJINSKY (1980)

Alan Bates
George de la Pena

Impresario Alan Bates looking for talent in Nijinsky.

Director Herbert Ross (*The Turning Point*) tries another movie with a ballet theme, this time based on the career of the legendary Vaslav Nijinsky, the great Russian dancer who ultimately descended into madness. The opulent but lethargic film basically dwells on Nijinsky's homosexual relationships. There isn't enough dancing to satisfy ballet fans, and de la Pena, who plays the title role, never sparks as an actor or a great dancer. Bates plays impresario Sergei Diaghilev. Also with Leslie Browne, Ronald Pickup, Alan Badel, Colin Blakely, Jeremy Irons, and Janet Suzman. **(R)** *129 minutes*

9½ WEEKS (1986)

Mickey Rourke
Kim Basinger

Mickey Rourke's and Kim Basinger's obsessive romance lasts 9½ Weeks.

Initially slated as a provocative and steamy love story, this film emerges as a dreary drama embroidered with a few tame, kinky sex scenes. Many of the raunchier love scenes had been cut by the studio before release. The title refers to the love affair's length. It could easily mean the time it seems to take to sit through the picture. Rourke stars as the charming New York stockbroker who introduces a strait-laced art dealer (Basinger) to sadomasochistic lovemaking. The videotape version runs 115 minutes and contains sexually explicit scenes not shown in the theatrical release print. The European theatrical version runs even longer and contains the most sexually graphic scenes. **Director**—Adrian Lyne. **(R)** *113 minutes*

976-EVIL (1989)

★½

Stephen Geoffreys

Those telephone information services are the inspiration for this dull and absurd horror picture. A nerdy teenager (Geoffreys) dials his "horror-scope," which gives him special powers to wreak revenge on his tormentors. The special effects are ineffective, and the plot is confusing. Robert Englund, Freddy Krueger of the *Nightmare on Elm Street* series, directed. Also with Sandy Dennis, Jim Metzler, and Patrick O'Bryan. **(R)** *92 minutes*

® This movie available with closed captions for the hearing impaired.

1900 (1977)

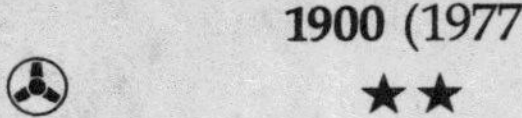

★★

Burt Lancaster
Robert De Niro
Gérard Depardieu
Romolo Valli

Director Bernardo Bertolucci's monumental chronicle of the struggle between the peasants and the landowners in Italy begins with grace and grandeur, but eventually withdraws into a Marxist tract. The story involves the sons of two families; one is the spoiled grandson of patriarch Lancaster, the other the illegitimate son of peasant farmers. The epic scope of the film makes for some lyrical and beautiful images, but the four-hour running time and the large cast can be overwhelming. Also stars Sterling Hayden, Donald Sutherland, Anna Marie Gherardi, Laura Betti, Stefania Sandrelli, Alida Valli, Francesca Bertini, and Dominique Sanda. The film contains some frontal nudity and disturbing violence. **(R)** *243 minutes*

1918 (1985)

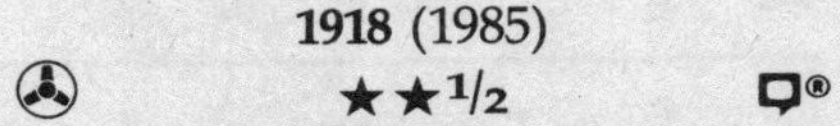

★★½

William Converse-Roberts
Hallie Foote
Matthew Broderick

Matthew Broderick reflects upon life beyond the limits of his small town in 1918.

Small-town life in Texas during the title year is examined in this restrained account based on Horton Foote's stage play. The characters cope with World War I on the home front and suffer through a deadly flu epidemic. While this literary film is often charming, the meager action and drama cannot sustain adequate interest. A competent ensemble cast delivers worthy performances. **Director**—Ken Harrison. **(No MPAA rating)** *91 minutes*

1941 (1979)

★★

Dan Aykroyd
John Belushi
Ned Beatty
Treat Williams

Steven Spielberg tries his hand at comedy and comes up with a film that's generous with style, but miserly with comic inspiration. This overblown, adolescent farce concerns a Japanese invasion of California on the heels of the Pearl Harbor attack. There's hysteria, brawling, silliness, destruction of buildings and vehicles, and lots of noise, but minimal humor and wit. Belushi, Aykroyd, Williams, and Beatty are essentially wasted. The film was Oscar-nominated for its visual effects. Also with Robert Stack, Tim Matheson, Christopher Lee, and Toshiro Mifune. **Academy Award Nomination**—William A. Fraker, cinematography. **(PG)** *118 minutes*

1984 (1955)

★★★

Michael Redgrave
Edmond O'Brien
Jan Sterling

A provocative screen version of George Orwell's prophetic tale of a sinister world, where people have limited freedom and live under the watchful eye of Big Brother. O'Brien and Sterling play lovers who try to rebel. The film, like the novel, is convoluted and not completely satisfying, but there are many thoughtful points in this absorbing drama. Also with David Kossoff, Mervyn Johns, and Donald Pleasence. **Director**—Michael Anderson. *91 minutes b&w*

1984 (1984)

★★★

John Hurt
Richard Burton

This second movie version of George Orwell's powerful novel captures the bleakness and monotony of his nightmarish vision of a totalitarian state. Hurt is convincing as the pitiful government drone who challenges the authority of Big Brother. And Burton, in his final screen performance, stands out as the ruthless inner-party torturer. Though well-produced (with an appropriately washed-out blue/gray look), the film is relentlessly depressing and difficult to watch. Also with Suzanna Hamilton and Cyril Cusack. **Director**—Michael Radford. **(R)** *117 minutes*

1969 (1988)

★★

Robert Downey, Jr.
Kiefer Sutherland

The title refers to the pivotal year of protest over the Vietnam War. The drama focuses on two college students (Downey and Sutherland) who try to avoid the draft, experiment with drugs, and clash with their parents. Ernest Thompson's direction is awkward and the script painfully trite. The Age of Aquarius certainly deserves better treatment than is provided here. Also with Winona Ryder, Joanna Cassidy, Bruce Dern, and Mariette Hartley. **(R)** *95 minutes*

9 TO 5 (1980)

★★

Jane Fonda
Lily Tomlin
Dolly Parton

Fonda, Tomlin, and Parton are secretaries who engineer an office revolt and wage war on their chauvinistic boss. With such a cast lineup and topical subject, the film should have been a rip-snorting comedy, but its potential is only partially realized. The half-baked screenplay erratically hops from farce to satire to drumbeating about the feminist movement. The leading ladies put in their 35-hour work week, but it's not worth anybody's overtime. Also with Dabney Coleman, Sterling Hayden, Henry Jones, and Marian Mercer. **Director**—Colin Higgins. **(PG)** *110 minutes*

92 IN THE SHADE (1975)

★★★

Peter Fonda

Thomas McGuane, who wrote *Rancho DeLuxe,* scripted and directed this cool and genuinely fascinating film. He again makes use of his favorite theme of youth and the pursuit of false values. Fonda delivers a stylish performance as a restless, spoiled, rich young man who

(Continued)

(Continued)
breaks into the charter-fishing business in Key West. Warren Oates, Burgess Meredith, and Elizabeth Ashley are excellent in their colorful roles. Also with Margot Kidder, Harry Dean Stanton, and Sylvia Miles. **(R)** *93 minutes*

NINOTCHKA (1939)

★★★★

Greta Garbo
Melvyn Douglas

Star power: Greta Garbo and Melvyn Douglas in the sophisticated Ninotchka.

This is one of Hollywood's brightest screen comedies, and represents the very best of two legendary screen artists—director Ernst Lubitsch and screenwriter Billy Wilder. An austere Russian agent, played by Garbo, is sent by the Soviet government to Paris to sell a former duchess's jewels. There she meets debonair playboy Douglas, who woos her desperately. Though at first she's all hard-edged ideology, she soon succumbs to both Paris and Douglas. The sparkling script celebrates love and spontaneity. The cast also includes Sig Ruman, Ina Clair, Felix Bressart, Alexander Granach, and Bela Lugosi. **Academy Award Nominations**—best picture; Garbo, best actress; Melchior Lengyel, original story; Charles Brackett, Walter Reisch, and Wilder, screenplay. *110 minutes b&w*

NOBODY'S FOOL (1986)

★★

Rosanna Arquette
Eric Roberts

An uneven romantic comedy about a kooky, small-town girl (Arquette) with a painful past, who is wooed by an equally unstable young man (Roberts). A few scenes are memorable, but the romance between the two leads is uninteresting. Surprisingly, the pairing of Arquette and Roberts fails to strike sparks, although both contribute good performances. Playwright Beth Henley (*Crimes of the Heart*) wrote the screenplay. Mare Winningham and Louise Fletcher appear in supporting roles. **Director**—Evelyn Purcell. **(PG-13)** *107 minutes*

NO MAN IS AN ISLAND (1962)

★★

Jeffrey Hunter

A Navy radioman, played by Hunter, is accidentally left behind on Guam after the Japanese attack, and chooses to fight the enemy as a guerrilla. This routine war adventure, based on a true story, suffers from mundane production values, but Hunter handles the acting well. Filmed on location in the Philippines. Supporting roles by Marshall Thompson, Barbara Perez, and Ronald Remy. **Directors**—John Monks, Jr., and Richard Goldstone. *114 minutes*

NO MAN'S LAND (1987)

★★½

Charlie Sheen
D.B. Sweeney
Lara Harris

A rookie cop (Sweeney) goes undercover to obtain evidence on the mastermind of a car theft ring (Sheen), who is also the prime suspect in the murder of a police detective. The plot thickens when the rookie becomes increasingly fond of the suspect, the fast-lane life he leads, and his attractive sister. Though there is a refreshing lack of hard-core violence in this police thriller, the film still substitutes car chases and action sequences for depth of character. An interesting supporting cast includes Randy Quaid, Bill Duke, Arlen Dean Snyder, and M. Emmet Walsh. **Director**—Peter Werner. **(R)** *106 minutes*

NO MERCY (1986)

★★½

Richard Gere
Kim Basinger

A great deal of style and intensity propels this uneven cop thriller, set mostly in Algiers, a seedy district across the river from New Orleans. Gere stars as a hard-boiled Chicago police detective who goes overboard to avenge the murder of his partner by a ruthless criminal kingpin. Gere delivers an energetic portrayal, but the script consists of all of the routine plot elements for a police thriller and the ultraviolent showdown at the end is thoroughly predictable. Dutch actor Jeroen Krabbe stands out as the ruthless villain. **Director**—Richard Pearce. **(R)** *107 minutes*

Richard Gere and Kim Basinger discover that the Louisiana bayou has No Mercy.

NONE BUT THE LONELY HEART (1944)

★★★

Cary Grant
Ethel Barrymore

An excellent drama directed by playwright Clifford Odets. Grant stars as a young cockney drifter seeking self-satisfaction as World War II approaches; Grant is astonishingly good in this straight dramatic part. Barrymore plays his dying mother. An excellent script, also by Odets, contributes to the film's quality. Also with June Duprez, Barry Fitzgerald, Jane Wyatt, George Coulouris, and Dan Duryea. **Academy Award**—Barrymore, best supporting actress. **Nomination**—Grant, best actor. *113 minutes b&w*

NO NUKES (1980)

★★½

A concert movie based on a series of Madison Square Garden performances by well-known rock stars protesting the use of nuclear power. Scattered among the musical segments are some brief antinuclear documentary footage and backstage conversations in which performers comment about the dangers of nuclear misuse; even Ralph Nader and Jane Fonda pop in for a few remarks. Fans of Bruce Springsteen will find an early appearance in this film by the noted rocker of particular interest.

® *This movie available with closed captions for the hearing impaired.*

Other singers and acts performing include the Doobie Brothers, Gil Scott-Heron, Bonnie Raitt, Carly Simon, James Taylor, Jackson Browne, Crosby, Stills & Nash, and John Hall. **Directors**—Julian Schlossberg, Danny Goldberg, and Anthony Potenza. **(PG)**
103 minutes

NORMA RAE (1979)

★★★★

Sally Field
Ron Leibman

Ron Liebman helps Sally Field unionize a textile factory in Norma Rae.

Field stars in the title role of this refreshing, gritty, and intelligent film about textile factory workers in a southern mill town. Under the superb direction of Martin Ritt, Field portrays a valiant young woman struggling to better her life. There are other excellent performances, including Leibman as a union organizer, and Beau Bridges as Norma Rae's husband. Also with Pat Hingle and Barbara Baxley. The film's theme song, "It Goes Like It Goes," won an Oscar. **(PG) Academy Award**—Field, best actress. **Nominations**—best picture; Irving Ravetch and Harriet Frank, Jr., best screenplay adapted from another medium. *113 minutes*

EL NORTE (1984)

★★★★

David Villalpando
Zaide Silvia Gutierrez

A remarkable, touching account of two young Guatemalan Indians (brother and sister) who make a torturous journey from their strife-torn country to the promised land of Los Angeles. Director Gregory Nava brings forth much sympathy for these complex and moving characters, played with amazing skill by Villalpando and Gutierrez. And the semidocumentary style offers a vivid contrast between the two cultures. Originally filmed in Spanish. **(R)**
139 minutes

THE NORTH AVENUE IRREGULARS (1979)

★★★

Edward Herrmann
Barbara Harris
Susan Clark
Karen Valentine

An eager-beaver minister and a posse of daffy housewives mop up local racketeers in this zany and frisky Walt Disney comedy. The formulaic plot is typical Disney, but there are plenty of clever gags to keep the whole family entertained. Herrmann makes a likable and amusing preacher, but Harris steals the film when she pursues the crooks in a station wagon bulging with pets and youngsters. Also with Michael Constantine, Cloris Leachman, and Patsy Kelly. **Director**—Bruce Bilson. **(G)**
99 minutes

NORTH BY NORTHWEST (1959)

★★★★

Cary Grant
Eva Marie Saint
James Mason

This comedy/thriller from director Alfred Hitchcock employs his characteristic theme of an innocent man mistakenly caught up in circumstances he can't control. Suave Grant plays a businessman who's pursued by foreign agents; they believe he's a spy. The excitement never slackens, and some scenes are unforgettable—especially Grant being menaced in a cornfield by a crop-dusting plane, and the climax atop Mt. Rushmore. The score by Bernard Herrmann is one of his most recognizable. First-class support from Leo G. Carroll, Martin Landau, and Jessie Royce Landis. **(PG) Academy Award Nomination**—Ernest Lehman, best story and screenplay written directly for the screen. *136 minutes*

NORTH DALLAS FORTY (1979)

★★★

Nick Nolte
Mac Davis

A hard-hitting, unglamorous look at the win-at-all-costs business of pro football. Nolte gives a powerful performance as an over-the-hill wide receiver who rebels against any notion of team spirit. G.D. Spradlin is frightening as a goading head coach, and Davis has never equaled his performance here as a cynical quarterback who knows how to play the game both on and off the field. It's a rough-and-tumble comedy that displays the anger and soul of the novel by Peter Gent. Also with Charles Durning, Dayle Haddon, and Steve Forrest. **Director**—Ted Kotcheff. **(R)**
119 minutes

NORTH SHORE (1987)

★★

Matt Adler
Gregory Harrison
Nia Peeples

Nia Peeples and Matt Adler find romance on the North Shore.

Adler stars as a youth caught between pursuing an art career in New York or riding the killer waves at Hawaii's famous North Shore surfing beach. Mixed in among the surfing footage is a coming-of-age romance with a local beauty, played by Peeples. The dialogue is heavy with adolescent expressions and words most familiar to surfers. Typical of such surfing sagas, a contest is featured as the spectacular climax. Nothing about this predictable film is particularly noteworthy, except for some of the surfing footage, which was probably directed by actor Harrison. A real-life surfing buff, he is credited as second-unit director. **Director**—William Phelps. **(PG)** *92 minutes*

NORTH TO ALASKA (1960)

★★★

John Wayne
Stewart Granger
Ernie Kovacs
Capucine

Wayne, Granger, and Fabian prospect for gold in the Yukon, and get mixed up

(Continued)

(Continued)
with dance-hall queen Capucine and con man Kovacs. A noisy action film from director Henry Hathaway, who's turned out some of the most entertaining of the genre for some 40 years. Not particularly sophisticated, but it is brash fun, with a wonderful barroom-brawl scene. With Mickey Shaughnessy, Joe Sawyer, and John Qualen.
122 minutes

NORTHWEST MOUNTED POLICE (1940)

Gary Cooper
Paulette Goddard
Robert Preston

Cecil B. De Mille directed this lavish action/adventure with typical style, though the story is unmoving and forgettable. The plot involves the efforts of a Texas Ranger, played by Cooper, to locate a criminal (Preston) hiding in Canada. Goddard plays a half-breed girl in love with the shady Preston. The production is hampered by the obvious use of indoor sets for outdoor scenes. Also with Preston Foster, Lynne Overman, Madeleine Carroll, George Bancroft, and Akim Tamiroff. **Academy Award Nomination**—Victor Milner and W. Howard Greene, cinematography.
125 minutes

NORTHWEST PASSAGE (1940)

★★★★

Spencer Tracy
Robert Young
Walter Brennan

Tracy is outstanding as frontier captain Robert Rogers of the Queen's Rangers in this rousing historical saga about adventurers seeking a route to the sea. Hardships and Indian attacks plague the group along the way. Young and Brennan play two recruits under Tracy's command. Also with Ruth Hussey, Nat Pendleton, and Donald MacBride. **Director**—King Vidor. **Academy Award Nomination**—Sidney Wagner and William V. Skall, cinematography.
126 minutes

NO SMALL AFFAIR (1984)

★★

Jon Cryer
Demi Moore

Jon Cryer falls for "older woman" Demi Moore in No Small Affair.

A labored romantic comedy about a square 16-year-old boy (Cryer) who is obsessed with a 22-year-old rock singer (Moore). This predictable film is only intermittently funny. Cryer is occasionally charming as the awkward adolescent. As a rites-of-passage film, it's no big deal. Also with George Wendt, Ann Wedgeworth, and Jeffrey Tambor. **Director**—Jerry Schatzberg. **(R)**
102 minutes

NOT AS A STRANGER (1955)

Robert Mitchum
Olivia de Havilland

Competent screen version of Morton Thompson's best-selling novel about a young physician who struggles with his career and his marriage. The story is much like a soap opera, but there are enough strong details about hospitals and operating procedures to give the film some depth. Mitchum does a credible job as a poor but bright medical student who becomes a country doctor. De Havilland is his wife, who supports him through medical school. Also with Broderick Crawford, Frank Sinatra, Charles Bickford, and Gloria Grahame. **Director**—Stanley Kramer.
125 minutes b&w

NOTHING IN COMMON (1986)

★★★

Jackie Gleason
Tom Hanks

A touching mixture of comedy and drama highlights this tale of a yuppie advertising executive (Hanks) whose career is suddenly sidetracked by his parents' marital difficulties. Gleason is excellent in his last film role, as the beleaguered, over-the-hill clothing salesman who for the first time needs his son's support. Witty, clever dialogue and tense domestic situations are shrewdly blended in this tribute to the strength and importance of families. As directed by television producer Garry Marshall, the film tends to rise and fall at 15-minute intervals, but Gleason's touching performance and Hanks' witticisms more than make up for it. Also with Eva Marie Saint and Bess Armstrong. **(PG)** *118 minutes*

NOTHING PERSONAL (1980)

★

Donald Sutherland
Suzanne Somers

Suzanne Somers and Donald Sutherland: all mixed up in Nothing Personal.

A hopeless romantic comedy that introduced Somers in her first major film feature. She plays a sexy lawyer who helps Sutherland, a professor, save baby seals from destruction. Somers is stiff in her role, and Sutherland looks as if he would rather be somewhere else. Direction, scripting, and editing are ragged and uninspired. Also with Dabney Coleman. **Director**—George Bloomfield. **(PG)** *96 minutes*

NOTHING SACRED (1937)

★★★½

Carole Lombard
Fredric March

Scriptwriter Ben Hecht, a one-time newspaperman, gave us two of the movies' greatest newspaper comedies. *The Front Page* (remade as *His Girl Friday*) was the first, and this is the second. Dazzling comedienne Lombard

This movie available with closed captions for the hearing impaired.

stars as a young woman who's said to have only six weeks to live as a result of radium poisoning. She's exploited by a small newspaper with big ambitions that drums up publicity by sending her to New York and turning her final days on Earth into a royal gala—only to find that the diagnosis was wrong. The pace is brisk, the dialogue cutting, the early Technicolor rich, and the score by Oscar Levant delectable. With Walter Connolly, Charles Winninger, Sig Ruman, Hedda Hopper, and Hattie McDaniel. **Director**—William Wellman.

77 minutes

NO TIME FOR SERGEANTS (1958)

★★★1/2

Andy Griffith

Griffith successfully repeats his Broadway role as the Georgia farm boy who joins the Army and cheerfully drives his superiors up the wall. It's Griffith's best screen performance, and his hilarious antics are a laugh a minute. Myron McCormick reprises his stage role as Griffith's hapless sergeant. Also with William Fawcett, Murray Hamilton, Nick Adams, and Don Knotts in his film debut. **Director**—Mervyn LeRoy. *111 minutes b&w*

NOTORIOUS (1946)

★★★★

Cary Grant
Ingrid Bergman
Claude Rains

Ingrid Bergman and Cary Grant discover a sinister wine cellar in Notorious.

Another gem from director Alfred Hitchcock. The setting is Rio de Janeiro just after World War II. Many surviving Nazis have fled to South America to avoid punishment for war crimes. Bergman is involved in an espionage scheme to trap a Nazi spy, played by Rains. American agent Grant is her contact in the dangerous caper. The atmosphere is heavily charged with sexual tension, tingling suspense, and high drama. Also with Louis Calhern, Leopoldine Konstantin, and Reinhold Schunzel. **Academy Award Nominations**—Rains, best supporting actor; Ben Hecht, original screenplay.

101 minutes b&w

NO WAY OUT (1987)

★★★

Kevin Costner
Gene Hackman
Sean Young

A high-voltage, political thriller set in the Pentagon, and loosely based on the novel *The Big Clock.* Naval hero Costner and defense secretary Hackman are rivals in a romantic triangle that leads to the murder of a young party girl, played by Young (in the film's only mediocre performance). A phony manhunt is set in motion by Hackman's aide to protect the actual killer. The complex plot with many twists and turns is kept exciting by the breathless pace and high-key performances. The superb cast also includes Will Patton, George Dzundza, and Howard Duff. **Director**—Roger Donaldson. **(R)** *114 minutes*

NO WAY TO TREAT A LADY (1968)

★★★

Rod Steiger
George Segal
Lee Remick

Rod Steiger doesn't know that murder is No Way to Treat a Lady.

A smart mixture of mystery, suspense, and black comedy, with Steiger excellent as a psychotic killer who murders only women. He traps his victims by the use of clever disguises. Segal plays a detective tracking down the elusive serial murderer. Steiger shows off his acting skills when he dons his many disguises. The production is uneven in spots, but is nonetheless scary and suspenseful. Also stars Eileen Heckart, Murray Hamilton, and Michael Dunn. **Director**—Jack Smight. *108 minutes*

NOW, VOYAGER (1942)

★★★

Bette Davis
Claude Rains
Paul Henreid

A star-studded soap opera that is absorbing because of the extraordinary skills of the performers. Davis is outstanding as a lonely spinster who's helped by a psychiatrist, played by Rains. She takes an ocean cruise to discover herself and becomes involved in a tragic romance with Henreid. Slickly produced for the utmost in sentimental, yet effective, drama. Other supporting roles by Gladys Cooper, Ilka Chase, Bonita Granville, John Loder, and Franklin Pangborn. **Director**—Irving Rapper. **Academy Award Nominations**—Davis, best actress; Cooper, best supporting actress. *117 minutes b&w*

NUNS ON THE RUN (1990)

★★1/2

Eric Idle
Robbie Coltrane

Eric Idle and Robbie Coltrane in the comedy Nuns on the Run.

Former Monty Python member Idle and sidekick Coltrane yuck it up as

(Continued)

This movie available on videotape and/or disc.

(Continued)
small-time bank robbers who evade some rival thugs by hiding out in a convent. The two hoods don full habit to impersonate Sister Euphemia of the Five Wounds and Sister Inviolata of the Immaculate Conception. Irreverent and off-color, the film is reminiscent of the British *Carry On* films of the 1950s. Fans of Monty Python–style humor will enjoy this hectic comedy more than most viewers. Also with Camille Coduri, Janet Suzman, Doris Hare, and Lila Kaye. **Director**—Jonathan Lynn. **(PG-13)**
90 minutes

THE NUN'S STORY (1959)

★★★★

Audrey Hepburn
Peter Finch

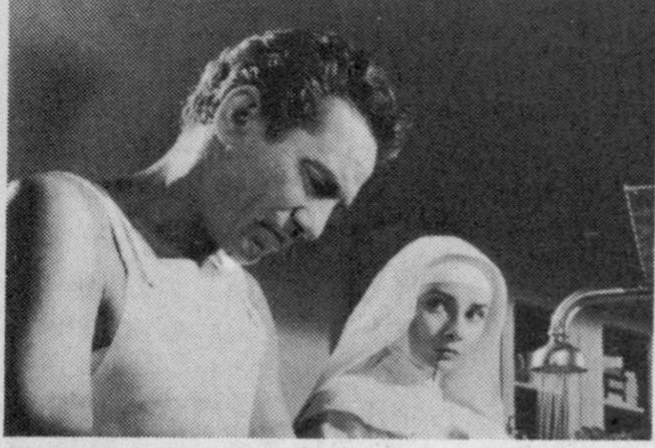

Peter Finch and Audrey Hepburn give excellent performances in The Nun's Story.

An exceptionally appealing story about a young nun, played by Hepburn, who serves under harsh conditions in the Belgian Congo and then quits the convent for an ordinary existence. The film, an intelligent rendition of Kathryn C. Hulme's book, is presented in a straightforward manner with outstanding performances. Finch plays a physician, and Colleen Dewhurst is a suicidal patient. Also with Edith Evans, Peggy Ashcroft, Dean Jagger, Mildred Dunnock, and Beatrice Straight. **Director**—Fred Zinnemann. **Academy Award Nominations**—best picture; Zinnemann, best director; Hepburn, best actress; Robert Anderson, best screenplay based on material from another medium; Franz Planer, cinematography.
151 minutes

NUNZIO (1978)

★★★

David Proval

Proval is convincing in his portrayal of a retarded Brooklyn grocery boy who's the object of ridicule, but eventually becomes the neighborhood hero. The sentimental story has elements of *Rocky* and *Marty,* and is an earnest and endearing film despite the reliance on emotional clichés. Also with James Andronica, Morgana King, Tovah Feldshuh, and Vincent Russo. **Director**—Paul Williams. **(R)** *87 minutes*

NUTS (1987)

★★★

Barbra Streisand
Richard Dreyfuss

Richard Dreyfuss helps Barbra Streisand have her day in court in Nuts.

Streisand returns to the screen in a dynamite performance as a strong-willed, eccentric prostitute trying to prove she is mentally fit to stand trial for manslaughter. Her parents and a court-appointed psychiatrist want her locked in a mental hospital, but a small-time, overworked public defender helps her get her day in court. Much of the drama occurs in the confined space of a near-empty courtroom, where Streisand must pass a competency hearing. This limited setting gives the film the appearance of a made-for-TV melodrama, but the performances of Streisand and Dreyfuss overcome the film's weaknesses. A cast of top supporting actors include Maureen Stapleton and Karl Malden as her parents and Eli Wallach as the hospital shrink. It's a vigorous, electrifying drama that dispels one's perceptions of insanity. **Director**—Martin Ritt. **(R)** *116 minutes*

THE NUTTY PROFESSOR (1963)

★★★

Jerry Lewis
Stella Stevens

The best of Lewis' solo comedies. The Jekyll-and-Hyde storyline provides an excellent vehicle for Lewis' physical comedy and gawky comic character. Shy, clumsy chemistry professor Julius Kelp mixes a formula that alters his personality into that of a brash, self-assured swinger named Buddy Love. Critics have noted that Buddy Love, a crooner with the perpetual cigarette in his hand, bears some resemblance to Dean Martin, Lewis' former straight man. Lewis, who also wrote and directed the film, proves that he didn't need Martin anymore because the storyline allows him to play both the comic and the straight man in one role. A fascinating film that goes much deeper than superficial comedy when considered with Lewis' other films. Also with Howard Morris, Kathleen Freeman, Henry Gibson, and Doodles Weaver. *107 minutes*

O

OBJECTIVE, BURMA! (1945)

★★★½

Errol Flynn
William Prince

A lively World War II adventure with Flynn leading American paratroopers against a Japanese radar station in Burma. Though the film is longer than most war films of this era, there are plenty of vivid action and combat scenes. Also with James Brown, George Tobias, Henry Hull, and Warner Anderson. **Director**—Raoul Walsh. **Academy Award Nomination**—Alvah Bessie, original story. *142 minutes b&w*

OBSESSION (1976)

★★½

Cliff Robertson
Geneviève Bujold

Director Brian De Palma's psychological mystery owes much to *Vertigo* in story and style, but it lacks the clarity of that Alfred Hitchcock classic. Screenwriter Paul Schrader leaves loose ends dangling everywhere. Yet there is adequate suspense and ample atmosphere in this story of a young New Orleans businessman who agonizes over the kidnapping and deaths of his wife and daughter. Vivid performances by Robertson and Bujold, and a powerful, Oscar-nominated score by Bernard Herrmann. Also with John Lithgow, Sylvia Kuumba Williams, and Wanda Blackman. **(PG)** *98 minutes*

® This movie available with closed captions for the hearing impaired.

THE OCTAGON (1980)

★★

Chuck Norris

A kung fu expert, played by Norris, comes out of retirement to put down a cult of international terrorists. Martial-arts fans won't be disappointed by the flashy finale when Norris dispatches a small army of bad guys in a blaze of flying fists. But for most of the movie, the audience will have to suffer through a complicated plot and boring dialogue that's akin to the Chinese water torture. **Director**—Eric Karson. **(R)**

103 minutes

OCTOPUSSY (1983)

★★★

Roger Moore

007 (Roger Moore) tracks international jewel thieves in Octopussy.

This 13th James Bond superspy adventure finds our dashing, tireless hero grappling yet again with treacherous villains, incredible gadgets, hair-raising escape schemes, and plenty of gorgeous women. Debonair Moore (in his sixth Bond film) handles the part with aplomb. His intrigues take place in sumptuous locations from Berlin to India. And once more the world is saved, this time from a madman Russian general who tries to explode a nuclear bomb. Also with Maud Adams, Louis Jourdan, Kristina Wayborn, and Stephen Berkoff. **Director**—John Glen. **(PG)**

130 minutes

THE ODD COUPLE (1968)

★★★1/2

Jack Lemmon
Walter Matthau

The excellent pairing of Lemmon and Matthau in this Neil Simon comedy adds up to loads of laughter. The two play recently divorced men—one meticulous and the other messy—who become roommates and quickly drive each other up the wall because of their contrasting habits. Simon's script, developed from his Broadway play, offers plenty of reliable comic material for the duo to chew on. Later adapted as a television series. Also with John Fiedler, Herb Edelman, Monica Evans, and Carole Shelley. **Director**—Gene Saks. **(G) Academy Award Nomination**—Simon, best screenplay based on material from another medium.

105 minutes

ODD MAN OUT (1947)

★★★★

James Mason
Robert Newton

Searing drama about a wounded Irish rebel and his desperate struggle to avoid capture following a daring holdup in Belfast. The suspenseful story is assembled with expert skill and vivid detail—an unforgettable man-on-the-run movie. Excellent performances by Mason, Newton, Kathleen Ryan, and Dan O'Herlihy. **Director**—Carol Reed. **Alternate Title**—*Gang War.*

115 minutes b&w

THE ODESSA FILE (1974)

★★

Jon Voight
Maria Schell
Maximilian Schell

Jon Voight is quite determined to find The Odessa File.

Voight does a convincing job portraying an eager German journalist who tracks down a Nazi war criminal. Unfortunately, the film is only a so-so screen adaptation of Frederick Forsyth's suspenseful novel. Maximilian Schell's portrayal of the sinister SS officer is the film's highlight. Also with Mary Tamm, Derek Jacobi, and Noel Willman. **Director**—Ronald Neame. **(PG)**

129 minutes

ODE TO BILLY JOE (1976)

★★

Robby Benson
Glynnis O'Connor

Singer Bobbie Gentry's successful 1967 ballad has been transformed into a dreamy and romantic film drama. This story of love and tragedy in Mississippi in 1953 fumbles a bit under the direction of actor Max Baer; there are just too many contradictions. Only a first-rate performance by O'Connor as a 15-year-old girl coming of age keeps the film moving. There are some appealing glimpses of southern family life. Benson stars in the title role. Also with Joan Hotchkis, Sandy McPeak, and James Best. **(PG)** *108 minutes*

OFF BEAT (1986)

★★

Judge Reinhold
Meg Tilly

Flat-footed romantic comedy starring Reinhold as a young library worker who impersonates a policeman and then falls in love with a female cop (Tilly). Little chemistry develops between the two actors, who turn in slack performances under the uninspired direction of Michael Dinner. The routine dialogue generates few real laughs and the film concludes on a predictable note. Cleavant Derricks and Joe Mantegna costar. Choreographer Jacques d'Amboise appears as himself. **(PG)**

93 minutes

AN OFFICER AND A GENTLEMAN (1982)

★★★

Richard Gere
Debra Winger
Lou Gossett, Jr.

A captivating love story about a young man (Gere) with a burning desire to be a Navy jet pilot, and a local girl (Winger) who yearns to escape the

(Continued)

Lou Gossett, Jr., tells Richard Gere he's all wet in An Officer and a Gentleman.

(Continued)
drudgery of her job in a paper mill. The engaging production is a fine example of old-fashioned Hollywood filmmaking, with believable characters and rich, romantic sentimentality. Gere and Winger make the most of their meaty roles, while Gossett shines as a brass-hearted drill instructor. Also with David Keith, Robert Loggia, and Lisa Eilbacher. **Director**—Taylor Hackford. **(R) Academy Award**—Gossett, best supporting actor; Jack Nitszche, Buffy Sainte-Marie, and Will Jennings, best original song ("Up Where We Belong"). **Nominations**—Winger, best actress; Douglas Day Stewart, best original screenplay. *126 minutes*

THE OFFICIAL STORY (1985)

★★★

Norma Aleandro
Hector Alterio

From Argentina, a harrowing film set during the 1970s when a military junta carried out a brutal counter-insurgency campaign in that country. The anguish is illuminated through the experiences of the wife (Aleandro) of a prominent businessman. She is suspicious and then convinced that her adopted daughter is the child of two victims of the notorious death squads. Though heavy viewing, the film makes a profound plea for human rights. Originally filmed in Spanish. **Director**—Luis Puenzo. **(No MPAA rating) Academy Award**—best foreign-language film. *112 minutes*

OFF LIMITS (1988)

★★ ®

Willem Dafoe
Gregory Hines

Dafoe and Hines play hard-edged criminal investigators for the Army, working in Saigon in 1968—the height of the Vietnam War. Their assignment is to track down an Army officer suspected of murdering prostitutes. Despite the exotic and turbulent locale, this cop thriller follows the conventions of the genre to the letter, making for a predictable storyline and familiar characters. Only occasionally does the film's sordid atmosphere add something unusual to the routine plot elements. Also with Fred Ward, Amanda Pays, and Scott Glenn. **Director**—Christopher Crowe. **(R)** *102 minutes*

OF HUMAN BONDAGE (1934)

★★★

Bette Davis
Leslie Howard
Frances Dee

A notable screen adaptation of a literary classic that also gave Davis the most critically acclaimed role of her early career. W. Somerset Maugham's novel tells of the emotional bondage of a lame young Englishman to a selfish waitress. Howard stars as the crippled medical student, and Davis plays the vulgar and steely-hearted young woman who uses him. Not exactly profound cinema, but a showcase for its stars and a much-discussed film of its day. With Reginald Owen, Reginald Denny, Kay Johnson, and Alan Hale. **Director**—John Cromwell. *83 minutes b&w*

OF HUMAN BONDAGE (1964)

★★

Laurence Harvey
Kim Novak

Harvey and Novak are miscast in this third film version of the classic Somerset Maugham story about a doctor's tragic affair with a waitress. The overall production is a disappointment and doesn't do justice to Maugham's novel. The 1934 version, with Bette Davis and Leslie Howard, is better. Costars Nanette Newman, Roger Livesey, and Robert Morley. **Director**—Ken Hughes. *105 minutes b&w*

OF MICE AND MEN (1939)

★★★★

Burgess Meredith
Lon Chaney, Jr.
Betty Field

Masterful filming of John Steinbeck's bittersweet tale of a migrant worker who protects his mentally retarded giant of a friend. The tragic story is persuasively told with much sensitivity. Chaney's performance as Lenny, the feeble-minded young man, is the best of his career. Matinee cowboy star Bob Steele gives an effective dramatic performance as Field's sadistic husband. Also with Charles Bickford and Noah Beery, Jr. **Director**—Lewis Milestone. **Academy Award Nomination**—best picture. *107 minutes b&w*

OF UNKNOWN ORIGIN (1983)

★★1/2

Peter Weller

Young executive Weller battles a super-rat that makes a shambles of his posh Manhattan townhouse. This unusual horror tale has a taut pace and is cleverly directed. The movie playfully educates the audience in the history, biology, and sociology of rats. Worthwhile thoughts on ambition, competition, and what gets lost in the drive to the top are illuminated as Weller's character gets trapped in more than one kind of rat race. Originally released in a longer version. Jennifer Dale and Shannon Tweed costar. **Director**—George Cosmatos. **(R)** *85 minutes*

OH, GOD! (1977)

★★★

George Burns
John Denver

George Burns is a down-to-earth sort of Almighty in Oh, God!

A schmaltzy, but entertaining, middlebrow comedy about a supermarket manager who is chosen by God to be a latter-day Moses. Denver, exuding his apple-pie good nature, debuts as the astonished storekeeper and does justice to the part. Burns plays the Almighty, and—well—he's George Burns. Carl Reiner's direction is adequate, but not

® *This movie available with closed captions for the hearing impaired.*

particularly interesting. Also with Teri Garr, Paul Sorvino, George Furth, and Ralph Bellamy. **(PG)** **Academy Award Nomination**—Larry Gelbart, best screenplay based on material from another medium. *104 minutes*

OH GOD! BOOK II (1980)

★★

George Burns
Suzanne Pleshette
David Birney
Louanne

Burns returns as the Almighty in this movie sequel, spreading his gospel via one-liners. John Denver, who clicked smartly with Burns in the first film, is replaced by Louanne—a cute kid—to help deliver God's message. Although she and some of her playmates exude innocent charm, the script is stale and most of the gags are familiar. Pleshette and Birney star as Louanne's estranged parents, who finally reconcile, thank God. **Director**—Gilbert Cates. **(PG)** *94 minutes*

OH, GOD! YOU DEVIL (1984)

★★1/2

George Burns
Ted Wass

Burns, America's senior citizen laureate, proves effective in a dual role as both God and the Devil in this schmaltzy but clever comedy, the third in the *Oh, God!* series. Burns as the Devil assumes the guise of a theatrical agent who transforms a so-so songwriter (Wass) into a rock superstar. The screenplay is maudlin at times, but the effervescent George, even at 88, keeps the material at a buoyant level. **Director**—Paul Bogart. **(PG)** *96 minutes*

OH, HEAVENLY DOG! (1980)

★

Chevy Chase
Jane Seymour

Benji, the cute pooch and delight of children, tracks down a killer in London in his third film. But this time, director Joe Camp aims at an older audience by throwing in some sexual innuendoes and a bit of mild profanity. The flea-bitten plot, which is reminiscent of *Heaven Can Wait*, features Chase as a murdered gumshoe and Benji as his reincarnation. The result includes

Chevy Chase, Jane Seymour, and canine friend in Oh, Heavenly Dog!

scenes such as Benji—with the mind of Chevy—jumping with glee into the bubble bath of an attractive magazine writer, played by Seymour. **(PG)** *103 minutes*

OH! WHAT A LOVELY WAR (1969)

★★★

Laurence Olivier
John Gielgud
Ralph Richardson

Uneven yet inspired antiwar movie, set to music and presented as a series of vignettes of events from World War I. Many of the musical sketches are impressive, but there are slow moments as well. The satire of man's fascination with war has sufficient bite. The large all-star cast of British players also includes Jack Hawkins, John Mills, Kenneth More, Susannah York, Dirk Bogarde, and Vanessa Redgrave. **Director**—Richard Attenborough. **(G)** *139 minutes*

OKLAHOMA! (1955)

★★★

Gordon MacRae
Shirley Jones
Rod Steiger

Appealing family entertainment in the form of Rodgers and Hammerstein's fanciful musical about the love affair between a cowboy and a country girl. The memorable hit songs that captivated Broadway come across on the screen with gusto, and the colorful sets help maintain the pleasant mood. MacRae and Jones are ideally cast in the key roles, and they do justice to such numbers as "Oh, What a Beautiful Morning" and "People Will Say We're in Love." Also with Gloria Grahame, Charlotte Greenwood, Gene Nelson, James Whitmore, and Eddie Albert. **Director**—Fred Zinnemann. **(G)** *143 minutes*

OKLAHOMA CRUDE (1973)

★★★

Faye Dunaway
George C. Scott

This predictable story about wildcat oil operators struggling against big-business interests at the turn of the century is nonetheless entertaining. Dunaway portrays a gritty, hard-driving oil-well owner desperately trying to hang on to her claim in the face of ruthless pressure from a giant petroleum company. Scott stars as a drifter who comes to her aid. Jack Palance is convincing as the sinister company representative trying to drive Dunaway off her land. Also with John Mills and Woodrow Parfrey. **Director**—Stanley Kramer. **(PG)** *108 minutes*

OLD BOYFRIENDS (1979)

★★

Talia Shire

Talia Shire listens to Richard Jordan, who is one of her Old Boyfriends.

Joan Tewkesbury, who wrote *Nashville*, tries her hand at directing and achieves only middling results. A young woman, played by Shire, tracks down old boyfriends in an effort to come to terms with herself. Some appealing moments—especially by Buck Henry as a private eye with an interest in his beautiful secretary—crop up, but the main character's motivations remain unclear. The script by Paul and Leonard Schrader is the film's major weakness. Richard Jordan, Keith Carradine, John Belushi, and John Houseman also star. **(R)** *103 minutes*

OLD GRINGO (1989)

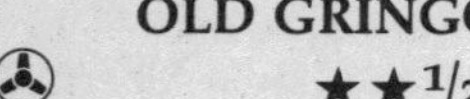

★★½

Jane Fonda
Gregory Peck
Jimmy Smits

Gregory Peck, Jane Fonda, and Jimmy Smits in Old Gringo.

Despite a powerful cast, this historical drama based on Carlos Fuentes' well-known novel is marred by a weak and unfocused script. Fonda stars as a straightlaced American governess caught up in the Mexican Revolution. She becomes involved in a love triangle with cynical journalist Ambrose Bierce, played by Peck, and a young Mexican general, played by Smits. Director Luis Puenzo, whose *The Official Story* won an Oscar for best foreign film, does not seem to have a grasp on the Hollywood movie-making system, because the story and the point get lost amid the scenery, the sets, and the thousands of extras. The acting, however, is generally impressive, and Peck's return to the big screen makes the film worth watching. Smits, who is one of the ensemble cast of *L.A. Law,* is especially winning as the smoldering army officer. Also with Patricio Contreras and Jenny Gago. **(R)**
119 minutes

THE OLD MAN AND THE SEA (1958)

★★★

Spencer Tracy

Tracy, who gives this Ernest Hemingway tale his best, plays an aging fisherman braving rough seas in hopes of catching a big fish. This one-character adventure isn't readily adaptable to the screen, but all hands try hard to sustain interest. Tracy's performance is really the main reason to see the film. Felipe Pazos and Harry Bellaver also star. **Director**—John Sturges. **Academy Award Nominations**—Tracy, best actor; James Wong Howe, cinematography.
89 minutes

OLD YELLER (1957)

★★★

Dorothy McGuire
Fess Parker
Tommy Kirk

A sentimental boy-and-his-dog tale from Walt Disney. Kirk plays a Texas farm boy in the mid-1800s who befriends a stalwart mongrel hound, and they become involved in numerous adventures. Based on Fred Gipson's novel, the film is excellent family fare. A classic Disney feature. McGuire and Parker play the parents. Also with Kevin Corcoran and Chuck Connors. **Director**—Robert Stevenson. **(G)**
83 minutes

OLIVER! (1968)

★★★★

Ron Moody
Oliver Reed
Mark Lester

Jack Wild and Mark Lester in the successful musical Oliver!

A first-class musical based on Charles Dickens' *Oliver Twist* and expertly adapted from the Broadway hit. The colorful production abounds with atmosphere, invigorating choreography, and memorable tunes by Lionel Bart. Child-star Lester is exceptionally good in the title role as the young orphan who becomes involved with a group of thieves led by the unsavory Fagin, played by Moody. Songs include "Consider Yourself" and "As Long as He Needs Me." Top supporting work by Reed, Shani Wallis, and Jack Wild. **Director**—Carol Reed. **(G) Academy Awards**—best picture; Reed, best director. **Nominations**—Moody, best actor; Wild, best supporting actor; Vernon Harris, best screenplay based on material from another medium; Oswald Morris, cinematography. *153 minutes*

OLIVER & COMPANY (1988)

★★★

The Disney studios have taken Charles Dickens' classic *Oliver Twist* and transplanted it to New York City. The result is a delightful children's cartoon adventure. The title character is an orange kitten who falls in with a gang of streetwise dogs. The colorful production is not quite at the top level of Disney animation, but an array of splendid voices including Billy Joel, Dom DeLuise, and Bette Midler, give life to the endearing characters. **Director—**George Scribner. **(G)** *72 minutes*

OLIVER'S STORY (1978)

★

Ryan O'Neal
Candice Bergen

Oliver (O'Neal) is numbed by the death of his young wife, and takes out his frustration by numbing the audience in this sequel to Erich Segal's *Love Story*. Oliver is now approaching middle age. He meets a rich girl, played by Bergen, but the romance soon falls apart. The movie is gloomy and far from the romantic mood of the first film. Also with Nicola Pagett, Edward Binns, and Ray Milland. **Director**—John Korty. **(PG)**
92 minutes

OLIVER TWIST (1948)

★★★★

Alec Guinness
Robert Newton
Francis L. Sullivan
Kay Walsh

This straightforward version of Charles Dickens' classic story is expertly crafted in all departments. Guinness portrays Fagin, the scoundrel who recruits the innocent orphan Oliver into a life of street crime. David Lean directs after the success of his *Great Expectations* (1946), which had also featured Guinness. Excellent supporting performances from John Howard Davies, Anthony Newley, Henry Stephenson, and Diana Dors. *116 minutes b&w*

® *This movie available with closed captions for the hearing impaired.*

O LUCKY MAN! (1973)

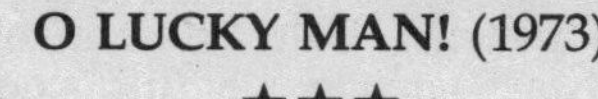

★★★

Malcolm McDowell
Arthur Lowe
Ralph Richardson
Rachel Roberts

It's *Candide* in the context of 1970s England, with McDowell as the lucky/unlucky youth who rises and falls again and again to the tune of some Alan Price songs. The storyline about a coffee salesman who is ruthless on his climb to the top is an allegory about the pitfalls of capitalism. A lot of corruption can be exposed in the film's interminable running time, but one feels the film has more adrenaline than passion, more weight and ambition than depth or emotion. The gifted actors—including Lowe, Richardson, Roberts, Helen Mirren, and Mona Washbourne—and veteran British director Lindsay Anderson do their energetic best with David Sherwin's script. **(R)** *173 minutes*

THE OMEN (1976)

★★1/2

Gregory Peck
Lee Remick

Peck and Remick unwittingly rear the son of Satan in this brutal and bloody horror film. The diabolical plot is implausible, but there are plenty of scare tactics to maintain tension and interest throughout. The purpose of the film, it seems, isn't to offer a meaningful story, but to make use of sensationalized images—a decapitation, creepy graveyards, mysterious hangings, attacks by mad dogs, howling baboons. The cast performs well, and Richard Donner's direction is slick. Also with David Warner, Billie Whitelaw, and Leo McKern. **(R)** *111 minutes*

ON A CLEAR DAY YOU CAN SEE FOREVER (1970)

★★★

Barbra Streisand
Yves Montand

Streisand is outstanding in this vibrant musical about a young woman who relives her past lives after undergoing hypnosis with a psychiatrist, played by Montand. The production isn't as invigorating as the Broadway show, but the music by Alan Jay Lerner and Burton Lane remains intact. Memorable songs include "He Wasn't You" and "Come Back to Me." Vincente Minnelli's direction is among his best. There's fine support from Bob Newhart, Jack Nicholson, Larry Blyden, and Simon Oakland. **(G)** *129 minutes*

ONCE BITTEN (1985)

★

Lauren Hutton
Karen Kopins
Jim Carrey

An anemic script and lackluster direction quickly sink this silly send-up of vampire and teen-sex movies. The glamorous Hutton is the female version of Dracula who must drink the blood of a young male virgin to stay youthful. This premise leads the film through a series of dull, juvenile sex jokes. Carrey and Kopins costar as the clean-cut high-school couple involved with the predatory countess. **Director**—Howard Storm. **(PG–13)** *93 minutes*

ONCE IN PARIS... (1978)

★★

Wayne Rogers
Gayle Hunnicutt
Jack Lenoir

A good-natured but sluggish movie about an American screenwriter (Rogers) who goes to Paris on a short assignment. He becomes involved with a colorful French chauffeur (Lenoir) and an attractive Englishwoman (Hunnicutt). Lenoir is particularly effective as the shady chauffeur. Though the location photography is beautiful, the episodic script lacks dramatic impact. Also with Clement Harari, Tanya Lopert, and Doris Roberts. Frank D. Gilroy wrote, directed, and produced. **(PG)** *100 minutes*

ONCE IS NOT ENOUGH (1975)

★

Kirk Douglas
Alexis Smith

A tawdry melodrama based on Jacqueline Susann's best-seller about the Hollywood, New York, and European jet set. The performances are mediocre and the screenplay is ludicrous and boring. Also with David Janssen, Deborah Raffin, George Hamilton, Melina Mercouri, and Brenda Vaccaro. **Director**—Guy Green. **(R)** **Academy Award Nomination**—Vaccaro, best supporting actress. *121 minutes*

ONCE MORE, WITH FEELING (1960)

★★★

Yul Brynner
Kay Kendall

Brynner and Kendall battle one another as husband and wife in this scrappy upper-crust comedy of marital blitz. Brynner is commanding as a tyrannical symphony orchestra conductor who seems to have more control over his musicians than he does over his gorgeous wife, who wants out of the marriage. Kendall, in her last film role, handles her part with skill and charm. Also with Geoffrey Toone, Maxwell Shaw, and Mervyn Johns. **Director**—Stanley Donen. *92 minutes*

ONCE UPON A TIME IN AMERICA (1984)

★★

Robert De Niro
James Woods
Elizabeth McGovern

Director Sergio Leone's sprawling film tapestry of American gangsters spans some 50 years, but unfolds in incoherent fits and starts because of the studio's decision to cut out over 90 minutes and reedit the rest (see below). The story, which has ambitions of being a Jewish *Godfather*, is overly contemplative and punctuated with moments of brutality. Yet the production, with its exquisite period details, is sumptuously photographed. An excellent cast is set adrift amid the fuzzy material. Also with Tuesday Weld, Larry Rapp, Joe Pesci, and Danny Aiello. **(R)** *135 minutes*

ONCE UPON A TIME IN AMERICA (1984)

★★★★

Robert De Niro
James Woods
Elizabeth McGovern

Restored, full-length version of Leone's epic (see above) seems like a completely different film. It reinstates the film's grandeur and fleshes out the story to true epic proportions. Don't pass judg-

(Continued)

Robert De Niro and James Woods attain power in Once upon a Time in America.

(Continued)

ment on this film until you've seen the long version. Also with Tuesday Weld, Larry Rapp, Treat Williams, Joe Pesci, Danny Aiello, William Forsythe, and James Hayden. **(R)** *227 minutes*

THE ONE AND ONLY (1978)

★★

Henry Winkler
Kim Darby

Winkler is amusing as a brassy show-off who fails to make it as a Broadway actor, but succeeds in the carnival world of professional wrestling. The storyline of the film, directed by Carl Reiner, has a sweet, upbeat flavor and a satisfying happy ending, but Winkler's character is too obnoxious at times. Darby, as Winkler's enduring wife, Herve Villechaize as a lascivious midget wrestler, and Gene Saks as a cynical promoter add warm and funny moments. Also with William Daniels and Polly Holliday. **(PG)** *98 minutes*

ONE CRAZY SUMMER (1986)

★1/2 ®

John Cusack
Demi Moore
Joel Murray

A throwaway teen comedy with jokes that are merely silly rather than funny. Two high-school graduates (Cusack and Murray) arrive on Nantucket for sun, surf, girls, and adventure. That's the trivial setup for a series of gags and routines that mainly fizzle. Moore costars as Cusack's romantic interest. The film's only highlight is the inclusion of a few animated sequences, which represent the inner thoughts of Cusack's character, an aspiring cartoonist. **Director**—Savage Steve Holland. **(PG)** *93 minutes*

ONE DAY IN THE LIFE OF IVAN DENISOVICH (1971)

★★

Tom Courtenay
Espen Skjonberg
Alfred Burke

Regardless of your literary tastes or politics, the Alexander Solzhenitsyn novel has more to offer than this film version indicates. Courtenay gives a novel respectable performance, and under Sven Nykvist's meticulous cinematographer's eye, the Arctic regions of Norway look a lot like Siberia might to western viewers. But however reverential you're prepared to be for a man's sufferings, you want to know more than the fact that it's a tough life laying bricks for ten years in a bone-chilling prison camp. The surfaces fail to reveal enough of the character's inner thoughts or the implications of his actions. **Director**—Caspar Wrede. **(G)** *100 minutes*

ONE-EYED JACKS (1961)

★★★

Marlon Brando
Karl Malden

Brando directed and stars in this tough western about an outlaw determined to settle a score with a buddy who was responsible for his imprisonment. A good psychological character study with vivid detail, but Brando overacts and the film is too long. Malden is convincing as the bandit's erstwhile friend turned sheriff. Also with Katy Jurado, Pina Pellicer, Slim Pickens, Ben Johnson, and Elisha Cook, Jr. **Academy Award Nomination**—Charles Lang, Jr., cinematography. *141 minutes*

ONE FLEW OVER THE CUCKOO'S NEST (1975)

★★★★

Jack Nicholson
Louise Fletcher

Ken Kesey's 1962 novel of rebellious insane asylum patients is the basis of director Milos Forman's stylish and moving film. Nicholson seems born to play the role of fast-talking R.P. McMurphy, the free-spirited fighter of the system. He's supported with excellent performances by Fletcher, as the heartless head nurse, and William Redfield, Danny DeVito, and Will Sampson as fellow patients. Dale Wasserman's off-Broadway version of this comedy/drama was popular among the young, mainly because of its antiestablishment theme. The first film since *It Happened One Night* to win the five top Oscars. Also with Brad Dourif, Michael Berryman, Peter Brocco, Scatman Crothers, and Christopher Lloyd. **(R) Academy Awards**—best picture; Nicholson, best actor; Fletcher, best actress; Forman, best director; Laurence Hauben and Bo Goldman, best screenplay adapted from another medium. **Nominations**—Dourif, best supporting actor; Haskell Wexler and Bill Butler, cinematography. *129 minutes*

ONE FOOT IN HEAVEN (1941)

★★★★

Fredric March
Martha Scott

A moving and charming story of a small-town minister and his wife trying to cope with fast-changing attitudes in America. Solid acting by March as the clergyman carries the film along despite an uncohesive plot. Scott is also good as his ever-faithful wife. A warm-hearted, well-handled movie. Costars Beulah Bondi, Gene Lockhart, Elizabeth Fraser, and Harry Davenport. **Director**—Irving Rapper. **Academy Award Nomination**—best picture. *108 minutes b&w*

ONE FROM THE HEART (1982)

★★1/2

Teri Garr
Frederic Forrest
Nastassja Kinski
Raul Julia

Lavish, dreamlike sets and dazzling effects swallow up both the story and the characters in this ambitious and misguided romantic musical by Francis Ford Coppola. The simplistic plot, set in Las Vegas, is reminiscent of 1940s and 1950s Hollywood musicals: Boy (Forrest) loses girl (Garr) and wins her back. The musical has always been an artificial-looking genre, with sets built on sound stages and characters bursting into song at any moment. Coppola's attempt to emphasize that artificiality by exaggerating his indoor sets to an almost abstract level is an interesting experiment, but it fails to make an entertaining film. The beautiful sets were designed by Dean Tavoularis; the

® *This movie available with closed captions for the hearing impaired.*

music is by Tom Waits and Crystal Gayle. Also with Harry Dean Stanton, Lainie Kazan, and Luana Anders. **(R)** *101 minutes*

ONE MAGIC CHRISTMAS (1985)

★★

Mary Steenburgen
Harry Dean Stanton

A struggling working mother (Steenburgen) has lost her Christmas spirit; her husband's out of a job and her mean-spirited boss leaves her little time for her kids. Can an angel (Stanton) convince her she really should be grateful? This downbeat Christmas carol is slow molasses with all its sugar at the bottom. Though the ending is uplifting, the emphasis on the protagonist's cheerlessness nearly leaves the audience cheerless as well. From the Disney studio. Also with Gary Basaraba, Arthur Hill, and Michelle Meyrink. **Director**—Philip Borsos. **(G)** *88 minutes*

ONE MILLON YEARS B.C. (1966)

Raquel Welch
John Richardson
Robert Brown

This is one of those films that actresses who are considered sex objects often articulate regrets over in later life, but, back in 1966, this film helped establish Welch as a household name. The gimmick in this Stone Age spectacular is that no English is spoken, just a guttural "primitive" language invented for the film's warring tribes. It's entertaining silliness, highlighted by Ray Harryhausen's stop-motion special effects. Carole Landis was certainly less statuesque then Welch in the original 1940 version, but then that film stressed beefcake (in the form of Victor Mature) over cheesecake. **Director**—Don Chaffey. *100 minutes*

ONE OF OUR AIRCRAFT IS MISSING (1942)

Godfrey Tearle
Eric Portman
Hugh Williams

Crackling wartime suspense film about the downed crew of an RAF bomber, trying to get back to England from occupied Holland with the aid of the Dutch resistance. This was the first credited screen collaboration of British filmmakers Michael Powell and Emeric Pressburger (*Black Narcissus; The Red Shoes*), and it was an impressive debut. Both the bombing mission over Stuttgart and the men's flight to freedom are excitingly depicted. With Bernard Miles, Pamela Brown, and Peter Ustinov. **Academy Award Nomination**—Powell and Pressburger, original screenplay. *106 minutes b&w*

ONE ON ONE (1977)

 ★★★

Robby Benson
Annette O'Toole

An engaging movie about big-time college basketball. Benson, who cowrote the script with Jerry Segal, is believable as a naive, small-town basketball player who challenges a sadistic coach and finally triumphs on the college courts. The story is a strong statement against the overcommercialized world of college athletics. Effective performances by G.D. Spradlin as the coach and O'Toole as Benson's romantic interest highlight the film. Also with Gail Strickland and Melanie Griffith. **Director**—Lamont Johnson. **(PG)** *98 minutes*

ONE TOUCH OF VENUS (1948)

 ★★★

Ava Gardner
Robert Walker

Pleasant and inventive romantic comedy about a statue of Venus that comes to life in a swank department store and becomes the love interest of a young employee. Gardner is exceptional as the beautiful Venus, and she sings "Speak Low" with passion. Walker plays the employee. Based on the Broadway play by S.J. Perelman. Also stars Eve Arden, Dick Haymes, Olga San Juan, and Tom Conway. **Director**—William A. Seiter. *82 minutes b&w*

ONE TRICK PONY (1980)

 ★★

Paul Simon
Blair Brown

Simon, one of the most influential singer/songwriters of the 1960s, wrote and stars in this personal story of a popular musician beset by a fading career and family problems. Simon also wrote the music, which is often more appealing than the laid-back dialogue or the colorless plot. Though detailed glimpses of the music industry are provided, overall there is not much excitement. Also with Rip Torn, Joan Hackett, Mare Winningham, Allen Goorwitz (Garfield), Lou Reed, Harry Shearer, and Tiny Tim. **Director**—Robert M. Young. **(R)** *98 minutes*

ONE, TWO, THREE (1961)

James Cagney

James Cagney in the world of business and finance in One, Two, Three.

Sophisticated, fast-paced Billy Wilder comedy set in West Berlin during the cold war. Cagney is excellent as a Coca-Cola executive trying to sell his product to the Communists. Complications arise when his boss's visiting daughter falls for a Communist from East Berlin. The invigorating plot offers nonstop satire heavily laced with clever one-liners. Andre Previn's music adds to the merriment. Cagney's last film before 1981's *Ragtime*. Also stars Horst Buchholz, Arlene Francis, Pamela Tiffin, Red Buttons, and Lilo Pulver. **Academy Award Nomination**—Daniel L. Fapp, cinematography. *115 minutes b&w*

ON GOLDEN POND (1981)

Henry Fonda
Katharine Hepburn
Jane Fonda

The drawing power of this sentimental drama is the magnificent casting of Henry Fonda and Hepburn as an elderly couple trying to enjoy what may be their last summer together. Family conflicts provide the core of the plot. Though the film is stagy and the plot

(Continued)

(Continued)
slight, the acting was critically acclaimed. Henry Fonda invests the story with pathos and humor as the crotchety retired professor who is forced at last to recognize his own vulnerability. Jane Fonda is outstanding as the resentful daughter. **Director**—Mark Rydell. **(PG)** **Academy Awards**—Henry Fonda, best actor; Hepburn, best actress; Ernest Thompson, best screenplay based on material from another medium. **Nominations**—best picture; Rydell, best director; Jane Fonda, best supporting actress; Filly Williams, cinematography. *109 minutes*

ON HER MAJESTY'S SECRET SERVICE (1969)

★★★½

George Lazenby
Diana Rigg
Telly Savalas

Lazenby substitutes for Sean Connery in this sixth James Bond adventure. Though highly criticized at the time, Lazenby is effective and appealing in the role. The movie is liberally salted with exciting action, tongue-in-cheek humor, and gorgeous women, which is typical of the series. This time 007 thwarts a group of scoundrels, led by Savalas, who are threatening to unleash a deadly virus. Breathtaking Switzerland provides a colorful backdrop as Bond encounters the bad guys on the snowy slopes. Rigg sparkles as a Spanish contessa. Also with Ilse Steppat, Gabriele Ferzetti, Bernard Lee, and Lois Maxwell. **Director**—Peter Hunt. **(PG)** *140 minutes*

THE ONION FIELD (1979)

★★★

John Savage
James Woods

Convicted killers James Woods and Jimmy Smith in The Onion Field.

This true story, about the abduction of two policemen and the murder of one of them by a couple of hoods, is based on a book by Joseph Wambaugh, who also wrote the screenplay. Decent acting and authentic detail are the major virtues of this absorbing portrayal of social, psychological, and moral decay. Also with Franklyn Seales, Ronny Cox, Ted Danson, and Dianne Hull. **Director**—Harold Becker. **(R)** *122 minutes*

ONLY TWO CAN PLAY (1962)

★★★★

Peter Sellers
Mai Zetterling

Sellers is at his comic best in this lively adult comedy with several outstanding scenes. Sellers portrays an assistant librarian in a Welsh town who is supposedly devoted to his wife. But he attempts an extramarital fling with a wealthy woman, and his bumbling efforts at lovemaking lead to many laughs. Zetterling is a riot as the desirable society woman. Also with Virginia Maskell, Richard Attenborough, Raymond Huntley, and Kenneth Griffith. **Director**—Sidney Gilliat. *106 minutes b&w*

ONLY WHEN I LAUGH (1981)

★★

Marsha Mason
Kristy McNichol

Neil Simon reworks his play *The Gingerbread Lady* into a comedy/drama for the screen. A Broadway actress, who is a reformed alcoholic, tries to reestablish her career and improve her relationship with her teenage daughter (McNichol). Mason is excellent in the lead, but the material is strictly soap opera. This showbiz story lacks Simon's usual humor. James Coco and Joan Hackett do well in supporting roles. **Director**—Glenn Jordan. **(R)** **Academy Award Nominations**—Mason, best actress; Coco, best supporting actor; Hackett, best supporting actress. *120 minutes*

ON MOONLIGHT BAY (1951)

★★★

Doris Day
Gordon MacRae

A syrupy musical, competently made and ideally suited for the wholesome talents of Day and MacRae, who play sweethearts in Indiana. The nostalgic story, based on Booth Tarkington's novel, is set just before World War I. It's a lighthearted family tale, with drama, music, and comedy. Also stars Leon Ames, Rosemary DeCamp, and Billy Gray. **Director**—Roy Del Ruth. *95 minutes*

ON THE BEACH (1959)

★★★

Gregory Peck
Ava Gardner
Fred Astaire
Anthony Perkins

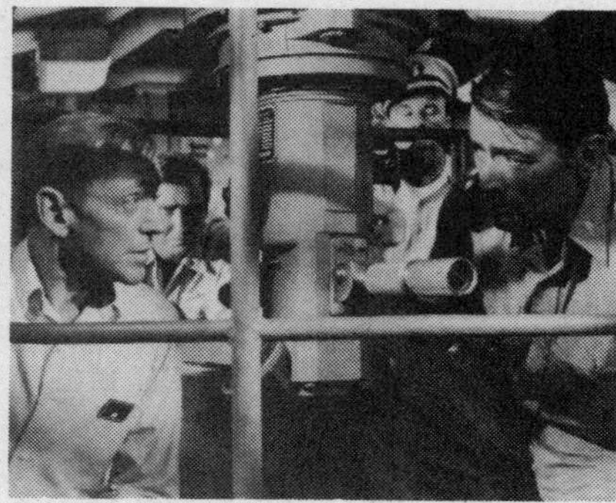

Gregory Peck in a tense moment from On the Beach.

Intelligent, thought-provoking account of survivors of a nuclear attack awaiting their fate in Australia. The film is enhanced by top performances from Peck and Gardner, and convincing supporting roles by Perkins and Astaire (in his first dramatic role). It's a grim subject, yet it presents a searing comment on atomic warfare and what could be the end of the world. Based faithfully on the novel by Nevil Shute. Also with Donna Anderson, John Tate, and Lola Brooks. **Director**—Stanley Kramer. *134 minutes b&w*

ON THE DOUBLE (1961)

★★

Danny Kaye

A typical vehicle for Kaye, who plays a private impersonating a high-ranking British officer during World War II. The dowdy script limits some of Kaye's comedic opportunities, but he has a good time with several funny scenes. Others in the cast are Dana Wynter, Wilfrid Hyde-White, Margaret Rutherford, Diana Dors, and Jesse White. **Director**—Melville Shavelson. *92 minutes*

® This movie available with closed captions for the hearing impaired.

ON THE EDGE (1986)

★★

Bruce Dern

The dichotomy of the physical difficulties and personal satisfaction of long-distance running provides the theme of this sports film set in northern California. Dern plays a determined marathon runner who enters the grueling competition at Cielo Sea despite official objections. Although the final race sequences are exciting, the preceding scenes are predictably sentimental, and include familiar *Rocky*-type shots that are supposed to inspire viewers. Though the film did not receive widespread distribution, it is available on videotape in two versions. The longer version, running 95 minutes, contains several scenes featuring black actress Pam Grier as Dern's lover. The shorter version, at 86 minutes, excludes Grier altogether. Also with John Marley and Bill Bailey. **Director**—Rob Nilsson. **(PG–13)** *91 minutes*

ON THE RIGHT TRACK (1981)

★★

Gary Coleman

TV child-star Coleman makes his film debut in this innocuous comedy about a shoeshine boy whose home is a locker in Chicago's Union Station. Coleman is predictably adorable as a pint-sized con man who can determine the outcome of horse races. The script is adequate, with its required number of romantic interludes, but this sort of material is basically just familiar TV fare. Also with Michael Lembeck, Lisa Eilbacher, and Maureen Stapleton. **Director**—Lee Philips. **(PG)** *97 minutes*

ON THE TOWN (1949)

★★★★

Gene Kelly
Frank Sinatra
Jules Munshin

Energetic, toe-tapping musical that's among the best of its kind. Three sailors—Kelly, Sinatra, and Munshin—make the most of their 24-hour liberty in New York City. Kelly and Sinatra head the exuberant cast, dancing and singing all over town, with lively choreography by Kelly and tuneful songs from the hit Broadway show by Leonard Bernstein, Betty Comden, and Adolph Green. Effective moments of comedy enhance the proceedings. An Oscar-winning score by Roger Edens and Lennie Hayton. Excellent supporting work by Vera-Ellen, Betty Garrett, Ann Miller, and Alice Pearce. **Directors**—Kelly and Stanley Donen. *98 minutes*

ON THE WATERFRONT (1954)

★★★★

Marlon Brando
Eva Marie Saint
Lee J. Cobb

Lee J. Cobb shows Marlon Brando a scar from his past in On the Waterfront.

Stark, powerful drama about corruption and despair among New York City longshoremen, brilliantly conceived and capped with a terrific performance by Brando. His portrayal of the young stevedore who bravely exposes the criminals who control the waterfront union is among the best of his distinguished career. Saint plays the girl he loves, and Cobb is Brando's waterfront boss. The pacing, the tense atmosphere, and the intelligent dialogue make for a powerful film. The screenplay by Budd Schulberg was based on a series of newpaper articles about corruption in the longshoremen's union. Excellent supporting performances by Rod Steiger, Karl Malden, Pat Henning, and Leif Erickson. **Director**—Elia Kazan. **Academy Awards**—best picture; Kazan, best director; Brando, best actor; Saint, best supporting actress; Schulberg, story and screenplay; Boris Kaufman, cinematography. **Nominations**—Cobb, Malden, and Steiger, best supporting actor. *108 minutes b&w*

ON THE YARD (1979)

★★½

John Heard
Thomas O. Waites
Mike Kellin

Day-to-day prison life is explored in this routine film, directed by Raphael D. Silver, about a power struggle among inmates. Convict Heard makes a mistake when he runs afoul of inmate leader Waites. Silver avoids the usual clichés of familiar big-house movies, but he also neglects drama and emotion. Nicely acted by Waites, Heard, and Kellin. The screenplay is based on a novel by Malcolm Braly, a former San Quentin inmate. Also with Joe Grifasi, Richard Bright, and Lane Smith. **(R)** *102 minutes*

ON VALENTINE'S DAY (1986)

★★

Hallie Foote
William Converse-Roberts

Lethargic, talkative period drama written by Horton Foote about his family in Texas in the early 1900s. It's a prequel to his *1918*. Although the acting is adequate and the atmosphere effective, the story seems to be of little consequence. Characters enter and exit exchanging small talk. All this nonaction is occasionally interrupted by some minor scandals and a suicide. Some of the cast of *1918*, including Hallie Foote and Converse-Roberts, reappear here. **Director**—Ken Harrison. **(PG)** *106 minutes*

OPERATION PETTICOAT (1959)

★★★

Cary Grant
Tony Curtis

Cary Grant listens to one of Tony Curtis' plans in Operation Petticoat.

An above-average comedy made better by the charming talent of Grant. As the skipper of a submarine in the South Pacific during World War II, he is desperately trying to reactivate his dilapidated

(Continued)

(Continued)
boat. Plenty of hilarious misadventures take place, but things really perk up when a group of nurses comes aboard. Curtis is perfectly cast as an officer with many outrageous schemes for getting the sub seaworthy. Also stars Dina Merrill, Gene Evans, Richard Sargent, Joan O'Brien and Arthur O'Connell. **Director**—Blake Edwards. **Academy Award Nominations**—Paul King and Joseph Stone (story), Stanley Shapiro and Maurice Richlin (screenplay), best story and screenplay written directly for the screen. *124 minutes*

OPERATION THUNDERBOLT (1977)

Klaus Kinski
Assaf Dayan
Yehoram Gaon

This Israeli-made film retells the events of the lightning commando raid on Entebbe, in which 104 hijacked passengers were rescued. There are occasional moments of suspense—especially the daring action sequences at the Ugandan airport—but the film smacks of official government propaganda. The characters are uninteresting, cardboard stereotypes. Perhaps the real-life episode that dominated the headlines that July day in 1976 is too thrilling to rehash for the screen. Also with Gila Almagor, Sybil Danning, and Shai K. Ophir. **Director**—Menahem Golan. **(PG)** *125 minutes*

OPPORTUNITY KNOCKS (1990)

★

Dana Carvey
Robert Loggia

Dana Carvey plays a confidence trickster in Opportunity Knocks.

Saturday Night Live cast member Carvey tries to follow the lead of other SNL alums by breaking into the feature-film market as a comic actor. Though Carvey has a talent for mimicry, he is not an actor. He is far too cute and inexperienced to make believable his character, slight as it is. He plays a con man who stumbles into the life of a wealthy businessman and then falls in love with his daughter. To call this a formula vehicle is an understatement, since the director and scriptwriter have followed every convention and used every cliché in the book. Even Carvey's famous impression of President Bush—his stock-in-trade on SNL—is thrown in. It is painful to watch Loggia, a highly respected character actor, in this trite material. Also with Todd Graff, Milo O'Shea, Julia Campbell, and James Tolkan. **Director**—Donald Petrie. **(PG-13)** *105 minutes*

ORCHESTRA WIVES (1942)

Glenn Miller
Ann Rutherford
George Montgomery

Miller and his orchestra take the spotlight in this backstage story about the private lives of the musicians and their spouses. The plot sustains adequate interest, but it's the wonderful swing music that keeps the film at a buoyant level. Miller and company belt out "I've Got a Gal in Kalamazoo," "Serenade in Blue," and more. Also with Lynn Bari, Jackie Gleason, Cesar Romero, and Carole Landis. **Director**—Archie Mayo. *97 minutes b&w*

ORDINARY PEOPLE (1980)

★★★

Donald Sutherland
Mary Tyler Moore
Timothy Hutton

Robert Redford, in his first time out as director, fashions a moving, intelligent, but cold film about family conflict as seen through the eyes of a troubled teenage boy. Based on Judith Guest's best-selling novel, this powerful movie examines human behavior with extraordinary sensitivity. Moore, Sutherland, and Hutton are excellent as members of an ordinary, affluent family who have difficulty expressing love. Also with Judd Hirsch, M. Emmet Walsh, Elizabeth McGovern, Adam Baldwin, and Dinah Manoff. **(R) Academy Awards**—best picture; Redford, best director; Hutton, best supporting actor; Alvin Sargent, best screenplay based on material from another medium. **Nominations**—Hirsch, best supporting actor; Moore, best actress. *123 minutes*

ORPHANS (1987)

Albert Finney
Matthew Modine
Kevin Anderson

Excellent acting highlights this film adaptation of Lyle Kessler's play about two young brothers who live alone in a ramshackle house in Newark, New Jersey. A big-time gangster (Finney) enters their shabby environment and transforms their lives for the better. Though somewhat stagy and slow-paced, the film moves toward an effective conclusion as complex emotions are revealed. All the performances are admirable, but Anderson, who appeared in the original play at Chicago's Steppenwolf Theater, stands out. **Director**—Alan J. Pakula. **(R)** *115 minutes*

OSCAR WILDE (1960)

Robert Morley

Adequate biography of the talented 19th-century playwright who was imprisoned on charges of being a sexual deviate. Morley, in the title role, repeats his stage portrayal and does a convincing job of interpreting Wilde's complex personality. A similar account, *The Trials of Oscar Wilde*, was filmed about the same time, but this version is better. Also stars Ralph Richardson and John Neville. **Director**—Gregory Ratoff. *96 minutes b&w*

THE OSTERMAN WEEKEND (1983)

Rutger Hauer
Burt Lancaster
John Hurt

Robert Ludlum's jumbled spy novel becomes even more confusing onscreen under the stylish but unsure direction of Sam Peckinpah. Dutch actor Hauer is a TV newscaster who conspires with the CIA to set up some of his friends believed to be Russian spies. The farfetched plot eventually goes out of con-

® *This movie available with closed captions for the hearing impaired.*

Rutger Hauer and Craig T. Nelson deliver a warning in The Osterman Weekend.

trol with an outrageous killing spree involving hunting bows, laser rays, explosions, and guns. And at the end we're still not sure who did what to whom—or why. Peckinpah's last film. Also with Craig T. Nelson, Dennis Hopper, Chris Sarandon, and Meg Foster. **(R)** *102 minutes*

OTHELLO (1965)

★★★½

Laurence Olivier

Magnificent screen version of Shakespeare's classic, with Olivier repeating his brilliant stage portrayal. This production isn't as effective as other cinematic depictions of Shakespeare's dramas, mostly because it is merely a filmed play and does not use the medium of film to its best advantage. However, Olivier's superb performance is considered one of the most innovative interpretations of this role. Excellent supporting work from Frank Finlay, Joyce Redman, Maggie Smith, and Derek Jacobi. **Director**—Stuart Burge. **Academy Award Nominations**—Olivier, best actor; Finlay, best supporting actor; Redman and Smith, best supporting actress. *166 minutes*

THE OTHER (1972)

★★★½ ®

Chris Udvarnoky
Martin Udvarnoky
Uta Hagen
Diana Muldaur

A brilliant supernatural thriller that is both a lyrical and a nightmarish paean to the powers of the imagination. In Connecticut during the mid-1930s, a pair of 10-year-old identical twins (Chris and Martin Udvarnoky) appear to be the cause behind a household's history of tragic and frightening incidents. The nature of that link, and how it relates to "The Game," is thrillingly unraveled in the course of the film. Probably the peak of director Robert Mulligan's career. Tom Tryon adapted the screenplay from his own novel. Photographed by the great Robert Surtees. Evocative supporting performances by Hagen and Muldaur. **(PG)** *100 minutes*

THE OTHER SIDE OF MIDNIGHT (1977)

★★

Marie-France Pisier
John Beck
Susan Sarandon

Marie-France Pisier doesn't want to talk to Raf Vallone in The Other Side of Midnight.

This slick adaptation of Sidney Sheldon's best-selling novel is a complex soap opera dripping with just about every movie cliché. Pisier plays a poor French girl who eventually attains wealth and fame, and then tries to get revenge on a dashing American cad, played by Beck, who abandoned her after a brief wartime romance. The corny plot spans some eight years and jumps between Europe and the United States. The title may have something to do with the film's length. Also with Raf Vallone, Clu Gulager, Christian Marquand, and Michael Lerner. **Director**—Charles Jarrott. **(R)** *165 minutes*

THE OTHER SIDE OF THE MOUNTAIN (1975)

 ★★

Marilyn Hassett
Beau Bridges

Hassett and Bridges star in this so-so tearjerker about Jill Kinmont, a promising young skier who was critically injured in 1956 while competing for the U.S. Olympic team. There are a few genuinely touching moments, but most of it is formula moviemaking. Bring plenty of handkerchiefs. Also with Belinda Montgomery, Nan Martin, and William Bryant. **Director**—Larry Peerce. **(PG)** *101 minutes*

THE OTHER SIDE OF THE MOUNTAIN PART 2 (1978)

 ★★

Marilyn Hassett
Timothy Bottoms

Part I told the tragic and true story of skier Jill Kinmont, who was crippled as the result of a downhill accident. Hassett is effective again as Jill in the second installment of this formula weepie, which has our heroine in love with a truck driver, played by Bottoms. The script, however, begs for interesting story angles. Director Larry Peerce manages to wring plenty of tears from moviegoers in the mood for a good cry. Also with Nan Martin, Belinda Montgomery, Gretchen Corbett, and William Bryant. **(PG)** *100 minutes*

OUR DAILY BREAD (1934)

 ★★★

Tom Keene
Karen Morley
John Qualen

Tom Keene and Karen Morley face the Depression together in Our Daily Bread.

Victims of the Depression from all walks of life pool their Herculean efforts to make a collective farm work. King Vidor directed and financed this impassioned, idealistic film, predating the populist fervor of Capra. It owes much to the Soviet rhapsodies of Sergei Eisenstein, especially Vidor's climactic

(Continued)

This movie available on videotape and/or disc.

(Continued)
irrigation scene, though it's quite powerful by itself. The actors aren't as effective as the images, and the drama isn't as strong as the message. Ironically, the film may be more interesting as a milestone in one artist's (Vidor's) career than as a collective vision; and, equally as ironic, the actors are more effective in scenes depicting rugged individualism than they are in those that depict dedicated collectivism. But all in all, very worthwhile. *74 minutes b&w*

OUR HEARTS WERE YOUNG AND GAY (1944)

★★★

Gail Russell
Diana Lynn

An appealing piece of adolescent froth about two young women—Russell and Lynn—who travel to Paris in 1923, where they have some romantic adventures. Not very deep, but a pleasant and scrubbed minor comedy, based on the book by Cornelia Otis Skinner. Also with Charles Ruggles, Dorothy Gish, Beulah Bondi, and James Brown. **Director**—Lewis Allen. *81 minutes b&w*

OUR MAN IN HAVANA (1960)

★★★★

Alec Guinness
Noel Coward

Guinness stars as the representative of a vacuum-cleaner shop in pre-Castro Cuba. He's recruited by British intelligence agent Coward to spy for England. Not knowing what is expected of him, Guinness makes up events and data to fill out his reports. The plot turns serious when people start getting killed as a result of Guinness' foolishness. The script was adapted by Graham Greene from his own novel. A complex blend of satire and suspense. Shot on location in Havana before Castro's takeover. Ernie Kovacs is good as a skeptical Cuban police chief. Adequate performances, too, from Burl Ives, Maureen O'Hara, Ralph Richardson, and Jo Morrow. **Director**—Carol Reed. *107 minutes b&w*

OUR TOWN (1940)

★★★★

Frank Craven
William Holden
Martha Scott

Thornton Wilder's classic story of life and love in a small New England community at the turn of the century is brought to the screen. An excellent production in all departments, with outstanding performances by a top cast. Music by Aaron Copland and production design by William Cameron Menzies. Also with Thomas Mitchell, Beulah Bondi, Guy Kibbee, and Fay Bainter. **Director**—Sam Wood. **Academy Award Nominations**—best picture; Scott, best actress. *90 minutes b&w*

OUR VINES HAVE TENDER GRAPES (1945)

★★½

Edward G. Robinson
Margaret O'Brien
Agnes Moorehead

This cozy look at life on the farm (specifically that of a Norwegian family in Wisconsin) is heartwarming and old-fashioned. It does, however, come perilously close to being too sentimental, and Robinson won't fit everyone's ideal of the kindly, bucolic patriarch. But if anyone can make the story meaningful, it's veteran screenwriter Dalton Trumbo. **Director**—Roy Rowland. *105 minutes*

OUT COLD (1989)

★★ ®

John Lithgow
Teri Garr
Bruce McGill
Randy Quaid

Lithgow stars as a timid butcher who finds his partner (McGill) frozen to death in the meat locker—the victim of foul play. A few chuckles surface when the dead man's wife (Garr) helps Lithgow try to dispose of the corpse. Otherwise, the proceedings are bland. Quaid co-stars as a bumbling private eye. **Director**—Malcolm Mowbray. **(R)** *87 minutes*

OUTLAND (1981)

★★½

Sean Connery
Peter Boyle

Connery plays a federal marshal of principle and determination who tries to crack a drug-smuggling ring at a remote mining camp on Jupiter's third moon. Boyle costars as the manager of

Sean Connery patrols the toughest reaches of space in Outland.

the mine colony. This rousing but frequently illogical space opera is close in storyline to the classic western *High Noon*. The chief selling points are the special effects and the art direction, which detail the bleak, synthetic outer-space environment and the rigors of working there. Also with James B. Sikking and Frances Sternhagen. **Director**—Peter Hyams. **(R)** *109 minutes*

THE OUTLAW (1943)

★★½

Jack Beutel
Jane Russell

The main attraction in this tongue-in-cheek western seems to be the bosom of a young Russell. Her low-cut blouses and the film's sexual undertones caused censorship problems that delayed the general release of the movie—shot in 1941—until 1947. But all of this hoopla aside, the storyline involving Billy the Kid and Doc Holliday packs some punch. There are decent performances by Beutel and Walter Huston as gunslingers who scrap over a half-breed beauty, played by Russell in her screen debut. Some prints are 95 minutes long; others run 103 minutes. Also with Thomas Mitchell and Joe Sawyer. **Directors**—Howard Hughes and Howard Hawks (uncredited). *117 minutes b&w*

OUTLAW BLUES (1977)

★★★

Peter Fonda
Susan Saint James

Fonda plays an ex-con who tries some picking and singing in this country music adventure. The lighthearted plot generates ample laughs and smiles, and even a few standard chase scenes are

® *This movie available with closed captions for the hearing impaired.*

appealing. Most of the performances are likable, making this energetic film palatable fare for country/western fans. Also stars John Crawford and James Callahan. **(PG)** *100 minutes*

THE OUTLAW JOSEY WALES (1976)

Clint Eastwood

A grim, violent post-Civil War western about lean, cool, tobacco-chewing Josey Wales, who embarks on a long trail of revenge and self-preservation after marauding Union soldiers kill his wife and son. Despite the excessive violence, the story is intriguing and suspenseful. Eastwood took over the direction from Philip Kaufman, and the result is a stylish, visually exciting film. Chief Dan George, Sondra Locke, Bill McKinney, and John Vernon also star. **(PG)** *135 minutes*

OUT OF AFRICA (1985)

★★★

Meryl Streep
Robert Redford
Klaus Maria Brandauer

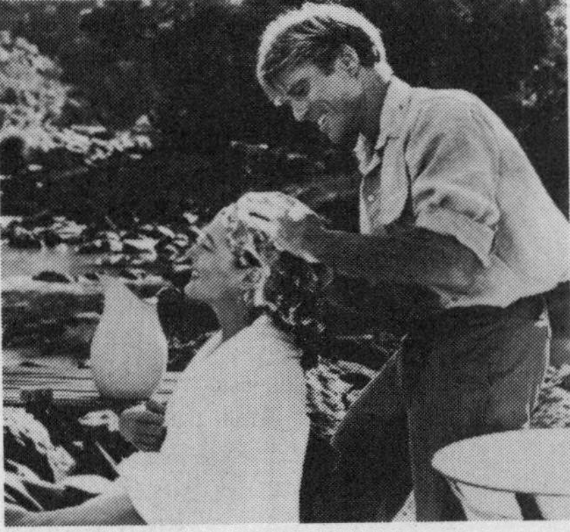

Meryl Streep and Robert Redford rest from the rigors of safari in Out of Africa.

A captivating, romantic film biography of a Danish noblewoman's intriguing but often tragic experiences in turn-of-the-century Africa. The period adventure is graced with appealing performances by Streep as the determined baroness and Brandauer as the irresponsible baron who marries her and squanders her money on a coffee farm in central Africa. Redford, however, is miscast as an aristocratic big-game hunter. Based on the memoirs of writer Isak Dinesen, the drama's languid pace and beautiful cinematography, filmed mostly in long shots, effectively suggest the nostalgic remembrances of someone recalling the distant past. **Director**—Sydney Pollack. **(PG) Academy Awards**—best picture; Pollack, best director; Kurt Luedtke, best screenplay based on material from another medium; David Watkin, cinematography. **Nominations**—Streep, best actress; Brandauer, best supporting actor. *150 minutes*

OUT OF BOUNDS (1986)

 ★★

Anthony Michael Hall
Jenny Wright

An Iowa farm boy (Hall) comes to big, bad Los Angeles, stumbles onto a heroin stash, and is pursued by both the cops and drug dealers. Despite a nonstop stream of car chases and shootouts, the cliché-strewn film quickly runs out of steam. The film is further hampered by Hall, who cannot shake his teenage-nerd image from previous films. Only Jeff Kober, as the drug kingpin, shows any depth in portraying his role. Also with Glynn Turman and Meat Loaf. **Director**—Richard Tuggle. **(R)** *93 minutes*

OUT OF THE PAST (1947)

★★★★

Robert Mitchum
Kirk Douglas
Jane Greer

This tough, crackling melodrama hits the heights of *film noir.* Mitchum plays a former private eye who is now the owner of a California gas station. Years before, he had been hired by hood Douglas to track down a sullen young woman (Greer) who had run out on the gangster. When Mitchum found the girl, he fell in love with her, and together they attempted to elude Douglas' grasp. After the fickle Greer left Mitchum, he assumed a new identity and occupation, until Douglas traced him to the service station. Now Mitchum must do an unsavory task for Douglas to make up for his mistake in the past. It's hard to keep up with all the double crosses, but the dialogue is sharp, Jacques Tourneur's direction is expressive, and the set design is moody and haunting. With Rhonda Fleming and Steve Brodie. The basis of the 1984 film *Against All Odds.*

97 minutes b&w

THE OUT-OF-TOWNERS (1970)

★★★

Jack Lemmon
Sandy Dennis

New York City is seen as a nightmare of mishaps in this darkly cynical Neil Simon comedy about an executive who comes to the Big Apple for a job interview. The comedy is uneven, but there are some funny moments, with Lemmon as the uptight visitor from Ohio involved in some hair-raising episodes. Dennis plays his wife. Also with Sandy Baron, Anne Meara, Billy Dee Williams, and Carlos Montalban. **Director**—Arthur Hiller. **(G)** *98 minutes*

OUTRAGEOUS! (1977)

 ★★★

Craig Russell
Hollis McLaren

Likable, energetic, but somewhat flawed film about an odd-couple relationship between a female impersonator and a beautiful schizophrenic girl. There's a winning, touching performance by McLaren as the troubled young woman. The highlights include the witty impersonations of famous women entertainers by Russell, who plays the transvestite. This funny Canadian film is more offbeat than it is outrageous. Written and directed by Richard Benner. **(R)** *100 minutes*

OUTRAGEOUS FORTUNE (1987)

Shelley Long
Bette Midler

Shelley Long and Bette Midler collaborate in Outrageous Fortune.

Brassy Midler and snooty Long trade one-liners and spout raunchy dialogue

(Continued)

This movie available on videotape and/or disc.

(Continued)
in this female buddy comedy. They star as aspiring actresses who discover they share the same lover (Peter Coyote) and chase him across the country in a fitful tangle of slapstick routines. The girls are as good a comic pair as Hope and Crosby, but this frantic romp bogs down in a swamp of silly clichés, car chases, and predictable shenanigans involving the CIA and KGB. Also with Robert Prosky, George Carlin, and John Schuck. **Director**—Arthur Hiller. **(R)**
96 minutes

THE OUTSIDERS (1983)

★★

C. Thomas Howell
Matt Dillon
Ralph Macchio
Diane Lane

Director Francis Ford Coppola mishandles this film adaptation of S.E. Hinton's novel about rival teenage gangs in Oklahoma during the 1960s. The production drips with sentimental slush about poor kids ("greasers") who are tormented by rich youths. The relatively simple story is puffed up to the point where it becomes pretentious and confusing. Coppola's reputation suffers. Also with Patrick Swayze, Rob Lowe, Emilio Estevez, Tom Cruise, and Tom Waits. **(PG)** *91 minutes*

OVERBOARD (1987)

★★1/2

Goldie Hawn
Kurt Russell

Kurt Russell and Goldie Hawn after she's fallen Overboard.

In this familiar but amusing romantic comedy, Hawn stars as a spoiled heiress who must suffer a bout with amnesia to learn the true meaning of love. After cheating carpenter Russell out of money that he earned, Hawn falls from her yacht, unnoticed by her husband and crew. When discovered, she cannot remember who she is or where she came from. Russell attempts to exact revenge by convincing her that she is his wife and the mother of his four monstrous kids. This latter-day version of *Taming of the Shrew* unfolds with warmth and charm, but may be too sentimental for some viewers. Also with Edward Herrmann, Katherine Helmond, Roddy McDowall, and Michael Hagerty. **Director**—Garry Marshall. **(PG)** *112 minutes*

OVER THE EDGE (1982)

★★

Michael Kramer
Pamela Ludwig
Matt Dillon

This vivid account of rebellious middle-class youths holds some fascination, but is routinely acted. The kids in the movie turn to vandalism and drugs because of the boring sterility of their environment and the benign neglect of their well-fixed parents. Their situations may be secure, but life offers little challenge. At times, the film seems as undramatic as the youths' banal existence. **Director**—Jonathan Kaplan. **(PG)**
95 minutes

OVER THE TOP (1987)

★★

Sylvester Stallone
David Mendenhall

Rick Zumwalt and Sylvester Stallone combat each other in Over the Top.

Stallone applies his *Rocky* formula to the world of arm wrestling in this sentimental drama. Stallone stars as a truck driver who tries to establish a rapport with his adolescent son on his way to some heavy competition at the arm-wrestling championship. He must actually face two challenges: To win custody of his son, he has to force his powerful father-in-law (Robert Loggia) to give the boy up; to win the competition, he must arm wrestle a most fierce opponent (Rick Zumwalt). Though the events are predictable, the carnival atmosphere surrounding the competition is amusing and colorful. Real-life arm wrestlers appear as themselves to create an air of authenticity. Also with Susan Blakely. **Director**—Menahem Golan. **(PG)** *92 minutes*

THE OWL AND THE PUSSYCAT (1970)

★★★

Barbra Streisand
George Segal

Streisand and Segal work well together and cook up some funny situations in this risqué comedy. She's a zany prostitute, and he's a stuffy bookstore clerk. They become roommates when she's ousted from her apartment. This odd-couple theme provokes déjà vu, but there are enough fresh antics to uphold interest. Witty dialogue and bawdy situations abound. Also with Robert Klein, Roz Kelly, and Allen Goorwitz (Garfield). **Director**—Herbert Ross. **(PG)** *96 minutes*

THE OX-BOW INCIDENT (1943)

★★★★

Henry Fonda
Dana Andrews

Powerful, authentic-looking western about a mob that lynches three men for murder despite the pleas of others who cry out for reason and justice. Fonda plays a cowboy with a conscience. The film is a strong statement against mob justice. Based on the well-known book by Walter Van Tilburg Clark. Also with Anthony Quinn, Henry Morgan, Mary Beth Hughes, William Blythe, and Jane Darwell. **Director**—William Wellman. **Academy Award Nomination**—best picture. *75 minutes b&w*

OXFORD BLUES (1984)

★★

Rob Lowe

A 1980s treatment of Robert Taylor's 1938 film *A Yank at Oxford*. Lowe plays a wise guy from Nevada who finagles his

® This movie available with closed captions for the hearing impaired.

way into the prestigious British university. There he pursues an aristocratic female student, joins the crew team, and adopts a flippant attitude toward his courses. Such events are hardly believable. Lowe's performance is constantly upstaged by various English character actors. Ally Sheedy, Julian Sands, and Amanda Pays costar. **Director**—Robert Boris. **(PG–13)** *96 minutes*

P

THE PACKAGE (1989)

 ★★★

Tommy Lee Jones
Gene Hackman

The Package *that Gene Hackman needs to deliver draws him into a deadly plot.*

This espionage, cold-war thriller follows the conventions of the spy genre fairly closely, but the smart direction and sharp performances by Jones and Hackman make for an interesting viewing experience. Hackman plays an army sergeant assigned to deliver a prisoner from Germany (the "package" of the title, played by Jones) to stand trial in the States. This detail draws him into an international assassination plot to sabotage *glasnost.* Surprising twists and turns keep the film suspenseful to the tense ending. Directed by Andrew Davis, whose *Code of Silence* and *Above the Law* proved to be superior examples of the action genre. Joanna Cassidy costars as Hackman's ex-wife, who outranks him in the military. Also with John Heard and Dennis Franz. **(R)** *107 minutes*

PAINT YOUR WAGON (1969)

★★

Lee Marvin
Clint Eastwood
Jean Seberg

Lavish but badly executed screen version of the Lerner and Loewe Broadway musical about a couple of gold rush prospectors who share the same wife. Marvin and Eastwood play the prospectors, and Seberg is the wife whom the two bought at an auction. The dancing is minimal, and some of the songs are forgettable, mostly because a majority of the cast are not musical performers. The script by Paddy Chayefsky is a bit off-color. "They Call the Wind Mariah" is among the songs. Some television prints run shorter. Also with Harve Presnell and Ray Walston. **Director**—Joshua Logan. **(PG)** *166 minutes*

PAISAN (1949)

★★★

Carmela Sazio
Gar Moore
Robert Van Loon

An extremely powerful compilation of six episodes depicting the Allied invasion of Italy during World War II. Directed and cowritten (with Federico Fellini) by Roberto Rossellini, the film is a masterpiece of neorealism, acted largely by nonprofessionals and filmed in a documentary style. The episodes emphasize the feelings associated with war—the anger, desperation, and fear—by focusing on the people that were affected on a day-to-day basis rather than depicting a group of larger-than-life heroes who seem invincible in battle, which was what most Hollywood productions did at that time. Rossellini's authentic characters—the assassinated Sicilian girl, the black GI and his urchin companion, and the partisans and O.S.S. men at the Po River—will both haunt and disturb the viewer. **Academy Award Nomination**—Alfred Hayes, Fellini, Sergio Amidei, Marcello Pagliero, and Rossellini, story and screenplay. *115 minutes b&w*

THE PAJAMA GAME (1957)

★★★

Doris Day
John Raitt

A labor/management dispute in a pajama factory is the subject of this lively movie musical, nicely adapted from the Broadway production. Day, well cast as the head of the grievance committee, falls in love with the factory manager, played by Raitt. The film is fast-paced, with some good songs, including "Hey There, You with the Stars in Your Eyes,"

John Raitt and Doris Day are happily playing The Pajama Game.

"Steam Heat," and "Hernando's Hideaway." The main point of the labor dispute is a 7½¢ pay raise, but the cast deserves more than that for its acting, singing, and dancing! Choreography by Bob Fosse. Also with Eddie Foy, Jr., Carol Haney, Reta Shaw, and Barbara Nichols. **Directors**—George Abbott and Stanley Donen. *101 minutes*

THE PALEFACE (1948)

★★★

Bob Hope
Jane Russell

Highly entertaining spoof of western films, with Hope cast as a bumbling frontier dentist who helps pistol-packing Calamity Jane, played by Russell, take on some bad guys. The Oscar-winning song "Buttons and Bows" is featured. Also stars Robert Armstrong, Iris Adrian, Robert Watson, and Jack Searle. This production led to a sequel, *Son of Paleface,* and a remake, *The Shakiest Gun in the West.* **Director**—Norman Z. McLeod. *91 minutes*

PALE RIDER (1985)

★★★

Clint Eastwood
Michael Moriarty
Carrie Snodgress

Eastwood stars as the mysterious, silent savior of a group of impoverished California gold prospectors who are being harassed by a ruthless mining baron. Eastwood also directed this classically structured western, whose storyline resembles that of *Shane.* Here, however, the mythic quality of the western story is emphasized over a traditional,

(Continued)

Clint Eastwood as Pale Rider, *the mysterious stranger who aids victimized miners.*

(Continued)
straightforward narrative through the religious overtones of the title character and the symbolism of the dialogue and imagery. Costars Christopher Penn, John Russell, Sydney Penny, and Richard Dysart. **(R)** *115 minutes*

PAL JOEY (1957)

★★★

Frank Sinatra
Rita Hayworth
Kim Novak

Sinatra is well cast in this slick musical as a nightclub operator who vacillates between being sincere and being a heel. Hayworth and Novak vie for Sinatra's attention. The film was specifically tailored for Sinatra's talents and isn't quite as vibrant as the Broadway production, but it's worthwhile viewing all the same. There are several classic Rodgers and Hart tunes, including "My Funny Valentine" and "The Lady Is a Tramp." The film was nominated for several minor Academy Awards, including editing, costumes, and art direction. Also with Barbara Nichols and Elizabeth Patterson. **Director**—George Sidney. *109 minutes*

THE PALM BEACH STORY (1942)

★★★★

Claudette Colbert
Joel McCrea
Rudy Vallee
Mary Astor

A classic screwball comedy with delightful zaniness, touching moments, and colorful characters. Colbert stars as the ambitious wife of a struggling engineer (McCrea). She runs away to the posh Florida city, where she becomes involved with an eccentric millionaire (Vallee) and his equally oddball sister (Astor). An inventive, well-made production representing a highlight in writer/director Preston Sturges' career. Also with William Demarest, Sig Arno, and Jack Norton. *88 minutes b&w*

THE PANIC IN NEEDLE PARK (1971)

Al Pacino
Kitty Winn

Hard-hitting account of a small-time thief (Pacino) and his girlfriend (Winn) who become involved with heroin and are dragged down into the gutter. The squalid atmosphere of Manhattan's Upper West Side is skillfully depicted, and the production is made more vivid by Pacino's astounding performance in his first major role. Also with Kiel Martin, Raul Julia, Paul Sorvino, Gil Rogers, Alan Vint, and Richard Bright. **Director**—Jerry Schatzberg. **(PG)** *110 minutes*

PANIC IN THE STREETS (1950)

★★★

Richard Widmark
Jack Palance

A tense story involving efforts to locate a gangster who is carrying the plague. Suspense mounts effectively in this authentic-looking, semidocumentary film, shot on the docks of New Orleans. Also with Zero Mostel, Paul Douglas, and Barbara Bel Geddes. **Director**—Elia Kazan. **Academy Award**—Edna and Edward Anhalt, motion picture story. *96 minutes b&w*

THE PAPER CHASE (1973)

★★★

Timothy Bottoms
Lindsay Wagner
John Houseman

Timothy Bottoms studies hard for his law degree in The Paper Chase.

A captivating and intense story of the agony and frustration of a graduate student trying to make it through Harvard Law School. His problems are compounded when he falls in love with the divorced daughter of a demanding and cynical law professor. Bottoms stars as the student, and Wagner is the daughter of the tyrannical Professor Kingsfield. Most of the performances are outstanding, and there are some realistic moments of classroom tension and humiliation. Houseman is exceptionally convincing as Kingsfield. Also with Graham Beckel, Edward Herrmann, and James Naughton. **Director**—James Bridges. **(PG) Academy Award**—Houseman, best supporting actor. **Nomination**—Bridges, best screenplay based on material from another medium. *111 minutes*

PAPERHOUSE (1989)

Charlotte Burke
Elliott Spiers
Glenne Headley

Drab psychological drama with a weird, muddled plot and a lot of Freudian references. Burke plays a lonely young girl whose drawings of a house haunt her dreams and then affect her real life. The young girl's switching from fantasy to dreams to reality often becomes confusing and is finally monotonous. On paper this project might have looked interesting, but it fails on the screen. **Director**—Bernard Rose. **(PG-13)** *94 minutes*

PAPER MOON (1973)

★★★1/2

Ryan O'Neal
Tatum O'Neal

An appealing, offbeat comedy set in mid-America in the 1930s. The story works to perfection, thanks in part to the pairing of Ryan O'Neal and his real-life daughter, Tatum, as a couple of Bible-selling con artists. The precocious and beguiling Tatum steals many a scene. Based on the novel *Addie Pray* by Joe David Brown. Costars Madeline Kahn, John Hillerman, and P.J. Johnson. **Director**—Peter Bogdanovich. **(PG) Academy Award**—Tatum O'Neal, best supporting actress. **Nominations**—Kahn, best supporting actress; Alvin Sargent, best screenplay based on material from another medium. *103 minutes b&w*

® This movie available with closed captions for the hearing impaired.

PAPER TIGER (1976)

★★

David Niven
Toshiro Mifune
Ando

Niven stars as a kindly English schoolmaster who daydreams of becoming a hero. He finally gets his chance when he and his pupil, the son of the Japanese ambassador, are kidnapped by terrorists. Ando plays the pupil, and Mifune plays his distraught father. The story, awash in sentiment, may have appeal for some. The direction by Ken Annakin lacks style. **(PG)**

99 minutes

PAPILLON (1973)

★★★

Steve McQueen
Dustin Hoffman

A tense, gut-wrenching tale of horrible conditions at the infamous Devil's Island prison colony, and of the daring escape of a man who claims he was falsely convicted of murder. McQueen plays the title role. There are several graphic scenes depicting the brutality of prison life—filthy living conditions, sadistic guards, and homosexuality among the inmates. The film's length and grueling sequences of prison life may tire some viewers. The script by veteran screenwriters Dalton Trumbo and Lorenzo Semple, Jr., is based on the book by Henri "Papillon" Charrière. Also with Victor Jory, Don Gordon, Anthony Zerbe, and Robert Deman. **Director**—Franklin J. Schaffner. **(PG)**

150 minutes

THE PARADINE CASE (1948)

★★★

Gregory Peck
Alida Valli
Charles Laughton

Though this Alfred Hitchcock film is better than its general reputation, it isn't for all tastes. A major portion of it consists of a courtroom trial, and the whole picture is too talky. Still, as shot and directed by the master of suspense, it's consistently absorbing. Peck stars as a married lawyer who finds himself falling for the seductive charms of his client (Valli), a woman accused of murdering her husband. From the novel by Robert Hitchens. With Laughton (excellent as a lecherous judge), Ann Todd, Louis Jourdan, Ethel Barrymore, and Charles Coburn. **Academy Award Nomination**—Barrymore, best supporting actress.

125 minutes b&w

PARADISE (1982)

★

Phoebe Cates
Willie Aames

If *The Blue Lagoon* only flirted with teenage sex, then this trashy look-alike gets right down to business, with innocence and loincloths tossed aside in quick succession. The story is set in the Middle East in 1823. Bright-eyed Cates and Aames play adolescent lovers on the run after the murder of both teens' parents. The youngsters find shelter at an oasis where they learn about lovemaking from the chimpanzees. **Director**—Stuart Gillard. **(R)** *100 minutes*

PARADISE ALLEY (1978)

★★★

Sylvester Stallone
Armand Assante
Lee Canalito

Sylvester Stallone both directs and stars in Paradise Alley.

Stallone, who triumphed with *Rocky*, directed and stars in this amusing and colorful film about three brothers who struggle to get out of New York's Hell's Kitchen shortly after World War II. Stallone skillfully draws winning performances from many promising new actors. The colorful characters, the smoky atmosphere of the setting, and the nostalgic re-creation of New York City in the 1940s highlight the film. Also with Anne Archer, Frank McRae, and Joyce Ingalls. **(PG)** *109 minutes*

THE PARALLAX VIEW (1974)

★★★

Warren Beatty
Paula Prentiss

Beatty stars as a determined reporter who investigates the assassination of a U.S. Senator. This gripping political thriller is executed with much style and skill by director Alan Pakula. Pakula would later team up with the cinematographer and production designer of this film for *All the President's Men.* Many subtle references to the Kennedys are apparent in the storyline. Also with William Daniels, Hume Cronyn, and Walter McGinn. **(R)** *102 minutes*

PARENTHOOD (1989)

★★★

Steve Martin
Mary Steenburgen
Dianne Wiest
Jason Robards

The uncertainty and strain of rearing children in a middle-class environment are explored in this frantic comedy. Martin heads an ensemble cast as a man with a high-pressure job who strives to be a superdad. Robards plays Martin's father, who is the patriarch of an extended four-generational family that includes Wiest, Steenburgen, Tom Hulce, Harley Kozak, Rick Moranis, Martha Plimpton, and Keanu Reeves. Though each of the actors has a dramatic, thought-provoking scene that reveals his or her character, the large cast makes for too many subplots. The story eventually meanders out of control. The contrast between Martin, who plays the fun-loving dad, and Moranis, who tries to turn his daughter into a genius child, adds much to the proceedings. Moments of dark-edged comedy blend with moments of true poignancy. **Director**—Ron Howard. **(PG-13) Academy Award Nominations**—Wiest, best supporting actress; Randy Newman, best song for "I Love to See You Smile."

124 minutes

PARENTS (1989)

★★

Randy Quaid
Mary Beth Hurt

Mom and Dad, who seem like a couple of squares right out of *Father Knows Best*

(Continued)

This movie available on videotape and/or disc.

A bourgeois suburban couple with unusual tastes in food—Parents.

(Continued)

sitcoms, are really suburban cannibals. This black comedy supposedly satirizes the 1950s as well as the horror genre, but the humor is bland. Quaid and Hurt try hard as the nice couple with the weird dinner menu, but their efforts are not enough to save this nightmarish, one-joke offering. Also with Sandy Dennis, Bryan Madorsky, and Graham Jarvis. **Director**—Bob Balaban. **(R)**

83 minutes

THE PARENT TRAP (1961)

★★★

Hayley Mills
Maureen O'Hara
Brian Keith

Mildly amusing and often clever adolescent romp from the Walt Disney studio, about twins who try to repair the broken marriage of their parents, played by O'Hara and Keith. Mills is likable in a dual role as the twin sisters who meet at a summer camp and discover they have the same mother and father. Some awkward slapstick scenes mar an otherwise entertaining family comedy. Also with Charles Ruggles, Leo G. Carroll, Una Merkel, and Joanna Barnes. **Director**—David Swift.

124 minutes

PARIS, TEXAS (1984)

★★★

Harry Dean Stanton
Dean Stockwell
Nastassja Kinski

Somber but poetic drama about a man who is reunited with his family after a mysterious four-year absence. German director Wim Wenders invests much tenderness and humanism into this gentle story of ordinary people who fail to communicate their emotions. The climactic reuniting of the estranged family is captivating indeed, but some of the film is slow-moving. Rich, convincing performances from Stanton, Stockwell, and Kinski. Also with Hunter Carson, Aurore Clement, and Bernhard Wicki. **(R)**

145 minutes

PARRISH (1961)

★★

Troy Donahue
Claudette Colbert
Karl Malden

Big-budget soap opera that provided early 1960s heartthrob Donahue with a vehicle for his lightweight talents. The story involves a Connecticut tobacco planter (Donahue) and his three romantic entanglements. Colbert plays Donahue's mother, who copes with wealthy suitor Malden. Writer/director Delmer Daves was adept at this type of melodrama, and he used the picture-postcard photography of Harry Stradling and the appropriately effusive performances of Connie Stevens, Diane McBain, Dean Jagger, Madeline Sherwood, and Sylvia Miles to their best advantage.

137 minutes

PARTNERS (1982)

★★

Ryan O'Neal
John Hurt

Partners: *Straight arrow Ryan O'Neal sizes up fellow cop John Hurt.*

French screenwriter Francis Veber (*La Cage aux Folles*) dishes up this unusual comedy about a homosexual cop and a straight cop who team up to solve murders in San Francisco's gay community. Though there are some funny and touching moments, the script offers mostly caricatures of homosexuals rather than fully understood characters. O'Neal is effective as the macho straight detective, but it is Hurt's delicate performance as the gentle homosexual cop that carries the film. Also with Kenneth McMillan, Robyn Douglass, and Rick Jason. **Director**—James Burrows. **(R)**

98 minutes

PASCALI'S ISLAND (1988)

★★½

Ben Kingsley
Charles Dance
Helen Mirren

A web of fraud and romance surrounds Ben Kingsley in Pascali's Island.

Kingsley is well cast as a Turkish spy on a Greek island in 1908 during the final phase of the Ottoman Empire. He gets caught up in a love triangle and a fraudulent scheme by a slick Britisher (Dance). Mirren is impressive as an Austrian painter who is the object of both men's passion. Despite the elegant production and fine performances, the complex film unfolds at a languid pace and lacks dramatic momentum. **Director**—James Dearden. **(PG-13)**

101 minutes

A PASSAGE TO INDIA (1984)

★★★

Judy Davis
Victor Banerjee
Peggy Ashcroft
James Fox
Alec Guinness

David Lean's eloquently crafted film adaptation of E.M. Forster's classic novel focuses on the clash of cultures in British-ruled India during the 1920s. Davis plays a young English woman, essentially critical of British policy, who accuses an Indian doctor (Banerjee) of raping her. The smugness of the British

This movie available with closed captions for the hearing impaired.

colonists is vividly illustrated in a tense courtroom drama. All characters are expertly portrayed by a top cast. Lean's first film after a 14-year absence from directing. **(PG) Academy Award**—Ashcroft, best supporting actress. **Nominations**—best picture; Lean, best director and best screenplay based on material from another medium; Davis, best actress. *160 minutes*

PASSAGE TO MARSEILLES (1944)

 ★★★

Humphrey Bogart
Michele Morgan
Claude Rains

Humphrey Bogart and Michele Morgan find each other in Passage to Marseilles.

A war drama starring Bogart as one of five convicts who escape from Devil's Island. His patriotism gets the best of him when he discovers that his homeland has been occupied by the Nazis. Few if any studios could boast of a director as prolific and successful as Michael Curtiz of Warner Bros. Here, he reunited four of the stars from *Casablanca*—Bogey, Rains, Sydney Greenstreet, and Peter Lorre—but with mixed results. A series of flashbacks within flashbacks muddles an otherwise interesting film. The excellent cast, however, which also includes Philip Dorn, Helmut Dantine, Eduardo Ciannelli, and John Loder, makes it all worthwhile. *110 minutes b&w*

LA PASSANTE (1983)

◉ ★★

Romy Schneider

Schneider plays two roles in this complex melodrama that interweaves the present with the past. In the modern-day sequences, she portrays the faithful wife of a wealthy Jewish activist, who kills a former Nazi collaborator; in the flashback scenes she is the wife of an anti-Nazi publisher in Germany during the Nazi occupation of Europe. Though Schneider is good, the story is difficult to follow and not particularly compelling. Michel Piccoli also stars. Originally filmed in French. **Director**—Jacques Rouffio. **(No MPAA rating)** *106 minutes*

PASSPORT TO PIMLICO (1949)

◉ ★★★

Stanley Holloway
Margaret Rutherford
Basil Radford

A postwar English comedy that has become a minor classic. Members of a neighborhood within London discover ancient documents indicating that the area really belongs to Burgundy. They then proclaim themselves free of current rationing rules, force riders of the Underground passing through the borders to declare customs, and generally throw the powers that be for a loop. T.E.B. Clarke's light but pointedly funny script was nominated for an Oscar. The excellent cast also includes Hermione Baddeley. It was the first film by English director Henry Cornelius, who died only nine years later at age 45. **Academy Award Nomination**—Clarke, story and screenplay. *84 minutes b&w*

PAT AND MIKE (1952)

◉ ★★★

Spencer Tracy
Katharine Hepburn

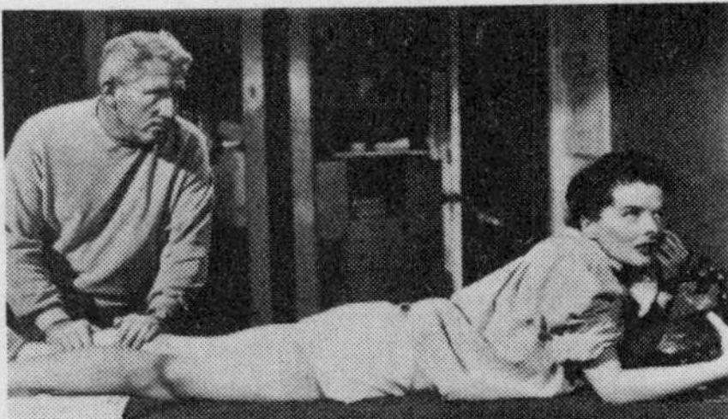

Katharine Hepburn has a leg up on Spencer Tracy in Pat and Mike.

The delightful teaming of Tracy and Hepburn transcends any minor drawbacks in this frothy comedy about the world of professional sports. Hepburn plays a champion athlete, and Tracy portrays her manager; their partnership leads to romance. Sporting greats appear in cameo roles. Also with Aldo Ray, Jim Backus, and Sammy White. **Director**—George Cukor. **Academy Award Nomination**—Ruth Gordon and Garson Kanin, story and screenplay. *95 minutes b&w*

A PATCH OF BLUE (1965)

★★★

Sidney Poitier
Elizabeth Hartman
Shelley Winters

A touching story about a poor, blind white girl who falls in love with a kind-hearted black man, but is unaware of his color. Hartman stars as the illiterate girl, and Poitier plays the well-educated man. The film is occasionally too sentimental, but the actors are excellent, particularly Winters as the girl's mean-spirited mother. Also with Wallace Ford, Ivan Dixon, and John Qualen. **Director**—Guy Green. **Academy Award**—Winters, best supporting actress. **Nominations**—Hartman, best actress; Robert Burks, cinematography. *105 minutes b&w*

PATERNITY (1982)

◉ ★★

Burt Reynolds
Beverly D'Angelo

Reynolds stars in this flat romantic comedy about a slightly sappy man-about-town looking for a woman to have his baby without the bother of marriage. The girl who agrees to the deal is a needy musician, played by D'Angelo. Now guess who's really in love and doesn't realize it? It's a predictable and sentimental script unevenly directed by stand-up comedian David Steinberg. Reynolds' charm isn't enough to carry the film. Also with Lauren Hutton. **(PG)** *94 minutes*

PATHS OF GLORY (1957)

◉ ★★★★

Kirk Douglas
Adolphe Menjou

A powerful tale about incompetence in the French Army's high command dur-

(Continued)

 *This movie available on videotape and/or disc.*

(Continued)
ing World War I. Douglas is excellent as an officer who treats his troops with dignity; Menjou plays a member of the high command. When the troops in the trenches are foolishly ordered into a battle in which they are hopelessly outnumbered, many casualties result and the troops are forced to retreat. Rather than admit to a mistake, the high command chooses three troops to execute for cowardly behavior. An early film by Stanley Kubrick and an effective antiwar statement. Also with George Macready, Wayne Morris, and Ralph Meeker. *86 minutes b&w*

PATTI ROCKS (1988)

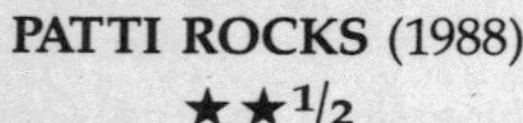

★★½

Karen Landry
John Jenkins
Chris Mulkey

Shrill, drawn-out dialogue spoils this potentially compelling account of an insecure male ego. Mulkey stars as a young married man who has a pregnant girlfriend in another state. On a trip to confront the girl—the "Patti Rocks" of the title—to confess his marital situation, this overaged adolescent brags about his sexual conquests to a friend he has dragged along. He discusses his experiences in the vulgar language men usually reserve for the locker room, making his character totally unsympathetic. When the men finally arrive at Patti's house, the friend is surprised to find that Patti (Landry) is tough and independent—not at all like she was described on the trip up. This low-budget independent feature serves as a working-class slice of life, but those offended by strong language and vulgar slang should steer clear. **Director**—David Burton Morris. **(R)** *86 minutes*

PATTON (1970)

★★★★

George C. Scott
Karl Malden

Expertly crafted screen biography of Gen. George S. Patton, the brilliant but quick-tempered Army commander who led American forces in Europe and North Africa during World War II. Scott is cast as the bombastic general, and he gives the performance of his career in this magnificent, bigger-than-life portrayal. Malden is also outstanding in the role of Gen. Omar Bradley, displaying an impressive contrast as the tactful military strategist. Many of the battle scenes are realistically staged. Also with Michael Bates, Stephen Young, Michael Strong, and Frank Latimore. **Director**—Franklin Schaffner. **(PG)** **Academy Awards**—best picture; Schaffner, best director; Scott, best actor (award declined); Francis Coppola and Edmund H. North, best story and screenplay based on factual material or material not previously published. **Nomination**—Fred Koenekamp, cinematography. *170 minutes*

George C. Scott plays the crusty Army general in Patton.

PATTY HEARST (1988)

★★

Natasha Richardson

A straightforward but detached account of the 1974 kidnapping of the publishing heiress by self-styled revolutionaries. The film is taken from Hearst's own 1982 book, *Every Secret Thing,* yet the telling here suggests there are many secrets unrevealed. Hearst's ordeal and subsequent cooperation with urban guerrillas is recounted from her point of view, complete with subjective camerawork. Yet, the effect is oddly numbing, or distanced—supposedly as Hearst herself felt throughout the ordeal. Richardson (Vanessa Redgrave's daughter) is impressive in the title role. Also with Dana Delaney, William Forsythe, Ving Rhamer, Francis Fisher, and Jodi Lang. **Director**—Paul Schrader. **(R)** *108 minutes*

PAULINE AT THE BEACH (1983)

★★★

Arielle Dombasle
Amanda Langlet

Director Eric Rohmer's playful comedy involves brief love affairs among six persons of various ages vacationing on the Normandy coast. At the center of this complex mating game is budding teenager Langlet, whose innocent summer romance contrasts with the childish behavior of the adults. Also with Pascal Greggory and Feodor Atkine. Originally filmed in French. **(R)** *94 minutes*

THE PAWNBROKER (1965)

★★★★

Rod Steiger

Steiger is memorable in the title role of this compelling melodrama about a Harlem hockshop owner haunted by the lingering memories of his experiences in a Nazi concentration camp. Steiger keeps the complex character in perfect control, and the result is an honest study of a distrustful man who struggles to regain faith in mankind. Directed by Sidney Lumet, well known for his socially conscious films. Fine supporting work from Brock Peters, Geraldine Fitzgerald, Jaime Sanchez, and Thelma Oliver. **Academy Award Nomination**—Steiger, best actor. *114 minutes b&w*

PEE-WEE'S BIG ADVENTURE (1985)

★★★

Paul Reubens

Paul Reubens and his beloved bike in Pee-Wee's Big Adventure.

"I know you are, but what am I?" What's childish, petulant, cute, clever, retro, and punk at the same time? Pee-Wee Herman, the man-child of the 1980s. Pee-Wee's act, which made the rounds of talk shows, nightclubs, and cable TV in the early part of the decade,

® This movie available with closed captions for the hearing impaired.

transfers to the big screen with remarkable ease. Credit goes equally to actor Reubens (who can probably do the character in his sleep by now) and novice director Tim Burton, who successfully creates both the vision and the world of a smart-alecky child. Reubens' act isn't for everyone, but suffice it to say that if you fell under Pee-Wee's spell on television, you'll be enchanted for the entire hour and a half. The plot? Don't be silly! **(PG)** *92 minutes*

PEGGY SUE GOT MARRIED (1986)

★★★

Kathleen Turner
Nicolas Cage

Francis Coppola's sentimental but thought-provoking comedy about a mature woman (Turner) who is transported back in time to her high-school years. Armed with adult hindsight, she attempts to alter her past decisions. Turner is excellent as the all-too-knowing adolescent and she manages some classic moments from the witty material. The film has some of the bittersweet quality of *It's a Wonderful Life.* Barry Miller and Catherine Hicks fare well in supporting roles. **(PG-13) Academy Award Nominations**—Turner, best actress; Jordan Cronenweth, cinematography; Theodora Van Runkle, best costume design. *103 minutes*

PELLE THE CONQUEROR (1988)

★★★★

Max von Sydow
Pelle Hvenegaard

Pelle Hvenegaard and Max von Sydow face many hardships in Pelle the Conqueror.

Absorbing drama about a poor Swedish widower (von Sydow) who comes to Denmark with his young son, Pelle (Hvenegaard), seeking a better life. Their lot as farmhands is bitterly hard, but they continue to strive to get ahead. The vivid vignettes of their experiences—of cruelty and compassion, disappointment and hope—make the drama engrossing despite its length. Von Sydow delivers a memorable performance. Originally filmed in Danish and Swedish. **Director**—Bille August. **(PG-13) Academy Award**—best foreign film. **Nomination**—Max von Sydow, best actor. *150 minutes*

PENITENTIARY (1979)

★★

Leon Isaac Kennedy

A rough, tough black prison drama, reminiscent of the black exploitation films of the 1960s and early 1970s. Kennedy plays a young convict who avoids sexual abuse in prison by becoming a competent boxer. There's a great deal of raw street language and several brutal encounters among the inmates. The film may be too violent for some viewers. Also with Thommy Pollard, Hazel Spears, and Badja Djola. **Director**—Jamaa Fanaka. **(R)** *99 minutes*

PENITENTIARY II (1982)

(no stars)

Leon Isaac Kennedy
Ernie Hudson
Glynn Turman

Kennedy returns for more violent confrontations in and out of the ring in this shabby and preposterous sequel. This exploitative, low-budget movie initially finds our young hero out of prison and supposedly through with boxing. Soon, however, an escaped convict is after him and Kennedy winds up fighting the champ back at the penitentiary. The brutality is nonstop; watching this bloody film is cruel and unusual punishment. **Director**—Jamaa Fanaka. **(R)** *103 minutes*

PENN & TELLER GET KILLED (1989)

★

Penn Jillette
Teller

A cavalcade of jokes in bad taste provides the basis for this bizarre comedy starring the bad boys of magic. The poor excuse for a plot revolves around Penn's statement that it would be interesting if he were stalked by a killer. The boys pull practical jokes on themselves by pretending there is a murderer after them: Then the action turns serious (supposedly) when a real killer becomes involved. Many pranks are either silly or sick, resulting in a film that will only appeal to a cult following. The film was directed by one of America's leading filmmakers in the 1960s, Arthur Penn *(Bonnie and Clyde; Little Big Man; Mickey One),* which seems a sad commentary on the state of the Hollywood industry. Also with Caitlin Clarke, David Patrick Kelly, and Leonardo Cimino. **(R)** *89 minutes*

PENNIES FROM HEAVEN (1981)

★★★

Steve Martin
Bernadette Peters

This movie is a strange mix of comedy and drama set to music. It's an ambitious attempt to contrast upbeat Hollywood musicals with the grim realities of the Depression era. Martin stars as a sheet-music salesman who lives the lyrics of his songs in his fantasies, even though his life is filled with doom and gloom—much of it of his own making. Many of the lavish musical numbers are inspired, but the film's unusual combination of tones and genres makes for an uneven—though frequently rewarding—viewing experience. Also stars Jessica Harper, Raul Julia, and Christopher Walken. Walken displays amazing skill in his song-and-dance number. **Director**—Herbert Ross. **(R) Academy Award Nomination—**Dennis Potter, best screenplay based on material from another medium. *107 minutes*

PENNY SERENADE (1941)

★★★

Cary Grant
Irene Dunne
Beulah Bondi

Grant and Dunne made audiences laugh by the millions as a married couple in *The Awful Truth;* they play a married couple once again in this classic tearjerker. Here, Dunne contemplates divorce, recollecting the joys and griefs she has shared with her husband, with a strong accent on their lives as parents. Effective work by director

(Continued)

(Continued)
George Stevens, writer Morrie Ryskind, the two leads, and costars Bondi and Edgar Buchanan. **Academy Award Nomination**—Grant, best actor.
120 minutes b&w

THE PEOPLE THAT TIME FORGOT (1977)

Patrick Wayne
Doug McClure

In 1919, a band of hardy adventurers attempts to rescue McClure—marooned several years earlier—from prehistoric monsters and unfriendly natives on a fictional Antarctic island. This comic-book movie, based on an Edgar Rice Burroughs fantasy, is a sequel to *The Land That Time Forgot*. The limited script and direction lack imagination, and the prehistoric trappings are as artificial as the acting. All in all, it's a forgettable film. Also with Dana Gillespie, Sarah Douglas, and Thorley Walters. **Director**—Kevin Connor. **(PG)** *90 minutes*

PEPPERMINT SODA (1979)

★★★

Eleanore Klarwein
Odile Michel

French director Diane Kurys made this understated yet effective film about the traumas of adolescence as seen through the eyes of two teenage sisters, played by Klarwein and Michel. It's a sensitive chronicle with vivid and engaging details. Klarwein stands out as the younger sister, encountering the familiar crises of growing up. Also with Anouk Ferjac. Originally filmed in French. **(PG)** *97 minutes*

PERFECT (1985)

John Travolta
Jamie Lee Curtis

Pretentious, labored nonsense starring Travolta as a *Rolling Stone* reporter who is doing a series on health spas as the singles bars of the 1980s. The manipulative plot touches on the issue of journalistic ethics, but the film eventually ends up glorifying what it intended to satirize. It's a glossy exhibition of well-formed bodies and aerobic dancing. Travolta and his love interest, Curtis, do display some chemistry together. Also with Marilu Henner, Laraine Newman, and Jann Wenner (the real-life editor of *Rolling Stone*). **Director**—James Bridges. **(R)** *125 minutes*

Jamie Lee Curtis tells John Travolta about the health-club scene in Perfect.

A PERFECT COUPLE (1979)

Paul Dooley
Marta Heflin

An intelligent film from director Robert Altman, about a man and a woman from contrasting backgrounds who meet via a computer dating service. The story occasionally lapses, but the many warm and funny moments make the film worthwhile. Dooley and Heflin are convincing as the unlikely lovers. Though not the best of Altman, it's a rousing social parody from an extraordinary filmmaker. Also with Henry Gibson, Belita Moreno, and Titos Vandis. **(PG)** *110 minutes*

PERFORMANCE (1970)

★★★

Mick Jagger
James Fox
Anita Pallenberg
Michele Breton

A vicious gangster (Fox) flees from the mob and holes up in the basement apartment of a townhouse owned by a former rock star turned recluse (Jagger). A complex relationship develops between landlord and tenant, and between both men and the two women also living in the residence. The film is a flashy drama of intertwined lives, characterized by mordant humor and visual virtuosity. However, its bizarreness and sadomasochism can ultimately be alienating. Jagger sings "Memo from Turner." **Directors**—Nicolas Roeg and Donald Cammell. **(R)** *105 minutes*

THE PERILS OF PAULINE (1947)

★★★

Betty Hutton
John Lund

The screen escapades of silent-film star Pearl White are fondly remembered in this energetic musical comedy, nicely adorned with Frank Loesser tunes. Hutton plunges into the title role as the frantic heroine who becomes involved in cliff-hanging predicaments. Several colorful slapstick scenes hark back to the days of Hollywood silents; but too much sentimentality mars an otherwise pleasant film. Others in the cast include Billy De Wolfe, William Demarest, and Constance Collier. **Director**—George Marshall. *96 minutes*

PERMANENT RECORD (1988)

Keanu Reaves
Alan Boyce

The sensitive issue of teenage suicide is explored here with good intentions, but this timely drama ultimately deteriorates into a somber monotone. Reaves stars as a high-school student who struggles with the stress caused by his friend's untimely death. Boyce plays the popular, talented, and ambitious classmate who inexplicably takes his own life. **Director**—Marisa Silver. **(PG–13)** *90 minutes*

PERSONAL BEST (1982)

Mariel Hemingway
Patrice Donnelly
Scott Glenn

Patrice Donnelly, Jodie Anderson, and Mariel Hemingway achieve their Personal Best.

Two female athletes (Hemingway and Donnelly) train hard for the Olympics

This movie available with closed captions for the hearing impaired.

and fall in love. The film avoids exploiting the lesbian relationship in favor of a close-up look at the intensity of athletes in training. Unlike most sports films, *Personal Best* implies that matches are really won in the training—in the endless hours of running, exercising, and sweating. The characters convey the amount of dedication and concentration required of world-class athletes. **Director**—Robert Towne. **(R)** *124 minutes*

PERSONAL SERVICES (1987)

★★★

Julie Walters
Alec McCowan

A droll English comedy loosely based on the experiences of Cynthia Payne, a working-class girl who became a well-known madam during the 1970s. Walters, who was a smash in *Educating Rita,* portrays Payne with a great deal of verve. Much of the humor derives from the eccentric requests of her upper-crust male clientele. Also with Danny Schiller, Shirley Stelfox, Victoria Hardcastle, Tim Woodward, and Dave Atkins. **Director**—Terry Jones. **(R)** *105 minutes*

PETE KELLY'S BLUES (1955)

★★

Jack Webb
Edmond O'Brien
Janet Leigh

The jazz world of the 1920s is re-created in this offbeat film. Webb directed and also plays the lead, though his minimalist acting technique—so effective in the TV series *Dragnet*—appears too wooden here. The music and the carefully reconstructed Jazz Age milieu are of most interest here, with the talents of Peggy Lee and Ella Fitzgerald highlighting the film. Lee has a rare dramatic role, and she displays some extraordinary acting skills. Also with Andy Devine, Lee Marvin, and Martin Milner. **Academy Award Nomination**—Lee, best supporting actress. *95 minutes*

PETE 'N' TILLIE (1972)

★★

Walter Matthau
Carol Burnett

Matthau and Burnett are nicely paired as middle-aged oddball characters who meet and then marry. The film begins as wry comedy but eventually lapses into sentimentality when the couple's son dies. The stars make the most of the material, but the script lets them down. Also with Geraldine Page, René Auberjonois, Barry Nelson, and Henry Jones. **Director**—Martin Ritt. **(PG)** **Academy Award Nominations**—Page, best supporting actress; Julius J. Epstein, best screenplay based on material from another medium. *100 minutes*

PETER PAN (1952)

★★★

Peter Pan *guides his young friends to enchanted adventure.*

Lively and colorful animated story from the Walt Disney studio, about the amazing boy who takes a trio of English children on an adventure to a magical land. There they meet Captain Hook, Tiger Lily, and Tinker Bell. Disney's imagination and the studio's animation skills are in evidence. Based on Sir J.M. Barrie's book, it's an exhilarating fantasy for the small fry, and for adults, too. **Directors**—Wilfred Jackson, Clyde Geronomi, and Hamilton Luske. **(G)** *76 minutes*

PETE'S DRAGON (1977)

★★

Helen Reddy
Jim Dale
Mickey Rooney
Red Buttons

What child could resist a jolly, cuddly green dragon—especially one with a potbelly and tiny pink wings? Elliot, the cartoon dragon in this Walt Disney romantic fantasy, is appealing as the companion and protector of Pete, a runaway orphan played by Sean Marshall. The voice of Pete is provided by comedian Charlie Callas. Though children will undoubtedly be entertained by this combination of animation and live action, adults will find its sentimental storyline too heavy-handed. Most of the cast overact shamelessly. Also with Shelley Winters and Jane Kean. **Director**—Don Chaffey. **(G)** *134 minutes*

THE PETRIFIED FOREST (1936)

★★★

Humphrey Bogart
Leslie Howard
Bette Davis

Humphrey Bogart re-created his Broadway role as vicious gangster Duke Mantee in this screen adaptation of the Robert E. Sherwood play. Fleeing from the law, Mantee and his gang hold a small group of people hostage at a desert cafe. Among those trapped at the Black Mesa Bar-B-Q are a dreamy-eyed intellectual, played by Howard (also recreating his stage role), and the waitress he falls for, played by Davis. Although it's a bit dusty after some 50 years, the film is still rife with tension, and the three luminous stars are excellent in their roles. Bogart's first major screen performance. **Director**—Archie Mayo. *83 minutes b&w*

PET SEMATARY (1989)

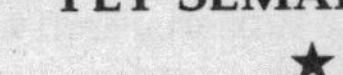

Dale Midkiff
Denise Crosby
Fred Gwynne

Ghoulish mayhem from the pen of horror master Stephen King. After the family cat is buried in a sacred Indian burial ground, it returns to harass Midkiff. But this is only the beginning of the family's problems. The story is predictable, and performances from a cast of relative unknowns are on the weak side. Midkiff and Crosby play the unsuspecting couple; Gwynne costars as the elderly neighbor. **Director**—Mary Lambert. **(R)** *102 minutes*

PETULIA (1968)

★★★

George C. Scott
Julie Christie
Shirley Knight
Richard Chamberlain

A flashy and often penetrating comedy/drama about a divorced doctor (Scott)

(Continued)

This movie available on videotape and/or disc.

(Continued)
who gets involved with a rich San Francisco kook (Christie), unhappily married to Chamberlain. The story is told in a fragmented, high-energy style, characteristic of its era and especially of its director, Richard Lester, who was highly successful during the 1960s. Very well acted by the entire cast (including Joseph Cotten, Arthur Hill, Kathleen Widdoes, and Pippa Scott), with excellent photography by Nicolas Roeg, and a notable score featuring music by John Barry and songs by the Grateful Dead, Big Brother and the Holding Company, and others. **(R)** *105 minutes*

PEYTON PLACE (1957)

Lana Turner
Arthur Kennedy
Hope Lange

What might have been only an average soap opera is elevated to an enjoyable melodrama by high production values and a cast of glamorous stars. Grace Metalious' sensational novel about scandalous activity in a small New Hampshire community is expertly adapted. Other Peyton Place residents include Diane Varsi, Lee Philips, Lloyd Nolan, Russ Tamblyn, Terry Moore, and Betty Field. The film inspired a sequel, a prime-time television series, and an afternoon soap opera. **Director**—Mark Robson. **Academy Award Nominations**—best picture; Robson, best director; Turner, best actress; Kennedy, best supporting actor; Lange and Varsi, best supporting actress; John Michael Hayes, best screenplay based on material from another medium; William Mellor, cinematography. *157 minutes*

PHANTASM (1979)

★★½

Michael Baldwin
Bill Thornbury

Wildly imaginative scare tactics and bloody gore dominate this ragged but frequently amusing horror story about strange happenings in a suburban mortuary. The plot is short on logic, but horror fans will appreciate the film's peculiar energy. Director/writer Don Coscarelli—in his early twenties at the time—has yet to live up to the promise indicated here. Also with Reggie Bannister, Kathy Lester, and Angus Scrimm. **(R)** *87 minutes*

PHANTASM II (1988)

Angus Scrimm
James Le Gros
Reggie Bannister

Violence and gore fill the screen in this sequel to the low-budget screamer released in 1979. The Tall Man (Scrimm), an evil mortician, continues his terror attacks on the living and the dead. The plot and acting are extraneous; such horrible scenes as embalming the living with acid, a chain saw ripping into flesh, and a flying metal ball that drills into people's skulls are the main focus. **Director—Don Coscarelli. (R)** *90 minutes*

THE PHANTOM OF THE OPERA (1943)

Claude Rains
Nelson Eddy
Susannah Foster

A worthy remake of the impressive 1925 silent melodrama that starred Lon Chaney. There are some colorful scenes in this well-produced version, with Rains in the title role as the mad and disfigured composer who hides in the sewers under the Paris Opera House and plots revenge. Many moments are devoted to Eddy and Foster singing. The art direction and cinematography won Academy Awards. Also stars Edgar Barrier, Leo Carrillo, and Hume Cronyn. **Director**—Arthur Lubin. **Academy Award**—Hal Mohr and W. Howard Greene, cinematography. *92 minutes*

PHANTOM OF THE OPERA (1989)

★½

Robert Englund

Robert Englund with another of his victims in Phantom of the Opera.

The classic story of love and compassion is presented here as just another hideous slasher movie. Englund, more familiar as Freddy Krueger, stars in the title role. Jill Schoelen costars as a young diva who is transported back in time to Victorian London. There, her opera work becomes entangled with the Phantom composer who stabs and decapitates assorted victims with ghastly relish. Part of Englund's grisly makeup involves his face coming apart at the seams. Obviously, the film was packaged in an attempt to cash in on the popularity of the hit Broadway musical. Also with Alex Hyde-White, Bill Nighy, and Stephanie Lawrence. **Director**—Dwight H. Little. **(R)** *90 minutes*

PHAR LAP (1983)

Tom Burlinson
Ron Leibman

Phar Lap *is the story of an Australian champion race horse.*

A horse-racing saga that follows in the hoof steps of similar outings, such as *National Velvet* and *The Story of Seabiscuit*. This true story traces the career of the scrawny colt from New Zealand who became Australia's legendary racing champion during the Depression era and then died mysteriously in California. Ample root-for-the-underdog elements and accounts of behind-the-scenes manipulation place this sports biography well above most others. Cut for American release by about ten minutes. **Director**—Simon Wincer. **(PG)** *107 minutes*

PHFFFT! (1954)

★★★

Jack Lemmon
Judy Holliday

Lemmon and Holliday sparkle in this buoyant romantic comedy as a couple

who separate and then discover they were happier when married. The situation is predictable and familiar, but Lemmon and Holliday make a good comic team. Also with Kim Novak, Jack Carson, Donald Randolph, and Luella Gear. **Director**—Mark Robson.
91 minutes b&w

THE PHILADELPHIA EXPERIMENT (1984)

Michael Paré
Bobby DiCicco

Two sailors engaged in a 1943 experiment to make a warship impervious to radar find themselves transported to the year 1984. This sci-fi time-warp adventure begins with some promise, but it eventually deteriorates to a predictable and unimpressive chain of events. The acting throughout is flat, and most of the special effects seem artificial. Yet the film is filled with ideas that could have been fascinating in a more inspired script. **Director**—Stewart Raffill. **(PG)** *101 minutes*

THE PHILADELPHIA STORY (1940)

Katharine Hepburn
Cary Grant
James Stewart

A top cast, expert direction, and a smooth script combine to make this witty romantic comedy, set among the upper crust of Philadelphia, worth viewing. The story, based on Philip Barry's play, involves a wealthy woman, played by Hepburn, who is about to be married for the second time. Grant plays her ex-husband, and Stewart is a reporter who falls in love with her. Also stars Ruth Hussey, Roland Young, John Howard, John Halliday, and Mary Nash. **Director**—George Cukor. **Academy Awards**—Stewart, best actor; Donald Ogden Stewart, screenplay. **Nominations**—best picture; Cukor, best director; Hepburn, best actress; Hussey, best supporting actress.
112 minutes b&w

PHYSICAL EVIDENCE (1989)

Burt Reynolds
Theresa Russell

Director Michael Crichton manufactures a familiar Hollywood mystery tale filled with standard plot elements. Reynolds plays a suspended cop with a reputation for violence who's suspected of murder. Russell is the public defender convinced of the policeman's innocence. There is no chemistry between the leads, and Russell (who actually has the bigger part) seems to be reading the script for the first time on screen. Kay Lenz and Ned Beatty are in supporting roles. **(R)** *99 minutes*

THE PICK-UP ARTIST (1987)

Molly Ringwald
Robert Downey, Jr.

Robert Downey, Jr., has finally met his match—Molly Ringwald—in The Pick-up Artist.

Downey plays a dauntless womanizer with an endless series of corny lines. He finally meets his match in Ringwald, who casually accepts his proposition and then just as casually dumps him. Consumed by her own problems involving her alcoholic father, she chooses not to get involved, which drives the lovestruck Downey to desperation. Although the characters are engaging, particulary Downey as the ladykiller, this lightweight romance suffers from a rambling script and an ending that simply fizzles out. Dennis Hopper is wasted in a small part as Ringwald's drunken father, while Harvey Keitel's role as an ill-tempered gangster seems to belong in another movie. **Director**—James Toback. **(PG–13)** *82 minutes*

PICKUP ON SOUTH STREET (1953)

Richard Widmark
Jean Peters

A well-crafted spy thriller about a pickpocket who steals a woman's wallet containing secret information; this small crime leads to his involvement with communist agents. Widmark is the light-fingered thief in this tough melodrama, which combines fast action and some violence. Excellent performances by a capable cast, which also includes Thelma Ritter and Richard Kiley. **Director**—Samuel Fuller. **Academy Award Nomination**—Ritter, best supporting actress. *80 minutes b&w*

PICNIC (1955)

 ★★★½

William Holden
Kim Novak
Rosalind Russell

A memorable movie about a drifter, played by Holden, who comes to a Kansas farming community and has a profound impact on the female residents. This smart psychological drama, based on William Inge's play, was adapted to the screen by Daniel Taradash. This depiction of small-town America is not the usual homespun stereotype, but a more provocative interpretation highlighted by Holden's smoldering presence. It's well-acted by a cast that also includes Susan Strasberg, Arthur O'Connell, Cliff Robertson, Betty Field, Verna Felton, and Nick Adams. **Director**—Joshua Logan. **Academy Award Nominations**—best picture; Logan, best director; O'Connell, best supporting actor.
113 minutes

PICNIC AT HANGING ROCK (1975)

Rachel Roberts
Dominic Guard

One of the breakthrough Australian films of the 1970s, directed by Peter Weir in his unique style. A group of schoolgirls and some of their teachers go off to the geological formation known as Hanging Rock for an innocent Valentine's Day outing in 1900. Three girls and a teacher decide to explore on their own, but only one of them ever returns—and she has no recollection of what happened. Though the film is more style than substance, and the mystery isn't resolved, the style is engrossing and the eerie, dreamlike atmosphere is hard to resist. Supposedly based on a true story. Also with Helen Morse, Jacki Weaver, Vivean Gray, Margaret Nelson, and Anne (Louise) Lambert. **(PG)** *110 minutes*

THE PICTURE OF DORIAN GRAY (1945)

 ★★★★

George Sanders
Hurd Hatfield

A clever and elegant Oscar Wilde tale about a man who remains forever young-looking while his portrait reveals his true age and evil nature. A stylish and sophisticated twist to the Jekyll and Hyde story, well acted and with good production values. Hatfield stars as Dorian. The film in its original release contained several color inserts, but television prints will not include those. Artists Ivan and Zsissly Albright painted the series of portraits. Narrated by Cedrick Hardwicke. The cast also includes Angela Lansbury, Peter Lawford, and Donna Reed. **Director**—Albert Lewin. **Academy Award**—Harry Stradling, cinematography. **Nomination**—Lansbury, best supporting actress. *111 minutes b&w*

A PIECE OF THE ACTION (1977)

★★

Sidney Poitier
Bill Cosby

Bill Cosby and Sidney Poitier must give up their bad habits in A Piece of the Action.

Poitier and Cosby team up for the third time in this comedy/adventure. The two play likable and successful con men who are blackmailed into helping delinquent youths. Despite the talented cast, the social commentary seems too obvious, the comedy is too shallow, and the pacing is out of step. Also stars James Earl Jones, Denise Nicholas, and Hope Clark. **Director**—Poitier. **(PG)** *135 minutes*

PILLOW TALK (1959)

 ★★★

Doris Day
Rock Hudson
Tony Randall

Hudson and Day are perfectly matched in this fluffy romantic comedy as two people who can't stand each other in person, but fall in love on a telephone party line, without realizing each other's true identity. Randall interferes with their romance. The lightweight story is fast paced and contains clever and witty dialogue. The successful teaming of Day and Hudson led to a series of similar films. Also with Thelma Ritter, Nick Adams, Julia Meade, and Lee Patrick. **Director**—Michael Gordon. **Academy Awards**—Russell Rouse and Clarence Greene (story); Stanley Shapiro and Maurice Richlin (screenplay), best story and screenplay written directly for the screen. **Nominations**—Day, best actress; Ritter, best supporting actress. *105 minutes*

PINK CADILLAC (1989)

Clint Eastwood
Bernadette Peters

Clint Eastwood holds Bernadette Peters' baby in Pink Cadillac.

A sluggish action/comedy starring the stone-faced Eastwood as a cunning skip tracer (a person who tracks down bail jumpers). Eastwood's quarry (Peters) is the wife of an ex-convict, and the chase leads to a nest of white supremacists who have kidnapped her baby. Most of the humor seems out of place in the face of the sinister, well-armed villains. This film is a lackluster combination of flimsy screwball antics and familiar shoot-'em-up action. Also with Timothy Carhart, Geoffrey Lewis, and William Hickey. **Director**—Buddy Van Horn. **(PG-13)** *122 minutes*

PINK FLOYD: THE WALL (1982)

★★

Bob Geldof

From director Alan Parker (*Fame*) comes this bizarre film based on the popular rock album. There's minimal dialogue; the teenage rantings about alienation and deterioration are conveyed via a flood of grisly, surreal imagery and overpowering rock music. The production is bold and tantalizing, but it is hard to follow and too often self-indulgent. Geldof stars as the crazy, burned-out rock performer. Also with Christine Hargreaves, James Laurenson, and Bob Hoskins. **(R)** *95 minutes*

THE PINK PANTHER (1964)

 ★★★½

David Niven
Peter Sellers

The incomparable Sellers is a riot as bumbling French Inspector Jacques Clouseau, who pursues a jewel thief in the Swiss Alps and, in the process, drives everyone around him up the wall. Niven plays the sophisticated thief, and Capucine is the inspector's wife. The film is a masterpiece of clever sight gags, pratfalls, and plot twists. Smartly directed by Blake Edwards, who went on to do several more *Panther* movies with Sellers. The familiar Henry Mancini score was nominated for an Oscar. Also with Claudia Cardinale and Robert Wagner. *113 minutes*

THE PINK PANTHER STRIKES AGAIN (1976)

Peter Sellers
Herbert Lom

French Inspector Jacques Clouseau, played by Sellers, bumbles through another chapter of comic misadventures. This time the zany Clouseau has driven his former superior—ex-Chief Inspector Dreyfus, played by Lom—insane. Lom gains control of a doomsday device and demands that Clouseau be turned over to him. The thin plot has many slow stretches, but the humor is solid. Also with Colin Blakely, Leonard Rossiter, Burt Kwouk, and Lesley-Anne Down. **Director**—Blake Edwards. **(PG)** *103 minutes*

® *This movie available with closed captions for the hearing impaired.*

PINKY (1949)

★★★

Jeanne Crain
Ethel Waters
Ethel Barrymore

Powerful drama about a light-skinned black girl, played by Crain, who passes for white and encounters assorted problems. The subject, which was daring at the time of the film's release, may be familiar now, but the story is still heartrending. Directed by Elia Kazan, the film reflects Kazan's notion that the cinema can be used to illustrate society's ills. The cast also includes William Lundigan and Nina Mae McKinney, who was a major star of several all-black productions in the 1930s. **Academy Award Nominations**—Crain, best actress; Barrymore and Waters, best supporting actress. *102 minutes b&w*

PINOCCHIO (1940)

★★★★

Walt Disney's Pinocchio, *featuring the little wooden boy and Jiminy Cricket.*

This children's classic from Walt Disney is considered by many critics to be the studio's greatest achievement. Based on the story by Carlo Collodi, the plot involves a poor, lonely woodcutter who builds a puppet, which comes to life only to fall in with bad company. When the puppet mends its ways, it becomes a real boy. The animation is colorful and lively, and the story brims with energy and charming characters. **Supervisors**—Ben Sharpsteen and Hamilton Luske. **(G) Academy Awards**—Leigh Harlin and Ned Washington, best song ("When You Wish upon a Star"); Harlin, Paul J. Smith, and Washington, original score. *77 minutes*

PINOCCHIO AND THE EMPEROR OF THE NIGHT (1988)

★★

This animated feature by Filmation based on the famous children's classic never comes close to the Disney Studios' spectacular 1940 masterpiece. Here the story centers on Pinocchio's efforts to become a star in a carnival. The production quality resembles Saturday morning TV fare. Ed Asner, Don Knotts, Tom Bosley, William Windom, and James Earl Jones supply some of the voices, but their expertise does little to overcome the film's flat texture. Strictly for small children. **Director**—Hal Sutherland. **(G)** *91 minutes*

PIRANHA (1978)

★★½

Bradford Dillman
Heather Menzies

Schools of deadly piranha are no match for one shark as another movie cashes in on the success of *Jaws*. Here, we find the toothy little critters escaping from a military experimental station into a nearby lake, where they put the bite on summer campers and school kids taking refreshing dips. A cut above most films inspired by the success of *Jaws*, this witty horror movie boasts a tongue-in-cheek script by writer/director John Sayles (*Brother from Another Planet*), a good cast, and some surprisingly effective scares. Also with Kevin McCarthy, Keenan Wynn, Dick Miller, and Barbara Steele. **Director**—Joe Dante. **(R)** *90 minutes*

THE PIRATE (1948)

★★★★

Gene Kelly
Judy Garland
Walter Slezak

MGM's golden age of musicals produced this colorful, tongue-in-cheek spectacular. The charismatic stars are terrific together. Garland plays a young woman of the West Indies with a richly romantic imagination; Kelly costars as the flamboyant traveling player who pretends to be a notorious Caribbean pirate to steal Garland away from the old windbag who intends to marry her. Top musical director Vincente Minnelli stages it all with tremendous panache, and Kelly does some of his most acrobatic dancing abetted by the Nicholas Brothers. The tuneful Cole Porter score includes "Be a Clown" and "Love of My Life." Also with Gladys Cooper, Reginald Owen and George Zucco. *102 minutes*

THE PIRATE MOVIE (1982)

★

Kristy McNichol
Christopher Atkins

McNichol and Atkins bumble and stumble through this foolish musical fantasy loosely based on Gilbert and Sullivan's operetta *The Pirates of Penzance*. The adolescent story, about a plain girl (McNichol) who dreams she is the love object of a young buccaneer (Atkins), bogs down in silly comic situations and innocuous song-and-dance numbers. Veteran director Ken Annakin (*The Longest Day*) fails to sustain a comic mood. An apology is owed to Gilbert and Sullivan. **(PG)** *98 minutes*

PIRATES (1986)

★★

Walter Matthau
Charlotte Lewis

This lavishly constructed takeoff of swashbuckling adventures directed by Roman Polanski quickly runs aground despite some good performances. The centerpiece of this uneven voyage is the delightful portrayal by Matthau of a rascally, peg-legged British pirate captain, who outfoxes some Spanish aristocrats. Unfortunately, the slow pacing and weak script take the wind out of the film's sails. Damien Thomas and Richard Pearson also are in the cast. **(PG–13) Academy Award Nomination**—Anthony Powell, best costume design. *124 minutes*

THE PIRATES OF PENZANCE (1983)

★★★

Kevin Kline
Linda Ronstadt
George Rose
Angela Lansbury

This latter-day film version of the classic Gilbert and Sullivan operetta comes off

(Continued)

(Continued)
with adequate charm, color, and good cheer. The stage production had more zip, but plenty of rousing musical numbers and lively dance routines are offered here. Most of the Broadway cast is on board: Kline swashbuckles as the Pirate King, and Ronstadt sings quite well as the delightful Mabel. Also with Rex Smith. **Director**—Edward Pressman. **(G)** *112 minutes*

THE PIT AND THE PENDULUM (1961)

★★★

Vincent Price
Barbara Steele
John Kerr

Vincent Price has a stranglehold on Barbara Steele in The Pit and the Pendulum.

Price is at his sinister best in this creepy horror tale, loosely based on the Edgar Allan Poe story. The setting is just after the Spanish Inquisition, and the film is well stocked with musty torture chambers, misty castles, thunder and lightning, entombed bodies, and so on. The storyline involves Price's belief that he is his father, an infamous member of the Inquisition known for viciously torturing his prisoners. The second of B-movie great Roger Corman's adaptations of Poe's stories. Scripted by Richard Matheson. Also with Luana Anders and Antony Carbone. *80 minutes*

PIXOTE (1980)

★★★

Fernando Ramos da Silva
Marília Pera

This Brazilian film is a grim account of abandoned São Paulo children who graduate from a squalid juvenile institution to a life of serious crime. Ten-year-old nonactor da Silva is convincing in the title role. He plays an innocent-looking lad who engages in purse snatching, dope dealing, and finally murder. Pera plays a prostitute who begins working for da Silva and his gang of preteen hoodlums. Graphic scenes of prison, rape, murder, and drug use will make this film difficult for many viewers to watch. Also with Jorge Juliano and Gilberto Moura. Originally filmed in Portugese. **Director**—Hector Babenco. **(R)** *127 minutes*

A PLACE IN THE SUN (1951)

★★★

Montgomery Clift
Elizabeth Taylor

Montgomery Clift pursues rich girl Elizabeth Taylor in A Place in the Sun.

A striking sociological/psychological drama based on Theodore Dreiser's novel *An American Tragedy*. Clift is outstanding as an ambitious blue-collar worker who shuns his poor working-class girlfriend for the love of the wealthy Taylor. The film emphasizes the contrasts between the wealthy and lower classes, though the representations of both now seem trite and out of date. The chemistry between Clift and Taylor makes the film a powerful love story. Also stars Shelley Winters, Raymond Burr, Anne Revere, Keefe Brasselle, and Fred Clark. **Director**—George Stevens. **Academy Awards**—Stevens, best director; Michael Wilson and Harry Brown, screenplay; William Mellor, cinematography. **Nominations**—best picture; Clift, best actor; Winters, best actress. *122 minutes b&w*

PLACES IN THE HEART (1984)

★★★★

Sally Field
John Malkovich
Danny Glover

A tender movie about a young widow in Depression-era Texas who struggles to support her two children and hold onto her heavily mortgaged home. Writer/director Robert Benton, reaching into his childhood memories, fashions an interesting story that is a mixture of melodrama, nostalgia, and heroism. The dreamlike ending will surprise some viewers, but is nonetheless thought-provoking. Malkovich costars as a blind boarder and Glover is a black laborer who helps Field plant cotton. Field, in the lead role, teaches a powerful lesson in the value of perseverance. Also with Amy Madigan, Lindsay Crouse, and Ed Harris. **(PG) Academy Awards**—Field, best actress; Benton, best screenplay written directly for the screen. **Nominations**—best picture; Benton, best director; Malkovich, best supporting actor. *113 minutes*

THE PLAINSMAN (1937)

★★★

Gary Cooper
James Ellison
Jean Arthur
Anthony Quinn

Cecil B. De Mille directed this western about the legendary Wild Bill Hickok (Cooper), Buffalo Bill (Ellison), and Calamity Jane (Arthur). Again De Mille makes use of historical personages and events in the narrative, which adds an air of believability to his sweeping epic style. Cooper and Arthur, who costarred the year before in *Mr. Deeds Goes to Town*, are just as good together here. Not an authentic look at the Old West, but an entertaining one. Also with Charles Bickford, Porter Hall, and Gabby Hayes. *113 minutes b&w*

PLANES, TRAINS AND AUTOMOBILES (1987)

★★★

Steve Martin
John Candy

Comedians Martin and Candy are perfectly cast as two businessmen thrown together when bad weather forces them to change their travel plans. Candy

® This movie available with closed captions for the hearing impaired.

Steve Martin and John Candy rendezvous in Planes, Trains and Automobiles.

plays a loud, blustery salesman who specializes in selling shower curtain rings, while Martin plays a straight-laced ad executive. Their paths fatefully cross when their plane trip from New York to Chicago is rerouted to Wichita. This sets off a chain reaction of such modern-day disasters as plane cancellations, car trouble, and horrid motel accommodations. Though the premise here is slight, the events progress at a rapid pace, and Martin and Candy handle the physical and verbal comedy with expert timing. Kevin Bacon, Michael McKean, Charles Tyner, and Edie McClurg are enjoyable in brief but hilarious cameo appearances. Also with Laila Robbins and William Windom. **Director**—John Hughes. **(R)** *90 minutes*

PLANET OF THE APES (1968)

★★★

Charlton Heston
Roddy McDowall
Kim Hunter

Innovative and thought-provoking science-fiction thriller about astronauts who land on an Earth-like planet where the apes have taken over and humans are subservient to them. The script, based on Pierre Boulle's novel *Monkey Planet*, is consistently engrossing. Special applause for the Oscar-nominated costumes by Morton Haack and the magnificent ape makeup by John Chambers. Also with Maurice Evans, James Whitmore, James Daly, and Linda Harrison. A slew of sequels and a TV series followed. **Director**—Franklin Schaffner. **(G)** *112 minutes*

PLATINUM BLONDE (1931)

★★★½

Loretta Young
Jean Harlow
Robert Williams

An early sound comedy written by Robert Riskin and Jo Swerling. Williams stars as a normally sharp newsman who loses his perspective when he marries constrictingly rich Harlow, leaving behind beautiful but unassuming coworker Young. Harlow takes the title role, but plays the least sympathetic character. Still an up-and-coming actress when she made this film, Harlow reached superstardom just a year or so later. Not a high point of director Frank Capra's career; it's really the writers' picture, with wonderfully amusing work by the unjustly forgotten Williams, who—like Harlow—died prematurely. *92 minutes b&w*

PLATOON (1986)

★★★★

Charlie Sheen
Tom Berenger
Willem Dafoe

Tom Berenger, Mark Moses, and Willem Dafoe in Platoon.

A powerful, gritty account of the Vietnam War as experienced by a platoon of "grunts" (infantryman) stationed near the Cambodian border. The sadism, frustration, horror, and inner conflicts among the troops are brilliantly captured by writer/director Oliver Stone, himself a Vietnam veteran. A vivid dramatization of an incident similar to the massacre at My Lai village is especially powerful. Stone's depiction of war deglamorizes combat partly by eliminating the glory and the larger-than-life heroics of standard war films. Stone's battle scenes seem frighteningly real because neither the soldiers nor the viewer knows when and from where the enemy will strike, emphasizing the chaos of battle. A grim but compelling account. Also with Kevin Dillon, Richard Edson, Forest Whitaker, and Francesco Quinn. **(R) Academy Awards**—best picture; Stone, best director; Claire Simpson, best editing. **Nominations**—Berenger and Dafoe, best supporting actor; Stone, best screenplay written directly for the screen; Robert Richardson, cinematography. *111 minutes*

PLAYERS (1979)

★

Ali MacGraw
Dean Paul Martin

Dean Paul Martin and Ali MacGraw in Players, *a film set in the world of pro tennis.*

The world of professional tennis is the backdrop to this tedious film marred by a love story so embarrassingly trite it draws unintentional laughter at every other line. Martin is convincing as the young man with tennis in his blood, but MacGraw looks shopworn as a rich, older woman torn between a wealthy man, played by Maximilian Schell, and our hero. Also with Pancho Gonzalez and Steve Guttenberg. **Director**—Anthony Harvey. **(PG)** *120 minutes*

PLAYING FOR KEEPS (1986)

Daniel Jordano
Matthew Penn
Leon W. Grant

This teen version of *Mr. Blandings Builds His Dream House* involves a group of city kids who struggle to fix up a crumbling country resort hotel while faced with resistance from hostile local residents and greedy industrialists. Despite all its energy and good intentions, the film is hampered by an unimaginative and cliché-strewn script. **Directors**—Bob Weinstein and Harvey Weinstein. **(PG–13)** *105 minutes*

PLAY IT AGAIN, SAM (1972)

Woody Allen
Diane Keaton

Allen mines some lively humor from the Bogart legend. He's an avid film fan who wants to revitalize his love life after

(Continued)

(Continued)
his wife, played by Susan Anspach, abandons him. Keaton plays the wife of Allen's best friend. Allen uses the Bogey and Bergman encounters from *Casablanca* to best advantage. Jerry Lacy does a remarkable Bogart imitation as the great actor's spirit, who counsels Allen about life and love. Also with Tony Roberts, Jennifer Salt, Joy Bang, and Viva. **Director**—Herbert Ross. **(PG)**
85 minutes

PLAY MISTY FOR ME (1971)

★★★

Clint Eastwood
Jessica Walter

Clint Eastwood tells Jessica Walter he can't do requests in Play Misty for Me.

An effective psychological shocker about a radio disc jockey, played by Eastwood, whose involvement with one of his female listeners leads to murder. This is Eastwood's first effort as director, and he does an impressive job of maintaining suspense and drama. Walter costars as the unhinged woman who repeatedly asks him to "play 'Misty' for me." Also with Donna Mills and John Larch. **(R)** *102 minutes*

PLAZA SUITE (1971)

★★★

Walter Matthau
Maureen Stapleton
Barbara Harris
Lee Grant

This Neil Simon comedy is among the best of his stage plays to be adapted for the screen. The film is composed of three vignettes about different people who stay at a particular room in the posh New York hotel. Matthau stars in all three segments in three different roles, and he scores in each situation. **Director**—Arthur Hiller. **(PG)**
114 minutes

PLEASE DON'T EAT THE DAISIES (1960)

Doris Day
David Niven

Buoyant situation comedy, based on Jean Kerr's play, about a drama critic who faces numerous problems with his job and his family when they move to the country. Cleverly executed with bright performances by the entire cast, which also includes Janis Paige, Spring Byington, Richard Haydn, and Patsy Kelly. Day sings the title song. **Director**—Charles Walters. *111 minutes*

PLENTY (1985)

Meryl Streep
John Gielgud
Sting
Tracey Ullman

Meryl Streep and Sting are torn by global events and personal values in Plenty.

Powerhouse performances by Streep, Gielgud, Sting, and Ullman are the main reasons to see this otherwise muddled film version of David Hare's stage play. Streep is excellent as an idealistic Englishwoman who served with the French Resistance during World War II. Later, she becomes disillusioned and neurotic over her assessment of British diplomacy as self-serving and shallow. In presenting this peculiar character, the story fails to generate adequate passion. **Director**—Fred Schepisi. **(R)** *119 minutes*

THE PLOT AGAINST HARRY (1969)

★★★

Martin Priest
Ben Lang

A quirky, deadpan comedy about a gruff, small-time Jewish gangster who is nudged into retiring to become a respectable family man. Originally shot and given a limited release in 1969, the film was forgotten until it was shown at the 1989 Toronto Film Festival, which resulted in its rerelease in 1990. Poignant observations on Jewish middle-class culture provide the strength of this modest satire, which not only holds up well alongside contemporary productions but also provides a guide to the thoughts and attitudes of another era. Priest performs well in the title role. Also with Maxine Woods, Henry Nemo, and Jacques Taylor. **Director**—Michael Roemer. **(No MPAA rating)**
81 minutes, b&w

POCKETFUL OF MIRACLES (1961)

Bette Davis
Glenn Ford

Director Frank Capra retreads his 1933 *Lady for a Day* into a slicker production for the wide screen. This version of the Damon Runyon tale isn't as bright as the earlier one, but it retains much of its charm and sentimentality. Davis plays the apple-seller who, with the help of good-hearted gangsters, poses as a rich lady to impress her visiting daughter. There are some bumpy moments, but the background settings are colorful. A talented cast handles the Runyonesque character parts competently. Also with Hope Lange, Arthur O'Connell, Peter Falk, Jack Elam, Sheldon Leonard, Thomas Mitchell, and—in her first film—Ann-Margret. **Academy Award Nomination**—Falk, best supporting actor. *136 minutes*

POLICE ACADEMY (1984)

Steve Guttenberg
George Gaynes
Kim Cattrall

The police department lowers its academy entrance requirements, setting the stage for some *Animal House* antics

® *This movie available with closed captions for the hearing impaired.*

among the new misfit recruits. The uneven, adolescent romp, which primarily pokes fun at authority figures, offers a few effective comic moments. But the bulk of the material is rather crude and commonplace. Guttenberg heads the cast as a young recruit who tries hard to get expelled but constantly bounces back. The film's success inspired several sequels. Also with G.W. Bailey, Bubba Smith, and Georgina Spelvin. **Director**—Hugh Wilson. **(R)** *96 minutes*

POLICE ACADEMY 2 (1985)

★½

Steve Guttenberg
Howard Hesseman
George Gaynes
Bubba Smith

The first sequel to the financially successful *Police Academy*. In this predictable but occasionally funny comedy, the Academy graduates are assigned to the worst inner-city precinct in the area. Many of the original cast members have returned, with Hesseman a new addition as their captain. As would be expected, the material is too familiar to generate the laughs that the original scored, but viewers who like broad comedy may be entertained. Also with Bobcat Goldthwait and Art Metrano. **Director**—Jerry Paris. **(PG–13)** *97 minutes*

POLICE ACADEMY 3: BACK IN TRAINING (1986)

★½

Steve Guttenberg
Bubba Smith

Steve Guttenberg and Shawn Weatherly in Police Academy 3: Back in Training.

Those latter-day Keystone Kops return for more slapstick antics in this third chapter of America's most unlikely law enforcement department. The gags revolve around two competing police academies. The one with the least blunders will survive the budget-cutting ax. The premise of this series has worn threadbare by now and the laughs are widely spaced. Guttenberg, Smith, David Graf and other original cast members are back in uniform. Also with Tim Kazurinsky and Shawn Weatherly. **Director**—Jerry Paris. **(PG)** *82 minutes*

POLICE ACADEMY 4: CITIZENS ON PATROL (1987)

★½

Steve Guttenburg
Tim Kazurinsky

This fourth installment finds the inept heroes in blue recruiting equally bumbling citizen volunteers to improve community relations and hopefully stop crime. Most of the original cast members are on board and handle the predictable slapstick gags with confidence, but the comic routines are too predictable and juvenile and the material is uninspired. Guttenberg returns as the cheerful group leader but adds nothing to the proceedings. Bubba Smith, Michael Winslow, Bobcat Goldthwait, and David Graf round out the cast. **Director**—Jim Drake. **(PG)** *90 minutes*

POLICE ACADEMY 5: ASSIGNMENT MIAMI BEACH (1988)

★

Bubba Smith
George Gaynes
David Graf

Those relentless latter-day Keystone Kops are in sunny Florida to honor their congenial commandant (Gaynes), who is facing mandatory retirement. The festivities are interrupted when he is kidnapped by diamond thieves. His rescue involves the expected round of slapstick antics, which are uniformly uninspired and unfunny in this least appealing episode of the well-worn series. Steve Guttenberg, who was the handsome star of the other four films, wisely declined to be in this sequel. Most of the other regulars do return, however, including Michael Winslow, the sound effects virtuoso. Also with Janet Jones and G.W. Bailey. **Director**—Alan Myerson. **(PG)** *90 minutes*

POLICE ACADEMY 6: CITY UNDER SIEGE (1989)

(no stars)

Bubba Smith
David Graf
Michael Winslow

The bungling men and women in blue break up a robbery gang. There's not much more excitement or originality than that in this installment of the now-worn-to-a-frazzle series. The antics of these latter-day Keystone Kops remain painfully predictable. Steve Guttenberg and Bob Goldthwait have departed from the ensemble cast, but the other familiar faces carry on. **Director**—Peter Bonerz. **(PG)** *83 minutes*

POLLYANNA (1960)

★★★

Hayley Mills
Jane Wyman
Adolphe Menjou

Thirteen-year-old Mills was at her most beguiling in her American film debut in Walt Disney's adaptation of the Eleanor Porter classic. She plays the ever-optimistic orphaned youngster who moves in with her Aunt Polly (Wyman), a wealthy New England spinster, circa 1912. "The glad girl" proceeds to lighten up the lives of everyone she meets in the small town that has become her new home. The film boasts an excellent supporting cast, including Karl Malden, Richard Egan, Agnes Moorehead, Donald Crisp, Kevin Corcoran, and James Drury. **Director**—David Swift. *134 minutes*

POLTERGEIST (1982)

★★★

Jobeth Williams
Craig T. Nelson

A visually spectacular, contemporary haunted-house movie, produced and cowritten by Steven Spielberg. Jolting, supernatural happenings occur when spirits take over a suburban California home. The hair-raising special effects are amazing, but much of the terror comes from the juxtaposition of the supernatural with the everyday setting of a typical suburban home. **Director**—Tobe Hooper. **(PG) Academy Award Nomination**—Richard Edlund, Michael Wood, and Bruce Nicholson, visual effects. *114 minutes*

POLTERGEIST II: THE OTHER SIDE (1986)

★★½

JoBeth Williams
Craig T. Nelson
Geraldine Fitzgerald

Another round of terror for Heather O'Rourke in Poltergeist II: The Other Side.

The young family whose suburban California home was destroyed by evil spirits in the original horror outing can't shake the menace in this film either, even when they move in with Grandma in Arizona. A confusing plot with a weak and sappy ending, which contradicts part of the storyline of the first film, makes this an unworthy sequel all the way around. Most of the original cast are back to deal with the mysterious ghosts and the mumbo-jumbo script. The elaborate special effects were nominated for an Oscar. **Director**—Brian Gibson. **(PG–13)** *90 minutes*

POLTERGEIST III (1988)

★★

Heather O'Rourke
Tom Skerrit
Nancy Allen
Zelda Rubinstein

This third installment of the horror series finds 12-year-old Carolanne followed by unwelcome, angry spirits when she visits her aunt and uncle in a Chicago high-rise. Film buffs will find the effects of interest because they are mostly mechanical effects done during the production phase rather than special effects done in post-production. Despite the city locale and the mechanical effects, however, this overworked horror tale has run out of energy and fresh ideas. Also with Lara Flynn Boyle, Kip Wentz, and Richard Fire. **Director**—Gary Sherman. **(PG-13)**

97 minutes

POLYESTER (1981)

★★

Divine
Tab Hunter

Writer/director John Waters (*Pink Flamingos*) made this fractured soap opera about the middle class, which is somewhat tamer than his previous outrageous comedies. Divine—actually a transvestite—plays an overweight housewife who cares for a family of degenerates, and the strain is driving her insane. At last she's rescued by debonair Hunter, the man of her dreams. There's a steady stream of tacky humor, but the campy farce begins to wear, and the garishness becomes annoying. **(R)**

86 minutes

PONY EXPRESS (1953)

★★★

Charlton Heston
Forrest Tucker

Better-than-average western, set in the 1860s, about the introduction of express mail service via a relay system of riders on horseback. The legendary Buffalo Bill Cody and Wild Bill Hickok lend a hand in establishing the mail service routes in this film. Adequate action scenes and decent acting enhance the production. Also with Rhonda Fleming and Jan Sterling. **Director**—Jerry Hopper. *101 minutes*

THE POPE OF GREENWICH VILLAGE (1984)

★★★

Mickey Rourke
Eric Roberts
Daryl Hannah

Schemers Eric Roberts and Mickey Rourke in The Pope of Greenwich Village.

This spicy tale of two small-time New York City hustlers falls somewhere between *The Bowery Boys* and Martin Scorsese's *Mean Streets*. Rourke and Roberts are the young hoods who burglarize a safe containing mob money and find themselves in big trouble with both Mafia types and the cops. Crude dialogue and strained situations abound, but rich characterizations and high-voltage acting sustain the film. Geraldine Page and Burt Young costar. **Director**—Stuart Rosenberg. **(R) Academy Award Nomination**—Page, best supporting actress.

122 minutes

POPEYE (1980)

★★★

Robin Williams
Shelley Duvall

Director Robert Altman based this strange musical on the lesser-known Popeye of the comic strip, and not the simpler character made famous in the animated cartoons. The result is a dark and atmospheric but quite entertaining film. Williams is perfect in the title role, decked out with huge forearms and muttering asides like W.C. Fields. Duvall is equally suited to the role of Olive Oyl, his sweetheart, and the songs by pop star Harry Nilsson are charming. Children expecting lots of action may be disappointed until the very end when Popeye finally downs some spinach, but adults should find the style and characters interesting throughout. Also with Paul L. Smith, Ray Walston, Paul Dooley, and Wesley Ivan Hurt. **(PG)**

114 minutes

POPI (1969)

Alan Arkin
Rita Moreno

A heartwarming story about the struggles of a Puerto Rican widower in Spanish Harlem trying to secure a better life for his young sons. Arkin is extremely convincing in the title role, as a determined man who works at multiple jobs and confronts the problems of ghetto life. The charming screenplay features an appropriate mixture of comedy and sentimentality. Miguel Alejandro and Ruben Figueroa perform in supporting roles. **Director**—Arthur Hiller. **(G)**

115 minutes

® This movie available with closed captions for the hearing impaired.

PORGY AND BESS (1959)

★★★

Sidney Poitier
Dorothy Dandridge

This film adaptation of George Gershwin's moving folk opera is stagy, but the memorable music makes the film worthwhile. Poitier plays the crippled denizen of Catfish Row who falls in love with a beautiful but vulnerable girl, played by Dandridge. Sammy Davis, Jr., stands out in the role of Sportin' Life. The unforgettable songs in the Academy Award-winning score include "Summertime" and "It Ain't Necessarily So." Pearl Bailey, Brock Peters, and Diahann Carroll are in supporting roles. **Director**—Otto Preminger. **Academy Award Nomination**—Leon Shamroy, cinematography.

138 minutes

PORK CHOP HILL (1959)

 ★★★

Gregory Peck
Harry Guardino

Gregory Peck is an officer in Korea facing tough decisions in Pork Chop Hill.

The film is among the best war movies about the Korean Conflict. American troops try to gain a foothold on a strategic position as negotiators seek a truce at Panmunjom. The authentic-looking battle scenes are embellished with rugged dialogue. Peck leads the fine cast, which also includes Rip Torn, George Peppard, George Shibata, Bob Steele, James Edwards, and Woody Strode. **Director**—Lewis Milestone.

97 minutes b&w

PORKY'S (1982)

 ★

Dan Monahan
Scott Colomby
Kaki Hunter
Kim Cattrall

A cavalcade of corny sex jokes and foolish pranks makes up this adolescent comedy about students at a Florida high school in the 1950s. The raunchy teenage romp features a relatively unknown but likable cast, though their good-natured energy is undermined by mindless and meandering material. The title refers to a local bar and bordello. Also with Susan Clark, Alex Karras, Wyatt Knight, Mark Herrier, and Roger Wilson. **Director**—Bob Clark. **(R)** *94 minutes*

PORKY'S II: THE NEXT DAY (1983)

  ★

Dan Monahan
Wyatt Knight

More adolescent high jinks from the raunchy gang at sun-drenched Angel Beach High School. Again, the students are involved with sex jokes, toilet jokes, and complex pranks. The teenagers, as usual, control every situation, while the adults are portrayed as buffoons. This time, the kids purportedly address social issues, but the film's prime concern is to cash in on the success of the original. Also with Mark Herrier, Roger Wilson, and Scott Colomby. **Director**—Bob Clark. **(R)**

95 minutes

PORKY'S REVENGE (1985)

 ★ 

Dan Monahan
Wyatt Knight

This third installment in the adventures of the rowdy male students at Angel Beach High offers more adolescent humor, which has become tired and predictable by now. The same characters are involved in childish pranks while any adults are made to look foolish. Porky, the crusty bar owner of the initial outing, now does business on a steamboat where a new confrontation with the kids takes place. Mark Herrier, Kaki Hunter, Scott Colomby, and Tony Ganjos star. **Director**—James Komack. **(R)**

94 minutes

PORTNOY'S COMPLAINT (1972)

 ★

Richard Benjamin
Karen Black
Lee Grant

Director Ernest Lehman mangles Philip Roth's sensational novel about a young Jewish man overwhelmed with hang-ups. Benjamin plays the role of the neurotic Portnoy. Most of the performances are undermined by poor handling of the production and an absurd screenplay. The satirical spirit of the novel is left on the shelf. Portnoy isn't the only one who should complain. Also with Jeannie Berlin, Jack Somack, and Jill Clayburgh. **(R)** *101 minutes*

PORTRAIT OF JENNIE (1948)

★★★½

Jennifer Jones
Joseph Cotten

Cotten stars as a poor artist who comes in contact with an unusual young woman, played by Jones. She becomes the subject of his paintings, they fall in love, and he wonders if she's the ghost of someone who died long ago. An unusual, haunting tale, smoothly produced with style and intrigue by David O. Selznick. The film was originally released with the last reel tinted green, and with the last shot in full Technicolor. Also with Ethel Barrymore, David Wayne, and Lillian Gish. **Director**—William Dieterle. **Academy Award Nomination**—Joseph August, cinematography. *86 minutes b&w*

THE POSEIDON ADVENTURE (1972)

  ★★★

Gene Hackman
Ernest Borgnine
Shelley Winters
Red Buttons

A Hollywood disaster extravaganza about trapped passengers in a capsized luxury liner who gallantly struggle to escape a watery tomb. The film is marred by an absurd script and numerous flimsy characters, but it does have some heroic moments that offer sufficient thrills. The special effects are the most entertaining attraction. Also with Carol Lynley, Leslie Nielsen, Arthur O'Connell, Pamela Sue Martin, Roddy

(Continued)

This movie available on videotape and/or disc.

McDowall, and Stella Stevens. **Director**—Ronald Neame. **(PG) Academy Award Nominations**—Winters, best supporting actress; Harold E. Stine, cinematography.

117 minutes

POSSE (1975)

 ★★★

Kirk Douglas
Bruce Dern

An ambitious Texas marshal, played by Douglas, stakes his campaign for the U.S. Senate on the capture of a notorious outlaw, played by Dern. A provocative and clever script, with excellent performances by Douglas and Dern. Douglas also directed this offbeat western. Also with Bo Hopkins, James Stacy, and Luke Askew. **(PG)**

94 minutes

POSSESSED (1931)

Joan Crawford
Clark Gable
Wallace Ford

Crawford and Gable were considered a hot romantic team in 1931. In this melodrama she plays a small-town girl who comes to New York in search of romance, and finds divorced lawyer Gable. This chronicle of the relationship between two unlikely people has lost its immediacy, but the stars are still charismatic. Also with Skeets Gallagher and Frank Conroy. **Director**—Clarence Brown.

77 minutes b&w

POSSESSED (1947)

Joan Crawford
Raymond Massey
Van Heflin

Crawford stars in this highly charged story about an emotionally unstable woman involved in several love affairs. Massey and Heflin are two of the men in her life. The script is heavy-handed, but Crawford excels in this type of material. This film is unrelated to the 1931 film also starring Crawford. Also with Geraldine Brooks. **Director**—Curtis Bernhardt. **Academy Award Nomination**—Crawford, best actress.

108 minutes b&w

THE POSTMAN ALWAYS RINGS TWICE (1946)

Lana Turner
John Garfield

Stylish, moody drama about a young woman who conspires with her lover to kill her husband. Turner and Garfield are perfectly matched as the lovers in this film version of the James M. Cain novel. Though several changes were made in the basic story to satisfy censorship requirements, it is still the best cinematic interpretation of Cain's steamy novel. Turner's bleached-blonde, "sweater girl" image was used to its best advantage, and she gives one of her best performances as the sultry adultress. Also with Cecil Kellaway, Hume Cronyn, and Leon Ames. **Director**—Tay Garnett. *113 minutes b&w*

THE POSTMAN ALWAYS RINGS TWICE (1981)

 ★★★

Jack Nicholson
Jessica Lange

The second Hollywood version of James M. Cain's 1941 novel of passion, greed, and murder stars Nicholson and Lange as the brooding, adulterous lovers. The film is well acted and beautifully photographed, with explicit detail of the Depression era. Nicholson is well suited to the role as the obsessive drifter who comes upon a dingy diner and lusts after the owner's wife. But keep your eye on the beautiful Lange as the sultry wife with murder on her mind; she makes the sparks fly. Also with John Colicos, Michael Lerner, and Anjelica Huston. **Director**—Bob Rafelson. **(R)** *122 minutes*

POWER (1986)

Richard Gere
Julie Christie
Gene Hackman

Sidney Lumet, a director noted for films about serious issues, takes on the packaging of political candidates by so-called media experts. It's an important topic that deserves scrutiny, but here, the case is overstated. Events fly by at such breakneck speed that characters are not adequately defined. Still, the

Media consultants Gene Hackman and Richard Gere are on opposite sides in Power.

subject matter is compelling. Gere stars as the high-powered image maker. Also with Kate Capshaw, Michael Lerner, Fritz Weaver, and Denzel Washington. **(R)** *111 minutes*

THE POWER AND THE GLORY (1933)

★★★

Spencer Tracy
Colleen Moore
Ralph Morgan

Widely acclaimed at the time of its release, and sometimes cited decades later as a forerunner of *Citizen Kane*, this film (bearing no relation to Graham Greene's novel) is a drama of a railroad magnate's rise to power. His story is told by various characters who knew him via flashbacks, and also in a narration by Morgan. Greatest credit for the film's impact must go to screenwriter Preston Sturges; this was one of his earliest scripts, and his most impressive until he turned director in the 1940s. Tracy stars as the powerful man with Moore as his wife. Also with Helen Vinson. *76 minutes b&w*

P.O.W. THE ESCAPE (1986)

 ★★

David Carradine

Prisoners in Vietnam fight for freedom in P.O.W. The Escape.

This movie available with closed captions for the hearing impaired.

Another flag-waving shoot-'em-up film about American soldiers who fight their way out of captivity near the end of the Vietnam War. Carradine is the tough colonel who leads his troops through enemy territory with minimal talk and much firepower. Scores of cardboard Vietnamese bite the dust. Also with Charles R. Floyd and Steve James. **Director**—Gideon Amir. **(R)** *90 minutes*

POWWOW HIGHWAY (1989)

★★

Gary Farmer
A Martinez

This road movie examines the current condition of American Indians in a lighthearted way. Farmer and Martinez are likable members of the Cheyenne tribe who drive from Montana to New Mexico, dwelling along the way on the lost glory and freedom of their tribal heritage. Though the humor is uneven and the odyssey loses its punch as the climax approaches, this independent effort is worthwhile viewing. **Director**—Jonathan Wacks. **(R)** *91 minutes*

PRANCER (1989)

★★½

Sam Elliott
Rebecca Harrell
Cloris Leachman

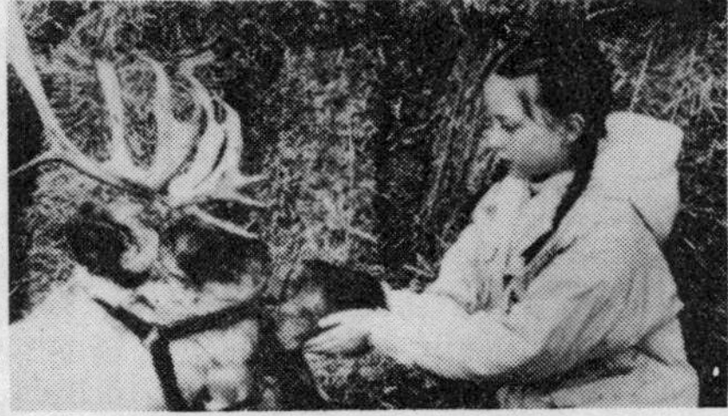

Rebecca Harrell believes that this reindeer is really Prancer.

An earnest but routine Christmas fantasy that pales beside the holiday film classics. Harrell stars as a farm girl who finds a wounded reindeer that she believes is a member of Santa's sleigh team. The youngster comes from a troubled household in which the father, played by Elliott, broods over the tragic loss of his wife. His daughter's determination to save the reindeer so that it can be ready for Christmas Eve is her way of overcoming her family's problems. Despite the fruitful material, John Hancock's direction lacks the spark of magic needed for fantasy, and the narrative rambles along with no suspense. Still, children should appreciate the tale, which emphasizes the special bond kids often share with animals. Also with Rutanya Alda, Abe Vigoda, Michael Constantine, and Ariana Richards. **(G)** *103 minutes*

A PRAYER FOR THE DYING (1987)

★★

Mickey Rourke
Alan Bates
Bob Hoskins

A moody melodrama about an ex-IRA terrorist who commits a murder witnessed by a priest. The priest cannot reveal the crime's details after the gunman shrewdly admits to the killing in the confessional. Some compelling moments emerge as the story examines the effect of constant violence on a man's soul, but the film tends to exploit the violence and action involved. Rourke seems ill at ease as the edgy killer, though Hoskins is convincing as the troubled priest. Rourke later denounced his role in this film, regretting the excessive violence. Also with Sammi Davis, Christopher Fulford, and Liam Neeson. **Director**—Mike Hodges. **(R)** *104 minutes*

PREDATOR (1987)

Arnold Schwarzenegger
Carl Weathers

Schwarzenegger and his elite squad of highly trained rescue specialists search the Central American jungle for missing comrades but stumble on a deadly space alien instead. The sophisticated creature hunts the team down and begins disposing of its members one by one. The tight direction, the effective use of jungle locales, and some innovative special effects make this a highly enjoyable, action-oriented science-fiction tale. A colorful cast breathes life into the roles of the squad members, including Bill Duke, Sonny Landham, writer Shane Black, and professional wrestler Jesse Ventura. Kevin Peter Hall, who played the creature in *Harry and the Hendersons,* plays the monster here as well. **Director**—John McTiernan. **(R)** **Academy Award Nomination**—Joel Hynek, Robert M. Greenberg, Richard Greenberg, and Stan Winston, visual effects. *106 minutes*

THE PRESIDENT'S ANALYST (1967)

★★★

James Coburn
Godfrey Cambridge
Severn Darden

A one-joke comedy about a psychiatrist who, after treating the President, finds himself pursued by special agents from the FBI and the CIA, and a slew of foreign spies, all of whom want to get at the secrets he's learned. Though imaginatively assembled by writer/director Theodore J. Flicker and enthusiastically played by Coburn, Cambridge, Darden, Pat Harrington, Joan Delaney, Eduard Franz, Will Geer, and William Daniels, it's not as consistently clever as it could be, and becomes muddled toward the end. *104 minutes*

THE PRESIDIO (1988)

★★

Sean Connery
Mark Harmon
Meg Ryan

A mediocre police thriller featuring a familiar storyline involving two mismatched detectives thrown together to solve a murder. Connery stars as the commander of the military police at an army base in San Francisco called the Presidio, where the murder took place. Harmon costars as a homicide detective who must rely on Connery's help in order to question any military personnel. Complications occur when Harmon finds himself falling in love with Connery's high-spirited daughter, played by Ryan. Though Connery and Harmon are an attractive team, the plot is convoluted and lacks any real mystery. Too many personal moments and family squabbles get in the way of the suspense. Also with Jack Warden and Dana Gladstone. **Director**—Peter Hyams. **(R)** *92 minutes*

PRESSURE POINT (1962)

★★★

Sidney Poitier
Bobby Darin

Captivating drama about a black prison psychiatrist, played by Poitier, struggling to deal with a violent inmate who's an American Nazi. The unusual story is quite engrossing, capturing the

(Continued)

(Continued)
tension surrounding a touchy subject. Darin is good as the hate-filled prisoner, and Poitier's professional and cool demeanor offers an effective contrast. Supporting roles by Peter Falk and Carl Benton Reid. **Director**—Hubert Cornfield. *91 minutes b&w*

PRESUMED INNOCENT (1990)

★★★

Harrison Ford
Bonnie Bedelia
Brian Dennehy
Raul Julia

A sharp, tension-filled whodunit based on Scott Turow's best-selling novel about a prosecutor who is tried for the murder of his ambitious female colleague. Ford stars as the luckless prosecutor, who wants to keep his affair with the woman, played by Greta Scacchi, out of the trial. As the provocative script unfolds, certain information is revealed about each of the characters, a device that serves as an exposé of the American judicial process. The key to the film's success is the tight script and intense performances by a top cast, including Paul Winfield and John Spencer in supporting roles. The film's major weakness is the heavy-handed framing device, which features a shot of a courtroom with Ford intoning about justice in voice-over narration. Alan J. Pakula directed the drama, which represents his most riveting work since *All the President's Men.* **(R)** *127 minutes*

PRETTY BABY (1978)

★★½

Brooke Shields
Keith Carradine

French director Louis Malle's first American film is about a 12-year-old prostitute (Shields) in New Orleans' legendary Storyville district in 1917. Carradine costars as Ernest James Bellocq, a real-life photographer known for his photos chronicling life in Storyville. The film relates a fictionalized account of Bellocq's relationship with the prostitutes he photographed, including marriage to the character played by Shields. The evocative cinematography by Sven Nykvist and set design by Polly Platt effectively recreate the era. The potentially shocking subject matter is handled tastefully. The title role is played with subtleness by Shields. Also with Susan Sarandon, Barbara Steele, Diana Scarwid, Francis Faye, and Antonio Fargas. **(R)** *109 minutes*

PRETTY IN PINK (1986)

Molly Ringwald
Andrew McCarthy
Jon Cryer

Molly Ringwald is romanced by Jon Cryer in Pretty in Pink.

Screenwriter/producer John Hughes, whose specialty is teens in turmoil, scores with this sensitive latter-day Cinderella story. Ringwald stars as the sweet but poor high-school senior who endures hostility from her wealthier classmates. She eventually attracts the attention of a charming and well-off boy (McCarthy). Adolescent insecurities are handled with sensitivity. Also with Annie Potts, Harry Dean Stanton, and James Spader. **Director**—Howard Deutsch. **(PG–13)** *96 minutes*

PRETTY WOMAN (1990)

★★★

Richard Gere
Julia Roberts

Though familiar plot elements abound, including echoes of *Pygmalion,* a touch of *Cinderella,* and the hooker-with-a-heart-of-gold story, this romantic comedy is topical, lighthearted, and thoroughly entertaining. Gere stars as a calculating corporate raider who falls in love with a young, unpretentious prostitute, played by Roberts. Both discover they have much in common, and their lives change for the better. Most of the comedy comes from Roberts' awkward attempts to fit in with the stuffy social set. The darker aspect of the material is diffused by keeping the sex scenes offscreen. The film exhibits the combination of sentiment and comedy that has always marked the work of director Garry Marshall *(Overboard; The Flamingo Kid; Nothing in Common).* The film ignited Roberts' career and helped revive Gere's. Also with Laura San Giacomo, Ralph Bellamy, Hector Elizondo, Jason Alexander, Alex Hyde-White, and Amy Yasbeck. **(R)** *119 minutes*

PRICK UP YOUR EARS (1987)

★★★

Gary Oldman
Alfred Molina

Young British playwright Joe Orton created a sensation in the mid-1960s with his controversial stage production *Entertaining Mr. Sloane.* He seemed at the start of a promising career when in 1967 he was brutally murdered by his male lover, Kenneth Halliwell. This sensitive film biography of Orton details his relationship with Halliwell and the events that led to his murder. Oldman, last seen as Sid Vicious in *Sid and Nancy,* is excellent as the ill-fated playwright, who was talented and witty but given to shockingly promiscuous behavior. What could have been sensationalistic material is here handled delicately and tastefully. Also with Vanessa Redgrave, Wallace Shawn, and Julie Walters. **Director**—Stephen Frears. **(R)** *108 minutes*

PRIDE AND PREJUDICE (1940)

★★★★

Laurence Olivier
Greer Garson

Delectable comedy of manners set in 19th-century England, about five sisters who want to get married. The film, based faithfully on the Jane Austen novel, sparkles with wit and effectively re-creates the period. Best of all, it features a splendid cast. Aldous Huxley was one of the screenwriters. Also with Edmund Gwenn, Mary Boland, Melville Cooper, Edna May Oliver, Ann Rutherford, and Maureen O'Sullivan. **Director**—Robert Z. Leonard. *116 minutes b&w*

THE PRIDE AND THE PASSION (1957)

Cary Grant
Sophia Loren
Frank Sinatra

This movie available with closed captions for the hearing impaired.

Slow historical adventure about Spanish guerrillas transporting a giant cannon across the countryside to use in the war against Napoleon. This adaptation of C.S. Forester's novel may not contain much humor the way the film version of his *The African Queen* did, but at least it's pictorially grand. Unfortunately, Grant, Sinatra, and Loren are miscast, and Stanley Kramer doesn't direct as much as organize. It's not kinetic but, as spectacle, it gives you your money's worth. Also with Theodore Bikel and Jay Novello. *132 minutes*

THE PRIDE OF ST. LOUIS (1952)

★★

Dan Dailey
Joanne Dru

Standard film biography of baseball great Jay Hanna Dean, better known as Dizzy Dean, with Dailey in the role of the extraordinary pitcher who later became a baseball announcer. Dailey's lanky physical appearance and easygoing image are well suited to the role, but the film is overly sentimental and not authentic. Also with Richard Haydn, Richard Crenna, and Hugh Sanders. **Director**—Harmon Jones. **Academy Award Nomination**—Guy Trosper, motion picture story. *93 minutes b&w*

PRIDE OF THE MARINES (1945)

★★★

John Garfield
Eleanor Parker
Dane Clark

Sentimental yet thoughtful account of a Marine who was blinded while fighting the Japanese during World War II. Garfield is convincing as brave fighting man Al Schmid, who struggles to adjust to his disability. Clark plays his buddy. An excellent production enhanced by fine performances. Also with John Ridgely, Rosemary DeCamp, and Tom D'Andrea. **Director**—Delmer Daves. **Academy Award Nomination**—Albert Maltz, screenplay. *119 minutes b&w*

THE PRIDE OF THE YANKEES (1942)

Gary Cooper
Teresa Wright

An exceptional film biography of Yankee baseball star Lou Gehrig. Cooper is just right in the role of the sports hero who died of amyotrophic lateral sclerosis (now commonly called Lou Gehrig's disease) at the peak of his astounding career; Wright plays Gehrig's wife. The film ends with Gehrig's emotional farewell in Yankee Stadium. The script by Jo Swerling and Herman Mankiewicz is touching but not maudlin. Also with Babe Ruth, Walter Brennan, Ludwig Stossel, Hardie Albright, and Dan Duryea. **Director**—Sam Wood. **Academy Award Nominations**—best picture; Cooper, best actor; Wright, best actress; Paul Gallico, original story; Mankiewicz and Swerling, screenplay; Rudolph Maté, cinematography. *128 minutes b&w*

PRIEST OF LOVE (1981)

Ian McKellen
Janet Suzman

A rather hollow film biography of controversial writer D.H. Lawrence, the author of *Lady Chatterley's Lover* and other much-censored novels. The story meanders from country to country as Lawrence, played adequately by McKellen, raves against the authorities and deals with a fatal case of tuberculosis. Of more interest is the role of his wife Frieda, played by Suzman, who was his inspiration and his protector. In any case, Lawrence's writings are far more engrossing than this story of his life. Also with Ava Gardner, Penelope Keith, Jorge Rivero, and John Gielgud. **Director**—Christopher Miles. **(R)** *125 minutes*

THE PRIME OF MISS JEAN BRODIE (1969)

Maggie Smith
Robert Stephens

Smith turns in an extraordinary, *tour-de-force* performance as an eccentric schoolteacher at a swank Edinburgh girls' school during the 1930s. The character's romantic ideals eventually lead to her downfall, and the film ends on a melancholy note. Represents Smith at the peak of her career. Based on the novel by Muriel Spark. Also stars Pamela Franklin, Gordon Jackson, and Celia Johnson. **Director**—Ronald Neame. **(PG) Academy Award**—Smith, best actress. *116 minutes*

THE PRIMROSE PATH (1940)

★★

Ginger Rogers
Joel McCrea
Marjorie Rambeau

Rogers stars as the scion of a family of hookers and boozers who wants to lead a virtuous life shared with hamburger-stand owner McCrea. An offbeat comedy/drama, directed unevenly by Gregory La Cava. Often humorous, the film eventually lapses into typical melodrama. **Academy Award Nomination**—Rambeau, best supporting actress. *93 minutes b&w*

THE PRINCE AND THE PAUPER (1978)

Mark Lester
Oliver Reed
Raquel Welch
Ernest Borgnine
George C. Scott
Rex Harrison
Charlton Heston

A robust costume adventure, based on Mark Twain's classic *The Prince and the Pauper.* An impressive cast enlivens the handsome saga about a ragged street urchin who trades identities with young Prince Edward of England. There's lots of derring-do and swashbuckling action to delight the kids and accompanying adults. Originally released as *Crossed Swords.* **Director**—Richard Fleischer. **(PG)** *113 minutes*

THE PRINCE AND THE SHOWGIRL (1957)

Laurence Olivier
Marilyn Monroe

(Continued)

Aristocrat Laurence Olivier and American Marilyn Monroe in The Prince and the Showgirl.

(Video icon) *This movie available on videotape and/or disc.*

(Continued)
Plush period comedy with Olivier and Monroe perfectly matched in contrasting roles. He plays a European aristocrat, and she's an American showgirl. The setting is the coronation of George V in London. They meet, and together they find love and understanding. The film's pace is slow, but the performances are delightful. The movie, based on Terence Rattigan's play *The Sleeping Prince*, costars Sybil Thorndike, Richard Wattis, and Jeremy Spencer. **Director**—Olivier. *127 minutes*

THE PRINCE OF DARKNESS (1987)

★★½

Donald Pleasence
Jameson Parker
Lisa Blount

Donald Pleasence as a priest who unlocks an evil force in The Prince of Darkness.

Director John Carpenter, whose classic *Halloween* changed the course of horror films, here fashions a modest supernatural thriller about the second coming of Satan. Pleasence stars as a Catholic priest who has uncovered something evil in the basement of an abandoned Los Angeles church. Character actor Victor Wong steals a few scenes as a physics professor who gathers a team of top graduate students to investigate the mysterious substance. Despite the potential of the premise, the dialogue is trite and lead actors Parker and Blount dull. Some interesting aspects of the storyline are doomed to the periphery, while the main plot focuses on turning the graduate students into zombies at a rapid rate. Still, fans of the horror genre should enjoy this latest entry by Carpenter. Also with Dennis Dun, Susan Blanchard, Dirk Blocker, and Alice Cooper. **(R)** *101 minutes*

THE PRINCE OF FOXES (1949)

★★

Tyrone Power
Orson Welles
Wanda Hendrix

Power plays a handsome adventurer who matches wits and arms against Cesare Borgia (Welles) in Renaissance Italy. The authentic costumes and settings are impressive, but except for the occasional duel or battle scene, the film is tedious. Technicolor would have enhanced this costume saga immensely. Also with Felix Aylmer, Everett Sloane, and Katina Paxinou. *107 minutes b&w*

THE PRINCE OF PENNSYLVANIA (1988)

★★

Keanu Reeves
Fred Ward
Amy Madigan

A confused drama about a sullen small-town teenager (Reeves) who rebels against his overbearing father (Ward). The familiar scenario becomes completely improbable when the boy and his girl friend (Madigan) kidnap the father to raise money for their escape from town. Also with Bonnie Bedelia, Jeff Hayenga, and Tracy Ellis. **Director**—Ron Nyswaner. **(R)** *87 minutes*

PRINCE OF THE CITY (1981)

★★★½

Treat Williams

Director Sidney Lumet's supercharged drama about a New York City undercover detective investigating corruption. The film evokes mixed emotions. The story is powerful and fascinating in its treatment of such issues as conscience, loyalty, and human emotions; yet it's too long and painfully complex. Williams excels as the double-agent cop who exposes his colleagues. There are good supporting performances from Jerry Orbach, Richard Foronjy, and Don Billett. **(R)** **Academy Award Nomination**—Jay Presson Allen and Lumet, best screenplay based on material from another medium. *167 minutes*

THE PRINCESS AND THE PIRATE (1944)

★★★

Bob Hope
Virginia Mayo

In this film, Hope and Mayo try to elude a sinister pirate, played by Victor McLaglen. Walter Slezak costars as a potentate. There's loads of wacky fun in this costume comedy. Other supporting roles are played by Walter Brennan, Marc Lawrence, and Hugo Maas. **Director**—David Butler. *94 minutes*

THE PRINCESS BRIDE (1987)

★★★ ®

Cary Elwes
Mandy Patinkin
Chris Sarandon

Cary Elwes and Robin Wright find true romantic love in The Princess Bride.

Director Rob Reiner fashions a postmodern fairy tale based on William Goldman's book. This romantic adventure has the necessary ingredients to be a typical children's fantasy—true love, swashbuckling sword fights, weird monsters, and a handful of special miracles—but they are presented in a self-conscious, tongue-in-cheek manner, making this enjoyable entertainment for adults. Lovely Robin Wright is ideally cast in the title role. An offbeat supporting cast, including comedian Billy Crystal, wrestler Andre the Giant, Wallace Shawn, and Christopher Guest, adds color to the tale. Reiner's flip humor and hip attitude toward the material, however, may put some viewers off. The film's theme song, "Storybook Love," by Willy DeVille was Oscar-nominated. **(PG)** *98 minutes*

® *This movie available with closed captions for the hearing impaired.*

THE PRINCIPAL (1987)

 ★★

James Belushi
Louis Gossett, Jr.

Troy Winbush, James Belushi, and J.J. Cohen in The Principal.

At Brandell High, a tough inner-city high school, the students major in drug dealing and extortion. Into this updated version of *The Blackboard Jungle* rides the new principal (Belushi) on his motorcycle to bring law and order to this alienated mob. After various bitter confrontations and a flurry of wisecracks, the job gets done. Gossett costars as the school's security chief, who agrees to help Belushi clean up Brandell High. Though the story lacks credibility and Belushi mugs a bit too much, there is enough action and humor to sustain some interest. Also with Rae Dawn Chong and Michael Wright. **Director**—Christopher Cain. **(R)** *110 minutes*

THE PRISONER OF ZENDA (1979)

 ★★

Peter Sellers
Lynne Frederick

Sellers plays multiple roles in this remake of the masquerade story about the king of Ruritania. Sellers reliably delivers some pleasing comedy and milks the listless material for more laughs than it's worth, but the film receives minimal help from director Richard Quine. Also with Lionel Jeffries, Elke Sommer, and Gregory Sierra. **(PG)** *101 minutes*

PRIVATE BENJAMIN (1980)

 ★★★

Goldie Hawn
Eileen Brennan

Hawn plays a pampered young woman who gets away from it all by joining the Army, where she wages comic warfare on the brass hats. Brennan plays her superior officer. The storyline is reminiscent of those "this is the Army" comedies popular in the 1940s and '50s. Here, however, the central characters are women instead of men. Hawn, who also served as coproducer, revitalized her career with this charming film, which contains a subtle message about women's need for independence. **Director**—Howard Zieff. **(R) Academy Award Nominations**—Hawn, best actress; Brennan, best supporting actress; Nancy Meyers, Charles Shyer, and Harvey Miller, best screenplay written directly for the screen. *110 minutes*

A PRIVATE FUNCTION (1985)

 ★★★

Michael Palin
Maggie Smith

Typically droll English comedy heightened by a fine cast of ensemble players. The setting is a Yorkshire village just after World War II when food rationing is in effect. A local chiropodist (Palin) kidnaps a pig destined for a banquet and hides it in his house, and raucous chaos develops. The film provides keen observations of the British lower class. Also with Denholm Elliott and Richard Griffiths. **Director**—Malcolm Mowbray. **(R)** *93 minutes*

PRIVATE LESSONS (1981)

 ★★

Eric Brown
Sylvia Kristel

A dubious comedy about a shy 15-year-old boy who's seduced by the family's attractive housekeeper. Brown stars as the naive boy, and Kristel plays the seductress. This low-budget film primarily exploits soft-core sex and contains frequent nude scenes. Howard Hesseman and Ed Begley, Jr., also star. **Director**—Alan Myerson. **(R)** *87 minutes*

THE PRIVATE LIFE OF HENRY VIII (1933)

 ★★★★

Charles Laughton
Elsa Lanchester

A classic movie about England's eccentric and much-married king. Laughton

Charles Laughton is the great Tudor king in The Private Life of Henry VIII.

is excellent as the 16th-century ruler who beheaded two wives and acquired four others. He adds dimension to the role by playing Henry VIII as both man and king. Lush production values also highlight this well-known historical drama. Lanchester plays Anne of Cleves. Other performances from Robert Donat, Miles Mander, Merle Oberon, and Binnie Barnes help make this film a gem. **Director**—Alexander Korda. **Academy Award**—Laughton, best actor. **Nomination**—best picture. *97 minutes b&w*

THE PRIVATE LIVES OF ELIZABETH AND ESSEX (1939)

 ★★★

Bette Davis
Errol Flynn
Olivia de Havilland

Davis stars as Queen Elizabeth I, a monarch in her 60s who is romantically involved, but politically at odds, with the Earl of Essex (Flynn), a man in his 20s. Maxwell Anderson's *Mary of Scotland* was a much more powerful historical film three years earlier; this was an adaptation of Anderson's *Elizabeth the Queen,* which became *Elizabeth and Essex* on the screen to accommodate costar Flynn, whose role was really subordinate (Davis wanted Laurence Olivier for the part). Though somewhat stodgy, the film boasts lush color photography and music, and a grand supporting cast including de Havilland, Donald Crisp as Francis Bacon, Vincent Price as Sir Walter Raleigh, Alan Hale, Henry Stephenson, Henry Daniell, Leo G. Carroll, and Nanette Fabray. Davis is well suited to the role she reprised in *The Virgin Queen.* **Academy Award Nomination**—Sol Polito and W. Howard Greene, cinematography. *106 minutes*

This movie available on videotape and/or disc.

PRIVATE SCHOOL (1983)

★

Phoebe Cates
Betsy Russell
Matthew Modine

A sleazy, threadbare, adolescent romp set in two private high schools, where the students are primarily concerned with sexual escapades. A deadpan Sylvia Kristel appears briefly as a sex education teacher. Other members of the cast are caught up in similar foolishness. This sort of teenage exploitation fare typically shows the kids in control while the adults appear foolish. Costars Martin Mull and Ray Walston. **Director**—Noel Black. **(R)** *82 minutes*

PRIVATES ON PARADE (1984)

★★★

John Cleese
Denis Quilley
Michael Elphick

A wacky entertainment troupe during World War II in Privates on Parade.

Wacky, witty English farce about the exploits of an Army entertainment troupe operating near Singapore just after World War II. Based on Peter Nichols' stage play, the uproarious film features sidesplitting song-and-dance numbers, clever dialogue, and excellent performances by a top cast of character actors. Cleese, of Monty Python fame, is droll and funny as the stuffy major in charge of this zany outfit. **Director**—Michael Blakemore. **(R)** *100 minutes*

PRIVATE'S PROGRESS (1956)

★★★

Ian Carmichael
Terry-Thomas

Delightful parody of the British Army, with plenty of good gags and lively scenes. An awkward young man is called to serve his country and everything goes haywire. This British version of *No Time for Sergeants* or *See Here, Private Hargrove* works effectively, thanks to a good script and a top cast of British actors. Also with Richard Attenborough, Dennis Price, Peter Jones, William Hartnett, and Ian Bannen. **Director**—John Boulting. *97 minutes b&w*

THE PRIZE (1963)

★★★

Paul Newman
Elke Sommer
Edward G. Robinson

Slick spy thriller set against the backdrop of the Nobel Prize awards in Stockholm. An American writer (Newman) finds himself involved in a plot to abduct a famous scientist (Robinson). The writer eventually becomes involved with the scientist's daughter (Sommer). The film, based on the Irving Wallace novel, is reminiscent in style of an Alfred Hitchcock thriller, but is too long to sustain suspense. The excellent cast also includes Diane Baker, Kevin McCarthy, and Leo G. Carroll. **Director**—Mark Robson. *135 minutes*

PRIZZI'S HONOR (1985)

★★★★

Jack Nicholson
Kathleen Turner

Kathleen Turner and Jack Nicholson share a demanding workload in Prizzi's Honor.

A Mafia hit man (Nicholson) and a hit woman (Turner) fall in love in this delectable, multilevel black comedy. Veteran director John Huston strikes the proper balance between satire and melodrama to fashion a bizarre, humorous film. Lead and supporting performances are consistently sensational. The complex plot is sometimes slow-moving. Not to everyone's taste. Costars Anjelica Huston (John's daughter), William Hickey, John Randolph, and Robert Loggia. **(R) Academy Award**—Anjelica Huston, best supporting actress. **Nominations**—best picture; John Huston, best director; Nicholson, best actor; Hickey, best supporting actor; Richard Condon and Janet Roach, best screenplay based on material from another medium. *130 minutes*

PROBLEM CHILD (1990)

John Ritter
Jack Warden
Amy Yasbeck
Gilbert Gottfried

A ridiculous comedy about the misadventures of a bratty seven-year-old boy who is adopted by a family right out of a television sitcom. Michael Oliver plays the red-haired devil, who photographs nuns in the shower, sets fire to his bedroom, drives the family car into a store window, and corresponds with a serial killer. The broad physical humor, which has the subtlety of a sledgehammer, fails to generate many laughs mostly because neither the screenwriters nor director Dennis Dugan could decide whether to make a dark satire or a warm-hearted tale with a lesson in love. **(PG)** *85 minutes*

THE PRODUCERS (1968)

Zero Mostel
Gene Wilder

The film is an audacious mixture of hilarity, brilliance, and bad taste; it's about a Broadway producer who cooks up a wild scheme to raise money from investors by staging a flop musical. He sells much more than 100 percent of the show, but the plan backfires when the production becomes a hit. The script is patchy, but there are some inventive, wild moments that keep the satire firmly afloat. The best scenes involve production of the play, entitled *Springtime for Hitler.* Mostel is funny as the hustling theater producer; Wilder plays Mostel's meek accountant. Good support, too, from Kenneth Mars, Dick Shawn, Renee Taylor, and Estelle Winwood. **Director**—Mel Brooks. **Academy Award**—Brooks, best story and screenplay written directly for the screen. **Nomination**—Wilder, best supporting actor. *88 minutes*

® This movie available with closed captions for the hearing impaired.

THE PROFESSIONALS (1966)

★★★1/2

Burt Lancaster
Lee Marvin
Ralph Bellamy
Claudia Cardinale

The Professionals *features Burt Lancaster and Lee Marvin as mercenaries.*

Rousing, spicy western about a band of mercenaries sent to Mexico to rescue the wife of a wealthy rancher from the clutches of a vile bandit. Bellamy plays the rancher, and Cardinale is his abducted wife. Lancaster and Marvin lead the band of mercenaries, and Jack Palance costars as the chief villain. The expedition across the border pits rugged men against rugged men, and the film bristles with excitement and suspense. An enjoyable latter-day western with some violent moments. Also with Robert Ryan and Woody Strode. **Director**—Richard Brooks. **(PG) Academy Award Nominations**—Brooks, best director and best screenplay based on material from another medium; Conrad Hall, cinematography. *117 minutes*

PROJECT X (1987)

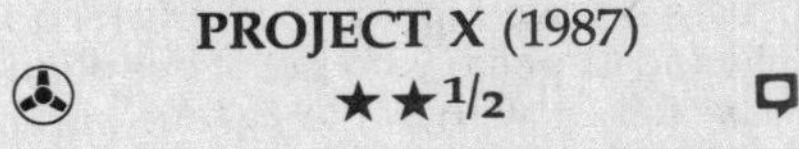

★★1/2

Matthew Broderick
Helen Hunt

Part animal-rights message and part suspense story, this film involves the plight of chimpanzees that are exposed to lethal doses of radiation at a Florida military base. Broderick stars as a young civil airman, assigned to care for the chimps, who questions the necessity of the Air Force research program that leads to the animals' deaths. To no one's surprise, the cute chimps upstage the human actors. Most of this monkey business is manipulative and pedestrian, except for a satisfying ending. **Director**—Jonathan Kaplan. **(PG)** *108 minutes*

PROMISED LAND (1988)

★★

Jason Gedrick
Tracy Pollan
Kiefer Sutherland
Meg Ryan

Meg Ryan, Kiefer Sutherland, Tracy Pollan, and Jason Gedrick in Promised Land.

The American dream does not live up to its promise in this labored melodrama about some small-town youths who face difficulties after completing high school. Gedrick stars as a former basketball star who becomes overwhelmed by college and decides to pursue a career as a cop. Sutherland costars as a shy young man who impulsively marries a wild girl with pink hair and a tattoo. Ryan stands out as this spaced-out wildcat. The thought-provoking premise involving unfulfilled lives and shattered dreams unfortunately gives way to a contrived ending with little dramatic tension. The video release runs 110 minutes. Also with Googy Gress and Jay Underwood. **Director**—Michael Hoffman. **(R)** *100 minutes*

PROMISES IN THE DARK (1979)

★★

Marsha Mason
Kathleen Beller

The right-to-die issue is taken up in this gloomy movie about a bright-eyed 17-year-old girl (Beller) who has terminal cancer. It's a difficult subject for a film, and here, the story is just a bland hype of tragic circumstances. The uninspired acting of Mason as the girl's gallant doctor also mars the film. Also with Ned Beatty, Susan Clark, Michael Brandon, and Paul Clemens. **Director**—Jerome Hellman. **(PG)** *115 minutes*

PROM NIGHT (1980)

★★

Jamie Lee Curtis
Leslie Nielsen

Curtis and veteran actor Nielsen star in this film about a masked killer who seeks revenge on teenagers attending a high-school prom. This Canadian-made melodrama smacks of such chillers as *Carrie* and *Halloween*. The murder scenes are gruesome, but they always seem to stop short of producing the shock effects expected of this sort of movie. Director Paul Lynch sets up a few tense moments, but most of the film is merely marking time while waiting for the killer to get into the act. Also with Eddie Benton. **(R)** *91 minutes*

PROTOCOL (1984)

★★

Goldie Hawn
Chris Sarandon
Cliff De Young

Goldie Hawn and Chris Sarandon star in Protocol.

This tailor-made Hawn vehicle gets off to a promising start but then falters at the halfway mark. Hawn plays a cocktail waitress in Washington who inadvertently becomes entangled in government diplomacy and Middle Eastern politics. It gets out of control when it turns to some "Miss Smith Goes to Washington" philosophizing. **Director**—Herbert Ross. **(PG)** *96 minutes*

PROVIDENCE (1977)

★

Dirk Bogarde
John Gielgud
Ellen Burstyn

French director Alain Resnais (*Last Year at Marienbad; Hiroshima, Mon Amour*)

(Continued)

This movie available on videotape and/or disc.

(Continued)
makes his first film in English with unfortunate results. The puzzling comedy is difficult to unravel. It's set inside the mind of a dying 78-year-old writer who drunkenly constructs a last novel about his family members. Most of the performances are feeble by way of miscasting or inadequate effort. The audience must work hard to fathom this film, which is actually a lot of fuss about nothing. Also with David Warner and Elaine Stritch. **(R)** *104 minutes*

PSYCHO (1960)

★★★★

Anthony Perkins
Vera Miles
John Gavin
Janet Leigh

Anthony Perkins and Janet Leigh at the Bates Motel in Psycho.

This classic horror story, based on the novel by Robert Bloch, is one of Alfred Hitchcock's masterpieces. Perkins plays the weird manager of a remote motel who isn't too accommodating to some of his guests. After a young woman and a private investigator hired to find her are killed, Perkins goes to great lengths to protect his mother. Watch for that legendary shower scene. An innovative film for the horror genre in terms of storyline and style. The fact that a major character (Leigh) was killed in the first third of the film was a shocking narrative device at that time. Even after three decades of imitations and parodies, the film is still effective. The recognizable musical score is by Bernard Herrmann. Also with John McIntire, Martin Balsam, and Simon Oakland. **(R) Academy Award Nominations**—Hitchcock, best director; Leigh, best supporting actress; John L. Russell, cinematography. *109 minutes b&w*

PSYCHO II (1983)

★★★

Anthony Perkins
Vera Miles
Meg Tilly

Anthony Perkins is back and looking for trouble in Psycho II.

This follow-up to the classic 1960 chiller is a workable spoof and a welcome homage to the master of suspense. Perkins once again portrays the frantic Norman Bates, now released from an insane asylum. He returns to the shabby motel and Victorian mansion seen in the original *Psycho,* and is soon up to his twitching eyebrows in murder and mystery. The inside jokes fall precisely into place, and there are ample shocks and eerie suprises. **Director**—Richard Franklin. **(R)** *113 minutes*

PSYCHO III (1986)

★★★

Anthony Perkins
Diana Scarwid
Jeff Fahey

The third installment in the saga of Norman Bates—this time directed by Perkins, who knows his character better than anyone. The original *Psycho* is such a familiar part of popular culture and has been emulated and parodied so many times that anything but a tongue-in-cheek approach to this film would have been anticlimactic. Here, Perkins' subtle mixture of horrific events, homage to the original film, and satire is perfectly suited to the material. The story involves a distressed young nun (Scarwid) who leaves a nearby convent after a horrible accident has killed one of her colleagues. The nun looks much like Marion Crane (Janet Leigh) of the original *Psycho,* and Norman is understandably shaken when she checks into his motel. Other events upset Norman as well, including a nosy reporter's snooping into Norman's past and present after the disappearance of a local resident, and the unsavory activities of an opportunistic drifter hired to help around the motel. Fans of the original film will appreciate this homage to Hitchcock's classic, while horror fans will be entertained by the witty dialogue and shocking murders. **(R)** *96 minutes*

PT 109 (1963)

★★

Cliff Robertson

Mildly interesting account of the wartime exploits of John F. Kennedy, who skippered a PT boat in the Pacific during World War II as a Navy lieutenant. The famous personality makes the story intriguing, but the film is long and routinely done. Robertson does well in the role of Kennedy. Also with Ty Hardin, Robert Blake, and James Gregory. **Director**—Leslie H. Martinson. *140 minutes*

PUBERTY BLUES (1981)

★★★

Nell Schofield
Jad Capelja

Australian Bruce Beresford (*Breaker Morant*) directed this poignant, sometimes humorous examination of adolescence. Set in a Sydney suburb, the film focuses on two high-school girls (Schofield and Capelja) who fret about popularity, fall in with some callous surfer boys, experiment with sex and drugs, and finally wise up. This subject has been thoroughly explored before, but Beresford offers a fresh and satisfying approach. **(R)** *86 minutes*

PUBLIC ENEMY (1931)

★★★★

James Cagney
Jean Harlow
Joan Blondell
Mae Clarke

Powerful, stunning gangster film starring Cagney, who starts out as a small-time hood but rises to the top as a notorious gangster. Cagney established his

® *This movie available with closed captions for the hearing impaired.*

reputation as a tough character in this film. The nerve-jangling story features some impressive and vivid scenes, including the scene where Cagney mashes a grapefruit into the face of Clarke. One of the three classic gangster films (along with *Scarface* and *Little Caesar*) that set the conventions of the genre. Costars Edward Woods and Donald Cook. **Director**—William Wellman. **Academy Award Nomination**—John Bright and Kubec Glasmon, original story. *85 minutes b&w*

PUMPING IRON (1977)

★★★

Arnold Schwarzenegger

This intelligent and lively documentary, about the subculture of bodybuilding, is based on the popular book by Charles Gaines and George Butler. It stars Schwarzenegger, that charming and spectacular champion of muscle men who calls himself a sculptor of his own body. There's a good deal of suspense about who will win the titles of Mr. Universe and Mr. Olympia. The film makes it clear that the object of all the strenuous and painful weight lifting isn't strength, but appearance. Stylishly directed by Butler and Robert Fiore. **(PG)** *85 minutes*

PUMPING IRON II: THE WOMEN (1985)

★★★

This sequel to the 1977 male bodybuilding documentary features women power lifters who compete for title recognition. The film follows the backstage maneuvering of four women who vie for the 1983 World Cup body-building championship at Caesar's Palace in Las Vegas. With Lori Bowen, Carla Dunlap, and Bev Francis. **Director**—George Butler. **(No MPAA rating)** *107 minutes*

THE PUMPKIN EATER (1964)

★★★

Anne Bancroft
Peter Finch

Solid acting by a fine cast enhances this melodramatic story about a thrice-married woman having husband trouble. Bancroft gives a superb performance as the bewildered and rather unstable mother of eight who finds yet another marriage falling apart. Finch costars as her u
film is executed
sitivity. Also with
Hardwicke, Magg
Porter. **Director**—Ja
emy Award Nom
best actress.

PUNCHLINE (1988)

★★

Tom Hanks
Sally Field

Sally Field and Tom Hanks ride the rough road of stand-up comedy in Punchline.

The painful underside of stand-up comedy is presented in this bittersweet comedy/drama. Hanks plays an unsuccessful medical student who wants to hit the big time as a comic; Field costars as a frustrated housewife with similar ambitions. They work at a Manhattan comedy club where fragile egos are hung out to dry. Both stars invest plenty of energy into their roles, but they can't do a lot with the second-rate screenplay and comedy routines. Also with Mark Rydell, Kim Greist, and Barry Sobel. **Director**—David Seltzer. **(R)** *123 minutes*

PURPLE HAZE (1983)

★★

Peter Nelson

Rambling, backward look at the volatile 1960s through the experiences of an alienated college dropout played by Nelson. The off-kilter story leans heavily on characters and situations similar to those in J.D. Salinger's *Catcher in the Rye;* the central character is even named Caulfield. Nothing new or interesting takes place and the film more or less lives up to its "hazy" title. Chuck McQuary and Bernard Baldan costar. **Director**—David Burton Morris. **(R)** *97 minutes*

...ARTS (1984)

te...
behind...
Anyone w...
mush deserve...
Sidney Furie. **(R)**

PURPLE RAIN (198...

★★★

Prince

Prince practices his come-hither look in this scene from Purple Rain.

Funk-rocker Prince sparkles when he's belting out the numerous songs in this semi-autobiographical musical. Otherwise, the backstage story is rather stiff, mean-spirited, and awkward. Various details of the young singer's tumultuous home life and a love affair with a beautiful vocalist (Apollonia Kotero) are highlighted. Yet Prince's Oscar-winning music takes center stage, with such hits as "When Doves Cry," "Darling Nikki," and the title song. Also with Jerome Benton, Clarence Williams III, Morris Day, and Olga Karlatos. **(R)** *113 minutes*

THE PURPLE ROSE OF CAIRO (1985)

★★★

Mia Farrow
Jeff Daniels

Woody Allen's delicate, comic oddity deftly explores the thin line between re-

(Continued)

This movie available on videotape and/or disc.

...s-
...a B-
...e screen
...h and witty
...ed by Farrow's
...ance. Also with
...ward Herrmann, and
... (PG) **Academy Award**
...**on**—Allen, best screenplay
...directly for the screen.
82 minutes

THE PURSUIT OF D. B. COOPER (1981)

★★★

Treat Williams
Robert Duvall

A spirited bit of tongue-in-cheek fiction based on the daredevil skyjacker who jumped from a 727 jet with $200,000 ransom and was never found. Williams is sensational as the slippery extortionist who leads an insurance company detective, played by Duvall, and other pursuers on a merry chase. The film owes much of its success to some slick energetic stunts. Also with Kathryn Harrold, Ed Flanders, R.G. Armstrong, and Paul Gleason. **Director**—Robert Spottiswoode. **(PG)** *100 minutes*

PUTNEY SWOPE (1969)

★★

Arnold Johnson
Allen Goorwitz (Garfield)
Antonio Fargas

Robert Downey was considered a counterculture director in the late 1960s and this is probably his funniest work. Johnson stars in the title role as a clever black advertising executive who leads a free-swinging, nonconforming agency to fame and fortune. It pokes fun at the materialist culture the 1960s generation was rebelling against. Also with Alan Abel and Mel Brooks. **(R)** *84 minutes*

PYGMALION (1938)

★★★★

Leslie Howard
Wendy Hiller
Wilfrid Lawson

George Bernard Shaw became the most illustrious Oscar winner in history ...e nabbed the award for his ...eenplay adaptation of his own de-...ightful comedy. Howard stars (and also codirected, with Anthony Asquith) as phonetics professor Henry Higgins, who tries to transform a common cockney flower seller (Hiller) into a dulcet-toned lady. Music by Arthur Honeggar. **Academy Awards**—Ian Dalrymple, Cecil Lewis, and W.P. Lipscomb, adaptation; Shaw, screenplay. **Nominations**—best picture; Howard, best actor; Hiller, best actress. *96 minutes b&w*

Q

Q (1982)

★★★

Michael Moriarty
David Carradine
Candy Clark

This is the kind of movie that *should* have been awful: It was directed by Larry Cohen, best known for *It's Alive!*; it has cheap, even ludicrous special effects; and it has a zany plot about a giant flying lizard that lives atop the Chrysler Building in New York City and eats rooftop sunbathers. Yet all the absurdity is tongue-in-cheek and is bolstered by first-rate acting. Moriarty plays an ex-junkie who discovers the lizard and employs it to eat his enemies. He brings a pathos to his part that is quite unexpected, and unnerving. Also with Richard Roundtree. **(R)** *92 minutes*

Q&A (1990)

★★★

Nick Nolte
Timothy Hutton
Armand Assante

Veteran director Sidney Lumet's penchant for socially conscious films is evidenced by this hard-hitting melodrama about corruption and racism within the New York City Police Department. Nolte gives a powerhouse performance as a tough, bigoted detective who murders a small-time Puerto Rican drug dealer, while Assante is magnificent as a Latin gangster. Hutton does well as a novice assistant D.A. who exposes the cover-up. Yet, this thoughtful film is weakened by a convoluted plot and a preachy point of view. Worth seeing for the performances and for Lumet's experienced direction. Also with Patrick O'Neal, Lee Richardson, Luis Guzman, Charles Dutton, Jenny Lumet, Leonard Cimino, and Paul Calderon. **(R)** *132 minutes*

QUADROPHENIA (1979)

★★★

Phil Daniels
Sting

Sting (center) with his group of mod young men in Quadrophenia.

This poignant British feature, with Daniels in the leading role, throbs with the music of the Who. But this isn't a rock-concert film; it's an entertaining drama that effectively illuminates the frustrations and conflicts of British youth in the 1960s. These are the disaffected young men and women who sought identity by joining such groups as the Mods or the Rockers. An excellent cast, which also includes Mark Wingett, Philip Davis, and Leslie Ash. **Director**—Franc Roddam. **(R)** *115 minutes*

QUEEN OF HEARTS (1989)

★★★ ®

Joseph Long
Anita Zagaria

A delightful, stylish family saga, which is told through the reminiscences of a young boy. A woman deserts an arranged marriage in Italy and then immigrates to London with her lover. There they build a large family, but the couple is later haunted by the woman's jilted fiancé. The film makes use of fantasy devices that serve as omens or pronouncements for the future, which may seem odd to viewers unaccustomed to foreign films. But the charming scenes of family members trying to make sense of life's mysteries are meaningful and worthwhile. Also with Vittorio Aman-

® *This movie available with closed captions for the hearing impaired.*

dola, Roberto Scateni, and Ian Hawkes. **Director**—Jon Amiel. **(PG)** *112 minutes*

QUEST FOR FIRE (1982)

★★★

Everett McGill
Ron Perlman
Rae Dawn Chong
Nameer El-Kadi

Both imagination and intelligence characterize this remarkable adventure of primitive people who inhabited the Earth 80,000 years ago. Unlike most films about prehistoric civilizations, this is an authentic-looking drama about man's struggle for survival and his acquisition of knowledge. The characters communicate by means of gestures and a guttural language developed by Anthony Burgess. A fascinating movie about early human life. **Director**—Jean-Jacques Annaud. **(R) Academy Award**—makeup. *97 minutes*

QUICK CHANGE (1990)

★★★

Bill Murray
Geena Davis
Randy Quaid

A low-key caper comedy starring Bill Murray as the ringleader of a funky trio of New York City bank robbers. The heist itself proves relatively easy, but the escape to the airport is complicated by problems found only in a big city—street crime, parking problems, street construction, cab drivers who can't speak English, surly clerks and service employees, etc. Fans of Murray may be somewhat disappointed in this quiet comedy, which lacks the physical humor usually associated with the comic actor *(Meatballs; Caddyshack)*. But the touch of farce in the misadventures of the unlucky thieves is sometimes amusing, sometimes charming. Based on the book by Jay Cronley. Also with Bob Elliott (formerly of the comedy team Bob and Ray), Phillip Bosco, Tony Shalhoub, and Jason Robards. **Directors**—Murray and Howard Franklin. **(R)** *88 minutes*

QUICKSILVER (1986)

★★

Kevin Bacon
Jami Gertz

Heavily contrived tale starring Bacon as a young, hotshot stockbroker who loses

Kevin Bacon rebounds from career disaster to become a bicycle messenger in Quicksilver.

a fortune in the market and then becomes a bicycle messenger. The film is overstuffed with various plot complications, and the farfetched story never develops believable characters or situations. A loud rock score and such gimmicks as bicycle break-dancing get in the way of the storyline. Paul Rodriguez and Rudy Ramos costar. **Director**—Tom Donnelly. **(PG)** *106 minutes*

THE QUIET AMERICAN (1958)

★★

Michael Redgrave
Audie Murphy

A diluted film version of Graham Greene's complex novel about an American who goes to Vietnam with vague plans for ending the fighting. Murphy is not particularly effective in the title role, but the film offers some notable performances by the rest of the cast. Redgrave plays the journalist who's deceived into betraying Murphy to the communists. Also with Claude Dauphin, Bruce Cabot, Giorgia Moll, and Richard Loo. **Director**—Joseph L. Mankiewicz. *122 minutes b&w*

QUIET COOL (1986)

★★1/2

James Remar
Adam Coleman Howard
Nick Cassavetes

Predictable but frequently exciting action/adventure featuring Remar as a New York City cop who becomes embroiled in a Pacific Northwest drug war. Murder, revenge, and other standard elements of this sort of melodrama are played out against a picturesque forest backdrop. Action fans won't be disappointed; the cop brandishes a .44 Magnum, while the backwoods youth (Howard) who becomes his ally is a terror with a longbow fitted with explosive arrows. Cassavetes, son of actors John Cassavetes and Gena Rowlands, is impressive as the stone-faced dope-grower who will do anything to protect his crop. Directed with visual flourish by Clay Borris. **(R)** *80 minutes*

THE QUIET MAN (1952)

John Wayne
Maureen O'Hara

John Wayne and Maureen O'Hara in The Quiet Man.

Highly entertaining story about an ex-prizefighter who settles down in his native Ireland and woos a willful Irish lass. One of director John Ford's most popular films, it boasts excellent production values, a beautiful score by Victor Young, and a winning combination of drama and humor. Wayne, who was often unappreciated by the critics, is perfectly suited to the title role. There are other outstanding performances from Barry Fitzgerald, Victor McLaglen, and Ward Bond. Also with Mildred Natwick, Francis Ford, and Arthur Shields. **Academy Awards**—Ford, best director; Winton C. Hoch and Archie Stout, cinematography. **Nominations**—best picture; McLaglen, best supporting actor; Frank S. Nugent, screenplay. *129 minutes*

QUINTET (1979)

★

Paul Newman

Director Robert Altman's fantasy of apocalypse. In a bleak, ice-crusted city, survivors play a deadly backgam-

(Continued)

This movie available on videotape and/or disc.

Paul Newman and Brigitte Fossey in their icy world in Quintet.

(Continued)

monlike game where the winners murder the losers. It's a tedious movie about a relentlessly gloomy world. Newman heads the international cast, which also includes Vittorio Gassman, Fernando Rey, Bibi Andersson, and Nina Van Pallandt. Even Altman devotees may have a hard time sitting through this one. **(R)** *110 minutes*

QUO VADIS (1951)

★★★

Robert Taylor
Deborah Kerr
Peter Ustinov

Lavish Hollywood extravaganza about the plight of Christians under the heavy hand of Roman Emperor Nero. Rome burns, the lions eat some Christians, and Taylor plays a Roman soldier who romances Kerr. The film is much too long for the material, and eventually becomes tedious, but there are moments of impressive acting and some spectacular scenes. Director Mervyn LeRoy was brought in to replace John Huston. Also with Leo Genn, Patricia Laffan, Finlay Currie, and Buddy Baer. **Academy Award Nominations**—best picture; Genn and Ustinov, best supporting actor; Robert Surtees and William V. Skall, cinematography. *171 minutes*

R

RACE FOR YOUR LIFE, CHARLIE BROWN (1977)

★★

The mere appearance of the lovable Peanuts gang should delight the kids, but this third animated screen feature of the famous comic strip is showing some wear. This time Charlie Brown and his pals are packed off to summer camp, where they give their neuroses the usual workout. The plot rambles, and the animation seems flat. Charles M. Schulz, creator of the comic strip, wrote the screenplay. **Director**—Bill Melendez. **(G)** *75 minutes*

RACE WITH THE DEVIL (1975)

★

Peter Fonda
Warren Oates

An adolescent, farfetched horror film about four vacationers who are chased by a group of devil-worshippers after stumbling upon a ritual killing in Texas. Fonda, Oates, Loretta Swit, and Lara Parker are the vacationers. Also with R.G. Armstrong. **Director**—Jack Starrett. **(PG)** *88 minutes*

RACHEL, RACHEL (1968)

★★★½

Joanne Woodward
Estelle Parsons

Joanne Woodward and James Olson star in Rachel, Rachel.

Woodward is splendid as a schoolteacher in this deeply moving portrait of a middle-aged spinster facing a midlife crisis. She's lonely, frustrated, and trapped in a small New England town. Parsons plays one of her colleagues. Under Paul Newman's direction, the film is a naturalistic slice of life rather than a melodramatic soap opera. Also with James Olson, Kate Harrington, Geraldine Fitzgerald, Donald Moffat, Terry Kiser, and Bernard Barrow. **Academy Award Nominations**—best picture; Woodward, best actress; Parsons, best supporting actress; Stewart Stern, best screenplay based on material from another medium. **(R)** *101 minutes*

RACING WITH THE MOON (1984)

★★★ Q®

Sean Penn
Elizabeth McGovern

Sean Penn finds that being young is not always easy in Racing with the Moon.

A sensitive and nostalgic romantic drama, which looks at the transition to adulthood among some youths in a small California town during World War II. Director Richard Benjamin expertly captures the flavor of the period, and the young, talented cast turns in some impressive performances. Penn and McGovern are appealing as lovers faced with dramatic changes in their lives because of the war. Nicolas Cage, John Karlen, Rutanya Alda, and Carol Kane costar. **(PG)** *110 minutes*

RADIO DAYS (1987)

★★★½

Mia Farrow
Julie Kavner
Michael Tucker
Dianne Wiest

Woody Allen takes us down memory lane to a time when radio dominated the airwaves and stirred our imaginations. This special comedy consists of insightful vignettes involving a Jewish, working-class family in Brooklyn during World War II. Allen, as narrator, writer, and director, weaves together several episodes illustrating radio's profound influence, while contrasting the lives of the hardworking family with the glamour of the radio stars. This film

Q® *This movie available with closed captions for the hearing impaired.*

should be especially appealing to those who lived during the era. Also with Seth Green, Josh Mostel, Danny Aiello, and Wallace Shawn. **Academy Award Nominations**—Allen, best original screenplay; Santo Loquasto, Carol Joffe, Les Bloom, and George DeTitta, Jr., best art direction. **(PG)** *88 minutes*

A RAGE TO LIVE (1965)

Suzanne Pleshette
Bradford Dillman
Ben Gazzara

This screen version of John O'Hara's popular novel about a woman of easy virtue has been marred by a heavy-handed Hollywood treatment. The film lacks the irony that characterizes most of O'Hara's work. Pleshette does as well as can be expected as the near-nymphomaniac who discovers she needs more in life than just a husband. Also with James Gregory, Peter Graves, Bethel Leslie, and Ruth White. **Director**—Walter Grauman.
101 minutes b&w

RAGGEDY ANN AND ANDY (1977)

This animated cartoon, based on Johnny Gruelle's famous children's stories, is a technical achievement of sorts—but the $4-million project fails to deliver enough satisfying entertainment for youngsters or adults. It's about two rag dolls who encounter a variety of unappealing creatures that screech and gurgle in a monotonous and ill-humored fashion. Songs by Joe Raposo of *Sesame Street* all seem to sound the same; they lack the lighthearted charm of those in Disney's cartoon features. **Director**—Richard Williams. **(G)**
87 minutes

RAGGEDY MAN (1981)

 ★★½

Sissy Spacek
Eric Roberts

Spacek is convincing as a lonely divorcée with two sons in a small Texas town in the mid-1940s. She has a brief affair with a sailor, played by Roberts. The film begins as a charming, sensitive love story, but events turn sour as the sailor abruptly leaves, and Spacek is at

Sissy Spacek is a divorced mother in Raggedy Man.

the mercy of two redneck brutes. Beautifully photographed and filled with meticulous detail, the film features an authentic and nostalgic re-creation of small-town life during the war. The violent ending, however, seems at odds with the rest of the film. Director Jack Fisk is an art director by trade, and also Spacek's husband in real life. Also with Sam Shepard and R.G. Armstrong. **(PG)** *94 minutes*

RAGING BULL (1980)

Robert De Niro
Cathy Moriarty
Joe Pesci

Director Martin Scorsese's hard-hitting, high-voltage characterization of middle-weight champ Jake La Motta is a brilliant study of brutality and torment in and out of the ring. De Niro, in the title role, stunningly portrays the Bronx Bull in a grim, unsentimental performance. There's credible support from Pesci and Moriarty in their first major film roles. The brief, supercharged boxing scenes are perhaps the best ever filmed, and are enhanced by the Oscar-winning editing of Thelma Schoonmaker. Also with Frank Vincent and Nicholas Colsanto. **(R) Academy Award**—De Niro, best actor. **Nominations**—best picture; Scorsese, best director; Pesci, best supporting actor; Moriarty, best supporting actress; Michael Chapman, cinematography. *128 minutes b&w*

RAGTIME (1981)

 ★★★

Brad Dourif
Howard E. Rollins, Jr.
James Cagney
Elizabeth McGovern
Mary Steenburgen

Exquisite period detail, impeccable photography, and impressive acting by a large, first-rate cast characterize this screen adaptation of E.L. Doctorow's multifaceted novel about America at the turn of the century. Despite these advantages, the movie is seriously hampered by the complications of the plot. The movie's running time isn't long enough to figure out the convoluted story, and much of the film's punch and style are lost in the confusion. Old pro Cagney plays a crusty police commissioner, and Rollins makes an impressive appearance as a young black piano player who takes extreme measures to soothe his wounded pride. The musical score was written by Randy Newman. Also with Moses Gunn, Donald O'Connor, Debbie Allen, Kenneth McMillan, James Olson, Mandy Patinkin, and Norman Mailer. **Director**—Milos Forman. **(PG) Academy Award Nominations**—Rollins, best supporting actor; McGovern, best supporting actress; Michael Weller, best screenplay based on material from another medium; Miroslav Ondricek, cinematography.
156 minutes

RAIDERS OF THE LOST ARK (1981)

 ★★★★

Harrison Ford
Karen Allen

Harrison Ford and Karen Allen remember the past in Raiders of the Lost Ark.

George (*Star Wars*) Lucas and Steven (*Jaws*) Spielberg joined talents to make this rip-roaring, thrill-a-minute adventure. Ford plays Indiana Jones, a stubborn, rough-and-ready archaeologist who races the Nazis to find a lost ark supposedly containing remnants of the Ten Commandments. Allen is the independent and strong-willed leading lady who helps him in this undertaking. The

(Continued)

This movie available on videotape and/or disc.

(Continued)
exotic, action-packed film harks back to those derring-do serials of the 1930s and 1940s, but this version is blessed with magnificent technical sophistication. It's the ultimate in escapist entertainment. The film won an Academy Award for its breathtaking editing by Michael Kahn. Also with Paul Freeman, Ronald Lacey, John Rhys-Davies, Wolf Kahler, and Denholm Elliott. **Director**—Spielberg. **(PG) Academy Award Nominations**—best picture; Spielberg, best director; Douglas Slocombe, cinematography. *115 minutes*

THE RAINBOW (1989)

★★★

Sammi Davis
Glenda Jackson

Director Ken Russell, who succeeded with a film version of D.H. Lawrence's *Women In Love* in 1969, continues on with this prequel to the story of the English farming family. The drama chronicles the struggles of Ursula Brangwen (Davis) to achieve personal and sexual independence. Impressive acting helps illuminate the motives of the characters. Although elegant and sincere, this film is not as compelling as the earlier drama. Jackson, an Oscar winner for *Women In Love,* effectively plays Ursula's mother. Also with Amanda Donohoe, Paul McGann, David Hemmings, Christopher Gable, and Ken Colley. **(R)** *104 minutes*

RAINBOW BRITE AND THE STAR STEALER (1985)

 ★ 

Nasty Toad Slurthie pursues our heroine in Rainbow Brite and the Star Stealer.

Syrupy-sweet children's fantasy based on animated characters created by Hallmark Properties. The heroine of the title is a cheerful little girl who brings happiness and rainbow colors to the world. She's challenged by an evil princess with contrary ambitions. The action is bland and the characters shallow in this below-average cartoon feature. **Director**—Bernard Deyries. **(G)** *97 minutes*

THE RAINMAKER (1956)

★★★

Katharine Hepburn
Burt Lancaster

Film adaptation of N. Richard Nash's hit play built around the character of Starbuck, a phoney rainmaker who's more successful at seducing a confirmed spinster than making rain. Lancaster is well suited to the charismatic title role as a dreamer who tries to make things happen simply by believing he can do so; Hepburn, by contrast, plays a spinster who has pragmatically accepted what she believes to be her lot in life. The film looks very much like a filmed play with stagy sets and broad acting styles, but that approach suits the material, which is laden with symbolism and metaphor. Also with Wendell Corey, Lloyd Bridges, Earl Holliman, and Wallace Ford. **Director**—Joseph Anthony. **Academy Award Nomination**—Hepburn, best actress. *121 minutes*

RAIN MAN (1988)

★★★★

Dustin Hoffman
Tom Cruise

Hoffman dominates this intriguing drama with a show-stopping performance as an autistic idiot savant. His character, although mentally retarded, is a walking calculator who can memorize the contents of a phone book. Cruise is effective as the slick younger brother who seeks to exploit his brother's abilities and grab part of the three-million-dollar inheritance left to his mentally deficient sibling. Certain sentimental scenes in this unorthodox road movie seem faintly contrived, but Hoffman's virtuoso performance compensates for any drawbacks. There are some fine moments of humor as well as a touching ending. **Director**—Barry Levinson. **(R) Academy Awards**—best picture; Levinson, best director; Hoffman, best actor; Ronald Bass and Barry Morrow, best original screenplay. **Nominations**—John Seale, cinematography; Ida Random and Linda DeScenna, art direction; Stu Linder, editing; Hans Zimmer, original score. *140 minutes*

RAINTREE COUNTY (1957)

★★★

Montgomery Clift
Elizabeth Taylor

Elizabeth Taylor is out to get her man in Raintree County.

Taylor and Clift, with the help of an excellent supporting cast, keep this rambling Civil War story from becoming too plodding. Taylor portrays a southern belle who stops at nothing to get what she wants. But when she gets her man, happiness still eludes her, and the war eventually tears her world apart. Clift plays her romantic interest. Originally released at 187 minutes. Also with Eva Marie Saint, Nigel Patrick, Lee Marvin, Rod Taylor, and Agnes Moorehead. **Director**—Edward Dmytryk. **Academy Award Nomination**—Taylor, best actress. *166 minutes*

RAISE THE TITANIC (1980)

★½

Jason Robards
Richard Jordan
Anne Archer

There are some striking visual effects to simulate the resurrection of the famous ocean liner from the deep, but the script and direction should be relegated to Davy Jones' locker. This bloated film wastes considerable time with cardboard characters who talk too much at the expense of the events surrounding the ship-raising. The plot concerns the urgent recovery of a mysterious ore on board the vessel so the Russians can't grab it. The film will seem dated since the discovery of the *Titanic* in 1985. Also with David Selby, Alec Guinness, and J.D. Cannon. **Director**—Jerry Jameson. **(PG)** *112 minutes*

RAISING ARIZONA (1987)

★★

Nicolas Cage
Holly Hunter

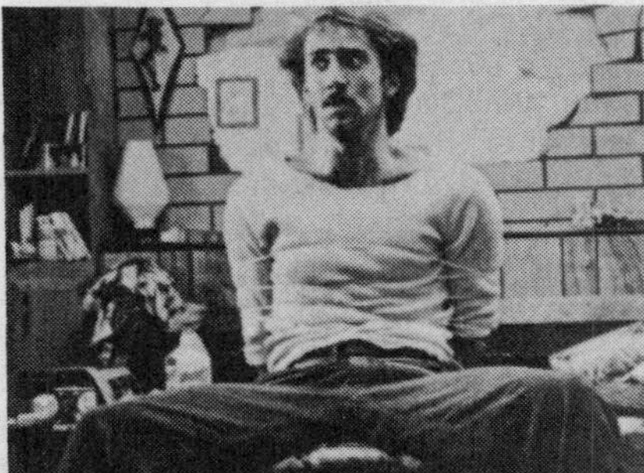

Nicolas Cage is all tied up in Raising Arizona.

Joel and Ethan Coen, who directed and produced the stylish *Blood Simple*, have difficulty here handling comedy. This comic adventure begins with a lively opening sequence but then sags in the middle and end. Cage plays a two-bit criminal who marries a cop (Hunter). Unable to have children, the couple kidnaps one of the infant quintuplets of a furniture-store magnate. Various characters intrude on the young family attempting to steal the valuable baby, and the film ends with a familiar car-chase sequence. Though some scenes are genuinely funny, most of the characters in this shrill comedy are exaggerated and presented as being incompetent or stupid, making the film seem smug and condescending. Also with Randall "Tex" Cobb, John Goodman, Trey Wilson, and William Forsythe. **(PG–13)** *94 minutes*

A RAISIN IN THE SUN (1961)

★★★★

Sidney Poitier
Ruby Dee
Claudia McNeil

This was one of the first commercial films to make an honest attempt to deal with the black experience in a realistic and sensitive manner. This tale of a black family in Chicago attempting to leave the ghetto to live in an all-white neighborhood is enhanced by the fine acting of Poitier, Dee, and McNeil. The movie doesn't differ much from Lorraine Hansberry's Broadway play; the dialogue still bristles, and the story makes a sharp impact. Also with Diana Sands, Ivan Dixon, John Fiedler, and Lou Gossett, Jr. **Director**—Daniel Petrie. *128 minutes b&w*

RALLY 'ROUND THE FLAG, BOYS! (1958)

★★

Paul Newman
Joanne Woodward

Hollywood mishandles this film version of Max Shulman's witty novel about Putnam's Landing, a small community upset over a proposed missile base. Newman and Woodward, who play a couple involved in the controversy, lack the comic acting touch needed to salvage this comedy. The script fails to bring the humor and charm of the book onto the screen. Jack Carson, Joan Collins, and Tuesday Weld also star. **Director**—Leo McCarey. *106 minutes*

RAMBO: FIRST BLOOD PART II (1985)

★★

Sylvester Stallone

Armed and dangerous: Sylvester Stallone in Rambo: First Blood Part II.

An orgy of blood, violence, and destruction overwhelms this mindless second installment in the saga of the sullen Vietnam veteran played by Stallone. This time, the alienated Green Beret is on a one-man commando mission in Vietnam to find missing Americans. He carries out his assignment with minimal dialogue and massive use of gunfire, explosions, and blood-spattering mayhem. Amid the noise, the film makes an absurd, shallow statement on America's involvement in the Vietnam War. Also with Steve Berkoff, Charles Napier, Richard Crenna, and Julia Nickson. **Director**—George P. Cosmatos. **(R)** *93 minutes*

RAMBO III (1988)

★★½

Sylvester Stallone
Richard Crenna

This third and expensive installment in Stallone's saga of the disillusioned Vietnam vet offers maximum bang for the buck. This time Rambo infiltrates a Russian stronghold in Afghanistan to rescue his friend and mentor, Col. Trautman (Crenna), who has been captured by the Russians as a spy. The plot and dialogue have been pared down to a minimum here, but this actually works to the film's advantage. A variety of choreographed action scenes—from a simple bout of stickfighting to the final confrontation involving complex, state-of-the-art weaponry—highlights the fast-paced film, which is much like a comic book brought to life. Fans of this type of action/adventure saga will not be disappointed; others may find the violence too extreme. Former cinematographer Peter MacDonald directs for the first time here and does an adequate, if not particularly memorable, job. Stallone also cowrote the script. Also with Marc de Jonge, Kurtwood Smith, Spiras Focas, Sasson Gabai, and Doudi Shoua. **(R)** *101 minutes*

RAMROD (1947)

★★

Veronica Lake
Joel McCrea
Charles Ruggles

Lake plays a ruthless rancher in this western story about a territorial dispute. She hires a rough and vicious foreman to assist her in a confrontation with her father, played by Ruggles. There are several deaths and a stampede before the issues are resolved. Also with Preston Foster and Lloyd Bridges. **Director**—Andrè De Toth. *94 minutes b&w*

RAN (1985)

★★★

Tatsuya Nakadai
Akira Terao

Peter (left) and Tatsuya Nakadai share a privileged moment in Ran.

Legendary Japanese filmmaker Akira Kurosawa borrows from the plot of Shakespeare's *King Lear* for this epic film set in 15th-century feudal Japan. An aging patriarch passes his power to the eldest of his three sons, losing the respect and loyalty of his youngest son in the process. A power struggle erupts among the three siblings, resulting in bloodshed, betrayal, and a loss of honor. Though slow-moving and long, the film is highlighted by beautiful cinematography and spectacular battle sequences, which are ballet-like in their artfully choreographed movements. The film was nominated for Oscars in several minor categories, including cinematography and best art direction, and won for best costume design. Also with Jinpachi Nezu, Daisuke Ryu, and Mieko Harada. **(R) Academy Award Nomination**—Kurosawa, best director. *160 minutes*

RANCHO DELUXE (1975)

★★★

Jeff Bridges
Sam Waterston

A kinky comedy of the tamed West, where modern buckaroos ride around in pickup trucks and fat-cat ranchers roam the range via helicopters. Bridges and Waterston star as aimless, latter-day cattle rustlers whose antics include sawing up steers with a chainsaw and holding a prize bull for ransom in a motel room. Screenwriter Thomas McGuane cleverly injects some offbeat dialogue into the script, and director Frank Perry emphasizes the freewheeling spirit of the characters, whose lives are essentially being wasted. Also with Elizabeth Ashley, Charlene Dallas, Clifton James, Harry Dean Stanton, and Slim Pickens. **(R)** *93 minutes*

RANDOM HARVEST (1942)

★★★

Ronald Colman
Greer Garson

Colman and Garson star in this sentimental romance about an amnesia sufferer who forgets the woman he loves. Colman plays a shell-shocked army officer who escapes from an asylum. Garson dutifully becomes his secretary as she attempts to rekindle the relationship he can't recall. The superior acting of this splendid duo prevents an unbelievable plot, based on a James Hilton novel, from becoming too maudlin. Also with Susan Peters, Philip Dorn, Reginald Owen, Una O'Connor, and Peter Lawford. **Director**—Mervyn LeRoy. **Academy Award Nominations**—best picture; LeRoy, best director; Colman, best actor; Peters, best supporting actress; George Froeschel, Claudine West, and Arthur Wimperis, screenplay. *126 minutes b&w*

RANSOM (1956)

★★

Glenn Ford
Donna Reed

Ford gives an uneven performance as an industrialist who debates whether to pay the ransom when his son is kidnapped. The story has been done better before and since, but there's enough suspense to keep the film interesting. Ford gets competent support from Leslie Nielsen, Juano Hernandez, Juanita Moore, and Robert Keith. **Director**—Alex Segal. *104 minutes b&w*

RASHOMON (1951)

★★★★

Toshiro Mifune
Machiko Kyo
Masayuki Mori
Takashi Shimura

This film, which brought director Akira Kurosawa international recognition, created a sensation at the Venice Film

Rashomon: *Machiko Kyo defends herself against bandit Toshiro Mifune.*

Festival and won the Oscar as best foreign film. It's a *tour de force*—built entirely around one incident. In medieval Japan, a merchant and his wife are attacked in the woods by a bandit. The merchant is killed, the wife raped. The incident is seen through the eyes of each of the protagonists—the three participants, and a woodcutter who witnessed the event. Each has a different version of the event, which emphasizes the main theme that truth is relative, not real. With unusually vivid imagery and soundtrack, the film probes into what motivates human behavior at its deepest level. Originally filmed in Japanese. **Academy Award**—best foreign-language film. *90 minutes b&w*

RATBOY (1986)

★

Sondra Locke
Robert Townsend
Christopher Hewett

The pitiful outcast called Ratboy *(S.L. Baird) takes refuge from the storm.*

An out-of-work journalist (Locke) discovers a woeful boy with ratlike features and attempts to turn him into a celebrity. Obviously a fable about the plight of an outsider in our sometimes rigid and heartless society, the film never fleshes out the character of this unlikely

hero and the story soon meanders out of control. Actress S.L. Baird in the title role has few lines, resulting in little sympathy for her character. This unsuccessful fable represents Locke's first directorial effort. The rat makeup was designed by Rick Baker. **(PG–13)**
104 minutes

THE RAT RACE (1960)

★★½

Tony Curtis
Debbie Reynolds

Curtis stars as a young jazz musician and Reynolds plays a dancer in this comedy/drama based on the Garson Kanin play. The story of show business people trying to make it in New York City has been told many times before, but the background settings, filmed on location, give the film an authentic look. In addition, Jack Oakie, Kay Medford, and Don Rickles deliver interesting characterizations of native New Yorkers. **Director**—Robert Mulligan.
105 minutes

THE RAVEN (1963)

★★

Vincent Price
Peter Lorre
Boris Karloff

The cast—Price, Lorre, Karloff, and Jack Nicholson—prevents this horror film from becoming a horrible bore. Though supposedly "inspired" by the Edgar Allan Poe poem, the plot, involving two sorcerers who team up against a fellow conjurer, has little to do with the poem. A climactic sorcerers' duel, in which the 15th-century conjurers battle each other in a deadly duel of magic, is the best part of the film. The wide-screen compositions will be lost on the small screen. Also with Hazel Court. **Director**—Roger Corman. **(G)** *86 minutes*

RAW DEAL (1986)

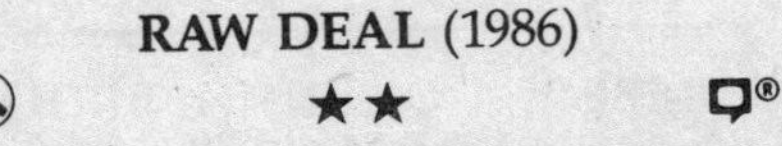

Arnold Schwarzenegger
Kathryn Harrold
Darren McGavin

Badly executed action drama starring Schwarzenegger as an ex-FBI agent on a special mission for his former supervisor (McGavin). Schwarzenegger must infiltrate the Chicago mob to discover

Arnold Schwarzenegger is on a special mission in Raw Deal.

how they are able to track down and execute the FBI's key witnesses in mob-related cases. Obviously there is a leak in the Bureau's ranks, and Schwarzenegger must find it. The story is similar in structure to Schwarzenegger's *Commando,* where a one-man army equipped with the latest in firepower is the only force capable of performing an impossible task. Here this plot formula is too familiar and unoriginal to elicit much excitement. The film is further hampered by trite dialogue weakly delivered by Schwarzenegger. The action scenes, on which films of this type are so dependent, are sloppy in terms of direction and editing. Also with Sam Wanamaker, Paul Shenar, Robert Davi, and Ed Lauter. **Director**—John Irvin. **(R)** *106 minutes*

RAWHIDE (1951)

★★

Tyrone Power
Susan Hayward

A gang of four desperate outlaws terrorizes Power and Hayward at a remote stagecoach station in this suspenseful but slow-moving western. The shootout at the end highlights this film. A remake of a gangster film entitled *Show Them No Mercy.* Hugh Marlowe, Jack Elam, Dean Jagger, George Tobias, Edgar Buchanan, and Jeff Corey also star. **Director**—Henry Hathaway. **Alternate Title**—*Desperate Siege.* *86 minutes b&w*

THE RAZOR'S EDGE (1946)

★★★

Tyrone Power
Gene Tierney

Long and glossy version of W. Somerset Maugham's famous philosophical novel about a wealthy young man's search for faith. It becomes a rambling and tedious film, but some fine acting salvages this long movie. Power portrays the hero seeking goodness in life; Tierney is a social climber who rejects Power; Anne Baxter plays an alcoholic; Herbert Marshall plays the author; and Elsa Lanchester sparkles in a small role as a social secretary. Clifton Webb and John Payne also star. **Director**—Edmund Goulding. **Academy Award**—Baxter, best supporting actress. **Nominations**—best picture; Webb, best supporting actor. *146 minutes b&w*

THE RAZOR'S EDGE (1984)

Bill Murray
Theresa Russell
Catherine Hicks

Scarred by World War I, Bill Murray traverses The Razor's Edge.

A glossy but uneven version of W. Somerset Maugham's novel, which was originally adapted to the screen in 1946. Funnyman Bill Murray plays the disillusioned World War I veteran who wanders through Europe and Asia seeking escape and inner peace. Murray tries his utmost to handle the serious drama, but his portrayal comes off as strained and awkward. The film is further hampered by its length and languid pace. Also with Denholm Elliott, James Keach, and Brian Doyle Murray. **Director**—John Byrum. **(PG-13)** *130 minutes*

REAL GENIUS (1985)

Val Kilmer

This loony comic adventure involves some young, off-the-wall science whiz-
(Continued)

Val Kilmer and Gabe Jarret try to foil their professor's plans in Real Genius.

zes at a technical college, who try to stop villainous government employees from using their research to develop a laser weapon. From this unpromising story, director Martha Coolidge pulls out many genuinely hilarious moments and characterizations. The film is enhanced by fine performances from young stars Kilmer, Gabe Jarret, and Michelle Meyrink. Real genius it's not, but it is a refreshingly appealing screwball comedy—1980s style. **(PG)**
108 minutes

REAL LIFE (1979)

★★

Albert Brooks
Charles Grodin

This comic satire is writer/director Brooks' attempt to parody the PBS-TV series called *American Family,* about the day-to-day events of the Louds, a typical middle-class family. Brooks—who also stars—acts silly and fires off corny jokes that sometimes fall flat. Though Brooks' parody may not be a funny one, it is interesting nonetheless because its fake documentary style unmasks the myth of objectivity about that form of filmmaking. Thought-provoking if not amusing. Also with Frances Lee McCain, J.A. Preston, and Matthew Tobin. **(PG)** *99 minutes*

RE-ANIMATOR (1985)

★★

Jeffrey Combs
Bruce Abbott

A medical student develops a serum that brings dead rabbits, cats, and inhabitants of the city morgue back to life—but the filmmakers are unable to do the same for this film. The movie does, however, answer the ageless question: Can a severed head make love, and if so, how? You may enjoy this self-spoofing horror endeavor if you have a taste for lopped-off limbs, splattered spleens, and bloodied heads. The film was originally rated R, but its rating certificate has been surrendered. **Director**—Stuart Gordon. **(No MPAA rating)**
86 minutes

REAP THE WILD WIND (1942)

★★★

John Wayne
Ray Milland
Paulette Goddard
Robert Preston

A rip-roaring Cecil B. De Mille adventure. In the 1840s, off the southern coast, Wayne operates a salvage vessel that recovers goods from sunken ships. Wayne vies for the affections of southern belle Goddard with the more sophisticated Milland. Raymond Massey plays a greedy villain who sinks ships on purpose for profit. The underwater segments photographed by Dewey Wrigley were an accomplishment for that time. Based on a story from the *Saturday Evening Post* by Thelma Strabel, the film won an Oscar for its special effects. Also with Charles Bickford, Walter Hampden, Hedda Hopper, and Louise Beavers. **Academy Award**—Farciot Edouart, Gordon Jennings, William L. Pereira, and Louis Mesenkop, special effects. **Nomination**—Victor Milner and William V. Skall, cinematography. *124 minutes*

REAR WINDOW (1954)

★★★★

James Stewart
Grace Kelly

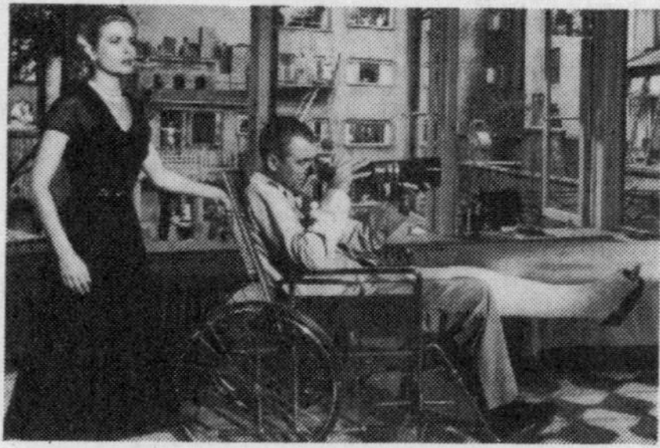

Grace Kelly and James Stewart peer at the neighbors in Rear Window.

One of director Alfred Hitchcock's masterpieces, about a news photographer confined to a wheelchair who witnesses a murder. Stewart's character, though ultimately the hero, is somewhat unlikable because of his unwholesome interest in voyeuristically watching his neighbors' activities—indicated by his switch from simple binoculars to a camera lens and then to a large telephoto lens. The confined setting plus the handicap of the main character makes for a heightened level of suspense. Kelly plays Stewart's society girlfriend and accomplice in his efforts to catch the murderer. The witty dialogue serves to break the relentless tension. Raymond Burr, Judith Evelyn, Wendell Corey, and Thelma Ritter perform well in supporting roles. **(PG)** **Academy Award Nominations**—Hitchcock, best director; John Michael Hayes, screenplay; Robert Burks, cinematography. *112 minutes*

REBECCA (1940)

★★★★

Laurence Olivier
Joan Fontaine
George Sanders
Judith Anderson

Director Alfred Hitchcock adapted this award-winning story from Daphne du Maurier's novel about a naive woman, played by Fontaine, who marries a brooding British nobleman, played by Olivier, and finds that she must live in the shadow of Rebecca—his beautiful first wife. Hitchcock deftly combines romance, comedy, suspense, and mystery in one of his most popular films—his first in America. Fontaine, Anderson, and Olivier perform superbly and receive excellent support from Sanders, Nigel Bruce, Gladys Cooper, Florence Bates, and Reginald Denny. C. Aubrey Smith and Leo G. Carroll are also in the cast. **Academy Awards**—best picture; George Barnes, cinematography. **Nominations**—Hitchcock, best director; Olivier, best actor; Fontaine, best actress; Anderson, best supporting actress; Robert E. Sherwood and Joan Harrison, screenplay. *130 minutes b&w*

REBECCA OF SUNNYBROOK FARM (1938)

★★★ ®

Shirley Temple
Randolph Scott
Jack Haley
Bill "Bojangles" Robinson

If you or the little ones worship at Shirley Temple, this is one of her better ve-

® *This movie available with closed captions for the hearing impaired.*

hicles, though it has hardly anything to do with the famous Kate Douglas Wiggins story. Auntie doesn't want her niece (Temple) to mingle with show-biz people, but the child gets mixed up with talent scout Scott anyway. Before you know it, she's on the radio performing such hits as "On the Good Ship Lollipop" and "Animal Crackers." With Bill "Bojangles" Robinson, she dances to "The Parade of the Wooden Soldiers." William Demarest, Slim Summerville, Gloria Stuart, and Franklin Pangborn costar. **Director**—Allan Dwan. *80 minutes b&w*

REBEL WITHOUT A CAUSE (1955)

★★★1/2

James Dean
Natalie Wood

The quintessential rebel: James Dean in Rebel Without a Cause.

Dean became a symbol to the younger generation after his role as a troubled teenager in this film. He plays a young man in conflict with the middle-class values of his parents. Dean finally finds some meaning in life when he befriends Wood and Sal Mineo, but their friendship is shattered in an exciting and tragic end. The film's themes involving lack of communication and alienation became suddenly relevant to a youthful audience who for the first time began to develop their own culture and their own values. Jim Backus, Ann Doran, Dennis Hopper, and Nick Adams also star. **Director**—Nicholas Ray. **Academy Award Nominations**—Mineo, best supporting actor; Wood, best supporting actress; Ray, motion picture story. *111 minutes*

RECKLESS (1984)

★★

Daryl Hannah
Aidan Quinn

Another film about restless youth, which leans too heavily on other youth films, from *Rebel Without a Cause* to *All the Right Moves.* Quinn seems to make all the wrong moves as the moody, motorcycle-riding, high-school senior who desires pampered Hannah. Quinn knocks himself out copying the mannerisms of James Dean, Marlon Brando, and Sylvester Stallone. Too derivative. **Director**—James Foley. **(R)** *93 minutes*

THE RED BADGE OF COURAGE (1951)

★★★★

Audie Murphy

Stephen Crane's classic Civil War novel becomes one of the greatest war films ever produced, thanks to the brilliant writing and direction of John Huston. Murphy, Bill Mauldin, and John Dierkes give naturalistic performances that enhance this authentic drama of combat as seen through the eyes of a new recruit. Before the young soldier becomes a brave soldier, he experiences fear, while the viewer gets a hint of the hell of war. Also with Douglas Dick, Royal Dano, Andy Devine, and Arthur Hunnicutt. *69 minutes b&w*

RED BALL EXPRESS (1952)

★★

Jeff Chandler
Alex Nicol
Judith Braun

Chandler plays the gruff but humane leader of an Army truck division—known as the Red Ball Express—that ferries war supplies from the beaches of Normandy to the outskirts of Paris during World War II. Sidney Poitier, Hugh O'Brian, Jack Kelly, and Jack Warden work well together in this conventional war story that has its share of action and adventure. **Director**—Budd Boetticher. *83 minutes b&w*

RED DAWN (1984)

★1/2

Patrick Swayze
C. Thomas Howell

Preposterous, violent war movie about the United States being invaded by Russian and Cuban troops. A band of all-American teenagers hightails it to the mountains to launch guerrilla counterattacks. It's the Pepsi generation versus the commies. Some of this nonsense may be considered tongue-in-cheek, but too much of it is badly written and overflowing with clichés. Also with Powers Boothe, Charlie Sheen, Ben Johnson, Harry Dean Stanton, and Lea Thompson. **Director**—John Milius. **(PG-13)** *114 minutes*

RED DUST (1932)

★★★1/2

Clark Gable
Jean Harlow
Mary Astor

This was considered steamy back in 1932, with Gable and Harlow burning up the screen as an Indochina plantation overseer and the Shanghai prostitute he admires. Astor plays a married woman who is romantically interested in Gable as well. Still provocative, with Harlow in one of her best roles. Gene Raymond, Donald Crisp, and Tully Marshall costar. Gable repeated his starring role in the 1953 remake, *Mogambo,* with Ava Gardner as the vamp and Grace Kelly as the cool but curious wife. *83 minutes b&w*

RED HEAT (1988)

★★★

Arnold Schwarzenegger
James Belushi

Two cops from different societies: Arnold Schwarzenegger and James Belushi in Red Heat.

An action-packed cop thriller featuring a familiar storyline but above-average production values. Two very different cops are thrown together by unusual circumstances to crack a tough case. Schwarzenegger stars as Ivan "Iron Jaw" Danko, a solemn Russian police detective who arrives in Chicago to take back a murderous drug dealer wanted

(Continued)

This movie available on videotape and/or disc.

(Continued)
in his country. The action heats up when the Russian criminal escapes into the mean streets of Chicago, and Art Ridzik, a wisecracking American detective played by Belushi, is assigned to assist Danko in his pursuit of this dangerous killer. The contrast between the personalities of the two cops adds humor to the tense proceedings much as it did in director Walter Hill's previous cop thriller, *48 HRS.* Hill, noted for his fast-paced and violent action movies, doesn't disappoint here, as many car chases and shoot-outs propel the film forward at a brisk pace. If the cinema had not been flooded with cop films during the late 1980s, this well-directed effort might have made a bigger impact. Also with Peter Boyle, Ed O'Ross, Larry Fishburne, and Gina Gershon. **(R)** *106 minutes*

RED RIVER (1948)

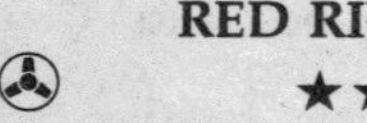

★★★★

John Wayne
Montgomery Clift

John Wayne and Montgomery Clift don't see eye to eye in Red River.

Wayne and Clift star in this classic western story about a cattle baron and the dynasty he builds. Clift rebels against his foster father, played by Wayne, and the empire Wayne has developed. Directed by Howard Hawks, the film features some of Hawks' familiar themes and characteristics—the tightly structured narrative, the pairing of opposites (here Clift and Wayne), the straightforward visual style. The photography by Russell Harlan is one of the film's highlights. Joanne Dru, Walter Brennan, Coleen Gray, John Ireland, and Noah Beery, Jr., appear in supporting roles. **Academy Award Nomination**—Borden Chase, motion picture story.
130 minutes b&w

REDS (1981)

★★★

Warren Beatty
Diane Keaton

Diane Keaton is caught up by Warren Beatty's political fervor in Reds.

A brilliant and passionate slice of history. Beatty is splendid as radical journalist John Reed, who chronicled the Russian Revolution in *Ten Days That Shook the World.* The epic historical drama also presents the stormy love affair between Reed and writer Louise Bryant, played by Keaton. Although the story deals heavily in radical politics, it's surprisingly lucid and invigorating. Interspersed within the narrative are interviews with real-life celebrities who were contemporaries of Reed, including Rebecca West, Henry Miller, George Jessell, and Dora Russell. An innovative film, and a triumph for Beatty, who also produced, wrote, and directed. He gets superb support from Jack Nicholson and Maureen Stapleton. Also with Edward Herrmann, Jerzy Kosinski, Paul Sorvino, and Gene Hackman. **(PG) Academy Awards**—Beatty, best director; Stapleton, best supporting actress; Vittorio Storaro, cinematography. **Nominations**—best picture; Beatty, best actor; Keaton, best actress; Nicholson, best supporting actor; Beatty and Trevor Griffiths, best screenplay written directly for the screen. *200 minutes*

RED SCORPION (1989)

★$^1/_2$

Dolph Lundgren

Scandinavian beefcake star Lundgren flexes some muscle, mumbles a bit of dialogue, and tackles Communist villains in this dull action adventure. This lackluster variant on the overworked one-man-army theme, set in a fictional African country, is bogged down by sluggish direction and unimpressive acting. M. Emmet Walsh has a supporting role of little consequence. **Director**—Joseph Zito. **(R)**
102 minutes

THE RED SHOES (1948)

★★★★

Anton Walbrook
Moira Shearer
Marius Goring

This sensitive and beautiful movie about a ballerina who gives up her romance with a composer to dedicate her life to ballet is enriched by superb dancing. The production offers an intimate and realistic slice-of-life view of the ballerina's backstage world. The title is based on a fairy tale by Hans Christian Andersen about a girl who puts on an enchanted pair of ballet slippers, which will not allow her to stop dancing. The girl dances herself to death. The film tells a similar story in more metaphorical terms. Also with Robert Helpmann, Albert Basserman, Frederick Ashton, and Léonide Massine. **Directors**—Michael Powell and Emeric Pressburger. **Academy Award Nominations**—best picture; Pressburger, motion picture story. *133 minutes*

RED SONJA (1985)

★★

Brigitte Nielsen
Arnold Schwarzenegger

Banging, clanging, sword-and-sorcery adventure featuring a tall, red-haired woman (Nielsen) as the chief blade swinger. She defeats hordes of armor-clad brutes in her mission to avenge the murder of her family. Such heroic feats are accomplished without smudging her makeup. Muscle man Schwarzenegger appears as her sidekick. Silly dialogue and stiff performances barely rise above the noise level. **Director**—Richard Fleischer. **(PG–13)** *89 minutes*

REFLECTIONS IN A GOLDEN EYE (1967)

★★

Marlon Brando
Elizabeth Taylor

A star-studded cast, which includes Brando, Taylor, Brian Keith, and Julie Harris, fails to salvage this clunker

This movie available with closed captions for the hearing impaired.

about a homosexual Army officer stationed in Georgia. Most of the characters are insane, or at least eccentric, in this debased film version of Carson McCullers' perceptive novel. Some of the acting, however, is quite good. Brando, despite the excesses wrought by his method acting, conveys the anguish of a homosexual Army officer. Robert Forster is the object of his affection, and Taylor plays Brando's wife. John Huston provides stylish but uneven direction. *108 minutes*

REFORM SCHOOL GIRLS (1986)

(no stars)

Sybil Danning
Wendy O. Williams
Pat Ast

This lame send-up of trashy women-behind-bars movies is itself just another exercise in schlock, low-budget filmmaking. Most of the clichés are present: scantily clad female inmates, brutal matrons, lesbian tormentors, brandings, beatings, and humiliations. Though supposedly a satire, the film swings from social commentary to spoof to straightforward storytelling, resulting in a widely uneven viewing experience. Ultimately, the film is merely a lot of bad taste and horrid acting. **Director**—Tom DeSimone. **(R)** *94 minutes*

THE REINCARNATION OF PETER PROUD (1975)

★★★

Michael Sarrazin
Jennifer O'Neill
Margot Kidder

A California college professor, played by Sarrazin, believes he led an earlier life that ended in violence. He searches for his past in a suburban Massachusetts town and finds more than he bargained for. A suspenseful and moody horror film, but no solid solution to the mystery is presented. Good performances by Sarrazin, O'Neill, and Kidder. Also with Cornelia Sharpe and Paul Hecht. **Director**—J. Lee Thompson. **(R)** *105 minutes*

THE REIVERS (1969)

★★★

Steve McQueen
Mitch Vogel
Sharon Farrell

This film no more gets to the heart of William Faulkner's novels than the other adaptations by Irving Ravetch and Harriet Frank, Jr., including *The Sound and the Fury* and *The Long Hot Summer.* However, it is an amusing film about an 11-year-old boy in Yoknapatawpha County, Mississippi, at the turn of the century, who takes off in the family car with two hired hands, and experiences a series of colorful adventures on the road to Memphis. Appealing performances by McQueen, Rupert Crosse, Vogel (as the boy), Farrell, Will Geer, Lonny Chapman, Michael Constantine, and Juano Hernandez. Narrated by Burgess Meredith. Music by John Williams. **Director**—Mark Rydell. **(M)** **Academy Award Nomination**—Crosse, best supporting actor. *107 minutes*

RELENTLESS (1989)

★★

Judd Nelson
Robert Loggia

Judd Nelson can't face rejection in the thriller Relentless.

A lackluster thriller starring Nelson as a psychopathic serial killer. The murder spree is touched off when Nelson's character is rejected as a candidate for the police force. His disciplinarian father groomed him from childhood to be a cop, and when he is rejected, he snaps. Loggia and Leo Rossie play the detectives assigned to the case. The gruesome killings and subsequent sleuthing unfold with no imagination and minimal suspense. Directed by William Lustig, who gave the world *Maniac Cop.* Also with Meg Foster. **(R)** *92 minutes*

THE RELUCTANT DEBUTANTE (1958)

Rex Harrison
Kay Kendall

Harrison and Kendall brighten this routine British drawing-room comedy about an unorthodox British couple who choose to permit their daughter, educated in America, to make her society debut in England. Sandra Dee plays the daughter. Despite such a lean plot, there are some pleasant moments that make the movie mildly enjoyable. Also with John Saxon, Peter Myers, and Angela Lansbury. **Director**—Vincente Minnelli. *96 minutes*

THE RELUCTANT DRAGON (1941)

★★★

Robert Benchley

This studio tour of the fantastic and magical universe of Walt Disney gives young and old moviegoers an excellent chance to see how cartoons of the 1930s and 1940s were made. During this Disney studio tour, the enjoyable mixture of short films presented includes *Baby Weems, How to Ride a Horse,* and the title story. Also, Clarence Nash (the voice of Donald Duck) and Florence Gill demonstrate various cartoon voices. The pleasant experience is enriched by the presence of Benchley, who's better known for his humorous essays. **Director**—Alfred Werker. *72 minutes*

THE REMARKABLE MR. PENNYPACKER (1959)

★★½

Clifton Webb
Dorothy McGuire
Charles Coburn

Webb stars in this mildly amusing story about a businessman who is married to two different women in different towns and is raising two families with a total of 17 children. Ray Stricklyn, Jill St. John, Ron Ely, and David Nelson also appear in this comedy, which takes place at the turn of the century. **Director**—Henry Levin. *87 minutes*

REMEMBER THE NIGHT (1940)

Barbara Stanwyck
Fred MacMurray

MacMurray and Stanwyck star in this delightful and sentimental story about an assistant district attorney who takes a shoplifter home with him when court

(Continued)

(Continued)
recesses for the Christmas holidays. MacMurray plays the attorney who falls in love with Stanwyck, the shoplifter. Under Mitchell Leisen's direction, the film is typical of the special blend of comedy, romance, and drama that some of the finer films of its era exhibited. The script was written by Preston Sturges. Also with Beulah Bondi, Elizabeth Patterson, Sterling Holloway, Paul Guilfoyle, and Willard Robertson.
86 minutes b&w

REMO WILLIAMS: THE ADVENTURE BEGINS (1985)

★★

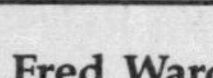

Fred Ward
Joel Grey

Guy Hamilton, who directed several successful James Bond films, is responsible for this cartoon-like adventure tale. However, this elaborate yet wobbly production never comes close to the fun of even the lesser Bond outings. Ward is in the title role as a New York cop reluctantly recruited to rid the country of corruption that the legal system can't handle. Some of the high-flying stunts are awesome, but a feeble script undermines this escapist material. Grey co-stars as a martial-arts master. Also with Wilford Brimley and Kate Mulgrew. **(PG–13)** *121 minutes*

RENALDO AND CLARA (1978)

★

Bob Dylan

Dylan devotees may find this film of interest; others will be frustrated by this four-hour mishmash of musical interludes and incoherent events. The movie mainly involves a 1975 concert tour by Dylan, Joan Baez, and friends. Dylan was the writer, director, and musical supervisor. The film was later edited to a 122-minute version, which was mostly concert footage. **(R)** *232 minutes*

RENEGADES (1989)

★★

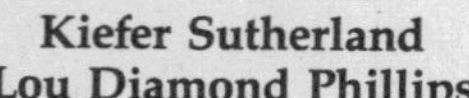

Kiefer Sutherland
Lou Diamond Phillips

Endless car chases, incredible shootouts, and other acts of mindless violence make up this preposterous cop thriller set in Philadelphia. The plot is

Kiefer Sutherland and Lou Diamond Phillips team up in Renegades.

superficial, and the characters are familiar stereotypes. Sutherland stars as a young cop assigned to infiltrate a gang of thugs who are in cahoots with crooked policemen. He teams up with a young Sioux Indian (Phillips) whose tribe falls victim to the villains. A romantic subplot featuring Jamie Gertz is inserted amid the predictable action and dialogue. **Director**—Jack Sholder. **(R)** *107 minutes*

RENT-A-COP (1988)

★★

Burt Reynolds
Liza Minnelli

Reynolds stars as an embattled police detective in this frantic comedy/cop thriller, while Minnelli portrays a perky prostitute with the proverbial heart of gold. They team up to chase around Chicago together in search of a murderous drug dealer. The strictly by-the-numbers plot trashes the efforts and talents of the stars, who seem to have taken their assignments out of desperation. *Rent-a-Cop* seems best suited to the rent-a-movie department. Also with James Remar, Richard Masur, Dionne Warwick, Bernie Casey, and Robby Benson. **Director**—Jerry London. **(R)**
100 minutes

REPO MAN (1984)

★★★

Harry Dean Stanton
Emilio Estevez

Bizarre farce that features punk-rockers, CIA agents, strange scientists, and other oddball characters looking for a used car with alien creatures in the trunk. The title refers to a sleazy repossessor of automobiles, played intensely by Stanton. The story is rife with off-the-wall material that produces laughs in spite of itself. The film seems destined for the midnight-movie circuit. Also with Vonetta McGee, Olivia Barash, and Sy Richardson. **Director**—Alex Cox. **(R)** *92 minutes*

REPORT TO THE COMMISSIONER (1975)

★★

Michael Moriarty
Yaphet Kotto
Susan Blakely

A rookie cop, played by Moriarty, becomes involved in a department cover-up after he shoots undercover policewoman Blakely. The theme of police corruption was handled brilliantly in *Serpico* and *The French Connection*, but here the suspense hardly gets off the ground. In addition, the plot bogs down in unlikely complications. Also with Hector Elizondo, Tony King, and Michael McGuire. **Director**—Milton Katselas. **(PG)** *112 minutes*

REPULSION (1965)

★★★½

Catherine Deneuve
Ian Hendry
Yvonne Furneaux

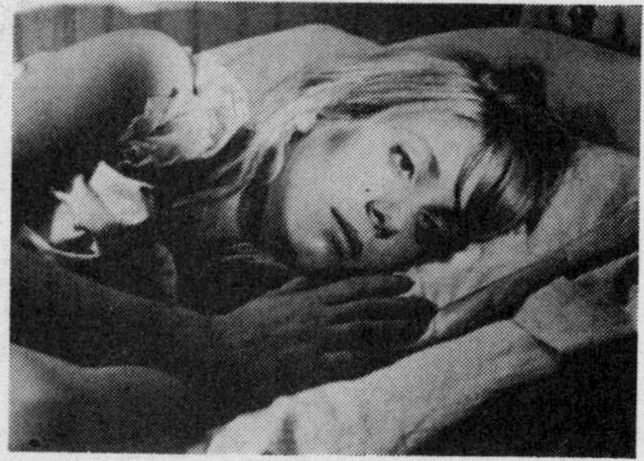

Catherine Deneuve is a repressed, isolated young woman in Repulsion.

Director Roman Polanski let his macabre imagination run wild, and the result is this nightmarish portrayal of young London beautician Deneuve's descent into madness. Isolating herself from the outside world, the beautiful, sexually repressed young woman murders those who try to reach out to her. With images of menacing arms bursting through walls, it's a grisly, often surrealistic visualization of a disturbed mind.
105 minutes b&w

® *This movie available with closed captions for the hearing impaired.*

REQUIEM FOR A HEAVYWEIGHT (1962)

★★★★

Anthony Quinn
Jackie Gleason
Mickey Rooney
Julie Harris

Excellent performances highlight this tough, hard-hitting drama about a prizefighter in the twilight of his career. Quinn stars as the washed-up boxer, Rooney plays a pathetic friend, and Harris is a social worker. The movie, based on Rod Serling's teleplay, contains realistic and harsh fight scenes. Some versions of the film run 100 minutes. Also with Nancy Cushman, Madame Spivy, and Stan Adams. **Director**—Ralph Nelson. *87 minutes b&w*

THE RESCUE (1988)

★½

Kevin Dillon
Christina Harnos

A preposterous adventure about a band of teenagers who infiltrate North Korea to free their captive fathers. Sylvester Stallone and Chuck Norris can get away with such heroics, but not these children. Aside from the absurdity of the plot, the supposedly daring exploits fall flat. Also with Ian Giatti, Charles Haid, Marc Price, Ned Vaughan, and Edward Albert. **Director**—Ferdinand Fairfax. **(PG)** *98 minutes*

THE RESCUERS (1977)

★★★

Imagination, expert craftsmanship, and a high budget have gone into this 22nd full-length animated feature by the Walt Disney studio. It's a lively and charming adventure about two brave mice who set out to rescue a kidnapped girl. The voices of Eva Gabor, Bob Newhart, Jim (Fibber McGee) Jordan, and Geraldine Page add delightful dimensions to the cartoon characters. **Directors**—Wolfgang Reitherman, John Lounsbery, and Art Stevens. **(G)** *76 minutes*

RESURRECTION (1980)

★★★½

Ellen Burstyn
Sam Shepard

Ellen Burstyn displays amazing spiritual power in Resurrection.

Burstyn dominates this unusual and uneven film with a glowing, virtuoso performance. She plays an ordinary woman who discovers after a serious accident that she can heal people by "the laying-on of hands." The slight story is neither an exposé of hokum nor a plug for divine faith. It is, instead, a beautifully acted fable. Also with Eva LeGallienne, Richard Farnsworth, Roberts Blossom, and Clifford David. **Director**—Daniel Petrie. **(PG) Academy Award Nominations**—Burstyn, best actress; LeGallienne, best supporting actress. *103 minutes*

RETREAT, HELL! (1952)

★★

Frank Lovejoy
Richard Carlson

Action scenes and a few tense moments enliven this run-of-the-mill war story about a Marine unit fighting in Korea. Lovejoy and Carlson, in starring roles, provide the rough-and-tough characterization that's typical of such movies. Also with Anita Louise and Russ Tamblyn. **Director**—Joseph H. Lewis. *95 minutes b&w*

RETURN FROM WITCH MOUNTAIN (1978)

★★★

Bette Davis
Christopher Lee
Kim Richards
Ike Eisenmann

Richards and Eisenmann play two appealing kids from outer space in this sequel to Walt Disney's *Escape to Witch Mountain.* Lee and Davis play a pair of villains who try to exploit the moppets for power and profit, but the two youngsters have dazzling Disney special effects on their side. The children will be enthralled; for adults, it's familiar and predictable. Also with Denver Pyle and Dick Bakalyan. **Director**—John Hough. **(G)** *93 minutes*

THE RETURN OF A MAN CALLED HORSE (1976)

★★

Richard Harris

Enrique Lucero and Richard Harris in The Return of a Man Called Horse.

Harris returns in this mystical sequel to *A Man Called Horse.* This time, the English nobleman (Harris) returns to South Dakota to rescue the Yellow Hand Sioux, his adopted tribe, from annihilation. Harris participates in yet another gruesome purification ritual in which his chest is pierced by small bones and then stretched. It's not for the squeamish. Fairly tedious viewing. Also with Gale Sondergaard, Geoffrey Lewis, Bill Lucking, and Jorge Luke. **Director**—Irvin Kershner. **(PG)** *129 minutes*

THE RETURN OF FRANK JAMES (1940)

★★★

Henry Fonda
Gene Tierney

Henry Fonda and Jackie Cooper in The Return of Frank James.

Fonda plays Frank James, who attempts to avenge brother Jesse's death in this

(Continued)

(Continued)
colorful and excellently photographed tale. Fritz Lang tautly directed this fast-paced western, which was Tierney's screen debut. Sequel to *Jesse James* (1939). Jackie Cooper, John Carradine, Henry Hull, J. Edward Bromberg, and Donald Meek costar. *92 minutes*

RETURN OF THE JEDI (1983)

Mark Hamill
Harrison Ford
Carrie Fisher

A tight spot for Harrison Ford, Mark Hamill, and Peter Mayhew in Return of the Jedi.

George Lucas' third chapter in the *Star Wars* saga offers the expected array of spectacular effects and colorful space creatures—including some we haven't met before. The elaborate space opera also provides the answers to the mystery involving Luke Skywalker's relationships with Darth Vader and Princess Leia. More sentimental than the other two entries in the trilogy, which ultimately mars the much-awaited finale. Also with Billy Dee Williams, Anthony Daniels, Peter Mayhew, David Prowse, and Kenny Baker. **Director**—Richard Marquand. **(PG)** **Academy Award**—Richard Edlund, Dennis Muren, Ken Ralston, and Phil Tippet, visual effects. *132 minutes*

THE RETURN OF THE LIVING DEAD (1985)

Clu Gulager
James Karen

Writer/director Dan O'Bannon spoofs the grisly horror films of George A. Romero with this energetic, frequently amusing takeoff that features an excess of ghoulish special effects. The result is certainly not to all tastes, but viewers predisposed to the idea that there is something funny about pushy zombies will have a fine time. Escaping gas from a medical warehouse stirs up numerous zombies, who go about eating the brains of the living. It's a fiendishly witty assault on the senses, accompanied by a soundtrack featuring various punk bands. **(R)** *91 minutes*

RETURN OF THE LIVING DEAD PART II (1988)

Michael Kenworthy
James Karen

This sequel has little to do with the original film and even less to do with George Romero's classic *Night of the Living Dead*. It merely provides an opportunity to resurrect a group of ghoulish, brain-eating zombies for a few scary moments as well as a few laughs. Fans of horror films might enjoy this mixture of comedy and grisly horror, which has become such a popular combination of late that this type of film constitutes a subgenre of its own. Just for the record, the plot begins when a chemical spill awakens the corpses in a cemetery. They crawl out of their graves and attack local citizens. Despite the routine storyline, great care is taken with the makeup, which was designed by Kenny Myers. Also with Thom Mathews, Suzanne Snyder, and Marsha Dietlein. **Director**—Ken Wiederhorn. **(R)** *89 minutes*

THE RETURN OF THE PINK PANTHER (1975)

Peter Sellers
Christopher Plummer
Herbert Lom

Inspector Clouseau (Peter Sellers) defends himself in The Return of the Pink Panther.

Funnyman Sellers once again plays the accident-prone Inspector Jacques Clouseau—hot on the trail of the fabled Pink Panther diamond, the national treasure of the State of Lugash, after it's stolen once more. Lom plays the Chief Inspector. It's slapstick carried to the most reckless degree, as the bumbling Clouseau drives those around him up the wall and gets himself into outrageous comic entanglements. Also with Catherine Schell, Bert Kwouk, Peter Arne, and Grégoire Aslan. **Director**—Blake Edwards. **(G)** *113 minutes*

THE RETURN OF THE SWAMP THING (1989)

Heather Locklear
Louis Jourdan
Dick Durock

Dick Durock, the vegetable monster, in The Return of the Swamp Thing.

This schlocky sequel to the 1982 original finds our vegetable monster (the result of a genetic experiment gone awry) romancing the stepdaughter (Locklear) of the fiendish Dr. Arcane (Jourdan), who conducts bizarre experiments at the edge of a Florida swamp. Based on the well-known comic book, this campy film bogs down in silly situations, and most of the laughs occur for the wrong reasons. Stuntman Durock plays the title character. **Director**—Jim Wynorski. **(PG-13)** *86 minutes*

THE RETURN OF THE VAMPIRE (1943)

Bela Lugosi
Miles Mander
Matt Willis

Lugosi stars in this horror tale about a vampire who appears during the Lon-

This movie available with closed captions for the hearing impaired.

don Blitz. The wartime setting is novel for the genre, making this film of particular interest to horror fans. Willis appears as Lugosi's werewolf accomplice. Lugosi is *not* Count Dracula in this film, but plays a vampire named Armand Tesla. *Dracula* was produced by Universal, while this film was made by Columbia. Thus, Columbia was not legally able to use the Dracula name. Also with Frieda Inescort and Nina Foch. **Directors**—Lew Landers and Kurt Neumann. *69 minutes b&w*

RETURN TO MACON COUNTY (1975)

Nick Nolte
Don Johnson
Robin Mattson

In this sequel to *Macon County Line,* two young racing-car enthusiasts (Nolte and Johnson) head for California in a bright yellow stock car, determined to become drag-racing champs. Along the way they pick up a young girl (Mattson), who wants to be a movie star. As in the earlier film, the unsuspecting travelers become involved in a violent confrontation with the law. Not as compelling as the original. Nolte's feature-film debut. Also with Robert Viharo and Eugene Daniels. Written and directed by Richard Compton. **(PG)** *90 minutes*

RETURN TO OZ (1985)

 ★★★

Fairuza Balk
Nicol Williamson

Anyone with predetermined expectations of this film having anything to do with the 1939 cinema classic can just pack up their predetermined disappointment without bothering to watch. However, those whose expectations go back to an earlier source—the original L. Frank Baum stories upon which the Judy Garland version was based—will find a deep satisfaction. This film is based upon two of the later volumes in Baum's *Oz* series, and it is quite true to his conceptions. The ragtag look of the characters and settings and the intensity of some of the villain's scenes may surprise those looking for a lighter interpretation. For parents willing to entrust their children to a wide range of emotions, however, this is a very good family film. Also with Piper Laurie and Jean Marsh. Directed by Walter Murch, who is well known for his innovative work as a sound technician. **(PG)** *109 minutes*

RETURN TO PEYTON PLACE (1961)

Jeff Chandler
Carol Lynley
Eleanor Parker
Mary Astor

Lackluster sequel to the well-made 1957 melodrama based on the best-selling novel. Parker, Astor, and Lynley perform competently, but the rest of the cast, including Chandler, Robert Sterling, Luciana Paluzzi, Brett Halsey, and Tuesday Weld, are wasted in this trite story. The action centers on the fallout after Allison Mackenzie, played by Lynley, writes a book about her notorious hometown and falls in love with her publisher. Directed by actor José Ferrer. *122 minutes*

RETURN TO SNOWY RIVER (1988)

 ★★½

Tom Burlinson
Sigrid Thornton
Brian Dennehy

Tom Burlinson and Sigrid Thornton in Return to Snowy River.

In this 19th-century western—Australian style—rugged horseman Jim Craig (Burlinson) returns home to claim his love (Thornton). The girl's father (Dennehy), however, has other plans for his beautiful daughter. The cinematography includes some beautiful location work and many effective scenes of galloping horses and courageous riders, but the predictable romance and the family conflict seem like plot elements left over from an old Disney film. Also with Nicholas Eadie, Bryan Marshall, and Rhys McConnochie. **Director**—Geoff Burrowes. **(PG)** *97 minutes*

REUBEN, REUBEN (1983)

Tom Conti
Kelly McGillis

Conti is believable as a boozing, baggy-pants Scottish poet who makes a career of seducing middle-aged women. The script is humorous, with witty dialogue by screenwriter Julius J. Epstein (*Casablanca*). But this one-man, one-note satire eventually goes astray when the slothful poet overindulges in self-pity and impregnates a beautiful girl (McGillis) half his age. Also with Roberts Blossom and Cynthia Harris. **Director**—Robert Ellis Miller. **(R) Academy Award Nominations**—Conti, best actor; Julius J. Epstein, best screenplay adaptation. *100 minutes*

REVENGE (1990)

Kevin Costner
Anthony Quinn
Madeleine Stowe

Madeleine Stowe and Kevin Costner have an adulterous affair in Revenge.

Costner served as executive producer and stars in this retrogressive, action-oriented romance about a young American who falls in love with the beautiful wife of a ruthless, wealthy Mexican. Veteran actor Quinn costars as the powerful tycoon, and Stowe plays his unfaithful wife. The adulterous affair touches off a brutal macho showdown. Instead of passion and tense drama, the film gives us a series of aimless con-

(Continued)

(Continued)
frontations among characters who appear for only a few minutes. So much misfortune befalls each character that the events have no impact on the story or the viewer. Stowe's character, as the cause of all the male posturing, suffers accordingly at the end. Such old-fashioned filmmaking belongs to another era, long since passed. Only Quinn, as the wounded old bull, seems interesting. Also with Tomas Milian, Joaquin Martinez, James Gammon, and Sally Kirkland. **Director**—Tony Scott. **(R)** *124 minutes*

THE REVENGE OF FRANKENSTEIN (1958)

★★½

Peter Cushing

In this well-made and well-acted sequel to *The Curse of Frankenstein*, Baron Von Frankenstein makes a new creation with the brain of a homicidal dwarf. Cushing is excellent as Dr. Frankenstein, and he gets able support from Michael Gwynn, Oscar Quitak, Lloyd Pack, Francis Matthews, Lionel Jeffries, John Welsh, and Eunice Gayson. The movie isn't without a message—especially in light of the recent advances in gene-splicing. **Director**—Terence Fisher. *89 minutes*

REVENGE OF THE NERDS (1984)

★★½

Robert Carradine
Anthony Edwards

Ted McGinley, Julie Montgomery, and Robert Carradine in Revenge of the Nerds.

The nerds get their day in the sun in this affable, yet predictable and uninspired, adolescent comedy. They are the ungainly and unattractive, but ever-resourceful, misfit college freshmen. Along with a sorority of sister outcasts, they fight for their dignity and better housing against the bullying jocks and their female counterparts who dominate the school. The appealing young cast often compensates for the crude gags. They turn at least one sequence—the obligatory party scene—into a genuine charmer. Also with Julie Montgomery, Curtis Armstrong, Michelle Meyrink, and Bernie Casey. **Director**—Jeff Kanew. **(R)** *89 minutes*

REVENGE OF THE NERDS II: NERDS IN PARADISE (1987)

★★

Robert Carradine
Curtis Armstrong

More misadventures with the socially awkward Tri-Lamb brothers, who attend a fraternity convention in Fort Lauderdale. Once again the nerds are able to triumph over the handsome but dim-witted jocks. This uninspired sequel features the expected array of scatological humor and low-brow physical comedy, with minimal results. Carradine returns as the head geek, and he's joined by other original cast members, including Armstrong, Larry B. Scott, and Timothy Busfield. **Director**—Joe Roth. **(PG-13)** *92 minutes*

REVENGE OF THE NINJA (1983)

★★

Sho Kosugi

A clean-cut Japanese artist/warrior (Kosugi) comes to America, where he's soon embroiled in an illegal drug operation. He then faces off with an old enemy. Our slightly built hero dispatches an assortment of brutes with kung-fu maneuvers and various weapons, including swords, daggers, darts, chains, clubs, claws, and axes. Excessive blood and gore is evident. The black-belt crowd may get a kick out of this martial-arts adventure. Others may merely wince. Also with Keith Vitali and Virgil Frye. **Director**—Sam Firstenberg. **(R)** *90 minutes*

REVENGE OF THE PINK PANTHER (1978)

★★★

Peter Sellers
Dyan Cannon
Robert Webber

Inspector Clouseau (Peter Sellers) in disarray in Revenge of the Pink Panther.

Sellers as the bumbling French Inspector Jacques Clouseau is as durable a comic persona as W.C. Fields or Jack Benny. In this fifth *Pink Panther* film, the "world's greatest detective" breaks up the French Connection drug ring while the audience breaks up with laughter. Sellers is helped by Cannon, who's well cast as the discarded mistress of the drug kingpin (Webber). **Director**—Blake Edwards. **(PG)** *99 minutes*

REVOLUTION (1986)

★

Al Pacino
Nastassja Kinski
Donald Sutherland

What is billed as an epic about the American Revolution is in fact a muddled cinematic disaster. If more attention had been devoted to character and script development, rather than costumes and scenery, the picture might have succeeded. The story is told primarily through the experiences of ordinary citizens. Pacino stars as a fur trapper, initially uninterested in the conflict, who finally becomes involved. His talents are wasted along with the efforts of Kinski and Sutherland. Also with Joan Plowright and Annie Lennox. **Director**—Hugh Hudson. **(PG)** *125 minutes*

RHAPSODY (1954)

Elizabeth Taylor
Vittorio Gassman
John Ericson

Taylor enlivens this romantic drama about a love triangle involving a

This movie available with closed captions for the hearing impaired.

wealthy woman (Taylor), a violinist (Gassman), and a pianist (Ericson). Taylor's wardrobe resembles a fashion show for stylish 1954 clothing. The musical interludes are pleasing, but the movie is below-average melodrama. Louis Calhern, Michael Chekhov, Barbara Bates, Celia Lovsky, and Richard Hageman also appear in supporting roles. **Director**—Charles Vidor.
116 minutes

RHAPSODY IN BLUE (1945)

★★★

Robert Alda
Joan Leslie

Alexis Smith and Robert Alda in Rhapsody in Blue, *a biography of George Gershwin.*

This biography of George Gershwin, starring Alda and Leslie, captures the great composer's enthusiasm for his work and reveals some of the conflicts he faced, but as a biography it's thin and shallow. Fortunately, the movie is sprinkled with Gershwin's wonderful music. The cast also includes Alexis Smith, Charles Coburn, Julie Bishop, Albert Basserman, Oscar Levant, Herbert Rudley, Al Jolson, Paul Whiteman, and Hazel Scott. **Director**—Irving Rapper. *139 minutes b&w*

RHINESTONE (1984)

★½

Sylvester Stallone
Dolly Parton

Corny, trumped-up comedy starring Stallone as a gruff New York cab driver trying to be a country singer under the guidance of Parton. Stallone merely looks foolish attempting the down-home songs. Only Parton manages a few good scenes with her perky charm and genuine singing ability. Parton bets

Sylvester Stallone tries to be a country singer like Dolly Parton in Rhinestone.

she can turn Sly into a successful rhinestone cowboy. Whatever the outcome, the audience loses. Also with Ron Leibman and Richard Farnsworth. **Director**—Bob Clark. **(PG)** *111 minutes*

RICH AND FAMOUS (1981)

★★

Jacqueline Bisset
Candice Bergen

Bisset and Bergen play old college friends who carry on a love-hate relationship over the years as they pursue separate literary careers. Veteran director George Cukor fashioned this woman's film, which is slickly produced but gradually deteriorates into soap opera. Gerald Ayres' irritating screenplay is loosely based on the 1943 film *Old Acquaintance,* which starred Bette Davis and Miriam Hopkins. Cukor's last film. Also with Michael Brandon, Steven Hill, David Selby, and Meg Ryan. **(R)**
117 minutes

RICHARD PRYOR HERE AND NOW (1983)

★★★

Richard Pryor

Satiric barbs and pointed wit from Richard Pryor Here and Now.

Pryor presents a cavalcade of sharp, satirical observations in his relentlessly shocking and streetwise style. His raucous monologue, peppered with expletives, embraces a wide range of subjects—sex, drugs, racism, poverty, and politics. This fourth Pryor concert movie was filmed before a live audience in New Orleans' French Quarter, with Pryor directing. Videotape versions of the film run shorter. **(R)**
94 minutes

RICHARD PRYOR LIVE ON THE SUNSET STRIP (1982)

★★½

Richard Pryor

The energetic comedian performs for over 80 minutes in this outrageous monologue. Lacing his routine with obscenities, he lashes out at a number of targets, particularly sex. Pryor, filmed at the Hollywood Palladium, is a gifted performer and there are some splendid moments of wit and hilarity; but the patter goes on too long, and the viewer runs out of endurance well before Pryor runs out of words. **Director**—Joe Layton. **(R)** *82 minutes*

RICHARD III (1956)

★★★★

Laurence Olivier

Olivier, one of the greatest actors of the century, turns in a magnificent performance in this film version of the Shakespeare play about Richard Crookback, the evil king. Olivier also directed this elaborate adaptation, which tells the story of Richard's seizure of the throne, his devious dealings in court, and his conquests on the battlefield. Superb performances are also delivered by Claire Bloom, Ralph Richardson, Cedric Hardwicke, John Gielgud, and Clive Morton. **Academy Award Nomination**—Olivier, best actor.
158 minutes

RICH KIDS (1979)

★★★

Trini Alvarado
Jeremy Levy

A warm, witty, and touching comedy about a disturbing and sad situation—the effect of divorce on children. Alvarado and Levy are remarkable as bright

(Continued)

(Continued)
New York adolescents who form a puppy-love relationship as shelter from their parents' ruined marriages. Robert M. Young directs from an appealing script by Judith Ross. Also with John Lithgow, Kathryn Walker, and Terry Kiser. **(PG)** *97 minutes*

THE RIDDLE OF THE SANDS (1979)

Michael York
Simon MacCorkindale

An unexciting spy adventure about two British men (York and MacCorkindale) who foil a German scheme to invade England. This drab drama, set at the turn of the century, has nothing to do with deserts; instead, the action unfolds at a seaside locale. Settings tend to be lavish, but the main riddle here is why so much money and effort was expended to prop up the weak script. **Director**—Tony Maylam. **(No MPAA rating)** *99 minutes*

RIDE A WILD PONY (1976)

Robert Bettles
Eva Griffith

A poor boy and a wealthy, handicapped girl struggle over the ownership of a pony in this mediocre melodrama from the Walt Disney organization. Youngsters Bettles and Griffith perform adequately in the pre-World War II Australian setting, but a sluggish plot fails them. Also with Michael Craig, John Meillon, and Graham Rouse. **Director**—Don Chaffey. **(G)** *91 minutes*

RIDE THE HIGH COUNTRY (1962)

Joel McCrea
Randolph Scott

Sam Peckinpah directed this classic western about two aging lawmen—Scott and McCrea—who are reunited after 20 years to deliver a gold shipment. Peckinpah, who later became known for more violent films, directed this story with sensitivity and subtlety. The film's theme about the passing of the Old West and the men who helped tame it adds a touch of melancholy and also prefigures Peckinpah's masterpiece, *The Wild Bunch.* Scott's last screen role. The movie was shot by Lucien Ballard on location at the beautiful Inyo National Forest in California. Also with Edgar Buchanan, Mariette Hartley, James Drury, and Warren Oates. *94 minutes*

THE RIGHT STUFF (1983)

Sam Shepard
Ed Harris
Scott Glenn

America's first astronauts meet the press in The Right Stuff.

Director/writer Philip Kaufman's overlong yet highly entertaining and exhilarating docudrama chronicles the evolution of America's space program. Based on Tom Wolfe's book, the high-flying film offers an intimate look at the much-publicized astronauts and the lesser-known test pilots who orbited the Earth and broke the sound barrier. Most prominently portrayed are Chuck Yeager (Shepard), Alan Shepard (Glenn), and John Glenn (Harris), with Shepard turning in the best performance of his acting career. Also with Dennis Quaid, Fred Ward, Barbara Hershey, Kim Stanley, Veronica Cartwright, Pamela Reed, Scott Wilson, and Levon Helm. **(PG) Academy Award Nominations**—best picture; Shepard, best supporting actor; Caleb Deschanel, cinematography. *193 minutes*

RIO BRAVO (1959)

 ★★★

John Wayne
Dean Martin
Ricky Nelson

Howard Hawks directed this story about a federal marshal trying to prevent a band of outlaws from helping a killer escape from the town jail. Hawks assembled a fine cast that includes Wayne as the marshal, Martin as the drunken town sheriff, and Nelson as a young cowhand ready to prove his manhood. Angie Dickinson plays the love interest. Hawks uses a combination of humor and western action to play with the conventions of the genre, making for a highly entertaining film. Also with Walter Brennan, Ward Bond, Claude Akins, and Bob Steele. *140 minutes*

RIO GRANDE (1950)

 ★★★

John Wayne
Maureen O'Hara

Wayne is excellent as a tough cavalry commander on the Mexican border in the 1880s, conducting a campaign against Indians on the warpath. O'Hara costars as his estranged wife who cannot accept his job or his way of life. After a 16-year absence, she arrives at the post to see their son, who is now a new recruit there. Wayne finds himself torn between his duty and the love for his family. Director John Ford fashioned a touching story involving the sacrifices made by the pioneers to secure the West for settlement. The last film in Ford's cavalry trilogy. Also with Ben Johnson, Harry Carey, Jr., Chill Wills, J. Carrol Naish, and Victor McLaglen. *105 minutes b&w*

RIO LOBO (1970)

John Wayne
Jennifer O'Neill

The usually surefire combination of Wayne and director Howard Hawks falls short in this rambling Civil War-era story. Wayne plays a Union colonel who recovers a gold shipment after it's stolen. The train robbery sequence at the beginning of the film is exciting, but afterward the movie bogs down and becomes a slow-moving bore. O'Neill is beautiful, but a below-average actress. The performances of Jorge Rivero, Jack Elam, and Chris Mitchum are adequate at best. **(G)** *114 minutes*

RISKY BUSINESS (1983)

Tom Cruise
Rebecca DeMornay

This movie available with closed captions for the hearing impaired.

While his parents are away, Tom Cruise starts a Risky Business.

A clever combination of teen comedy and social satire about an upper-middle-class youth (Cruise) who turns his swank, suburban home into a temporary brothel while his parents are on vacation. Debuting director/writer Paul Brickman manages some insights into youthful rebellion. Cruise, in his first starring role, is admirable as the innocent but enterprising youth. Also with Curtis Armstrong, Bronson Pinchot, Raphael Sbarge, Joe Pantoliano, and Richard Masur. **(R)** *99 minutes*

RITA, SUE AND BOB TOO (1987)

★★★

George Costigan
Siobhan Finneran
Michelle Holmes

From England comes this sharp, hard-edged sex comedy, which serves as a social satire on the plight and character of modern industrial Britain. The background is England's depressed area to the north, where teenagers Rita and Sue (Finneran and Holmes) eke out a meager wage as babysitters. They agree to join their less-than-romantic employer (Costigan) in a *ménage à trois* affair for no other reason than to ease their dreary lives. The total lack of morality of the three central characters may be shocking to some viewers, but that in itself makes a statement about the environment in which these characters must live. **Director**—Alan Clarke. **(R)** *95 minutes*

THE RITZ (1976)

★★★

Jack Weston
Rita Moreno

Moreno steals the show in this rip-roaring film version of the brassy Broadway comedy by Terence McNally about high jinks in a homosexual bathhouse. Moreno, who was in the stage production, delivers the same energetic and madcap portrayal of Googie Gomez, the fiery Puerto Rican singer yearning for discovery. Weston plays a man fleeing from his brother-in-law. Richard Lester's direction is uneven, but the film is entertaining nevertheless. Also with Jerry Stiller, Kaye Ballard, Bessie Love, Treat Williams, and George Couloris. **(R)** *91 minutes*

THE RIVER (1984)

★★

Mel Gibson
Sissy Spacek
Scott Glenn

Mel Gibson and Sissy Spacek are determined to protect their farm in The River.

Gibson and Spacek play a Tennessee farm couple stalwartly struggling with crops, bank debts, and the menacing river that borders their fields. Their lives and hardships seem authentic, yet the sentimental, uneven plot is only an accumulation of hard-luck experiences. Also, the occasional attempts at symbolism seem out of place given the film's efforts to make the couple's problems realistic and topical. The actors turn in good performances, with Spacek faring especially well. Mark Rydell's direction is below par. **(PG–13) Academy Award Nomination**—Spacek, best actress. *124 minutes*

THE RIVER NIGER (1976)

★★

James Earl Jones
Cicely Tyson

The moving, award-winning Broadway play by Joseph A. Walker loses its punch on the screen. Much of the fault belongs to the uneven direction by Krishna Shah, and to the script, which has too much unnecessary dialogue. The story is about a black family's struggle to survive in contemporary America. Jones stars as a house painter who writes poetry. Also with Glynn Turman, Lou Gossett, Jr., and Roger E. Mosley. **(R)** *104 minutes*

RIVER OF NO RETURN (1954)

★★½

Robert Mitchum
Marilyn Monroe

Robert Mitchum and Marilyn Monroe in River of No Return.

The chemistry between Monroe and Mitchum, under the direction of Otto Preminger, and the excellent location photography make this film worthwhile viewing. Monroe, a saloon singer, and Mitchum, a widower with a 10-year-old son, search for the gambler who deserted her. The action occurs during the California gold rush. The CinemaScope photography will be lost on a small screen. Tommy Rettig, Rory Calhoun, and Murvyn Vye also star. *91 minutes*

THE RIVER'S EDGE (1956)

★★★

Ray Milland
Anthony Quinn
Deborah Paget

Milland delivers an excellent portrayal of a fugitive bank robber who menaces his former girlfriend (Paget) and threatens her husband (Quinn) during his attempt to escape over the mountains into Mexico with a fortune. Also with Byron Foulger. **Director**—Allan Dwan. *87 minutes*

RIVER'S EDGE (1987)

 ★★★ ®

Crispin Glover
Keanu Reeves
Ione Skye Leitch
Dennis Hopper

Moral responsibility weighs heavily on the plot of this unsettling film about a teenage boy who murders his girlfriend. The shocking aspect of this story is the casual reaction among the boy's young friends, who learn about the crime and even view the dead body, but do nothing about it. The reason behind their total alienation from adults remains ambiguous, but the film hints that the fault lies with the parents. The filmmakers pressure the audience to feel the compassion obviously lacking in the spaced-out youths, and the result is a compelling and disturbing experience. Based on a true story, which makes the events in the film that much more frightening. Also with Roxana Zal, Daniel Roebuck, and Jim Metzler. **Director**—Tim Hunter. **(R)**

99 minutes

ROAD GAMES (1981)

 ★★★

Stacy Keach
Jamie Lee Curtis

Jamie Lee Curtis hitchhikes through Australia in Road Games.

Keach plays a poetry-quoting truck driver in this above-average Australian chase thriller. The cops suspect Keach of being a latter-day Jack the Ripper, and he attempts to clear himself by nabbing the real killer. He encounters a number of strange characters, among them Curtis as a damsel in distress whom he rescues. **Director**—Richard Franklin. **(PG)** *100 minutes*

ROAD HOUSE (1989)

 ★★

Patrick Swayze
Ben Gazzara

This violence-filled action drama exists only to show off Swayze's sex appeal. The plot is essentially an updated version of a western: Swayze plays a bouncer called in to clean up a sleazy bar in a town run by a vile businessman (Gazzara). Fight scenes—and there are plenty—are choreographed as tightly as dance routines. Too much violence destroys what little interest the film holds. Also with Sam Elliott, Kelly Lynch, Marshall Teague, and Red West. Video versions run several minutes longer. **Director**—Rowdy Herrington. **(R)**

108 minutes

ROADIE (1980)

Meat Loaf

This energetic, madcap parody of the rock 'n' roll scene stars popular rock star Meat Loaf in an effective nonsinging role. The screwball story features a number of slapstick escapades, but its nonstop, earsplitting rock music may not be for all tastes. The music is by Blondie, Alice Cooper, and Hank Williams, Jr., among others. Also with Art Carney and Roy Orbison. **Director**—Alan Rudolph. **(PG)** *106 minutes*

ROAD TO MOROCCO (1942)

Bob Hope
Bing Crosby
Dorothy Lamour

Bing gets ready to sock Bob in Road to Morocco, *one of the team's great comedies.*

One of the best of the Hope and Crosby *Road* films. Here, Bing sells Bob into slavery in exotic Morocco. Lamour is present for romantic high jinks, and Monte Blue, Yvonne De Carlo, Anthony Quinn, and Dona Drake join in the silliness. A few good songs, including "Moonlight Becomes You," and a talking camel add to the entertainment value of this fun-filled movie. **Director**—David Butler. **Academy Award Nomination**—Frank Butler and Don Hartman, original screenplay.

83 minutes b&w

ROAD TO SINGAPORE (1940)

Bob Hope
Bing Crosby
Dorothy Lamour

Hope and Crosby are rich playboys who swear off women, but when they meet a Singapore maiden, played by Lamour, they quarrel over her. Many contemporary viewers may not realize that Hope and Crosby's *Road* series was designed to parody the exotic adventure movies that were popular then, but forgotten now. However, the chemistry between the two stars plus the witty, clever dialogue still makes this film most amusing. Also with Charles Coburn, Judith Barrett, Anthony Quinn, and Jerry Colonna. **Director**—Victor Schertzinger. *84 minutes b&w*

ROAD TO UTOPIA (1946)

 ★★★

Bob Hope
Bing Crosby
Dorothy Lamour

Bing Crosby, Dorothy Lamour, and Bob Hope on the Road to Utopia.

One of the most entertaining of the Hope/Crosby *Road* pictures, with the comic and the crooner going north to Alaska. In the course of their hunt for a

® *This movie available with closed captions for the hearing impaired.*

Skagway gold mine, they're pursued by bad guys and mistaken for desperados. Lamour sings "Personality"; Robert Benchley narrates—with footnotes on the art of filmmaking; Hope and Crosby trade gags, sing "Put It There Pal," and take audiences along for a rollicking good ride. With Hillary Brooke, Jack LaRue, Douglass Dumbrille. **Director**—Hal Walker. **Academy Award Nomination**—Norman Panama and Melvin Frank, original screenplay.
90 minutes b&w

ROAD TO ZANZIBAR (1941)

★★★

Bob Hope
Bing Crosby
Dorothy Lamour

Anything goes in this satire of jungle pictures. Hope and Crosby play carnival hustlers on a safari in Africa. They are joined again by Lamour, and the trio searches for a diamond mine. The cast also includes Una Merkel, Eric Blore, Luis Alberni, and Douglass Dumbrille. **Director**—Victor Schertzinger.
92 minutes b&w

THE ROAD WARRIOR (1982)

★★★★

Mel Gibson

Mel Gibson strides across the bleak landscape of the future in The Road Warrior.

Essentially, this Australian feature is B-movie, comic-book fare, but it is accomplished with exceptional imagination and skillful direction and editing. In this post-World War III story, a handful of scrubby survivors fight over dwindling gasoline supplies. Gibson stars as a loner who helps an oil-producing colony defend itself against crazed marauders. The high-powered climax is carried off with such dazzling skill that it outshines some of the key action scenes in *Raiders of the Lost Ark*. Also with Emil Minty, Bruce Spense, and Virginia Hay. **Director**—George Miller. **(R)**
95 minutes

THE ROARING TWENTIES (1939)

★★★★

James Cagney
Humphrey Bogart
Jeffrey Lynn

Frank McHugh, James Cagney, and Humphrey Bogart in The Roaring Twenties.

This film version of the Mark Hellinger story, about a World War I veteran who becomes involved in crime during Prohibition, has a familiar plot, but Cagney is fantastic as the New York bootlegger who finds success in the underworld. Bogart costars as a childhood pal who becomes Cagney's rival in the rackets; Lynn appears as Cagney's army buddy. The film's rapid-fire action and charismatic but morally corrupt characters are typical of the genre. Also with Priscilla Lane, Gladys George, and Frank McHugh. **Director**—Raoul Walsh.
106 minutes b&w

THE ROBE (1953)

★★★

Richard Burton
Jean Simmons
Michael Rennie
Victor Mature

This Bible epic features Burton as Gallio, a Roman tribune put in charge of the execution of Jesus Christ. Burton later converts to Christianity when he dons Christ's robe. Burton is joined by a large cast, which also includes Richard Boone, Dawn Addams, and Dean Jagger. The movie, the first feature film made in the CinemaScope process, is impressively produced, but the plot does not stand the test of time. **Director**—Henry Koster. **Academy Award Nominations**—best picture; Burton, best actor; Leon Shamroy, cinematography.
133 minutes

ROBERTA (1935)

★★★

Irene Dunne
Randolph Scott
Fred Astaire
Ginger Rogers

Astaire and Rogers were still getting second billing at this point in their careers, but they're the major reason for seeing the film. An All-American gridiron star travels to Paris to contend with the very chic shop he's inherited from his late aunt. There's entertainment throughout, but when the dancing begins, there are fireworks. Top Jerome Kern songs include "Smoke Gets in Your Eyes," "Lovely to Look At," and "I Won't Dance." **Director**—William A. Seiter.
105 minutes b&w

ROBIN AND MARIAN (1976)

★★★

Sean Connery
Audrey Hepburn
Robert Shaw

Audrey Hepburn, Sean Connery, and Nicol Williamson in Robin and Marian.

The legend of Robin Hood is revised in this film. A middle-aged and battle-scarred Robin, played by Connery, returns to Sherwood Forest after fighting

(Continued)

This movie available on videotape and/or disc.

(Continued)
in the Crusades for 20 years. He locates Maid Marian (Hepburn), who is now an abbess. The unscrupulous Sheriff of Nottingham (Shaw) still controls the countryside. Robin takes him on, and summons the reserves of his strength and heroism. The acting and photography are impressive, and screenwriter James Goldman has turned the colorful myth of Robin Hood and his merry men into a story with contemporary relevance. Also with Richard Harris, Nicol Williamson, and Ian Holm. **Director**—Richard Lester. **(PG)** *106 minutes*

ROBIN AND THE SEVEN HOODS (1964)

★★★

Frank Sinatra
Dean Martin
Bing Crosby
Sammy Davis, Jr.
Peter Falk

An entertaining musical spoof set during Prohibition in Chicago. Sinatra and his friends—dubbed the "Rat Pack" in the early 1960s by gossip columnists—are well suited to their roles as small-time hoods who work as Chicago-style Robin Hoods; they steal from the rich and give to the poor. "My Kind of Town" and "Style" highlight the music. The cast also includes Barbara Rush, Edward G. Robinson, Victor Buono, Jack LaRue, and Hans Conried. **Director**—Gordon Douglas. *123 minutes*

ROBOCOP (1987)

★★★

Peter Weller
Nancy Allen

Robocop *(Peter Weller) gets the goods on criminal mastermind Kurtwood Smith.*

A comic-book-style science-fiction thriller about a half-human, half-robot character, who proves to be a relentless crimestopper. Weller, an actor who has spent his career playing offbeat characters in an off-center fashion, is well cast in the title role. Devised by an unscrupulous corporation, the figure of Robocop is actually the remains of an idealistic street cop—brutally killed by a gang of thugs—added to a huge mechanized body. Though the film is strangely cold and distant at times, the friendship between Robocop and a young policewoman (Allen) is poignant, giving this fast-paced action thriller some much-needed emotion. The special effects are outstanding, with the Robocop figure created by Rob Bottin. Also with Daniel O'Herlihy, Ronny Cox, Kurtwood Smith, and Miguel Ferrer. **(R) Academy Award Nominations**—Frank J. Vrioste, best editing; Michael J. Kohut, Carlos DeLarios, Aaron Rochin, and Robert Wald, best sound. *103 minutes*

ROBOCOP 2 (1990)

★★

Peter Weller
Nancy Allen

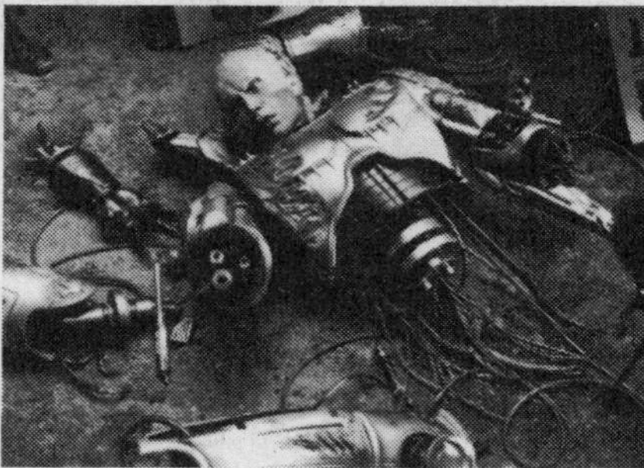

Temporarily out of order: Peter Weller in Robocop 2.

Mayhem and gore dominate this unworthy sequel about the dauntless cyborg police officer. Laced with cynical but flat humor, the violence is sometimes repellent, sometimes numbing. Weller dons the metallic costume once again to battle a corrupt conglomerate that wants to control a futuristic Detroit (though the film was shot in Texas). In addition, he must confront an ever larger and more sinister version of himself. The inventive satire and colorful villains of the original have been brushed aside in favor of graphic violence and sensational characters. Original director Paul Verhoeven moved on to greener pastures *(Total Recall)*; veteran Irvin Kershner directs by the numbers. Also with Daniel O'Herlihy, Belinda Bauer, Tom Noonan, Patricia Charbonneau, John Glover, Felton Perry, and Gabriel Damon. **(R)** *118 minutes*

ROCK AROUND THE CLOCK (1956)

★★½

Bill Haley and His Comets
Johnny Johnston
The Platters

This may be a low-budget B-movie, but it definitely takes you back to the pioneer days of Alan Freed, Bill Haley and His Comets, the Platters, Little Richard, Lisa Gaye, and Freddie Bell and the Bellboys. This picture was shot on a shoestring to cash in on the huge and sudden success of rock music in the mid-1950s, and it does convey that early excitement. Everything else about it, including its rudimentary tale of an unknown band that surges to success in the Big Apple, is fairly routine. **Director**—Fred F. Sears. *77 minutes b&w*

ROCKET GIBRALTAR (1988)

★★½

Burt Lancaster
Suzy Amis
Patricia Clarkson

Burt Lancaster hugs grandson Macaulay Culkin in Rocket Gibraltar.

Lancaster plays the grizzled patriarch whose family honors him on his 77th birthday at his Long Island beach home. Though his grown children love him, they don't understand him the way his grandchildren do. It is the kids who vow to carry out his last wish. A talented ensemble cast makes the most of the less-than-credible material. Also with John Glover, Francis Conroy, Sinead Cusack, Bill Pullman, and Marcy Culkin. **Director**—Daniel Petrie. **(PG)** *100 minutes*

® This movie available with closed captions for the hearing impaired.

ROCK 'N' ROLL HIGH SCHOOL (1979)

 ★★★

P.J. Soles
Vincent Van Patten
Clint Howard

Silliness and exuberance characterize this youth fantasy. Riff Randell (Soles) leads the kids at her high school in assorted escapades to provoke the displeasure of the school's stern principal; all this is carried out against a booming soundtrack of rock music, much of it by the hard-rocking band the Ramones, who also have speaking roles. The film celebrates the rebellious nature of rock music and its fans. Also with Paul Bartel and Alix Elias. **Director**—Allan Arkush. **(PG)** *94 minutes*

ROCKY (1976)

 ★★★★

Sylvester Stallone
Talia Shire

Rocky *(Sylvester Stallone) finds fulfillment and love with Adrian (Talia Shire).*

This gritty Cinderella story of a luckless Philadelphia boxer who gets a chance at the world heavyweight championship is uplifting to the human spirit. Stallone, who wrote the film script, plays the prizefighter in one of the best performances of his career. The schmaltzy plot owes much to *Marty,* yet the cliché takes on new life in this updated version. Excellent use of Philadelphia locales. Also with Burt Young, Carl Weathers, Burgess Meredith, and Thayer David. Crisply directed by John G. Avildsen. **(PG) Academy Awards**—best picture; Avildsen, best director. **Nominations**—Stallone, best actor; Shire, best actress; Meredith and Young, best supporting actor; Stallone, best screenplay written directly for the screen. *119 minutes*

ROCKY II (1979)

 ★★★

Sylvester Stallone
Talia Shire

Sequels seldom live up to the original, but this second chapter in the life of underdog boxer Rocky Balboa is an exception. The plot is overly sentimental in spots, but the training sequences and final fight scene are well crafted by Stallone, who both directed and stars in this popular sequel. The same supporting cast is back, including Carl Weathers, Burgess Meredith, and Burt Young. **(PG)** *119 minutes*

ROCKY III (1982)

★★★

Sylvester Stallone
Carl Weathers
Mr. T

This is the third installment in the film series about the champion boxer from Philadelphia. Writer/director/star Stallone continues the schmaltzy formula with Rocky struggling hard to keep his title when faced by snarling challenger Clubber Lang (Mr. T). This time, former opponent Apollo Creed (Weathers) has an important role as the champ's trainer and source of inspiration. Also with Talia Shire and Burt Young. **(PG)** *100 minutes*

ROCKY IV (1985)

★★

Sylvester Stallone
Dolph Lundgren

Sylvester Stallone enjoys the adulation of the crowd in Rocky IV.

It's round four for the Italian Stallion, and the dauntless heavyweight champ can still pack a walloping punch. Yet the story by now is too familiar and predictable. Rocky (Stallone) takes on a mammoth Russian boxer (Lundgren) at a match staged in the Soviet Union. This magnificent and brutal fight sequence is the centerpiece of the movie. Talia Shire, Burt Young, and Carl Weathers also star. **Director**—Stallone. **(PG)** *91 minutes*

ROGER AND ME (1989)

★★★½

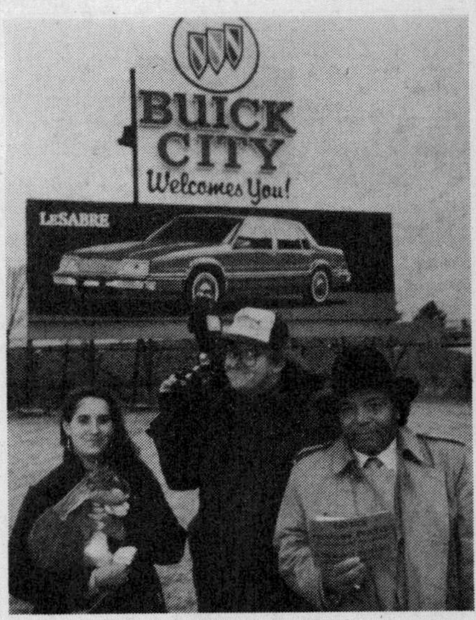

Filmmaker Michael Moore (center) with two of his cohorts on Roger and Me.

Filmmaker Michael Moore attacks General Motors, in particular, and big business, in general, in this low-budget documentary that uses humor as a weapon. The title refers to Moore's futile attempts to interview GM chairman Roger Smith about the plant shutdowns in Moore's hometown of Flint, Michigan. Often, Moore tries to track Smith down at the haunts of the rich and powerful, making a subtle statement about the wealthy lifestyle of executives versus the meager existence of the unemployed workers. Moore received some criticism because his documentary is not the factual "truth" about the massive GM layoffs in Flint. However, most documentaries do not present truth, only a point of view. Though Moore's point of view is obvious, his points about the human tragedy caused by the plant closings should be taken seriously. **(No MPAA rating)** *90 minutes*

ROGUES OF SHERWOOD FOREST (1950)

John Derek
Diana Lynn

The son of Robin Hood, played by Derek, helps the barons force the signing of the Magna Carta. The film's theme is tiresome and familiar, but the production is well done, and the sets and costumes are splendid. The competent cast also includes George Macready, Alan Hale, and Billy House. **Director**—Gordon Douglas. *80 minutes*

ROLLERBALL (1975)

★★

James Caan
John Beck

James Caan works out his aggressions playing Rollerball.

This futuristic sci-fi film, based on William Harrison's story, revolves around a sport that combines hockey, roller derby, motorcycle racing, and gladiatorial combat. Supposedly, this violent sport vicariously works out the aggressions of the masses, keeping billions of people glued to their TV sets and out of trouble. The setting is the 21st century, and all other forms of violence have been outlawed. The planet has come under the control of the "major corporate conglomerates," but one man—Caan—attempts to regain individual freedom in this brave new world. The derivative script offers few surprises, but clever art direction and slick cinematography nearly compensate. Also with John Houseman, Ralph Richardson, Maud Adams, and Moses Gunn. **Director**—Norman Jewison. **(R)** *123 minutes*

ROLLERCOASTER (1977)

★★½

George Segal
Richard Widmark
Timothy Bottoms
Henry Fonda

Ups and downs in amusement parks in Rollercoaster.

A clever extortionist, played by Bottoms, sabotages roller coasters to blackmail amusement-park owners. Segal is amusing and relaxed as a safety inspector who pursues the wily terrorist from coast to coast. The plot is straightforward but predictable. Originally released in theaters in high-vibration Sensurround. Also with Harry Guardino and Susan Strasberg. **Director**—James Goldstone. **(PG)** *119 minutes*

ROLLING THUNDER (1977)

★★★

William Devane

A finely crafted film about a Vietnam veteran, played by Devane, who hunts down the killers of his wife and son. Scriptwriter Paul Schrader, who wrote *Taxi Driver,* again uses an explosive and complicated character as the protagonist. The acting is excellent, and there's a convincing portrayal of small-town Middle America. The considerable amount of blood and gore may be too heavy for some viewers. Also with Tommy Lee Jones, Linda Haynes, James Best, and Dabney Coleman. **Director**—John Flynn. **(R)** *99 minutes*

ROLLOVER (1981)

★★

Jane Fonda
Kris Kristofferson

Fonda and Kristofferson star in this meandering, socially relevant movie about the vulnerability of the world's monetary system. The romantic thriller, set against the backdrop of banking and multinational corporations, is burdened with technical economic jargon. Fonda, dressed to the nines, plays a widow who takes over a petrochemical company after her husband's murder and tries to save the business from financial ruin. The film and Fonda look elegant, but the bottom line is confusion. Also stars Hume Cronyn, Josef Sommer, and Bob Gunton. **Director**—Alan J. Pakula. **(R)** *118 minutes*

ROMANCING THE STONE (1984)

★★★★ ®

Kathleen Turner
Michael Douglas
Danny DeVito

Michael Douglas and Kathleen Turner get a dunking while Romancing the Stone.

Slam-bang romantic adventure with many winning elements: a steamy love affair, cliff-hanging suspense, twinkling humor, colorful scoundrels, and a mad dash for buried treasure. Turner stars as a lonely pulp-fiction writer suddenly thrust into her own hair-raising escapade when her sister is kidnapped in Colombia. In the jungle, Turner teams up with an American wildlife entrepreneur, played by Douglas, for some rousing excitement. Also with Zack Norman, Alfonso Arau, and Manuel Ojeda. **Director**—Robert Zemeckis. **(PG)** *106 minutes*

ROMAN HOLIDAY (1953)

★★★★

Gregory Peck
Audrey Hepburn

Peck and Hepburn star in this story of a lonely princess who runs away from her official duties, meets a newspaperman, and falls in love with him. This captivating comedy—filmed in Rome—

® *This movie available with closed captions for the hearing impaired.*

A princess (Audrey Hepburn) and a newspaperman (Gregory Peck) are on a Roman Holiday.

made Hepburn a movie star, and set a fashion trend called the "Hepburn look." William Wyler directed from a script by Ian McLellan Hunter and John Dighton. The film also stars Eddie Albert, Hartley Power, and Harcourt Williams. **Academy Awards**—Hepburn, best actress; Hunter, motion picture story. **Nominations**—best picture; Wyler, best director; Albert, best supporting actor; Hunter and Dighton, screenplay; Franz Planer and Henry Alekan, cinematography.

118 minutes b&w

ROMANOFF AND JULIET (1961)

★★★

Peter Ustinov
Sandra Dee
John Gavin

Ustinov wrote, directed, and acted in this satire, set in the mythical Concordia, where the daughter of the U.S. ambassador falls in love with the Russian ambassador's son. Dee and Gavin play the loving couple. Some of the comic-strip action falls flat, and, at times, it seems that perhaps Ustinov took on too much; but his wit and the cold-war satire make this movie worthwhile. Ustinov gets solid support from Akim Tamiroff, Tamara Shayne, and Peter Jones. *103 minutes*

THE ROMAN SPRING OF MRS. STONE (1961)

Vivien Leigh
Warren Beatty
Jill St. John
Lotte Lenya

An aging, widowed actress (Leigh), who feels that her finest hours, both romantically and professionally, are all behind her, becomes romantically involved with her hired male companion (Beatty). Gavin Lambert adapted the script from a Tennessee Williams novella, but the usual Williams sensitivity is lost. More dominant is the sparkle of the Rome backdrop, and the unhappiness or downright ugliness in many of its denizens' lives. Lenya gives a compelling display of decadence. Frequent Williams stage director Jose Quintero gets adequate performances from a cast that also includes Jeremy Spenser and Coral Browne. **Academy Award Nomination**—Lenya, best supporting actress. *104 minutes*

ROMANTIC COMEDY (1983)

Dudley Moore
Mary Steenburgen

Mary Steenburgen and Dudley Moore are a team in Romantic Comedy.

Moore and Steenburgen, highly respected for their acting in previous romantic comedies, can't save this charmless production. They star as a successful play-writing team whose long-standing collaboration keeps threatening to blossom into a hot romance. Moore and Steenburgen try hard, but Bernard Slade's adaptation of his own play doesn't spark any fireworks. With Ron Leibman and Frances Sternhagen. **Director**—Arthur Hiller. **(PG)** *102 minutes*

THE ROMANTIC ENGLISHWOMAN (1975)

Glenda Jackson
Michael Caine

Joseph Losey directed this sophisticated yet complicated love story about a successful paperback novelist whose money and intense love fail to fulfill his wife, who runs away with a gigolo poet. Jackson plays the would-be liberated housewife; Caine is her novelist husband. There's lavish scenery and some witty dialogue, but the confusing love-triangle plot and poor casting override the assets. Also with Helmut Berger, Marcus Richardson, and Kate Nelligan. **(R)** *117 minutes*

ROMEO AND JULIET (1936)

★★★★

Norma Shearer
Leslie Howard
John Barrymore
Basil Rathbone

Well-crafted film version of the Shakespeare classic. Purists may object that scenarist Talbot Jennings has left out big chunks of the original (though he didn't add words of his own), or that Olivia Hussey and Leonard Whiting of the 1968 version (see below) are much closer in age to the protagonists Shakespeare had in mind than are Shearer (producer Irving Thalberg's wife) and Howard. Still, this remains one of the best filmed versions of a Shakespeare play, charged by the direction of George Cukor, the luminous performances, and the stylish studio sets. **Academy Award Nominations**—best picture; Shearer, best actress; Rathbone, best supporting actor.

126 minutes b&w

ROMEO AND JULIET (1968)

 ★★★

Leonard Whiting
Olivia Hussey

Director Franco Zeffirelli has a flair for bringing dazzling élan to classic theater and opera pieces, without unduly altering the original text. For this lush, breathlessly paced and acted production, he cast two youngsters—Whiting and Hussey—in the lead roles, and they do a fine job as Shakespeare's star-crossed lovers of Verona. They look sensational (as does the entire production), and their performances are quite moving. The film has an exciting, contemporary feel to it, with an outstanding score by Nino Rota. Also with Michael York, Milo O'Shea, John McEnery, and Robert Stephens. **(PG) Academy Award**—Pasquale De Santis, cinematography. **Nominations**—best picture; Zeffirelli, best director.

138 minutes

This movie available on videotape and/or disc.

ROMERO (1989)

★★1/2

Richard Jordan
Raul Julia

A moving but flawed account of the life of Oscar Romero, the archbishop of El Salvador who was assassinated in 1980 on orders of the military junta. The shy priest initially was expected to serve as a passive tool of the powerful, but his startling opposition to the brutal deeds of the government led to his death. Julia stars in the title role, while a competent supporting cast, including Ana Alicia and Eddie Valez, adds weight to the other characters. Unfortunately, too much reverence for Romero results in a two-dimensional depiction of the heroic priest. The film is not so much a biography that follows a man's life but a series of solemn, stately scenes that present Romero as a candidate for sainthood. Written by John Sacret Young, creator of television's *China Beach*. **Director**—John Duigan. **(PG-13)**

105 minutes

ROOFTOPS (1989)

★★

Jason Gedrick
Troy Beyer

Jason Gedrick (left) fights against gang leader Eddie Velez in Rooftops.

Inner-city youngsters fight, fall in love, and survive in a strange rooftop world among crumbling tenements. Gedrick plays the young hero who resides in a water tower and battles vicious crack dealers. Beyer provides the love interest. There are some energetic moments—notably a lively Brazilian dance—but this formulaic drama unfolds in routine fashion and offers minimal excitement. Also with Eddie Velez, Tisha Campbell, Alexis Cruz, and Allen Payne. **Director**—Robert Wise. **(R)**

95 minutes

ROOM AT THE TOP (1959)

★★★★

Laurence Harvey
Simone Signoret

Despite Harvey's wooden performance, this drama is a vivid and realistic look at the British working class. Harvey plays an egotistical, selfish clerk in a factory who jilts the woman who loves him to marry the daughter of the factory owner. Signoret plays Harvey's jilted mistress. Heather Sears, Donald Wolfit, Raymond Huntley, Donald Houston, Mary Peach, and Hermione Baddeley also star in this skillful screen adaptation of John Braine's novel. **Director**—Jack Clayton. **Academy Awards**—Signoret, best actress; Neil Paterson, best screenplay based on material from another medium. **Nominations**—best picture; Clayton, best director; Harvey, best actor; Baddeley, best supporting actress. *117 minutes b&w*

ROOM SERVICE (1938)

★★★

The Marx Brothers
Lucille Ball
Ann Miller
Donald MacBride

This attempt to meld the inspired, anarchic humor of the Marx Brothers with the tight, stage-bound humor of the John Murray/Allen Boretz play resulted in a box-office flop that was neither vintage Marx Brothers nor a good adaptation of the theatrical hit. Still, it is a funny portrayal of a producer and his company struggling to get financing for their show, and holing up in the White Way Hotel—which wants to evict them because they have no money. Hardly among the Brothers' best but still a lark. Also with Frank Albertson. **Director**—William A. Seiter. *78 minutes b&w*

A ROOM WITH A VIEW (1986)

★★★ ®

Helena Bonham Carter
Julian Sands

An insightful and subtly amusing film about members of the English upper crust during the Edwardian era. Based

Julian Sands comforts Helena Bonham Carter in A Room with a View.

on E.M. Forster's novel, the story concerns the "outrage" committed when a socially improper young man (Sands) falls in love with a genteel young woman (Bonham Carter). Though slow-moving and occasionally pompous, the film boasts an excellent cast and high production values. Also with Maggie Smith, Denholm Elliott, and Daniel Day-Lewis. **Director**—James Ivory. **Academy Awards**—Ruth Prawer Jhabvala, best screenplay based on material from another medium; Gianna Quaranta, Brian Ackland-Snow, Brian Savegar, and Elio Altramura, best art direction and set decoration; Jenny Beaven and John Bright, best costume design. **Nominations**—best picture; James Ivory, best director; Elliott, best supporting actor; Smith, best supporting actress; Tony Pierce-Roberts, cinematography. **(No MPAA rating)**

115 minutes

ROOSTER COGBURN (1975)

★★

John Wayne
Katharine Hepburn

Katharine Hepburn and John Wayne are on the trail in Rooster Cogburn.

Wayne—a one-eyed, booze-guzzling U.S. marshal—is on the trail of outlaws. Hepburn—the pastor's daughter—is at his side in this less-than-successful se-

® *This movie available with closed captions for the hearing impaired.*

quel to *True Grit*. Watching such legendary actors as Wayne and Hepburn may be entertaining for some, but the movie itself is only a run-of-the-mill western. Also with Anthony Zerbe, John McIntire, Strother Martin, and Richard Jordan. **Director**—Stuart Millar. **(PG)** *107 minutes*

ROPE (1948)

★★★

James Stewart
John Dall
Farley Granger

Alfred Hitchcock directed this stagy film about two young men who kill a college friend as part of a thrill-seeking experiment. As the movie unfolds, the men ghoulishly reveal clues to the crime. The interesting but static-looking mystery tale was inspired by the Leopold/Loeb murder case. It was also Hitchcock's first color film, and he experimented with 10-minute takes in an effort to perfect a seamless movie, one in which none of the editing would be apparent. Also with Cedric Hardwicke, Joan Chandler, and Douglas Dick. **(PG)** *81 minutes*

ROPE OF SAND (1949)

★★★

Burt Lancaster
Corinne Calvet
Claude Rains
Peter Lorre

Bristling adventure about a stash of diamonds, hidden in the South African desert, and a sultry siren, played by Calvet in her film debut. Those vying for the booty include Lancaster, as an adventurer; Rains, as a villainous diamond company man; and Paul Henreid, as the chief of police. Also with Sam Jaffe and Mike Mazurki. **Director**—William Dieterle. *104 minutes b&w*

ROSALIE GOES SHOPPING (1989)

★★½

Marianne Sagebrecht
Brad Davis

This quirky satire revolves around a merry housewife who fills her family's surroundings with state-of-the-art gadgets, fancy food, and new cars. Her materialistic binge is carried out via phoney credit cards, juggled bank accounts, and unbridled gall. Sagebrecht, the queen-sized German actress, approaches the role as a doting, overprotective mother who would do anything for her family. Davis costars as her trusting husband. German filmmaker Percy Adlon fashions a cinematic statement that criticizes Americans as gross consumers, a view held by many European intellectuals. Also with Judge Reinhold, Alex Winter, and John Hawkes. **(PG)** *94 minutes*

THE ROSARY MURDERS (1987)

Donald Sutherland
Charles Durning

The Catholic clergy of Detroit fall prey to a serial killer. A good-natured priest (Sutherland) who hears the murderer's confession is faced with the dilemma of saving innocent lives while upholding religious confidentiality. He also butts heads with Durning, a colorful but more traditional priest who goes strictly by the book. This suspense tale gets off to an interesting start, but the tension subsides as the mystery unfolds. Sutherland seems to walk through his performance, while Durning fares better in a more clearly drawn role. Predictable and ultimately shallow. Also with Belinda Dauer and Josef Somer. **Director**—Fred Walton. **(R)** *105 minutes*

THE ROSE (1979)

★★½

Bette Midler
Alan Bates
Frederic Forrest

Bette Midler puts across a song with plenty of punch in The Rose.

Midler, in her screen acting debut, plays a rock 'n' roll queen who self-destructs on alcohol, drugs, and the stresses of stardom. Forrest is good as her lover, who wants her to quit the business. The screenplay is obviously based on the career of the late Janis Joplin. The film's hysterical, hair-pulling pitch helps compensate for a shallow script, as does Midler's rendition of the songs. Also with Harry Dean Stanton, Barry Primus, and David Keith. **Director**—Mark Rydell. **(R) Academy Award Nominations**—Midler, best actress; Forrest, best supporting actor. *134 minutes*

ROSELAND (1977)

Lou Jacobi
Teresa Wright

This study of loneliness, set in New York City's famous Roseland dance hall, is divided into three interlocking vignettes and has a made-for-TV quality. There's pathos here, but it barely transcends the soft script. First-rate performances carry the film—especially those in a touching segment with Jacobi and Wright. Also with Christopher Walken, Helen Gallagher, Geraldine Chaplin, and Lilia Skala. **Director**—James Ivory. **(PG)** *103 minutes*

ROSEMARY'S BABY (1968)

Mia Farrow
John Cassavetes

A new apartment with new neighbors means trouble for Mia Farrow in Rosemary's Baby.

An excellent cast combined with Roman Polanski's deft direction yields a top-notch thriller about a coven of witches in New York City. Farrow and her overly ambitious husband, played

(Continued)

This movie available on videotape and/or disc.

(Continued)
by Cassavetes, become involved with diabolical neighbors—Ruth Gordon and Sidney Blackmer—resulting in devilish consequences. Produced by William Castle, well known for his horror films of the 1950s and 1960s. The cast also includes Ralph Bellamy, Patsy Kelly, Maurice Evans, Charles Grodin, and Elisha Cook, Jr. Based on the novel by Ira Levin. **(R) Academy Award**—Gordon, best supporting actress. **Nomination**—Polanski, best screenplay based on material from another medium. *137 minutes*

THE ROSE TATTOO (1955)

★★★★

Anna Magnani
Burt Lancaster

Anna Magnani portrays a troubled widow who finds love again in The Rose Tattoo.

Magnani gives a robust and earthy performance as a troubled widow who finds love again when she meets a rough-and-tumble truck driver, played by Lancaster. At times she seems larger than life and appears to be too powerful for the screen. This movie version of the Tennessee Williams play was ably directed by Daniel Mann and well photographed, with excellent supporting efforts from Virginia Grey, Jo Van Fleet, Ben Cooper, and Marisa Pavan. **Academy Awards**—Magnani, best actress; James Wong Howe, cinematography. **Nominations**—best picture; Pavan, best supporting actress. *117 minutes b&w*

ROUGH CUT (1980)

★★

Burt Reynolds
Lesley-Anne Down

Reynolds stars as a smooth-talking American jewel thief who stages a diamond heist in Europe and seduces the beautiful woman (Down) sent to lure him into the crime. Reynolds displays his reliable charm, but he's saddled with a hopeless script and wooden dialogue. The story springs to action in the final quarter, but it's too late—interest has flagged by that time. The troubled production went through four directors, and scriptwriter Larry Gelbart did not use his real name in the credits. Also with David Niven, Patrick Magee, and Timothy West. **Director**—Don Siegel. **(PG)** *111 minutes*

THE ROUNDERS (1965)

★★

Henry Fonda
Glenn Ford

Fonda and Ford are congenial modern cowboys in this comedy/western. The two are foiled by a stubborn horse that refuses to be trained. The horse gives them plenty of trouble and is the source of many of the gags. Although the story is slight, this film, written and directed by Burt Kennedy, is pleasant fare for the entire family. Also with Sue Ane Langdon, Edgar Buchanan, Chill Wills, and Denver Pyle. *85 minutes*

'ROUND MIDNIGHT (1986)

★★★

Dexter Gordon
Francois Cluzet

Dexter Gordon plays jazz musician Bud Powell in 'Round Midnight.

Inspired by the career of jazz great Bud Powell, this atmospheric drama concerns the struggles of an American saxophonist living in Paris during the late 1950s. Directed by French filmmaker Bertrand Tavernier (*A Sunday in the Country; Coup de Torchon*), the film stars an English-speaking cast headed by real-life musician Gordon in the main role. Cluzet costars as a devoted jazz fan who takes in the aged, alcoholic musician and nurtures what remains of the old man's career. The recreation of the jazz milieu and the score by Herbie Hancock highlight this poignant film, which conveys the improvisational and emotional nature of American jazz music. Gabrielle Haker, Lonette McKee, and Herbie Hancock appear in supporting roles. Originally filmed in French and English. **(R) Academy Award**—Hancock, best original score. **Nomination**—Gordon, best actor. *131 minutes*

ROXANNE (1987)

★★★

Steve Martin
Daryl Hannah
Rick Rossovich

Steve Martin is a latter-day Cyrano de Bergerac; Daryl Hannah is Roxanne.

Martin stars in his best comedy to date in this breezy, updated version of Edmond Rostand's *Cyrano de Bergerac*. He plays a small-town fire chief endowed with an oversized nose, who writes beautiful love letters to the lovely Roxanne (Hannah) on behalf of a shy, awkward suitor (Rossovich). While doing so, he too falls in love with her, setting off the famous love triangle. The low-key antics and the emphasis on clever dialogue give the film an endearing quality that is hard to resist. The secondary characters add some physical humor to the proceedings. Also with Shelley Duvall, Michael J. Pollard, and Fred Willard. **Director**—Fred Schepisi. **(PG)** *107 minutes*

® This movie available with closed captions for the hearing impaired.

ROYAL FLASH (1975)

★★

Malcolm McDowell
Alan Bates
Oliver Reed

This film about the misadventures of Captain Harry Paget Flashman is a spoof of Victorian England, but it comes off as low-grade slapstick. Leading man McDowell tries hard, but director Richard Lester has exploited this swashbuckling theme before in *The Three Musketeers* and *The Four Musketeers*. The outcome this time is overkill; it's more of a flush. Based on the enjoyable novel by George MacDonald Fraser. With Lionel Jeffries, Britt Ekland, and Florinda Bolkan. **(PG)**

98 minutes

ROYAL WEDDING (1951)

 ★★★

Fred Astaire
Jane Powell

Astaire's brilliant dancing and Powell's delightful singing overcome a pedestrian plot in which the two stars—who play brother and sister—perform in London at the time of Queen Elizabeth II's marriage to Prince Philip. Alan Jay Lerner, of *My Fair Lady* fame, and Burton Lane wrote the songs. Watch for Astaire's famous dance sequence on the ceiling. Produced by Arthur Freed. Sarah Churchill, Peter Lawford, and Keenan Wynn also star. **Director**—Stanley Donen. *100 minutes*

RUBY GENTRY (1952)

 ★★★

Jennifer Jones
Charlton Heston
Karl Malden

Jones was never better than as the title character, a sultry North Carolina woman from the wrong side of the tracks. When the blueblood she loves (Heston) won't have her, she marries the town's wealthiest man (Malden), and avenges herself against those who have spurned her. Passion has seldom been more vividly incarnated on the screen. The title song became a popular tune of the era. Also with Josephine Hutchison and Tom Tully. Expertly directed by King Vidor.

82 minutes b&w

RUDE AWAKENING (1989)

 ★★

Eric Roberts
Cheech Marin

A loosely structured satire about two career hippies (Marin and Roberts) who return from Central America to live in Manhattan, where they confront the yuppie culture. Though a plot whose time has come, the story crudely meanders from scene to scene. The film offers a bit of nostalgia about the 1960s counterculture but little else. Julie Hagerty, Cliff DeYoung, and Robert Carradine costar. Andrea Martin, Louise Lasser, and Buck Henry fare better in bit roles. **Directors**—Aaron Russo and David Greenwalt. **(R)** *100 minutes*

RUGGLES OF RED GAP (1935)

 ★★★★

Charles Laughton
Charles Ruggles
Roland Young
Mary Boland

Uproarious 1930s comedy, beautifully acted by an offbeat cast and well directed by Leo McCarey. The Earl of Brunstead (Young) loses his butler, Marmaduke Ruggles (Laughton), to an American hick (Ruggles) during a poker game. Accompanying his new employer back to his new home in the wild and woolly West, the stiff-upper-lipped Ruggles has trouble adjusting to this informal, downright raucous environment. Laughton won the New York Film Critics Award for his work in this film and in *Mutiny on the Bounty*, both released in the same year. He's quite touching in the famous scene in which he astonishes barroom patrons with an emotional recitation of the Gettysburg Address. Also with Zasu Pitts and Lucien Littlefield. **Director**—Leo McCarey. **Academy Award Nomination**—best picture. *92 minutes b&w*

THE RULING CLASS (1972)

 ★★★

Peter O'Toole
Alastair Sim
Harry Andrews

Smartly acted British satire from Peter Barnes' stage success. O'Toole plays the mad (or is he really?) young gentleman

Peter O'Toole suffers from a delusion in The Ruling Class.

whose father, the 13th Earl of Gurney, dies, leaving him the vast wealth and title of the 14th Earl of Gurney. This inheritance may not mean as much to the bereaved son—who fancies himself to be Jesus Christ and has spent time in a mental institution—as to other members of the family, who would love to share the booty. As directed by Peter Medak, the film itself is too self-consciously stylized, but it's delectably acted by O'Toole, Sim, Andrews, Arthur Lowe, and Coral Browne. Some prints run 130 minutes; others are 141 minutes. **(PG) Academy Award Nomination**—O'Toole, best actor.

154 minutes

RUMBLE FISH (1983)

★★★

Matt Dillon
Mickey Rourke

Struggle and disillusionment with Matt Dillon and Mickey Rourke in Rumble Fish.

One of the finest and most overlooked films in Francis Coppola's brilliant career. He calls it his "art film for kids," but this downbeat, surreal story is probably too wrenching for most kids.

(Continued)

This movie available on videotape and/or disc.

(Continued)
Adapted from S.E. Hinton's novel, the plot is derived from Greek tragedy and concerns the disillusionment of street-punk Dillon and the fall of the older brother he idolizes (played with grace and feeling by Rourke). A unique, jarring style is evident everywhere, from Coppola's dreamlike direction to the percussive soundtrack by rock musician Stewart Copeland. Tom Waits and Diane Lane are superb in their supporting roles. **(R)** *94 minutes b&w/color*

RUNAWAY (1984)

★★

Tom Selleck
Cynthia Rhodes

Sabotaged robots go on the rampage and kill people. Selleck plays the high-tech police detective who has the task of stopping the mechanical murders. It's a clever idea that unfolds with little style or energy. Unfortunately, the human characters seem as mechanical as the robots. Gene Simmons (of the pop group KISS) and Kirstie Alley also star. **Director**—Michael Crichton. **(PG–13)** *100 minutes*

RUNAWAY TRAIN (1985)

★★★

Jon Voight
Eric Roberts
Rebecca DeMornay

Eric Roberts, Rebecca DeMornay, and Jon Voight in Runaway Train.

Two escaped convicts stow away on a train that runs out of control when the engineer dies of a heart attack. The story begins at an Alaskan maximum-security prison, from which the prisoners make their escape, and then follows the duo's attempts to stop the speeding train after they discover their dilemma. The prison scenes are authentic looking, though the brutality among the convicts is difficult to watch. Less convincing are the train sequences, which strive too hard for suspense and symbolism. Voight is excellent as a cynical convicted killer. Directed by Russian Andrei Konchalovsky from a story by Japanese filmmaker Akira Kurosawa, shot in Canada, and starring an American cast—the film is truly an international production. **(R)** **Academy Award Nominations**—Voight, best actor; Roberts, best supporting actor. *111 minutes*

THE RUNNER STUMBLES (1979)

★★

Dick Van Dyke
Kathleen Quinlan

Forbidden romance: Dick Van Dyke and Kathleen Quinlan in The Runner Stumbles.

Director Stanley Kramer, known for tackling touchy subjects, presents this film about a priest's romantic interest in a young, vivacious nun. Van Dyke plays the distraught priest too self-consciously; Quinlan plays the perky nun. Celibacy is perhaps a bit too touchy even for Kramer, who seems overly cautious about treating the issue with depth or passion. The movie merely drifts along, and the story is never convincing. Also with Maureen Stapleton, Ray Bolger, Tammy Grimes, and Beau Bridges. **(PG)** *99 minutes*

RUNNING (1979)

★★

Michael Douglas
Susan Anspach

Douglas plays a chronic loser who seeks redemption by competing for the United States Olympic running team. This is yet another sports film that parallels *Rocky,* but can't match the spirit of Sylvester Stallone's popular film series. Douglas is too good for the mediocre material, which merely runs its course with minimal suspense and drama; Anspach is wasted as Douglas' ex-wife. Also with Lawrence Dane and Eugene Levy. **Director**—Steven Hilliard Stern. **(PG)** *103 minutes*

THE RUNNING MAN (1987)

★★★

Arnold Schwarzenegger
Richard Dawson
Maria Conchita Alonso

In the year 2017, America is a totalitarian state where a vicious, bloody TV game show is the most popular program on the air. Each week a convict is given a chance to be pardoned if he can defeat a gang of ruthless killers in a series of brutal confrontations. When Schwarzenegger is given his opportunity to be on the program, he makes short work of the ferocious futuristic gladiators who wield flame throwers, chainsaws, and other exotic weaponry. Though a somewhat hyped-up mixture of *Rollerball* and *Mad Max,* this action-packed science-fiction tale also serves as a provocative spoof of television. Clever casting gives the film much of its color. Dawson almost steals the film as the unctious game-show host, while ex-football star Jim Brown, wrestlers Toru Tanaka and Jesse Ventura, and weight-lifter Gus Rethwisch appear as the boob-tube gladiators. **Director**—Paul Michael Glaser. **(R)** *101 minutes*

RUNNING ON EMPTY (1988)

★★★

Christine Lahti
River Phoenix
Judd Hirsch

River Phoenix, Christine Lahti, and the rest of the family are Running on Empty.

® This movie available with closed captions for the hearing impaired.

A drama about a teenager (Phoenix) struggling for his adulthood in a family still beset by the turmoil of the 1960s. Phoenix is exceptionally convincing as the adolescent son of politically radical parents who have been on the lam for 15 years. His love affair with a local girl (Martha Plimpton) and his future as a promising pianist are tragically at odds with his family's precarious predicament. The film revolves around the dangers and rewards of strong family loyalty. Lahti and Hirsch are excellent as the embattled parents. Also with Jonas Arby, Ed Crowley, L.M. Kit Carson, and Steven Hill. **Director**—Sidney Lumet. **(PG-13) Academy Award Nominations**—Phoenix, best supporting actor; Naomi Foner, best original screenplay. *115 minutes*

RUNNING SCARED (1986)

★★

Gregory Hines
Billy Crystal

Two undercover cops flush out a noted drug dealer in this action comedy with a too-familiar storyline and mediocre production values. Only the Chicago locales provide any freshness. Much was made at the time of the film's release of the rapport between Hines and Crystal, but their mostly improvised dialogue is frequently adolescent and tries too hard to be hip. The set dressing and cinematography are below par—the fake snow clings to the sides of buildings and characters' clothing like shaving cream! Obviously inspired by the success of *48 HRS.*, but without that film's style and wicked humor. Also with Steven Bauer, Joe Pantoliano, Darlanne Fluegel, Tracy Reed, Jonathan Gries, and Dan Hedaya. **Director**—Peter Hyams. **(R)** *110 minutes*

RUN SILENT, RUN DEEP (1958)

★★★

Clark Gable
Burt Lancaster

Gable, as the commander of a U.S. submarine, and Lancaster, as his lieutenant, provide competent portrayals in this suspenseful World War II drama. Besides the larger conflict with the Japanese Navy in Tokyo Bay, there's feuding between the two naval officers. There are also excellent sea-fighting sequences—an improvement over most submarine movies. Also with Jack Warden, Brad Dexter, Nick Cravat, Joe Maross, and Don Rickles. **Director**—Robert Wise. *93 minutes b&w*

THE RUSSIANS ARE COMING! THE RUSSIANS ARE COMING! (1966)

★★½

Carl Reiner
Eva Marie Saint
Alan Arkin

There are enough stars in this cold-war farce about the forced landing of a Russian submarine off the shore of Nantucket to keep the plot from sinking into oblivion. Arkin, Reiner, and Jonathan Winters provide excellent comic acting, and are helped by the competent performances of Saint, John Phillip Law, Paul Ford, Tessie O'Shea, Brian Keith, Theodore Bikel, and Ben Blue. If you don't expect too much and are willing to laugh about the Cold War, this is a mildly enjoyable movie. The perceptive viewer will also notice that the movie was not photographed off Nantucket and that the scenery is that of northern California. **Director**—Norman Jewison. **Academy Award Nominations**—best picture; Arkin, best actor; William Rose, best screenplay based on material from another medium. *120 minutes*

RUSSKIES (1987)

★★

Whip Hubley
Leaf Phoenix
Peter Billingsley
Stefan DeSalle

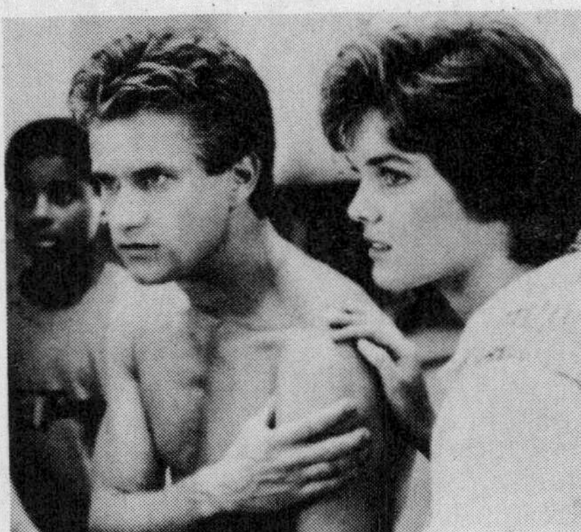

Whip Hubley, who is a stranded Russian sailor, and Susan Walters in Russkies.

A Russian sailor is washed ashore on a Florida beach where he is found by three adolescents. At first they suspect him to be part of a secret Soviet invasion—just like in the action-packed comic books they have been reading all summer. But they soon grow fond of their new-found friend and decide to help him return to his own country. Despite the good intentions of the plot, the film is overly sentimental and predictable right from the opening shots. Young viewers may find the film of interest, but adults should steer clear. Also with Susan Walters, Patrick Kilpatrick, Susan Blanchard, and Summer Phoenix. **Director**—Rick Rosenthal. **(PG)** *99 minutes*

RUSTLER'S RHAPSODY (1985)

★★

Tom Berenger

This rhapsody is the familiar old song—the overplayed western spoof, offkey at that, and without any novel orchestrations. Berenger plays nattily dressed singing cowboy Rex O'Herlihan, who trots into town on his wonder horse and gets mixed up in a clash between sheepherders and cattlemen. It has its moments, but it will be appreciated only by those too young to remember *Blazing Saddles*. You've been warned, pardners. Costars Andy Griffith, Marilu Henner, and Fernando Rey. **Director**—Hugh Wilson. **(PG)** *89 minutes*

RUTHLESS PEOPLE (1986)

★★★

Bette Midler
Danny DeVito
Judge Reinhold
Helen Slater

Bette Midler makes the most of a bad situation in Ruthless People.

An outrageous farce directed by Jim Abrahams, David Zucker, and Jerry Zucker, the trio who brought us *Airplane!* Midler stars as the gauche, over-

(Continued)

(Continued)
weight wife of millionaire clothing manufacturer DeVito. She is kidnapped by a cute couple (Slater and Reinhold) and held for a ransom of several million dollars. The couple are riled at DeVito because he stole their clothing designs and made a fortune from their hard work. Complications occur when DeVito refuses to pay the ransom because he cannot stand his spouse, and was about to kill her when the kidnapping occurred. The storyline (reminiscent of O. Henry's "The Ransom of Red Chief") is a complex series of plot twists and turns that neatly comes together for a surprise ending. Midler and DeVito are both excellent comic actors, and Dale Launer's screenplay contains clever commentary on the culture of Los Angeles' *nouveaux riches.* Also with Anita Morris and Art Evans. **(R)**
93 minutes

RYAN'S DAUGHTER (1970)

★★★

Sarah Miles
Robert Mitchum
Chris Jones

The beautiful Irish scenery, superbly photographed, makes this simple love story seem more majestic than it really is. The story, about a schoolteacher's wife who falls in love with a British officer in 1916 Ireland, is too long and fails to attain the greatness sought by director David Lean. His filmmaking technique is excellent, however, and the acting is above average. Miles plays the romantic adulteress, Mitchum is the moody schoolteacher, and Jones plays the soldier. John Mills, Trevor Howard, and Leo McKern also star. Originally released at 206 minutes; videotape versions are 194 minutes. **(PG) Academy Awards**—Mills, best supporting actor; Freddie Young, cinematography. **Nominations**—Miles, best actress.
176 minutes

S

SABOTAGE (1937)

★★★1/2

Sylvia Sidney
John Loder
Oscar Homolka

One of the best of Alfred Hitchcock's 1930s films, this is a tight reworking of

Oscar Homolka and Sylvia Sidney in Alfred Hitchcock's Sabotage.

Joseph Conrad's novel *The Secret Agent* (and not to be confused with Hitchcock's earlier film, *The Secret Agent,* which had nothing to do with Conrad). Sidney stars as the wife of a movie theater manager (Homolka) who is unaware her husband is a saboteur. The film includes the famous sequence in which the heroine's younger brother dawdles as he makes a delivery across London—not realizing the package he's carrying is a time bomb.
76 minutes b&w

SABOTEUR (1942)

★★★1/2

Robert Cummings
Priscilla Lane
Otto Kruger

Robert Cummings and Priscilla Lane are under scrutiny in Saboteur.

A gripping Alfred Hitchcock thriller, starring Cummings as a wartime worker in a California aircraft factory who falls under suspicion of sabotage. He can clear himself only by tracking the real villains—a cross-country pursuit that involves him with Lane and Kruger, and takes him through some tingling moments at Radio City Music Hall and on top of the Statue of Liberty. Dorothy Parker contributed to the screenplay. Norman Lloyd and Alan Baxter costar. **(PG)** *108 minutes b&w*

SABRINA (1954)

★★★

Humphrey Bogart
William Holden
Audrey Hepburn

Hepburn is delightful in this excellent comedy about a chauffeur's daughter. She's romanced by Bogart, who plays a middle-aged tycoon, and by Holden, who is Bogart's playboy brother. Based on *Sabrina Fair,* a popular play at the time by Samuel Taylor, the film makes good use of an offbeat cast. Director Billy Wilder also served as producer and screenwriter on the film. Although not one of his most significant efforts, this sophisticated romantic comedy is well crafted and entertaining. **Academy Award Nominations**—Wilder, best director; Hepburn, best actress; Wilder, Samuel Taylor, and Ernest Lehman, screenplay; Charles Lang, Jr., cinematography. *113 minutes b&w*

THE SAD SACK (1957)

★★

Jerry Lewis
David Wayne

In this uneven comic effort, inspired by the George Baker comic strip, Lewis plays a woebegone soldier who gets involved with spies and Arabian intrigues. Aside from Peter Lorre, who appears as an Arab in the latter part of the film, the rest of the cast is 4F. Also with Mary Treen, Gene Evans, and Joe Mantell. **Director**—George Marshall.
98 minutes b&w

SAHARA (1943)

★★★

Humphrey Bogart
Dan Duryea

Bogart stars in this action-packed war story, with an all-male supporting cast, including J. Carrol Naish and Rex Ingram. Bogart heads a British-American tank unit stranded in the Sahara Desert. Typical of other war films about a small unit of men, the characters represent a cross-section of types and classes—the Southerner, the Brooklyn native, a black man, etc. Also with

This movie available with closed captions for the hearing impaired.

Humphrey Bogart heads an Allied tank unit stranded in the Sahara.

Bruce Bennett, Lloyd Bridges, and Kurt Kreuger. **Director**—Zoltan Korda. **Academy Award Nominations**—Naish, best supporting actor; Rudolph Maté, cinematography. *97 minutes b&w*

SAILOR BEWARE (1951)

★★½

Dean Martin
Jerry Lewis

This is one of the funnier movies Martin and Lewis made before going their separate ways. Here the duo join the Navy and become involved with its boxing tournament. And, as unlikely as it sounds, Lewis gets a reputation as a suave man among the ladies. The boxing and Naval induction scenes are the highlights in this comedy, which also includes Robert Strauss, Leif Erickson, Marion Marshall, and Corinne Calvet. James Dean appears in one of the crowd scenes during a boxing match. **Director**—Hal Walker. *108 minutes b&w*

THE SAILOR WHO FELL FROM GRACE WITH THE SEA (1976)

★★

Sarah Miles
Kris Kristofferson

Miles and Kristofferson star in this film adaptation of an erotic novel by the Japanese writer Yukio Mishima. The setting is transplanted from Yokohama to Dartmouth, England, with less than successful results, and Mishima's chilling story becomes merely grotesque as a movie. The story involves a sailor who gives up the sea for domestic tranquility—an affair with a widow—and is gruesomely killed by a band of teenage boys, who determine he has violated the "perfect order of things." Miles plays the widow and Kristofferson co-stars as the sailor. Beautiful cinematography by Douglas Slocombe. Also with Jonathan Kahn, Margo Cunningham, and Earl Rhodes. **Director**—Lewis John Carlino. **(R)** *105 minutes*

ST. ELMO'S FIRE (1985)

★★

Rob Lowe
Demi Moore
Emilio Estevez
Andrew McCarthy

Is there life after college graduation? Four buddies find out in St. Elmo's Fire.

Recent college graduates sort out their love affairs and other life crises in this erratic, trendy ensemble drama that resembles *The Big Chill*. (It was sarcastically labeled *The Little Chill* by critics upon its release.) While the various post-adolescent problems appear real, the thin script never adopts a particular viewpoint. The attractive young performers don't have the opportunity to display their talents to best advantage. Also with Mare Winningham, Judd Nelson, and Ally Sheedy. **Director**—Joel Schumaker. **(R)** *110 minutes*

ST. IVES (1976)

★★★

Charles Bronson
John Houseman
Jacqueline Bisset

Bronson plays an ex-crime reporter who suddenly finds himself involved as a go-between for an eccentric millionaire seeking the return of his stolen and incriminating journals. It's a change of pace for Bronson, who usually appears in action/adventure films characterized by violence. This witty and low-key film manages to entertain despite an excessively complicated plot that eventually unravels toward the end. Also with Harry Guardino, Maximilian Schell, and Elisha Cook, Jr. **Director**—J. Lee Thompson. **(PG)** *94 minutes*

SAINT JACK (1979)

★★

Ben Gazzara
Denholm Elliott

A low-key melodrama by Peter Bogdanovich set in Singapore in the early 1970s. Jack Flowers, played by Gazzara, is a pimp with a heart of gold and a sense of honor, who's determined to run the best brothel in town. There are masterful performances by Gazzara and Elliott, who plays a woebegone Englishman. Their acting towers over the sparse material. The exotic locale provides a colorful atmosphere. Also with James Villiers, Rodney Bewes, George Lazenby, Joss Ackland, and Lisa Lu. **(R)** *112 minutes*

SAINT JOAN (1957)

Jean Seberg

Although novelist Graham Greene wrote the screenplay from a George Bernard Shaw play, this screen adaptation is a clunker. Most of the impressive cast is wasted, but Seberg is simply miscast as the Maid of Orleans. John Gielgud, Anton Walbrook, Richard Todd, Harry Andrews, Richard Widmark, and Felix Aylmer make the film tolerable viewing. A financial and critical failure upon its release. **Director**—Otto Preminger. *110 minutes b&w*

THE ST. VALENTINE'S DAY MASSACRE (1967)

Jason Robards
George Segal

Robards stars as Al Capone in B-movie king Roger Corman's semidocumentary interpretation of the notorious Chicago massacre and the events leading to it. The film is violent, and perhaps too episodic, but also perversely amusing. Robards is physically miscast as Capone, but gives a forcefully energetic performance. Despite the deliberate buildup, the climactic shoot-out is genuinely shocking. The performances of Ralph

(Continued)

This movie available on videotape and/or disc.

(Continued)
Meeker, Jean Hale, Bruce Dern, Clint Ritchie, Jack Nicholson, and Reed Hadley help make this an enjoyable viewing experience. *100 minutes*

SALAAM BOMBAY! (1988)

★★★1/2

Shafiq Syed

Indian director Mira Nair examines Bombay's squalid underbelly—a world of prostitutes, drug dealers, and con artists—through the eyes of street urchins. Syed is remarkable as the 10-year-old boy struggling to survive amid this urban chaos. The other nonprofessional child players are also good. The drama was shot mainly in the brothels and on the crowded streets of Bombay. Originally filmed in Hindi.
(No MPAA rating) *113 minutes*

SALSA (1988)

★★

Robby Rosa
Rodney Harvey
Angela Alvarado

Robby Rosa and Angela Alvarado dance with a Latin beat in Salsa.

Rosa, a former member of the adolescent pop group Menudo, dances up a storm in this obvious imitation of *Dirty Dancing* with a Latin beat. The thin plot involves a handsome lad who wants to win a Los Angeles salsa contest and a trip to Puerto Rico to be crowned "King of Salsa." Along the way to certain victory, the youth experiences a number of romantic adventures. The many flashy dance sequences and production numbers take center stage in this lightweight production, making the film seem like a series of music videos edited together. Also with Magali Alvarado, Miranda Garrison, Moon Orona, and Loyda Ramos. **Director**—Boaz Davidson. **(PG)** *96 minutes*

SALTY O'ROURKE (1945)

Alan Ladd
Stanley Clements
Gail Russell

Brisk racetrack picture starring Ladd as a Runyonesque gambler who, despite his dishonest efforts, can't seem to hit pay dirt. Clements costars as a jockey hired by Ladd to throw races. Russell plays a schoolteacher who provides the romantic interest. Also with William Demarest, Bruce Cabot, and Spring Byington. A minor effort by veteran Hollywood director Raoul Walsh. **Academy Award Nomination**—Milton Holmes, original screenplay. *97 minutes b&w*

SALVADOR (1986)

★★★1/2

James Woods
Jim Belushi
John Savage
Elpedia Carrillo

A vivid, highly charged story, based on fact, about a selfish, down-and-out photojournalist (Woods) who redeems himself while covering El Salvador's civil war. This is a jittery, nervous movie that shifts back and forth between irreverent humor and sobering realism. Although Woods' initial obnoxiousness may annoy some viewers, the character's journey to altruistic self-awareness is fascinating. The script is politically preachy but intelligent and heartfelt. Woods is cocky and passionate; Belushi registers strongly as the journalist's deceptively heroic friend. The fine supporting cast also includes Michael Murphy as the ethical U.S. ambassador. **Director**—Oliver Stone. **(R) Academy Award Nominations**—Woods, best actor; Stone and (real-life journalist) Richard Boyle, best screenplay written directly for the screen. *123 minutes*

SAME TIME, NEXT YEAR (1978)

★★

Ellen Burstyn
Alan Alda

Though this movie version of Bernard Slade's two-character Broadway hit looks stagy, some of the warmth, humor, and appeal of the original play remain intact on the screen. Burstyn—repeating her stage role—and Alda give engaging performances as adulterers who meet for one weekend a year for 26 years. The scant plot is merely a contrivance to comment on the changes in American society from the 1950s to the 1970s, which are reflected in the dialogue, clothing, and attitudes of the two characters. Unfortunately, some of the observations are too superficial to be in any way insightful. **Director**—Robert Mulligan. **(PG) Academy Award Nominations**—Burstyn, best actress; Slade, best screenplay adaptation. *119 minutes*

SAM MARLOWE, PRIVATE EYE (1980)

Robert Sacchi

A mystery/comedy that pays homage to Humphrey Bogart and private-eye films of the 1940s. Sacchi plays a man who undergoes plastic surgery to resemble Bogart. He then becomes involved in a caper on the order of *The Maltese Falcon*. Sacchi does a convincing Bogart imitation, and there's a delightful takeoff by Misty Rowe as a dumb blonde secretary. Also with Michelle Phillips, Olivia Hussey, Victor Buono, Herbert Lom, George Raft, Sybil Danning, Yvonne De Carlo, Mike Mazurki, and Franco Nero. Raft's last film. **Director**—Robert Day. **(PG) Alternate Title**—*The Man with Bogart's Face.* *111 minutes*

SAMSON AND DELILAH (1949)

Hedy Lamarr
Victor Mature

Fans of epic films should enjoy this biblical story about Samson, whose strength is sapped after devious Delilah cuts his curls. Mature and Lamarr play the title roles. Despite the epic theme, grand photography, and spectacular special effects—including the destruc-

This movie available with closed captions for the hearing impaired.

tion of the temple and Samson's fight with a lion—the movie lacks the reputation of some of director Cecil B. DeMille's biblical adaptations. The cast also includes Angela Lansbury, George Sanders, Fay Holden, Russ Tamblyn, and Olive Deering. **Academy Award Nomination**—George Barnes, cinematography. *128 minutes*

THE SAND PEBBLES (1966)

★★★

Steve McQueen
Richard Crenna

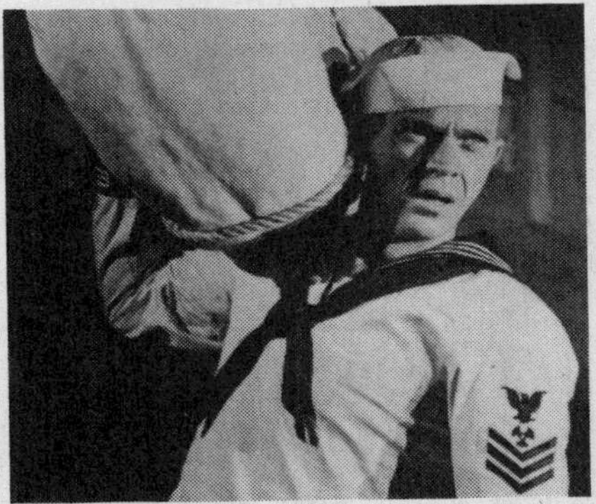

Steve McQueen sees a dangerous situation in The Sand Pebbles.

McQueen is superb as a sailor aboard a gunboat who quarrels with his superiors and tries to warn them of the potential diplomatic pitfalls in dealing with Chinese warlords. Crenna plays the captain of the vessel. The movie, based on Richard McKenna's best-selling novel, is set on the Yangtze River during the 1920s, but the script's criticisms of American imperialism could have been aimed at the Vietnam situation. Though overlong, the film is an interesting reflection of the times. Also with Candice Bergen, Richard Attenborough, Marayat Andriane, Mako, and Simon Oakland. **Director**—Robert Wise. **Academy Award Nominations**—best picture; McQueen, best actor; Mako, best supporting actor; Joseph MacDonald, cinematography. *193 minutes*

THE SANDPIPER (1965)

 ★★

Elizabeth Taylor
Richard Burton
Eva Marie Saint

A superficial tale concocted to capitalize on the real-life romance of Taylor and Burton. The Big Sur scenery has more redeeming quality than the trite plot. Taylor, a liberated artist with an illegitimate son, has a romance with Burton, who's an errant minister. Saint plays Burton's wife. The Oscar-winning theme song "The Shadow of Your Smile" was a hit tune of the era. Also with Charles Bronson, Robert Webber, and Torin Thatcher. **Director**—Vincente Minnelli. *117 minutes*

SANDS OF IWO JIMA (1949)

 ★★★

John Wayne
John Agar

Hard-hitting Pacific battle action with John Wayne (left) in Sands of Iwo Jima.

Wayne stars as a tough and capable Marine sergeant who trains young recruits and turns them into disciplined combat troops during World War II. Although some of the characterizations in this terse drama are stereotypes of the genre, Wayne's larger-than-life persona adds color to his portrayal. The battle scenes are among the best ever filmed for that time. The cast also includes Forrest Tucker, Arthur Franz, Adele Mara, Richard Jaeckel, and Julie Bishop. **Director**—Allan Dwan. **Academy Award Nominations**—Wayne, best actor; Harry Brown, motion picture story. *109 minutes b&w*

SAN FRANCISCO (1936)

Clark Gable
Jeanette MacDonald
Spencer Tracy

Entertaining tale of the Barbary Coast at the turn of the century. Gable stars as saloon owner Blackie Norton, who falls for the toast of San Francisco, Jeanette MacDonald. Tracy costars as fighting Father Mullin. The film ends with the famous earthquake, a sequence that is still exciting after 50 years. An excellent example of classic Hollywood filmmaking, featuring major stars, a colorful recreation of a historical setting, lavish production values, and a director—W.S. Van Dyke—at the peak of his feature-film career. Scripted by Anita Loos. Also with Jack Holt, Jessie Ralph, Ted Healy, Shirley Ross, and Al Shean. **Academy Award Nominations**—best picture; Van Dyke, best director; Tracy, best actor; Robert Hopkins, original story. *115 minutes b&w*

San Francisco *of another era, with Clark Gable and Jeanette MacDonald.*

SANTA CLAUS: THE MOVIE (1985)

 ★★ 

David Huddleston
Dudley Moore
John Lithgow

Lavish and overblown attempt to explain the origins of the Santa legend. It's aimed at the preschool set, who just might enjoy the glitzy scenes of elves at work and Santa's Christmas Eve delivery ride over Manhattan. For the adult Scrooges, there's nothing here to produce a ho-ho-ho. Huddleston is well suited to the role of jolly St. Nick. Moore plays a wayward elf, while Lithgow is convincing as a greedy toy manufacturer. **Director**—Jeannot Szwarc. **(PG)** *112 minutes*

SANTA FE TRAIL (1940)

 ★★

Errol Flynn
Olivia de Havilland
Raymond Massey

Flynn and de Havilland top the cast of this formula western, but the weak

(Continued)

This movie available on videotape and/or disc.

(Continued)
plot, indecisive direction, and slow pace spoil a potentially good tale. Flynn plays cavalry officer Jeb Stuart, and the action focuses on his efforts to capture John Brown, played by Massey. The supporting cast also includes Alan Hale, Gene Reynolds, Van Heflin, Ward Bond, and Ronald Reagan. **Director**—Michael Curtiz. *110 minutes b&w*

SARATOGA TRUNK (1945)

Ingrid Bergman
Gary Cooper

An overlong and miscast film based on the novel by Pulitzer Prize-winning author Edna Ferber. Bergman plays a notorious Creole woman who returns to New Orleans. She falls in love with Texan Cooper, who portrays a millionaire involved in a squabble among railroad owners. Supporting actors include Florence Bates, Flora Robson, and John Warburton. **Director**—Sam Wood. **Academy Award Nomination**—Robson, best supporting actress. *135 minutes b&w*

SATISFACTION (1988)

Justine Bateman
Liam Neeson

Justine Bateman (center) expresses herself with rock 'n' roll in Satisfaction.

Bateman, of television's long-running sit-com *Family Ties*, stars in this lightweight teen comedy as a singer in an all-female rock band. She and her group of scruffy, working-class musicians land a gig at a summer beach resort where they encounter snobby, up-and-coming law students. As the determined singer, Bateman latches onto an older composer who shakes off the blues to write her a ballad. Though obviously low-budget teen fare, the film features a group of likable young actresses. The familiar coming-of-age plot gets a slight twist this time, because it is presented from the female point of view. Also with Trini Alvarado, Scott Coffey, Britta Phillips, Julia Roberts, and Debbie Harry. **Director**—Joan Freeman. **(R)** *92 minutes*

SATURDAY NIGHT AND SUNDAY MORNING (1960)

Albert Finney
Rachel Roberts
Shirley Anne Field

Finney rose to stardom in this stark depiction of working-class lifestyles in an English industrial community. Finney plays an impish, devious nonconformist who's unhappy as a factory worker. He also has an affair with a married woman, until he eventually settles for a more conventional existence. Roberts, as the married woman, and Field, as Finney's girlfriend, give excellent supporting performances in this finely crafted drama. Adapted by Alan Sillitoe from his novel—one of the best-known examples of literature from Britain's "angry young man" era of the late 1950s. Other actors include Hylda Baker and Norman Rossington. **Director**—Karel Reisz. *89 minutes b&w*

SATURDAY NIGHT FEVER (1977)

John Travolta
Karen Lynn Gorney
Barry Miller

The glitter of disco dancing: Saturday Night Fever, *starring John Travolta.*

Travolta stars as a young disco dancer in this pivotal film about a tough, poverty-stricken Brooklyn teenager, whose only glorious moments come on the dance floor of the local disco. Travolta is excellent in his first starring role and has yet to live up to the potential indicated here. The pulsing music of the Bee Gees set the standard for this trend in music for the next few years. The film also exists in a PG-version with much of the offensive language excised and some of the sexually explicit scenes edited out. Also with Joseph Cali, Paul Pape, and Donna Pescow. **Director**—John Badham. **(R) Academy Award Nomination**—Travolta, best actor. *118 minutes*

SATURN 3 (1980)

Kirk Douglas
Farrah Fawcett

Kirk Douglas and Farrah Fawcett fight an enemy in Saturn 3.

Two research scientists—Douglas and Fawcett—are growing food in outer space when their spaceship is invaded by a madman, played by Harvey Keitel. That's the extent of the flimsy plot in this unappealing movie, which suffers from mediocrity from beginning to end. The outer space setting is peculiarly vast and gaudy, and seems out of place in contrast with the routine action. Also with Douglas Lambert. **Director**—Stanley Donen. **(R)** *88 minutes*

SAVAGE STREETS (1984)

 ★★

Linda Blair
John Vernon
Robert Dryer

High-school gang members do battle on the streets of Los Angeles. Blair tops the untalented cast as a female gang leader who seeks revenge for the rape of her mute younger sister. The film goes overboard to exploit violence and tough-sounding, vulgar dialogue. **Director**—Danny Steinmann. **(R)** *93 minutes*

This movie available with closed captions for the hearing impaired.

SAVE THE TIGER (1973)

★★★

Jack Lemmon
Jack Gilford

This honest effort—by Hollywood standards—to examine contemporary business ethics created a stir at the time of the film's release, but seems pretentious in retrospect. Lemmon, however, is excellent as a troubled businessman at the breaking point because of financial difficulties. In desperation, he decides to torch his warehouse so he can collect the insurance money. Gilford plays his long-suffering partner. Also with Laurie Heineman, Thayer David, and Norman Burton. **Director**—John G. Avildsen. **(R) Academy Award**—Lemmon, best actor. **Nominations**—Gilford, best supporting actor; Steve Shagan, best story and screenplay based on factual material or material not previously published. *100 minutes*

SAY ANYTHING (1989)

★★★

John Cusack
Ione Skye

An enchanting romantic comedy/drama about two adolescent lovers. A nonconforming high-school boy falls in love with a shy girl primed from infancy to achieve. When the illegal activities of the girl's overprotective father are revealed, the boy becomes the stabilizing influence in her life. Cusack and Skye are exceptionally charming in this melodramatic but warmhearted story of young love. Also with John Mahoney, Lili Taylor, Joan Cusack, and Eric Stoltz. **Director**—Cameron Crowe. **(PG-13)** *100 minutes*

SAYONARA (1957)

★★★

Marlon Brando
Miyoshi Umeki
Red Buttons
Miiko Taka

Brando plays an Air Force pilot who falls in love with Taka, a Japanese entertainer. Based on a novel by James Michener, the script by Paul Osborn emphasizes sentiment over insight, but is nonetheless effective. A talented supporting cast helps sustain interest throughout the lengthy film. Also with Ricardo Montalban, James Garner, Patricia Owens, Kent Smith, and Martha Scott. **Director**—Joshua Logan. **Academy Awards**—Buttons, best supporting actor; Umeki, best supporting actress. **Nominations**—best picture; Logan, best director; Brando, best actor; Osborn, best screenplay based on material from another medium; Ellsworth Fredericks, cinematography. *147 minutes*

Marlon Brando and Miiko Taka have a passionate affair in Sayonara.

THE SCALPHUNTERS (1968)

★★

Burt Lancaster
Ossie Davis
Shelley Winters
Telly Savalas

A revisionist western from the late 1960s, with Lancaster and Davis starring as a trapper and a runaway slave. The two make uneasy sidekicks who travel through a land of hostile Indians and white scalp-hunters. Savalas costars as a renegade marauder, with Winters playing his female companion. An uneven film by director Sydney Pollack, though the offbeat cast makes the film worthwhile viewing. Good score by Elmer Bernstein. Also with Nick Cravat and Dabney Coleman. *102 minutes*

SCANDAL (1989)

★★★½

John Hurt
Joanne Whalley-Kilmer
Bridget Fonda

The steamy and explosive sexual affair between party girl Christine Keeler and British war minister John Profumo is told with compelling intensity. Fine acting gives dimension to the characters who engaged in the hanky-panky that brought down the conservative Macmillan government in 1963. Hurt sensitively plays Stephen Ward, the socially ambitious osteopath who served as catalyst for the sordid goings-on. Whalley-Kilmer is vulnerable and appealing as the sexy young Keeler. Fonda brings a saucy impertinence to her performance as Keeler's cohort, Mandy Rice-Davies. Also with Ian McKellen, Britt Ekland, Daniel Massey, Roland Gift, and Jeroen Krabbé. Original 114-minute British version was trimmed to avoid and X rating in America. Both versions are available on video. **Director**—Michael Caton-Jones. **(R)** *106 minutes*

SCANDALOUS (1984)

★

John Gielgud
Robert Hays
Jim Dale

This perky spy spoof begins promisingly, but soon falls apart as it turns into a muddled murder mystery. Hays plays a TV journalist suspected of killing his wife. He tangles at first with London con artists Gielgud and Pamela Stephenson, and then with a giddy Scotland Yard inspector played by Dale. If the opportunity to see Gielgud in punk regalia doesn't seem worth the effort, skip this film. It's probably the best of the film's handful of bright moments. **Director**—Rob Cohen. **(PG)** *93 minutes*

SCANNERS (1981)

★★★

Patrick McGoohan
Jennifer O'Neill
Stephen Lack

An ambitious sci-fi/horror film with some grisly shock effects. Scanners are seemingly normal people with telepathic superpowers who can physically manipulate and even kill other humans. In one gory scene, for example, a man's head literally explodes. McGoohan plays a pompous scientist, and O'Neill is cast as a scanner. The real stars, however, are the makeup artists responsible for some incredible effects. **Director**—David Cronenberg. **(R)** *102 minutes*

SCARAMOUCHE (1952)

★★★

Stewart Granger
Eleanor Parker
Janet Leigh

The near-perfect casting of Granger as a swashbuckler determined to avenge the

(Continued)

(Continued)
death of his brother highlights this exciting adventure story based on Rafael Sabatini's novel set in 18th-century France. Granger is ably joined by two beauties—Parker and Leigh—who vie for his love. Mel Ferrer, Nina Foch, Henry Wilcoxon, Robert Coote, and Lewis Stone also star. **Director**—George Sidney. *118 minutes*

SCARED STIFF (1953)

★★★

Dean Martin
Jerry Lewis
Lizabeth Scott

One of Martin and Lewis' best comedies, featuring Martin as a nightclub singer who gets mixed up with busboy Lewis. After the two are falsely accused of murder, they escape to a mysterious Caribbean island. The combination of escape, escapades, romance, and a spooky castle spawns enough laughs to please fans of this zany duo. A remake of *Ghost Breakers* with Bob Hope. Also with George Dolenz, Dorothy Malone, Jack Lambert, and William Ching. **Director**—George Marshall.
108 minutes b&w

SCARFACE (1932)

★★★★

Paul Muni
Ann Dvorak
George Raft

Underworld violence: Paul Muni in the first version of Scarface.

One of the first and most powerful of the great gangster films. Muni is excellent as a Capone-like Chicago mobster named Tony Camonte. He ruthlessly pushes his way to the top to become king of the underworld. The compelling, hard-edged script was written by five screenwriters, including W.R. Burnett and Ben Hecht. The film is fast-paced, with raw, harsh scenes involving Camonte's crude tactics in dealing with both his enemies and his associates. Much has been written about the symbolism, which foreshadows later events in the film. The film was originally released in 1930, but was shelved for censorship reasons. It's the film that forever linked Raft to his coin-tossing gesture. Directed by the great Howard Hawks. Also with Boris Karloff, Karen Morley, Vince Barnett, Osgood Perkins, and C. Henry Gordon. Reworked in a 1983 version starring Al Pacino. **(PG)**
90 minutes b&w

SCARFACE (1983)

★★★

Al Pacino
Steven Bauer
Michelle Pfeiffer

As Scarface, Al Pacino copes with pressures of life at the top of the drug trade.

Savage gangster epic that follows in the footsteps of Howard Hawks' 1932 crime drama. The locale has been shifted from Chicago to Miami, and the booty from alcohol to cocaine. Pacino stars as the Cuban refugee who machine-guns his way to the top as the czar of a lucrative drug empire. The story is a bloody, sometimes comical, study in greed, with Pacino's character eventually wallowing in excess until his demise. Director Brian De Palma employs a great deal of violence and many brutal murder scenes to drive home his point about the American dream gone sour, but the beautiful set designs and charismatic performances make the film worthwhile viewing. Also with Robert Loggia, F. Murray Abraham, and Mary Elizabeth Mastrantonio. **(R)**
170 minutes

SCARLET STREET (1946)

★★★

Edward G. Robinson
Joan Bennett
Dan Duryea

A dark, brooding, beautifully realized *film noir* of illicit desire, directed by Fritz Lang. Robinson plays a henpecked middle-aged husband who leads a quiet life as a cashier and amateur painter. That life is torn apart when *femme fatale* Bennett walks into it; she stirs up the man's long-buried passions, and conspires with a boyfriend (Duryea) to extort money from him. The film initially won some notoriety when it was briefly banned by New York State censors because the protagonist is shown getting away with a crime (although he's also portrayed as tortured by his guilt). Dudley Nichols adapted Georges de la Fouchardiere's play *La Chienne*, which had previously been filmed by Jean Renoir.
103 minutes b&w

SCAVENGER HUNT (1980)

(no stars)

Richard Benjamin
James Coco
Tony Randall
Cloris Leachman

A noisy and absurd comedy that features a large cast of familiar names in brief but embarrassing roles. Benjamin, Leachman, Coco, Randall, and others greedily scramble for strange objects, after Vincent Price, who plays an eccentric game manufacturer, wills $200 million to the winner of a scavenger hunt. The callous humor delights in degrading people with physical impairments. Also with Scatman Crothers, Ruth Gordon, Roddy McDowall, and Cleavon Little. Director Michael Schultz seems to have gone to the limits of bad taste. **(PG)** *117 minutes*

SCENE OF THE CRIME (1986)

★★★

Catherine Deneuve
Danielle Darrieux

A stylish psychological drama starring Deneuve as a divorced mother struggling with family problems. Her life is completely turned around after a criminal assaults her young son, touching off a suspenseful chain of events. Excellent acting by the entire cast and an interesting screenplay, filled with violent passions and strange coincidences, enliven this unusual and compelling thriller. Nicolas Girauldi and Wadeck Stanczak costar. **Director**—André Techine. **(No MPAA rating)** *90 minutes*

SCENES FROM A MARRIAGE (1973)

Liv Ullmann
Erland Josephson
Bibi Andersson

Ingmar Bergman's introspective dissection of a marriage. Bergman's fans will admire this 168-minute condensation of what was originally six 50-minute episodes made for Swedish television. Ullmann and Josephson play wife and husband who split up to marry others, but find themselves drawn together in an attempt to renew their relationship. Intimate and touching, but occasionally painful. Originally filmed in Swedish. **(PG)** *168 minutes*

SCENES FROM THE CLASS STRUGGLE IN BEVERLY HILLS (1989)

Ray Sharkey
Robert Beltran

Director Paul Bartel presents a bubbly sex farce that parodies the glossy lifestyle of California's mecca for the rich and famous. The story revolves around a bet by two houseboys (Sharkey and Beltran) as to who will be the first to seduce Sharkey's female boss. Some scenes wear thin, but the performances are uniformly good. Jacqueline Bisset is notable as a pampered, newly widowed queen of second-rate sitcoms. Also with Mary Woronov, Ed Begley, Jr., Paul Mazursky, and Wallace Shawn. **(R)** *102 minutes*

SCHOOL DAZE (1988)

 ★★1/2 

Larry Fishburne
Giancarlo Esposito
Tisha Campbell
Kyme

Writer/director Spike Lee, who received critical acclaim for his low-budget *She's Gotta Have It,* attempts a more ambi-

Spike Lee (right) resists Giancarlo Esposito's needling in School Daze.

tious project with less successful results. A musical that takes place on homecoming weekend at an all-black university, the film seems rambling and choppy. Lee's unique talent does show through occasionally, and the subject matter deals with issues relevant to the black audience. But the snappy production numbers aren't well integrated into the storyline, interrupting the film's rhythm. **(R)** *120 minutes*

SCHOOL FOR SCOUNDRELS (1960)

Ian Carmichael
Alastair Sim
Terry-Thomas

Capable performances by Carmichael, Sim, and Terry-Thomas make this a school worth attending. The film is based on Stephen Potter's books. Here, a training school teaches one-upmanship so that graduates can always come out on top in the game of life. Janette Scott, Dennis Price, Peter Jones, John LeMesurier, and Edward Chapman also star in this amusing and enjoyable British romp. **Director**—Robert Hamer. *94 minutes b&w*

SCROOGE (1970)

 ★1/2

Albert Finney

Unsatisfying musical interpretation of Dickens' classic novel *A Christmas Carol.* Finney stars as the title character, a miserly misanthrope, who learns a lesson from the ghosts of Christmases past, present, and future. At times, the talents of Finney and the supporting cast almost make this version seem bearable, but then the characters burst into song, and the spirit of tolerance dissipates. Also with Michael Medwin, Alec Guinness, Kay Walsh, David Collings, Laurence Naismith, Edith Evans, and Kenneth More. **Director**—Ronald Neame. **(G)** *118 minutes*

SCROOGED (1988)

★★★

Bill Murray
Alfre Woodard
Karen Allen

Charles Dickens' *A Christmas Carol* receives a contemporary comedic treatment starring Murray as the latter-day skinflint. He plays a heartless TV network president who confronts the ghosts of Christmas past, present, and future. There are many funny moments on the way to acquiring the Christmas spirit, but the sentimental ending is out of place compared to the rest of the material. Many good cameos cap the fun: Among them, Bob Goldthwait plays a fired yes-man, and Mary Lou Retton is an agile Tiny Tim. Also with John Forsythe, John Glover, David Johansen, Carol Kane, Robert Mitchum, John Houseman, and Buddy Hackett. **Director**—Richard Donner. **(PG-13) Academy Award Nomination**—Tom Burman and Bari Drieband-Burman, makeup. *101 minutes*

THE SEA CHASE (1955)

John Wayne
Lana Turner

A sea voyage to Germany for Lana Turner and John Wayne in The Sea Chase.

Wayne stars as the German captain of a fugitive freighter trying to reach the fatherland from Australia, but it seems odd to have Wayne toiling for the other side in this World War II adventure. Other aspects of the melodrama are

(Continued)

(Continued)
standard, including Turner as the romantic interest in Wayne's life. The assorted crew of supporting actors includes David Farrar, Tab Hunter, Dick Davalos, Lyle Bettger, and James Arness. **Director**—John Farrow.
117 minutes

THE SEA GYPSIES (1978)

★★★

Robert Logan
Heather Rattray
Mikki Jamison-Olsen

Beautiful location photography, effective acting, and a lively plot enhance this engaging family adventure film. A man, his two daughters, and a photographer are marooned on the Alaskan coast and learn to survive among the wild bear, moose, caribou, and sea lions. The story is predictable, but there's enough excitement to delight the youngsters and involve the adults. Also with Shannon Saylor. **Director**—Stewart Raffill. **(G)**
101 minutes

THE SEA HAWK (1940)

★★★

Errol Flynn
Claude Rains
Flora Robson

Flynn stars in this entertaining swashbuckler as a privateer rooting out treacherous Spaniards on the high seas and in the court of Queen Elizabeth I. Colorful action dominates this loose adaptation of the novel by Rafael Sabatini, which was directed by Warner Bros. stalwart Michael Curtiz. Curtiz had successfully teamed with Flynn two years earlier for the classic *The Adventures of Robin Hood.* Also with Henry Daniell, Donald Crisp, Brenda Marshall, Alan Hale, and Gilbert Roland.
127 minutes b&w

SEANCE ON A WET AFTERNOON (1964)

★★★

Kim Stanley
Richard Attenborough
Nanette Newman

Stanley stars as a fake medium who involves her seemingly weak hubby in the kidnapping of a child in this high-powered chiller. She plans to win attention and money by helping to find the missing girl through her clairvoyant abilities. Attenborough costars as the husband. British director Bryan Forbes steers the film toward the artsy side, but it's a well-crafted suspense drama. Also with Patrick Magee, Maria Kazan, and Judith Donner. **Academy Award Nomination**—Stanley, best actress.
121 minutes b&w

SEA OF LOVE (1989)

★★★

Al Pacino
Ellen Barkin
John Goodman

Dangerous attraction: Ellen Barkin and Al Pacino in Sea of Love.

A tightly crafted police thriller starring Pacino as an aging New York City detective. He falls in love with the prime suspect in a serial-killer case in which the murderer finds the victims through lonely hearts ads. Barkin costars as the key suspect, a beautiful but bitter woman who has been used by men once too often. Goodman relieves the unbearable tension with some much-needed comic relief as a fellow detective who helps Pacino on the case. Gritty dialogue, graphic love scenes, and a wicked killer help raise this thriller above the ordinary. Also with Michael Rooker, William Hickey, Christine Estabrook, Patricia Barry, and Barbara Baxley. **Director**—Harold Becker. **(R)**
110 minutes

THE SEARCHERS (1956)

★★★★

John Wayne
Jeffrey Hunter
Natalie Wood

John Ford's most famous western, and one of the most influential films in the history of American cinema. Wayne's image as the ultimate western hero was used perfectly by Ford to convey both the admirable qualities of that character—such as individualism and courage—as well as the darker side, marked by intolerance and savagery. The storyline involves Wayne and Hunter's search for Wayne's niece (Wood), who was captured by the Indians after her family was massacred. His relentless pursuit against insurmountable odds is courageous, yet his determination to kill his niece because she has been contaminated by the Indians is disturbing. *The Searchers* marks the beginning of Ford's interest in the darker side of the western myth, more evident in *The Man Who Shot Liberty Valance.* The poetic imagery of the desert landscapes seems at odds with the brutality of the environment. A cast of Ford's favorite character actors, including Ward Bond, John Qualen, Ken Curtis, Harry Carey, Jr., and Hank Worden, are excellent in supporting roles. Also with Vera Miles, Olive Carey, and Lana Wood.
119 minutes

Natalie Wood, John Wayne, and Jeffrey Hunter in The Searchers.

THE SEA WOLF (1941)

★★★

Edward G. Robinson
John Garfield
Ida Lupino

This film version of Jack London's novel about a sadistic sea captain emphasizes what makes the captain, played by Robinson, tick. The story deals with how the captain brutally treats the survivors he has rescued from a ferry boat collision in San Francisco Bay. Among the survivors are such excellent supporting actors as Alexander Knox, Gene Lockhart, Barry Fitzgerald, Howard Da Silva, and David Bruce. **Director**—Michael Curtiz.
90 minutes b&w

® *This movie available with closed captions for the hearing impaired.*

THE SEA WOLVES (1980)

★★★

Roger Moore
Gregory Peck
David Niven
Trevor Howard

A group of polo-playing, British businessmen form a commando team and destroy a secret Nazi radio transmitter somewhere in the Indian Ocean. This daring charge of the geriatric brigade is a likable World War II adventure. Peck, Niven, and Howard, who appeared in films of this genre in the past, play the grand old men, but the film really belongs to Moore, who, as a British officer, adds the right amount of dashing romance. **Director**—Andrew V. McLaglen. **(PG)** *120 minutes*

SECOND SIGHT (1989)

★½

John Larroquette
Bronson Pinchot
Stuart Pankin

Stuart Pankin, Bronson Pinchot, and John Larroquette in Second Sight.

A very dim comedy about a detective agency run by an embittered private detective who works with a goofy psychic. The film features television stars Larroquette and Pinchot as characters obviously patterned after their TV personas. Pinchot is the flaky seer who is helped through his psychic episodes by Pankin. Larroquette plays the cranky investigator with a penchant for dry, witty one-liners. The nonsensical plot involves the team's efforts to find out who damaged a car belonging to the secretary of a powerful Catholic cardinal. This is the first feature assignment for Joel Zwick, who made his name as a director of TV sitcoms. It shows. Also with Bess Armstrong, John Schuck, James Tolkan, and Christine Estabrook. **(PG)** *83 minutes*

SECRET ADMIRER (1985)

★

C. Thomas Howell
Lori Loughlin
Kelly Preston

Lori Loughlin and C. Thomas Howell in Secret Admirer.

A leering, teen sex comedy loaded with inept dialogue and silly situations that portray young people as callous and materialistic slobs. A round robin of romantic mix-ups is touched off when an anonymous love letter is delivered to a high-school boy. Eventually, the kid's parents become involved in the confusion. This lowbrow, screwball nonsense is hardly entertaining and far from admirable. Also with Dee Wallace Stone, Cliff De Young, and Leigh Taylor-Young. **Director**—David Greenwalt. **(R)** *90 minutes*

SECRET AGENT (1936)

★★★

John Gielgud
Madeleine Carroll
Robert Young
Peter Lorre

Robert Young and Madeleine Carroll in Hitchcock's Secret Agent.

One of director Alfred Hitchcock's less focused spy films, but still an engrossing thriller. Posing as husband and wife, Gielgud and Carroll are actually two secret agents. Their lives are considerably complicated by mountainside killer Lorre as well as other agents. The famous climactic sequence takes place in a chocolate factory. From a play based on Somerset Maugham's "Ashenden" stories. *93 minutes b&w*

THE SECRET LIFE OF AN AMERICAN WIFE (1968)

★

Walter Matthau
Anne Jackson

Jackson portrays a bored suburban housewife who decides to seduce a movie star in this insipid and unsatisfying comedy, which has a message lurking somewhere concerning suburban lifestyles of the 1960s. Matthau plays the cinema sex idol. Both stars seem miscast in this production. Patrick O'Neal, Edy Williams, Richard Bull, and Paul Napier appear in supporting roles. **Director**—George Axelrod. **(R)** *92 minutes*

THE SECRET LIFE OF WALTER MITTY (1947)

★★★½

Danny Kaye
Virginia Mayo

Virginia Mayo and Danny Kaye find real-life adventure in The Secret Life of Walter Mitty.

Kaye is charming in this entertaining story about a man who lives in a fantasy world where he leads an exciting life. In the real world, he's mild-mannered and cowardly. Viewers expecting a faithful film version of James Thurber's story will be disappointed, but excellent songs—including Kaye's rendition of his famed "Anatole of Paris"—and enjoyable comedy sequences make this a movie the whole

(Continued)

(Continued)
family will enjoy. Also with Boris Karloff, Reginald Denny, Florence Bates, Ann Rutherford, and Fay Bainter. **Director**—Norman Z. McLeod.

110 minutes

THE SECRET OF MY SUCCESS (1987)

★★1/2

Michael J. Fox
Helen Slater

Michael J. Fox falls for executive Helen Slater in The Secret of My Success.

A frothy, yuppie comedy about a young man (Fox) who bluffs his way from the mail room to an executive position in a New York conglomerate. The script and gags are reminiscent of various comedies from the 1950s and early 1960s that spoofed corporate executives and their mad dash to power, particularly *How to Succeed in Business Without Really Trying.* The film also takes comic aim at other topics more relevant to the 1980s—casual sex, hostile takeovers—but with much less success. Also with Richard Jordan and Margaret Whitton. **Director**—Herbert Ross. **(PG–13)**

109 minutes

THE SECRET OF NIMH (1982)

★★★

A group of former Disney animators have made an animated feature reminiscent of Disney's classic cartoons of past decades. The story concerns a poor widowed mouse caught in the path of man's progress and struggling to save her family. More than one and a half million individual drawings were used in the production. The film is a dazzling display of mirth, charm, and color—and it has its moments of terror, as well. Dom DeLuise, Elizabeth Hartman, Peter Strauss, and John Carradine are some of the voices behind the characters. **Director**—Don Bluth. **(G)**

83 minutes

THE SECRET OF SANTA VITTORIA (1969)

★★★

Anthony Quinn
Anna Magnani

An offbeat comedy that takes place in an Italian village during the last months of World War II. The storyline concerns the efforts of the villagers to save their precious hoard—one million bottles of wine—from German soldiers during the occupation. The story, based on Robert Crichton's novel, is interesting at times, but the film is ultimately too long. Hardy Kruger is excellent as a German officer. Also with Virna Lisi, Sergio Franchi, and Renato Rascel. **Director**—Stanley Kramer. **(PG)**

140 minutes

THE SEDUCTION (1982)

(no stars)

Morgan Fairchild
Andrew Stevens

This amateurishly made thriller features television star Fairchild as a glamorous news reporter who's pursued by a Peeping-Tom photographer (Stevens). Fairchild displays plenty of flesh, but her "Barbie Doll" beauty is as plastic as her acting. Writer/director David Schmoeller's idea of suspense is cheap fright tactics embellished with purring telephone conversations. It's a trite, aimless effort that hardly lives up to its title. Michael Sarrazin and Vince Edwards also star. **(R)**

104 minutes

THE SEDUCTION OF JOE TYNAN (1979)

★★

Alan Alda
Barbara Harris
Meryl Streep

Alda, in the title role, plays a liberal New York senator ambitiously pursuing his career and struggling with his domestic life. Harris plays the senator's attractive wife, and Streep is a southern labor lawyer who has an affair with the senator. Alda, Harris, and Streep deliver some remarkable performances, but the flat script, written by Alda, fails to offer badly needed excitement and drama. Also with Rip Torn, Charles Kimbrough, and Melvyn Douglas. **Director**—Jerry Schatzberg. **(R)**

107 minutes

SEE HERE, PRIVATE HARGROVE (1944)

★★★

Robert Walker
Donna Reed
Keenan Wynn

Entertaining comedy about a raw recruit going through his paces in the U.S. Army. Walker, Reed, and Wynn star in this film adaptation of Marion Hargrove's best-selling novel. Also with Robert Benchley, Bob Crosby, Chill Wills, Ray Collins, and Grant Mitchell. **Director**—Wesley Ruggles.

102 minutes b&w

SEEMS LIKE OLD TIMES (1980)

★★

Goldie Hawn
Chevy Chase
Charles Grodin

Hawn plays an affluent, liberal lawyer with a soft spot for stray dogs, her down-and-out clients, and her ex-husband, played by Chase, who's on the lam after two criminals force him to help them rob a bank. Grodin plays her current husband, a district attorney. Hawn, making the most of this broad comedy, is as zany as ever, and she works well with Chase. Unfortunately, Neil Simon's uneven screenplay contains too many uninspired one-liners. **Director**—Jay Sandrich. **(PG)**

121 minutes

SEE NO EVIL, HEAR NO EVIL (1989)

★★

Richard Pryor
Gene Wilder

Pryor and Wilder team up for their third comedy together. Pryor plays a blind man; Wilder a deaf newsstand operator. Using their available senses, they witness a murder that is tied to industrial espionage. Although the stars' rapport and talent are obvious, they are saddled with a gimmicky script loaded with unimaginative comic setups and stock characters. Predictable chases with cops and various villains provide

® This movie available with closed captions for the hearing impaired.

Richard Pryor and Gene Wilder are unlikely pals in See No Evil, Hear No Evil.

only a minimum of laughs amid the chaos. Also with Joan Severance, Kevin Spacey, and Anthony Zerbe. **Director**—Arthur Hiller. **(R)** *103 minutes*

SEE YOU IN THE MORNING (1989)

★★

Jeff Bridges
Alice Krige
Farrah Fawcett

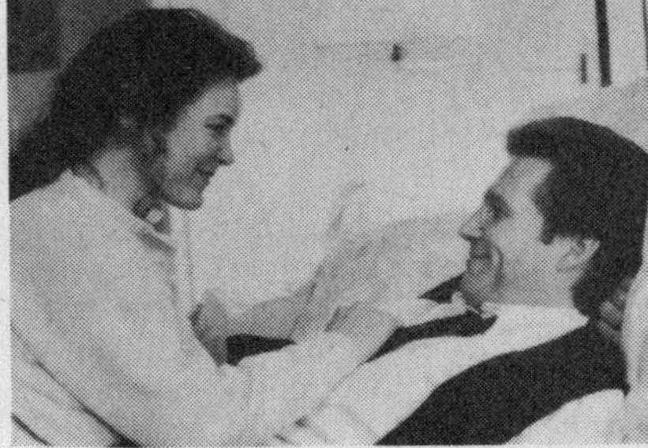

A second chance: Alice Krige and Jeff Bridges in See You in the Morning.

Director Alan J. Pakula's romantic comedy about divorce and remarriage is smothered in angst and extended dialogue. Bridges stars as a Manhattan psychiatrist struggling to adjust to living with his second wife (Krige) and her children. Most of the film seems like an overlong group therapy session. The cast is talented but saddled with material that's phoney. Also with Linda Lavin, Drew Barrymore, Lukas Haas, and David Dukes. **(PG-13)** *119 minutes*

SEMI-TOUGH (1977)

★★★

Burt Reynolds
Kris Kristofferson
Jill Clayburgh

A lively satire that demolishes professional football and self-improvement fads. Reynolds, Kristofferson, and Clayburgh work well together as a low-key *ménage à trois.* Director Michael Ritchie (*Smile; Bad News Bears*) makes the most of this material, which tosses barbs at various hypocrisies. The script by Ring Lardner, Jr., and Walter Bernstein contains a great deal of locker-room language. Also with Robert Preston, Bert Convy, and Lotte Lenya. **(R)** *107 minutes*

THE SENDER (1982)

★★

Kathryn Harrold
Zeljko Ivanek
Shirley Knight

Eerie, convoluted horror film that exploits its storyline about mental telepathy. Harrold stars as an attractive psychiatrist involved with a suicidal, amnesiac patient (Ivanek). Soon she's sharing the young man's hallucinations and nightmares. There are enough spooky gimmicks to keep the viewer absorbed, but many of the events in the plot are absurd. **Director**—Roger Christian. **(R)** *92 minutes*

THE SENTINEL (1977)

★★★

Cristina Raines
Ava Gardner
Chris Sarandon
Burgess Meredith

An effective horror film about a fashion model, played by Raines, who rents a room in an old Brooklyn brownstone that's actually a gateway to Hell. Director Michael Winner assembles a horrifying assortment of grotesque characters and nerve-jangling effects. There's a final scene so gruesome that you may lose your appetite. Also with Sylvia Miles, José Ferrer, Arthur Kennedy, and John Carradine. **(R)** *92 minutes*

A SEPARATE PEACE (1972)

★

Parker Stevenson
John Heyl
William Roerick

John Knowles' coming-of-age classic does not translate well to the screen. Stevenson and Heyl play two prep-school roommates during World War II, who learn some very tough lessons about adult emotions and moral compromise. Director Larry Peerce emphasizes surface details over interior conflict. The period flavor, derived from the on-location photography at Phillips Exeter Academy in New Hampshire, is more convincing than the thrashing melodrama. **(PG)** *104 minutes*

SEPARATE TABLES (1958)

★★★★

Burt Lancaster
Rita Hayworth
David Niven
Deborah Kerr

Brilliant acting and excellent direction smooth the transition of Terence Rattigan's play from the stage to the screen. Under Delbert Mann's direction, the characterizations are sensitive, and the emotional conflicts are deftly portrayed in this story about the guests at a British seaside resort. Among the stars are Kerr, who plays a spinster; Niven, a troubled ex-colonel; and Wendy Hiller, the owner of the resort as well as Lancaster's mistress. Hayworth is surprisingly good as Lancaster's ex-wife who begs him for another chance. Also with Gladys Cooper, Cathleen Nesbitt, Felix Aylmer, Rod Taylor, May Hallat, and Audrey Dalton. **Academy Awards**—Niven, best actor; Hiller, best supporting actress. **Nominations**—best picture; Kerr, best actress; Rattigan and John Gay, best screenplay based on material from another medium; Charles Lang, Jr., cinematography. *98 minutes b&w*

SEPTEMBER (1987)

★★

Mia Farrow
Dianne Wiest
Denholm Elliott
Sam Waterston

Woody Allen directed this dreary drama, set in a Vermont country home, about unrequited love. Howard (Elliott), an older man, loves Lane (Farrow), a suicidal woman who loves Peter (Waterston), a frustrated writer who loves Stephanie (Wiest), Lane's married friend. The film emphasizes brittle and piercing dialogue as each character reveals his innermost self to another, only to be rejected in the long run. The film contains some great acting, particularly by Elaine Stritch as Lane's estranged mother, but the melancholy mood and

(Continued)

(Continued)
grim outcome are difficult to bear. Also with Jack Warden, Ira Wheeler, Jane Cecil, and Rosemary Murphy. **(PG)** *82 minutes*

SEPTEMBER 30, 1955 (1978)

Richard Thomas
Susan Tyrrell

The title has to do with the day actor James Dean died in a car crash. This tedious 1950s youth film tells how Arkansas college student Jimmy J. becomes despondent over the news of Dean's death. It's difficult to identify with such a peculiar and naive adolescent character. Thomas, who played John-Boy on TV's *The Waltons*, gives an unconvincing and bland performance as Jimmy J. Also with Deborah Benson and Lisa Blount. **Director**—James Bridges. **(PG)** *101 minutes*

SGT. PEPPER'S LONELY HEARTS CLUB BAND (1978)

Peter Frampton
The Bee Gees

This loosely constructed film is based on the music of the Beatles and stars Frampton, the Bee Gees, and dozens of other rock performers. A few scenes are outstanding, but the outcome is a garish mishmash. The silly plot—what there is of it—is merely a vehicle for introducing the musical numbers. Most of the musicians aren't particularly good actors. Also with George Burns, Frankie Howard, Donald Pleasence, and Steve Martin. **Director**—Michael Schultz. **(PG)** *113 minutes*

SERGEANTS 3 (1962)

Frank Sinatra
Dean Martin
Peter Lawford
Sammy Davis, Jr.
Joey Bishop

Sinatra and some of his real-life cohorts—Martin, Davis, Lawford, and Bishop—star in this adventure yarn that resembles a western parody of *Gunga Din*. In this movie, Davis turns heroic in Gunga Din fashion. The story is set just after the Civil War, when three cavalry sergeants—Sinatra, Martin, and Lawford, with the assistance of Davis—dispose of hostile Indians. There's more than enough spirited action and fun for fans of this quintet, but the plot is trite, and much of the story is boring. Ruta Lee and Henry Silva also appear. **Director**—John Sturges. *112 minutes*

SERGEANT YORK (1941)

★★★★

Gary Cooper
Walter Brennan

In Sergeant York, *Gary Cooper portrays a pacifist who must fight in World War I.*

Cooper is perfectly cast as the backwoods farm boy—a pacifist—who is drafted into the Army and becomes the greatest U.S. hero of World War I. Under Howard Hawks' intelligent direction, the portrait of York is sensitive and compassionate. Hawks keeps the film fast-paced, which is typical of his directorial style. The excellent cast also includes Joan Leslie, George Tobias, David Bruce, Ward Bond, Margaret Wycherly, and Dickie Moore. **Academy Award**—Cooper, best actor. **Nominations**—best picture; Hawks, best director; Brennan, best supporting actor; Wycherly, best supporting actress; Harry Chandlee, Abem Finkel, John Huston, and Howard Koch, original screenplay; Sol Polito, cinematography. *134 minutes b&w*

SERIAL (1980)

★★

Martin Mull
Tuesday Weld

Mull and Weld star as a me-generation couple in this silly satire of trendy lifestyles in affluent Marin County, California. The rapid-fire dialogue seems as if it were gleaned from *Psychology Today* magazine. The soap-opera screenplay delves into hot tubs, open marriages, cult religions, consciousness-raising, and organic foods. There are some amusing moments amid the smorgasbord of pop jargon, but a lot of it is just dead air. Based on the book by Cyra McFadden. Also with Sally Kellerman, Bill Macy, Peter Bonerz, Christopher Lee, and Tom Smothers. **Director**—Bill Persky. **(R)** *92 minutes*

THE SERPENT AND THE RAINBOW (1988)

★★★

Bill Pullman
Cathy Tyson

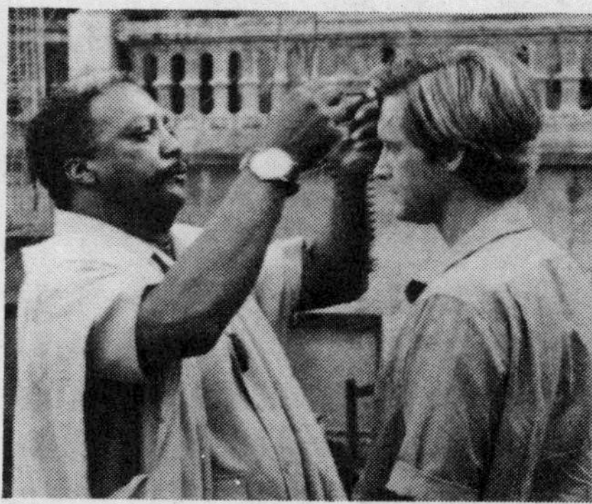

Paul Winfield gives Bill Pullman a symbolic necklace in The Serpent and the Rainbow.

Wes Craven, the director of the original *A Nightmare on Elm Street*, fashions a visually compelling horror film about the voodoo religion and culture of Haiti. Loosely inspired by a study of zombification by Harvard anthropologist Wade Davis, the film stars Pullman as a scientist hired by a drug company to track down the potion used by voodoo priests to turn humans into zombies. Pullman eventually pushes too far in his quest and evokes the wrath of a black magician, who invades Pullman's dreams and causes him much physical and psychic pain. The eerie, atmospheric setting is an effective backdrop for the supernatural elements of the story, while the poverty and oppression depicted here is a reminder of the political horror Haiti has experienced recently. Also with Zakes Mokae, Paul Winfield, Brent Jennings, and Conrad Roberts. **(R)** *98 minutes*

THE SERPENT'S EGG (1978)

Liv Ullmann
David Carradine

® This movie available with closed captions for the hearing impaired.

This film is set in Berlin during the 1920s, when poverty, fear, and despair haunted the populace on the eve of Hitler's rise to power. In this English-language film, director Ingmar Bergman captures the grim and depressing mood in his usual intelligent fashion, but the point of the story is unclear. Bergman, who also wrote the screenplay, leaves unanswered questions dangling everywhere. Carradine plays an out-of-work American circus performer floundering among the demoralized Germans, and Ullmann is a cabaret performer—both roles lack depth. Also with Gert Frobe, Glynn Turman, and James Whitmore. **(R)**

119 minutes

SERPICO (1973)

★★★

Al Pacino
John Randolph

A dedicated, honest cop: Al Pacino in Serpico.

Pacino is brilliant as Frank Serpico, a dedicated New York City cop who's appalled by police corruption and decides to expose the sleazy practices. The story, based on a book by Peter Maas, is about the problems and adventures of this honest nonconformist, but there's enough hard-hitting action for fans of police procedural tales. On-location filming gives the production an authentic feel under the excellent direction of Sidney Lumet. Also with Jack Kehoe, Biff McGuire, Barbara Eda-Young, Cornelia Sharpe, and Tony Roberts. **(R) Academy Award Nominations**—Pacino, best actor; Waldo Salt and Norman Wexler, best screenplay based on material from another medium.

130 minutes

SEVEN BEAUTIES (1976)

★★★★

Giancarlo Giannini
Shirley Stoler
Fernando Rey

Director Lina Wertmuller's fifth movie is a masterpiece; it's rich with irony, paradox, and humor, and deals with the fundamental theme of survival. Giannini, in one of his best performances, plays a small-time hood from Naples, nicknamed "Seven Beauties," who deserts the Italian Army and is sent to a concentration camp by the Germans. To survive, he desperately attempts to seduce the camp's hefty and ferocious female commandant, played effectively by Stoler. The movie is Wertmuller's best effort to date, as she reaffirms her political and philosophical beliefs. Also with Elena Fiore and Enzo Vitale. Originally filmed in Italian. **(R) Academy Award Nominations**—best foreign-language film; Wertmuller, best director; Giannini, best actor; Wertmuller, best screenplay written directly for the screen. *116 minutes*

SEVEN BRIDES FOR SEVEN BROTHERS (1954)

★★★★

Howard Keel
Jane Powell

The energetic cast of Seven Brides for Seven Brothers *with Jane Powell and Howard Keel.*

Powell and Keel star in this delightful MGM musical. When Keel meets and marries Powell after one trip to town, his six rowdy brothers resolve to find wives for themselves. They come down from their mountain cabin and kidnap six girls to take back home. An avalanche closes the mountain pass, forcing the girls to remain there until spring. The pleasant score by Johnny Mercer and Gene DePaul is surpassed only by Michael Kidd's exuberant choreography, topped by the barn-raising scene. The production, inspired by a Stephen Vincent Benét story, also stars Jeff Richards, Russ Tamblyn, and Jacques d'Amboise. **Director**—Stanley Donen. **(G) Academy Award Nominations**—best picture; Albert Hackett, Frances Goodrich, and Dorothy Kingsley, screenplay; George Folsey, cinematography. *103 minutes*

SEVEN DAYS IN MAY (1964)

★★★

Kirk Douglas
Burt Lancaster
Fredric March

Ava Gardner and Kirk Douglas in Seven Days in May.

This tense and exciting political drama about a plot by the military to overthrow the United States government is enhanced by a fine cast, solid direction, and a first-rate script. Lancaster and Douglas play military leaders, and March is outstanding as the President who must confront the plotters. Rod Serling wrote the taut, intelligent screenplay, which, under John Frankenheimer's direction, moves briskly to a suspenseful climax. Also with Ava Gardner, John Houseman, Edmond O'Brien, George Macready, and Martin Balsam. **Academy Award Nomination**—O'Brien, best supporting actor.

120 minutes b&w

THE SEVEN LITTLE FOYS (1955)

★★★

Bob Hope
George Tobias
Milly Vitale

Hope stars in this spirited musical biography of vaudevillian Eddie Foy and his

(Continued)

This movie available on videotape and/or disc.

(Continued)
family of performers. Hope is well suited to his role; he began his career as a song-and-dance man in vaudeville. He's aided by above-average production numbers and James Cagney's guest appearance as George M. Cohan. Herbert Heyes and Angela Clark also star. **Director**—Melville Shavelson. **Academy Award Nomination**—Shavelson and Jack Rose, story and screenplay.
95 minutes

THE SEVEN-PERCENT SOLUTION (1976)

★★★

Nicol Williamson
Alan Arkin
Robert Duvall

Nicol Williamson, Robert Duvall, and Alan Arkin in The Seven-Percent Solution.

Nicholas Meyer wrote the screenplay for this film, based on his own bestseller about the imaginary collaboration between Sherlock Holmes and Sigmund Freud on a criminal investigation. A star-studded cast adds class—Williamson plays Holmes, Arkin is Dr. Freud, and Duvall is Dr. Watson. Also with Vanessa Redgrave, Laurence Olivier, Joel Grey, and Samantha Eggar. **Director**—Herbert Ross. **(PG) Academy Award Nomination**—Meyer, best screenplay based on material from another medium.
113 minutes

THE SEVEN SAMURAI (1954)

Toshiro Mifune
Takashi Shimura

This epic Japanese film is one of director Akira Kurosawa's masterpieces. In 16th-century Japan, a lethal gang of 40 bandits threatens to wreak havoc on a farming village. The menaced citizens hire seven professional soldiers—the samurai—who agree to ward off the invaders. The film has been duly celebrated by fans and critics around the world for its humor, heroism, and humanity. Kurosawa's samurai films are similar in terms of characters and narrative structure to American westerns. In 1960, *The Seven Samurai* was remade into the popular Hollywood western *The Magnificent Seven*. Originally filmed in Japanese.
204 minutes b&w

SEVEN SINNERS (1940)

★★★

Marlene Dietrich
John Wayne
Broderick Crawford
Albert Dekker

Tropical romance: Marlene Dietrich and John Wayne in Seven Sinners.

The hot South Seas island of Boni-Komba is made steamier by the presence of saloon queen Bijou Blanche (Dietrich). When a U.S. Navy lieutenant (Wayne) becomes thoroughly enthralled with her, he is ready to throw away his career for the hot chanteuse. Mischa Auer, Billy Gilbert, Oscar Homolka, and Anna Lee appear in supporting roles. **Director**—Tay Garnett.
87 minutes b&w

1776 (1972)

★★★

William Daniels
Howard Da Silva

Peter Stone's Pulitzer Prize-winning musical about the heroes involved in America's struggle for independence is competently adapted to the screen. Though the subject is an odd choice for a musical, the film is entertaining and quite moving, particularly near the end when all the characters step forward to sign the Declaration of Independence. Almost all of the original Broadway cast members appear, with Daniels as John Adams and Da Silva as Ben Franklin. Donald Madden, David Ford, Ron Holgate, Virginia Vestoff, Blythe Danner, and Ken Howard star in supporting roles. **Director**—Peter H. Hunt. **(G) Academy Award Nomination**—Harry Stradling, Jr., cinematography.
141 minutes

THE SEVENTH SEAL (1957)

★★★★

Max Von Sydow
Gunnar Bjornstrand
Bibi Andersson

Ingmar Bergman's haunting, allegorical drama is a one-of-a-kind masterpiece. As plague sweeps across 14th-century Sweden, black-robed Death comes to claim a knight who's just returned from the Crusades. The knight challenges the Grim Reaper to a game of chess, which leads to a contemplation of life's meaning. It's heavy viewing, and sometimes elusive, but full of striking images, and a seminal work in the director's career. Originally filmed in Swedish.
96 minutes b&w

THE SEVENTH SIGN (1988)

★★ ®

Demi Moore
Michael Biehn
Jürgen Prochnow

Demi Moore has more to worry about than just bad weather in The Seventh Sign.

A lot of ambiguous references to the apocalypse make up the bulk of this horror film, which unfolds with a lack of credibility and no impact. The pretentious story jumps around the globe before finally settling in California, where a young woman (Moore) awaits the birth of her child. A mysterious stranger (Prochnow) arrives to rent the room above her garage, and the young

® *This movie available with closed captions for the hearing impaired.*

mother soon figures out that her soon-to-be-born child is destined to save the world from destruction. Only the delivery room scene carries any suspense. Also with Peter Friedman, Manny Jacobs, and John Taylor. **Director**—Carl Schultz. **(R)** *97 minutes*

THE SEVENTH VEIL (1946)

★★★

James Mason
Ann Todd

Mason and Todd star in this romantic drama about a woman who leaves her family to become a concert pianist. She's romantically torn between her psychiatrist, her guardian, and two other men. Mason plays the role of her guardian. Though bordering on soap opera, the film's excellent production values and performances raise the level of the material. Also with Herbert Lom, Yvonne Owen, Manning Whiley, David Horne, Albert Lieven, and Hugh McDermott. **Director**—Compton Bennett. **Academy Award**—Muriel Box and Sydney Box, original screenplay. *91 minutes b&w*

THE SEVEN YEAR ITCH (1955)

★★★★

Tom Ewell
Marilyn Monroe

Ewell and Monroe are a delightful combination in this comedy about a married man who becomes infatuated with a model. She moves into his apartment building while his wife is away on a long summer vacation. Ewell's male fantasies of possible encounters with Monroe, contrasted with what really happens, makes for a sophisticated romantic comedy. Robert Strauss, Marguerite Chapman, Evelyn Keyes, Sonny Tufts, Victor Moore, Carolyn Jones, and Oscar Homolka appear in supporting roles. **Director**—Billy Wilder. *105 minutes*

SEX AND THE SINGLE GIRL (1964)

Natalie Wood
Tony Curtis
Lauren Bacall
Henry Fonda

This splashy comedy features several major stars, but the lame script lets them down. Curtis plays a writer for a smut magazine who woos Wood, a psychologist. Bacall and Fonda costar as an embattled married couple. Otto Kruger, Mel Ferrer, Edward Everett Horton, and Fran Jeffries also appear in this sexcapade based on the successful book by Helen Gurley Brown. The dated material further mars this mediocre film. **Director**—Richard Quine. *114 minutes*

SEX, LIES AND VIDEOTAPE (1989)

James Spader
Andie MacDowell
Peter Gallagher
Laura San Giacomo

Andie MacDowell is the frosty wife in sex, lies and videotape.

Writer/director Steven Soderbergh debuts with a brilliant sex comedy that deftly explores the sexual problems and psychological makeup of a group of young adults. The icy Ann (MacDowell) is married to John (Gallagher) who is having a loveless but passionate affair with Ann's sister, Cynthia (San Giacomo). The tense triangle is broken when the mysterious Graham (Spader) arrives. A drifter who is painfully honest, Graham is selectively impotent—he can only function sexually by viewing his collection of videotaped interviews with beautiful women. How Graham's visit interrupts and changes the lives of the others provides the core of the plot. Despite the premise, the most erotic scenes in the film are those in which the characters engage in conversation—a testimony to Soderbergh's abilities as a writer. The film takes place in Baton Rouge, Louisiana, which adds a proper backdrop to the steamy sexual encounters. Spader's performance as the provocative Graham won the best actor award at the 1989 Cannes Film Festival. **(R) Academy Award Nomination**—Soderbergh, best original screenplay. *104 minutes*

SHADOW OF A DOUBT (1943)

★★★★

Joseph Cotten
Teresa Wright

Alfred Hitchcock directed this excellent film about a psychopathic killer known as the Merry Widow murderer. The killer, played by Cotten, visits relatives in a small California town in a desperate effort to escape the police. Wright costars as Cotten's niece, who suspects her uncle is the murderer. The horrifying plotline involving a killer on the loose is contrasted with the background setting emphasizing the noble values and virtues of small-town America. Cotten is marvelous as the glib and devious killer, posing as a congenial relative. He gets excellent support from Wright, Hume Cronyn, Henry Travers, Wallace Ford, Patricia Collinge, and Macdonald Carey. The script was well written by Thornton Wilder, Sally Benson, and Alma Reville. **(PG) Academy Award Nomination**—Gordon McDonell, original story. *108 minutes b&w*

SHAFT (1971)

★★★

Richard Roundtree

Roundtree plays John Shaft—a tough, cool black private eye—in this action-packed thriller. It remains an interesting action movie, although there are heavy doses of sex and violence. Gwenn Mitchell, Moses Gunn, Charles Cioffi, and Christopher St. John appear in supporting roles. Isaac Hayes' hip theme song won an Oscar. The film inspired two sequels—*Shaft's Big Score* and *Shaft in Africa*. **Director**—Gordon Parks. **(R)** *98 minutes*

SHAG (1989)

Phoebe Cates
Annabeth Gish
Bridget Fonda
Page Hannah

Cates heads an ensemble cast in this well-acted coming-of-age comedy. Told from the female point of view, the film

(Continued)

(*Continued*)
revolves around the adventures of four teenage girls who find romance in the resort town of Myrtle Beach, South Carolina. Set in 1963, the story substitutes nostalgia for depth and period costumes for character, but the sparkling performances of the four young actresses make the film worthwhile viewing. The "shag" of the title refers to one of the more elaborate dances of that era, and a shag contest provides the conclusion for the loosely constructed film. The male roles in the film are all secondary but are amply acted by Tyrone Power, Jr., Scott Coffey, and Robert Rusler. **Director**—Zelda Barron. **(PG)**
98 minutes

THE SHAGGY D.A. (1977)

Dean Jones
Suzanne Pleshette

Suzanne Pleshette's husband is a dog in The Shaggy D.A.

The Walt Disney studio attempted to repeat the success of their 1959 comedy, *The Shaggy Dog*, with this uninspired sequel. Jones plays a man who is miraculously transformed into the canine while running for district attorney against a corrupt incumbent. All the familiar slapstick tricks—pie-throwing, auto chases, shoot-outs, and so on—are here en masse, though such scenes appear dated now. Tim Conway, Keenan Wynn, and Jo Ann Worley also star. **Director**—Robert Stevenson. **(G)**
90 minutes

THE SHAGGY DOG (1959)

Fred MacMurray
Tommy Kirk
Jean Hagen
Annette Funicello

This enjoyable Walt Disney fantasy about a boy who changes into a shaggy Old English sheepdog by means of a magical device is pleasant film fare for the whole family. Disney's first truly slapstick comedy features two of the studio's top stars at that time—Kirk and Funicello. A huge financial and popular success at the time. The cast also includes Jack Albertson, Tim Considine, and Alexander Scourby. **Director**—Charles Barton. **(G)** *101 minutes b&w*

SHAKEDOWN (1988)

Peter Weller
Sam Elliott

Peter Weller and Sam Elliot are on the chase in Shakedown.

This supercharged cop thriller is overloaded with intense action sequences, jazzy dialogue, and larger-than-life characters. Weller stars as a slick legal-aid lawyer who goes all out to defend a small-time drug dealer falsely charged with murdering a policeman. Elliott almost steals the film as a burned-out street detective who assists Weller with the case. The film's momentum is incredible with high-powered shootouts, hectic car chases, and spectacular stunts propelling the film forward toward a farfetched conclusion, which almost reaches the level of parody. Only a silly romance brings the film down. Patricia Charbonneau, Antonio Fargas, and Blanche Baker costar. **Director**—James Glickenhaus. **(R)** *105 minutes*

SHAKE HANDS WITH THE DEVIL (1959)

James Cagney
Don Murray
Dana Wynter

Cagney stars as the leader of a group of rebels in this action-packed drama about Ireland during the rebellion of the 1920s. Murray plays a young American who tries to stay out of the conflict, but eventually joins Cagney and his gang. Despite the fine acting and vivid photography, the weak script detracts from the film's effectiveness. Filmed on location. Also with Glynis Johns, Michael Redgrave, Richard Harris, Noel Purcell, Cyril Cusack, and Sybil Thorndike. **Director**—Michael Anderson.
110 minutes b&w

SHALL WE DANCE (1937)

Fred Astaire
Ginger Rogers
Edward Everett Horton

Astaire and Rogers play, respectively, a phoney Russian in ballet shoes and a ballroom dancer, who journey together on an ocean liner bound for America. A web of intrigue leads them to pretend to be husband and wife. The film features George and Ira Gershwin's only score for Astaire and Rogers, with such wonderful songs as "They Can't Take That Away from Me," "Let's Call the Whole Thing Off," "They All Laughed," and "Slap That Bass." Bright, breezy fun. **Director**—Mark Sandrich.
116 minutes b&w

SHAMPOO (1975)

★★★ ®

Warren Beatty
Julie Christie
Goldie Hawn

Beatty plays a hedonistic Beverly Hills hairdresser whose clients like to get into his bed as well as under his dryer. It's witty, pointed, and sometimes disturbing cynical mayhem, set against the backdrop of Nixon's 1968 election victory. Also with Lee Grant, Jack Warden, Tony Bill, and Carrie Fisher. **Director**—Hal Ashby. **(R) Academy Award**—Grant, best supporting actress. **Nominations**—Warden, best supporting actor; Robert Towne and Beatty, best original screenplay. *112 minutes*

SHAMUS (1972)

Burt Reynolds
Dyan Cannon

® *This movie available with closed captions for the hearing impaired.*

Reynolds stars in this simpleminded, confusing, and violent updating of private-eye films. Reynolds is hired to recover stolen jewels and find a killer. In the process, he performs numerous heroic feats and tries to recover from a number of beatings. Cannon plays one of his girlfriends. John Ryan, Joe Santos, Giorgio Tozzi, and Ron Weyland are also in the cast, but everyone is overshadowed by Reynolds. **Director**—Buzz Kulik. **(PG)** *91 minutes*

SHANE (1953)

★★★★

Alan Ladd
Jean Arthur
Van Heflin
Brandon De Wilde

This story about a mysterious ex-gunfighter who helps a family of homesteaders is one of the finest westerns ever made. Under the skilled direction of George Stevens, the film unfolds slowly, but builds to a tense, climactic gunfight. The film is a classic because it is mythic in scope: The gunfighter Shane (Ladd) represents the wilderness of the Wild West while the settlers are symbolic of encroaching civilization. It is ironic and sad that Shane can never belong to the civilized West because of his reputation as a gunfighter, although it is his skill with a gun that allows the settlers to remain there. The excellent story and cast are enhanced by superb, Oscar-winning photography. Also with Jack Palance, Ben Johnson, Edgar Buchanan, and Elisha Cook, Jr. **Academy Award**—Loyal Griggs, cinematography. **Nominations**—best picture; Stevens, best director; De Wilde and Palance, best supporting actor; A.B. Guthrie, Jr., screenplay. *117 minutes*

SHANGHAI EXPRESS (1932)

★★★★

Marlene Dietrich
Clive Brook
Warner Oland
Anna May Wong

The impassioned, creative partnership between director Josef von Sternberg and his star, Dietrich, was at its zenith in artistic power and commercial popularity when they turned out this romantic adventure of an eventful train ride through a China devastated by civil war. Dietrich plays the mysterious temptress Shanghai Lily, who runs into old flame Brook during a trip from Peking to Shanghai. Their rekindled liaison is interrupted by bandits (led by Oland), who set upon the train. Solid script by Jules Furthman. Also with Eugene Pallette. **Academy Award**—Lee Garmes, cinematography. **Nominations**—best picture; von Sternberg, best director. *80 minutes b&w*

Marlene Dietrich and Clive Brook take a journey on a Shanghai Express.

SHANGHAI SURPRISE (1986)

★★

Sean Penn
Madonna

A hopeless throwback to those type of thrillers popular during the 1930s, which were set in the mysterious Orient. Madonna stars as an uptight missionary who hires an American adventurer (Penn) to track down a supply of opium. Though filmed on location with glossy production values, this romantic comedy fails, mostly due to the incomprehensible screenplay and poor direction. Surprisingly, Mr. and Mrs. Penn fail to strike any sparks onscreen. **Director**—Jim Goddard. **(PG–13)** *97 minutes*

SHARKY'S MACHINE (1981)

★★★

Burt Reynolds
Rachel Ward

Reynolds directed and stars in this gripping, action-packed police thriller. He plays a wily undercover cop who cracks a high-flying prostitution and drug operation while encountering an overwhelming amount of blood, gore, and brutality in the process. Sharky bears a likeness to Clint Eastwood's Dirty Harry character, but Reynolds accomplishes the feat with more glamour. Reminiscent of the classic *film noir Laura*. Also with Vittorio Gassman, Brian Keith, Charles Durning, Earl Holliman, Bernie Casey, and Henry Silva. **(R)** *119 minutes*

SHE (1965)

Ursula Andress
John Richardson

Andress and Richardson spark enough energy in this story about the search for the Flame of Eternal Life to please fans of African adventure films. Andress plays Ayesha, the queen who never grows old. Richardson leads the quest for the Flame. The production, based on the H. Rider Haggard novel, takes itself too seriously, however, and would have been more effective as a fantasy. Peter Cushing, Christopher Lee, Bernard Cribbins, Rosenda Monteros, and André Morell appear in supporting roles. **Director**—Robert Day. *105 minutes*

SHE-DEVIL (1989)

★★½ 

Meryl Streep
Roseanne Barr

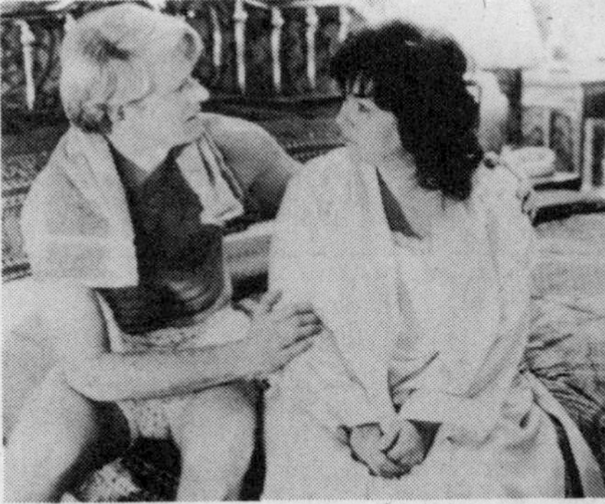

Ed Begley, Jr. has his problems with wife Roseanne Barr in She-Devil.

An unfaithful accountant leaves his dumpy wife and runs straight into the arms of a man-stealing romance novelist in this uneven revenge comedy. But, the downtrodden housewife doesn't get mad—she gets even. She systematically wrecks their house, his career, and his philandering love affair. Barr is believable as the jilted wife and Streep, in her first major comedy role, fares well as the egocentric writer. Unfortunately, the two have no scenes together, deny-

(Continued)

(Continued)
ing the audience the humor inherent in the offbeat casting. Most of the film's problems seem to be the result of bad choices on the part of director Susan Seidelman *(Desperately Seeking Susan; Cookie; Making Mr. Right)*. Ed Begley, Jr. plays the hapless husband. Also with Linda Hunt, Sylvia Miles, and A Martinez. **(PG-13)** *99 minutes*

SHE DONE HIM WRONG (1933)

★★★

Mae West
Cary Grant
Gilbert Roland

Go West, young man; go *Mae* West. This was her second film, where she advises Grant to come up and see her sometime. West scripted (along with a few other hired hands) from her Broadway sensation *Diamond Lil*, and her lines still crackle with sexy wit. Grant plays a cop posing as a Salvation Army man, trying to expose, as it were, a notorious lady saloon keeper's corruption. Though now considered a comedy classic, it was an unlikely Oscar nominee as best picture. A good supporting cast includes Roland, Owen Moore, Noah Beery, and Louise Beavers. Charles Lang photographed. **Director**—Lowell Sherman. **Academy Award Nomination**—best picture.

66 minutes b&w

SHEENA (1984)

★

Tanya Roberts
Ted Wass

Campy, comic-book trifle that features scantily clad Roberts in the title role as the female answer to Tarzan. The story, set in Africa, is filled with two-dimensional characters and corny, melodramatic events, including a military coup, a romance between Sheena and a TV reporter (Wass), and the expected communication with the jungle animals. The production is taken far too seriously—a situation that provokes unintentional laughter. **Director**—John Guillermin. **(PG)** *117 minutes*

SHENANDOAH (1965)

★★★

James Stewart
Rosemary Forsyth

Stewart portrays the head of a Virginia household disrupted by the Civil War in this well-acted and competently directed western. A sentimental storyline is enhanced by the fine performance of Stewart and quality supporting efforts of Doug McClure, Katharine Ross, George Kennedy, Patrick Wayne, Glenn Corbett, and Philip Alford. **Director**—Andrew V. McLaglen. *105 minutes*

SHENANIGANS

See The Great Bank Hoax

SHE'S GOTTA HAVE IT (1986)

★★★

Tracy Camilla Johns
Tommy Redmond Hicks
Spike Lee

Tracy Camilla Johns pleads with Tommy Redmond Hicks in She's Gotta Have It.

Actor/director/writer Lee displays genuine talent with this social comedy made on a shoestring budget. Despite its rough edges, this poignant, oddball film is an original work about sexual manners and male-female role-playing. Johns stars as a young, independent woman who is involved with three men. All three of them eventually become exasperated by her lack of commitment. Hicks, Lee, and John Canada Terrell costar as the unfortunate suitors. **(R)** *84 minutes b&w*

SHE'S HAVING A BABY (1988)

★★½

Kevin Bacon
Elizabeth McGovern

Director John Hughes, who began his career specializing in teenage angst, takes on modern marriage in this uneven social satire. Bacon is appealing as a newlywed at odds with his career in advertising and his sterile suburban lifestyle. Influenced by his best friend, played by Alec Baldwin in the film's best performance, Bacon longs for a more carefree existence. Only after his wife (McGovern) becomes pregnant and bears a child does he finally mature. By that time, however, the film has subjected the audience to many gimmicky comic sequences and whiney monologues by Bacon on what he perceives as a dull life. Also with William Windom, Cathryn Damon, James Ray, and Holland Taylor. **(PG–13)**

106 minutes

SHE'S OUT OF CONTROL (1989)

★½

Tony Danza
Ami Dolenz

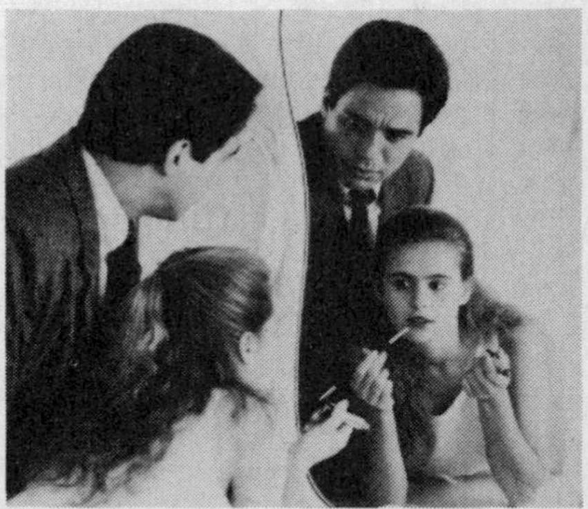

Tony Danza can't handle Ami Dolenz— She's Out of Control.

This comedy is merely an extended sitcom loaded with clichés, gimmicks, and stock characters. Danza, of TV's *Who's The Boss?*, plays a divorced father who can't quite cope with the transformation of his young daughter (Dolenz) into an attractive woman. Wallace Shawn steals some scenes as a dubious shrink. Also with Catherine Hicks, Dick O'Neill, and Dana Ashbrook. **Director**—Stan Dragoti. **(PG)** *97 minutes*

SHE WORE A YELLOW RIBBON (1949)

★★★

John Wayne
Joanne Dru
John Agar

Wayne is excellent as a rugged cavalry officer about to retire. Before he can leave the army, he faces a last encounter with some rampaging Indians. A touch of melancholy pervades this western as Wayne's character seems to have nowhere to go after he retires; his wife has died, and the cavalry has taken the place of a family. The film makes use of one of director John Ford's favorite themes—the passing of the Old West, represented by Wayne, to make way for civilization. Ben Johnson, Harry Carey, Jr., Mildred Natwick, Arthur Shields, Victor McLaglen, and George O'Brien also star. **Academy Award**—Winton Hock, cinematography. *103 minutes*

SHINE ON HARVEST MOON (1944)

★★

Ann Sheridan
Dennis Morgan

Some enjoyable tunes make this lightweight musical about the lives of vaudevillians Nora Bayes and Jack Norworth worthwhile. If you want to learn the real story about these famous entertainers, you won't find it in this film. But the performances of Sheridan and Morgan, as Bayes and Norworth, are pleasant enough, and they receive competent support from S.Z. Sakall, Marie Wilson, the Step Brothers, Robert Shayne, Jack Carson, and Irene Manning. The finale was shot in color. **Director**—David Butler.

112 minutes b&w/color

THE SHINING (1980)

✇ ★★★

Jack Nicholson
Shelley Duvall

Jack Nicholson shows another side of his personality in The Shining.

Director Stanley Kubrick's horror film about a haunted hotel, based on Stephen King's best-selling novel, is a fascinating thriller about horror, rage, and frustration. Yet as sumptuous and spellbinding as the film is, many of its horror scenes wind up as puzzling dead ends. Nicholson gives an impressive but wildly overplayed performance as a congenial father who is gradually transformed into a snarling demon bent on killing his family with an ax. Duvall plays his wife, and Danny Lloyd is his son. Also with Scatman Crothers and Anne Jackson. **(R)**

143 minutes

SHIP OF FOOLS (1965)

✇ ★★★ 🗨®

Vivien Leigh
Simone Signoret
Oskar Werner
Heinz Ruhmann

Director Stanley Kramer tries hard to be faithful to the best-selling novel by Katherine Anne Porter, but far too often he fails to do the book justice. Fortunately, superior performances keep the ship from sinking. The movie is about a voyage in 1933 from Vera Cruz to Bremerhaven and the eccentricities of its various passengers. Leigh plays a divorcée, and Signoret and Werner are lovers. Also with Michael Dunn, Lee Marvin, José Ferrer, Elizabeth Ashley, Lilia Skala, José Greco, George Segal, and Kaaren Verne. **Academy Award**—Ernest Laszlo, cinematography. **Nominations**—best picture; Werner, best actor; Signoret, best actress; Dunn, best supporting actor; Abby Mann, best screenplay based on material from another medium.

149 minutes b&w

SHIRLEY VALENTINE (1989)

✇ ★★★ 🗨®

Pauline Collins
Tom Conti

Collins reprises her stage role as a frustrated Liverpool housewife in this delightful comedy about the importance of finding oneself. The original stage play was structured as a one-woman show, with Collins taking the parts of all the characters. Director Lewis Gilbert retains the feel of a one-person show but opens the story up by including a small cast of skilled supporting players. Shirley eventually rebels against her bleak family life and achieves rejuvenation on a romantic Greek island—a welcome change from the recent flux of melodramas that emphasize traditional roles as the most gratifying options for women. It's a funny, spirited valentine indeed. Also with Julia McKenzie, Alison Steadman, Bernard Hill, and Tracie Bennett. **(R) Academy Award Nominations**—Collins, best actress; Marvin Hamlisch and Alan and Marilyn Bergman, best song for "The Girl Who Used to Be Me." *108 minutes*

SHOAH (1985)

✇ ★★★★

Nazi death camp survivors, guards, and bystanders tell their stories in this engrossing, unique, and masterful documentary about the Holocaust. French filmmaker Claude Lanzmann spent more than 10 years locating and filming subjects who remember the tragic details. The result is a powerful and extraordinary oral history made without any archival film footage. The work is about 9½ hours long, but the unfolding is so compelling that the time spent watching is worthwhile. **(No MPAA rating)** *570 minutes*

A SHOCK TO THE SYSTEM (1990)

✇ ★★

Michael Caine
Elizabeth McGovern
Peter Riegert

The durable Caine highlights this dark satire about corporate politics. He plays a likable advertising executive who, when passed over for promotion, rises to the firm's top by killing his adversaries. Though not as humorous as it was meant to be, the film succeeds as a portrait of greed and power. The film's weaknesses are its lackluster direction by Jan Egleson and poorly drawn characters; its strengths are the performances by a well-chosen cast. Also with Swoosie Kurtz, Will Patton, Jenny Wright, and Barbara Baxley. **(R)**

90 minutes

SHOCKER (1989)

✇ ★★½

Michael Murphy
Peter Berg
Mitch Pileggi

Wes Craven, the director of the original *A Nightmare on Elm Street* and the man who breathed live into Freddy Krueger, brings to the screen a second hideous fiend—Horace Pinker. Pinker, a TV

(Continued)

Mitch Pileggi gets a charge out of the situation in Shocker.

(Continued)
repairman turned mass murderer, is executed in the electric chair. Not surprisingly, Horace continues on after death as a disembodied spirit who possesses the bodies of others. The twist is that he gains access to his victims when they absent-mindedly turn on the tube to watch mindless programs. Though not the mass-market hit the producers had hoped for, the film will be of interest to horror fans. Craven makes use of some of the elements that have made him a hit among horror patrons, including the wicked one-liners that spill forth from the mouth of the monster and an emphasis on dreams as the vehicle that connects the monster with the protagonist. Also with Cami Cooper, Richard Brooks, John Tesh, and Dr. Timothy Leary. **(R)** *107 minutes*

SHOCK TREATMENT (1982)

Cliff De Young
Richard O'Brien

A failed effort to capture the magic of *The Rocky Horror Picture Show* by the same folks who conceived the earlier cult classic. This musical tries to lampoon TV game shows and soap operas; the result is a dull, witless, and confusing production that isn't worth viewing. The attempt at camp is all too obvious and strained. **Director**—Jim Sharman. **(PG)** *94 minutes*

THE SHOES OF THE FISHERMAN (1969)

Anthony Quinn
David Janssen
Laurence Olivier

A fine cast can't salvage this confusing, boring, and long saga of a Russian cardinal who becomes the Pope. Quinn plays the pontiff, Janssen is a journalist, and Olivier is the Russian premier. The story is supposedly based on Morris L. West's best-selling novel; but while the book was a thoughtful and sensitive effort to explore complex life and death issues, the movie is superficial and fails to be of interest to either Christians or non-Christians. Also with Vittorio De Sica, Clive Revill, Paul Rogers, Oskar Werner, Barbara Jefford, and Leo McKern. **Director**—Michael Anderson. **(G)** *157 minutes*

SHOGUN ASSASSIN (1980)

★★

Tomisaburo Wakayama

This is an exceedingly gory film set in medieval Japan. A samurai warrior, played by Wakayama, has been exiled, so he's forced to wander around the countryside, pushing his small son in a cart. Periodically, they're attacked by bands of ninja. Heads, hands, and feet are whacked off with abandon and blood gushes freely—all to the tune of disco music. The samurai manages to leave plenty of bodies in his wake, while his son tries to keep an accurate body count. It appears that at least two Japanese films were spliced together and redubbed to create *Shogun Assassin*. The film should be seen as a grisly parody of the ninja films, many of which have been recently imported from Japan. Brilliantly edited, though the fight scenes may be too bloody for some. **Director**—Robert Houston. **(R)** *86 minutes*

SHOOT (1976)

★

Cliff Robertson
Ernest Borgnine

Robertson and Borgnine star in this farfetched movie about two groups of weekend hunters who engage in a military-type shoot-out. The film is supposed to be a statement favoring gun control, but it's too simplistic and unbelievable to be taken seriously. The performances are dreary, and the direction is lackluster. *Shoot* is way off target. Also with Larry Reynolds, Henry Silva, and James Blendick. **Director**—Harvey Hart. **(R)** *98 minutes*

THE SHOOTING PARTY (1985)

★★★

James Mason
John Gielgud

An elegant, sophisticated British period drama that details the end of the Edwardian era and the start of World War I. Events take place at a country estate where aristocrats gather for a pheasant hunt. The film is populated with numerous characters played by some of England's best thespians. Mason in his last screen role stands out as a wise and wealthy country squire. Gielgud is appropriately dignified as an animal-rights defender. Also with Dorothy Tutin, Edward Fox, and Gordon Jackson. **Director**—Alan Bridges. **(No MPAA rating)** *108 minutes*

THE SHOOTIST (1976)

★★★

John Wayne
Lauren Bacall
James Stewart
Ron Howard

Ron Howard is a young man who comes to know a dying gunfighter in The Shootist.

A moving, final film performance by Wayne as an aging frontier gunfighter who's dying of cancer. He wants to die in peace, but his reputation won't let him. Bacall plays the owner of a rooming house, and Stewart is a doctor who befriends Wayne. The way the film's plot parallels Wayne's own career is uncanny. Wayne himself was dying of cancer while shooting this film. Also, director Don Siegel uses a montage of film clips from Wayne's old movies to visually suggest the early life of the gunfighter Wayne is portraying. The parallels make this last Wayne film all the more poignant. Also with Richard

® *This movie available with closed captions for the hearing impaired.*

Boone, Hugh O'Brian, Harry Morgan, John Carradine, and Scatman Crothers. **(PG)** *100 minutes*

SHOOT THE MOON (1982)

★★★

Albert Finney
Diane Keaton

An honest drama about the breakup of a 15-year marriage and the devastating effect on family members. Finney and Keaton are exceptionally good as the estranged couple, and many scenes are moving. Director Alan Parker (*Fame*) lingers on the pain, but does arrive at some telling revelations about what keeps people together and what drives them apart. Also with Karen Allen, Dana Hill, and Peter Weller. **(R)** *124 minutes*

SHOOT TO KILL (1988)

★★1/2

Sidney Poitier
Tom Berenger

Kirstie Alley and Tom Berenger in the detective thriller Shoot to Kill.

Poitier, after an absence of over a decade, returned to the big screen in 1988 with two detective thrillers, *Little Nikita* and this moderately entertaining action drama. As a veteran FBI agent, Poitier chases a vicious killer from San Francisco to the wilderness of the American Northwest. There the big-city detective is forced to accept the help of tough backwoodsman Berenger in order to traverse the rugged terrain. The film focuses on the contrast between the sophisticated Poitier, with his high-tech forensic approach to apprehending the criminal, and the rough-hewn Berenger, who tracks the killer much like a mountian man of yesteryear. The film's highpoint involves some exciting action sequences played out against the beautiful mountain scenery, but the story quickly turns predictable when it returns to an urban locale. Also with Kirstie Alley, Clancy Brown, Richard Masur, and Andrew Robinson. **Director**—Roger Spottiswoode. **(R)** *106 minutes*

THE SHOP AROUND THE CORNER (1940)

★★★

James Stewart
Margaret Sullavan

James Stewart and Margaret Sullavan fall in love in The Shop Around the Corner.

In quaint old Budapest two employees of the shop around the corner—Stewart and Sullavan—feel they can't stand each other. Neither realizes that each is the anonymous pen pal with whom the other has been romantically corresponding. Vintage Hollywood champagne from director Ernst Lubitsch, a master of mixing comedy and sentiment. Stewart and Sullavan are wonderful, as are cast members Frank Morgan, Felix Bressart, and Joseph Schildkraut. Lovely script by Samson Raphelson. *97 minutes b&w*

SHORT CIRCUIT (1986)

★★

Ally Sheedy
Steve Guttenberg

A lethal military robot is struck by lightning and comes alive—literally. The electronic machine becomes a playful, peace-loving, nuts-and-bolts being that befriends free spirit Sheedy and astounds its own inventor, Guttenberg. The film isn't well written or acted, but the robot with personality does some amusing celebrity impersonations. The film should win fans among preteens and those who like their movies glossy and light. However, Fisher Stevens' interpretation of an Eastern Indian scientist who butchers the English language borders on the offensive. **Director**—John Badham. **(PG)** *99 minutes*

SHORT CIRCUIT 2 (1988)

★★

Fisher Stevens
Michael McKean

A run-down sequel to the 1986 comedy about the almost-human robot with extraordinary talents. The mechanical wonder, named Johnny Five, comes to the big city to help Stevens, who is now in the toy business. Complications occur when crooks want to use the robot's abilities to steal jewels. Despite the robot's stiff and labored movements, Johnny is less mechanical that his human friends, played by Stevens and McKean. Also with Cynthia Gibb, Jack Weston, and the voice of Tim Blaney. **Director**—Kenneth Johnson. **(PG)** *112 minutes*

SHORT EYES (1977)

★★★

Bruce Davison
José Perez
Joe Carberry

Davison, Perez, and Carberry star in this tough-talking semidocumentary based on Miguel Pinero's award-winning play about prison life. It has a raw quality that steers clear of the usual prison-movie sentimentality. The cast—a mixture of ex-cons, street people, and professional actors—performs well. Filmed entirely in The Tombs, which is New York City's Men's House of Detention. Also with Don Blakely and Nathan George. **Director**—Robert M. Young. **(R)** *100 minutes*

SHORT TIME (1990)

Dabney Coleman
Matt Frewer
Teri Garr

Coleman stars as a policeman close to retirement who mistakenly believes he has a fatal disease. He tries to get killed in the line of duty so his survivors will collect a large life insurance settlement. Though a good idea for a black comedy, the premise is poorly executed. Filled with stale gimmicks, routine car chases, and an odd combination of cruelty and sentiment, the film lacks the smart dialogue and quirky characters needed for farce. First-time director Gregg Cham-

(Continued)

(Continued)
pion overdoes the action and violence. Also with Barry Corbin, Joe Pantoliano, and Rob Roy. **(PG-13)** *97 minutes*

A SHOT IN THE DARK (1964)

★★★½

Peter Sellers
Elke Sommer
George Sanders

Sellers excels in this comic adventure as the inept French police inspector Jacques Clouseau. Sommer, Clouseau's partner in this comic romp through Paris, is a murder suspect in a crime at the home of Sanders. Well-paced under the direction of Blake Edwards. The sequence at a nudist colony is hilarious. Also with Herbert Lom, Tracy Reed, and Graham Stark. **(PG)** *101 minutes*

THE SHOUT (1979)

★★

Alan Bates
Susannah York
John Hurt

An eerie but muddled movie about a strange madman who can kill someone by yelling loudly. Bates delivers a keen performance as a mental patient who acquired his terrifying knack from Australian aborigines. Hurt plays a composer, and York is his wife. The film's material is difficult to understand, and the soundtrack, as if to emphasize the point of the film, is extra loud. Also with Tim Curry and Robert Stephens. **Director**—Jerzy Skolimowski. **(R)** *87 minutes*

SHOUT AT THE DEVIL (1976)

★★½

Lee Marvin
Roger Moore

Action fans should like this old-fashioned African adventure with sea battles, run-ins with hungry crocodiles, narrow escapes, aerial derring-do, and hand-to-hand combat. It's based on a novel by Wilbur Smith. Marvin plays a gin-soaked ivory poacher who feuds with the local German commissioner on the eve of World War I. Moore co-stars as Marvin's very British partner. The film is too long, and the plot sags in places, but it is nonetheless acceptable entertainment. Also with Barbara Perkins, René Kolldehoff, Karl Michael Vogler, Ian Holm, and George Coulouris. **Director**—Peter Hunt. **(PG)** *128 minutes*

SHOW BOAT (1951)

★★★

Kathryn Grayson
Howard Keel

Howard Keel (far right) goes for broke in Show Boat, *as Adele Jergens looks on.*

Some excellent Jerome Kern songs and energetic dancing highlight this musical. The movie, based on Edna Ferber's novel about life on the Mississippi River in the 1900s, is enriched by the performances of Grayson, Keel, and Joe E. Brown. Marge and Gower Champion, Ava Gardner, William Warfield, Agnes Moorehead, and Robert Sterling appear in supporting roles. Songs include "My Bill," "Can't Help Loving That Man," and "Old Man River." **Director**—George Sidney. **Academy Award Nomination**—Charles Rosher, cinematography. *115 minutes*

SHY PEOPLE (1987)

★★★½

Jill Clayburgh
Barbara Hershey

A writer for *Cosmopolitan* magazine (Clayburgh) travels with her young daughter to the bayous of Louisiana to search for part of her family. There she finds a distant cousin (Hershey), who heads a small clan of backwoods people, including three rough-looking sons. The differences between the two women and the lifestyles they represent provide the basis for the film. Director Andrei Konchalovsky depicts the unusual tale with a dark atmosphere of foreboding through repeated shots of the swampland, the fog, and the dense foliage characteristic of the area. Despite its limited theatrical distribution, the film was critically acclaimed and Hershey won the best actress award at the Cannes Film Festival for her role. Also with Martha Plimpton, Merritt Butrick, John Philbin, Mare Winningham, and Don Swayze. **(R)** *120 minutes*

THE SICILIAN (1987)

★½

Christopher Lambert
Terence Stamp

Director Michael Cimino's epic drama about the Sicilian bandit Salvatore Giuliano is a ponderous mess. Saddled with a confusing script, mediocre performances from a miscast group of actors, and trite stylistic devices, the film doesn't have a chance. Lambert, in the title role, offers little appeal as the brooding young rebel who supposedly fights for land reform but seems more interested in contemplating his place in Italian history. The sweeping vistas of the Sicilian countryside are impressive but not enough to sustain interest in this flat production. Cut by almost 30 minutes for its theatrical release, the film is offered on video in both its restored 146-minute version and the original 115-minute version. Based on Mario Puzo's novel. Also with Joss Ackland, John Turturro, Barbara Sukowa, and Richard Bauer. **(R)** *115 minutes*

SID AND NANCY (1986)

★★★½

Gary Oldman
Chloe Webb

Rock 'n' roll nightmare: Gary Oldman and Chloe Webb play the ill-fated Sid and Nancy.

® *This movie available with closed captions for the hearing impaired.*

Alex Cox (*Repo Man*) directed this excellent account of the destructive relationship between punk-rocker Sid Vicious of the Sex Pistols and his groupie girlfriend Nancy Spungen. Cox manages to bring warmth and sympathy to this story despite the couple's brutal and warped existence, which included heroin addiction and physical abuse. Through Sid and Nancy's story, Cox reveals the raw, manic energy behind punk-rock music as well as the sociopolitical conditions that gave birth to it. It was a movement destined by its very nature to self-destruct. The total lack of values and disregard for human life exhibited by the punk-rockers will shock some audiences, but more daring viewers will appreciate the performances by Oldman and Webb as well as the thought-provoking message. Drew Schofield plays Johnny Rotten, the Sex Pistols' notorious lead singer. **(R)**
111 minutes

SIDEWALK STORIES (1989)
★★★½

Charles Lane
Nicole Alysia

In this era of big-budgeted action films with phenomenal special effects, filmmaker Lane directs a gentle *silent* comedy, shot in black and white. Lane stars as a poor, shy street artist who helps a lost child (Alysia) find her mother. The artist, who lives in an abandoned tenement, loses his home completely when the dilapidated building is torn down. Writer/director/actor Lane has fashioned a sharp social statement about homelessness using the conventions of the silent comedy. As such, he is a modern-day successor to Charlie Chaplin, whose films often featured keen observations about society's ills amidst the comic bits. Shot on a shoestring budget using real New York locations, Lane's film is a must-see for cinephiles as well as for those with a social conscience. **(R)** *97 minutes b&w*

SIDNEY SHELDON'S BLOODLINE
See Bloodline

SIESTA (1988)
★★

Ellen Barkin
Gabriel Byrne
Julian Sands

Ellen Barkin is obsessed with Gabriel Byrne in Siesta.

Barkin, who most often appears in costarring roles (*Diner; The Big Easy; Desert Bloom*), is the star of this offbeat story with a foreign flavor. She portrays a stuntwoman who becomes unduly upset when she hears of a former lover's decision to marry. Hoping to track him down for a possible reconciliation, she boards a plane for Spain where her life spirals downward into an abyss of emotional turmoil. Unable to separate fantasy from reality from nightmare, Barkin soon becomes lost in a maze of memories and illusions. Despite a complex and intriguing beginning, this surrealistic drama eventually becomes too tangled to sustain suspense. Also with Isabella Rossellini, Jodie Foster, Martin Sheen, and Grace Jones. **(R)**
97 minutes

THE SIGN OF THE CROSS (1932)
★★½

Fredric March
Claudette Colbert
Charles Laughton
Elissa Landi

A below-standard biblical epic from Cecil B. De Mille. The storyline involves the persecution of Christians under the reign of Emperor Nero, portrayed in a grandiose manner by Laughton. The film falls under the weight of its slow-moving, ponderous script, though the performances, particularly those by March as Marcus Superbus and Colbert as the seductive Poppaea, are above average. Originally released at 123 minutes, and rereleased in 1944 with a special prologue designed for World War II audiences. Also with Ian Keith, Vivian Tobin, Nat Pendleton, and Joe Bonomo. **Academy Award Nomination**—Karl Struss, cinematography.
120 minutes b&w

SIGN O' THE TIMES (1987)
★★★

Prince

Prince performs in the concert film Sign O' the Times.

This colorful, high-key concert film shot in Rotterdam and in a recording studio in Minnesota features the outrageous rock singer in all his glory, performing from his album *Sign O' the Times.* Not an ordinary concert performance, the film captures Prince's attempt to illustrate, through dance and staging, the mood and theme of each song. Dancer Cat Glover's sensual interpretation of some of the music is compelling, while regular band member Sheila E. performs an energetic drum solo. Singer Sheena Easton is featured performing "U Got the Look." Other songs include "Little Red Corvette," "Now's the Time," and "If I Was Your Girlfriend." **Director**—Prince. **(PG-13)** *85 minutes*

SIGNS OF LIFE (1989)
★★

Beau Bridges
Arthur Kennedy
Kevin J. O'Connor

A melancholy fable set in a Maine fishing village starring Bridges as an underpaid boat-yard worker who has trouble supporting his growing family. The drama offers uninspired vignettes that revolve around the closing of a boat-building business and its effect on employees who must find other work. A good cast tries hard with the thin material. Kennedy returns after a ten-year absence from the screen. Also with Vincent Philip D'Onofrio, Kate Reid, and Mary Louise Parker. **Director**—John David. **(PG-13)** *91 minutes*

SILENCE OF THE NORTH (1982)

★★

Ellen Burstyn
Tom Skerritt

Ellen Burstyn and Tom Skerritt float downstream to the Silence of the North.

Burstyn portrays an independent woman who survives harrowing experiences and brutal conditions in the northern Canadian territory of the early 1900s. The story, based on the life of Olive Fredrickson, is presented as an undramatic series of episodes. The film seems to work best as a travelogue, with breathtaking wilderness scenery upstaging everything else. Costars Gordon Pinsent, Jennifer McKinney, and Donna Dobrijevic. **Director**—Allan Winton King. **(PG)** *94 minutes*

THE SILENCERS (1966)

★★

Dean Martin
Stella Stevens

Martin plays secret agent Matt Helm in this effort to capitalize on the success of James Bond films. However, this movie lacks the cleverness and budget of the Bond productions. Stevens perks up the movie slightly, but the film suffers from too much emphasis on obvious sexual innuendo at the expense of more colorful villains and an interesting plot. Arthur O'Connell, Cyd Charisse, Robert Webber, James Gregory, Victor Buono, and Dahlia Lavi appear in supporting roles. **Director**—Phil Karlson. *103 minutes*

SILENT MOVIE (1976)

★★★

Mel Brooks
Marty Feldman
Dom DeLuise

Comedy king Brooks proves that silence is golden by taking a chance and making a silent comedy. The result is a procession of hilarious sight gags, on the order of the broad physical humor of the Marx Brothers and the Three Stooges. The film also conveys warmth, so don't expect the scatological jokes and sexual antics of Brooks' *Blazing Saddles*. Here, Brooks plays a director named Mel Funn who tries to save a film studio from a takeover by a New York-based conglomerate. DeLuise and Feldman are his lunatic sidekicks. Splendid cameo appearances by Paul Newman, Burt Reynolds, and Liza Minnelli, and an uproarious nightclub tango routine with Anne Bancroft highlight the film. With subtitles. **(PG)** *88 minutes*

THE SILENT PARTNER (1979)

★★★

Elliott Gould
Christopher Plummer

A drab bank teller (Gould) and a vicious, psychotic bank robber (Plummer) engage in a battle of wits in this suspense film from Canada. The story moves briskly with intriguing plot twists, while detailing the monotonous lives of the central characters. Gould is excellent as a man constantly teetering on the brink of disaster or victory. Also with Susannah York, Celine Lomez, Michael Kirby, and John Candy. **Director**—Daryl Duke. **(R)** *103 minutes*

SILENT RAGE (1982)

Chuck Norris
Ron Silver

Chuck Norris comforts Toni Kalem following a harrowing night in Silent Rage.

Karate champ Norris plays a Texas sheriff in pursuit of a mad killer, whom genetic engineering has made virtually indestructible. There's an interesting science-fiction theme here, but it's handled awkwardly in the slow-paced story. Norris kicks and chops with his usual proficiency, and finally dumps the psychopath down a well. But is the vicious murderer really dead? The ending seems like a setup for a sequel, but fortunately one has not materialized yet. **Director**—Michael Miller. **(R)** *100 minutes*

SILENT RUNNING (1971)

★★★

Bruce Dern
Cliff Potts

Bruce Dern aboard a spaceship carrying the plants of Earth in Silent Running.

A well-made science-fiction adventure about a 21st-century space-station crew trying to keep the last of Earth's vegetation from being destroyed. Dern is outstanding as the leader of the scientists aboard the verdant space ark. Two charming robots, named Huey and Dewey, provide some clever comic relief. The big star of this movie is the magnificent special effects, handled skillfully by director Douglas Trumbull, who did the effects for *2001: A Space Odyssey*. Also with Ron Rifkin and Jesse Vint. **(G)** *90 minutes*

SILK STOCKINGS (1957)

Fred Astaire
Cyd Charisse

Astaire and Charisse star in this musical version of the famous film comedy *Ninotchka*, which starred Greta Garbo. Charisse plays a Russian agent trying to bring a Russian composer living in Paris

This movie available with closed captions for the hearing impaired.

back to Moscow. Astaire is a dapper Hollywood producer who sidetracks Charisse from her mission. The Garbo film was better, but the personable team of Astaire and Charisse, and the Cole Porter music, make this a highly acceptable substitute. Janis Paige, Peter Lorre, George Tobias, Jules Munshin, and Joseph Buloff also star. **Director**—Rouben Mamoulian. *117 minutes*

SILKWOOD (1983)

★★★

Meryl Streep
Cher
Kurt Russell

Kurt Russell and Meryl Streep reflect about their future in Silkwood.

An often compelling biography of courageous Karen Silkwood, an Oklahoma plutonium-plant worker who died mysteriously in an auto crash as she was about to expose nuclear safety violations. Though Streep gives a brilliant portrayal in the title role, and the film examines the plight of many workers who toil under dangerous conditions, many complex circumstances are never adequately resolved. A flawed, but moving film. **Director**—Mike Nichols. **(R) Academy Award Nominations**—Nichols, best director; Streep, best actress; Cher, best supporting actress; Nora Ephron and Alice Arlen, best original screenplay. *131 minutes*

SILVERADO (1985)

★★½

Kevin Kline
Scott Glenn
Danny Glover
Kevin Costner

This sweeping sagebrush saga takes a latter-day approach to the classic west-

Gunfighter Kevin Costner launches himself into the fray in Silverado.

ern genre. Unfortunately, the film is burdened with a complex storyline, involving numerous subplots that ramble off in various directions. Many undefined characters get lost in the shuffle. The film is essentially about four drifters who arrive in a desert town and try to free the small community from the corrupt local law enforcement officials. Each cowboy has his own subplot within that larger framework, which results in too much confusion. Also with Rosanna Arquette and Brian Dennehy. **Director**—Lawrence Kasdan. **(PG–13)** *132 minutes*

SILVER BULLET (1985)

★★

Corey Haim
Gary Busey
Megan Follows

A lackluster horror movie based on Stephen King's novelette *Cycle of the Werewolf*. A small town experiences a sudden series of brutal murders and only a plucky 11-year-old boy (Haim), confined to a wheelchair, believes a werewolf is the culprit. If this was the first werewolf movie, it might have some impact, but such tales are so commonplace that every frame is predictable. Everett McGill and Terry O'Quinn also stars. **Director**—Daniel Attias. **(R)** *95 minutes*

THE SILVER CHALICE (1954)

★★

Paul Newman
Pier Angeli
Jack Palance
Virginia Mayo

Newman made an unspectacular film debut in this biblical epic as a Greek slave freed by the apostle Luke. The slave later went on to craft the chalice that held the wine that Christ drank at the Last Supper. The cast includes Angeli, Palance, Mayo, Natalie Wood, Walter Hampden, E.G. Marshall, Lorne Greene, Alexander Scourby, and Albert Dekker. **Director**—Victor Saville. **Academy Award Nomination**—Wiliam V. Skall, cinematography. *137 minutes*

SILVER STREAK (1976)

★★½

Gene Wilder
Richard Pryor
Jill Clayburgh

An entertaining comedy/adventure set aboard a Los Angeles-to-Chicago train. Wilder plays a meek editor who becomes involved in an art forgery scheme that leads to murder. Most of the laughs are provided by Pryor, who enters the film about midway through. The violence is a bit heavy-handed considering the film is a comedy. Colin Higgins' screenplay is directed by Arthur Hiller. Also with Patrick McGoohan, Ned Beatty, Ray Walston, and Scatman Crothers. **(PG)** *113 minutes*

SIMON (1980)

★★

Alan Arkin

Writer/director Marshall Brickman, who collaborated with Woody Allen on several films, solos with this droll comedy. It's about a group of scientific geniuses who, out of boredom, brainwash a psychology professor into believing he's an alien from outer space. The professor is played by Arkin, in another of his roles as the offbeat outsider. The Brickman script comments on the absurdities of contemporary civilization, but after a while, the comments become sanctimonious and preachy. Also with Madeline Kahn, Austin Pendleton, Fred Gwynne, William Finley, and Judy Graubart. **(PG)** *97 minutes*

SINBAD AND THE EYE OF THE TIGER (1977)

★★★

Patrick Wayne
Jane Seymour

Dazzling special effects are the mainstay of this third Arabian Nights film adventure. This time, Sinbad, played

(Continued)

(Continued)
by Wayne (John Wayne's son), is joined by Princess Farah, played by Seymour. The couple embarks on a dangerous journey to rescue her brother, who has been changed into a baboon. They battle supernatural creatures and prehistoric monsters animated by special effects wizard Ray Harryhausen. Also with Taryn Power (daughter of Tyrone) and Margaret Whiting. **Director**—Sam Wanamaker. **(G)** *113 minutes*

SINBAD THE SAILOR (1947)

★★★

Douglas Fairbanks, Jr.
Maureen O'Hara

With Fairbanks as the swashbuckling hero, this high-seas adventure is great tongue-in-cheek entertainment. Here Sinbad seeks the lost treasure of Alexander, with the support of a lovely princess, played by O'Hara. Walter Slezak, Jane Greer, Anthony Quinn, Sheldon Leonard, George Tobias, and Mike Mazurki appear in supporting roles. **Director**—Richard Wallace.

117 minutes

SINCE YOU WENT AWAY (1944)

★★★

Claudette Colbert
Joseph Cotten
Jennifer Jones
Shirley Temple

Robert Walker, Jennifer Jones, and Guy Madison in Since You Went Away.

Star-studded melodrama about the effects of World War II on the home front. Colbert stars as the mother who holds her middle-class family together when her husband is listed as missing in action. Jones and Temple play her daughters. Though often criticized in retrospect for being too sentimental, the film was an effective morale booster at the time of its release, and represents part of Hollywood's contribution to the war effort. Produced by David O. Selznick, who also wrote the screenplay. Also with Lionel Barrymore, Guy Madison, Agnes Moorehead, Monty Woolley, Robert Walker, Hattie McDaniel, Albert Basserman, Keenan Wynn, and Craig Stevens. **Director**—John Cromwell. **Academy Award Nominations**—best picture; Colbert, best actress; Woolley, best supporting actor; Jones, best supporting actress; Stanley Cortez and Lee Garmes, cinematography. *172 minutes b&w*

SING (1989)

★½

Lorraine Bracco
Peter Dobson
Jessica Steen
Louise Lasser

Peter Dobson and the girls put together a musical number in Sing.

A ragged musical about high-school students in a tough Brooklyn neighborhood. The school is about to be closed because of limited funds, but should the annual song-and-dance competition go on anyway? The answer is obvious and so are the familiar characters: a determined teacher (Bracco), a delinquent student with dancing talent (Dobson), and a plucky girl (Steen) who wants to reform the delinquent. Nothing more than recycled bits and pieces of *Dirty Dancing* and *Fame*, but without the competent acting that made those films above the ordinary. **Director**—Richard Baskin. **(PG-13)**

98 minutes

SINGIN' IN THE RAIN (1952)

★★★★ ®

Gene Kelly
Donald O'Connor
Debbie Reynolds
Jean Hagen

What a glorious feeling: Gene Kelly is Singin' in the Rain.

A marvelous musical spoof of Hollywood during the period when talkies first replaced silent films. Kelly and Hagen appear as silent-film stars who must make the transition to sound or lose their careers. Among the hit songs are "Make 'em Laugh," "My Lucky Star," "Broadway Melody," "Good Morning," and the title tune. The film is considered by some critics to be the greatest Hollywood musical of all time. Part of the reason is the screenplay by Betty Comden and Adolph Green, which spoofs the Hollywood of another era while remaining nostalgic for it. The songs were chosen from a catalogue of tunes by Arthur Freed and Nacio Herb Brown that had been used in earlier films. **Directors**—Kelly and Stanley Donen. **Academy Award Nomination**—Hagen, best supporting actress.

103 minutes

SINK THE BISMARCK! (1960)

★★★

Kenneth More
Dana Wynter

Exciting sea battles and solid acting make this semidocumentary about the British hunt for the famed WWII German battleship worthwhile viewing. Besides the search for and eventual sinking of the German man-of-war, the

® *This movie available with closed captions for the hearing impaired.*

personal dramas of the British sailors make the film more involving. Also with Karel Stepanek, Geoffrey Keen, Esmond Knight, Michael Hordern, Maurice Denham, Laurence Naismith, and Carl Mohner in supporting roles. **Director**—Lewis Gilbert.

97 minutes b&w

SIROCCO (1951)

★★

Humphrey Bogart
Marta Toren
Lee J. Cobb

Bogart manages to make this melodrama about gunrunning in the 1920s mildly interesting. Toren and Cobb also give adequate performances, but the slow-moving story, set in Damascus, lacks firepower. Comic actor Zero Mostel appears in a supporting role. Also with Gerald Mohr, Onslow Stevens, and Everett Sloane. **Director**—Curtis Bernhardt. *98 minutes b&w*

SITTING PRETTY (1948)

★★★

Clifton Webb
Robert Young
Maureen O'Hara

Dignified babysitter Clifton Webb has the last laugh in Sitting Pretty.

Webb is delightful as Mr. Belvedere, an eccentric genius who works as a babysitter for Young and O'Hara. When he writes a successful novel about his experiences, he throws gossipy neighbors into a tizzy. Webb became famous in this role, and two other Mr. Belvedere films followed. Also with Richard Haydn, Larry Olsen, Ed Begley, Randy Stewart, and Louise Allbritton. **Director**—Walter Lang. **Academy Award Nomination**—Webb, best actor.

84 minutes b&w

SIX BRIDGES TO CROSS (1955)

★★

Tony Curtis

Apparently inspired by the Boston Brink's robbery, this well-made film depicts the life and hard times of a Boston gangster in the 1930s. Curtis is at his best as the hoodlum who gets involved with crime and can't abide by the law no matter how hard he tries to go straight. He finally masterminds a robbery involving more than two-and-a-half million dollars. George Nader, Sal Mineo, Jan Merlin, Julie Adams, and Jay C. Flippen appear in supporting roles. **Director**—Joseph Pevney.

96 minutes b&w

SIX PACK (1982)

★★

Kenny Rogers
Diane Lane
Erin Gray

Country singer Rogers stars in this lightweight family film as a racing-car driver trying to make a comeback with the help of six orphans. Rogers is charming, but not an impressive actor. He can't do much with the shallow material. One of the film's songs became a hit for Rogers. Also with Barry Corbin, Terry Kiser, and Bob Hannah. **Director**—Daniel Petrie. **(PG)** *108 minutes*

SIXTEEN CANDLES (1984)

★★★

Molly Ringwald
Anthony Michael Hall
Michael Schoeffling

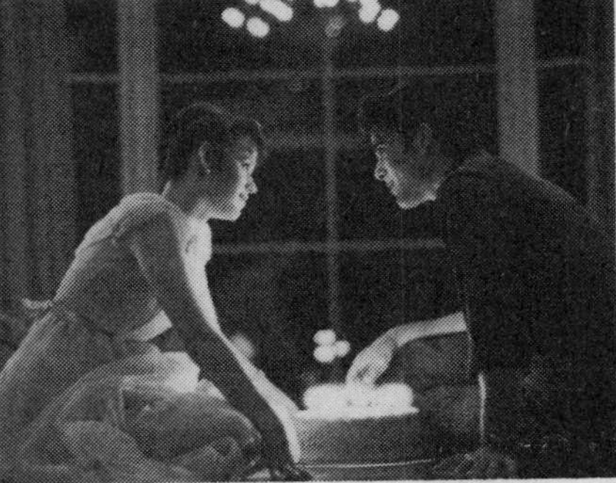

Michael Schoeffling is Molly Ringwald's birthday wish in Sixteen Candles.

Ringwald stars as a teen whose sixteenth birthday is upstaged by her sister's wedding. This touches off a series of disappointing experiences for her, including her crush on the school dreamboat and the efforts of the class "geek" to seduce her. The young actors do well with the material, which is presented from the point of view of the teens. Some offensive language and stereotyped characters mar an otherwise charming film. Also with Paul Dooley, Gedde Watanabe, and Edward Andrews. **Director**—John Hughes. **(PG)**

93 minutes

SIX WEEKS (1982)

★

Mary Tyler Moore
Dudley Moore
Katherine Healy

Katherine Healy, Dudley Moore, and Mary Tyler Moore share a remarkable Six Weeks.

Dreary tearjerker with a plot so contrived as to defy belief. A cosmetic tycoon (Mary Tyler Moore) and her precocious daughter (Healy), who has leukemia, strike up a sentimental friendship with a California politician (Dudley Moore). Soon these unlikely chums are off to New York City, where the 12-year-old heroine skates at Rockefeller Center, assumes the lead in *The Nutcracker* ballet, and dies on the subway all in a single weekend. Preposterous nonsense, and manipulative as well. **Director**—Tony Bill. **(PG)**

107 minutes

SKIN DEEP (1989)

★★½

John Ritter
Vincent Gardenia
Alyson Reed

Blake Edwards directed this mean-spirited comedy that relies heavily on

(Continued)

(Continued)
material from his previous movies. Ritter stars as a prize-winning author suffering from writer's block, which leads to too much boozing and womanizing. Ritter's character is supposed to be sympathetic, but his attitude toward women is from the Dark Ages, while his self-destructive habits come off as self-pity. One memorable scene involving glow-in-the-dark condoms stands out. Also with Joel Brooks, Julianne Phillips, Denise Crosby, and Chelsea Field. **(R)** *102 minutes*

SKI PATROL (1990)

★

Ray Walston
T.K. Carter

Roger Rose points the way to Tess in Ski Patrol.

An unfunny juvenile comedy from the folks who brought us *Police Academy.* The silly plot involves a group of land developers who try to undermine the success of a local ski lodge, owned by kindly old Pops, played by Walston. Pops relies on the support of a group of young skiers who battle for the land in a skiing contest. Except for Walston, the cast is made up of a group of unknowns who do nothing with their cardboard parts in this forgettable farce. To say that this film is formulaic and predictable is an understatement. Also with Roger Rose and Yvette Nipar. **Director**—Richard Correll. **(PG)**
91 minutes

SKY RIDERS (1976)

★★★

James Coburn
Susannah York
Robert Culp

Daredevil hang-gliding stunts highlight this well-photographed action drama filmed in Greece. A wealthy industrialist's wife and children are kidnapped by political terrorists and held at a remote mountain fortress. The wife's ex-husband, played by Coburn, tracks down the hideaway and hires a group of hang-gliding commandos for the thrilling rescue. Director Douglas Hickox does his best with the farfetched plot, but Bob and Chris Wills and their hang-glider team fly away with the movie. Also with Charles Aznavour, Werner Pochath, and Harry Andrews. **(PG)** *93 minutes*

SLAMDANCE (1987)

★★½

Tom Hulce
Virginia Madsen
Mary Elizabeth Mastrantonio

A striking visual style dominates this offbeat thriller, which stars Hulce as an underground cartoonist trying to shake loose from a murder rap. A hard-edged vice cop, played by Harry Dean Stanton, believes that the bumbling cartoonist has killed his lover, and, true to the genre, Hulce must prove his innocence. A convoluted storyline prevents this likable mystery tale from being totally successful. Director Wayne Wang, who made the critically acclaimed low-budget *Chan Is Missing,* concentrates on the flashy visuals at the expense of the plot. Also with Adam Ant and Millie Perkins. **(R)**
100 minutes

SLAP SHOT (1977)

★★★

Paul Newman
Michael Ontkean
Lindsay Crouse

A freewheeling comedy that probes the violence of professional ice hockey. Newman stars as a broken-down player/coach of a fourth-rate minor-league team, which suddenly becomes popular by playing dirty. The zestful screenplay by Nancy Dowd presents some lively and believable characters, although several subplots get in the way. The film is well salted with locker-room humor and expletives. Also with Melinda Dillon, Jennifer Warren, and Strother Martin. Directed by George Roy Hill (*Butch Cassidy and the Sundance Kid; The Sting*). **(R)**
123 minutes

SLAUGHTERHOUSE FIVE (1972)

★★★

Michael Sacks
Ron Leibman
Sharon Gans

Michael Sacks and Valerie Perrine greet their alien captors in Slaughterhouse Five.

The very bizarre—almost mystical—antiwar novel by Kurt Vonnegut, Jr., was difficult to transfer to the screen. However, there are still many good moments in this complex film about a New York optometrist who has fantasies about a strange futuristic planet and nightmares about Nazi prisoner-of-war camps. Many of the images are brilliant, but the movie is hard to follow, even for those who read the book. Eugene Roche, Valerie Perrine, John Dehner, and Sorrell Booke appear in supporting roles. **Director**—George Roy Hill. **(R)**
104 minutes

SLAUGHTER ON TENTH AVENUE (1957)

★★★

Richard Egan
Jan Sterling
Dan Duryea
Walter Matthau

Better-than-average drama about murder and corruption on the New York City waterfront. The storyline concerns an assistant district attorney struggling to convict gangsters who control the waterfront. Obviously derivative of *On the Waterfront,* but still an effective film with an excellent supporting cast, including Julie Adams, Mickey Shaughnessy, Charles McGraw, Sam Levene, and Harry Bellaver. **Director**—Arnold Laven. *103 minutes b&w*

SLAVES OF NEW YORK (1989)

★★

Bernadette Peters
Adam Coleman Howard

® *This movie available with closed captions for the hearing impaired.*

Bernadette Peters and Adam Coleman Howard live an arty life in Slaves of New York.

A flat film adaptation of Tama Janowitz's best-selling collection of short stories about self-centered New York artists. These bohemians are slaves of fashion, just as Peters is emotionally enslaved to her insensitive boyfriend (Howard). While the film has some quirky charm, it lacks the sharp wit of the book and is hurt by too many ill-defined characters. Brief performances by Mary Beth Hurt and Mercedes Ruehl stand out. **Director**—James Ivory. **(R)** *121 minutes*

SLAYGROUND (1984)

Peter Coyote
Philip Sayer
Bill Luhr

Drab, poorly made crime melodrama that is excessively violent. Coyote plays a gangster who is blamed for killing a child during a holdup. The child's wealthy father hires a hit man to avenge the death. This unappealing scenario leads to numerous shootings and a great deal of violence. Mel Smith and Billie Whitelaw have supporting roles. **Director**—Terry Bedford. **(R)** *89 minutes*

SLEEPER (1973)

 ★★★★ ◘®

Woody Allen
Diane Keaton

Allen wrote, directed, and stars in this film about a health-food storekeeper who is frozen after an operation and awakened 200 years later in the year 2173. He is shocked to discover that Earth has become a weird police state. Keaton is charming as his love interest of the future. The futuristic setting allows for some effective sight gags, and there is entertaining background music by the Preservation Hall Band. John Beck, Mary Gregory, Don Keefer, and John McLiam are in supporting roles. **(PG)** *88 minutes*

SLEEPING BEAUTY (1959)

This classic fairy tale has been impressively rendered by the Walt Disney studios. By and large, the original story, about a beautiful princess put to sleep by an evil sorceress, remains intact. The drawing style has been criticized by animation critics for its angularity, but the cartoon attempted to capture the look of French medieval manuscripts. With the voices of Mary Costa, Bill Shirley, and Vera Vague. **Directors**—Clyde Geronimi, Les Clark, Eric Larsen, and Wolfgang Reitherman. **(G)** *75 minutes*

SLEEPING DOGS (1977)

Sam Neill
Warren Oates

An intriguing political thriller made in New Zealand. Neill stars as a man unwittingly caught between revolutionaries and a repressive government. Though well-paced with an intriguing storyline, the haphazard direction mars the film. Neill fares well as a frantic man-on-the-run; Oates turns in an impressive performance as an American officer who's in league with the military regime. The first film from New Zealand ever to open in the U.S. **Director**—Roger Donaldson. **(No MPAA rating)** *107 minutes*

SLEUTH (1972)

★★★

Laurence Olivier
Michael Caine

Director Joseph L. Mankiewicz brings Anthony Shaffer's *tour de force* Broadway thriller to the stage, with smashing success. Mystery writer Olivier invites his wife's lover (Caine) to his English country house—ostensibly to propose an unusual scheme that would benefit both of them. Plot twists abound in this clever mystery, which was a popular success at the time of its release. The production design by Ken Adam effectively re-creates the quaintness of the old English manor house. **(PG) Academy Award Nominations**—Mankiewicz, best director; Caine and Olivier, best actor. *138 minutes*

SLITHER (1972)

★★½

James Caan
Sally Kellerman
Peter Boyle
Louise Lasser

James Caan and Peter Boyle eye one another in Slither.

A zany romp about a search—by means of trailers and campers—for a cache of money in California. At times the movie is too shrill, and the glib blend of violence and comedy is disturbing, but the inspired lunacy of the whole production makes for worthwhile viewing. Allen Garfield and Richard B. Shull appear in supporting roles. **Director**—Howard Zieff. **(PG)** *96 minutes*

SLOW DANCING IN THE BIG CITY (1978)

★★

Paul Sorvino
Anne Ditchburn

A cliché-ridden romantic drama set in New York City. As directed by John G. Avildsen, who brought us *Rocky*, the film emphasizes sentimentality over any attempt at a complex or lifelike story. Sorvino is well cast as a gruff newspaper columnist who falls for a struggling but ailing young ballerina, played by Ditchburn. Also with Nicolas Coster, Anita Dangler, and Hector Jaime Mercado. **(PG)** *101 minutes*

This movie available on videotape and/or disc.

THE SLUGGER'S WIFE (1985)

★★

Michael O'Keefe
Rebecca DeMornay

Ballplayer Michael O'Keefe is dazzled by Rebecca DeMornay in The Slugger's Wife.

A clash of careers between a professional baseball player (O'Keefe) and a rock singer (DeMornay) is the basis of this mildly amusing comedy written by Neil Simon. The acting, direction, and particularly the script are only routine, though the beat picks up toward the film's latter half as efforts are made to reunite the estranged couple. Martin Ritt, better known as a director, steals scenes as the crusty, ambitious team manager. **Director**—Hal Ashby. **(PG–13)**
105 minutes

SLUMBER PARTY MASSACRE (1982)

★★

Michele Michaels
Robin Stille

Two women filmmakers—director Amy Jones and screenwriter Rita Mae Brown—are responsible for this horror film, made quickly on a low budget. The standard maniac is running loose, this time doing his bloody deeds with a power drill. Scores of scantily clad coeds and a few adolescent boys get slaughtered. At first glance it all seems very mechanical, but it can also be viewed as a parody. **(R)** *84 minutes*

SMALL CHANGE (1976)

★★★★

Eva Truffaut
Philippe Goldman

François Truffaut cowrote and directed this endearing and entertaining celebra-

The young charmers in François Truffaut's delightful Small Change.

tion of childhood. The film consists of a series of vignettes about a group of French children in a small village and how they manage to survive in an adult world. Truffaut lovingly treats his children as human beings—not as pawns for entertainment or exploitation. Also with Jean-François Stevenin, Claudio Deluca, and Frank Deluca. Originally filmed in French. **(PG)** *104 minutes*

A SMALL CIRCLE OF FRIENDS (1980)

★★

Brad Davis
Karen Allen
Jameson Parker

A romanticized look at student life in the late 1960s, when Vietnam War protests, drugs, and the sexual revolution made news. The story follows the college careers of three students, played enthusiastically by Davis, Allen, and Parker. Unfortunately, Rob Cohen directs at such a frantic pace that the story loses its perspective and burns out in the final segments. Perhaps the principals in this venture were too close to this period to effectively reflect on the times. **(R)** *113 minutes*

SMALL TOWN GIRL (1953)

★★

Jane Powell
Farley Granger
Ann Miller
Bobby Van

Powell falls in love with Granger, a handsome playboy who gets arrested in her Connecticut hometown for speeding. This musical version of the 1936 film of the same title lacks the dynamic pace and tempo of the better musicals, but it's still enjoyable. Miller almost steals the show with "I've Gotta Hear That Beat," staged by Busby Berkeley. S.Z. Sakall, Billie Burke, Robert Keith, Nat King Cole, and Fay Wray also appear. **Director**—Leslie Kardos.
93 minutes

A SMALL TOWN IN TEXAS (1976)

★★

Timothy Bottoms
Susan George
Bo Hopkins

A young man comes home after serving time in prison on a drug conviction and seeks revenge on the sheriff who busted him. The approach to the film is that of a B-picture melodrama, with plenty of car chases and stunt crashes. Given the subject matter and action-packed sequences, the film was apparently aimed at a younger audience. Hopkins performs rather well as the mean sheriff, upstaging Bottoms in the lead. **Director**—Jack Starrett. **(PG)**
96 minutes

SMASH PALACE (1981)

★★★★

Bruno Lawrence
Anna Jemison

A straightforward story from New Zealand about the marital breakup of a young couple. A frantic auto mechanic (Lawrence) kidnaps his daughter after his wife (Jemison) walks out on him. Director Roger Donaldson depicts the various emotional confrontations with restraint. The bleak background provides ample cause for Jemison to walk out on her spouse. **(No MPAA rating)**
100 minutes

SMILE (1975)

★★★½

Barbara Feldon
Bruce Dern

This satirical film, directed by Michael Ritchie, dissects the callousness and competitiveness of beauty contests, while also taking a hard look at small-town life in America. Shot in a documentary style, the film is alternately amusing and tragic. Dern plays the

This movie available with closed captions for the hearing impaired.

pageant's sponsor—a used-car salesman—and Feldon is the woman who takes care of the contestants. Famed choreographer Michael Kidd costars as a washed-up dance director working for the pageant. Also with Geoffrey Lewis, Nicholas Pryor, Colleen Camp, and Melanie Griffith. **(PG)**
113 minutes

SMILIN' THROUGH (1932)

 ★★½

Norma Shearer
Fredric March
Leslie Howard

This 1932 version of Jane Cowl and Jane Murfin's stage play is an improvement over the silent vehicle starring Norma Talmadge. When a bride is slain by a jealous lover on her wedding day, descendants of the romantic triangle pay the price. Remade again in 1941. **Director**—Frank Borzage. **Academy Award Nomination**—best picture.
97 minutes b&w

SMITHEREENS (1982)

 ★★

Susan Berman
Richard Hell
Brad Rinn

Susan Berman struggles to be noticed in Smithereens.

Director Susan Seidelman's (*Desperately Seeking Susan*) first feature film concerns an eccentric, footloose teenage girl (Berman) trying to establish contact in New York's world of punk rock. A fair amount of energy has gone into this low-budget production, but the story, like the heroine's life, is haphazard and appears to go nowhere. Hell was the leader of the real-life punk band Richard Hell and the Void-Oids. **(R)**
90 minutes

SMOKEY AND THE BANDIT (1977)

★★½

Burt Reynolds
Sally Field
Jackie Gleason
Jerry Reed

Fast cars and an 18-wheel trailer truck are the stars of this comedy about a couple of good ol' boys who try to bootleg 400 cases of beer from Texas to Georgia under the noses of the cops. The film evolves into a drawn-out car chase, punctuated with predictable crash stunts and laced with CB jargon. Reynolds and country singer Reed are likable as the happy-go-lucky bootleggers, and Gleason is in top form as the stereotypical southern sheriff in hot pursuit. Field, a damsel in distress, shows an adeptness for light comedy. Well edited, with some amazing stunt work. Directed by former stunt coordinator Hal Needham. Also with Mike Henry, Paul Williams, and Pat McCormick. **(PG)** *96 minutes*

SMOKEY AND THE BANDIT II (1980)

 ★★

Burt Reynolds
Sally Field
Jackie Gleason
Dom DeLuise

Once again frustrated Sheriff Buford T. Justice, played by Gleason, is in pursuit of the Bandit (Reynolds), the Frog (Field), and their pals, who are transporting a pregnant elephant to Dallas to earn $400,000. There are fewer laughs and fewer spectacular stunts here, but the cast carries on in good-natured harmony. Also with Paul Williams. **Director**—Hal Needham. **(PG)** *104 minutes*

SMOKEY AND THE BANDIT III (1983)

 ★

Jackie Gleason
Jerry Reed

Gleason, as Sheriff Buford T. Justice, is the star of this third in the series of nonstop chases and smashups. Here the storyline involves a race from Florida to Texas to deliver a large plastic fish. The characters and corny jokes wore thin long ago. Colleen Camp and Paul Williams are in supporting roles. **Director**—Dick Lowry. **(PG)** *86 minutes*

SMOOTH TALK (1986)

 ★★★

Laura Dern
Treat Willams

A languid, confined drama, based on a Joyce Carol Oates story, about the sexual awakening of a 15-year-old girl (Dern). The film unfolds at an awkward pace as we observe various adolescent encounters at shopping malls and hamburger drive-ins. After Williams appears as an older, seductive figure, the atmosphere turns menacing. An eerie tale, with an ambiguous but fascinating conclusion. Also with Mary Kay Place and Levon Helm. **Director**—Joyce Chopra. **(PG–13)** *92 minutes*

THE SNAKE PIT (1948)

Olivia de Havilland

Olivia de Havilland and Mark Stevens in The Snake Pit.

This drama about life in a crowded mental hospital is an example of the socially conscious melodrama prevalent in Hollywood filmmaking after World War II. (Other examples include *Pinky* and *Gentleman's Agreement*.) De Havilland is excellent as a woman trying to overcome mental illness who has horrifying experiences in the institution to which she is committed. Leo Genn, Mark Stevens, Celeste Holm, Lee Patrick, Natalie Schafer, Glenn Langan, Beulah Bondi, and Leif Erickson are good in supporting roles. **Director**—
(Continued)

This movie available on videotape and/or disc.

(Continued)
Anatole Litvak. **Academy Award Nominations**—best picture; Litvak, best director; de Havilland, best actress; Frank Partos and Millen Brand, screenplay. *108 minutes b&w*

THE SNOWS OF KILIMANJARO (1952)

Gregory Peck
Susan Hayward
Ava Gardner

Hollywood gives the star treatment to this Ernest Hemingway short story about an adventurous writer contemplating his own life as he awaits death on the African mountain. Unfortunately, most of the performers are less than stirring, although Peck is competent as the dying man. Hayward and Gardner are less than satisfactory, and a weak script doesn't help them overcome their limitations. Also with Leo G. Carroll, Marcel Dalio, Torin Thatcher, and Hildegard Neff. **Director**—Henry King. **Academy Award Nomination**—Leon Shamroy, cinematography. *117 minutes*

SNOW WHITE AND THE SEVEN DWARFS (1937)

This classic cartoon—Disney's first full-length feature—is as fresh and delightful now as when it was made. Besides the excellence of the production, the superb filming, and the wonderful songs, there's the well-known story about the beautiful maiden and her little friends confronting the evil Queen. Eight Disney writers worked on the Brothers Grimm fairy tale, with Larry Morey and Frank Churchill writing the songs. **Supervising Director**—David Hand. **(G)** *82 minutes*

S.O.B. (1981)

★★

Julie Andrews
Richard Mulligan
William Holden
Robert Preston

Director Blake Edwards (*The Pink Panther* series; *10*) fries the Hollywood establishment in a cauldron of bitter comedy that often backfires, and peters out midway. This pointed satire comes off basically as an inside joke. Mulligan plays a producer who makes a $30-million musical flop, which he salvages by turning it into a soft-core porn extravaganza. Squeaky-clean Andrews, the star of the movie-within-the-movie, goes topless to salvage the project. The event is a cheap shot. Also with Robert Vaughn, Loretta Swit, Larry Hagman, Robert Webber, Shelley Winters, and Craig Stevens. **(R)** *121 minutes*

SO DEAR TO MY HEART (1948)

Burl Ives
Beulah Bondi

Luana Patten and Bobby Driscoll with a feathered friend in So Dear to My Heart.

Adults may find this Walt Disney story about a boy's determination to tame a black sheep and enter it in the competition at the state fair too nostalgic and sentimental, but it should appeal to young children. The film, which includes some animated sequences, manages to capture the mood and charm of the American heartland in the early 1900s. The cast also includes Harry Carey, Bobby Driscoll, and Luana Patten. **Director**—Harold Schuster. *84 minutes*

SODOM AND GOMORRAH (1963)

Stewart Granger
Stanley Baker
Pier Angeli
Anouk Aimée

A made-in-Italy biblical extravaganza about the Helamite plot to take over the wicked cities of Sodom and Gomorrah. Fortunately, the acting has merit, because the overly long story becomes boring despite the vice and gore. Truly an international production, with French and Italian producers and an American director. Also with Rossana Podesta. **Director**—Robert Aldrich. *154 minutes*

SO FINE (1981)

★★

Ryan O'Neal
Jack Warden

O'Neal seems out of place in this uneven comedy involving New York City's garment industry. He plays a tweedy college professor who improves his father's faltering clothing business by accidentally introducing a new style of jeans with pink plastic seats designed to look like the human anatomy. The improbable story wavers between sophisticated humor and broad, physical comedy. Warden stands above the rest of the cast as the unrefined, huffing and puffing dress-factory owner. Mariangela Melato and Richard Kiel also star. **Director**—Andrew Bergman. **(R)** *91 minutes*

SOLARBABIES (1986)

★

Jami Gertz
Richard Jordan
Charles Durning

A barren script, with an incoherent plot and ludicrous dialogue, characterizes this teenage derivative of the *Road Warrior* movies. The unappealing setting is Earth in the distant future where water is scarce. A group of roller-skating youths, held in a mysterious orphanage, try to escape from their tyrannical supervisors to discover what the world is like on the outside. Also with Lukas Haas, Jason Patric, and Peter DeLuise. **Director**—Alan Johnson **(PG–13)** *95 minutes*

THE SOLDIER (1982)

Ken Wahl
Alberta Watson
Jeremiah Sullivan

Stone-faced Wahl stars as a romantic superhero who saves humanity from an international terrorist plot to destroy half the world's oil supply. The lavish production is styled on the order of a

® *This movie available with closed captions for the hearing impaired.*

Efficient antiterrorist Ken Wahl takes deadly aim in The Soldier.

James Bond adventure, but it pales in comparison. A humorless, globe-hopping plot bogs down in unnecessary complications and grisly killings. The acting is no more than average, and for action the film relies mainly on hokey stunts and effects. Also with Klaus Kinski and William Prince. **Director**—James Glickenhaus. **(R)** *90 minutes*

SOLDIER BLUE (1970)

★★★

Candice Bergen
Peter Strauss
Donald Pleasence

Violent, controversial western, loosely based on an actual page of American history. The incident—the Sand Creek Massacre of 1864—led to the wholesale killing of Indian women and children by Colorado militia, an event that eerily paralleled the My Lai, Vietnam, tragedy when the film was released. Bergen is particularly effective as the spunky fiancée of an Army officer and a former Cheyenne captive. She learns about the Cavalry's plan to wipe out the inhabitants of an Indian village, and tries to prevent the slaughter. She doesn't succeed, and we're witnesses to the graphic results of her failure. Though this pro-Indian western is often self-righteous and over-stylized, and carries an inflated reputation in some circles, it's certainly worth seeing. **Director**—Ralph Nelson. **(PG)** *109 minutes*

SOLDIER IN THE RAIN (1963)

★★★

Steve McQueen
Jackie Gleason

McQueen and Gleason star in this tragicomedy about the friendship between an Army sergeant and an enlisted man. Gleason effectively underplays his role as a wise but melancholy career man, who seems an unlikely friend to the boisterous, conniving McQueen. The script by Blake Edwards and Maurice Richlin is based on a novel by William Goldman. A low-key, but touching, film with an excellent supporting cast, including Tuesday Weld, Tom Poston, John Hubbard, Tony Bill, and Ed Nelson. **Director**—Ralph Nelson. *88 minutes b&w*

SOLDIER OF FORTUNE (1955)

★★

Clark Gable
Susan Hayward

Gable and Hayward are better than average in this adventure film set in Hong Kong. Gable, a smuggler, is hired to find Hayward's photographer husband, played by Gene Barry, who's missing in Red China. The excellent photography and the adventure sequences make this worthwhile viewing. Also with Anna Sten, Michael Rennie, Leo Gordon, Russell Collins, Tom Tully, and Alex D'Arcy. **Director**—Edward Dmytryk. *96 minutes*

A SOLDIER'S STORY (1984)

★★★1/2

Howard Rollins, Jr.
Adolph Caesar
Denzel Washington

Adolph Caesar (right) disciplines Larry Riley (center) in A Soldier's Story.

Tense drama and mystery characterize this superb film adaptation of Charles Fuller's prize-winning play about internal conflicts among black soldiers. Set at an Army base in Louisiana during World War II, the literate and intriguing plot follows the investigation of the murder of a tyrannical black sergeant. Yet the story explores, in a deeper sense, the pain and outrage inflicted by racial prejudice. Powerhouse ensemble acting. Also with Larry Riley, Art Evans, and Patti LaBelle. **Director**—Norman Jewison. **(PG) Academy Award Nominations**—best picture; Caesar, best supporting actor; Fuller, best screenplay based on material from another medium. *101 minutes*

THE SOLID GOLD CADILLAC (1956)

★★★

Judy Holliday
Paul Douglas

The comic genius of Holliday combines with the brilliant acting skills of Douglas in this enjoyable comedy. She plays a minor stockholder in a big company who tries to fire a corrupt board of directors. The movie is based on the play by George S. Kaufman and Howard Teichman, with the screen version written by Abe Burrows. John Williams, Fred Clark, Neva Patterson, Ray Collins, and Arthur O'Connell also star; George Burns narrates. Originally, the final scene was in color. **Director**—Richard Quine. *99 minutes b&w/color*

SOLOMON AND SHEBA (1959)

★★

Yul Brynner
Gina Lollobrigida

This well-produced biblical spectacle, photographed in Spain, tells the story of Solomon, David's eldest son, who plots revenge after learning that David has named Solomon's younger brother heir. This film is basically escapist action fare, with Lollobrigida as the alluring Queen of Sheba and Brynner as King Solomon. The large cast includes George Sanders, David Farrar, Marisa Pavan, Harry Andrews, and Alejandro Rey. **Director**—King Vidor. *139 minutes*

SO LONG AT THE FAIR (1950)

★★★

Jean Simmons
Dirk Bogarde

Simmons and Bogarde star in this mystery, set during the 1889 Paris Exposition. A woman searches for her brother, who has mysteriously vanished with-

(Continued)

This movie available on videotape and/or disc.

(Continued)
out a trace during their visit to the exposition. Appropriately atmospheric. David Tomlinson, Marcel Poncin, Cathleen Nesbitt, Felix Aylmer, André Morell, and Honor Blackman costar in supporting roles. **Director**—Terence Fisher. *86 minutes b&w*

SOMEBODY KILLED HER HUSBAND (1978)

Farrah Fawcett-Majors
Jeff Bridges

Farrah Fawcett-Majors goes sleuthing in Somebody Killed Her Husband.

Fawcett-Majors proves her competence as a screen actress in this glossy mystery/comedy set in New York City. Fawcett-Majors and her friend, played by Bridges, set out to solve the murder of her estranged husband. However, the script is tedious, and director Lamont Johnson fails to maintain tension. Also with John Wood, Tammy Grimes, Patricia Elliott, and John Glover. **(PG)** *97 minutes*

SOMEBODY UP THERE LIKES ME (1956)

 ★★★ ▢®

Paul Newman
Pier Angeli

Boxer Rocky Graziano rose from the slums of New York City and reform school to become the middleweight boxing champion of the world. Newman does a memorable job of portraying Graziano in this film biography. Angeli is excellent as his wife. A top supporting cast includes Joseph Buloff as an earthy, streetwise philosopher; Eileen Heckart as Rocky's mom; and Everett Sloane as a fight promoter. Beautifully photographed by Joseph Ruttenberg, the film is sentimental at times, but the depiction of the fight game is appropriately gritty. Script by Ernest Lehman. Sal Mineo, Robert Loggia, and Steve McQueen appear in supporting roles. **Director**—Robert Wise. **Academy Award**—Ruttenberg, cinematography. *112 minutes b&w*

SOME CAME RUNNING (1958)

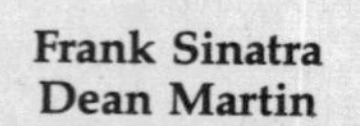

Frank Sinatra
Dean Martin
Shirley MacLaine

A melancholy story based on a novel by James Jones about a moody writer trying to adjust to his small hometown in the Midwest after returning from World War II. Though less hard-hitting than Jones' novel, the film is worth seeing for the excellent performances by Sinatra, MacLaine, and Martha Hyer. Nancy Gates, Leora Dana, and Arthur Kennedy appear in supporting roles. **Director**—Vincente Minnelli. **Academy Award Nominations**—MacLaine, best actress; Kennedy, best supporting actor; Hyer, best supporting actress. *136 minutes*

SOME KIND OF HERO (1982)

Richard Pryor
Margot Kidder
Ray Sharkey

Pryor's versatile and engaging performance is the only respectable asset that this otherwise second-rate movie can lay claim to. Pryor plays a Vietnam veteran who returns home to face a barrage of personal problems. At times, the film comes off as serious drama, then abruptly switches to comedy; and this baffling vacillation destroys both the movie's impact and its credibility. Pryor's extraordinary talent deserves better material than this. **Director**—Michael Pressman. **(R)** *97 minutes*

SOME KIND OF WONDERFUL (1987)

 ★★½ ▢®

Eric Stoltz
Mary Stuart Masterson
Lea Thompson

Young love: Eric Stoltz and Mary Stuart Masterson in Some Kind of Wonderful.

Writer/producer John Hughes reworks his teen-angst formula: A poor but gallant high-school senior competes with a wealthy boy for the affections of a popular girl. It's more or less the reverse of Hughes' *Pretty in Pink.* Good performances and tender moments compensate a bit for the well-worn plot. Stoltz stars as the love-struck youth; Masterson excels in a supporting role. Also with Craig Sheffer and John Ashton. **Director**—Howard Deutch. **(PG–13)** *93 minutes*

SOME LIKE IT HOT (1959)

 ▢®

Jack Lemmon
Tony Curtis
Marilyn Monroe

Lemmon, Curtis, and Monroe form an excellent comic trio in this clever comedy about two unemployed musicians—Lemmon and Curtis—on the run from mobsters after they witness a gangland slaying much like the St. Valentine's Day Massacre. Disguised as women, the two join an all-girl orchestra. Much of the comedy is based on this gender reversal, though Curtis also poses as a wealthy yachtsman, who speaks remarkably like Cary Grant. The trio gets fine support from Joe E. Brown, Joan Shawlee, Pat O'Brien, Nehemiah Persoff, and George E. Stone. George Raft does a takeoff on his coin-tossing gangster role from *Scarface.* For extra measure, Monroe sings "Running Wild," and widemouthed Brown delivers the film's classic closing line. **Director**—Billy Wilder. **Academy Award Nominations**—Wilder, best director; Lemmon, best actor; Wilder and I.A.L. Diamond, best screenplay based on material from another medium; Charles Lang, Jr., cinematography. *119 minutes b&w*

▢® *This movie available with closed captions for the hearing impaired.*

SOMEONE TO WATCH OVER ME (1987)

★★½

Tom Berenger
Mimi Rogers

Tom Berenger protects Mimi Rogers in Someone to Watch over Me.

This glossy romantic thriller features Berenger as a working-class cop from Queens who is assigned to protect a wealthy, Manhattan socialite from a vicious killer. The pair fall in love, but the difference between their two worlds represents a culture gap too wide to bridge. The story emphasizes the romance between the main characters, while the mystery is merely a plot device to throw the couple together. The result is a predictable soap opera with no suspense and a disappointing ending. Only the character of the cop's feisty wife, played by Lorraine Bracco, offers sufficient appeal. Also with Jerry Orbach, John Rubinstein and Andreas Katsulas. **Director**—Ridley Scott. **(R)** *106 minutes*

SOMETHING SHORT OF PARADISE (1979)

 ★★

Susan Sarandon
David Steinberg

This contemporary romantic comedy is about an on-again, off-again affair between a klutzy movie theater proprietor and a magazine writer. Sarandon is the writer, and Steinberg is the theater manager. There are some funny moments here, although the humor is generally low-key. Marilyn Sokol is excellent as a cunning member of the singles jungle. Also with Robert Hitt, Jean-Pierre Aumont, and Joe Grifasi. **Director**—David Helpern, Jr. **(PG)** *91 minutes*

SOMETHING WICKED THIS WAY COMES (1983)

 ★★

Vidal Peterson
Shawn Carson
Jason Robards
Jonathan Pryce

Jason Robards realizes evil is afoot in Something Wicked This Way Comes.

Disappointing film adaptation of Ray Bradbury's novel about a sinister carnival that causes havoc in a small midwestern town. Peterson and Carson do reasonably well with their roles as adventuresome boys, and Robards is effective as the meek librarian who gathers his courage to save them from their fate. Unfortunately, the straightforward script, adapted by Bradbury himself, lacks the ambiguity and complexity of the novel. However, the recreation of the turn-of-the-century Midwest and the appropriately eerie atmosphere make the film enjoyable to watch. Also with Pam Grier, Diane Ladd, and Royal Dano. **Director**—Jack Clayton. **(PG)** *94 minutes*

SOMETHING WILD (1986)

★★★½

Melanie Griffith
Jeff Daniels

Unpredictability characterizes this vibrant, offbeat romantic comedy/drama about an unlikely couple involved in unusual circumstances. Excellent performances by Daniels and Griffith highlight this tale of a straight-arrow, Wall Street accountant who embarks on a madcap joyride with an alluring seductress. As the film progresses, the element of danger lurking behind the comic adventures of the couple subtly changes to a prevailing sense of menace and doom. Their excursion out of the city into America's heartland turns frightening as they become involved with a sinister character, played chillingly by Ray Liotta. Like *Blue Velvet*, released at the same time, this film reveals the darker side of small-town America. **Director**—Jonathan Demme. **(R)** *114 minutes*

SOMETIMES A GREAT NOTION (1971)

★★★

Paul Newman
Henry Fonda
Michael Sarrazin
Richard Jaeckel

Newman directed and stars in this beautifully filmed story about a logging family in Oregon. The members of the family believe in individuality, so they defy a local strike by staying on the job. The father is played by Fonda; Newman, Sarrazin, and Jaeckel are his sons. The movie isn't particularly faithful to Ken Kesey's novel, but the acting is excellent. The star-studded cast also includes Lee Remick, Cliff Potts, and Linda Lawson. **(PG)** **Academy Award Nomination**—Jaeckel, best supporting actor. **Alternate Title**—*Never Give an Inch.* *115 minutes*

SOMEWHERE IN TIME (1980)

★★★

Christopher Reeve
Jane Seymour
Christopher Plummer

Somewhere in Time: *Predestined romance with Jane Seymour and Christopher Reeve.*

A young playwright becomes obsessed with the image of a beautiful actress

(Continued)

(Continued)

who found fame before World War I, and travels through time to find her. Literal-minded viewers may not buy the film's novel concept of time travel, or the story's unshakable romanticism; but viewers willing to suspend their disbelief will be enchanted by the picture's bittersweet portrait of a predestined love. Reeve is earnest and appealing as the smitten playwright, while Seymour is ideally cast as the tenderhearted actress. A *Svengali*-like subplot casts Plummer as a sympathetic heavy. The sensitive, often clever script is by Richard Matheson from his novel *Bid Time Return*. Gracefully directed by Jeannot Szwarc on stunning Mackinac Island locations. Also with Teresa Wright and George Voskovec. **(PG)**
103 minutes

A SONG IS BORN (1948)

Danny Kaye
Virginia Mayo

Kaye and Mayo are well supported by jazz greats Benny Goodman, Charlie Barnet, Louis Armstrong, Lionel Hampton, and Tommy Dorsey in this musical remake of the screwball comedy *Ball of Fire*, but the weak script sinks the whole show. Hugh Herbert, Edward Bromberg, Mary Field, Steve Cochran, Felix Bressart, and Mel Powell appear in supporting roles. **Director**—Howard Hawks. *113 minutes*

THE SONG OF BERNADETTE (1943)

Jennifer Jones
William Eythe
Charles Bickford

Jennifer Jones witnesses a beautiful vision in The Song of Bernadette.

Jones became a star after her portrayal of Bernadette, a pious French girl who had a vision of the Virgin Mary at Lourdes, a site that later became a shrine. Although the movie is long and the handling of a sensitive religious subject is heavy-handed, the film's virtues—the beautiful production values and critically acclaimed acting—outweigh its faults. Also with Vincent Price, Lee J. Cobb, Sig Ruman, Gladys Cooper, and Anne Revere. **Director**—Henry King. **Academy Awards**—Jones, best actress; Arthur Miller, cinematography. **Nominations**—best picture; King, best director; Bickford, best supporting actor; Cooper and Revere, best supporting actress; George Seaton, screenplay. *156 minutes b&w*

SONG OF THE SOUTH (1947)

Ruth Warrick
James Baskett
Bobby Driscoll

This charming children's story about Uncle Remus and Brer Rabbit is interspersed with animated segments. Driscoll stars as a small boy in the pre-Civil War South who is upset to learn that his parents are separating. He decides to run away from his southern mansion home, but Uncle Remus lures him back into the fold with his allegories about Brer Rabbit, Brer Fox, and the rest. Though well crafted and touching in parts, the film has been criticized in recent years for perpetrating the stereotype of the indolent black servant. The cast also includes Lucile Watson, Hattie McDaniel, and Luana Patten. **Director**—Harve Foster.
94 minutes

THE SONG REMAINS THE SAME (1976)

(no stars)

Led Zeppelin

This long, ear-shattering feature covers rock group Led Zeppelin's 1973 Madison Square Garden appearance. Going to this movie is supposed to be the equivalent of attending such a concert but, the sense of physical presence and the excitement of the audience are gone. What's left is an unbearable sound assault, which may leave you with a headache. Interspersed with trite fantasy segments, featuring members of the band. **Directors**—Peter Clifton and Joe Massot. **(PG)** *136 minutes*

A SONG TO REMEMBER (1945)

★★

Cornel Wilde
Paul Muni
Merle Oberon

The music is memorable in this colorful biography of Chopin. The composer is played by Wilde; his music is played by José Iturbi. Muni costars as Chopin's teacher. The film was quite popular when first released in 1945. With Oberon (as George Sand), Nina Foch, George Coulouris, and George Macready. **Director**—Charles Vidor. **Academy Award Nominations**—Wilde, best actor; Ernst Marischka, original story.
113 minutes

SON OF DRACULA (1943)

★★★

Lon Chaney, Jr.
Louise Allbritton

A superior cast, including Allbritton, Chaney, Frank Craven, Samuel S. Hinds, Robert Paige, J. Edward Bromberg, and Evelyn Ankers, enhances this low-budget horror film. The story involves Count Alucard—"Dracula" spelled backward—who visits a southern plantation and terrorizes much of the countryside. The production design and atmospheric black-and-white photography are appropriately eerie. The offbeat setting—that of America's Deep South—may be of interest to horror-film fans. **Director**—Robert Siodmak.
80 minutes b&w

SON OF FRANKENSTEIN (1939)

★★★

Basil Rathbone
Boris Karloff
Bela Lugosi
Lionel Atwill

Classic horror-film actors, including Rathbone, Karloff, Lugosi, Atwill, and Edgar Norton, make this a top-rated entry of the genre. There are numerous tense, spine-tingling moments as the son of Dr. Frankenstein tries to capture an old monster created by his father. The production is well staged, with unusual sets by Jack Otterson. Lawrence Grant, Donnie Dunagan, Josephine Hutchinson, and Emma Dunn appear in supporting roles. Karloff's last performance as the monster. **Director**—Rowland V. Lee. *93 minutes b&w*

SON OF PALEFACE
(1952)

★★★

Bob Hope
Roy Rogers
Jane Russell

Hope stars in this wacky comedy about a bumbling fellow who goes West to collect his inheritance. Some of the bids at humor are a bit strained, but there's enough fun to make viewing worthwhile. Russell is a pleasant addition and an inspiration for Hope. Rogers and his famous horse, Trigger, also make an appearance. Bill Williams, Harry Von Zell, Iron Eyes Cody, Douglass Dumbrille, and Lloyd Corrigan appear in supporting roles. **Director**—Frank Tashlin. *95 minutes*

SONS AND LOVERS
(1960)

★★★★

Dean Stockwell
Trevor Howard
Wendy Hiller

Heather Sears, Dean Stockwell, and Wendy Hiller in Sons and Lovers.

D.H. Lawrence's autobiographical novel about a sensitive youth pushed by his mother to make a life for himself away from the Nottingham coal mines is faithfully brought to the screen by director Jack Cardiff. Stockwell stars as the youth; Hiller plays his mother. The movie is enhanced by the performances of Howard as the boy's gruff father, and Mary Ure as the woman in the life of this would-be artist. The photography beautifully conveys a mood appropriate for the material. Heather Sears, Donald Pleasence, Ernest Thesiger, and William Lucas also star. **Academy Award**—Freddie Francis, cinematography. **Nominations**—best picture; Cardiff, best director; Howard, best actor; Ure, best supporting actress; Gavin Lambert and T.E.B. Clark, best screenplay based on material from another medium. *103 minutes b&w*

THE SONS OF KATIE ELDER
(1965)

 ★★

John Wayne
Dean Martin
Michael Anderson, Jr.
Earl Holliman

Wayne, Martin, Anderson, and Holliman—the sons of frontier woman Katie Elder—set out to avenge their mother's death, but town thugs and other villains give them trouble. Much of the action is predictable, but the stars make the film worthwhile and entertaining for western fans. George Kennedy, Martha Hyer, James Gregory, Paul Fix, and Jeremy Slate appear in supporting roles. **Director**—Henry Hathaway. *122 minutes*

SOPHIE'S CHOICE (1982)

★★★

Meryl Streep
Kevin Kline
Peter MacNicol

Heavy emotion with Meryl Streep and Kevin Kline in Sophie's Choice.

An unforgettable performance by Streep in the title role dominates this film adaptation of William Styron's haunting novel. She plays a guilt-ridden survivor of a Nazi concentration camp, and her subtle mannerisms and Polish-accented English contribute to a heartrending portrait of a tragic heroine. The lengthy film often lapses into staginess, but the many powerful moments compensate for the slow passages. **Director**—Alan J. Pakula. **(R) Academy Award**—Streep, best actress. **Nominations**—Pakula, best screenplay based on material from another medium; Nestor Almendros, cinematography. *157 minutes*

SO PROUDLY WE HAIL! (1943)

Claudette Colbert
Paulette Goddard
Veronica Lake

This patriotic film about Army nurses serving bravely on Bataan during World War II is conscientiously done and makes a valiant bid to give another view of the hell of war. However, it now seems dated, particularly because of the melodramatic approach. The performances of Colbert, Goddard, and Lake were well received at the time the movie was released. The cast also includes George Reeves, Barbara Britton, Walter Abel, Sonny Tufts, and John Litel. **Director**—Mark Sandrich. **Academy Award Nominations**—Goddard, best supporting actress; Allan Scott, original screenplay; Charles Lang, cinematography. *125 minutes b&w*

SORCERER (1977)

★★★

Roy Scheider
Bruno Cremer
Francisco Rabal

Director William Friedkin has done a masterful job of building suspense and capturing despair in this intense thriller, which is a remake of Henri-Georges Clouzot's *The Wages of Fear.* The film is about four desperate men, stuck in a squalid South American country, who drive two truckloads of nitroglycerin on bumpy roads through 200 miles of steaming jungle. Scheider stands out as one of the antiheroes. Also with Amidou, Ramon Bieri, and Peter Capell. **(PG)** *122 minutes*

This movie available on videotape and/or disc.

SORROWFUL JONES
(1949)

★★

Bob Hope
Lucille Ball

Bob Hope, William Demarest, Lucille Ball, and a little orphan in Sorrowful Jones.

Hope and Ball star in this overly sentimental Damon Runyon comedy about a bookie, deeply involved with mobsters, who unofficially adopts an orphan. Hope stars in the title role as the bookie. There are some pleasant moments and occasional laughs, but an earlier version of the story, *Little Miss Marker,* with Shirley Temple, was superior. Also with William Demarest, Thomas Gomez, Houseley Stevenson, Bruce Cabot, Mary Jane Saunders, and Tom Pedi. **Director**—Sidney Lanfield.

88 minutes b&w

SORRY, WRONG NUMBER
(1948)

 ★★★

Barbara Stanwyck
Burt Lancaster

A tense thriller, starring Stanwyck as a bedridden neurotic who overhears a plot to murder her on the telephone. Based on a well-known radio drama, the film lacks the relentless suspense that an aural production might generate, but is still frightening because of the vulnerability of the main character. Wendell Corey, Ed Begley, Leif Erickson, William Conrad, Harold Vermilyea, and Ann Richards also star. **Director**—Anatole Litvak. **Academy Award Nomination**—Stanwyck, best actress.

89 minutes b&w

SOUL MAN (1986)

★★

C. Thomas Howell
Rae Dawn Chong
James Earl Jones

Rae Dawn Chong with C. Thomas Howell, who becomes the Soul Man.

Howell stars as an upper-middle-class college graduate who darkens his skin to win a scholarship—available only to black students—to Harvard Law School. He supposedly learns what it is like to be black in a world dominated by whites. Though perhaps unintentionally, the film is subtly racist. Howell's character gets the scholarship because no other black student in his area received it, implying that no black students were qualified enough to win it. Just as Dustin Hoffman's role in *Tootsie* suggested that men make the best feminists, here Howell's role suggests that white men make the best blacks. A few good laughs can't compensate for the offensive premise. Also with Ayre Gross. **Director**—Steve Miner. **(PG–13)**

101 minutes

THE SOUND AND THE FURY
(1959)

★★

Yul Brynner
Joanne Woodward

There's too much misspent fury and not enough sound filmmaking in this strange production based on William Faulkner's novel. Hollywood tries to convey the decadence of the South in this story of a young lady seeking independence from her strict family, but the result is a misinterpretation of the Faulkner novel. Brynner, Woodward, Margaret Leighton, Stuart Whitman, Ethel Waters, Jack Warden, and Françoise Rosay create some fine moments amid the rubble. **Director**—Martin Ritt.

117 minutes

SOUNDER (1972)

★★★★

Paul Winfield
Cicely Tyson

Brilliant performances by Winfield and Tyson help to make this Depression-era story about a family of sharecroppers in Louisiana one of the finest movies ever made. The excellent direction of Martin Ritt and splendid supporting performances by Kevin Hooks, Carmen Mathews, James Best, and Taj Mahal make the experiences of the family authentic and compelling. A warm and compassionate movie for the whole family. **(G) Academy Award Nominations**—best picture; Winfield, best actor; Tyson, best actress; Lonne Elder III, best screenplay based on material from another medium.

105 minutes

SOUNDER, PART 2 (1976)

★★

Harold Sylvester
Ebony Wright

This sequel about the struggles of poor black sharecroppers in Louisiana during the 1930s isn't in the same league with the popular and moving 1972 film. This episode has the Morgan family involved with building a schoolhouse for the neighborhood. The idea is embarrassingly drowned in sentimentality and gloominess, and the film has nothing to do with the family's battered hound dog, Sounder, who remains entirely in the background. Also with Darryl Young, Annazette Chase, and Taj Mahal. **Director**—William Graham. **(G)**

98 minutes

THE SOUND OF MUSIC (1965)

★★★★

Julie Andrews
Christopher Plummer

Julie Andrews portrays Maria Von Trapp in the popular The Sound of Music.

Andrews sings and acts with such vitality that her performance overshadows the sugary excesses in this overlong

This movie available with closed captions for the hearing impaired.

film. The beautiful scenery and excellent score also highlight this popular musical. The movie is based on the life of the Von Trapp family. Andrews plays Maria Von Trapp, who escapes from the Nazis in Austria along with her children. Other stars in this Rodgers and Hammerstein musical include Peggy Wood, Richard Haydn, Anna Lee, Eleanor Parker, and Marni Nixon. Television prints are usually 145 minutes in length. **Director**—Robert Wise. **(G) Academy Awards**—best picture; Wise, best director. **Nominations**—Andrews, best actress; Wood, best supporting actress; Ted McCord, cinematography.

174 minutes

SOUP FOR ONE (1982)

★★

Saul Rubinek
Marcia Strassman
Gerrit Graham

There's a similarity to Woody Allen's comedies in this attempted satire on the singles scene, written and directed by novice filmmaker Jonathan Kaufer. The film contains some clever scenes, but Kaufer cannot sustain the necessary degree of wit. The amateurish acting matches the material, which is generally inept and pretentious. Rubinek stars as the desperate young man pursuing the girl of his dreams (Strassman). **(R)** *87 minutes*

SOUTHERN COMFORT (1981)

★★★

Keith Carradine
Powers Boothe

Nine weekend warriors in the National Guard become lost in the Louisiana bayous and wind up in a war with local Cajun hunters. The story is mean-spirited, but the direction by Walter Hill is taut, and the suspense is nerve-racking. An excellent cast of supporting actors portray the characters that make up the platoon, which is a collection of types—the fiery-tempered hothead, the slow-witted and loyal soldier, the irresponsible but likable clown, and the cynical and intelligent outsiders, played by Carradine and Boothe. Violent and unnerving to watch, this survival-of-the-fittest story, in which no one wins, has been cited as an allegory for America's involvement in Vietnam. Also with T.K. Carter, Franklyn Seales, Fred Ward, and Peter Coyote. **(R)**

106 minutes

THE SOUTHERNER (1945)

★★★

Zachary Scott
Betty Field
J. Carrol Naish
Beulah Bondi

Poetic drama of a poor southern farmer's struggle to raise his crops and support his family. Despite a never-ending succession of natural and man-made problems, he goes on...like nature. Probably the best of the films French director Jean Renoir made in America, although it's more compelling visually than dramatically—possibly because its documentary-like style was atypical of the filmmaker. Renoir produced the film independently with Burgess Meredith, among others; Hugo Butler helped write the script. Also with Percy Kilbride. **Academy Award Nomination**—Renoir, best director.

91 minutes b&w

SOUTH PACIFIC (1958)

★★½

Mitzi Gaynor
Rossano Brazzi

This film version of the musical about the South Pacific during World War II, involving the love story of an American Navy nurse and a middle-aged French planter, lacks the superstars needed to make it a production with clout. However, the photography is beautiful, and the Rodgers and Hammerstein music is delightful; the numbers include "Some Enchanted Evening," "Younger Than Springtime," "There Is Nothing Like a Dame," "Bali Ha'i," and "You've Got to Be Taught." Gaynor is perky but not dynamic enough as the nurse, and Brazzi is dull as the planter. Other performers in this overly long musical are France Nuyen, John Kerr, Ray Walston, and Juanita Hall. **Director**—Joshua Logan. **Academy Award Nomination**—Leon Shamroy, cinematography.

171 minutes

SOYLENT GREEN (1973)

★★

Charlton Heston
Joseph Cotten
Edward G. Robinson
Leigh Taylor-Young

Food is the key to this futuristic mystery, set in an overpolluted, overpopulated Big Apple, where the populace survives on a synthetic food called Soylent Green. An investigation into the murder of an exec at the Soylent Green manufacturing company gradually leads to a shocking revelation of just what that unappetizing mess really is. An entertaining science-fiction tale, if you like this sort of dish. Also with Chuck Connors and Brock Peters. Robinson, at age 80, appears in his last screen role. **Director**—Richard Fleischer. **(PG)** *95 minutes*

Joseph Cotten knows the secret of Soylent Green, *but he isn't telling.*

SPACEBALLS (1987)

★★

Mel Brooks
John Candy
Rick Moranis

Spaceballs: *Galactic panic with George Wyner, Rick Moranis, and Mel Brooks.*

Brooks' lavish spoof of *Star Wars* is a moderately amusing effort featuring an array of talented comic actors. Brooks stars as the president of the evil planet Spaceballs who, with his warrior chief Dark Helmet (Moranis), plots to kidnap Princess Vespa of Druidia (Daphne Zuniga). Though the *Star Wars* saga would seem a natural subject for par-

(Continued)

This movie available on videotape and/or disc.

(Continued)
ody, the timing is much too late. The original film is a decade old and has already been lampooned on television, in magazines, and in other films. Though there are a few truly inspired comic bits in this film, the best moments make you wish there weren't so many flat ones. **Director**—Brooks. **(PG)**
96 minutes

SPACECAMP (1986)

★★

Kate Capshaw
Lea Thompson
Kelly Preston

Surprise! Up into the air—and beyond—in the comedy Spacecamp.

Five teenagers and their instructor accidentally blast into orbit aboard the space shuttle. Though there are a few moments of suspense as the youths attempt to land the shuttle, much of this drama is riddled with clichés and predictable situations. Capshaw stars as the space-age den mother who is in charge of the astro-teens, but her performance lacks depth or believability. If it had not been released a few months after the shuttle disaster, this film would have been forgotten. As it is, it merely raises unpleasant memories. **Director**—Harry Winer. **(PG)**
107 minutes

SPACED INVADERS (1990)

★★

Douglas Barr
Royal Dano

This science-fiction comedy, aimed at children, features a group of cute green Martians who travel to Earth after intercepting a radio broadcast of *The War of the Worlds*. They land in a small Midwestern town, where they attempt to make sense of life on our planet. The film's slapstick humor, predictable conclusion, and cute creature design relegate it to strictly children's fare, though adults may get a kick out of Blaznee, the alien who affects a Jack Nicholson persona. Directed by special-effects supervisor Patrick Read Johnson. Also with Ariana Richards, J.J. Anderson, Gregg Berger, and Kevin Thompson. **(PG)** *100 minutes*

SPACEHUNTER: ADVENTURES IN THE FORBIDDEN ZONE (1983)

★½ ®

Peter Strauss
Molly Ringwald
Ernie Hudson

Strauss and Ringwald in Spacehunter: Adventures in the Forbidden Zone.

This grubby-looking space opera, shot in 3-D, features Strauss as a man-about-planets on a mission to rescue three damsels. Strauss pursues his objective at the wheel of a futuristic junk-mobile. A great deal of lavish technical background in 21st-century junkyard chic graces this noisy production, but the script is strictly third-rate. **Director**—Lamont Johnson. **(PG)** *90 minutes*

THE SPANISH MAIN (1945)

★★★

Paul Henreid
Maureen O'Hara
Walter Slezak

In this pirate movie, a dashing adventurer (Henreid) confronts the villain (Slezak) and eventually wins the hand of the beautiful maiden (O'Hara). Though predictable, these classic swashbuckling adventures are always plenty of fun. Supporting actors include Jack LaRue, Victor Kilian, Binnie Barnes, Barton MacLane, Fritz Leiber, Nancy Gates, Mike Mazurki, and J.M. Kerrigan. **Director**—Frank Borzage. **Academy Award Nomination**—George Barnes, cinematography. *101 minutes*

SPARKLE (1976)

★★

Lonette McKee
Irene Cara
Philip M. Thomas

A familiar melodrama about three Harlem sisters who become pop singers in the 1950s. Aside from scattered bright moments, the story and acting are routine and shallow, following well-worn paths of violence, drug addiction, and family crisis. The music of Curtis Mayfield helps, as do the well-composed scenes of murky nightclubs. Thomas later gained recognition under the name "Philip Michael Thomas" in NBC-TV's *Miami Vice*. Also with Dwan Smith, Mary Alice, Tony King, and Dorian Harewood. **Director**—Sam O'Steen. **(PG)** *100 minutes*

SPARTACUS (1960)

★★★

Kirk Douglas
Laurence Olivier
Peter Ustinov

Between the gaudy scenes and the trite moments, there are several thoughtful sequences and excellent characterizations in this long and, at times, thrilling historical epic about slaves in revolt in ancient Rome. Douglas, Olivier, and Ustinov are superb in major parts; Douglas plays the title role. The script by Dalton Trumbo is intelligent. The large cast also includes Charles Laughton, John Gavin, Nina Foch, Jean Simmons, Tony Curtis, Woody Strode, Herbert Lom, and John Ireland. Some prints run 185 minutes. **Director**—Stanley Kubrick. **Academy Awards**—Ustinov, best supporting actor; Russell Metty, cinematography. *196 minutes*

A SPECIAL DAY (1977)

★★

Sophia Loren
Marcello Mastroianni

Loren plays a bedraggled Italian housewife who finds a brief moment of passion with an intellectual, homosexual neighbor, played by Mastroianni. As always, the two stars work well together,

® *This movie available with closed captions for the hearing impaired.*

but the syrupy, two-character drama is as shabby as the downtrodden apartment setting. This brief encounter takes place in 1938 on a day when all Rome turned out to rally for Hitler. Also with John Vernon, Nicole Magny, and Françoise Berd. Originally filmed in Italian. **Director**—Ettore Scola. **(No MPAA rating) Academy Award Nominations**—best foreign-language film; Mastroianni, best actor.
105 minutes

SPECIAL DELIVERY (1976)

Bo Svenson
Cybill Shepherd

Shepherd plays a divorcée who cuts herself in on a bank heist pulled off by an ex-Marine, played by Svenson. The comic melodrama maintains a degree of suspense as other bystanders try to horn in on the loot. It's a better-than-average B-movie, with some interesting performances and a touch of humor. The adventure ends with a screeching car chase that's become the standard climax for such fare. Also with Tom Atkins, Vic Tayback, Michael Gwynne, and Sorrell Booke. **Director**—Paul Wendkos. **(PG)** *99 minutes*

SPECIAL SECTION (1975)

Louis Seigner
Michel Lonsdale
Jacques Perrin

A political drama about the Vichy government in France, which set up special courts to force Frenchmen to appease the Nazis. The film, which is directed by Constantin Costa-Gavras, lacks the drive and emotional impact of Z and *State of Siege*. Characters come and go rather mechanically, and the cast consists mostly of unfamiliar actors. The story is based on an actual event—the killing of a German officer by young Marxists in a Paris subway. Also with Ivo Garrani, Bruno Cremer, Pierre Dux, and Henri Serre. Originally filmed in French. **(PG)** *110 minutes*

SPEED ZONE (1989)

★

John Candy
Peter Boyle
Donna Dixon

Candy leads a cast of celebrities driving a variety of vehicles on a cross-country car race from Washington, D.C., to Santa Monica, California. The Smothers Brothers, Brooke Shields, Tim Matheson, and others waste their talents in throwaway parts. There are few effective gags, and be forewarned that good taste is nowhere to be found. Burt Reynolds' *Cannonball Run* films are similar but somewhat better. **Director**—Jim Drake **(PG)** *95 minutes*

SPELLBOUND (1945)

Ingrid Bergman
Gregory Peck

In Spellbound, *Ingrid Bergman hides a psychiatric patient from the law.*

Bergman portrays a psychiatrist who protects a patient accused of murder from the police until she's able to solve his emotional problems. There are many fascinating aspects to this Alfred Hitchcock mystery, including the idea of searching for the clues to a murder within someone's dreams. The film garnered much publicity at the time because of the collaboration of artist Salvador Dali on the dream sequences. Michael Chekhov, Rhonda Fleming, Leo G. Carroll, Steve Geray, Wallace Ford, and Norman Lloyd also star. **Academy Award Nominations**—best picture; Hitchcock, best director; Chekhov, best supporting actor; George Barnes, cinematography.
111 minutes b&w

SPENCER'S MOUNTAIN (1963)

Henry Fonda
Maureen O'Hara
James MacArthur

A talented cast is saddled with an inferior script in this soap opera about a Wyoming landowner who keeps promising to build another house for his family of nine. Despite its faults, this sentimental entry, set in the 1930s, proved popular enough to be the basis for the TV series *The Waltons*. Also with Donald Crisp, Mimsy Farmer, and Lillian Bronson. **Director**—Delmer Daves.
119 minutes

SPHINX (1981)

Lesley-Anne Down
Frank Langella

Egyptologist Erica Baron, played by Down, goes to the land of the pharaohs, where she witnesses a murder, dodges bullets, fends off a rape attack, gets thrown into a dungeon, and—believe it or not—falls through the floor of a men's room into a tomb filled with ancient treasures. She's out of breath by the second reel, and so is the audience. Langella, playing an Egyptian diplomat, pops up now and then in his worst film performance to date. Franklin Schaffner lamely directed this idiotic gibberish. **(PG)** *118 minutes*

SPIES LIKE US (1985)

Chevy Chase
Dan Aykroyd

Chevy Chase and Dan Aykroyd travel far afield in Spies Like Us.

Chase and Aykroyd team up as government agents in this strained, bedraggled spoof of international espionage. The two are so incompetent that they are chosen as expendable decoys and sent on a dangerous, globe-trotting mission. The direction, script, and acting are all weak, and the film is further marred by the inclusion of some tasteless jokes. Also with Steve Forrest and Donna Dixon. **Director**—John Landis. **(PG)** *103 minutes*

SPIKE OF BENSONHURST (1988)

★★½

Sasha Mitchell
Ernest Borgnine

A loosely constructed comedy set in a Brooklyn working-class neighborhood. Teenage boxer Mitchell tries to focus on his future ambitions while dealing with a local Mafia boss, various romances, and family problems. The film is rich with colorful characters and ethnic references, but the jumbled plot is hard to follow. Borgnine costars as a Mafia elder statesman. Also with Anne DeSalvo, Sylvia Miles, Talisa Soto, and Rick Aviles. **Director**—Paul Morrissey. **(R)** *91 minutes*

THE SPIRAL STAIRCASE (1946)

★★★★

Dorothy McGuire
George Brent
Ethel Barrymore

A taut and well-directed suspense film about a killer who terrorizes physically flawed girls. McGuire is brilliant as a mute servant girl trying to avoid the killer's evil clutches. The visual conventions of the horror genre—the stormy-night setting and the high contrast of lights and darks—create the expected eerie effect, which is enhanced by the portrayal of the psychopath as outwardly normal. Kent Smith, James Bell, Sara Allgood, Gordon Oliver, and Rhonda Fleming appear in supporting roles. **Director**—Robert Siodmak. **Academy Award Nomination**—Barrymore, best supporting actress. *83 minutes b&w*

THE SPIRIT OF ST. LOUIS (1957)

★★

James Stewart

Stewart is well cast as Charles Lindbergh in this biopic, but there are too many trite and dull scenes. The production seems overly long because there are so many sequences showing Lindy flying solo, especially on his 3,600-mile, 33½-hour New York-to-Paris flight in 1927. There just isn't enough action to keep the film interesting. An unusual departure for director Billy Wilder. Marc Connelly, Patricia Smith, and Murray Hamilton are competent in supporting roles. *137 minutes*

SPLASH (1984)

★★★

Tom Hanks
Daryl Hannah
John Candy

A predictable man-meets-mermaid romantic comedy made more interesting by the use of clever satire. Hanks plays a lonely New York bachelor who falls in love with winsome mermaid Hannah. In the big city, she must cope with the sophisticated urban lifestyle as well as ambitious scientists who seek to exploit her. Ron Howard's direction wrings the most out of some very funny visual and verbal gags. Candy in particular is a delight. **(PG)** *109 minutes*

SPLENDOR IN THE GRASS (1961)

★★★

Natalie Wood
Warren Beatty

Natalie Wood and Warren Beatty experience first love in Splendor in the Grass.

Elia Kazan skillfully directed this love story from an original script by playwright William Inge. The storyline involves two young high-school students who fall in love and have difficulties controlling their passions. Kazan has captured the feel of a small Kansas town in the 1920s superbly, but the approach to the material is occasionally melodramatic. Beatty—in his film debut—and Wood are excellent as the young lovers. Also with Pat Hingle, Audrey Christie, Sean Garrison, Phyllis Diller, Sandy Dennis, Zohra Lampert, and Barbara Loden. **Academy Award**—Inge, best story and screenplay written directly for the screen. **Nomination**—Wood, best actress. *124 minutes*

SPLIT IMAGE (1982)

★★

Michael O'Keefe
James Woods

A bright, clean-cut college student (O'Keefe) gets caught up in a religious cult and his distraught parents hire a de-programmer to break the spell. The film, directed by Ted Kotcheff, offers some engrossing moments of suspense and drama. Dangling loose ends, however, weaken the story's effectiveness. **(R)** *113 minutes*

THE SPOILERS (1942)

★★½

Marlene Dietrich
John Wayne
Randolph Scott
Richard Barthelmess

Marlene Dietrich, John Wayne, and Margaret Lindsay in The Spoilers.

Rex Beach's frontier novel has been filmed many times, and this version is perhaps the best known, if not the best made. Two rugged adventurers are at odds over a gold mine and a saloon singer in the Yukon territory. Wayne, Scott, and Dietrich rise to the occasion in this version, and give the material some luster. There's also the famous climactic fight, which is the highlight of the film. With William Farnum, Margaret Lindsay, and Harry Carey. **Director**—Ray Enright. *84 minutes b&w*

SPRING BREAK (1983)

David Knell
Perry Lang
Paul Land
Steve Bassett

This movie available with closed captions for the hearing impaired.

A noisy, mindless, adolescent comedy about college students living it up in Fort Lauderdale during spring recess. Typical high jinks include beer guzzling, girl chasing, and a wet T-shirt contest. These escapades seldom produce any laughs, and the performances by the unfamiliar cast are forgettable. Sean Cunningham (*Friday the 13th*) directed this nonsense halfheartedly. **(R)**

101 minutes

THE SPY WHO CAME IN FROM THE COLD (1965)

★★★

Richard Burton
Claire Bloom
Oskar Werner

Mood, tempo, and tension highlight this film based on the best-selling John Le Carré spy novel, though the plot becomes needlessly complicated. Burton is well cast as the bitter agent who goes undercover in a bid to infiltrate the communists. At the time of release, the lighthearted James Bond spy movies were hitting their peak in terms of style and influence. This movie puts the grisly trade of espionage into another perspective, particularly with the gritty, low-key photography of Oswald Morris. Rupert Davies, Peter Van Eyck, Sam Wanamaker, Cyril Cusack, Beatrix Ichmann, Bernard Lee, and George Voskovec appear in supporting roles. **Director**—Martin Ritt. **Academy Award Nomination**—Burton, best actor.

112 minutes b&w

THE SPY WHO LOVED ME (1977)

★★★

Roger Moore
Curt Jurgens

Ready for action: Barbara Bach and Roger Moore in The Spy Who Loved Me.

British superspy James Bond is back for his tenth action-packed screen adventure. Debonair Moore is enjoyable as agent 007, who has one hour to overcome Karl Stromberg, a villain deluxe, who wants to rule the world by gaining control of the seas. Jurgens is the heavy in this thriller. As usual, the special gadgets are fascinating, the locales are exotically stunning, and the women are fetching. Also with Barbara Bach, Richard Kiel, Caroline Munro, and Bernard Lee. Classy direction by Lewis Gilbert. **(PG)**

125 minutes

SQUARE DANCE (1987)

★★½

Rob Lowe
Winona Ryder
Jane Alexander

A sweet-natured teenage girl (Ryder) leaves her grandfather's farm in rural Texas to seek her identity amid Fort Worth's glitter. There, while living with her floozy mother (Alexander), she finds romance with a mentally disabled young man (Lowe). Most of the performances are first-rate and the harsh Texas backdrop is well drawn, but the film is stilted and lacks dramatic impact. Released to network television as *Home Is Where the Heart Is.* Also with Jason Robards and Guich Koock. **Director**—Daniel Petrie. **(PG–13)**

112 minutes

THE SQUEEZE (1987)

★½

Michael Keaton
Rae Dawn Chong

Keaton, a high-key actor with a sort of manic charm, stars as an artist who spends a great deal of money but owes much more in alimony. Chong costars as a bill collector who tracks down deadbeats. They meet, fall in love, and stumble onto a scheme to fix the New York State Lottery. Though Keaton and Chong are both appealing performers, this action comedy gives them nothing to work with: The script is ridiculous, the dialogue unmemorable, and the direction mediocre. Originally titled *Skip Tracer*, the film was held back for several months and then never given a full theatrical release—and rightfully so. John Davidson and Meat Loaf appear in supporting roles. **Director**—Roger Young. **(PG–13)**

102 minutes

SQUEEZE PLAY (1980)

★★

Jim Harris
Jenni Hetrick

The men are using all their free time to play softball, so the women fight back by forming their own team in this goofy but lively low-level comedy. There are plenty of harmless pranks, slapstick happenings, and sexual shenanigans, which manage to provoke a few laughs. The actors—mostly unknowns—frolic through their routines with ample energy. It ends with a predictable softball game between the sexes. **Director**—Samuel Weil. **(R)**

92 minutes

STACKING (1987)

★★½

Christine Lahti
Megan Follows

Some striking scenes of the Montana landscape highlight this independently made drama about a struggling farm family in the 1950s. Lahti stars as a bored farm wife who yearns for a more exciting lifestyle, while Follows plays her spunky young daughter determined to rebuild a haying truck so the family farm can continue to operate. Despite the good intentions and some excellent acting, the film lacks the spark of originality of most independent features and gets bogged down in its depiction of the hardships of such a lifestyle. Also with Frederic Forrest, Jason Gedrick, Ray Baker, and Peter Coyote. **Director**—Martin Rosen. **(PG)**

111 minutes

STAGECOACH (1939)

★★★★

John Wayne
Claire Trevor
Thomas Mitchell
George Bancroft

John Wayne shares a bite with Claire Trevor in Stagecoach.

This movie available on videotape and/or disc.

(Continued)

This film by director John Ford, about the relationships among passengers on a stagecoach under the stress of an Indian attack, is the quintessential classic western. Each character represents a type that would later become a staple of the genre, including the untamed hero, who symbolizes the uncivilized West; the saloon girl; the prim woman from the East, who symbolizes advancing civilization; and the drunken "doc." Wayne stars as the Ringo Kid, whose self-sacrifice and heroism against the Indians assure the passengers of their safety. The role helped make Wayne an icon of the genre. Shot in Ford's beloved Monument Valley. Andy Devine, Louise Platt, Tim Holt, and Chris-Pin Martin also star. **Academy Award**—Mitchell, best supporting actor. **Nominations**—best picture; Ford, best director; Bert Glennon, cinematography. *100 minutes b&w*

STAGECOACH (1966)

Ann-Margret
Alex Cord
Bing Crosby
Van Heflin

Although there's still plenty of action and some vivid scenery in this remake of *Stagecoach*, it's barely half as good as the 1939 John Ford classic. This time around, Cord has the John Wayne role. Cord, Ann-Margret, Crosby, Heflin, and Red Buttons do a conscientious job, but the characterizations are much weaker than those in the earlier film. Also with Slim Pickens, Robert Cummings, Michael Connors, Stefanie Powers, and Keenan Wynn. **Director**—Gordon Douglas. *114 minutes*

STAGE DOOR (1937)

★★★

Katharine Hepburn
Ginger Rogers
Adolphe Menjou
Lucille Ball

An entertaining backstage comedy/drama based on the Edna Ferber/George S. Kaufman play about a New York boarding house inhabited by young women struggling for the chance to make it in the theater. Hepburn is well cast as a wealthy girl trying to make it on the stage without the help of her family's money. Menjou is a leering

Katharine Hepburn, Lucille Ball, and Ginger Rogers in Stage Door.

producer, and Andrea Leeds is memorable as a high-strung actress. Also with Gail Patrick, Eve Arden, Constance Collier, Ann Miller, Samuel S. Hinds, Grady Sutton, and Franklin Pangborn. **Director**—Gregory La Cava. **Academy Award Nominations**—best picture; La Cava, best director; Leeds, best supporting actress; Morris Ryskind and Anthony Veiller, screenplay. *92 minutes b&w*

STAGE FRIGHT (1950)

★★★

Marlene Dietrich
Jane Wyman
Michael Wilding
Alastair Sim

Although generally considered a weaker effort by Hitchcock, this film remains delectably atmospheric entertainment. A young man is suspected of murder, so his girlfriend (Wyman)—a drama student—poses as a maid to gain entry into the home of the star (Dietrich) whose spouse was the murder victim. The suspense and the London backstage milieu make the film worthwhile viewing. The outstanding cast also includes Richard Todd, Sybil Thorndike, Joyce Grenfell, and Kay Walsh. *110 minutes b&w*

STAIRWAY TO HEAVEN (1946)

David Niven
Kim Hunter
Raymond Massey

Michael Powell and Emeric Pressburger, who gave us *The Red Shoes*, among other stylish screen entertainments, wrote and directed this lovely British fantasy. Pilot Niven bails out over the English Channel during World War II. He should be dead, but isn't—and he finds himself before a heavenly court, arguing that he was wrongly chosen to die. The film is colorful and charming, with animated performances by the entire cast, including Roger Livesey, Robert Coote, and Richard Attenborough. *104 minutes*

STAKEOUT (1987)

★★★½ ®

Richard Dreyfuss
Emilio Estevez

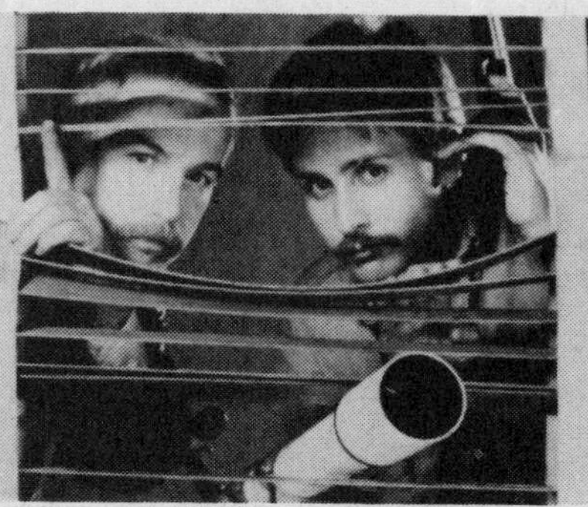

Richard Dreyfuss and Emilio Estevez are detectives on a Stakeout.

The performance of Dreyfuss, who made a career comeback during the mid-1980s, highlights this cop thriller featuring snappy dialogue, clever plot complications, tight pacing, and a touch of humor. He plays a freewheeling detective assigned, along with his youthful partner (Estevez), to watch the girlfriend (Madeleine Stowe) of an escaped convict in the hopes of nabbing the murderer. Despite the repeated warnings of the practical-minded Estevez, Dreyfuss falls in love with the attractive woman. Many anxious situations arise as Dreyfuss and Estevez try to keep the affair from the other cops involved in the stakeout. Aidan Quinn is appropriately menacing as the cold-blooded killer, while Forest Whitaker and Dan Lauria provide the humor as the rival policemen on the stakeout. **Director**—John Badham. **(R)** *115 minutes*

STALAG 17 (1953)

★★★★

William Holden
Don Taylor
Otto Preminger

One of the most popular American movies of all time. The story of U.S. prisoners in a Nazi POW camp has all

® *This movie available with closed captions for the hearing impaired.*

the necessary ingredients for a quality viewing experience—good acting, a well-crafted plot, tension, expert characterization, a well-written script, a mixture of humor and drama, and action. Holden heads the list of stars, but Taylor, Preminger, Robert Strauss, Sig Ruman, and Harvey Lembeck are as good. Holden's character—a cynical, independent loner—was not the typical Hollywood hero at the time of the film's release, but proved to be a forerunner of the antihero, popular in the 1960s. **Director**—Billy Wilder. **Academy Award**—Holden, best actor. **Nominations**—Wilder, best director; Strauss, best supporting actor. *120 minutes b&w*

STAND AND DELIVER (1988)

★★★

Edward James Olmos
Lou Diamond Phillips

Edward James Olmos is a dedicated high school teacher in Stand and Deliver.

A simple, straightforward, and inspiring story based closely on fact. Olmos, who gained attention on television's *Miami Vice,* stars as a gifted teacher in an embattled East Los Angeles high school, who motivates his poverty-stricken Hispanic students to take the advanced placement test in calculus. A small, low-budget film, this slice-of-life story depends on the excellent acting of the principal players for its drama and impact. The film should work well on the small screen because of its intimate scale and restricted locales. Also with Rosana De Soto and Andy Garcia. **Director**—Ramon Menendez. **(PG) Academy Award Nomination**—Olmos, best actor. *102 minutes*

STAND BY ME (1986)

★★★½

River Phoenix
Wil Wheaton
Corey Feldman
Jerry O'Connell

Jerry O'Connell, River Phoenix, Wil Wheaton, and Corey Feldman in Stand by Me.

A well-crafted coming-of-age movie, sensitively directed by Rob Reiner. Based on Stephen King's novella *The Body,* the story concerns four preteen boys who heroically trek through the woods to find the body of a teenager reportedly killed by a train. The youths discover much about themselves in the process. Reiner obtains remarkable performances from the young actors and evokes some warm but bittersweet memories about growing up. The film includes Richard Dreyfuss and John Cusack in small but significant roles. **(R) Academy Award Nomination**—Raymond Gideon and Bruce A. Evans, best screenplay based on material from another medium. *87 minutes*

STAND-IN (1937)

★★★

Joan Blondell
Leslie Howard
Humphrey Bogart

A satire of Hollywood moviemaking directed by Tay Garnett. Colossal Studios is about to come tumbling down unless efficiency expert Howard can save it. The mild-mannered accountant sets out to learn all he can about the ways of Tinseltown from stand-in Blondell, who teaches him more than he bargained for. With Bogart playing a studio director, none of the stars is in a typical role—which may explain why the film is as funny as it is. *90 minutes b&w*

STAND UP AND CHEER (1934)

★★

Warner Baxter
Madge Evans
Shirley Temple
James Dunn

A thoroughly entertaining piece of fluff starring Baxter as a producer who is appointed by the President to the newly created cabinet post of Secretary of Amusement. The idea is to cheer up the Depression-affected populace with a great big happy revue, which features a bright little entertainer named Shirley Temple. She sings "Baby Take a Bow," and you better believe people stood up and cheered. Fox signed Temple to a contract immediately, and she quickly became Hollywood's top box-office attraction. With Nigel Bruce, Ralph Morgan, John Boles, and Stepin Fetchit. **Director**—Hamilton MacFadden. *80 minutes b&w*

STANLEY & IRIS (1989)

★★½

Jane Fonda
Robert De Niro

Despite the high-powered talent of De Niro and Fonda in the title roles, this blue-collar romance makes for a low-energy drama. De Niro plays Stanley, a gentle, illiterate cafeteria worker; Fonda stars as Iris, who toils on a bakery production line. Iris takes on the responsibility of teaching Stanley how to read and, predictably, they fall in love. The screenplay touches on some contemporary social problems, including illiteracy, unemployment, teenage pregnancy, and affordable care for the elderly, yet offers no insight into any of them. Their slight treatment makes them seem more like gimmicks than subject matter. The film also suffers from a change in tone and plot about half way through—as though some changes were forced on the production. From the team that brought *Norma Rae* to the screen. Also with Martha Plimpton, Swoosie Kurtz, and Harley Cross. **Director**—Martin Ritt. **(PG-13)** *104 minutes*

THE STAR CHAMBER (1983)

★★

Michael Douglas
Hal Holbrook

A group of California judges, frustrated with loopholes in the legal system, resorts to vigilante justice to dispose of some vile criminals. This thinking-man's version of *Death Wish* begins with promise, but soon turns pretentious and preposterous. Douglas stars as one of the justices who wrestles with his conscience, though he seems far too young for the part. Sharon Gless and Yaphet Kotto perform well in supporting roles. **Director**—Peter Hyams. **(R)** *109 minutes*

This movie available on videotape and/or disc.

STARCHASER: THE LEGEND OF ORIN (1985)

 ★★

This animated sci-fi adventure in 3-D tells of a boy's attempt to rescue the human race from oppressive robots. He carries out his noble mission armed with a magical, jewel-studded sword. The high-tech production and animation are impressive, and the 3-D effect enhances the action with minimal eyestrain. The story brims with creative characters, yet the screenplay, which is remarkably similar to that of *Star Wars*, is essentially banal. **Director**—Steven Hahn. **(PG)** *107 minutes*

STARDUST (1975)

★★½

David Essex
Adam Faith

Essex and Faith star in this story about a young, working-class British rock musician who finally makes it to the big time and becomes a victim of his own success. The story seems to accurately parallel the world of Jimi Hendrix or Janis Joplin—a dazzling display of money, screaming groupies, unscrupulous promoters, internal squabbles, and finally death from a drug overdose. Yet instead of probing deeply, the movie skips from one situation to another. Also, it's difficult to understand much of the cockney dialect. Also with Larry Hagman and Dave Edmunds. **Director**—Michael Apted. **(R)** *97 minutes*

STARDUST MEMORIES (1980)

★★★

Woody Allen
Charlotte Rampling

Stardust Memories, *Woody Allen's bittersweet reflection on the price of fame.*

This uneven film is Allen's version of Federico Fellini's *8½*. Allen plays a harassed celebrity filmmaker who discovers there's meager satisfaction in such adoration. The movie is filled with numerous harried crowd scenes, which produce a desperate and overheated tone well suited to the serious material. Also with Jessica Harper and Marie-Christine Barrault. **(PG)** *89 minutes b&w*

STAR 80 (1983)

★★★

Mariel Hemingway
Eric Roberts

Compelling and uncompromising film about the rise and horrid murder of centerfold model Dorothy Stratten. Hemingway appropriately plays Stratten as an exploited pinup doll, but the story's focal point is her sleazy manager/husband, Paul Snider (Roberts). He turns a shotgun on Dorothy and then on himself after he is left in the dust of her rocketing career. Roberts' *tour de force* performance underscores the rage and frustration of this unsavory character. Director Bob Fosse successfully duplicates the documentary style he introduced in *Lenny*. **(R)** *104 minutes*

A STAR IS BORN (1937)

★★★½

Janet Gaynor
Fredric March
Adolphe Menjou
Lionel Stander

The first of the three versions of this story, and one of the best of the behind-the-scenes Hollywood dramas. Gaynor stars as the young actress discovered by a screen giant (March), whose own career is on the decline. She becomes a sensation; he sinks deeper into alcoholism. Not as lively as the Judy Garland musical version, but much sharper than the Streisand film. Dorothy Parker collaborated on the script. Good early color cinematography. Also with Andy Devine, May Robson, Franklin Pangborn, Edgar Kennedy, and Peggy Wood. **Director**—William A. Wellman. **Academy Award**—Wellman and Robert Carson, original story. **Nominations**—best picture; Wellman, best director; March, best actor; Gaynor, best actress; Alan Campbell, Robert Carson, and Parker, screenplay. *111 minutes*

A STAR IS BORN (1954)

★★★½

Judy Garland
James Mason

Judy Garland sizzles as a rising Hollywood actress in A Star Is Born.

This musical version of the 1937 David O. Selznick movie is excellent entertainment, but it loses some of its dramatic force in the shift to music. Garland is the power behind the film as she belts out such songs as "Born in a Trunk" and "The Man That Got Away." The script was written by Moss Hart. The film was rereleased in 1984 with several minutes of restored footage, including some musical numbers. The restored version is available on tape and runs 175 minutes. Also with Charles Bickford, Jack Carson, Tommy Noonan, Lucy Marlow, and Amanda Blake. **Director**—George Cukor. **(PG) Academy Award Nominations**—Mason, best actor; Garland, best actress. *154 minutes*

A STAR IS BORN (1976)

 ★★

Barbra Streisand
Kris Kristofferson

Streisand dominates this third telling of the show-biz soap opera. In this rock version about an unknown singer's rise to fame, Streisand is billed as the star, executive producer, cosongwriter, and wardrobe consultant; rumor has it that she usurped the direction from Frank Pierson, and also had a hand in the editing. The result is a lukewarm movie hardly the caliber of the 1954 Judy Garland/James Mason production. Kristofferson has a major part, but he is upstaged. The theme song, "Evergreen," won an Academy Award. Also with Gary Busey, Paul Mazursky, and Oliver Clark. **(R)** *140 minutes*

STARMAN (1984)

★★★

Jeff Bridges
Karen Allen

Jeff Bridges shares the secret of eternal life with Karen Allen in Starman.

Bridges stars in the title role of this sci-fi romantic adventure as an alien who falls to Earth. He assumes the human form of a dead man, and falls in love with the widow (Allen). The story's theme echos those of *E.T.* and *Close Encounters*—that visitors from space can be gentle and even helpful. The structure of the narrative takes on that of a chase film, with scores of cops and federal officials trying to nab the alien before he can rendezvous with a spaceship. **Director**—John Carpenter. **(PG) Academy Award Nomination**—Bridges, best actor. *115 minutes*

STARS AND BARS (1988)

★1/2

Daniel Day-Lewis
Harry Dean Stanton

A frazzled farce starring Day-Lewis as a snooty English art dealer who has moved to America to escape his own prim and proper origins. He travels to the Deep South to appraise and purchase a valuable Renoir in the possession of a rural Georgia family headed by Stanton. His attempts to deal with these unsophisticated characters lead to numerous misadventures, which ultimately prove more embarrassing than funny. The film, for the most part, engages in a bashing of American pop culture and American stereotypes, which is not surprising considering it was directed by Englishman Pat O'Connor and based on English writer William Boyd's novel. An offbeat American cast, including Martha Plimpton, Joan Cusack, Will Patton, Steven Wright, Glenne Headly, and Maury Chaykin, is totally wasted. **(R)** *94 minutes*

STARS AND STRIPES FOREVER (1952)

★★

Clifton Webb
Debra Paget
Ruth Hussey

Webb is well suited to the role of march king John Philip Sousa, a musician who wanted to write ballads, but eventually found success as a bandmaster and writer of rousing marches. Some of the march music gets a bit tedious and jarring after a while, but the band plays on, and the music is expertly spliced into the plot. Robert Wagner, Lester Matthews, and Finlay Currie appear in supporting roles. **Director**—Henry Koster. *89 minutes*

STAR SPANGLED RHYTHM (1942)

★★★

Bing Crosby
Betty Hutton
Victor Moore
Walter Abel

This movie must be taken on its own terms. If you expect a plot or any degree of meaningful characterization, you'll be disappointed. However, if you accept the fact that it's a star-studded variety show, you'll find a great deal of enjoyment in this World War II song-and-dance fest. Tunes include "Time to Hit the Road to Dreamland" and "That Old Black Magic." Some of those included in this galaxy of stars are Preston Sturges, Eddie Bracken, Bob Hope, Paulette Goddard, Veronica Lake, Dorothy Lamour, Ray Milland, William Bendix, Arthur Treacher, Eddie "Rochester" Anderson, Alan Ladd, and Susan Hayward. **Director**—George Marshall. *99 minutes b&w*

STARTING OVER (1979)

★★★★

Burt Reynolds
Jill Clayburgh
Candice Bergen

Reynolds casts aside his good-ol'-boy image for a superb, sympathetic role in this thoroughly enjoyable romantic comedy, which views the man's side of divorce. There's a witty script, crisp direction by Alan J. Pakula, and rich satire. Other first-rate performances are turned in by Clayburgh and Bergen. Clayburgh plays a nursery-school teacher who establishes a romance with Reynolds. Bergen is his ex-wife, who tries to become famous as a pop singer. Also with Charles Durning, Frances Sternhagen, Paul Sorvino, Mary Kay Place, and Austin Pendleton. **(R) Academy Award Nominations**—Clayburgh, best actress; Bergen, best supporting actress. *105 minutes*

STAR TREK—THE MOTION PICTURE (1979)

★★

William Shatner
Leonard Nimoy

The producers lavished millions of dollars on hardware and special effects for this epic, based on the popular television series. But they seemed to have run out of funds when it came to character and script development. The spaceship U.S.S. *Enterprise* is back in action with Captain Kirk (Shatner), Mr. Spock (Nimoy), and other familiar crew members combating a menacing force in space. The super gadgetry blasts away while the story—reminiscent of an old TV episode—lacks warmth. Strictly for Trekkies. Also with Stephen Collins, Persis Khambatta, DeForest Kelley, George Takei, James Doohan, and Nichelle Nichols. **Director**—Robert Wise. **(G)** *132 minutes*

STAR TREK II: THE WRATH OF KHAN (1982)

★★★

William Shatner
Leonard Nimoy
Ricardo Montalban

William Shatner and Leonard Nimoy in Star Trek II: The Wrath of Khan.

This movie available on videotape and/or disc.

(Continued)
A beautifully made sequel to the first big-budget space adventure based on the popular television series. This time, the affecting story superbly captures the spirit of the original series. Admiral Kirk (Shatner), Mr. Spock (Nimoy), and the familiar crew aboard the U.S. Starship *Enterprise* are gallantly protecting the frontiers of space from the evil ambitions of Khan, played impressively by Montalban. Based on "Space Seed," an episode that aired in the series' second season. Also with DeForest Kelley, James Doohan, George Takei, Walter Koenig, Nichelle Nichols, and Kirstie Alley. **Director**—Nicholas Meyer. **(PG)**
113 minutes

STAR TREK III: THE SEARCH FOR SPOCK (1984)

★★★

William Shatner
Christopher Lloyd
Leonard Nimoy

The second *Star Trek* movie sequel, which explores the fate of Mr. Spock, who was seemingly killed in the 1982 sequel. The Starship *Enterprise* is spared an ignominious forced retirement in order to search for the intriguing Vulcan. The journey takes the *Enterprise* crew to a planet on the verge of self-destruction. All of the regulars—including James Doohan, DeForest Kelley, Walter Koenig, Nichelle Nichols, and George Takei—return. Also with Dame Judith Anderson, Mark Lenard, James B. Sikking, John Larroquette, and Robin Curtis. Directed by Nimoy. **(PG)**
105 minutes

STAR TREK IV: THE VOYAGE HOME (1986)

★★★

William Shatner
Leonard Nimoy
DeForest Kelley
James Doohan

This fourth *Star Trek* film is as well-crafted and entertaining as the previous sequels. The adventure begins with a long special-effects sequence involving high-tech equipment and elaborate vessels moving through space. But when the *Enterprise* crew returns to 20th-century Earth to save the whales, the story perks up, takes on a good-humored, human dimension, and soars on all thrusters. All the *Star Trek* regulars, including George Takei, Walter Koenig, and Nichelle Nichols, are on board once again. **Director**—Nimoy. **(PG) Academy Award Nominations**—Don Peterman, cinematography; Leonard Rosenman, best original score; Terry Porter, Dave Hudson, Mel Metcalfe, and Gene S. Cantamessa, best sound; Mark Mangini, best sound effects editing.
119 minutes

STAR TREK V: THE FINAL FRONTIER (1989)

★★

William Shatner
Leonard Nimoy
DeForest Kelley

The series runs low on energy in this chapter. The familiar crew, with Shatner holding the director's reins, is comfortably on board as the Enterprise is hijacked for a journey to the end of the universe. Unfortunately, the ambitious mission ends up wallowing in metaphors about God and leaving a lot of loose ends. The villains are ill-defined, and suspense is sorely lacking. Also with James Doohan, Nichelle Nichols, Walter Koenig, George Takei, David Warner, and Laurence Luckinbill. **(PG)**
105 minutes

STAR WARS (1977)

★★★$^1/_2$

Mark Hamill
Harrison Ford
Alec Guinness
Carrie Fisher

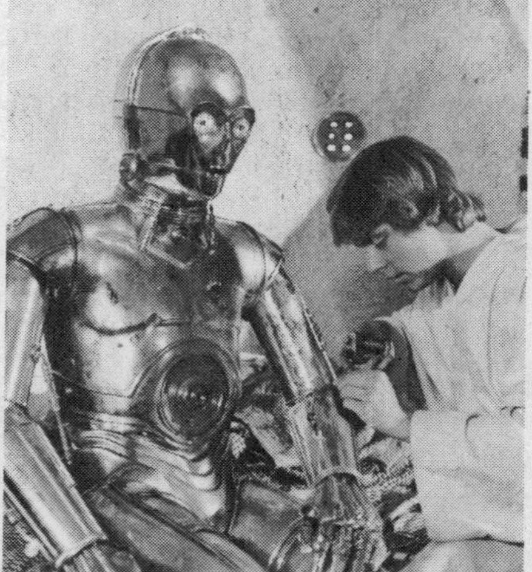

Luke Skywalker (Mark Hamill) repairs C3PO's arm in Star Wars.

A magnificent intergalactic adventure with innovative special effects, an equally effective soundtrack, and archetypal characters that embody good or evil. Though similar in storyline and approach to the old-time science-fiction serials it pays homage to, the film is far more sophisticated and hip than that type of film fare. Writer/director George Lucas built an empire on the success of this film, which spawned two sequels and breathed life into the science-fiction genre. The film made stars of its principals, and became a pop-culture artifact of the 1970s. Winner of several technical Academy Awards, plus one for John Williams' highly recognizable score. Also with Anthony Daniels, Kenny Baker, Peter Cushing, and David Prowse. **(PG) Academy Award Nominations**—best picture; Lucas, best director; Guinness, best supporting actor; Lucas, best screenplay based on original material.
121 minutes

STATE FAIR (1945)

★★★

Charles Winninger
Jeanne Crain
Dana Andrews

The fine songs of Rodgers and Hammerstein highlight this entertaining musical about a family's experiences at the Iowa State fair. The script and plot lack substance, but the small-town atmosphere and nostalgia for an era long past make for an appealing and charming film. Tunes include "Grand Night for Singing" and "It Might As Well Be Spring." Fay Bainter, Frank McHugh, Vivian Blaine, Donald Meek, and Dick Haymes also star. **Director**—Walter Lang. **Alternate Title**—*It Happened One Summer.*
100 minutes

STATE OF THE UNION (1948)

★★★★

Spencer Tracy
Katharine Hepburn

Tracy and Hepburn click in this political comedy about a man who runs for President, and almost loses both his ideals and his wife. Tracy and Hepburn are the estranged couple. Angela Lansbury plays a millionairess who bankrolls the campaign, and Van Johnson costars as the campaign manager. This film version of the Howard Lindsay/Russel Crouse play is expertly directed by Frank Capra. Lewis Stone, Howard Smith, Charles Dingle, Raymond Walburn, and Adolphe Menjou appear in supporting roles. *124 minutes b&w*

® This movie available with closed captions for the hearing impaired.

STAY HUNGRY (1976)

★★½

Jeff Bridges
Sally Field

A thought-provoking story, set in the contemporary South, about a wealthy young man who becomes involved with the freaky world of bodybuilders when he invests in a gym. The rich heir is played by Bridges; and Field costars as the working-class woman he gets involved with. Muscle-man Arnold Schwarzenegger plays a weight lifter, whose gentle demeanor belies his bigger-than-life build. The film is a mulligan stew of plots, subplots, characters, and themes that ultimately becomes too confusing. Also with Joe Santo, Scatman Crothers, Roger Mosley, and R.G. Armstrong. **Director**—Bob Rafelson. **(R)** *102 minutes*

STAYING ALIVE (1983)

★★

John Travolta
Cynthia Rhodes
Finola Hughes

Despite the potential powerhouse combination of Sylvester Stallone's direction and Travolta's performance, this sequel to the popular *Saturday Night Fever* is an inferior product. Our young dancing hero, Tony Manero (Travolta), has left Brooklyn and now wants to make it big on Broadway. Songs by the Bee Gees and Stallone's brother Frank are forgettable, and the contrived dance numbers irritate more often than they excite. Given this limp script, the audience may have difficulty staying awake. **(PG)** *96 minutes*

STAYING TOGETHER (1989)

★★½

Sean Astin
Stockard Channing
Melinda Dillon
Tim Quill
Dermot Mulroney

A sentimental comedy/drama set in small-town America. When a father (Jim Haynie) sells the family's fast-food business to land developers, his three sons find it difficult to deal with the change. A series of crises are set off, which the characters resolve in an uneven and often unrealistic manner. Astin, Mulroney, and Quill offer solid performances as the three brothers who experience life's changes—which in this film take the form of romance. A somewhat clichéd story that is nonetheless entertaining. Also with Levon Helm, Dinah Manoff, Keith Szarabajka, Daphne Zuniga, and Sheila Kelley. **Director**—Lee Grant. **(R)** *91 minutes*

STEALING HEAVEN (1989)

★★½

Derek de Lint
Kim Thompson

A ponderous and uneven telling of the steamy real-life love affair between 12th-century French philosopher Peter Abelard (de Lint) and his bright and beautiful student Heloise (Thompson). Impressive acting and elaborate period settings are real assets, but the drama seems stilted; it's difficult to understand the angst and passion of these ill-fated lovers. Also with Denholm Elliott and Mark Jax. **Director**—Clive Donner. **(R)** *116 minutes*

STEALING HOME (1988)

★★ 

Mark Harmon
Jodie Foster

Lifelong friends Harold Ramis and Mark Harmon in Stealing Home.

A disordered, syrupy melodrama about a young man's adolescence among Philadelphia's upper class. Harmon plays a washed-up minor league baseball player called home because of the suicide of a childhood friend. Foster plays the friend in numerous flashbacks, which merely confuse the story. The nostalgic tale evokes a mood similar to *Summer of '42.* Also with Jonathan Silverman, William McNamara, Harold Ramis, John Shea, Blair Brown, and Helen Hunt. **Directors**—Steven Kampmann and Will Aldis. **(PG-13)** *98 minutes*

STEAMBOAT 'ROUND THE BEND (1935)

★★★

Will Rogers
Anne Shirley
Eugene Pallette

Between star Rogers and director John Ford, there's a lot of irresistible humor floating down this Mississippi excursion. In a Mark Twain-like tale (actually from a novel by Ben Lucien Berman, as scripted by Dudley Nichols and Lamar Trotti), an easygoing riverboat captain must steam up to defeat a rival captain in a race and clear his nephew of a murder charge. Rogers is dandy in one of his last roles (the film opened after his death in 1935). With John McGuire, Stepin Fetchit, Francis Ford, and Irvin S. Cobb. *96 minutes b&w*

STEEL (1980)

★★★

Lee Majors
Jennifer O'Neill

High drama on a high-rise building, as tough, gritty steelworkers rush to complete a skyscraper before the bank forecloses. The uncomplicated script is reminiscent of those 1930s formula melodramas from Warner Bros. Majors, O'Neill, Art Carney, and George Kennedy turn in good performances, along with several supporting players who portray courageous construction men. **Director**—Steven Carver. **(PG)** *100 minutes*

STEEL DAWN (1987)

★★

Patrick Swayze
Lisa Niemi

Swayze and real-life wife Niemi star in this post-apocalyptic action/adventure film, which never rises above its low-budget origins. Swayze plays a mysterious soldier of fortune who comes to the aid of a widow and her young son when a ruthless farmer (Anthony Zerbe) wants to take over the widow's land and water supply. It's a futuristic *Shane* story adorned with gory sword fights and savage karate contests. The flimsy script is predictable, and the bloody action sequences add nothing. Also with Brion James, Christopher Neame, and Brett Hool. **Director**—Lance Hool. **(R)** *100 minutes*

STEELE JUSTICE (1987)

 ★★

Martin Kove

Submachine guns blaze away in this hyped-up, comic-book-style action film, which is so absurd it becomes unintentionally comical. Kove plays a Rambo-like character—a washed-up Vietnam veteran with a penchant for revenge—who goes to extremes to settle an old debt with a Vietnamese drug kingpin. The beefy vet takes on the cardboard villains at a rapid rate, but emerges as bullet proof, snake bite proof, and poison dart proof. Also with Sela Ward, Ronny Cox, Astrid Plane, Sarah Douglas, Shannon Tweed, Bernie Casey, and Joseph Campanella. **Director**—Robert Boris. **(R)**

95 minutes

STEEL MAGNOLIAS (1989)

★★1/2

Sally Field
Dolly Parton
Shirley MacLaine
Daryl Hannah
Olympia Dukakis
Julia Roberts

The intertwining lives of five Southern women in Steel Magnolias.

Robert Harling's play about six Southern women who meet each week at the local beauty parlor is expanded for the screen. The result is a long-winded soap opera with elements of comedy. The main story involves Roberts' decision to have a baby despite the health threat it poses. Expanding the narrative outside of the beauty shop adds nothing to the story. Director Herbert Ross' version of the South is so homogenized that the setting means nothing. In Harling's play, it was integral to the characters' personalities. Only Parton retains any Southern flavor, while the feeble attempts at a Louisiana accent by Dukakis and MacLaine will make some cringe. Still, the high-profile star turns by big-name actors should please some viewers. The male roles are well acted by Sam Shepard, Tom Skerritt, Dylan McDermott, Kevin J. O'Connor, and Bill McCutcheon. **(PG-13) Academy Award Nomination**—Roberts, best supporting actress.

118 minutes

THE STEEL TRAP (1952)

Joseph Cotten
Teresa Wright

Cotten is ideally cast as a bank manager who steals a half-million dollars from his bank on Friday, but decides to return it by Monday because his conscience troubles him. This twist on the common crime caper is pleasant viewing and well done, with plenty of suspense and an element of doubt until the conclusion. Also stars Jonathan Hale and Walter Sande. **Director**—Andrew L. Stone.

85 minutes b&w

STEELYARD BLUES (1973)

Donald Sutherland
Jane Fonda
Peter Boyle

Donald Sutherland and Jane Fonda are united in a cause in Steelyard Blues.

With stars such as Sutherland, Fonda, and Boyle in the same film, you might expect more than what is produced here. Still, despite the trio's failure to deliver as expected in this antiestablishment yarn, there are some funny moments as they try a bizarre plan to get an abandoned airplane working again. John Savage, Garry Goodrow, and Howard Hesseman appear in supporting roles. **Director**—Alan Myerson. **(PG)**

93 minutes

STELLA (1990)

 ★★

Bette Midler
Trini Alvarado

This baroque remake of the classic Barbara Stanwyck tearjerker *Stella Dallas* has been updated to modern times, but the poignancy and power of the original is absent. Midler, in the title role, plays the character too broadly to be effective. The story remains the same as the 1937 original. A poor unwed mother refuses the financial aid of the wealthy man who fathered the child. When the daughter grows up, the mother lets her go so the girl can have the financial advantages offered by the father's family. The class differences between mother and father are underplayed in favor of superficial sentiment, which is emphasized by the overbearing score. John Goodman does well in a supporting role as the good-natured bartender involved with Midler. Alvarado costars as the daughter. Also with Stephen Collins, Marsha Mason, Eileen Brennan, and Linda Hart. **Director**—John Erman. **(PG-13)**

106 minutes

STELLA DALLAS (1937)

Barbara Stanwyck
John Boles
Anne Shirley
Alan Hale

John Boles and Anne Shirley in Stella Dallas.

One of the screen's most popular tearjerkers. Stanwyck gives an outstanding performance as the title character, who marries into money but never escapes her lower-middle-class ways. She not only loses her husband, but gives up her daughter (Shirley) so

® This movie available with closed captions for the hearing impaired.

she will not be in the way of her child's own social and romantic aspirations. This solid adaptation of the well-known Olive Higgins Prouty novel is beautifully directed by King Vidor. Also with Marjorie Main and Tim Holt. **Academy Award Nominations**—Stanwyck, best actress; Shirley, best supporting actress. *111 minutes b&w*

THE STEPFORD WIVES (1975)

★★

Katharine Ross
Paula Prentiss

Men who feel threatened by the women's liberation movement may take mild delight in this suspense film about suburban Connecticut men who replace their wives with android replicas designed to be eternally beautiful and mindlessly obedient. The obvious, shallow script by William Goldman is based on Ira Levin's best-selling novel. The performances of Ross, Prentiss, and Tina Louise sustain the movie. Peter Masterson, Nanette Newman, and Patrick O'Neal appear in supporting roles. **Director**—Bryan Forbes. **(PG)** *115 minutes*

THE STERILE CUCKOO (1969)

★★★

Liza Minnelli
Wendell Burton

Liza Minnelli and Wendell Burton have a fragile first affair in The Sterile Cuckoo.

Minnelli steals the show in this story about Pookie Adams, a neurotic college student who finds love on campus with Burton. Minnelli's performance is light-years ahead of the material, which is often trite and has not aged well. Also with Tim McIntire, Austin Green, and Sandra Faison. **Director**—Alan J. Pakula. **(PG) Academy Award Nomination**—Minnelli, best actress. *108 minutes*

STEVIE (1978)

★★★

Glenda Jackson

Jackson, in the title role, delivers a spellbinding performance straight from the heart in this screen adaptation of Hugh Whitemore's play about the late British poet Stevie Smith. The film is static and stagy, but the extraordinary acting and characterizations more than make up for any drawbacks. Jackson's acute portrayal of the gentle woman's life is enhanced with expert reading of her verses. Mona Washbourne is remarkable as Stevie's stalwart spinster aunt. Also with Trevor Howard and Alec McCowen. **Director**—Robert Enders. **(PG)** *102 minutes*

STICK (1985)

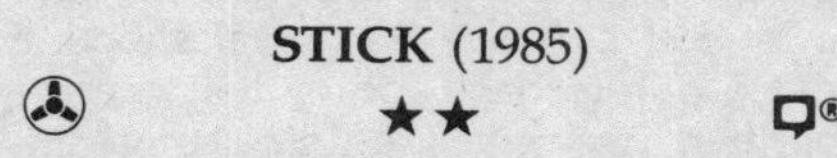

★★

Burt Reynolds
Candice Bergen

Burt Reynolds becomes mixed up with the underworld in Stick.

Reynolds is disappointing as an ex-con mixed up with slimy drug dealers in Florida. This box-office failure, based on Elmore Leonard's novel, finds Burt hobnobbing with the *nouveau riche* and romancing Bergen, who plays a classy investment counselor. George Segal and Charles Durning ham it up in supporting roles. **Director**—Reynolds. **(R)** *109 minutes*

STICKY FINGERS (1988)

★★

Helen Slater
Melanie Mayron

Two wacky female roommates come across a $1 million stash of illicit cash in this broad buddy comedy. The girls shop, shop, and shop some more as they try hard to squander all the loot. Though the plot is paper thin and the comedy uninspired, the two female leads are likable. Veteran character actresses Eileen Brennan and Carol Kane appear in supporting roles, adding some flavor to the film. This low-brow comedy did not experience a wide theatrical release. **Director**—Catlin Adams. **(PG–13)** *96 minutes*

STILL OF THE NIGHT (1982)

★★

Roy Scheider
Meryl Streep
Jessica Tandy
Joseph Summer

A sleek psychological thriller, similar in story and style to Hitchcock's films, about a pensive New York shrink (Scheider) who falls in love with the fidgety blonde (Streep) who's suspected of murdering one of his patients. Director Robert Benton (*Kramer vs. Kramer*) depicts some tingling, intelligent scenes, but the electricity between the two leads is practically nonexistent. The conclusion is also a letdown. **(PG)** *91 minutes*

STILL SMOKIN' (1983)

★

Cheech Marin
Thomas Chong

Those maharajas of marijuana, Cheech and Chong, frolic about Amsterdam pursuing various fantasies, usually involving sex and drugs. Some sketches generate modest chuckles, but the construction of the film is loose and lazy, and the boys seem drained of energy. Their drug-related routines are now dated and out of touch. **Director**—Chong. **(R)** *91 minutes*

THE STING (1973)

★★★½

Paul Newman
Robert Redford
Robert Shaw

This story of two small-time Chicago con men who avenge the death of a friend by tricking, or "stinging," a big-time mobster sparkles with vibrant action. Newman and Redford play the

(Continued)

(Continued)
con men, and Shaw is the subject of the sting. The plot is complex, but that doesn't really spoil the overall enjoyment of the film. More important, the key scenes at the end, when the swindle of the mobster takes place, are unpredictable. Eileen Brennan, Ray Walston, Harold Gould, and Charles Durning also star. Scott Joplin's ragtime music is another plus. **Director**—George Roy Hill. **(PG) Academy Awards**—best picture; Hill, best director; David S. Ward, best story and screenplay based on factual material or material not previously published. **Nominations**—Redford, best actor; Robert Surtees, cinematography.
129 minutes

THE STING II (1983)

★★

Jackie Gleason
Mac Davis
Teri Garr
Karl Malden
Oliver Reed

Teri Garr steps out with Jackie Gleason in The Sting II.

Gleason and Davis take over the Newman and Redford roles in this lukewarm follow-up to the popular, bouncy film about con men and their own brand of artistry. This time the scam, which is not much different from the original, unfolds at a painfully slow pace despite all the twists and turns of the plot. This *Sting* packs only a mild punch; there's not much of the charm that made the original work so well. **Director**—Jeremy Kagan. **(PG)**
102 minutes

STIR CRAZY (1980)

★★1/2

Gene Wilder
Richard Pryor

Wilder and Pryor mug and bumble through this uneven but funny comedy about two buddies who land in the slammer because they're mistaken for bank robbers. Wilder and Pryor work well as a team, as they try to outmaneuver prison officials and fellow inmates. As directed by Sidney Poitier, this comedy is not particularly innovative, but fans of Wilder and Pryor will enjoy the physical humor and clever one-liners. Also with Georg Stanford Brown, JoBeth Williams, and Craig T. Nelson. **(R)** *111 minutes*

THE STONE BOY (1984)

★★

Jason Presson
Robert Duvall

Dour, harrowing account of a rural family's grief over the accidental shooting death of a teenage son by his younger brother. Twelve-year-old Presson is impressive as the lad who bottles up his emotions following the tragedy, but the film unfolds at a strained, slow pace with characterizations that are far too studied and repressed to be wholly effective. Frederic Forrest and Glenn Close also star. **Director**—Chris Cain. **(PG)** *93 minutes*

STORMY MONDAY (1988)

★★★

Tommy Lee Jones
Melanie Griffith
Sean Bean

A visually stylish, modern-day *film noir* revolving around four unusual characters who cross paths over a three-day period in Newcastle, England. Jones stars as a ruthless Texas businessman who plans to reshape Newcastle into a complex of office buildings and shopping centers. Griffith plays his former girlfriend, who entertains the politicians and local business people important to Jones' deals. Rock musician Sting has a colorful secondary role as the owner of a jazz club who refuses to sell out to Jones. Into this tense arena walks Bean, an innocent drifter who gets a job in Sting's club but soon finds himself in the middle of open warfare between the two entrepreneurs. The beautiful, lush cinematography and the tasteful jazz tunes in the background set the cool tone for this low-key drama, which is long on atmosphere and mood. **Director**—Mike Figgis. **(R)**
93 minutes

STORMY WEATHER (1943)

★★★

Bill Robinson
Lena Horne

Ever-elegant Lena Horne romances Eddie "Rochester" Anderson in Stormy Weather.

Many musicals have silly plots, and this all-black talent show based on the life of Bill Robinson is no exception. But the delightful performers overshadow any triteness in this movie. The stars include Fats Waller, Ada Brown, Eddie "Rochester" Anderson, Flournoy Miller, Dooley Wilson, Cab Calloway, and Katherine Dunham. Horne sings the title song, and Waller does "Ain't Misbehavin'." **Director**—Andrew L. Stone.
77 minutes b&w

STORY OF ADELE H (1975)

★★★★

Isabelle Adjani
Bruce Robinson
Sylvia Marriott

Director François Truffaut has created a passionate and intelligent movie, based on the life of the youngest daughter of French writer Victor Hugo, about a woman obsessed with love itself. When the young woman is rejected by a British officer, her love becomes more intense and devastating. Adjani plays the lead role with impact and grace, and the film is beautifully photographed. Also with Joseph Blatchley and Reubin Dorey. Originally filmed in French. **(PG) Academy Award Nomination**—Adjani, best actress. *97 minutes*

THE STORY OF G.I. JOE (1945)

★★★

Burgess Meredith
Robert Mitchum

® *This movie available with closed captions for the hearing impaired.*

Meredith gives a stirring performance as Ernie Pyle, the famed war correspondent, in this drama set during the Italian campaign of World War II. Pyle earned a reputation as a friend of the typical infantry soldier and lived with them in the foxholes and on the front lines. The movie offers thoughtful characterizations, with Mitchum outstanding in his first major role. With Freddie Steele, Wally Cassell, Jimmy Lloyd, and Jack Reilly in supporting roles. **Director**—William Wellman.

108 minutes b&w

THE STORY OF LOUIS PASTEUR (1936)

★★★

Paul Muni
Josephine Hutchinson
Akim Tamiroff

Paul Muni (center) battles an outbreak of anthrax in The Story of Louis Pasteur.

Muni gives a strong portrayal of the famous 19th-century scientist who developed the anthrax vaccine and the toxin/antitoxin to cure rabies. A surprise hit of its day, it draws out the human side of Pasteur's life as well as his historic achievements. It shows him to be a man of incredible dedication, who was largely unappreciated for much of his life. The film breathed new life into the genre of biographical drama at that time. Also with Anita Louise, and Donald Woods. **Director**—William Dieterle. **Academy Awards**—Muni, best actor; Pierre Collings and Sheridan Gibney, screenplay; Collings and Gibney, original story. **Nomination**—best picture. *87 minutes b&w*

THE STORY OF SEABISCUIT (1949)

★★

Shirley Temple
Barry Fitzgerald

Fitzgerald is believable as a crusty horse trainer in this sentimental movie about the famous racehorse. Though this below-average picture does star Temple and has several excellently photographed racing scenes, neither is enough to make it a winner. Donald McBride, Lon McCallister, Pierre Watkin, and Rosemary DeCamp appear in supporting roles. **Director**—David Butler. *93 minutes*

STRAIGHT TIME (1978)

★★★

Dustin Hoffman
Theresa Russell

Hoffman portrays Max Dumbo, an ex-con who is his own worst enemy and is following a course of self-destruction. The film is based on a novel by ex-convict Edward Bunker. Harry Dean Stanton, M. Emmet Walsh, and Gary Busey are excellent in supporting roles. The film's release was tainted by rumors of hatchet editing, and Hoffman's attempt at direction before Ulu Grosbard took over further mars the film. Also with Rita Taggart. **(R)** *114 minutes*

STRAIGHT TO HELL (1987)

★½

Sy Richardson
Joe Strummer
Dick Rude

Joe Strummer, Sy Richardson, and Dick Rude are hit men in Straight to Hell.

The title tells it all in this low-budget send-up of spaghetti westerns actually shot on a Sergio Leone set. Directed by independent filmmaker Alex Cox (*Repo Man; Sid and Nancy*), this punk western attempts to tell the story of a gang of bumbling robbers who wander into a hostile town and engage in a lot of shootings and just as many silly gags. The film is self-indulgent and a good example of what happens when a filmmaker allows himself too much freedom. The comedy seems like one long in-joke with most of the viewers left on the outside. Costar Strummer is formerly of the rock group The Clash, and is just one of several members of an offbeat cast. Also with Jim Jarmusch, Elvis Costello, Dennis Hopper, Grace Jones, and Courtney Love. **(R)** *86 minutes*

STRANGE BEHAVIOR (1981)

★★½

Michael Murphy
Louise Fletcher
Fiona Lewis

A slightly addled, offbeat horror/drama about a series of teenage murders in a small midwestern college town. The film, which is similar to a 1950s-style thriller, offers some impressive special effects and a bit of campy horror, but the plot is filled with the usual predictable, gruesome killings. Michael Laughlin debuted as director with this film, and he shows promise of better work to come. **(R)** *99 minutes*

STRANGE BREW (1983)

★

Dave Thomas
Rick Moranis
Max Von Sydow

It's hard to believe that two comedians so talented could make such a stupid, witless movie. SCTV's Thomas and Moranis have tossed off an inconsequential, slapstick comedy involving the takeover of a brewery by madman Von Sydow, who wants to control the world with spiked beer. After a lot of beer-guzzling and chasing around, the film fizzles out with hardly a decent laugh. Von Sydow seems especially out of place amid the sophomoric humor. **Directors**—Thomas and Moranis. **(PG)**

90 minutes

STRANGE CARGO (1940)

★★

Clark Gable
Joan Crawford

An adventure story about a group of convicts who escape from Devil's Island. They are forced to choose between good in the form of Ian Hunter or evil in the form of Paul Lukas. Crawford and Gable, who often costarred together, are both fine here; although, unlike most of their vehicles, this

(Continued)

(Continued)
strange allegorical fantasy has a distinctly unglamorous atmosphere. Peter Lorre, J. Edward Bromberg, Eduardo Ciannelli, and Albert Dekker highlight the cast of characters. **Director**—Frank Borzage. *105 minutes b&w*

STRANGE INVADERS (1983)

Paul LeMat
Nancy Allen
Diana Scarwid

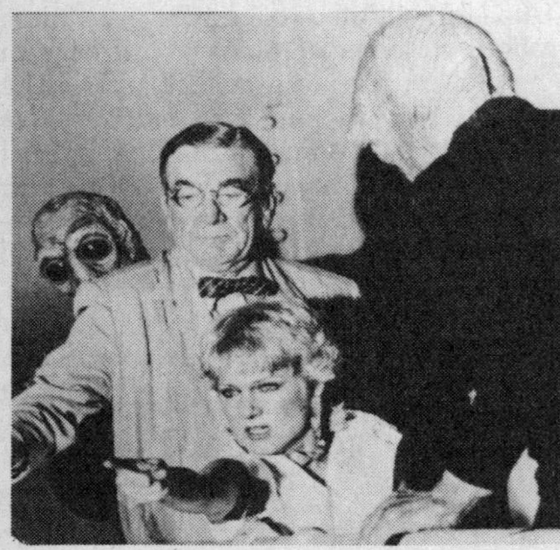

Kenneth Robey and Diana Scarwid, embroiled in the climax of Strange Invaders.

Outer-space movies of the 1950s are spoofed in this droll satire starring LeMat as a New York professor who wants to rescue his daughter from aliens. The creatures from space landed in a small Illinois town 25 years ago, and though it's 1983, the creatures still adopt the styles and manners of the Eisenhower era. The film seems to be mostly style with little substance, but it draws laughter as it manages to pay homage to and emulate the sci-fi films of the 1950s. Louise Fletcher and Wallace Shawn costar. **Director**—Michael Laughlin. **(PG)** *94 minutes*

THE STRANGE LOVE OF MARTHA IVERS (1946)

Barbara Stanwyck
Kirk Douglas
Van Heflin
Lizabeth Scott

Satisfying mystery/thriller, with Stanwyck and Douglas as a married couple hiding a dark secret. When Martha Ivers' ex-heartthrob Heflin breezes into town, the questions arise. A team of able Hollywood pros—screenwriter Robert Rossen, director Lewis Milestone, and producer Hal Wallis—connect with this one. Douglas is impressive in his screen debut, as is the rest of the cast, including Scott, Judith Anderson, Darryl Hickman, and Ann Doran. **Academy Award Nomination**—Jack Patrick, original story. *117 minutes b&w*

THE STRANGER (1946)

Edward G. Robinson
Orson Welles
Loretta Young

Robinson is well cast as a government agent with a keen mind who's tracking down a Nazi, played by Welles. The trail ends in a small Connecticut town, where the Nazi is posing as a respectable professor. Young plays the Nazi's wife, who is unaware of her husband's past. Welles' skilled direction and the vivid photography sweeten this melodrama, which seems slightly dated now. Richard Long and Philip Merivale also star. **Academy Award Nomination**—Victor Trivas, original story. *95 minutes b&w*

THE STRANGER (1967)

Marcello Mastroianni

Mastroianni is superb as the antihero estranged from society in this film version of Albert Camus' existential tale *L'Etranger.* Although the French author and existentialism were more popular at the time of the filming, under Luchino Visconti's direction the story is still meaningful and relevant to our times. Also with Anna Karina, Bernard Blier, Bruno Cremer, and Georges Wilson. Originally filmed in French and Italian. *105 minutes*

A STRANGER IS WATCHING (1982)

Rip Torn
Kate Mulgrew

Director Sean Cunningham, best known for his low-budget *Friday the 13th* bloodbath, tones down the gore in this shocker, but it's still a routine movie at best. The complex plot involves a brutal criminal who holds a

Rip Torn holds Kate Mulgrew hostage in A Stranger Is Watching.

child and a female TV reporter hostage in the murky bowels of Grand Central Station. Torn is convincing as the nasty kidnapper, but other cast members perform rather woodenly. Mulgrew plays the reporter. Also with James Naughton and Shawn Von Schreiber. **(R)** *92 minutes*

STRANGERS KISS (1984)

Victoria Tennant
Blaine Novak
Peter Coyote

An offbeat love story set in Hollywood during the 1950s. The clever plot involves two young movie stars whose offscreen romance parallels their roles before the cameras. The story is supposedly based on the real-life filming of Stanley Kubrick's *Killer's Kiss,* during which Kubrick encouraged an affair between the principals in order to enhance their performances onscreen. Aside from the unique plot, the melancholy mood and nostalgic re-creation of another time and place make the film enjoyable. **Director**—Matthew Chapman. **(R)** *93 minutes*

STRANGERS ON A TRAIN (1951)

Farley Granger
Robert Walker

This excellent Alfred Hitchcock suspense film is about two strangers who meet on a train and become involved in a hypothetical discussion about swapping murders. If each murdered the other's designated victim, then the authorities would find it difficult to catch either killer. The success of the movie

This movie available with closed captions for the hearing impaired.

Farley Granger listens to Robert Walker's bizarre plan in Strangers on a Train.

relies on Walker's brilliant performance as the psychotic who promptly acts on what he believes to be his part of the murder deal. Granger plays a tennis star who can't believe Walker took the proposal seriously. Superb script by Raymond Chandler. Also with Ruth Roman, Marion Lorne, Laura Elliott, Leo G. Carroll, and Howard St. John. **Academy Award Nomination**—Robert Burks, cinematography. *101 minutes b&w*

STRANGER THAN PARADISE (1984)

★★★

John Lurie
Eszter Balint
Richard Edson

Despite its meager budget, this quirky, droll comedy has a luxurious charm all its own. Innovative filmmaker Jim Jarmusch weaves a gritty, original story about the American scene as viewed by an American, a Hungarian immigrant, and the latter's visiting cousin, who drift from New York to Cleveland to Florida. The film excels because of a strong emphasis on well-defined characters, and intriguing performances by Lurie, Balint, and Edson. **(R)** *90 minutes b&w*

STRAPLESS (1989)

★★½

Blair Brown
Bruno Ganz
Bridget Fonda

From English playwright David Hare comes this serious story about two American sisters living in London. Brown (of TV's *The Days and Nights of Molly Dodd*) stars as the older sister, a physician who is eventually abandoned by her irresponsible lover. The story features stern political overtones about the deterioration of Britain's social services—a heavy viewing experience for American audiences. Fonda costars as the flighty younger sister. Similar in tone to Hare's plays *(Plenty; Wetherby)*. Also with Michael Gough and Constantin Alexandrov. **Director**—James Scott. **(R)** *103 minutes*

STRATEGIC AIR COMMAND (1955)

★★

James Stewart
June Allyson
Frank Lovejoy

Stewart, Allyson, and Lovejoy are vibrant and wholesome in this story about a baseball star (Stewart) who interrupts his career to return to the U.S. Air Force and the Strategic Air Command. Allyson costars as his wife, who tries to be understanding. Though the film is ordinary at best, the flying sequences make it worth viewing. Also with Jay C. Flippen, Alex Nicol, Barry Sullivan, and Bruce Bennett. **Director**—Anthony Mann. **Academy Award Nomination**—Beirne Lay, Jr., motion picture story. *114 minutes*

THE STRAWBERRY BLONDE (1941)

★★★

James Cagney
Olivia de Havilland
Rita Hayworth

James Cagney on an outing with Rita Hayworth in The Strawberry Blonde.

Cagney is at his best in this 1890s love story about a Brooklyn dentist who falls for the charms of *femme fatale* Hayworth. When she jilts him, he marries demure, shy de Havilland. A bittersweet comedy that depends on the personas of the principals—Cagney's energetic gruffness, Hayworth's allure, and de Havilland's sweetness—to make the story work. Also with Alan Hale, Jack Carson, George Tobias, Una O'Connor, and George Reeves. **Director**—Raoul Walsh. *97 minutes b&w*

STRAW DOGS (1971)

★★★½

Dustin Hoffman
Susan George

Violence reigns in this controversial film, in which director Sam Peckinpah pushes his themes to their limits. Hoffman plays a pacifist American professor living in England who's provoked into violence by the men of a remote Cornish village. George plays his wife, and her rape by villagers triggers a series of vengeful events. Despite its faults, the movie is well conceived and deftly executed; Hoffman and George give good performances. Also with T.P. McKenna, Colin Welland, Peter Vaughan, and David Warner. **(R)** *114 minutes*

STREAMERS (1983)

★★★

Matthew Modine
Michael Wright
Guy Boyd
David Alan Grier

Riveting film version of David Rabe's stage play about friction among Army misfits awaiting assignment to Vietnam. Director Robert Altman coaxes powerful ensemble acting from a virtually unknown yet talented cast. The film provides a close-cropped portrait of charged hostility in a claustrophobic barracks setting that reaches a violent and breathtaking conclusion. George Dzunda and Mitchell Lichtenstein also star. **(R)** *118 minutes*

A STREETCAR NAMED DESIRE (1951)

★★★★

Marlon Brando
Vivien Leigh
Kim Hunter
Karl Malden

Brando is masterful in this Tennessee Williams story about a brute who's in conflict with his wife's neurotic sister, played by Leigh. The theme may seem dated, as Williams attempts to contrast the new cultural values (personified by

(Continued)

Clash of culture—Vivien Leigh and Marlon Brando in A Streetcar Named Desire.

(Continued)
Brando) with the decaying values of the Old South (Leigh), but the acting is among the best in American cinema history. Harry Stradling's on-location photography of a hot, humid New Orleans blends vividly with the sultry performances of the actors. **Director**—Elia Kazan. **(PG) Academy Awards**—Leigh, best actress; Malden, best supporting actor; Hunter, best supporting actress. **Nominations**—best picture; Kazan, best director; Brando, best actor; Williams, screenplay; Stradling, cinematography. *122 minutes b&w*

STREET SMART (1987)

★★★

Christopher Reeve
Morgan Freeman

A compelling urban drama about sleazy journalism and an ambitious reporter who sacrifices his ethics for a good story. Reeve plays a magazine reporter who fakes a cover story about a flashy Times Square pimp. This sensational concoction leads to intriguing complications with a real pimp who fits the fictional profile. Some scenes are too contrived to be plausible, but powerful performances (especially Freeman as the pimp) and some clever twists compensate. Also with Mimi Rogers and Kathy Baker. **Director**—Jerry Schatzberg. **(R) Academy Award Nomination**— Freeman, best supporting actor. *97 minutes*

STREETS OF FIRE (1984)

★★½

Michael Paré
Amy Madigan
Diane Lane

A stylish but noisy film described by director Walter Hill as a rock 'n' roll fable. A young outsider (Paré) and a female mercenary soldier battle motorcycle thugs over the abduction of a beautiful rock singer. The atmosphere is dark urban decay, embellished with tough-talking dialogue. The powerful rock score by Ry Cooder and the state-of-the-art production design rise above the uneven story and mediocre acting. Beautifully photographed by Andrew Laszlo. **(PG)** *93 minutes*

STREETS OF GOLD (1986)

★★½

Klaus Maria Brandauer
Adrian Pasdar
Wesley Snipes

A well-acted, richly textured drama about three losers from the boxing world who combine their efforts to become winners. Brandauer stars as a former Soviet boxing champ who discovers two talented young street fighters and develops their boxing skills. The film comes closer to the original *Rocky* than any of that blockbuster's sequels, but its predictability destroys any dramatic tension. Also with Angela Molina. **Director**—Joe Roth. **(R)** *98 minutes*

STREETS OF LAREDO (1949)

★★★

William Holden
Macdonald Carey
William Bendix

Two former outlaws, who have become law-abiding citizens and have joined the Texas rangers, confront an old friend who has remained an outlaw. A remake of the 1936 film *The Texas Rangers*, though not as well directed as that earlier effort. Mona Freeman appears in a supporting role. **Director**—Leslie Fenton. *92 minutes*

STRIKE IT RICH (1989)

★★

Molly Ringwald
Robert Lindsay

Ringwald heads the cast of this disappointing adaptation of Graham Greene's novel *Loser Takes All*. She stars as a young woman who becomes engaged to an accountant, played by the uncharismatic Lindsay. At the request of his eccentric boss, played by John Gielgud, the couple are married in Monte Carlo, which they can ill afford. To defray expenses, Lindsay comes up with a system to win at the roulette wheel. Ironically, it prevents him from spending time with his new wife. Little about this film proves entertaining: There's no chemistry between the leads and the story meanders aimlessly. Stylish direction by James Scott is not enough to overcome the film's weaknesses. Also with Margi Clarke, Max Wall, and Simon de la Brosse. **(PG)** *87 minutes*

STRIKE UP THE BAND (1940)

★★★

Judy Garland
Mickey Rooney

Garland and Rooney energize what otherwise might be a dated and trite musical. Rooney leads a high-school band competing in Paul Whiteman's nationwide radio contest, and Garland is his female vocalist. Songs include "Our Love Affair," "Nell of New Rochelle," and "Do the Conga." William Tracy, Larry Nunn, and June Preisser costar. Director Busby Berkeley adds his usual bizarre touches to the musical numbers, including a marionette orchestra made out of pieces of fruit. *120 minutes b&w*

STRIPES (1981)

★★½

Bill Murray
Harold Ramis

P.J. Soles arrests an obviously repentant Bill Murray in Stripes.

Murray stars in this typical Army comedy, which pits reluctant privates against sergeants and officers. The film is composed of inconsistent episodes strung together with Murray's wise-guy humor. After bungling their way through basic training, Murray and his fellow misfits are stationed in Europe, where they inadvertently create havoc in Czechoslovakia. Also with Sean Young, P.J. Soles, and John Candy. **Director**—Ivan Reitman. **(R)** *105 minutes*

STRIPPER (1986)

★★★

Although this semidocumentary features many scenes of women stripping professionally, the film emphasizes the personal lives of the stripteasers. The women talk frankly about why they chose this profession, combining an innocence with street savvy. The First Annual Strippers' Convention that concludes the documentary is actually an invention of the filmmaker, Jerome Gary, for inclusion in this film. The remainder is an authentic look at an occupation society scorns, but allows. **(R)** *90 minutes*

STROKER ACE (1983)

★

Burt Reynolds
Loni Anderson

Good ol' boy Reynolds sleepwalks through this dreary comedy that mixes stock-car racing with fast-food retailing. When Reynolds isn't zooming around the track, he's chasing bright-eyed Anderson, a public relations worker for a fried-chicken king (Ned Beatty). Burt even dresses up in an oversized chicken outfit, but the desperate gag merely lays an egg. Also with Parker Stevenson, Bubba Smith, and John Byner. **Director**—Hal Needham. **(PG)** *96 minutes*

THE STUDENT PRINCE (1954)

★★

Edmund Purdom
Ann Blyth

The music of Sigmund Romberg and the singing of Mario Lanza brighten this otherwise dull operetta about a young prince who falls in love with a beautiful barmaid in old Heidelberg. Though Purdom portrays the prince, Lanza dubbed his singing voice. Blyth costars as the barmaid. Also with John Williams, Evelyn Varden, Louis Calhern, Betta St. John, Edmund Gwenn, and S.Z. Sakall. **Director**—Richard Thorpe. **(G)** *107 minutes*

THE STUFF (1985)

★★1/2

Michael Moriarty

An uneven, sometimes mildly amusing spoof of 1950s horror films that also skewers heavily advertised and packaged foods. The title villain is a yogurtlike goo that is addictive to consumers and can get out of control and kill. Moriarty heads the cast as a cynical industrial spy hired to find the source of this popular but deadly dessert. Also with Andrea Marcovicci, Paul Sorvino, and Scott Bloom. **Director**—Larry Cohen. **(R)** *88 minutes*

THE STUNT MAN (1980)

Peter O'Toole
Steve Railsback

Crazed director Peter O'Toole embraces Steve Railsback, who is The Stunt Man.

A rowdy, offbeat movie-within-a-movie about a fugitive, played by Railsback, who stumbles onto a film set and becomes a stunt man. The busy script is cluttered with riddles and tricky illusions, but such drawbacks are overcome by the film's amazing energy and subtle humor. O'Toole, playing the omnipotent and fey director, gives a virtuoso comic performance—his best in years. The film offers several hair-raising stunts. Also with Barbara Hershey. **Director**—Richard Rush. **(R)** **Academy Award Nominations**—Rush, best director; O'Toole, best actor; Rush and Lawrence T. Marcus, best screenplay adapted from another medium. *129 minutes*

THE SUBJECT WAS ROSES (1968)

★★★

Patricia Neal
Jack Albertson
Martin Sheen

Frank D. Gilroy's Pulitzer Prize-winning play is weakened when it is transferred to the big screen, but the story of a young veteran trying to cope with his quarreling parents is still vivid and compelling. Neal and Albertson play Sheen's parents. This was Neal's first appearance in a movie after a near-fatal stroke. Elaine Williams, Don Saxon, and Grant Gordon star in supporting roles. **Director**—Ulu Grosbard. **(G)** **Academy Award**—Albertson, best supporting actor. **Nomination**—Neal, best actress. *107 minutes*

SUDDEN IMPACT (1983)

★★★

Clint Eastwood
Sondra Locke

Eastwood returns as Dirty Harry Callahan in this fourth installment of the film series about the brutal police detective who takes an eye-for-an-eye approach toward crime control. Harry pursues a female killer (Locke) with personality traits similar to his own. Yet the violence-saturated film is disturbing to watch. The final sequence in an empty amusement park is an exciting combination of action, symbolism, and irony. **Director**—Eastwood. **(R)** *117 minutes*

SUDDENLY, LAST SUMMER (1959)

★★1/2

Katharine Hepburn
Elizabeth Taylor
Montgomery Clift

Hepburn and Clift's excellent acting salvages this pretentious film based on Tennessee Williams' play. Clift plays a neurosurgeon thrust into the position of pretending to be a psychiatrist so he can determine what has caused Hepburn's niece, played by Taylor, to have a nervous breakdown. Also with Gary Raymond, Albert Dekker, and Mercedes McCambridge. **Director**—Joseph L. Mankiewicz. **Academy Award Nominations**—Hepburn and Taylor, best actress. *114 minutes b&w*

This movie available on videotape and/or disc.

SUEZ (1938)

Tyrone Power
Loretta Young
Annabella

Fictionalized biographical drama about French architect/engineer Ferdinand de Lesseps and the building of the Suez Canal in mid-19th century Egypt. Good production values, including the lavish sets and costumes and the excellent photography, highlight this overblown Darryl F. Zanuck epic. Unfortunately, the romantic triangle between Power, Young, and Annabella takes precedence over the interesting historical drama. Impressive casting also includes Edward Bromberg, Joseph Schildkraut, Henry Stephenson, and Sidney Blackmer. **Director**—Allan Dwan.

104 minutes b&w

THE SUGARLAND EXPRESS (1974)

Goldie Hawn
William Atherton

Hawn and Atherton star in this comedy/drama about fugitive parents trying to reclaim their baby from foster guardians. Much of the film, based on a true incident, centers on the pursuit of the couple by Texas state police. The production is deftly handled, and the chase sequence builds slowly to a suspenseful conclusion. Hawn and Atherton are superb, with fine support from Ben Johnson and Michael Sacks. Director Steven Spielberg's first theatrical film. **(PG)** *109 minutes*

SULLIVAN'S TRAVELS (1941)

Joel McCrea
Veronica Lake

McCrea is splendid in this charming, satirical story about a disgruntled film director who goes out into the real world to learn how the events of the Great Depression have affected the lives of America's people. He feels the lightweight musicals and comedies that have garnered him critical acclaim are too trite considering the state of the world. The first half of the film details his adventures in a humorous fashion, but the latter half is surprisingly dark and sinister. The juxtaposition of comedy with the more serious events is jarring, but ultimately memorable. Robert Warwick, Jimmy Conlin, Franklin Pangborn, Eric Blore, Margaret Hayes, and Porter Hall also star. **Director**—Preston Sturges. *90 minutes b&w*

SUMMER HEAT (1987)

Lori Singer
Anthony Edwards
Bruce Abbott

Passion, adultery, and eventually murder come to a boil on Tobacco Road in the summer of 1937. Despite such explosive elements, this small-town drama is listless and lifeless from beginning to end. Singer stars as the bored wife of a tobacco farmer (Edwards) who has an affair with a handsome drifter (Abbott). The story is presented with a first-person narrative and is supposedly from Singer's point of view, but her actions seem unmotivated and without cause. The period settings are impressive, but this drama lacks the sultry, languid atmosphere of such southern potboilers as *The Long Hot Summer.* Also with Clu Gulager and Kathy Bates. **Director**—Michie Gleason. **(R)**

90 minutes

SUMMER LOVERS (1982)

Daryl Hannah
Peter Gallagher
Valerie Quennessen

Daryl Hannah, Peter Gallagher, and Valerie Quennessen are the Summer Lovers.

Dreary nonsense about a young college man and two young women involved in a *ménage à trois* on a sunny Greek island. It's hard to believe that Randal Kleiser, the director of the energetic *Grease,* is responsible for this exercise in tedium. The thin plot meanders, the characters are shallow, and the acting is an embarrassment. A total washout. **(R)** *98 minutes*

SUMMER OF '42 (1971)

★★½

Jennifer O'Neill
Gary Grimes

Gary Grimes and Jennifer O'Neill in Summer of '42.

This story of young love is expertly produced and photographed, but the emphasis on nostalgia approaches nausea at times. Herman Raucher's autobiographical screenplay also makes the mistake of projecting the permissive sexual attitudes of the late 1960s and 1970s onto the 1940s. Grimes plays a teenager of 15 who's infatuated with a 22-year-old war bride, played by O'Neill; both are superior to the material. When the subject isn't sex, the mood and tempo of the early 1940s are superbly evoked. Jerry Houser, Oliver Conant, Christopher Norris, Katherine Allentuck, and Lou Frizell appear in supporting roles. **Director**—Robert Mulligan. **(PG) Academy Award Nominations**—Raucher, best story and screenplay based on factual material or material not previously published; Robert Surtees, cinematography.

102 minutes

A SUMMER PLACE (1959)

Richard Egan
Dorothy McGuire
Sandra Dee
Troy Donahue

Novelist Sloan Wilson has an unerring instinct when it comes to portrayals of middle-class people and their value systems. This film version of his novel captures that aspect expertly, but the script and plot don't measure up to the characterizations. The storyline concerns the pain caused by an adulterous

® This movie available with closed captions for the hearing impaired.

Dorothy McGuire, Troy Donahue, Richard Egan, and Sandra Dee in A Summer Place.

love affair contrasted with the innocence of teenage love. Arthur Kennedy, Beulah Bondi, and Constance Ford also star. The film's theme song was a popular hit at the time of release. **Director**—Delmer Daves. *130 minutes*

SUMMER RENTAL (1985)

★★

John Candy

Candy heads the cast of this routine comedy as an air traffic controller who discovers his Florida vacation is as stressful as his high-pressure job. Director Carl Reiner manages to put over a few clever scenes, but too many gags fall flat. Costars Karen Austin, Rip Torn, and Richard Crenna. **(PG)** *88 minutes*

SUMMER SCHOOL (1987)

★★

Mark Harmon

Summer School *means job satisfaction for goof-off teacher Mark Harmon.*

The affable Harmon stars in this low-brow comedy as an irresponsible high-school gym teacher who is pressured into teaching remedial English to a summer class of problem students. The film strains to make us sympathetic toward these students as it probes their various personal problems—one boy moonlights as a male stripper, one girl is pregnant and unwed, one girl is dyslexic, etc. But these characters have been drawn primarily to generate laughs, and as such, remain superficial. The storyline is so lightweight that few truly funny bits emerge. Kirstie Alley, Robin Thomas, Dean Cameron, and Gary Riley also star. **Director**—Carl Reiner. **(PG-13)** *94 minutes*

A SUMMER STORY (1988)

★★★

James Wilby
Imogen Stubbs

A misty-eyed pastoral romance set in England in 1902, based on John Galsworthy's novella *The Apple Tree.* A British aristocrat (Wilby) meets a beautiful country lass (Stubbs), and they fall in love. The drama intensifies when the lovers part and the refined gentleman chooses a new romantic interest from his own class. Well acted and well directed. **Director**—Piers Haggard. **(PG-13)** *95 minutes*

SUMMERTIME (1955)

★★★

Katharine Hepburn
Rossano Brazzi

Katharine Hepburn and Rossano Brazzi share a memorable Summertime.

Romantic drama about an American spinster who has a love affair with a handsome married Italian while vacationing in Venice. Hepburn expertly portrays a woman past her prime, who blossoms and glows with newfound love, and takes the biggest chance of her life, knowing she will lose. She enjoys life to the fullest for one summer. From the play *The Time of the Cuckoo* by Arthur Laurents, with good support from Isa Miranda, Darren McGavin, and Marie Aldon. **Director**—David Lean. **Academy Award Nominations**—Lean, best director; Hepburn, best actress. *100 minutes*

SUMMER WISHES, WINTER DREAMS (1973)

★★★

Joanne Woodward
Martin Balsam
Sylvia Sidney

Woodward is captivating as a troubled housewife who's disturbed by the death of her mother, played by Sidney. Despite the kindness of Balsam, her understanding husband, Woodward lives in the past. She then finds new meaning in life when she accompanies her husband to sites where he served during World War II. The movie has its weaknesses, but the superior acting of this trio makes it a worthwhile viewing experience. **Director**—Gilbert Cates. **(PG) Academy Award Nominations**—Woodward, best actress; Sidney, best supporting actress. *95 minutes*

THE SUN ALSO RISES (1957)

★★

Tyrone Power
Ava Gardner
Errol Flynn

Ernest Hemingway's story of the Lost Generation loses much of its impact in this screen version. The characters seem to be hollow shells, and many incidents in the plot have been eliminated or toned down. Some of the scenery—filmed in Mexico—is attractive, although the setting is supposed to be Spain and Paris in the 1920s. Flynn almost steals the show from the weaker acting efforts of Power and Gardner. Gregory Ratoff, Henry Daniell, Eddie Albert, Juliette Greco, Mel Ferrer, and Robert Evans are also in the cast. **Director**—Henry King. *129 minutes*

SUNBURN (1979)

★

Farrah Fawcett-Majors
Charles Grodin
Art Carney

A silly comic mystery starring Grodin and Carney as oddball insurance investigators who crack a blackmail caper. The film is mostly a setup for Fawcett-Majors, who plays a model posing as

(Continued)

(*Continued*)
Grodin's wife. The film suffers from poor production values as well as a mediocre script. Also with Joan Collins, Alejandro Rey, and William Daniels. **Director**—Richard C. Sarafian. **(PG)** *100 minutes*

SUNDAY, BLOODY SUNDAY (1971)

Glenda Jackson
Peter Finch
Murray Head

A complex and unusual story about a bisexual triangle, in which Finch and Jackson are both in love with Head. Surprisingly, the risque subject matter is handled in a casual and low-key manner. Most of the movie is tastefully and superbly crafted. Also with Tony Britton, Peggy Ashcroft, Maurice Denham, Harold Goldblatt, and Vivian Pickles. **Director**—John Schlesinger. **(R) Academy Award Nominations**—Schlesinger, best director; Finch, best actor; Jackson, best actress; Penelope Gilliatt, best story and screenplay based on factual material or material not previously published. *110 minutes*

A SUNDAY IN THE COUNTRY (1984)

Louis Ducreux
Sabine Azema
Michel Aumont

Louis Ducreux and Sabine Azema share a dance in A Sunday in the Country.

Elegant, thoughtful French film set during a summer day in 1912, when an elderly painter invites his children and grandchildren to his country home. The screenplay, based on a Pierre Bost novel, is filled with wise observations about family relations and the contrasts in outlook between the old artist and his offspring. Worthy performances from the entire cast. Originally filmed in French. **Director**—Bertrand Tavernier. **(G)** *94 minutes*

THE SUNDOWNERS (1960)

★★★

Robert Mitchum
Deborah Kerr
Glynis Johns
Peter Ustinov

Deborah Kerr, Robert Mitchum, and Peter Ustinov in The Sundowners.

A splendid cast and excellent on-location photography in Australia brighten this tale about the struggles of a sheepherding family in the 1920s. The well-written script by Isobel Lennart is enhanced by the emphasis on visual detail. Dina Merrill, Chips Rafferty, and Michael Anderson, Jr., perform well in supporting roles. Despite some faults, it's a film the entire family will enjoy. **Director**—Fred Zinnemann. **Academy Award Nominations**—best picture; Zinnemann, best director; Kerr, best actress; Johns, best supporting actress; Lennart, best screenplay based on material from another medium. *113 minutes*

SUNRISE AT CAMPOBELLO (1960)

 ★★★

Ralph Bellamy
Greer Garson

Bellamy and Garson give convincing performances as Franklin Delano Roosevelt and Eleanor Roosevelt in this biography about the early years of FDR's adult life, as he enters politics and confronts polio. This moving drama, however, worked better as a Broadway play. Also with Hume Cronyn, Jean Hagen, Lyle Talbot, Tim Considine, and Ann Shoemaker. **Director**—Vincent J. Donehue. **Academy Award Nomination**—Garson, best actress. *143 minutes*

SUNSET (1988)

★★★

Bruce Willis
James Garner

Wyatt Earp (James Garner) confers with Tom Mix (Bruce Willis) in Sunset.

Director Blake Edwards fashions a complicated and ultimately serious comedy, which combines both fact and myth in an allegory about Hollywood's predilection for making myth out of history. The always-appealing Garner plays the legendary marshal Wyatt Earp, who during the cinema's silent era was hired as a consultant to Hollywood westerns. Here, Earp has been hired to make sure that a western starring legendary screen cowboy Tom Mix (Willis) is authentic. The two become fast friends while working together and combine their skills to solve the murder of a high-class Hollywood prostitute. The way that the truth is manipulated to make a better story in Tom Mix's western is symbolic of the complex weaving of fiction and history used by Edwards throughout all of *Sunset*. Viewers unfamiliar with Hollywood history may have a difficult time sifting through this often convoluted tale, while film buffs will enjoy Edwards' somewhat personal statement on the Hollywood cinema. Also with Malcolm McDowell, Mariel Hemingway, and Kathleen Quinlan. **(R) Academy Award Nomination**—Patricia Norris, costume design. *107 minutes*

This movie available with closed captions for the hearing impaired.

SUNSET BOULEVARD (1950)

★★★★

Gloria Swanson
William Holden
Erich von Stroheim

Gloria Swanson, as an aging movie queen, engineers a comeback in Sunset Boulevard.

An impoverished screenwriter, played by Holden, becomes the kept man of an aging movie queen, played by Swanson, in this memorable drama. The cynical and acid commentary on Hollywood morality highlights the gothic storyline. The baroque details of the setting and plot—the burial of a pet chimpanzee, the empty swimming pool, the gaudy decor of Swanson's home—emphasize the theme of death and decay. A brittle portrait of Hollywood. Fred Clark, Nancy Olson, Buster Keaton, Hedda Hopper, Jack Webb, and Cecil B. De Mille star in supporting roles. **Director**—Billy Wilder. **Academy Award**—Charles Brackett, Wilder, and D.M. Marsham, Jr., story and screenplay. **Nominations**—best picture; Wilder, best director; Holden, best actor; Swanson, best actress; von Stroheim, best supporting actor; Olson, best supporting actress; John F. Seitz, cinematography.
110 minutes b&w

THE SUNSHINE BOYS (1975)

★★★

Walter Matthau
George Burns

Matthau and Burns play two aging and feuding vaudeville partners who are reunited for a TV special after an 11-year separation. The lightweight comedy by Neil Simon is based on his Broadway play. Matthau and Burns are an effective comic combination, exuding warmth and charm as they bat their one-liners back and forth. Also with Richard Benjamin and Carol Arthur. **Director**—Herbert Ross. **(PG) Academy Award**—Burns, best supporting actor. **Nominations**—Matthau, best actor; Simon, best screenplay adapted from another medium. *109 minutes*

SUPERFLY (1972)

★★

Ron O'Neal
Carl Lee

O'Neal and Lee star in this vulgar tale glorifying Harlem drug traffic. It's about a drug dealer who vows to make one last big score before retiring. Admittedly, there's a lot of action in this well-made film, and there are comic moments, but there is also excessive violence. Also with Julius W. Harris. **Director**—Gordon Parks, Jr. **(R)**
98 minutes

SUPERGIRL (1984)

★★

Faye Dunaway
Brenda Vaccaro
Helen Slater

She manages to fly but fails to soar. And whenever the characters open their mouths, the leaden banter nearly sinks this comic-book adventure from the producers of the *Superman* movies. Slater is in the title role as the schoolgirl from inner space who tangles with two forces of evil (Dunaway and Vaccaro) over a magical source of power. Like the movie, the heroine is pretty to look at but lacks the easy charm found in Christopher Reeve's high-flying adventures. **Director**—Jeannot Szwarc. **(PG)**
114 minutes

SUPERMAN (1978)

★★★½

Christopher Reeve
Margot Kidder
Marlon Brando
Gene Hackman

That durable comic-book hero comes to the screen in this elaborate, $35-million production; it's great fun, and the special effects are well done. However, the movie seems almost too extravagant for such mindless material. Reeve is physically well suited to the role of the Man of Steel who busily fights crime, saves airplanes, and courts Lois Lane (Kidder). Brando received top billing—and top dollar—as Superman's father, but

Superman *(Christopher Reeve) and reporter Lois Lane (Margot Kidder).*

he's on and off the screen faster than a speeding bullet. Also with Ned Beatty, Jackie Cooper, Glenn Ford, and Valerie Perrine. **Director**—Richard Donner. **(PG)** *144 minutes*

SUPERMAN II (1981)

★★★

Christopher Reeve
Margot Kidder
Gene Hackman

The Man of Steel, played by Reeve, is smitten by love for Lois Lane in this thrilling sequel that some critics preferred over the 1978 original. Lois is once again played by Kidder. The film brims with exquisite special effects, heroic splendor, and some warm, human touches. This time, Earth is threatened by three power-crazed villains from the planet Krypton, but our hero triumphs over evil in a glorious battle amid Metropolis' skyscrapers. Also with Jackie Cooper, Valerie Perrine, and Susannah York. **Director**—Richard Lester. **(PG)**
127 minutes

SUPERMAN III (1983)

★★

Richard Pryor
Christopher Reeve

Pryor, playing a bumbling computer programmer, adds some welcome comic touches to this third adventure about the Man of Steel. Reeve is still Superman, this time battling a sinister conglomerate boss (Robert Vaughn) who wants to destroy the world's coffee crop. Annette O'Toole costars as Superman's new love interest while Lois Lane (Margot Kidder) takes a back seat. Unfortunately, this Superman adventure lacks the zip of its predecessors. **Director**—Richard Lester. **(PG)**
125 minutes

This movie available on videotape and/or disc.

SUPERMAN IV: THE QUEST FOR PEACE (1987)

★★

Christopher Reeve
Gene Hackman
Margot Kidder
Mariel Hemingway

Christopher Reeve reaffirms his love for Margot Kidder in Superman IV.

This fourth installment of the Superman series finds the Man of Steel struggling for nuclear disarmament, while the bespectacled Clark Kent deals with a new publisher who wants to change the *Daily Planet* into a sleazy tabloid. Reeve, who cowrote the script, is effective as ever in the dual role, but this episode lacks the wit and style of previous outings. The message, the predictable storyline, and the cardboard characters are less tolerable this time, and none of the special effects stand out. Hackman returns as the diabolical Lex Luthor. Also with Jackie Cooper, Jon Cryer, and Mark Pillow. **Director**—Sidney J. Furie. **(R)** *90 minutes*

SUPPORT YOUR LOCAL GUNFIGHTER (1971)

James Garner

Garner fans might enjoy this weak and silly movie about a gambler who flees from a woman who wants to marry him. Many of the attempts at laughs are keyed to Garner's plight when he's mistaken for a professional gunfighter. The supporting cast includes Harry Morgan, Suzanne Pleshette, Joan Blondell, Jack Elam, and Chuck Connors. **Director**—Burt Kennedy. **(G)** *92 minutes*

SUPPORT YOUR LOCAL SHERIFF! (1969)

★★★

James Garner
Joan Hackett

In this amusing spoof of conventional westerns, Garner becomes sheriff of a town, outwitting the bad guys while romancing Hackett. Garner has just the right comic touch for such a farce, and the performances of Hackett and Walter Brennan (as the main villain) enhance the production. Jack Elam, Bruce Dern, Henry Jones, and Harry Morgan appear in supporting roles. **Director**—Burt Kennedy. **(G)** *92 minutes*

THE SURE THING (1985)

★★★

John Cusack
Daphne Zuniga

John Cusack is tutored by Daphne Zuniga in The Sure Thing.

A refreshing, adolescent romantic comedy skillfully directed by Rob Reiner. The story involves two mismatched college students (Cusack and Zuniga), who fall in love while on a cross-country trip to Los Angeles. This refurbishing of *It Happened One Night* maintains traditional values while wisely blending in contemporary attitudes. Both leads appear comfortable and confident in their challenging roles. Also with Anthony Edwards, Lisa Jane Persky, and Viveca Lindfors. **(PG-13)** *94 minutes*

SURRENDER (1987)

★★★

Michael Caine
Sally Field

Michael Caine is delighted when Sally Field wins a jackpot in Surrender.

An amusing battle-of-the-sexes comedy, which looks at love in a material world. Caine plays a wealthy, twice-divorced novelist, who begins a budding romance with an impoverished painter, played by Field. To avoid getting taken to the cleaners one more time, he pretends to be broke. Field and Caine make a likable couple, and Steve Guttenberg is better than usual as Field's yuppie boyfriend. The relationship between the main characters, however, eventually gets lost in a series of subplots about winning a million-dollar jackpot, communing on a mountain top with a lone wolf, and being robbed by an armed transvestite. Also with Peter Boyle, Julie Kavner, and Jackie Cooper. **Director**—Jerry Belson. *96 minutes*

THE SURVIVORS (1983)

★

Walter Matthau
Robin Williams

Matthau and Williams flounder about in this aimless social satire that takes potshots at Reaganomics. The overloaded, rickety plot concerns an unemployed executive (Williams) and a dismissed gas-station manager (Matthau) who get involved with a cockeyed paramilitary training organization after they encounter a desperate hit man (Jerry Reed). Williams digs into his role with desperation while Matthau appears continually bored. **Director**—Michael Ritchie. **(R)** *102 minutes*

SUSAN LENOX, HER FALL AND RISE (1931)

Greta Garbo
Clark Gable

® *This movie available with closed captions for the hearing impaired.*

This two-star vehicle featuring Garbo and Gable is surprisingly disappointing. Garbo is beautiful but uninspired as a farm girl who runs away from her tyrant father and a forced marriage. Gable is handsome as the big-city heavy who leads her astray. The contrived and farfetched film does not make the most of its charismatic stars. **Director**—Robert Z. Leonard. *76 minutes b&w*

SUSAN SLEPT HERE (1954)

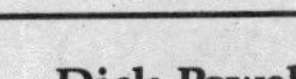

★★

Dick Powell
Debbie Reynolds

Powell and Reynolds star in this comedy about a Hollywood scriptwriter who's doing a movie about juvenile delinquency. He's given custody of a problem child, and that development is supposed to be the foundation for the comedy and the romance. Instead, the production crumbles. Powell plays the scriptwriter, and Reynolds costars as the delinquent. Also with Anne Francis, Horace MacMahon, Alvy Moore, and Glenda Farrell. **Director**—Frank Tashlin. *98 minutes*

SUSPECT (1987)

★★★

Dennis Quaid
Cher

Dennis Quaid gives Cher crucial information in Suspect.

Cher stars as a public defender assigned to represent a homeless Vietnam veteran accused of killing a legal secretary. Quaid costars as a dairy lobbyist on the jury, who helps her find the real murderer. As the mystery unfolds, several plot twists complicate the proceedings and lead to a surprise climax. Cher and Quaid are engaging as the two lonely people, who are highly successful in their careers but lead empty personal lives. Liam Neeson fares well in the tricky role of the deaf-mute veteran who has lost all faith in society. Also with John Mahoney, Joe Mantegna, and Philip Bosco. **Director**—Peter Yates. **(R)** *118 minutes*

SUSPICION (1941)

★★★½

Joan Fontaine
Cary Grant

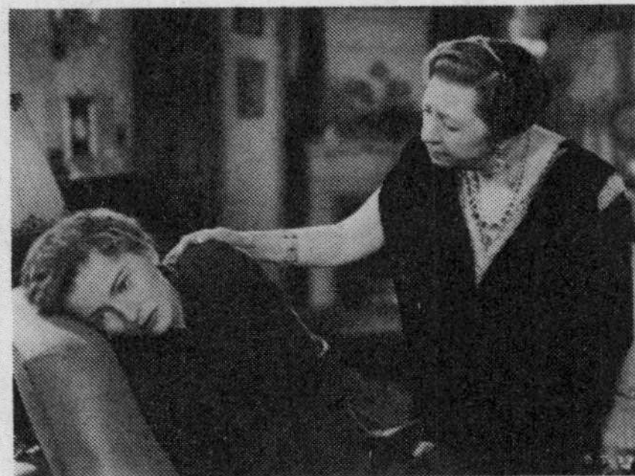

May Whitty discovers that Joan Fontaine is just sick from Suspicion.

Classic Alfred Hitchcock suspense thriller about a young woman who suspects her husband is planning to murder her. Fontaine stars as a prim British woman who falls for and marries a dashing but slightly scandalous roué, superbly played by Grant. The tension mounts as the audience identifies with the heroine's fears. An excellent supporting cast includes Nigel Bruce as Beaky, Cedric Hardwicke, May Whitty, and many more. **Academy Award**—Fontaine, best actress. **Nomination**—best picture. *99 minutes*

SWAMP THING (1982)

★★

Ray Wise
Adrienne Barbeau
Louis Jourdan

Adrienne Barbeau doesn't like the looks of what she sees in Swamp Thing.

The DC Comics horror/adventure is translated to the screen; but the filmmakers lack the courage of their camp convictions, and the story does not have the outrageous dialogue and absurd situations that it needs. The plot concerns a scientist who is changed into a walking vegetable and hides in the swamp, where he battles the villains and pines away for his girlfriend. **Director**—Wes Craven. **(PG)** *91 minutes*

THE SWAN (1956)

Grace Kelly
Alec Guinness
Louis Jourdan

Aside from the always welcome presence of Kelly, this film lacks any other mark of distinction—despite the fine acting of Guinness and Jourdan. The story involves the search by a prince for a wife. Guinness plays the prince. Based on the play by Ferenc Molnar. Also with Agnes Moorehead, Estelle Winwood, Robert Coote, Leo G. Carroll, and Jessie Royce Landis. **Director**—Charles Vidor. *112 minutes*

THE SWARM (1978)

Michael Caine
Katharine Ross

Zillions of African killer bees are on the rampage in this movie by director Irwin Allen (*The Towering Inferno*). The enraged insects attack an Air Force ICBM base and a nearby town, but they can't measure up in scariness to man-eating sharks or overgrown gorillas. The movie plods on with dull dialogue, questionable credibility, and not much sting. An all-star cast, which seems to number as many players as there are bees, also includes Richard Widmark, Henry Fonda, Olivia de Havilland, Fred MacMurray, Richard Chamberlain, Lee Grant, Ben Johnson, and José Ferrer. **(PG)** *116 minutes*

SWEET BIRD OF YOUTH (1962)

Paul Newman
Geraldine Page
Ed Begley

A film version of Tennessee Williams' play about a Hollywood actor who re-

(Continued)

This movie available on videotape and/or disc.

(Continued)
turns to his hometown with an aging and neurotic film star. Newman stars as the actor, and Page is the aging glamour queen. Newman is at odds with the boss of the corrupt southern town, a feud that goes back many years. Much of the original Williams play has been emasculated in this screen adaptation. Nonetheless, there are vivid characterizations, crisp dialogue, and memorable scenes. Also with Rip Torn, Madeleine Sherwood, and Shirley Knight. **Director**—Richard Brooks. **Academy Award**—Begley, best supporting actor. **Nominations**—Page, best actress; Knight, best supporting actress.
120 minutes

SWEET DREAMS (1985)

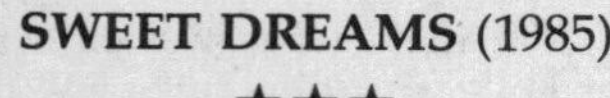

★★★

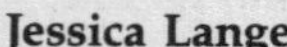

Jessica Lange

Patsy Cline (Jessica Lange) has a new suitor (Ed Harris) in Sweet Dreams.

Warm, intelligent biopic of country singer Patsy Cline's rise to stardom. Between the songs, there is a richly felt human drama of a young woman trying to build a better life for herself and her loved ones. Unfortunately, director Karel Reisz has no feel for the South, an integral part of Cline's background and life. This omission mars the film. Lange's performance, however, is excellent. Other high-caliber performances include those by Ed Harris as her husband and Ann Wedgeworth as her mom. **(PG-13) Academy Award Nomination**—Lange, best actress.
115 minutes

SWEET HEART'S DANCE (1988)

★★½

Don Johnson
Susan Sarandon
Jeff Daniels

Don Johnson, Susan Sarandon, Jeff Daniels, and Elizabeth Perkins in Sweet Heart's Dance.

The pitfalls of love and marriage are examined in this drama set in a small Vermont town. Johnson stars as a construction contractor tired of his long marriage to his high-school sweetheart, Sarandon. Daniels, Johnson's bachelor friend, is just getting his love life off the ground. The clumsy plot meanders over well-worn territory, but the cast does a good job with the material. Also with Elizabeth Perkins, Kate Reid, Justin Henry, and Holly Marie Combs. **Director**—Robert Greenwald. **(R)**
102 minutes

SWEETIE (1990)

★★★

Genevieve Lemon
Karen Colston
Tom Lycos

Sibling rivalry: Genevieve Lemon and Karen Colston in Sweetie.

This moody comedy from Australia may be difficult viewing for some audiences, but it represents original and audacious filmmaking nevertheless. The story involves two sisters of contrasting temperament: The skittish Kay (Colston) is superstitious and repressed, while the title character (Lemon) is outrageously freewheeling. Sweetie's disposition threatens to destroy her parents' lives as well as her sister's romance. Lurking in the background is a dark secret that has affected the entire family, but director Jane Campion keeps the details under wraps. The viewer is not privy to that private information, making for a tense viewing experience. Campion displays a remarkable flair for depicting the startling aspects of the sisters' complex personalities. Also with Jon Darling, Dorothy Barry, Michael Lake, and Andre Pataczek. **(R)** *100 minutes*

SWEET LIBERTY (1986)

★★★

Alan Alda
Michelle Pfeiffer

American history gets taken for a ride: Alan Alda in Sweet Liberty.

Alda served as the writer, director, and star of this send-up of Hollywood moviemaking. The result is a saucy adult comedy enhanced by some fine performances. Alda portrays a history professor who has written a novel about actual historical personages who were key figures during the American Revolution. When a film studio attempts to turn his literary treasure into a teen comedy, the author gets a lesson in "show business." Michael Caine, Lillian Gish, and Bob Hoskins costar. **(PG)**
107 minutes

SWEET LORRAINE (1987)

★★½

Maureen Stapleton
Trini Alvarado

The "Lorraine" of the title is not a woman, but a sweet, charming Catskill resort hotel that is long past its time. Stapleton portrays the matriarch proprietor who presides with motherly authority over the loyal help. Alvarado plays her young granddaughter who

® This movie available with closed captions for the hearing impaired.

spends a summer working in the kitchen, but finds time to experience her first summer romance. A small, independently made film, this slice-of-life comedy/drama will work well on the small screen. In a film like this, the secondary roles often provide a wealth of comic bits and touching performances. Here the supporting cast includes Lee Richardson, Todd Graff, Edith Falco, John Bedford Lloyd, and Giancarlo Espositor. **Director**—Steve Gomer. **(PG–13)** *91 minutes*

SWEET ROSIE O'GRADY (1943)

★★

Betty Grable
Adolphe Menjou

Menjou is suave, debonair, and charming in this enjoyable musical about a former burlesque star and a reporter's efforts to dig into her past. Grable plays the burlesque star. Unfortunately, most of the movie's songs are second-rate. Robert Young, Alan Dinehart, Reginald Gardiner, Virginia Grey, and Phil Regan appear in supporting roles. **Director**—Irving Cummings. *74 minutes*

SWEET SMELL OF SUCCESS (1957)

★★★

Burt Lancaster
Tony Curtis

The characterizations are stunning in this startling drama of the rough-and-tumble world of a New York-based newspaper columnist and his dealings with a vile press agent. Curtis is superb as the scheming PR man, while Lancaster is competent but less convincing as the vicious columnist. The gritty black-and-white photography of James Wong Howe enhances the brittle storyline. Also with Barbara Nichols, Emile Meyer, Martin Milner, Susan Harrison, and Sam Levene. **Director**—Alexander Mackendrick. *96 minutes b&w*

SWEPT AWAY...BY AN UNUSUAL DESTINY IN THE BLUE SEA OF AUGUST (1975)

★★★

Giancarlo Giannini
Mariangela Melato

Melato plays a spoiled, arrogant, and wealthy capitalist. Giannini is a communist deckhand on the yacht she has chartered. They become shipwrecked on an island, and the tables are turned as he dominates her in this gripping, political film about the battle of the classes and sexes. Originally filmed in Italian. **Director**—Lina Wertmuller. **(R)** *116 minutes*

THE SWIMMER (1968)

★★★

Burt Lancaster

The Swimmer *(Burt Lancaster) searches for truth and finds Janet Landgard.*

Unusual drama about a man's attempt to journey home via the swimming pools of his wealthy Connecticut friends. Based on a John Cheever short story, the Eleanor Perry script reveals the collapse of the American dream and the emptiness of material possessions. Lancaster gives a thoughtful performance as a former member of this suburban set whose past life is revealed as he swims to the remains of his estate. Some of the people he encounters on his trip include Janice Rule, Kim Hunter, Diana Muldaur, Cornelia Otis Skinner, and Marge Champion. **Director**—Frank Perry. **(PG)** *94 minutes*

SWIMMING TO CAMBODIA (1987)

★★★1/2

Spalding Gray

A unique cinematic experience consisting only of Gray sitting behind a desk and talking for an hour and a half. As directed by Jonathan Demme, however, the film remains compelling and Gray's monologue absorbing. Gray, a New York actor who has been performing his

Spalding Gray performs a compelling monologue in Swimming to Cambodia.

personal monologues for almost ten years, here discusses his experiences as an actor during the filming of Roland Joffe's *The Killing Fields* in Cambodia. His stories range from the comic to the tragic, with only occasional clips from the film and Laurie Anderson's music to supplement Gray's narration. **(No MPAA rating)** *87 minutes*

SWING SHIFT (1984)

★★

Goldie Hawn
Kurt Russell

Goldie Hawn and Kurt Russell keep the boys flying by working the Swing Shift.

Hawn plays a riveter at an aircraft factory in this sweet, nostalgic comedy/drama that looks at America's home front during World War II. The period details are sharply defined, but the sluggish plot bogs down in mushy melodramatics over Hawn's guilt-ridden love affair with a coworker (Russell). Christine Lahti and Ed Harris also star. **Director**—Jonathan Demme. **(PG)** *112 minutes*

SWING TIME (1936)

★★★★

Fred Astaire
Ginger Rogers
Victor Moore

Swing Time: *Fred Astaire forsakes a fortune in favor of Ginger Rogers.*

Mandatory viewing to chase away the blues and to see the screen's greatest dancing couple at their best. Astaire stars as a professional dancer and gambler, who must earn $25,000 before he can marry his hometown fiancée. Then, the debonair hoofer falls in love with Rogers, and does everything possible to avoid coming into money. The Oscar-winning "The Way You Look Tonight" and the famous "Bojangles in Harlem" number—in which Fred tap-dances along with three huge silhouettes—top the fine Jerome Kern score, which also includes "A Fine Romance," "Pick Yourself Up," and "Never Gonna Dance." Betty Furness and Eric Blore costar. **Director**—George Stevens.

103 minutes b&w

THE SWISS FAMILY ROBINSON (1960)

★★★

John Mills
Dorothy McGuire
James MacArthur

This Walt Disney version of the famed Johann Wyss children's classic is a total escape into a fantasy world. The movie shows how a family—shipwrecked en route to New Guinea—adjusts superbly to life on a desert island, as they build a paradise of their own and dispatch pirate invaders. Also with Sessue Hayakawa, Janet Munro, Tommy Kirk, Cecil Parker, and Kevin Corcoran. **Director**—Ken Annakin. **(G)** *126 minutes*

John Mills and Dorothy McGuire in The Swiss Family Robinson.

SWITCHING CHANNELS (1988)

★★

Burt Reynolds
Kathleen Turner
Christopher Reeve

Christopher Reeve, Burt Reynolds, and Kathleen Turner in Switching Channels.

Another screen version of the classic Charles McArthur-Ben Hecht comedy, *The Front Page.* This time, the story has been updated to involve a Chicago-based satellite TV network. A hot-shot news reporter (Turner) wants to quit her job to marry a rich milquetoast (Christopher Reeve), but her boss—who is also her ex-husband (Reynolds)—assigns her to a major story in an effort to convince her to stay. Unfortunately, clichés fly instead of sparks. The cast does have some chemistry together, but, whereas the original snapped and crackled, this remake wheezes and fizzles. Also with Ned Beatty, Henry Gibson, George Newbern, and Al Waxman. **Director**—Ted Kotcheff. **(PG–13)** *105 minutes*

THE SWORD AND THE SORCERER (1982)

★★

Lee Horsley
Richard Lynch

Nonstop sword-fighting, torture, and other shenanigans dominate this hectic action/adventure set in the Middle Ages. Some of the special effects are hair-raising, but the jumbled story abandons logic and the acting is strictly second-rate. Horsley heads the unfamiliar cast as an invincible warrior who takes revenge on a wicked conqueror (Lynch). A spectacular mix of nonsense and fast-paced carnage. **Director**—Albert Pyun. **(R)** *100 minutes*

SYLVESTER (1985)

★★

Melissa Gilbert

Melissa Gilbert astride future champion Sylvester.

Gilbert plays a spunky 16-year-old tomboy who breaks wild horses for a living. She falls in love with a spirited white gelding (the film's title horse) and enters him in a ritzy steeplechase competition in Kentucky. This sentimental film covers similar ground as *National Velvet*, but the acting is below par. Even the horse doesn't seem to have much heart for the task. Also with Richard Farnsworth and Michael Schoeffling. **Director**—Tim Hunter. **(PG)**

104 minutes

This movie available with closed captions for the hearing impaired.

T

TABLE FOR FIVE (1983)

★

Jon Voight
Richard Crenna

Custody struggle: Jon Voight and Richard Crenna in Table for Five.

This strained and sentimental tale stars Voight as an immature, divorced father who struggles to reestablish relations with his three children by taking them on a luxurious ocean cruise. While they're in mid-voyage, the children's mother dies in a car crash, and Voight and the stepfather (Crenna) fight for custody of the kids. Too banal to be effective. Also with Marie-Christine Barrault and Millie Perkins. **Director**—Robert Lieberman. **(PG)** *120 minutes*

TAI–PAN (1986)

★

Bryan Brown
John Stanton
Joan Chen

Bryan Brown (right) finds dangerous adventure in Tai-Pan.

An overlong historical costume adventure, set in 19th-century China, about the opium trade and the establishment of the colony of Hong Kong. Steamy romances, sword fights, beheadings, male rivalries, and a typhoon are all jumbled together in this ridiculous saga. Characters appear and fade like so many travelers passing through an airline terminal and the script is filled with meaningless episodes. A waste of Brown's considerable talents. **Director**—Daryl Duke. **(R)** *127 minutes*

TAKE A HARD RIDE (1975)

★★

Jim Brown
Jim Kelly
Lee Van Cleef
Fred Williamson

A familiar western starring Brown and Van Cleef as rivals. The story involves the transporting of $86,000 from Texas across hundreds of miles to a family in Mexico. Several unscrupulous types, ready to grab the loot, pop out of the brush along the way. Also with Catherine Spaak, Dana Andrews, Barry Sullivan, and Harry Carey, Jr. **Director**—Anthony M. Dawson. **(PG)** *109 minutes*

TAKE CARE OF MY LITTLE GIRL (1951)

★★

Jeanne Crain
Mitzi Gaynor
Dale Robertson

Crain, Gaynor, and Robertson star in this melodrama about university life and the dynamics and demerits of belonging to a campus sorority. Even viewers who recall their school days with fondness will probably find this movie too routine. Other cast members include George Nader, Jean Peters, Jeffrey Hunter, and Helen Westcott. **Director**—Jean Negulesco. *93 minutes*

TAKE ME OUT TO THE BALL GAME (1949)

★★★

Gene Kelly
Frank Sinatra
Esther Williams
Betty Garrett

An unpretentious musical set at the turn of the century about a woman who owns a baseball team. The plot is innocuous and the songs are not classics, but the stars put enough of their energy into the show to make it pleasant. "The Hat My Father Wore on St. Patrick's Day" and "O'Brien to Ryan to Goldberg" are two of the livelier songs. Also with Richard Lane, Tom Dugan, Edward Arnold, and Jules Munshin. **Director**—Busby Berkeley. *93 minutes*

TAKE THE MONEY AND RUN (1969)

★★★

Woody Allen
Janet Margolin
Marcel Hillaire
Jacquelyn Hyde

Allen is excellent as writer, director, and actor in this documentary spoof about the life of an inept thief. Some of the jokes fail and not all of the sight gags work, but the concept behind the comedy—a satire on film forms—is thought provoking and prefigures ideas explored in Allen's later films. Louise Lasser, Lonny Chapman, and Mark Gordon also appear, with Jackson Beck as the narrator of the documentary-style sequences. **(PG)** *85 minutes*

TAKE THIS JOB AND SHOVE IT (1981)

★★

Robert Hays
Barbara Hershey

Barbara Hershey and Robert Hays agree to Take This Job and Shove It.

Hays stars as a young man on the way up the corporate ladder who joins brewery workers protesting the takeover of their local brewery. The title is based on a popular country/western

(Continued)

(Continued)
song, but the film doesn't live up to its potential of effectively revealing the tensions between labor and management. Some well-known country music singers make cameo appearances, including Lacey J. Dalton, David Allan Coe, and Johnny Paycheck, who wrote the title song. Also with Art Carney, David Keith, Martin Mull, and Tim Thomerson. **Director**—Gus Trikonis. **(PG)** *100 minutes*

THE TAKING OF PELHAM ONE TWO THREE (1974)

★★★

Walter Matthau
Robert Shaw

A story about four gangsters who hold the passengers of a New York City subway car hostage. The well-crafted script has frequent moments of cynical humor, and enough suspense to keep viewers interested. Matthau, who plays a transit detective, and Shaw, as a ruthless gang leader, bring an effective edge to their performances. Martin Balsam, James Broderick, Hector Elizondo, Tony Roberts, and Earl Hindman appear in supporting roles. **Director**—Joseph Sargent. **(R)** *102 minutes*

A TALE OF TWO CITIES (1935)

★★★★

Ronald Colman

A tremendous cast fortifies this film version of the classic Charles Dickens tale of the French Revolution. Although the production has the glossy look of a Hollywood adaptation of a historical or literary classic, it's a faithful rendition of Dickens' masterpiece. Colman stars as the British lawyer who aids victims of the Reign of Terror and sacrifices his life to save another man from the guillotine. Also with Edna May Oliver, Elizabeth Allan, Fritz Leiber, Basil Rathbone, Claude Gillingwater, H.B. Warner, and Donald Woods. **Director**—Jack Conway. **Academy Award Nomination**—best picture. *128 minutes b&w*

TALES FROM THE DARKSIDE: THE MOVIE (1990)

★★1/2

Deborah Harry
Christian Slater
David Johansen

Appropriately moody settings, sharp acting, and clever screenplays make this trio of creepy stories worthwhile viewing for horror fans. Though the title is derived from the anthology series shown on syndicated television, these tales are more gory and offer better production values than their small-screen counterparts. "Cat from Hell" is perhaps the best of the bunch. It tells the story of a kitten that seeks revenge on a pharmaceutical executive (William Hickey) whose firm used animal testing to develop a drug. "Lot 249" is based on an Arthur Conan Doyle story about an ancient mummy, and "Lover's Vow" is the story of an artist (James Remar) who tells a deep, dark secret to his beautiful wife (Rae Dawn Chong). Harry appears in the opening and closing segments as a demonic housewife who plans to cook and eat a small boy. The boy puts off his execution by telling Harry this trio of tall tales. **Director**—John Harrison. **(R)** *93 minutes*

THE TALK OF THE TOWN (1942)

★★★★

Ronald Colman
Cary Grant
Jean Arthur

Cary Grant, Ronald Colman, and Jean Arthur in Talk of the Town.

A compelling tale about a woman in love with a suspected murderer and the attorney who defends him. This charming and intelligent comedy about civil liberties is a fine example of Hollywood studio filmmaking at its best. Script by Irwin Shaw and Sidney Buchman. The talented cast includes Charles Dingle, Rex Ingram, Glenda Farrell, Edgar Buchanan, and Emma Dunn. **Director**—George Stevens. **Academy Award Nominations**—best picture; Sidney Harmon, original story; Buchman and Shaw, screenplay; Ted Tetzlaff, cinematography. *118 minutes b&w*

TALK RADIO (1988)

★★★

Eric Bogosian

Eric Bogosian unleashes his acid tongue over the airwaves in Talk Radio.

Bogosian is spellbinding as a caustic radio talk-show host who baits hatemongers, toys with assorted weirdos, and soothes the lonely, on his late-night radio show. Based on Bogosian's off-Broadway play, the film is based on Alan Berg, the Denver talk-show personality who was murdered in 1984. Under the sure direction of Oliver Stone, the penetrating drama focuses on the media's penchant for exploiting the darker side of human nature. Also with Alec Baldwin, Ellen Greene, Leslie Hope, John Pankow, Michael Wincott, and John C. McGinley. **(R)** *110 minutes*

TALL IN THE SADDLE (1944)

★★★

John Wayne
Ella Raines

Ward Bond (right) learns the hard way why John Wayne sits Tall in the Saddle.

This movie available with closed captions for the hearing impaired.

Wayne plays a cowpoke who hates women, but changes his mind when a spinster (Raines) and her young niece take over the ownership of the ranch where Wayne is foreman. Despite the predictable twists and turns in the plot, this is an enjoyable film. Also with Ward Bond, Gabby Hayes, Elisabeth Risdon, Raymond Hatton, Russell Wade, Paul Fix, and Audrey Long. **Director**—Edwin L. Marin.
87 minutes b&w

THE TALL MEN (1955)

★★

Clark Gable
Jane Russell
Robert Ryan

Gable, Russell, and Ryan bolster the appeal of this standard western tale, but it doesn't offer much beyond some well-executed action scenes. Gable and Ryan play two Texans who head to Montana after the Civil War in search of their fortunes and meet many hazards along the way. Also with Cameron Mitchell, Emile Meyer, Juan Garcia, Mae Marsh, and Harry Shannon. **Director**—Raoul Walsh. *122 minutes*

THE TAMARIND SEED (1974)

★★

Julie Andrews
Omar Sharif

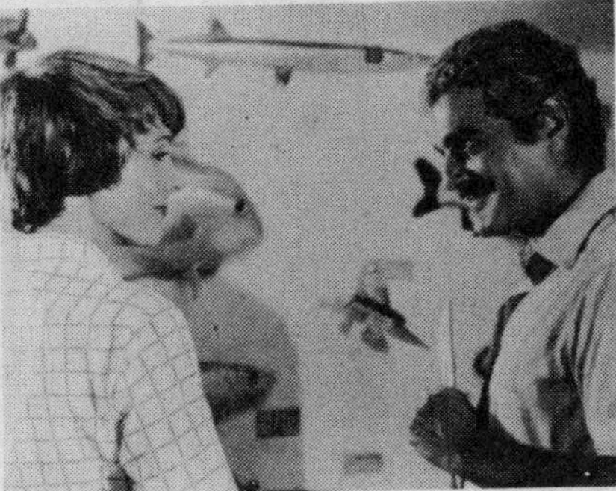

Julie Andrews falls for KGB agent Omar Sharif in The Tamarind Seed.

Andrews and Sharif star in this romance with an international backdrop—London, Paris, and Barbados—and an espionage storyline. Andrews plays a British widow who falls in love with a Russian agent, played by Sharif. The plot substitutes confusion for suspense, but the stars are appealing enough to keep the story interesting. The cast includes Anthony Quayle, Oscar Homolka, Daniel O'Herlihy, and Sylvia Sims. **Director**—Blake Edwards. **(PG)** *123 minutes*

THE TAMING OF THE SHREW (1967)

★★★

Richard Burton
Elizabeth Taylor

A boisterous version of Shakespeare's comedy. Burton and Taylor were at the peak of their careers when this film was made, and their interpretations of the roles are accessible and delightful to watch. An unpretentious and cinematic presentation of a Shakespeare play. The supporting actors include Michael York, Cyril Cusack, Victor Spinetti, Michael Hordern, Vernon Dobtcheff, Natasha Pyne, and Alan Webb. **Director**—Franco Zeffirelli. *122 minutes*

TAMMY AND THE BACHELOR (1957)

★★½

Debbie Reynolds
Leslie Nielsen

Country girl Debbie Reynolds looks for a boyfriend in Tammy and the Bachelor.

Reynolds, in the title role, nurses an injured pilot, played by Nielsen, back to health in this lightweight romantic comedy. The performance by Reynolds is spirited, energetic, and contagious enough so that the whole cast gets into step and makes the best of average material. The theme song, "Tammy," was a hit song for Reynolds. Also with Walter Brennan, Fay Wray, Mala Powers, Louise Beavers, Sidney Blackmer, and Mildred Natwick. **Director**—Joseph Pevney. *89 minutes*

TANGO AND CASH (1989)

★★½

Sylvester Stallone
Kurt Russell

Sylvester Stallone and Kurt Russell are forced into partnership in Tango and Cash.

Stallone dons glasses and a three-piece suit for this buddy film about two cops who are falsely accused of murder and sent to prison. Russell costars as his rumpled, sloppy cohort. Despite the adjustment to Stallone's familiar image, this action thriller features familiar villains and a predictable outcome. Though fans of the genre will enjoy the pairing of the two swaggering leads, the story is so slight as to be nonexistent and the dialogue lacks the clever banter of other films of this genre *(Lethal Weapon; Midnight Run)*. Competent direction from Andrei Konchalovsky helps compensate for the film's weaknesses. Jack Palance, the perennial heavy, costars as a brutal drug kingpin bent on annihilating the two heroes. Also with Teri Hatcher, Brion James, and Michael J. Pollard. **(R)** *98 minutes*

TANGO BAR (1988)

★★½

Raul Julia
Ruben Juarez
Valeria Lynch

This musical is for tango fans everywhere. The flimsy plot concerns a lounge act, a love triangle, and references to Argentina's repressive military government. There are delightful film clips of Fred Astaire, Charlie Chaplin, and even Fred Flintstone doing the tango. Julia is charming as a cabaret piano player. Originally filmed in Spanish. **Director**—Marcos Zurinaga.
(No MPAA rating) *90 minutes*

This movie available on videotape and/or disc.

TANK (1984)

★★½

James Garner
Shirley Jones
C. Thomas Howell

On the defensive: Jenilee Harrison and C. Thomas Howell in Tank.

Garner plays an Army sergeant major who owns his own Sherman battle tank, which he uses to rescue his teenage son from the clutches of a red-neck sheriff. The implausible story wavers from social commentary to yahoo farce, but Garner's performance and quiet air of authority carry the film. Worth watching. Also with Dorian Harewood and Jenilee Harrison. **Director**—Marvin J. Chomsky. **(PG)** *113 minutes*

TAP (1989)

★★★

Gregory Hines

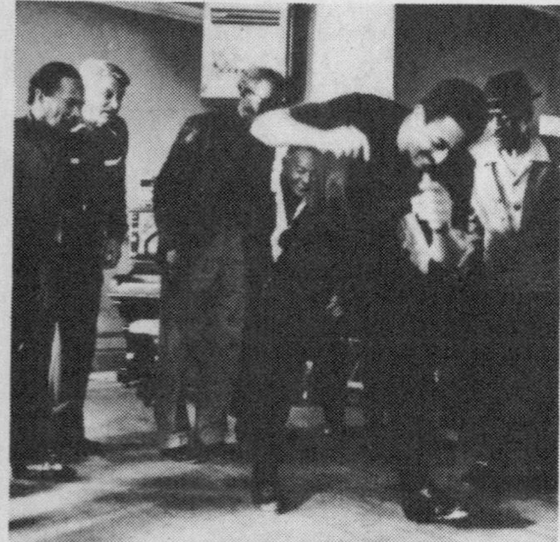

With joy in his step, Gregory Hines shows the others he can Tap.

This foot-stomping, energetic musical is a worthy tribute to tap dancing, which dominated musicals of the 1930s and 1940s. Hines stars as an ex-con struggling to revive his tap dancing career and start a romance with an ambitious dance teacher (Suzzanne Douglas). The major highlight is a sequence in which legendary hoofers Sandman Sims, Bunny Briggs, and others display their amazing talents. Sammy Davis, Jr., makes his final screen appearance here, which is a worthy finale to his legendary career as a song-and-dance man. **Director**—Nick Castle. **(PG-13)** *110 minutes*

TAPEHEADS (1988)

★★★

John Cusack
Tim Robbins

Tapeheads: *Tim Robbins and John Cusack size up the options in the music video biz.*

Cusack and Robbins play pals working as security guards who decide to strike it big with music videos. The plot has its weak moments, but the script is clever and the two stars well cast. The snappy music carries the picture: Soul singers Junior Walker and Sam Moore are on board, as are blues legends Bo Diddley and King Cotton. **Director**—Bill Fishman. **(R)** *97 minutes*

TAPS (1981)

★★

George C. Scott
Timothy Hutton

An ambiguous and farfetched drama about military-school cadets who take up arms to defend their academy and prevent it from being converted to a condominium development. Essentially, the film is a sentimental analogy of the attitude that led to involvement in Vietnam. The ponderous and predictable story stars Hutton as a gung ho and misguided cadet leader; Scott is impressive as the school's superintendent, but he fades away before the film is half over. Also with Ronny Cox, Tom Cruise, and Sean Penn. **Director**—Harold Becker. **(PG)** *118 minutes*

TARAS BULBA (1962)

★★

Yul Brynner
Tony Curtis

Action, violence, and superior photography highlight this Nikolai Gogol tale of a 16th-century revolt in Poland. Brynner portrays Taras Bulba, the famed Cossack leader, and Curtis plays one of the Cossack's sons. They give the conventional performances such films require. Also with Sam Wanamaker, Guy Rolfe, Abraham Sofaer, Christine Kaufmann, and Vladimir Sokoloff. **Director**—J. Lee Thompson. *122 minutes*

TARGET (1985)

★★★

Gene Hackman
Gayle Hunnicutt
Matt Dillon

Ex-CIA agent Gene Hackman springs to the defense of son Matt Dillon in Target.

A unique and pleasant father-son relationship is at the heart of this spy thriller set mostly in Europe. Hackman plays a stodgy lumberyard owner from Texas whose colorful CIA past is revealed when his wife (Hunnicutt) is kidnapped in Paris. Son Dillon gets in on the cloak-and-dagger action and discovers a new side to his father. Some routine car-chase scenes mar an otherwise involving film. **Director**—Arthur Penn. **(R)** *117 minutes*

® This movie available with closed captions for the hearing impaired.

TARZAN, THE APE MAN (1932)

★★★½

Johnny Weissmuller
Maureen O'Sullivan

The most popular of all the Tarzan movies remains the best. An expedition searching for ivory treasure discovers instead the great man of the jungle, convincingly portrayed by Olympic swimmer Weissmuller. He escapes into the jungle with Jane (O'Sullivan), and the two discover love, high above in the treetops. The film is full of well-known bits that are great fun to rediscover—especially Tarzan's first appearance, and the scene in which he discovers his attraction to Jane. From the novel by Edgar Rice Burroughs. With Neil Hamilton and C. Aubrey Smith. **Director**—W.S. Van Dyke. *104 minutes b&w*

TARZAN, THE APE MAN (1981)

(no stars)

Bo Derek
Miles O'Keeffe
Richard Harris

A Jane by any other name: Bo Derek goes native in Tarzan, the Ape Man.

The lord of the jungle is dethroned and relegated to the role of a silent sex symbol in this labored and shabby remake, which looks more like a pinup calendar than a movie. Practically all the attention is on Jane, played by beautiful Derek, who's frequently photographed in various stages of undress. Jane loses her way in the jungle, where she finds the magnificent ape-man, played by O'Keeffe, and the two "monkey around" together. Tarzan doesn't say a word, which is probably wise because everyone else is saddled with silly dialogue. **Director**—John Derek. **(R)** *112 minutes*

TATTOO (1981)

Bruce Dern
Maud Adams

Dern once again portrays an offbeat character. This time he's a tormented tattoo artist who kidnaps a glamorous model, played by Adams, and applies needlework all over her beautiful body. The story, which borrows heavily from *The Collector*, starts with some promise, but soon becomes sour and predictable. With Adams nearly nude through much of the ordeal, the film eventually resembles a sleazy soft-core skin flick. **Director**—Bob Brooks. **(R)** *103 minutes*

TAXI DRIVER (1976)

★★★★

Robert De Niro
Jodie Foster
Harvey Keitel

Taxi Driver *Robert De Niro struggles to establish a relationship with Cybill Shepherd.*

One of the ten best American films of the 1970s. Director Martin Scorsese depicts a brutally disturbing account of a lonely and psychotic New York cabbie. The experience evokes mixed emotions; it's depressing, violent, and cynical—yet undeniably brilliant. Paul Schrader's screenplay is his finest so far, and there's a dazzling performance by De Niro as the quietly unhinged Travis Bickle, who stalks a presidential candidate, but turns his sudden fury on the pimp of a young prostitute. Foster is impressive as a 12-year-old hustler, as is Keitel, who plays her pimp. The film is haunting and unforgettable. A dark comment on the confusing post-Watergate, post-Vietnam era. Also with Cybill Shepherd, Peter Boyle, and Albert Brooks. **(R) Academy Award Nominations**—best picture; De Niro, best actor; Foster, best supporting actress. *112 minutes*

TEA AND SYMPATHY (1956)

Deborah Kerr
John Kerr

Deborah Kerr and John Kerr—they're not related—give sensitive performances in this movie about a troubled schoolboy's affair with a teacher's wife. This film version of Robert Anderson's successful Broadway play is stagy at times, but the superior acting and characterizations more than compensate for the pace of the production. Leif Erickson, Edward Andrews, Norma Crane, Dean Jones, and Darryl Hickman also star. **Director**—Vincente Minnelli. *122 minutes*

TEACHERS (1984)

Nick Nolte
JoBeth Williams
Judd Hirsch
Ralph Macchio

Nick Nolte, Judd Hirsch, and JoBeth Williams in Teachers.

The odd mixture of comedy and drama ultimately mars this film about dedicated teachers who try hard to reject both bureaucratic nonsense and self-serving interests. Nolte plays a high-minded high-school teacher in this occasionally effective film, which tackles the chaotic state of public education in much the same way that director Arthur Hiller's *The Hospital* dealt with the world of medicine. Give Nolte and

(Continued)

This movie available on videotape and/or disc.

(Continued)
other good cast members high marks for fine acting. Also with Lee Grant, Art Metrano, and Allen Garfield. **Director**—Hiller. **(R)** *106 minutes*

TEACHER'S PET (1958)

★★★

Clark Gable
Doris Day
Gig Young

Clark Gable is trying to be Doris Day's Teacher's Pet.

Gable, Day, and Young star in this unpretentious and enjoyable comedy. Gable plays a tough newspaper editor who enrolls in Day's journalism course, but does not reveal his true identity. He tries to romance her, but is in competition with the intellectual and eccentric Young. The supporting cast includes Nick Adams, Mamie Van Doren, and Charles Lane. **Director**—George Seaton. **Academy Award Nominations**—Young, best supporting actor; Fay and Michael Kanin, best story and screenplay written directly for the screen. *120 minutes b&w*

TEA FOR TWO (1950)

★★

Doris Day
Gordon MacRae

A congenial cast, including Day, MacRae, Eve Arden, and Billy De Wolfe, keeps this musical, inspired by the play *No, No, Nanette,* wholesome and energetic. Although amusing and enjoyable, the predictable production lacks substance. Most of the activity centers on Day's decision to become interested in show business. Gene Nelson, Patrice Wymore, Bill Goodwin, and S.Z. Sakall round out the cast. **Director**—David Butler. *97 minutes*

THE TEAHOUSE OF THE AUGUST MOON (1956)

Marlon Brando
Glenn Ford

Brando is miscast as a cunning native interpreter in this pleasing film version of John Patrick's successful Broadway play. Fortunately, Ford, who plays a U.S. Army captain in charge of the rehabilitation of an Okinawan village in 1944, has a keen comic touch and carries the film, which was critically and financially successful in its day. Also with Machiko Kyo, Paul Ford, Henry Morgan, and Eddie Albert. **Director**—Daniel Mann. *123 minutes*

TEENAGE MUTANT NINJA TURTLES (1990)

★★1/2

Judith Hoag
Elias Koteas

A surprise attack on Judith Hoag and her green buddies, the Teenage Mutant Ninja Turtles.

An enjoyable though uneven live-action version of the *Teenage Mutant Ninja Turtles* cartoon series. Jim Henson's Creature Shop designed marvelous renditions of the titular tortoises for this film, which unfortunately suffers from mediocre direction and unexciting production design. The film is visually dark but not necessarily for reasons of style. Whether the intent was to hide any faults in the turtle suits, or whether it was the result of bad choices by director Steve Barron, is not known. In their first major screen outing, the Turtles try to stop a gang of thieves called the Foot Clan from turning New York's teenagers into juvenile criminals. They are helped by ace reporter April O'Neil, played by Hoag, who acts in that broad style usually found in high-school productions. The Turtles are entertaining, well designed, and colorful; the human actors pale in comparison. A must-see for children; worthwhile viewing for adults. A variety of human actors inhabit the Turtle costumes, including Joch Pais, Leif Tilden, Michelan Sisti, and David Forman. Corey Feldman provided the voice of one of the Turtles. **(PG)** *93 minutes*

TEEN WOLF (1985)

★★

Michael J. Fox

Uninspired, low-budget teen comedy about a high-school student (Fox) who discovers he's a werewolf. When the lad grows heavy hair all over and sprouts fangs, he scores with the girls and wins on the basketball court. Fox is pleasant enough in this lightweight role. The rest of the unknown cast strains with the weak material. Nothing to howl about. Also with James Hampton and Susan Ursitti. **Director**—Rod Daniel. **(PG)** *92 minutes*

TEEN WOLF TOO (1987)

★

Jason Bateman
Kim Darby

For this incredibly dull sequel to the 1985 box-office hit, *Teen Wolf,* Bateman takes over the adolescent werewolf role initially played by Michael J. Fox. Bateman, who portrays a cousin to the original teen werewolf, enters college on an athletic scholarship. There his secret is revealed and he deals with the familiar problems of self-esteem and love relationships in a virtual carbon copy of the original film's script. The acting is dreadful—Bateman, a popular TV actor, simply doesn't have the charm and comic timing of Fox, and the direction is leaden. John Astin, Paul Sand, and James Hampton appear in secondary roles. **Director**—Christopher Leitch. **(PG)** *95 minutes*

TELEFON (1977)

★★★

Charles Bronson
Lee Remick

Bronson stars as a Russian agent who pursues a deranged defector to the United States because the crazed man is trying to trigger World War III. The plot, which owes much to *The Manchurian Candidate,* is based on Walter Wa-

® This movie available with closed captions for the hearing impaired.

ger's novel. Remick costars as an innocent woman who is accidentally caught up in the intrigue. Bronson maintains his usual stone face amid the numerous action sequences, but his persona suits his role as a man taught to serve only his state. A captivating storyline and well-developed script by Stirling Silliphant and Peter Hyams. Locations range all over the globe—Moscow, Canada, and several cities in the United States. Also with Donald Pleasence, Tyne Daly, Patrick Magee, and Alan Badel. **Director**—Don Siegel. **(PG)** *102 minutes*

TELL ME A RIDDLE (1980)

★★★

Melvyn Douglas
Lila Kedrova

Melvyn Douglas and Lila Kedrova come to terms in Tell Me a Riddle.

Douglas and Kedrova star in this low-key film about an elderly couple who reconcile their long, quarrelsome marriage. Douglas and Kedrova create heartwarming, memorable characterizations. The film is often lacking in dramatic momentum, but there are many moments of beauty and sensitivity. Based on Tillie Olsen's acclaimed 1961 novella. Lee Grant, in her first time out as director, handles the job in a straightforward manner. Also with Brooke Adams, Bob Elross, and Joan Harris. **(PG)** *90 minutes*

TELL ME THAT YOU LOVE ME, JUNIE MOON (1970)

★★★

Liza Minnelli
Ken Howard
Robert Moore

There are some superb and moving moments in this strange tragicomedy about three handicapped people who decide to live together. The excellent acting of Minnelli (facially scarred), Howard (an epileptic), and Moore (a homosexual paraplegic) helps to carry the film over its rough spots. There are many flaws in this movie, but the sensitive treatment of the difficult and touching subject matter makes the film worthwhile viewing. The supporting cast includes James Coco, Fred Williamson, Kay Thompson, and Leonard Frey. **Director**—Otto Preminger. **(PG)** *113 minutes*

TELL THEM WILLIE BOY IS HERE (1969)

★★★

Robert Redford
Robert Blake

Redford and Blake star in this turn-of-the-century western about an Indian who flees after killing a man in self-defense. The film, under the excellent writing and direction of Abraham Polonsky, explores the cruel treatment of the American Indian by whites. Redford plays the sheriff who hunts down the Indian, played brilliantly by Blake. Also with Susan Clark, Barry Sullivan, Katharine Ross, John Vernon, Charles McGraw, and Charles Aidman. **(PG)** *98 minutes*

TEMPEST (1982)

★★

John Cassavetes
Gena Rowlands
Susan Sarandon
Vittorio Gassman

Molly Ringwald, Susan Sarandon, and John Cassavetes in Tempest.

Director Paul Mazursky (*An Unmarried Woman*) fashions a latter-day, middle-class comedy after Shakespeare's magical play. The result is a movie that's simultaneously intelligent and overblown. Though there are some good moments, pretension prevails. Cassavetes stars as a successful New York architect who retreats to an isolated Greek island to sort out his midlife crises. Rowlands portrays his actress wife. Also with Molly Ringwald and Raul Julia. **(PG)** *140 minutes*

10 (1979)

★★★

Dudley Moore
Julie Andrews
Bo Derek

Bo Derek became an overnight celebrity as the desirable beauty who rates a 10.

Moore stars as a middle-aged Hollywood songwriter in this romantic comedy about the frustrations involved in the pursuit of happiness. Director Blake Edwards skillfully sets up a number of funny situations for Moore, who stumbles and bumbles after a vision of beauty and youth, played by Derek. There are some slow spots, but Moore manages to keep the comic momentum rolling along. Andrews plays Moore's longtime girlfriend. Also with Robert Webber, Sam Jones, Dee Wallace, Max Showalter, and Brian Dennehy. **(R)** *123 minutes*

THE TENANT (1976)

★★★

Roman Polanski
Isabelle Adjani
Melvyn Douglas
Shelley Winters

Polanski directed and stars in this horror tale about a mild-mannered young

(Continued)

(Continued)
Pole who rents a Paris apartment and believes he's being persecuted by his neighbors. Polanski delivers some striking shock effects and an intense portrait of a man creating his own torture. However, the film doesn't reach the same degree of suspense or polish as Polanski's *Rosemary's Baby* or *Chinatown*. Also with Jo Van Fleet, Bernard Fresson, and Claude Dauphin. Be aware of the poor English dubbing of French-speaking cast members. **(R)** *126 minutes*

THE TEN COMMANDMENTS (1956)

★★★1/2

Charlton Heston
Yul Brynner

Moses (Charlton Heston) cradles the word of God in The Ten Commandments.

This biblical extravaganza about the life of Moses, culminating with his leading the Jews out of Egypt to the Promised Land, is the best known of the genre. Though not particularly thought-provoking, the film features a star-studded cast, lush photography, and brilliant dramatic moments. Heston, who plays Moses, and Brynner, as the pharaoh Ramses, head the huge cast, with Anne Baxter, Edward G. Robinson, Yvonne De Carlo, Martha Scott, Vincent Price, John Carradine, Cedric Hardwicke, John Derek, and Nina Foch among the many supporting actors. **Director**—Cecil B. De Mille. **(G) Academy Award Nominations**—best picture; Loyal Griggs, cinematography.
219 minutes

TENDER MERCIES (1983)

★★★★

Robert Duvall
Tess Harper

Tender Mercies: *Robert Duvall rebuilds his life with Tess Harper and Allan Hubbard.*

Australian Bruce Beresford's (*Breaker Morant*) outstanding American directorial debut. This extraordinary film concerns a has-been, drunken country singer (Duvall) who reclaims his self-respect when he marries a shy widow (Harper) with a young son. Duvall's brilliant performance projects an honest grittiness. Harper is magnificent in her first screen role, and the supporting players are equally as appealing. It's a compassionate, dignified portrait of loneliness, hope, and the tender mercies that help people deal with their lives. Also with Betty Buckley and Ellen Barkin. **(PG) Academy Awards**—Duvall, best actor; Horton Foote, best original screenplay written directly for the screen. **Nominations**—best picture; Beresford, best director. *93 minutes*

THE TENDER TRAP (1955)

Frank Sinatra
Debbie Reynolds
David Wayne
Celeste Holm

Delightful performances by Sinatra, Reynolds, Wayne, and Holm vitalize this ordinary comedy and make it worth viewing. Sinatra plays a New York agent who has a way with women until he eventually falls for the trap of marriage set by Reynolds. Lola Albright, Tom Helmore, and Carolyn Jones appear in supporting roles. **Director**—Charles Walters. *111 minutes*

TEN NORTH FREDERICK (1958)

Gary Cooper
Geraldine Fitzgerald

Cooper plays a wealthy man pushed by his domineering wife (Fitzgerald) into national politics. His bid for a shot at the vice-presidential nomination of his party never gets off the ground because of his family problems. The melodramatic approach to the material keeps the film from making any profound points. Based on John O'Hara's novel. Also with Diane Varsi, Suzy Parker, Stuart Whitman, Ray Stricklyn, and Tom Tully. **Director**—Philip Dunne.
102 minutes b&w

TEN TO MIDNIGHT (1983)

★★

Charles Bronson
Lisa Eilbacher

Tight-lipped Bronson portrays a veteran homicide detective trailing a psychopath who murders young women. The action heats up when the killer turns his attention to the detective's lovely daughter (Eilbacher). The lively screenplay packs in an unusual amount of suspense and some clever plot twists. Ultimately, however, the film yields to reactionary attitudes that advocate eye-for-an-eye punishment. **Director**—J. Lee Thompson. **(R)**
101 minutes

TEQUILA SUNRISE (1988)

Mel Gibson
Kurt Russell
Michelle Pfeiffer

Drug dealer Mel Gibson and policeman Kurt Russell are old buddies in Tequila Sunrise.

This slick crime melodrama is awash in style, but the twisting plot makes little sense. Gibson and Russell play childhood friends on opposite sides of the law—one is a retired drug dealer, the other a cop. Both vie for the attention of Pfeiffer. Director Robert Towne, noted for his scripts *Chinatown* and *The Last Detail*, keeps the audience in the dark with his muddled screenplay and un-

® This movie available with closed captions for the hearing impaired.

steady direction. The beautiful *film noir* cinematography and the star turns may attract some viewers. Also with Raul Julia, Arliss Howard, J.T. Walsh, Ayre Gross, and Ann Magnuson. **(R) Academy Award Nomination**—Conrad Hall, cinematography. *116 minutes*

THE TERMINATOR (1984)

★★★1/2

Arnold Schwarzenegger
Michael Biehn
Linda Hamilton

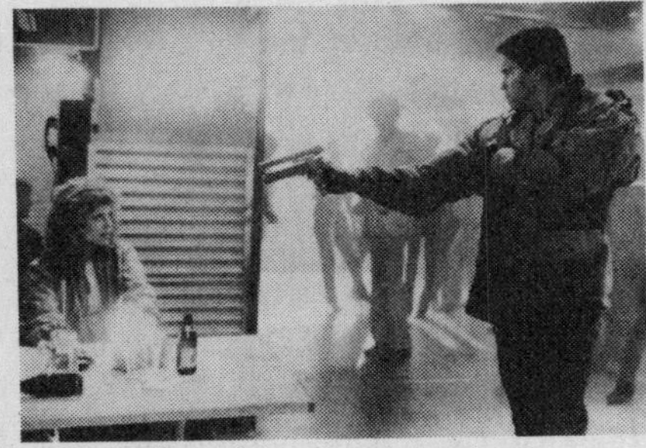

*Linda Hamilton is threatened by Arnold Schwarzenegger—*The Terminator.

Muscle-man Schwarzenegger plays a computer-controlled android from a future century who arrives in Los Angeles to assassinate a young waitress. A nonstop series of action scenes involving the android's relentless pursuit of the young girl makes for an exhilarating viewing experience. Though made on a low budget, this sci-fi thriller—one of the best in recent years—is well crafted by novice director James Cameron, who went on to greater success with *Aliens*. Schwarzenegger's role contains few lines, but his physical presence is overpowering. **(R)** *108 minutes*

TERMS OF ENDEARMENT (1983)

★★1/2

Shirley MacLaine
Debra Winger
Jack Nicholson

This tearjerker explores the love-hate relationship between a neurotic mother (MacLaine) and her strong-willed daughter (Winger). The plot meanders through emotional problems, funny situations, and the inevitable concluding tragedy. The film is blessed with some endearing, lifelike characters expertly portrayed by the top cast. Not surprisingly, Nicholson, in a supporting role, steals several scenes as a womanizing, over-the-hill astronaut. The simplistic storyline is manipulative, without being particularly profound or meaningful. Overrated at the time of release, the film will ultimately be remembered only as a boost to MacLaine's sagging cinematic career. **Director**—James L. Brooks. **(PG) Academy Awards**—best picture; Brooks, best director; MacLaine, best actress; Nicholson, best supporting actor; Brooks, best screenplay. **Nomination**—Winger, best actress. *129 minutes*

Shirley MacLaine and Debra Winger bring a touch of class to Terms of Endearment.

TERROR IN THE AISLES (1984)

★★

A haphazardly assembled compilation of scenes from such suspense classics as *Psycho* and *Rosemary's Baby,* as well as from more recent horror films, including *Halloween* and *Scanners*. The juxtaposition of the different types of horror films has little thought behind it, which lessens the impact of many sequences. Scenes of shock and grisly terror are highlighted over more traditional horror fare. Narrated by Donald Pleasence and Nancy Allen. **Director**—Andrew Kuehn. **(R)** *84 minutes*

TESS (1979)

★★★

Nastassja Kinski
Peter Firth
Leigh Lawson

Director Roman Polanski's excellent screen adaptation of the classic Victorian novel by Thomas Hardy is physically beautiful. Kinski plays the heroine, an exploited peasant girl who resorts to murder. Polanski remains faithful to the novel and the historic period, and there are authentic settings and striking costumes. Firth and Lawson costar. Also with John Colin. **(PG) Academy Award Nominations**—best picture; Polanski, best director. *170 minutes*

Nastassja Kinski steps up in class by marrying gentleman Peter Firth in Tess.

TESTAMENT (1983)

★★★★

Jane Alexander
William Devane

What happens to a small American community after a nuclear bomb destroys a nearby city? This grim film deals with this "unthinkable" situation with an amazing lack of sensationalism and still manages to be emotionally effective, unlike the similar, made-for-TV film *The Day After*. Alexander stars as a stalwart housewife who witnesses the deterioration of her community and the gradual deaths of her children and neighbors from radiation sickness. First-time director Lynne Littman handles this devastating subject with intelligence. **(PG) Academy Award Nomination**—Alexander, best actress. *90 minutes*

TEX (1982)

★★★

Matt Dillon
Jim Metzler

Walt Disney studios broke out of their familiar, naive style of storytelling with this engaging and straightforward story based on the S.E. Hinton novel. Two adolescent brothers (Dillon and Metzler) grow up in rural Oklahoma without parental support. The film touches on episodes involving sex,

(Continued)

This movie available on videotape and/or disc.

Troubled teen Matt Dillon struggles with life's passages in Tex.

(Continued)

drugs, and violence. Well acted by Dillon. Also with Emilio Estevez, Meg Tilly, Ben Johnson, and Bill McKinney. **Director**—Tim Hunter. **(PG)** *103 minutes*

THE TEXAS CHAINSAW MASSACRE (1974)

★★★

Marilyn Burns
Allen Danzinger

A brutal but fascinating horror film, which has attracted a cult following among midnight-movie fans, critics, and such directors as Steven Spielberg. A family of brutes in rural Texas engages in grisly mayhem against a group of innocent teens. The tension is almost unbearable with the frequent screams of the victims and the incessant buzzing of chainsaws. The screenplay is loosely based on the story of murderer Ed Gein, a Wisconsin maniac who collected body parts. **Director**—Tobe Hooper. **(R)** *86 minutes*

THE TEXAS CHAINSAW MASSACRE PART 2 (1986)

★1/2

Dennis Hopper
Caroline Williams

A grisly, disappointing sequel to the notorious 1974 cult film, which has spawned a cavalcade of splatter movies over the years. The crazy Sawyer family is now in the chili-making business, and their secret ingredient should come as no surprise to anyone who saw the original. Williams plays a disc jockey who is drawn into the Sawyers' bloody business. Hopper costars as a quirky Texas Ranger seeking revenge for his brother's children, who were killed in the first film. Bill Johnson stars as the hideous Leatherface. The sequel tries to employ the same gallows humor that made the original so controversial, but here the humor is overshadowed by too many drawn-out scenes of dismemberings, skinnings, and body organs flying about. Also with Jim Siedow and Bill Moseley. **Director**—Tobe Hooper. **(No MPAA rating)** *95 minutes*

THAT CHAMPIONSHIP SEASON (1982)

★★1/2

Robert Mitchum
Stacy Keach
Paul Sorvino
Bruce Dern
Martin Sheen

Keach, Dern, Mitchum, Sorvino, and Sheen: the solid cast of That Championship Season.

Jason Miller's screen version of his prizewinning play is less successful than the Broadway stage production. This portrait of four middle-aged men, who reveal their failures and frustrations during a 25th reunion of their championship high-school basketball team, is too talky and lacks drama. Some decent performances come through, however, with Mitchum especially effective as the aging coach. **Director**—Miller. **(R)** *110 minutes*

THAT DARN CAT! (1965)

★★★

Hayley Mills
Dean Jones

An entertaining movie about a talented cat who leads an FBI agent, played by Jones, to a gangsters' hideout to rescue a kidnapped woman. The film represents the Walt Disney studios at the height of their live-action filmmaking. The talented cast also includes Roddy McDowall, Ed Wynn, Dorothy Provine, and Elsa Lanchester. **Director**—Robert Stevenson. **(G)** *115 minutes*

THAT FORSYTE WOMAN (1949)

★★1/2

Greer Garson
Errol Flynn
Robert Young

Garson, Flynn, and Young make a valiant effort to bring John Galsworthy's novel *A Man of Property* to the screen with style and vitality. Unfortunately, this adaptation of Galsworthy's book is a fairly dull achievement. Garson is excellent as Irene Forsyte, an unhappily married woman, who falls in love with the young man (Young) her niece plans to marry. There are competent supporting performances from Walter Pidgeon, Janet Leigh, Aubrey Mather, and Harry Davenport. **Director**—Compton Bennett. *114 minutes*

THAT HAMILTON WOMAN (1941)

★★★

Laurence Olivier
Vivien Leigh

Star power: Laurence Olivier and Vivien Leigh in That Hamilton Woman.

Olivier and Leigh star in this costume drama, detailing the tragic romance of British naval hero Lord Nelson and Lady Emma Hamilton. The movie is too long, but many attractive scenes and the excellent acting make the movie worthwhile. The cast also includes Gladys Cooper, Alan Mowbray, Sara Allgood, Henry Wilcoxon, Halliwell Hobbes, and Heather Angel. **Director**—

® *This movie available with closed captions for the hearing impaired.*

Alexander Korda. **Academy Award Nomination**—Rudolph Maté, cinematography. **Alternate Title**—*Lady Hamilton.* *125 minutes b&w*

THAT OBSCURE OBJECT OF DESIRE (1977)

Fernando Rey
Carole Bouquet
Angela Molina

A symbolic drama about man's sexual and spiritual fantasies from the refined hand of Spanish director Luis Buñuel. A middle-aged man, played by Rey, pursues and is rebuffed by the object of his dreams. Elusively, his fantasy woman alternates between two different women (played by two different actresses, Bouquet and Molina), both of whom succeed in taunting and debasing him. The humor is wry and highly sophisticated, and the script, from a French novel, is witty and devastating in its satire. **(R) Academy Award Nominations**—best foreign-language film; Buñuel and Jean-Claude Carriere, best screenplay based on material from another medium. *100 minutes*

THAT'S DANCING (1985)

Paula Kella and Shirley MacLaine in a scene from That's Dancing.

A sparkling compilation of memorable movie dance scenes featuring the fancy footwork of such greats as Gene Kelly, Fred Astaire, Ginger Rogers, Ray Bolger, Cyd Charisse, Bill "Bojangles" Robinson, and Eleanor Powell. Latter-day hoofers John Travolta and Michael Jackson also display their talent. Kelly, Bolger, Sammy Davis, Jr., Mikhail Baryshnikov, Liza Minnelli, and others handle the narration. **Director**—Jack Haley, Jr. **(G)** *104 minutes*

THAT'S ENTERTAINMENT (1974)

Fred Astaire
Gene Kelly
Bing Crosby
Liza Minnelli

Astaire, Kelly, and several other film stars narrate segments of this compilation documentary that includes both well-known and unknown song-and-dance numbers from MGM's musicals. Such excellent musical productions as the final ballet from *An American in Paris* are included along with such lesser-known and awkward numbers as Clark Gable singing "Puttin' on the Ritz." The film is a valuable documentation of a genre no longer considered financially viable in Hollywood, as well as an opportunity for younger generations to see why Astaire, Kelly, Mickey Rooney, Judy Garland, etc., are now considered legendary figures in cinema. **Director**—Jack Haley, Jr. **(G)** *90 minutes*

THAT'S ENTERTAINMENT, PART 2 (1976)

Fred Astaire
Gene Kelly

This is another delightful stroll down Hollywood's memory lane, with more snippets from MGM's classic movies. The experience is like a visit with friends you haven't seen in 20 years. The well-constructed compilation of scenes is taken from more than 70 musicals, dramas, and comedy treasures from the MGM library. Some 100 top performers are featured. Kelly and Astaire narrate to bridge the footage. It was, and still is, great entertainment. **Director**—Kelly. **(G)** *113 minutes*

THAT'S LIFE (1986)

 ★★1/2

Jack Lemmon
Julie Andrews

Blake Edwards directed this heartfelt comedy about a well-heeled architect facing a midlife crisis. Lemmon stars as the sputtering, whining hypochondriac who goes to pieces on the threshold of his 60th birthday. Andrews costars as his supportive wife, who faces a more serious threat to her life. Though Lem-

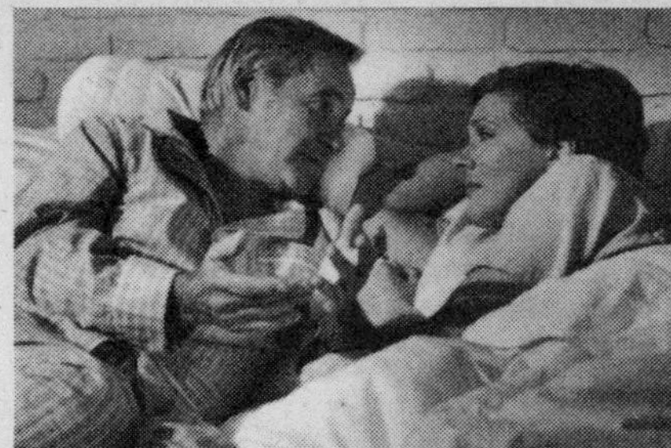

Jack Lemmon explains his life crisis to Julie Andrews in That's Life.

mon and Andrews are well cast in the main roles, Lemmon's character is unsympathetic; the film bogs down in the self-indulgent whinings of his character. Also with Chris Lemmon (Jack's son), Robert Loggia, Sally Kellerman, and Felicia Farr. **(PG–13) Academy Award Nomination**—Henry Mancini and Leslie Bricusse, best song ("Life in a Looking Glass"). *102 minutes*

THAT'S MY BOY (1951)

Dean Martin
Jerry Lewis

This early Martin and Lewis comedy concerns a clumsy son pushed by his father into becoming a football player just like the old man. Lewis is the teenage son, and Eddie Mayehoff is his father. Martin is hired to coach Lewis. Fans of Martin and Lewis might find something of merit here, but otherwise it is predictable entertainment. Also with Marion Marshall, Polly Bergen, and John McIntire. **Director**—Hal Walker. *98 minutes b&w*

THAT TOUCH OF MINK (1962)

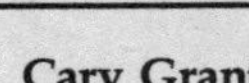

Cary Grant
Doris Day

Grant is so suave and debonair in this lightweight story, about a wealthy businessman who romances an unemployed secretary, that it doesn't matter that the plot is silly and the script flimsy. Day costars as the secretary. Gig Young, John Astin, Audrey Meadows, and Dick Sargent appear in supporting roles. **Director**—Delbert Mann. **Academy Award Nomination**—Stanley Shapiro and Nate Monaster, best story and screenplay written directly for the screen. *99 minutes*

THAT WAS THEN...THIS IS NOW (1985)

★★

Emilio Estevez
Craig Sheffer
Kim Delaney

Teen angst with Craig Sheffer and Emilio Estevez in That Was Then . . . This Is Now.

An earnest but dour teen drama rife with numerous shortcomings. Estevez stars as a troubled youth engaged in joyriding, fighting, goofing off, and resisting adulthood. Sheffer plays his best friend, whose interests take him in other directions. This brooding portrait of the adolescent world was adapted by Estevez from an S.E. Hinton novel. **Director**—Christopher Cain. **(R)**
102 minutes

THEATRE OF BLOOD (1973)

★★★

Vincent Price
Diana Rigg

The actor's revenge: Vincent Price and a mustachioed Diana Rigg in Theatre of Blood.

Price portrays a Shakespearean actor who gets even with eight critics, who have panned his performances, by killing them. His clever methods of disposal are re-creations of death scenes from the plays he has appeared in. Rigg plays his daughter. Price is perfectly cast as the demented thespian, and the fine supporting cast includes Robert Morley, Ian Hendry, Harry Andrews, Robert Coote, Jack Hawkins, Diana Dors, Milo O'Shea, Dennis Price, Eric Sykes, and Joan Hickson. **Director**—Douglas Hickox. **(R)** *104 minutes*

THEM! (1954)

★★★½

Edmund Gwenn
James Whitmore

Joan Weldon meets one of Them! *in Gordon Douglas' sci-fi classic.*

The giant ants are so vivid in this science-fiction film you might want to avoid picnics for a while. The mutated ants have grown to enormous proportions because of atomic radiation, and are running amok in the southwestern part of the United States. The movie is well crafted, and some of the scenes are truly startling—especially the tense climax in the sewers of Los Angeles. Joan Weldon, Fess Parker, James Arness, and Onslow Stevens do their share in supporting roles. **Director**—Gordon Douglas. *93 minutes b&w*

THERE'S A GIRL IN MY SOUP (1970)

★★

Peter Sellers
Goldie Hawn
Tony Britton

A mediocre movie version of the successful play by Terence Frisby. Sellers plays a television gourmet in search of

What a big bowl! Peter Sellers and Goldie Hawn in There's a Girl in My Soup.

fun, and Hawn becomes the disruptive force in his life. The trite and dated material manages only a few laughs. Diana Dors, Judy Campbell, Nicky Henson, and John Comer appear in supporting roles. **Director**—Roy Boulting. **(R)**
95 minutes

THERESE (1986)

★★

Catherine Mouchet

A curious, complicated interpretation of the life of St. Therese of Lisieux, the 19th-century French nun who was eventually canonized and became known as "The Little Flower of Jesus." The film presents a sober, close-up view of convent life and the attitudes and aspirations of the sisters, yet it unfolds with an obvious lack of continuity and clarity. Mouchet stars in the title role with supporting performances by Aurore Prieto and Sylvie Habault. Originally filmed in French. **Director**—Alain Cavalier. **(No MPAA rating)**
90 minutes

THERE'S NO BUSINESS LIKE SHOW BUSINESS (1954)

★★½

Ethel Merman
Dan Dailey
Marilyn Monroe
Donald O'Connor

Vibrant Irving Berlin music props up this weak musical about a family of vaudevillians and their struggles on and offstage. Merman and Dailey play the parents; O'Connor is one of their children and Monroe is O'Connor's girlfriend. The rest of the cast includes Mitzi Gaynor, Hugh O'Brian, Frank

This movie available with closed captions for the hearing impaired.

McHugh, and Johnny Ray. Merman sings the title song with spirit. Other tunes include "Play a Simple Melody" and "Heat Wave." **Director**—Walter Lang. **Academy Award Nomination**—Lamar Trotti, motion picture story.
117 minutes

THESE THREE (1936)

★★★★

Joel McCrea
Miriam Hopkins
Merle Oberon

A stirring drama about two women who operate a private girls' school. Their reputations are ruined by the malicious slander of a student. Based on the Lillian Hellman play *The Children's Hour*. The play's lesbian theme has been replaced with a conventional romantic triangle, but the drama is still effective. Highlighted by the riveting performances of Oberon and Hopkins as the teachers, and especially that of Bonita Granville as the vicious student. Also starring McCrea, Margaret Hamilton, and Walter Brennan. Remade by the same director in 1962 as *The Children's Hour*. **Director**—William Wyler. **Academy Award Nomination**—Granville, best supporting actress.
92 minutes b&w

THEY ALL LAUGHED (1981)

★★

Audrey Hepburn
Ben Gazzara
Patti Hansen

Ben Gazzara pursues Audrey Hepburn in the charming They All Laughed.

Director/writer Peter Bogdanovich misfires with this meandering comedy starring Hepburn and Gazzara. Essentially, it's about four inept private detectives in New York City who specialize in trailing various good-looking women married to jealous husbands. Yet nothing of great interest happens in this overstuffed sex farce; it has a hodgepodge of forgettable characters chasing around Manhattan. Also with John Ritter and Dorothy Stratten. **(PG)**
115 minutes

THEY CALL ME BRUCE? (1982)

★★

Johnny Yune
Margaux Hemingway
Ralph Mauro

Korean comic Yune squeezes a few laughs from this breezy send-up of martial-arts films. He's likable in his screen debut as a Walter Mitty type who pretends he has the prowess of kung-fu champ Bruce Lee. Some of the gags are humorous, but many of the comic situations are clichéd. This is a lighthearted affair, easy to digest, and just as easy to forget. **Director**—Elliot Hong. **(PG)** *88 minutes*

THEY DIED WITH THEIR BOOTS ON (1941)

★★★

Errol Flynn

Olivia de Havilland and Erroll Flynn in They Died with Their Boots On.

A lavish Hollywood treatment of General George Armstrong Custer's fight at the Little Bighorn. Flynn is dashing as the defeated general, though the film lacks historical accuracy. Olivia de Havilland, Arthur Kennedy, Anthony Quinn, Gene Lockhart, Sydney Greenstreet, Charles Grapewin, Hattie McDaniel, Stanley Ridges, and Walter Hampden appear in supporting roles. **Director**—Raoul Walsh.
141 minutes b&w

THEY DRIVE BY NIGHT (1940)

★★★

George Raft
Humphrey Bogart
Ann Sheridan
Ida Lupino

Trucker Humphrey Bogart is wearied by life on the road in They Drive by Night.

A well-crafted melodrama about honest truck drivers battling corruption in the trucking industry. An engrossing murder trial will hold your interest in the film's second half. The excellent script is by Jerry Wald and Richard Macaulay. Also with Alan Hale, Gale Page, George Tobias, and John Litel. **Director**—Raoul Walsh. *97 minutes b&w*

THEY LIVE (1988)

★★½

Roddy Piper
Keith David
Meg Foster

Keith David and Roddy Piper go after alien invaders in They Live.

A down-on-his-luck construction worker (Piper) discovers special eye-

(Continued)

(Continued)
glasses that reveal the presence of hideous aliens. The invaders' mission? Domination of Earth via subliminal thought control. An intriguingly paranoid premise, disquieting visuals, and dark humor compensate for this thriller's flat dialogue and lapses into absurd violence. Ex-wrestler Piper is quietly effective as the tough loner who becomes a "freedom fighter" almost against his will. Also with Raymond St. Jacques, Jason Robards III, and Peter Jason. **Director**—John Carpenter. **(R)**
115 minutes

THEY LIVE BY NIGHT (1949)

★★★½

Farley Granger
Cathy O'Donnell
Howard Da Silva

Captivating melodrama about the plight of two young lovers tragically involved with criminals during the Great Depression. Director Nicholas Ray, in his debut effort, handles the assignment with sensitivity and steers clear of clichés. Based on the novel *Thieves Like Us* and remade under that title in 1974 by Robert Altman. *95 minutes b&w*

THEY SHOOT HORSES, DON'T THEY? (1969)

Gig Young
Jane Fonda
Michael Sarrazin
Susannah York

This movie about a six-day marathon dance exquisitely captures the impoverished mood of the Great Depression. The production is well conceived and expertly staged, with excellent acting. The dance hall is actually a microcosm of the world, with the characters representing types or ideas: Fonda is a self-destructive cynic, Sarrazin is an aimless everyman who takes it all in, and York plays an innocent changed forever by the events of the marathon. Young won an Oscar as the coldhearted master of ceremonies. Also with Bruce Dern, Bonnie Bedelia, and Allyn Ann McLerie. **Director**—Sydney Pollack. **(PG) Academy Award**—Young, best supporting actor. **Nominations**—Pollack, best director; Fonda, best actress; York, best supporting actress; James Poe and Robert E. Thompson, best screenplay based on material from another medium. *123 minutes*

THEY WERE EXPENDABLE (1945)

★★★★

John Wayne
Robert Montgomery
Donna Reed

PT-boat skipper John Wayne confronts a landlubber in They Were Expendable.

Stirring World War II drama about fighting men on PT boats in the Pacific. An old-fashioned, straightforward film well directed by John Ford. Unlike many war dramas of this era, Ford's film exhibits a sense of perspective on the war, albeit a patriotic one. Ward Bond, Jack Holt, Marshall Thompson, Leon Ames, and Cameron Mitchell also star. *135 minutes b&w*

THIEF (1981)

★★★

James Caan
Tuesday Weld

Caan stars as a free-lance safecracker who pursues the American dream with passion and daring. One of Caan's best roles, this gripping character study is hard hitting, but still evokes sympathy from the viewer. Director/writer Michael Mann impressively executes his first feature film. Also with Willie Nelson, James Belushi, and Robert Prosky. **(R)** *126 minutes*

THE THIEF OF BAGDAD (1940)

★★★

Conrad Veidt
Sabu

This enchanting fairy tale involves a young thief, played by Sabu, who prevails over the forces of evil. Veidt is well cast as an evil magician. The tale remains fresh for those who don't take the story too seriously. The excellent photography and the acting by Sabu, Veidt, and Rex Ingram capture the quality of *Arabian Nights* on film. The cast also includes John Justin, June Duprez, Mary Morris, and Miles Malleson. **Directors**—Michael Powell, Ludwig Berger, and Tim Whelan. **Academy Award**—George Perinal, cinematography. *106 minutes*

THIEF OF HEARTS (1984)

★★

Steven Bauer
Barbara Williams

Barbara Williams takes target practice with Steven Bauer, the Thief of Hearts.

A cat burglar (Bauer) steals the secret diaries of a frustrated married woman (Williams). The contents describe her innermost sexual fantasies. Such privileged knowledge paves the way for seduction. While this setup has potential for suspense and steamy passion, the story concludes in a dead end. Williams' performance lacks passion, which this film needed in order to make the story believable. **Director**—Douglas Day Stewart. **(R)**
100 minutes

THE THIN BLUE LINE (1988)

★★★½

A riveting documentary that reexamines the 1976 murder of a Dallas policeman. The film strongly suggests that the wrong man was convicted of the crime. Filmmaker Errol Morris painstakingly interviews many of the witnesses and other figures in the case. Elements of the shooting are chillingly reconstructed to dramatize the possible

® This movie available with closed captions for the hearing impaired.

miscarriage of justice. Tension is relentless as Morris builds his case for exonerating the convicted man, who spent more than 11 years in prison before being released, largely due to this film. **(No MPAA rating)** *96 minutes*

THE THING (1982)

★★★

Kurt Russell

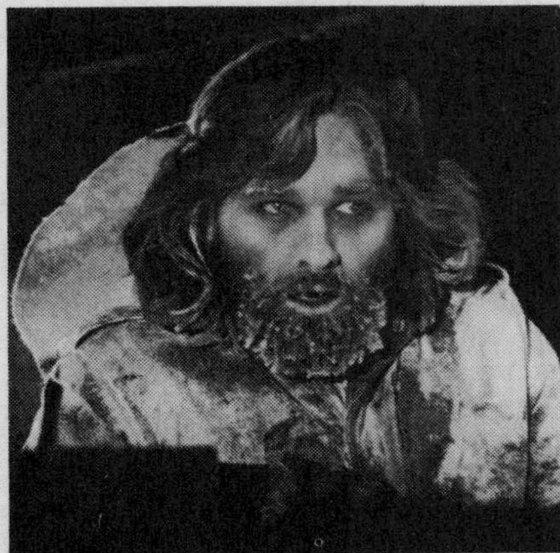

The nippy Antarctic climate is nearly as hard on Kurt Russell as The Thing.

John Carpenter's moody remake of the 1951 B-movie classic concentrates on outrageous, stomach-turning special effects, but does not ignore character or story. The plot involves scientists in Antarctica who stumble on a buried spaceship that contains a strange, frozen organism. When the creature thaws out, it escapes, killing and impersonating every life form within reach. Makeup wizard Rob Bottin deserves some credit for the success of the film, but it is Carpenter who manages to add depth to the fright through a sustained sense of isolation and alienation. Also with Wilford Brimley, Richard Dysart, Richard Masur, Donald Moffat, and T.K. Carter. **(R)** *108 minutes*

THINGS ARE TOUGH ALL OVER (1982)

★★

Cheech Marin
Tommy Chong

Cheech and Chong take a break from their familiar drug-oriented routine here, but they fail to provide much humor in its place. The laid-back twosome's adventure begins in a car wash and takes them to Las Vegas, where they connect with some wealthy Arabs. The boys play dual roles as themselves and as Middle Easterners. Director Thomas Avildsen handles the assignment with a steady hand but fails to contribute any freshness. Things are tough, indeed. **(R)** *87 minutes*

THINGS CHANGE (1988)

★★★1/2

Don Ameche
Joe Mantegna

Things Change *unexpectedly for innocent Don Ameche and small-time hood Joe Mantegna.*

Director David Mamet has created an endearing and well-drawn character—an elderly shoeshine man who becomes mixed up with the Mafia. A mob boss is in trouble for murder, and the gangsters convince Ameche to take the rap for the crime in exchange for a boat—the old man's lifelong dream. Ameche is absolutely perfect as the sweet, innocent Italian-American. Mantegna is marvelous as a young hoodlum who must keep an eye on the old man. Also with Robert Prosky, J.T. Walsh, and J.J. Johnson. **(PG)** *100 minutes*

THE THIN MAN (1934)

★★★★

William Powell
Myrna Loy
Maureen O'Sullivan

Highly enjoyable and entertaining combination of sophisticated humor and mystery, distilled from a Dashiell Hammett detective story. Powell and Loy are perfect in the roles of Nick and Nora Charles, the fun-loving, charming couple adept at handling the sleuthing chores. In their first screen caper, the pair solve the murder of a screwball inventor. Its success led the way to the ever-popular series of Thin Man adventures, which continued for more than 10 years. **Director**—W.S. Van Dyke. **Academy Award Nominations**—best picture; Van Dyke, best director; Powell, best actor; Frances Goodrich and Albert Hackett, adaptation. *93 minutes b&w*

THE THIRD MAN (1949)

★★★★

Joseph Cotten
Trevor Howard
Orson Welles
Alida Valli

Alida Valli and Joseph Cotten in the thriller The Third Man.

One of the best thrillers in the history of cinema. Graham Greene's story about a vile black-market operation in Vienna after World War II is excellently directed by Carol Reed. Cotten stars as an American writer of westerns, who comes to Vienna upon hearing of the death of his childhood friend Harry Lime, played by Welles. As Cotten begins to investigate, he learns what really happened to Harry. Welles' portrayal of the complex and unscrupulous Harry Lime dominates the film. Welles wrote much of his own dialogue, and some of the visuals in the film are reflective of Welles' own directorial style. The score by Anton Karas, emphasizing zither music, and the black-and-white photography by Robert Krasker also highlight the film. Also with Wilfrid Hyde-White, Bernard Lee, Paul Hoerbiger, and Siegfried Breuer. **Academy Award**—Krasker, cinematography. **Nomination**—Reed, best director. *104 minutes b&w*

THE 39 STEPS (1935)

★★★★

Robert Donat
Madeleine Carroll

Donat stars as an innocent man who becomes involved in international espi-

(Continued)

(Continued)

onage. He flees from England to Scotland before he is able to find the real villains and clear his name. Carroll plays a woman who believes Donat to be the real criminal. Perhaps Alfred Hitchcock's best film from his early years, the story represents one of his most familiar themes—that of an innocent man caught in circumstances not of his making, which he cannot control. The film also exhibits some of the visual motifs that would later become part of the Hitchcock style. Godfrey Tearle, Wylie Watson, and Peggy Ashcroft also star in this classic thriller.

81 minutes b&w

THIRTY SECONDS OVER TOKYO (1944)

Van Johnson
Spencer Tracy

Van Johnson and Spencer Tracy in Thirty Seconds over Tokyo.

Johnson and Tracy star in this exciting World War II film about the first attack on the Japanese mainland by the U.S. Army Air Force. Tracy plays Col. James Doolittle. Dalton Trumbo's excellent screenplay highlights this semidocumentary film. Robert Walker, Phyllis Thaxter, Robert Mitchum, Louis Jean Heydt, Paul Langton, Stephen McNally, and Scott McKay appear in supporting roles. **Director**—Mervyn LeRoy. **Academy Award Nomination**—Robert Surtees and Harold Rosson, cinematography. *132 minutes b&w*

THIS GUN FOR HIRE (1942)

★★★1/2

Alan Ladd
Veronica Lake

Ladd and Lake rose to stardom in this film version of the Graham Greene novel *A Gun for Sale*, about a hired killer who seeks revenge after being double-crossed. Ladd plays the professional killer. Laird Cregar, Robert Preston, and Tully Marshall also star in this well-made production. An atmospheric mystery tale, which exhibits the visual conventions of *film noir.* **Director**—Frank Tuttle. *81 minutes b&w*

THIS IS ELVIS (1981)

★★★

A blend of newsreels, videotapes, re-created scenes, and home movies provides an absorbing sociological portrait of the rock 'n' roll hero and his era. The fascinating documentary segments are effective in charting Elvis Presley's rise and decline. Though some may be surprised at the use of actors portraying Elvis to re-create key sequences from the pop idol's life, the ruse doesn't really mar the overall effect. Those acquainted with Elvis lore will realize that the film adds no new information or insights to the legend, but merely perpetrates the existing mythology surrounding his life. Some brief candid moments and the 38 musical numbers make this unique film well worth viewing. An interesting example of documentary filmmaking. **Directors**—Malcolm Leo and Andrew Solt. **(PG)**

88 minutes

THIS IS SPINAL TAP (1984)

Michael McKean
Christopher Guest

This Is Spinal Tap, *featuring the sublimely bad boys of rock.*

An unusual lampoon of rock music constructed as a mock documentary of a fading British heavy-metal band on tour in the United States. Rob Reiner, the film's director, appears as the deadpan interviewer of the far-out musicians. The humor is droll indeed, but the off-the-wall dialogue occasionally lapses into babble that becomes tiresome. McKean and Guest play the lead rockers with tongue-in-cheek playfulness. Also with Harry Shearer, Tony Hendra, and David Kaff. **(R)**

82 minutes

THIS IS THE ARMY (1943)

George Murphy
Joan Leslie

Song-and-dance man Murphy gets top billing in this wartime musical about soldiers during World War II who stage a show with the songs of Irving Berlin. Some of the material is dated now, and even at the time of its production much of it was mediocre, but there are still some entertaining moments. Among the many performers are Ronald Reagan, Alan Hale, Irving Berlin, Joe Louis, Kate Smith, George Tobias, Una Merkel, and Rosemary DeCamp. **Director**—Michael Curtiz. *121 minutes*

THIS THING CALLED LOVE (1941)

Rosalind Russell
Melvyn Douglas

Russell and Douglas star in this slightly saucy adult comedy about newlyweds who agree to test their marriage by not sleeping together for the first three months. Although the movie seems tame now and just mildly delightful, it was banned by the Legion of Decency upon its release. Binnie Barnes and Lee J. Cobb also star, with Allyn Josyln, Gloria Dickson, Don Beddoe, and Gloria Holden in supporting roles. **Director**—Alexander Hall. *98 minutes b&w*

THE THOMAS CROWN AFFAIR (1968)

Steve McQueen
Faye Dunaway

McQueen stars as a debonair millionaire who engineers a bank robbery because he's bored. Dunaway plays a glamorous investigator for an insurance company who stalks the suave thief. Unfortunately, the slick production lacks substance, aside from Dunaway's

This movie available with closed captions for the hearing impaired.

pursuit of McQueen. Jack Weston, Biff McGuire, and Paul Burke also appear. **Director**—Norman Jewison. **(R)**
102 minutes

THOROUGHLY MODERN MILLIE (1967)

★★1/2

Julie Andrews
Carol Channing
Mary Tyler Moore

Beatrice Lillie sums up the 1920s in Thoroughly Modern Millie.

Andrews stars in this musical spoof about a young lady who comes to New York City in the 1920s, falls in love with her boss, and becomes modern in the process. Even Andrews' immense talent, however, cannot sustain the production beyond the first hour. Despite its faults, the film contains some fine songs and dancing, plus quality supporting performances by Beatrice Lillie and James Fox. The cast also includes John Gavin, Anthony Dexter, and Jack Soo. **Director**—George Roy Hill. **(G) Academy Award Nomination**—Channing, best supporting actress.
138 minutes

THOSE LIPS, THOSE EYES (1980)

★★★

Frank Langella

Langella stars as a charming, second-rate actor who dreams of making it big on Broadway in this 1950s backstage romance. Langella's performance exudes poise and confidence and evokes pathos. Although limited in scope, this film is a tribute to those striving and hopeful thespians performing in summer stock and other byways of the theater. Also with Glynnis O'Connor and Thomas Hulce. **Director**—Michael Pressman. **(R)**
106 minutes

THOSE MAGNIFICENT MEN IN THEIR FLYING MACHINES, OR HOW I FLEW FROM LONDON TO PARIS IN 25 HOURS AND 11 MINUTES (1965)

★★★

Stuart Whitman
Robert Morley
Sarah Miles
Terry-Thomas

This long, lavish comedy/adventure film, with its superb photography and many stars, begins well, but becomes muddled toward the end. The story concerns a 1910 airplane race from London to Paris, with some cunning characters vying for the top prize. Whitman plays an American cowboy turned pilot, and Terry-Thomas portrays a devious rogue out to win at any cost. Red Skelton does a pleasant prologue to the film, detailing the early history of aviation. The large cast also includes Eric Sykes, Alberto Sordi, Gert Frobe, James Fox, Benny Hill, and Sam Wanamaker. **Director**—Ken Annakin. **(G) Academy Award Nomination**—Jack Davies and Annakin, best story and screenplay written directly for the screen.
138 minutes

A THOUSAND CLOWNS (1965)

★★★

Jason Robards
Martin Balsam
Barry Gordon
Barbara Harris

The splendid acting of Robards and Balsam sustains this strange comedy about a nonconformist New Yorker (Robards) who has dropped out of society's rat race for a life of philosophical introspection. The plot thickens when a social worker, played by Harris, pressures him to conform again for the sake of Gordon, who plays his teenage ward. Balsam costars as Robards' wealthy and successful brother. Also with William Daniels and Gene Saks. **Director**—Fred Coe. **Academy Award**—Balsam, best supporting actor. **Nominations**—best picture; Herb Gardner, best screenplay based on material from another medium.
118 minutes b&w

THOUSANDS CHEER (1943)

★★★

Kathryn Grayson
Gene Kelly

Grayson and Kelly head an all-star cast in this World War II musical about an Army base that stages a variety show. Although the plot is flimsy, the entertainment is tops. The large cast of stars includes Red Skelton, Lena Horne, Mary Astor, Margaret O'Brien, Judy Garland, June Allyson, Mickey Rooney, Eleanor Powell, and Lionel Barrymore. **Director**—George Sidney. **Academy Award Nomination**—George Folsey, cinematography. *126 minutes*

THREE AMIGOS (1986)

★★

Steve Martin
Chevy Chase
Martin Short

Martin Short, Chevy Chase, and Steve Martin are the Three Amigos.

This spoof of B-westerns stars Chase, Martin, and Short as movie cowboys who travel South of the Border under the assumption the trip is a publicity gig for their fans. Instead, they encounter real outlaws who fire real bullets. Though the hapless gringo characters are likable enough, the script and the performances are shallow and predictable. The three comedians are upstaged by Alfonso Arau, who plays the vilest of banditos. **Director**—John Landis. **(PG)** *103 minutes*

THREE COINS IN THE FOUNTAIN (1954)

★★★

Clifton Webb
Dorothy McGuire
Louis Jourdan
Jean Peters

This romantic melodrama, set in Rome, is about the search for love by three

(Continued)

(Continued)
American secretaries—McGuire, Peters, and Maggie McNamara. It's a pleasant film with no pretentions. The superior acting of Webb and Jourdan adds to the production's competence, as does the splendid on-location photography. Also with Rossano Brazzi, Howard St. John, and Cathleen Nesbitt. **Director**—Jean Negulesco. **Academy Awards**—Milton Krasner, cinematography; Jule Styne and Sammy Cahn, best song ("Three Coins in the Fountain"). **Nomination**—best picture. *102 minutes*

THREE COMRADES (1938)

★★★★

Margaret Sullavan
Franchot Tone
Robert Taylor
Robert Young

A searing portrait of post-World War I Germany conveyed symbolically through the story of three friends and their hopeless love for a young woman dying of tuberculosis. From the Erich Maria Remarque novel, this deeply moving and poignant tale of a shattered country ripe for fascism as reflected in the tragic lives of its young men still evokes tears from the viewer. Sullavan is wonderful as the life-loving but doomed girl. Beautifully photographed and directed. The fine supporting cast includes Guy Kibbee, Lionel Atwill, Henry Hull, George Zucco, Charley Grapewin, and Monty Woolley. **Director**—Frank Borzage. **Academy Award Nomination**—Sullavan, best actress. *98 minutes b&w*

THREE DAYS OF THE CONDOR (1975)

★★★

Robert Redford
Faye Dunaway

Redford stars as a researcher working for an information bureau of a CIA department in New York. One day he finds all his coworkers mysteriously murdered. He flees for his life, pursued by several different factions of the espionage network. Dunaway is the girl who protects him. The movie is both slick and exciting. Based on James Grady's novel *Six Days of the Condor.* Also with Cliff Robertson, Max Von Sydow, John Houseman, and Walter McGinn. **Director**—Sydney Pollack. **(R)** *118 minutes*

THE THREE FACES OF EVE (1957)

Joanne Woodward
Lee J. Cobb

Woodward stars as a troubled woman with three different personalities in this well-made drama. Cobb is excellent as a psychiatrist who tries to cure her so she can lead a normal life, but Alistair Cooke almost spoils the movie with his typically pompous narration. David Wayne, Edwin Jerome, Nancy Kulp, and Vince Edwards appear in supporting roles. **Director**—Nunnally Johnson. **Academy Award**—Woodward, best actress. *91 minutes b&w*

3:15: THE MOMENT OF TRUTH (1986)

Adam Baldwin
Deborah Foreman
Danny De La Paz

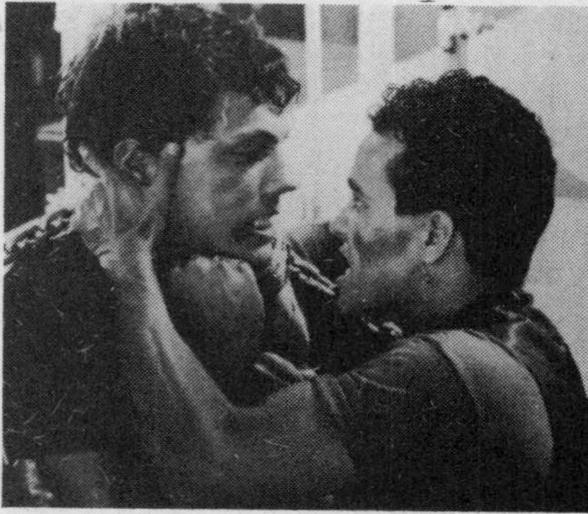

Gang violence between Adam Baldwin and Danny De La Paz in 3:15: The Moment of Truth.

Sleazy gang movie, set in an embattled high school, where switchblade-wielding punks run wild. The predictable plot features the traditional former gang member (Baldwin) who must face a showdown with the new hoodlum leader. The film works up to a familiar, violent climax with much snarling and trumped-up tension. **Director**—Larry Gross. **(R)** *86 minutes*

THREE FOR THE ROAD (1987)

Charlie Sheen
Kerri Green
Alan Ruck

Sheen almost permanently detoured his acting career with this frivolous road comedy. He plays a political aid assigned to escort a senator's headstrong daughter (Green) to a restrictive boarding school. Ruck costars as Sheen's friend and sidekick. Uninspired car chases and stale jokes litter the highway as the youths make their way to their destination. The direction is flat, the dialogue is dumb, and the acting is awkward at best. Raymond J. Barry appears as the blowhard senator; Sally Kellerman also appears in a small role. **Director**—B.W.L. Norton. **(PG)** *88 minutes*

THREE FUGITIVES (1989)

Nick Nolte
Martin Short
Sarah Rowland Doroff

Martin Short, Sarah Rowland Doroff, and Nick Nolte in Three Fugitives.

This american version of the French farce *Les Fugitifs* loses the comic punch of the original. Nolte, an ex-con who wants to go straight, is taken hostage during a holdup by a bumbling bank robber, played by comedian Short. The comedy consists of a series of chases and obvious slapstick. Doroff plays Short's daughter, but her cuteness can't compensate for the dumb escapades. Director Francis Veber adapted and directed his own film, *Les Fugitifs,* to make this unsuccessful remake. Also with James Earl Jones, Allan Ruck, Bruce McGill, and Kenneth McMillan. **(PG-13)** *96 minutes*

THE THREE GODFATHERS (1948)

John Wayne
Pedro Armendariz
Harry Carey, Jr.

This movie available with closed captions for the hearing impaired.

The best version of this frequently remade Christmas parable about three outlaws who find a newborn baby in the desert and adopt it. John Ford handles this sentimental story with respect and dignity, creating a moving drama. The three "wise men" are flawlessly played by Wayne, Armendariz, and Carey. Mildred Natwick, Ward Bond, Mae Marsh, Jane Darwell, and Ben Johnson costar. *106 minutes*

THREE LITTLE WORDS (1950)

★★★

Fred Astaire
Red Skelton

Fred Astaire and Red Skelton find fame as songwriters in Three Little Words.

This musical about famed songwriters Bert Kalmar and Harry Ruby features good dancing and snappy songs. Astaire and Skelton play the tunesmiths with charm and vitality, but the thin plot mars the film. The supporting cast includes Vera-Ellen, Arlene Dahl, Gale Robbins, Debbie Reynolds, and Gloria DeHaven. Also with Keenan Wynn and Phil Regan. **Director**—Richard Thorpe. *102 minutes*

THREE MEN AND A BABY (1987)

★★★

Tom Selleck
Steve Guttenberg
Ted Danson

This heartwarming comedy involves the misadventures of three swinging bachelors who care for a baby girl left unexpectedly on their doorstep. The plot becomes a bit more complicated when a second package containing cocaine also arrives. Their attempts to protect themselves and the baby from

Steve Guttenberg tends to his young charge in Three Men and a Baby.

both the drug dealers and the police make up the bulk of the storyline. But it is the scenes involving the three handsome, macho men trying to cope with a helpless baby that provide the most laughs and the best interaction between the actors. Based on the popular French comedy, *Trois Hommes et un Couffin*, the film was a long-running box-office success. Directed by actor Leonard Nimoy and featuring Nancy Travis, Philip Bosco, and Celeste Holm in supporting roles. Twins Lisa and Michelle Blair play the baby. **(PG)** *102 minutes*

THE THREE MUSKETEERS (1939)

★★★

Don Ameche
The Ritz Brothers
Binnie Barnes

There are at least four versions of Alexandre Dumas' classic adventure tale, and some cinema historians claim there might be as many as ten. This film with Ameche, the Ritz Brothers, Barnes, and Joseph Schildkraut in the key roles is good, lively fare. There's vibrant music, and the original story remains intact with the proper dose of romance and chivalric tradition. Also with Lionel Atwill, Miles Mander, and John Carradine. **Director**—Allan Dwan. *73 minutes b&w*

THREE O'CLOCK HIGH (1987)

★★

Casey Siemaszko
Richard Tyson

This *High Noon* for the teen set was directed by newcomer Phil Joanou, a Steven Spielberg protegé. Unfortunately, the material is trite and the film has little to offer that differs from countless other teen sagas. A bookish student (Siemaszko) is assigned to interview a fearsome bully (Tyson) for the school newspaper. During the course of events, Siemaszko accidently angers Tyson, resulting in the bully's declaration that he will beat the kid up after school. A number of subplots involving minor characters detract from the suspense. Also with Anne Ryan, Stacey Glick, Jonathan Wise, and Jeffrey Tambor. **(PG–13)** *90 minutes*

THREE WOMEN (1977)

★★★★

Sissy Spacek
Shelley Duvall
Janice Rule
Robert Fortier

Sissy Spacek and Shelley Duvall share an unusual relationship in Three Women.

Director Robert Altman's daring and absorbing psychological excursion of soul and character is an innovative film. Duvall's memorable and striking performance as the lonely and ostracized Millie Lammoreaux is the cornerstone of this examination of the quality of American life. Brilliant acting and characterizations from Spacek and Fortier add to the emotion and poetry. It's one of Altman's best films, and Duvall emerges as a major actress. Also with Ruth Nelson and John Cromwell. **(PG)** *125 minutes*

THRESHOLD (1981)

★★★

Donald Sutherland
Jeff Goldblum
Mare Winningham

A straightforward drama about a group of doctors who attempt the first self-contained artificial heart transplant.

(Continued)

(Continued)
The story lacks suspense, but the documentary approach and the avoidance of sentiment are appropriate to the subject matter. Sutherland is confident and dignified as one of the pioneering cardiac surgeons. Some of the operating-room scenes are startlingly realistic. Videotape versions of the film run 97 minutes. **Director**—Richard Pearce. **(PG)** *106 minutes*

THE THRILL OF IT ALL (1963)

★★★

Doris Day
James Garner

Day brightens this farce about a doctor's wife who becomes a star in television commercials. Garner is appealing as her husband. Carl Reiner wrote the script, which satirizes television ads and effectively captures their lunacy. Also with Arlene Francis, Zasu Pitts, Edward Andrews, Elliot Reid, and Reginald Owen. **Director**—Norman Jewison. *108 minutes*

THROUGH A GLASS DARKLY (1962)

 ★★★★

Harriet Andersson
Gunnar Bjornstrand
Max Von Sydow

Brilliant study of insanity set on the bleak island landscapes off the coast of Sweden. Writer/director Ingmar Bergman philosophically probes and questions man's relation to God through the tortured eyes of an emotionally disturbed young woman, hauntingly played by Andersson. Her husband, father, and brother—superbly portrayed by Bjornstrand, Von Sydow, and Lars Passgard—share the island with her for a summer, and experience a devastating descent into hell as Andersson goes beyond the brink. Originally filmed in Swedish. **Academy Awards**—best foreign-language film; Bergman, best story and screenplay written directly for the screen. *91 minutes b&w*

THROW MOMMA FROM THE TRAIN (1987)

 ★★½ 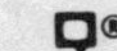

Danny DeVito
Billy Crystal

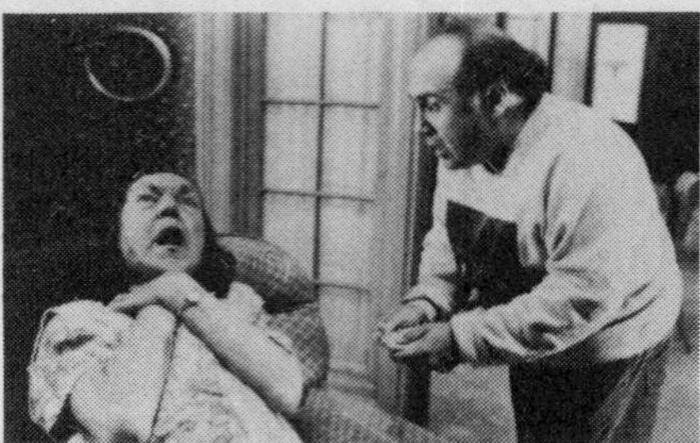

Anne Ramsey is driving Danny DeVito to Throw Momma from the Train.

Alfred Hitchcock's famed murder mystery *Strangers on a Train* provides the basis for this mildly amusing farce. DeVito portrays a particularly untalented writing student who wishes his ill-tempered mother (Anne Ramsey, in an Oscar-nominated performance) were dead. Crystal costars as DeVito's writing teacher, who fantasizes about bumping off his conniving ex-wife. The unlikely pair end up attempting to commit each other's murder to eliminate the appearance of motive, just like in the Hitchcock film. DeVito, who also directed the film, is excellent at creating eccentric comic characters and making them believable. His performance is the highpoint of this comic effort, which is too gloomy for lighthearted laughs and too soft for a wicked black comedy. Also with Kate Mulgrew. **(PG–13) Academy Award Nomination**—Ramsey, best supporting actress. *88 minutes*

THUNDERBALL (1965)

Sean Connery
Adolfo Celi

Connery stars as James Bond, and Celi appears as the archvillain who cleverly matches secret agent 007 step for step in this fourth Bond tale. SPECTRE plans to destroy the city of Miami if a huge ransom isn't paid. The plot is weak, but there are many slick gimmicks and the usual bevy of beautiful girls. The cast also includes Claudine Auger, Lois Maxwell, Luciana Paluzzi, and Bernard Lee. **Director**—Terence Young. **(PG)** *127 minutes*

THUNDER BAY (1953)

 ★★★

James Stewart
Joanne Dru

In this action-packed film, Stewart stars as an engineer who's convinced oil can be pumped from the sea off the coast of Louisiana. The conflicts between oil prospectors and shrimp fishermen provide the tension and action in the movie. Marcia Henderson, Dan Duryea, Gilbert Roland, Jay C. Flippen, and Anthony Moreno also appear in supporting roles. **Director**—Anthony Mann. *102 minutes*

THUNDER ROAD (1958)

Robert Mitchum
Keely Smith
James Mitchum

Robert Mitchum and Smith star in this exciting story about moonshiners and bootleggers in Kentucky. Robert Mitchum's low-key acting style is well suited to the role of a man who returns from prison to the only life he knows—bootlegging moonshine across county and state lines. James Mitchum (Robert's son) costars as a younger brother who wants to follow in big brother's footsteps, though his family wants him to go to engineering school. An air of doom and inevitability hangs over the film as Robert Mitchum's fate is sealed when he makes his first liquor run. A well-made B-movie that has attained a cult status. Robert Mitchum also cowrote and produced the film, in addition to writing the theme song. Gene Barry and Jacques Aubuchon also star. **Director**—Arthur Ripley. *92 minutes b&w*

THX-1138 (1971)

Robert Duvall
Donald Pleasence

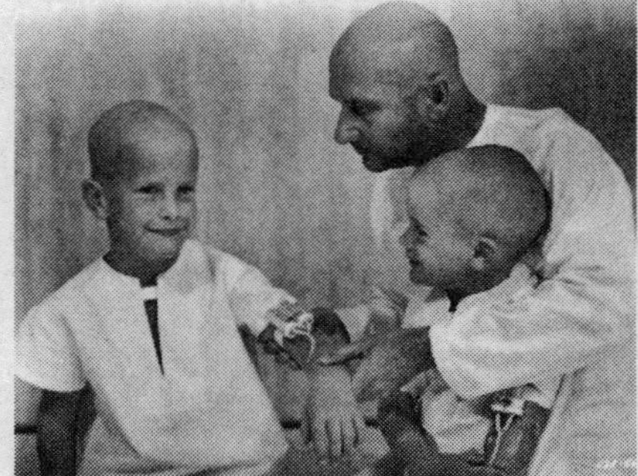

Donald Pleasence and two children in the sci-fi adventure THX-1138.

This early sci-fi effort by director George Lucas (*Star Wars*) is surprisingly mature. The cold, eerie, Orwellian set-

This movie available with closed captions for the hearing impaired.

ting is impressive, as is the cast, headed by Duvall. The film is set in the 25th century, where an autocratic regime presides over a population of robotlike humans. Also with Johnny Weissmuller, Jr., and Maggie McOmie. **(PG)** *88 minutes*

TICKET TO HEAVEN (1981)

 ★★★

Nick Mancuso
Meg Foster
Saul Rubinek

A hard-hitting docudrama about religious cults as experienced by a young Toronto schoolteacher, played by Mancuso. He joins a cult in California and is eventually rescued by friends and family. The film vividly details the young man's transformation into a near-robot through powerful indoctrination methods and concludes with a gut-wrenching deprogramming session. The film is engrossing despite the lack of sufficient background information. Also stars R.H. Thomson. **Director**—Ralph L. Thomas. **(PG)** *109 minutes*

THE TIGER MAKES OUT (1967)

Eli Wallach
Anne Jackson

Wallach is excellent as a frustrated postman turned kidnapper, and Jackson is good as the suburban housewife Wallach holds captive. Charles Nelson Reilly, Elizabeth Wilson, Bob Dishy, Ruth White, and John Harkins give solid supporting performances, but quality acting can't overcome the obtuse subject matter. Dustin Hoffman made his film debut in a bit part in this wacky and uneven comedy. **Director**—Arthur Hiller. *94 minutes*

TIGER WARSAW (1988)

 ★★

Patrick Swayze

Swayze, who lit up *Dirty Dancing*, is bogged down by a listless script in this maudlin family drama. He portrays a former drug addict who returns to his native working-class community in hopes of getting his life back on track. Fifteen years earlier he had abruptly left town after shooting his father during a violent confrontation. The story is little more than a soap opera, with synthetic dialogue and plodding direction. Also with Piper Laurie, Lee Richardson, Bobby DiCicco, and Kaye Ballard. **Director**—Amin Q. Chaudhri. **(R)** *92 minutes*

TIGHT LITTLE ISLAND

See Whisky Galore

TIGHTROPE (1984)

 ★★★

Clint Eastwood
Geneviève Bujold
Dan Hedaya

Clint Eastwood and Dan Hedaya investigate a homicide in Tightrope.

Eastwood once again portrays a tough cop, this time tracking a relentless sex killer in New Orleans. The result is a compelling police drama that concentrates on the complex character traits of both the hunter and the hunted. Much of the movie's appeal comes from the focus on Eastwood's character's fascination with the seamy side of life. Also with Alison Eastwood. **Director**—Richard Tuggle. **(R)** *115 minutes*

A TIGER'S TALE (1988)

 ★★

Ann-Margret
C. Thomas Howell

Howell stars as a teenage boy who falls in love with his girlfriend's beautiful mother in this tepid and absurd drama. Ann-Margret costars as the divorced nurse who eventually becomes romantically entangled with the starry-eyed youth. Both actors are worthy of better material. The film is set in Texas, and the local color is laid on a bit thick. Howell's father, played by Charles Durning, operates an exotic animal menagerie behind his gas station, which includes the tiger of the title. Everyone talks in an exaggerated accent, and the characters have names like "Bubber." Also with Kelly Preston, Ann Wedgeworth, and William Zabka. **Director**—Peter Douglas. **(R)** *97 minutes*

TILL THE CLOUDS ROLL BY (1946)

 ★★

Robert Walker

The entertaining songs of Jerome Kern make this star-studded movie about the life of the composer worthwhile viewing. Walker is adequate as Kern. June Allyson, Judy Garland, Van Johnson, Lena Horne, Tony Martin, Lucille Bremer, Kathryn Grayson, Frank Sinatra, Virginia O'Brien, Dinah Shore, Van Heflin, and Mary Nash are delightful in guest appearances, but too much of the movie is overly sentimental. **Director**—Richard Whorf. *137 minutes*

TILL THE END OF TIME (1946)

 ★★★

Dorothy McGuire
Guy Madison
Robert Mitchum
Bill Williams

This powerful drama about the romances and adjustment problems of three GIs returning to their hometown after service in World War II seems slightly dated now. Despite this, the excellent acting of McGuire, Madison, Williams, and Mitchum keeps the story fresh for contemporary viewers. Also with William Gargan, Jean Porter, and Tom Tully. **Director**—Edward Dmytryk. *105 minutes b&w*

TILL WE MEET AGAIN (1944)

Ray Milland
Barbara Britton

Britton plays a French nun who helps Milland, an American pilot, elude the Nazis and return to the Allies in this World War II drama. The good intentions surpass the weak plot, and the performances by the actors, who were in the prime of their careers, are excel-

(Continued)

(Continued)
lent. Also with Mona Freeman, Walter Slezak, Vladimir Sokoloff, Lucile Watson, and Konstantin Shayne. **Director**—Frank Borzage. *88 minutes b&w*

TIME AFTER TIME (1979)

★★★

Malcolm McDowell
David Warner

H.G. Wells and Jack the Ripper travel via time machine to contemporary San Francisco, where the Ripper resumes his penchant for carving up prostitutes. Wells' vision of a future Utopia is dashed when he realizes the Ripper's bloodthirsty behavior is small potatoes compared with the violence wrought by modern technology. A clever idea, well executed by writer/director Nicholas Meyer. McDowell, as Wells, is enjoyable. Similar in concept to Meyer's *The Seven-Percent Solution*, which featured the fictional character of Sherlock Holmes in a storyline with the historical Sigmund Freud. Warner plays the Ripper. Also with Mary Steenburgen, Charles Cioffi, and Kent Williams. **(PG)**
112 minutes

TIME BANDITS (1981)

★★★

John Cleese
Sean Connery
Shelley Duvall
Ian Holm

Sean Connery is the lusty King Agamemnon in Time Bandits.

A lively fantasy film, done in an imaginative style, which mocks science-fiction stories, history, and good-vs.-evil conflicts. An 11-year-old English lad, played by Craig Warnock, joins a band of dwarfs in a rollicking romp through time holes in space, where they meet such historical figures as Napoleon (Holm), Greek warrior Agamemnon (Connery), and Robin Hood (Cleese). The film will appeal to children of all ages, and it boasts a playful script, tasteful direction, and splendid special effects. Also with Katherine Helmond, Michael Palin, Ralph Richardson, Peter Vaughn, and David Warner. **Director**—Terry Gilliam. **(PG)** *110 minutes*

A TIME OF DESTINY (1988)

★★

William Hurt
Timothy Hutton
Melissa Leo

A Time of Destiny: *William Hurt and Timothy Hutton during World War II.*

A preposterous melodrama about family conflicts, set against the backdrop of World War II. The story begins when the daughter (Leo) of an old-world rancher elopes with her all-American boyfriend (Hutton). While trying to retrieve the daughter home, the father dies in an accident. Hurt, as the eldest son of the old gentleman, seeks revenge on Hutton in an extreme fashion. Many twists and turns of the plot plus a great deal of frantic activity characterize the film, yet it is still painfully dull. The big-name cast miscalculated with this soap-opera drama. Also with Francisco Rabal, Concha Hidalgo, and Stockard Channing. **Director**—Gregory Nava. **(PG–13)**
118 minutes

THE TIME OF THEIR LIVES (1946)

★★★

Bud Abbott
Lou Costello
Marjorie Reynolds

A seance turns up two Revolutionary ghosts in The Time of Their Lives.

This imaginative comedy about ghosts haunting a country estate is one of the best Abbott and Costello films. Costello and Reynolds play ghosts from Revolutionary times. They complicate life for Abbott and his friends. Interestingly, in this movie, Bud and Lou don't work as a team. Fine supporting performances by Binnie Barnes, and Gale Sondergaard help to make this a pleasant viewing experience. **Director**—Charles Barton. *82 minutes b&w*

THE TIME OF YOUR LIFE (1948)

★★★

James Cagney
William Bendix

Excellent acting by Cagney and Bendix sparks this film version of the prize-winning play by William Saroyan. Broderick Crawford and Ward Bond also star in this whimsical story about a group of offbeat characters who discuss their lives and the nature of things as they sit and drink in a small saloon in San Francisco. Although there's little action, the film is nonetheless fascinating. **Director**—H.C. Potter.
109 minutes b&w

TIMERIDER (1983)

★★

Fred Ward
Belinda Bauer

An absurd mixture of contemporary motorcycle movies and horse operas. Ward is a hotshot biker who, through the help of a time machine, finds himself and his motorcycle in Mexico in the year 1875. There he gets involved with a gang of outlaws in shoot-'em-up confrontations. The characters are cardboard and the tongue-in-cheek dialogue is frequently annoying. Also with Richard Masur, Peter Coyote, Ed

Lauter, and L.Q. Jones. **Director**—William Dear. **(PG)** *93 minutes*

TIMES SQUARE (1980)

★★

Trini Alvarado
Robin Johnson
Tim Curry

Alvarado plays a runaway teenager whose land of Oz is the glittering sleaze of New York City's 42nd Street. She teams up with a streetwise urchin, played by Johnson, and together they perform in a strip joint (without stripping), put on a punk-rock concert, and engage in various pranks. Curry plays a disc jockey. The film, aimed at teenagers, has ample energy, but the story is hardly convincing. The production seems to be mostly a promotion for the soundtrack. **Director**—Alan Moyle. **(R)** *111 minutes*

A TIME TO LOVE AND A TIME TO DIE (1958)

★★★

John Gavin
Lilo Pulver

Gavin stars as a German officer who falls in love with a woman (Pulver) during a furlough. The acting in this film version of Erich Maria Remarque's novel is above average, and some effective scenes near the beginning highlight this love story set against the backdrop of WWII Germany. The cast also includes Remarque, Keenan Wynn, and Jock Mahoney. **Director**—Douglas Sirk. *132 minutes*

THE TIN DRUM (1979)

★★★

Angela Winkler
Mario Adorf
Daniel Olbrychski
David Bennent

The Tin Drum: *Troubling allegory with David Bennent (left) and Mario Adorf.*

Artistic, stirring, yet complex allegory based on the epic German novel by Günter Grass. Bennent, who was 12 when filming began, is extraordinary as a dwarf who refused—from the age of three—to grow any more as a protest against the absurdities and obscenities of the adult world. Director Volker Schlöndorff captures much of the anguish of the Nazi period with haunting pictorial splendor. Yet the film is as puzzling as it is moving. Originally filmed in German. **(R) Academy Award**—best foreign-language film. *141 minutes*

TIN MEN (1987)

★★★

Danny DeVito
Richard Dreyfuss
Barbara Hershey

Rival siding salesmen Richard Dreyfuss and Danny DeVito have at it in Tin Men.

An intelligent and colorful comedy about feuding, flimflamming aluminum-siding salesmen. Writer/director Barry Levinson captures the patter, camaraderie, and lifestyle of these con men, who operate among vulnerable Baltimore homeowners in the early 1960s. Dreyfuss and DeVito star as rival tin men (slang for siding salesmen), who compete for the affections of Hershey as the ultimate test of who is the better man. The production design and attention to detail perfectly evoke the era. Comic Jackie Gayle and John Mahoney costar as fellow siding-pitchmen. **(R)** *108 minutes*

TIN PAN ALLEY (1940)

★★★

Alice Faye
Betty Grable
John Payne
Jack Oakie

Familiar musical about two struggling songwriters of the pre-World War I era. The music and dancing are so delightful it doesn't matter that the story is trite. Inspired performances by Faye, Grable, Payne, and Oakie are the main reason the production sparkles. The cast also includes Elisha Cook, Jr., Esther Ralston, Allen Jenkins, Billy Gilbert, and John Loder. **Director**—Walter Lang. *95 minutes b&w*

TITANIC (1953)

★★

Clifton Webb
Barbara Stanwyck
Robert Wagner

Another film version about the destruction of the famous ship in 1912. The plot consists mostly of personal stories involving the many passengers on board. Not as effective as other films on the subject, such as *A Night to Remember.* Also with Audrey Dalton, Brian Aherne, and Allyn Joslyn. **Director**—Jean Negulesco. **Academy Award**—Charles Brackett, Walter Reisch, and Richard Breen, story and screenplay. *98 minutes b&w*

TOBACCO ROAD (1941)

★★★

Charley Grapewin
Elizabeth Patterson

This film version of Erskine Caldwell's famed novel and play loses some of its punch in its translation to the screen. Some vivid scenes do remain, however, in this tragicomedy about poor whites in Georgia being pushed off their land. Grapewin and Patterson star, with Dana Andrews, Marjorie Rambeau, Gene Tierney, William Tracy, Russell Simpson, and Grant Mitchell in supporting roles. **Director**—John Ford. *84 minutes b&w*

TO BE OR NOT TO BE (1942)

★★★★

Jack Benny
Carole Lombard

This brilliant black comedy concerns a group of actors in Poland during WWII who get involved in a plot to outwit the invading Nazis. At the time of its release, some critics thought this propaganda movie was in bad taste, but it's

(Continued)

This movie available on videotape and/or disc.

Carole Lombard assists Jack Benny's impersonation of a Nazi in To Be or Not to Be.

(Continued)
now considered a classic comedy. Its difficult subject matter was handled in a sympathetic and effective manner. It was Lombard's last movie. Skillfully directed by Ernst Lubitsch. Also with Lionel Atwill, Sig Rumann, Tom Dugan, Robert Stack, Stanley Ridges, and Felix Bressart. *100 minutes b&w*

TO BE OR NOT TO BE (1983)

★★½

Mel Brooks
Anne Bancroft

Brooks and Bancroft star in this remake of the 1942 classic Ernst Lubitsch comedy. Although not as droll as the original, the sequel, produced by Brooks, is still entertaining, as Brooks and Bancroft apply their own brand of farcical humor to the misadventures of a second-rate acting troupe in wartime Poland. Tim Matheson, Charles Durning, and José Ferrer are in supporting roles. **Director**—Alan Johnson. **(PG) Academy Award Nomination**—Durning, best supporting actor. *108 minutes*

TOBRUK (1967)

★★

Rock Hudson
George Peppard

Hudson and Peppard are well cast in this adventure tale about a small band of soldiers assigned to destroy German Field Marshal Erwin Rommel's fuel supply at Tobruk in North Africa during World War II. Nigel Green, Jack Watson, Liam Redmond, Guy Stockwell, Percy Herbert, and Leo Gordon appear in supporting roles. The acting is passable and the production is well done, but there's nothing about this movie to distinguish it from dozens of other war films. **Director**—Arthur Hiller. *110 minutes*

TO CATCH A THIEF (1955)

★★★

Cary Grant
Grace Kelly

Elegant Grace Kelly awaits her larcenous paramour in To Catch a Thief.

A jewel thief, who has retired to the French Riviera, is suspected of returning to his trade. Grant, who plays the reformed thief, and Kelly, as the woman in his life, account for much of the film's enchanting quality. Though more lighthearted than the usual Hitchcock fare, the film still exhibits his taut visual style and key thematic element—that of a man falsely accused. Jessie Royce Landis, Charles Vanel, Brigitte Auber, and John Williams are in supporting roles. **Academy Award**—Robert Burks, cinematography. *97 minutes*

TO HAVE AND HAVE NOT (1945)

★★★½

Humphrey Bogart
Lauren Bacall

Bogart and Bacall are marvelous in this story about a fishing-boat captain who reluctantly gets involved in fighting the Nazis. The movie is loosely based on one of Ernest Hemingway's novels. This was Bacall's film debut, and the attraction between Bogart and Bacall onscreen reflected that in real life. The script by Jules Furthman and gritty black-and-white photography by Sid Hickox highlight the film, but ultimately it is the Bogart/Bacall romance for which the film will be remembered. Supporting cast includes Walter Brennan, Marcel Dalio, Sheldon Leonard, Dolores Moran, and Hoagy Carmichael. **Director**—Howard Hawks. *100 minutes b&w*

Humphrey Bogart and Lauren Bacall foil the Nazis in To Have and Have Not.

TO HELL AND BACK (1955)

★★½

Audie Murphy

Murphy stars in this story based on his military career in World War II; he was the nation's most decorated soldier. Murphy is surprisingly good and doesn't overdo the heroics. The battle sequences are superior to the weak story. The above-average supporting performances of Susan Kohner, Marshall Thompson, Charles Drake, Paul Picerni, Jack Kelly, and David Janssen enhance the film. **Director**—Jesse Hibbs. *106 minutes*

TO KILL A MOCKINGBIRD (1962)

★★★★

Gregory Peck
Mary Badham

Peck stars as a lawyer in a small southern town who defends a black man accused of rape. Peck gets top-notch acting support from Philip Alford, John Megna, Robert Duvall, and Brock Peters. Screenwriter Horton Foote did an excellent job of translating Harper Lee's novel to the screen, and much of the atmosphere of the time and place remains intact. **Director**—Robert Mulligan. **Academy Awards**—Peck, best actor; Foote, best screenplay based on material from another medium. **Nom-**

® This movie available with closed captions for the hearing impaired.

Gregory Peck and Frank Overton (rear) defy their neighbors in To Kill a Mockingbird.

inations—best picture; Mulligan, best director; Badham, best supporting actress; Russell Harlan, cinematography. *129 minutes b&w*

TOKYO JOE (1949)

★★

Humphrey Bogart

Bogart stars in this dull, slow melodrama about an ex-nightclub owner who returns to Tokyo after World War II and becomes involved in smuggling and blackmail to protect his ex-wife and child. There are occasional moments that are reminiscent of Bogart's better films, but they are few and far between. Also with Sessue Hayakawa, Florence Marly, Alexander Knox, Jerome Courtland, and Lora Lee Michel. **Director**—Stuart Heisler. *88 minutes b&w*

TO LIVE AND DIE IN L.A. (1985)

★★1/2

William Petersen
Willem Dafoe
John Pankow

John Pankow (left) and William Petersen go bad in To Live and Die in L.A.

William Friedkin, who directed the action-packed *The French Connection* on location in New York, here uses similar tactics in a West Coast locale. The cynical story concerns the all-out, brutal efforts of a Secret Service agent to nab a counterfeiter/murderer. Friedkin makes use of exciting car chases and several overblown effects to heighten excitement. However, the lack of any likable characters and the overly intense acting deprive the film of emotional appeal. The style of the film is slick and modern, which unfortunately overshadows the grim story. **(R)** *116 minutes*

TOM HORN (1980)

★★

Steve McQueen
Richard Farnsworth
Linda Evans

Ready to show his skill as a marksman, Steve McQueen is Tom Horn.

McQueen stars as the title character, a real-life gunfighter who was hanged at the turn of the century for killing a boy. The film was based on Horn's letters from prison in which he claimed he had been framed for the murder. Though the letters might have provided some interesting details on the life of this legendary western folk-hero, this disappointing film features nothing spectacular. Some attempt at portraying Horn as a man past his era is evident, but the romance with Evans interferes with that theme. Also with Billy Green Bush and Slim Pickens. **Director**—William Wiard. **(R)** *98 minutes*

TOM JONES (1963)

★★★1/2

Albert Finney

Finney is splendid as the impish, free-spirited 18th-century hero of Henry Fielding's novel. At times, there's too much emphasis on the bawdy humor. But the joy of the story prevails, and the sexual high jinks and culinary exploits of Tom Jones are exhilarating. Finney gets royal acting support from Susannah York, Edith Evans, Diane Cilento, Joan Greenwood, Joyce Redman, Rachel Kempson, Wildfrid Lawson, and Hugh Griffith. **Director**—Tony Richardson. **Academy Awards**—best picture; Richardson, best director; John Osborne, best screenplay based on material from another medium. **Nominations**—Finney, best actor; Griffith, best supporting actor; Cilento, Evans, and Redman, best supporting actress. *129 minutes*

TOMMY (1975)

★★★

Ann-Margret
Oliver Reed
Roger Daltrey

Ann-Margret and the blind, deaf-mute pinball champion, Tommy.

This celebrated rock opera by the Who is a clamorous, energetic film about a child who becomes deaf, mute, and blind after seeing his father killed. He grows up to become pinball champion of the world and a messiah figure. The colorful cast also includes Elton John, Jack Nicholson, Eric Clapton, Keith Moon, and Tina Turner. **Director**—Ken Russell. **(PG) Academy Award Nomination**—Ann-Margret, best actress. *108 minutes*

TOM SAWYER (1973)

★★

Johnnie Whitaker
Jeff East
Jodie Foster

This musical version of the Mark Twain classic is too squeaky-clean to have

(Continued)

This movie available on videotape and/or disc.

(Continued)
much appeal for adults, but kids might find it enjoyable. Whitaker and East play Tom Sawyer and Huck Finn, respectively. Although they haven't captured the magic of the characters, Foster plays Becky Thatcher with energy. Celeste Holm costars as Aunt Polly and Warren Oates plays the colorful Muff Potter. Filmed on location in Missouri. **Director**—Don Taylor. **(G)**
104 minutes

TONY ROME (1967)

★★★

Frank Sinatra

A well-paced detective tale featuring Miami private eye Tony Rome, who tries to solve a jewel robbery and the murder of a beautiful woman. In some ways, it's reminiscent of the 1940s *films noirs*, but Sinatra lacks the melancholy and depth of Bogart's detectives. Still, the intricate story and tough dialogue make the film appealing. The cast also includes Simon Oakland, Sue Lyon, Jill St. John, Richard Conte, Lloyd Gough, Lloyd Bochner, Jeffrey Lynn, and Gena Rowlands. **Director**—Gordon Douglas.
110 minutes

TOOTSIE (1982)

★★★½

Dustin Hoffman
Teri Garr
Jessica Lange
Dabney Coleman
Charles Durning
Bill Murray

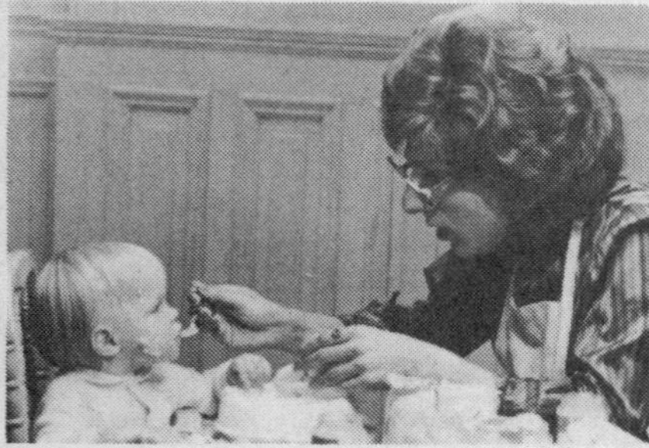

Dustin Hoffman discovers the fulfillment of "women's work" in Tootsie.

Hoffman is charming, funny, and touching as a desperate actor who masquerades as a middle-aged woman to win a role in a soap opera. His character is so extraordinary that he (she) becomes a media celebrity. He also becomes wiser for his experiences as a woman. The engaging comedy is filled with delicious complications and original humor. Though an acting triumph for Hoffman, his role in the film was criticized by feminists for implying that men make the best women. Lange is terrific as the woman who befriends him as a woman. **Director**—Sydney Pollack. **(PG) Academy Award**—Lange, best supporting actress. **Nominations**—best picture; Pollack, best director; Hoffman, best actor; Garr, best supporting actress; Larry Gelbart, Murray Schisgal, and Don McGuire, best screenplay written directly for the screen; Owen Roizman, cinematography.
110 minutes

TOPAZ (1969)

★★

Frederick Stafford
John Forsythe

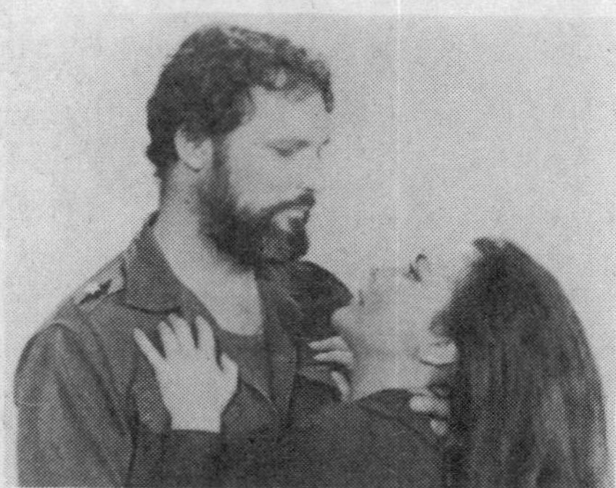

John Vernon and Karin Dor in supporting roles in Topaz.

A dated espionage adventure about a French intelligence agent who works with an American agent to get information about Russia's involvement in Cuba. Stafford plays the French spy, and Forsythe is the U.S. agent. John Vernon, Michel Piccoli, Philippe Noiret, Karin Dor, Roscoe Lee Browne, and Dany Robin give competent supporting performances in this rather routine enterprise, based on the Leon Uris novel. One of director Alfred Hitchcock's lesser efforts. **(PG)** *126 minutes*

TOP GUN (1986)

★★★

Tom Cruise
Kelly McGillis
Anthony Edwards

A well-crafted movie about jet fighter-pilots, starring teen idol Cruise in a role that helped him break into more mature films. Cruise plays a pilot nicknamed "Maverick," who is assigned to "Top Gun," a special flight school designed to hone the skills of the finest pilots. Maverick's nickname is derived from his inability to work with a team; and the themes of individual glory vs. teamwork, discipline vs. frivolous derring-do, and responsibility vs. rivalry are at the core of the narrative. Though a subplot involving a romance between Cruise and McGillis, one of his instructors, is predictable, it does highlight an interesting element of the film: Director Tony Scott presents Cruise and the other handsome young men as the sex objects, rather than McGillis. The well-toned bodies of the pilots are frequently shown in various states of undress, while warm, glowing light flows over their rippling muscles. Excellent visuals enhance the film, which was a box-office smash at the time of its release. Also with Val Kilmer, Meg Ryan, Michael Ironside, and Tom Skerritt. **(PG) Academy Award**—Giorgio Moroder and Tom Whitlock, best song ("Take My Breath Away"). **Nominations**—Billy Weber and Chris Lebenzon, best editing; Donald Mitchell, Keven O'Connell, Rick Kline, and William Kaplan, best sound; Cecilia Hall and George Watters II, best sound effects editing. **(PG)** *109 minutes*

TOP HAT (1935)

★★★★

Fred Astaire
Ginger Rogers

Sophisticated: Fred Astaire and Ginger Rogers in Top Hat.

Astaire and Rogers are magnificent in this musical about a case of mistaken identity. Astaire pursues the love of his

® This movie available with closed captions for the hearing impaired.

life from England to Italy, but she thinks he's married to her best friend. The performances of Edward Everett Horton, Erik Rhodes, Helen Broderick, and Eric Blore add to this film's charm and vibrancy. The Irving Berlin songs include "Top Hat, White Tie and Tails," and "Cheek to Cheek." Some prints are 93 minutes. **Director**—Mark Sandrich. **Academy Award Nomination**—best picture. *100 minutes b&w*

TOPKAPI (1964)

★★★

Melina Mercouri
Maximilian Schell
Peter Ustinov
Robert Morley

This movie, based on Eric Ambler's novel *The Light of Day*, is about an international gang after jewels in the Topkapi Museum in Istanbul. A lighthearted crime caper, the film inspired many imitators in the 1960s. The excellent acting by Ustinov, Morley, Mercouri, Schell, and Akim Tamiroff highlights the film. **Director**—Jules Dassin. **Academy Award**—Ustinov, best supporting actor. *122 minutes*

TOPPER (1937)

★★★1/2

Cary Grant
Constance Bennett
Roland Young

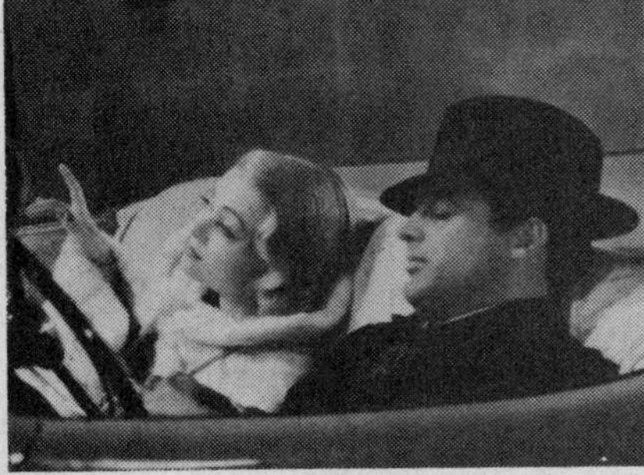

The party couple, Constance Bennett and Cary Grant, are the ghosts in Topper.

Charming comedy of a meek banker haunted by his swinging neighbors, who die in a car accident and reappear to Topper at awkward moments. This film classic gave rise to several sequels as well as the famous TV series, but the original is still a gem. Grant and Bennett are the irreverent and madcap ghosts who take pleasure in haunting and embarrassing Young as Topper, the gentle, bumbling banker. Billie Burke is superb as Mrs. Topper, as are Alan Mowbray, Eugene Pallette, Arthur Lake, and Hedda Hopper. **Director**—Norman Z. McLeod. **Academy Award Nomination**—Young, best supporting actor. *97 minutes b&w*

TOP SECRET (1984)

★★★

Val Kilmer
Lucy Gutteridge
Jim Carter
Omar Sharif

Lucy Gutteridge and Val Kilmer trapped in a plot in Top Secret.

Directors Jim Abrahams, David Zucker, and Jerry Zucker, the creators of *Airplane!*, spoof World War II spy movies with smart sight gags and funny dialogue. It doesn't fly as high as *Airplane!*, but it's fun all the same. Kilmer stars as an Elvis-style rock singer caught up in a dastardly plot to unite East and West Germany by force. **(PG)** *90 minutes*

TORA! TORA! TORA! (1970)

★★1/2

Martin Balsam
Jason Robards
Joseph Cotten

At the time of its release, some critics quipped that this movie about the attack on Pearl Harbor cost more than the actual military operation; the cost of the movie was estimated at about $25 million. Aside from the expense, this is an above-average war movie, but others with lower budgets have been much better. The film is at its best when it documents—from both sides—historical events, such as mistakes by those in charge, and when it reproduces the horrors of the infamous attack. Also with James Whitmore, E.G. Marshall, Soh Yamamura, Edward Andrews, Leon Ames, and Takahiro Tamura. **Directors**—Richard Fleischer, Ray Kellogg, Toshio Masuda, and Kinji Fukasaku. **(G) Academy Award Nomination**—Charles F. Wheeler, Osami Furuya, Sinsaku Himeda, and Masamichi Satoh, cinematography. *144 minutes*

TORCHLIGHT (1985)

★

Pamela Sue Martin
Steve Railsback

Pamela Sue Martin and Steve Railsback confront the specter of cocaine in Torchlight.

The tragic failure of a marriage because of cocaine addiction is examined with an unfortunate lack of determination and dramatic momentum. Martin (who cowrote the screenplay) plays an accomplished artist who marries a successful construction executive (Railsback). When he becomes heavily involved in the drug scene, he predictably goes down the drain and the movie heads in the same direction. Also with Ian McShane and Al Corley. **Director**—Tom Wright. **(R)** *90 minutes*

TORCH SONG TRILOGY (1988)

★★1/2

Harvey Fierstein
Anne Bancroft
Brian Kerwin
Matthew Broderick

Fierstein's award-winning play is adapted for the screen. He reprises his likable role as a mournful drag queen in search of love and respect. Unfortunately, the film reduces this sympathetic character to a chronic whiner, and much of the comic energy of the play is missing. Bancroft is convincing as his voluble Jewish mother who has diffi-

(Continued)

This movie available on videotape and/or disc.

(Continued)
culty with her son's life-style. Also with Karen Young and Charles Pierce. **Director**—Paul Bogart. **(R)** *117 minutes*

TORN APART (1990)

★★½

Adrian Pasdar
Cecilia Peck

Pasdar and Peck (Gregory Peck's daughter) star in a Middle East version of *Romeo and Juliet*. Pasdar stars as an Israeli soldier; Peck plays an Arab schoolteacher. Their relationship is made impossible by the conflict between the Palestinians and the Israelis. This well-intentioned film poignantly conveys the tragedy of the ongoing war, but the structure is awkward. Too much of the outcome depends on the age-old narrative device of the undelivered letter, while Pasdar's reminiscences get in the way. Still, the fine performances, evocative photography, and stirring music will win over some viewers. Also with Machram Huri, Arnon Zadok, Barry Primus, and Margrit Polak. **Director**—Jack Fisher. **(R)** *96 minutes*

TORN CURTAIN (1966)

★★½

Paul Newman
Julie Andrews

Director Alfred Hitchcock's 50th film, about an American science professor who becomes involved with espionage by undertaking a secret mission in East Germany, is strangely flat and devoid of depth for a film by the "Master of Suspense." Newman, who plays the professor, is competent in his role, but Andrews is dull as his secretary and lover. Also with Lila Kedrova, Ludwig Donath, Wolfgang Kieling, Tamara Toumanova, and David Opatoshu. **(PG)** *125 minutes*

TORPEDO RUN (1958)

★★★

Glenn Ford
Ernest Borgnine

Ford and Borgnine star in this well-made submarine adventure. Ford plays a sub commander who sinks an enemy ship carrying members of his own family and must live with the knowledge. Dean Jones and Diane Brewster appear in supporting roles. **Director**—Joseph Pevney. *98 minutes*

TORRID ZONE (1940)

★★★

James Cagney
Pat O'Brien
Ann Sheridan

An entertaining period piece featuring action and romance on a banana plantation in Central America. Cagney and O'Brien are rivals for Sheridan's affections. Sharp dialogue hides some of the holes in the plot and helps the trio brighten the movie. Also with George Tobias, George Reeves, Helen Vinson, Jerome Cowan, and Andy Devine. **Director**—William Keighley. *88 minutes b&w*

TORTILLA FLAT (1942)

★★★

Spencer Tracy
Hedy Lamarr
John Garfield
Frank Morgan

This uneven film version of John Steinbeck's novel is too philosophical and slow-moving to be a great film, but outstanding performances by Tracy, Garfield, and Morgan make the movie worth viewing. The story concerns the joys and sorrows of a group of poor Mexicans in a California fishing community. The three stars get excellent support from Akim Tamiroff, Connie Gilchrist, Henry O'Neill, Sheldon Leonard, John Qualen, and Donald Meek. **Director**—Victor Fleming. **Academy Award Nomination**—Morgan, best supporting actor. *106 minutes b&w*

TO SIR, WITH LOVE (1967)

★★★

Sidney Poitier
Judy Geeson
Lulu

Poitier is charming as a West Indian schoolteacher who's assigned to instruct tough white pupils in London's rough East End. The story is sentimental at times, as Poitier copes with the problems of his students, but the supporting performances by Geeson, Suzy Kendall, Christian Roberts, Patricia Routledge, and Faith Brook prevent the movie from becoming too maudlin. Lulu sings the title song, which became a pop classic. **Director**—James Clavell. *105 minutes*

TOTAL RECALL (1990)

★★★

Arnold Schwarzenegger
Rachel Ticotin
Sharon Stone

Schwarzenegger stars in this big-budget science-fiction thriller as an ordinary worker in the 21st century. His life seems pleasant until he uncovers information that confuses him: He discovers that he is either a pawn in a Martian struggle against a vicious tyrant, or he has simply been programmed to believe that. Either way, his enemies pursue him with the latest in lethal weapons. Based on a story by sci-fi great Philip K. Dick, the slight plot is fleshed out with much violence and mayhem. But, as directed by Paul Verhoeven (the original *Robocop*), the violence is exciting and the pace is breathtaking. Some will find the violence disturbing; others will see it as standard fare for action films. The production design—which emphasizes a cold, steely gray and blood red—enhances the themes of repressive institutions and the need to rebel against them. Also with Ronny Cox, Michael Ironside, Marshall Bell, Michael Champion, Mel Johnson, Jr., and Roy Brocksmith. **(R)** *109 minutes*

TOUCH AND GO (1987)

★★ ®

Michael Keaton
Maria Conchita Alonso

An offbeat romantic comedy starring Keaton as a pro hockey player who falls in love with a poor Hispanic single mother (Alonso) after being mugged by her delinquent son (Ajay Naidu). Although the relationship with the mother is touching, the film is slowly paced and saddled with bland dialogue. The hockey scenes do little to enliven the slack story. **Director**—Robert Mandel. **(R)** *101 minutes*

A TOUCH OF CLASS (1973)

★★

Glenda Jackson
George Segal

Without the performances of Jackson and Segal, this production would seem

® *This movie available with closed captions for the hearing impaired.*

Glenda Jackson and George Segal make music together in A Touch of Class.

more like a touch of trash. The story is about an American insurance broker, played by Segal, who has an affair with Jackson, a British dress designer. There isn't much more to the story of this romantic comedy, and even with the acting of the twosome, the tale falters at times. Paul Sorvino and Hildegard Neil appear in supporting roles. **Director**—Melvin Frank. **(PG) Academy Award**—Jackson, best actress. **Nominations**—best picture; Frank and Jack Rose, best story and screenplay based on factual material or material not previously published. *105 minutes*

TOUCH OF EVIL (1958)

★★★★

Orson Welles
Charlton Heston
Janet Leigh

A highly stylized film by Orson Welles about a narcotics agent, played by Heston, who attempts to foil a crime while in Mexico on his honeymoon. Welles also stars in the film, as the corrupt chief of police in a seedy Mexican border town. The tawdry village is the perfect background for the cavalcade of prostitutes, thieves, drunks, and ruffians who populate it. The visual style—including the use of wide-angle lenses to distort the image, the high-angle shots, and the pervasive use of shadows—reflects the twisted corruption of Welles' character and his town. An excellent example of how style complements and enhances a storyline. A 108-minute version also exists, which is the version available on videotape. Marlene Dietrich, Mercedes McCambridge, Joseph Calleia, Akim Tamiroff, Dennis Weaver, Joanna Moore, and Zsa Zsa Gabor are also in the cast. *93 minutes b&w*

TOUGH ENOUGH (1983)

★

Dennis Quaid
Warren Oates
Carlene Watkins
Stan Shaw

Dennis Quaid hopes he's Tough Enough *to practice the sweet science.*

Repetitive and unimaginative boxing bouts dominate this imitation of *Rocky.* The story is set in Texas and Detroit, and Quaid is not very impressive as a country singer who turns to amateur prizefighting to meet the mortgage payments. The script is shot full of clichés, and it's obvious from the start that Quaid will dispose appropriately of his various ring opponents. **Director**—Richard Fleischer. **(PG)** *107 minutes*

TOUGH GUYS (1986)

★★½

Burt Lancaster
Kirk Douglas

They've still got what it takes: Burt Lancaster and Kirk Douglas are Tough Guys.

Old pros Lancaster and Douglas have a good time portraying senior-citizen train robbers who emerge from the slammer after 30 years. The two face many difficulties adjusting to contemporary society, which is the setup for much of the humor. Eventually they become tired of being patronized and return to their crooked ways. Sadly, the trite material does not do justice to the legendary stars. Each gag and comic episode is predictable and often childish. Eli Wallach steals a few scenes as an over-the-hill, half-blind hit man. Also with Charles Durning, Darlanne Fluegel, and Alexis Smith. **Director**—Jeff Kanew. **(PG)** *100 minutes*

TOUGH GUYS DON'T DANCE (1987)

★½

Ryan O'Neal
Isabella Rossellini

Ryan O'Neal and Isabella Rossellini in Tough Guys Don't Dance.

Celebrated author Norman Mailer wrote and directed this mystery thriller set in Provincetown, and his lack of filmmaking experience is painfully obvious. O'Neal stars as an ex-con and sometimes writer heavily involved in such self-destructive practices as drug dealing and wife swapping. His hedonistic lifestyle is interrupted when he discovers a severed head in his house. Though many rich and interesting characters come and go in the film, the meandering plot is almost incoherent. The past and present mingle without any indication which characters belong where. It is apparent that Mailer was less interested in the storyline than he was with character and mood, but the viewer is not given enough straightforward information to get involved with the film on any level. Also with Debra Sandlund, Wings Hauser, John Bedford Lloyd, and Lawrence Tierney. **(R)** *109 minutes*

THE TOWERING INFERNO (1974)

★★1/2

Paul Newman
Steve McQueen
William Holden
Faye Dunaway
Fred Astaire

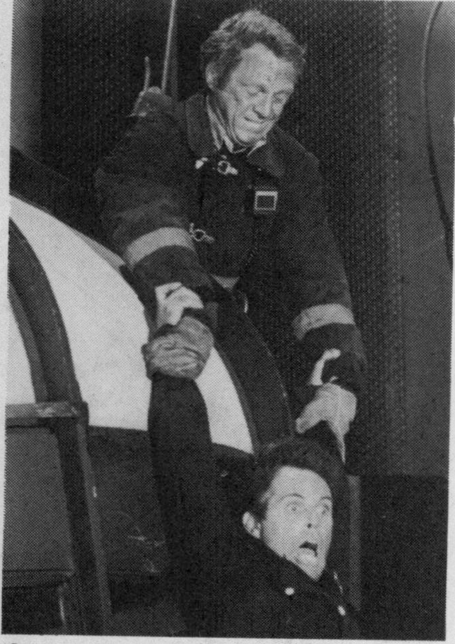

Steve McQueen attempts to rescue Ernie Orsatti from The Towering Inferno.

This mediocre production about a raging fire in the world's tallest building boasts some brilliant special effects and an all-star cast, but the film emphasizes the many gruesome ways there are to die a fiery death. The cast also includes Susan Blakely, O.J. Simpson, Robert Wagner, Richard Chamberlain, Robert Vaughn, and Jennifer Jones. **Directors**—John Guillermin and Irwin Allen. **(PG)** **Academy Award**—Fred Koenekamp and Joseph Biroc, cinematography. **Nominations**—best picture; Astaire, best supporting actor. *165 minutes*

TOWER OF LONDON (1939)

★★1/2

Basil Rathbone
Boris Karloff

Rathbone and Karloff star in this historical melodrama, which distorts British history to give an account of the return to the throne of an exiled king—apparently Richard III. Also with Nan Grey, Barbara O'Neil, Ian Hunter, Vincent Price, and Leo G. Carroll. **Director**—Rowland V. Lee. *92 minutes b&w*

TOWER OF LONDON (1962)

★

Vincent Price
Joan Freeman

There are no towering performances in this flat remake of the 1939 movie, about a wicked king trying to return to power. Price, who played the Duke of Clarence in the earlier film, does an adequate job of portraying Richard III in this effort. Aside from Price and the vivid addition of ghostly visions, there's little to warrant the price of admission. The cast also includes Robert Brown, Michael Pate, Bruce Gordon, Sara Salby, and Justice Eatson. **Director**—Roger Corman. *79 minutes b&w*

THE TOXIC AVENGER (1986)

★★

Andree Maranda
Mitchell Cohen

One solution to the toxic waste problem is this spoof of superhero movies. A timid young man falls into some toxic sludge and is transformed into a powerful avenger of evil in a small town. Although the film is amateurish, with too much emphasis on violence and gore, there are enough likable moments to make it worthwhile for undiscriminating viewers. **Directors**—Michael Herz and Samuel Weil. **(R)** *90 minutes*

THE TOXIC AVENGER, PART II (1989)

★

Ron Fazio
John Altamura

The mutant is back, in The Toxic Avenger, Part II.

A foul parody of horror exploitation films from Troma, Inc., the leading purveyor of sleaze. The horribly deformed mutant of the title again champions the fight against illegal toxic chemicals. The subject is prime for satire, but this low-budget sequel to the 1986 original misses the mark. Bad acting, a dull screenplay, and sloppy direction characterize this bomb. Also with Phoebe Legere and Rick Collins. **Directors**—Michael Herz and Lloyd Kaufman. **(R)** *95 minutes*

THE TOXIC AVENGER, PART III: THE LAST TEMPTATION OF TOXIE (1989)

★★

Ron Fazio
John Altamura
Phoebe Legere

This third chapter in the Toxie series is somewhat slicker than the previous two, and it boasts the usual portions of schlock horror effects and gore. Toxie, the unlikely hero who was deformed by toxic waste in the original film, confronts the evil conglomerate Apocalypse, Inc., this time around. Apocalypse serves as a front for a company that is literally from Hell, and Toxie infiltrates the evil corporation to uncover their sinister deeds. The premise serves as a setup for a number of good jokes about the corporate lifestyle, but a little of this film goes a long way. The low budget, the deliberately bad jokes, the weak acting, and the cheap special effects make this film strictly for fans. Altamura and Fazio alternate in the title role. **Directors**—Michael Herz and Lloyd Kaufman. **(R)**

89 minutes

THE TOY (1982)

★

Richard Pryor
Jackie Gleason
Scott Schwartz

The talents of Pryor and Gleason are shamelessly thrown away here. Pryor plays an unemployed journalist who is so desperate that he takes a job as playmate to the bratty nine-year-old son of a heartless tycoon (Gleason). Countless poor-little-rich-kid clichés are mixed in with stale slapstick routines. Predictably, Pryor becomes the surrogate father to the affection-starved youngster. Also with Teresa Ganzel, Ned Beatty,

® This movie available with closed captions for the hearing impaired.

Wilfrid Hyde-White, and Annazette Chase. **Director**—Richard Donner. **(PG)** *99 minutes*

TOYS IN THE ATTIC (1963)

Geraldine Page
Wendy Hiller
Dean Martin

Lillian Hellman's stimulating and provocative play becomes an uninteresting soap opera in this film treatment. Page and Hiller star as two spinster sisters who must deal with their roguish brother when he brings home his childlike bride. Martin is miscast as the brother, but Gene Tierney, Larry Gates, Yvette Mimieux, and Nan Martin are superior to the material they have to work with. **Director**—George Roy Hill. *90 minutes b&w*

TRADER HORN (1931)

Harry Carey

An innovative jungle drama from the early sound era, featuring some much-publicized on-location shooting in Africa. The authentic setting made this a box-office hit in its day; however, time has dulled much of its impact. Carey stars as the trader who overcomes the hostile natives. He is supported by Edwina Booth, Duncan Renaldo, and C. Aubrey Smith. **Director**—W.S. Van Dyke. **Academy Award Nomination**—best picture. *120 minutes b&w*

TRADING PLACES (1983)

Eddie Murphy
Dan Aykroyd
Jamie Lee Curtis

Eddie Murphy and Dan Aykroyd become unlikely allies in Trading Places.

Murphy stars as a glib street-hustler who switches roles with a prissy, stuffed-shirt commodities trader, played by Aykroyd. This sharp screwball comedy is hilarious. Murphy demonstrates extraordinary comic talent and steals many of the scenes. Curtis stars as a hooker with a heart of gold who wins Aykroyd's affections. Ralph Bellamy, Don Ameche, Denholm Elliott, and Jim Belushi stand out in supporting roles. **Director**—John Landis. **(R)** *106 minutes*

TRAIL OF THE PINK PANTHER (1982)

Peter Sellers
David Niven
Capucine

Adieu, Clouseau: Peter Sellers and Capucine in Trail of the Pink Panther.

This sixth adventure of bumbling French detective Clouseau (Sellers) is a letdown. A wisp of a plot features the inscrutable inspector preparing to investigate yet another theft of the "Pink Panther" diamond. Most of the film consists of snippets of earlier Panther movies, assembled after Sellers' untimely death, as a tribute to Sellers' Clouseau character. **Director**—Blake Edwards. **(PG)** *97 minutes*

THE TRAIN (1965)

★★★1/2

Burt Lancaster
Paul Scofield
Michel Simon

This is a simple but exciting story about the efforts of the French Resistance to prevent the Nazis from removing French art treasures by train in 1944. Under John Frankenheimer's deft direction, there isn't a wasted moment, just nerve-racking tension right up to the final sequence in a railroad yard. Lancaster plays a railroad boss, Scofield is a German officer, and Simon is a train engineer. Also with Albert Remy, Wolfgang Preiss, Jeanne Moreau, and Suzanne Flon. **Academy Award Nomination**—Franklin Coen and Frank Davis, best story and screenplay written directly for the screen. *113 minutes b&w*

THE TRAIN ROBBERS (1973)

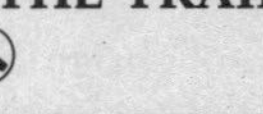 

John Wayne
Ann-Margret

John Wayne tries to help widow Ann-Margret in The Train Robbers.

Wayne and Ann-Margret head the cast of this dismal western, in which the Duke is enlisted to help a widow recover gold stolen by her late husband. Ann-Margret plays the widow. They should have gotten on the train and ridden off the set rather than tarnish their acting reputations with this worthless enterprise. There's some action, but not enough to interest fans of blazing guns and ambushes. Rod Taylor, Ben Johnson, Christopher George, Ricardo Montalban, and Bobby Vinton appear in supporting roles. **Director**—Burt Kennedy. **(PG)** *92 minutes*

TRANSYLVANIA 6-5000 (1985)

Jeff Goldblum
Ed Begley, Jr.

There are neither laughs nor screams in this labored, sophomoric send-up of classic horror movies. Goldblum and Begley play supermarket-tabloid reporters who journey to the infamous

(Continued)

This movie available on videotape and/or disc.

(Continued)
East European land in quest of Frankenstein's monster. There, they find the place has become a tourist trap populated by various horror-film characters who utter nonsense. Perhaps the funniest feature of this film is its title. **Director**—Rudy DeLuca. **(PG)** *94 minutes*

TRAPEZE (1956)

Burt Lancaster
Tony Curtis
Gina Lollobrigida

Lancaster, Curtis, and Lollobrigida star in this suspenseful, tightly directed circus movie. Lancaster portrays an experienced aerialist, who makes a high-wire star of newcomer Curtis. Lollobrigida is the woman they both fall in love with. The film is noteworthy because Lancaster, a former trapeze artist in real life, did many of his own stunts. The cast also includes Katy Jurado, Sidney James, Albert Evans, Thomas Gomez, and John Puleo. **Director**—Carol Reed. *105 minutes*

TRAVELLING NORTH (1988)

Leo McKern
Julia Blake
Graham Kennedy

McKern is exceptional in this colorful character study about a crusty Australian who retires from his job as a civil engineer and marries for a second time. A former Communist and a tough-minded union organizer in his prime, McKern and his gentle bride decide to move to the north country along Australia's coast and lead a quieter life. When he experiences a heart attack, he puts up a brave fight against his deteriorating health, but ultimately makes those close to him suffer as much as he does. Not many large-scale events occur in this small, low-budget drama, but as a bittersweet slice of life, it is both funny and poignant. Also with Henri Szeps, Michele Fawdon, and Diane Craig. **Director**—Carl Schultz. **(PG-13)** *98 minutes*

LA TRAVIATA (1982)

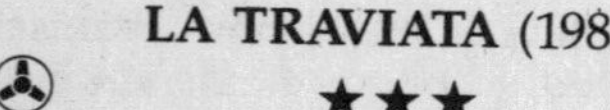

Placido Domingo
Teresa Stratas

Tenor Placido Domingo dominates the screen in La Traviata.

One of the finest film productions of grand opera ever brought to America. The sumptuous spectacle is directed by Franco Zeffirelli (*Romeo and Juliet*) with an attention to authentic detail and emotional effectiveness. Noted opera stars Stratas and Domingo sing beautifully and bring new life to Verdi's tragic romance. A refreshing interpretation. **(G)** *105 minutes*

TREASURE ISLAND (1950)

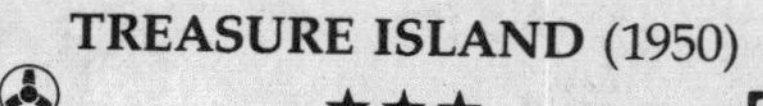

Robert Newton
Bobby Driscoll

Newton is splendid as Long John Silver, and Driscoll is competent as Jim Hawkins in this Walt Disney version of the Robert Louis Stevenson tale about the discovery of a pirate map that leads to a search for buried treasure. A notable version because the film changes the ending of the original novel. In 1975, the film was rereleased in an 87-minute version, with some objectionably violent scenes edited out. Basil Sydney, Denis O'Dea, Ralph Truman, Walter Fitzgerald, Finlay Currie, and Geoffrey Wilkinson appear in supporting roles. **Director**—Byron Haskin. **(G)** *96 minutes*

THE TREASURE OF THE SIERRA MADRE (1948)

★★★★

Humphrey Bogart
Walter Huston
Tim Holt

Obsessed with gold: Humphrey Bogart in The Treasure of the Sierra Madre.

A Hollywood classic with excellent direction and screenwriting by John Huston, superb photography by Ted McCord, and stunning acting by Bogart, Walter Huston, and Holt. The three star as prospectors who find gold, but are done in by their own greed. Like many other Huston films, the theme involves the quest for wealth or power, but the fulfillment of that quest results in the characters' destruction or downfall. Walter Huston, John's father, won an Oscar for his portrayal of the eldest prospector, while John won for both writing and direction. Barton MacLane, Bruce Bennett, and Alfonso Bedoya star in supporting roles. **Academy Awards**—John Huston, best director; Walter Huston, best supporting actor; John Huston, screenplay. **Nomination**—best picture. *126 minutes b&w*

A TREE GROWS IN BROOKLYN (1945)

Peggy Ann Garner
James Dunn

Peggy Ann Garner, James Dunn, and Dorothy McGuire in A Tree Grows in Brooklyn.

Garner and Dunn star in this sensitive story about a troubled Irish family in the Brooklyn tenements at the turn of the century. Dunn plays an alcoholic father, and Garner plays a young lady

® This movie available with closed captions for the hearing impaired.

trying to mature despite her dismal surroundings. Joan Blondell, Lloyd Nolan, Dorothy McGuire, James Gleason, Charles Halton, Ted Donaldson, Ruth Nelson, and John Alexander provide fine supporting performances in this excellently directed film. **Director**—Elia Kazan. **Academy Awards**—Dunn, best supporting actor; Garner, a special award for "outstanding child actress of 1945." **Nomination**—Frank Davis and Tess Slesinger, screenplay.
128 minutes b&w

TREMORS (1990)

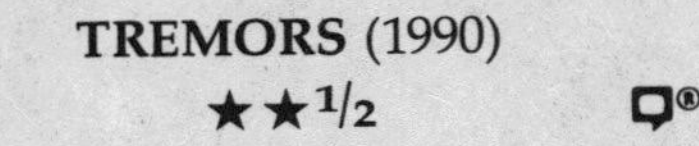

★★½

Kevin Bacon
Fred Ward

Creatures from under the earth menace Fred Ward and Finn Carter in Tremors.

Giant, carnivorous earthworms menace a Nevada desert community. Although the terrors from underground are innovative, their discovery and demise evolve in familiar creature-feature fashion. Yet, it is not the monsters that make this film a cut above most science-fiction tales, it is the focus on the offbeat characters and the allusions to those 1950s B-pictures. The clever humor, the careful pacing, and the use of western references and landscapes will entice film buffs. Bacon and Ward head the cast as handymen who become the unlikely heroes. Country singer Reva McEntire costars as the wife of survivalist Michael Gross (from TV's *Family Ties*). Also with Finn Carter, Conrad Bachman, and Bibi Besch. **Director**—Ron Underwood. **(PG-13)** *96 minutes*

TRENCHCOAT (1983)

Margot Kidder
Robert Hays

Kidder plays a court stenographer turned mystery writer turned detective

Would-be mystery writer Margot Kidder, caught up in real-life intrigue in Trenchcoat.

in this Disney-made spoof of gumshoe movies. While on vacation in Malta, where she's trying to write a detective story, Kidder becomes tangled in a cocaine-smuggling scheme and a murder. Kidder turns in an energetic performance, but the chain of events is predictable and labored. Hays costars as the object of her affections. Also with Daniel Faraldo, David Suchet, and Ronald Lacey. **Director**—Michael Tuchner. **(PG)** *95 minutes*

TRIAL (1955)

★★★

Glenn Ford
Dorothy McGuire

This taut courtroom melodrama about a Mexican boy accused of rape and murder had many racial and political implications in a Hollywood fraught with McCarthyism. The deft adaptation of the Don Mankiewicz novel plays on the hysteria of the 1950s by using both procommunist and anticommunist factors as manipulators in the trial. Stirring performances from Ford, McGuire, John Hodiak, and especially Arthur Kennedy; with Katy Jurado, Robert Middleton, and Rafael Campos in supporting roles. **Director**—Mark Robson. **Academy Award Nomination**—Kennedy, best supporting actor.
109 minutes b&w

THE TRIALS OF OSCAR WILDE (1960)

Peter Finch
James Mason
Nigel Patrick
John Fraser

Excellent performances by Finch, Mason, Patrick, and Fraser sustain this flat account of the eccentric playwright's libel trial and subsequent prosecution for sodomy. Finch's portrayal of Wilde is a full and vivid characterization. Yvonne Mitchell, Lionel Jeffries, James Booth, Maxine Audley, and Emrys Jones appear in supporting roles. **Director**—Ken Hughes. *123 minutes*

TRIBUTE (1980)

Jack Lemmon
Robby Benson

Robby Benson and Jack Lemmon reach a truce on Broadway in Tribute.

Bernard Slade's play, about a strained relationship between father and son, doesn't transfer well to the screen. This emotionally unrewarding film provides a *tour-de-force* role for Lemmon, who mugs away as the clownish father dying of cancer. But what is supposed to be drama is merely a string of self-pitying temper tantrums. Benson, as the priggish and obnoxious son, performs mechanically and unevenly. Also with Lee Remick. **Director**—Bob Clark. **(PG) Academy Award Nomination**—Lemmon, best actor. *123 minutes*

THE TRIP TO BOUNTIFUL (1985)

Geraldine Page
Rebecca DeMornay

A small, sweet movie, set in the late 1940s, about ordinary people. Page demonstrates magnificent acting craftsmanship in the central role of Horton Foote's screenplay. She portrays a determined elderly woman who briefly es-
(Continued)

Geraldine Page (right) meets a new friend in The Trip to Bountiful.

(Continued)

capes from her nagging daughter-in-law to visit the godforsaken hometown of her youth. John Heard and Carlin Glynn stand out in supporting roles. **Director**—Peter Masterson. **(PG) Academy Award**—Page, best actress. **Nomination**—Foote, best screenplay adapted to the screen from another medium.
105 minutes

TRIUMPH OF THE SPIRIT (1989)

★★1/2

Willem Dafoe
Edward James Olmos

Willem Dafoe witnesses terror from the Nazis in Triumph of the Spirit.

The horrors of the Holocaust are represented in this fact-based story about a young Greek boxing champion (Dafoe) who fought for his life in bouts with other prisoners at a Nazi death camp. The subject is harrowing, and a number of scenes are compelling. Unfortunately, the many recent films and television dramas about the Holocaust will dull the impact of this independent effort. A pedestrian screenplay that does not give Dafoe enough to work with and a redundant voice-over narration weaken the film further. Filmed on location at Auschwitz-Birkenau. Also with Robert Loggia, Wendy Gazelle, Kelly Wolf, Costas Mandylor, Kario Salem, Edward Zentara, and Hartmut Becker. **Director**—Robert M. Young. **(R)**
120 minutes

TROLL (1986)

★★

Michael Moriarty
Shelley Hack

A typical American family moves into an apartment building. . .and the troll there promptly possesses their daughter, intending to transform the building into a troll kingdom. This threadbare likeness to *Gremlins* features a generous assortment of slimy creatures that should satisfy fans of the genre. But the intermittent tongue-in-cheek approach and offbeat casting (including Sonny Bono) should keep nonfans interested as well. **Director**—John Buechler. **(PG–13)**
86 minutes

TRON (1982)

★★

Jeff Bridges
Bruce Boxleitner

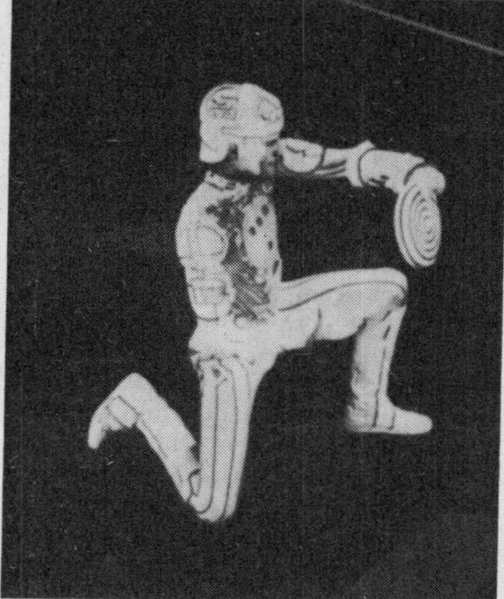

High-tech video warrior Bruce Boxleitner braces for attack in Tron.

The Disney studio presents a mechanical, garish sci-fi adventure that takes place inside of a computerized videogame. The computer-generated effects are splashy, but the characters are neither credible nor interesting, and what passes for dialogue is mostly technical jargon. **Director**—Steven Lisberger. **(PG)**
96 minutes

TROOP BEVERLY HILLS (1989)

★★

Shelley Long
Craig T. Nelson

Shelley Long is an upscale den mother in Troop Beverly Hills.

Meet the Wilderness Girls of posh Beverly Hills: They earn merit badges for sushi tasting, arrive at campsites in limos, and repair to lavish hotels when it rains. This one-joke send-up of spoiled rich kids and their equally spoiled parents is only mildly amusing. Long, as the effervescent den mother in the designer uniform, gives the role her best shot. Also stars Betty Thomas, Mary Gross, Audra Linley, Edd Byrnes, Stephanie Beacham, Ami Foster, and Jenny Lewis. **Director**—Jeff Kanew. **(PG)**
100 minutes

TROUBLE IN MIND (1985)

★★★★

Kris Kristofferson
Geneviève Bujold
Keith Carradine

Alan Rudolph's highly original film is characterized by moodiness and stylish eccentricities. Kristofferson stars as an ex-con who returns to his old surroundings and becomes involved in a romantic triangle. The storyline is really incidental to the melancholy atmosphere and symbolic production design in this film, which is a combination of fantasy and *film noir* sensibilities. The colorful characters also include Wanda

® *This movie available with closed captions for the hearing impaired.*

Country hick Keith Carradine adjusts to the big city in Trouble in Mind.

(Bujold), the owner of a run-down café; a petty thief looking for a big score (Carradine); and the thief's young wife, whose innocence Kristofferson falls in love with. The cast makes the most of the savory material. Also with Divine, George Kirby, and Joe Morton. **(R)**
111 minutes

THE TROUBLE WITH ANGELS (1966)

 ★★

Rosalind Russell
Hayley Mills
June Harding

Mills and Harding give enthusiastic performances in this mild comedy about the fun and pranks that occur at a convent school, where Russell is the Mother Superior. Mary Wickes, Margalo Gillmore, Binnie Barnes, Gypsy Rose Lee, and Marge Redmond appear in supporting roles. **Director**—Ida Lupino.
112 minutes

THE TROUBLE WITH HARRY (1955)

 ★★★

Shirley MacLaine
John Forsythe

The Trouble with Harry *is that he crops up in the most embarrassing places.*

Charmingly offbeat black comedy about a corpse that is an embarrassment to a community because people are repeatedly burying it and digging it up. The exquisite color photography of the autumnal Vermont forests provides a sharp contrast to the ghoulish events. Excellent performances by Edmund Gwenn, Mildred Natwick, Forsythe, and MacLaine. The whimsical wit and humor never falter in this delightful masterpiece by Alfred Hitchcock. **(PG)**
90 minutes

THE TROUBLE WITH SPIES (1987)

 ★ 

Donald Sutherland
Ned Beatty
Ruth Gordon

Despite an impressive star lineup, this dreary spy comedy proves to be an embarrassment to all involved. The inane plot involves a bumbling British agent (Sutherland) who is sent to the Mediterranean island of Ibiza to retrieve the formula for a new truth serum, recently perfected by the Russians. This stale, incoherent spoof was produced in 1984, but no distributor would touch it until the DeLaurentitis Entertainment Group picked it up three years later for a limited theatrical run. Michael Hordern, Robert Morley, and Gregory Sierra also damage their reputations by appearing in supporting roles. **Director**—Burt Kennedy. **(PG)**
91 minutes

TRUE BELIEVER (1989)

★★★ ❑®

James Woods
Robert Downey, Jr.

James Woods, Robert Downey, Jr., and Yuji Okumoto in True Believer.

Woods stars in this crackling mystery/drama as a celebrated civil rights lawyer, now disenchanted, who rediscovers his former passion when he defends an Asian immigrant wrongly imprisoned for murder. The finely tuned script is filled with surprises and thrills, and it culminates in a tingling courtroom showdown. Woods delivers a fierce and gripping performance, and Downey does a good job as a young associate lawyer. Also with Yuji Okumoto, Margaret Colin, and Kurtwood Smith. **Director**—Joseph Ruben. **(R)**
104 minutes

TRUE CONFESSIONS (1981)

 ★★★

Robert De Niro
Robert Duvall

Robert Duvall is a homicide detective in True Confessions.

De Niro and Duvall star as two brothers—De Niro as a priest, Duvall as a police detective—who are brought into conflict over a prostitute's murder. The grisly crime leads to the core of this engrossing film, based on John Gregory Dunne's novel about hypocrisy among high-level church officials. The 1940s settings create a rich atmosphere. It's a tough, intriguing film, masterfully directed by Ulu Grosbard. Also with Charles Durning, Ed Flanders, and Burgess Meredith. **(R)** *110 minutes*

TRUE GRIT (1969)

 ★★★½

John Wayne
Kim Darby

Although Wayne turned in many excellent performances, this movie was a

(Continued)

Glen Campbell is part of the cast of True Grit.

(Continued)
high point in his career because he received critical recognition, in the form of an Academy Award. Wayne plays Rooster Cogburn, a one-eyed, tough old marshal, who responds to the plea of a young girl, played by Darby, to avenge the slaying of her father. Dennis Hopper, Robert Duvall, Jeff Corey, Strother Martin, and Jeremy Slate provide polished supporting performances. The weak performance of pop singer Glen Campbell is the movie's only major distraction. **Director**—Henry Hathaway. **(G) Academy Award**—Wayne, best actor.

128 minutes

TRUE STORIES (1986)

★★

David Byrne
Swoosie Kurtz

David Byrne is ready to tell you some True Stories *about a town in Texas.*

An oddball collection of vignettes about a small Texas town, directed and narrated by David Byrne (of the rock group the Talking Heads). The peculiar film takes a close look at such absurdities as the laziest woman in the world (Kurtz), lawn mowers and baby strollers on parade, and a perpetual liar who claims to have met the real Rambo. This up-close study of what Byrne sees as contemporary life tends to make a big deal out of the trivial, and is condescending to those who live in small-town America. **(PG)**

88 minutes

TUCKER: THE MAN AND HIS DREAMS (1988)

★★★

Jeff Bridges
Joan Allen
Martin Landau

Maverick auto designer Preston Tucker introduced such automobile features as disc brakes, fuel injection, and seat belts just after World War II. Director Francis Ford Coppola's stylish drama reveals how the big Detroit auto companies conspired to destroy this visionary man and the progressive vehicle he created. Bridges provides a colorful, booming performance as the man who believed in American free enterprise but was ground down by the establishment. Coppola's production at times recalls the style and conventions of the 1940s magazines and movies. Also with Frederic Forrest, Mako, Dean Stockwell, Elias Koteas, Christian Slater, and Llyod Bridges. **(PG) Academy Award Nominations**—Landau, best supporting actor; Dean Tavoularis and Armin Ganz, art direction; Milena Canonero, costumes.

105 minutes

TUFF TURF (1985)

★★

James Spader

James Spader comes up against some difficult times in Tuff Turf.

An overheated youth-exploitation film. Spader plays the out-of-place preppie from Connecticut who antagonizes a vicious teen gang-leader by taking a shine to his girlfriend. Various fights, car chases, and tense confrontations progress in prescribed order. The film ends with a predictable showdown. Also with Kim Richards and Paul Mones. **Director**—Fritz Kersch. **(R)**

113 minutes

TURK 182 (1985)

★★

Timothy Hutton
Robert Urich

Robert Urich explains his problem to Timothy Hutton in Turk 182.

The common man who fights City Hall provides the theme for this comedy/drama that is hardly believable. Hutton plays the young rebel who plasters the big city with the title phrase. His graffiti campaign is designed to attract attention to the plight of Hutton's injured fireman brother (Urich), and also to embarrass the pompous and corrupt mayor. Such outrageous heroics come off as preposterous. Costars Kim Cattrall, Robert Culp, and Peter Boyle. **Director**—Bob Clark. **(PG–13)**

96 minutes

TURNER & HOOCH (1989)

★★

Tom Hanks
Mare Winningham

It took five scriptwriters to concoct this formulaic movie with three familiar elements—an odd-couple premise, a wide array of action scenes, and a quirky romance. Hanks and a drooling, jowly canine are the mismatched buddies who bust a drug-smuggling ring that also involves murder. Both leads find time for romantic interludes—Hanks with a veterinarian (Winningham) and the dog with a frisky collie. Hooch the pooch chews the

® *This movie available with closed captions for the hearing impaired.*

Tom Hanks and his sad-faced friend star in Turner & Hooch.

scenery—literally. Hanks and Hooch salvage the film with a few comic scenes, which makes the film's tragic ending seem out of place. Also with Reginald VelJohnson, Craig T. Nelson, Scott Paulin, J.C. Quinn, and John McIntire. **Director**—Roger Spottiswoode. **(PG)** *98 minutes*

THE TURNING POINT (1977)

★★

Anne Bancroft
Shirley MacLaine

Anne Bancroft is a prima ballerina in The Turning Point.

Bancroft and MacLaine play old rivals who are reunited in this backstage ballet drama. The melodramatic approach to the material is a significant drawback. In addition, the script is mechanical; only the dance scenes perk up portions of the film. Russian-born dancer Mikhail Baryshnikov steals a few scenes with his acting as well as his ballet performances. Also with Tom Skerritt, Martha Scott, and Leslie Browne. **Director**—Herbert Ross. **(PG) Academy Award Nominations**—best picture; Ross, best director; Bancroft and MacLaine, best actress; Baryshnikov, best supporting actor; Browne, best supporting actress; Arthur Laurents, best screenplay written directly for the screen. *119 minutes*

TWELVE ANGRY MEN (1957)

★★★★

Henry Fonda
Lee J. Cobb
E.G. Marshall
Jack Warden

The jurors debate in Sidney Lumet's compelling film Twelve Angry Men.

Fonda plays a conscientious and moral juror in the trial of a teenager accused of killing his father. He prevails on the eleven other jurors not to rush into a quick judgment. Each juror gets an opportunity to express his opinion on the law and the boy's guilt or innocence, revealing something about himself and his life in the process. Though the setting is limited to the courtroom and the deliberation room, the intensity of the performances and material makes for a compelling viewing experience. Director Sidney Lumet's first feature film. The script was based on a television play by Reginald Rose. The sensational cast also includes Ed Begley, Martin Balsam, Jack Klugman, Edward Binns, Joseph Sweeney, Robert Webber, George Voskovec, and John Fiedler. **Director**—Sidney Lumet. **Academy Award Nominations**—best picture; Lumet, best director; Rose, best screenplay based on material from another medium. *95 minutes b&w*

TWELVE O'CLOCK HIGH (1949)

★★★½

Gregory Peck
Dean Jagger

Gregory Peck undergoes the stress of battle in Twelve O'Clock High.

Peck and Jagger star in this story about the stress experienced by officers who must lead U.S. fliers into combat during World War II. Peck plays the commander of a bomber unit based in England. The characterizations are superior to the two-dimensional portraits seen in most war films. Hugh Marlowe, Gary Merrill, Millard Mitchell, John Kellogg, Paul Stewart, and Robert Arthur are among the fine supporting actors. **Director**—Henry King. **Academy Award**—Jagger, best supporting actor. **Nominations**—best picture; Peck, best actor. *132 minutes b&w*

TWENTIETH CENTURY (1934)

★★★★

John Barrymore
Carole Lombard

The famous New York-to-Chicago passenger train serves as part of the setting for this top-notch screwball comedy taken from the popular play by Ben Hecht and Charles MacArthur. The backstage story involves egotistical producer Barrymore, who makes a star of novice actress Lombard. Plenty of delightful complications develop. Director Howard Hawks' fast-paced style enhances the energetic performances and biting dialogue. Also with Étienne Girardot, Edgar Kennedy, Charles Levinson (Lane), Roscoe Karns, and Walter Connolly. *91 minutes b&w*

This movie available on videotape and/or disc.

20,000 LEAGUES UNDER THE SEA (1954)

★★★½

Kirk Douglas
James Mason

Undersea divers like what they find 20,000 Leagues Under the Sea.

The universe of novelist Jules Verne springs to life in this exciting Walt Disney production about life aboard a futuristic submarine during the Victorian era. Douglas, Peter Lorre, and Paul Lukas get aboard Captain Nemo's sub for scintillating adventures. Nemo is played by Mason. The film is noteworthy for its innovative special effects, which won an Academy Award, as did the production design. Carleton Young, Ted De Corsia, and Robert J. Wilke appear in supporting roles. **Director**—Richard Fleischer. **(G)** *127 minutes*

TWICE IN A LIFETIME (1985)

★★★

Gene Hackman
Ann-Margret
Ellen Burstyn
Amy Madigan

Gene Hackman gives away daughter Ally Sheedy in Twice in a Lifetime.

Midlife crisis and marital breakup provide the plot of this uneven and sentimental film. A stalwart cast and some affecting performances help overcome the film's flaws. Hackman is convincing as the steelworker who abandons his wife of 30 years for a barmaid, skillfully played by Ann-Margret. Burstyn is unforgettable as the rejected wife. **Director**—Bud Yorkin. **(R) Academy Award Nomination**—Madigan, best supporting actress. *117 minutes*

TWILIGHT'S LAST GLEAMING (1977)

★★★

Burt Lancaster
Richard Widmark
Charles Durning

This political thriller stars Lancaster as a disgruntled U.S. Air Force general who blackmails the government by threatening to unleash nuclear missiles on Russia. Director Robert Aldrich forcefully fashions ample suspense and taut confrontations through his use of split-screen sequences. Lancaster and other Hollywood elder statesmen, such as Melvyn Douglas, Joseph Cotten, and Widmark, move the action along energetically. Durning plays the President. The compelling screenplay stirs the conscience about the Vietnam War era, though there are some lapses in credibility. Also with Paul Winfield, Richard Jaeckel, Burt Young, and Roscoe Lee Browne. **(R)** *146 minutes*

TWILIGHT ZONE: THE MOVIE (1983)

★★½

Vic Morrow
Scatman Crothers
John Lithgow
Dan Aykroyd

Remus Peets, Vic Morrow, and Kai Wulff in Twilight Zone: The Movie.

Rod Serling's eerie and thought-provoking TV series inspired this film, made up of four different tales. John Landis directed the least satisfactory vignette, about a hostile bigot (Morrow, who was killed while this movie was being made) who gets his comeuppance. Steven Spielberg does somewhat better with a tale of old people who become young again. A zany family trapped in a nightmare is the subject of Joe Dante's segment. And George Miller (*The Road Warrior*) skillfully directs a story about a hysterical airline passenger (Lithgow). The result is an uneven viewing experience. Also with Selma Diamond, Bill Quinn, Kathleen Quinlan, Kevin McCarthy, and William Schallert. **(PG)** *101 minutes*

TWINS (1988)

★★½

Arnold Schwarzenegger
Danny DeVito

An example of biology gone bad: Twins *Danny DeVito and Arnold Schwarzenegger.*

Just the idea of Schwarzenegger and DeVito as identical twins is funny. But the humor involving these unlikely brothers—the result of a botched biological experiment—soon wears away, and the comedy turns into a routine road film. The boys become involved with gangsters, romance, and money as they search for their roots. Also with Chloe Webb, Kelly Preston, Bonnie

Bartlett, Trey Wilson, and Hugh O'Brian. **Director**—Ivan Reitman.
(PG-13) *115 minutes*

TWO FOR THE ROAD (1967)

 ★★★★

Audrey Hepburn
Albert Finney

A sophisticated comedy/drama with pointed dialogue and a thought-provoking theme. The story concerns a fashionable and successful married couple motoring through Europe and reviewing their 12-year marriage in flashback. Director Stanley Donen paints a realistic portrait of the 1950s and 1960s with all the social changes presented in microcosm. Hepburn and Finney are perfect as the couple who see their failures but cannot overcome them. An exceptional script from Frederic Raphael provides many insights. **Academy Award Nomination**—Raphael, best story and screenplay written directly for the screen.
113 minutes

THE TWO JAKES (1990)

★★★

Jack Nicholson
Harvey Keitel

This follow-up to Roman Polanski's *Chinatown* had a rocky road from inception to release. The project had been in the works for several years, and the actual production was plagued by delays and personnel changes. Nicholson stars in and directs the final version from a script by *Chinatown* writer Robert Towne. The story does not follow the clear-cut path that Polanski's original does, and viewers who like their mysteries neatly solved will get bogged down in the jumbled plotline. Truer to the conventions of *film noir*, this film makes use of a quiet, all-pervasive corruption, which affects each character. Set in the late 1940s, the film finds Nicholson's character Jake Gittes operating a prosperous detective agency. He agrees to take on a divorce case against his better judgment, and the case ends up in murder. Along the way, Jake is haunted by the events of the earlier film, which have some bearing on his current case. Meg Tilly and Madeleine Stowe costar as the corrupted and corruptible *noir*-like heroines. Also with Eli Wallach, Frederic Forrest, David Keith, Richard Farnsworth, and Ruben Blades.
(R) *128 minutes*

TWO-MINUTE WARNING (1976)

Charlton Heston
John Cassavetes

A sniper, perched above the scoreboard of the Los Angeles Coliseum, opens fire on fans watching a championship football game. This gory action sequence takes place during the last 15 minutes of the movie. The rest is filled with tedious slice-of-life vignettes about selected spectators, who are eventually killed or injured. An unimaginative and unaffecting viewing experience. The large cast also includes Martin Balsam, Beau Bridges, David Janssen, Jack Klugman, and Gena Rowlands. **Director**—Larry Peerce. **(R)** *115 minutes*

TWO MOON JUNCTION (1988)

★★

Sherilyn Fenn
Richard Tyson

Class conflict: Sherilyn Fenn and Richard Tyson in Two Moon Junction.

A sultry, sometimes sordid tale of a carnival roustabout who has a steamy affair with the daughter of a wealthy southern senator. Tyson, who appears throughout this cliché-ridden melodrama in various states of undress, stars as the muscular carny worker who falls for the white-blonde innocence of Sherilyn Fenn. Fenn is torn between her desire for Tyson and her commitment to marry a successful local boy. The intense and sometimes frank love scenes dominate this film, which seems to be an erotic version of a Harlequin novel—a formulaic story about a passionate romance presented from the female point of view. Some interesting actors show up in oddball supporting roles, including Kristy McNichol, Louise Fletcher, and Burl Ives. **Director**—Zalman King. **(R)** *104 minutes*

THE TWO MRS. CARROLLS (1947)

Humphrey Bogart
Barbara Stanwyck

This psychological melodrama about a murderous artist who paints his wives' portraits before killing them is stilted and awkward. Bogart, ill-cast and uncomfortable as the psychopath, runs into problems when his latest victim, Stanwyck, realizes the pattern of his crimes. The first-rate cast, including Alexis Smith, Nigel Bruce, and Isobel Elsom, still makes the film fun to watch. **Director**—Peter Godfrey.
99 minutes b&w

TWO OF A KIND (1983)

John Travolta
Olivia Newton-John

Olivia Newton-John and John Travolta in Two of a Kind.

This ridiculous romantic comedy is a desperate excuse for bringing Travolta and Newton-John together again after the success of *Grease.* He plays a wacky inventor who resorts to robbing a bank to pay off some loan sharks. She's the flaky teller who makes goo-goo eyes at him during the heist. If they fall madly in love, they will please God and save the world. All they do is damage their acting careers and bore the audience into a stupor with this tacky mess. Also with Charles Durning, Oliver Reed, Beatrice Straight, Scatman Crothers, and James Stephens. **Director**—John Herzfeld. **(PG)** *90 minutes*

TWO RODE TOGETHER (1961)

★★★

James Stewart
Richard Widmark

Western saga about a Texas marshal and an army commander leading a wagon train into Comanche territory to negotiate for the return of captive pioneers. Director John Ford depicts the thorny relationship between two strong men with differing points of view who are pitted against a greater enemy. Stewart and Widmark add stature to their stereotyped characters. Strong support from Shirley Jones, Linda Cristal, Andy Devine, and John McIntire.

109 minutes

2001: A SPACE ODYSSEY (1968)

★★★★

Keir Dullea
William Sylvester
Gary Lockwood

2001: A Space Odyssey is a futuristic view of the universe.

This film about a journey into another realm of thought and time is a one-of-a-kind masterpiece. There are so many special effects and visually stunning scenes that at times it seems that actors aren't necessary, but Dullea and Lockwood are effective as two astronauts traveling to Jupiter with a complex and disturbed computer called HAL. Director Stanley Kubrick has fashioned a profound and deeply moving meditation on the meaning of the universe. Based on Arthur C. Clarke's short story "The Sentinel," the film lifted the science-fiction genre to a new level of complexity. The innovative special effects by Douglas Trumball won an Academy Award. Also with Daniel Richter. **(G) Academy Award Nominations**—Kubrick, best director; Kubrick and Clarke, best story and screenplay written directly for the screen.

141 minutes

2010 (1984)

★★

Roy Scheider
John Lithgow
Bob Balaban

Bob Balaban, Roy Scheider, and John Lithgow confer in 2010.

Dazzling special effects and fancy space hardware dominate this follow-up to Stanley Kubrick's *2001: A Space Odyssey*. Yet there's no feeling of awe, mystery, or imagination as a joint American and Russian space crew try to find out what went wrong with the spacecraft *Discovery*, lost in space some nine years before. This high-tech misfire winds down with many loose ends dangling and a lot of trite talk about peace among the superpowers. Originally released at 157 minutes. Also with Helen Mirren, Keir Dullea, and Savely Kramarov. **Director**—Peter Hyams. **(PG)**

116 minutes

TWO WEEKS IN ANOTHER TOWN (1962)

Kirk Douglas
Edward G. Robinson

Douglas stars in this solid melodrama as a former alcoholic trying to make a comeback in the film industry. The movie is based on Irwin Shaw's best-selling novel. Douglas does his best to capture the better aspects of the book's main character but the story remains a glorified soap opera. Also with Cyd Charisse, Claire Trevor, George Hamilton, Constance Ford, Dahlia Lavi, George Macready, and Rosanna Schiaffino. **Director**—Vincente Minnelli.

107 minutes

TWO WOMEN (1961)

★★★★

Sophia Loren

Assault aftermath: Sophia Loren comforts daughter Eleanora Brown in Two Women.

Profound, moving drama about an Italian mother and her daughter emigrating south from Rome during the Allied invasion. Loren gives her best performance as the courageous and distraught woman who endures her own rape and that of her young daughter at the hands of invading soldiers, but carries on. Beautifully scripted from an Alberto Moravia novel with restrained direction by Vittorio De Sica. Loren deservedly won the Oscar for her intense portrayal and was ably supported by Eleanora Brown, Jean-Paul Belmondo, and Raf Vallone. Originally filmed in Italian. **Academy Award**—Loren, best actress.

110 minutes b&w

TYPHOON (1940)

Dorothy Lamour
Lynne Overman

Sailors discover Lamour on an island and learn that she has been there since childhood; the story builds from there. One of several movies Lamour made after her success in *The Hurricane,* in which the story was secondary to her sarong. J. Carrol Naish, Robert Preston, Frank Reicher, and Jack Carson handle the supporting roles. **Director**—Louis King.

70 minutes

® This movie available with closed captions for the hearing impaired.

U

THE UGLY AMERICAN (1963)

★★1/2

Marlon Brando
Sandra Church

Marlon Brando confronts unsavory politics as The Ugly American.

By Hollywood standards, this movie was a sincere effort to deal with America's confrontation with communism in Southeast Asia. Unfortunately, the story, based on a Eugene Burdick and William J. Lederer novel, has been watered down for the screen. Brando makes the most of his role as the U.S. Ambassador who fumbles his assignment and causes new problems in an Asian country despite his good intentions. Eiji Okada, Arthur Hill, Jocelyn Brando, and Pat Hingle appear in supporting roles. **Director**—George H. Englund. *120 minutes*

UHF (1989)

★1/2

Al Yankovic
Victoria Jackson
Kevin McCarthy

A frivolous vehicle tailored to the comic style of "Weird Al" Yankovic. Weird Al plays a nerdy character who becomes the manager of a marginal TV station, which he helps turn around by programming such innovative shows as *Wheel of Fish* and *Raul's Wild Kingdom*. The plot is merely a loose framework for a number of sketches that lampoon typical television fare. As such, it is reminiscent of *The Groove Tube* but with-

David Bowe gets a treat from "Weird Al" Yankovic in UHF.

out that film's satiric bite. A few spoofs, including those of the films *Gandhi* and *Rambo*, are humorous, but most of Yankovic's humor revolves around violence, death, and doing disgusting things with food. Also with Michael Richards, Trinidad Silver, Gedde Watanabe, and David Bowe. **Director**—Jay Levey. **(PG-13)** *97 minutes*

THE UMBRELLAS OF CHERBOURG (1964)

★★★

Catherine Deneuve

A French operatic love story by director Jacques Demy with haunting music by Michel Legrand. The film was beautifully photographed in Cherbourg in a dreamy visual style that suits the ill-fated romance of the story. Deneuve is perfect as the tragic heroine, adding much beauty to an already attractive film. A highly stylized work, this musical holds up well today. Originally filmed in French. **Academy Award Nominations**—best foreign-language film; Demy, best story and screenplay written directly for the screen. *90 minutes*

THE UNBEARABLE LIGHTNESS OF BEING (1988)

★★1/2

Daniel Day-Lewis
Juliette Binoche
Lina Olin

This ambitious film adaptation of Milan Kundera's impressive novel ranges from eroticism to high drama. The striking love story, set against the 1968 Russian takeover of Czechoslovakia, involves the experiences of a prominent surgeon who is also a notorious womanizer (Day-Lewis). Though he marries the in-

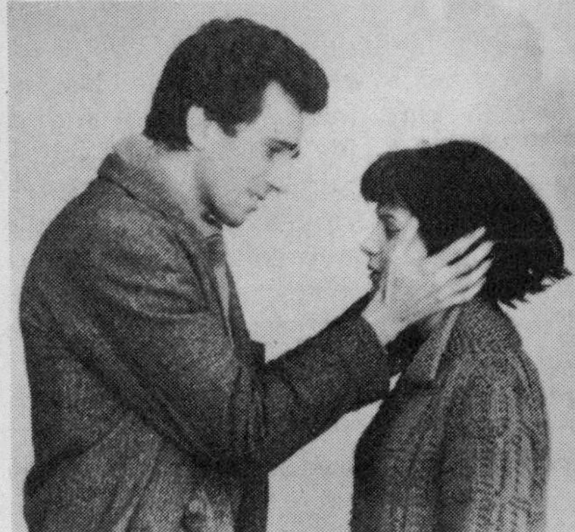

Daniel Day-Lewis and Lena Olin in The Unbearable Lightness of Being.

nocent Binoche, he still carries on a sordid affair with the voluptuous Olin. This romantic drama may be too long and is sometimes difficult to follow, but it often bristles with passion. Though directed by American Philip Kaufman, the film has the fragmented structure and allegorical storyline of a European film. Critical reaction to the film was mixed: Critics either loved it or hated it, indicating that viewers' reaction to this unique effort will be a matter of taste. **(R) Academy Award Nominations**—Kaufman and Jean-Claude Carriere, best screenplay adaptation; Sven Nykvist, cinematography. *172 minutes*

UNCLE BUCK (1989)

★★1/2

John Candy
Jean Kelly
Gaby Hoffman
Macaulay Culkin

John Candy is Uncle Buck, *a babysitter with a difference.*

(Continued)
Candy was made for the role of a ne'er-do-well uncle who is called as a last resort to care for two nieces and a nephew. The kids transform him into a responsible person, and he emerges as an effective surrogate parent. Though the outcome is predictable, the film thrives on the comic scenes involving Candy's inexperience with kids and the middle-class, suburban lifestyle. Directed by John Hughes, who seems to bring out the best in Candy *(Planes, Trains, and Automobiles)*. If the material seems suited to a television sitcom, then it will come as no surprise that the premise was later adapted to the small screen. Also with Amy Madigan, Laurie Metcalf, Elaine Bromka, Garrett M. Brown, and Jay Underwood. **(PG)** *100 minutes*

UNCOMMON VALOR (1983)

★★★

Gene Hackman
Robert Stack
Fred Ward
Patrick Swayze

Gene Hackman attempts a rescue mission in Uncommon Valor.

Hackman stars as a tough Marine colonel who leads a gung ho band of veterans through the Laotian jungles to rescue American troops listed as missing during the Vietnam War. The film features a great deal of well-choreographed action, although it celebrates violence under the pretense of nobility. Hackman is excellent, as are Reb Brown and Randall "Tex" Cobb in supporting roles. **Director**—Ted Kotcheff. **(R)** *105 minutes*

THE UNDEFEATED (1969)

★★

John Wayne
Rock Hudson

Rock Hudson and John Wayne team up together in The Undefeated.

Wayne plays an ex-Union colonel in the horse-trading business who confronts Hudson, a former Confederate colonel. They mend their past differences in time to fight together against Mexican marauders in this mediocre Civil War-era western. Tony Aguilar, Lee Meriwether, Bruce Cabot, Roman Gabriel, Merlin Olsen, and Ben Johnson appear in supporting roles. **Director**—Andrew V. McLaglen. **(G)** *119 minutes*

UNDER CAPRICORN (1949)

★★

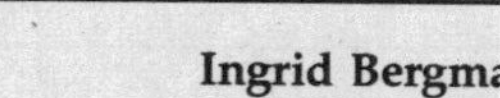

Ingrid Bergman
Joseph Cotten

This disappointing suspense melodrama by Alfred Hitchcock takes place in Australia during the 1830s. Bergman plays the alcoholic wife of domineering Cotten, a wealthy landowner, who is visited by an English cousin, played by Michael Wilding. The stagy sets and pregnant pauses detract from the timing of the drama and overburden the suspense. The excellent acting helps, particularly the fine performance from Margaret Leighton. *117 minutes*

UNDERCURRENT (1946)

★★

Katharine Hepburn
Robert Taylor
Robert Mitchum

Katharine Hepburn and Robert Taylor star in Undercurrent.

A melodrama about a woman who gradually discovers that her husband is an evil man. Unfortunately, the high production values, typical of MGM films, cannot make up for the predictable story. Modern viewers may see it in a feminist light, although that doesn't make this a better movie. Also with Edmund Gwenn, Marjorie Main, Dan Tobin, and Jayne Meadows. **Director**—Vincente Minnelli. *116 minutes b&w*

UNDER FIRE (1983)

★★★½

Nick Nolte
Gene Hackman
Joanna Cassidy

Nick Nolte and Joanna Cassidy are caught Under Fire *during Nicaragua's 1979 revolution.*

Tough, gripping historical drama about events that toppled Nicaraguan dictator Anastasio Somoza. The action is seen through the eyes and camera of freelance photographer Nolte, who compromises his journalistic ethics by siding with the Sandinista rebels. The acting and pacing are first-rate, but the newsman's abrupt radicalization and the occasional Hollywood treatment of the revolution lessen the film's impact. Also with Ed Harris, Jean-Louis Trintignant, Richard Masur, and Rene Enriquez. **Director**—Roger Spottiswood. **(R)** *128 minutes*

UNDER THE CHERRY MOON (1986)

★½

Prince
Kristin Scott-Thomas

An amateurish ego trip featuring rock star Prince as the centerpiece of this

® *This movie available with closed captions for the hearing impaired.*

Rock star Prince performs in Under the Cherry Moon.

foolish love story. He plays a struggling musician, working on the French Riviera, who falls in love with an unhappy heiress (Scott-Thomas) much to the dismay of her father. Prince, who also directed this nonsense, primps, pouts, dresses up in fancy outfits, and utters meaningless dialogue. The film's only highlight is the luscious black-and-white photography, purposefully reminiscent of films of the 1940s. Also with Jerome Benton. **(PG–13)**

98 minutes b&w

UNDER THE RAINBOW (1981)

★½

Chevy Chase
Carrie Fisher

Hollywood confusion with Carrie Fisher and Chevy Chase in Under the Rainbow.

Chase and Fisher star in this meandering comedy about the problems caused by the scores of midgets hired as Munchkins for *The Wizard of Oz*. Involved with the various cornball incidents are Japanese and German spies, touring Japanese photographers, and a duke and duchess threatened with assassination. Though much goes on throughout the film, none of it produces any laughs. Also with Eve Arden, Joseph Maher, Adam Arkin, Mako, and Billy Barty. **(PG)** *97 minutes*

UNDER THE VOLCANO (1984)

★★★½

Albert Finney
Jacqueline Bisset
Anthony Andrews

Anthony Andrews and Jacqueline Bisset are lovers in Under the Volcano.

Malcom Lowry's difficult novel about an alcoholic British ex-diplomat residing in Mexico is brought to the screen under the skillful direction of John Huston. Finney pours out his soul as the former consul drowning in booze. Bisset costars as his estranged wife, whose affair with the ex-consul's half-brother, played by Andrews, drives him over the edge. Lowry's novel, told from the ex-consul's point of view, was given a more straightforward interpretation in the screenplay (cowritten by Huston), which ultimately proved the best approach to the complex material. Finney gives the best performance of his career to date. Also with Katy Jurado and Ignacio Lopez Tarso. **(R)** *112 minutes*

UNDER THE YUM YUM TREE (1963)

★★

Jack Lemmon
Carol Lynley
Dean Jones

The comic talents of Lemmon are the highlight of this comedy about a lecherous landlord who has designs on a cute coed tenant, played by Lynley. She, in turn, wants to live with her fiancé, played by Jones, without benefit of wedlock, to determine if they are physically compatible for marriage. The dated attitudes toward love and sex make this romantic comedy nothing more than routine entertainment. Paul Lynde, Robert Lansing, Imogene Coca, and Edie Adams appear in supporting roles. **Director**—David Swift.

110 minutes

UNFAITHFULLY YOURS (1948)

★★★★

Rex Harrison
Linda Darnell

Rex Harrison plots the murder of wife Linda Darnell in Unfaithfully Yours.

Hilarious comic farce about a jealous orchestra conductor who imagines his wife to be unfaithful and fantasizes his revenge while performing at a concert. Harrison combines wit with bumbling clumsiness in a riotous performance. Don't miss his calamitous attempt to use a complicated recording machine to trick Darnell, his beautiful and loving wife, and falsify evidence as he plots her murder. One of the best movies by first-rate writer/director Preston Sturges. *105 minutes b&w*

UNFAITHFULLY YOURS (1984)

★★

Dudley Moore
Natassja Kinski

This reworking of the 1948 Preston Sturges black comedy unfolds laboriously at first, but the humorous final sequence makes the film worthwhile. Moore, a jealous symphony conductor, tries to fulfill his fantasy of murdering his kittenish young wife (Kinski), who

(Continued)

Dudley Moore toasts Nastassja Kinski and Armand Assante in Unfaithfully Yours.

(Continued)

he suspects is being unfaithful. Moore's bumbling attempts to get revenge on Kinski are the comic highlights of the film. Also with Armand Assante and Richard Libertini. **Director**—Howard Zieff. **(PG)** *96 minutes*

UNFINISHED BUSINESS (1941)

Irene Dunne
Robert Montgomery

Dunne and Montgomery star in this romantic comedy/drama about a small-town girl's search for love and adventure in the big city. Dunne plays a singer who marries foolishly and lives to regret it. The familiar story has been told many times before, with this version one of the least successful. The film lacks energy and style. Eugene Pallette, Preston Foster, Esther Dale, Dick Foran, Samuel S. Hinds, and June Clyde star in supporting roles. **Director**—Gregory La Cava. *95 minutes b&w*

THE UNFORGIVEN (1960)

Burt Lancaster
Audrey Hepburn
Charles Bickford
Lillian Gish

Lancaster and Hepburn star in this uneven western, which is marred by conflicting elements. Though the cast is filled with excellent performers, only Bickford and Gish seem at home in a western setting. The others seem miscast. John Huston is usually an excellent director, and there are some vivid scenes here, including the climactic Indian attack. However, much of the film is unevenly executed. The story is about a woman living with whites, who's suspected of being an Indian. *125 minutes*

THE UNINVITED (1944)

Ray Milland
Ruth Hussey
Gail Russell

Fans of horror films will find this to be one of the best in cinema history. Russell stars as a woman who is haunted by her dead mother. Milland and Hussey costar as the couple who try to help Russell solve the mystery. The film's theme song is the well-known "Stella by Starlight." Also with Donald Crisp, Alan Napier, Cornelia Otis Skinner, Dorothy Stickney, and Barbara Everest. **Director**—Lewis Allen. **Academy Award Nomination**—Charles Lang, cinematography. *98 minutes b&w*

UNION STATION (1950)

★★★

William Holden
Barry Fitzgerald

Actual locations and well-paced action enliven this suspense film starring Holden and Fitzgerald. The story concerns the kidnapping of a blind girl, played by Allene Roberts. The title refers to the crowded train station that the kidnappers decide to use as the ransom collection point. Also with Lyle Bettger, Nancy Olson, Robert Preston, and Jan Sterling. **Director**—Rudolph Maté. *80 minutes b&w*

AN UNMARRIED WOMAN (1978)

Jill Clayburgh

This bittersweet melodrama, concerning a woman's struggle to piece her life together after her husband walks out, is witty and sensitive. Clayburgh gives a triumphant performance in the title role. Writer/director Paul Mazursky skillfully explores America's rootless affluent society in this uncompromising film. Also stars Alan Bates, Michael Murphy, Lisa Lucas, Cliff Gorman, Pat Quinn, and Kelly Bishop. **(R) Academy Award Nominations**—best picture; Clayburgh, best actress; Mazursky, best screenplay written directly for the screen. *124 minutes*

Jill Clayburgh and Alan Bates in the bittersweet An Unmarried Woman.

THE UNSINKABLE MOLLY BROWN (1964)

Debbie Reynolds
Harve Presnell

The effervescent Debbie Reynolds in The Unsinkable Molly Brown.

Reynolds is delightful in this lively comedy/musical, based on a true story, about a country girl who rises to social prominence and wealth in Denver. She plays the title role and gets able support from Presnell, who portrays her gold-prospecting husband. The production is well-staged, and the music by Meredith Willson is entertaining, although unsensational. Ed Begley, Martita Hunt, Jack Kruschen, and Hermione Baddeley also star. **Director**—Charles Walters. **Academy Award Nominations**—Reynolds, best actress; Daniel L. Fapp, cinematography. *128 minutes*

® This movie available with closed captions for the hearing impaired.

UNTIL SEPTEMBER (1984)

★★

Karen Allen
Thierry Lhermitte

American Karen Allen falls hard for Frenchman Thierry Lhermitte in Until September.

Syrupy soap-opera romance about a bright-eyed girl from the Midwest (Allen), temporarily stranded in Paris, who falls in love with a Frenchman (Lhermitte). Much of the story is devoted to drawn-out, conversational sparring between the lovers, who gradually reveal details of their backgrounds—he's married, she's divorced. The overwrought ending is all too predictable. **Director**—Richard Marquand. **(R)** *96 minutes*

THE UNTOUCHABLES (1987)

★★★★

Kevin Costner
Sean Connery
Robert De Niro

Violence in Chicago during Prohibition: The Untouchables.

An elegant gangster saga based on the story of federal agent Eliot Ness, who worked hard to bring down the powerful Al Capone during Prohibition-era Chicago. Costner plays the honest, incorruptible Ness, and De Niro costars as the pompous, brutal Capone. Connery, however, steals the film with his energetic portrayal of honest street cop Jimmy Malone, who gives Ness the method, inspiration, and courage to "get Capone the Chicago way." Director Brian De Palma fashions a large-scale epic, with some larger-than-life characters, violent action, and mythic overtones. The script was written by acclaimed playwright David Mamet. Andy Garcia, Charles Martin Smith, and Billy Drago are effective in supporting roles. **(R) Academy Award**—Connery, best supporting actor. **Nominations**—Ennio Morricone, best music score, Patrizia von Brandenstein and Hal Gausman, best art direction; Marilyn Vance-Straker, best costume design. *120 minutes*

UP IN SMOKE (1978)

★★

Cheech Marin
Tommy Chong

Cheech and Chong make their feature-film debut in this uneven comedy, which is dependent on the drug subculture of the past generation for its humor. The story is no more than a concoction of the pair's familiar routines involving bathroom humor and slapstick sketches, and just about everyone onscreen gets high on marijuana. Also with Stacy Keach, Tom Skerritt, Edie Adams, and Strother Martin. **Director**—Lou Adler. **(R)** *87 minutes*

UP THE ACADEMY (1980)

★★

Ron Leibman
Wendell Brown
Tim Citera

This uneven comedy, presented by *Mad* magazine, lampoons the military, blacks, women, Arabs, and other vulnerable targets. The mediocre screenplay concerns the misadventures of four students at the unlikely Sheldon R. Weinberg Military Academy. The students tangle with Major Liceman, the school's scowling disciplinarian, played with relish by Leibman. When he's on the screen, the film occasionally perks

Hutch Parker, Tom Citera, and Ralph Macchio in Up the Academy.

up; otherwise, it merely stumbles along. Also with Ralph Macchio, Tom Poston, and Barbara Bach. **Director**—Robert Downey. **(R)** *88 minutes*

UP THE CREEK (1984)

★★

Tim Matheson
Stephen Furst
Dan Monahan

Tim Matheson and Stephen Furst find that they are Up the Creek.

Sophomoric humor dominates this absurd comedy in the tradition of *Animal House.* Matheson stars as a smart-aleck student who leads other misfits on a white-water rafting race in hopes of bringing notoriety to their unsung, third-rate college. The kids also engage in the expected girl chasing and boozing. Worn-out slapstick gags and amateurish acting eventually send this silly mess down the tubes. Bright spot: the pooch who plays charades. **Director**—Robert Butler. **(R)** *95 minutes*

UP THE DOWN STAIRCASE
(1967)

★★★

Sandy Dennis
Patrick Bedford
Eileen Heckart

Sandy Dennis ponders the plight of her students in Up the Down Staircase.

Dennis is sensational as a beleaguered schoolteacher in the New York City school system who tries to overcome the negativism of administrators while solving the problems of her high-school students. Although there are weak parts with an inappropriate emphasis on comedy, it's still one of the best motion pictures about the failings of modern-day inner-city school systems. Also with Ellen O'Mara, Jean Stapleton, Patrick Bedford, Ruth White, Roy Poole, and Sorrell Booke. **Director**—Robert Mulligan. *124 minutes*

UP THE SANDBOX (1972)

★★★

Barbra Streisand

Barbra Streisand tries to get control of her life in Up the Sandbox.

Touching and wryly amusing story, told in a mixture of fantasy and reality, about a Manhattan housewife who is pregnant and trapped by circumstances. Streisand, in a nonmusical role, is effective as the woman who makes a valiant effort to gain control of her life in this modern-day version of *A Doll's House*. Adroitly adapted by Paul Zindel from Anne Richardson Roiphe's best-seller with all the intelligence and humor of the original still intact. David Selby plays Streisand's philandering husband. Ariane Heller and Jane Hoffman are also featured. **Director**—Irwin Kershner. **(R)** *98 minutes*

UPTOWN SATURDAY NIGHT
(1974)

★★★

Sidney Poitier
Bill Cosby

Bill Cosby and Harry Belafonte in Uptown Saturday Night.

Poitier and Cosby star in this uninhibited comedy about the efforts of two friends to recover stolen money and a winning lottery ticket before their wives discover that the items are missing. The good-natured performances of this pair get pleasant support from Harry Belafonte, who does an imitation of Marlon Brando's *Godfather* role. The movie also stars Richard Pryor, Flip Wilson, Roscoe Lee Browne, Paula Kelly, and Rosalind Cash. **Director**—Poitier. **(PG)** *104 minutes*

URBAN COWBOY (1980)

★★★

John Travolta
Debra Winger
Scott Glenn

Travolta plays a refinery worker who spends his nights at a huge honky-tonk on the outskirts of Houston, where he

John Travolta lives a working-class macho fantasy as the Urban Cowboy.

acts out his macho cowboy fantasies. Travolta is well suited to the title role in this film version of Aaron Latham's magazine story. The irony surrounding the plot about a group of young people who emulate the dress and attitudes of an Old West long dead is magnified by the impact the film itself had on trends and singles' bars. Also with Bonnie Raitt and the Charlie Daniels Band. **Director**—James Bridges. **(PG)** *135 minutes*

USED CARS (1980)

★★½

Kurt Russell
Jack Warden

A tasteless but bitterly funny comedy about the unscrupulous competition between neighboring used-car dealers. Writer/director Robert Zemeckis fashions an outrageous film, in which nothing is sacred. Russell stars in an atypical role as a slimy used-car salesman, but David Lander and Michael McKean steal the film as broadcasting pirates who splice into the President's televised address to present an unauthorized commercial. Also with Gerrit Graham and Deborah Harmon. **(R)** *113 minutes*

U2: RATTLE AND HUM (1988)

★★★

A straightforward but stylistically scattered documentary about the Irish rock band's 1987 tour of America. Phil Janou directs part of the film in black and white and part of it in color, though his reasons for doing so are not readily ap-

® This movie available with closed captions for the hearing impaired.

Larry Mullen, Jr., Adam Clayton, The Edge, and Bono in U2: Battle and Hum.

parent. He also employs a number of stylistic devices, which reveal nothing about the band or their music. The music makes the film worthwhile viewing, however, as does a segment on the band members' side trip to Elvis Presley's Graceland. **(PG-13)** *99 minutes*

VAGABOND (1985)

★★★1/2

Sandrine Bonnaire
Macha Meril
Stephane Freiss

Downbeat study of a young, working-class French woman (Bonnaire) who chucks a soul-killing job in order to take to the road as a drifter. Although structurally similar to traditional "road pictures," *Vagabond* is no *Sullivan's Travels,* but rather a bleak look at a world of disaffection, alienation, and victimization. Bonnaire gives a moving performance as a courageous but vulnerable woman who comes to understand the limits imposed on members of her class—and gender—by an uncaring, often predatory society. Thoughtful and provocative viewing; sensitively directed by Agnes Varda. Originally filmed in French. **(No MPAA rating)**
105 minutes

THE VALACHI PAPERS (1972)

★1/2

Charles Bronson
Lino Ventura
Jill Ireland

Instead of drawing from the available factual information on the life of Mafia informer Joseph Valachi, director Terence Young mistakenly decided to make just another cliché-ridden gangster film. Bronson is competent as Va-

Charles Bronson and Jill Ireland play husband and wife in The Valachi Papers.

lachi, the gangster who talked about his career in the mob, and Ventura is good in the role of Vito Genovese, but the other performances are as mediocre as the rest of this violent movie. Also with Joseph Wiseman, Walter Chiari, Fred Valleca, and Gerald S. O'Laughlin. **(PG)**
127 minutes

VALLEY GIRL (1983)

★★★

Deborah Foreman
Nicolas Cage

An exceptional and funny teenage comedy, smartly directed by Martha Coolidge. Foreman plays a giddy, pampered denizen of the sprawling San Fernando Valley. She agonizes over her precarious involvement with a Hollywood punker—portrayed by Cage in a solid performance. The script is liberally salted with hip jargon. This film is far superior to the typical teen exploitation movie. Also with Colleen Camp, Frederic Forrest, Elizabeth Daily, and Lee Purcell. **(R)** *95 minutes*

THE VALLEY OF DECISION (1945)

★★

Greer Garson
Gregory Peck

Garson portrays a young woman who becomes a servant in the home of an industrialist and later marries his son, played by Peck. Though Garson and Peck are good in this rags-to-riches tale set in Pittsburgh, the film is neither profound nor powerful. Solid supporting performances by Donald Crisp, Lionel Barrymore, Preston Foster, Gladys Cooper, and Marsha Hunt. **Director**—Tay Garnett. **Academy Award Nomination**—Garson, best actress.
111 minutes b&w

VALLEY OF THE DOLLS (1967)

Barbara Parkins
Patty Duke
Sharon Tate

Three young women—Parkins, Duke, and Tate—decide on a career in show business in this trashy film version of Jacqueline Susann's pulp novel. The high melodrama of this badly written film often draws unintentional laughter, and the shallow performances did nothing for the careers of the actresses involved. Sadly, this is one of Tate's few well-known roles. Also with Susan Hayward, Paul Burke, Martin Milner, Charles Drake, and Lee Grant. **Director**—Mark Robson. **(PG)** *123 minutes*

VALMONT (1989)

★★1/2

Colin Firth
Annette Bening
Meg Tilly

Meg Tilly as Madame de Tourvel and Colin Firth as Valmont.

Milos Forman's version of *Les Liaisons Dangereuses* is well acted by a multinational cast but suffers from a formal style and slow pacing. The plot from Choderlos de Laclos' 18th-century novel centers around a bet between two French aristocrats. The Marquise de Merteuil (Bening) wants Valmont to seduce the innocent Cecile (Fairuza Balk), but he counters by betting the Marquise

(Continued)

This movie available on videotape and/or disc.

(Continued)
that he can win the favors of timid Madame De Tourvel (Tilly). Anyone who saw Stephen Frears' 1988 hit film *Dangerous Liaisons* or Christopher Hampton's stage production is familiar with the story. The release of this film just one year after Frears' interpretation dulls the impact of Forman's meticulous but weighty version. Also with Sian Phillips, Jeffrey Jones, Henry Thomas, and Fabia Drake. **(R) Academy Award Nomination**—Theodor Pistek, costume design. *137 minutes*

VAMP (1986)

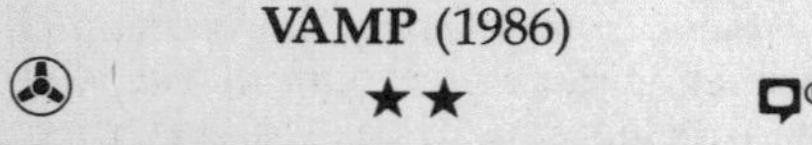

★★

Grace Jones
Robert Rusler
Chris Makepeace

Dedee Pfeiffer and Robert Rusler are horrified by the After Dark Club in Vamp.

Makepeace, Rusler, and Gedde Watanabe play three college students who set out to find a stripper for a fraternity party in this unsuccessful horror/comedy. Their candidate turns out to be Jones, a deadly vampire working in a seedy nightclub. Jones looks outrageous as the sensual Katrina, but her performing talents go unused. Deprived of dialogue, she merely hisses and spats through most of her scenes. Though the eerie, back-alley setting is colorful, it can't compensate for the haphazard script, which jumps from comic adventures to horror-filled scenes with loose abandon. **Director**—Richard Wenk. **(R)** *99 minutes*

VAMPIRE'S KISS (1989)

★★

Nicolas Cage
Jennifer Beals

Cage is wild and frantic as a literary agent who believes he has turned into a vampire. Beals costars as his lover, who puts the bite on his neck that triggers his outrageous antics. This silly outing is billed as a horror/comedy, but the story is absurd and Cage's over-the-edge performance is inappropriate. Also with Maria Conchita Alonso. **Director**—Robert Bierman. **(R)** *105 minutes*

VANISHING POINT (1971)

★★

Barry Newman
Cleavon Little

There are enough serious moments in this unusual story about a long car chase from Colorado to California to make one wonder what director Richard C. Sarafian had in mind. Newman stars as the driver of the car, and Little plays a blind, black disc jockey who helps him avoid the police. Victoria Medlin, Dean Jagger, Bob Donner, and Paul Koslo appear in supporting roles. Fans of rock music will appreciate the exceptional soundtrack. Some versions of the film run shorter. **(PG)** *107 minutes*

VASECTOMY: A DELICATE MATTER (1986)

★

Paul Sorvino
Cassandra Edwards
Abe Vigoda

A silly, lowbrow comedy devoid of wit or intelligence and amply supplied with offensive sex gags. Sorvino plays a bank manager with eight children. His beleaguered wife urges him to undergo a vasectomy or else. As for this film, it should never have been born. **Director**—Robert Burge. **(PG–13)** *90 minutes*

VERA CRUZ (1954)

★★★

Gary Cooper
Burt Lancaster

Cooper and Lancaster provide the energy and appeal that keep this western from being ordinary. They play adventurers who become involved in the plot to unseat Emperor Maximilian from power in Mexico. Cesar Romero, George Macready, Ernest Borgnine, Denise Darcel, Charles Bronson, and Sarita Montiel appear in supporting roles. **Director**—Robert Aldrich. *94 minutes*

THE VERDICT (1946)

★★½

Sydney Greenstreet
Peter Lorre

Many tricky twists and turns highlight this murder mystery. Greenstreet and Lorre are excellent in this film about an ex-Scotland Yard inspector, played by Greenstreet, who continues to work on a strange case despite his forced retirement. Unfortunately, the storyline is contrived and predictable. The cast also includes Joan Lorring, Arthur Shields, George Coulouris, Paul Cavanagh, Rosalind Ivan, and Holmes Herbert. **Director**—Don Siegel. *86 minutes b&w*

THE VERDICT (1982)

★★★★

Paul Newman
Jack Warden
Charlotte Rampling

Paul Newman stars as an attorney who regains his self-esteem in The Verdict.

Newman stars as a down-and-out lawyer who is presented with one final chance to regain his self-esteem—a lawsuit involving negligence in a Catholic hospital. Newman is superb as he comes alive with compassion and conviction in the courtroom. Director Sidney Lumet creates tension and maintains a vigorous pace even though the action is limited to only a few lo-

This movie available with closed captions for the hearing impaired.

cales. The impressive supporting cast includes Lindsay Crouse, Milo O'Shea, and James Mason. Script by David Mamet. **(R) Academy Award Nominations**—best picture; Lumet, best director; Newman, best actor; Mason, best supporting actor; Mamet, best screenplay adapted from another medium.

129 minutes

VERTIGO (1958)

★★★★

James Stewart
Kim Novak

James Stewart becomes obsessed with mysterious Kim Novak in Vertigo.

This Alfred Hitchcock thriller about a detective who's drawn into a complex plot, which is indirectly involved with his fear of heights, is one of the director's most discussed films. Stewart plays the acrophobic detective hired by an old friend to watch his wife, played by Novak. Stewart falls in love with the mysterious woman, who is preoccupied with the life of a 19th-century beauty. An unusual role for Stewart, whose humble, good-guy image is at odds with his character here—an obsessed, guilt-ridden man driven to extreme actions. Enhanced by Bernard Herrmann's haunting score. Barbara Bel Geddes, Henry Jones, and Tom Helmore costar. **(PG)** *128 minutes*

VIBES (1988)

★★

Cyndi Lauper
Jeff Goldblum
Peter Falk

In her first starring role, rock singer Lauper plays a wacky psychic. She and fellow medium Goldblum become en-

Jeff Goldblum and Cyndi Lauper are two psychics in Vibes.

tangled in a wild scheme to find gold in the Andes. Falk costars as the instigator of the adventure. The film seems a pale imitation of *Romancing the Stone* that never reaches its full comic potential. Also with Julian Sands, Michael Lerner, and Elizabeth Peña. **Director**—Ken Kwapis. **(PG)** *99 minutes*

VICE SQUAD (1982)

★★½

Season Hubley
Gary Swanson

Gary Swanson points a finger of blame at Season Hubley in Vice Squad.

This gripping police drama, set against the seedy underworld of nocturnal Los Angeles, is typical sensational fare designed to exploit violence. But there are some remarkable virtues amid the grim torture and killing—an imaginative, fast-paced script and decent acting by an unknown cast. Hubley performs ably as a "good girl" prostitute who's threatened by a sadistic lunatic, played by Wings Hauser. Swanson is convincing as a cynical vice-squad cop. **Director**—Gary A. Sherman. **(R)**

97 minutes

VICE VERSA (1988)

★★½

Judge Reinhold
Fred Savage

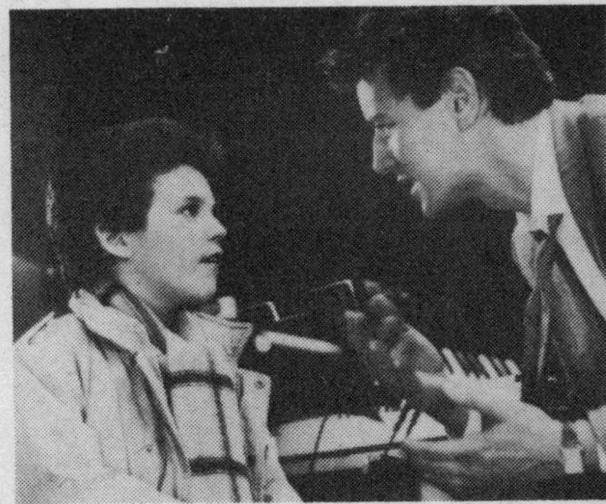

Fred Savage and Judge Reinhold have switched bodies in Vice Versa.

An uptight department store executive (Reinhold) and his 11-year-old son (Savage) temporarily switch bodies in this strained comedy, imitative of other films from this same subgenre (*Like Father, Like Son; 18 Again*). Each then assumes the other's daily roles and routines; a tall, gangly Reinhold attends school, while the diminutive son conducts business at the office. These awkward circumstances lead to a few funny moments, but the film is ultimately contrived and silly. Also with Corinne Bohrer, Swoosie Kurtz, Jane Kaczmarek, David Proval, and William Prince. **Director**—Brian Gilbert. **(PG)**

97 minutes

VICTOR/VICTORIA (1982)

★★★

Julie Andrews
Robert Preston
James Garner
Lesley Ann Warren

Blake Edwards' spicy, breezy farce stars Andrews as a down-and-out singer in Paris in 1934, who impersonates a man impersonating a woman. That's heady material for the once prim Andrews, and although she can't really convince us that she's a man, she gives an effective performance just the same. There are fine supporting performances, too,

(Continued)

Julie Andrews breezily sends up sexual manners and mores in Victor/Victoria.

(Continued)
by Preston as a gay nightclub entertainer and Garner as an American gangster. Warren steals several scenes as Garner's dumb blonde girlfriend. **(PG) Academy Award Nominations**—Andrews, best actress; Preston, best supporting actor; Warren, best supporting actress; Edwards, best screenplay based on material from another medium. *133 minutes*

VICTORY (1981)

★★

Michael Caine
Sylvester Stallone

Max von Sydow is a German propaganda officer in Victory.

Allied POWs and a professional German soccer team vie for athletic victory in a jam-packed Paris stadium in this World War II escape drama. The banal screenplay smacks of *Hogan's Heroes,* and the sentimental attitudes about winning the game strain credibility. However, the film, directed by John Huston, comes to life when the players take the field with legendary soccer great Pelé going through his extraordinary maneuvers. Also with Max Von Sydow, Daniel Massey, and Carole Laure. **(PG)**

110 minutes

VICTORY AT SEA (1954)

★★★

This rousing documentary of World War II battles at sea has been edited down from the TV documentary series. Alexander Scourby narrates these stirring descriptions of Allied encounters, with a musical score by Richard Rodgers. Throughout, the photography is superior and the editing skillful. Real-life drama is captured and preserved with vivid style. **Director**—Henry Salomon.

108 minutes b&w

VIDEODROME (1983)

★★½

James Woods
Deborah Harry

James Woods has a high-tech conversation with Deborah Harry in Videodrome.

This complex shocker about futuristic TV revels in high-tech horror and lurid effects. Woods stars as an unconventional TV executive seeking the source of a sadistic video program that causes hallucinations and brain tumors. The frantic story begins well enough, but concludes in a barrage of sensationalistic gore. Pop singer Harry costars as a bizarre radio talk-show guru. **Director**—David Cronenberg. **(R)**

87 minutes

THE VIEW FROM POMPEY'S HEAD (1955)

★★★

Richard Egan
Dana Wynter

This movie, about a New York City-based lawyer who returns to his small southern hometown on business and falls in love again with an old girlfriend, touches on the eternal issues of love and death, albeit melodramatically. Egan plays the lawyer, and Wynter is his sweetheart. Sidney Blackmer, Marjorie Rambeau, and Cameron Mitchell are fine in supporting performances. **Director**—Philip Dunne. *97 minutes*

A VIEW TO A KILL (1985)

★★ ®

Roger Moore
Grace Jones

Roger Moore and Tanya Roberts hang on for dear life in A View to Kill.

This tired chapter in the James Bond superspy series is just barely entertaining. Moore, in his seventh Agent 007 portrayal, saves the world and California's Silicon Valley from the evil scheme of a nasty industrialist who wants to monopolize the microchip market. Hair-raising escapes, thrilling stunts, and lavish scenery are in abundance. Yet, in comparison with most Bond outings, the execution here is sloppy and the momentum falters. Moore's last outing as James Bond. Christopher Walken and Tanya Roberts costar. **Director**—John Glen. **(PG)** *120 minutes*

® *This movie available with closed captions for the hearing impaired.*

THE VIKINGS (1958)

★★★

Kirk Douglas
Tony Curtis
Janet Leigh

A strong cast and vivid, on-location photography highlight this predictable Viking tale. Action fans should enjoy the battle sequences and the invasion of England by the Vikings. Also with Ernest Borgnine, Maxine Audley, and Frank Thring. Narrated by Orson Welles. **Director**—Richard Fleischer. *116 minutes*

VILLAGE OF THE DAMNED (1960)

★★★½

George Sanders
Barbara Shelley
Martin Stephens

Martin Stephens leads the unearthly children in Village of the Damned.

A subtly horrifying adaptation of *The Midwich Cuckoos,* John Wyndham's novel about an English village that mysteriously stops dead. Its population is quietly rendered unconscious while its women are impregnated by a sinister alien life-force. The brilliant but emotionless children who result from the cosmic rape eventually control the entire village. Their goal? World domination. Eleven-year-old Stephens is terrifying as the *un*human child who leads the others. A science-fiction classic; intelligently understated direction by Wolf Rilla. Also with Michael Gwynn, Laurence Naismith, John Phillips, and Richard Vernon. *78 minutes b&w*

VIOLETS ARE BLUE (1986)

★★½

Sissy Spacek
Kevin Kline

Kevin Kline and Sissy Spacek resume an old romance in Violets Are Blue.

Spacek plays a globe-trotting photojournalist who returns to her hometown and rekindles a love affair with her now married high-school sweetheart (Kline). The stars turn in noble performances, but what could have been a red-hot romance turns out to be a wilted affair. Character development is glossed over and the script is never profound. Bonnie Bedelia stands out as the all-suffering spouse. Directed by Spacek's real-life husband, production designer Jack Fisk. **(PG–13)** *88 minutes*

THE V.I.P.s (1963)

★★★

Richard Burton
Elizabeth Taylor
Maggie Smith
Rod Taylor

Louis Jourdan, Richard Burton, and Elizabeth Taylor are stranded in London in The V.I.P.s.

Quality acting and an excellent script by famed British writer Terence Rattigan make this story, about passengers stranded at a London airport because of fog, excellent entertainment. The glossy approach is appropriate for the multi-plotted storyline. Margaret Rutherford is the star among stars, but Burton, Elizabeth Taylor, Smith, Rod Taylor, Louis Jourdan, Orson Welles, and Elsa Martinelli are also appealing. **Director**—Anthony Asquith. **Academy Award**—Rutherford, best supporting actress. *119 minutes*

VIRGINIA CITY (1940)

★★½

Errol Flynn
Randolph Scott
Miriam Hopkins
Humphrey Bogart

This Civil War western concerns a plot to steal a gold shipment for the Confederate cause. Rebel spy Hopkins poses as a saloon girl to help the southern war effort. Bogart costars as a Mexican bandit. The casting is interesting, but the direction uneven. Also with Frank McHugh, Alan Hale, Douglass Dumbrille, and Guinn Williams. **Director**—Michael Curtiz. *121 minutes b&w*

THE VIRGIN SPRING (1960)

★★★★

Max Von Sydow
Brigitta Valberg
Gunnel Lindblom

Ingmar Bergman's The Virgin Spring *is a drama of the rape and murder of an innocent girl.*

A brooding, symbolic drama based on a 14th-century Swedish fable about the rape and murder of an innocent girl. After her killers are caught and executed, a natural spring bursts forth to cleanse and purify the land. Director Ingmar Bergman, in one of his finest

(Continued)

This movie available on videotape and/or disc.

(Continued)
films, has captured the passion and brutality of primitive emotions in a stunningly pictorial manner. Long-time Bergman cinematographer Sven Nykvist handles the black-and-white photography masterfully. The excellent cast includes Brigitta Pettersson and Axel Duberg. Originally filmed in Swedish. **Academy Award**—best foreign-language film.
87 minutes b&w

VISION QUEST (1985)

★★★

Matthew Modine
Linda Fiorentino

Matthew Modine with older woman Linda Fiorentino in Vision Quest.

Modine stars as a teenage *Rocky* in this romantic teen comedy about a young man coming of age. Modine's sport is wrestling, and he must lose weight in order to compete against the champion brute—while at the same time he falls hopelessly in love with an older woman (Fiorentino). The movie pulls off both the quest and the predictable romance with believability. **Director**—Harold Becker. **(R)** *102 minutes*

VISITING HOURS (1982)

★★

Lee Grant
Michael Ironside
William Shatner

Grant stars as an opinionated television reporter who is relentlessly pursued by a knife-wielding psychotic (Ironside). The madman is so determined to kill Grant that he tracks her to a hospital where she is recovering from his earlier assault. The cliché-rife suspense story has its tense moments, but the hackneyed plot is strictly déjà vu. There are occasional references to the slasher's troubles with his mother. Nothing new or astounding here. **Director**—Jean-Claude Lord. **(R)** *101 minutes*

VISIT TO A SMALL PLANET (1960)

★★½

Jerry Lewis

This Lewis film is based on an urbane, satirical Gore Vidal play, in which a being from outer space visits Earth to get an insight into our strange habits. Lewis is the alien creature, and he plays the part for heavy-handed laughs as slapstick prevails. Joan Blackman, Earl Holliman, Fred Clark, Lee Patrick, Gale Gordon, John Williams, and Jerome Cowan appear in supporting roles. **Director**—Norman Taurog.
87 minutes b&w

VITAL SIGNS (1990)

★★

Adrian Pasdar
Diane Lane
Jack Gwaltney
Laura San Giacomo

The group of medical students in the film Vital Signs.

Operating rooms are filled, patients cry out for emergency treatment, and love blossoms not far from the intensive care unit. So it goes for the group of tense third-year medical students who populate this glossy hospital melodrama. Despite the urgent situations frequently faced by the characters, the film seems drained of energy, and the characters have been stolen from prime-time television. Also with Jimmy Smits, Norma Aleandro, Jane Adams, Tim Ransom, and Bradley Whitford. **Director**—Marisa Silver. **(R)** *103 minutes*

VIVA LAS VEGAS (1964)

★★★

Elvis Presley
Ann-Margret

Ann-Margret and Elvis Presley heat things up in Viva Las Vegas!

A better-than-average star vehicle for Presley, who plays a singing race-car driver. The glitter of the gambling city and some exciting racing scenes perk up the proceedings. Ann-Margret is excellent as a cabaret dancer who attracts Presley's attention. Excellent production numbers. Cesare Danova and William Demarest are also in the cast. **Director**—George Sidney. *85 minutes*

VIVA ZAPATA! (1952)

★★★★

Marlon Brando
Jean Peters
Anthony Quinn

Marlon Brando plays the hero of the Mexican Revolution in Viva Zapata!

® This movie available with closed captions for the hearing impaired.

Elia Kazan's classic about a Mexican peasant who becomes the president of his country during the Mexican Revolution. Brando plays Emiliano Zapata, and Quinn plays his brother. John Steinbeck's script is provocative without being preachy, and under Kazan's superb direction the agony as well as the glory of the revolution is clearly presented. Joseph Wiseman, Arnold Moss, Frank Silvera, Margo, and Mildred Dunnock appear in supporting roles. **Academy Award**—Quinn, best supporting actor. **Nominations**—Brando, best actor; Steinbeck, story and screenplay.
112 minutes b&w

VOICES (1979)

Michael Ontkean
Amy Irving

A lackluster romantic melodrama about a young musician who falls in love with an overprotected deaf woman. The film is cluttered with contrived subplots. Ontkean, as the struggling rock singer, seems stifled in his role. The film's only appeal is the performance of Irving as the girl who realizes her dream to become a ballerina despite her handicap. Also with Alex Rocco, Barry Miller, and Viveca Lindfors. **Director**—Robert Markowitz. **(PG)**
107 minutes

VOLUNTEERS (1985)

 ★★

Tom Hanks
John Candy

A plodding, tasteless comedy that spoofs the youthful idealism of the 1960s. Hanks stars as a snooty rich kid who joins the Peace Corps to avoid a gambling debt. He winds up in Thailand, where he and his fellow corpsmen are assigned to build a bridge. Black marketers, Chinese Communists, and CIA operatives get tangled in the misadventure, which lapses into silliness. Rita Wilson appears in a supporting role. **Director**—Nicholas Meyer. **(R)**
107 minutes

VON RYAN'S EXPRESS (1965)

 ★★★1/2

Frank Sinatra
Trevor Howard

Frank Sinatra and Trevor Howard in the adventure Von Ryan's Express.

This exciting action film is about a group of prisoners who escape from an Italian POW camp. The most memorable sequence involves the prisoners' takeover of a German freight train, which they need to complete their escape. Sinatra is splendidly cast as a cynical but ultimately heroic American colonel, who leads the English prisoners in their escape. Howard plays an English officer outranked by Sinatra. There are good performances as well from Sergio Fantoni, Edward Mulhare, Raffaella Carra, and Brad Dexter. **Director**—Mark Robson. *117 minutes*

VOYAGE OF THE DAMNED (1976)

Faye Dunaway
Oskar Werner
Max Von Sydow
Orson Welles

Faye Dunaway and Oskar Werner journey on the Voyage of the Damned.

This compelling melodrama deals with a tragic World War II episode, when a shipload of Jews sailed from Germany to Cuba only to be returned to face death. The film plods through a parade of melodramatic vignettes, yet the historical subject matter is so vital and absorbing that the ponderous format can be forgiven. A huge all-star cast portrays the doomed passengers and the onshore characters. Such luminaries as Welles and José Ferrer are there for fleeting moments. Dunaway and Von Sydow are outstanding in more significant roles. Also with Malcolm McDowell, James Mason, and Lee Grant. **Director**—Stuart Rosenberg. **(PG) Academy Award Nominations**—Grant, best supporting actress; Steve Shagan and David Butler, best screenplay based on material from another medium.
134 minutes

VOYAGE TO THE BOTTOM OF THE SEA (1961)

Walter Pidgeon
Robert Sterling
Joan Fontaine

Excellent trick photography and entertaining action sequences make this science-fiction tale worthwhile for fans. The adventures of the atomic submarine assigned to destroy a radiation belt that threatens the planet are superficial by and large, but the acting of Pidgeon, Sterling, Fontaine, Peter Lorre, Frankie Avalon, and Barbara Eden make the sub's mission seem believable. **Director**—Irwin Allen.
106 minutes

W

WABASH AVENUE (1950)

Betty Grable
Victor Mature
Phil Harris

Mature and Harris both have designs on Grable in this musical set during the 1892 Chicago World's Fair. Grable sparkles as she sings, dances, and tries to decide which man she'll choose in this colorful production. A remake of *Coney Island* (1934), which also starred Grable. The cast also includes Reginald Gar-
(Continued)

(Continued)
diner, Margaret Hamilton, James Barton, and Barry Kelley. **Director**—Henry Koster. *92 minutes*

THE WACKIEST SHIP IN THE ARMY (1960)

Jack Lemmon
Ricky Nelson

This entertaining movie, starring Lemmon and Nelson, treads a thin line between comedy and drama. The story involves the World War II adventures of a reconditioned sailing ship commissioned by the Army, which is manned by an inexperienced crew. Lemmon heads the brave but offbeat group. The story intensifies when the ship is used as a decoy to land an agent behind Japanese lines in the South Pacific. Also with John Lund, Chips Rafferty, Joby Baker, and Tom Tully. **Director**—Richard Murphy. *99 minutes*

WAGONMASTER (1950)

 ★★★1/2

Ben Johnson
Harry Carey, Jr.

An excellent western about a wagon train of Mormons heading for Utah in 1879. Johnson and Carey, two drifting cowboys, join up to help guide the settlers, who are led by a no-nonsense wagonmaster, played by Ward Bond. Director John Ford's eloquence in depicting simple virtues raises this adventure to classic stature and infuses the film with the poetry of the West. Writer Frank Nugent infuses the simple story with sensitivity and poetry. The film served as the basis for the TV series *Wagon Train*. Also with Joanne Dru, James Arness, and Jane Darwell. *85 minutes b&w*

THE WAGONS ROLL AT NIGHT (1941)

Humphrey Bogart
Sylvia Sidney

Bogart stars in this mediocre film as the manager of a small circus. Sidney costars as his girlfriend who takes a sudden interest in the new lion tamer, Eddie Albert. The familiar story about a love triangle offers nothing new, though Bogart's fans may enjoy him in a lesser-known role. A few comic bits derive from the naiveté of Albert's character. **Director**—Ray Enright. *83 minutes b&w*

WAIT UNTIL DARK (1967)

Alan Arkin
Audrey Hepburn

Spine-tingling thriller set in a Greenwich Village brownstone where a blind woman is terrorized by a psychopathic killer. Hepburn is superb as the fast-thinking victim who uses her blindness against her pursuer by darkening the house and fighting him on equal terms. Arkin's performance as the vicious intruder is a mixture of menace and good humor, making him a memorable villain. The action rarely moves outside the house, but the deft direction turns this into an asset. From the Frederick Knott play, the drama also features Richard Crenna and Efrem Zimbalist, Jr. **Director**—Terence Young. **Academy Award Nomination**—Hepburn, best actress. *105 minutes*

WAKE OF THE RED WITCH (1948)

John Wayne
Luther Adler

Gig Young, Paul Fix, and John Wayne in Wake of the Red Witch.

Missing pearls, combative treasure seekers, and an alluring woman yield a standard adventure film with several good action scenes. Wayne and Adler play two treasure hunters who seek their fortune in the East Indies. Though the story is sometimes confusing, there are enough exciting sequences to make the viewing worthwhile. Gail Russell, Gig Young, Dennis Hoey, Henry Daniell, and Paul Fix also appear in supporting roles. **Director**—Edward Ludwig. *106 minutes b&w*

WALK, DON'T RUN (1966)

Cary Grant
Samantha Eggar
Jim Hutton

Only the charm and comic acting skills of Grant salvage this witless farce about two men and a young woman who share an apartment in Tokyo during the 1964 Olympics. Instead of winning the girl, this time Grant is a matchmaker who helps Eggar and Hutton find love; the viewer will find boredom. After this film, Grant retired from movies. John Standing, Ted Hartley, and Miiko Taka appear in supporting roles. A remake of the delightful 1943 film *The More the Merrier.* **Director**—Charles Walters. *114 minutes*

WALKER (1987)

Ed Harris
Richard Masur

Ed Harris (center) is temporarily master of all he surveys in Walker.

This jumbled satire tells the supposedly true story of 19th-century mercenary William Walker, who invaded Nicaragua with a ragtag platoon of gunslingers. From 1856-1857, he served as that country's president and was supported in his ambitions by American tycoon Cornelius Vanderbilt. Harris stars in the title role and plays his part—as do all the actors—fairly broadly, which suits the absurdist, mocking approach to the material taken by director Alex Cox (*Repo Man; Sid and Nancy*). The film is laced with anachronisms—characters reading *People* magazine, scenes with Coke bottles, etc.—as a means to connect the Walker fiaso with America's involvement with Nicaragua in the 1980's.

Such heavy-handed techniques are daring, but often make for difficult viewing: There's no sympathy for the characters involved and the sardonic tone is monotonous. Also with Marlee Matlin, Rene Auberjonois, Sy Richardson, John Diehl, Peter Boyle, Gerrit Graham, and Pedro Armendariz. **(R)**
95 minutes

WALKING MY BABY BACK HOME (1953)

★★

Donald O'Connor
Janet Leigh
Buddy Hackett

O'Connor, Leigh, and Hackett brighten this lightweight musical, but they can't quite overcome the trite material. The plot involves two army buddies (O'Connor and Hackett) who put together a Dixieland band. The dancing of O'Connor and Leigh is pleasant, and the music is fairly entertaining, although the score contains no classics. Also with Lori Nelson, Scatman Crothers, John Hubbard, and Kathleen Lockhart. **Director**—Lloyd Bacon.
95 minutes

WALKING TALL (1973)

 ★★★

Joe Don Baker
Elizabeth Hartman

Joe Don Baker and Elizabeth Hartman stand firm in Walking Tall.

This highly successful but violent movie vividly depicts the courageous stand of Tennessee sheriff Buford Pusser against local mobsters. The movie exploits blood and violence, but the story of the real-life hero remains effective. Baker is believable in the role of Pusser; Hartman portrays his wife, who is murdered by the local mob. Noah Beery, Jr., Gene Evans, and Felton Perry appear in supporting roles. **Director**—Phil Karlson. **(R)** *126 minutes*

WALKING TALL—PART 2 (1975)

 ★★

Bo Svenson

A continuation of the legend of Buford Pusser, the Tennessee sheriff who was determined to rid his community of corruption. Svenson replaces Joe Don Baker in the lead role of this watered-down sequel to the popular and financially successful original film. Shot on location in Tennessee. Also with Luke Askew, Richard Jaeckel, Noah Beery, Jr., and Robert DoQui. **Director**—Earl Bellamy. **(PG)** *109 minutes*

A WALK IN THE SUN (1945)

★★★★

Dana Andrews
Richard Conte
Sterling Holloway
John Ireland

In A Walk in the Sun, *Dana Andrews comes to the aid of a frightened Lloyd Bridges.*

Excellent acting and authentic settings make this one of the finest war films in cinema history. Andrews, Conte, Holloway, and Ireland star in the story of an Army platoon of infantrymen in Italy who must attack a German-held farmhouse. The production avoids the superficiality of so many war movies by stressing the human element over battlefield action. Also with George Tyne, Herbert Rudley, Richard Benedict, Norman Lloyd, Lloyd Bridges, and Huntz Hall. **Director**—Lewis Milestone.
117 minutes b&w

WALK ON THE WILD SIDE (1962)

 ★★

Jane Fonda
Capucine
Barbara Stanwyck
Laurence Harvey

Stanwyck plays a lesbian madam of a brothel, Fonda and Capucine portray prostitutes, and Harvey is a troubled man in search of his lost love in this sordid melodrama. The movie is based on one of Nelson Algren's novels; unfortunately, the story was left behind, and just the seamy elements were brought to the screen. The opening title sequence, designed by Saul Bass, is original and memorable. Also with Anne Baxter and Richard Rust. **Director**—Edward Dmytryk. *114 minutes b&w*

WALK PROUD (1979)

 ★★

Robby Benson
Sarah Holcomb

Robby Benson plays a troubled member of a Chicano street gang in Walk Proud.

Soft-spoken, clean-cut Benson plays a tough Chicano youth in this gang movie that leans heavily on *West Side Story*. Despite heavy makeup and an accent, Benson is still unconvincing in this portrayal, which is far removed from his typical wholesome characters. The predictable plot focuses on Benson's conflict between his love for an Anglo girl, played by Holcomb, and his loyalty to his gang friends. Also with Henry Darrow, Domingo Ambriz, and Pepe Serna. **Director**—Robert Collins. **(PG)** *102 minutes*

This movie available on videotape and/or disc.

WALK THE PROUD LAND (1956)

Audie Murphy

Murphy stars in this sensitive western as an Indian agent attempting to bring peace between the Apaches and white settlers. Some of the dialogue is riddled with clichés, but the acting and direction are competent enough to keep most viewers interested. Also with Anne Bancroft, Pat Crowley, Robert Warwick, Charles Drake, Tommy Rall, and Jay Silverheels. **Director**—Jesse Hibbs. *88 minutes*

WALL STREET (1987)

★★★ [CC]

Charlie Sheen
Michael Douglas
Martin Sheen

Charlie Sheen in the high-pressure world of big money in Wall Street.

Director Oliver Stone's melodrama hammers fiercely away at amoral corporate types, inside trading, stock manipulation, and questionable practices involving contemporary big business. Douglas had the role of a lifetime as Gordon Gekko, a corrupt corporate raider who manipulates a novice stockbroker, played by Charlie Sheen. Martin Sheen plays the young broker's father, who sees his son being lured by the money and advantages of Gekko's extravagant lifestyle. The topical subject matter lent the film an immediacy at the time of the film's release, coming shortly after the October 1987 market crash and the Ivan Boesky trading scandal. But the simplistic characters, who are either good or villainous, and the moralizing ending make the film nothing more than a well-done soap opera. Actors in secondary parts are burdened with characters drawn too superficially to be effective, including Daryl Hannah, Sean Young, James Spader, Hal Holbrook, and Terence Stamp. **Academy Award**—Douglas, best actor. **(R)** *124 minutes.*

WALTZ OF THE TOREADORS (1962)

 ★★

Peter Sellers

General Peter Sellers suspects the help in Waltz of the Toreadors.

The translation of Jean Anouilh's saucy comedy from stage to the screen is mishandled. However, Sellers, playing a lecherous retired general, is memorable as he tries to keep his young mistress away from his son. The movie is interesting, although the vibrancy of the play is missing. Also with Margaret Leighton, Dany Robin, John Fraser, Prunella Scales, and Cyril Cusack. **Director**—John Guillermin. *105 minutes*

THE WANDERERS (1979)

Ken Wahl
John Friedrich
Karen Allen

Though not widely distributed upon initial release, this film about growing up in the Bronx in the 1960s has since gained a respectable following. The story, based on the novel by Richard Price, is a series of vignettes involving a group of Italian youths who try to survive in the city jungle among the fearsome Irish Ducky Boys, the grotesque Fordham Baldies, and other adversaries. A nostalgic but uncompromising look at an era long gone. An effective re-creation of a specific time and place. Also with Alan Rosenberg, Linda Manz, and Toni Kalem. **Director**—Philip Kaufman. **(R)** *113 minutes*

THE WANNSEE CONFERENCE (1987)

 ★★★

Gerd Bockmann

A chilling, true-to-life account of the infamous meeting in Germany on January 20, 1942, where plans for "the Final Solution" were engineered. As though at a board meeting of a large corporation, 14 Nazi leaders gather at a charming house in a Berlin suburb. With infinite good humor, the group calls for the systematic annihilation of European Jews—some 11 million persons. The actual meeting lasted 85 minutes, as does this provocative film. **Director**—Heinz Schirk. **(No MPAA rating)** *85 minutes*

WANTED: DEAD OR ALIVE (1987)

  [CC]

Rutger Hauer

Rutger Hauer confronts Gene Simmons in Wanted: Dead or Alive.

A predictable but smartly directed action thriller about a bounty hunter on the trail of an Arab terrorist who is wreaking havoc on Los Angeles. The gimmick of this film is that the main character, played by Dutch actor Hauer, is the great-grandson of the character that Steve McQueen established on the 1950s TV western series *Wanted: Dead or Alive.* McQueen's character was a bounty hunter as well. The rest of the cast includes Gene Simmons (formerly of the rock group KISS) as the terrorist and Robert Guillaume as a cop. Though the plot and main character are familiar, the link to another character from another medium offers an unusual twist. **Director**—Gary Sherman. **(R)** *104 minutes*

[CC] *This movie available with closed captions for the hearing impaired.*

WAR AND PEACE (1956)

★★

Audrey Hepburn
Henry Fonda
Mel Ferrer
Herbert Lom
John Mills

Mai Britt and Helmut Dantine in the sweeping epic War and Peace.

This film version of Leo Tolstoy's great novel about Russia during the time of Napoleon's invasion is presented like a Cecil B. De Mille epic—there's too much emphasis on sweeping battle scenes and other spectacles. Because of this misplaced focus, Tolstoy's brilliant characterizations are lost despite an excellent cast of actors that also includes Barry Jones, Oscar Homolka, Wilfrid Lawson, Vittorio Gassman, Anita Ekberg, Helmut Dantine, and Mai Britt. **Directors**—King Vidor and Mario Soldati. **Academy Award Nominations**—Vidor, best director; Jack Cardiff, cinematography. *208 minutes*

WARGAMES (1983)

★★★

Matthew Broderick
Ally Sheedy
Dabney Coleman

A timely comedy/drama about a high-school computer whiz (Broderick) who accidentally accesses the military's air-defense computer system and touches off a panic. It's an exciting movie that offers much thought about thermonuclear war as the ultimate no-win situation. The story is presented from the teens' point of view, with the younger set depicted as having all the answers,

Matthew Broderick and Ally Sheedy inadvertently imperil the world in WarGames.

while the adults are objects of ridicule or scorn. The tense, final sequence is well paced by director John Badham. **(PG) Academy Award Nominations**—Lawrence Lasker and Walter F. Parkes, best original screenplay written directly for the screen; William A. Fraker, cinematography. *110 minutes*

WARLOCK (1959)

★★★

Henry Fonda
Richard Widmark
Anthony Quinn

Gunfighter Henry Fonda makes his play to clean up the town called Warlock.

Fonda plays a gunfighter hired to bring law and order to a small western town. The movie follows his success as a lawman when he ousts the villains, and then details his fall from grace after his friend, played by Quinn, betrays him. Some may find the use of some obvious symbolism and the excessive number of subplots a detriment to an otherwise straightforward story. Also with Dorothy Malone, Richard Arlen, and Regis Toomey. **Director**—Edward Dmytryk. *122 minutes*

WARNING SIGN (1985)

★★

Sam Waterston
Kathleen Quinlan
Yaphet Kotto

Kathleen Quinlan and Sam Waterston have received a Warning Sign.

Deadly microbes are the stars of this shrill, high-tech melodrama that takes a dim view of genetic engineering and biological warfare. Tension builds effectively when killer germs are accidentally spilled at a research lab, causing the facility to be sealed and trapping workers inside. The film becomes unconvincing, however, when rescue efforts begin and a scientist desperately whips up a last-minute miracle cure. **Director**—Hal Barwood. **(R)** *99 minutes*

THE WAR OF THE ROSES (1989)

★★★

Michael Douglas
Kathleen Turner
Danny DeVito

Douglas and Turner star as Oliver and Barbara Rose, a yuppie couple locked in a bitter divorce battle. Told in flashback by Douglas' attorney, played by DeVito, the film follows the course of their seemingly idyllic marriage and then emphasizes their vindictive behavior during the divorce. Douglas, Turner, and DeVito are reteamed after their success in *Romancing the Stone* and *Jewel of the Nile*, but don't expect a romantic comedy with a neatly packaged happy ending. This film is a black comedy, with a vicious undertone to the couple's attempts to outdo each other's dirty

(Continued)

Kathleen Turner and Michael Douglas are about to embark on The War of the Roses.

(Continued)

tricks. DeVito's directorial style features obvious lighting effects and self-conscious camera moves, but it is more distinctive than those found in most big-budget star vehicles. Not for everyone's taste. Also with Marianne Sagebrecht, Sean Astin, Heather Fairfield, G.D. Spradlin, and Peter Donat. **(R)**

116 minutes

WAR OF THE WORLDS (1953)

★★★½

Gene Barry
Les Tremayne
Ann Robinson

Spectacular special effects mark this sci-fi/drama about a Martian invasion of Earth. Adapted from the H.G. Wells story, the plot offers little more than the initial premise of the confrontation between Earthlings and Martians. However, the simulated eradication of the city of Los Angeles was enough to win the Oscar for best special effects. Exciting and entertaining visuals compensate for any lapse in the drama. Produced by legendary science-fiction director/producer George Pal. Also with Robert Cornthwaite and Henry Brandon. **Director**—Byron Haskin. **(G)** *85 minutes*

WAR PARTY (1989)

★★ ®

Billy Wirth
Kevin Dillon
Tim Sampson

In modern-day Montana, American Indians battle bigoted whites in this pretentious action film that makes a feeble statement on contemporary race relations. A revengeful white man shoots an Indian during a mock historic battle between the U.S. Cavalry and Blackfoot tribesmen, triggering a bloodbath between the two groups. The Indians escape into the wilderness with a posse in pursuit. The film's attempts at a socially conscious statement are muted by the stereotyped characters that populate both sides of the confrontation. The use of the action genre, with an emphasis on blood and violence, seems inappropriate as well. Also with Jimmie Ray Weeks, Kevyn Major Howard, Jerry Hardin, and Tantoo Cardinal. **Director**—Frank Roddam. **(R)**

96 minutes

THE WARRIORS (1979)

★★★

Michael Beck
Thomas Waites

Youth gangs roam New York City's streets and subways in this glossy film that looks similar to *A Clockwork Orange.* The story focuses on one gang, which is falsely accused of murder. They spend the movie making a dash for their home turf in Coney Island while being chased by rival gangs and the cops. Walter Hill's direction is slick and spectacular. Also with Dorsey Wright, Brian Tyler, and Deborah Van Valkenburgh. **(R)**

94 minutes

THE WAR WAGON (1967)

★★★

John Wayne
Kirk Douglas

John Wayne and Kirk Douglas team up to knock over The War Wagon.

Wayne and Douglas star in this western about an ex-con, played by Wayne, bent on revenge. Wayne teams up with Douglas to rob an armored wagon filled with gold, which he believes rightfully belongs to him. The plot is predictable, but the action and solid performances will keep your interest. The excellent cast also includes Howard Keel, Robert Walker, Keenan Wynn, Bruce Dern, Gene Evans, Bruce Cabot, and Joanna Barnes. **Director**—Burt Kennedy.

101 minutes

THE WATCHER IN THE WOODS (1980)

★★

Bette Davis
Carroll Baker

A flimsy and silly suspense movie from the Walt Disney studio. The film involves an American family that rents an old house in England and becomes involved with a supernatural mystery. The film maintains tension, but it's full of contrived scare-effects that strain credibility. Davis has a minor role as the crusty landlady whose daughter mysteriously vanished from the strange house 30 years ago. She's terrific despite the nonsensical material. Originally released at 100 minutes. Also with Lynn-Holly Johnson, Kyle Richards, and David McCallum. **Director**—John Hough. **(PG)** *84 minutes*

WATCH ON THE RHINE (1943)

★★★

Paul Lukas
Bette Davis

Bette Davis and Paul Lukas are pursued by dogged Nazi agents in Watch on the Rhine.

The propaganda aspects of this film seem obvious in retrospect, but the brilliant performances of Lukas and Davis still brighten the movie. Lukas portrays a German underground leader confronted by Nazis wherever he goes—

® *This movie available with closed captions for the hearing impaired.*

even in Washington, D.C. Davis plays his wife. The movie is based on Lillian Hellman's play, and the film script was written by Dashiell Hammett. The excellent cast also includes Lucile Watson, George Coulouris, Henry Daniell, Donald Woods, and Geraldine Fitzgerald. **Director**—Herman Shumlin. **Academy Award**—Lukas, best actor. **Nominations**—best picture; Watson, best supporting actress; Hammett, screenplay. *113 minutes b&w*

WATER (1986)

★★

Michael Caine
Brenda Vaccaro

This effervescent but uneven political satire, set on an unimportant British Caribbean island, does include a humorous, well-timed conclusion. Caine stars as the laid-back governor, who must deal with renewed interest in the local economy after a Perrier-like mineral water is discovered. Vaccaro is amusing as the governor's outrageous wife. Valerie Perrine and Leonard Rossiter also star. **Director**—Dick Clement. **(PG-13)** *95 minutes*

WATERLOO BRIDGE (1940)

★★★

Vivien Leigh
Robert Taylor

Wartime romance with Vivien Leigh and Robert Taylor in Waterloo Bridge.

Tearful but effective wartime love story about a dancer and an officer who meet and fall in love during World War I. When he is reported missing, she resorts to prostitution to earn a living. Leigh is stunning as the haunted heroine who uses the train station at Waterloo Bridge as her meeting place for customers. Her reunion with Taylor on the same spot is a highly charged emotional *tour de force* despite the contrivance, and is worthy of several handkerchiefs. Also with Lucile Watson, Maria Ouspenskaya, and C. Aubrey Smith. **Director**—Mervyn LeRoy. *109 minutes b&w*

WATERMELON MAN (1970)

★★½

Godfrey Cambridge
Estelle Parsons

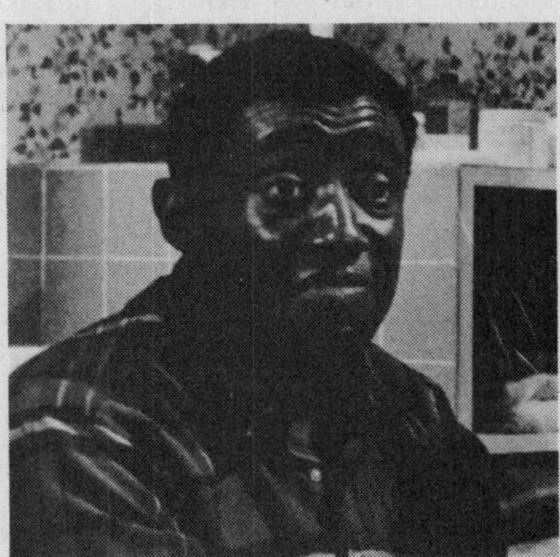

Godfrey Cambridge gets a big surprise in Watermelon Man.

Cambridge stars in this comedy about a bigoted white insurance salesman who wakes up one morning to discover he's suddenly black. Once the impact of the funny and preposterous premise subsides, the movie drags, and some of the inherent social satire is weakened. Also with Howard Caine, Mantan Moreland, Kay Kimberly, and D'Urville Martin. **Director**—Melvin Van Peebles. **(R)** *100 minutes*

WATERSHIP DOWN (1978)

★★★

An animated fantasy about a family of rabbits, based on Richard Adams' best-selling novel. This is a serious story, with the cottontails fleeing their burrow because of man's encroachment. In their painful search for a new home, the rabbits are attacked by dogs, snared, ravaged by hawks, and set upon by other rabbits. The beautiful animation and the allegorical story make this feature meaningful for adults as well as children. Sir Ralph Richardson and Zero Mostel provide some of the voices. **Director**—Martin Rosen. **(PG)** *92 minutes*

THE WAY WE WERE (1973)

★★★

Barbra Streisand
Robert Redford

Barbra Streisand and Robert Redford in the nostalgic The Way We Were.

The splendid performances of Streisand and Redford sustain this nostalgic journey from the 1930s to the 1950s, including a sequence involving the McCarthy era. Parts of the film are particularly effective, including the scenes in which Streisand and Redford fall in love. But some of the nostalgia is too maudlin. Interestingly, some of the subplot involving McCarthyism was edited out just before the film was released, thereby weakening the storyline. Bradford Dillman, Lois Chiles, Murray Hamilton, Patrick O'Neal, and Viveca Lindfors are in supporting roles. **Director**—Sydney Pollack. **(PG) Academy Award Nominations**—Streisand, best actress; Harry Stradling, Jr., cinematography. *118 minutes*

A WEDDING (1978)

★★★

Carol Burnett
Desi Arnaz, Jr.
Amy Stryker

Innovative director Robert Altman reveals a host of family emotions and crises during an extraordinary wedding day. The tart, energetic comedy is rich with Altman's gems of insight and sat-

(Continued)

This movie available on videotape and/or disc.

Desi Arnaz, Jr., and Mia Farrow get together in A Wedding.

(Continued)
ire about marriage, religion, and middle-class values. A first-rate cast includes many newcomers along with a number of film veterans. Altman fans won't be disappointed. Also with Vittorio Gassman, Geraldine Chaplin, Mia Farrow, Paul Dooley, Lillian Gish, and Howard Duff. **(PG)** *125 minutes*

WEEDS (1987)

★★★

Nick Nolte
Lane Smith

Nolte gives a powerful performance as a convict who discovers he has an interest in theater. After his release from prison, he organizes a traveling theater group composed of fellow inmates, and eventually ends up off-Broadway. The film unfolds with humor, cynicism, and suspense as an embezzler, a shoplifter, a pimp, and other seasoned cons evolve into an effective stage group. The enthusiasm and inspiration of the small troupe propels the movie to an upbeat if somewhat unconvincing conclusion. Loosely based on the actual experiences of Rick Cluchey, a playwright and former convict. Also with Joe Mantegna, William Forsythe, John Toles-Baye, Ernie Hudson, and Rita Taggart. **Director**—John Hancock. **(R)** *115 minutes*

WEEKEND AT BERNIE'S (1989)

★

Andrew McCarthy
Jonathan Silverman

A colorless one-joke farce that recycles the worn-out comic bit about disguising a corpse as a living human being. McCarthy and Silverman play young in-

The host's dead body proves a source of embarrassment during a Weekend at Bernie's.

surance company executives who are invited to a party at their boss' beach house in the Hamptons. There they discover his dead body and then spend the rest of the film carting the corpse around under the noses of easily fooled guests and associates. Terry Kiser fares well as the stiff of the title, mainly because he does not have to utter the poorly written lines or actively participate in the foolish situations. Also with Catherine Mary Stewart, Catherine Parks, and Don Calfa. **Director**—Ted Kotcheff. **(PG-13)** *99 minutes*

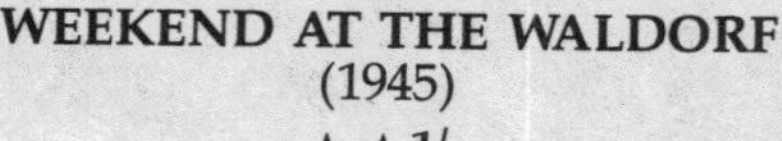

WEEKEND AT THE WALDORF (1945)

★★½

Ginger Rogers
Walter Pidgeon
Van Johnson
Lana Turner

This pleasant entertainment is a weak imitation of the famous *Grand Hotel*, with less compelling acting and less subtle characterizations. If the viewer doesn't expect too much, these characters and their experiences at New York's largest hotel make for an entertaining viewing experience. The cast also includes Keenan Wynn, Robert Benchley, Edward Arnold, and Phyllis Thaxter. **Director**—Robert Z. Leonard. *130 minutes b&w*

WEE WILLIE WINKIE (1937)

★★★

Shirley Temple

This loose adaptation of the Rudyard Kipling story features Temple as Priscilla Williams, who joins her grandfather (C. Aubrey Smith), a British officer stationed in India. The young heroine eventually charms the entire regiment, including a gruff sergeant played by

Shirley Temple joins the regiment in Wee Willie Winkle.

Victor McLaglen. Though overly syrupy family entertainment, this lushly set production teamed Temple and McLaglen to both their advantages. Originally released at 99 minutes. Also featured are Cesar Romero, Constance Collier, and Michael Whalen. **Director**—John Ford. *74 minutes b&w*

WEIRD SCIENCE (1985)

★

Anthony Michael Hall
Ilan Mitchell-Smith
Kelly LeBrock

Obnoxious, mean-spirited teen comedy/fantasy filled with desperate gimmicks and vulgar dialogue. Hall and Mitchell-Smith play high-school nerds who use a computer to create their ultimate female playmate in the form of sensuous LeBrock. The film then goes overboard as a Pershing missile penetrates their bedroom floor, a wild house party is invaded by motorcycle bullies, and an intimidating older brother is turned into a frog. Weird indeed. **Director**—John Hughes. **(PG-13)** *94 minutes*

WELCOME HOME (1989)

★★

Kris Kristofferson
JoBeth Williams

Franklin Schaffner's final film is a muddled soap opera about the heartbreak-

® This movie available with closed captions for the hearing impaired.

ing aftereffects of the Vietnam War. Kristofferson stars as an Air Force pilot who returns to the United States after being classified as missing in action for 17 years. His sudden reappearance provokes conflicts with his remarried American wife (Williams), his teenage son (Thomas Wilson Brown), and certain military officials. Kristofferson performs poorly in the lead role, while the other actors seem unable to add any life to their characters. The main emotion in the film is anguish, and characters consistently wring their hands and look soulfully at each other. It's unfortunate that such a competent director as Schaffner *(Planet of the Apes; Papillon; Patton)* ended his career with such a poor film. Also with Trey Wilson, Sam Waterston, and Brian Keith. **(R)**

96 minutes

WE OF THE NEVER NEVER (1983)

Angela Punch McGregor
Arthur Dignam
Tony Barry

Angela Punch McGregor comes to the Australian outback in We of the Never Never.

From Australia, a visually magnificent film with a plot reminiscent of many westerns. McGregor stars as the city-reared bride who follows her cattleman husband to the outback. There she struggles to overcome the prejudices of both the aborigines and the white ranch hands. Unfortunately, director Igor Auzins concentrates on majestic scenery and period details at the expense of dramatic involvement. **(G)**

132 minutes

WE'RE NO ANGELS (1955)

  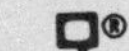

Humphrey Bogart
Peter Ustinov
Aldo Ray

Bad boys: Humphrey Bogart, Peter Ustinov, and Aldo Ray in We're No Angels.

Bogart, Ustinov, and Ray are delightful in this lighthearted story about three escapees from Devil's Island who help a beleaguered shopkeeper prosper and outwit his foes. The production, based on the Albert Husson play, is stagy but warm and humorous. Joan Bennett, Basil Rathbone, John Smith, and Leo G. Carroll star in supporting roles. **Director**—Michael Curtiz. *106 minutes*

WE'RE NO ANGELS (1989)

Robert De Niro
Sean Penn

De Niro and Penn mug their way through this unsuccessful comedy loosely based on the 1955 film starring Humphrey Bogart. They play dim-witted convicts who escape to a small town near the Canadian border and evade the cops by disguising themselves as priests. Though the script was adapted by writer/director David Mamet *(Glenglarry Glen Ross; House of Games)*, the material is overly sentimental. Played broadly by the two principals, the film ends up as a one-joke story that becomes progressively tiresome. Demi Moore costars as a local resident who becomes romantically involved with De Niro. Also with Hoyt Axton, Bruno Kirby, Ray McAnally, James Russo, and Wallace Shawn. **Director**—Neil Jordan. **(PG-13)**

101 minutes

WE'RE NOT MARRIED (1952)

★★★

Ginger Rogers
Fred Allen
Victor Moore
Paul Douglas

The ingenious premise of this film—six married couples are advised that their marriages are not legal—provides the basis for a fine comedy with a provocative message. The film, written by well-known screenwriter Nunnally Johnson, is constructed as a series of vignettes, with the Allen and Rogers scene surpassing the others. The all-star cast also includes Eddie Bracken, James Gleason, Jane Darwell, Eve Arden, Marilyn Monroe, David Wayne, Louis Calhern, Mitzi Gaynor, and Zsa Zsa Gabor. **Director**—Edmund Goulding.

85 minutes b&w

THE WESTERNER (1940)

 ★★★

Gary Cooper
Walter Brennan

The Westerner *(Gary Cooper) astounds pal Walter Brennan.*

Brennan won his third Oscar for his role as the infamous Judge Roy Bean in this excellent western involving land disputes that turn bloody and violent. The film is interesting in its use of historical personages—Bean and singer Lillie Langtry—who interact with the fictional characters. William Wyler's detailed and meticulous depiction of the West contrasts with the boisterous characters and events. Also with Fred Stone, Dana Andrews, Chill Wills, Doris Davenport, Forrest Tucker, Tom Tyler, Charles Halton, and Lillian Bond. **Director**—Wyler. **Academy Award**—Brennan, best supporting actor. **Nomination**—Stuart N. Lake, original story.

100 minutes b&w

WESTERN UNION (1941)

Randolph Scott
Robert Young
Dean Jagger

This intelligent western, based on the Zane Grey novel, pinpoints the prob-

(Continued)

(Continued)
lems involved in constructing the first coast-to-coast Western Union wire in 1861. Scott, Young, and Jagger give polished performances, with Virginia Gilmore, Barton MacLane, John Carradine, and Chill Wills in supporting roles. **Director**—Fritz Lang.

94 minutes

WEST SIDE STORY (1961)

★★★★

Natalie Wood
Richard Beymer
Russ Tamblyn
Rita Moreno
George Chakiris

Natalie Wood and Oscar-winner George Chakiris in the exuberant West Side Story.

This dynamite musical, which won ten Academy Awards, remains fresh and vibrant many years after its release. Wood and Beymer are miscast in this story about rival gangs in a New York ghetto, but Moreno, Chakiris, and Tamblyn are superb. The excellent on-location photography enhances the Romeo and Juliet theme, and the Leonard Bernstein/Stephen Sondheim music was innovative and influential in terms of the history of the Broadway musical. Boisterous and exhilarating choreography by Jerome Robbins. **Directors**—Robert Wise and Jerome Robbins. **Academy Awards**—best picture; Wise and Robbins, best director; Chakiris, best supporting actor; Moreno, best supporting actress; Daniel L. Fapp, cinematography. **Nomination**—Ernest Lehman, best screenplay based on material from another medium.

151 minutes

WESTWORLD (1973)

★★★

Yul Brynner
Richard Benjamin
James Brolin

Deadly android Yul Brynner shoots to kill in Westworld.

In this engaging science-fiction tale, Brynner portrays a robot who runs amok at a futuristic vacation resort, which offers its visitors the opportunity to live out their fantasies. Benjamin and Brolin costar as 21st-century men whose fantasy about the Wild West becomes real when the gunfighter robot starts to stalk them. Victoria Shaw, Norman Bartold, and Alan Oppenheimer appear in supporting roles. **Director**—Michael Crichton. **(PG)** *90 minutes*

WE THINK THE WORLD OF YOU (1988)

★★

Alan Bates
Gary Oldman

This tedious British comedy, based on J.R. Ackerley's novel, revolves around two homosexual men, their class differences, and their mutual concern for a German shepherd dog. An upper-class man (Bates) falls in love with a working-class chap (Oldman) in jail for burglary. A great deal of screen time is spent on how to take care of the dog. Even the actors don't appear to have their hearts in this project. **Director**—Colin Gregg. **(PG)** *94 minutes*

THE WHALES OF AUGUST (1987)

★★½

Bette Davis
Lillian Gish

Movie legends Davis and Gish star as elderly sisters, residing on the Maine coast, who must learn to deal with their twilight years. The two sisters are as different as night and day—Davis is bitter and cynical, while Gish is introspective and optimistic. It's a pleasure to watch these two great actresses, but the film progresses at a deliberately slow pace and lacks a compelling storyline. Other former cinematic greats appear in supporting roles, including Vincent Price as a Russian gentleman, Ann Sothern as a nosy neighbor, and Harry Carey, Jr., as a fumbling handyman. **Director**—Lindsay Anderson. **(No MPAA rating) Academy Award Nomination**—Sothern, best supporting actress.

90 minutes

WHAT EVER HAPPENED TO BABY JANE? (1962)

★★★

Bette Davis
Joan Crawford
Victor Buono

Bette Davis plans more mischief in Whatever Happened to Baby Jane?

This grim and chilling black comedy about an ex-child movie star who tortures her crippled sister is made interesting by the excellent acting of Davis, Crawford, and Buono. The film revitalized the career of Davis, and helped usher in a trend in horror films that utilized older actresses in key roles. Also with Anna Lee and Marjorie Bennett. **Director**—Robert Aldrich. **Academy Award Nominations**—Davis, best actress; Buono, best supporting actor; Ernest Haller, cinematography.

132 minutes b&w

WHAT PRICE GLORY? (1952)

★★

James Cagney
Dan Dailey
Corinne Calvet

® This movie available with closed captions for the hearing impaired.

Energetic performances by Cagney and Dailey brighten this remake of the silent film classic about two tough Marines in love with the same woman in France during World War I. Calvet is the woman they love. The original film, made in 1926 and based on a play by Maxwell Anderson and Laurence Stallings, was effective because of its antiwar statement, but this remake emphasizes the high jinks of the two principals. The result is a shallow interpretation of the material. The cast also includes James Gleason, William Demarest, and Marisa Pavan. **Director**—John Ford. *111 minutes*

WHAT PRICE HOLLYWOOD? (1932)

★★★

Lowell Sherman
Constance Bennett

Well-scripted Hollywood drama that served as the basis for *A Star Is Born.* Sherman stars as an alcoholic director who turns waitress Bennett into a star. Eventually, his own career collapses in ruin and he takes his life. The Adela Rogers St. John story provides a sharp look at the early studio system and reveals insights rarely publicized at that time. Director George Cukor handles the material and the fine cast with expertise. **Academy Award Nomination**—Rogers St. John, original story. *87 minutes b&w*

WHAT'S NEW, PUSSYCAT? (1965)

 ★★

Peter Sellers
Peter O'Toole
Woody Allen

A tasteless and dated production about an eccentric psychiatrist (Sellers) and a troubled fashion editor (O'Toole), who's obsessed with women. The cast includes Ursula Andress, Capucine, Romy Schneider, Louise Lasser, and Paula Prentiss, who are exploited here for their good looks. Allen's first feature film as a writer and actor. **Director**—Clive Donner. *108 minutes*

WHAT'S UP, DOC? (1972)

◈ ★★★

Barbra Streisand
Ryan O'Neal

Screwball comedy with Barbra Streisand and Ryan O'Neal in What's Up, Doc?

Director Peter Bogdanovich successfully captures the uninhibited quality of the 1930s screwball comedies with this hilarious film. A vibrant performance by Streisand as a wacky coed who manages to disrupt the lifestyles of a square musicologist (O'Neal) and his fiancée (Madeline Kahn) highlights this romantic comedy. The well-edited chase sequence that concludes the film was emulated in other romantic comedies throughout the decade. Kenneth Mars, Austin Pendleton, Sorrell Booke, Michael Murphy, and Mabel Albertson appear in supporting roles. **(G)** *94 minutes*

THE WHEELER DEALERS (1963)

★★

James Garner
Lee Remick

Garner and Remick star in this comedy about a Texas oil millionaire who decides to have some fun on Wall Street with the stock market. Solid performances by Remick, Jim Backus, Phil Harris, and Louis Nye highlight the film. The cast also includes John Astin, Shelley Berman, and Chill Wills. **Director**—Arthur Hiller. *106 minutes*

WHEN A STRANGER CALLS (1979)

 ★★

Carol Kane
Charles Durning

This suspense thriller gets off to a promising start. A babysitter, played by Kane, is alone in a dark house and receives threatening phone calls. The film soon goes rapidly downhill, however. Even a psychopathic killer, played by Tony Beckley, needs some kind of motive to give the story meaning. Instead, events unfold with little more than shock effect in mind. Durning has a skimpy role as a police detective in this mediocre film. Also with Colleen Dewhurst, Rachel Roberts, and Ron O'Neal. **Director**—Fred Walton. **(R)** *97 minutes*

WHEN HARRY MET SALLY (1989)

◈ ★★★ 

Billy Crystal
Meg Ryan

Meg Ryan and Billy Crystal eventually become a couple in When Harry Met Sally.

Rob Reiner directs this soft romantic comedy that is reminiscent of Woody Allen's work from the 1970s. The title characters, played by Crystal and Ryan, meet at the University of Chicago when they team up to share the drive to New York. They reconnect several years later when they bump into each other at an airport. They finally become friends when they meet in a book store a few years after that. Gradually and reluctantly, the two fall in love. Though some of the dialogue and situations are genuinely witty, this talky film seems too much like a clever sitcom. Still, the film struck a chord with audiences the summer it was released, and it became one of that year's biggest hits. Also with Carrie Fisher, Bruno Kirby, Steven Ford, Lisa Jane Persky, and Michelle Nicastro. **(R) Academy Award Nomination**—Nora Ephron, best original screenplay. *95 minutes*

WHEN MY BABY SMILES AT ME (1948)

★★½

Dan Dailey
Betty Grable

This musical version of the play *Burlesque* traces the downfall and rehabilitation of a vaudeville comic. Dailey and Grable are a married couple who per-

(Continued)

Dan Dailey clowns it up in When My Baby Smiles at Me.

Paul Newman and Jacqueline Bisset in the disaster movie "When Time Ran Out . . . ."

(Continued)

form as a team. When she gets a chance to star on Broadway, his career takes a turn for the worse. The story is familiar, and no one will be surprised when the pair is reunited and his career is reestablished. The cast, including Jack Oakie, June Havoc, Richard Arlen, and James Gleason, all seasoned pros, make the film reasonably entertaining. **Director**—Walter Lang. **Academy Award Nomination**—Dailey, best actor.
98 minutes

WHEN THE WHALES CAME (1989)

★★

Helen Mirren
Paul Scofield

A sentimental tale revolving around the inhabitants of a dreary island off the English coast just prior to World War I. The central action concerns the efforts of the island's eccentric recluse and two children to save a rare narwhal from being butchered by the townsfolk after it is washed up on shore. By saving the whale, the three succeed in lifting a curse that has left the island poverty-stricken for many years. Though the direction by Clive Rees is competent and the cast performs well, this maudlin fable is too shallow for seasoned moviegoers. Based on a book by Michael Morpurgo. Also with Fergus Rees, Max Rennie, and Helen Pearce. **(PG)**
100 minutes

WHEN TIME RAN OUT... (1980)

Paul Newman
Jacqueline Bisset

Irwin Allen, who brought us *The Towering Inferno* and other disaster movies, this time unleashes an erupting volcano on a Hawaiian resort. Newman and other well-known stars struggle through a dull script. Most of the cast is killed off by the force of nature, but a few make it to safety. Allen seems to have run out of fresh ideas. Also with William Holden, Red Buttons, Ernest Borgnine, and James Franciscus. **Director**—James Goldstone. **(PG)**
121 minutes

WHEN WORLDS COLLIDE (1951)

★★★

Richard Derr
Barbara Rush

Vivid and spectacular effects make this science-fiction tale, about the rush to build a spaceship before another planet collides with Earth, one of the most memorable of the decade. The only hope for the survival of mankind is the escape of a chosen few to another world. Based on a novel by Edwin Balmer and Philip Wylie, the film was produced by George Pal. Gordon Jennings won an Oscar for the special effects. Peter Hanson, John Hoyt, and Larry Keating appear in supporting roles. **Director**—Rudolph Maté. **Academy Award Nomination**—John F. Seitz and W. Howard Greene, cinematography.
82 minutes

WHEN YOU COMIN' BACK, RED RYDER? (1979)

Marjoe Gortner
Peter Firth
Hal Linden
Lee Grant

Gortner stars as an enraged Vietnam veteran who terrorizes some nice folks in a sleepy New Mexico diner. There are some decent performances by Gortner, Firth, and Stephanie Faracy. However, the story, which was taken from the 1973 stage production, loses much of its sizzle by dwelling too long on the various characters before the action in the diner begins. The finale has its taut moments, but the outcome leaves a bad aftertaste. Also with Audra Lindley, Bill McKinney, Candy Clark, and Pat Hingle. **Director**—Milton Katselas. **(R)**
118 minutes

WHERE ANGELS GO, TROUBLE FOLLOWS (1968)

Rosalind Russell
Stella Stevens

This cute and simplistic story about nuns in frequent conflict with their pupils holds moderate interest. Russell plays a Mother Superior who's challenged by Stevens, a younger and more progressive nun, in this sequel to *The Trouble with Angels.* The supporting cast of Binnie Barnes, Susan Saint James, Milton Berle, Arthur Godfrey, William Lundigan, Van Johnson, Robert Taylor, Mary Wickes, and Barbara Hunter brightens the production. **Director**—James Neilson. **(G)** *95 minutes*

WHERE EAGLES DARE (1969)

★★★

Richard Burton
Clint Eastwood

This old-fashioned adventure story about a dangerous mission to rescue an American officer from an escape-proof German prison is highlighted by its action sequences and nerve-racking tension. Burton and Eastwood star as the leaders of the rescue expedition, with Patrick Wymark, Michael Hordern, Robert Beatty, Mary Ure, Donald Houston, and Peter Barkworth in supporting roles. Director Brian G. Hutton had the good sense not to take the movie too seriously. Based on the novel by Alistair MacLean. **(PG)**
156 minutes

WHERE'S CHARLEY? (1952)

★★★

Ray Bolger

This movie available with closed captions for the hearing impaired.

Bolger sparkles in this musical version of *Charley's Aunt*, the story of an Oxford student who impersonates his best friend's rich aunt to solve problems only to end up causing new complications. Bolger is at his best singing "Once in Love with Amy," and the other Frank Loesser songs are appealing as well. The cast also includes Robert Shackleton, Allyn Ann McLerie, Horace Cooper, Mary Germaine, and Margaretta Scott. **Director**—David Butler. *95 minutes*

WHERE THE BOYS ARE (1960)

★★½

George Hamilton
Dolores Hart
Paula Prentiss
Jim Hutton

A popular comedy about college boys and girls on vacation in Fort Lauderdale, Florida. The movie never pretends to be anything other than what it is—a teenage beach movie. A clever mixture of comedy, pop music, and melodrama. Barbara Nichols is hilarious in a secondary role as a show girl who has been around. The cast also includes Yvette Mimieux, Connie Francis, Chill Wills, and Frank Gorshin. **Director**—Henry Levin. *99 minutes*

WHERE THE BOYS ARE '84 (1984)

Lisa Hartman
Lorna Luft
Lynn-Holly Johnson
Wendy Schaal

Guys 'n' gals 'n' fun 'n' sun in Where the Boys Are '84.

A charmless rehash of the 1960 film of the same name about the spring frolic of college students on the sun-drenched beaches of Fort Lauderdale. This less innocent version features four coeds on the make, who get involved in assorted silly escapades. The plot is frequently interrupted by scenes of briefly clad young women and men showing off on the sands. An interesting role reversal, with the girls leering at the boys for a change, but the offensive jokes and stereotyped characters are tacky. Also with Alana Stewart, Russell Todd, and Louise Sorel. **Director**—Hy Averback. **(R)** *93 minutes*

WHERE THE BUFFALO ROAM (1980)

★★

Bill Murray
Peter Boyle

Gonzo journalism—and weak laughs—with Bill Murray in Where the Buffalo Roam.

Low comedy about the high jinks of outrageous gonzo journalist Hunter Thompson, who ruffled the establishment's feathers in the late 1960s. Murray, playing the role of Thompson, generates a few laughs as he covers a marijuana trial, the Super Bowl, and the Presidential election. But it's mostly preposterous slapstick that wears thin as the movie progresses. Also with Bruno Kirby and R.G. Armstrong. **Director**—Art Linson. **(R)** *98 minutes*

WHERE THE HEART IS (1990)

★½

Dabney Coleman
Uma Thurman
Joanna Cassidy

Coleman stars as a successful Manhattan building demolition contractor who tries to teach his spoiled children a lesson in life. He does so by forcing them to live in a run-down Brooklyn apartment building. Little about this misguided comedy makes for worthwhile viewing: The dialogue is coarse and awkward, the acting is wildly uneven, and the ending is ridiculous. Director John Boorman, who scored so well with *Hope and Glory*, misfires with this shallow comedy that is reminiscent of a little-known film he made 20 years ago called *Leo the Last*. Also with Crispin Glover, Suzy Amis, Christopher Plummer, David Hewlett, and Dylan Walsh. **(R)** *94 minutes*

WHERE THE RIVER RUNS BLACK (1986)

★★½

Alessandro Rabelo

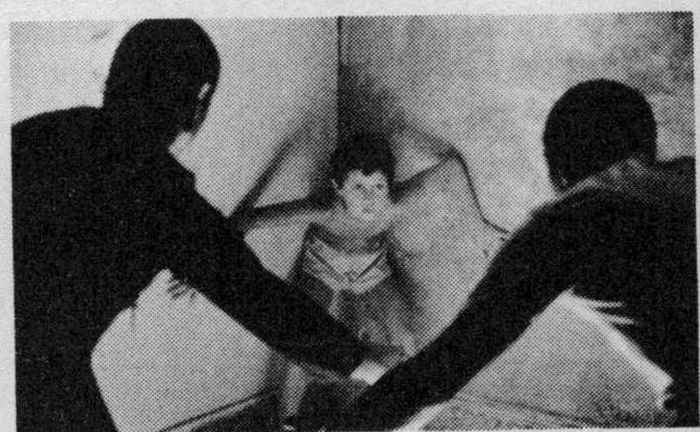

Where the River Runs Black: *Alessandro Rabelo is trapped by a chaotic society.*

Offbeat but slow-moving tale of a Brazilian jungle boy (Rabelo) who finds modern civilization distasteful and longs to return to his peaceful, primitive origins. The film, based on David Kendall's novel, unfolds at a too-languid pace to arouse much interest in the plight of the wide-eyed lad. Most of the acting is unimpressive, but there are colorful scenes of life on the Rio Negro. Charles Durning and Ajay Naidu also star. **Director**—Christopher Cain. **(PG)** *96 minutes*

WHICH WAY IS UP? (1977)

★

Richard Pryor

Comic Pryor, generally successful in even the weakest of screen endeavors, takes a step backward in this crude adaptation of Lina Wertmuller's Italian comedy *The Seduction of Mimi*. Pryor plays three roles, but is primarily featured as a poor fruit picker who becomes a farm union organizer. Most of the material is shallow, and ruined by

(Continued)

This movie available on videotape and/or disc.

(Continued)
unnecessary vulgar language. Also with Lonette McKee, Margaret Avery, and Dewayne Jessie. **Director**—Michael Schultz. **(R)** *94 minutes*

WHISKY GALORE (1949)

★★★★

Basil Radford
Joan Greenwood

A droll British comedy about a cargo of whisky that is shipwrecked off a Scottish island during World War II. The thirsty natives covet the cargo, and humorous problems and situations are created as they confront the local customs agent. Radford and Greenwood star in this fast-paced delight, with Jean Cadel, Catherine Lacey, Bruce Seton, Wylie Watson, Gordon Jackson, A.E. Matthews, and Compton Mackenzie starring in supporting roles. **Director**—Alexander Mackendrick.

82 minutes b&w

WHISPERING SMITH (1948)

★★★

Alan Ladd
Robert Preston
Brenda Marshall

Robert Preston (center) and Donald Crisp await the arrival of Whispering Smith.

Ladd, Preston, and Marshall star in this western about a government detective who discovers that a friend is involved in a series of robberies. The cast also includes Donald Crisp, William Demarest, Frank Faylen, Fay Holden, and Murvyn Vye. **Director**—Leslie Fenton.

88 minutes

THE WHISTLE BLOWER (1987)

★★★

Michael Caine
James Fox
John Gielgud

Nigel Havers (left) explains to Michael Caine why he's become The Whistleblower.

Caine gives a full-bodied performance as a middle-aged Britisher seeking the truth about his son, who was caught up in a spy scandal and then mysteriously killed in an accident. The film is as much about class distinctions as it is about spying, but that adds a humanistic touch sometimes missing from espionage dramas. A weak ending hampers the otherwise suspenseful film. A top supporting cast is featured, with exceptional work from Fox, Gielgud, and Nigel Havers as the son. Also with Felicity Dean, Gordon Jackson, and Barry Foster. **Director**—Simon Langton. **(PG)**

104 minutes

WHITE CHRISTMAS (1954)

★★★

Bing Crosby
Danny Kaye
Dean Jagger

Danny Kaye and Bing Crosby burst forth with song in White Christmas.

A star-studded cast brightens this musical package about two old Army friends—Crosby and Kaye—who help Jagger, an ex-officer, make his winter resort a financial success. Though the storyline may seem lightweight, it provides the perfect framework to showcase the 15 Irving Berlin songs. Highlights include the title song, which will always be associated with Crosby, and the popular "Snow," "The Best Things Happen While You're Dancing," and "Sisters." Rosemary Clooney, Vera-Ellen, Grady Sutton, Sig Ruman, and Mary Wickes also star. **Director**—Michael Curtiz. *120 minutes*

WHITE HEAT (1949)

★★★★

James Cagney
Edmond O'Brien

James Cagney faces Edmond O'Brien in the explosive White Heat.

Cagney stars in this hard-boiled story of a psychopathic gangster. The movie vividly depicts his violent lifestyle and his penchant for running his gang with a cruel hand and blaring gun. O'Brien plays the clever cop who infiltrates Cagney's gang and finally collars him. One of the last great gangster sagas, the film also utilizes such *film noir* conventions as a psychologically disturbed character and the idea that the world is a dark and corrupt one that ultimately destroys the individual. The excellent cast also includes Margaret Wycherly, Virginia Mayo, John Archer, and Steve Cochran. **Director**—Raoul Walsh. **Academy Award Nomination**—Virginia Kellogg, motion picture story.

114 minutes b&w

WHITE LINE FEVER (1975)

★★★

Jan-Michael Vincent
Kay Lenz

This action drama focuses on the independent trucking business. The story concerns a young Vietnam veteran who returns home, purchases a diesel truck, and battles the corruption of the bigger interests who want him to smuggle con-

This movie available with closed captions for the hearing impaired.

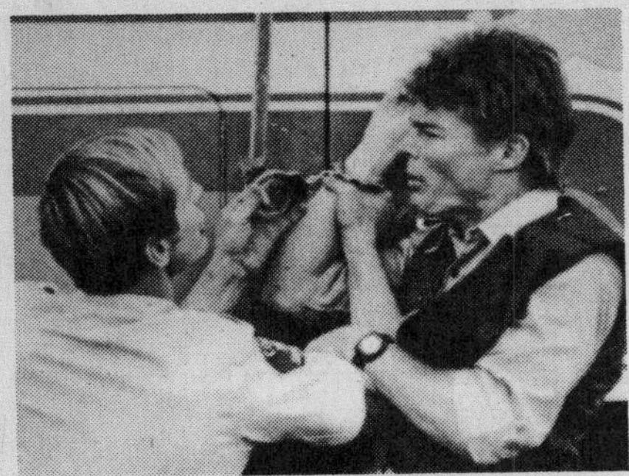

Jan-Michael Vincent battles a corrupt system in the exciting White Line Fever.

traband across state lines. Although the plot is loaded down with clichés, the huge, barreling trucks are a show in themselves, and one crash scene is rumored to have cost $130,000. The title refers to the tiring, hypnotic effect of the highway's white center line on drivers during long trips. Also with Slim Pickens, L.Q. Jones, and Don Porter. **Director**—Jonathan Kaplan. **(PG)**

92 minutes

WHITE MISCHIEF (1987)

★★½

Sarah Miles
Joss Ackland
John Hurt
Greta Scacchi

Joss Ackland, Greta Scacchi, and Trevor Howard in White Mischief.

While World War II rages in Europe, some British aristocrats in Kenya engage in scandalous love affairs and a hedonistic lifestyle that leads to murder. Scacchi stars as the stunning young wife of a wealthy planter who carries on with a dashing but notoriously promiscuous earl. Based on the real-life scandal and murder of the 22nd Earl of Erroll, the exposé of the amoral rich and famous tries to criticize the characters involved—and the world they represent—but ends up wallowing in their sordidness. The result is neither sufficiently titillating nor is it pointed social commentary. Also with Charles Dance, Geraldine Chaplin, and Trevor Howard (in his final screen appearance). **Director**—Michael Radford. **(R)**

100 minutes

WHITE NIGHTS (1985)

★★½

Mikhail Baryshnikov
Gregory Hines
Isabella Rossellini

Terrific dancing is the primary asset of this glossy but wildly improbable thriller. Baryshnikov plays a Russian ballet star who defected to the U.S. eight years earlier; Hines is an American tap dancer who took up residence in the U.S.S.R. during the Vietnam War. When Baryshnikov's plane crashes over Russia, he's captured by the KGB and put under Hines' guardianship. But Hines has had it with Soviet life, and plots with Baryshnikov to escape to the West. We know you won't swallow this plot—just enjoy the stars' fancy stepping and the gorgeous Eastern European scenery. Also with Geraldine Page, Helen Mirren, and Jerzy Skolimowski. **Director**—Taylor Hackford. **(PG-13)**

135 minutes

WHO FRAMED ROGER RABBIT? (1988)

★★★★

Bob Hoskins
Christopher Lloyd

Bob Hoskins becomes attached to Toons in Who Framed Roger Rabbit?

An unparalleled achievement in animation from Walt Disney Productions and Steven Spielberg's Amblin Entertainment. Years in the making, this comedy spoof of *film noir* detective stories combines live actors and animated characters with a startling degree of realism. The story involves a down-and-out detective, played by Bob Hoskins, who reluctantly takes a job involving "Toons." These are the animated characters in the film (cartoons), who live on the wrong side of the tracks in "Toontown." True to the genre, Hoskins' detective work uncovers more than he bargained for, and he finds himself helping Roger Rabbit—a particularly annoying Toon—clear his name of a murder rap. The best scenes involve the "cameo appearances" of many familiar cartoon characters of the past and present. Donald Duck and Daffy Duck perform a piano solo in a nightclub; Mickey Mouse and Bugs Bunny collaborate on a practical joke; Betty Boop appears as a barmaid. Enjoyable for all, this is a cinematic achievement not to be missed. Also with Stubby Kaye and Joanna Cassidy. **Director**—Bob Zemeckis. **Animation director**—Richard Williams. **(PG) Academy Awards**—Arthur Schmidt, editing; Ken Ralston, Richard Williams, Edward Jones, and George Gibbs, visual effects; Charles L. Campbell and Louis L. Edemann, sound effects editing. **Nominations**—Elliot Scott and Peter Hewitt, art direction; Dean Cundey, cinematography; Robert Knudsen, John Boyd, Don Digirolamo, and Tony Dawe, sound.

103 minutes

WHO IS KILLING THE GREAT CHEFS OF EUROPE? (1978)

★★★

George Segal
Jacqueline Bisset
Robert Morley

Segal and Bisset get top billing in this mystery/comedy, but the film belongs to Morley, who provides most of the laughs with his caustic dialogue. The story is set in several famous European hotels and elegant restaurants, with many shots of fancy, delicious dishes. It's entertaining, funny, suspenseful, and mouth-watering, too. Also with Jean-Pierre Cassel, Philippe Noiret, Jean Rochefort, and Madge Ryan. **Director**—Ted Kotcheff. **(PG)**

112 minutes

THE WHOLE TOWN'S TALKING (1935)

★★★

Edward G. Robinson
Jean Arthur

Sparkling comedy/drama about two look-alikes—one a gangster, the other a soft-spoken bookkeeper—who trade places. Robinson handles both characters with charm and wit. Arthur costars as the girl pursuing one of the pair—but which? The pacing and staging are in-

(Continued)

(Continued)
dicative of director John Ford's attention to detail. Donald Meek and Wallace Ford add to the pleasure of this film.
95 minutes b&w

WHO'LL STOP THE RAIN? (1978)

Nick Nolte
Tuesday Weld

This hard-hitting action drama about a couple on the lam is based on *Dog Soldiers,* Robert Stone's emotional novel about the backwash of the Vietnam War. Nolte is terrific as an ex-Marine whose friend has smuggled heroin into the U.S. Nolte protects and then falls in love with his friend's wife (Weld) when she is relentlessly pursued by three sadistic villains because of her husband's foolishness. The film, like the novel, reflects on the war's impact on America. Also with Michael Moriarty, Anthony Zerbe, Richard Masur, and Ray Sharkey. **Director**—Karel Reisz. **(R)**
126 minutes

WHOLLY MOSES (1980)

Dudley Moore

Moore stars in this sporadically funny Bible tale that seems to be inspired by *The Life of Brian,* but is not nearly as outrageous. Moore plays a shepherd who is always two steps behind Moses when a famous incident occurs. Though the film is below average, Dom DeLuise, Madeline Kahn, John Houseman, and Richard Pryor contribute some nice cameo performances—especially Pryor as a formidable pharaoh. **Director**—Gary Weis. **(PG)** *109 minutes*

WHO'S AFRAID OF VIRGINIA WOOLF? (1966)

Richard Burton
Elizabeth Taylor
George Segal
Sandy Dennis

The famous Edward Albee play successfully makes the transition to the screen. Burton and Taylor are excellent as the troubled middle-aged couple who impose on an innocent younger couple (Segal and Dennis). The film is loud, vulgar, and wrenching, but also

A moment of anguish in Who's Afraid of Virginia Woolf?

sadly truthful about the pitfalls of life. The film is historically significant because it broke new ground in the presentation of adult material, pushing the limits of censorship. The claustrophobic set adds to the tension of the drama. Beautiful, Academy Award-winning cinematography by Haskell Wexler. **Director**—Mike Nichols. **Academy Awards**—Taylor, best actress; Dennis, best supporting actress; Wexler, cinematography. **Nominations**—best picture; Nichols, best director; Burton, best actor; Segal, best supporting actor; Ernest Lehman, best screenplay based on material from another medium.
127 minutes b&w

WHO'S BEEN SLEEPING IN MY BED? (1963)

Dean Martin
Elizabeth Montgomery

In this innocuous comedy, Martin plays a TV star who is pushed to the altar by his fiancée because she's worried about the competition. Montgomery plays his pretty but insecure bride-to-be. Some bright dialogue sparks this very ordinary story, as do the solid supporting efforts by Carol Burnett, Louis Nye, Elizabeth Fraser, and Richard Conte. **Director**—Daniel Mann. *103 minutes*

WHOSE LIFE IS IT, ANYWAY? (1981)

Richard Dreyfuss
John Cassavetes

A quadriplegic with no chance of recovery fights for his right to die with dignity. This amazing film is handled with such warmth, wit, and humanity that it transcends any morbidity. The performance by Dreyfuss as the courageous, paralyzed sculptor is spellbinding. There's masterful support from Janet Eilber, Christine Lahti, and Bob Balaban. **Director**—John Badham. **(R)**
118 minutes

WHO'S HARRY CRUMB? (1989)

★★ ®

John Candy
Jeffrey Jones
Annie Potts

Detective John Candy undercover as the world's fattest jockey in Who's Harry Crumb?

Candy stars in the title role of this mildly amusing comedy. He plays a bumbling detective hired to solve the case of a kidnapped heiress. The comedy is flimsy: Candy deals with a runaway car, mangles his necktie in a paper shredder, and sneaks around in various disguises. Strictly for fans. Also with Barry Corbin, Shawnee Smith, Joe Flaherty, and Jim Belushi. **Director**—Paul Flaherty. **(PG-13)** *87 minutes*

WHO'S THAT GIRL (1987)

★1/2 ®

Madonna
Griffin Dunne

Singer/actress Madonna stars in this wildly uneven comedy spoof, which was specially tailored to her style. She plays a young woman, recently paroled from prison, who seeks revenge on the people who framed her. Dunne costars as a yuppie lawyer who reluctantly helps her. The charismatic rock singer, as well as the rest of the cast, are drowned out by the frantic, noisy production, which includes hyped-up car chases, ridiculous shoot-outs, and too many characters. By the time the commotion subsides, viewers will have real-

® *This movie available with closed captions for the hearing impaired.*

ized that the plot made no sense, there were very few laughs, and Madonna's costumes are unbelievably ridiculous. Also with John Mills, Haviland Morris, and John McMartin. **Director**—James Foley. **(PG)** *94 minutes*

WHO WAS THAT LADY? (1960)

★★

Tony Curtis
Dean Martin
Janet Leigh

Curtis and Martin star in this entertaining farce. They pretend to be FBI agents to fool Leigh, who plays Curtis' wife, but new problems arise when foreign spies become interested in their identities. The entertaining premise is let down by the predictable screenplay. The cast also includes James Whitmore, Larry Keating, John McIntire, and Barbara Nichols. **Director**—George Sidney. *115 minutes b&w*

THE WICKED LADY (1983)

★★

Faye Dunaway
John Gielgud

Dunaway plays a 17th-century noblewoman who becomes a highway robber in this frothy remake of the 1945 British costume drama. The result is a send-up of the original, with various comic scenes conveyed awkwardly. Most of the budget seems to have been squandered on elaborate costumes and period settings. Apparently the producers couldn't afford a script. The distinguished cast, which also includes Denholm Elliott and Alan Bates, is shamelessly wasted. **Director**—Michael Winner. **(R)** *98 minutes*

THE WILBY CONSPIRACY (1975)

★★★

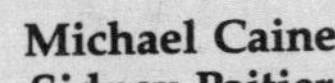

Michael Caine
Sidney Poitier

Poitier plays a political activist on the lam from the police in Cape Town, South Africa. His fate is intertwined with that of a white businessman, played by Caine, in a situation reminiscent of *The Defiant Ones*. The film is set against the backdrop of South Africa's racist regime. Filmed mostly in Kenya. Also with Nicol Williamson and Persis Khambatta. **Director**—Ralph Nelson. **(PG)** *101 minutes*

THE WILD BUNCH (1969)

★★★★

William Holden
Ernest Borgnine
Robert Ryan

A ground-breaking modern western, characterized by explicit violence and innovative editing. An aging group of gunfighters confronts the law as well as the Mexican Army in 1914 along the Texas-Mexico border. Though critics were harsh on the film at the time of release, in retrospect it is considered director Sam Peckinpah's best work. The multicamera setups used in the action sequences and the inclusion of six times as many cuts as the average film of that time make this western an exhilarating visual experience. Peckinpah's theme about the civilizing of the Old West at the expense of rugged individualism is here a bitter one, effectively conveyed by Holden, Borgnine, and Ryan in the major roles. Edmond O'Brien, Warren Oates, Albert Dekker, Ben Johnson, Jaime Sanchez, Strother Martin, and L.Q. Jones appear in supporting roles. **(R) Academy Award Nomination**—Walon Green, Roy N. Sickner, and Peckinpah, best story and screenplay based on material not previously published or produced. *134 minutes*

WILDCATS (1986)

★★★

Goldie Hawn

Hawn scores as a girls' track coach who always wanted to coach boys' football. She finally gets her chance with the hostile losers at tough Central High. The film is uneven, but at times amusing and heartwarming. It gets much better as it picks up steam with Hawn trying to win the loyalty of a group of inner-city tough guys. Swoosie Kurtz, Nipsey Russell, and James Keach each have some priceless moments. **Director**—Michael Ritchie. **(R)** *107 minutes*

THE WILD GEESE (1978)

★★★

Richard Burton
Roger Moore
Richard Harris

Burton, Moore, and Harris lead a mercenary army to Africa to rescue a kidnapped African president. The story is routine, but it's filled with exciting action and adventure. The high-caliber cast does an effective job of portraying some interesting characters and giving the audience their money's worth. Also with Hardy Kruger, Stewart Granger, Jack Watson, and Frank Finlay. **Director**—Andrew V. McLaglen. **(R)** *132 minutes*

THE WILD LIFE (1984)

★

Christopher Penn
Ilan Mitchell-Smith
Jenny Wright

A moronic, adolescent romp, constructed along the lines of *Fast Times at Ridgemont High*. The movie is populated with slobs, nerds, and jerks who engage in partying, girl chasing, and assorted reckless pranks. In its desperate attempt to be outrageous and funny, the film is actually tame stuff. **Director**—Art Linson. **(R)** *96 minutes*

THE WILD ONE (1954)

★★★

Marlon Brando
Lee Marvin

One of the first motorcycle films, and one that set the conventions for the genre. Brando stars in the title role as the leader of a gang of youths rebelling against nothing and yet everything. The film is significant less for its script or style than for its recognition that the youth of America were not content with the values of their parents. Fine performances by Marvin, Mary Murphy, Robert Keith, and Jay C. Flippen. **Director**—Laslo Benedek. *79 minutes b&w*

WILD ORCHID (1990)

★$^1/_2$

Mickey Rourke
Jacqueline Bisset
Carre Otis

A sleazy drama that strives to be erotic but is really little more than soft-core pornography. Set mostly in Rio de Janeiro during the city's famous carnival, the story revolves around the sex lives of three characters. Otis plays an innocent, small-time lawyer who is seduced

(Continued)

This movie available on videotape and/or disc.

(Continued)
by a wealthy scoundrel, played by Rourke. Bisset costars as an arrogant businesswoman who shares in the many embarrassing moments of this dreadful film. Otis is utterly dreadful in her role, but the film is so bad that few will notice. The film was initially given an X rating, but the director made some last-minute cuts to secure an R. Also with Assumpta Serna and Bruce Greenwood. **Director**—Zalman King. **(R)** *103 minutes*

WILD STRAWBERRIES (1957)

★★★★

Victor Sjostrom

Profoundly probing and brilliant study of an aging professor reviewing his life in flashbacks. Sjostrom, the great Swedish director, plays the professor with an astute knowledge of what it means to grow old. Writer/director Ingmar Bergman lucidly presents one of the finest studies of the stages of man from childhood to the grave. Riveting performances from Ingrid Thulin, Gunnar Bjornstrand, and Bibi Andersson. Originally filmed in Swedish. **Academy Award Nomination**—Bergman, best story and screenplay written directly for the screen. *90 minutes b&w*

WILD THING (1987)

Ron Knepper
Kathleen Quinlan

The Tarzan legend is transplanted to the American urban jungle in this tame story hampered by cardboard characters and silly dialogue. The title character (Knepper) is an abandoned boy who has grown up on his own amid the mean streets of dope dealers, bag ladies, and hookers. Amid this squalor, he becomes a mysterious street warrior who despises the establishment, fights criminals, and comes to the rescue of a social worker named Jane (Quinlan). The screenplay was written by writer/director John Sayles (*Lianna; Brother from Another Planet*). **Director**—Max Reid. **(PG–13)** *92 minutes*

WILLARD (1971)

Bruce Davison
Ernest Borgnine

A box-office hit about a sensitive young man who wreaks revenge on the world with his collection of trained rats. Anyone with a revulsion of rodents should steer clear of this one, but others may find it modestly entertaining. Davison, Borgnine, Elsa Lanchester, and Sondra Locke star, but they all get second billing to the rats. **Director**—Daniel Mann. **(PG)** *95 minutes*

WILLIE & PHIL (1980)

Michael Ontkean
Ray Sharkey
Margot Kidder

Ontkean, Sharkey, and Kidder are appealing bohemian types who develop a deep friendship in this comic romance that satirizes life in the 1970s. Paul Mazursky directs with the same skill he showed in *An Unmarried Woman,* but the weakness here is the shallow screenplay. Mazursky's characters are charming stereotypes; the more serious their story becomes, the less believable they are. A loose remake of the French New Wave classic *Jules and Jim.* **(R)** *116 minutes*

WILLOW (1988)

★★$^1/_2$ 

Warwick Davis
Val Kilmer
Joanne Whalley

Warwick Davis tries to save a baby from evil forces in Willow.

This big-budget sword-and-sorcery epic produced by George Lucas proves to be a major disappointment. Various plot elements from well-known fables and movie fantasies—from *The Wizard of Oz* to Lucas' own *Star Wars*—are jammed together into a ponderous production. The story centers on the title character, a member of a race of little people, who tries to save a baby from the clutches of an evil queen. He is aided in his self-appointed task by a cynical adventurer, a couple of miniature beings called Brownies, and other assorted magical characters. The special effects are impressive, the action sequences exciting, and the main characters generally likable, but the script is derivative and the concept calculated to appeal to the same fans of the *Star Wars* saga. That, plus the fact that the characters were marketed *ad nauseum* even before the film's release, leaves a bad taste in the mouth. Also with Billy Barty, Jean Marsh, Patricia Hayes, David Steinberg, and Pat Roach. **Director**—Ron Howard. **(PG) Academy Award Nominations**—Ben Burtt and Richard Hymns, sound effects editing; Dennis Muren, Michael McAllister, Phil Tipper, and Chris Evans, visual effects. *126 minutes*

WILL SUCCESS SPOIL ROCK HUNTER? (1957)

Jayne Mansfield
Tony Randall

Mansfield and Randall star in this successful satire that ridicules TV commercials and the world of advertising. The plot, about an ad man who attempts to persuade a glamorous movie star to endorse a product he is representing, provides the framework with which to comment on the values, trends, and lifestyles of the 1950s. Directed by Frank Tashlin, who specialized in pointed social satire and high comedy. The film represents Mansfield's best effort. Costarring Betsy Drake, Mickey Hargitay, Joan Blondell, John Williams, Henry Jones, and Groucho Marx. *95 minutes*

WINCHESTER '73 (1950)

★★★★

James Stewart
Shelley Winters

Stewart and Winters star in this marvelous western about Stewart's search for an old foe and a stolen rifle. The film is episodic in structure but builds to a suspenseful shoot-out. One of director Anthony Mann's best westerns, which are more action-filled and darker than those of John Ford. The success of this film led to a rise in popularity for west-

This movie available with closed captions for the hearing impaired.

erns in the 1950s. The excellent cast also includes Dan Duryea, Rock Hudson, Tony Curtis, Steve Brodie, Stephen McNally, Millard Mitchell, and John McIntire. *92 minutes b&w*

THE WIND AND THE LION (1975)

 ★★★

Sean Connery
Candice Bergen

In 1904, Teddy Roosevelt sent the U.S. Marines to Morocco to rescue an American widow and her children, who had been kidnapped by a sheik and his band of ruthless nomads. Connery is charming as the sheik in this romanticized version of the real-life adventure, though Bergen is weak as the captive widow. Brian Keith excellently portrays Roosevelt. Beautiful cinematography and a rousing score enhance this exotic story. Also with John Huston, Geoffrey Lewis, and Steve Kanaly. **Director**—John Milius. **(PG)** *119 minutes*

THE WINDOW (1949)

 ★★★

Bobby Driscoll

This compelling thriller about a slum kid who witnesses a murder, but can't convince his parents about what he saw, is deftly executed and excruciatingly tense as the boy and murderer parry. Driscoll is excellent in the role of a boy who is often caught telling tales. And there are fine supporting performances by Arthur Kennedy, Ruth Roman, Barbara Hale, and Paul Stewart. The photography of William Steiner sets the mood and tempo of the story. **Director**—Ted Tetzlaff. *73 minutes b&w*

WINDOWS (1980)

 ★

Talia Shire
Elizabeth Ashley

A gloomy, would-be thriller about a young woman, played by Shire, who's harassed by a psychotic lesbian, played by Ashley. The shoddy screenplay quickly deteriorates into a stale and predictable story. Low-key and overwrought performances misfire, resulting in unintentional humor. Gordon Willis, the noted cinematographer (*The Godfather; Manhattan*), debuts as director with this movie. He offers some stunning views of New York City, but the rest of the movie is ridiculous. Also with Joseph Cortese. **(R)** *96 minutes*

WINDWALKER (1981)

 ★★

Trevor Howard

Howard plays a dying Cheyenne warrior who relates the tragic adventures of his life, much of it dealing with feuding between his tribe and the neighboring Crows. With the exception of Howard, who's unconvincing in the title role, cast members are Indians who perform adequately. The sentimental story, however, never develops with sufficient clarity or impact. Even the various battles involving revengeful Indians and wild animals become tiresome and exceedingly violent. Originally filmed in Crow and Cheyenne with English titles. **Director**—Keith Merrill. **(PG)** *108 minutes*

WINDY CITY (1984)

 ★1/2

John Shea
Kate Capshaw
Josh Mostel

An overly self-conscious, sentimental drama of friendships, unfulfilled ambitions, and lost romance among a group of young men residing in Chicago. The film emulates in theme and storyline both *Diner* and *The Big Chill*, but the characters are banal and unspontaneous. The dialogue is trite and unintentionally funny. Also with Lewis Stadlen and Jim Borrelli. **Director**—Armyan Bernstein. **(R)** *103 minutes*

THE WINSLOW BOY (1950)

★★★★

Robert Donat
Cedric Hardwicke
Margaret Leighton
Frank Lawton

The splendid acting of Donat, Hardwicke, Leighton, and Lawton make this real-life story a gem. An attorney, played by Donat, defends a naval cadet falsely accused of stealing. Based on a play by Terence Rattigan, the production brilliantly depicts British society and details of that country's legal system. The excellent cast also includes Ernest Thesiger, Neil North, Jack Watling, and Basil Radford. **Director**—Anthony Asquith. *117 minutes*

WINTER KILLS (1979)

★★

Jeff Bridges
John Huston
Anthony Perkins

Bridges plays the half-brother of an American president who was assassinated 19 years ago. He attempts to solve the crime alone, but is dependent on the information of CIA operatives, organized crime figures, eccentric industrial tycoons, and a Jack Ruby-like character to put the pieces together. The film, based on the Richard Condon novel, is frequently confusing, and only mildly entertaining. Reedited and rereleased in 1983. Belinda Bauer, Eli Wallach, and Sterling Hayden make the most of their supporting roles. Also with Richard Boone, Ralph Meeker, and Dorothy Malone. **Director**—William Richert. **(R)** *97 minutes*

WINTER PEOPLE (1989)

 ★★

Kurt Russell
Kelly McGillis

Kelly McGillis is caught in a backwoods feud in Winter People.

A Depression-era melodrama set in the North Carolina hill country. Russell stars as a gentle traveling clockmaker who falls in love with a rural unwed mother, played by McGillis. The unlikely romance sets off a feud among a family of backwoods people. The stars appear mismatched, the villains are stereotypes, and too many characters have too little to do. Also with Lloyd Bridges and Mitchell Ryan. **Director**—Ted Kotcheff. **(PG-13)** *110 minutes*

WIRED (1989)

★

Michael Chiklis
Ray Sharkey
J.T. Walsh
Patti D'Arbanville

Michael Chiklis plays the role of John Belushi in Wired.

Bob Woodward's best-selling book translates onscreen as a disappointing and confused fantasy/biography of the late comedian John Belushi, who died of a drug overdose. The film is structured mainly as a series of flashbacks and dream sequences in which Belushi reassesses his life. The gimmick fails miserably. The producers are merely exploiting Belushi's tragic death to make money. To add insult to injury, Belushi's *Saturday Night Live* routines are recreated with disastrous results. Chiklis takes on the role with determination, but he's working with dreadful material. Not a fitting way to remember an entertainer who spoke to a generation. Also with Lucinda Jenney, Alex Rocco, and Gary Groomes. **Director**—Larry Peerce. **(R)** *108 minutes*

WISDOM (1987)

★★

Emilio Estevez
Demi Moore

This contemporary version of *Bonnie and Clyde* features Estevez and Moore as a bright, middle-class couple who roam the western United States robbing banks. The film is unintentionally funny at first as it presents these unlikely criminals as do-gooders who primarily destroy mortgage records to benefit financially strapped farmers. But the film eventually becomes too predictable, relying on familiar car chases and bloody shoot-outs to keep the action moving. **Director**—Estevez. **(R)** *109 minutes*

WISE BLOOD (1979)

★★★

Brad Dourif

Director John Huston's 33rd feature film is a puzzling, offbeat story about Bible Belt evangelism. The film was shot in Georgia, but the setting seems to be the private world of some very eccentric characters. Dourif, who played the stutterer in *One Flew Over the Cuckoo's Nest*, turns in an intense performance as a preacher who's also an atheist. Huston's direction of this adaptation of Flannery O'Connor's novella carries impact. Also with Amy Wright and Harry Dean Stanton. **(PG)** *106 minutes*

WISE GUYS (1986)

★★

Danny DeVito
Joe Piscopo
Dan Hedaya

Brian De Palma's ethnic comedy is a series of noisy, routine, slapstick gags that barely generate a few smiles. DeVito and Piscopo appear constantly frantic in their portrayal of bumbling hoodlums. They spend most of the film trying to escape execution for fouling up their boss's track wager. The stars are more often upstaged by wrestler-turned-actor Captain Lou Albano, who plays a particularly ferocious hit man. DeVito's timing and familiar comic persona provide the film's only energy. Piscopo's wooden performance proves he is no comic actor. **(R)** *92 minutes*

WISH YOU WERE HERE (1987)

★★★

Emily Lloyd

A breezy comedy/drama from England about a spirited 15-year-old girl who seeks love and recognition in unconventional ways. Set in a stuffy seaside community in 1951, this poignant film suggests that the girl's underlying unhappiness is due to her father's lack of affection. Her attempts to annoy or get back at her father include having an affair with his friend. Lloyd plays the spunky adolescent with exceptional charm and energy, though some viewers may find her behavior too scandalous to warrant sympathy for her plight. A fine supporting cast includes Geoffrey Hutchings and Tom Bell. **Director**—David Leland. **(R)** *92 minutes*

THE WITCHES OF EASTWICK (1987)

★★★

Jack Nicholson
Cher
Susan Sarandon
Michelle Pfeiffer

Devilish Jack Nicholson answers the prayers of The Witches of Eastwick.

Nicholson stars as the Devil—the role he was born to play—and seduces three bored, unmarried women in a small New England town. The modern-day "witches" are played by Cher, Sarandon, and Pfeiffer. The women experience the various stages of a relationship with Nicholson—seduction, fulfillment, disappointment, and rejection—before getting back at him at the end. Despite Nicholson's entertaining performance and some colorful scenes, the screenplay seems ragged and the special effects at the end are out of place. Also with Veronica Cartwright, Richard Jenkins, Keith Jochim, and Carel Struycken. **Director**—George Miller. **(R)** **Academy Award Nomination**—Wayne Artman, Tom Beckert, Tom Dahl, and Art Rochester, best sound.

118 minutes

WITH A SONG IN MY HEART (1952)

★★

Susan Hayward
David Wayne
Rory Calhoun

This movie available with closed captions for the hearing impaired.

Hayward gives a vivid portrayal of Jane Froman, a singer who struggles to return to show business after being seriously injured in an airplane crash. Hayward is convincing as the crippled singer, but the songs were actually sung by Froman. Thelma Ritter, Helen Westcott, Una Merkel, and Robert Wagner appear in supporting roles. **Director**—Walter Lang. **Academy Award Nominations**—Hayward, best actress; Ritter, best supporting actress. *117 minutes*

WITHOUT A CLUE (1988)

★★1/2

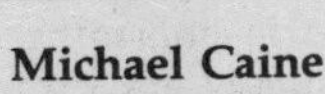

Michael Caine
Ben Kingsley

Ben Kingsley is Watson and Michael Caine is Holmes in Without a Clue.

In this dry comedy, the venerable Sherlock Holmes is actually a dim-witted, drunken actor hired to play the legendary supersleuth. Dr. Watson is the behind-the-scenes brain who really solves the cases. Caine, as the bumbling Holmes, and Kingsley, as the exasperated Watson, have a good time with this role-reversal spoof. There are several slow spots, but fans of Sherlock Holmes will enjoy this twist. Also with Jeffrey Jones, Nigel Davenport, and Peter Cook. **Director**—Thom Eberhardt. **(PG)** *107 minutes*

WITHOUT A TRACE (1983)

★★★

Kate Nelligan
Judd Hirsch

A six-year-old boy vanishes on his way to school. The police and the media descend on the frantic household, and the investigation bogs down in false leads. Director Stanley Jaffe skillfully builds suspense and comes up with plausible details and a jolting ending. The melodrama is graced by top performances from Nelligan as the distraught, determined mother, and Hirsch as a sympathetic detective. Also with David Dukes, Stockard Channing, and Daniel Bryan Corkill. **(PG)** *119 minutes*

WITNESS (1985)

★★★1/2

Harrison Ford
Kelly McGillis

Australian director Peter Weir fashions a remarkable, unique police thriller, a fascinating love story, and a thoughtful statement on violence. Ford shucks his familiar larger-than-life image to play a streetwise Philadelphia detective who hides from his enemies by living among the peaceful, pastoral Amish. McGillis fills the screen with her beauty and charm as the young Amish widow who falls in love with him. The gentle Amish life is effectively contrasted with contemporary society. **(R) Academy Awards**—William Kelly, Pamela Wallace, and Earl Wallace, best original screenplay written directly for the screen. **Nominations**—best picture; Weir, best director; Ford, best actor; John Seale, cinematography. *112 minutes*

WITNESS FOR THE PROSECUTION (1958)

★★★★

Charles Laughton
Tyrone Power
Marlene Dietrich

Clever dialogue, brilliant acting by Laughton, and some devious twists and turns in the plot make this an intriguing mystery tale. Dietrich plays the wife of Power, an alleged killer whom Laughton is hired to defend. Based on a play by Agatha Christie. Like most of Christie's tales, there is inevitably one trick too many, thus lessening any chance an intelligent viewer has to solve the crime. **Director**—Billy Wilder. **Academy Award Nominations**—best picture; Wilder, best director; Laughton, best actor; Elsa Lanchester, best supporting actress. *114 minutes b&w*

THE WIZ (1978)

★★

Diana Ross
Michael Jackson
Nipsey Russell
Ted Ross
Richard Pryor

Somewhere over the Brooklyn Bridge, skies are blue. Dorothy (Diana Ross), the Scarecrow (Jackson), the Tin Man (Russell), and the Cowardly Lion (Ted Ross) follow the Yellow Brick Road in search of miracles from the Wiz, played by Pryor, ensconced in the World Trade Center. This extravagant film musical, a black version of *The Wizard of Oz* adapted from the smash Broadway production, offers some rousing singing and dancing, but Ross is too old to be believable as Dorothy. Also, trite dialogue and overproduced musical numbers detract from the play's freshness. Also with Mabel King and Theresa Merritt. **Director**—Sidney Lumet. **(G) Academy Award Nomination**—Oswald Morris, cinematography. *133 minutes*

THE WIZARD (1989)

★1/2

Fred Savage
Beau Bridges
Christian Slater

A shabby children's film that exploits its intended audience because it is filled with plugs for the Nintendo video game and the Universal City studio tour. The screenplay is reminiscent of *Rain Man:* A 13-year-old boy helps his young handicapped brother run away from a hospital to California, where they enter a video-game tournament. The afflicted brother is a real ace at such games. Savage (of TV's *The Wonder Years*) stars as the older brother, and Luke Edwards costars as the near-catatonic video wizard. In addition to its offensive premise, the film is predictable and overly sentimental. Also with Jenny Lewis, Will Seltzer, Sam McMurray, and Wendy Phillips. **Director**—Todd Holland. **(PG)** *99 minutes*

THE WIZARD OF LONELINESS (1988)

★★

Lukas Haas
Lea Thompson

A weakly constructed coming-of-age drama set during World War II. A young California boy (Haas) grows up quickly while living with his relatives in a quaint Vermont town. Many individual performances rise above the slow-paced plot, but overall, the film has little magic. Thompson is commend-

(Continued)

(Continued)
able as the boy's stalwart aunt. Also with John Randolph, Anne Pitoniak, Lance Guest, and Dylan Baker. **Director**—Jenny Bowen. **(PG-13)**
110 minutes

THE WIZARD OF OZ (1939)
★★★★

Judy Garland
Frank Morgan
Ray Bolger
Jack Haley
Bert Lahr
Margaret Hamilton

This fantastic tale about a Kansas farm girl named Dorothy, who's spirited off to the land of Oz, still tingles with freshness. Garland stars as Dorothy in the role that made her immortal. Though based on the novel by L. Frank Baum, the film has taken on a life of its own. The scenes that take place in Kansas are in black and white, while the magical land of Oz is filmed in the beautiful three-color Technicolor process. The well-known score by E.Y. Harburg and Harold Arlen gave Garland her theme song—"Over the Rainbow." An example of the Hollywood studio system at its best. Clara Blandick, Charley Grapewin, and Billie Burke costar. **Director**—Victor Fleming. **(G) Academy Awards**—Arlen and Harburg, best song ("Over the Rainbow"); Garland, special award for her performance as a screen juvenile. **Nomination**—best picture.
101 minutes b&w/color

WOLF AT THE DOOR (1987)
★★

Donald Sutherland
Max Von Sydow

Sutherland gives a colorful portrayal of celebrated French painter Paul Gauguin. The story centers on Gauguin's return to Paris in 1893 from Tahiti, his difficulties in the art world, and his predilection for teenage girls. A Danish-French coproduction, the film was calculated to appeal to the foreign market, with Sutherland in the lead role to appeal to Americans, and Von Sydow as playwright August Strindberg to appeal to the Scandinavian crowd. The remainder of the cast, consisting mostly of Danish actors, are dubbed with British accents. The film suffers as a result, with this presentation of Gauguin never attaining the passion of Anthony Quinn's interpretation in *Lust for Life.* Valerie Morea and Merete Volstedlund are in supporting roles. **Director**—Henning Carlsen. **(R)**
90 minutes

WOLFEN (1981)
★★½

Albert Finney
Gregory Hines

This is a stunning, nerve-jangling horror film with many attributes, but unfortunately, a muddled and preposterous conclusion cancels out some of the thrills. Finney gives a classy performance as a shrewd New York City homicide detective who connects some brutal murders to a marauding pack of superwolves. Director Michael Wadleigh creates an extraordinarily eerie atmosphere, but the film becomes bogged down with unclear rationalizations about man's callousness toward nature. **(R)** *115 minutes*

THE WOLF MAN (1941)

★★★

Lon Chaney, Jr.
Claude Rains

Chaney, Rains, Bela Lugosi, and Maria Ouspenskaya appear in this grim, intelligent, and well-made horror classic about Larry Talbot, an ordinary man who turns peculiar whenever there's a full moon. Chaney, of course, is the troubled man; Rains plays his father. The eerie atmosphere and beautiful production values from Universal studios increase the tension and enhance the storyline. The outstanding cast also includes Ralph Bellamy, Warren William, Patric Knowles, Evelyn Ankers, and Fay Helm. **Director**—George Waggner. *70 minutes b&w*

A WOMAN IN FLAMES (1982)
★★

Gudrun Landgrebe

Eva (Landgrebe) is a lousy conversationalist and a bad cook. She walks out on her bourgeois husband and sets up shop as a prostitute specializing in kinky sex. She then experiences a series of mechanical encounters with masochistic men. Though an interesting comment on the status of women in modern society, the cold approach to the material may offend some viewers. Not for all tastes. Mathieu Carriere costars. **Director**—Robert van Ackeren. **(No MPAA rating)** *106 minutes*

THE WOMAN IN RED (1984)
★★★

Gene Wilder
Kelly LeBrock
Judith Ivey

Lightweight comedy about the misadventures of a philandering advertising manager. The film reworks the French comedy *Pardon Mon Affaire* and owes much to *The Seven Year Itch*. Mop-haired Wilder, as the smitten middle-aged family man, is charming as he awkwardly pursues a gorgeous model (LeBrock) while keeping his wife (Ivey) in the dark. Charles Grodin, Joseph Bologna, and Gilda Radner are in supporting roles. **Director**—Wilder. **(PG–13)**
87 minutes

WOMAN IN THE DUNES (1964)
★★★½

Eiji Okada
Kyoto Kishida

A beautifully moving allegory about alienation, which depicts a man trapped and held prisoner by a woman in a sandpit among the dunes. This poetically depicted Japanese drama, based on the novel by Kobo Abe, is superbly acted by Okada and Kishida. Director Hiroshi Teshigahara sensitively captures the scenes of erotic lovemaking with taste and beauty. The photography of Hiroshi Segawa is memorable and haunting. **Academy Award Nominations**—best foreign-language film; Teshigahara, best director.
127 minutes b&w

THE WOMAN IN THE WINDOW (1944)
★★★½

Edward G. Robinson
Joan Bennett

Robinson and Bennett star in this taut, frequently funny, thriller about a professor, played by Robinson, who befriends a beautiful woman, played by Bennett, while his family is on vacation. He is then drawn into a complex murder case. A well-crafted B-movie, with excellent production values. The film exhibits some of the conventions of *film noir,* such as the high contrast black-and-white photography, the

® *This movie available with closed captions for the hearing impaired.*

heavy use of shadows, and the *femme fatale* character. Raymond Massey, Dan Duryea, Arthur Loft, Bobby Blake, Edmund Breon, and Dorothy Peterson also star. **Director**—Fritz Lang.
99 minutes b&w

WOMAN OF THE YEAR (1942)

★★★

Spencer Tracy
Katharine Hepburn

Tracy and Hepburn are charming in this story about a sportswriter and a well-known political columnist, who seems to know about everything except sports. Tracy is the sports reporter, and Hepburn plays the political commentator. The acting and dialogue are superior, as the couple struggles to keep their romance free from the intrusion of world events. Fay Bainter, William Bendix, Reginald Owen, Roscoe Karns, Minor Watson, and Dan Tobin are in supporting roles. This was the first pairing of Tracy and Hepburn on the screen. **Director**—George Stevens. **Academy Award**—Michael Kanin and Ring Lardner, Jr., original screenplay. **Nomination**—Hepburn, best actress.
114 minutes b&w

A WOMAN UNDER THE INFLUENCE (1974)

Gena Rowlands
Peter Falk

Ambitious but flawed character study of a blue-collar marriage breaking up, focusing on the wife's self-examination. Writer/director John Cassavetes elicits powerful performances from Rowlands and Falk as the troubled couple. The film, which makes good use of improvisation, tends to drag out certain scenes, relying too heavily on emotional excess for resolution. Despite the problems, the virtues outweigh the vices. **(R)** **Academy Award Nominations**—Cassavetes, best director; Rowlands, best actress.
155 minutes

THE WOMEN (1939)

★★★

Norma Shearer
Joan Crawford
Rosalind Russell

This comedy/drama has a cast of more than 125 women. It seems tame now, but sparks and barbs in the complex plot are still entertaining. The large cast also includes Paulette Goddard, Mary Boland, Margaret Dumont, Hedda Hopper, Ruth Hussey, and Marjorie Main. Anita Loos and Jane Murfin wrote the script of this film version of the Clare Boothe Luce play and kept much of the original dialogue intact. The story concerns the divorce of a well-known socialite. **Director**—George Cukor.
133 minutes b&w/color

WOMEN IN LOVE (1970)

★★★

Oliver Reed
Glenda Jackson
Jennie Linden
Alan Bates

Jackson, Reed, Linden, and Bates star in this film version of D.H. Lawrence's celebrated novel. Though director Ken Russell's approach to the material is self-conscious and even ostentatious, the period sets of the Midlands of England during the 1920s, the excellent acting, and a provocative nude wrestling scene make the film worthwhile. Eleanor Bron, Alan Webb, and Michael Gough appear in supporting roles. **(R)** **Academy Award**—Jackson, best actress. **Nominations**—Russell, best director; Larry Kramer, best screenplay based on material from another medium.
129 minutes

WOMEN ON THE VERGE OF A NERVOUS BREAKDOWN (1988)

★★1/2

Carmen Maura

Carmen Maura in Women on the Verge of a Nervous Breakdown.

From Spain comes this energetic, slapstick spoof of contemporary romance. Maura stars as a wildly erratic TV actress who loses control because of her philandering lover. Most of the action centers on her gadget-crammed apartment, which becomes a haven for an assortment of oddball characters. The film was highly popular upon its initial release, though some viewers may find the curious episodes in this farce are disconnected and difficult to comprehend. Originally filmed in Spanish. **Director**—Pedro Almodovar. **(R)**
88 minutes

WONDER MAN (1945)

★★★

Danny Kaye

Kaye is sensational in this story about twins. Kaye, of course, plays both of them—one a quiet, studious type, the other a brash nightclub entertainer. The action and comic pace pick up when the entertainer is killed, and the bookish twin must replace him. Virginia Mayo, Vera-Ellen, S.Z. Sakall, Donald Woods, Ed Brophy, and Steve Cochran also appear in this colorful and delightful production. **Director**—H. Bruce Humberstone. **Academy Award**—John Fulton and A.W. Johns, special effects.
96 minutes

WOODSTOCK (1970)

★★★★

Brilliant documentary of the historic four-day rock festival that climaxed the 1960s in America and labeled a generation. Michael Wadleigh's direction effectively balances the stunning array of top performers with the equally entertaining audience. Skilled use of multiscreen camera shots and quadraphonic sound effects add to the high-tech style that signaled the 1970s. The extraordinary lineup features Jimi Hendrix, Joan Baez, Joe Cocker, Arlo Guthrie, Richie Havens, the Who, Jefferson Airplane, Crosby, Stills and Nash, and more. **(R)** **Academy Award**—best feature documentary.
180 minutes

WORKING GIRL (1988)

★★★1/2

Melanie Griffith
Harrison Ford
Sigourney Weaver

Honesty triumphs over duplicity in this bright comedy about a secretary who gamely climbs into the upper echelons of the corporate world. Griffith plays

(Continued)

This movie available on videotape and/or disc.

Melanie Griffith and Harrison Ford take a meeting in Working Girl.

(Continued)
the savvy secretary—which is the role that made her a true star. Weaver plays the conniving boss who steals Griffith's idea for a corporate merger. Ford costars as the ambitious broker romantically involved with both women. The screenplay is often cute and farfetched, but this modern Cinderella story is both charming and witty. Joan Cusack is effective as Griffith's good pal. **Director**—Mike Nichols. **(R) Academy Award**—Carly Simon, best song for "Let the River Run." **Nominations**—best picture; Nichols, best director; Griffith, best actress; Cusack, best supporting actress; Weaver, best supporting actress.

115 minutes

THE WORLD ACCORDING TO GARP (1982)

Robin Williams
Mary Beth Hurt
Glenn Close
John Lithgow

John Irving's trendy novel translates to the screen with difficulty. The story of a gentle writer (Williams), overwhelmed by eccentric characters and bizarre events, is disjointed and lacking in dramatic weight. The actors are impressive, but even their skill can't help this shallow film. **Director**—George Roy Hill. **(R) Academy Award Nominations**—Lithgow, best supporting actor; Close, best supporting actress.

136 minutes

A WORLD APART (1988)

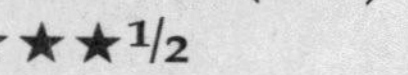

Barbara Hershey
Jodhi May

This anti-apartheid drama, set in the early 1960s, should have a profound impact on viewers despite some flaws. The real-life story, told through the experiences of a South African teenager, concerns the wrenching efforts of a white activist family to combat the discriminatory racial policies of South Africa. Also involved is the unintentional neglect of the family's children by the intensely committed mother (Hershey). Powerful performances illuminate family conflicts against a backdrop of social and political tensions. Based on a true story. Also with David Suchet, Jeroen Krabbé, Paul Freeman, and Tim Roth. **Director**—Chris Menges. **(PG)**

113 minutes

THE WORLD OF HENRY ORIENT (1964)

★★★

Tippy Walker
Merri Spaeth
Peter Sellers

Walker and Spaeth play two rich New York teenagers who adore an eccentric pianist, played by Sellers, in this congenial yet sensitive comedy. The young duo just about steal the show from Sellers and other veterans as they harass the pianist by following him around New York City. The teens idolize him because love is missing in their own lives. The theme of misplaced love is touchingly portrayed. The cast also includes Paula Prentiss, Phyllis Thaxter, Angela Lansbury, and Tom Bosley. **Director**—George Roy Hill. *106 minutes*

THE WORLD OF SUZIE WONG (1960)

★★

William Holden
Nancy Kwan

The world in the title is that of a prostitute in Hong Kong, but in this insensitive Hollywood treatment, everything is presented as merely offbeat. Holden gives a wooden performance as an artist who falls in love with Suzie, played competently by Kwan. The story lacks credibility. Sylvia Syms, Michael Wilding, Laurence Naismith, and Jackie Chan appear in supporting roles. **Director**—Richard Quine. *129 minutes*

THE WORLD'S GREATEST LOVER (1978)

★

Gene Wilder

Wilder wrote, directed, and stars in this frantic tale about a Milwaukee baker who longs to become a silent-screen star in the 1920s. Wilder fails on all three counts. The movie's silly gags produce too few laughs, and the pacing is choppy. Wilder, who studied at the Mel Brooks comedy school, doesn't come close to the level of his mentor. Also with Dom DeLuise, Carol Kane, Fritz Feld, and Carl Ballantine. **(PG)**

89 minutes

WORTH WINNING (1989)

★½

Mark Harmon
Madeleine Stowe
Lesley Ann Warren
Maria Holvoe

Mark Harmon decides that all three beautiful women are Worth Winning.

Harmon is utterly without charm in this frivolous romantic comedy. He plays an attractive, smug TV weatherman who accepts a bet that he can get three beautiful women to agree to marry him within a three-month period. Harmon's character is shallow and insulting, while the three women run the gamut from abrasive to stupid. The script is hopelessly outdated, the direction is mechanical, and Harmon's acting skills leave much to be desired. Also with Mark Blum, Andrea Martin, and David Brenner. **Director**—Will Mackenzie. **(PG-13)** *102 minutes*

THE WRAITH (1986)

★

Charlie Sheen
Nick Cassavetes
Griffin O'Neal
Matthew Barry

® This movie available with closed captions for the hearing impaired.

Numerous souped-up cars charging up and down the highways provide the only thrills in this pedestrian teen adventure. The plot involves a mysterious youth who shows up in a super-hot-rod to challenge a group of small-time car thieves. The plot is paper-thin and the many crashes and explosions eventually become tedious. Many of the young cast members are the offspring of some famous personalities: Sheen is the son of actor Martin Sheen; Cassavetes of actor/director John Cassavetes; O'Neal of actor Ryan O'Neal; and Barry of playwright Phillip James Barry. **Director**—Mike Marvin. **(PG–13)**

92 minutes

WRITTEN ON THE WIND (1956)

★★★

Lauren Bacall
Robert Stack
Dorothy Malone

Bacall, Stack, and Malone star in this melodrama about the many problems within a wealthy oil family. Though the film is melodramatic, its innovative production design, with its dramatic use of color, is ahead of its time. Director Douglas Sirk, who specialized in this type of exaggerated drama, is now considered one of the most talented and influential directors of the 1950s. The cast also includes Rock Hudson, Robert Keith, and Grant Williams. **Academy Award**—Malone, best supporting actress. **Nomination**—Stack, best supporting actor.

100 minutes

WUTHERING HEIGHTS (1939)

★★★★

Laurence Olivier
Merle Oberon

An excellent cast transforms the classic Victorian novel by Emily Brontë into a memorable motion picture. Olivier plays the brooding Heathcliff, and Oberon is the spoiled but passionate Cathy. David Niven, Flora Robson, Geraldine Fitzgerald, Donald Crisp, Miles Mander, and Leo G. Carroll also star. Under William Wyler's sensitive direction and with a well-written script by Ben Hecht and Charles MacArthur, this great love story is worthy of its reputation as one of Olivier's best films. **Academy Award**—Gregg Toland, cinematography. **Nominations**—best picture; Wyler, best director; Olivier, best actor; Fitzgerald, best supporting actress; Hecht and MacArthur, screenplay.

104 minutes b&w

W.W. AND THE DIXIE DANCEKINGS (1975)

Burt Reynolds
Art Carney

A friendly holdup man, played by Reynolds, gets involved with a third-rate country-and-western music group and leads them on to Nashville for a crack at Grand Ol' Opry stardom. The movie, set in the 1950s, has ample good humor and energy, but an empty script. Carney plays an amusing preacher/detective. Also with Conny Van Dyke, Jerry Reed, and Ned Beatty. **Director**—John Avildsen. **(PG)**

91 minutes

XANADU (1980)

Gene Kelly
Olivia Newton-John
Michael Beck

Newton-John plays a glowing, singing, rollerskating muse who inspires a young artist, played by Beck, to open a disco. The plot is absurd, even for a musical. The most worthwhile aspect of this mediocre movie is some fine singing and dancing, primarily by Newton-John. The always charming Kelly plays a former clarinetist who was once smitten by the same muse; he does a charming number or two with Olivia. Why he came out of retirement for this gig, however, is puzzling. Cable television and videotape prints run 96 minutes. **Director**—Robert Greenwald. **(PG)**

88 minutes

Y

YANKEE DOODLE DANDY (1942)

 ★★★★

James Cagney
Joan Leslie
Walter Huston

A stunning musical about the life and times of George M. Cohan, the famed song-and-dance man. Cagney, in an Oscar-winning performance, is superb as Cohan. Released during World War II, the film is an excellent example of Hollywood's contribution to the war effort. Cohan's songs and plays were unabashedly patriotic, and Hollywood's presentation of Cohan as a man who served his country through his artistic endeavors boosted the morale on the home front. The film's narrative structure, with Cohan telling his life story in flashback to Franklin Delano Roosevelt, reinforces the patriotic approach. Also with Rosemary DeCamp, Richard Whorf, Jeanne Cagney, S.Z. Sakall, Captain Jack Manning, George Tobias, Eddie Foy, Jr., and Frances Langford. **Director**—Michael Curtiz; Ray Heindorf and Heinz Roemheld, music score. **Academy Award**—Cagney, best actor. **Nominations**—best picture; Curtiz, best director; Huston, best supporting actor; Robert Buckner, original story.

126 minutes b&w

YANKS (1979)

★★½

Richard Gere
Lisa Eichhorn
Vanessa Redgrave
William Devane

A sentimental account about the effect American soldiers had on an English community during their brief stay during World War II. The film is rich in detail and beautifully photographed, but the script suffers from a lack of action and conviction. The film is also too long given the familiar material. Also with Chick Vennera, Rachel Roberts, and Wendy Morgan. **Director**—John Schlesinger. **(R)** *139 minutes*

THE YEARLING (1946)

★★★½

Gregory Peck
Jane Wyman
Claude Jarman, Jr.

This sensitive story about a young farm boy who is devoted to a pet fawn that his father must destroy is one of the most beloved family films of all time. Filmed on location, with Academy Award-winning cinematography by Charles Rosher, Leonard Smith, and Arthur Arling. Adapted from the novel by Marjorie Kinnan Rawlings. Chill Wills, Clem Bevans, June Lockhart, Forrest Tucker, and Henry Travers appear

(Continued)

This movie available on videotape and/or disc.

(Continued)
in supporting roles. **Director**—Clarence Brown. **Academy Award**—Jarman, special miniature award as outstanding child actor of 1946. **Nominations**—best picture; Brown, best director; Peck, best actor; Wyman, best actress.

134 minutes

THE YEAR MY VOICE BROKE (1987)

★★½

Noah Taylor
Loene Carmen
Graeme Blundell
Lynette Curran

A routine coming-of-age film from Australia. The story is set in New South Wales during the early 1960s. Taylor stars as an awkward 15-year-old boy who loves a slightly older girl (Carmen). The youngster feels the pain and frustration of lost love as the girl falls for a more mature boy who is a star athlete and local troublemaker. A touching script and natural performances by the young cast make for worthwhile viewing. **Director**—John Duigan. **(PG-13)**

103 minutes

THE YEAR OF LIVING DANGEROUSLY (1983)

★★★

Mel Gibson
Sigourney Weaver
Linda Hunt

Mel Gibson and Sigourney Weaver in The Year of Living Dangerously.

Stylish and atmospheric romantic adventure by Australian director Peter Weir (*Gallipoli*). Set in Indonesia in 1965, the poverty and political turmoil of Southeast Asia is seen through the eyes of an eager journalist (Gibson). He's aided by a provocative, pint-size cameraman—an extraordinary performance by actress Hunt. A love affair between Gibson and a mysterious British embassy assistant (Weaver) adds to the conflict. The theme of the clash between two very different cultures—here represented by the western journalists and the victimized Asians—is a recurring one in Weir's work. **(PG) Academy Award**—Hunt, best supporting actress.

114 minutes

YEAR OF THE DRAGON (1985)

★★★

Mickey Rourke
John Lone
Ariane

An uneven film in which the main character is unlikable and the plot often jumps off the track. Despite such annoying flaws, this elaborate and chaotic crime melodrama about New York's Chinatown underworld frequently brims with excitement, dazzling detail, and mystery. Rourke stars as a supercop who risks all to bust up the Chinese Mafia. Though touted as a comeback for director Michael Cimino (*Heaven's Gate*), the film was a commercial and critical failure. **(R)** *136 minutes*

YELLOWBEARD (1983)

★

Graham Chapman
Marty Feldman

A mediocre send-up of pirate movies, with a large cast of zanies in pursuit of buried treasure. Chapman, of the Monty Python troupe, is in the title role as a foul, incorrigible buccaneer who wants to reclaim his booty. Unfortunately, none of the Python magic is evident here. Many of the individual performances are amusing, but the movie doesn't work as a whole. How sad for Feldman that his last performance should be in so lame a film. Peter Boyle, Madeline Kahn, James Mason, and Cheech & Chong also are on board. Director Mel Damski seems to have had trouble even matching his shots, let alone displaying any style. **(PG)**

97 minutes

YENTL (1983)

★★★

Barbra Streisand
Mandy Patinkin
Amy Irving

Streisand is the star, director, producer, and cowriter of this controversial version of Isaac Bashevis Singer's fable set in the early 1900s. Streisand, in the title role, plays a rabbi's daughter who masquerades as a boy to attend an all-male yeshiva (religious school). Although the charade becomes preposterous, the film is generally warm and engaging. Streisand sings 12 soliloquy songs in her usual style. **(PG) Academy Award Nomination**—Irving, best supporting actress.

134 minutes

YES, GIORGIO (1982)

★★

Luciano Pavarotti
Kathryn Harrold

Opera great Pavarotti fills the screen with beautiful music in this old-fashioned romantic comedy. This may be a treat for opera lovers, but all Pavarotti's charm and talent cannot make up for the film's flimsy story. It's about the egotistical tenor's pursuit of a woman physician (Harrold) during an American tour. A rousing "yes" for the masterful arias and popular songs. A resolute "no" for the hokey, paper-thin screenplay. **Director**—Franklin Schaffner. **(PG)** *111 minutes*

YOU CAN'T CHEAT AN HONEST MAN (1939)

★★★

W.C. Fields
Edgar Bergen

A bit of inspired lunacy about beleaguered circus owner Larson E. Whipsnade, who must elude the law and deal with Bergen's pals Charlie McCarthy and Mortimer Snerd. One of Fields' classic comedies, it includes the memorable Ping-Pong game. Many of Fields' scenes were directed by his friend Edward Cline. The cast also includes Constance Moore, James Bush, Mary Forbes, Edward Brophy, Thurston Hall, and Charles Coleman. **Director**—George Marshall.

79 minutes b&w

YOU CAN'T HURRY LOVE (1988)

★★

David Packer
David Leisure

This movie available with closed captions for the hearing impaired.

Newcomer Packer stars as a naive young man from Ohio who moves to Los Angeles after his fiancée leaves him at the altar. A friend helps him find a job, and a video dating service helps him find girls. Packer misrepresents himself on his videotapes, however, as first a filmmaker, then a race-car driver, and finally a rock musician. Predictably, his dates are endless disasters with a series of oddball women. This familiar romantic comedy is too routine to offer many laughs or inspired characterizations, though Leisure (of the Izusu auto commercials) has a few moments of inspired lunacy as Packer's boss. Also with Scott McGinnis, Bridget Fonda (Jane Fonda's niece), and Frank Bonner. **Director**—Richard Martini. **(R)**

101 minutes

YOU CAN'T TAKE IT WITH YOU (1938)

 ★★★★ 

James Stewart
Jean Arthur

Warm and exhilarating comedy based on the Pulitzer Prize-winning play by Moss Hart and George S. Kaufman. Fireworks occur when a poor, eccentric family and a rich, conservative family are united by the engagement of their daughter and son. Director Frank Capra adds dimension to the stage characters, as well as a touch of serious philosophizing, making the film version grander than the original. Stewart and Arthur are delightfully sincere as the young lovers, but they are topped by Lionel Barrymore as Grandpa. Spring Byington, Edward Arnold, Mischa Auer, Ann Miller, and Donald Meek are appealing in supporting roles. **Academy Awards**—best picture; Capra, best director. **Nominations**—Byington, best supporting actress; Robert Riskin, screenplay. *127 minutes b&w*

YOU LIGHT UP MY LIFE (1977)

★

Didi Conn
Joe Silver

This melodrama about a young girl's struggle to become a pop singer is supposed to be a warm and touching film, but is too trite to be effective. Former ad man Joseph Brooks, who produced, directed, and wrote the screenplay, emphasizes sentimental episodes over originality or profound insights. Conn in the lead role, however, manages to exude some appeal. Silver, who plays the girl's father—a mediocre stand-up comedian—does well among a cast of unknowns. Unbelievably, the film's title song won an Academy Award. Also with Michael Zaslow and Melanie Mayron. **(PG)** *90 minutes*

YOU'LL NEVER GET RICH (1941)

Fred Astaire
Rita Hayworth

Astaire and Hayworth sparkle in this comedy/musical about an entertainer who's still able to put on his show and land the girl of his dreams even though he's drafted into the Army. The plot is as limp as those of most musicals, but the dancing is excellent and the Cole Porter music is classic. John Hubbard, Robert Benchley, Osa Massen, Frieda Inescort, and Guinn Williams appear in supporting roles. **Director**—Sidney Lanfield. *88 minutes b&w*

YOUNG AND INNOCENT (1937)

★★★

Nova Pilbeam
Derrick de Marney

Charming chase thriller about a man wrongly accused of murder, who flees the police to pursue the real killer. Based on a Josephine Tey novel, *A Shilling for Candles,* the story has many clever twists and turns. Although this is one of director Alfred Hitchcock's slighter pieces, his unique touches are evident. The cast also includes Mary Clare and Edward Rigby. **Alternate Title**—*The Girl Was Young.*

80 minutes b&w

YOUNG AT HEART (1954)

 ★★★

Doris Day
Frank Sinatra
Gig Young

Sinatra romances Day in this polished musical version of *Four Daughters,* a story about the problems of a musical family in a small town. Fine supporting performances by Ethel Barrymore, Robert Keith, Alan Hale, Jr., and Dorothy Malone. Sinatra steals the film with his renditions of "One More for the Road" and "Just One of Those Things." **Director**—Gordon Douglas. *117 minutes*

YOUNGBLOOD (1986)

 ★★½

Rob Lowe
Cynthia Gibb

Rob Lowe and Patrick Swayze experience the rigors of pro hockey in Youngblood.

The violence-prone world of professional ice hockey is illustrated through the experiences of a young player (Lowe). While the scenes of hockey matches are arresting, the formula plot follows the Rocky movies with predictable results. Lowe takes his role seriously, yet he appears too pretty to be believable as an aggressive hockey star. Also with Patrick Swayze and Ed Lauter. **Director**—Peter Markle. **(R)**

110 minutes

YOUNG DOCTORS IN LOVE (1982)

Michael McKean
Sean Young

A send-up of TV soap operas. The slapdash plot, set in a big city hospital, offers a steady stream of sight gags, scatological humor, and sick jokes. A few skits manage to be funny, but the bulk of the satire is too episodic to be effective. Garry Marshall, of TV sitcom fame, directed with an unsure hand. Familiar faces from long-running daytime soaps make cameo performances. Also with Harry Dean Stanton, Hector Elizondo, Dabney Coleman, Pamela Reed, and Patrick Macnee. **(R)**

95 minutes

YOUNG EINSTEIN (1989)

  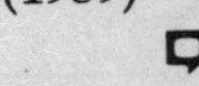

Yahoo Serious

In this uneven satire from Australia, Albert Einstein invents the surfboard and

(Continued)

This movie available on videotape and/or disc.

Comedian Yahoo Serious as the great inventor in Young Einstein.

(Continued)
rock 'n' roll, and his theory of relativity leads to brewing a better beer. Comedian Yahoo Serious stars in the title role of this unusual farce, which he also wrote and directed. His version of history is often cheerful and sometimes funny, but it is also filled with too many adolescent gags. The humor is reminiscent of that of Monty Python's Flying Circus, particularly the emphasis on physical comedy, the reliance on costumes, and the obtuse quality that comes from lampooning deadly serious historical personages. Yet it lacks the sophistication and edge of the famed British comedy troupe. Odile Le Clezio costars as Marie Curie. **(PG)** *91 minutes*

YOUNG FRANKENSTEIN (1974)

★★★

Gene Wilder
Marty Feldman

Mel Brooks directed but does not star in this zany send-up of monster movies. Brooks regulars Wilder, Feldman, Madeline Kahn, and Cloris Leachman are well suited to the material, which contains some delirious moments. Wilder is in the title role as the grandson of the venerable doctor, who returns to Transylvania to stir up more mischief. The moody black-and-white photography, reminiscent of the well-known horror films of Universal Studios, enhances the film. **(PG)** *108 minutes b&w*

YOUNG GUNS (1988)

★★½

Emilio Estevez
Kiefer Sutherland
Lou Diamond Phillips
Charlie Sheen
Jack Palance

A violent western designed to showcase the youthful ensemble cast. Billy the Kid (Estevez) and five young gunslingers called the Regulators battle a wealthy landowner (Palance) bent on owning the town. This western has a contemporary feel because of the youthful cast and their modern attitudes and appearance. Traditionalists may balk at the "hunks on horseback," but the popularity of this film introduced the western to a new generation. Unfortunately, Christopher Cain's direction is amateurish and marred by bad choices. Also with Dermot Mulroney, Casey Siemaszko, Patrick Wayne, Terence Stamp, Terry O'Quinn, Brian Keith, and Sharon Thomas. **Director**—Christopher Cain. **(R)** *97 minutes*

YOUNG GUNS II (1990)

★★½

Emilio Estevez
Kiefer Sutherland
Lou Diamond Phillips
Christian Slater
Alan Ruck
Balthazar Getty

Billy the Kid (Emilio Estevez) and his gang are back in Young Guns.

Half of the original cast are back in the saddle again for this glossy sequel that takes the story of Billy the Kid to its inevitable conclusion. Though the opening suggests an ambitious sequel, the film eventually lapses into a virtual copy of the original. Told in flashback, the story follows Billy and his gang (with new members Slater, Ruck, and Getty) as they try to escape across the West to the perceived safety of Mexico. Once again, the young actors bring their modern appearances and mannerisms to their characters, which at once updates the genre but makes the film seem too much like young punks out for a good time. This time around, William Petersen replaces Patrick Wayne as Pat Garrett. Also with R.D. Call, James Coburn, and Jack Kehoe. **(PG-13)** *103 minutes*

THE YOUNG LIONS (1958)

★★★

Marlon Brando
Montgomery Clift
Dean Martin

Brando, Clift, and Martin star in this complex World War II tale comparing the war experience of the Americans (Clift and Martin) with that of the Germans (Brando as a Nazi officer). Based on the novel by Irwin Shaw as adapted by Edward Anhalt. The cast also includes Hope Lange, Maximilian Schell, May Britt, Barbara Rush, and Lee Van Cleef. **Director**—Edward Dmytryk. **Academy Award Nomination**—Joe MacDonald, cinematography. *167 minutes b&w*

YOUNG MAN WITH A HORN (1950)

★★★

Kirk Douglas
Lauren Bacall
Doris Day

Douglas stars as a troubled and compulsive trumpet player in this story loosely based on the life of famed jazz musician Bix Beiderbecke. Bacall and Day portray the women in his life. Douglas' trumpet licks were dubbed by the great Harry James. Hoagy Carmichael, Juano Hernandez, Nestor Paiva, Mary Beth Hughes, and Jerome Cowan appear in supporting roles. **Director**—Michael Curtiz. *112 minutes b&w*

YOUNG MR. LINCOLN (1939)

★★★★

Henry Fonda
Alice Brady
Marjorie Weaver
Donald Meek

Fonda excels in the role of young Abraham Lincoln in this story about the early years of the 16th President of the United States. Under John Ford's excellent direction, the attention to period detail, such as a log-splitting contest and a tug-of-war, enhances the quality of the movie. Eddie Quillan, Spencer Charters, Ward Bond, Francis Ford, and

Arleen Whelan also star in supporting roles. **Academy Award Nomination**—Lamar Trotti, original story.
100 minutes b&w

THE YOUNG PHILADELPHIANS (1959)

★★½

Paul Newman
Barbara Rush

Despite the "young" in the title, this story about a lawyer from humble beginnings, who is on the make in Philadelphia society, has been told many times before. Newman plays the role of the lawyer; Rush is a society girl he's pursuing. Solid performances by Alexis Smith, Robert Vaughn, Otto Kruger, Brian Keith, and Diane Brewster buoy this conventional potboiler. **Director**—Vincent Sherman. **Academy Award Nominations**—Vaughn, best supporting actor; Harry Stradling, Sr., cinematography.
136 minutes b&w

YOUNG SHERLOCK HOLMES (1985)

★★★

Nicholas Rowe
Alan Cox

Much imagination and inspiration went into this portrayal of the fictional master sleuth as a prep-school student in Victorian England. Lanky Rowe is perfectly cast as the brilliant and self-assured adolescent who cracks the mystery of strange murders by a bizarre Egyptian cult. And Cox is good as the bumbling aspiring physician, John Watson. Scary special effects sometimes enhance the film, but occasionally intrude when adopting an "Indiana Jones" style. **Director**—Barry Levinson. **(PG–13)**
109 minutes

YOUNG TOM EDISON (1940)

Mickey Rooney
Fay Bainter
George Bancroft

Rooney in the title role curtails his usual exuberance to play this modest biography conventionally. The movie traces the brilliant inventor's early experiments and details the problems he faced. Although the story is less than complete—some facts are out of focus—it's the kind of motion picture that is often inspiring. Solid performances by Rooney, Bainter, Bancroft, Victor Kilian, and Virginia Weidler. **Director**—Norman Taurog.
82 minutes b&w

YOU ONLY LIVE TWICE (1967)

★★★½

Sean Connery
Donald Pleasence
Mie Hama
Akiko Wakabayashi

This, the most extravagant of the James Bond adventures with Connery, takes 007 to Japan, where he goes undercover to disrupt a SPECTRE scheme to incite World War III with hijacks of Russian and American space capsules. Although Bond is as steely here as in earlier films in the series, ingenious gadgetry and sheer spectacle reach an apex. Bond remains stalwart in the face of guns, piranha, ninja warriors, and archvillain Ernst Blofeld (Pleasence). Big entertainment, with *two* leading ladies (as well as a curvaceous villainess), and a climax that makes the battle for Okinawa seem puny. The outstanding score is by John Barry; lavish set designs by Ken Adam. Also with Karin Dor, Bernard Lee, and Lois Maxwell. **Director**—Lewis Gilbert. **(PG)**
115 minutes

YOU'RE A BIG BOY NOW (1966)

★★★

Peter Kastner
Elizabeth Hartman

This far-out comedy marked the beginning of the mainstream career of director Francis Coppola, who coaxed some fine acting from the cast. He also wrote the screenplay, about a mama's boy (Kastner) who learns about life and love the hard way from nightclub dancer Hartman. The pace is lively and the characters interesting. Geraldine Page, Rip Torn, and Karen Black are in supporting roles. **Academy Award Nomination**—Page, best supporting actress.
96 minutes

YOURS, MINE AND OURS (1968)

★★½

Lucille Ball
Henry Fonda

Ball and Fonda star in this well-made farce about a widow and widower—both with large families—who marry. The problems encountered when two large families live in the same house create the comic situations in this movie. At times, the problems are so obvious they fail to bring laughs, but there are enough good moments to make this film mildly entertaining. Van Johnson and Tom Bosley appear in supporting roles. **Director**—Melville Shavelson.
111 minutes

YOU WERE NEVER LOVELIER (1942)

★★★

Fred Astaire
Rita Hayworth
Adolphe Menjou

Menjou plays a matchmaking father trying to marry off his daughter, played by Hayworth. Astaire, of course, is the man Hayworth falls in love with. A Latin American setting adds some sparks to the proceedings. The rest of the cast includes Leslie Brooks, Larry Parks, Adele Mara, and Xavier Cugat and his orchestra. The songs include "I'm Old-Fashioned," "Dearly Beloved," and the title tune. **Director**—William A. Seiter.
98 minutes b&w

Z

Z (1969)

★★★★

Yves Montand
Jean-Louis Trintignant

This French-made thriller about the killing of a peace-movement leader in Greece in 1963 is a brilliant film and an insightful piece of political commentary. Trintignant, who heads the investigation of the crime, uncovers a right-wing terrorist faction infiltrating the government with far-reaching effects. Montand is well cast as the popular leader assassinated at a rally, and he is ably supported by Jacques Perrin, Irene Papas, and Charles Denner. Director Constantin Costa-Gavras creates a taut and chilling drama, all the more riveting because of its authenticity. **(PG) Academy Award**—best foreign-language film. **Nominations**—best picture; Costa-Gavras, best director; Jorge Semprum and Costa-Gavras, best screenplay based on material from another medium.
128 minutes

This movie available on videotape and/or disc.

Z

ZAPPED! (1982)

★

Scott Baio
Willie Aames
Felice Schachter
Scatman Crothers

The telekinesis gimmick is recycled in this sophomoric teenage comedy, starring Baio as a whiz kid who acquires the amazing power. Baio's accidentally acquired talent permits him to move objects, fix the basketball game, and remove girls' clothing (to the delight of adolescent boys). The youngsters are portrayed as cute and clever; the adults come off as bumbling and absurd. **Director**—Robert J. Rosenthal. **(R)**

98 minutes

ZELIG (1983)

★★★1/2

Woody Allen
Mia Farrow

Allen plays a fictional character with the power to miraculously assume the personality traits of others, including celebrities. Farrow plays a psychiatrist who falls in love with Allen when she tries to cure him of his chameleonlike tendencies. The satirical film is a well-crafted curiosity, expertly blending old newsreel footage with near-perfect simulations that position Allen in the midst of historical situations. Allen's unique wit abounds, and the original period-style songs by Dick Hyman are hilarious. A unique technical and creative triumph from director/writer Allen and cinematographer Gordon Willis. **(PG)** **Academy Award Nomination**—Willis, cinematography. *79 minutes b&w/color*

ZELLY AND ME (1988)

★1/2

Isabella Rossellini
Alexandra Johnes

The psychological damage a neurotic adult can inflict on a child is the subject of this flat drama set in Virginia during the late 1950's. An 11-year-old girl (Johnes) is tormented by her wealthy and possessive grandmother (Glynis Johns), and the child's only comfort comes from her sweet French nanny (Rossellini). Though the premise offers some interest, the story progresses with a lack of dramatic energy and many bland, syrupy scenes between Johnes and Rossellini. Director David Lynch (*Blue Velvet*) makes his acting debut as Rossellini's suitor. **Director**—Tina Rathborn. **(PG)**

87 minutes

ZIEGFELD FOLLIES (1946)

★★

Fred Astaire
Lucille Ball
William Powell

An all-star musical, starring Powell as Florenz Ziegfeld, who narrates the affair from Heaven. The movie has some splendid production numbers and some mediocre ones, but there are so many stars that you're bound to find someone you like. Besides Astaire, Ball, and Powell, the cast includes Jimmy Durante, Fanny Brice, Lena Horne, Gene Kelly, Hume Cronyn, Judy Garland, Red Skelton, Lucille Bremer, Victor Moore, and Edward Arnold. **Director**—Vincente Minnelli.

109 minutes

ZIEGFELD GIRL (1941)

★★

James Stewart
Judy Garland
Hedy Lamarr
Lana Turner

A charming musical about the problems and triumphs of three typical Ziegfeld girls, whose lives are changed when they join the legendary showman's Follies. Though the film eventually becomes bogged down in melodrama, the musical numbers, as choreographed by Busby Berkeley, are excellent. The rest of the cast includes Tony Martin, Jackie Cooper, Charles Winninger, Al Shean, Dan Dailey, Eve Arden, and Edward Everett Horton. The movie is noted for Garland's renditions of "Minnie from Trinidad" and "I'm Always Chasing Rainbows," but the Berkeley number called "You Stepped out of a Dream" is the best in the show. **Director**—Robert Z. Leonard.

131 minutes b&w

ZOOT SUIT (1981)

★★★

Daniel Valdez
Edward James Olmos
Tyne Daly

A powerful and colorful musical/drama that captures the Chicano spirit and presents a compelling social message about racial prejudice. This worthy screen version of Luis Valdez's play involves a group of Mexican-Americans in 1942 Los Angeles, who were sent to prison on trumped-up charges. Even when the drama falters the characters remain memorable. Olmos, who later became known for his Emmy-winning role as Lt. Castillo on NBC-TV's *Miami Vice,* is remarkable as the narrator and personification of the Latino machismo. **Director**—Luis Valdez. **(R)** *103 minutes*

ZORBA THE GREEK (1964)

★★★

Anthony Quinn
Alan Bates
Lila Kedrova

The mood and atmosphere of Nikos Kazantzakis' great novel are captured in this visually beautiful production, but the major character remains elusive onscreen. Quinn makes a commendable effort as the congenial Greek peasant, and Bates is excellent as the English writer who befriends him on Crete. Kedrova and Irene Papas also deliver solid performances in supporting roles. **Director**—Michael Cacoyannis. **Academy Awards**—Kedrova, best supporting actress; Walter Lassally, cinematography. **Nominations**—best picture; Cacoyannis, best director; Quinn, best actor; Cacoyannis, best screenplay based on material from another medium.

146 minutes b&w

ZORRO, THE GAY BLADE (1981)

★★

George Hamilton

Following *Love at First Bite,* Hamilton starred in this wild spoof about the legendary masked man's adventures, made famous in earlier decades by Douglas Fairbanks, Sr., and Tyrone Power. Hamilton hams it up with a mock Spanish accent as he plays the role of Don Diego Vega, a champion of "the poor pipples" of Los Angeles. He also takes a turn playing foppish twin brother Bunny Wigglesworth, a swashbuckler indeed. Unfortunately, this humorous premise is let down by the mediocre and occasionally offensive material. Ron Leibman and Brenda Vacarro costar. **Director**—Peter Medak. **(PG)** *96 minutes*

® This movie available with closed captions for the hearing impaired.